KEY TO WORLD MAP PAGES

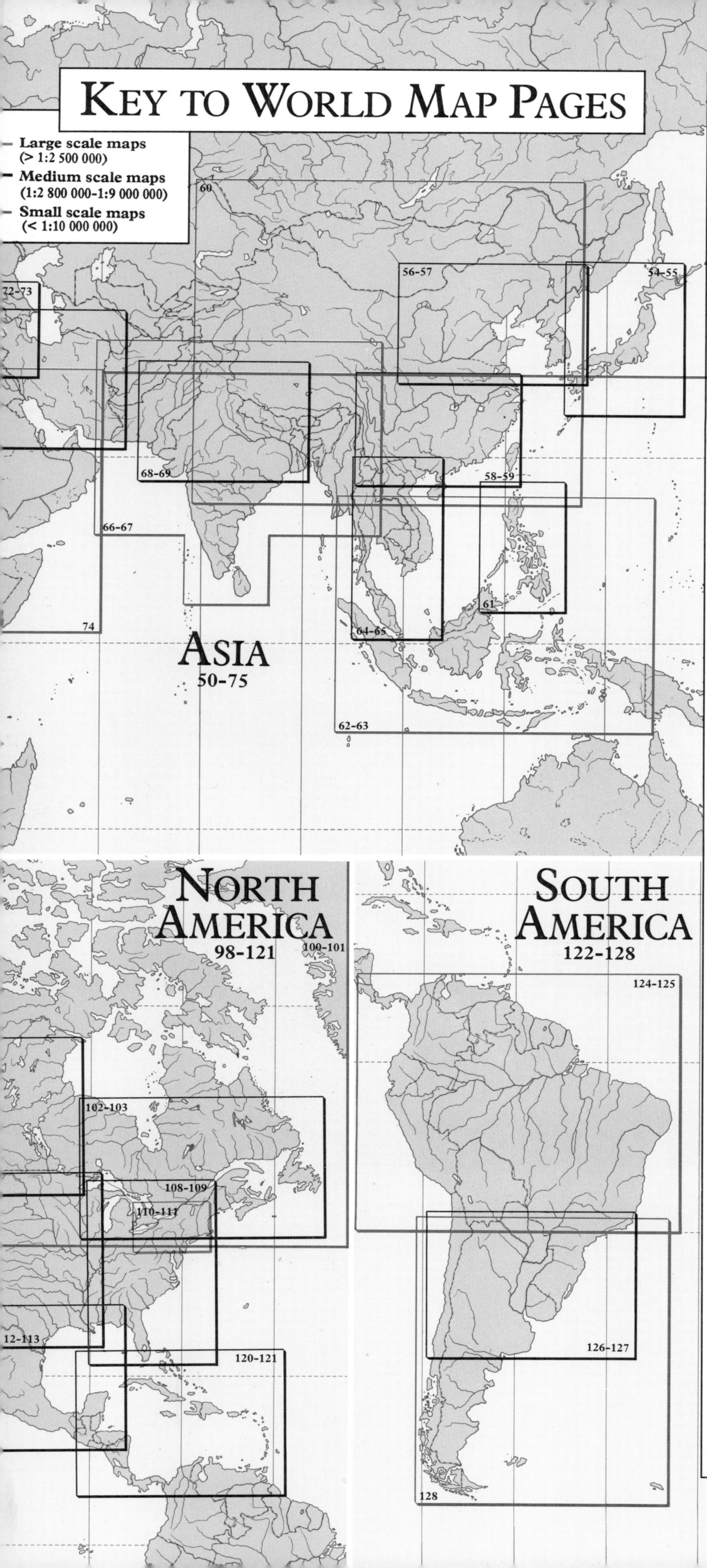

COUNTRY INDEX

Afghanistan 66
Albania 40
Algeria 78
Angola 84–85
Argentina 126, 128
Armenia 73
Australia 92-95
Austria 26-27
Azerbaijan 73

Bahamas 120–121
Bahrain 71
Bangladesh 67
Barbados 121
Belarus 46–47
Belgium 17
Belize 120
Benin 83
Bhutan 67
Bolivia 124
Bosnia-Herzegovina 29, 40
Botswana 88-89
Brazil 124–127
Brunei 78
Bulgaria 40–41
Burkina Faso 82–83
Burma 67
Burundi 86

Cambodia 64–65
Cameroon 84
Canada 100–101
Central African Republic 84
Chad 79
Chile 124, 128
China 56–60
Colombia 124
Congo 84
Congo, Dem. Rep. of the 84–85
Costa Rica 120
Croatia 29, 42
Cuba 120–121
Cyprus 36
Czech Republic 26–27

Denmark 11
Djibouti 74
Dominican Republic 121

Ecuador 124
Egypt 80
El Salvador 120
England 12–13
Equatorial Guinea 84
Eritrea 80–81
Estonia 46
Ethiopia 74, 81

Fiji 91
Finland 8–9
France 18–21
French Guiana 125

Gabon 84
Gambia 82
Georgia 73
Germany 24–25
Ghana 82-83
Greece 38–41
Greenland 4
Guatemala 120
Guinea 82
Guinea-Bissau 82
Guyana 124

Haiti 121
Honduras 120
Hungary 42

Iceland 8
India 66–69
Indonesia 62–63
Iran 70–71
Iraq 70–71
Irish Republic 15
Israel 75
Italy 28–31
Ivory Coast 82

Jamaica 120
Japan 54–55
Jordan 75

Kazakstan 50
Kenya 86
Korea, North 57
Korea, South 57
Kuwait 70–71
Kyrgyzstan 50

Laos 64
Latvia 46
Lebanon 75
Lesotho 88–89
Liberia 82
Libya 79
Lithuania 46
Luxembourg 17

Macedonia 40
Madagascar 89
Malawi 87
Malaysia 62–63
Mali 78, 82–83
Malta 36
Mauritania 78, 82
Mauritius 77
Mexico 118–119
Moldova 43
Mongolia 60
Morocco 78
Mozambique 85, 87

Namibia 88
Nepal 69
Netherlands 17
New Zealand 91
Nicaragua 120
Niger 83
Nigeria 83
Northern Ireland 15
Norway 8–9

Oman 74

Pakistan 68
Panama 120
Papua New Guinea 90
Paraguay 126–127
Peru 124
Philippines 61
Poland 44–45
Portugal 34–35
Puerto Rico 121

Qatar 71

Romania 42–43
Russia 50–51
Rwanda 86

Saudi Arabia 74
Scotland 14
Senegal 82
Sierra Leone 82
Singapore 65
Slovak Republic 27
Slovenia 29
Somali Republic 74
South Africa 88–89
Spain 32–35, 37
Sri Lanka 66
Sudan 79, 81
Surinam 124–125
Swaziland 89
Sweden 8–9
Switzerland 25
Syria 72–73

Taiwan 59
Tajikistan 50
Tanzania 86–87
Thailand 64–65
Togo 83
Trinidad and Tobago 121
Tunisia 78–79
Turkey 72–73
Turkmenistan 50

Uganda 86
Ukraine 47
United Arab Emirates 71
United Kingdom 12–15
USA 106–117
Uruguay 126–127
Uzbekistan 50

Venezuela 124
Vietnam 64–65

Wales 12–13

Yemen 74
Yugoslavia 40, 42

Zambia 84–85, 87
Zimbabwe 87

PHILIP'S

WORLD ATLAS

TED SMART

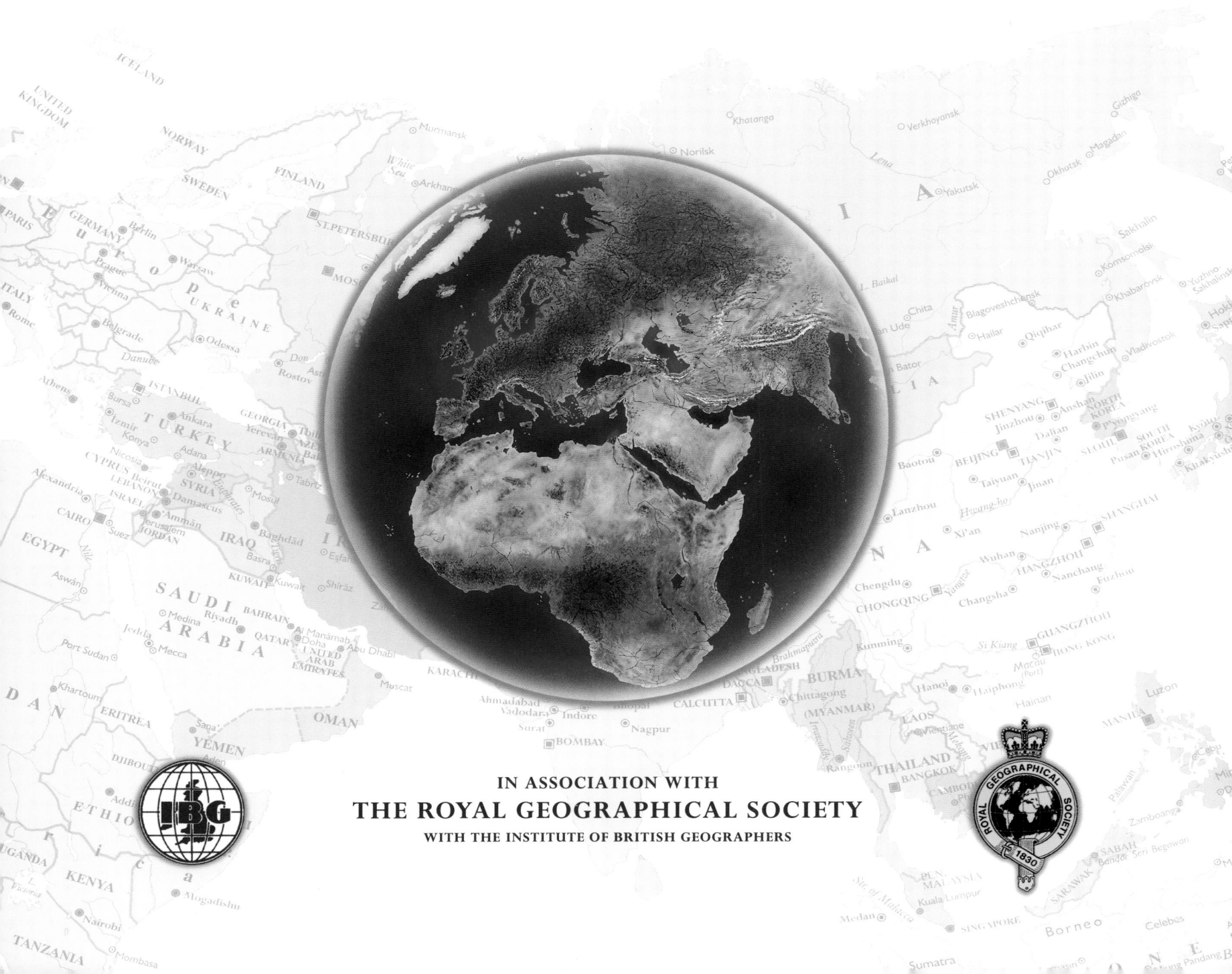

PHILIP'S

WORLD ATLAS

IN ASSOCIATION WITH
THE ROYAL GEOGRAPHICAL SOCIETY
WITH THE INSTITUTE OF BRITISH GEOGRAPHERS

THE EARTH IN SPACE
Cartography by Philip's

Text
Keith Lye

Illustrations
Stefan Chabluk

Star Charts
John Cox
Richard Monkhouse

PICTURE ACKNOWLEDGEMENTS
Robert Harding Picture Library /PHOTRI 13, /Bill Ross 41, /Adam Woolfitt 43
Hutchison Library /Melanie Friend 47, /John Hatt 46
Image Bank /Peter Hendrie 20, /Daniel Hummel 34, /Image Makers 8 top, /Pete Turner 39
Images Colour Library Limited 15
Japan National Tourist Organisation 45
NASA/Galaxy Picture Library 8 bottom left
Panos Pictures /Howard Davies 35
Chris Rayner 19 top
Rex Features /SIPA Press /Scott Andrews 12
Science Photo Library /Martin Bond 14, /CNES, 1992 Distribution Spot Image 27 top, /Luke Dodd 3, 6, /Earth Satellite Corporation 25 bottom, /NASA 9 centre right, 9 top, 22, 23, 24, /David Parker 26, /Peter Ryan 27 below, /Jerry Schad 4, /Space Telescope Science Institute /NASA 9 centre left, 9 bottom right, /US Geological Survey 8 centre right
Space Telescope Science Institute /R. Williams /NASA 2
Starland Picture Library /NASA 8 centre left
Still Pictures /Francois Pierrel 28, /Heine Pedersen 31, 40
Tony Stone Images 33, /Glen Allison 38, /James Balog 16, /John Beatty 21, /Neil Beer 30, /Kristin Finnegan 11, /Jeremy Horner 42, /Gary Norman 36, /Frank Oberle 25 top, /Dennis Oda 17, /Nigel Press 37, /Donovan Reese 18, 19, /Hugh Sitton 32, /Richard Surman 44, /Michael Townsend 29, /World Perspectives 10
Telegraph Colour Library /Space Frontiers 9 bottom left

Published in Great Britain in 1998
by George Philip Limited,
an imprint of Reed Consumer Books Limited,
Michelin House, 81 Fulham Road, London SW3 6RB,
and Auckland and Melbourne

This edition produced for
The Book People Limited,
Hall Wood Avenue,
Haydock,
St Helens WA11 9UL

Cartography by Philip's

ISBN 1–85613–491–1

A CIP catalogue record for this book is available from the British Library.

Printed in China

Philip's World Maps

The reference maps which form the main body of this atlas have been prepared in accordance with the highest standards of international cartography to provide an accurate and detailed representation of the Earth. The scales and projections used have been carefully chosen to give balanced coverage of the world, while emphasizing the most densely populated and economically significant regions. A hallmark of Philip's mapping is the use of hill shading and relief colouring to create a graphic impression of landforms: this makes the maps exceptionally easy to read. However, knowledge of the key features employed in the construction and presentation of the maps will enable the reader to derive the fullest benefit from the atlas.

MAP SEQUENCE

The atlas covers the Earth continent by continent: first Europe; then its land neighbour Asia (mapped north before south, in a clockwise sequence), then Africa, Australia and Oceania, North America and South America. This is the classic arrangement adopted by most cartographers since the 16th century. For each continent, there are maps at a variety of scales. First, physical relief and political maps of the whole continent; then a series of larger-scale maps

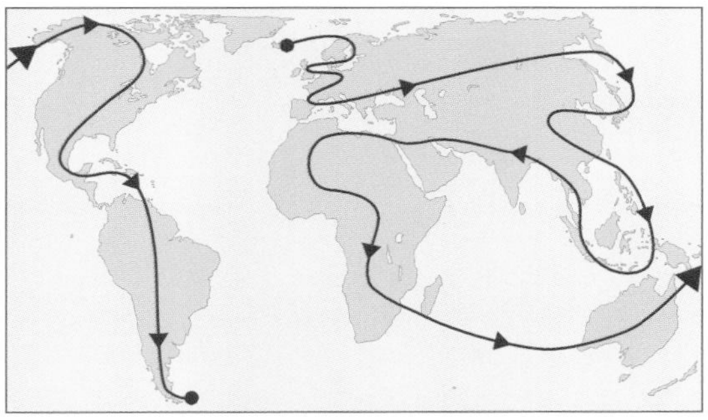

of the regions within the continent, each followed, where required, by still larger-scale maps of the most important or densely populated areas. The governing principle is that by turning the pages of the atlas, the reader moves steadily from north to south through each continent, with each map overlapping its neighbours. A key map showing this sequence, and the area covered by each map, can be found on the endpapers of the atlas.

MAP PRESENTATION

With very few exceptions (e.g. for the Arctic and Antarctic), the maps are drawn with north at the top, regardless of whether they are presented upright or sideways on the page. In the borders will be found the map title; a locator diagram showing the area covered and the page numbers for maps of adjacent areas; the scale; the projection used; the degrees of latitude and longitude; and the letters and figures used in the index for locating place names and geographical features. Physical relief maps also have a height reference panel identifying the colours used for each layer of contouring.

MAP SYMBOLS

Each map contains a vast amount of detail which can only be conveyed clearly and accurately by the use of symbols. Points and circles of varying sizes locate and identify the relative importance of towns and cities; different styles of type are employed for administrative, geographical and regional place names to aid identification. A variety of pictorial symbols denote landscape features such as glaciers, marshes and coral reefs, and man-made structures including roads, railways, airports, canals and dams. International borders are shown by red lines. Where neighbouring countries are in dispute, for example in parts of the Middle East, the maps show the *de facto* boundary between nations, regardless of the legal or historical situation. The symbols are explained on the first page of the World Maps section of the atlas.

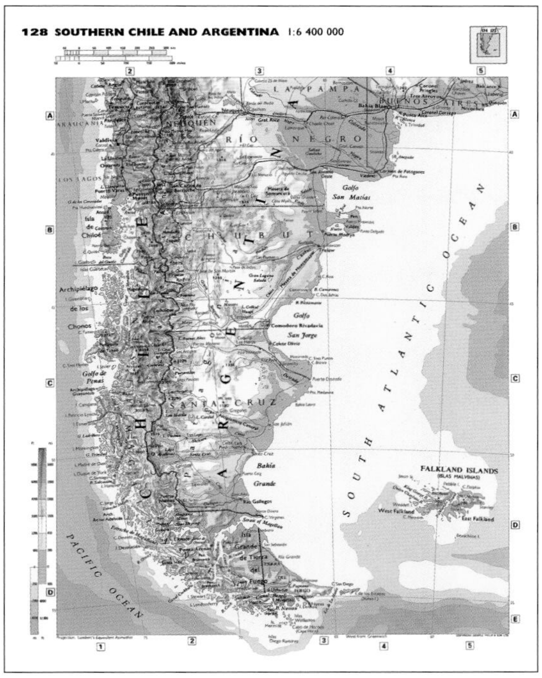

MAP SCALES

1:16 000 000
1 inch = 252 statute miles

The scale of each map is given in the numerical form known as the 'representative fraction'. The first figure is always one, signifying one unit of distance on the map; the second figure, usually in millions, is the number by which the map unit must be multiplied to give the equivalent distance on the Earth's surface. Calculations can easily be made in centimetres and kilometres, by dividing the Earth units figure by 100 000 (i.e. deleting the last five 0s). Thus 1:1 000 000 means 1 cm = 10 km. The calculation for inches and miles is more laborious, but 1 000 000 divided by 63 360 (the number of inches in a mile) shows that 1:1 000 000 means approximately 1 inch = 16 miles. The table below provides distance equivalents for scales down to 1:50 000 000.

LARGE SCALE

1:1 000 000	1 cm = 10 km	1 inch = 16 miles
1:2 500 000	1 cm = 25 km	1 inch = 39.5 miles
1:5 000 000	1 cm = 50 km	1 inch = 79 miles
1:6 000 000	1 cm = 60 km	1 inch = 95 miles
1:8 000 000	1 cm = 80 km	1 inch = 126 miles
1:10 000 000	1 cm = 100 km	1 inch = 158 miles
1:15 000 000	1 cm = 150 km	1 inch = 237 miles
1:20 000 000	1 cm = 200 km	1 inch = 316 miles
1:50 000 000	1 cm = 500 km	1 inch = 790 miles

SMALL SCALE

MEASURING DISTANCES

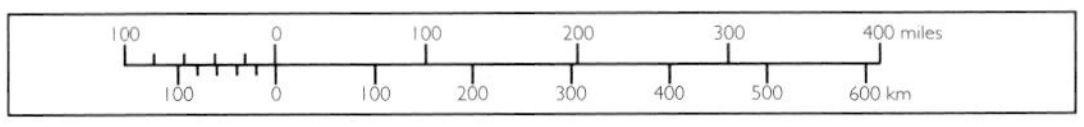

Although each map is accompanied by a scale bar, distances cannot always be measured with confidence because of the distortions involved in portraying the curved surface of the Earth on a flat page. As a general rule, the larger the map scale (i.e. the lower the number of Earth units in the representative fraction), the more accurate and reliable will be the distance measured. On small-scale maps such as those of the world and of entire continents, measurement may only be accurate along the 'standard parallels', or central axes, and should not be attempted without considering the map projection.

MAP PROJECTIONS

Unlike a globe, no flat map can give a true scale representation of the world in terms of area, shape and position of every region. Each of the numerous systems that have been devised for projecting the curved surface of the Earth on to a flat page involves the sacrifice of accuracy in one or more of these elements. The variations in shape and position of landmasses such as Alaska, Greenland and Australia, for example, can be quite dramatic when different projections are compared.

For this atlas, the guiding principle has been to select projections that involve the least distortion of size and distance. The projection used for each map is noted in the border. Most fall into one of three categories – conic, cylindrical or azimuthal – whose basic concepts are shown above. Each involves plotting the forms of the Earth's surface on a grid of latitude and longitude lines, which may be shown as parallels, curves or radiating spokes.

LATITUDE AND LONGITUDE

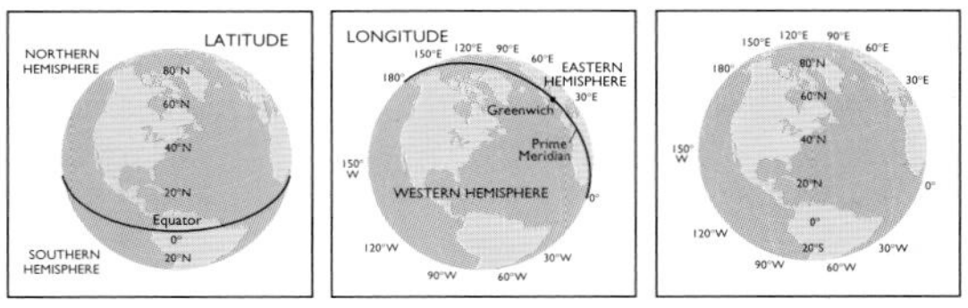

Accurate positioning of individual points on the Earth's surface is made possible by reference to the geometrical system of latitude and longitude. Latitude *parallels* are drawn west–east around the Earth and numbered by degrees north and south of the Equator, which is designated 0° of latitude. Longitude *meridians* are drawn north–south and numbered by degrees east and west of the *prime meridian*, 0° of longitude, which passes through Greenwich in England. By referring to these co-ordinates and their subdivisions of minutes (1/60th of a degree) and seconds (1/60th of a minute), any place on Earth can be located to within a few hundred yards. Latitude and longitude are indicated by blue lines on the maps; they are straight or curved according to the projection employed. Reference to these lines is the easiest way of determining the relative positions of places on different maps, and for plotting compass directions.

NAME FORMS

For ease of reference, both English and local name forms appear in the atlas. Oceans, seas and countries are shown in English throughout the atlas; country names may be abbreviated to their commonly accepted form (e.g. Germany, not The Federal Republic of Germany). Conventional English forms are also used for place names on the smaller-scale maps of the continents. However, local name forms are used on all large-scale and regional maps, with the English form given in brackets only for important cities – the large-scale map of Russia and Central Asia thus shows Moskva (Moscow). For countries which do not use a Roman script, place names have been transcribed according to the systems adopted by the British and US Geographic Names Authorities. For China, the Pin Yin system has been used, with some more widely known forms appearing in brackets, as with Beijing (Peking). Both English and local names appear in the index, the English form being cross-referenced to the local form.

Contents

World Statistics

Countries	x
Cities	xi
Climate	xii
Physical Dimensions	xiv
Regions in the News	xvi

The Earth In Space

The Universe	2–3
Star Charts and Constellations	4–7
The Solar System	8–9
The Earth: Time and Motion	10–11
The Earth From Space	12–13
The Dynamic Earth	14–15
Earthquakes and Volcanoes	16–17
Forces of Nature	18–19
Oceans and Ice	20–21
The Earth's Atmosphere	22–23
Climate and Weather	24–25
Water and Land Use	26–27
The Natural World	28–29
The Human World	30–31
Languages and Religions	32–33
International Organizations	34–35
Agriculture	36–37
Energy and Minerals	38–39
World Economies	40–41
Trade and Commerce	42–43
Travel and Communications	44–45
The World Today	46–47
Glossary of Terms	48

World Maps

Map Symbols	**1**
The World: Political 1:71 100 000	**2–3**
Arctic Ocean 1:31 100 000	**4**
Antarctica 1:31 100 000	**5**

Europe

Europe: Physical
1:17 800 000 6

Europe: Political
1:17 800 000 7

Scandinavia
1:4 400 000

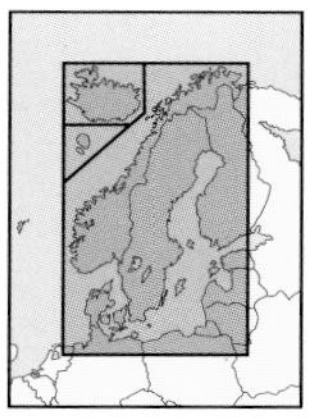

8–9

Denmark and Southern Sweden
1:2 200 000

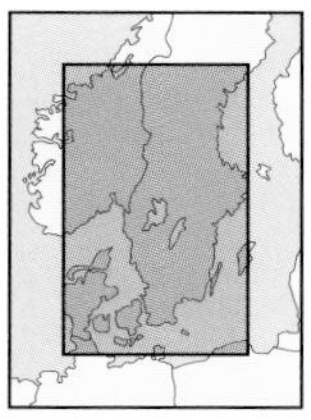

10–11

England and Wales
1:1 800 000

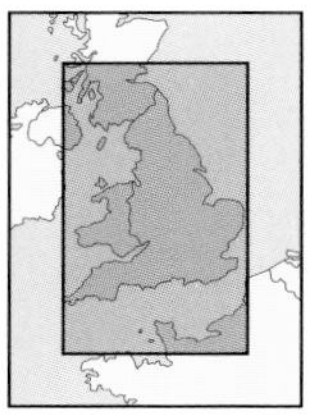

12–13

Scotland
1:1 800 000

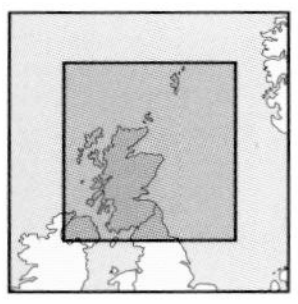

14

Ireland
1:1 800 000

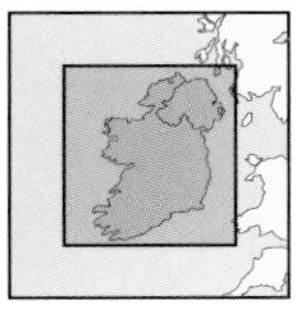

15

British Isles
1:4 400 000

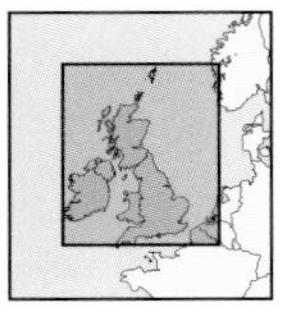

16

Netherlands, Belgium and Luxembourg
1:2 200 000

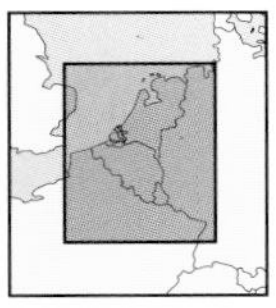

17

Northern France
1:2 200 000

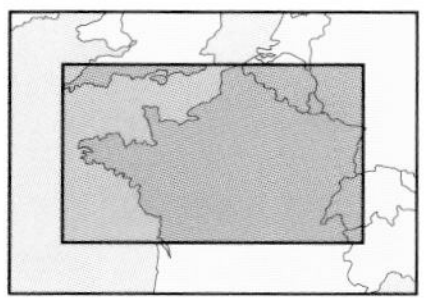

18–19

Southern France
1:2 200 000

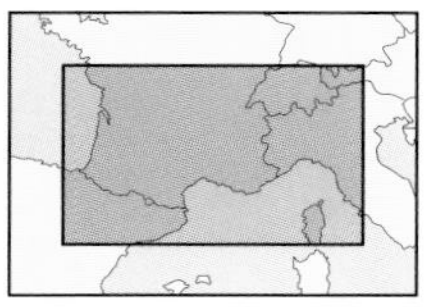

20–21

Middle Europe
1:4 400 000

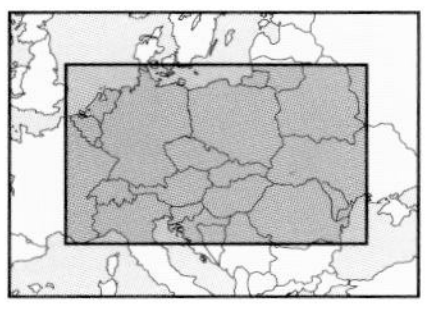

22–23

Germany and Switzerland
1:2 200 000

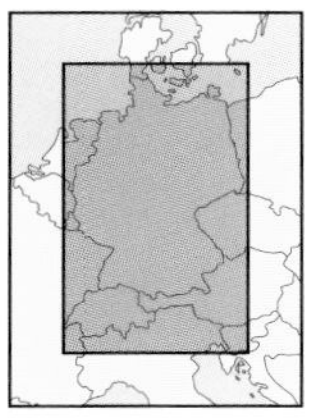

24–25

Austria, Czech Republic and Slovak Republic
1:2 200 000

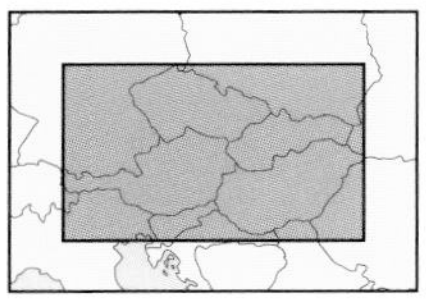

26–27

Northern Italy, Slovenia and Croatia
1:2 200 000

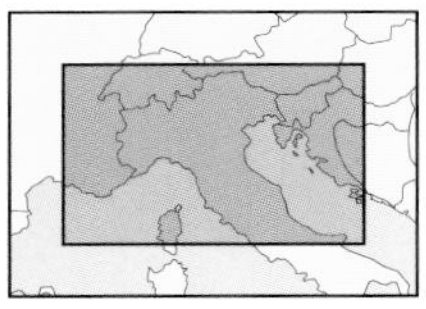

28–29

Southern Italy
1:2 200 000

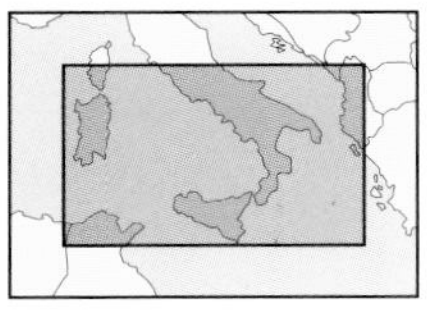

30–31

Eastern Spain
1:2 200 000

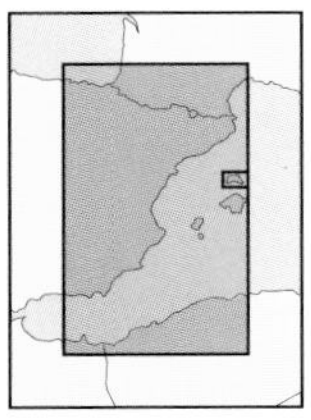

32–33

Western Spain and Portugal
1:2 200 000

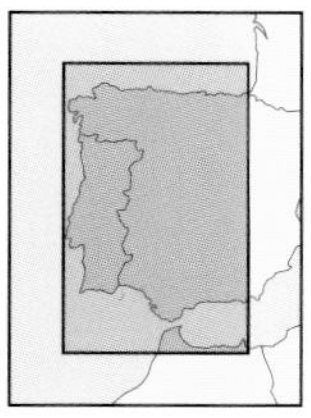

34–35

Malta, Crete, Corfu, Rhodes and Cyprus
1:900 000 / 1:1 200 000

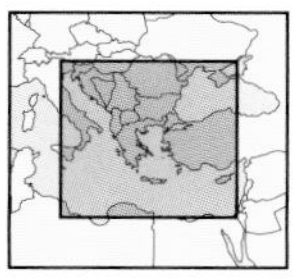

36

Balearics, Canaries and Madeira
1:900 000 / 1:1 800 000

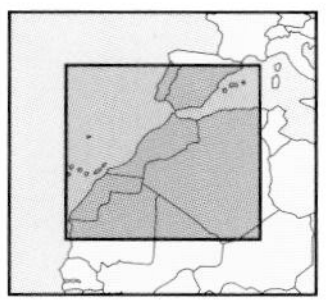

37

Southern Greece
1:2 200 000

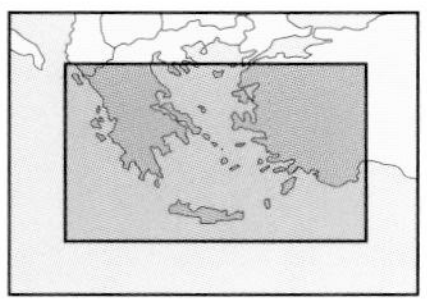

38–39

Northern Greece, Bulgaria and Albania
1:2 200 000

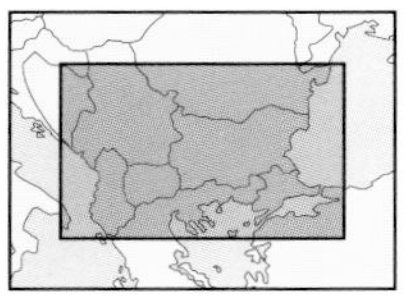

40–41

Hungary, Romania and the Lower Danube
1:2 200 000

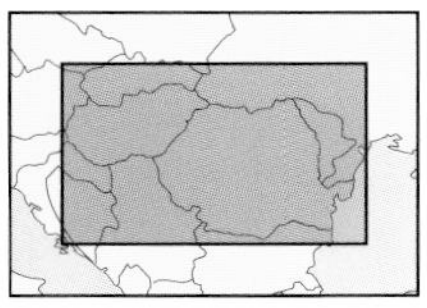

42–43

Poland and the Southern Baltic
1:2 200 000

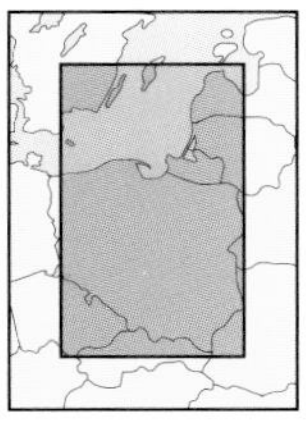

44–45

Australia and Oceania

North America

South America

Index to World Maps

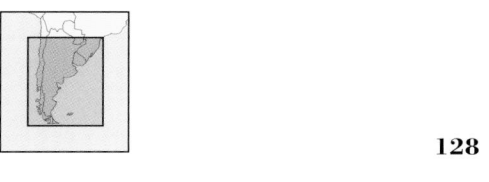

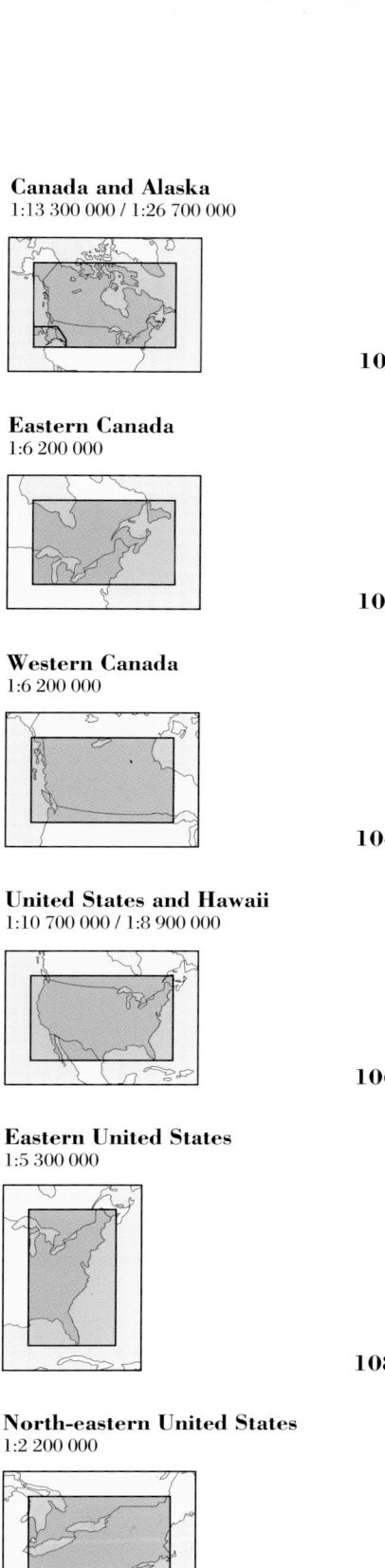

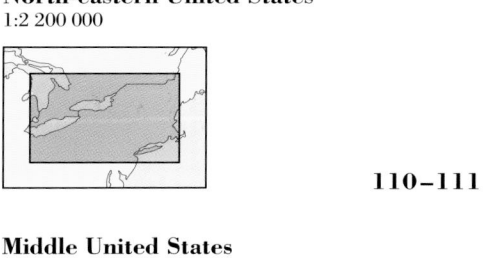

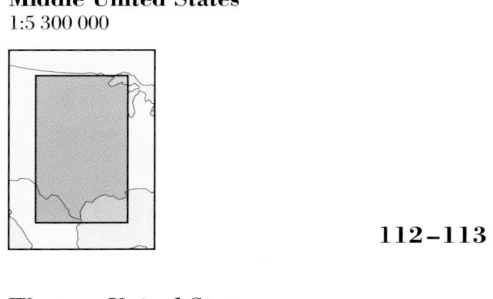

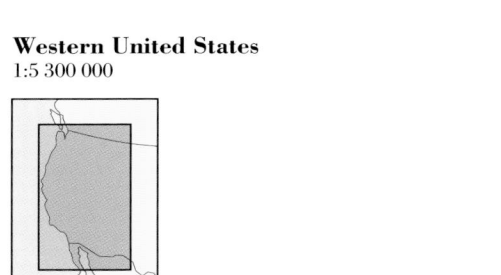

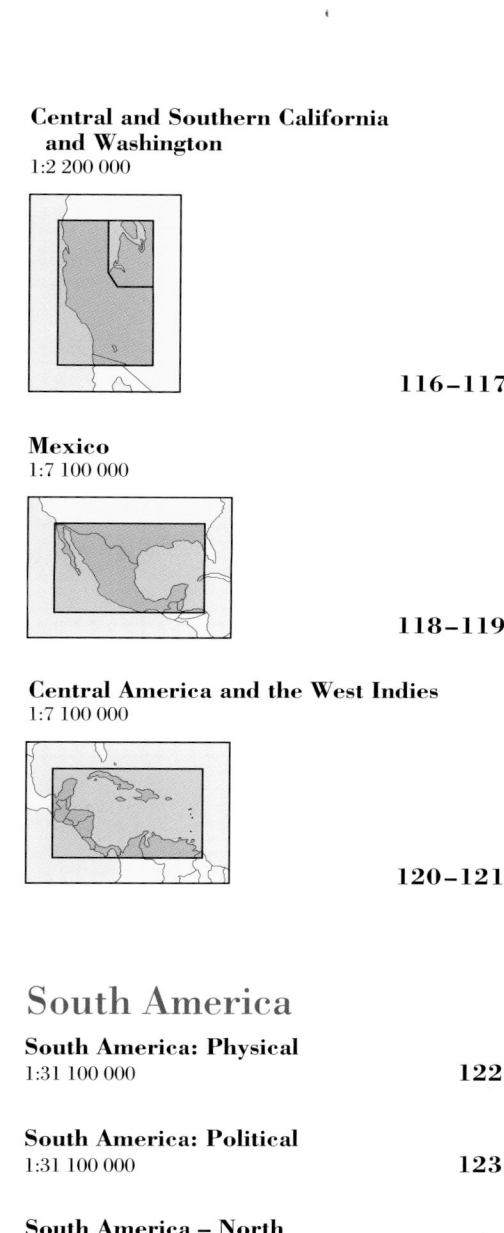

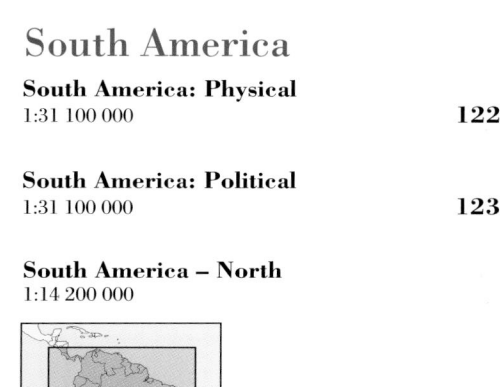

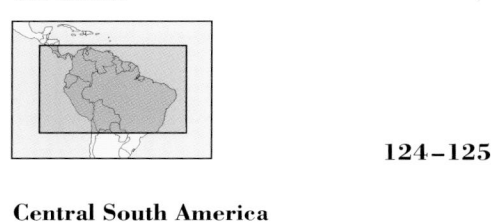

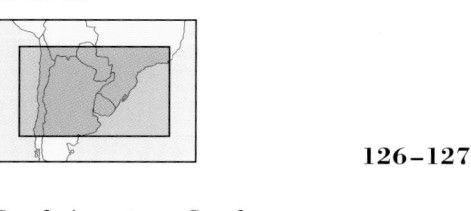

World Statistics: Countries

This alphabetical list includes all the countries and territories of the world. If a territory is not completely independent, then the country it is associated with is named. The area figures give the total area of land, inland water and ice. Units for areas and populations are thousands. The population figures are 1997 estimates. The annual income is the Gross National Product per capita in US dollars. The figures are the latest available, usually 1995.

Country/Territory	Area km² Thousands	Area miles² Thousands	Population Thousands	Capital	Annual Income US $
Afghanistan	652	252	23,000	Kabul	300
Albania	28.8	11.1	3,600	Tirana	670
Algeria	2,382	920	29,300	Algiers	1,600
American Samoa (US)	0.20	0.08	62	Pago Pago	2,600
Andorra	0.45	0.17	75	Andorra-la-Vella	14,000
Angola	1,247	481	11,200	Luanda	410
Anguilla (UK)	0.1	0.04	10	The Valley	6,800
Antigua & Barbuda	0.44	0.17	66	St John's	6,390
Argentina	2,767	1,068	35,400	Buenos Aires	8,030
Armenia	29.8	11.5	3,800	Yerevan	730
Aruba (Netherlands)	0.19	0.07	70	Oranjestad	17,500
Australia	7,687	2,968	18,400	Canberra	18,720
Austria	83.9	32.4	8,200	Vienna	26,890
Azerbaijan	86.6	33.4	7,700	Baku	480
Azores (Portugal)	2.2	0.87	238	Ponta Delgada	–
Bahamas	13.9	5.4	280	Nassau	11,940
Bahrain	0.68	0.26	605	Manama	7,840
Bangladesh	144	56	124,000	Dhaka	240
Barbados	0.43	0.17	265	Bridgetown	6,560
Belarus	207.6	80.1	10,500	Minsk	2,070
Belgium	30.5	11.8	10,200	Brussels	24,710
Belize	23	8.9	228	Belmopan	2,630
Benin	113	43	5,800	Porto-Novo	370
Bermuda (UK)	0.05	0.02	65	Hamilton	27,000
Bhutan	47	18.1	1,790	Thimphu	420
Bolivia	1,099	424	7,700	La Paz/Sucre	800
Bosnia-Herzegovina	51	20	3,600	Sarajevo	2,600
Botswana	582	225	1,500	Gaborone	3,020
Brazil	8,512	3,286	159,500	Brasília	3,640
Brunei	5.8	2.2	300	Bandar Seri Begawan	14,500
Bulgaria	111	43	8,600	Sofia	1,330
Burkina Faso	274	106	10,900	Ouagadougou	230
Burma (= Myanmar)	677	261	47,500	Rangoon	1,000
Burundi	27.8	10.7	6,300	Bujumbura	160
Cambodia	181	70	10,500	Phnom Penh	270
Cameroon	475	184	13,800	Yaoundé	650
Canada	9,976	3,852	30,200	Ottawa	19,380
Canary Is. (Spain)	7.3	2.8	1,494	Las Palmas/Santa Cruz	–
Cape Verde Is.	4	1.6	410	Praia	960
Cayman Is. (UK)	0.26	0.10	35	George Town	20,000
Central African Republic	623	241	3,400	Bangui	340
Chad	1,284	496	6,800	Ndjaména	180
Chile	757	292	14,700	Santiago	4,160
China	9,597	3,705	1,210,000	Beijing	620
Colombia	1,139	440	35,900	Bogotá	1,910
Comoros	2.2	0.86	630	Moroni	470
Congo	342	132	2,700	Brazzaville	680
Congo (= Zaïre)	2,345	905	47,200	Kinshasa	120
Cook Is. (NZ)	0.24	0.09	20	Avarua	900
Costa Rica	51.1	19.7	3,500	San José	2,610
Croatia	56.5	21.8	4,900	Zagreb	3,250
Cuba	111	43	11,300	Havana	1,250
Cyprus	9.3	3.6	800	Nicosia	11,500
Czech Republic	78.9	30.4	10,500	Prague	3,870
Denmark	43.1	16.6	5,400	Copenhagen	29,890
Djibouti	23.2	9	650	Djibouti	1,000
Dominica	0.75	0.29	78	Roseau	2,990
Dominican Republic	48.7	18.8	8,200	Santo Domingo	1,460
Ecuador	284	109	11,800	Quito	1,390
Egypt	1,001	387	63,000	Cairo	790
El Salvador	21	8.1	6,000	San Salvador	1,610
Equatorial Guinea	28.1	10.8	420	Malabo	380
Eritrea	94	36	3,500	Asmara	500
Estonia	44.7	17.3	1,500	Tallinn	2,860
Ethiopia	1,128	436	58,500	Addis Ababa	100
Faroe Is. (Denmark)	1.4	0.54	45	Tórshavn	23,660
Fiji	18.3	7.1	800	Suva	2,440
Finland	338	131	5,200	Helsinki	20,580
France	552	213	58,800	Paris	24,990
French Guiana (France)	90	34.7	155	Cayenne	6,500
French Polynesia (France)	4	1.5	226	Papeete	7,500
Gabon	268	103	1,200	Libreville	3,490
Gambia, The	11.3	4.4	1,200	Banjul	320
Georgia	69.7	26.9	5,500	Tbilisi	440
Germany	357	138	82,300	Berlin/Bonn	27,510
Ghana	239	92	18,100	Accra	390
Gibraltar (UK)	0.007	0.003	28	Gibraltar Town	5,000
Greece	132	51	10,600	Athens	8,210
Greenland (Denmark)	2,176	840	57	Nuuk (Godthåb)	9,000
Grenada	0.34	0.13	99	St George's	2,980
Guadeloupe (France)	1.7	0.66	440	Basse-Terre	9,500
Guam (US)	0.55	0.21	161	Agana	6,000
Guatemala	109	42	11,300	Guatemala City	1,340
Guinea	246	95	7,500	Conakry	550
Guinea-Bissau	36.1	13.9	1,200	Bissau	250
Guyana	215	83	820	Georgetown	590
Haiti	27.8	10.7	7,400	Port-au-Prince	250
Honduras	112	43	6,300	Tegucigalpa	600
Hong Kong (China)	1.1	0.40	6,500	–	22,990
Hungary	93	35.9	10,200	Budapest	4,120
Iceland	103	40	275	Reykjavik	24,950
India	3,288	1,269	980,000	New Delhi	340
Indonesia	1,905	735	203,500	Jakarta	980
Iran	1,648	636	69,500	Tehran	4,800
Iraq	438	169	22,500	Baghdad	1,800
Ireland	70.3	27.1	3,600	Dublin	14,710
Israel	27	10.3	5,900	Jerusalem	15,920
Italy	301	116	57,800	Rome	19,020
Ivory Coast	322	125	15,100	Yamoussoukro	660
Jamaica	11	4.2	2,600	Kingston	1,510
Japan	378	146	125,900	Tokyo	39,640
Jordan	89.2	34.4	5,600	Amman	1,510
Kazakstan	2,717	1,049	17,000	Aqmola	1,330
Kenya	580	224	31,900	Nairobi	280
Kiribati	0.72	0.28	85	Tarawa	710
Korea, North	121	47	24,500	Pyŏngyang	1,000
Korea, South	99	38.2	46,100	Seoul	9,700
Kuwait	17.8	6.9	2,050	Kuwait City	17,390
Kyrgyzstan	198.5	76.6	4,700	Bishkek	700
Laos	237	91	5,200	Vientiane	350
Latvia	65	25	2,500	Riga	2,270
Lebanon	10.4	4	3,200	Beirut	2,660
Lesotho	30.4	11.7	2,100	Maseru	770
Liberia	111	43	3,000	Monrovia	850
Libya	1,760	679	5,500	Tripoli	7,000
Liechtenstein	0.16	0.06	32	Vaduz	33,500
Lithuania	65.2	25.2	3,700	Vilnius	1,900
Luxembourg	2.6	1	400	Luxembourg	41,210
Macau (Portugal)	0.02	0.006	450	Macau	7,500
Macedonia	25.7	9.9	2,200	Skopje	860
Madagascar	587	227	15,500	Antananarivo	230
Madeira (Portugal)	0.81	0.31	253	Funchal	–
Malawi	118	46	10,300	Lilongwe	170
Malaysia	330	127	20,900	Kuala Lumpur	3,890
Maldives	0.30	0.12	275	Malé	990
Mali	1,240	479	11,000	Bamako	250
Malta	0.32	0.12	400	Valletta	11,000
Marshall Is.	0.18	0.07	60	Dalap-Uliga-Darrit	1,500
Martinique (France)	1.1	0.42	405	Fort-de-France	10,000
Mauritania	1,030	412	2,400	Nouakchott	460
Mauritius	2.0	0.72	1,200	Port Louis	3,380
Mayotte (France)	0.37	0.14	105	Mamoundzou	1,430
Mexico	1,958	756	97,400	Mexico City	3,320
Micronesia, Fed. States of	0.70	0.27	127	Palikir	1,560
Moldova	33.7	13	4,500	Chişinău	920
Monaco	0.002	0.0001	33	Monaco	16,000
Mongolia	1,567	605	2,500	Ulan Bator	310
Montserrat (UK)	0.10	0.04	12	Plymouth	4,500
Morocco	447	172	28,100	Rabat	1,110
Mozambique	802	309	19,100	Maputo	80
Namibia	825	318	1,700	Windhoek	2,000
Nauru	0.02	0.008	12	Yaren District	10,000
Nepal	141	54	22,100	Katmandu	200
Netherlands	41.5	16	15,900	Amsterdam/The Hague	24,000
Netherlands Antilles (Neths)	0.99	0.38	210	Willemstad	10,500
New Caledonia (France)	18.6	7.2	192	Nouméa	16,000
New Zealand	269	104	3,700	Wellington	14,340
Nicaragua	130	50	4,600	Managua	380
Niger	1,267	489	9,700	Niamey	220
Nigeria	924	357	118,000	Abuja	260
Northern Mariana Is. (US)	0.48	0.18	50	Saipan	11,500
Norway	324	125	4,400	Oslo	31,250
Oman	212	82	2,400	Muscat	4,820
Pakistan	796	307	136,000	Islamabad	460
Palau	0.46	0.18	17	Koror	2,260
Panama	77.1	29.8	2,700	Panama City	2,750
Papua New Guinea	463	179	4,400	Port Moresby	1,160
Paraguay	407	157	5,200	Asunción	1,690
Peru	1,285	496	24,500	Lima	2,310
Philippines	300	116	73,500	Manila	1,050
Poland	313	121	38,800	Warsaw	2,790
Portugal	92.4	35.7	10,100	Lisbon	9,740
Puerto Rico (US)	9	3.5	3,800	San Juan	7,500
Qatar	11	4.2	620	Doha	11,600
Réunion (France)	2.5	0.97	680	Saint-Denis	4,500
Romania	238	92	22,600	Bucharest	1,480
Russia	17,075	6,592	147,800	Moscow	2,240
Rwanda	26.3	10.2	7,000	Kigali	180
St Kitts & Nevis	0.36	0.14	42	Basseterre	4,470
St Lucia	0.62	0.24	150	Castries	3,370
St Vincent & Grenadines	0.39	0.15	114	Kingstown	2,280
San Marino	0.06	0.02	26	San Marino	20,000
São Tomé & Príncipe	0.96	0.37	135	São Tomé	350
Saudi Arabia	2,150	830	19,100	Riyadh	7,040
Senegal	197	76	8,900	Dakar	600
Seychelles	0.46	0.18	78	Victoria	6,370
Sierra Leone	71.7	27.7	4,600	Freetown	180
Singapore	0.62	0.24	3,200	Singapore	26,730
Slovak Republic	49	18.9	5,400	Bratislava	2,950
Slovenia	20.3	7.8	2,000	Ljubljana	8,200
Solomon Is.	28.9	11.2	410	Honiara	910
Somalia	638	246	9,900	Mogadishu	500
South Africa	1,220	471	42,300	C. Town/Pretoria/Bloem.	3,160
Spain	505	195	39,300	Madrid	13,580
Sri Lanka	65.6	25.3	18,700	Colombo	700
Sudan	2,506	967	31,000	Khartoum	750
Surinam	163	63	500	Paramaribo	880
Swaziland	17.4	6.7	1,000	Mbabane	1,170
Sweden	450	174	8,900	Stockholm	23,750
Switzerland	41.3	15.9	7,100	Bern	40,630
Syria	185	71	15,300	Damascus	1,120
Taiwan	36	13.9	21,700	Taipei	12,000
Tajikistan	143.1	55.2	6,000	Dushanbe	340
Tanzania	945	365	31,200	Dodoma	120
Thailand	513	198	60,800	Bangkok	2,740
Togo	56.8	21.9	4,500	Lomé	310
Tonga	0.75	0.29	107	Nuku'alofa	1,610
Trinidad & Tobago	5.1	2	1,300	Port of Spain	3,770
Tunisia	164	63	9,200	Tunis	1,820
Turkey	779	301	63,500	Ankara	2,780
Turkmenistan	488.1	188.5	4,800	Ashkhabad	920
Turks & Caicos Is. (UK)	0.43	0.17	15	Cockburn Town	5,000
Tuvalu	0.03	0.01	10	Fongafale	600
Uganda	236	91	20,800	Kampala	240
Ukraine	603.7	233.1	51,500	Kiev	1,630
United Arab Emirates	83.6	32.3	2,400	Abu Dhabi	17,400
United Kingdom	243.3	94	58,600	London	18,700
United States of America	9,373	3,619	268,000	Washington, DC	26,980
Uruguay	177	68	3,300	Montevideo	5,170
Uzbekistan	447.4	172.7	23,800	Tashkent	970
Vanuatu	12.2	4.7	175	Port-Vila	1,200
Venezuela	912	352	22,500	Caracas	3,020
Vietnam	332	127	77,100	Hanoi	240
Virgin Is. (UK)	0.15	0.06	13	Road Town	–
Virgin Is. (US)	0.34	0.13	105	Charlotte Amalie	12,000
Wallis & Futuna Is. (France)	0.20	0.08	15	Mata-Utu	–
Western Sahara	266	103	280	El Aaiún	980
Western Samoa	2.8	1.1	175	Apia	1,120
Yemen	528	204	16,500	Sana	260
Yugoslavia	102.3	39.5	10,500	Belgrade	1,400
Zambia	753	291	9,500	Lusaka	400
Zimbabwe	391	151	12,100	Harare	540

At the time of going to press, the government of Kazakstan planned to rename the capital Aqmola to Astana.

World Statistics: Cities

This list shows the principal cities with more than 500,000 inhabitants (for China and India only cities with more than 1 million inhabitants are included). The figures are taken from the most recent census or population estimate available, and as far as possible are the population of the metropolitan area, e.g. greater New York, Mexico or Paris. All the figures are in thousands. Local name forms have been used for the smaller cities (e.g. Kraków).

AFGHANISTAN	
Kabul	1,565
ALGERIA	
Algiers	1,722
Oran	664
ANGOLA	
Luanda	2,250
ARGENTINA	
Buenos Aires	10,990
Córdoba	1,198
Rosario	1,096
Mendoza	775
La Plata	640
San Miguel de Tucumán	622
Mar del Plata	520
ARMENIA	
Yerevan	1,226
AUSTRALIA	
Sydney	3,713
Melbourne	3,189
Brisbane	1,422
Perth	1,221
Adelaide	1,071
AUSTRIA	
Vienna	1,560
AZERBAIJAN	
Baku	1,081
BANGLADESH	
Dhaka	7,832
Chittagong	2,041
Khulna	877
Rajshahi	517
BELARUS	
Minsk	1,700
Homyel	512
BELGIUM	
Brussels	952
BENIN	
Cotonou	537
BOLIVIA	
La Paz	1,126
Santa Cruz	767
BOSNIA-HERZEGOVINA	
Sarajevo	526
BRAZIL	
São Paulo	16,417
Rio de Janeiro	9,888
Salvador	2,056
Belo Horizonte	2,049
Fortaleza	1,758
Brasília	1,596
Curitiba	1,290
Recife	1,290
Nova Iguaçu	1,286
Pôrto Alegre	1,263
Belém	1,246
Manaus	1,011
Goiânia	921
Campinas	846
Guarulhos	781
São Gonçalo	748
São Luís	696
Duque de Caxias	665
Maceió	628
Santo André	614
Natal	607
Teresina	598
São Bernado de Campo	565
Osasco	563
Campo Grande	526
BULGARIA	
Sofia	1,117
BURKINA FASO	
Ouagadougou	690
BURMA (MYANMAR)	
Rangoon	2,513
Mandalay	533
CAMBODIA	
Phnom Penh	920
CAMEROON	
Douala	884
Yaoundé	750
CANADA	
Toronto	4,264
Montréal	3,327
Vancouver	1,832
Ottawa–Hull	1,010
Edmonton	863
Calgary	822
Québec	672
Winnipeg	667
Hamilton	624
CENTRAL AFRICAN REP.	
Bangui	706
CHAD	
Ndjaména	530
CHILE	
Santiago	5,077
CHINA	
Shanghai	15,082
Beijing	12,362
Tianjin	10,687
Hong Kong (SAR)[1]	6,205
Chongqing	3,870
Shenyang	3,762
Wuhan	3,520
Guangzhou	3,114
Harbin	2,505
Nanjing	2,211
Xi'an	2,115
Chengdu	1,933
Dalian	1,855
Changchun	1,810
Jinan	1,660
Taiyuan	1,642
Qingdao	1,584
Fuzhou, Fujian	1,380
Zibo	1,346
Zhengzhou	1,324
Lanzhou	1,296
Anshan	1,252
Fushun	1,246
Kunming	1,242
Changsha	1,198
Hangzhou	1,185
Nanchang	1,169
Shijiazhuang	1,159
Guiyang	1,131
Ürümqi	1,130
Jilin	1,118
Hefei	1,110
Tangshan	1,110
Baotou	1,033
COLOMBIA	
Bogotá	5,026
Cali	1,719
Medellín	1,621
Barranquilla	1,064
Cartagena	746
CONGO	
Brazzaville	938
Pointe-Noire	576
CONGO (ZAÏRE)	
Kinshasa	3,804
Lubumbashi	739
Mbuji-Mayi	613
Kolwezi	544
COSTA RICA	
San José	1,186
CROATIA	
Zagreb	931
CUBA	
Havana	2,143
CZECH REPUBLIC	
Prague	1,217
DENMARK	
Copenhagen	1,353
DOMINICAN REPUBLIC	
Santo Domingo	2,135
Santiago	691
ECUADOR	
Guayaquil	1,925
Quito	1,444
EGYPT	
Cairo	9,656
Alexandria	3,380
El Gîza	2,144
Shubra el Kheima	834
EL SALVADOR	
San Salvador	1,522
ETHIOPIA	
Addis Ababa	2,316
FINLAND	
Helsinki	525
FRANCE	
Paris	9,469
Lyon	1,262
Marseille	1,087
Lille	959
Bordeaux	696
Toulouse	650
Nice	516
GEORGIA	
Tbilisi	1,279
GERMANY	
Berlin	3,472
Hamburg	1,706
Munich	1,245
Cologne	964
Frankfurt	652
Essen	618
Dortmund	601
Stuttgart	588
Düsseldorf	573
Bremen	549
Duisburg	536
Hanover	526
GHANA	
Accra	1,781
Kumasi	540
GREECE	
Athens	3,097
GUATEMALA	
Guatemala	1,814
GUINEA	
Conakry	1,508
HAITI	
Port-au-Prince	1,402
HONDURAS	
Tegucigalpa	739
HUNGARY	
Budapest	1,909
INDIA	
Bombay (Mumbai)	15,093
Calcutta	11,673
Delhi	9,882
Madras (Chennai)	5,361
Hyderabad	4,280
Bangalore	4,087
Ahmadabad	3,298
Pune	2,485
Kanpur	2,111
Nagpur	1,661
Lucknow	1,642
Surat	1,517
Jaipur	1,514
Coimbatore	1,136
Vadodara	1,115
Indore	1,104
Patna	1,099
Madurai	1,094
Bhopal	1,064
Vishakhapatnam	1,052
Varanasi	1,026
Ludhiana	1,012
INDONESIA	
Jakarta	11,500
Surabaya	2,701
Bandung	2,368
Medan	1,910
Semarang	1,366
Palembang	1,352
Ujung Pandang	1,092
Bandar Lampung	832
Malang	763
IRAN	
Tehran	6,750
Mashhad	1,964
Esfahan	1,221
Tabriz	1,166
Shiraz	1,043
Ahvaz	828
Qom	780
Bakhtaran	666
Karaj	588
IRAQ	
Baghdad	3,841
Diyala	961
As Sulaymaniyah	952
Arbil	770
Al Mawsil	644
Kadhimain	521
IRELAND	
Dublin	1,024
ISRAEL	
Tel Aviv	1,880
Jerusalem	562
ITALY	
Rome	2,688
Milan	1,334
Naples	1,062
Turin	946
Palermo	695
Genoa	660
IVORY COAST	
Abidjan	2,500
JAMAICA	
Kingston	644
JAPAN	
Tokyo–Yokohama	26,836
Osaka	10,601
Nagoya	2,159
Sapporo	1,732
Kobe	1,509
Kyoto	1,452
Fukuoka	1,269
Kawasaki	1,200
Hiroshima	1,102
Kitakyushu	1,020
Sendai	951
Chiba	851
Sakai	806
Kumamoto	640
Okayama	605
Hamamatsu	561
Sagamihara	560
Funabashi	540
Kagoshima	540
Higashiosaka	515
JORDAN	
Amman	1,300
Az-Zarqā	609
KAZAKSTAN	
Almaty	1,151
Qaraghandy	613
KENYA	
Nairobi	2,000
Mombasa	600
KOREA, NORTH	
Pyŏngyang	2,639
Hamhung	775
Chŏngjin	754
Chinnampo	691
Sinŭiju	500
KOREA, SOUTH	
Seoul	11,641
Pusan	3,814
Taegu	2,449
Inchon	2,308
Taejŏn	1,272
Kwangju	1,258
Ulsan	967
Sŏngnam	869
Puch'on	779
Suwŏn	756
Chŏnju	563
KYRGYZSTAN	
Bishkek	584
LATVIA	
Riga	840
LEBANON	
Beirut	1,500
Tripoli	500
LIBYA	
Tripoli	960
LITHUANIA	
Vilnius	576
MACEDONIA	
Skopje	541
MADAGASCAR	
Antananarivo	1,053
MALAYSIA	
Kuala Lumpur	1,145
MALI	
Bamako	746
MAURITANIA	
Nouakchott	600
MEXICO	
Mexico City	15,643
Guadalajara	2,847
Monterrey	2,522
Puebla	1,055
León	872
Ciudad Juárez	798
Tijuana	743
Culiacán Rosales	602
Mexicali	602
Acapulco de Juárez	592
Mérida	557
Chihuahua	530
San Luis Potosí	526
Aguascalientés	506
MOLDOVA	
Chişinău	700
MONGOLIA	
Ulan Bator	619
MOROCCO	
Casablanca	2,943
Rabat-Salé	1,220
Marrakesh	602
Fès	564
MOZAMBIQUE	
Maputo	2,000
NEPAL	
Katmandu	535
NETHERLANDS	
Amsterdam	1,100
Rotterdam	1,074
The Hague	695
Utrecht	546
NEW ZEALAND	
Auckland	929
NICARAGUA	
Managua	974
NIGERIA	
Lagos	10,287
Ibadan	1,365
Ogbomosho	712
Kano	657
NORWAY	
Oslo	714
PAKISTAN	
Karachi	9,863
Lahore	5,085
Faisalabad	1,875
Peshawar	1,676
Gujranwala	1,663
Rawalpindi	1,290
Multan	1,257
Hyderabad	1,107
PARAGUAY	
Asunción	945
PERU	
Lima–Callao	6,601
Callao	638
Arequipa	620
Trujillo	509
PHILIPPINES	
Manila	9,280
Quezon City	1,677
Davao	961
Cebu	688
Caloocan	643
POLAND	
Warsaw	1,638
Lódz	826
Kraków	745
Wroclaw	643
Poznań	582
PORTUGAL	
Lisbon	2,561
Oporto	1,174
ROMANIA	
Bucharest	2,061
RUSSIA	
Moscow	9,233
Petersburg	4,883
Nizhniy Novgorod	1,425
Novosibirsk	1,418
Yekaterinburg	1,347
Samara	1,223
Omsk	1,161
Chelyabinsk	1,125
Kazan	1,092
Ufa	1,092
Perm	1,086
Rostov	1,023
Volgograd	1,000
Krasnoyarsk	914
Voronezh	905
Saratov	899
Togliatti	689
Simbirsk	670
Izhevsk	653
Krasnodar	638
Vladivostok	637
Irkutsk	632
Yaroslavl	631
Khabarovsk	609
Barnaul	596
Novokuznetsk	593
Orenburg	558
Penza	551
Tyumen	550
Tula	535
Ryazan	526
Naberezhnyye-Chelny	524
Kemerovo	513
Astrakhan	512
SAUDI ARABIA	
Riyadh	2,000
Jedda	1,400
Mecca	618
Medina	500
SENEGAL	
Dakar	1,729
SIERRA LEONE	
Freetown	505
SINGAPORE	
Singapore	2,874
SOMALIA	
Mogadishu	1,000
SOUTH AFRICA	
Cape Town	2,350
East Rand	1,379
Johannesburg	1,196
Durban	1,137
Pretoria	1,080
West Rand	870
Port Elizabeth	853
Vanderbijlpark–Vereeniging	774
Soweto	597
Sasolburg	540
SPAIN	
Madrid	3,041
Barcelona	1,631
Valencia	764
Sevilla	714
Zaragoza	607
Málaga	531
SRI LANKA	
Colombo	1,863
SUDAN	
Khartoum	561
Omdurman	526
SWEDEN	
Stockholm	1,553
Göteburg	788
SWITZERLAND	
Zürich	915
SYRIA	
Damascus	2,230
Aleppo	1,640
Homs	644
TAIWAN	
Taipei	2,653
Kaohsiung	1,405
Taichung	817
Tainan	700
Panchiao	544
TAJIKISTAN	
Dushanbe	602
TANZANIA	
Dar-es-Salaam	1,361
THAILAND	
Bangkok	5,876
TOGO	
Lomé	590
TUNISIA	
Tunis	1,827
TURKEY	
Istanbul	7,490
Ankara	3,028
Izmir	2,333
Adana	1,472
Bursa	1,317
Konya	1,040
Gaziantep	930
Icel	908
Antalya	734
Diyarbakir	677
Kocaeli	661
Urfa	649
Kayseri	648
Manisa	641
Hatay	561
Samsun	557
Eskisehir	508
Balikesir	501
UGANDA	
Kampala	773
UKRAINE	
Kiev	2,630
Kharkiv	1,555
Dnipropetrovsk	1,147
Donetsk	1,088
Odesa	1,046
Zaporizhzhya	887
Lviv	802
Kryvyy Rih	720
Mariupol	510
Mykolayiv	508
UNITED KINGDOM	
London	8,089
Birmingham	2,373
Manchester	2,353
Liverpool	852
Glasgow	832
Leeds	529
Newcastle	525
UNITED STATES	
New York	16,329
Los Angeles	12,410
Chicago	7,668
Philadelphia	4,949
Washington, DC	4,466
Detroit	4,307
Houston	3,653
Atlanta	3,331
Boston	3,240
Dallas	2,898
Minneapolis–St Paul	2,688
San Diego	2,632
St Louis	2,536
Phoenix	2,473
Baltimore	2,458
Pittsburgh	2,402
Cleveland	2,222
San Francisco	2,182
Seattle	2,180
Tampa	2,157
Miami	2,025
Denver	1,796
Portland (Or.)	1,676
Kansas City (Mo.)	1,647
Cincinnati	1,581
San Jose	1,557
Norfolk	1,529
Indianapolis	1,462
Milwaukee	1,456
Sacramento	1,441
San Antonio	1,437
Columbus (Oh.)	1,423
New Orleans	1,309
Charlotte	1,260
Buffalo	1,189
Salt Lake City	1,178
Hartford	1,151
Oklahoma	1,007
Jacksonville	665
Omaha	663
Memphis	614
El Paso	579
Austin	514
Nashville	505
URUGUAY	
Montevideo	1,326
UZBEKISTAN	
Tashkent	2,106
VENEZUELA	
Caracas	2,784
Maracaibo	1,364
Valencia	1,032
Maracay	800
Barquisimeto	745
Ciudad Guayana	524
VIETNAM	
Ho Chi Minh City	4,322
Hanoi	3,056
Haiphong	783
YEMEN	
Sana	972
YUGOSLAVIA	
Belgrade	1,137
ZAMBIA	
Lusaka	982
ZIMBABWE	
Harare	1,189
Bulawayo	622

[1] SAR = Special Administrative Region of China

World Statistics: Climate

Rainfall and temperature figures are provided for more than 70 cities around the world. As climate is affected by altitude, the height of each city is shown in metres beneath its name. For each location, the top row of figures shows the total rainfall or snow in millimetres, and the bottom row the average temperature in degrees Celsius; the average annual temperature and total annual rainfall are at the end of the rows. The map opposite shows the city locations.

CITY	JAN.	FEB.	MAR.	APR.	MAY	JUNE	JULY	AUG.	SEPT.	OCT.	NOV.	DEC.	YEAR
EUROPE													
Athens, Greece	62	37	37	23	23	14	6	7	15	51	56	71	402
107 m	10	10	12	16	20	25	28	28	24	20	15	11	18
Berlin, Germany	46	40	33	42	49	65	73	69	48	49	46	43	603
55 m	–1	0	4	9	14	17	19	18	15	9	5	1	9
Istanbul, Turkey	109	92	72	46	38	34	34	30	58	81	103	119	816
14 m	5	6	7	11	16	20	23	23	20	16	12	8	14
Lisbon, Portugal	111	76	109	54	44	16	3	4	33	62	93	103	708
77 m	11	12	14	16	17	20	22	23	21	18	14	12	17
London, UK	54	40	37	37	46	45	57	59	49	57	64	48	593
5 m	4	5	7	9	12	16	18	17	15	11	8	5	11
Málaga, Spain	61	51	62	46	26	5	1	3	29	64	64	62	474
33 m	12	13	16	17	19	29	25	26	23	20	16	13	18
Moscow, Russia	39	38	36	37	53	58	88	71	58	45	47	54	624
156 m	13	–10	–4	6	13	16	18	17	12	6	–1	–7	4
Odesa, Ukraine	57	62	30	21	34	34	42	37	37	13	35	71	473
64 m	–3	–1	2	9	15	20	22	22	18	12	9	1	10
Paris, France	56	46	35	42	57	54	59	64	55	50	51	50	619
75 m	3	4	8	11	15	18	20	19	17	12	7	4	12
Rome, Italy	71	62	57	51	46	37	15	21	63	99	129	93	744
17 m	8	9	11	14	18	22	25	25	22	17	13	10	16
Shannon, Ireland	94	67	56	53	61	57	77	79	86	86	96	117	929
2 m	5	5	7	9	12	14	16	16	14	11	8	6	10
Stockholm, Sweden	43	30	25	31	34	45	61	76	60	48	53	48	554
44 m	–3	–3	–1	5	10	15	18	17	12	7	3	0	7
ASIA													
Bahrain	8	18	13	8	<3	0	0	0	0	0	18	18	81
5 m	17	18	21	25	29	32	33	34	31	28	24	19	26
Bangkok, Thailand	8	20	36	58	198	160	160	175	305	206	66	5	1,397
2 m	26	28	29	30	29	29	28	28	28	28	26	25	28
Beirut, Lebanon	191	158	94	53	18	3	<3	<3	5	51	132	185	892
34 m	14	14	16	18	22	24	27	28	26	24	19	16	21
Bombay (Mumbai), India	3	3	3	<3	18	485	617	340	264	64	13	3	1,809
11 m	24	24	26	28	30	29	27	27	27	28	27	26	27
Calcutta, India	10	31	36	43	140	297	325	328	252	114	20	5	1,600
6 m	20	22	27	30	30	30	29	29	29	28	23	19	26
Colombo, Sri Lanka	89	69	147	231	371	224	135	109	160	348	315	147	2,365
7 m	26	26	27	28	28	27	27	27	27	27	26	26	27
Harbin, China	6	5	10	23	43	94	112	104	46	33	8	5	488
160 m	–18	–15	–5	6	13	19	22	21	14	4	–6	–16	3

CITY	JAN.	FEB.	MAR.	APR.	MAY	JUNE	JULY	AUG.	SEPT.	OCT.	NOV.	DEC.	YEAR
ASIA (continued)													
Ho Chi Minh, Vietnam	15	3	13	43	221	330	315	269	335	269	114	56	1,984
9 m	26	27	29	30	29	28	28	28	27	27	27	26	28
Hong Kong, China	33	46	74	137	292	394	381	361	257	114	43	31	2,162
33 m	16	15	18	22	26	28	28	28	27	25	21	18	23
Jakarta, Indonesia	300	300	211	147	114	97	64	43	66	112	142	203	1,798
8 m	26	26	27	27	27	27	27	27	27	27	27	26	27
Kabul, Afghanistan	31	36	94	102	20	5	3	3	<3	15	20	10	338
1,815 m	–3	–1	6	13	18	22	25	24	20	14	7	3	12
Karachi, Pakistan	13	10	8	3	3	18	81	41	13	<3	3	5	196
4 m	19	20	24	28	30	31	30	29	28	28	24	20	26
Kazalinsk, Kazakstan	10	10	13	13	15	5	5	8	8	10	13	15	125
63 m	–12	–11	–3	6	18	23	25	23	16	8	–1	–7	7
New Delhi, India	23	18	13	8	13	74	180	172	117	10	3	10	640
218 m	14	17	23	28	33	34	31	30	29	26	20	15	25
Omsk, Russia	15	8	8	13	31	51	51	51	28	25	18	20	318
85 m	–22	–19	–12	–1	10	16	18	16	10	1	–11	–18	–1
Shanghai, China	48	58	84	94	94	180	147	142	130	71	51	36	1,135
7 m	4	5	9	14	20	24	28	28	23	19	12	7	16
Singapore	252	173	193	188	173	173	170	196	178	208	254	257	2,413
10 m	26	27	28	28	28	28	28	27	27	27	27	27	27
Tehran, Iran	46	38	46	36	13	3	3	3	3	8	20	31	246
1,220 m	2	5	9	16	21	26	30	29	25	18	12	6	17
Tokyo, Japan	48	74	107	135	147	165	142	152	234	208	97	56	1,565
6 m	3	4	7	13	17	21	25	26	23	17	11	6	14
Ulan Bator, Mongolia	<3	<3	3	5	10	28	76	51	23	5	5	3	208
1,325 m	–26	–21	–13	–1	6	14	16	14	8	–1	–13	–22	–3
Verkhoyansk, Russia	5	5	3	5	8	23	28	25	13	8	8	5	134
100 m	–50	–45	–32	–15	0	12	14	9	2	–15	–38	–48	–17
AFRICA													
Addis Ababa, Ethiopia	<3	3	25	135	213	201	206	239	102	28	<3	0	1,151
2,450 m	19	20	20	20	19	18	18	19	21	22	21	20	20
Antananarivo, Madag.	300	279	178	53	18	8	8	10	18	61	135	287	1,356
1,372 m	21	21	21	19	18	15	14	15	17	19	21	21	19
Cairo, Egypt	5	5	5	3	3	<3	0	0	<3	<3	3	5	28
116 m	13	15	18	21	25	28	28	28	26	24	20	15	22
Cape Town, S. Africa	15	8	18	48	79	84	89	66	43	31	18	10	508
17 m	21	21	20	17	14	13	12	13	14	16	18	19	17
Jo'burg, S. Africa	114	109	89	38	25	8	8	8	23	56	107	125	709
1,665 m	20	20	18	16	13	10	11	13	16	18	19	20	16

CITY	JAN.	FEB.	MAR.	APR.	MAY	JUNE	JULY	AUG.	SEPT.	OCT.	NOV.	DEC.	YEAR
AFRICA (continued)													
Khartoum, Sudan	<3	<3	<3	<3	3	8	53	71	18	5	<3	0	158
390 m	24	25	28	31	33	34	32	31	32	32	28	25	29
Kinshasa, Congo (Z.)	135	145	196	196	158	8	3	3	31	119	221	142	1,354
325 m	26	26	27	27	26	24	23	24	25	26	26	26	25
Lagos, Nigeria	28	46	102	150	269	460	279	64	140	206	69	25	1,836
3 m	27	28	29	28	28	26	26	25	26	26	28	28	27
Lusaka, Zambia	231	191	142	18	3	<3	<3	0	<3	10	91	150	836
1,277 m	21	22	21	21	19	16	16	18	22	24	23	22	21
Monrovia, Liberia	31	56	97	216	516	973	996	373	744	772	236	130	5,138
23 m	26	26	27	27	26	25	24	25	25	25	26	26	26
Nairobi, Kenya	38	64	125	211	158	46	15	23	31	53	109	86	958
820 m	19	19	19	19	18	16	16	16	18	19	18	18	18
Timbuktu, Mali	<3	<3	3	<3	5	23	79	81	38	3	<3	<3	231
301 m	22	24	28	32	34	35	32	30	32	31	28	23	29
Tunis, Tunisia	64	51	41	36	18	8	3	8	33	51	48	61	419
66 m	10	11	13	16	19	23	26	27	25	20	16	11	18
Walvis Bay, Namibia	<3	5	8	3	3	<3	<3	3	<3	<3	<3	<3	23
7 m	19	19	19	18	17	16	15	14	14	15	17	18	18
AUSTRALIA, NEW ZEALAND AND ANTARCTICA													
Alice Springs, Aust.	43	33	28	10	15	13	8	8	8	18	31	38	252
579 m	29	28	25	20	15	12	12	14	18	23	26	28	21
Christchurch, N.Z.	56	43	48	48	66	66	69	48	46	43	48	56	638
10 m	16	16	14	12	9	6	6	7	9	12	14	16	11
Darwin, Australia	386	312	254	97	15	3	<3	3	13	51	119	239	1,491
30 m	29	29	29	29	28	26	25	26	28	29	30	29	28
Mawson, Antarctica	11	30	20	10	44	180	4	40	3	20	0	0	362
14 m	0	–5	–10	–14	–15	–16	–18	–18	–19	–13	–5	–1	–11
Perth, Australia	8	10	20	43	130	180	170	149	86	56	20	13	881
60 m	23	23	22	19	16	14	13	13	15	16	19	22	18
Sydney, Australia	89	102	127	135	127	117	117	76	73	71	73	73	1,181
42 m	22	22	21	18	15	13	12	13	15	18	19	21	17
NORTH AMERICA													
Anchorage, USA	20	18	15	10	13	18	41	66	66	56	25	23	371
40 m	–11	–8	–5	2	7	12	14	13	9	2	–5	–11	2
Chicago, USA	51	51	66	71	86	89	84	81	79	66	61	51	836
251 m	–4	–3	2	9	14	20	23	22	19	12	5	–1	10
Churchill, Canada	15	13	18	23	32	44	46	58	51	43	39	21	402
13 m	–28	–26	–20	–10	–2	6	12	11	5	–2	–12	–22	–7
Edmonton, Canada	25	19	19	22	43	77	89	78	39	17	16	25	466
676 m	–15	–10	–5	4	11	15	17	16	11	6	–4	–10	3
Honolulu, USA	104	66	79	48	25	18	23	28	36	48	64	104	643
12 m	23	18	19	20	22	24	25	26	26	24	22	19	22
Houston, USA	89	76	84	91	119	117	99	99	104	94	89	109	1,171
12 m	12	13	17	21	24	27	28	29	26	22	16	12	21

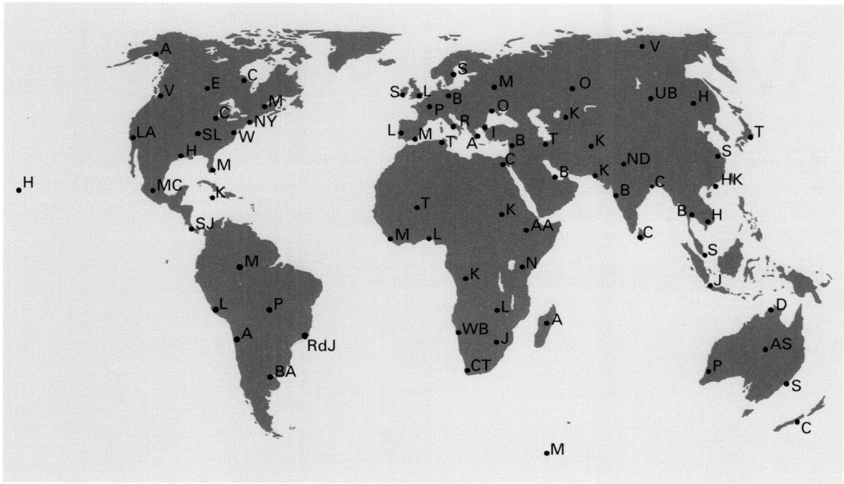

CITY	JAN.	FEB.	MAR.	APR.	MAY	JUNE	JULY	AUG.	SEPT.	OCT.	NOV.	DEC.	YEAR
NORTH AMERICA (continued)													
Kingston, Jamaica	23	15	23	31	102	89	38	91	99	180	74	36	800
34 m	25	25	25	26	26	28	28	28	27	27	26	26	26
Los Angeles, USA	79	76	71	25	10	3	<3	<3	5	15	31	66	381
95 m	13	14	14	16	17	19	21	22	21	18	16	14	17
Mexico City, Mexico	13	5	10	20	53	119	170	152	130	51	18	8	747
2,309 m	12	13	16	18	19	19	17	18	18	16	14	13	16
Miami, USA	71	53	64	81	173	178	155	160	203	234	71	51	1,516
8 m	20	20	22	23	25	27	28	28	27	25	22	21	24
Montréal, Canada	72	65	74	74	66	82	90	92	88	76	81	87	946
57 m	–10	–9	–3	–6	13	18	21	20	15	9	2	–7	6
New York City, USA	94	97	91	81	81	84	107	109	86	89	76	91	1,092
96 m	–1	–1	3	10	16	20	23	23	21	15	7	2	11
St Louis, USA	58	64	89	97	114	114	89	86	81	74	71	64	1,001
173 m	0	1	7	13	19	24	26	26	22	15	8	2	14
San José, Costa Rica	15	5	20	46	229	241	211	241	305	300	145	41	1,798
1,146 m	19	19	21	21	22	21	21	21	21	20	20	19	20
Vancouver, Canada	154	115	101	60	52	45	32	41	67	114	150	182	1,113
14 m	3	5	6	9	12	15	17	17	14	10	6	4	10
Washington, DC, USA	86	76	91	84	94	99	112	109	94	74	66	79	1,064
22 m	1	2	7	12	18	23	25	24	20	14	8	3	13
SOUTH AMERICA													
Antofagasta, Chile	0	0	0	<3	<3	3	5	3	<3	3	<3	0	13
94 m	21	21	20	18	16	15	14	14	15	16	18	19	17
Buenos Aires, Arg.	79	71	109	89	76	61	56	61	79	86	84	99	950
27 m	23	23	21	17	13	9	10	11	13	15	19	22	16
Lima, Peru	3	<3	<3	<3	5	5	8	8	8	3	3	<3	41
120 m	23	24	24	22	19	17	17	16	17	18	19	21	20
Manaus, Brazil	249	231	262	221	170	84	58	38	46	107	142	203	1,811
44 m	28	28	28	27	28	28	28	28	29	29	29	28	28
Paraná, Brazil	287	236	239	102	13	<3	3	5	28	127	231	310	1,582
260 m	23	23	23	23	23	21	21	22	24	24	24	23	23
Rio de Janeiro, Brazil	125	122	130	107	79	53	41	43	66	79	104	137	1,082
61 m	26	26	25	24	22	21	21	21	21	22	23	25	23

World Statistics: Physical Dimensions

Each topic list is divided into continents and within a continent the items are listed in order of size. The order of the continents is as in the atlas, Europe through to South America. The lists down to this mark > are complete; below they are selective. The world top ten are shown in square brackets; in the case of mountains this has not been done because the world top 30 are all in Asia. The figures are rounded as appropriate.

WORLD, CONTINENTS, OCEANS

THE WORLD	km²	miles²	%
The World	509,450,000	196,672,000	–
Land	149,450,000	57,688,000	29.3
Water	360,000,000	138,984,000	70.7
Asia	44,500,000	17,177,000	29.8
Africa	30,302,000	11,697,000	20.3
North America	24,241,000	9,357,000	16.2
South America	17,793,000	6,868,000	11.9
Antarctica	14,100,000	5,443,000	9.4
Europe	9,957,000	3,843,000	6.7
Australia & Oceania	8,557,000	3,303,000	5.7
Pacific Ocean	179,679,000	69,356,000	49.9
Atlantic Ocean	92,373,000	35,657,000	25.7
Indian Ocean	73,917,000	28,532,000	20.5
Arctic Ocean	14,090,000	5,439,000	3.9

SEAS

	km²	miles²
South China Sea	2,974,600	1,148,500
Bering Sea	2,268,000	875,000
Sea of Okhotsk	1,528,000	590,000
East China & Yellow	1,249,000	482,000
Sea of Japan	1,008,000	389,000
Gulf of California	162,000	62,500
Bass Strait	75,000	29,000

ATLANTIC	km²	miles²
Caribbean Sea	2,766,000	1,068,000
Mediterranean Sea	2,516,000	971,000
Gulf of Mexico	1,543,000	596,000
Hudson Bay	1,232,000	476,000
North Sea	575,000	223,000
Black Sea	462,000	178,000
Baltic Sea	422,170	163,000
Gulf of St Lawrence	238,000	92,000

INDIAN	km²	miles²
Red Sea	438,000	169,000
The Gulf	239,000	92,000

MOUNTAINS

EUROPE		m	ft
Mont Blanc	France/Italy	4,807	15,771
Monte Rosa	Italy/Switzerland	4,634	15,203
Dom	Switzerland	4,545	14,911
Liskamm	Switzerland	4,527	14,852
Weisshorn	Switzerland	4,505	14,780
Taschorn	Switzerland	4,490	14,730
Matterhorn/Cervino	Italy/Switz.	4,478	14,691
Mont Maudit	France/Italy	4,465	14,649
Dent Blanche	Switzerland	4,356	14,291
Nadelhorn	Switzerland	4,327	14,196
> Grandes Jorasses	France/Italy	4,208	13,806
Jungfrau	Switzerland	4,158	13,642
Barre des Ecrins	France	4,103	13,461
Gran Paradiso	Italy	4,061	13,323
Piz Bernina	Italy/Switzerland	4,049	13,284
Eiger	Switzerland	3,970	13,025
Monte Viso	Italy	3,841	12,602
Grossglockner	Austria	3,797	12,457
Wildspitze	Austria	3,772	12,382
Monte Disgrazia	Italy	3,678	12,066
Mulhacén	Spain	3,478	11,411
Pico de Aneto	Spain	3,404	11,168
Marmolada	Italy	3,342	10,964
Etna	Italy	3,340	10,958
Zugspitze	Germany	2,962	9,718
Musala	Bulgaria	2,925	9,596
Olympus	Greece	2,917	9,570
Triglav	Slovenia	2,863	9,393
Monte Cinto	France (Corsica)	2,710	8,891
Gerlachovka	Slovak Republic	2,655	8,711
Galdhöpiggen	Norway	2,468	8,100
Hvannadalshnúkur	Iceland	2,119	6,952
Kebnekaise	Sweden	2,117	6,946
Ben Nevis	UK	1,343	4,406

ASIA		m	ft
Everest	China/Nepal	8,848	29,029
K2 (Godwin Austen)	China/Kashmir	8,611	28,251
Kanchenjunga	India/Nepal	8,598	28,208
Lhotse	China/Nepal	8,516	27,939
Makalu	China/Nepal	8,481	27,824
Cho Oyu	China/Nepal	8,201	26,906
Dhaulagiri	Nepal	8,172	26,811
Manaslu	Nepal	8,156	26,758
Nanga Parbat	Kashmir	8,126	26,660
Annapurna	Nepal	8,078	26,502
Gasherbrum	China/Kashmir	8,068	26,469
Broad Peak	China/Kashmir	8,051	26,414
Xixabangma	China	8,012	26,286
Kangbachen	India/Nepal	7,902	25,925
Jannu	India/Nepal	7,902	25,925
Gayachung Kang	Nepal	7,897	25,909
Himalchuli	Nepal	7,893	25,896
Disteghil Sar	Kashmir	7,885	25,869
Nuptse	Nepal	7,879	25,849
Khunyang Chhish	Kashmir	7,852	25,761
Masherbrum	Kashmir	7,821	25,659
Nanda Devi	India	7,817	25,646
Rakaposhi	Kashmir	7,788	25,551
Batura	Kashmir	7,785	25,541
Namche Barwa	China	7,756	25,446
Kamet	India	7,756	25,446
Soltoro Kangri	Kashmir	7,742	25,400
Gurla Mandhata	China	7,728	25,354
Trivor	Pakistan	7,720	25,328
> Kongur Shan	China	7,719	25,324
Tirich Mir	Pakistan	7,690	25,229
K'ula Shan	Bhutan/China	7,543	24,747
Pik Kommunizma	Tajikistan	7,495	24,590
Elbrus	Russia	5,642	18,510
Demavend	Iran	5,604	18,386
Ararat	Turkey	5,165	16,945
Gunong Kinabalu	Malaysia (Borneo)	4,101	13,455
Yu Shan	Taiwan	3,997	13,113
Fuji-San	Japan	3,776	12,388

AFRICA		m	ft
Kilimanjaro	Tanzania	5,895	19,340
Mt Kenya	Kenya	5,199	17,057
Ruwenzori (Margherita)	Uganda/Congo (Z.)	5,109	16,762
Ras Dashan	Ethiopia	4,620	15,157
Meru	Tanzania	4,565	14,977
Karisimbi	Rwanda/Congo (Z.)	4,507	14,787
Mt Elgon	Kenya/Uganda	4,321	14,176
Batu	Ethiopia	4,307	14,130
Guna	Ethiopia	4,231	13,882
Toubkal	Morocco	4,165	13,665
Irhil Mgoun	Morocco	4,071	13,356
Mt Cameroon	Cameroon	4,070	13,353
Amba Ferit	Ethiopia	3,875	13,042
Pico del Teide	Spain (Tenerife)	3,718	12,198
Thabana Ntlenyana	Lesotho	3,482	11,424
Emi Koussi	Chad	3,415	11,204
> Mt aux Sources	Lesotho/S. Africa	3,282	10,768
Mt Piton	Réunion	3,069	10,069

OCEANIA		m	ft
Puncak Jaya	Indonesia	5,029	16,499
Puncak Trikora	Indonesia	4,750	15,584
Puncak Mandala	Indonesia	4,702	15,427
Mt Wilhelm	Papua NG	4,508	14,790
> Mauna Kea	USA (Hawaii)	4,205	13,796
Mauna Loa	USA (Hawaii)	4,170	13,681
Mt Cook (Aoraki)	New Zealand	3,753	12,313
Mt Balbi	Solomon Is.	2,439	8,002
Orohena	Tahiti	2,241	7,352
Mt Kosciuszko	Australia	2,237	7,339

NORTH AMERICA		m	ft
Mt McKinley (Denali)	USA (Alaska)	6,194	20,321
Mt Logan	Canada	5,959	19,551
Citlaltepetl	Mexico	5,700	18,701
Mt St Elias	USA/Canada	5,489	18,008
Popocatepetl	Mexico	5,452	17,887
Mt Foraker	USA (Alaska)	5,304	17,401
Ixtaccihuatl	Mexico	5,286	17,342
Lucania	Canada	5,227	17,149
Mt Steele	Canada	5,073	16,644
Mt Bona	USA (Alaska)	5,005	16,420
Mt Blackburn	USA (Alaska)	4,996	16,391
Mt Sanford	USA (Alaska)	4,940	16,207
Mt Wood	Canada	4,848	15,905
Nevado de Toluca	Mexico	4,670	15,321
Mt Fairweather	USA (Alaska)	4,663	15,298
Mt Hunter	USA (Alaska)	4,442	15,573
Mt Whitney	USA	4,418	14,495
Mt Elbert	USA	4,399	14,432
Mt Harvard	USA	4,395	14,419
Mt Rainier	USA	4,392	14,409
Blanca Peak	USA	4,372	14,344
> Longs Peak	USA	4,345	14,255
Tajumulco	Guatemala	4,220	13,845
Grand Teton	USA	4,197	13,770
Mt Waddington	Canada	3,994	13,104
Mt Robson	Canada	3,954	12,972
Chirripó Grande	Costa Rica	3,837	12,589
Pico Duarte	Dominican Rep.	3,175	10,417

SOUTH AMERICA		m	ft
Aconcagua	Argentina	6,960	22,834
Bonete	Argentina	6,872	22,546
Ojos del Salado	Argentina/Chile	6,863	22,516
Pissis	Argentina	6,779	22,241
Mercedario	Argentina/Chile	6,770	22,211
Huascaran	Peru	6,768	22,204
Llullaillaco	Argentina/Chile	6,723	22,057
Nudo de Cachi	Argentina	6,720	22,047
Yerupaja	Peru	6,632	21,758
N. de Tres Cruces	Argentina/Chile	6,620	21,719
Incahuasi	Argentina/Chile	6,601	21,654
Cerro Galan	Argentina	6,600	21,654
Tupungato	Argentina/Chile	6,570	21,555
Sajama	Bolivia	6,542	21,463
> Illimani	Bolivia	6,485	21,276
Coropuna	Peru	6,425	21,079
Ausangate	Peru	6,384	20,945
Cerro del Toro	Argentina	6,380	20,932
Siula Grande	Peru	6,356	20,853
Chimborazo	Ecuador	6,267	20,561
Alpamayo	Peru	5,947	19,511
Cotapaxi	Ecuador	5,896	19,344
Pico Colon	Colombia	5,800	19,029
Pico Bolivar	Venezuela	5,007	16,427

ANTARCTICA	m	ft
Vinson Massif	4,897	16,066
Mt Kirkpatrick	4,528	14,855
Mt Markham	4,349	14,268

OCEAN DEPTHS

ATLANTIC OCEAN	m	ft	
Puerto Rico (Milwaukee) Deep	9,220	30,249	[7]
Cayman Trench	7,680	25,197	[10]
Gulf of Mexico	5,203	17,070	
Mediterranean Sea	5,121	16,801	
Black Sea	2,211	7,254	
North Sea	660	2,165	
Baltic Sea	463	1,519	
Hudson Bay	258	846	

INDIAN OCEAN	m	ft
Java Trench	7,450	24,442
Red Sea	2,635	8,454
Persian Gulf	73	239

PACIFIC OCEAN	m	ft	
Mariana Trench	11,022	36,161	[1]
Tonga Trench	10,882	35,702	[2]
Japan Trench	10,554	34,626	[3]
Kuril Trench	10,542	34,587	[4]
Mindanao Trench	10,497	34,439	[5]
Kermadec Trench	10,047	32,962	[6]

PACIFIC OCEAN (continued)	m	ft	
Peru–Chile Trench	8,050	26,410	[8]
Aleutian Trench	7,822	25,662	[9]

ARCTIC OCEAN	m	ft
Molloy Deep	5,608	18,399

LAND LOWS

		m	ft
Caspian Sea	Europe	–28	–92
Dead Sea	Asia	–403	–1,322
Lake Asale	Africa	–116	–381
Lake Eyre North	Oceania	–16	–52
Death Valley	N. America	–86	–282
Valdés Peninsula	S. America	–40	–131

RIVERS

EUROPE		km	miles
Volga	Caspian Sea	3,700	2,300
Danube	Black Sea	2,850	1,770
Ural	Caspian Sea	2,535	1,575
Dnepr (Dnipro)	Black Sea	2,285	1,420
Kama	Volga	2,030	1,260
Don	Black Sea	1,990	1,240
Petchora	Arctic Ocean	1,790	1,110
Oka	Volga	1,480	920
Belaya	Kama	1,420	880
Dnister (Dniester)	Black Sea	1,400	870
Vyatka	Kama	1,370	850
Rhine	North Sea	1,320	820
N. Dvina	Arctic Ocean	1,290	800
Desna	Dnepr (Dnipro)	1,190	740
Elbe	North Sea	1,145	710
Wisla	Baltic Sea	1,090	675
Loire	Atlantic Ocean	1,020	635

ASIA		km	miles	
Yangtze	Pacific Ocean	6,380	3,960	[3]
Yenisey–Angara	Arctic Ocean	5,550	3,445	[5]
Huang He	Pacific Ocean	5,464	3,395	[6]
Ob–Irtysh	Arctic Ocean	5,410	3,360	[7]
Mekong	Pacific Ocean	4,500	2,795	[9]
Amur	Pacific Ocean	4,400	2,730	[10]
Lena	Arctic Ocean	4,400	2,730	
Irtysh	Ob	4,250	2,640	
Yenisey	Arctic Ocean	4,090	2,540	
Ob	Arctic Ocean	3,680	2,285	
Indus	Indian Ocean	3,100	1,925	
Brahmaputra	Indian Ocean	2,900	1,800	
Syrdarya	Aral Sea	2,860	1,775	
Salween	Indian Ocean	2,800	1,740	
Euphrates	Indian Ocean	2,700	1,675	
Vilyuy	Lena	2,650	1,645	
Kolyma	Arctic Ocean	2,600	1,615	
Amudarya	Aral Sea	2,540	1,575	
Ural	Caspian Sea	2,535	1,575	
Ganges	Indian Ocean	2,510	1,560	
Si Kiang	Pacific Ocean	2,100	1,305	
Irrawaddy	Indian Ocean	2,010	1,250	
Tarim–Yarkand	Lop Nor	2,000	1,240	
Tigris	Indian Ocean	1,900	1,180	

AFRICA		km	miles	
Nile	Mediterranean	6,670	4,140	[1]
Congo	Atlantic Ocean	4,670	2,900	[8]
Niger	Atlantic Ocean	4,180	2,595	
Zambezi	Indian Ocean	3,540	2,200	
Oubangi/Uele	Congo (Zaïre)	2,250	1,400	
Kasai	Congo (Zaïre)	1,950	1,210	
Shaballe	Indian Ocean	1,930	1,200	
Orange	Atlantic Ocean	1,860	1,155	
Cubango	Okavango Swamps	1,800	1,120	
Limpopo	Indian Ocean	1,600	995	
Senegal	Atlantic Ocean	1,600	995	
Volta	Atlantic Ocean	1,500	930	

AUSTRALIA		km	miles
Murray–Darling	Indian Ocean	3,750	2,330
Darling	Murray	3,070	1,905
Murray	Indian Ocean	2,575	1,600
Murrumbidgee	Murray	1,690	1,050

NORTH AMERICA		km	miles	
Mississippi–Missouri	Gulf of Mexico	6,020	3,740	[4]
Mackenzie	Arctic Ocean	4,240	2,630	
Mississippi	Gulf of Mexico	3,780	2,350	
Missouri	Mississippi	3,780	2,350	
Yukon	Pacific Ocean	3,185	1,980	
Rio Grande	Gulf of Mexico	3,030	1,880	

NORTH AMERICA (continued)		km	miles
Arkansas	Mississippi	2,340	1,450
Colorado	Pacific Ocean	2,330	1,445
Red	Mississippi	2,040	1,270
Columbia	Pacific Ocean	1,950	1,210
Saskatchewan	Lake Winnipeg	1,940	1,205
Snake	Columbia	1,670	1,040
Churchill	Hudson Bay	1,600	990
Ohio	Mississippi	1,580	980
Brazos	Gulf of Mexico	1,400	870
St Lawrence	Atlantic Ocean	1,170	730

SOUTH AMERICA		km	miles	
Amazon	Atlantic Ocean	6,450	4,010	[2]
Paraná–Plate	Atlantic Ocean	4,500	2,800	
Purus	Amazon	3,350	2,080	
Madeira	Amazon	3,200	1,990	
São Francisco	Atlantic Ocean	2,900	1,800	
Paraná	Plate	2,800	1,740	
Tocantins	Atlantic Ocean	2,750	1,710	
Paraguay	Paraná	2,550	1,580	
Orinoco	Atlantic Ocean	2,500	1,550	
Pilcomayo	Paraná	2,500	1,550	
Araguaia	Tocantins	2,250	1,400	
Juruá	Amazon	2,000	1,240	
Xingu	Amazon	1,980	1,230	
Ucayali	Amazon	1,900	1,180	
Maranón	Amazon	1,600	990	
Uruguay	Plate	1,600	990	

LAKES

EUROPE		km²	miles²
Lake Ladoga	Russia	17,700	6,800
Lake Onega	Russia	9,700	3,700
Saimaa system	Finland	8,000	3,100
Vänern	Sweden	5,500	2,100
Rybinskoye Res.	Russia	4,700	1,800

ASIA		km²	miles²	
Caspian Sea	Asia	371,800	143,550	[1]
Aral Sea	Kazakstan/Uzbekistan	33,640	13,000	[6]
Lake Baykal	Russia	30,500	11,780	[9]
Tonlé Sap	Cambodia	20,000	7,700	
Lake Balqash	Kazakstan	18,500	7,100	
Lake Dongting	China	12,000	4,600	
Lake Ysyk	Kyrgyzstan	6,200	2,400	
Lake Orumiyeh	Iran	5,900	2,300	
Lake Koko	China	5,700	2,200	
Lake Poyang	China	5,000	1,900	
Lake Khanka	China/Russia	4,400	1,700	
Lake Van	Turkey	3,500	1,400	

AFRICA		km²	miles²	
Lake Victoria	E. Africa	68,000	26,000	[3]
Lake Tanganyika	C. Africa	33,000	13,000	[7]
Lake Malawi/Nyasa	E. Africa	29,600	11,430	[10]
Lake Chad	C. Africa	25,000	9,700	
Lake Turkana	Ethiopia/Kenya	8,500	3,300	
Lake Volta	Ghana	8,500	3,300	
Lake Bangweulu	Zambia	8,000	3,100	
Lake Rukwa	Tanzania	7,000	2,700	
Lake Mai-Ndombe	Congo (Zaïre)	6,500	2,500	
Lake Kariba	Zambia/Zimbabwe	5,300	2,000	
Lake Albert	Uganda/Congo (Z.)	5,300	2,000	
Lake Nasser	Egypt/Sudan	5,200	2,000	
Lake Mweru	Zambia/Congo (Z.)	4,900	1,900	
Lake Cabora Bassa	Mozambique	4,500	1,700	
Lake Kyoga	Uganda	4,400	1,700	
Lake Tana	Ethiopia	3,630	1,400	

AUSTRALIA		km²	miles²
Lake Eyre	Australia	8,900	3,400
Lake Torrens	Australia	5,800	2,200
Lake Gairdner	Australia	4,800	1,900

NORTH AMERICA		km²	miles²	
Lake Superior	Canada/USA	82,350	31,800	[2]
Lake Huron	Canada/USA	59,600	23,010	[4]
Lake Michigan	USA	58,000	22,400	[5]
Great Bear Lake	Canada	31,800	12,280	[8]
Great Slave Lake	Canada	28,500	11,000	
Lake Erie	Canada/USA	25,700	9,900	
Lake Winnipeg	Canada	24,400	9,400	
Lake Ontario	Canada/USA	19,500	7,500	
Lake Nicaragua	Nicaragua	8,200	3,200	
Lake Athabasca	Canada	8,100	3,100	
Smallwood Reservoir	Canada	6,530	2,520	
Reindeer Lake	Canada	6,400	2,500	
Lake Winnipegosis	Canada	5,400	2,100	
Nettilling Lake	Canada	5,500	2,100	

SOUTH AMERICA		km²	miles²
Lake Titicaca	Bolivia/Peru	8,300	3,200
Lake Poopo	Peru	2,800	1,100

ISLANDS

EUROPE		km²	miles²	
Great Britain	UK	229,880	88,700	[8]
Iceland	Atlantic Ocean	103,000	39,800	
Ireland	Ireland/UK	84,400	32,600	
Novaya Zemlya (N.)	Russia	48,200	18,600	
W. Spitzbergen	Norway	39,000	15,100	
Novaya Zemlya (S.)	Russia	33,200	12,800	
Sicily	Italy	25,500	9,800	
Sardinia	Italy	24,000	9,300	
N.E. Spitzbergen	Norway	15,000	5,600	
Corsica	France	8,700	3,400	
Crete	Greece	8,350	3,200	
Zealand	Denmark	6,850	2,600	

ASIA		km²	miles²	
Borneo	S. E. Asia	744,360	287,400	[3]
Sumatra	Indonesia	473,600	182,860	[6]
Honshu	Japan	230,500	88,980	[7]
Sulawesi (Celebes)	Indonesia	189,000	73,000	
Java	Indonesia	126,700	48,900	
Luzon	Philippines	104,700	40,400	
Mindanao	Philippines	101,500	39,200	
Hokkaido	Japan	78,400	30,300	
Sakhalin	Russia	74,060	28,600	
Sri Lanka	Indian Ocean	65,600	25,300	
Taiwan	Pacific Ocean	36,000	13,900	
Kyushu	Japan	35,700	13,800	
Hainan	China	34,000	13,100	
Timor	Indonesia	33,600	13,000	
Shikoku	Japan	18,800	7,300	
Halmahera	Indonesia	18,000	6,900	
Ceram	Indonesia	17,150	6,600	
Sumbawa	Indonesia	15,450	6,000	
Flores	Indonesia	15,200	5,900	
Samar	Philippines	13,100	5,100	
Negros	Philippines	12,700	4,900	
Bangka	Indonesia	12,000	4,600	
Palawan	Philippines	12,000	4,600	
Panay	Philippines	11,500	4,400	
Sumba	Indonesia	11,100	4,300	
Mindoro	Philippines	9,750	3,800	

AFRICA		km²	miles²	
Madagascar	Indian Ocean	587,040	226,660	[4]
Socotra	Indian Ocean	3,600	1,400	
Réunion	Indian Ocean	2,500	965	
Tenerife	Atlantic Ocean	2,350	900	
Mauritius	Indian Ocean	1,865	720	

OCEANIA		km²	miles²	
New Guinea	Indon./Papua NG	821,030	317,000	[2]
New Zealand (S.)	Pacific Ocean	150,500	58,100	
New Zealand (N.)	Pacific Ocean	114,700	44,300	
Tasmania	Australia	67,800	26,200	
New Britain	Papua NG	37,800	14,600	
New Caledonia	Pacific Ocean	19,100	7,400	
Viti Levu	Fiji	10,500	4,100	
Hawaii	Pacific Ocean	10,450	4,000	
Bougainville	Papua NG	9,600	3,700	
Guadalcanal	Solomon Is.	6,500	2,500	
Vanua Levu	Fiji	5,550	2,100	
New Ireland	Papua NG	3,200	1,200	

NORTH AMERICA		km²	miles²	
Greenland	Atlantic Ocean	2,175,600	839,800	[1]
Baffin Is.	Canada	508,000	196,100	[5]
Victoria Is.	Canada	212,200	81,900	[9]
Ellesmere Is.	Canada	212,000	81,800	[10]
Cuba	Caribbean Sea	110,860	42,800	
Newfoundland	Canada	110,680	42,700	
Hispaniola	Dom. Rep./Haiti	76,200	29,400	
Banks Is.	Canada	67,000	25,900	
Devon Is.	Canada	54,500	21,000	
Melville Is.	Canada	42,400	16,400	
Vancouver Is.	Canada	32,150	12,400	
Somerset Is.	Canada	24,300	9,400	
Jamaica	Caribbean Sea	11,400	4,400	
Puerto Rico	Atlantic Ocean	8,900	3,400	
Cape Breton Is.	Canada	4,000	1,500	

SOUTH AMERICA		km²	miles²
Tierra del Fuego	Argentina/Chile	47,000	18,100
Falkland Is. (East)	Atlantic Ocean	6,800	2,600
South Georgia	Atlantic Ocean	4,200	1,600
Galapagos (Isabela)	Pacific Ocean	2,250	870

Regions in the News

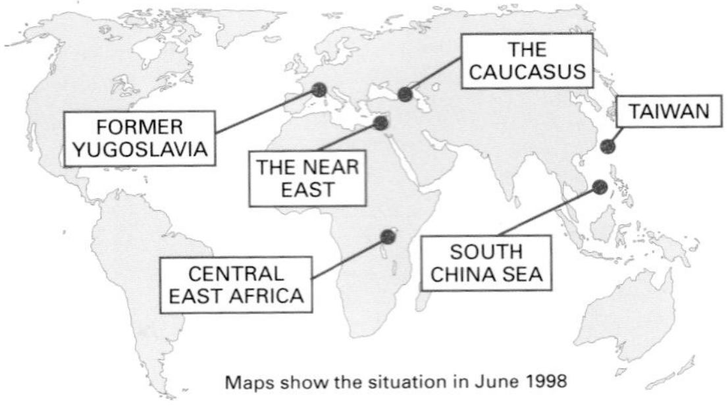

THE BREAK-UP OF YUGOSLAVIA
The former country of Yugoslavia comprised six republics. In 1991 Slovenia and Croatia declared independence. Bosnia-Herzegovina followed in 1992 and Macedonia in 1993. Yugoslavia now comprises the remaining two republics, Serbia and Montenegro.

YUGOSLAVIA
Population: 10,881,000 (Serb 62.6%, Albanian 16.5%, Montenegrin 5%, Hungarian 3.3%, Muslim 3.2%)

Serbia Population: 6,060,000 (Serb 87.7%, excluding the provinces of Kosovo and Vojvodina)

Kosovo Population: 1,989,050 (Albanian 81.6%, Serb 9.9%)

Vojvodina Population: 2,131,900 (Serb 56.8%, Hungarian 16.9%)

Montenegro Population: 700,050 (Montenegrin 61.9%, Muslim 14.6%, Albanian 7%)

CROATIA
Population: 4,850,000 (Croat 78.1%, Serb 12.2%)

SLOVENIA
Population: 2,000,000 (Slovene 88%)

MACEDONIA (F. Y. R. O. M.)
Population: 2,150,000 (Macedonian 64%, Albanian 21.7%, Turkish 5%)

BOSNIA-HERZEGOVINA
Population: 3,600,000 (Muslim 49%, Serb 31.2%, Croat 17.2%)

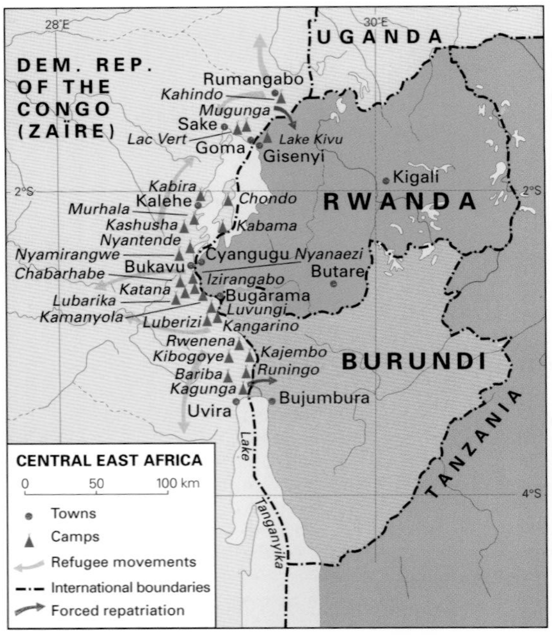

COUNTRIES AND REPUBLICS OF THE CAUCASUS REGION

RUSSIA

North Ossetia (Alania)
Population: 695,000 (Ossetian 53%, Russian 29%, Chechen 5.2%)

Chechenia Population: 1,308,000 (Chechen and Ingush 70.7%, Russian 23.1%, Armenian 1.2%)

Ingushetia (Split from Chechenia in June 1993) Population: 250,000

GEORGIA
Population: 5,450,000 (Georgian 70.1%, Armenian 8.1%, Russian 6.3%, Azerbaijani 5.7%, Ossetian 3%, Greek 2%, Abkhazian 2%)

Abkhazia Population: 537,500 (Georgian 45.7%, Abkhazian 17.8%, Armenian 14.6%, Russian 14.3%)

Ajaria Population: 382,000 (Georgian 82.8%, Russian 7.7%, Armenian 4%)

ARMENIA
Population: 3,800,000 (Armenian 93%, Azerbaijani 3%)

Nagorno-Karabakh Population: 192,400 (Armenian 76.9%, Azerbaijani 21.5%)

AZERBAIJAN
Population: 7,650,000 (Azerbaijani 83%, Russian 6%, Armenian 6%)

Naxçivan Population: 300,400 (Azerbaijani 95.9%)

ISRAEL
Population: 5,900,000 (inc. East Jerusalem and Jewish settlers in the areas under Israeli administration. (Jewish 82%, Arab Muslim 13.8%)

West Bank
Population: 1,122,900 (Palestinian Arabs 97% [of whom Arab Muslim 85%, Jewish 7%, Christian 8%])

Gaza Strip
Population: 748,400 (Arab 98%)

JORDAN
Population: 5,600,000 (Arab 99% [of whom about 50% are Palestinian Arab])

LEBANON
Population: 3,200,000 (Arab 93% [of whom 83% are Lebanese Arab and 10% Palestinian Arab])

The Earth in Space

The Universe 2

Star Charts and Constellations 4

The Solar System 8

The Earth: Time and Motion 10

The Earth from Space 12

The Dynamic Earth 14

Earthquakes and Volcanoes 16

Forces of Nature 18

Oceans and Ice 20

The Earth's Atmosphere 22

Climate and Weather 24

Water and Land Use 26

The Natural World 28

The Human World 30

Languages and Religions 32

International Organizations 34

Agriculture 36

Energy and Minerals 38

World Economies 40

Trade and Commerce 42

Travel and Communications 44

The World Today 46

Glossary of Terms 48

The Universe

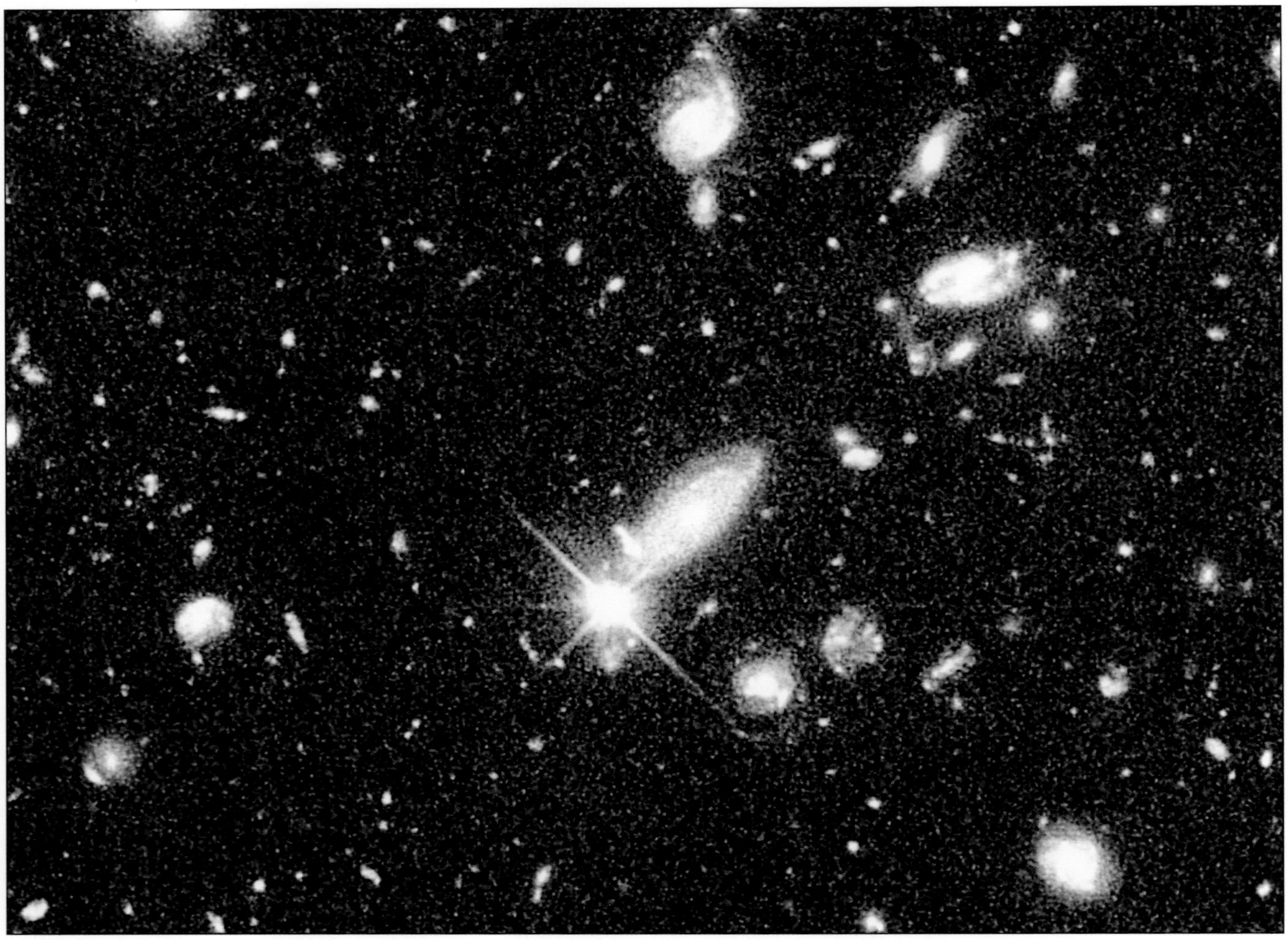

The depths of the Universe

This photograph shows some of the 1,500 or more galaxies that were recorded in the montage of photographs taken by the Hubble Space Telescope in 1995.

THE NEAREST STARS

The 20 nearest stars, excluding the Sun, with their distance from the Earth in light-years.*

Proxima Centauri	4.2
Alpha Centauri A	4.3
Alpha Centauri B	4.3
Barnard's Star	6.0
Wolf 359	7.8
Lalande 21185	8.3
Sirius A	8.7
Sirius B	8.7
UV Ceti A	8.7
UV Ceti B	8.7
Ross 154	9.4
Ross 248	10.3
Epsilon Eridani	10.7
Ross 128	10.9
61 Cygni A	11.1
61 Cygni B	11.1
Epsilon Indi	11.2
Groombridge 34 A	11.2
Groombridge 34 B	11.2
L789-6	11.2

** A light-year equals approximately 9,500 billion km [5,900 billion miles].*

Just before Christmas 1995, the Hubble Space Telescope, which is in orbit about 580 km [360 miles] above the Earth, focused on a tiny area in distant space. Over a ten-day period, photographs taken by the telescope revealed unknown galaxies billions of times fainter than the human eye can see.

Because the light from these distant objects has taken so long to reach us, the photographs transmitted from the telescope and released to the media were the deepest look into space that astronomers have ever seen. The features they revealed were in existence when the Universe was less than a billion years old.

The Hubble Space Telescope is operated by the Space Telescope Science Institute in America and was launched in April 1990. The photographs it took of the Hubble Deep Field have been described by NASA as the biggest advance in astronomy since the work of the Italian scientist Galileo in the early 17th century. US scientists have graphically described the astonishing photographs received from the Telescope as 'postcards from the edge of space and time'.

The Big Bang

According to the latest theories, the Universe was created, and 'time' began, about 15,000 million (or 15 billion) years ago, though other estimates range from 8 to 24 billion years. Following a colossal explosion, called the 'Big Bang', the Universe expanded in the first millionth of a

The End of the Universe

The diagram shows two theories concerning the fate of the Universe. One theory, top, suggests that the Universe will expand indefinitely, moving into an immense dark graveyard. Another theory, bottom, suggests that the galaxies will fall back until everything is again concentrated in one point in a so-called 'Big Crunch'. This might then be followed by a new 'Big Bang'.

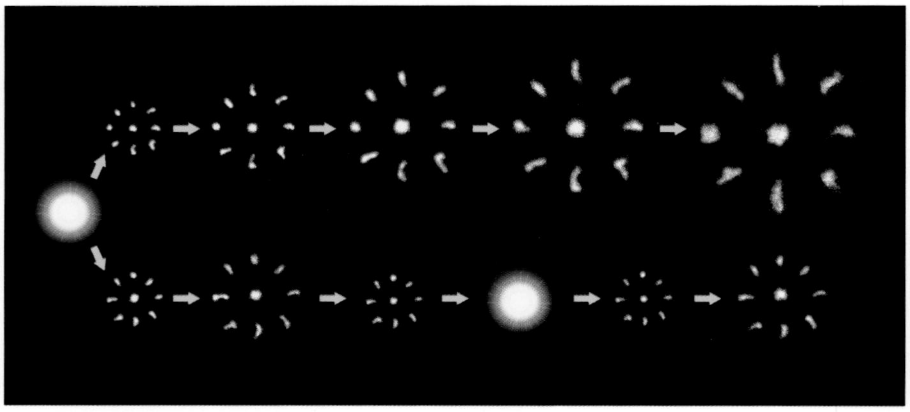

second of its existence from a dimensionless point of infinite mass and density into a fireball, about 30 billion km [19 billion miles] across. The Universe has been expanding ever since, as demonstrated in the 1920s by Edwin Hubble, the American astronomer after whom the Hubble Space Telescope was named.

The temperature at the end of the first second was perhaps 10 billion degrees – far too hot for composite atomic nuclei to exist. As a result, the fireball consisted mainly of radiation mixed with microscopic particles of matter. Almost a million years passed before the Universe was cool enough for atoms to form.

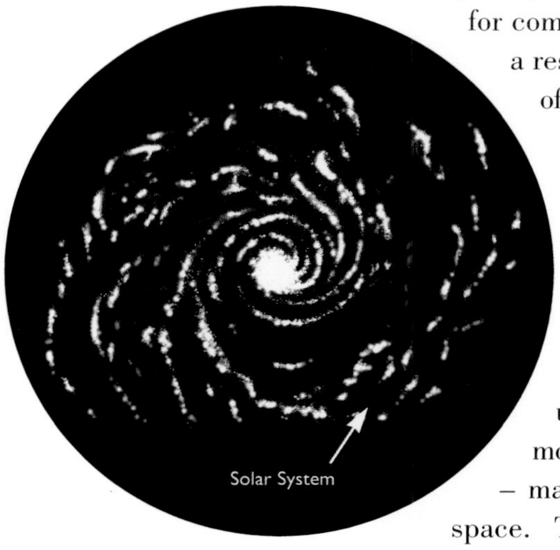

The Home Galaxy
This schematic plan shows that our Solar System is located in one of the spiral arms of the Milky Way galaxy, a little less than 30,000 light-years from its centre. The centre of the Milky Way galaxy is not visible from Earth. Instead, it is masked by light-absorbing clouds of interstellar dust.

A few billion years later, atoms in regions where matter was relatively dense began, under the influence of gravity, to move together to form proto-galaxies – masses of gas separated by empty space. The proto-galaxies were dark, because the Universe had cooled. But a few billion years later, stars began to form within the proto-galaxies as particles were drawn together. The internal pressure produced as matter condensed created the high temperatures required to cause nuclear fusion. Stars were born and later destroyed. Each generation of stars fed on the debris of extinct ones. Each generation produced larger atoms, increasing the number of different chemical elements.

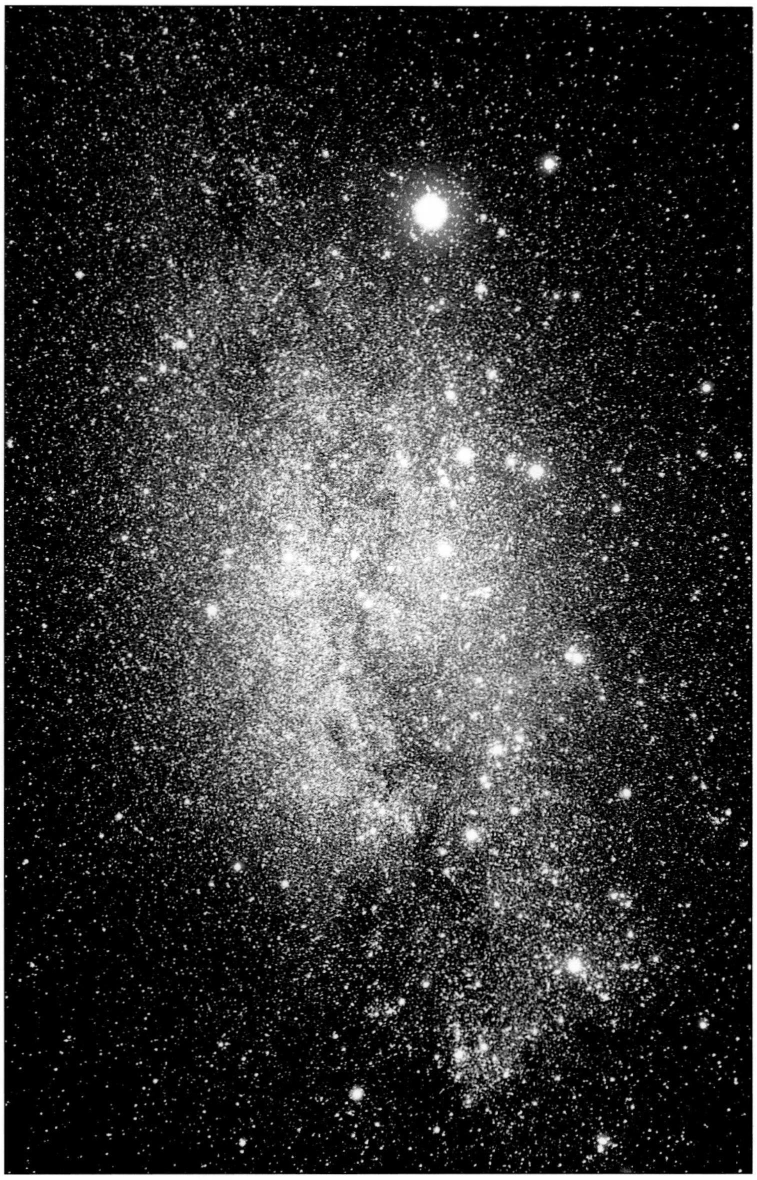

The Milky Way
This section of the Milky Way is dominated by Sirius, the Dog Star, top centre, in the constellation of Canis Major. Sirius is the brightest star in the sky.

The Galaxies

At least a billion galaxies are scattered through the Universe, though the discoveries made by the Hubble Space Telescope suggest that there may be far more than once thought, and some estimates are as high as 100 billion. The largest galaxies contain trillions of stars, while small ones contain less than a billion.

Galaxies tend to occur in groups or clusters, while some clusters appear to be grouped in vast superclusters. Our Local Cluster includes the spiral Milky Way galaxy, whose diameter is about 100,000 light-years; one light-year, the distance that light travels in one year, measures about 9,500 billion km [5,900 billion miles]. The Milky Way is a huge galaxy, shaped like a disk with a bulge at the centre. It is larger, brighter and more massive than many other known galaxies. It contains about 100 billion stars which rotate around the centre of the galaxy in the same direction as the Sun does.

One medium-sized star in the Milky Way galaxy is the Sun. After its formation, about 5 billion years ago, there was enough leftover matter around it to create the planets, asteroids, moons and other bodies that together form our Solar System. The Solar System rotates around the centre of the Milky Way galaxy approximately every 225 million years.

Recent discoveries suggest that other stars similar to our Sun have planets orbiting around them, while evidence from the Hubble Space Telescope suggests that the raw materials from which planets are formed is common in dusty disks around many stars. This provokes one of the most intriguing of all the questions that has ever faced humanity. If there are other planets in the Universe, then do living organisms exist elsewhere?

Before the time of Galileo, people thought that the Earth lay at the centre of the Universe. But we now know that our Solar System and even the Milky Way galaxy are tiny specks in the Universe as a whole. Perhaps our planet is also not unique in being the only one to support intelligent life.

Star Charts and Constellations

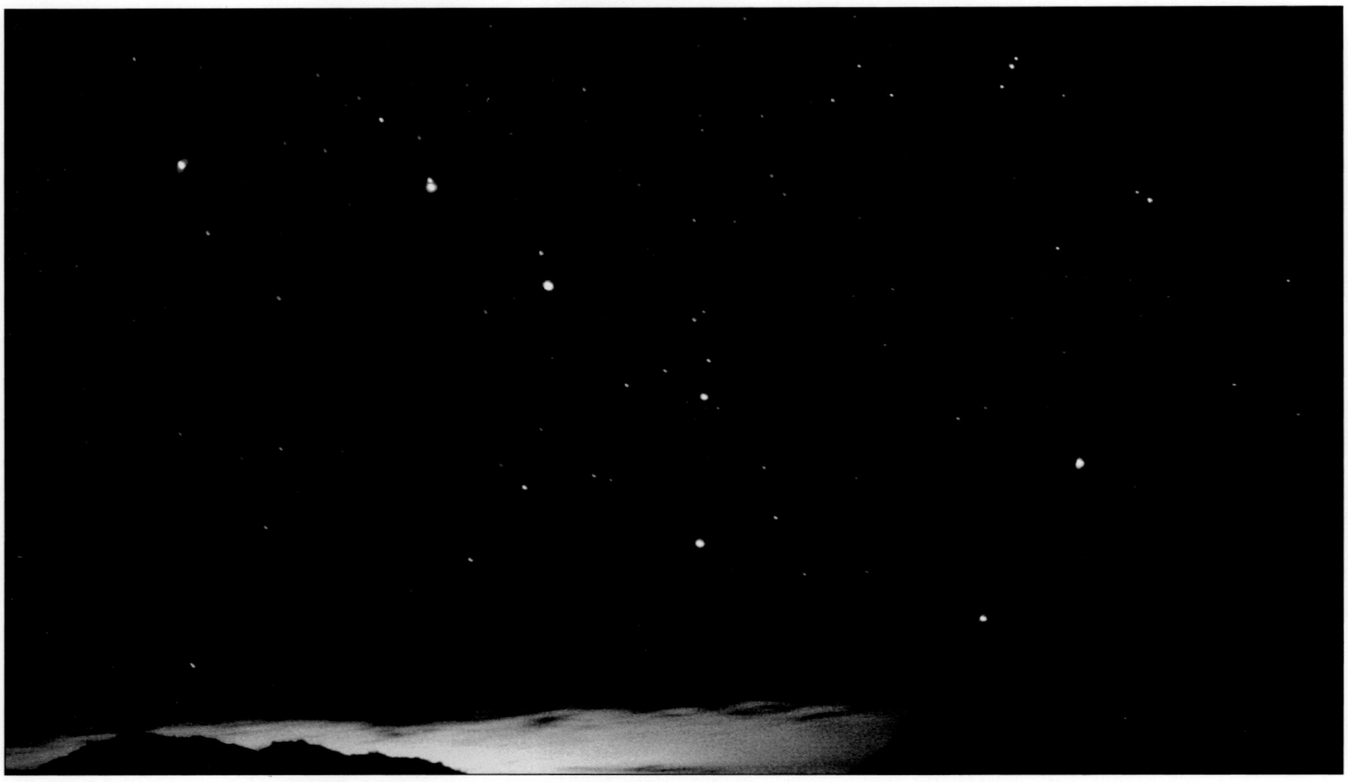

The Plough

The Plough, or Big Dipper, above glowing yellow clouds lit by city lights. It is part of a larger group called Ursa Major one of the best-known constellations of the northern hemisphere. The two bright stars to the lower right of the photograph (Merak and Dubhe) are known as the Pointers because they show the way to the Pole Star.

THE BRIGHTEST STARS

The 15 brightest stars visible from northern Europe. Magnitudes are given to the nearest tenth.

Sirius	−1.5
Arcturus	0.0
Vega	0.0
Capella	0.1
Rigel	0.1
Procyon	0.4
Betelgeuse	0.4
Altair	0.8
Aldebaran	0.8
Antares	1.0
Spica	1.0
Pollux	1.1
Fomalhaut	1.2
Deneb	1.2
Regulus	1.3

On a clear night, under the best conditions and far away from the glare of city lights, a person in northern Europe can look up and see about 2,500 stars. In a town, however, light pollution can reduce visibility to 200 stars or less. Over the whole celestial sphere it is possible to see about 8,500 stars with the naked eye and it is only when you look through a telescope that you begin to realize that the number of stars is countless.

Small and Large Stars

Stars come in several sizes. Some, called neutron stars, are compact, with the same mass as the Sun but with diameters of only about 20 km [12 miles]. Larger than neutron stars are the small white dwarfs. Our Sun is a medium-sized star, but many visible stars in the night sky are giants with diameters between 10 and 100 times that of the Sun, or supergiants with diameters over 100 times that of the Sun.

Two bright stars in the constellation Orion are Betelgeuse (also known as Alpha Orionis) and Rigel (or Beta Orionis). Betelgeuse is an orange-red supergiant, whose diameter is about 400 times that of the Sun. Rigel is also a supergiant. Its diameter is about 50 times that of the Sun, but its luminosity is estimated to be over 100,000 times that of the Sun.

The stars we see in the night sky all belong to our home galaxy, the Milky Way. This name is also used for the faint, silvery band that arches across the sky. This band, a slice through our

THE CONSTELLATIONS

The constellations and their English names. Constellations visible from both hemispheres are listed.

Andromeda	Andromeda	Delphinus	Dolphin	Perseus	Perseus
Antlia	Air Pump	Dorado	Swordfish	Phoenix	Phoenix
Apus	Bird of Paradise	Draco	Dragon	Pictor	Easel
Aquarius	Water Carrier	Equuleus	Little Horse	Pisces	Fishes
Aquila	Eagle	Eridanus	River Eridanus	Piscis Austrinus	Southern Fish
Ara	Altar	Fornax	Furnace	Puppis	Ship's Stern
Aries	Ram	Gemini	Twins	Pyxis	Mariner's Compass
Auriga	Charioteer	Grus	Crane	Reticulum	Net
Boötes	Herdsman	Hercules	Hercules	Sagitta	Arrow
Caelum	Chisel	Horologium	Clock	Sagittarius	Archer
Camelopardalis	Giraffe	Hydra	Water Snake	Scorpius	Scorpion
Cancer	Crab	Hydrus	Sea Serpent	Sculptor	Sculptor
Canes Venatici	Hunting Dogs	Indus	Indian	Scutum	Shield
Canis Major	Great Dog	Lacerta	Lizard	Serpens*	Serpent
Canis Minor	Little Dog	Leo	Lion	Sextans	Sextant
Capricornus	Sea Goat	Leo Minor	Little Lion	Taurus	Bull
Carina	Ship's Keel	Lepus	Hare	Telescopium	Telescope
Cassiopeia	Cassiopeia	Libra	Scales	Triangulum	Triangle
Centaurus	Centaur	Lupus	Wolf	Triangulum Australe	Southern Triangle
Cepheus	Cepheus	Lynx	Lynx		
Cetus	Whale	Lyra	Lyre	Tucana	Toucan
Chamaeleon	Chameleon	Mensa	Table	Ursa Major	Great Bear
Circinus	Compasses	Microscopium	Microscope	Ursa Minor	Little Bear
Columba	Dove	Monoceros	Unicorn	Vela	Ship's Sails
Coma Berenices	Berenice's Hair	Musca	Fly	Virgo	Virgin
Corona Australis	Southern Crown	Norma	Level	Volans	Flying Fish
Corona Borealis	Northern Crown	Octans	Octant	Vulpecula	Fox
Corvus	Crow	Ophiuchus	Serpent Bearer		
Crater	Cup	Orion	Hunter		
Crux	Southern Cross	Pavo	Peacock		
Cygnus	Swan	Pegasus	Winged Horse		

** In two halves: Serpens Caput, the head, and Serpens Cauda, the tail.*

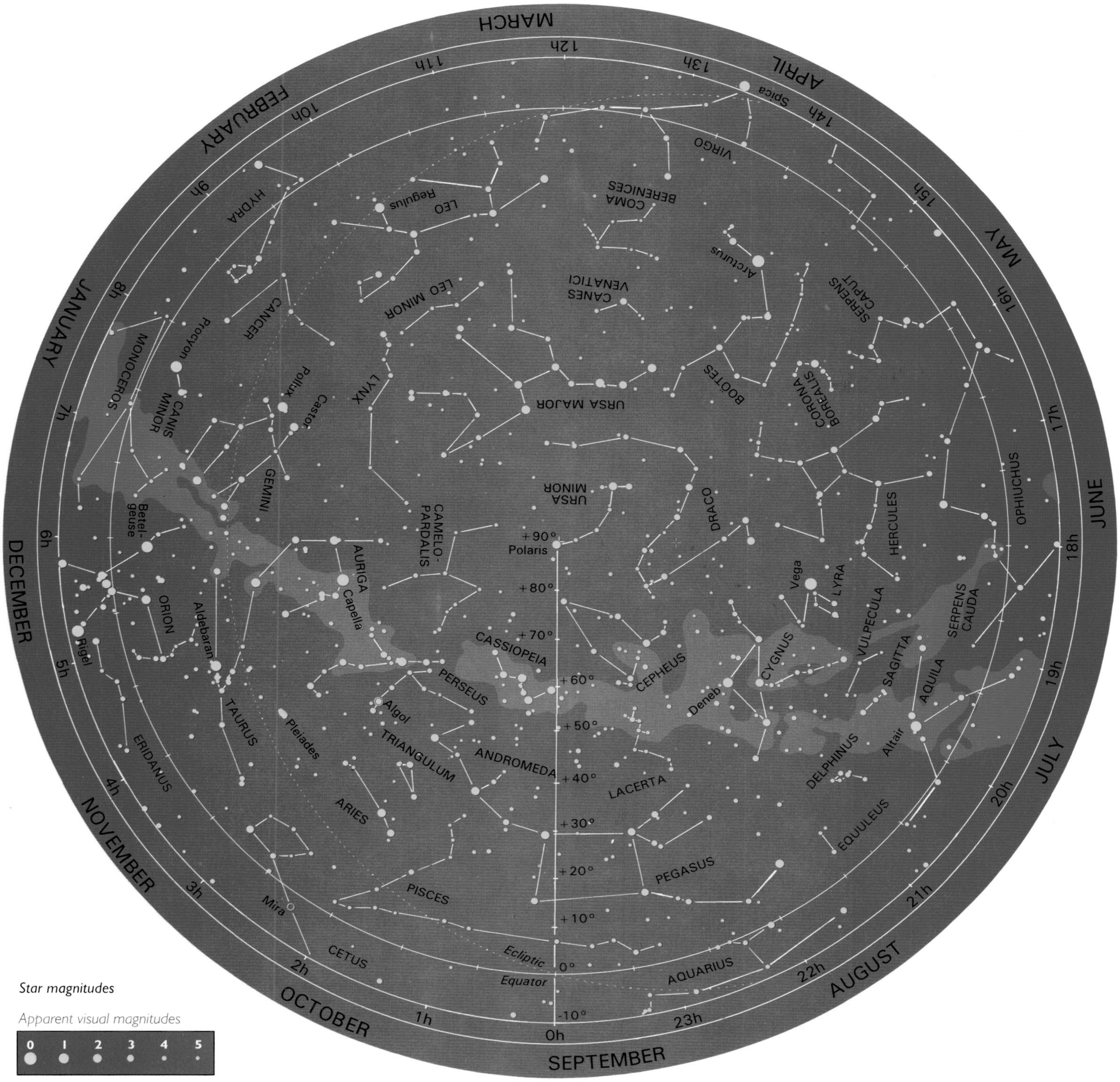

Star magnitudes

Apparent visual magnitudes

0 1 2 3 4 5

The Milky Way is shown in light blue on the above chart.

Star chart of the northern hemisphere

When you look into the sky, the stars seem to be on the inside of a huge dome. This gives astronomers a way of mapping them. This chart shows the sky as it would appear from the North Pole. To use the star chart above, an observer in the northern hemisphere should face south and turn the chart so that the current month appears at the bottom. The chart will then show the constellations on view at approximately 11pm Greenwich Mean Time. The map should be rotated clockwise 15° for each hour before 11pm and anticlockwise for each hour after 11pm.

galaxy, contains an enormous number of stars. The nucleus of the Milky Way galaxy cannot be seen from Earth. Lying in the direction of the constellation Sagittarius in the southern hemisphere, it is masked by clouds of dust.

The Brightness of Stars

Astronomers use a scale of magnitudes to measure the brightness of stars. The brightest visible to the naked eye were originally known as first-magnitude stars, ones not so bright were second-magnitude, down to the faintest visible, which were rated as sixth-magnitude. The brighter the star, the lower the magnitude. With the advent of telescopes and the development of accurate instruments for measuring birightnesses, the magnitude scale has been refined and extended. Very bright bodies such as Sirius, Venus and the Sun have negative magnitudes. The nearest star is Proxima Centauri, part of a multiple star system, which is 4.2 light-years away. Proxima Centauri is very faint and has a magnitude of 11.3. Alpha Centauri A, one of the two brighter members of the system, is the nearest visible star to Earth. It has a magnitude of 1.7.

These magnitudes are what are called apparent magnitudes – measures of the brightnesses of the stars as they appear to us. These are the magnitudes shown on the charts on these pages. But the stars are at very different distances. The star Deneb, in the constellation Cygnus, for example, is over 1,200 light-years away. So astronomers also use absolute magnitudes – measures of how bright the stars really are. A star's absolute magnitude is the apparent magnitude it would have if it could be placed 32.6 light-years away. So Deneb, with an apparent magnitude of 1.2, has an absolute magnitude of –7.2.

The brightest star in the night sky is Sirius, the Dog Star, with a magnitude of –1.5. This medium-sized star is 8.64 light-years distant but it gives out about 20 times as much light as the Sun. After the Sun and the Moon, the brightest objects in the sky are the planets Venus, Mars and Jupiter. For example, Venus has a magnitude of up to –4. The planets have no light of their own however, and shine only because they reflect the Sun's rays. But whilst stars have fixed positions, the planets shift nightly in relation to the constellations, following a path called the Ecliptic (shown on the star charts). As they follow their orbits around the Sun, their distances from the Earth vary, and therefore so also do their magnitudes.

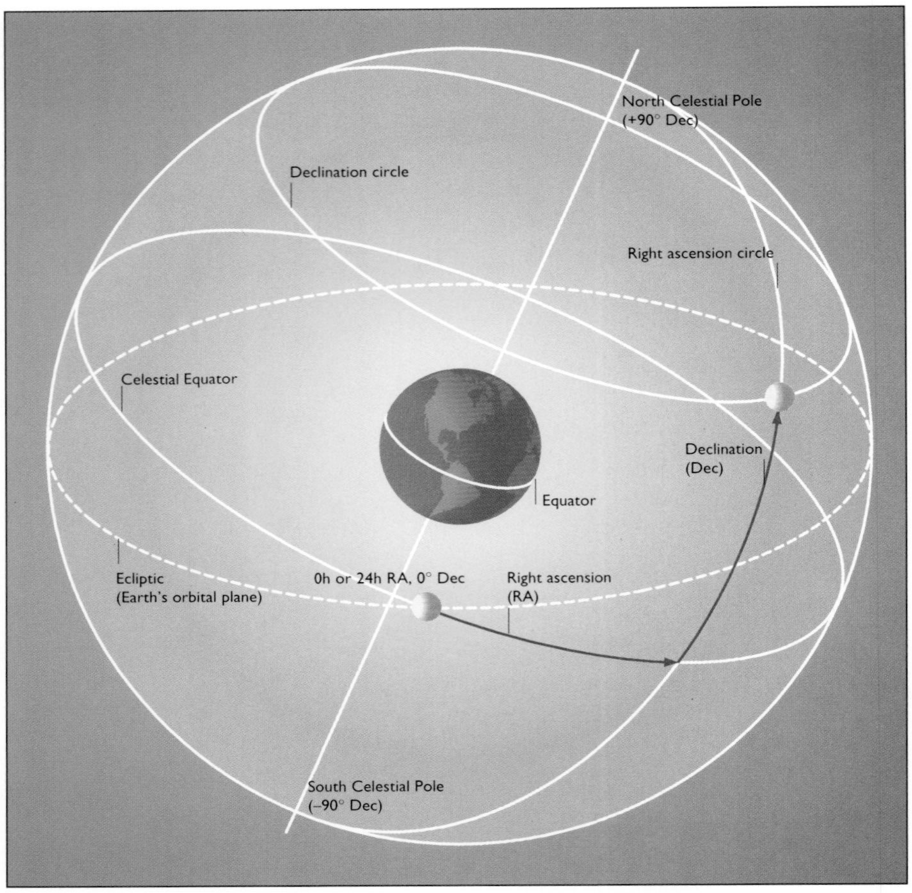

Celestial sphere

The diagram shows the imaginary surface on which astronomical positions are measured. The celestial sphere appears to rotate about the celestial poles, as though an extension of the Earth's own axis. The Earth's axis points towards the celestial poles.

The Southern Cross

The Southern Cross, or Crux, in the southern hemisphere, was classified as a constellation in the 17th century. It is as familiar to Australians and New Zealanders as the Plough is to people in the northern hemisphere. The vertical axis of the Southern Cross points towards the South Celestial Pole.

While atlas maps record the details of the Earth's surface, star charts are a guide to the heavens. An observer at the Equator can see the entire sky at some time during the year, but an observer at the poles can see only the stars in a single hemisphere. As a result, star charts of both hemispheres are produced. The northern hemisphere chart is centred on the North Celestial Pole, while the southern hemisphere chart is centred on the South Celestial Pole.

In the northern hemisphere, the North Pole is marked by the star Polaris, or North Star. Polaris lies within a degree of the point where an extension of the Earth's axis meets the sky. Polaris appears to be stationary and navigators throughout history have used it as a guide. Unfortunately, the South Pole has no convenient reference point.

Star charts of the two hemispheres are bounded by the Celestial Equator, an imaginary line in the sky directly above the terrestrial Equator. Astronomical co-ordinates, which give the location of stars, are normally stated in terms of right ascension (the equivalent of longitude) and declination (the equivalent of latitude). Because the stars appear to rotate around the Earth every 24 hours, right ascension is measured eastwards in hours and minutes. Declination is measured in degrees north or south of the Celestial Equator.

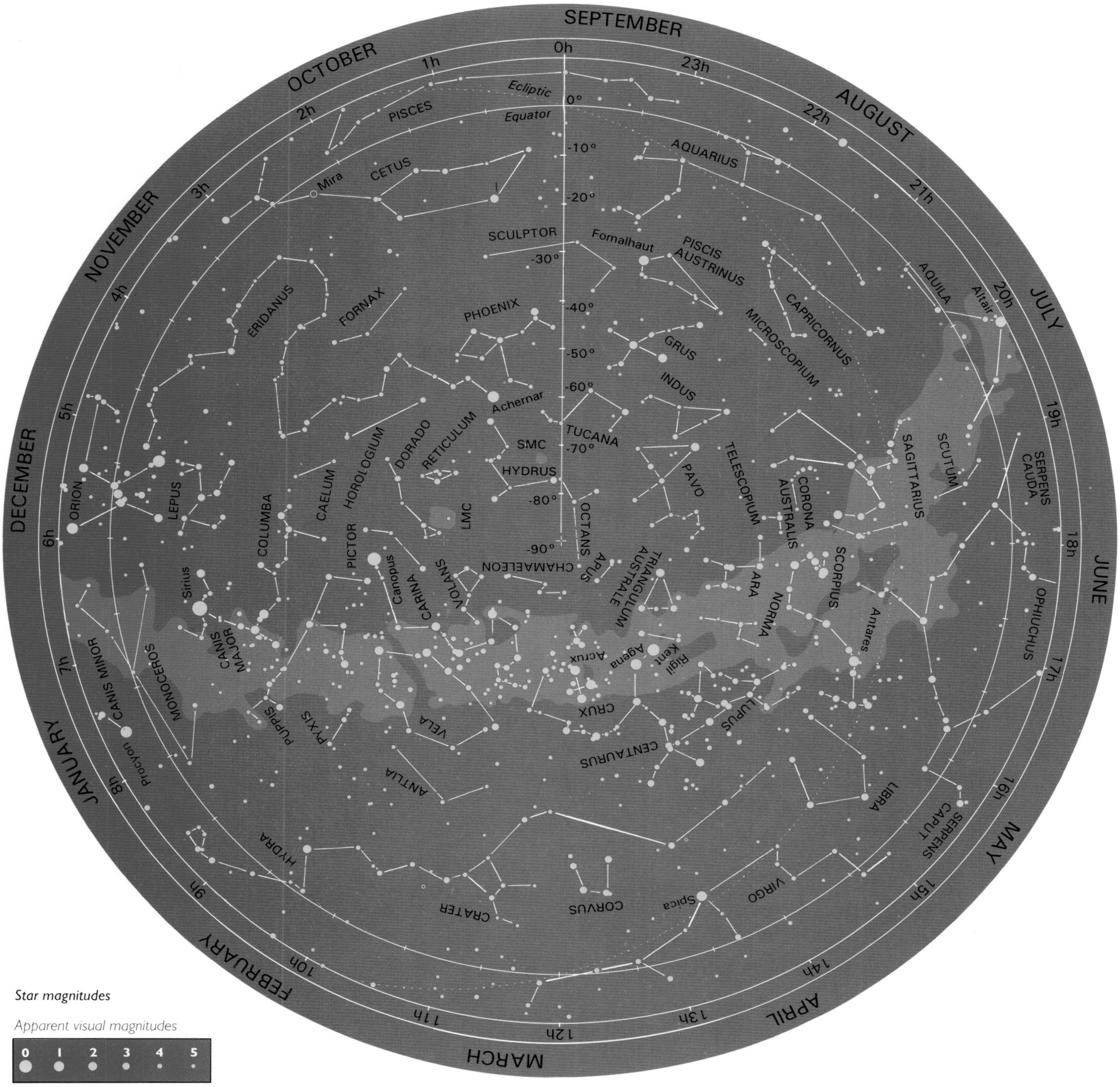

Star magnitudes

Apparent visual magnitudes

0	1	2	3	4	5

The Milky Way is shown in light blue on the above chart.

Star chart of the southern hemisphere

Many constellations in the southern hemisphere were named not by the ancients but by later astronomers. Some, including Antila (Air Pump) and Microscopium (Microscope), have modern names. The Large and Small Magellanic Clouds (LMC, SMC) are small 'satellite' galaxies of the Milky Way. To use the chart, an observer in the southern hemisphere should face north and turn the chart so that the current month appears at the bottom. The map will then show the constellations on view at approximately 11pm Greenwich Mean Time. The chart should be rotated clockwise 15° for each hour before 11pm and anticlockwise for each hour after 11pm.

Constellations

Every star is identifiable as a member of a constellation. The night sky contains 88 constellations, many of which were named by the ancient Greeks, Romans and other early peoples after animals and mythological characters, such as Orion and Perseus. More recently, astronomers invented names for constellations seen in the southern hemisphere, in areas not visible around the Mediterranean Sea.

Some groups of easily recognizable stars form parts of a constellation. For example, seven stars form the shape of the Plough or Big Dipper within the constellation Ursa Major. Such groups are called asterisms.

The stars in constellations lie in the same direction in space, but normally at vastly different distances. Hence, there is no real connection between them. The positions of stars seem fixed, but in fact the shapes of the constellations are changing slowly over very long periods of time. This is because the stars have their own 'proper motions', which because of the huge distances involved are imperceptible to the naked eye.

The Solar System

Although the origins of the Solar System are still a matter of debate, many scientists believe that it was formed from a cloud of gas and dust, the debris from some long-lost, exploded star. Around 5 billion years ago, material was drawn towards the hub of the rotating disk of gas and dust, where it was compressed to thermonuclear fusion temperatures. A new star, the Sun, was born, containing 99.8% of the mass of the Solar System. The remaining material was later drawn together to form the planets and the other bodies in the Solar System. Spacecraft, manned and unmanned, have greatly increased our knowledge of the Solar System since the start of the Space Age in 1957, when the Soviet Union launched the satellite Sputnik I.

The Planets

Mercury is the closest planet to the Sun and the fastest moving. Space probes have revealed that its surface is covered by craters, and looks much like our Moon. Mercury is a hostile place, with no significant atmosphere and temperatures ranging between 400°C [750°F] by day and –170°C [–275°F] by night. It seems unlikely that anyone will ever want to visit this planet.

Venus is much the same size as Earth. But it is the hottest of the planets, with temperatures reaching 475°C [885°F], even at night. The reason for this scorching heat is the atmosphere, which consists mainly of carbon dioxide, a gas that traps heat thus creating a greenhouse effect. The density of the atmosphere is about 90 times that of Earth and dense clouds permanently mask the surface. Active volcanic regions discharging sulphur dioxide may account for the haze of sulphuric acid droplets in the upper atmosphere.

From planet Earth, Venus is brighter than any other star or planet and is easy to spot. It is often the first object to be seen in the evening sky and the last to be seen in the morning sky. It can even be seen in daylight.

Earth, seen from space, looks blue (because of the oceans which cover more than 70% of the planet) and white (a result of clouds in the atmosphere). The atmosphere and water make Earth the only planet known to support life. The Earth's hard outer layers, including the crust and the top of the mantle, are divided into rigid plates. Forces inside the Earth move the plates, modifying the landscape and causing earthquakes and volcanic activity. Weathering and erosion also change the surface.

Mars has many features in common with Earth, including an atmosphere with clouds and polar caps that partly melt in summer. Scientists once considered that it was the most likely planet on which other life might exist, but the two Viking space probes that went there in the 1970s found only a barren rocky surface with no trace of water. But Mars did have flowing water at one time and there are many dry channels – but these are not the fictitious 'canals'. There are also giant, dormant volcanoes.

PLANETARY DATA

Planet	Mean distance from Sun (million km)	Mass (Earth=1)	Period of orbit (Earth yrs)	Period of rotation (Earth days)	Equatorial diameter (km)	Average density (water=1)	Surface gravity (Earth=1)	Number of known satellites
Sun	–	333,000	–	25.38	1,392,000	1.41	28	–
Mercury	57.9	0.055	0.2406	58.67	4,878	5.43	0.38	0
Venus	108.2	0.815	0.6152	243.0	12,100	5.24	0.90	0
Earth	149.6	1.0	1.00	1.00	12,756	5.52	1.00	1
Mars	227.9	0.107	1.88	1.028	6,794	3.93	0.38	2
Jupiter	778.3	317.8	11.86	0.411	142,800	1.33	2.69	18
Saturn	1,426.8	95.2	29.46	0.427	120,000	0.69	1.19	20
Uranus	2,869.4	14.5	84.01	0.748	52,400	1.25	0.93	15
Neptune	4,496.3	17.1	164.8	0.710	48,400	1.64	0.98	8
Pluto	5,900.1	0.002	2447.7	6.39	2,445	1.40	0.05	1

Asteroids are small, rocky bodies. Most of them orbit the Sun between Mars and Jupiter, but some small ones can approach the Earth. The largest is Ceres, 913 km [567 miles] in diameter. There may be around a million asteroids bigger than 1 km [0.6 miles].

Jupiter, the giant planet, lies beyond Mars and the asteroid belt. Its mass is almost three times as much as all the other planets combined and, because of its size, it shines more brightly than any other planet apart from Venus and, occasionally, Mars. The four largest moons of Jupiter were discovered by Galileo. Jupiter is made up mostly of hydrogen and helium, covered by a layer of clouds. Its Great Red Spot is a high-pressure storm. Jupiter made headline news when it was struck by fragments of Comet Shoemaker–Levy 9 in July 1994. This was the greatest collision ever seen by scientists between a planet and another heavenly body. The fragments of the comet that crashed into Jupiter created huge fireballs that caused scars on the planet that remained visible for months after the event.

Saturn is structurally similar to Jupiter but it is best known for its rings. The rings measure about 270,000 km [170,000 miles] across, yet they are no more than a few hundred metres thick. Seen from Earth, the rings seem divided into three main bands of varying brightness, but photographs sent back by the *Voyager* space probes in 1980 and 1981 showed that they are broken up into thousands of thin ringlets composed of ice particles ranging in size from a snowball to an iceberg. The origin of the rings is still a matter of debate.

Uranus was discovered in 1781 by William Herschel who first thought it was a comet. It is broadly similar to Jupiter and Saturn in composition, though its distance from the Sun makes its surface even colder. Uranus is circled by thin rings which were discovered in 1977. Unlike the rings of Saturn, the rings of Uranus are black, which explains why they cannot be seen from Earth.

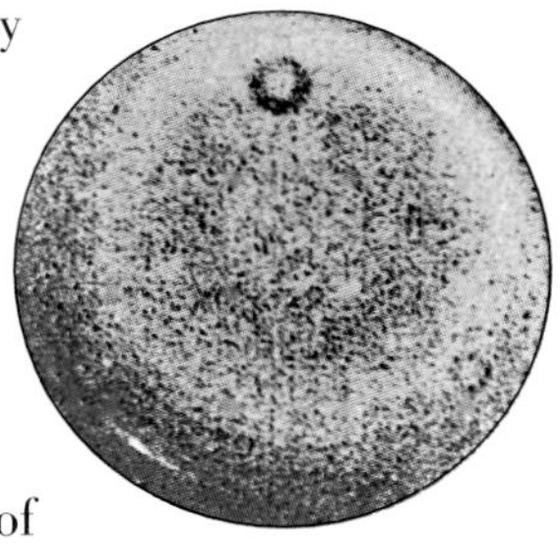

Neptune, named after the mythological sea god, was discovered in 1846 as the result of mathematical predictions made by astronomers to explain irregularities in the orbit of Uranus, its near twin. Little was known about this distant body until *Voyager 2* came close to it in 1989. Neptune has thin rings, like those of Uranus. Among its blue-green clouds is a prominent dark spot, which rotates anticlockwise every 18 hours or so.

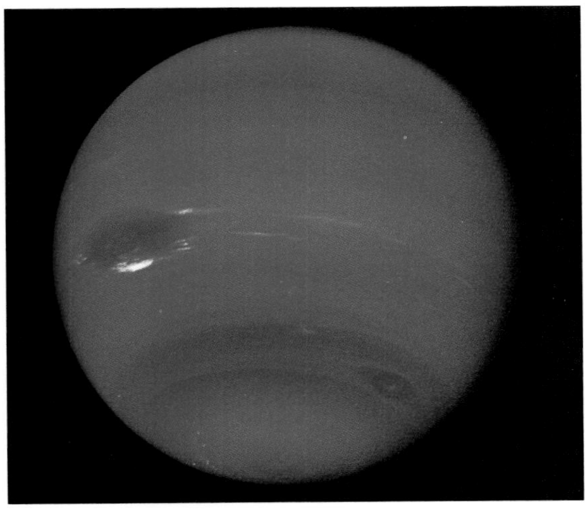

Pluto is the smallest planet in the Solar System, even smaller than our Moon. The American astronomer Clyde Tombaugh discovered Pluto in 1930. Its orbit is odd and it sometimes comes closer to the Sun than Neptune. The nature of Pluto, a gloomy planet appropriately named after the Greek and Roman god of the underworld, is uncertain. At Pluto's distance and beyond are many small, asteroid-like bodies the first of which was found in 1992.

Comets are small icy bodies that orbit the Sun in highly elliptical orbits. When a comet swings in towards the Sun some of its ice evaporates, and the comet brightens and may become visible from Earth. The best known is Halley's Comet, which takes 76 years to orbit the Sun.

The Earth: Time and Motion

The Earth is constantly moving through space like a huge, self-sufficient spaceship. First, with the rest of the Solar System, it moves around the centre of the Milky Way galaxy. Second, it rotates around the Sun at a speed of more than 100,000 km/h [more than 60,000 mph], covering a distance of nearly 1,000 million km [600 million miles] in a little over 365 days. The Earth also spins on its axis, an imaginary line joining the North and South Poles, via the centre of the Earth, completing one turn in a day. The Earth's movements around the Sun determine our calendar, though accurate observations of the stars made by astronomers help to keep our clocks in step with the rotation of the Earth around the Sun.

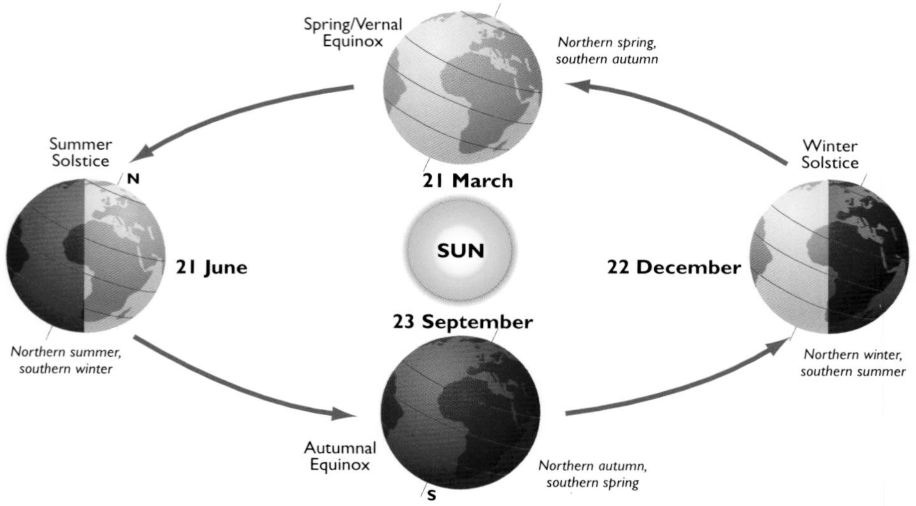

The Seasons

The 23½° tilt of the Earth's axis remains constant as the Earth orbits around the Sun. As a result, first the northern and then the southern hemispheres lean towards the Sun. Annual variations in the amount of sunlight received in turn by each hemisphere are responsible for the four seasons experienced in the middle latitudes.

The Earth from the Moon

In 1969, Neil Armstrong and Edwin 'Buzz' Aldrin Junior were the first people to set foot on the Moon. This superb view of the Earth was taken by the crew of Apollo 11.

The Changing Year

The Earth takes 365 days, 6 hours, 9 minutes and 9.54 seconds to complete one orbit around the Sun. We have a calendar year of 365 days, so allowance has to be made for the extra time over and above the 365 days. This is allowed for by introducing leap years of 366 days. Leap years are generally those, such as 1992 and 1996, which are divisible by four. Century years, however, are not leap years unless they are divisible by 400. Hence, 1700, 1800 and 1900 were not leap years, but the year 2000 will be one. Leap years help to make the calendar conform with the solar year.

Because the Earth's axis is tilted by 23½°, the middle latitudes enjoy four distinct seasons. On 21 March, the vernal or spring equinox in the northern hemisphere, the Sun is directly overhead at the Equator and everywhere on Earth has about 12 hours of daylight and 12 hours of darkness. But as the Earth continues on its journey around the Sun, the northern hemisphere tilts more and more towards the Sun. Finally, on 21 June, the Sun is overhead at the Tropic of Cancer (latitude 23½° North). This is

Tides

The daily rises and falls of the ocean's waters are caused by the gravitational pull of the Moon and the Sun. The effect is greatest on the hemisphere facing the Moon, causing a 'tidal bulge'. The diagram below shows that the Sun, Moon and Earth are in line when the spring tides occur. This causes the greatest tidal ranges. On the other hand, the neap tides occur when the pull of the Moon and the Sun are opposed. Neap tides, when tidal ranges are at their lowest, occur near the Moon's first and third quarters.

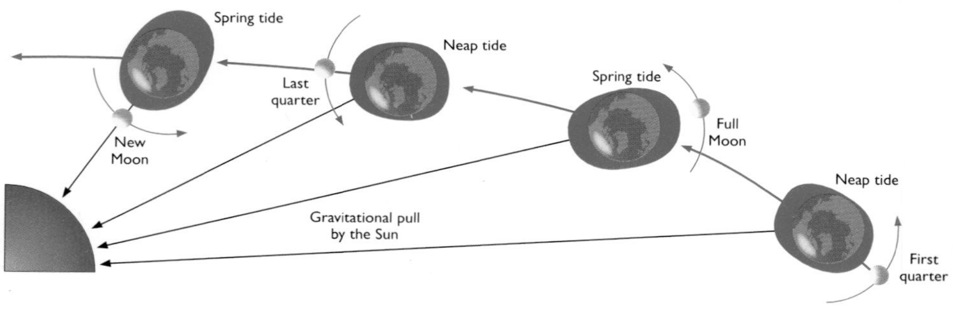

SUN DATA

DIAMETER	1.392×10^{6} km
VOLUME	1.412×10^{18} km^{3}
VOLUME (EARTH = 1)	1.303×10^{6}
MASS	1.989×10^{30} kg
MASS (EARTH = 1)	3.329×10^{6}
MEAN DENSITY (WATER = 1)	1.409
ROTATION PERIOD	
AT EQUATOR	24.25 days
AT POLES	about 35 days
SURFACE GRAVITY (EARTH = 1)	27.9
MAGNITUDE	
APPARENT	–26.9
ABSOLUTE	+4.71
TEMPERATURE	
AT SURFACE	5,400°C [5,700 K]
AT CORE	14×10^{16} K

MOON DATA

DIAMETER	3,476 km
MASS (EARTH = 1)	0.0123
DENSITY (WATER = 1)	3.34
MEAN DISTANCE FROM EARTH	384,402 km
MAXIMUM DISTANCE (APOGEE)	406,740 km
MINIMUM DISTANCE (PERIGEE)	356,410 km
SIDERIAL ROTATION AND REVOLUTION PERIOD	27.322 days
SYNODIC MONTH (NEW MOON TO NEW MOON)	29.531 days
SURFACE GRAVITY (EARTH = 1)	0.165
MAXIMUM SURFACE TEMPERATURE	+130°C [403 K]
MINIMUM SURFACE TEMPERATURE	–158°C [115 K]

the summer solstice in the northern hemisphere.

The overhead Sun then moves south again until on 23 September, the autumn equinox in the northern hemisphere, the Sun is again overhead at the Equator. The overhead Sun then moves south until, on around 22 December, it is overhead at the Tropic of Capricorn. This is the winter solstice in the northern hemisphere, and the summer solstice in the southern, where the seasons are reversed.

At the poles, there are two seasons. During half of the year, one of the poles leans towards the Sun and has continuous sunlight. For the other six months, the pole leans away from the Sun and is in continuous darkness.

Regions around the Equator do not have marked seasons. Because the Sun is high in the sky throughout the year, it is always hot or warm. When people talk of seasons in the tropics, they are usually referring to other factors, such as rainy and dry periods.

Day, Night and Tides

As the Earth rotates on its axis every 24 hours, first one side of the planet and then the other faces the Sun and enjoys daylight, while the opposite side is in darkness.

The length of daylight varies throughout the year. The longest day in the northern hemisphere falls on the summer solstice, 21 June, while the longest day in the southern hemisphere is on 22 December. At 40° latitude, the length of daylight on the longest day is 14 hours, 30 minutes. At 60° latitude, daylight on that day lasts 18 hours, 30 minutes. On the shortest day, 22 December in the northern hemisphere and 21 June in the southern, daylight hours at 40° latitude total 9 hours and 9 minutes. At latitude 60°, daylight lasts only 5 hours, 30 minutes in the 24-hour period.

Tides are caused by the gravitational pull of the Moon and, to a lesser extent, the Sun on the waters in the world's oceans. Tides occur twice every 24 hours, 50 minutes – one complete orbit of the Moon around the Earth.

The highest tides, the spring tides, occur when the Earth, Moon and Sun are in a straight line, so that the gravitational pulls of the Moon and Sun are combined. The lowest, or neap, tides occur when the Moon, Earth and Sun form a right angle. The gravitational pull of the Moon is then opposed by the gravitational pull of the Sun. The greatest tidal ranges occur in the Bay of Fundy in North America. The greatest mean spring range is 14.5 m [47.5 ft].

The speed at which the Earth is spinning on its axis is gradually slowing down, because of the movement of tides. As a result, experts have calculated that, in about about 200 million years, the day will be 25 hours long.

Total eclipse of the Sun

A total eclipse is caused when the Moon passes between the Sun and the Earth. With the Sun's bright disk completely obscured, the Sun's corona, or outer atmosphere, can be viewed.

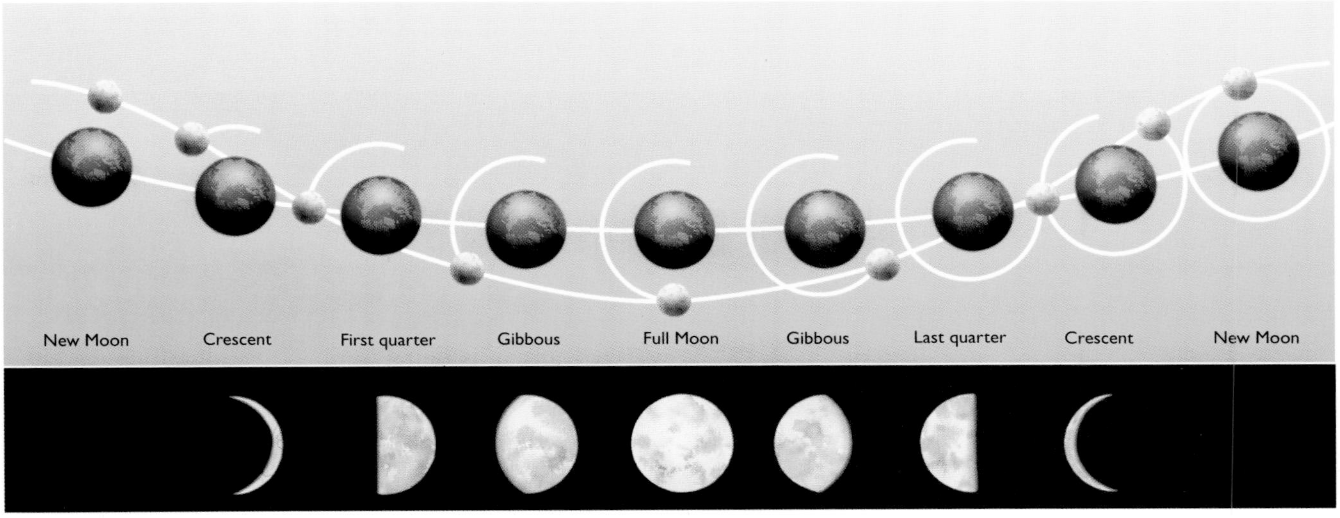

Phases of the Moon

The Moon rotates more slowly than the Earth, making one complete turn on its axis in just over 27 days. This corresponds to its period of revolution around the Earth and, hence, the same hemisphere always faces us. The interval between one full Moon and the next (and also between new Moons) is about 29½ days, or one lunar month. The apparent changes in the appearance of the Moon are caused by its changing position in relation to Earth. Like the planets, the Moon produces no light of its own. It shines by reflecting the Sun's rays, varying from a slim crescent to a full circle and back again.

The Earth from Space

Any last doubts about whether the Earth was round or flat were finally resolved by the appearance of the first photographs of our planet taken at the start of the Space Age. Satellite images also confirmed that map- and globe-makers had correctly worked out the shapes of the continents and the oceans.

More importantly, images of our beautiful, blue, white and brown planet from space impressed on many people that the Earth and its resources are finite. They made people realize that if we allow our planet to be damaged by such factors as overpopulation, pollution and irresponsible over-use of resources, then its future and the survival of all the living things upon it may be threatened.

Views from Above

The first aerial photographs were taken from balloons in the mid-19th century and their importance in military reconnaissance was recognized as early as the 1860s during the American Civil War.

Launch of the Space Shuttle Atlantis

Space Shuttles transport astronauts and equipment into orbit around the Earth. The American Space Shuttle Atlantis, *shown below, launched the Magellan probe, which undertook a radar mapping programme of the surface of Venus in the early 1990s.*

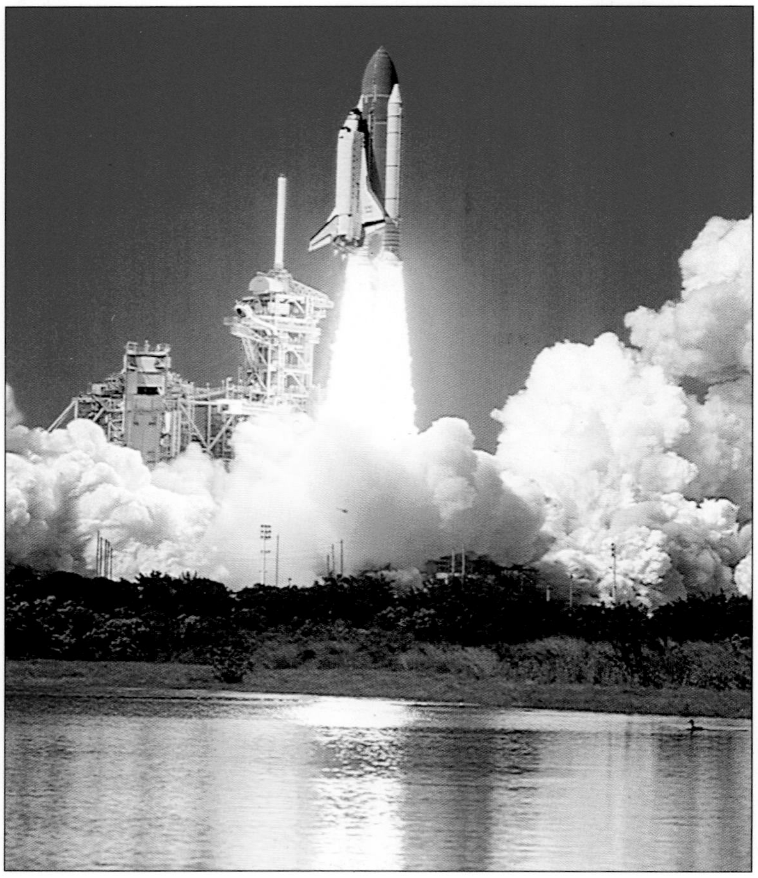

Since the end of World War II, photographs taken by aircraft have been widely used in map-making. The use of air photographs has greatly speeded up the laborious process of mapping land details and they have enabled cartographers to produce maps of the most remote parts of the world.

Aerial photographs have also proved useful because they reveal features that are not visible at ground level. For example, circles that appear on many air photographs do not correspond to visible features on the ground. Many of these mysterious shapes have turned out to be the sites of ancient settlements previously unknown to archaeologists.

Images from Space

Space probes equipped with cameras and a variety of remote sensing instruments have sent back images of distant planets and moons. From these images, detailed maps have been produced, rapidly expanding our knowledge of the Solar System.

Photographs from space are also proving invaluable in the study of the Earth. One of the best known uses of space imagery is the study of the atmosphere. Polar-orbiting weather satellites that circle the Earth, together with geostationary satellites, whose motion is synchronized with the Earth's rotation, now regularly transmit images showing the changing patterns of weather systems from above. Forecasters use these images to track the development and the paths taken by hurricanes, enabling them to issue storm warnings to endangered areas, saving lives and reducing damage to property.

Remote sensing devices are now monitoring changes in temperatures over the land and sea, while photographs indicate the melting of ice sheets. Such evidence is vital in the study of global warming. Other devices reveal polluted areas, patterns of vegetation growth, and areas suffering deforestation.

In recent years, remote sensing devices have been used to monitor the damage being done to the ozone layer in the stratosphere, which prevents most of the Sun's harmful ultraviolet radiation from reaching the surface. The discovery of 'ozone holes', where the protective layer of ozone is being thinned by chlorofluorocarbons (CFCs), chemicals used in the manufacture of such things as air conditioners and refrigerators, has enabled governments to take concerted action to save our planet from imminent danger.

Earth Data

MAXIMUM DISTANCE FROM SUN (APHELION)
152,007,016 km

MINIMUM DISTANCE FROM SUN (PERIHELION)
147,000,830 km

LENGTH OF YEAR – SOLAR TROPICAL (EQUINOX TO EQUINOX)
365.24 days

LENGTH OF YEAR – SIDEREAL (FIXED STAR TO FIXED STAR)
365.26 days

LENGTH OF DAY – MEAN SOLAR DAY
24 hours, 03 minutes, 56 seconds

LENGTH OF DAY – MEAN SIDEREAL DAY
23 hours, 56 minutes, 4 seconds

SUPERFICIAL AREA
510,000,000 km^2

LAND SURFACE
149,000,000 km^2 (29.3%)

WATER SURFACE
361,000,000 km^2 (70.7%)

EQUATORIAL CIRCUMFERENCE
40,077 km

POLAR CIRCUMFERENCE
40,009 km

EQUATORIAL DIAMETER
12,756.8 km

POLAR DIAMETER
12,713.8 km

EQUATORIAL RADIUS
6,378.4 km

POLAR RADIUS
6,356.9 km

VOLUME OF THE EARTH
1,083,230 $\times 10^6$ km^3

MASS OF THE EARTH
5.9 $\times 10^{21}$ tonnes

Satellite image of San Francisco Bay

Unmanned scientific satellites called ERTS (Earth Resources Technology Satellites), or Landsats, were designed to collect information about the Earth's resources. The satellites transmitted images of the land using different wavelengths of light in order to identify, in false colours, such subtle features as areas that contain minerals or areas covered with growing crops, that are not identifiable on simple photographs using the visible range of the spectrum. They were also equipped to monitor conditions in the atmosphere and oceans, and also to detect pollution levels. This Landsat image of San Francisco Bay covers an area of great interest to geologists because it lies in an earthquake zone in the path of the San Andreas fault.

The Dynamic Earth

The Earth was formed about 4.6 billion years ago from the ring of gas and dust left over after the formation of the Sun. As the Earth took shape, lighter elements, such as silicon, rose to the surface, while heavy elements, notably iron, sank towards the centre.

Gradually, the outer layers cooled to form a hard crust. The crust enclosed the dense mantle which, in turn, surrounded the even denser liquid outer and solid inner core. Around the Earth was an atmosphere, which contained abundant water vapour. When the surface cooled, rainwater began to fill hollows, forming the first lakes and seas. Since that time, our planet has been subject to constant change – the result of powerful internal and external forces that still operate today.

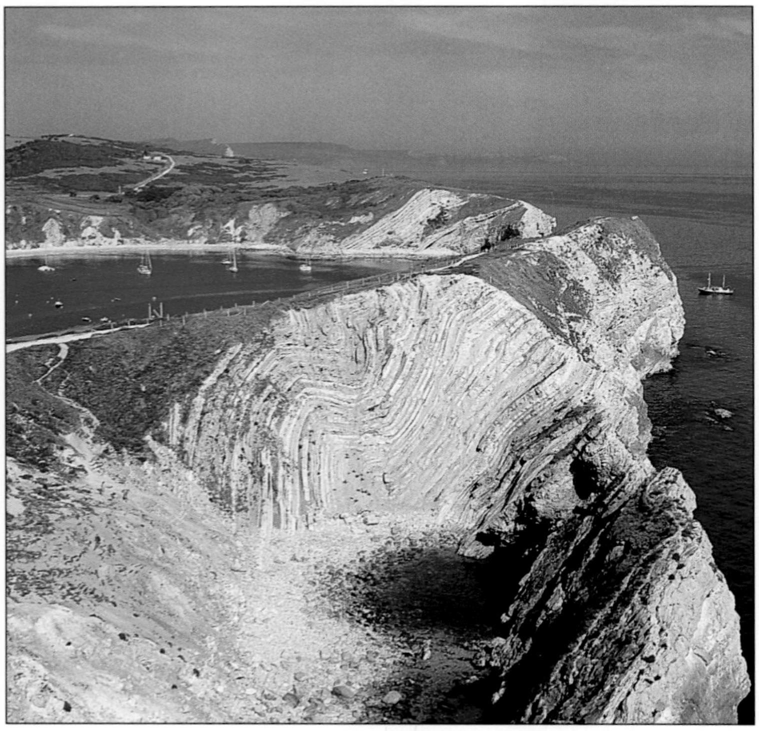

Lulworth Cove, southern England

When undisturbed by earth movements, sedimentary rock strata are generally horizontal. But lateral pressure has squeezed the Jurassic strata at Lulworth Cove into complex folds.

The History of the Earth

From their study of rocks, geologists have pieced together the history of our planet and the life forms that evolved upon it. They have dated the oldest known crystals, composed of the mineral zircon, at 4.2 billion years. But the oldest rocks are younger, less than 4 billion years old. This is because older rocks have been weathered away by natural processes.

The oldest rocks that contain fossils, which are evidence of once-living organisms, are around 3.5 billion years old. But fossils are rare in rocks formed in the first 4 billion years of Earth history. This vast expanse of time is called the Precambrian. This is because it precedes the Cambrian period, at the start of which, about 590 million years ago, life was abundant in the seas.

The Cambrian is the first period in the Paleozoic (or ancient life) era. The Paleozoic era is followed by the Mesozoic (middle life) era, which witnessed the spectacular rise and fall of the dinosaurs, and the Cenozoic (recent life) era, which was dominated by the evolution of mammals. Each of the eras is divided into periods, and the periods in the Cenozoic era, covering the last 65 million years, are further divided into epochs.

The Earth's Changing Face

While life was gradually evolving, the face of the Earth was constantly changing. By piecing together evidence of rock structures and fossils, geologists have demonstrated that around 250 million years ago, all the world's land areas were grouped together in one huge landmass called Pangaea. Around 180 million years ago, the supercontinent Pangaea, began to break up. New oceans opened up as the continents began to move towards their present positions.

Evidence of how continents drift came from studies of the ocean floor in the 1950s and 1960s. Scientists discovered that the oceans are young features. By contrast with the continents, no part of the ocean floor is more than 200 million years old. The floors of oceans older than 200 million years have completely vanished.

Studies of long undersea ranges, called ocean ridges, revealed that the youngest rocks occur along their centres, which are the edges of huge plates – rigid blocks of the Earth's lithosphere, which is made up of the crust and the solid upper layer of the mantle. The Earth's lithosphere is split into six large and several smaller

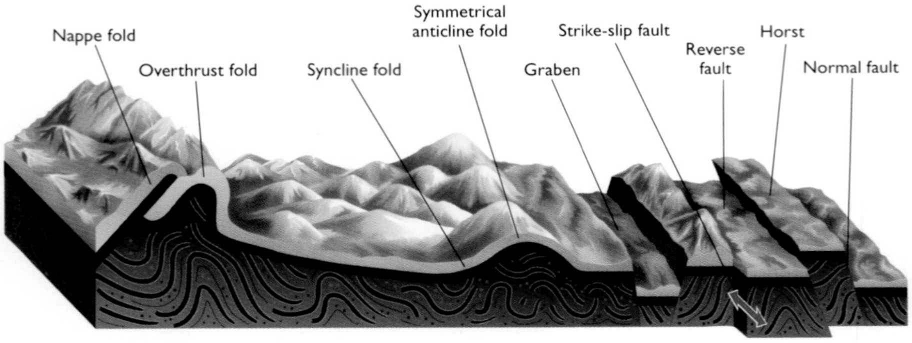

Mountain building

Lateral pressure, which occurs when plates collide, squeezes and compresses rocks into folds. Simple symmetrical upfolds are called anticlines, while downfolds are synclines. As the pressure builds up, strata become asymmetrical and they may be tilted over to form recumbent folds. The rocks often crack under the intense pressure and the folds are sheared away and pushed forward over other rocks. These features are called overthrust folds or nappes. Plate movements also create faults along which rocks move upwards, downwards and sideways. The diagram shows a downfaulted graben, or rift valley, and an uplifted horst, or block mountain.

The Himalayas seen from Nepal
The Himalayas are a young fold mountain range formed by a collision between two plates. The earthquakes felt in the region testify that the plate movements are still continuing.

plates. The ocean ridges are 'constructive' plate margins, because new crustal rock is being formed there from magma that wells up from the mantle as the plates gradually move apart. By contrast, the deep ocean trenches are 'destructive' plate edges. Here, two plates are pushing against each other and one plate is descending beneath the other into the mantle where it is melted and destroyed. Geologists call these areas subduction zones.

A third type of plate edge is called a transform fault. Here two plates are moving alongside each other. The best known of these plate edges is the San Andreas fault in California, which separates the Pacific plate from the North American plate.

Slow-moving currents in the partly molten asthenosphere, which underlies the solid lithosphere, are responsible for moving the plates, a process called plate tectonics.

Geological time scale
The geological time scale was first constructed by a study of the stratigraphic, or relative, ages of layers of rock. But the absolute ages of rock strata could not be fixed until the discovery of radioactivity in the early 20th century. Some names of periods, such as Cambrian (Latin for Wales), come from places where the rocks were first studied. Others, such as Carboniferous, refer to the nature of the rocks formed during the period. For example, coal seams (containing carbon) were formed from decayed plant matter during the Carboniferous period.

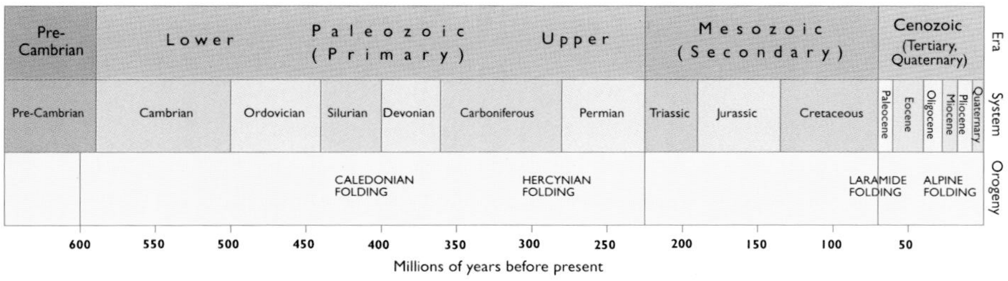

Mountain Building

The study of plate tectonics has helped geologists to understand the mechanisms that are responsible for the creation of mountains. Many of the world's greatest ranges were created by the collision of two plates and the bending of the intervening strata into huge loops, or folds. For example, the Himalayas began to rise around 50 million years ago, when a plate supporting India collided with the huge Eurasian plate. Rocks on the floor of the intervening and long-vanished Tethys Sea were squeezed up to form the Himalayan Mountain Range.

Plate movements also create tension that cracks rocks, producing long faults along which rocks move upwards, downwards or sideways. Block mountains are formed when blocks of rock are pushed upwards along faults. Steep-sided rift valleys are formed when blocks of land sink down between faults. For example, the basin and range region of the south-western United States has both block mountains and down-faulted basins, such as Death Valley.

Earthquakes and Volcanoes

On 4 February 1998, the remote province of Takhar in northern Afghanistan was struck by a devastating earthquake which razed 30 villages to the ground. More than 4,200 people died, and 15,000 more were made homeless. Relief efforts were hampered by strong aftershocks, difficult terrain, poor weather and continuing civil war.

The Restless Earth

Earthquakes can occur anywhere, whenever rocks move along faults. But the most severe and most numerous earthquakes occur near the edges of the plates that make up the Earth's lithosphere. Japan, for example, lies in a particularly unstable region above subduction zones, where plates are descending into the Earth's mantle. It lies in a zone encircling the Pacific Ocean, called the 'Pacific ring of fire'.

Plates do not move smoothly. Their edges are jagged and for most of the time they are locked together. However, pressure gradually builds up until the rocks break and the plates lurch forwards, setting off vibrations ranging from tremors that are recorded only by sensitive instruments to terrifying earthquakes. The greater the pressure released, the more destructive the earthquake.

Earthquakes are also common along the ocean trenches where plates are moving apart, but they mostly occur so far from land that they do little damage. Far more destructive are the earthquakes that occur where plates are moving alongside each other. For example, the earthquakes that periodically rock south-western California are caused by movements along the San Andreas Fault.

The spot where an earthquake originates is called the focus, while the point on the Earth's surface directly above the focus is called the epicentre. Two kinds of waves, P-waves or compressional waves and S-waves or shear waves, travel from the focus to the surface where they make the ground shake. P-waves travel faster than S-waves and the time difference between their arrival at recording stations enables scientists to calculate the distance from a station to the epicentre.

Earthquakes are measured on the Richter scale, which indicates the magnitude of the shock. The most destructive earthquakes are shallow-focus, that is, the focus is within 60 km [37 miles] of the surface. A magnitude of 7.0 is a major earthquake, but earthquakes with a somewhat lower magnitude can cause tremendous damage if their epicentres are on or close to densely populated areas.

San Andreas Fault, United States

Geologists call the San Andreas fault in south-western California a transform, or strike-slip, fault. Sudden movements along it cause earthquakes. In 1906, shifts of about 4.5 metres [15 ft] occurred near San Francisco, causing a massive earthquake.

NOTABLE EARTHQUAKES *(since 1900)*

Year	Location	Mag.
1906	San Francisco, USA	8.3
1906	Valparaiso, Chile	8.6
1908	Messina, Italy	7.5
1915	Avezzano, Italy	7.5
1920	Gansu, China	8.6
1923	Yokohama, Japan	8.3
1927	Nan Shan, China	8.3
1932	Gansu, China	7.6
1934	Bihar, India/Nepal	8.4
1935	Quetta, India†	7.5
1939	Chillan, Chile	8.3
1939	Erzincan, Turkey	7.9
1964	Anchorage, Alaska	8.4
1968	N. E. Iran	7.4
1970	N. Peru	7.7
1976	Guatemala	7.5
1976	Tangshan, China	8.2
1978	Tabas, Iran	7.7
1980	El Asnam, Algeria	7.3
1980	S. Italy	7.2
1985	Mexico City, Mexico	8.1
1988	N. W. Armenia	6.8
1990	N. Iran	7.7
1993	Maharashtra, India	6.4
1994	Los Angeles, USA	6.4
1995	Kobe, Japan	7.2
1995	Sakhalin Is., Russia	7.5
1996	Yunnan, China	7.0
1997	N. E. Iran	7.1
1998	N. Afghanistan	6.1

† now Pakistan

Earthquakes in subduction zones

Along subduction zones, one plate is descending beneath another. The plates are locked together until the rocks break and the descending plate lurches forwards. From the point where the plate moves – the origin – seismic waves spread through the lithosphere, making the ground shake. The earthquake in Mexico City in 1985 occurred in this way.

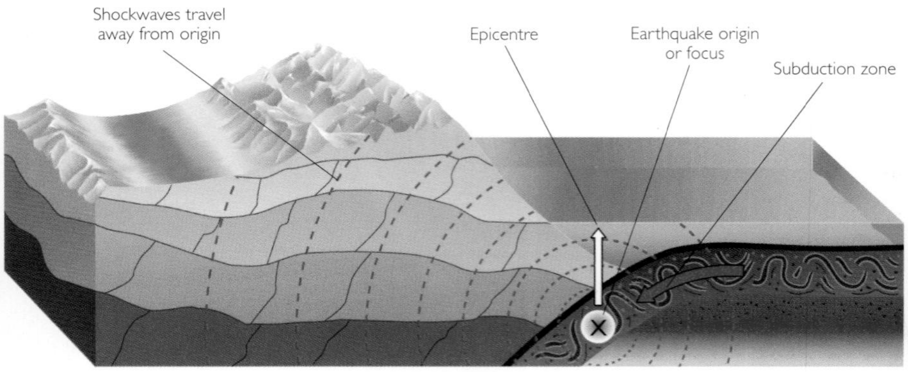

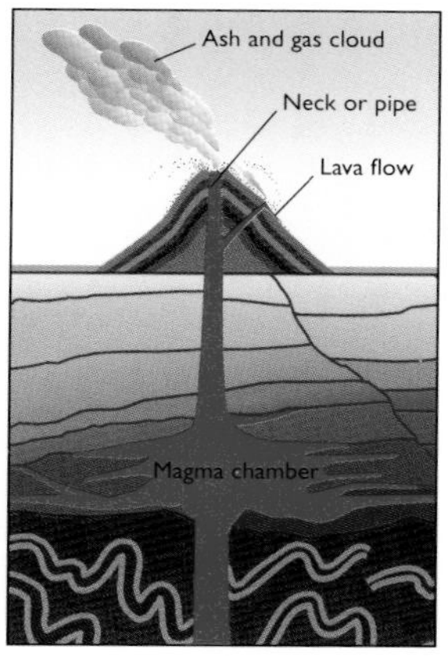

Cross-section of a volcano

Volcanoes are vents in the ground, through which magma reaches the surface. The term volcano is also used for the mountains formed from volcanic rocks. Beneath volcanoes are pockets of magma derived from the semi-molten asthenosphere in the mantle. The magma rises under pressure through the overlying rocks until it reaches the surface. There it emerges through vents as pyroclasts, ranging in size from large lumps of magma, called volcanic bombs, to fine volcanic ash and dust. In quiet eruptions, streams of liquid lava run down the side of the mountain. Side vents sometimes appear on the flanks of existing volcanoes.

Scientists have been working for years to find effective ways of forecasting earthquakes but with very limited success. Following the Kobe earthquake in 1995, many experts argued that they would be better employed developing techniques of reducing the damage caused by earthquakes, rather than pursuing an apparently vain attempt to predict them.

Volcanic Eruptions

Most active volcanoes also occur on or near plate edges. Many undersea volcanoes along the ocean ridges are formed from magma that wells up from the asthenosphere to fill the gaps created as the plates, on the opposite sides of the ridges, move apart. Some of these volcanoes reach the surface to form islands. Iceland is a country which straddles the Mid-Atlantic Ocean Ridge. It is gradually becoming wider as magma rises to the surface through faults and vents. Other volcanoes lie alongside subduction zones. The magma that fuels them comes from the melted edges of the descending plates.

A few volcanoes lie far from plate edges. For example, Mauna Loa and Kilauea on Hawaii are situated near the centre of the huge Pacific plate. The molten magma that reaches the surface is created by a source of heat, called a 'hot spot', in the Earth's mantle.

Magma is molten rock at temperatures of about 1,100°C to 1,200°C [2,012°F to 2,192°F]. It contains gases and superheated steam. The chemical composition of magma varies. Viscous magma is rich in silica and superheated steam, while runny magma contains less silica and steam. The chemical composition of the magma affects the nature of volcanic eruptions.

Explosive volcanoes contain thick, viscous magma. When they erupt, they usually hurl clouds of ash (shattered fragments of cooled magma) into the air. By contrast, quiet volcanoes emit long streams of runny magma, or lava. However, many volcanoes are intermediate in type, sometimes erupting explosively and sometimes emitting streams of fluid lava. Explosive and intermediate volcanoes usually have a conical shape, while quiet volcanoes are flattened, resembling upturned saucers. They are often called shield volcanoes.

One dangerous type of eruption is called a *nuée ardente*, or 'glowing cloud'. It occurs when a cloud of intensely hot volcanic gases and dust particles and superheated steam are exploded from a volcano. They move rapidly downhill, burning everything in their path and choking animals and people. The blast that creates the *nuée ardente* may release the pressure inside the volcano, resulting in a tremendous explosion that hurls tall columns of ash into the air.

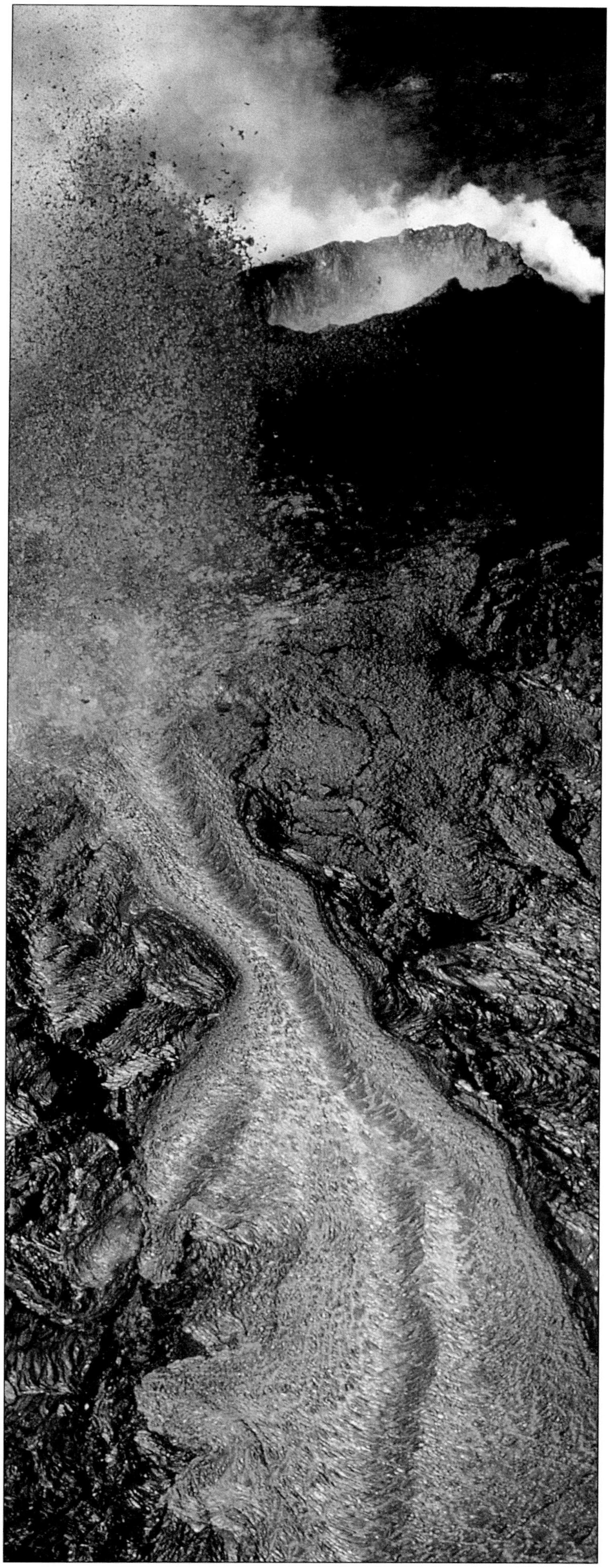

Kilauea Volcano, Hawaii

The volcanic Hawaiian islands in the North Pacific Ocean were formed as the Pacific plate moved over a 'hot spot' in the Earth's mantle. Kilauea on Hawaii emits blazing streams of liquid lava.

Forces of Nature

When the volcano Mount Pinatubo erupted in the Philippines in 1991, large areas around the mountain were covered by ash. Later, rainwater mixed with the loose ash on sloping land, created lahars, or mudflows, which swept down river valleys burying many areas. Such incidents are not only reminders of the great forces that operate inside our planet but also of those natural forces operating on the surface, which can have dramatic effects on the land.

The chief forces acting on the surface of the Earth are weathering, running water, ice and winds. The forces of erosion seem to act slowly. One estimate suggests that an average of only 3.5 cm [1.4 in] of land is removed by natural processes every 1,000 years. This may not sound much, but over millions of years, it can reduce mountains to almost flat surfaces.

RATES OF EROSION

	SLOW ◄	WEATHERING RATE	► FAST
Mineral solubility	low (e.g. quartz)	moderate (e.g. feldspar)	high (e.g. calcite)
Rainfall	low	moderate	heavy
Temperature	cold	temperate	hot
Vegetation	sparse	moderate	lush
Soil cover	bare rock	thin to moderate soil	thick soil

Weathering is the breakdown and decay of rocks in situ. It may be mechanical (physical), chemical or biological.

Rates of erosion
The chart shows that the rates at which weathering takes place depend on the chemistry and hardness of rocks, climatic factors, especially rainfall and temperature, the vegetation and the nature of the soil cover in any area. The effects of weathering are increased by human action, particularly the removal of vegetation and the exposure of soils to the rain and wind.

WEATHERING

Weathering occurs in all parts of the world, but the most effective type of weathering in any area depends on the climate and the nature of the rocks. For example, in cold mountain areas, when water freezes in cracks in rocks, the ice occupies 9% more space than the water. This exerts a force which, when repeated over and over again, can split boulders apart. By contrast, in hot deserts, intense heating by day and cooling by night causes the outer layers of rocks to expand and contract until they break up and peel away like layers of an onion. These are examples of what is called mechanical weathering.

Other kinds of weathering include chemical reactions usually involving water. Rainwater containing carbon dioxide dissolved from the air or the soil is a weak acid which reacts with limestone, wearing out pits, tunnels and networks of caves in layers of limestone rock. Water also combines with some minerals, such as the feldspars in granite, to create kaolin, a white

Grand Canyon, Arizona, at dusk
The Grand Canyon in the United States is one of the world's natural wonders. Eroded by the Colorado River and its tributaries, it is up to 1.6 km [1 mile] deep and 29 km [18 miles] wide.

clay. These are examples of chemical weathering which constantly wears away rock.

Running Water, Ice and Wind

In moist regions, rivers are effective in shaping the land. They transport material worn away by weathering and erode the land. They wear out V-shaped valleys in upland regions, while vigorous meanders widen their middle courses. The work of rivers is at its most spectacular when earth movements lift up flat areas and rejuvenate the rivers, giving them a new erosive power capable of wearing out such features as the Grand Canyon. Rivers also have a constructive role. Some of the world's most fertile regions are deltas and flood plains composed of sediments periodically dumped there by such rivers as the Ganges, Mississippi and Nile.

Glaciers

During Ice Ages, ice spreads over large areas and the effect of glacial erosion on landscapes is enormous. However, during warm periods, the world's ice sheets and glaciers retreat. The chart shows that in recent years, the volumes of many glaciers around the world have been decreasing, possibly as a result of global warming.

ANNUAL FLUCTUATIONS FOR SELECTED GLACIERS

Glacier name and location	Changes in the annual mass balance † 1970–1	1990–1	Cumulative total 1970–90
Alfotbreen, Norway	+940	+790	+12,110
Wolverine, USA	+770	–410	+2,320
Storglaciaren, Sweden	–190	+170	–120
Djankuat, Russia	–230	–310	–1,890
Grasubreen, Norway	+470	–520	–2,530
Ürümqi, China	+102	–706	–3,828
Golubin, Kyrgyzstan	–90	–722	–7,105
Hintereisferner, Austria	–600	–1,325	–9,081
Gries, Switzerland	–970	–1,480	–10,600
Careser, Italy	–650	–1,730	–11,610
Abramov, Tajikistan	–890	–420	–13,700
Sarennes, France	–1,100	–1,360	–15,020
Place, Canada	–343	–990	–15,175

† The annual mass balance is defined as the difference between glacier accumulation and ablation (melting) averaged over the whole glacier. Balances are expressed as water equivalent in millimetres. A plus indicates an increase in the depth or length of the glacier; a minus indicates a reduction.

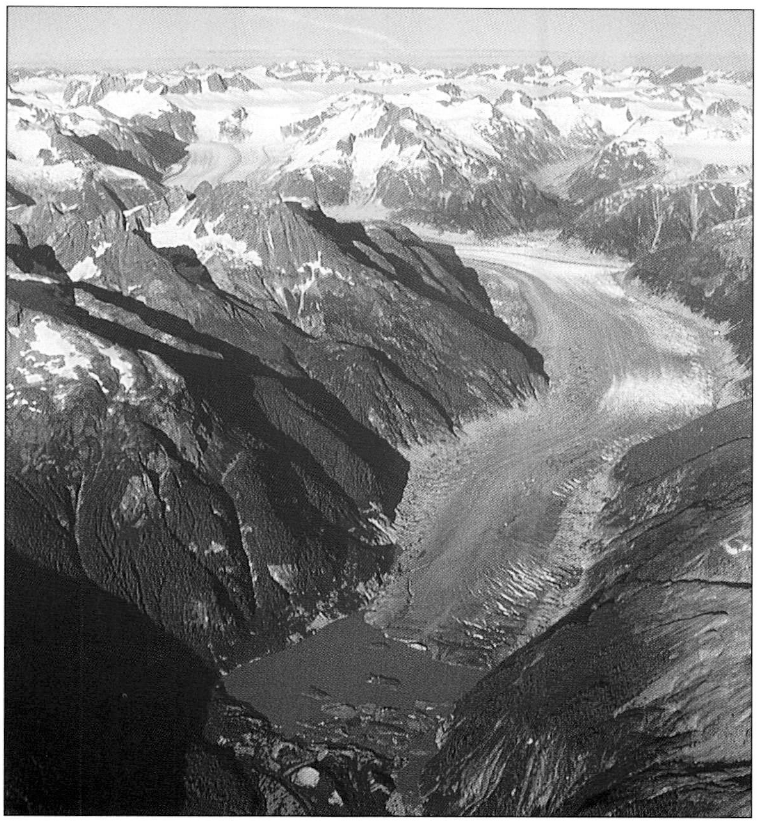

Juneau Glacier, Alaska

Like huge conveyor belts, glaciers transport weathered debris from mountain regions. Rocks frozen in the ice give the glaciers teeth, enabling them to wear out typical glaciated land features.

Running water in the form of sea waves and currents shapes coastlines, wearing out caves, natural arches, and stacks. The sea also transports and deposits worn material to form such features as spits and bars.

Glaciers in cold mountain regions flow downhill, gradually deepening valleys and shaping dramatic landscapes. They erode steep-sided U-shaped valleys, into which rivers often plunge in large waterfalls. Other features include cirques, armchair-shaped basins bounded by knife-edged ridges called *arêtes*. When several glacial cirques erode to form radial *arêtes*, pyramidal peaks like the Matterhorn are created. Deposits of moraine, rock material dumped by the glacier, are further evidence that ice once covered large areas. The work of glaciers, like other agents of erosion, varies with the climate. In recent years, global warming has been making glaciers retreat in many areas, while several of the ice shelves in Antarctica have been breaking up.

Many land features in deserts were formed by running water at a time when the climate was much rainier than it is today. Water erosion also occurs when flash floods are caused by rare thunderstorms. But the chief agent of erosion in dry areas is wind-blown sand, which can strip the paint from cars, and undercut boulders to create mushroom-shaped rocks.

Oceans and Ice

Since the 1970s, oceanographers have found numerous hot vents on the ocean ridges. Called black smokers, the vents emit dark, mineral-rich water reaching 350°C [662°F]. Around the vents are chimney-like structures formed from minerals deposited from the hot water. The discovery of black smokers did not surprise scientists who already knew that the ridges were plate edges, where new crustal rock was being formed as molten magma welled up to the surface. But what was astonishing was that the hot water contained vast numbers of bacteria, which provided the base of a food chain that included many strange creatures, such as giant worms, eyeless shrimps and white clams. Many species were unknown to science.

Little was known about the dark world beneath the waves until about 50 years ago. But through the use of modern technology such as echo-sounders, magnetometers, research ships equipped with huge drills, submersibles that can carry scientists down to the ocean floor, and satellites, the secrets of the oceans have been gradually revealed.

The study of the ocean floor led to the discovery that the oceans are geologically young features – no more than 200 million years old. It also revealed evidence as to how oceans form and continents drift because of the action of plate tectonics.

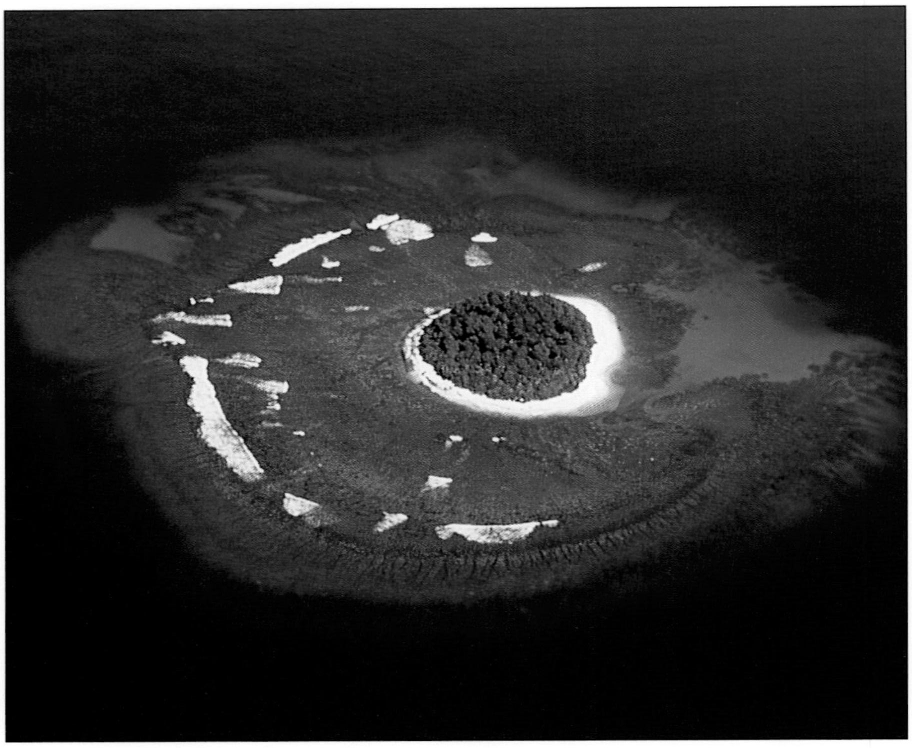

Vava'u Island, Tonga

This small coral atoll in northern Tonga consists of a central island covered by rainforest. Low coral reefs washed by the waves surround a shallow central lagoon.

The Blue Planet

Water covers almost 71% of the Earth, which makes it look blue when viewed from space. Although the oceans are interconnected, geographers divide them into four main areas: the Pacific, Atlantic, Indian and Arctic oceans. The average depth of the oceans is 3,370 m [12,238 ft], but they are divided into several zones.

Around most continents are gently sloping continental shelves, which are flooded parts of the continents. The shelves end at the continental slope, at a depth of about 200 m [656 ft]. This slope leads steeply down to the abyss. The deepest parts of the oceans are the trenches, which reach a maximum depth of 11,033 m [36,198 ft] in the Mariana Trench in the western Pacific.

Most marine life is found in the top 200 m [656 ft], where there is sufficient sunlight for plants, called phytoplankton, to grow. Below this zone, life becomes more and more scarce, though no part of the ocean, even at the bottom of the deepest trenches, is completely without living things.

Continental islands, such as the British Isles, are high parts of the continental shelves. For example, until about 7,500 years ago, when the ice sheets formed during the Ice Ages were melting, raising the sea level and filling the North Sea and the Strait of Dover, Britain was linked to mainland Europe.

By contrast, oceanic islands, such as the Hawaiian chain in the North Pacific Ocean, rise from the ocean floor. All oceanic islands are of volcanic origin, although many of them in warm parts of the oceans have sunk and are capped by layers of coral to form ring- or horseshoe-shaped atolls and coral reefs.

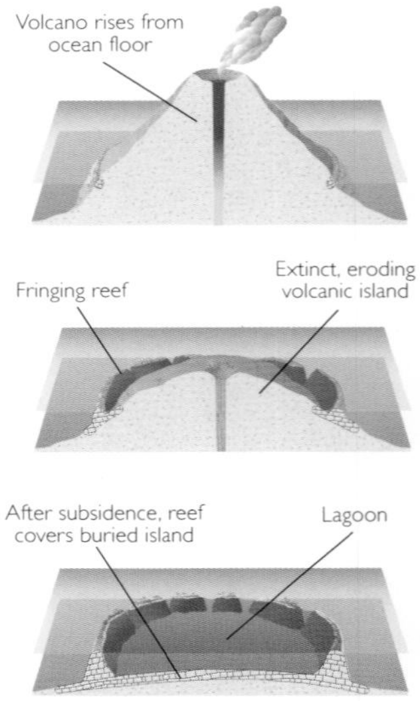

Development of an atoll

Some of the volcanoes that rise from the ocean floor reach the surface to form islands. Some of these islands subside and become submerged. As an island sinks, coral starts to grow around the rim of the volcano, building up layer upon layer of limestone deposits to form fringing reefs. Sometimes coral grows on the tip of a central cone to form an island in the middle of the atoll.

Ocean Water

The oceans contain about 97% of the world's water. Seawater contains more than 70 dissolved elements, but chloride and sodium make up 85% of the total. Sodium chloride is common salt and it makes seawater salty. The salinity of the oceans is mostly between 3.3–3.7%. Ocean water fed by icebergs or large rivers is less saline than shallow seas in the tropics, where the evaporation rate is high. Seawater is a source of salt but the water is useless for agriculture or drinking unless it is desalinated. However, land

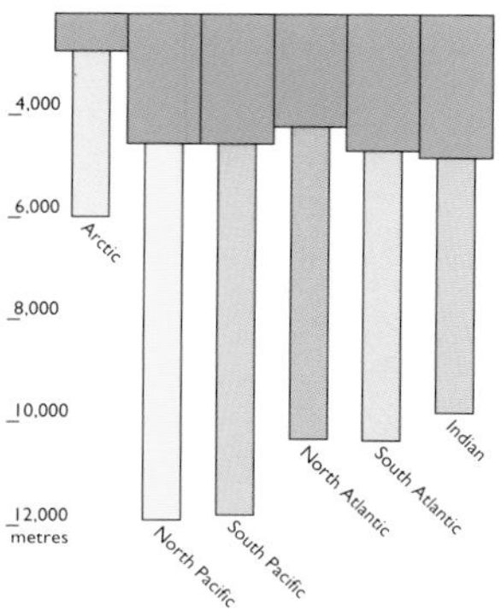

The ocean depths

The diagram shows the average depths (in dark blue) and the greatest depths in the four oceans. The North Pacific Ocean contains the world's deepest trenches, including the Mariana Trench, where the deepest manned descent was made by the bathyscaphe Trieste *in 1960. It reached a depth of 10,916 metres [35,813 ft].*

Relative sizes of the world's oceans:

PACIFIC	49%	ATLANTIC	26%
INDIAN	21%	ARCTIC	4%

Some geographers distinguish a fifth ocean, the Southern or Antarctic Ocean, but most authorities regard these waters as the southern extension of the Pacific, Atlantic and Indian oceans.

areas get a regular supply of fresh water through the hydrological cycle (see page 26).

The density of seawater depends on its salinity and temperature. Temperatures vary from –2°C [28°F], the freezing point of seawater at the poles, to around 30°C [86°F] in parts of the tropics. Density differences help to maintain the circulation of the world's oceans, especially deep-sea currents. But the main cause of currents within 350 m [1,148 ft] of the surface is the wind. Because of the Earth's rotation, currents are deflected, creating huge circular motions of surface water – clockwise in the northern hemisphere and anticlockwise in the southern hemisphere.

Ocean currents transport heat from the tropics to the polar regions and thus form part of the heat engine that drives the Earth's climates. Ocean currents have an especially marked effect on coastal climates, such as north-western Europe. In the mid-1990s, scientists warned that global warming may be weakening currents, including the warm Gulf Stream which is responsible for the mild winters experienced in north-western Europe.

Ice Sheets, Ice Caps and Glaciers

Global warming is also a threat to the world's ice sheets, ice caps and glaciers that together account for about 2% of the world's water. There are two ice sheets in the world, the largest covers most of Antarctica. With the ice reaching maximum depths of 4,800 m [15,748 ft], the Antarctic ice sheet contains about 70% of the world's fresh water, with a total volume about nine times greater than the Greenland ice sheet. Smaller bodies of ice include ice caps in northern Canada, Iceland and Scandinavia. Also throughout the world in high ranges are many valley glaciers, which help to shape dramatic mountain scenery.

Only about 11,000 years ago, during the final phase of the Pleistocene Ice Age, ice covered much of the northern hemisphere. The Ice Age, which began about 1.8 million years ago, was not a continuous period of cold. Instead, it consisted of glacial periods when the ice advanced and warmer interglacial periods when temperatures rose and the ice retreated.

Some scientists believe that we are now living in an inter-glacial period, and that glacial conditions will recur at some time in the future. Others fear the opposite, that global warming, caused mainly by pollution, may melt the world's ice, raising sea levels by up to 55 m [180 ft]. Many fertile and densely populated coastal plains, islands and great cities would vanish from the map.

Weddell Sea, Antarctica

Antarctica contains two huge bays, occupied by the Ross and Weddell seas. Ice shelves extend from the ice sheet across parts of these seas. Pack ice covers the open sea in winter.

The Earth's Atmosphere

Since the discovery in 1985 of a thinning of the ozone layer, creating a so-called 'ozone hole', over Antarctica, many governments have worked to reduce the emissions of ozone-eating substances, notably the chlorofluorocarbons (CFCs) used in aerosols, refrigeration, air conditioning and dry cleaning.

Following forecasts that the ozone layer would rapidly repair itself as a result of controls on these emissions, scientists were surprised in early 1996 when a marked thinning of the ozone layer occurred over the Arctic, northern Europe, Russia and Canada. The damage, which was recorded as far south as southern Britain, was due to pollution combined with intense cold in the stratosphere. It was another sharp reminder of the dangers humanity faces when it interferes with and harms the environment.

The ozone layer in the stratosphere blocks out most of the dangerous ultraviolet B radiation in the Sun's rays. This radiation causes skin cancer and cataracts, as well as harming plants on the land and plankton in the oceans. The ozone layer is only one way in which the atmosphere protects life on Earth. The atmosphere also provides the air we breathe and the carbon dioxide required by plants. It is also a shield against meteors and it acts as a blanket to prevent heat radiated from the Earth escaping into space.

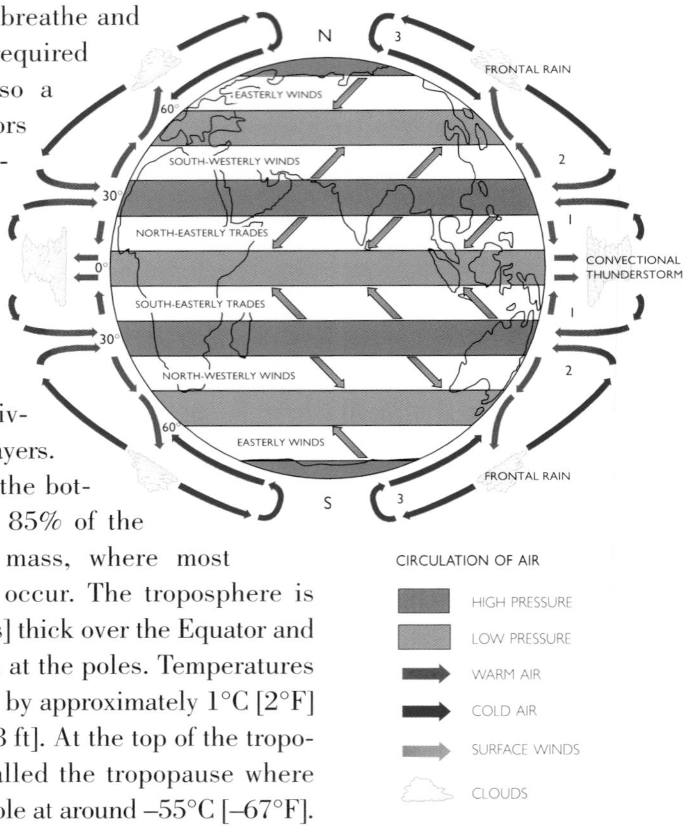

The circulation of the atmosphere can be divided into three rotating but interconnected air systems, or cells. The Hadley cell (figure 1 on the above diagram) is in the tropics; the Ferrel cell (2) lies between the subtropics and the mid-latitudes, and the Polar cell (3) is in the high latitudes.

Layers of Air

The atmosphere is divided into four main layers. The troposphere at the bottom contains about 85% of the atmosphere's total mass, where most weather conditions occur. The troposphere is about 15 km [9 miles] thick over the Equator and 8 km [5 miles] thick at the poles. Temperatures decrease with height by approximately 1°C [2°F] for every 100 m [328 ft]. At the top of the troposphere is a level called the tropopause where temperatures are stable at around –55°C [–67°F]. Above the tropopause is the stratosphere, which contains the ozone layer. Here, at about 50 km [31 miles] above the Earth's surface, temperatures rise to about 0°C [32°F].

The ionosphere extends from the stratopause to about 600 km [373 miles] above the surface. Here temperatures fall up to about 80 km

Moonrise seen from orbit

This photograph taken by an orbiting Shuttle shows the crescent of the Moon. Silhouetted at the horizon is a dense cloud layer. The reddish-brown band is the tropopause, which separates the blue-white stratosphere from the yellow troposphere.

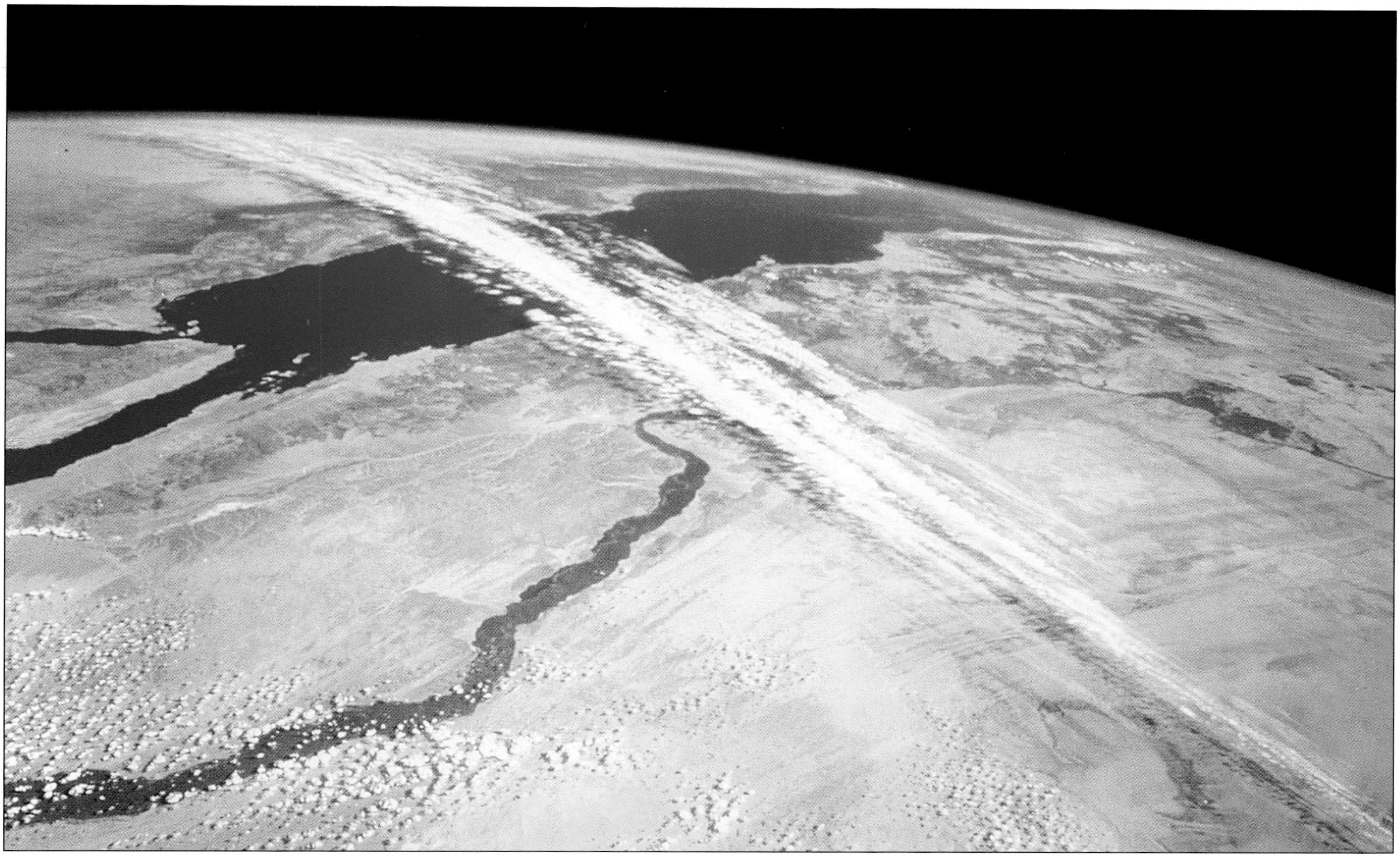

Jetstream from space
Jetstreams are strong winds that normally blow near the tropopause. Cirrus clouds mark the route of the jet stream in this photograph, which shows the Red Sea, North Africa and the Nile valley, which appears as a dark band crossing the desert.

[50 miles], but then rise. The aurorae, which occur in the ionosphere when charged particles from the Sun interact with the Earth's magnetic field, are strongest near the poles. In the exosphere, the outermost layer, the atmosphere merges into space.

Circulation of the Atmosphere

The heating of the Earth is most intense around the Equator where the Sun is high in the sky. Here warm, moist air rises in strong currents, creating a zone of low air pressure: the doldrums. The rising air eventually cools and spreads out north and south until it sinks back to the ground around latitudes 30° North and 30° South. This forms two zones of high air pressure called the horse latitudes.

From the horse latitudes, trade winds blow back across the surface towards the Equator, while westerly winds blow towards the poles. The warm westerlies finally meet the polar easterlies (cold dense air flowing from the poles). The line along which the warm and cold air streams meet is called the polar front. Depressions (or cyclones) are low air pressure frontal systems that form along the polar front.

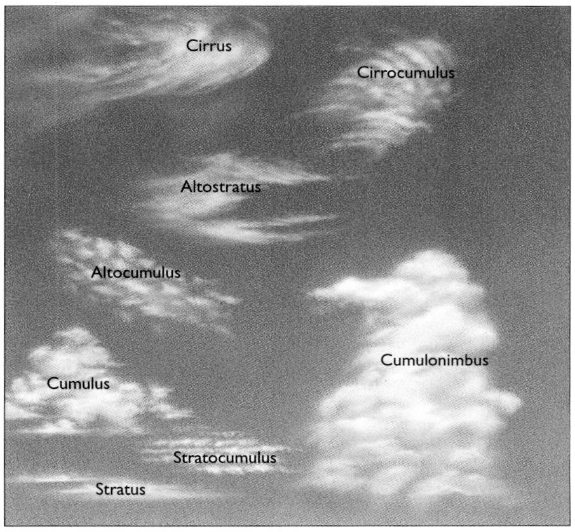

Classification of clouds
Clouds are classified broadly into cumuliform, or 'heap' clouds, and stratiform, or 'layer' clouds. Both types occur at all levels. The highest clouds, composed of ice crystals, are cirrus, cirrostratus and cirrocumulus. Medium-height clouds include altostratus, a grey cloud that often indicates the approach of a depression, and altocumulus, a thicker and fluffier version of cirrocumulus. Low clouds include stratus, which forms dull, overcast skies; nimbostratus, a dark grey layer cloud which brings almost continuous rain and snow; cumulus, a brilliant white heap cloud; and stratocumulus, a layer cloud arranged in globular masses or rolls. Cumulonimbus, a cloud associated with thunderstorms, lightning and heavy rain, often extends from low to medium altitudes. It has a flat base, a fluffy outline and often an anvil-shaped top.

Composition of the Atmosphere

The air in the troposphere is made up mainly of nitrogen (78%) and oxygen (21%). Argon makes up more than 0.9% and there are also minute amounts of carbon dioxide, helium, hydrogen, krypton, methane, ozone and xenon. The atmosphere also contains water vapour, the gaseous form of water, which, when it condenses around minute specks of dust and salt, forms tiny water droplets or ice crystals. Large masses of water droplets or ice crystals form clouds.

Climate and Weather

In April 1989, a tornado destroyed the town of Shaturia in Bangladesh, killing 1,300 people. In April 1991, at least 139,000 people died when a tropical cyclone (known also as a hurricane, a typhoon or a willy-willy) struck Bangladesh. In June and July 1993, record floods in the North American Midwest did enormous damage. And in May 1998, a series of mudslides caused by unusually heavy and prolonged rainfall killed over 100 people in the southern Italian region of Campania.

Every year, exceptional weather conditions cause disasters around the world. Modern forecasting techniques now give people warning of advancing storms, but the toll of human deaths continues as people are powerless in the face of the awesome forces of nature.

Weather is the day-to-day condition of the atmosphere. In some places, the weather is nomally stable, but in other areas, especially the middle latitudes, it is highly variable, changing from hour to hour with the passing of a depression. By contrast, climate is the average, or usual weather of a place, based on data obtained over a long period.

Hurricane Elena, 1995

Hurricanes form over warm oceans north and south of the Equator. Their movements are tracked by satellites, enabling forecasters to issue storm warnings as they approach land. In North America, forecasters identify them with boys' and girls' names.

Climatic Factors

Climate depends basically on the unequal heating of the Sun between the Equator and the poles. But ocean currents and terrain also affect climate. For example, despite their northerly positions, Norway's ports remain ice-free in winter. This is because of the warming effect of the North Atlantic Drift, an extension of the Gulf Stream which flows across the Atlantic Ocean from the Gulf of Mexico.

By contrast, the cold Benguela current which flows up the coast of south-western Africa cools the coast and causes arid conditions. This is because the cold onshore winds are warmed as they pass over the land. The warm air can hold more water vapour than cold air, giving the winds a drying effect.

The terrain affects climate in several ways. Because temperatures fall with altitude, highlands are cooler than lowlands in the same

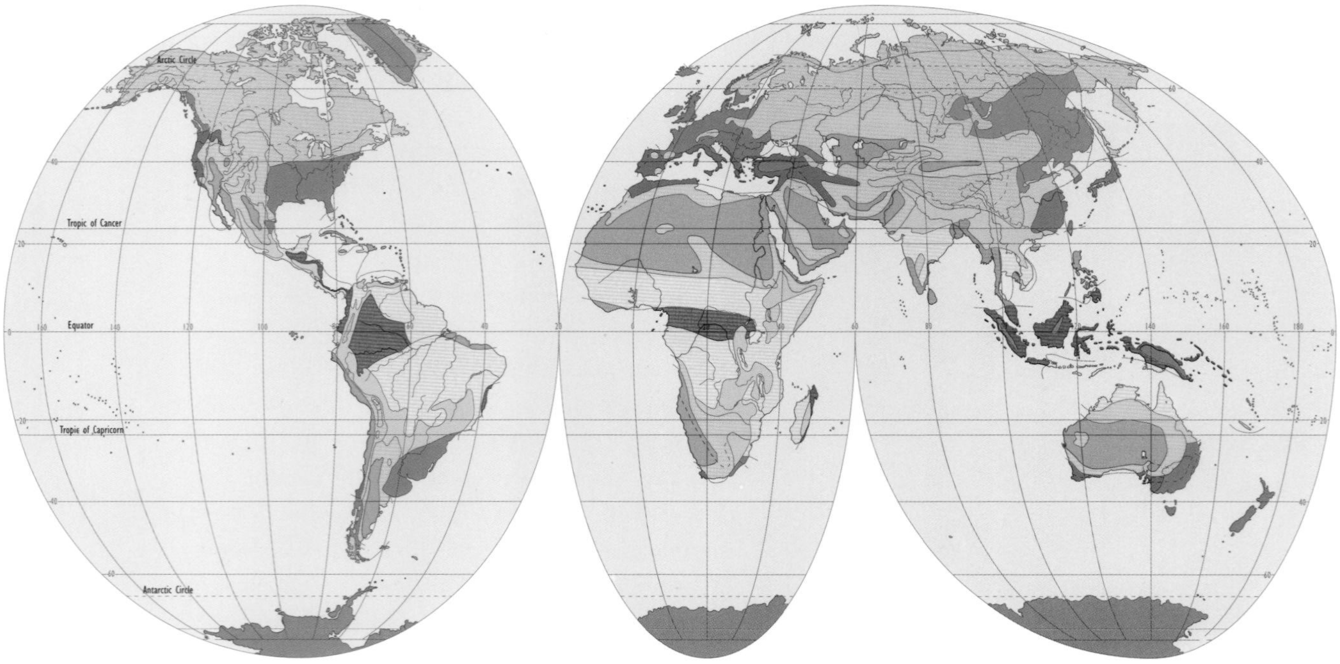

CLIMATIC REGIONS

Tropical rainy climates
All mean monthly temperatures above 18°C [64°F].

- RAINFOREST CLIMATE
- MONSOON CLIMATE
- SAVANNA CLIMATE

Dry climates
Low rainfall combined with a wide range of temperatures.

- STEPPE CLIMATE
- DESERT CLIMATE

Warm temperate rainy climates
The mean temperature is below 18°C [64°F] but above –3°C [26°F] and that of the warmest month is over 10°C [50°F].

- DRY WINTER CLIMATE
- DRY SUMMER CLIMATE
- CLIMATE WITH NO DRY SEASON

Cold temperate rainy climates
The mean temperature of the coldest month is below 3°C [37°F] but the warmest month is over 10°C [50°F].

- DRY WINTER CLIMATE
- CLIMATE WITH NO DRY SEASON

Polar climates
The temperature of the warmest month is below 10°C [50°F], giving permanently frozen subsoil.

- TUNDRA CLIMATE
- POLAR CLIMATE

Flood damage in the United States
In June and July 1993, the Mississippi River basin suffered record floods. The photograph shows a sunken church in Illinois. The flooding along the Mississippi, Missouri and other rivers caused great damage, amounting to about $12 billion. At least 48 people died in the floods.

Floods in St Louis, United States
The satellite image, right, shows the extent of the floods at St Louis at the confluence of the Mississippi and the Missouri rivers in June and July 1993. The floods occurred when very heavy rainfall raised river levels by up to 14 m [46 ft]. The floods reached their greatest extent between Minneapolis in the north and a point approximately 150 km [93 miles] south of St Louis. In places, the width of the Mississippi increased to nearly 11 km [7 miles], while the Missouri reached widths of 32 km [20 miles]. In all, more than 28,000 sq km [10,800 sq miles] were inundated and hundreds of towns and cities were flooded. Damage to crops was estimated at $8 billion. The USA was hit again by flooding in early 1997, when heavy rainfall in North Dakota and Minnesota caused the Red River to flood. The flooding had a catastrophic effect on the city of Grand Forks, which was inundated for months.

latitude. Terrain also affects rainfall. When moist onshore winds pass over mountain ranges, they are chilled as they are forced to rise and the water vapour they contain condenses to form clouds which bring rain and snow. After the winds have crossed the mountains, the air descends and is warmed. These warm, dry winds create rain shadow (arid) regions on the lee side of the mountains.

Climatic Regions

The two major factors that affect climate are temperature and precipitation, including rain and snow. In addition, seasonal variations and other climatic features are also taken into account. Climatic classifications vary because of the weighting given to various features. Yet most classifications are based on five main climatic types: tropical rainy climates; dry climates; warm temperate rainy climates; cold temperate rainy climates; and very cold polar climates. Some classifications also allow for the effect of altitude. The main climatic regions are subdivided according to seasonal variations and also to the kind of vegetation associated with the climatic conditions. Thus, the rainforest climate, with rain throughout the year, differs from monsoon and savanna climates, which have marked dry seasons. Similarly, parched desert climates differ from steppe climates which have enough moisture for grasses to grow.

Water and Land Use

All life on land depends on fresh water. Yet about 80 countries now face acute water shortages. The world demand for fresh water is increasing by about 2.3% a year and this demand will double every 21 years. About a billion people, mainly in developing countries, do not have access to clean drinking water and around 10 million die every year from drinking dirty water. This problem is made worse in many countries by the pollution of rivers and lakes.

In 1995, a World Bank report suggested that wars will be fought over water in the 21st century. Relations between several countries are already soured by disputes over water resources. Egypt fears that Sudan and Ethiopia will appropriate the waters of the Nile, while Syria and Iraq are concerned that Turkish dams will hold back the waters of the Euphrates.

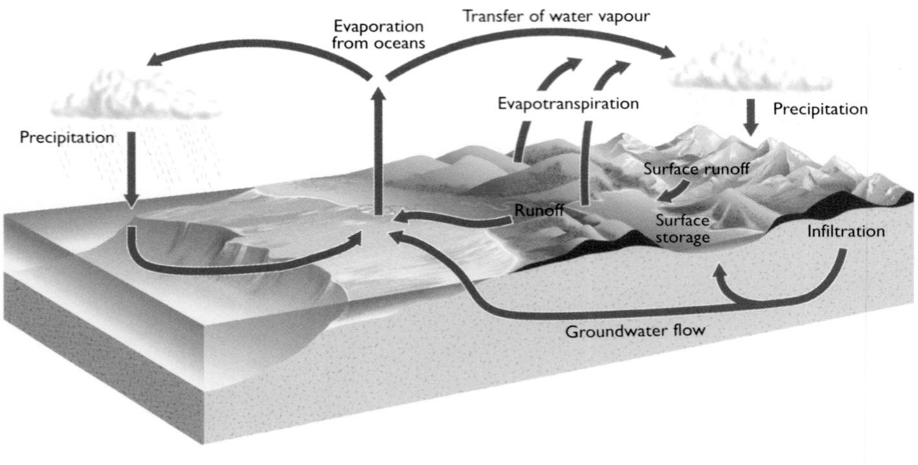

The hydrological cycle

The hydrological cycle is responsible for the continuous circulation of water around the planet. Water vapour contains and transports latent heat, or latent energy. When the water vapour condenses back into water (and falls as rain, hail or snow), the heat is released. When condensation takes place on cold nights, the cooling effect associated with nightfall is offset by the liberation of latent heat.

Hoover Dam, United States

The Hoover Dam in Arizona controls the Colorado River's flood waters. Its reservoir supplies domestic and irrigation water to the south-west, while a hydroelectric plant produces electricity.

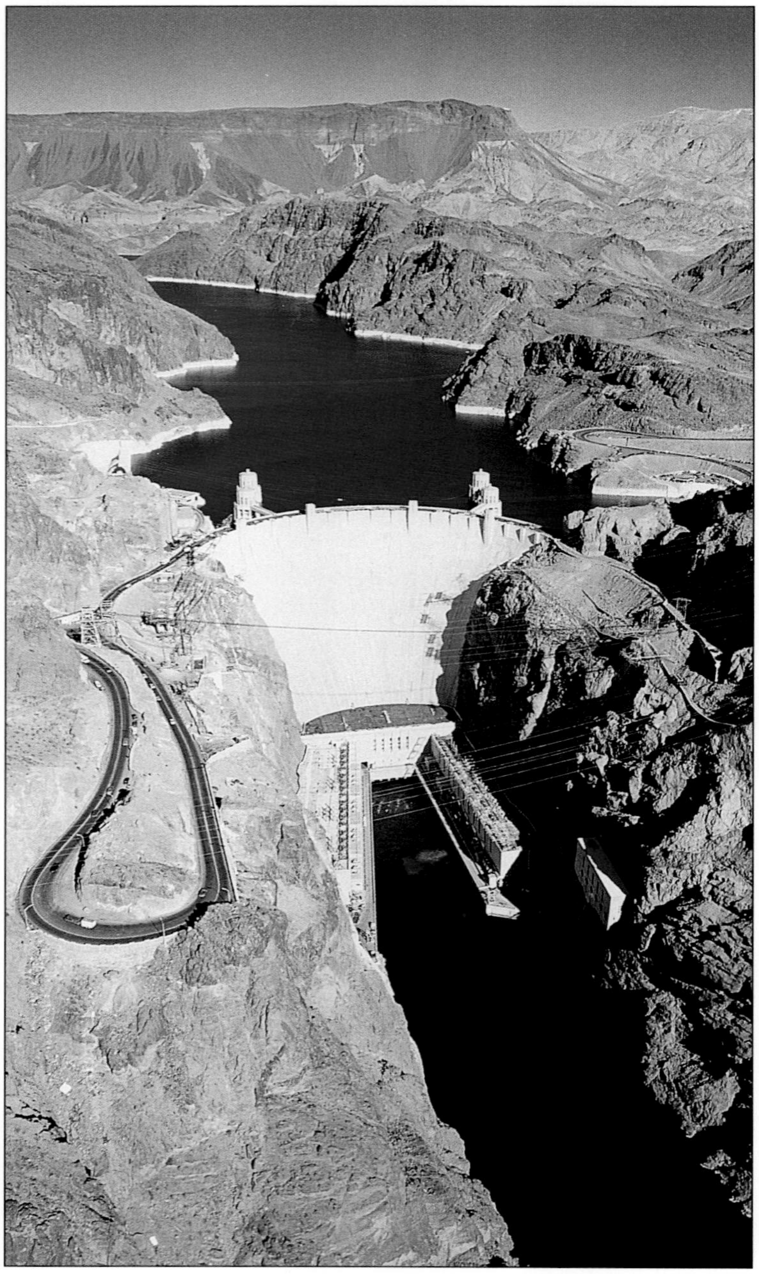

However, experts stress that while individual countries face water crises, there is no global crisis. The chief global problems are the uneven distribution of water and its inefficient and wasteful use.

The World's Water Supply

Of the world's total water supply, 99.4% is in the oceans or frozen in bodies of ice. Most of the rest circulates through the rocks beneath our feet as ground water. Water in rivers and lakes, in the soil and in the atmosphere together make up only 0.013% of the world's water.

The freshwater supply on land is dependent on the hydrological, or water cycle which is driven by the Sun's heat. Water is evaporated from the oceans and carried into the air as invisible water vapour. Although this vapour averages less than 2% of the total mass of the atmosphere, it is the chief component from the standpoint of weather.

When air rises, water vapour condenses into visible water droplets or ice crystals, which eventually fall to earth as rain, snow, sleet, hail or frost. Some of the precipitation that reaches the ground returns directly to the atmosphere through evaporation or transpiration via plants. Much of the rest of the water flows into the rocks to become ground water or across the surface into rivers and, eventually, back to the oceans, so completing the hydrological cycle.

WATER DISTRIBUTION

The distribution of planetary water, by percentage.

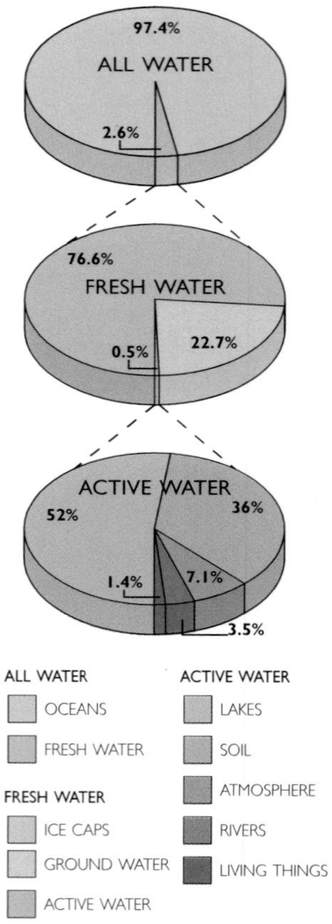

Water and Agriculture

Only about a third of the world's land area is used for growing crops, while another third

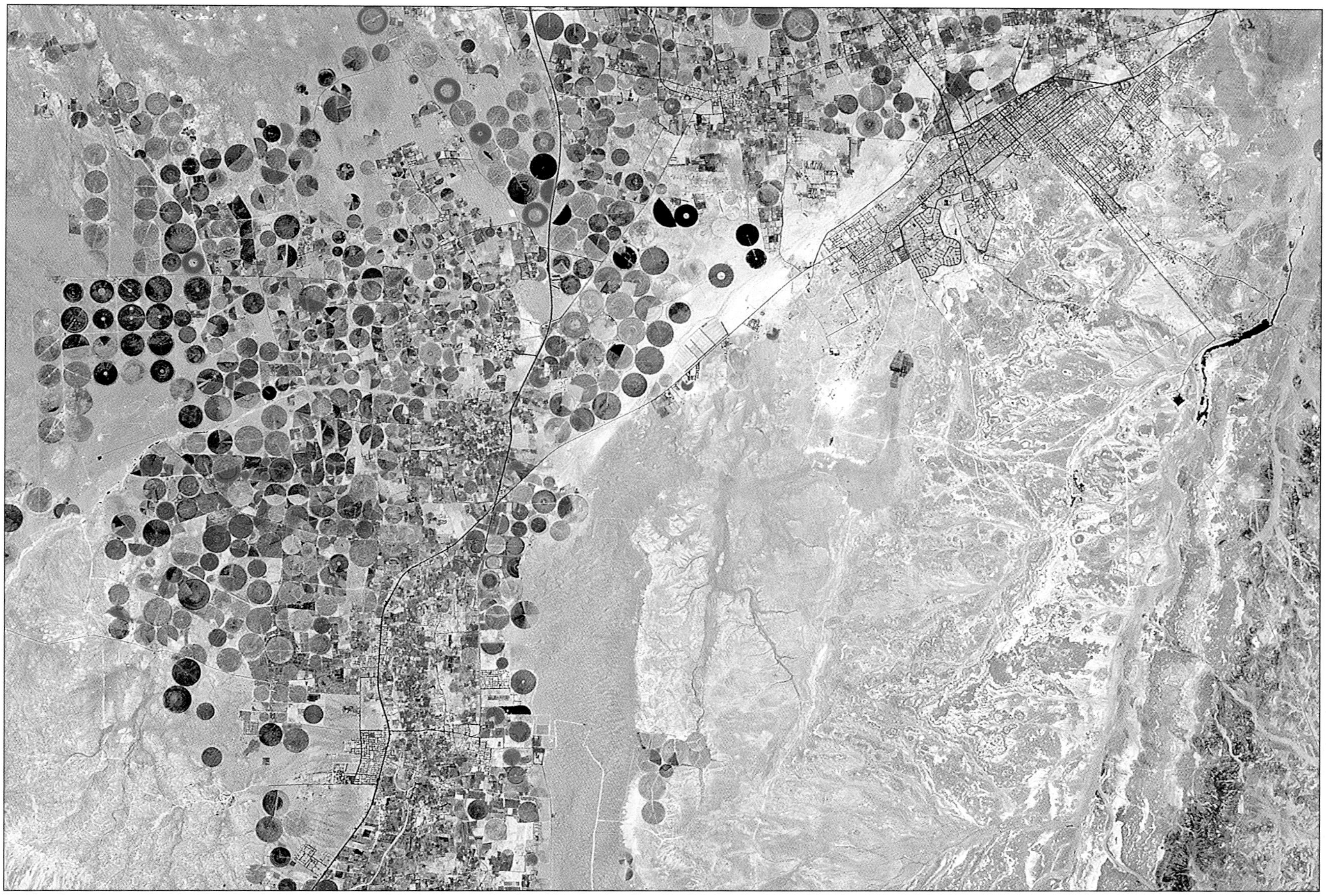

Irrigation in Saudi Arabia

Saudi Arabia is a desert country which gets its water from oases, which tap ground water supplies, and desalination plants. The sale of oil has enabled the arid countries of south-western Asia to develop their agriculture. In the above satellite image, vegetation appears brown and red.

Irrigation boom

The photograph shows a pivotal irrigation boom used to sprinkle water over a wheat field in Saudi Arabia. Irrigation in hot countries often takes place at night so that water loss through evaporation is reduced. Irrigation techniques vary from place to place. In monsoon areas with abundant water, the fields are often flooded, or the water is led to the crops along straight furrows. Sprinkler irrigation has become important since the 1940s. In other types of irrigation, the water is led through pipes which are on or under the ground. Underground pipes supply water directly to the plant roots and, as a result, water loss through evaporation is minimized.

consists of meadows and pasture. The rest of the world is unsuitable for farming, being too dry, too cold, too mountainous, or covered by dense forests. Although the demand for food increases every year, problems arise when attempts are made to increase the existing area of farmland. For example, the soils and climates of tropical forest and semi-arid regions of Africa and South America are not ideal for farming. Attempts to work such areas usually end in failure. To increase the world's food supply, scientists now concentrate on making existing farmland more productive rather than farming marginal land.

To grow crops, farmers need fertile, workable land, an equable climate, including a frost-free growing period, and an adequate supply of fresh water. In some areas, the water falls directly as rain. But many other regions depend on irrigation.

Irrigation involves water conservation through the building of dams which hold back storage reservoirs. In some areas, irrigation water comes from underground aquifers, layers of permeable and porous rocks through which ground water percolates. But in many cases, the water in the aquifers has been there for thousands of years, having accumulated at a time when the rainfall was much greater than it is today. As a result, these aquifers are not being renewed and will, one day, dry up.

Other sources of irrigation water are desalination plants, which remove salt from seawater and pump it to farms. This is a highly expensive process and is employed in areas where water supplies are extremely low, such as the island of Malta, or in the oil-rich desert countries around the Gulf, which can afford to build huge desalination plants.

LAND USE BY CONTINENT

	Forest	Permanent pasture	Permanent crops	Arable	Non-productive
North America	32.2%	17.3%	0.3%	12.6%	37.6%
South America	51.8%	26.7%	1.5%	6.6%	13.4%
Europe	33.4%	17.5%	3.0%	26.8%	19.3%
Africa	23.2%	26.6%	0.6%	5.6%	44.0%
Asia	20.2%	25.0%	1.2%	16.0%	37.8%
Oceania	23.5%	52.2%	0.1%	5.7%	18.5%

The Natural World

In 1995, a United Nations Environment Programme report stated that 11% of all mammal species, 18% of birds and 5% of fish are now threatened with extinction. Furthermore, it predicted that half of all bird and mammal species will become extinct within 300 years, or sooner if current trends continue. This will greatly reduce the biodiversity of our planet, causing the disappearance of unique combinations of genes that could be vital in improving food yields on farms or in the production of drugs to combat diseases.

Extinctions of species have occurred throughout Earth history, but today the extinction rate is estimated to be about 10,000 times the natural average. Some scientists have even compared it with the mass extinction that wiped out the dinosaurs 65 million years ago. However, the main cause of today's high extinction rate is not some natural disaster, such as the impact of an asteroid a few kilometres across, but it is the result of human actions, most notably the destruction of natural habitats for farming and other purposes. In some densely populated areas, such as Western Europe, the natural habitats were destroyed long ago. Today, the greatest damage is occurring in tropical rainforests, which contain more than half of the world's known species.

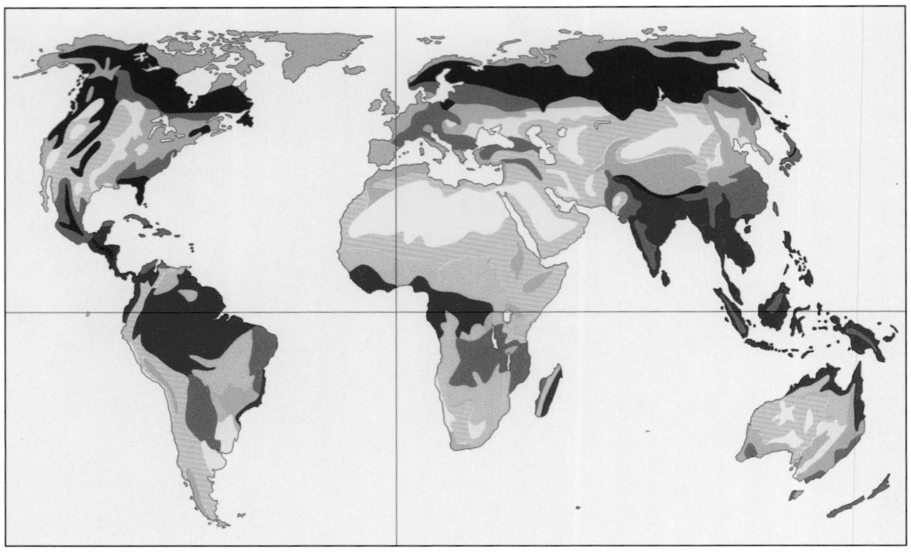

NATURAL VEGETATION

- TUNDRA & MOUNTAIN VEGETATION
- NEEDLELEAF EVERGREEN FOREST
- MIXED NEEDLELEAF EVERGREEN & BROADLEAF DECIDUOUS TREES
- BROADLEAF DECIDUOUS WOODLAND
- MID-LATITUDE GRASSLAND
- EVERGREEN BROADLEAF & DECIDUOUS TREES & SHRUBS
- SEMI-DESERT SCRUB
- DESERT
- TROPICAL GRASSLAND (SAVANNA)
- TROPICAL BROADLEAF RAINFOREST & MONSOON FOREST
- SUBTROPICAL BROADLEAF & NEEDLELEAF FOREST

The map shows the world's main biomes. The classification is based on the natural 'climax' vegetation of regions a result of the climate and the terrain. But human activities have greatly modified this basic division. For example, the original deciduous forests of Western Europe and the eastern United States have largely disappeared. In recent times, human development of some semi-arid areas has turned former dry grasslands into barren desert.

Rainforest in Rwanda

Rainforests are the most threatened of the world's biomes. Effective conservation policies must demonstrate to poor local people that they can benefit from the survival of the forests.

Modern technology has enabled people to live comfortably almost anywhere on Earth. But most plants and many animals are adapted to particular climatic conditions, and they live in association with and dependent on each other. Plant and animal communities that cover large areas are called biomes.

The World's Biomes

The world's biomes are defined mainly by climate and vegetation. They range from the tundra, in polar regions and high mountain regions, to the lush equatorial rainforests.

The Arctic tundra covers large areas in the polar regions of the northern hemisphere. Snow covers the land for more than half of the year and the subsoil, called permafrost, is permanently frozen. Comparatively few species can survive in this harsh, treeless environment. The main plants are hardy mosses, lichens, grasses, sedges and low shrubs. However, in summer, the tundra plays an important part in world animal geography, when its growing plants and swarms of insects provide food for migrating animals and birds that arrive from the south.

The tundra of the northern hemisphere merges in the south into a vast region of needleleaf evergreen forest, called the boreal forest or taiga. Such trees as fir, larch, pine and spruce are adapted to survive the long, bitterly cold winters of this region, but the number of plant and animal species is again small. South of the boreal forests is a zone of mixed needleleaf evergreens and broadleaf deciduous trees, which

Tundra in subarctic Alaska
The Denali National Park, Alaska, contains magnificent mountain scenery and tundra vegetation which flourishes during the brief summer. The park is open between 1 June and 15 September.

shed their leaves in winter. In warmer areas, this mixed forest merges into broadleaf deciduous forest, where the number and diversity of plant species is much greater.

Deciduous forests are adapted to temperate, humid regions. Evergreen broadleaf and deciduous trees grow in Mediterranean regions, with their hot, dry summers. But much of the original deciduous forest has been cut down and has given way to scrub and heathland. Grasslands occupy large areas in the middle latitudes, where the rainfall is insufficient to support forest growth. The moister grasslands are often called prairies, while drier areas are called steppe.

The tropics also contain vast dry areas of semi-desert scrub which merges into desert, as well as large areas of savanna, which is grassland with scattered trees. Savanna regions, with their marked dry season, support a wide range of mammals.

Tropical and subtropical regions contain three types of forest biomes. The tropical rainforest, the world's richest biome measured by its plant and animal species, experiences rain and high temperatures throughout the year. Similar forests occur in monsoon regions, which have a season of very heavy rainfall. They, too, are rich in plant species, though less so than the tropical rainforest. A third type of forest is the subtropical broadleaf and needleleaf forest, found in such places as south-eastern China, south-central Africa and eastern Brazil.

NET PRIMARY PRODUCTION OF EIGHT MAJOR BIOMES

- TROPICAL RAINFORESTS
- DECIDUOUS FORESTS
- TROPICAL GRASSLANDS
- CONIFEROUS FORESTS
- MEDITERRANEAN
- TEMPERATE GRASSLANDS
- TUNDRA
- DESERTS

The net primary production of eight major biomes is expressed in grams of dry organic matter per square metre per year. The tropical rainforests produce the greatest amount of organic material. The tundra and deserts produce the least.

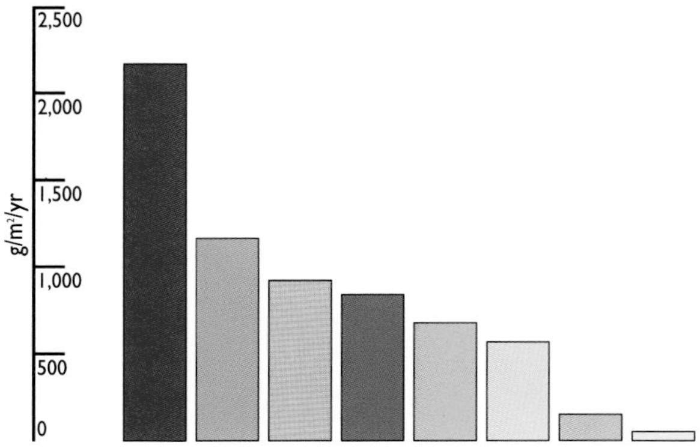

The Human World

Every minute, the world's population increases by between 160 and 170. While forecasts of future growth are difficult to make, most demographers are in agreement that the world's population is likely to increase from around 5.8 billion in 1997 to 10 billion by 2050, reaching a peak of around 11 billion by 2075. It is then expected to level out or even decline a little towards the year 2100. The fastest rates of increase will take place in the developing countries of Africa, Asia and Latin America – the places least able to afford the costs incurred by such a rapidly expanding population.

Average world population growth rates have declined from about 2% a year in the early 1960s to 1.3% in 1997. This was partly due to a decline in fertility rates – that is, the number of births to the number of women of child-bearing age – especially in developed countries where, as income has risen, the average size of families has fallen.

Declining fertility rates were also evident in many developing countries. Even Africa shows signs of such change, though its population is expected to triple before it begins to fall. Population growth is also dependent on death rates, which are affected by such factors as famine, disease and the quality of medical care.

The Population Explosion

The world's population has grown steadily throughout most of human history, though certain events triggered periods of population growth. The invention of agriculture around 10,000 years ago, led to great changes in human society. Before then, most people had obtained food by hunting animals and gathering plants. Average life expectancies were probably no more than 20 years and life was hard. However, when farmers began to produce food surpluses, people began to live settled lives. This major milestone in human history led to the development of the first cities and the emergence of the early civilizations.

From an estimated 8 million in 8000 BC, the world population rose to about 300 million by AD 1000. Between 1000 and 1750, the rate of world population increase was around 0.1% per year, but another period of major economic and social change – the Industrial Revolution – began in the late 18th century. The Industrial Revolution led to improvements in farm technology and increases in food production. The world population began to increase quickly as industrialization spread across Europe and into North America. By 1850, it had reached 1.2 billion. The 2 billion mark was passed in the 1920s, and then the population rapidly doubled to 4 billion by the 1970s.

Population Features

Population growth affects the structure of societies. In developing countries with high annual rates of population increase, the large majority of the people are young and soon to become parents themselves. For example, in Kenya, which had until recently an annual rate of population growth of around 4%, just over half

Elevated view of Ki Lung Street, Hong Kong

Urban areas of Hong Kong, a Special Administrative Region on the southern coast of China, contain busy streets overlooked by crowded apartments. They reflect the early days of urbanization in China.

Largest Cities

Within 10 years, for the first time ever, the majority of the world's population will live in urban areas. Almost all the urban growth will be in developing countries. Below is a list of cities with their estimated populations in the year 2015, in millions.

1	Tokyo	28.7
2	Bombay (Mumbai)	27.4
3	Lagos	24.1
4	Shanghai	23.2
5	Jakarta	21.5
6	São Paulo	21.0
7	Karachi	20.6
8	Beijing	19.6
9	Dhaka	19.2
10	Mexico City	19.1
11	Calcutta	17.6
12	Delhi	17.5
13	New York City	17.4
14	Tianjin	17.1
15	Metro Manila	14.9
16	Cairo	14.7
17	Los Angeles	14.5
18	Seoul	13.1
19	Buenos Aires	12.5
20	Istanbul	12.1

These city populations are based on figures for urban agglomerations rather than actual city limits.

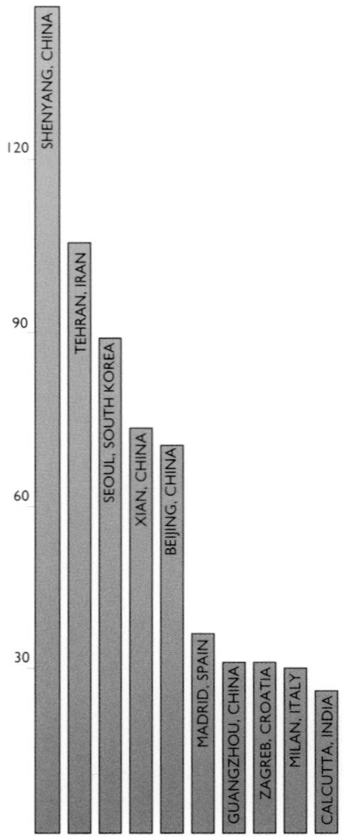

Urban air pollution

This diagram of the world's most polluted cities indicates the number of days per year when sulphur dioxide levels exceed the WHO threshhold of 150 micrograms per cubic metre.

Hong Kong's business district

By contrast with the picturesque old streets of Hong Kong, the business district of Hong Kong City, on the northern shore of Hong Kong Island, is a cluster of modern high-rise buildings. The glittering skyscrapers reflect the success of this tiny region, which has one of the strongest economies in Asia.

of the population is under 15 years of age. On the other hand, the populations of developed countries, with low population growth rates, have a fairly even spread across age groups.

Such differences are reflected in average life expectancies at birth. In rich countries, such as Australia and the United States, the average life expectancy is 77 years (74 years for men and 80 for women; women live longer, on average, than their male counterparts). As a result, an increasing proportion of the people are elderly and retired, contributing little to the economy. The reverse applies in many of the poorer countries, where average life expectancies are below 60 years. In more than a dozen countries in Africa, the average life expectancy is less than 50.

Paralleling the population explosion has been a rapid growth in the number and size of cities and towns, which contained nearly half of the world's people by the 1990s. This proportion is expected to rise to nearly two-thirds by 2025.

Urbanization occurred first in areas undergoing the industrialization of their economies, but today it is also a feature of the developing world. In developing countries, people are leaving impoverished rural areas hoping to gain access to the education, health and other services available in cities. But many cities are unable to provide the housing and other facilities necessitated by rapid population growth. As a result, slums grow up around the cities. Pollution, crime and disease become features of everyday life.

The population explosion poses another probem for the entire world. No one knows how many people the world can support or how consumer demand will damage the fragile environments on our planet. The British economist Thomas Malthus argued in the late 18th century that overpopulation would lead to famine and war. But an increase in farm technology in the 19th and 20th centuries, combined with a green revolution, in which scientists developed high-yield crop varieties, has greatly increased food production since Malthus' time.

However, some modern scientists argue that overpopulation may become a problem in the 21st century. They argue that food shortages leading to disastrous famines will result unless population growth can be halted. Such people argue in favour of birth control programmes. China, the only country with more than a billion people, has introduced a one-child family policy. Their action has slowed the growth of China's huge population, though rising living standards seem to be the most effective brakes on rapid population growth.

POPULATION CHANGE 1990–2000

The predicted population change for the years 1990–2000.

- OVER 40% POPULATION GAIN
- 30–40% POPULATION GAIN
- 20–30% POPULATION GAIN
- 10–20% POPULATION GAIN
- 0–10% POPULATION GAIN
- NO CHANGE OR LOSS

TOP 5 COUNTRIES	
Kuwait	+75.0%
Namibia	+62.5%
Afghanistan	+60.1%
Mali	+55.5%
Tanzania	+54.6%

BOTTOM 5 COUNTRIES	
Belgium	–0.1%
Hungary	–0.2%
Grenada	–2.4%
Germany	–3.2%
Tonga	–3.2%

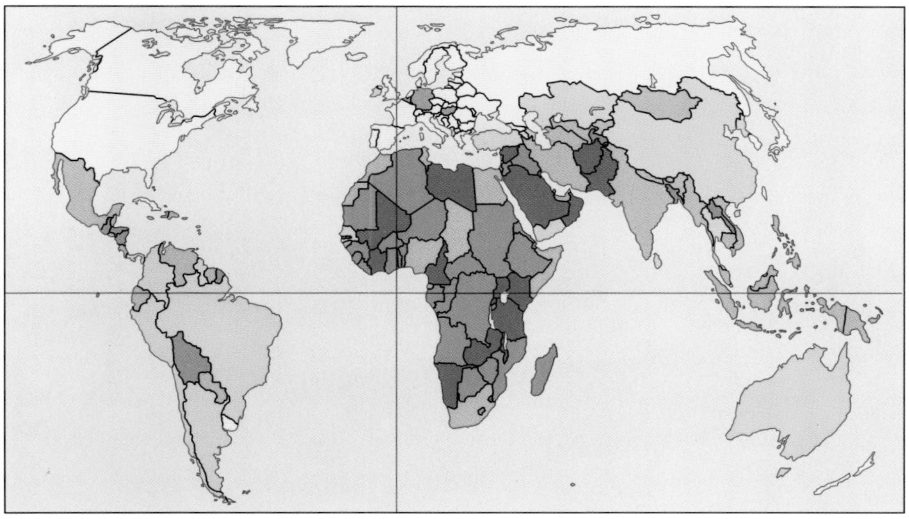

Languages and Religions

In 1995, 90-year-old Edna Guerro died in northern California. She was the last person able to speak Northern Pomo, one of about 50 Native American languages spoken in the state. Her death marked the extinction of one of the world's languages.

This event is not an isolated incident. Language experts regularly report the disappearance of languages and some of them predict that between 20 to 50% of the world's languages will no longer exist by the end of the next century. Improved transport and communications are partly to blame, because they bring people from various cultures into closer and closer contact. Many children no longer speak the language of their parents, preferring instead to learn the language used at their schools. The pressures on children to speak dominant rather than minority languages are often great. In the first part of the 20th century, Native American children were punished if they spoke their native language.

The disappearance of a language represents the extinction of a way of thinking, a unique expression of the experiences and knowledge of a group of people. Language and religion together give people an identity and a sense of belonging. However, there are others who argue that the disappearance of minority languages is a step towards international understanding and economic efficiency.

The World's Languages

Definitions of what is a language or a dialect vary and, hence, estimates of the number of languages spoken around the world range from about 3,000 to 6,000. But whatever the figure, it is clear that the number of languages far exceeds the number of countries.

RELIGIOUS ADHERENTS

The number of adherents to the world's major religions, in millions.

Christian	1,667
Roman Catholic	952
Protestant	337
Orthodox	162
Anglican	70
Other Christian	148
Muslim	881
Sunni	841
Shia	40
Hindu	663
Buddhist	312
Chinese Folk	172
Tribal	92
Jewish	18
Sikhs	17

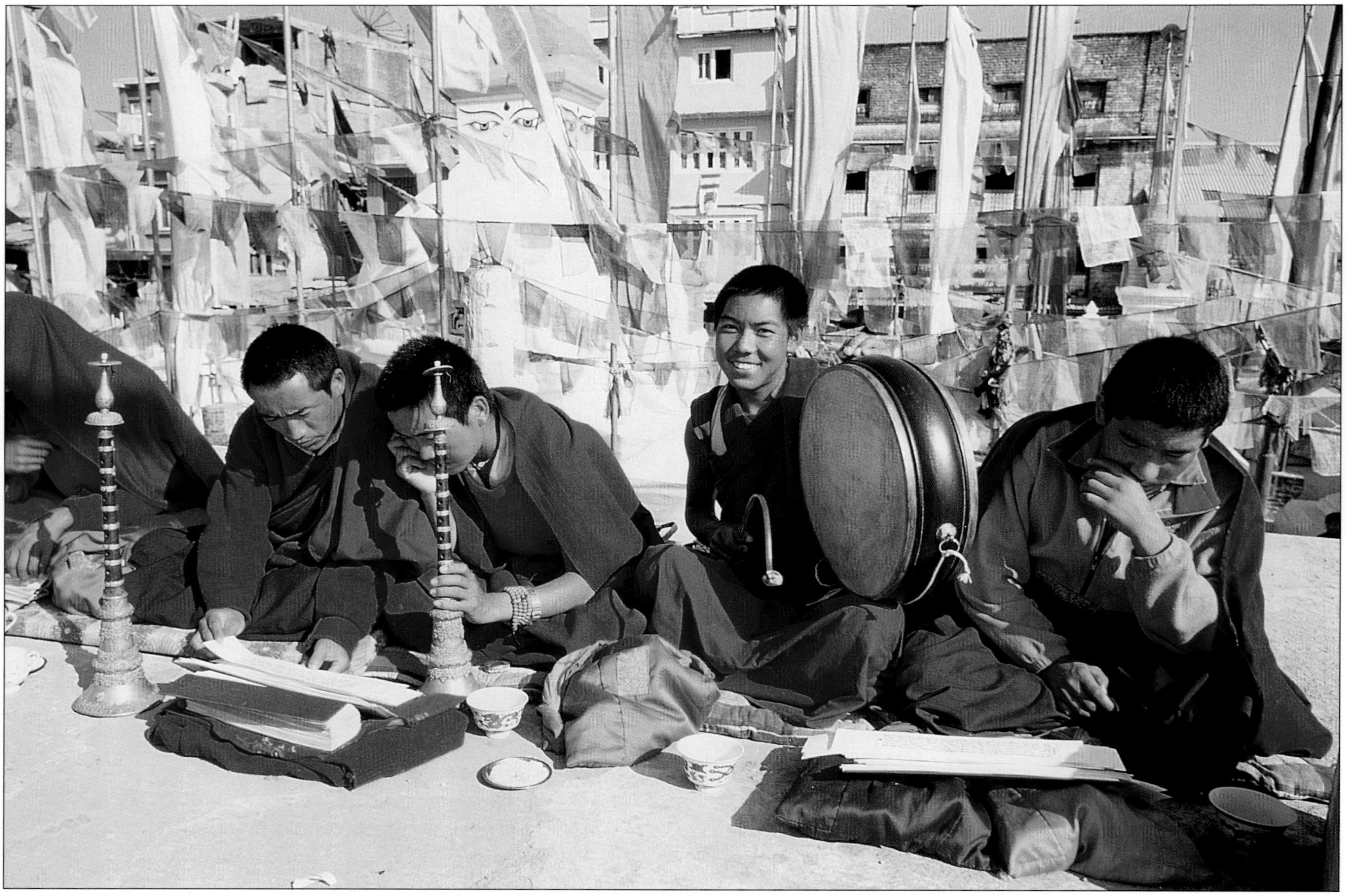

Buddhist monks in Katmandu, Nepal

Hinduism is Nepal's official religion, but the Nepalese observe the festivals of both Hinduism and Buddhism. They also regard Buddhist shrines and Hindu temples as equally sacred.

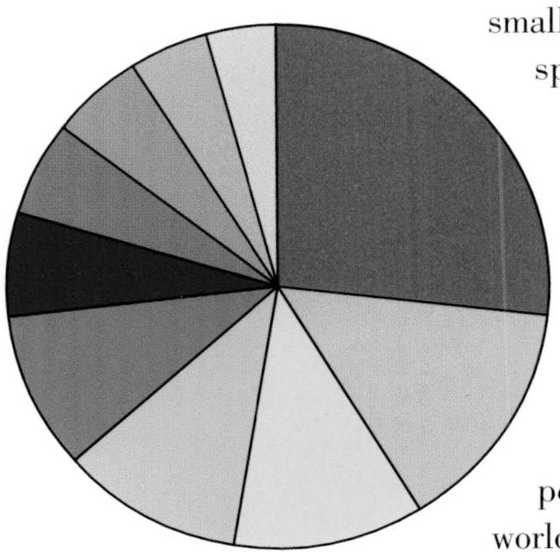

MOTHER TONGUES

Native speakers of the major languages, in millions (1990).

- MANDARIN CHINESE 834M
- ENGLISH 443M
- HINDI 352M
- SPANISH 341M
- RUSSIAN 293M
- ARABIC 197M
- BENGALI 184M
- PORTUGUESE 173M
- MALAY 142M
- JAPANESE 125M

Countries with only one language tend to be small. For example, in Liechtenstein, everyone speaks German. By contrast, more than 860 languages have been identified in Papua New Guinea, whose population is only about 4.3 million people. Hence, many of its languages are spoken by only small groups of people. In fact, scientists have estimated that about a third of the world's languages are now spoken by less than 1,000 people. By contrast, more than half of the world's population speak just seven languages.

The world's languages are grouped into families. The Indo-European family consists of languages spoken between Europe and the Indian subcontinent. The growth of European empires over the last 300 years led several Indo-European languages, most notably English, French, Portuguese and Spanish, to spread throughout much of North and South America, Africa, Australia and New Zealand.

English has become the official language in many countries which together contain more than a quarter of the world's population. It is now a major international language, surpassing in importance Mandarin Chinese, a member of the Sino-Tibetan family, which is the world's leading first language. Without a knowledge of English, businessmen face many problems when conducting international trade, especially with the United States or other English-speaking countries. But proposals that English, French, Russian or some other language should become a world language seem unlikely to be acceptable to a majority of the world's peoples.

The Church of San Giovanni, Dolomites, Italy

Christianity has done much to shape Western civilization. Christian churches were built as places of worship, but many of them are among the finest achievements of world architecture.

World Religions

Religion is another fundamental aspect of human culture. It has inspired much of the world's finest architecture, literature, music and painting. It has also helped to shape human cultures since prehistoric times and is responsible for the codes of ethics by which most people live.

The world's major religions were all founded in Asia. Judaism, one of the first faiths to teach that there is only one god, is one of the world's oldest. Founded in south-western Asia, it influenced the more recent Christianity and Islam, two other monotheistic religions which now have the greatest number of followers. Hinduism, the third leading faith in terms of the numbers of followers, originated in the Indian subcontinent and most Hindus are now found in India. Another major religion, Buddhism, was founded in the subcontinent partly as a reaction to certain aspects of Hinduism. But unlike Hinduism, it has spread from India throughout much of eastern Asia.

Religion and language are powerful creative forces. They are also essential features of nationalism, which gives people a sense of belonging and pride. But nationalism is often also a cause of rivalry and tension. Cultural differences have led to racial hatred, the persecution of minorities, and to war between national groups.

OFFICIAL LANGUAGES: % OF WORLD POPULATION

English	27.0%
Chinese	19.0%
Hindi	13.5%
Spanish	5.4%
Russian	5.2%
French	4.2%
Arabic	3.3%
Portuguese	3.0%
Malay	3.0%
Bengali	2.9%
Japanese	2.3%

Polyglot nations

The graph, right, shows countries of the world with more than 200 languages. Although it has only about 4.3 million people, Papua New Guinea holds the record for the number of languages spoken.

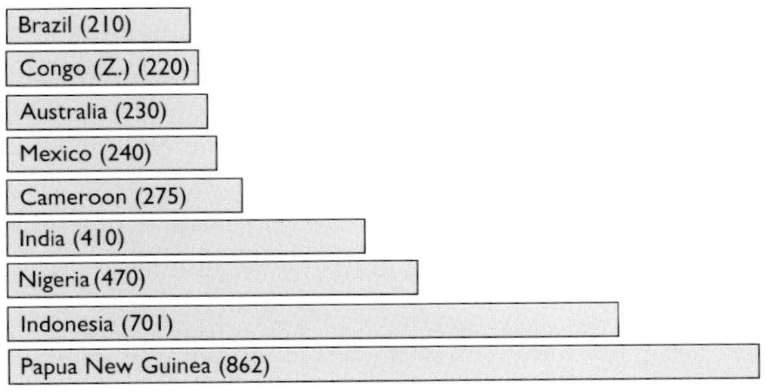

International Organizations

Twelve days before the surrender of Germany and four months before the final end of World War II, representatives of 50 nations met in San Francisco to create a plan to set up a peace-keeping organization, the United Nations. Since its birth on 24 October 1945, its membership has grown from 51 to 185.

Its first 50 years have been marked by failures as well as successes. While it has helped to prevent some disputes from flaring up into full-scale wars, the Blue Berets, as the UN troops are called, have been forced, because of their policy of neutrality, to stand by when atrocities are committed by rival warring groups.

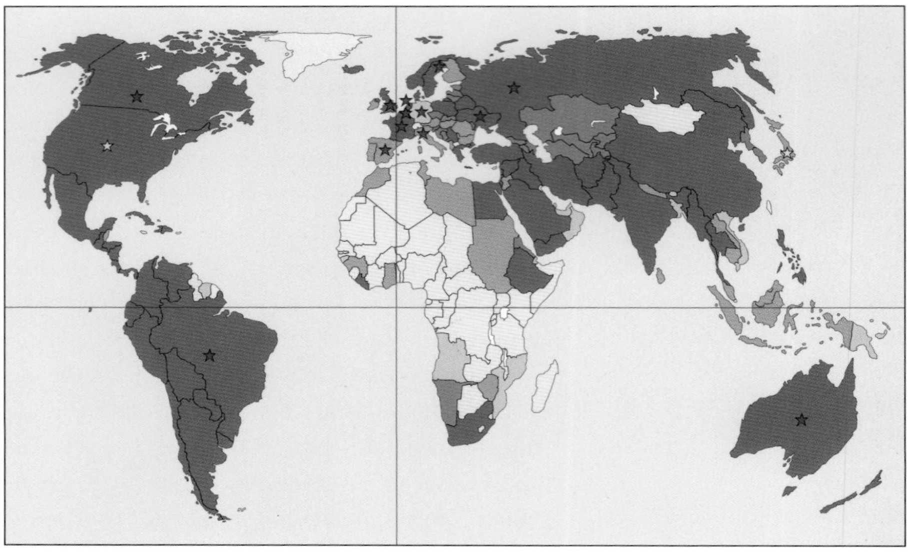

MEMBERS OF THE UN
Year of joining.

- 1940s
- 1950s
- 1960s
- 1970s
- 1980s
- 1990s
- NON–MEMBERS
- ★ 1% – 10% CONTRIBUTION TO FUNDING
- ★ OVER 10% CONTRIBUTION TO FUNDING

The Work of the UN

The United Nations has six main organs. They include the General Assembly, where member states meet to discuss issues concerned with peace, security and development. The Security Council, containing 15 members, is concerned with maintaining world peace. The Secretariat, under the Secretary-General, helps the other organs to do their jobs effectively, while the Economic and Social Council works with specialized agencies to implement policies concerned with such matters as development, education and health. The International Court of Justice, or World Court, helps to settle disputes between member nations. The sixth organ of the UN, the Trusteeship Council, was designed to bring 11 UN trust territories to independence. Its task has now been completed.

The specialized agencies do much important work. For example, UNICEF (United Nations International Children's Fund) has provided health care and aid for children in many parts of the world. The ILO (International Labour Organization) has improved working conditions in many areas, while the FAO (Food and Agricultural Organization) has worked to improve the production and distribution of food. Among the other agencies are organizations to help refugees, to further human rights and to control the environment. The latest agency, set up in 1995, is the WTO (World Trade Organization), which took over the work of GATT (General Agreement on Tariffs and Trade).

Food aid to Bosnia-Herzegovina

International organizations supply aid to people living in areas suffering from war or famine. In Bosnia-Herzegovina, the UN Protection Force supervised the movements of food aid.

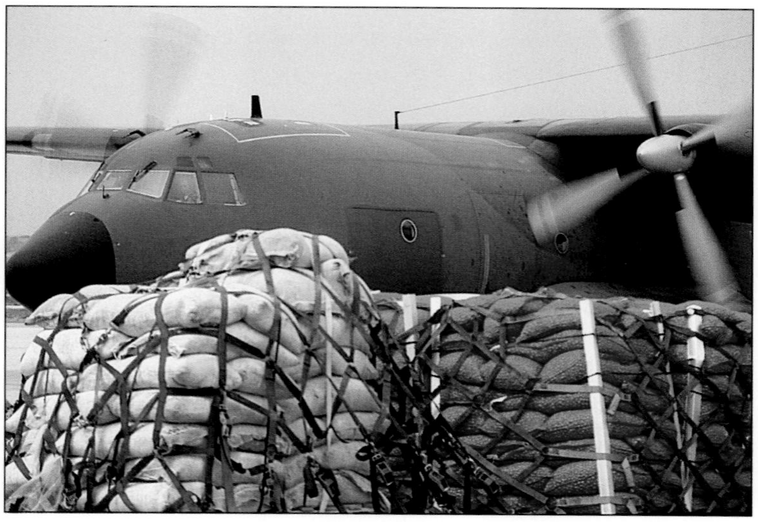

Other Organizations

In a world in which nations have become increasingly interdependent, many other organizations have been set up to deal with a variety of problems. Some, such as NATO (the North Atlantic Treaty Organization), are defence alliances. In the early 1990s, the end of the Cold War suggested that NATO's role might be finished, but the civil war in the former Yugoslavia showed that it still has a role in maintaining peace and security.

Other organizations encourage social and economic co-operation in various regions. Some are NGOs (non-governmental organizations), such as the Red Cross and its Muslim equivalent, the Red Crescent. Other NGOs raise funds to provide aid to countries facing major crises, such as famine.

Some major international organizations aim at economic co-operation and the removal of trade barriers. The best known of these organizations is the European Union, which has 15 members. Its

INTERNATIONAL AID AND GNP
Aid provided as a percentage of GNP, with total aid in brackets (1995).

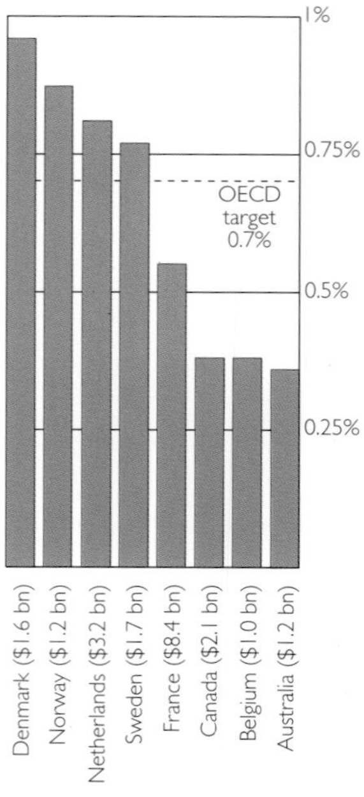

UNHCR-funded jetty, Sri Lanka

In 1994, the UN High Commission for Refugees was responsible for 23 million people. Sometimes, it has to provide transport facilities, such as this jetty, to get aid to the refugees.

economic success has led some people to support the idea of setting up a federal Europe. Others oppose such developments, they fear that a 'United States of Europe' would lead to a loss of national identity among the member states.

Other groupings include ASEAN (the Association of South-east Asian Nations) which aims at reducing trade barriers between its members (Brunei, Burma, Indonesia, Laos, Malaysia, the Philippines, Singapore, Thailand and Vietnam). APEC (the Asia-Pacific Co-operation Group) was founded in 1989 with the aim of creating a free trade zone between the countries of eastern Asia, North America, Australia and New Zealand by 2020. Meanwhile, Canada, Mexico and the United States have formed NAFTA (the North American Free Trade Agreement), while other economic groupings link most of the countries in Latin America. Another grouping with a more limited but important objective is OPEC (the Organization of Oil-Exporting Countries). OPEC works to unify policies concerning trade in oil on the world markets.

Some organizations exist to discuss matters of common interest between groups of nations. The Commonwealth of Nations, for example, initially developed from links created by the British Empire. In North and South America, the OAS (Organization of American States) aims at increasing understanding in the Western hemisphere. The OAU (Organization of African Unity) has a similar role in Africa, while the Arab League represents the Arab nations of North Africa and the Middle East.

COUNTRIES OF THE EUROPEAN UNION

	Total land area (sq km)	Total population (1997)	GNP per capita, US$ (1995)	Unemployment rate, % (1994)	Year of accession to the EU	Seats in EU parliament (1998)
Austria	83,850	8,200,000	26,890	4.3%	1995	21
Belgium	30,510	10,225,000	24,710	9.7%	1958	25
Denmark	43,070	5,350,000	29,890	10.7%	1973	16
Finland	338,130	5,180,000	20,580	18.4%	1995	16
France	551,500	58,800,000	24,990	12.2%	1958	87
Germany	356,910	82,300,000	27,510	8.6%	1958	99
Greece	131,990	10,600,000	8,210	9.4%	1981	25
Ireland	70,280	3,625,000	14,710	15.2%	1973	15
Italy	301,270	57,750,000	19,020	11.4%	1958	87
Luxembourg	2,590	425,000	41,210	3.4%	1958	6
Netherlands	41,526	15,900,000	24,000	7.6%	1958	31
Portugal	92,390	10,100,000	9,740	6.7%	1986	25
Spain	504,780	39,300,000	13,580	24.4%	1986	64
Sweden	449,960	8,850,000	23,750	7.4%	1995	22
United Kingdom	243,368	58,600,000	18,700	9.7%	1973	87

Agriculture

In 1995, the world production of grains was lower than average – the result mainly of a wet spring in the United States, and bad weather combined with economic turmoil in the former Soviet Union. Downward trends in world food production in the 1990s reopened an old debate – whether food production will be able to keep pace with a rapidly rising world population in the 21st century.

Some experts argue that the lower than expected production figures in the 1990s herald a period of relative scarcity and high prices of food, which will be felt most in the poorer developing countries. Others are more optimistic. They point to the successes of the 'green revolution' which, through the use of new crop varieties produced by scientists, irrigation and the extensive use of fertilizers and pesticides, has revolutionized food production since the 1950s and 1960s.

The green revolution has led to a great expansion in the production of many crops, including such basic foods as rice, maize and wheat. In India, its effects have been spectacular. Between 1955 and 1995, grain production trebled, giving the country sufficient food reserves to prevent famine in years when droughts or floods reduce the harvest. While once India had to import food, it is now self-sufficient.

Food Production

Agriculture, which supplies most of our food, together with materials to make clothes and other products, is the world's most important economic activity. But its relative importance has declined in comparison with manufacturing and service industries. As a result, the end of the 20th century marked the first time for 10,000 years when the vast majority of the people no longer had to depend for their living on growing crops and herding animals.

However, agriculture remains the dominant economic activity in many developing countries in Africa and Asia. For example, in the late 1990s, 90% or more of the people of Bhutan, Burundi, Nepal and Rwanda depended on farming for their living.

Many people in developing countries eke out the barest of livings by nomadic herding or shifting cultivation, combined with hunting, fishing and gathering plant foods. A large proportion of farmers live at subsistence level, producing little more than they require to provide the basic needs of their families.

The world's largest food producer and exporter is the United States, although agriculture employs

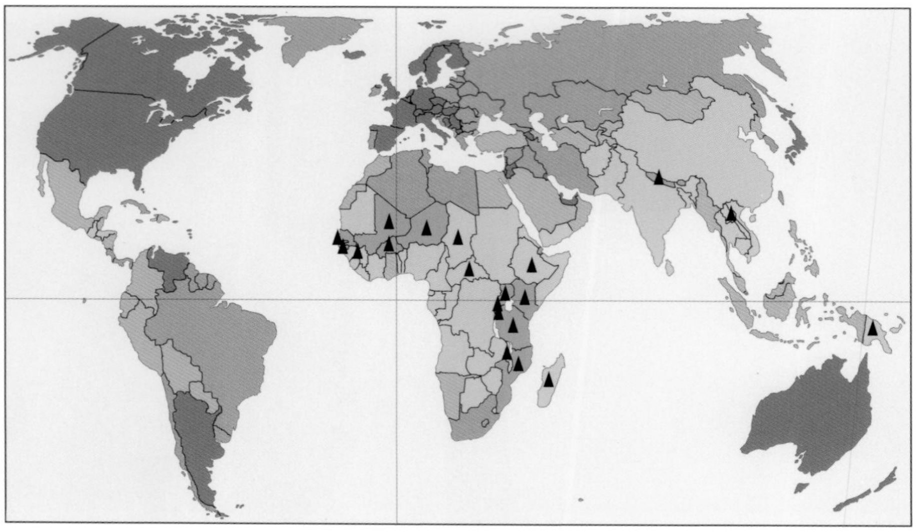

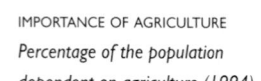

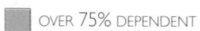

IMPORTANCE OF AGRICULTURE

Percentage of the population dependent on agriculture (1994).

- OVER 75% DEPENDENT
- 50–75% DEPENDENT
- 25–50% DEPENDENT
- 10–25% DEPENDENT
- UNDER 10% DEPENDENT
- ▲ *Over 75% of the total workforce employed in agriculture, forestry and fishing in 1995*

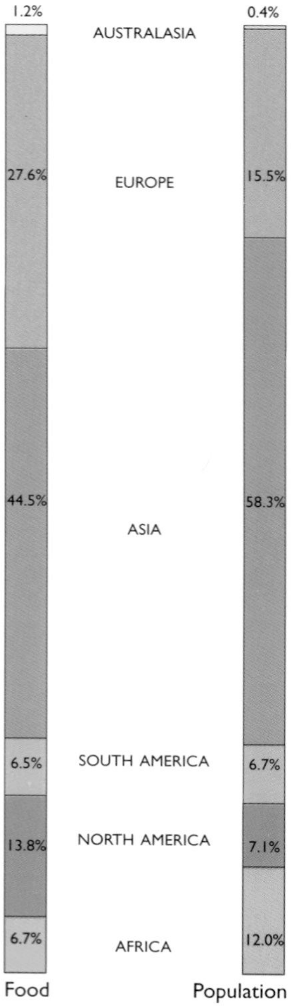

A comparison of world food production and population by continent.

Rice harvest, Bali, Indonesia

More than half of the world's people eat rice as their basic food. Rice grows well in tropical and subtropical regions, such as in Indonesia, India and south-eastern China.

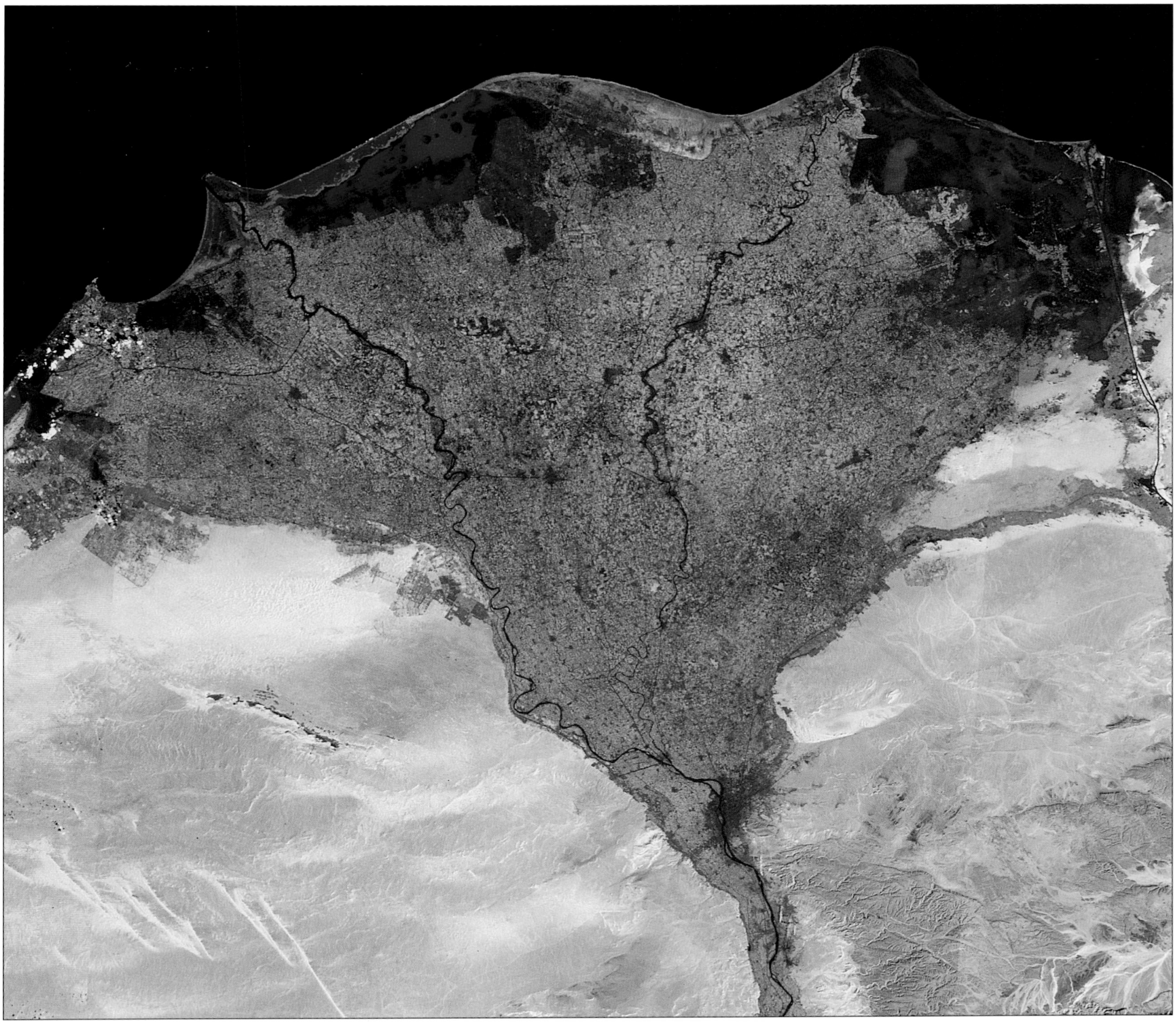

Landsat *image of the Nile delta, Egypt*

Most Egyptians live in the Nile valley and on its delta. Because much of the silt carried by the Nile now ends up on the floor of Lake Nasser, upstream of the Aswan Dam, the delta is now retreating and seawater is seeping inland. This eventuality was not foreseen when the Aswan High Dam was built in the 1960s.

WHEAT

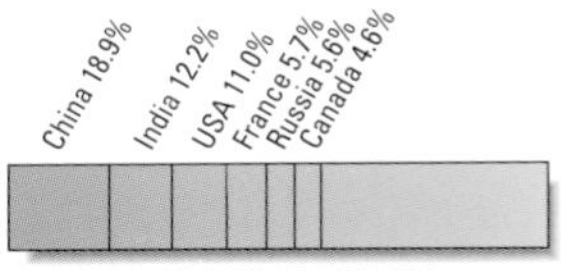

World total (1996): 584,874,000 tonnes

RICE

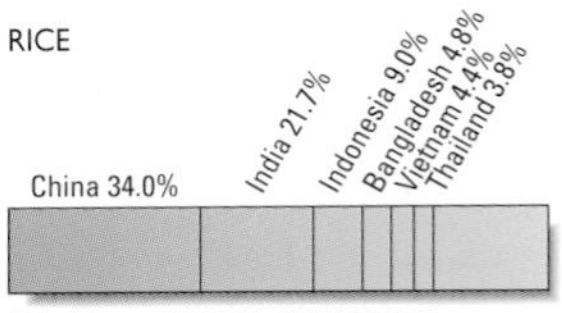

World total (1996): 562,259,000 tonnes

CASSAVA

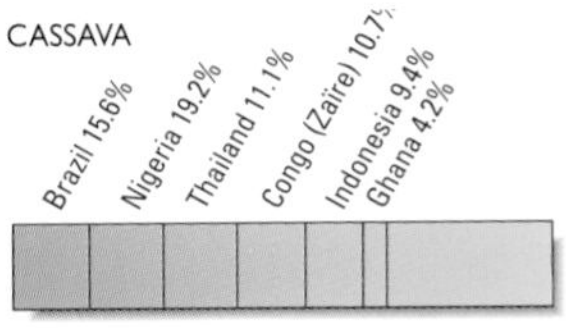

World total (1996): 162,942,000 tonnes

less than 3% of its total workforce. The high production of the United States is explained by its use of scientific methods and mechanization, which are features of agriculture throughout the developed world.

Intensive or Organic Farming

By the late 20th century, some people were beginning to question the dependence of farmers on chemical fertilizers and pesticides. Many people became concerned that the widespread use of chemicals was seriously polluting and damaging the environment.

Others objected to the intensive farming of animals to raise production and lower prices. For example, the suggestion in Britain in 1996 that BSE, or 'mad cow disease', might be passed on to people causing CJD (Creuzfeldt-Jakob Disease) caused widespread alarm.

Such problems have led some farmers to return to organic farming, which is based on animal-welfare principles and the banning of chemical fertilizers and pesticides. The costs of organic foods are certainly higher than those produced by intensive farming, but an increasing number of consumers in the Western world are beginning to demand organic products from their retailers.

Energy and Minerals

In March 1996, floods in Ukraine carried radioactive waste dumped near Chernobyl hundreds of kilometres downstream. This was the latest chapter in the disaster caused by the explosion at the Chernobyl nuclear power station in 1986, the worst nuclear accident in history. Nuclear power now provides about 17% of the world's electricity and experts once thought that it would eventually supply much of the world's energy supply. But concern about safety and worries about the high costs involved make this seem unlikely. Several developed countries have already abandoned their nuclear programmes.

Fossil Fuels

Huge amounts of energy are needed for heating, generating electricity and for transport. In the early years of the Industrial Revolution, coal formed from organic matter buried beneath the Earth's surface, was the leading source of energy. It remains important as a raw material in the manufacture of drugs and other products and also as a fuel, despite the fact that burning coal causes air pollution and gives off carbon dioxide, an important greenhouse gas.

However, oil and natural gas, which came into wide use in the 20th century, are cheaper to produce and easier to handle than coal, while, kilogram for kilogram, they give out more heat. Oil is especially important in moving transport, supplying about 97% of the fuel required.

In 1995, proven reserves of oil were sufficient to supply the world, at current rates of production, for 43 years, while supplies of natural gas stood at about 66 years. Coal reserves are more abundant and known reserves would last 200 years at present rates of use. Although these figures must be regarded with caution, because they do not allow for future discoveries, it is clear that fossil fuel reserves will one day run out.

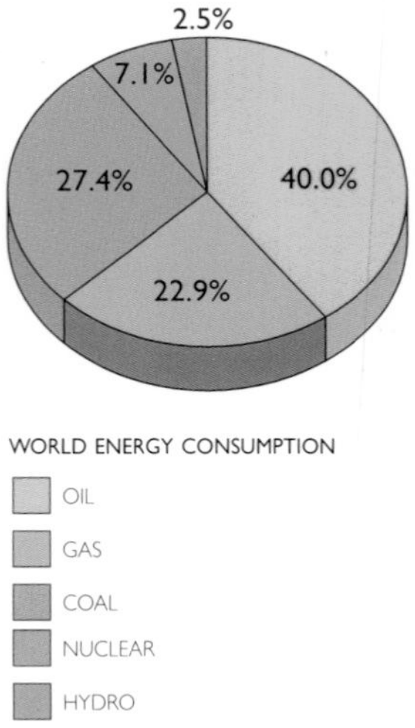

The diagram shows the proportion of world energy consumption in 1993 by type. Total energy consumption was 7,804 million tonnes of oil equivalent. Such fuels as wood, peat and animal wastes, together with renewable forms of energy, such as wind and geothermal power, are not included, although they are important in some areas.

Wind farms in California, United States

Wind farms using giant turbines can produce electricity at a lower cost than conventional power stations. But in many areas, winds are too light or too strong for wind farms to be effective.

SELECTED MINERAL PRODUCTION STATISTICS (1995)

Bauxite		Diamonds	
Australia	38%	Australia	38%
Guinea	13%	Congo (Zaïre)	18%
Jamaica	10%	Botswana	16%
Brazil	9%	Russia	12%
China	6%	South Africa	8%
Gold		**Iron ore**	
South Africa	23%	China	15%
USA	14%	Brazil	12%
Australia	11%	Australia	9%
Canada	7%	Russia	4%
Russia	6%	India	4%
Potash		**Zinc**	
Canada	37%	China	12%
Germany	13%	Canada	8%
Belarus	11%	Japan	8%
Russia	11%	USA	7%
USA	6%	Germany	5%

Potash mines in Utah, United States

Potash is a mineral used mainly to make fertilizers. Much of it comes from mines where deposits formed when ancient seas dried up are exploited. Potash is also extracted from salt lakes.

Alternative Energy

Other sources of energy are therefore required. Besides nuclear energy, the main alternative to fossil fuels is water power. The costs of building dams and hydroelectric power stations is high, though hydroelectric production is comparatively cheap and it does not cause pollution. But the creation of reservoirs uproots people and, in tropical rainforests, it destroys natural habitats. Hydroelectricity is also suitable only in areas with plenty of rivers and steep slopes, such as Norway, while it is unsuitable in flat areas, such as the Netherlands.

In Brazil, alcohol made from sugar has been used to fuel cars. Initially, this government-backed policy met with great success, but it has proved to be extremely expensive. Battery-run, electric cars have also been developed in the United States, but they appear to have limited use, because of the problems involved in regular and time-consuming recharging.

Other forms of energy, which are renewable and cleaner than fossil fuels, are winds, sea waves, the rise and fall of tides, and geothermal power. These forms of energy are already used to some extent. However, their contribution in global terms seems likely to remain small in the immediate future.

MINERAL DISTRIBUTION

Location of the principal mines and deposits.

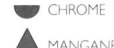

IRON & FERRO-ALLOYS
- IRON
- CHROME
- MANGANESE
- NICKEL

PRECIOUS METALS
- GOLD
- SILVER

PRECIOUS STONES
- DIAMONDS

LIGHT METALS
- BAUXITE

BASE METALS
- COPPER
- LEAD
- MERCURY
- TIN
- ZINC

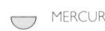

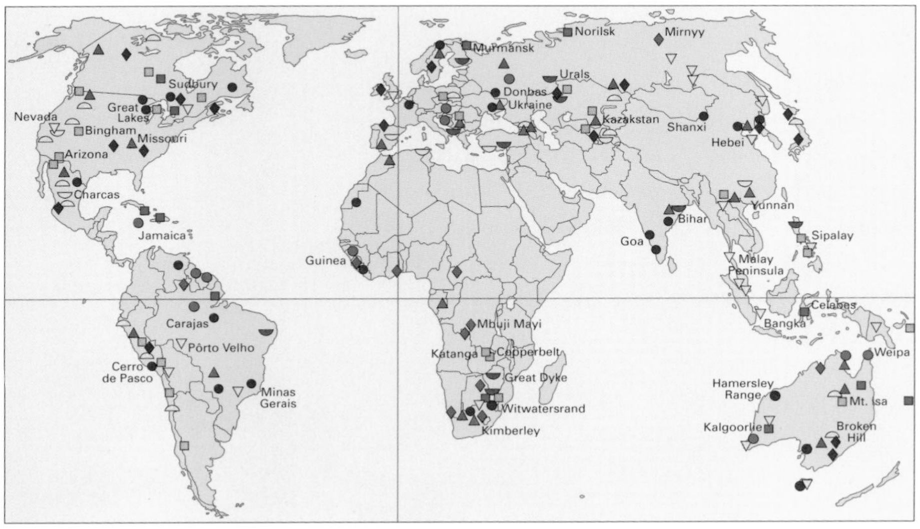

Minerals for Industry

In addition to energy, manufacturing industries need raw materials, including minerals, and these natural resources, like fossil fuels, are being used in such huge quantities that some experts have predicted shortages of some of them before long.

Manufacturers depend on supplies of about 80 minerals. Some, such as bauxite (aluminium ore) and iron, are abundant, but others are scarce or are found only in deposits that are uneconomical to mine. Many experts advocate a policy of recycling scrap metal, including aluminium, chromium, copper, lead, nickel and zinc. This practice would reduce pollution and conserve the energy required for extracting and refining mineral ores.

World Economies

In 1995, Tanzania had a per capita GNP (Gross National Product) of US$120, as compared with Switzerland, whose per capita GNP stood at $40,630. These figures indicate the vast gap between the economies and standards of living of the two countries.

The GNP includes the GDP (Gross Domestic Product), which consists of the total output of goods and services in a country in a given year, plus net exports – that is, the value of goods and services sold abroad less the value of foreign goods and services used in the country in the same year. The GNP divided by the population gives a country's GNP per capita. In low-income developing countries, agriculture makes a high contribution to the GNP. For example, in Tanzania, 56% of the GDP in 1995 came from agriculture. On the other hand, manufacturing was small-scale and contributed only 5% of the GDP. By comparison, in high-income economies, the percentage contribution of manufacturing far exceeds that of agriculture.

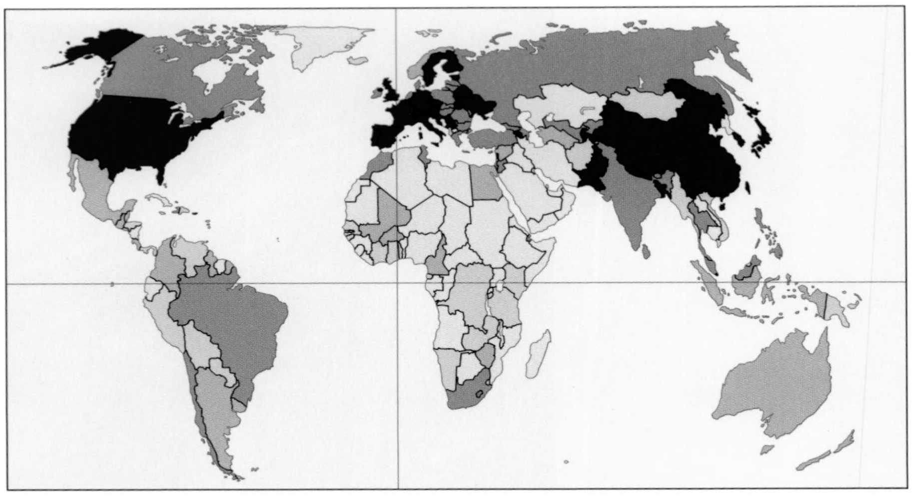

INDUSTRY AND TRADE

Manufactured goods (including machinery and transport) as a percentage of total exports.

- OVER 75%
- 50–75%
- 25–50%
- 10–25%
- UNDER 10%

Eastern Asia, including Japan (98.3%), Taiwan (92.7%) and Hong Kong (93.0%), contains countries whose exports are most dominated by manufactures. But some countries in Europe, such as Slovenia (92.5%), are also heavily dependent on manufacturing.

Microchip production, Taiwan

Despite its lack of resources, Taiwan is one of eastern Asia's 'tiger' economies. Its high-tech industies have helped it to achieve fast economic growth and to compete on the world market.

Industrialization

The Industrial Revolution began in Britain in the late 18th century. Before that time, most people worked on farms. But with the Industrial Revolution came factories, using machines that could manufacture goods much faster and more cheaply than those made by cottage industries which already existed.

The Industrial Revolution soon spread to several countries in mainland Europe and the United States and, by the late 19th century, it had reached Canada, Japan and Russia. At first, industrial development was based on such areas as coalfields or ironfields. But in the 20th century, the use of oil, which is easy to transport along pipelines, made it possible for industries to be set up anywhere.

Some nations, such as Switzerland, became industrialized even though they lacked natural resources. They depended instead on the specialized skills of their workers. This same pattern applies today. Some countries with rich natural resources, such as Mexico (with a per capita GNP in 1995 of $3,320), lag far behind Japan ($39,640) and South Korea ($9,700), which lack resources and have to import many of the materials they need for their manufacturing industries.

Service Industries

Experts often refer to high-income countries as industrial economies. But manufacturing employs only one in six workers in the United

GROSS NATIONAL PRODUCT PER CAPITA US$ (1995)

1	Luxembourg	41,210
2	Switzerland	40,630
3	Japan	39,640
4	Norway	31,250
5	Denmark	29,890
6	Germany	27,510
7	USA	26,980
8	Austria	26,890
9	Singapore	26,730
10	France	24,990
11	Iceland	24,950
12	Belgium	24,710
13	Netherlands	24,000
14	Sweden	23,750
15	Hong Kong	22,990
16	Finland	20,580
17	Canada	19,380
18	Italy	19,020
19	Australia	18,720
20	UK	18,700

New cars awaiting transportation, Los Angeles, United States
Cars are the most important single manufactured item in world trade, followed by vehicle parts and engines. The world's leading car producers are Japan, the United States, Germany and France.

States, one in five in Britain, and one in three in Germany and Japan.

In most developed economies, the percentage of manufacturing jobs has fallen in recent years, while jobs in service industries have risen. For example, in Britain, the proportion of jobs in manufacturing fell from 37% in 1970 to 21% in 1995, while jobs in the service sector rose from just under 50% to 66%. While change in Britain was especially rapid, similar changes were taking place in most industrial economies. By 1995, service industries accounted for well over half the jobs in the generally prosperous countries that made up the OECD (Organization for Economic Co-operation and Development). Instead of being called the 'industrial' economies, these countries might be better named the 'service' economies.

Service industries offer a wide range of jobs and many of them require high educational qualifications. These include finance, insurance and high-tech industries, such as computer programming, entertainment and telecommunications. Service industries also include marketing and advertising, which are essential if the cars and television sets made by manufacturers are to be sold. Another valuable service industry is tourism; in some countries, such as the Gambia, it is the major foreign exchange earner. Trade in services now plays an important part in world economics. The share of services in world trade rose from 17% in 1980 to 22% in 1992.

THE WORKFORCE
Percentage of men and women between 15 and 64 years old in employment, selected countries (latest available year).

MEN
WOMEN

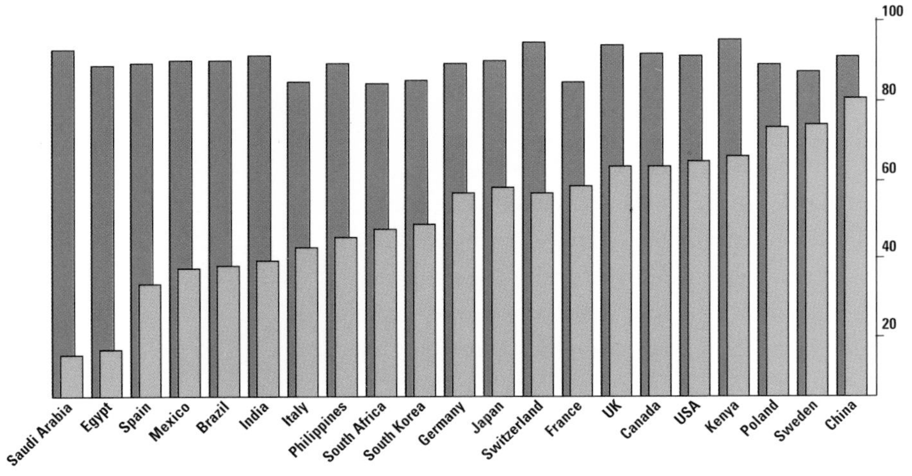

Trade and Commerce

The establishment of the WTO (World Trade Organization) on 1 January 1995 was the latest step in the long history of world trade. The WTO was set up by the eighth round of negotiations, popularly called the 'Uruguay round', conducted by the General Agreement on Tariffs and Trade (GATT). This treaty was signed by representatives of 125 governments in April 1994 after many difficulties.

GATT was first established in 1948. Its initial aim was to produce a charter to create a body called the International Trade Organization. This body never came into being. Instead, GATT, acting as an *ad hoc* agency, pioneered a series of agreements aimed at liberalizing world trade by reducing tariffs on imports and other obstacles to free trade.

GATT's objectives were based on the belief that international trade creates wealth. Trade occurs because the world's resources are not distributed evenly between countries, and, in theory, free trade means that every country should concentrate on what it can do best and purchase from others goods and services that they can supply more cheaply. In practice, however, free trade may cause unemployment when imported goods are cheaper than those produced within the country.

Trade is sometimes an important factor in world politics, especially when trade sanctions are applied against countries whose actions incur the disapproval of the international community. For example, in the 1990s, worldwide trade sanctions were imposed on Serbia because of its involvement in the civil war in Bosnia-Herzegovina.

CHANGING TRADE PATTERNS

The early 16th century, when Europeans began to divide the world into huge empires, opened up a new era in international trade. By the 19th century, the colonial powers, who were among the first industrial powers, promoted trade with their colonies, from which they obtained unprocessed raw materials, such as food, natural fibres, minerals and timber. In return, they shipped clothes, shoes and other cheap items to the colonies.

From the late 19th century until the early 1950s, primary products dominated world trade, with oil becoming the leading item in the later part of this period. Many developing countries still depend heavily on the export of one or two primary products, such as coffee or iron ore, but overall the proportion of primary products in world trade has fallen since the 1950s. Today the most important elements in world trade are

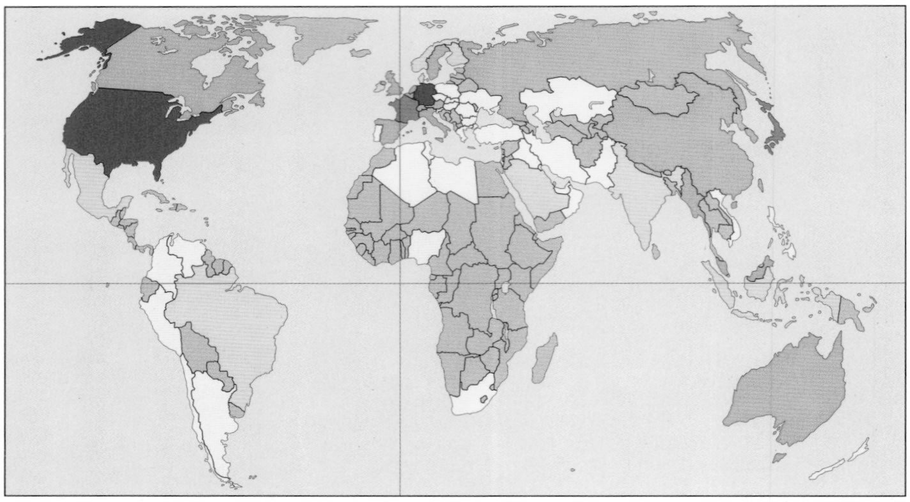

WORLD TRADE

Percentage share of total world exports by value (1995).

- OVER 10% OF WORLD TRADE
- 5–10% OF WORLD TRADE
- 1–5% OF WORLD TRADE
- 0.5–1% OF WORLD TRADE
- 0.1–0.5% OF WORLD TRADE
- UNDER 0.1% OF WORLD TRADE

The world's leading trading nations, according to the combined value of their exports and imports, are the United States, Germany, Japan, France and the United Kingdom.

New York City Stock Exchange, United States

Stock exchanges, where stocks and shares are sold and bought, are important in channelling savings and investments to companies and governments. The world's largest stock exchange is in Tokyo, Japan.

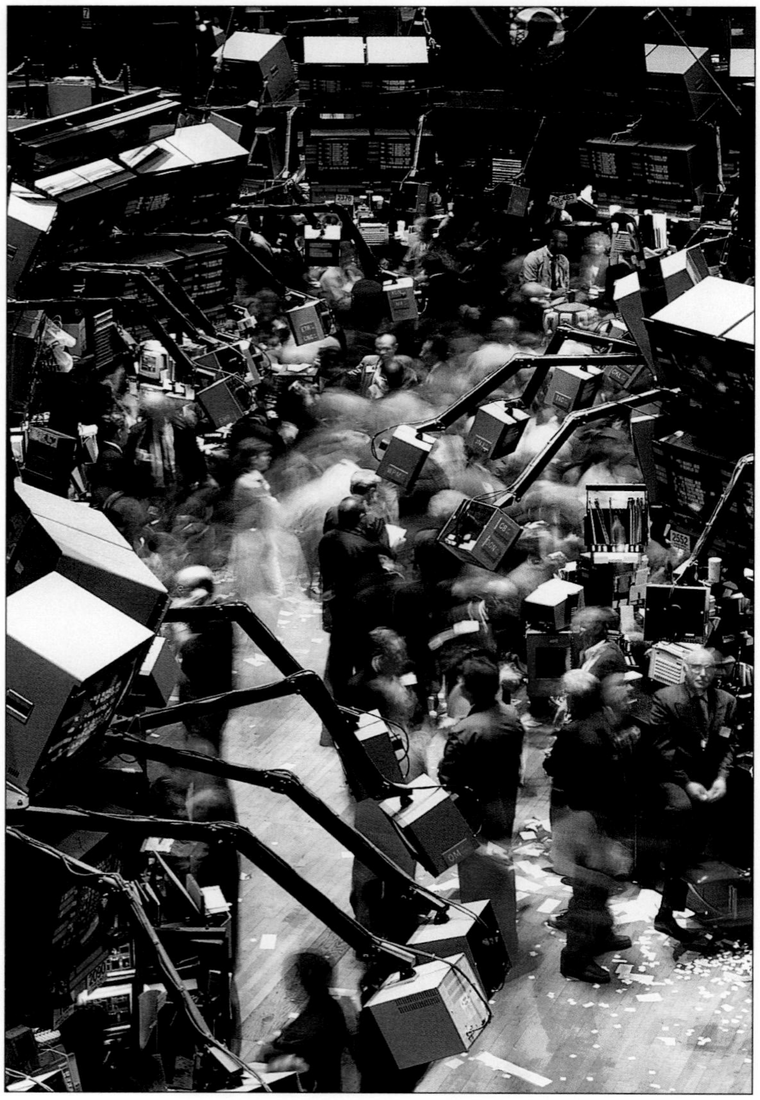

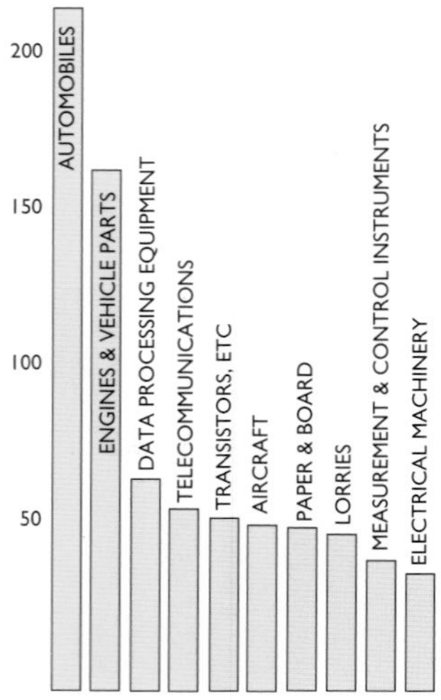

Traded products

Top ten manufactures traded by value in billions of US$ (latest available year).

Rotterdam, Netherlands

World trade depends on transport. Rotterdam, the world's largest port, serves not only the Netherlands, but also industrial areas in parts of Germany, France and Switzerland.

manufactures and semi-manufactures, exchanged mainly between the industrialized nations.

The World's Markets

Private companies conduct most of world trade, but government policies affect it. Governments which believe that certain industries are strategic, or essential for the country's future, may impose tariffs on imports, or import quotas to limit the volume of imports, if they are thought to be undercutting the domestic industries.

For example, the United States has argued that Japan has greater access to its markets than the United States has to Japan's. This might have led the United States to resort to protectionism, but instead the United States remains committed to free trade.

Other problems in international trade occur when governments give subsidies to its producers, who can then export products at low prices. Another difficulty, called 'dumping', occurs when products are sold at below the market price in order to gain a market share. One of the aims of the newly-created WTO is the phasing out of government subsidies for agricultural products, though the world's poorest countries will be exempt from many of the WTO's most severe regulations.

Governments are also concerned about the volume of imports and exports and most countries keep records of international transactions. When the total value of goods and services imported exceeds the value of goods and services exported, then the country has a deficit in its balance of payments. Large deficits can weaken a country's economy.

DEPENDENCE ON TRADE

Value of exports as a percentage of GNP (1995).

- OVER 50% GNP FROM EXPORTS
- 40–50% GNP FROM EXPORTS
- 30–40% GNP FROM EXPORTS
- 20–30% GNP FROM EXPORTS
- 10–20% GNP FROM EXPORTS
- UNDER 10% GNP FROM EXPORTS
- MOST DEPENDENT ON INDUSTRIAL EXPORTS (OVER 75% OF TOTAL)
- MOST DEPENDENT ON FUEL EXPORTS (OVER 75% OF TOTAL)
- MOST DEPENDENT ON METAL & MINERAL EXPORTS (OVER 75% OF TOTAL)

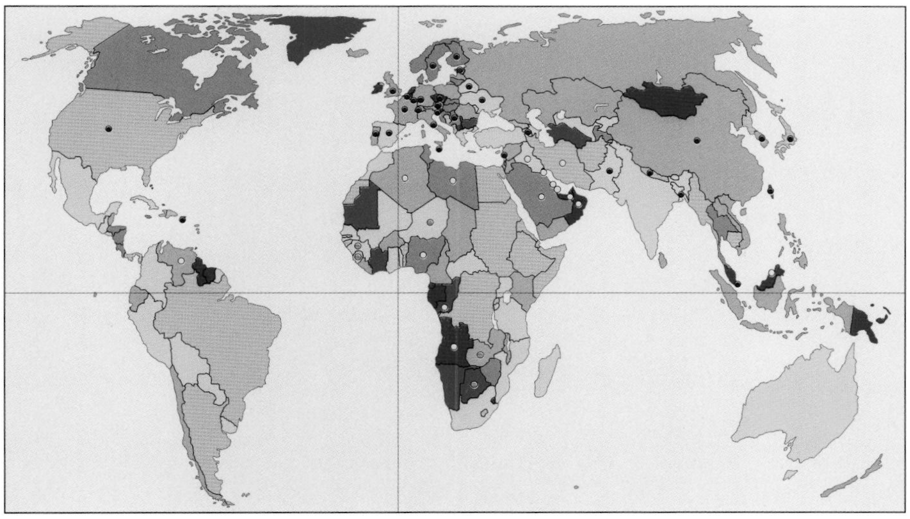

Travel and Communications

In the 1990s, millions of people became linked into an 'information superhighway' called the Internet. Equipped with a personal computer, an electricity supply, a telephone and a modem, people are able to communicate with others all over the world. People can now send messages by e-mail (electronic mail), they can engage in electronic discussions, contacting people with similar interests, and engage in 'chat lines', which are the latest equivalent of telephone conferences.

These new developments are likely to affect the working lives of people everywhere, enabling them to work at home whilst having many of the facilities that are available in an office. The Internet is part of an ongoing and astonishingly rapid evolution in the fields of communications and transport.

Transport

Around 200 years ago, most people never travelled far from their birthplace, but today we are much more mobile. Cars and buses now provide convenient forms of transport for many millions of people, huge ships transport massive cargoes around the world, and jet airliners, some travelling faster than the speed of sound, can transport high-value goods as well as holiday-makers to almost any part of the world.

Land transport of freight has developed greatly since the start of the Industrial Revolution. Canals, which became important in the 18th century, could not compete with rail transport in the 19th century. Rail transport remains important, but, in the 20th century, it has suffered from competition with road transport (especially in the United Kingdom), which is cheaper and has the advantage of carrying materials and goods from door to door.

Road transport causes pollution and the burning of fuels creates greenhouse gases that contribute to global warming. Yet privately owned cars are now the leading form of passenger traffic in developed nations, especially for journeys of less than about 400 km [250 miles]. Car owners do not have to suffer the inconvenience of waiting for public transport, such as buses, though they often have to endure traffic jams at peak travel times.

Ocean passenger traffic is now modest, but ships carry the bulk of international trade. Huge oil tankers and bulk grain carriers now ply the oceans with their cargoes, while container ships

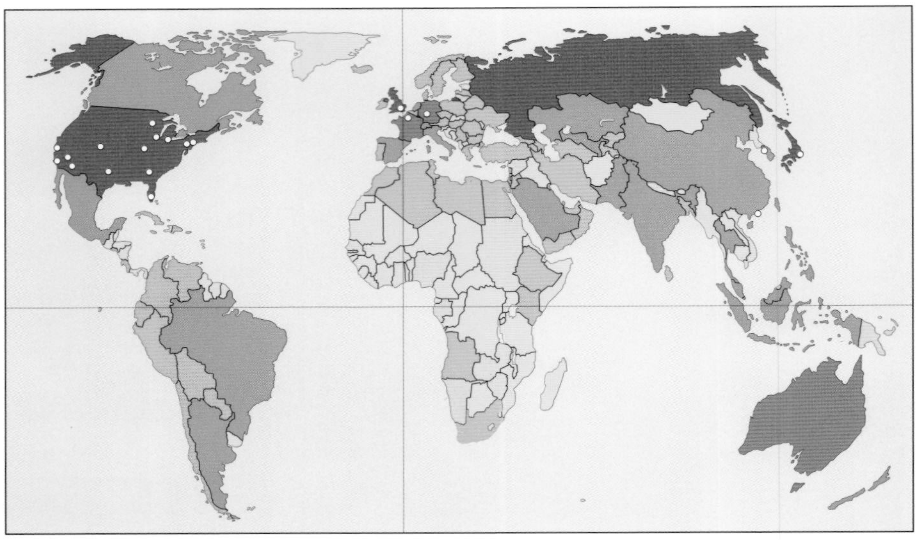

AIR TRAVEL – PASSENGER KILOMETRES* FLOWN (*1994*).

- OVER 100,000 MILLION
- 50,000–100,000 MILLION
- 10,000–50,000 MILLION
- 1,000–10,000 MILLION
- 500–1,000 MILLION
- UNDER 500 MILLION
- ◦ MAJOR AIRPORTS (HANDLING OVER 25 MILLION PASSENGERS IN 1995)

** Passenger kilometres are the number of passengers (both international and domestic) multiplied by the distance flown by each passenger from the airport of origin.*

Jodrell Bank Observatory, Cheshire, England

The world's first giant radio telescope began operations at Jodrell Bank in 1957. Radio telescopes can explore the Universe as far as 16 billion light-years away.

SELECTED NEWSPAPER CIRCULATION FIGURES (1995)

France		
Le Monde		357,362
Le Figaro		350,000
Germany		
Bild		4,500,000
Süddeutsche Zeitung		402,866
Italy		
Corriera Della Sella		676,904
La Republica		655,321
La Stampa		436,047
Japan		
Yomiuri Shimbun	(a.m. edition)	9,800,000
	(p.m. edition)	4,400,000
Manichi Shimbun	(a.m. edition)	3,200,000
	(p.m. edition)	1,900,000
Russia		
Pravda		1,373,795
Ivestia		700,000
Spain		
El Pais		407,629
United Kingdom		
The Sun		4,061,253
Daily Mirror		2,525,000
Daily Express		1,270,642
The Times		672,802
The Guardian		402,214
United States		
New York Times		1,724,705
Chicago Tribune		1,110,552
Houston Chronicle		605,343

Kansai International Airport, Japan
The new airport, opened in September 1994, is built on an artificial island in Osaka Bay. The island holds the world's biggest airport terminal at nearly 2 km [1.2 miles] long.

carry mixed cargoes. Containers are boxes built to international standards that contain cargo. Containers are easy to handle, and so they reduce shipping costs, speed up deliveries and cut losses caused by breakages. Most large ports now have the facilities to handle containers.

Air transport is suitable for carrying goods that are expensive, light and compact, or perishable. However, because of the high costs of air freight, it is most suitable for carrying passengers along long-distance routes around the world. Through air travel, international tourism, with people sometimes flying considerable distances, has become a major and rapidly expanding industry.

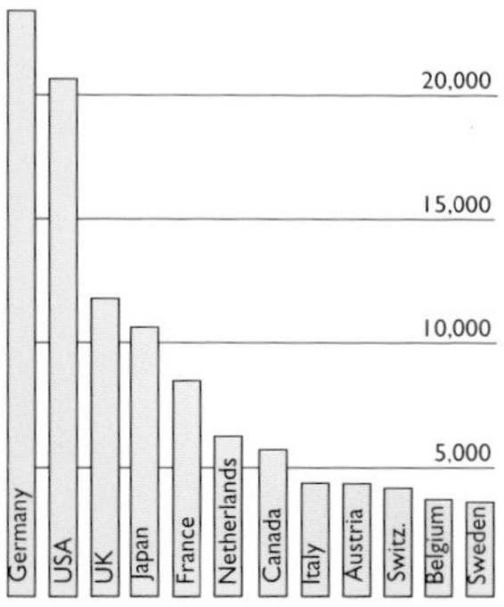

Spending on tourism
Countries spending the most on overseas tourism, US$ million (latest available year).

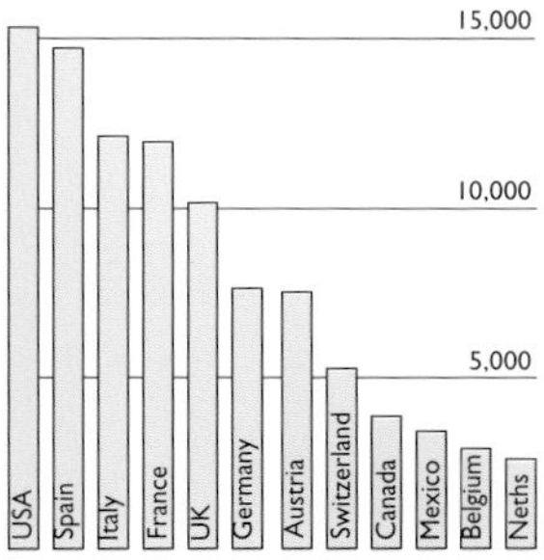

Receipts from tourism
Countries receiving the most from overseas tourism, US$ million (latest available year).

Communications

After humans first began to communicate by using the spoken word, the next great stage in the development of communications was the invention of writing around 5,500 years ago.

The invention of movable type in the mid 15th century led to the mass production of books and, in the early 17th century, the first newspapers. Newspapers now play an important part in the mass communication of information, although today radio and, even more important, television have led to a decline in the circulation of newspapers in many parts of the world.

The most recent developments have occurred in the field of electronics. Artificial communications satellites now circle the planet, relaying radio, television, telegraph and telephone signals. This enables people to watch events on the far side of the globe as they are happening. Electronic equipment is also used in many other ways, such as in navigation systems used in air, sea and space, and also in modern weaponry, as shown vividly in the television coverage of the 1991 Gulf War.

The Age of Computers

One of the most remarkable applications of electronics is in the field of computers. Computers are now making a huge contribution to communications. They are able to process data at incredibly high speeds and can store vast quantities of information. For example, the work of weather forecasters has been greatly improved now that computers can process the enormous amount of data required for a single weather forecast. They also have many other applications in such fields as business, government, science and medicine.

Through the Internet, computers provide a free interchange of news and views around the world. But the dangers of misuse, such as the exchange of pornographic images, have led to calls for censorship. Censorship, however, is a blunt weapon, which can be used by authoritarian governments to suppress the free exchange of information that the new information superhighway makes possible.

The World Today

The early years of the 20th century witnessed the exploration of Antarctica, the last uncharted continent. Today, less than 100 years later, tourists are able to take cruises to the icy southern continent, while almost no part of the globe is inaccessible to the determined traveller. Improved transport and images from space have made our world seem smaller.

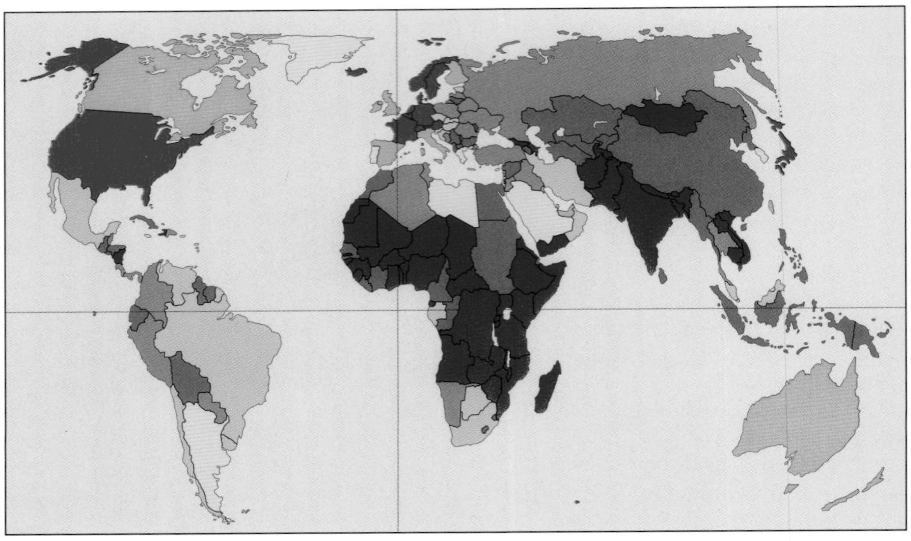

GROSS NATIONAL PRODUCT PER CAPITA

The value of total production divided by the population (1995).

- OVER 400% OF WORLD AVERAGE
- 200–400% OF WORLD AVERAGE
- 100–200% OF WORLD AVERAGE

[WORLD AVERAGE WEALTH PER PERSON US$5,714]

- 50–100% OF WORLD AVERAGE
- 25–50% OF WORLD AVERAGE
- 10–25% OF WORLD AVERAGE
- UNDER 10% OF WORLD AVERAGE

RICHEST COUNTRIES	
Luxembourg	$41,210
Switzerland	$40,630
Japan	$39,640
Norway	$31,250

POOREST COUNTRIES	
Mozambique	$80
Ethiopia	$100
Congo (Zaïre)	$120
Tanzania	$120

A Divided World

Between the end of World War II in 1945 and the late 1980s, the world was divided, politically and economically, into three main groups: the developed countries or Western democracies, with their free enterprise or mixed economies; the centrally planned or Communist countries; and the developing countries or Third World.

This division became obsolete when the former Soviet Union and its old European allies, together with the 'special economic zones' in eastern China, began the transition from centrally planned to free enterprise economies. This left the world divided into two broad camps: the prosperous developed countries and the poorer developing countries. The simplest way of distinguishing between the groups is with reference to their per capita Gross National Products (per capita GNPs).

The World Bank divides the developing countries into three main groups. At the bottom are the low-income economies, which include China, India and most of sub-Saharan Africa. This group contains about 56% of the world's population but its average per capita GNP in 1994 was only US$390. The other two groups are the lower-middle-income economies with an average GNP per capita of $1,650, and the upper-middle-income economies, with an average GNP per capita of $4,640. By contrast, the high-income economies, also called the developed countries, contain less than 15% of the world's population but have the high (and rising) average GNP per capita of $24,170.

Economic and Social Contrasts

Economic differences are coupled with other factors, such as rates of population growth. For example, in 1980–93, the low-income economies had a high rate of population growth of 2% per year, while the populations of the middle-income economies were increasing by 1.7%. By contrast, the populations of countries in the high-income category were increasing by only 0.6%.

Stark contrasts exist worldwide in the quality

Porters carrying luggage for tourists, Selous Park, Tanzania

Improved and cheaper transport has led to a boom in tourism in many developing countries. Tourism provides jobs and foreign exchange, though it can undermine local cultures.

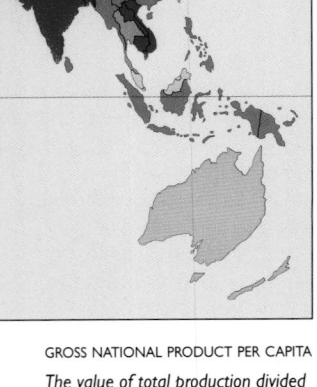

Birth control poster, China
China is the only country with more than a billion people. Central to its economic development policies is population control. Posters exhort the advantages of one-child families.

of life. Generally, the people in Western Europe and North America are better fed, healthier and have more cars and better homes than the people in low- and middle-income economies.

The average life expectancy at birth in low-income economies in 1993 was 62 years, 15 years less than in the high-income economies. Illiteracy in countries in the low-income category is high, at 42% in 1992, while for women, who get fewer opportunities, the percentage of those who could not read and write stood at 54%. By contrast, illiteracy is relatively rare in the high-income economies.

Future Development

In the last 50 years, despite all the aid supplied to developing countries, much of the world still suffers from poverty and economic backwardness. Some countries are even poorer now than they were a generation ago while others have become substantially richer.

The most remarkable success has been achieved in eastern Asia. Japan and the 'tiger economies' of Hong Kong, Indonesia, Malaysia, Singapore, South Korea, Thailand and Taiwan had an average annual economic growth rate of 5.5% between 1965 and 1993, while their share in the exports of manufactured goods more than doubled in the same period. In 1997, however, an Asian market crash temporarily halted this dramatic economic expansion.

Reasons advanced to explain the success of the eastern Asian countries include low wage scales, strong family structures, low state expenditure on welfare and large investment in education for both sexes. Some of the arguments are contradictory. For example, while some argue that the success of Hong Kong is due to free enterprise, the governments of Japan and South Korea have intervened substantially in the development of their economies.

Eastern Asia's economic growth has been exceptional and probably cannot be regarded as a model for the developing world. But several factors suggest that poor countries may find progress easier in the 21st century. For example, technology is now more readily transferable between countries, while improved transport and communications make it easier for countries to take part in the world economy. But industrial development and rising living standards could lead to an increase in global pollution. Hence, any strategy for global economic expansion must also take account of environmental factors.

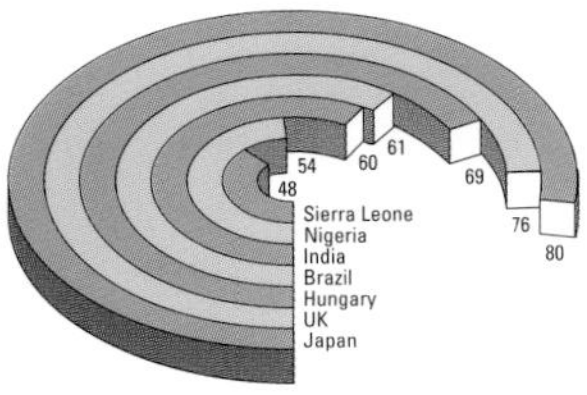

Years of life expectancy at birth, selected countries (1997).
The chart shows the contrasting range of average life expectancies at birth for a range of countries, including both low-income and high-income economies. Generally, improved health services are raising life expectancies. On average, women live longer than men, even in the poorer developing countries.

Glossary

Abyss The lowest part of the oceans, at the foot of the continental slope, which forms the true edge of the continents.

Apparent magnitude The magnitude of a star as seen from Earth; it depends on the absolute magnitude (the apparent magnitude if the star was observed from a standard distance of 32.6 light-years) and the distance of the star from the Earth.

Aquifer A layer of rock which contains water and allows water to percolate through it. It may be porous, as in sandstone, or fissured, as in limestone.

Atmosphere The layer of air which surrounds the Earth, which includes gases, such as nitrogen and oxygen, and water vapour.

Biome A major type of plant and animal community, such as tundra, taiga (boreal forest) or tropical rainforest.

Comet A body in the Solar System consisting of a nucleus and a tail. It is composed of ice particles, gases and dust.

Declination How far north or south a star is above the Celestial Equator, an imaginary line in the sky directly above the Equator. It is measured in degrees.

Delta An area of land at the mouths of some rivers which is made up of sediment deposited there by the river. It gets its name from the triangular Greek letter delta (Δ), though some deltas are not triangular.

Demographers People who study human populations, such as their numbers and distribution.

Developed country A country with a balanced economy, including a major manufacturing sector.

Developing country A poor country in which agriculture (often at subsistence level) is usually the mainstay of the economy.

Element A basic chemical substance which cannot be broken down into other substances by chemical means.

Equinox Two days during the year when the Sun is overhead at the Equator and everywhere on Earth has 12 hours of darkness. The equinoxes occur on or around 21 March and 23 September.

Erosion The processes by which natural forces, including weathering, running water, ice and winds, constantly modify the land.

Fault A crack or fracture in the Earth's crust along along which the rocks have moved so that the rocks on either side are displaced.

Fold Bends in rock strata caused by enormous lateral pressure.

Fossil fuel Any non-renewable fuel formed from once-living plant or animal matter, including peat and coal, oil and natural gas.

Glacier A body of ice which flows down a valley. It is composed of compacted snow.

Ice Age A period in history when global temperatures fell and ice covered large areas that are now ice-free.

Ice sheet A huge body of ice covering a large area. The world's two ice sheets cover Antarctica and Greenland. Small ice sheets are called ice caps.

Internet A global network of interconnected computer networks. Until the late 1980s the Internet was used only by governments and universities. By the mid-1990s, millions of home computers were connected.

Lithosphere The hard outer layer of the Earth, consisting of the crust and the hard upper layer of the mantle.

Monsoon A seasonal wind, especially in southern Asia, where the prevailing north-easterly trade winds in winter are replaced in summer by moist south-westerly winds which bring heavy rain.

Moraine Eroded rock ranging from clay to large boulders, that is transported and deposited by glaciers and other bodies of ice.

Neutron star A star made up almost entirely of atomic particles called neutrons.

Nuclear fision The process in stars by which hydrogen nuclei change into helium nuclei, creating energy which escapes in the form of light.

Ozone layer A layer of the gas ozone in the stratosphere that blocks out most of the Sun's harmful ultraviolet radiation.

Population growth A change in human population caused by natural increase (the difference between births and deaths) and migration.

Primary products Raw materials, such as crops, minerals or timber, that have not been processed.

Pyroclasts Fragments of magma thrown out by explosions during volcanic activity.

Porous rock A rock, such as sandstone, that contains pores through which water can percolate.

Right ascension A measure in hours of the position of a star east of the place where the Sun crosses the Celestial Equator on 21 March. One hour represents 15 degrees.

Solstice Two days during the year when the overhead Sun reaches either its northernmost point (the Tropic of Cancer) or its southernmost point (the Tropic of Capricorn).

Special economic zones Areas in eastern China where the government has encouraged foreign investment and where economic growth has been exceptionally rapid.

'Tiger' economies The name given to the developing economies of rapidly industrializing countries of eastern Asia, including Indonesia, Malaysia, South Korea, Singapore, Thailand and Taiwan.

Tornado A small, but violent whirlwind which occurs over land areas.

Trade wind A prevailing wind that blows from the high-pressure horse latitudes towards the low-pressure doldrums around the Equator.

Tropical cyclone A large storm which forms over warm seas north and south of the Equator. It may cause great damage to coastal areas, but it dies out quickly when it reaches land. Other names for this kind of storm are hurricane (in North America), typhoon (in Asia) and willy-willy (in Australia).

WORLD MAPS

MAP SYMBOLS

SETTLEMENTS

PARIS | Berne | Livorno | Brugge | *Algeciras* | *Fréjus* | *Oberammergau* | *Thira*

Settlement symbols and type styles vary according to the scale of each map and indicate the importance of towns on the map rather than specific population figures

∴ Ruins or Archæological Sites

Wells in Desert

ADMINISTRATION

International Boundaries

International Boundaries (Undefined or Disputed)

Internal Boundaries

National Parks

Country Names

NICARAGUA

Administrative Area Names

KENT

CALABRIA

International boundaries show the *de facto* situation where there are rival claims to territory

COMMUNICATIONS

Principal Roads

Other Roads

Trails and Seasonal Roads

Passes

Airfields

Principal Railways

Railways Under Construction

Other Railways

Railway Tunnels

Principal Canals

PHYSICAL FEATURES

Perennial Streams

Intermittent Streams

Perennial Lakes

Intermittent Lakes

Swamps and Marshes

Permanent Ice and Glaciers

▲ 8848 Elevations in metres

▼ 8050 Sea Depths in metres

1134 Height of Lake Surface Above Sea Level in metres

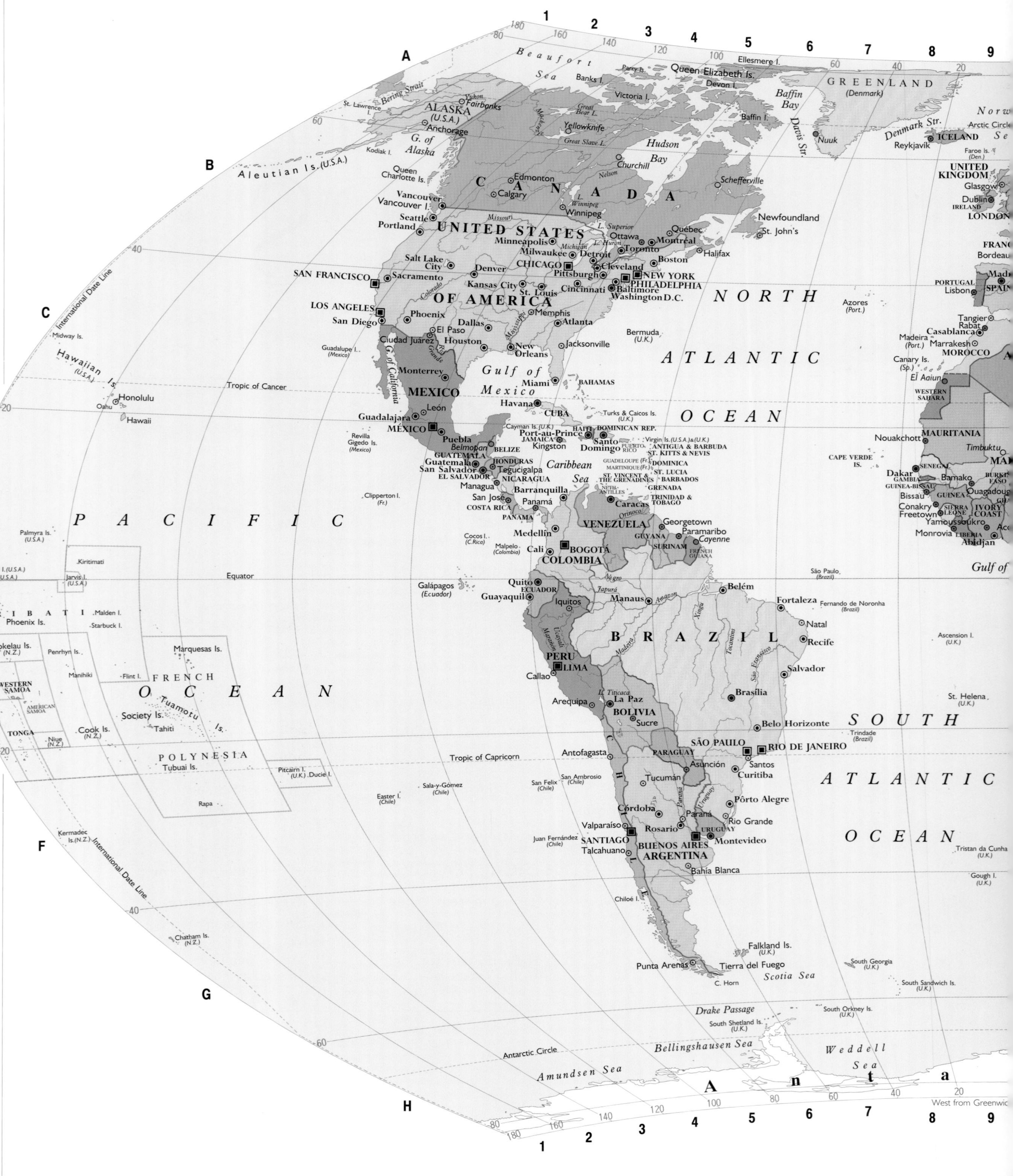

Projection: *Hammer Equal Area*

Hanoi ◉ Capital Cities

ARCTIC OCEAN 1:31 100 000

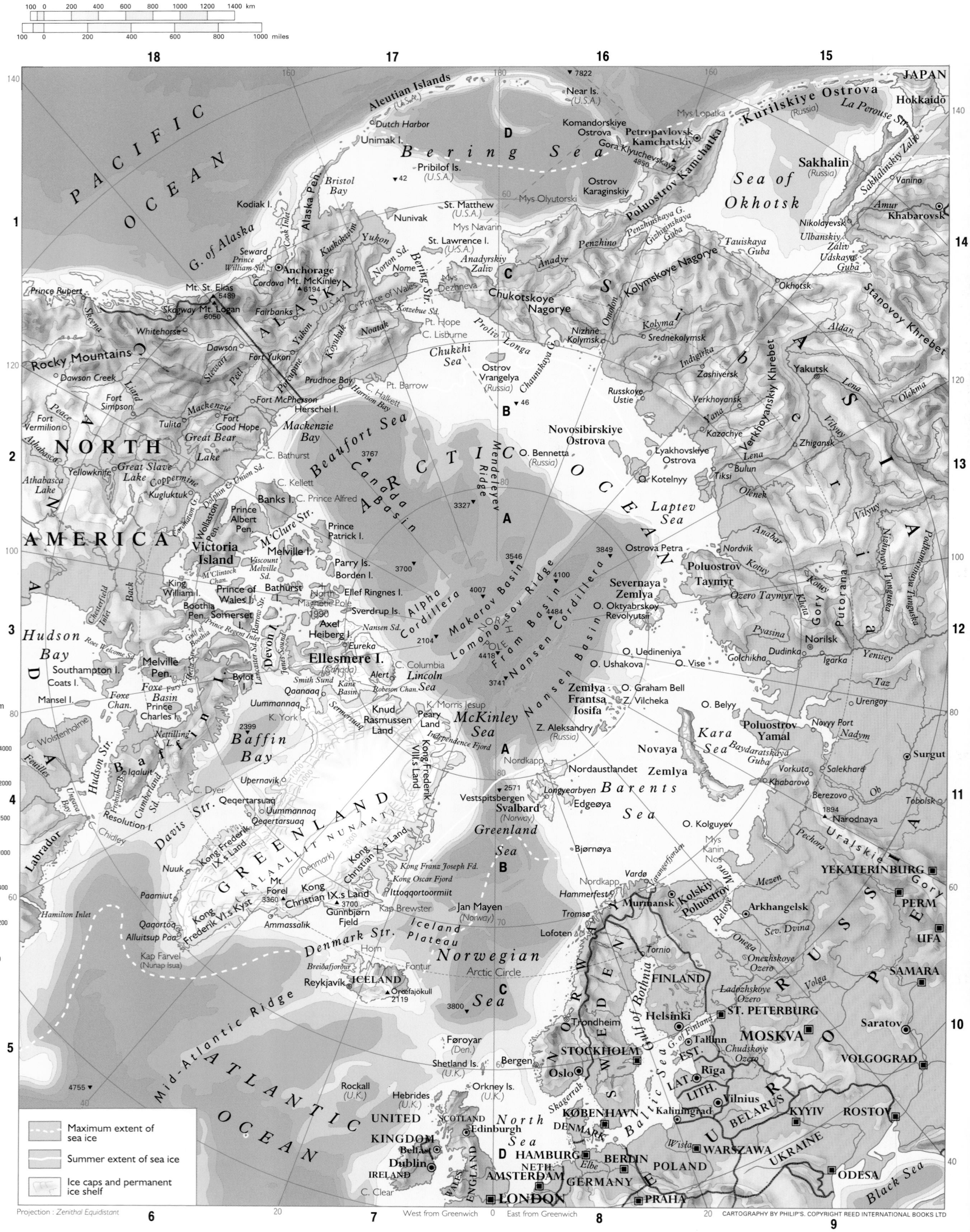

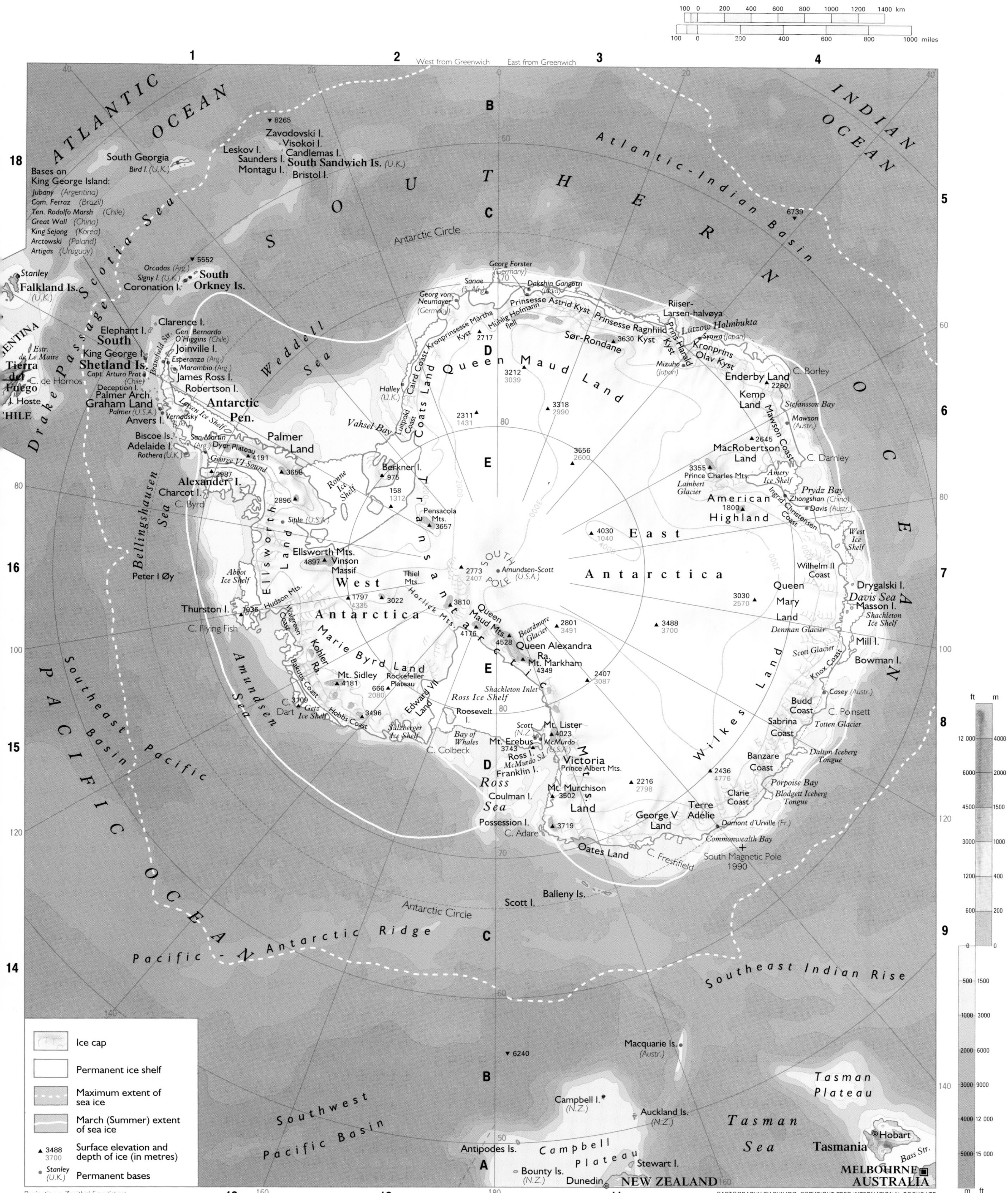

Projection: *Zenithal Equidistant*

CARTOGRAPHY BY PHILIP'S. COPYRIGHT REED INTERNATIONAL BOOKS LTD

The Antarctic Treaty was signed in Washington in 1959 so that scientific and technical research could continue unhampered by international politics.

All territorial claims covering land areas south of latitude 60°S have been suspended. Those claims were:

Norwegian claim	45°E - 20°W	French claim	136°E - 142°E	British claim	80°W - 20°W
Australian claims	45°E - 136°E	New Zealand claim	160°E - 150°W	Argentine claim	74°W - 53°W
	142°E - 160°E	Chilean claim	90°W - 53°W		

6 EUROPE : Physical 1:17 800 000

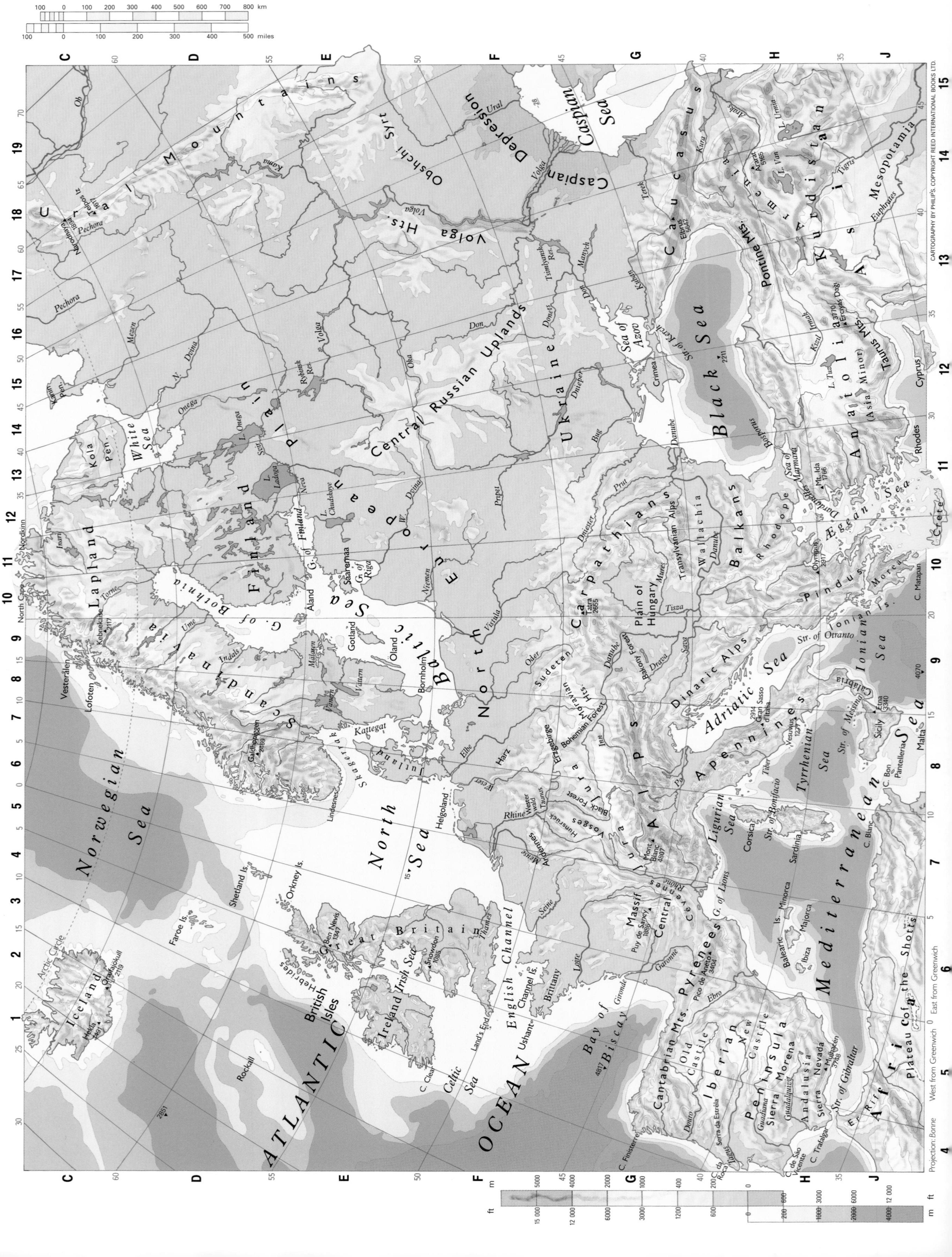

100 0 100 200 300 400 500 600 700 800 km

100 0 100 200 300 400 500 miles

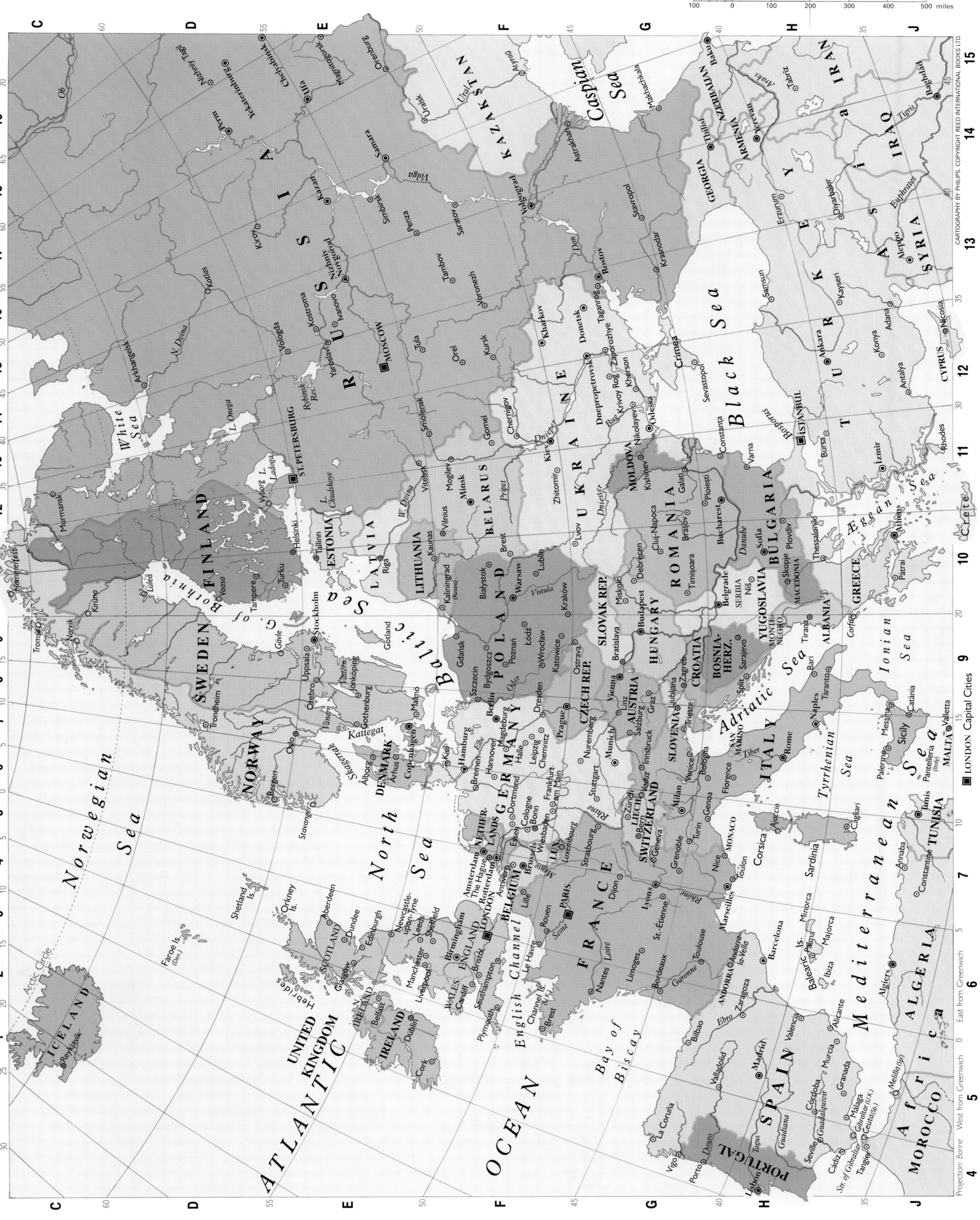

SCANDINAVIA 1:4 400 000

50 0 25 50 75 100 125 150 175 km

50 0 25 50 75 100 125 miles

FINLAND

RUSSIA

LAPLAND

NORWAY

SWEDEN

NORWEGIAN SEA

Finnmark

Maanselkä

Koillismaa

Kainuu

Peräpohjola

Norrbotten

Västerbotten

Ångermanland

Jämtland

Trøndelag

Nordland

Lofoten

Vesterålen

Vestfjorden

Varangerhalvøya

Varangerfjorden

Tanafjorden

Nordkinnhalvøya

Laksefjorden

Porsangen

Nordkapp

Magerøya

Hammerfest

Altafjorden

Alta

Sørøya

Seiland

Stjernøya

Loppthavet

Kvænangen

Arnøy

Vanna

Tromsø

Ringvassøy

Kvaløy

Malangen

Senja

Andøya

Andfjorden

Hinnøya

Harstad

Narvik

Ofotfjorden

Tysfjorden

Austvågøy

Vestvågøy

Moskenesøya

Moskenstraumen

Værøy

Røst

Bodø

Saltfjorden

Fauske

Sulitjelma

Mo i Rana

Mosjøen

Vefsna

Dønna

Alsten

Vega

Brønnøysund

Vikna

Namsos

Steinkjer

Levanger

Trondheim

Trondheimsfjorden

Fosna

Frøya

Hitra

Smøla

Kristiansund

Kirkenes

Vardø

Vadsø

Utsjoki

Inari

Inarijärvi

Ivalo

Sodankylä

Kemijärvi

Rovaniemi

Kemi

Tornio

Haparanda

Oulu

Oulujärvi

Kajaani

Kuopio

Kokkola

Raahe

Hailuoto

Kittilä

Muonio

Enontekiö

Kautokeino

Karasjok

Lakselv

Kiruna

Gällivare

Jokkmokk

Stora Lulevatten

Kebnekaise 2117

Luleå

Boden

Kalix

Piteå

Skellefteå

Umeå

Örnsköldsvik

Vindeln

Lycksele

Vilhelmina

Storuman

Sorsele

Arjeplog

Arvidsjaur

Hornavan

Uddjaur

Torneträsk

Torne älv

Lule älv

Råne älv

Pite älv

Skellefte älv

Ume älv

Vindelälven

Ångermanälven

Sollefteå

Strömsund

Hoting

Dorotea

Storsjön

Kallsjön

Gulf of Bothnia

ICELAND on same scale

FÆROE ISLANDS on same scale

Vatnajökull

Hofsjökull

Langjökull

Mýrdalsjökull

Akureyri

Reykjavík

Keflavík

Hafnarfjörður

Kópavogur

Akranes

Borgarnes

Ísafjörður

Húsavík

Vopnafjörður

Seyðisfjörður

Egilsstaðir

Höfn

Vík

Heimaey

Selfoss

Hekla 1491

Geysir

Þingvallavatn

Snæfellsjökull 1446

Grímsey

Raufarhöfn

Þórshöfn

Drangajökull 925

Hvannadalshnúkur 2119

Tórshavn

Streymoy

Eysturoy

Vágar

Sandoy

Suðuroy

Norðoyar

Føroyar (Den.) (Færoe Is.)

Arctic Circle

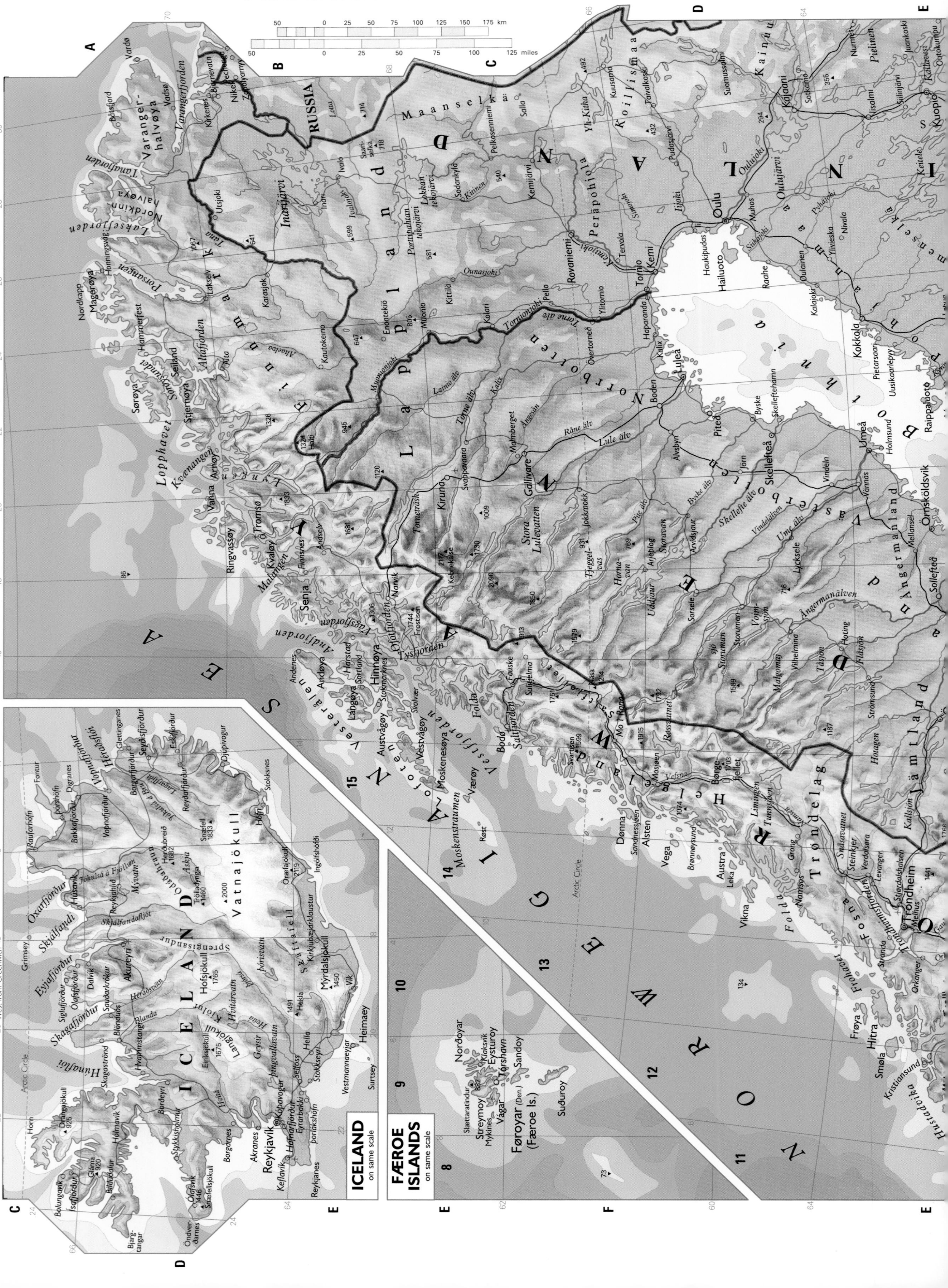

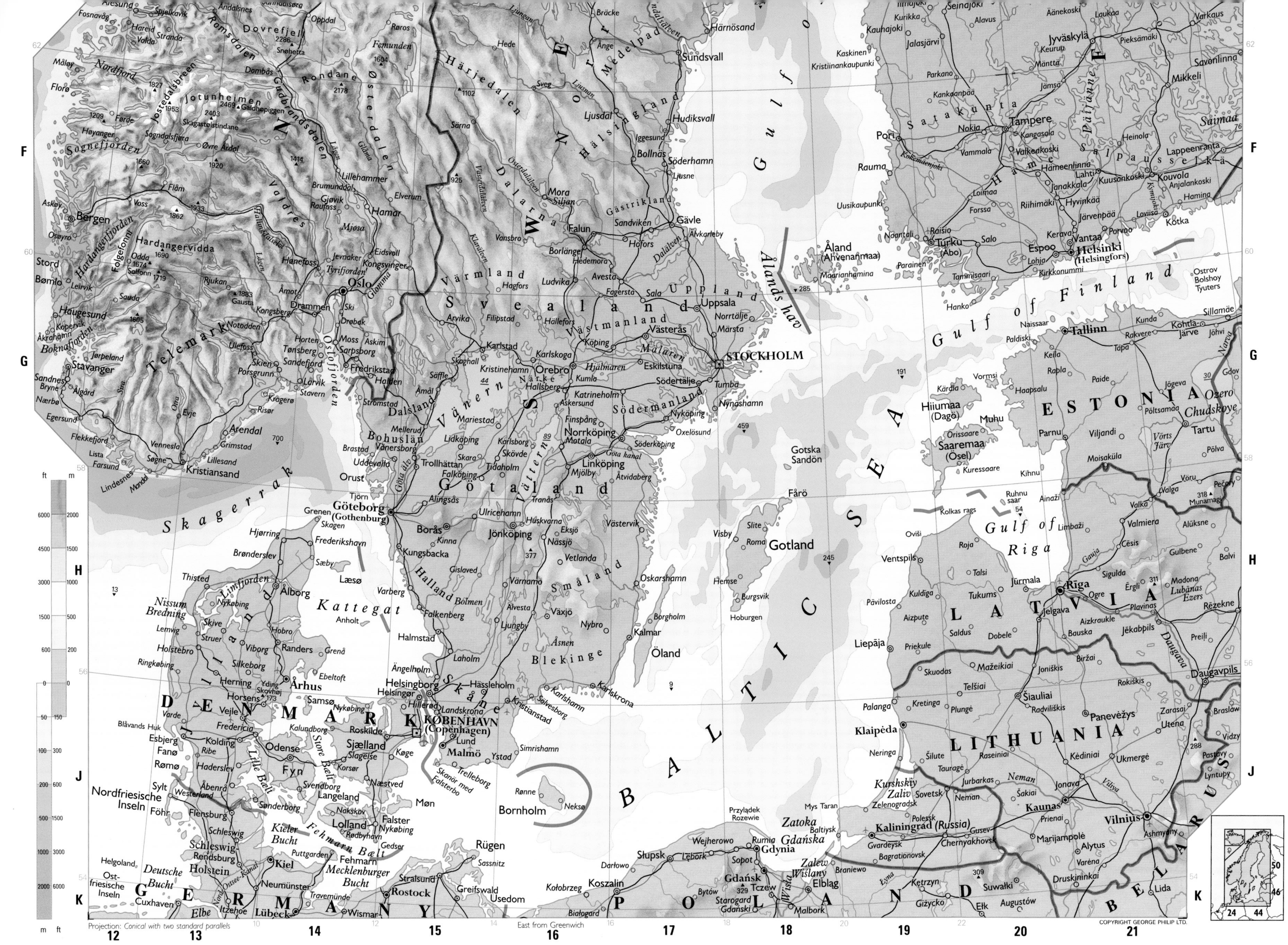
NORWAY
SWEDEN
FINLAND
ESTONIA
LATVIA
LITHUANIA
BELARUS
POLAND
GERMANY
DENMARK
BALTIC SEA
Gulf of Bothnia
Gulf of Finland
Gulf of Riga
Ålands hav
Skagerrak
Kattegat
Zatoka Gdańska
Svealand
Götaland
Norrland
Dalarna
Värmland
Telemark
Jylland
Skåne
Småland
Blekinge
Halland
Bohuslän
Hälsingland
Medelpad
Uppland
Västmanland
Södermanland
Gästrikland
Härjedalen
Satakunta
Häme
Salpausselkä
Päijänne
Saimaa
Jotunheimen
Hardangervidda
Rondane
Dovrefjell
Østerdalen
Gudbrandsdalen
Valdres
Vänern
Vättern
Mälaren
Hjälmaren
Oslofjorden
Sognefjorden
Hardangerfjorden
Limfjorden
Gotland
Öland
Bornholm
Sjælland
Fyn
Lolland
Falster
Møn
Rügen
Hiiumaa (Dagö)
Saaremaa (Ösel)
Åland (Ahvenanmaa)
Kieler Bucht
Mecklenburger Bucht
Fehmarn Bælt
Store Bælt
Lille Bælt
Nordfriesische Inseln
Ostfriesische Inseln
Deutsche Bucht
Kurshskiy Zaliv
Zalew Wiślany
Ozero Chudskoye
STOCKHOLM
Oslo
KØBENHAVN (Copenhagen)
Helsinki (Helsingfors)
Tallinn
Riga
Vilnius
Göteborg (Gothenburg)
Malmö
Uppsala
Västerås
Örebro
Norrköping
Linköping
Jönköping
Gävle
Sundsvall
Bergen
Stavanger
Kristiansand
Drammen
Århus
Ålborg
Odense
Turku (Åbo)
Tampere
Pori
Tartu
Pärnu
Liepāja
Ventspils
Daugavpils
Klaipėda
Kaunas
Šiauliai
Panevėžys
Kaliningrad (Russia)
Gdańsk
Gdynia
Elbląg
Koszalin
Słupsk
Rostock
Kiel
Lübeck
Flensburg
Schleswig
Rendsburg
Neumünster
Stralsund
Greifswald
Cuxhaven
Holstein
Elbe
F
G
H
J
K
12
13
14
15
16
17
18
19
20
21
East from Greenwich
Projection: Conical with two standard parallels
COPYRIGHT GEORGE PHILIP LTD.
ft
m
6000
4500
3000
1500
600
0
2000
1500
1000
500
200
0
50
150
100
300
200
600
500
1500
1000
3000
2000
6000
m
ft

DENMARK AND SOUTHERN SWEDEN 1:2 200 000

km
miles
Gulf of Bothnia
STOCKHOLM
Uppsala
Gävle
Falun
Borlänge
Örebro
Karlstad
Oslo
Drammen
Trondheim
Östersund
Sundsvall
Hudiksvall
Härnösand
Lillehammer
Hamar
Fredrikstad
Halden
JÄMTLANDS LÄN
GÄVLEBORGS LÄN
KOPPARBERGS LÄN
VÄRMLANDS LÄN
ÖREBRO LÄN
VÄSTMANLANDS LÄN
UPPSALA LÄN
STOCKHOLMS LÄN
SÖDERMANLANDS LÄN
VÄSTERNORRLANDS LÄN
HEDMARK
OPPLAND
BUSKERUD
TELEMARK
VESTFOLD
ØSTFOLD
AKERSHUS
SØR TRØNDELAG
MØRE OG ROMSDAL
Dovrefjell
Rondane
Jotunheimen
Mjøsa
Siljan
Klarälven
Västerdalälven
Österdalälven
ft

Skagerrak
Kattegat
BALTIC SEA
DENMARK
SWEDEN
GERMANY
POLAND
Göteborg
KØBENHAVN
Malmö
Århus
Ålborg
Odense
Jönköping
Norrköping
Linköping
Helsingborg
Kalmar
Karlskrona
Öland (Sweden)
Gotland (Sweden)
Bornholm (Denmark)
Anholt (Denmark)
Læsø (Denmark)
Flensburg
Schleswig
Słupsk
Lolland
Falster
Sjælland
Fyn
Jylland
Skåne
Småland
Götaland
Vättern
Hanöbukten
Fehmarn Belt
Store Bælt
Lille Bælt
Öresund
Projection : Lambert's Conformal Conic
East from Greenwich
COPYRIGHT GEORGE PHILIP LTD.

ENGLAND AND WALES 1:1 800 000

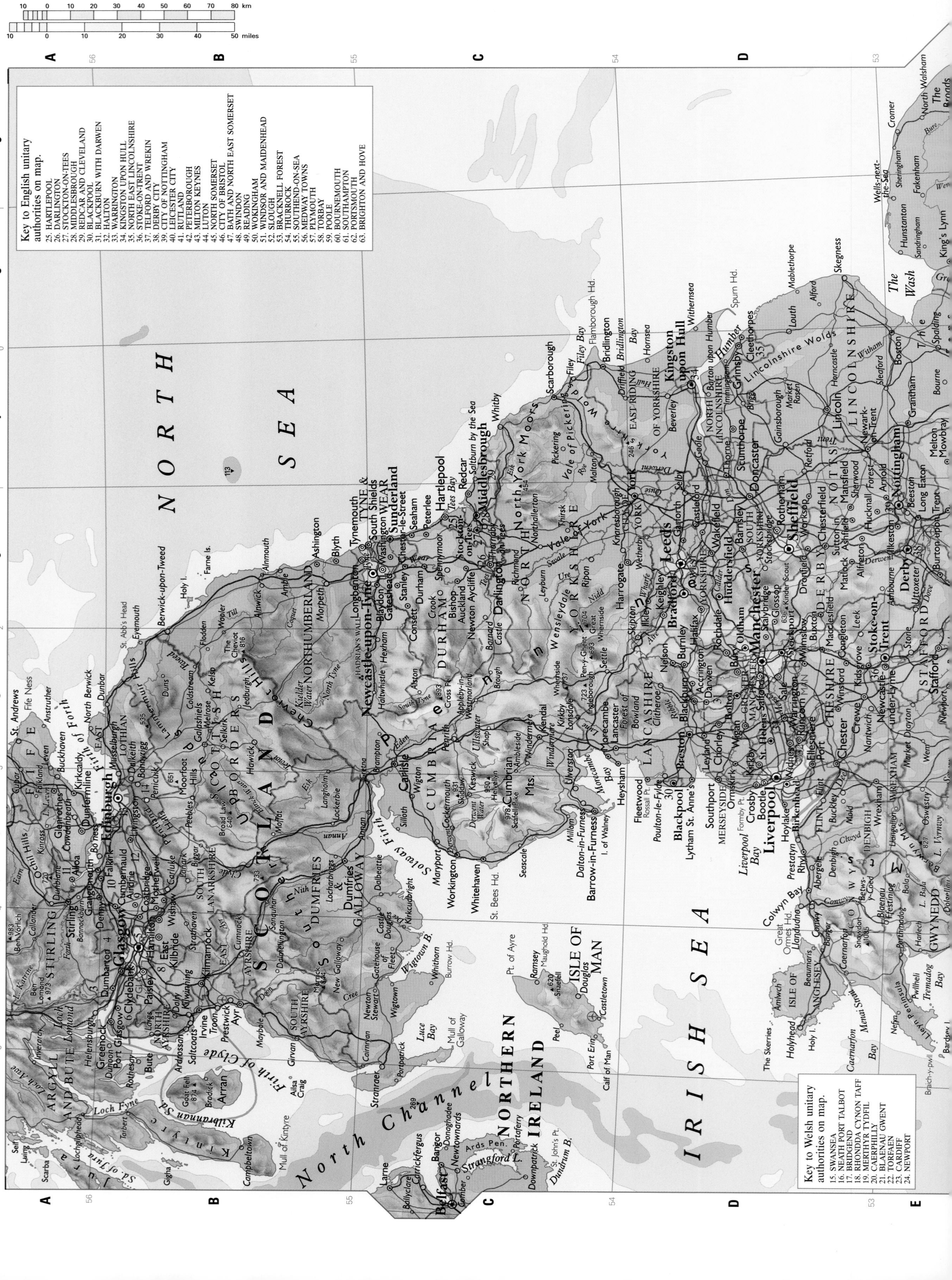

WALES
ENGLAND
FRANCE
ENGLISH CHANNEL
Bristol Channel
Cardigan Bay
Strait of Dover
Thames Estuary
Baie de la Seine
Baie de la Somme
Lyme Bay
CHANNEL ISLANDS (U.K.)
Alderney
Guernsey
St. Peter Port
Herm
Sark
Jersey
St. Helier
ISLE OF WIGHT
Isles of Scilly
On same scale
Tresco
St. Mary's
LONDON
BIRMINGHAM
Bristol
Cardiff
Southampton
Portsmouth
Brighton
Plymouth
Bournemouth
Reading
Oxford
Cambridge
Northampton
Coventry
Wolverhampton
Peterborough
Ipswich
Swansea
Newport
Exeter
Gloucester
Swindon
Le Havre
Rouen
Caen
Cherbourg
Dieppe
Calais
Boulogne-sur-Mer
CORNWALL
DEVON
DORSET
SOMERSET
WILTSHIRE
HANTS
SUSSEX
SURREY
KENT
ESSEX
SUFFOLK
NORFOLK
CAMBRIDGE
NORTHAMPTON
BEDFORD
HERTS
BUCKS
OXFORD
BERKSHIRE
GLOUCS
WARWICK
WORCESTER
HEREFORD
SHROPSHIRE
POWYS
CEREDIGION
CARMARTHENSHIRE
PEMBROKESHIRE
SEINE-MARITIME
HAUTE-NORMANDIE
CALVADOS
MANCHE
Projection : Lambert's Conformal Conic
West from Greenwich
East from Greenwich
COPYRIGHT GEORGE PHILIP LTD.

10 0 10 20 30 40 50 60 70 80 km
10 0 10 20 30 40 50 miles
Key to Scottish unitary authorities on map
1. CITY OF ABERDEEN
2. DUNDEE CITY
3. WEST DUNBARTONSHIRE
4. EAST DUNBARTONSHIRE
5. CITY OF GLASGOW
6. INVERCLYDE
7. RENFREWSHIRE
8. EAST RENFREWSHIRE
9. NORTH LANARKSHIRE
10. FALKIRK
11. CLACKMANNANSHIRE
12. WEST LOTHIAN
13. CITY OF EDINBURGH
14. MIDLOTHIAN
ORKNEY IS.
On same scale
ORKNEY
Mainland
North Ronaldsay
Papa Westray
Westray
Eday
Sanday
Rousay
Stronsay
Shapinsay
Kirkwall
Stromness
Hoy
Scapa Flow
Burray
Burwick
South Ronaldsay
Pentland Firth
Dunnet Hd.
Stroma
Duncansby Head
John o' Groats
Thurso
Sinclair's Bay
SHETLAND IS.
On same scale
SHETLAND
Unst
Haroldswick
Yell
Yell Sound
Fetlar
Ulsta
Esha Ness
St. Magnus Bay
Whalsay
Voe
Papa Stour
Walls
Lerwick
Scalloway
Bressay
Foula
West Burra
Boddam
Sumburgh Hd.
Mainland
SCOTLAND
ENGLAND
NORTHERN IRELAND
ATLANTIC OCEAN
NORTH SEA
North Channel
Outer Hebrides
Inner Hebrides
North Minch
Little Minch
Pentland Firth
Moray Firth
Firth of Forth
Firth of Tay
Firth of Clyde
Firth of Lorn
Solway Firth
WESTERN ISLES
Lewis
Harris
North Uist
South Uist
Benbecula
Barra
Skye
Mull
Islay
Jura
Arran
Kintyre
Tiree
Coll
Rhum
Eigg
Stornoway
Butt of Lewis
Flannan Is.
Ullapool
Inverness
Fort William
Oban
Aberdeen
Dundee
Perth
Stirling
Edinburgh
Glasgow
Kilmarnock
Ayr
Dumfries
Carlisle
Newcastle-upon-Tyne
Belfast
Wick
Thurso
Elgin
Peterhead
Fraserburgh
Montrose
Arbroath
Forfar
St. Andrews
Kirkcaldy
Dunfermline
Falkirk
Greenock
Paisley
Hamilton
Motherwell
Stranraer
Campbeltown
Girvan
Hawick
Galashiels
Berwick-upon-Tweed
Ben Nevis 1342
Ben Macdhui 1309
Cairn Gorm 1245
Ben Lawers 1214
Ben More 1174
HIGHLAND
MORAY
ABERDEENSHIRE
ANGUS
PERTH AND KINROSS
FIFE
STIRLING
ARGYLL AND BUTE
EAST LOTHIAN
SCOTTISH BORDERS
DUMFRIES & GALLOWAY
SOUTH AYRSHIRE
EAST AYRSHIRE
NORTH AYRSHIRE
SOUTH LANARKSHIRE
NORTHUMBERLAND
CUMBRIA
DURHAM
North West Highlands
Grampian Mountains
Cairngorm Mts.
Monadhliath Mts.
Southern Uplands
Cheviot Hills
Lammermuir Hills
Pentland Hills
Galloway
Glen More
Loch Ness
Loch Lomond
Loch Fyne
Loch Awe
Kielder Water
Projection : Lambert's Conformal Conic
West from Greenwich
COPYRIGHT GEORGE PHILIP LTD.

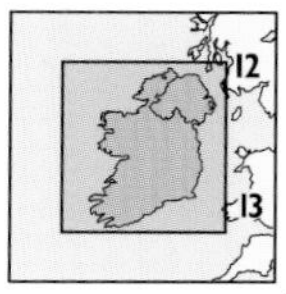

10 0 10 20 30 40 50 60 70 80 km
10 0 10 20 30 40 50 miles

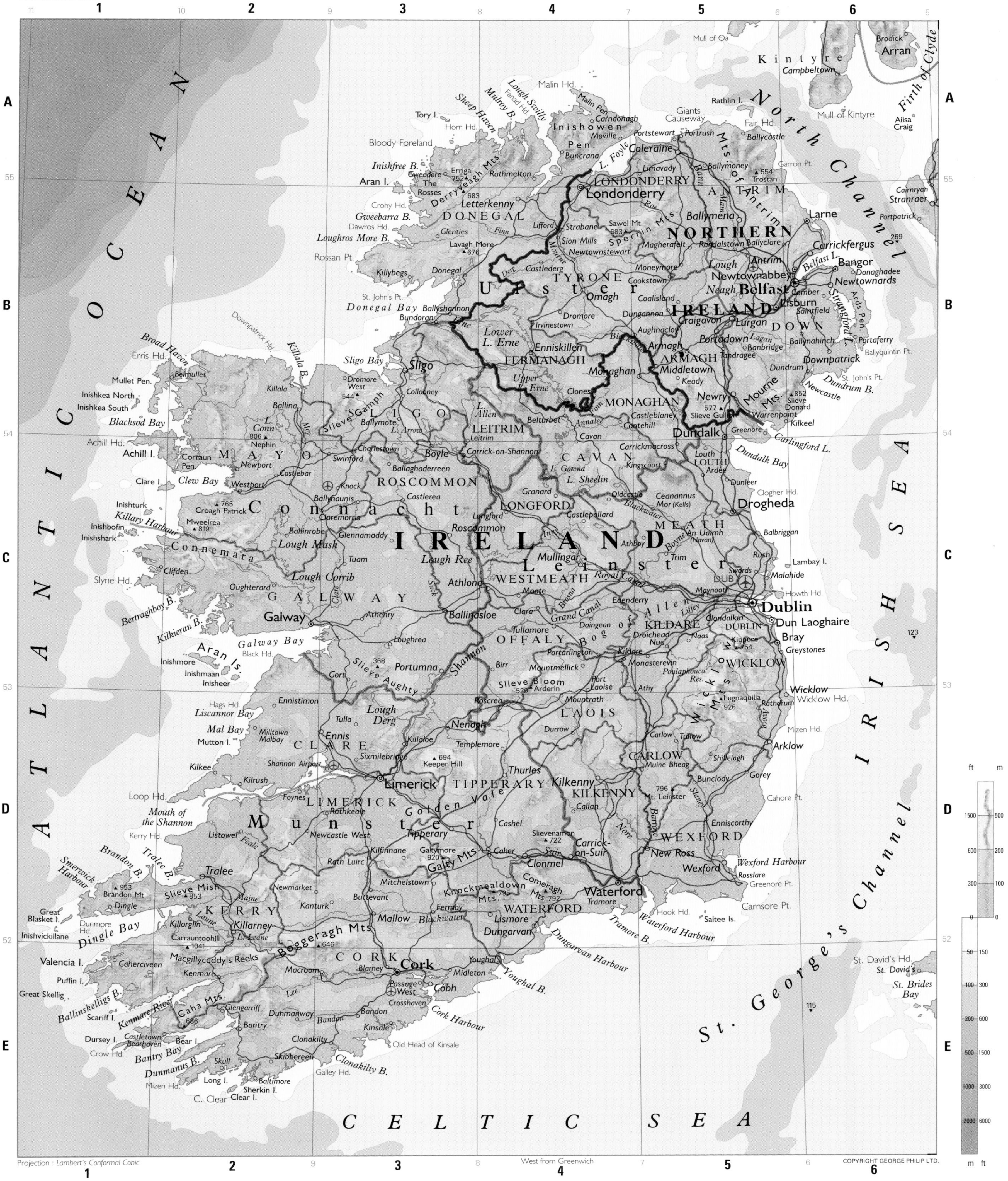

50 0 25 50 75 100 125 150 175 km
50 0 25 50 75 100 125 miles
ATLANTIC OCEAN
NORTH SEA
CELTIC SEA
IRISH SEA
English Channel
Bristol Channel
St. George's Channel
North Channel
Firth of Clyde
Pentland Firth
Moray Firth
North Minch
The Wash
Shetland Is.
Unst
Yell
Fetlar
Mainland
Lerwick
Foula
Fair Isle
Orkney Is.
Westray
Sanday
Stronsay
Kirkwall
Hoy
South Ronaldsay
Outer Hebrides
Inner Hebrides
Lewis
Stornoway
Harris
St. Kilda
North Uist
Benbecula
South Uist
Barra
Skye
Rhum
Eigg
Coll
Tiree
Mull
Colonsay
Jura
Islay
Arran
C. Wrath
Thurso
Wick
Helmsdale
Lairg
Golspie
Tain
Ullapool
Invergordon
Dingwall
Inverness
Nairn
Elgin
Buckie
Banff
Fraserburgh
Peterhead
Huntly
Inverurie
Aberdeen
Stonehaven
Portree
Mallaig
Fort William
Ben Nevis
Tobermory
Oban
Aviemore
North West Highlands
Grampian Mts.
SCOTLAND
L. Ness
Ballater
Forfar
Montrose
Arbroath
Dundee
St. Andrews
Perth
L. Lomond
Stirling
Glenrothes
Kirkcaldy
Dunfermline
Dunbar
Greenock
Glasgow
Edinburgh
Paisley
East Kilbride
Hamilton
Irvine
Kilmarnock
Ayr
Campbeltown
Girvan
Southern Uplands
Galashiels
Jedburgh
Hawick
Berwick-upon-Tweed
Alnwick
Cheviot Hills
Dumfries
Kirkcudbright
Stranraer
Annan
Carlisle
Malin Hd.
Aran I.
Buncrana
Letterkenny
Coleraine
Londonderry
Ballymena
Larne
Lifford
Donegal
Ulster
NORTHERN IRELAND
Antrim
Bangor
Lough Neagh
Belfast
Omagh
Bundoran
Lower L. Erne
Portadown
Lisburn
Lurgan
Armagh
Enniskillen
Clones
Newry
Sligo
Ballina
Achill I.
Castlebar
L. Conn
Leitrim
Cavan
Castleblaney
Dundalk
Westport
Lough Mask
Roscommon
Connacht
Longford
Ceanannus Mor
Drogheda
Connemara
Lough Corrib
Athlone
Lough Ree
Mullingar
Galway
Galway B.
Ballinasloe
Tullamore
Dublin
Dun Laoghaire
Bray
Aran Is.
IRELAND
Birr
Port Laoise
Athy
Leinster
Wicklow Mts.
Lough Derg
Ennis
Nenagh
Carlow
Kilkenny
Arklow
Kilrush
Limerick
Thurles
Shannon
Listowel
Tipperary
Tralee
Munster
Clonmel
Carrick-on-Suir
Wexford
Rosslare
Dingle
Killarney
Mallow
Waterford
Carrauntoohill
Macgillycuddy's Reeks
Blackwater
Dungarvan
Valencia I.
Cork
Cobh
Youghal
Bantry
Bandon
Kinsale
C. Clear
UNITED KINGDOM
Mull of Galloway
Workington
Whitehaven
Cumbrian Mts.
Pennines
Douglas
I. of Man
Barrow-in-Furness
Lancaster
Newcastle-upon-Tyne
South Shields
Sunderland
Hexham
Gateshead
Durham
Hartlepool
Redcar
Middlesbrough
Darlington
Stockton-on-Tees
Scarborough
Bridlington
Harrogate
York
Leeds
Bradford
Beverley
Kingston upon Hull
Keighley
Burnley
Blackpool
Preston
Blackburn
Bolton
Halifax
Huddersfield
Barnsley
Scunthorpe
Humber
Grimsby
Manchester
Oldham
Doncaster
Rotherham
Liverpool
Warrington
Stockport
Sheffield
Lincoln
Louth
Skegness
Holyhead
Anglesey
Bangor
Colwyn Bay
Chester
Crewe
Chesterfield
Mansfield
Nottingham
Snowdon
Wrexham
Stoke on Trent
Derby
Stafford
Trent
Grantham
Boston
Pwllheli
Shrewsbury
Telford
ENGLAND
King's Lynn
Norwich
Cromer
Great Yarmouth
Lowestoft
Cardigan Bay
Aberystwyth
Cambrian Mts.
Welshpool
Wolverhampton
BIRMINGHAM
Nuneaton
Leicester
Corby
Peterborough
Thetford
Coventry
Rugby
Ely
Bury St. Edmunds
Redditch
Worcester
Royal Leamington Spa
Northampton
Bedford
Cambridge
Ipswich
Felixstowe
Harwich
Colchester
Hereford
Milton Keynes
Stevenage
WALES
Fishguard
Carmarthen
Brecon
Cheltenham
Gloucester
Cotswold Hills
Luton
Harlow
Chelmsford
Haverfordwest
Milford Haven
Pembroke
Merthyr Tydfil
Neath
Llanelli
Swansea
Port Talbot
Rhondda
Cwmbran
Newport
Cardiff
Barry
Oxford
Hemel Hempstead
High Wycombe
Watford
Basildon
Southend-on-Sea
Bristol
Bath
Swindon
Newbury
Slough
Reading
LONDON
Thames
Chatham
Margate
Canterbury
Maidstone
Dover
Reigate
Guildford
Basingstoke
Weston-super-Mare
Exmoor
Barnstaple
Taunton
Salisbury
Winchester
Crawley
Ashford
Folkestone
Str. of Dover
Yeovil
Southampton
Fareham
Havant
Hastings
Brighton
Worthing
Eastbourne
Portsmouth
Bude
Exeter
Dartmoor
Bournemouth
Poole
Weymouth
Newport
Isle of Wight
Exmouth
Torbay
Newquay
Truro
St. Austell
Plymouth
Falmouth
Penzance
Land's End
Isles of Scilly
Alderney
Guernsey
St. Peter Port
Sark
Channel Is. (U.K.)
Jersey
St. Helier
C. de la Hague
Cotentin
Pte. de Barfleur
Cherbourg
Valognes
Bayeux
Le Havre
Fécamp
Pays de Caux
Bolbec
Trouville-sur-Mer
Caen
Lisieux
Elbeuf
Seine
Rouen
FRANCE
Dieppe
Le Tréport
Abbeville
Amiens
Somme
Picardie
St-Quentin
Cambrai
Valenciennes
Lens
Bruay-la-Buissière
Béthune
Lille
Villeneuve-d'Ascq
Tourcoing
Tournai
Le Touquet-Paris-Plage
Boulogne-sur-Mer
C. Gris Nez
Calais
St-Omer
Dunkerque
Oostende
Zeebrugge
Brugge
Gent
Mechelen
Antwerpen
BELGIUM
BRUSSEL (Bruxelles)
Flandre
Vlissingen
NETHERLANDS
's-Gravenhage (Den Haag)
Hoek van Holland
ROTTERDAM
Dordrecht
Haarlem
Alkmaa
Den Helder
Texel
NORWAY
Askøy
Bergen
Osøyro
Stord
Bømlo
Leirvik
Haugesund
Kopervik
Åkrahamn
Boknafjorden
Stavanger
Sandnes
Bryne
Nærbø
Projection: Conical with two standard parallels
East from Greenwich
West from Greenwich
COPYRIGHT GEORGE PHILIP LTD.
ft m
3000 1000
1500 500
600 200
0 0
50 150
100 300
200 600
500 1500
1000 3000
2000 6000
m ft

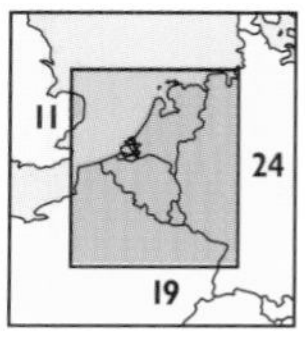

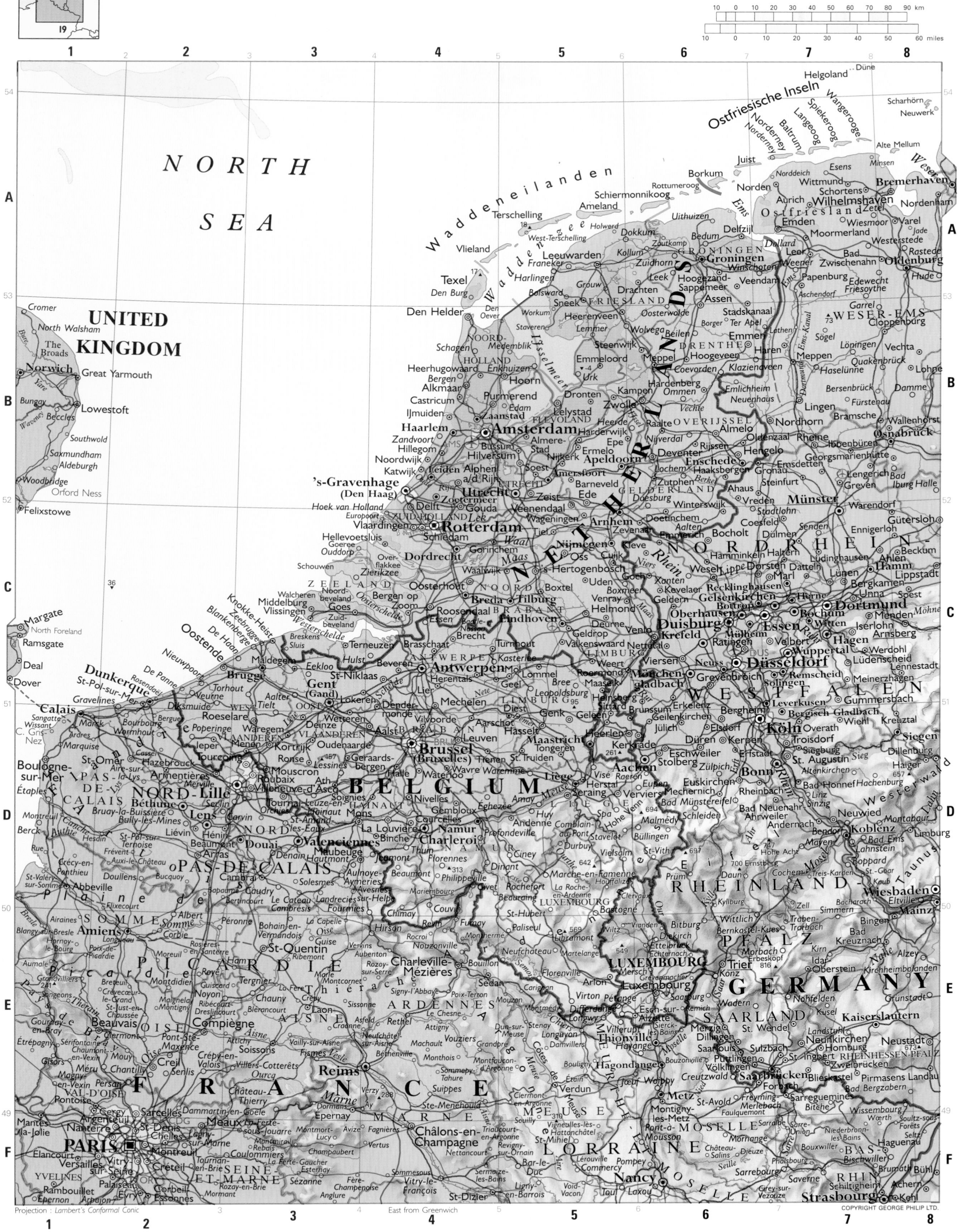

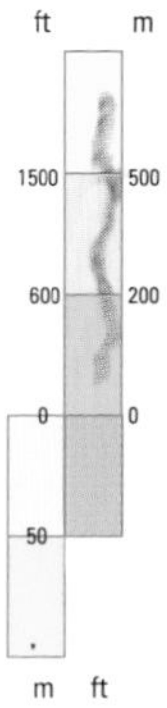

Underlined towns give their name to the administrative area in which they stand.

NORTHERN FRANCE 1:2 200 000

DÉPARTEMENTS IN THE PARIS AREA

1. Ville de Paris
2. Seine-St-Denis
3. Val-de-Marne
4. Hauts-de-Seine

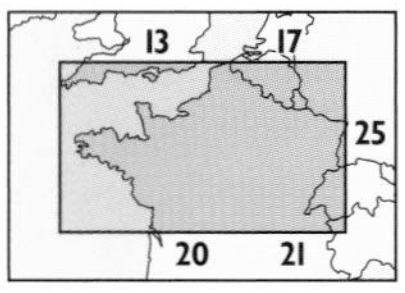

Underlined towns give their name to the administrative area in which they stand.

SOUTHERN FRANCE 1:2 200 000

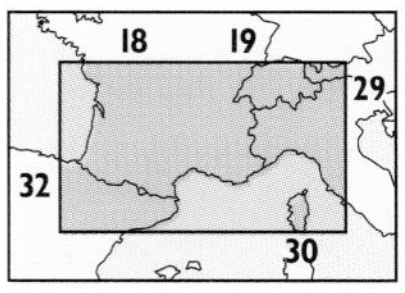
18
19
29
32
30

SWITZERLAND
ITALY
FRANCE
LIGURIAN SEA
MEDITERRANEAN SEA
Golfo di Génova
Riviera di Ponente
Riviera di Levante
Côte d'Azur
CÔTE D'AZUR
PROVENCE-ALPES-
RHÔNE-ALPES
PIEMONTE
LOMBARDIA
LIGURIA
VALLE D'AOSTA
CORSE
HAUTE-CORSE
CORSE-DU-SUD
Alpi Pennine
Alpes Maritimes
Alpi Lepontine
Berner Alpen
Mts. du Jura
L. Léman
L. Maggiore
Genève
Lausanne
Bern
Luzern
Lyon
St-Étienne
Grenoble
Chambéry
Annecy
Valence
Avignon
Marseille
Toulon
Nice
MONACO
Cannes
Torino
Milano
Génova
Novara
Piacenza
Parma
La Spézia
Livorno
Pisa
Lucca
Brescia
Bérgamo
Cremona
Pavia
Alessándria
Asti
Cúneo
Savona
San Remo
Impéria
Ajaccio
Bastia
Elba
Arcipelago Toscano
Bouches de Bonifacio
Îs. d'Hyères
Gorgona
Capraia
Pianosa
Montecristo
2940
2650

50 0 25 50 75 100 125 150 175 km
50 0 25 50 75 100 125 miles
NORTH SEA
BALTIC SEA
UNITED KINGDOM
NETHERLANDS
BELGIUM
LUXEMBOURG
GERMANY
DENMARK
FRANCE
SWITZERLAND
LIECHTENSTEIN
AUSTRIA
CZECH R.
SLOVENIA
ITALY
MONACO
SAN MARINO
ADRIATIC SEA
Golfo di Génova
Golfo di Venézia
Norwich
Great Yarmouth
Lowestoft
Ipswich
Felixstowe
Harwich
Cromer
Margate
Dover
AMSTERDAM
's-Gravenhage (Den Haag)
ROTTERDAM
Utrecht
Groningen
Antwerpen
BRUSSEL (Bruxelles)
Gent
Brugge
Liège
Lille
Calais
Dunkerque
Oostende
PARIS
Reims
Amiens
Troyes
Dijon
Metz
Nancy
Strasbourg
Besançon
Lyon
Grenoble
Saint-Étienne
Avignon
Nîmes
Aix-en-Provence
MARSEILLE
Toulon
Nice
Cannes
Luxembourg
HAMBURG
Bremen
Kiel
Lübeck
Rostock
Hannover
BERLIN
Magdeburg
Leipzig
Dresden
Halle
Köln (Cologne)
Bonn
Düsseldorf
Dortmund
Essen
Duisburg
Frankfurt
Mannheim
Stuttgart
Nürnberg
MÜNCHEN (Munich)
Augsburg
Regensburg
Basel
Zürich
Bern
Genève
Lausanne
Luzern
Innsbruck
Salzburg
Linz
Graz
PRAHA (Prague)
Plzeň
Ljubljana
Trieste
MILANO
TORINO (Turin)
Genova
Venézia (Venice)
Verona
Pádova
Bologna
Firenze (Florence)
Parma
Ferrara
Ravenna
Szczecin
Zagreb
Rijeka
Projection: Conical with two standard parallels

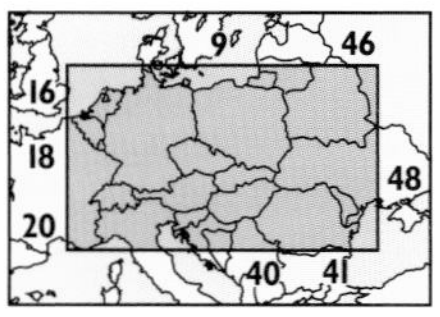

9
10
11
12
13
14
15
16
B
C
D
E
F
G
LITHUANIA
B E L A R U S
P O L A N D
U K R A I N E
SLOVAK REP.
H U N G A R Y
R O M A N I A
M O L D O V A
YUGOSLAVIA
BOSNIA-HERZEGOVINA
B U L G A R I A
C a r p a t h i a n s
T r a n s i l v a n i a
W a l l a c h i a
D o b r u j a
P o d i l s k a   v y s o c h y n a
P r i p e t   M a r s h e s
Zatoka Gdańska
Kaliningrad (Russia)
Gdynia
Gdańsk
Elbląg
Vilnius
Minsk
Hrodna
Białystok
Olsztyn
Bydgoszcz
Toruń
Włocławek
Płock
WARSZAWA (Warsaw)
Łódź
Poznań
Radom
Lublin
Kielce
Częstochowa
Wrocław
Opole
Katowice
Kraków
Rzeszów
Brest
Pinsk
Baranavichy
Babruysk
Mahilyow
Homyel
Mazyr
Lutsk
Rivne
Lviv (Lvov)
Ternopil
Khmelnytskyy
Vinnytsya
Zhytomyr
KYYIV (Kiev)
Bila Tserkva
Ivano-Frankivsk
Chernivtsi
Uzhhorod
Košice
Bratislava
Miskolc
Nyíregyháza
Debrecen
BUDAPEST
Győr
Szeged
Pécs
Oradea
Cluj-Napoca
Satu Mare
Baia Mare
Suceava
Iaşi
Chişinău
Tiraspol
Bacău
Braşov
Sibiu
Timişoara
Arad
Galaţi
Brăila
Constanţa
BUCUREŞTI (Bucharest)
Ploieşti
Craiova
Ruse
Varna
Dobrich
Subotica
Novi Sad
BEOGRAD (Belgrade)
Sarajevo
Osijek
Tuzla
Wisła (Vistula)
Dunaj
Tisza
Dnister
Prut
Siret
Mureş
Olt
Dunărea (Danube)
Balaton
Vf. Moldoveanu 2543
East from Greenwich
COPYRIGHT GEORGE PHILIP LTD.

10 0 10 20 30 40 50 60 70 80 90 km
10 0 10 20 30 40 50 60 miles
NORTH SEA
BALTIC SEA
DENMARK
POLAND
GERMANY
SCHLESWIG-HOLSTEIN
MECKLENBURG-VORPOMMERN
BRANDENBURG
SACHSEN-ANHALT
NIEDERSACHSEN
NORDRHEIN-WESTFALEN
THÜRINGEN
SACHSEN
Deutsche Bucht
Mecklenburger Bucht
Kieler Bucht
Ostfriesische Inseln
Nordfriesische Inseln
BERLIN
HAMBURG
Bremen
Hannover
Kiel
Lübeck
Rostock
Szczecin
Magdeburg
Leipzig
Dresden
Halle
Erfurt
Dortmund
Düsseldorf
Köln
Münster
Osnabrück
Bielefeld
Kassel
Braunschweig
Potsdam
Chemnitz
Rügen
Fehmarn
Lolland
Flensburg

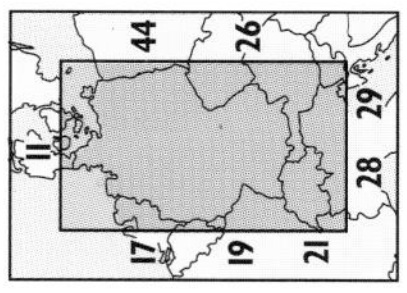

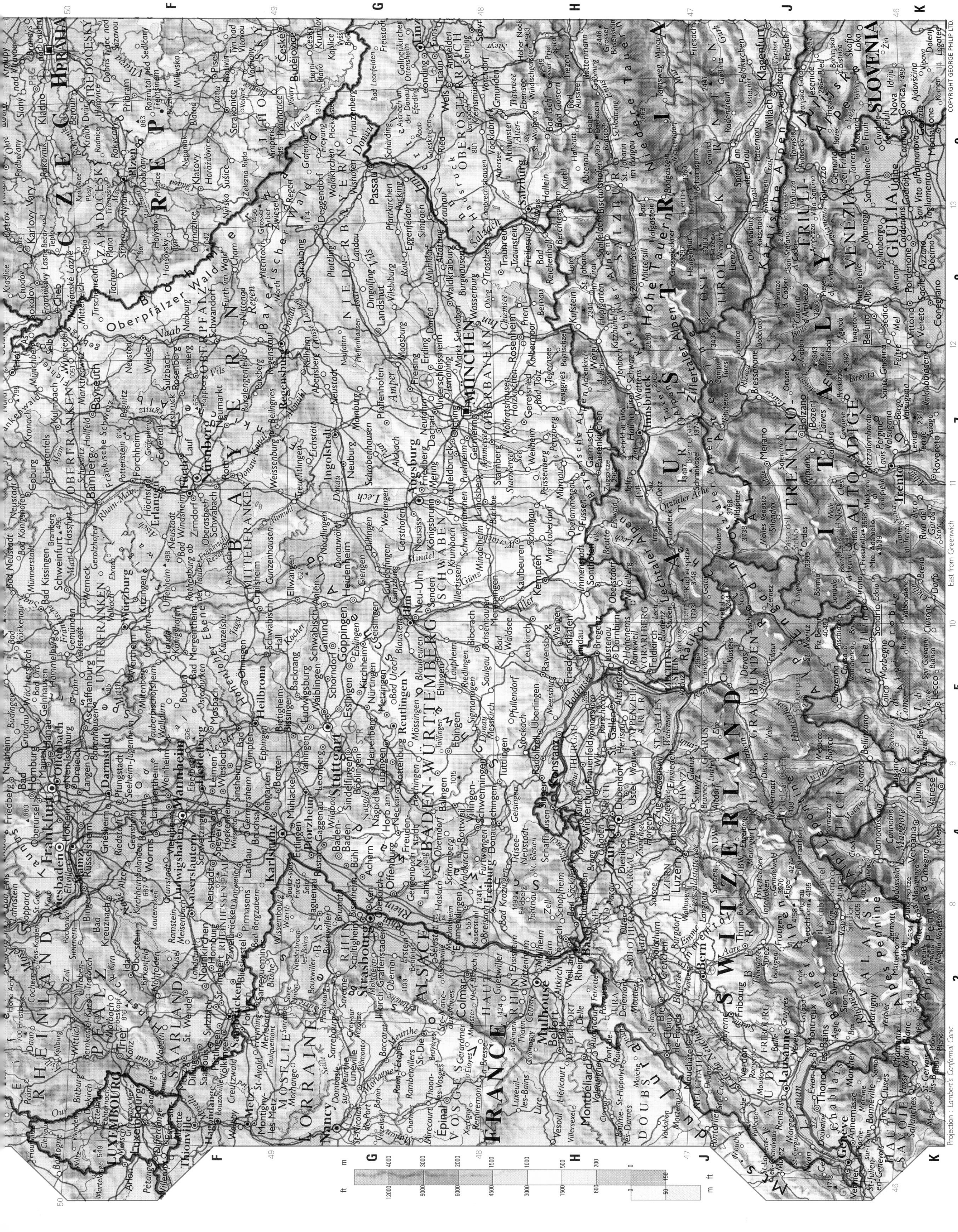

Underlined towns give their name to the administrative area in which they stand.
Projection : Lambert's Conformal Conic
COPYRIGHT GEORGE PHILIP LTD.
East from Greenwich
FRANCE
SWITZERLAND
ITALY
AUSTRIA
SLOVENIA
LUXEMBOURG

10 0 10 20 30 40 50 60 70 80 90 km
10 0 10 20 30 40 50 60 miles
GERMANY
THÜRINGEN
OBERFRANKEN
UNTERFRANKEN
MITTELFRANKEN
BAYERN
OBERPFALZ
NIEDERBAYERN
OBERBAYERN
SCHWABEN
CZECH REP.
ZÁPADOČESKÝ
STŘEDOČESKÝ
SEVEROČESKÝ
JIHOČESKÝ
NIEDERÖSTERREICH
OBERÖSTERREICH
SALZBURG
STEIERMARK
KÄRNTEN
OST-TIROL
VORARLBERG
AUSTRIA
SWITZERLAND
ITALY
TRENTINO-ALTO ADIGE
FRIULI-VENEZIA GIULIA
VENETO
LOMBARDIA
SLOVENIA
Dresden
Chemnitz
Erfurt
Praha
Plzeň
Nürnberg
Würzburg
Regensburg
Stuttgart
Augsburg
München
Ulm
Ingolstadt
Passau
Linz
Salzburg
Innsbruck
Graz
Klagenfurt
Ljubljana
Zagreb
Trieste
Venézia
Bolzano
Trento
Golfo di Venézia
Projection : Lambert's Conformal Conic
ft m

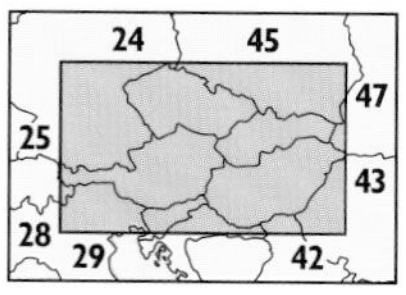

Underlined towns give their name to the administrative area in which they stand.

NORTHERN ITALY, SLOVENIA AND CROATIA 1:2 200 000

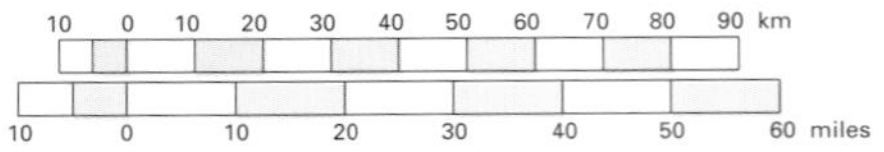

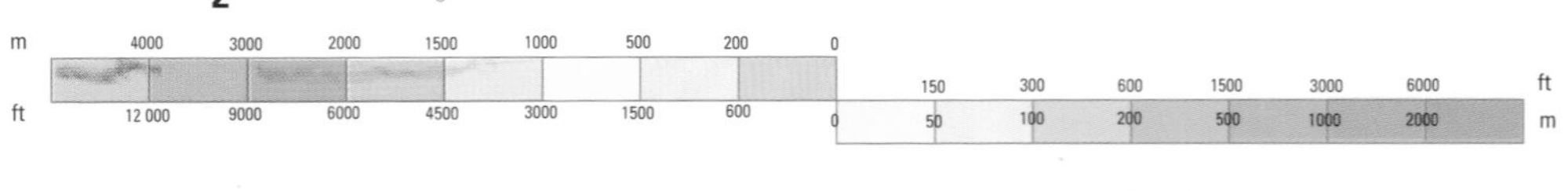

Underlined towns give their name to th
administrative area in which they stand.

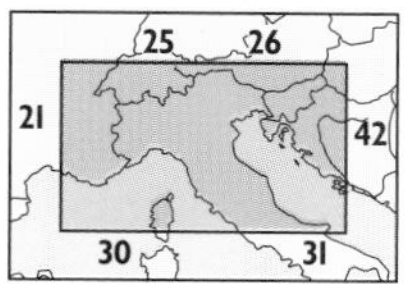

ministrative divisions in Croatia:

rodsko-Posavska
oprivničko-Križevačka
rapinsko-Zagorska
4. Medimurska
6. Požeško-Slavonska
7. Varaždinska
8. Virovitičko-Podravska
10. Zagrebačka

Inter-entity boundaries as agreed at the 1995 Dayton Peace Agreement.

SOUTHERN ITALY 1:2 200 000

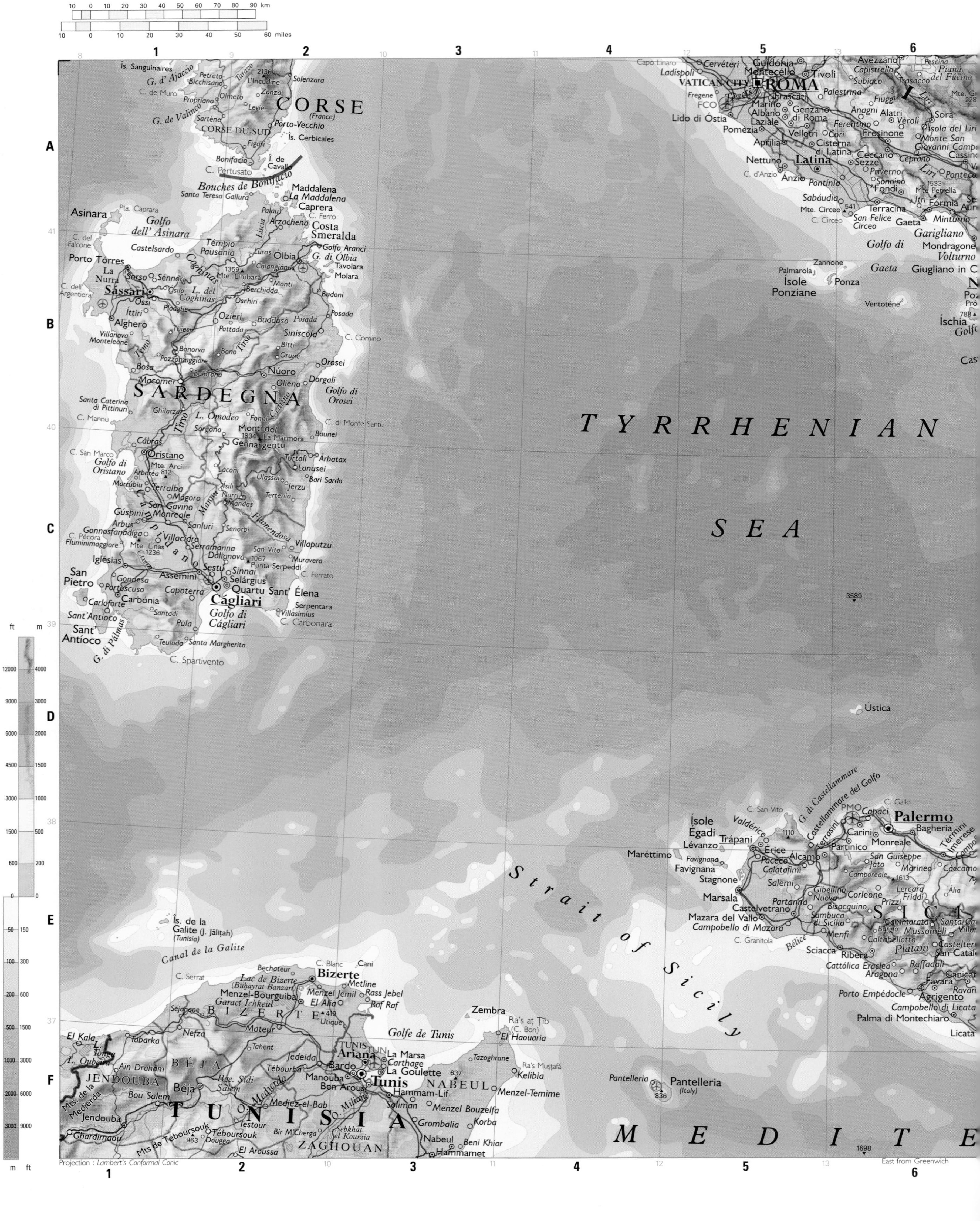

CORSE
(France)
SARDEGNA
TYRRHENIAN SEA
Strait of Sicily
TUNISIA
MEDITE
Cágliari
Sássari
Olbia
Núoro
Oristano
ROMA
VATICAN CITY
Latina
Palermo
Trápani
Marsala
Agrigento
Tunis
Bizerte
Pantelleria
Ústica
Ísole Ponziane
Ísole Égadi
Golfo di Cágliari
Golfo di Orosei
Golfo di Oristano
Golfe de Tunis
Bouches de Bonifacio
Canal de la Galite
Projection : Lambert's Conformal Conic
East from Greenwich

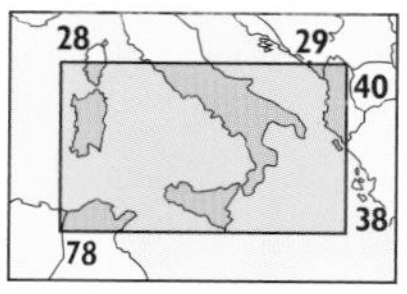

Underlined towns give their name to the administrative area in which they stand.

10 0 10 20 30 40 50 60 70 80 90 km
10 0 10 20 30 40 50 60 miles
FRANCE
ESPAÑA
MIDI-PYRÉNÉES
LANGUEDOC-ROUSSILLON
AQUITAINE
ANDORRA
CATALUÑA
ARAGÓN
NAVARRA
PAÍS VASCO
LA RIOJA
CASTILLA Y LEÓN
MADRID
BALEARES
Golfe de Gascogne
Golfe du Lion
Costa Brava
Costa del Azahar
Costa Dorada
Toulouse
Perpignan
Carcassonne
Narbonne
Béziers
Pau
Tarbes
Bayonne
Biarritz
Donostia-San Sebastián
Bilbao
Vitoria-Gasteiz
Pamplona
Logroño
Burgos
Santander
Zaragoza
Huesca
Lleida (Lérida)
Tarragona
BARCELONA
Girona
Teruel
Castelló de la Plana
Guadalajara
Soria
Andorra la Vella
Figueres
Manresa
Sabadell
Terrassa
Reus
Tortosa
Calatayud
Tudela
Cuenca
Ebro
Segre
Cinca
Duero
Tajo
Garonne
Sierra de Albarracín
Montes Universales
Serranía de Cuenca
Sa. del Moncayo
MENORCA
MALLORCA
Ciudadela de Menorca
Maó (Mahón)
Palma de Mallorca

M E D I T E R R A N E A N S E A
A L G E R I A
CASTILLA-LA MANCHA
VALENCIA
ALICANTE
MURCIA
ALMERÍA
GRANADA
JAÉN
CIUDAD REAL
ALBACETE
Golfo de Valencia
Costa Blanca
Costa del Sol
Valencia
Alicante
Murcia
Cartagena
Almería
Granada
Albacete
Elche
Lorca
Eivissa (Ibiza)
Formentera
Alger (Algiers)
Blida
Médéa
Ech Chelif
Mostaganem
Oran (Ouahran)
Sidi-bel-Abbès
Mascara
Tiaret
Relizane
Melilla (Sp.)
Nador
Alborán (Sp.)
Golfe d'Arzew
G. de Almería
G. de Mazarrón
Sierra Nevada
Sierra de Segura
Projection: Lambert's Conformal Conic
COPYRIGHT GEORGE PHILIP LTD.
West from Greenwich
East from Greenwich

10 0 10 20 30 40 50 60 70 80 90 km
10 0 10 20 30 40 50 60 miles
Bay of Biscay
Costa Verde
GALICIA
ASTURIAS
CANTABRIA
PAÍS VASCO
LA RIOJA
CASTILLA Y LEÓN
MADRID
ESPAÑA
PORTUGAL
Cordillera Cantábrica
Sierra de Guadarrama
Sierra de Gredos
Montes de León
Sierra de la Demanda
Tierra de Campos
Donostia-San Sebastián
Bilbao
Vitoria-Gasteiz
Santander
Gijón
Oviedo
Avilés
León
Burgos
Logroño
Palencia
Valladolid
Zamora
Salamanca
Segovia
Ávila
Soria
Guadalajara
Alcalá de Henares
Toledo
Talavera de la Reina
Plasencia
Ponferrada
Lugo
Ourense (Orense)
Pontevedra
Vigo
Santiago de Compostela
A Coruña (La Coruña)
Ferrol
Braga
Porto
Vila Nova de Gaia
Viseu
Aveiro
Coimbra
Guarda
Castelo Branco
Figueira da Foz
Duero
Douro
Miño
Ebro
Pisuerga
Tajo

ATLANTIC OCEAN

MEDITERRANEAN SEA

MOROCCO

EXTREMADURA

CASTILLA - LA MANCHA

ANDALUCÍA

Costa del Sol

Golfo de Cádiz

Strait of Gibraltar

Projection: Lambert's Conformal Conic

COPYRIGHT GEORGE PHILIP LTD.

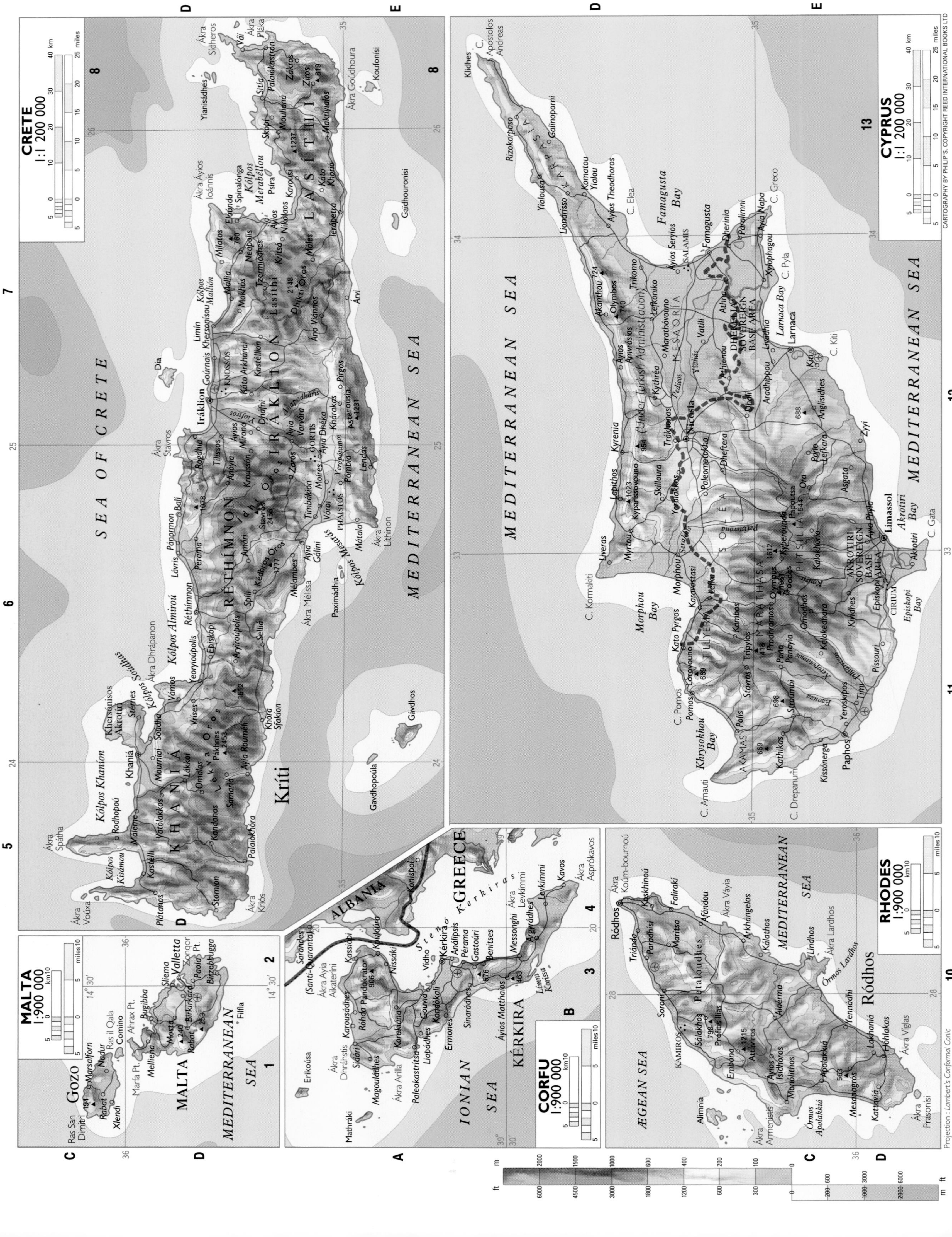
CRETE
1:1 200 000
SEA OF CRETE
MEDITERRANEAN SEA
Kríti
CYPRUS
1:1 200 000
MEDITERRANEAN SEA
RHODES
1:900 000
ÆGEAN SEA
MEDITERRANEAN SEA
Ródhos
CORFU
1:900 000
IONIAN SEA
KÉRKIRA
ALBANIA
GREECE
MALTA
1:900 000
GOZO
MALTA
MEDITERRANEAN SEA
Projection : Lambert's Conformal Conic
CARTOGRAPHY BY PHILIP'S. COPYRIGHT REED INTERNATIONAL BOOKS LTD

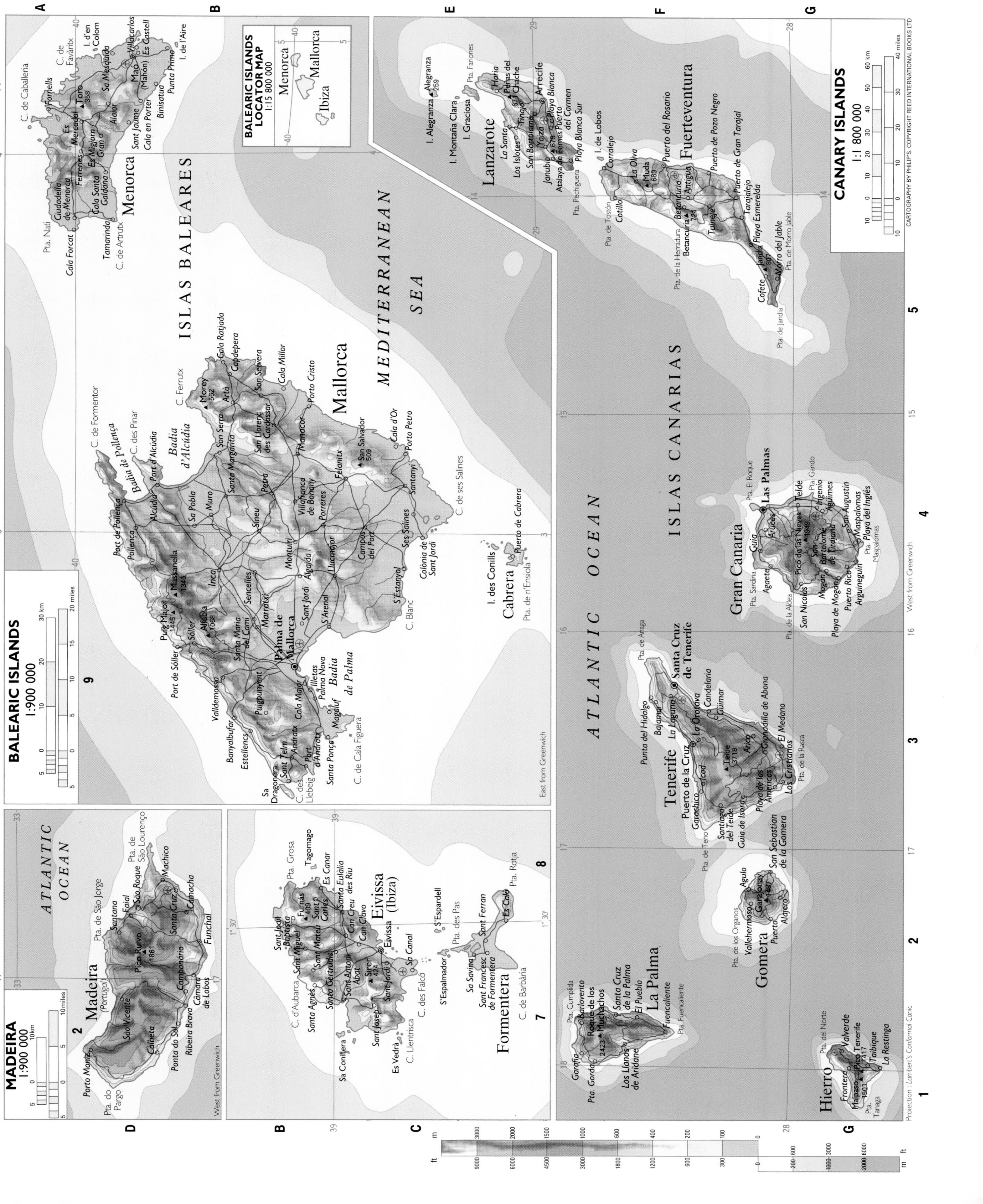
BALEARIC ISLANDS
1:900 000
BALEARIC ISLANDS LOCATOR MAP
1:15 800 000
ISLAS BALEARES
MEDITERRANEAN SEA
Mallorca
Menorca
Eivissa (Ibiza)
Formentera
Cabrera
Palma de Mallorca
MADEIRA
1:900 000
Madeira (Portugal)
ATLANTIC OCEAN
CANARY ISLANDS
1:1 800 000
ISLAS CANARIAS
Lanzarote
Fuerteventura
Gran Canaria
Tenerife
Gomera
La Palma
Hierro
Santa Cruz de Tenerife
Las Palmas
Projection : Lambert's Conformal Conic
CARTOGRAPHY BY PHILIPS. COPYRIGHT REED INTERNATIONAL BOOKS LTD

SOUTHERN GREECE 1:2 200 000

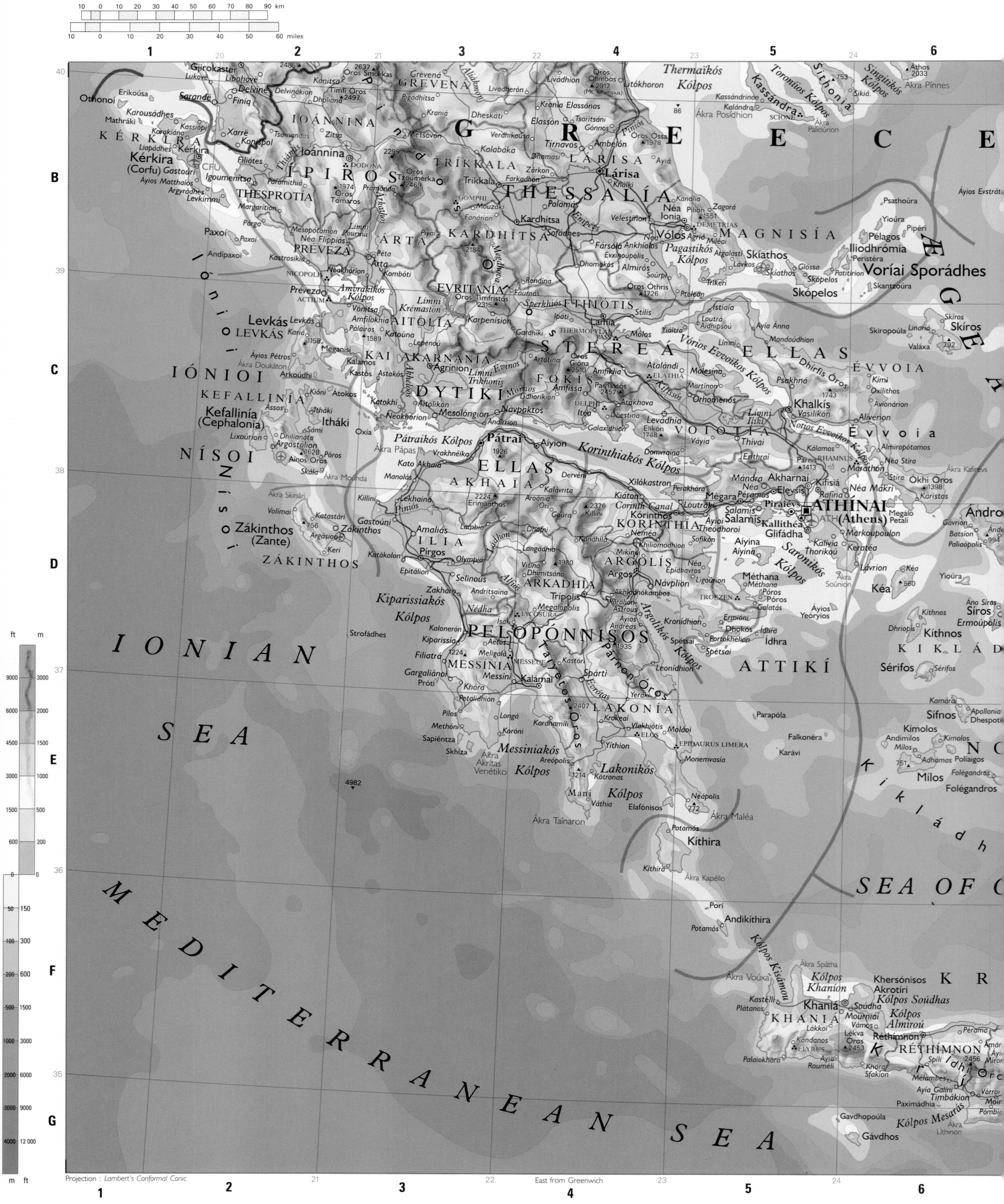

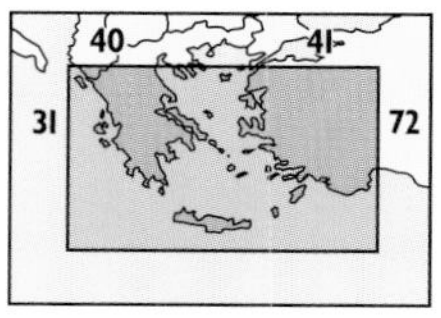

7 8 9 10 11 12

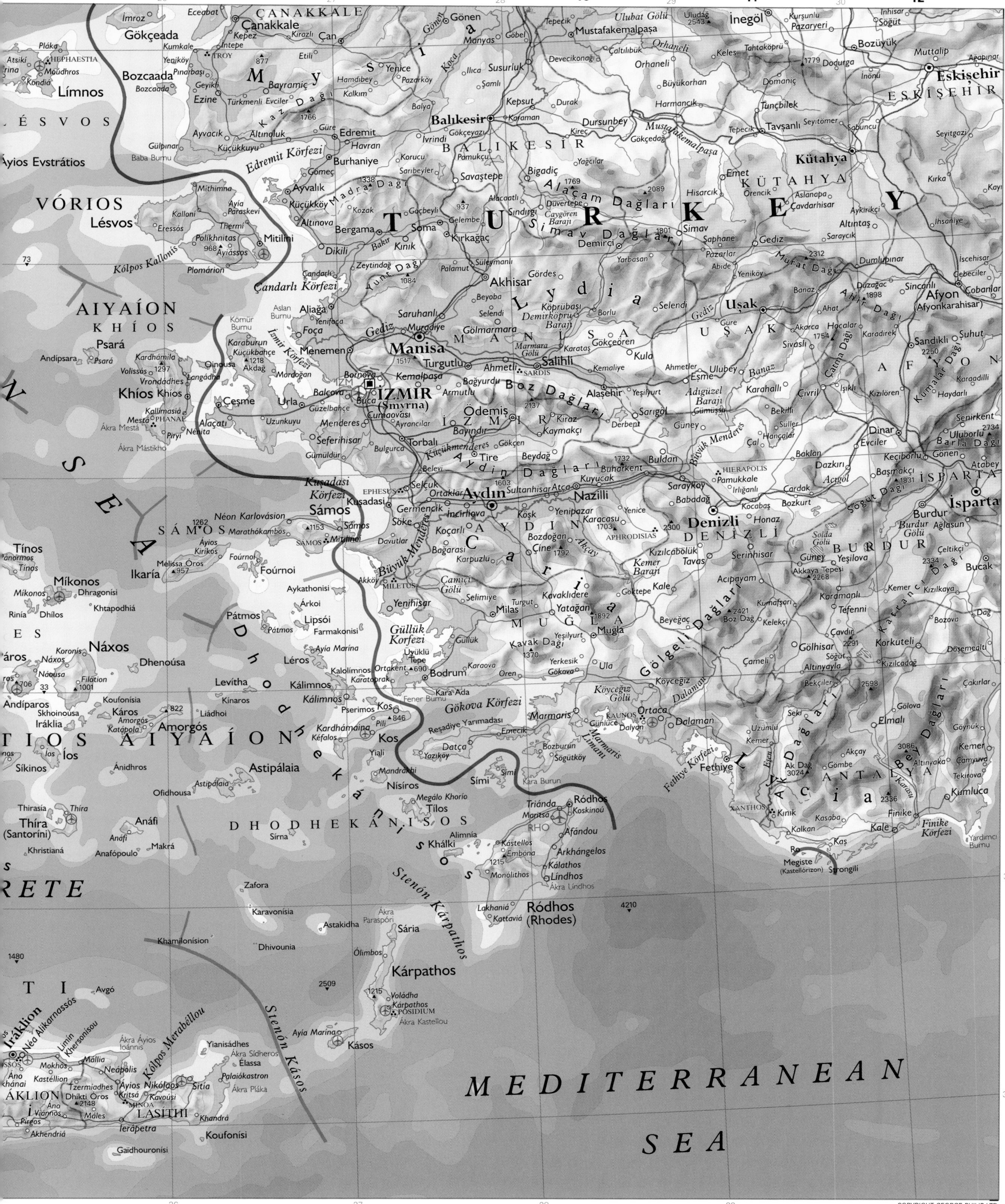

7 8 9 10 11 12

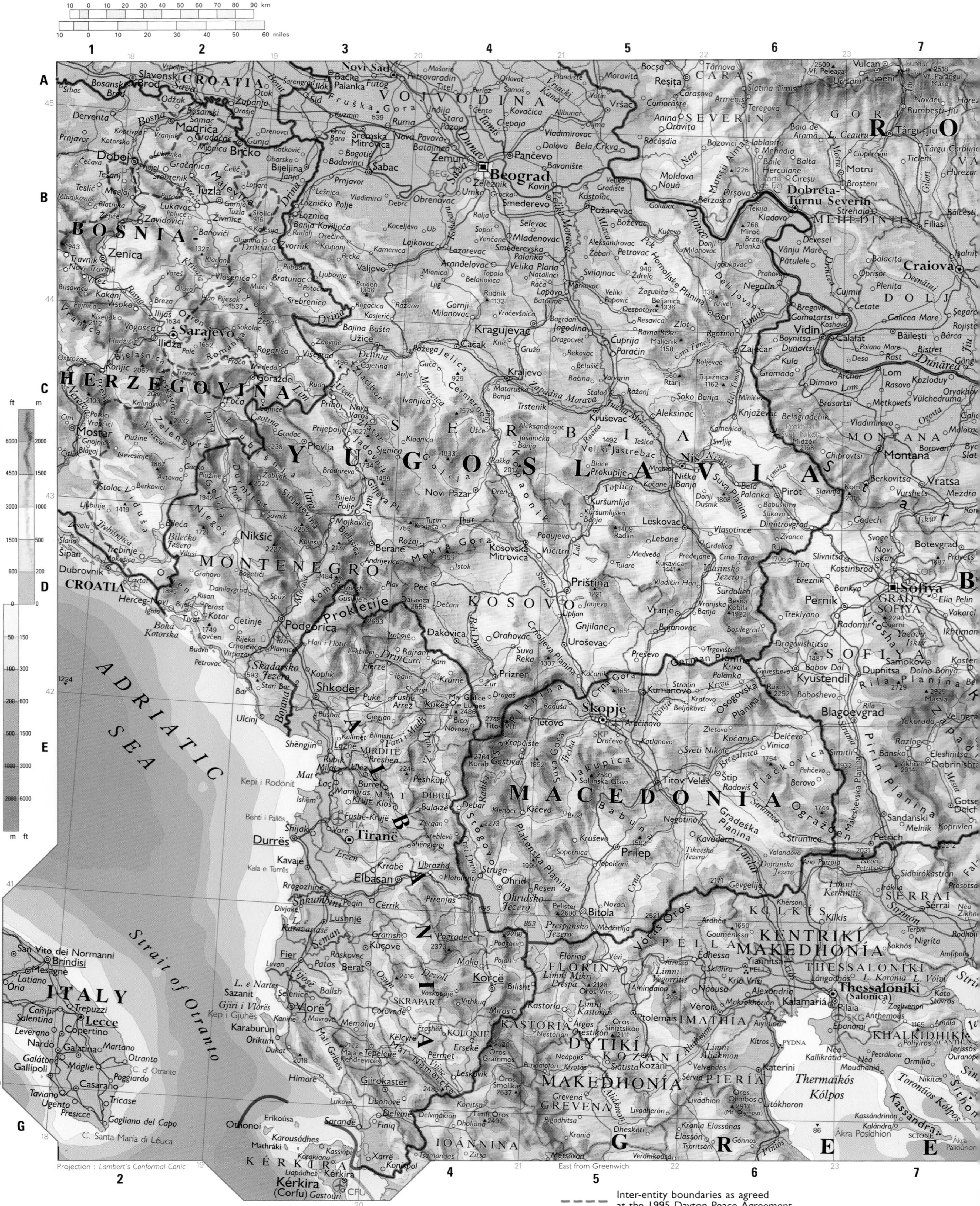

Inter-entity boundaries as agreed at the 1995 Dayton Peace Agreement.

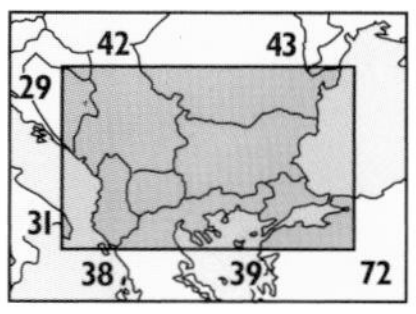

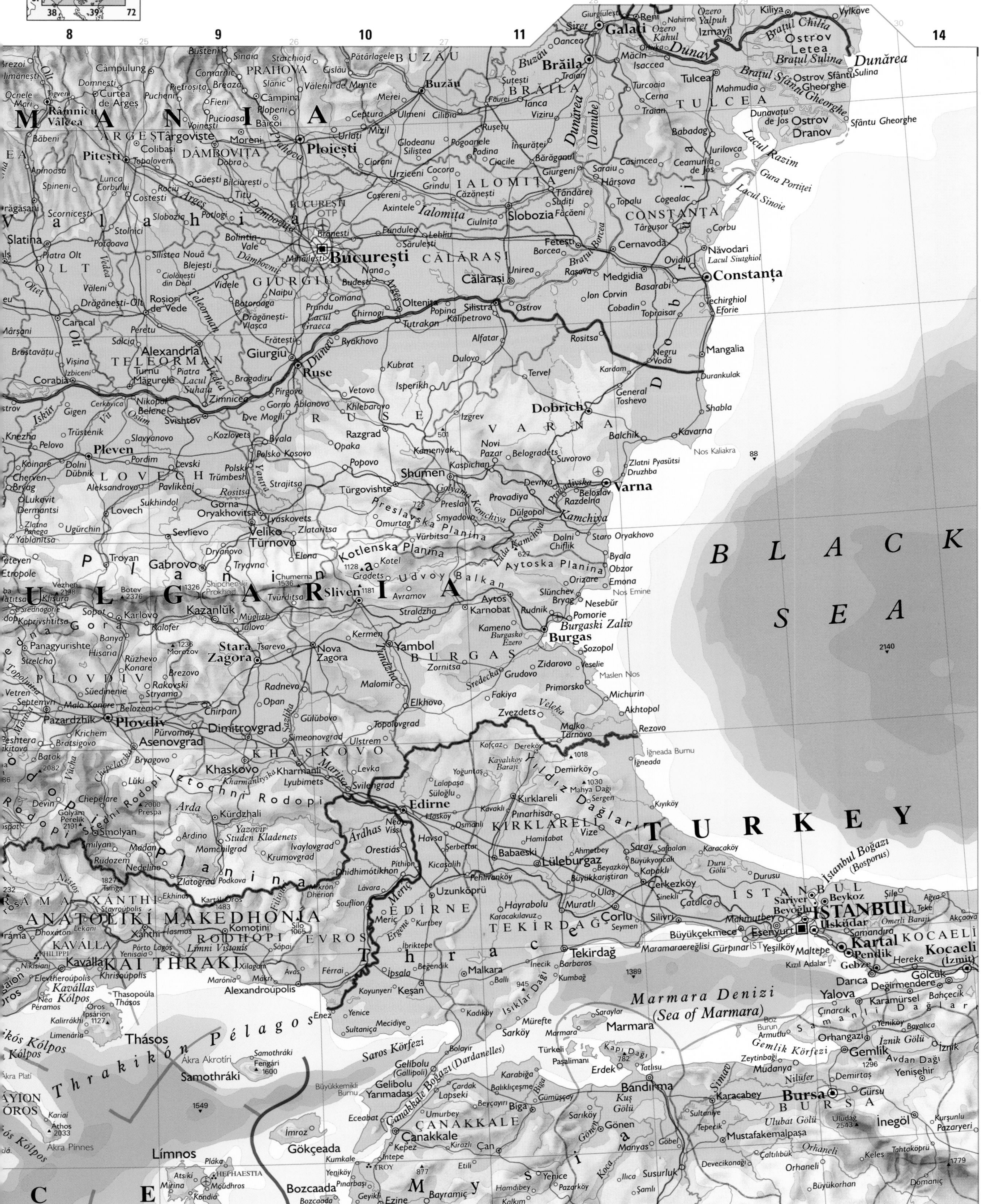

Underlined towns give their name to the administrative area in which they stand.

Administrative divisions in Croatia:

1. Brodsko-Posavska
2. Koprivničko-Križevačka
4. Međimurska
5. Osječko-Baranjska
6. Požeško-Slavonska
8. Virovitičko-Podravska
9. Vukovarsko-Srijemska

Inter-entity boundaries as agreed at the 1995 Dayton Peace Agreement.

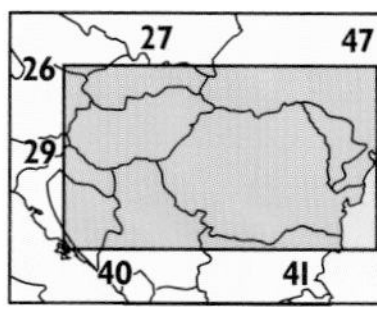

Underlined towns give their name to the administrative area in which they stand.

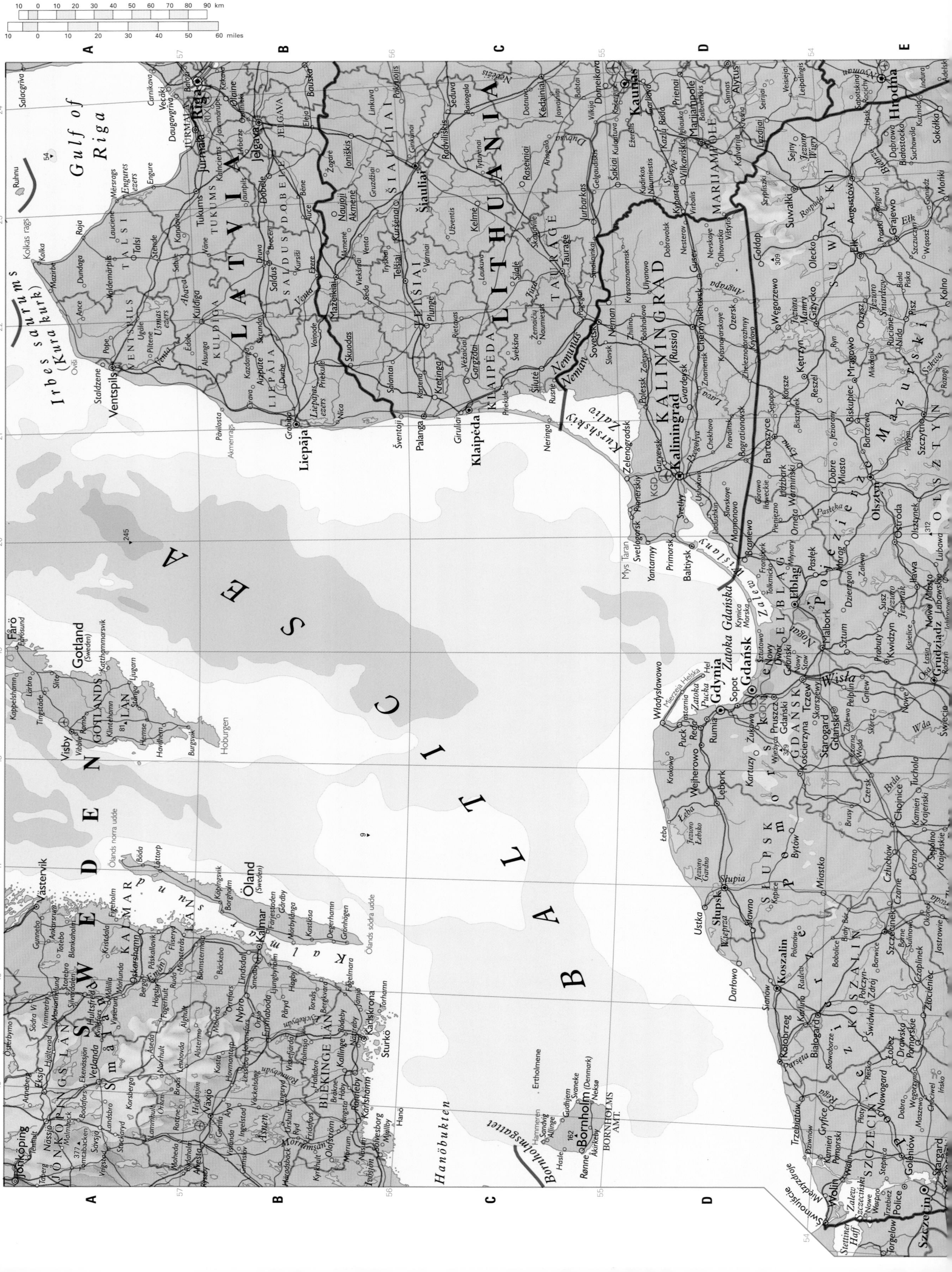
10 0 10 20 30 40 50 60 70 80 90 km
10 0 10 20 30 40 50 60 miles
BALTIC SEA
Gulf of Riga
SWEDEN
LATVIA
LITHUANIA
KALININGRAD (Russia)
Gotland (Sweden)
Öland (Sweden)
Bornholm (Denmark)
Riga
Ventspils
Liepāja
Klaipėda
Kaunas
Šiauliai
Kaliningrad
Gdańsk
Gdynia
Elbląg
Olsztyn
Słupsk
Koszalin
Kołobrzeg
Szczecin
Kalmar
Karlskrona
Växjö
Jönköping
Visby
Hanöbukten
Kurshskiy Zaliv
Zatoka Gdańska

Projection : Lambert's Conformal Conic

Underlined towns give their name to the administrative area in which they stand.

BALTIC STATES, BELARUS AND UKRAINE 1:4 400 000

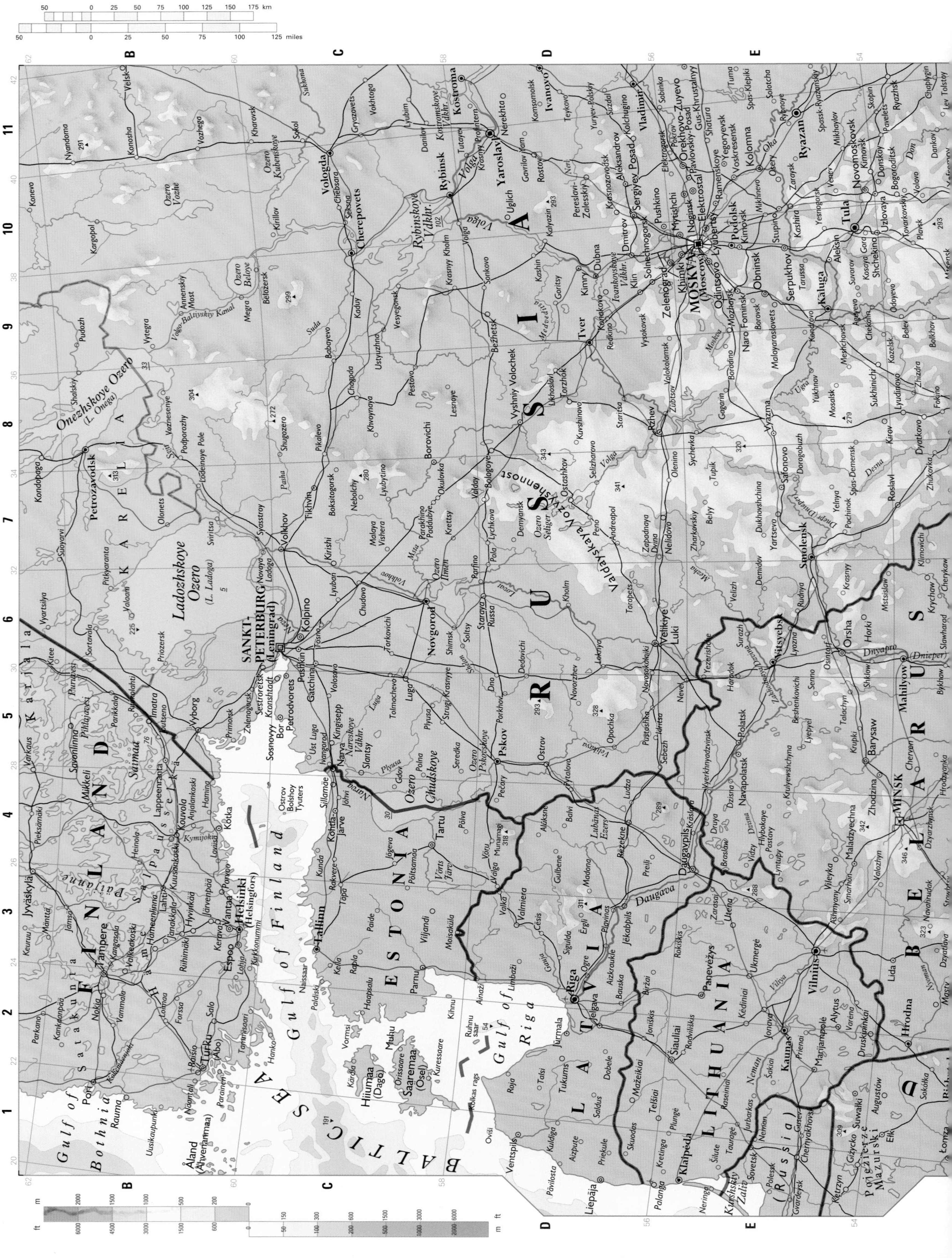

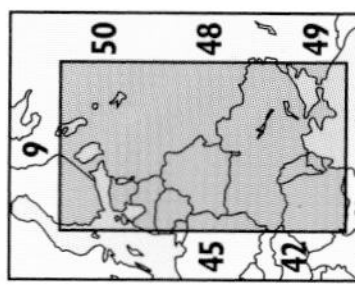

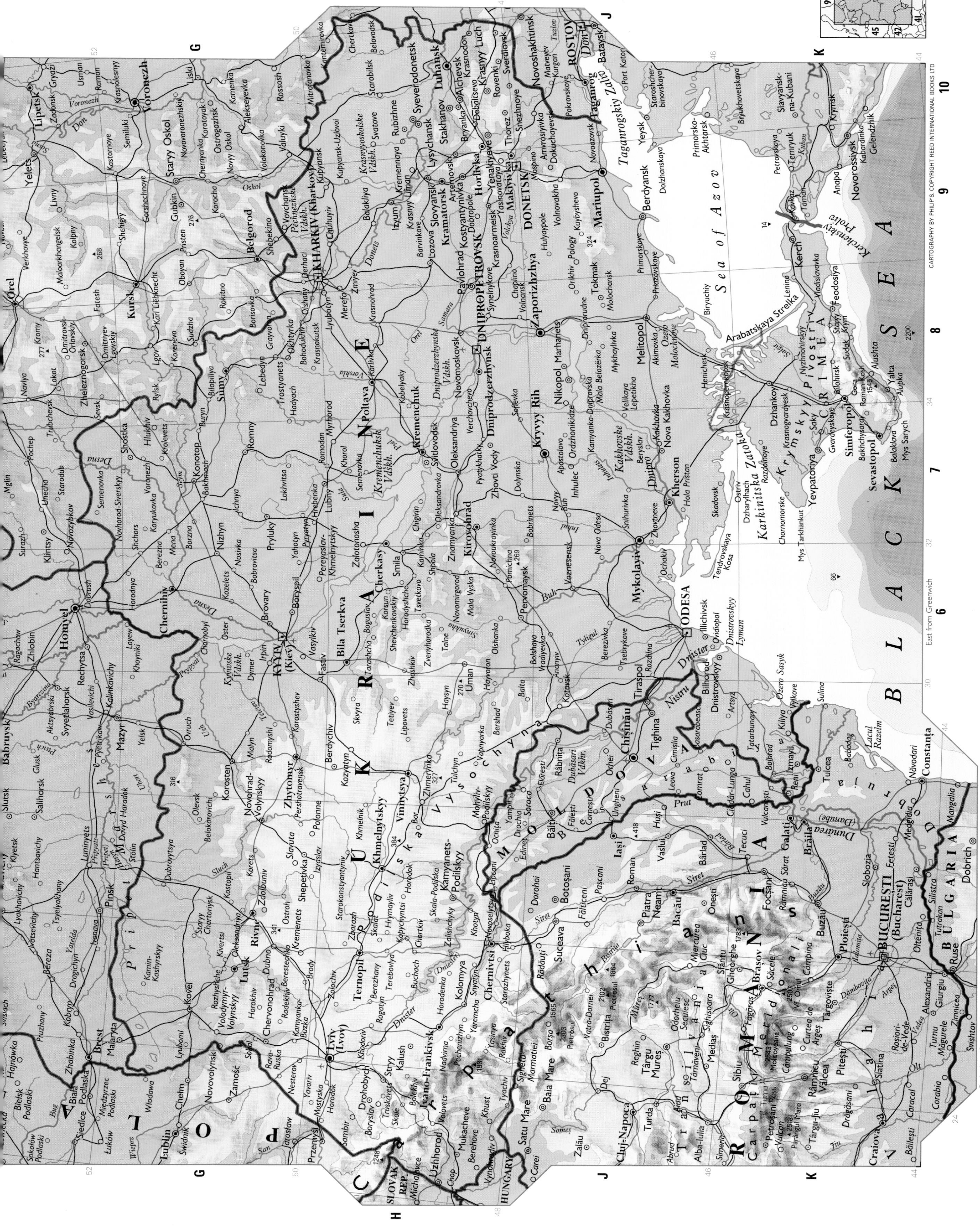

BLACK SEA
Sea of Azov
UKRAINE
CRIMEA
MOLDOVA
ROMANIA
BULGARIA
POLAND
HUNGARY
SLOVAK REP.
KYIV (Kiev)
KHARKIV (Kharkov)
DNIPROPETROVSK
DONETSK
ODESA
LVIV (Lvov)
CHIȘINĂU
BUCUREȘTI (Bucharest)
ROSTOV
Voronezh
Kursk
Belgorod
Homyel
Zaporizhzhya
Mykolayiv
Kherson
Sevastopol
Simferopol
Constanța
Carpații Meridionali
East from Greenwich
Projection: Conical with two standard parallels

50 0 25 50 75 100 125 150 175 km

50 0 25 50 75 100 125 miles

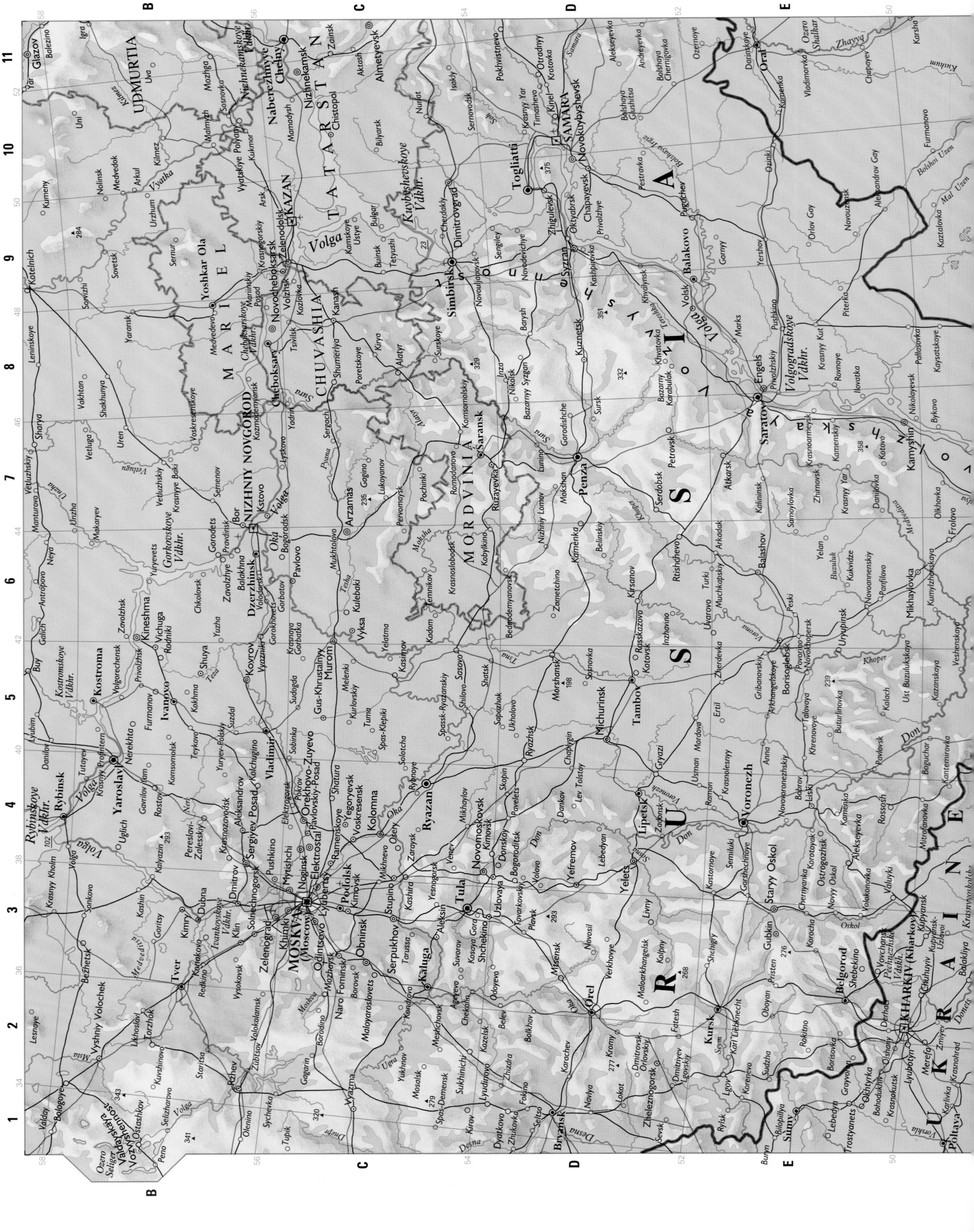

KAZAKSTAN
Caspian Depression
Ryn Peski
KALMYKIA
Chernyye Zemli
Ergeni Vozvyshennost
CASPIAN SEA
BLACK SEA
Sea of Azov
Taganrogskiy Zaliv
Prikubanskaya Nizmennost
CRIMEA
ADYGEA
KARACHEY-CHERKESSIA
KABARDINO-BALKARIA
NORTH OSSETIA
INGUSHETIA
CHECHENIA
DAGESTAN
ABKHAZIA
South Ossetia
AJARIA
GEORGIA
ARMENIA
AZERBAIJAN
TURKEY
Caucasus Mountains
Kuzey Anadolu Dağları
Samurskiy Khrebet
Agrakhanskiy Poluostrov
Volga
Don
Kuban
Manych
Terek
Kür
Elbrus 5642
VOLGOGRAD
ROSTOV
DONETSK
DNIPROPETROVSK
TBILISI
YEREVAN
BAKI
Astrakhan
Volzhskiy
Elista
Stavropol
Krasnodar
Novorossiysk
Sochi
Sokhumi
Nalchik
Vladikavkaz
Groznyy
Makhachkala
Derbent
Kutaisi
Batumi
Rustavi
Gyumri
Gäncä
Sumqayit
Trabzon
Samsun
Mariupol
Taganrog
Zaporizhzhya
Luhansk
Kerch
Melitopol
Berdyansk
Projection: Conical with two standard parallels
East from Greenwich
CARTOGRAPHY BY PHILIP'S. COPYRIGHT REED INTERNATIONAL BOOKS LTD
ft
m
12000
9000
6000
4500
3000
1500
600
0
4000
3000
2000
1500
1000
500
200
0
50
100
200
500
1000
2000
150
300
600
1500
3000
6000

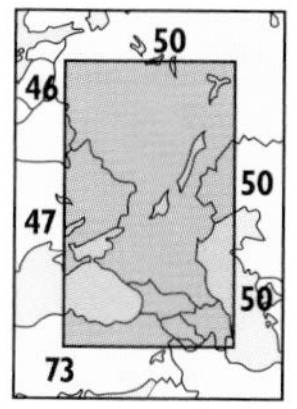

100 0 100 200 300 400 500 600 700 800 km
100 0 100 200 300 400 500 miles
RUSSIA
1 Adygea
2 Karachey-Cherkessia
3 Kabardino-Balkaria
4 North Ossetia
5 Ingushetia
6 Chechenia
7 Dagestan
8 Mordvinia
9 Chuvashia
10 Mari El
11 Tatarstan
12 Udmurtia
13 Khakassia
AZERBAIJAN
14 Naxçıvan
GEORGIA
15 Ajaria
16 Abkhazia
UKRAINE
17 Crimea
ft m
12 000 4000
6000 2000
3000 1000
1200 400
600 200
0 0
200 600
m ft
NORWAY
SWEDEN
FINLAND
ESTONIA
LATVIA
LITHUANIA
POLAND
BELARUS
UKRAINE
MOLDOVA
ROMANIA
GERMANY
DENMARK
RUSSIA
KAZAKSTAN
GEORGIA
ARMENIA
AZERBAIJAN
TURKEY
IRAQ
IRAN
TURKMENISTAN
UZBEKISTAN
KYRGYZSTAN
TAJIKISTAN
AFGHANISTAN
MOSKVA
SANKT-PETERBURG
KYYIV
MINSK
WARSZAWA
STOCKHOLM
HELSINKI
TALLINN
RIGA
VILNIUS
KØBENHAVN
BERLIN
BAKI (Baku)
TBILISI
YEREVAN
TEHRAN
BAGHDAD
TOSHKENT
BISHKEK
ALMATY
DUSHANBE
ÜRÜMQI
Barents Sea
Kara Sea
Black Sea
Caspian Sea
Aral Sea
Gulf of Bothnia
Baltic Sea
Beloye More
Sea of Azov
Zemlya Frantsa Iosifa
Novaya Zemlya
Ustyurt Plateau
Kara Kum
Kyzyl Kum
Projection: Conical Orthomorphic with two standard parallels
East from Greenwich

A
B
C
D
E
F
8
9
10
11
12
13
14
15
16
17
18
19
Ostrov Shmidta
Mys Arkticheskiy
Ostrov Komsomolets
Ostrov Pioner
Ostrov Oktyabrskoy Revolyutsii
965
Ostrov Bolshevik
Severnaya Zemlya
Proliv Vilkitskogo
Mys Chelyuskin
Byrranga
1146
Poluostrov
Gory
Taymyr
Oz. Taymyr
Nordvik
Ostrov Bolshoy Begichev
O C E A N
Laptev
Sea
3800
Ostrov Genriyetty
Ostrov Zhannetty
Ostrova Delonga
Ostrov Zhokhova
Ostrov Bennetta
Novosibirskiye Ostrova
Ostrov Faddeyevskiy
Ostrov Novaya Sibir
374
Ostrov Belkovskiy
Ostrov Kotelnyy
Ostrov Malyy Lyakhovskiy
Ostrov Bolshoy Lyakhovskiy
Ostrov Stolbovoy
Lyakhovskiye Ostrova
Proliv Dmitriya Lapteva
East Siberian Sea
Ostrov Vrangelya
Chukchi Sea
Mys Dezhneva (East C.)
Uelen
Vankarem
1843
Chukotskoye Nagorye
Pevek
Egvekinot
Provideniya
Anadyrskiy Zaliv
St. Lawrence I. (U.S.A.)
Beringovskiy
Ostrova Medvezhi
Ostrov Ayon
Ust Chaun
Bilibino
1853
Ambarchik
Chersky
Anadyr
Khatyrka
Bolshoy Anyuy
Yeropol
Markovo
Penzhino
1752
2562
Koryakskoye Nagorye
Kovacha
Bering Sea
Nizhne Kolymsk
Oloy
Omolon
Kamenskoye
Tilichiki
Chokurdakh
Indigirka
Srednekolymsk
Kolymskoye Nagorye
Paren
Gizhiga
Penzhinskaya Guba
Ossora
Ostrov Karaginskiy
Komandorskiye Ostrova
Mys Buorkhaya
Tiksi
Kazachye
Ust Kuyga
Ust Olenek
Tit-Ary
Olenek
Bulun
Kyusyur
Saskylakh
Anabar
Novorybnoye
Khatanga
Pyasina
Volochanka
Kheta
Kotuy
Zhilinda
Yana
Deputatskiy
Druzhina
Khonuu
Zyryanka
Kolyma
Pobeda 3147
Verkhoyansk
Batagai
2389
Gora Chen 2682
Ust-Nera
Taskan
Omsukchan
Orotukan
Evensk
Nayakhan
Gizhiginskaya Guba
Zaliv Shelikhova
Palana
Tigil
Sredinnyy
Ust-Kamchatsk
Nikolskoye
Ukа
Khrebet Cherskogo
Yagodnoye
Susuman
Atka
Palatka
Magadan
Poluostrov Kamchatka
Gora Klyuchevskaya 4750
Norilsk
Gory Putorana
1701
Olenek
Kystatyam
Verkhoyanskiy Khrebet
Oymyakon
2959
Ust-Omchug
Ust Khayryuzovo
3621
Kamchatka
Khrebet
3456
Petropavlovsk-Kamchatskiy
Yessey
Kotuy
Moyero
Zhigansk
Khandyga
Ust-Bolsheretsk
Kirovskiy
Severo-Kurilsk
962
Arctic Circle
Sangar
Lena
Batamay
Borogontsy
Okhotskiy Perevoz
Arka
Okhotsk
Ulya
Sea of Okhotsk
Turukhansk
Vilyuy
Vilyuysk
Verkhnevilyuysk
Namtsy
Yakutsk
Ytyk Kyuyel
Mayya
Amga
Ust Maya
Noginsk
Nizhnyaya Tunguska
Tura
Yukta
Chernyshevskiy
Mirnyy
Nyurba
Suntar
Pokrovsk
Sinsk
Amga
Ust-Mil
Aim
Maya
Nelkan
Dzhugdzur
1780
Ostrov Paramushir
Ostrov Onekotan
Yerbogachen
Olekminsk
Tommot
Chagda
Uchur
Ayan
Ostrov Bolshoy Shantar
Sakhalinskiy Zaliv
Okha
Sakhalin
Ostrov Simushir
Kurilskiye Ostrova
Podkamennaya Tunguska
Kuyumba
Motoray
Lensk
Aldan
2246
Aleksandrovsk-Sakhalinskiy
Gora Lopatina 1609
Vanavara
Severo-Yeniseyskiy
Vitim
Yenyuka
Olekma
Neryungri
Stanovoy Khrebet
Chumikan
Tugur
Nikolayevsk-na-Amur
Amgun
Poronaysk
Ostrov Urup
Kezhma
Korshunovo
Mama
Bodaybo
Chara
2999
Nagornyy
Uda
Zeya
Yeniseysk
Strelka
Angara
Boguchany
Ust-Ilimsk
Kirensk
Kalakan
Karalon
Ust-Nyukzha
Tynda
Selemdzha
Uglegorsk
Yuzhno-Sakhalinsk
Kurilsk
Ostrov Iturup
Ostrov Kunashir
Chuna
Kondratyevo
Makarovo
Zheleznogorsk-Ilimskiy
Ust-Kut
Magistralnyy
Skovorodino
Dzhalinda
Ushumun
Norsk
Bureya
Komsomolsk
2640
Amursk
Vanino
Kholmsk
Korsakov
Achinsk
Kansk
Ilanskiy
Krasnoyarsk
Tayshet
Bratsk
Lena
2840
Bagdarin
Yablonovyy Khrebet
Mogocha
Amur
Gulian
Shimanovsk
Svobodnyy
Belogorsk
Chegdomyn
2078
Khabarovsk
Wakkanai
Nizhneudinsk
Artemovsk
Vostochnyy Sayan
Chernogorsk
Minusinsk
Abakan
Tulun
Zima
Barguzin
Vitim
Bukachacha
Chita
Shilka
Sretensk
Nerchinsk
Argun
1054
Da Hinggan Ling
Blagoveshchensk
Zavitinsk
Raychikhinsk
Obluchye
Birobidzhan
Smidovich
Khrebet Sikhote Alin
Rumoi
Abashiri
2290
Kushiro
Obihiro
SAPPORO
Hokkaidō
Otaru
Hakodate
Zapadnyy Sayan
Cheremkhovo
Usolye Sibirskoye
Munku-Sardyk 3491
Angarsk
Irkutsk
1620
2456
Ulan Ude
Aginskoye
Poyarkovo
Nenjiang
Hegang
Jiamusi
Songhua Jiang
Vyazemskiy
Bikin
Amgu
Terney
Dalnegorsk
3669
Lesozavodsk
Spassk Dalniy
Dalnerechensk
Turan
Kyzyl
Toora-Khem
Chadan
Slyudyanka
Petrovsk-Zabaykalskiy
Khilok
Olovyannaya
Borzya
Zabaykalsk
Hailar
QIQIHAR
Samagaltay
Hövsgöl Nuur
Gusinoozersk
Kyakhta
Khapcheranga
Manzhouli
Hulun Nur
Tannu Ola
Uvs Nuur
Erzin
Hatgal
Zakamensk
Darhan
HARBIN
Lake Khanka
Ussuriysk
Artem
Vladivostok
Nakhodka
Olga
Hangayn Nuruu
Hentiyn Nuruu
Onon
Choybalsan
Ang'angxi
Nen Jiang
Dongbei
Mudanjiang
Aomori
Hachinohe
Hyargas Nuur
2800
Ulaanbaatar
Tamsagbulag
Tao'an
Yanji
Kraskino
Akita
Döröö Nuur
Ulyasutay
Tsetserleg
Lun
Öndörhaan
Chŏngjin
CHANGCHUN
JILIN
Songhua Hu
2744
Sea of Japan
Honshū
MONGOLIA
Altay
1949
Linxi
Siping
FUSHUN
Tonghua
Niigata
Saynshand
Xilinhot
Chifeng
SHENYANG
ANSHAN
NORTH KOREA
Dandong
Wŏnsan
3957
Gobi
CHINA
Erenhot
Kansŏng
Kanazawa
Fuji-San 3776
4266
Dalandzadgad
Chengde
Yingkou
P'YŎNGYANG
Nampo
SŎUL (Seoul)
JAPAN
Hami
Zhangjiakou
BEIJING
DALIAN
INCH'ŎN
SOUTH KOREA
TAEJŎN
TAEGU
PUSAN
Gaxun Nur
Baotou
Hohhot
ŌSAKA
60
50
40
70
80
90
100
110
120
130
140
150
170

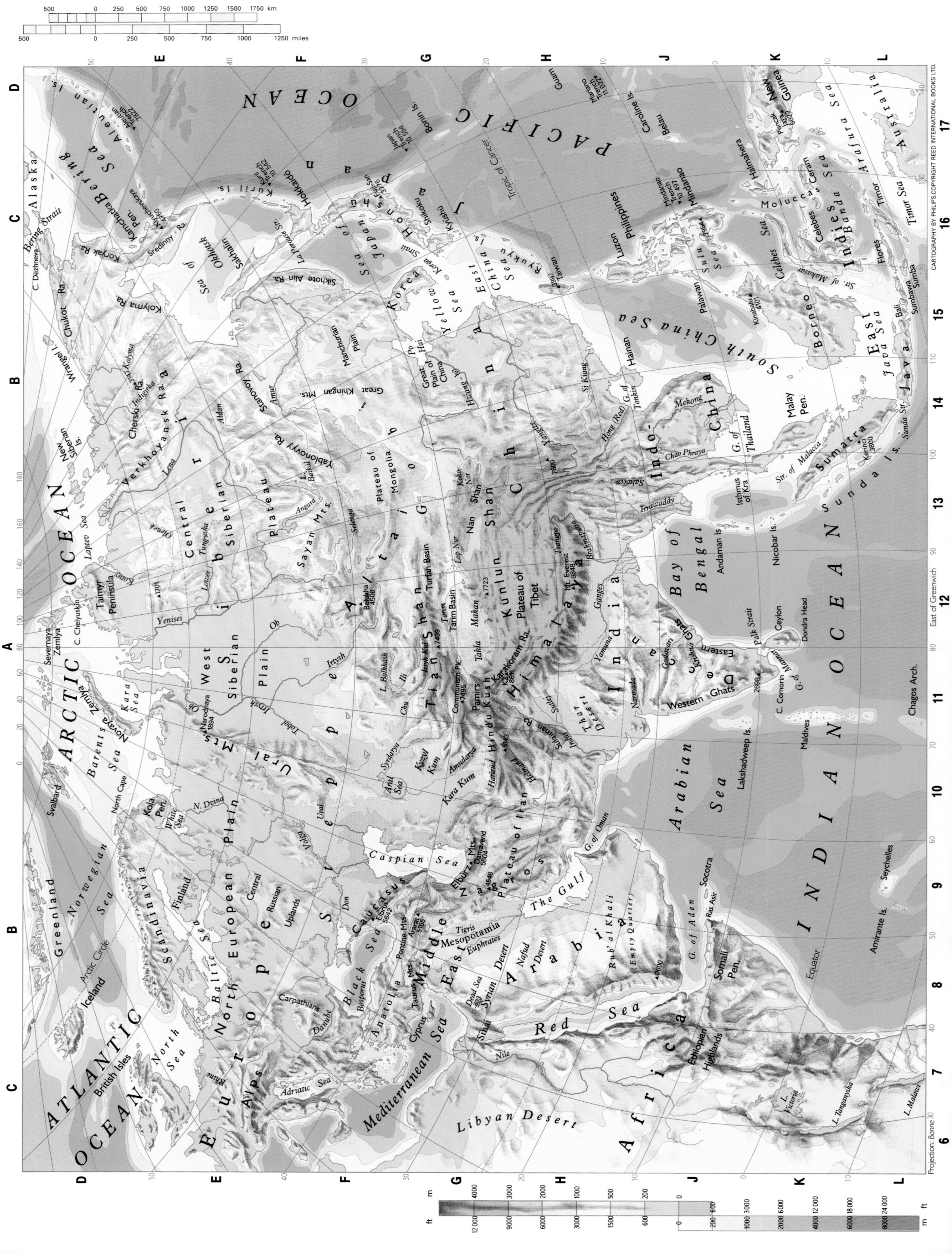
500 0 250 500 750 1000 1250 1500 1750 km
500 0 250 500 750 1000 1250 miles
ARCTIC OCEAN
PACIFIC OCEAN
INDIAN OCEAN
ATLANTIC OCEAN
Bering Sea
Sea of Okhotsk
Sea of Japan
Yellow Sea
East China Sea
South China Sea
Philippines
Celebes Sea
Banda Sea
Arafura Sea
Timor Sea
Java Sea
Bay of Bengal
Arabian Sea
Caspian Sea
Black Sea
Mediterranean Sea
Red Sea
The Gulf
G. of Oman
G. of Aden
Barents Sea
Kara Sea
Laptev Sea
Norwegian Sea
North Sea
Baltic Sea
White Sea
Adriatic Sea
Aral Sea
L. Balkhash
L. Baikal
Lop Nur
Koko Nor
West Siberian Plain
Central Siberian Plateau
Plateau of Mongolia
Plateau of Tibet
Plateau of Iran
Manchurian Plain
Great Plain of China
North European Plain
Central Russian Uplands
Ural Mts.
Caucasus
Elburz Mts.
Zagros
Hindu Kush
Pamirs
Karakoram Ra.
Himalaya
Kunlun Shan
Nan Shan
Tian Shan
Altai
Sayan Mts.
Yablonovyy Ra.
Stanovoy Ra.
Great Khingan Mts.
Verkhoyansk Ra.
Cherski Ra.
Kolyma Ra.
Koryak Ra.
Sredinny Ra.
Sikhote Alin Ra.
Chukot Ra.
Takla Makan
Tarim Basin
Turfan Basin
Gobi
Kara Kum
Kyzyl Kum
Thar Desert
Rub' al Khali (Empty Quarter)
Nafud Desert
Syrian Desert
Libyan Desert
Arabia
Mesopotamia
Anatolia
Middle East
Indo-China
India
Deccan
Western Ghats
Eastern Ghats
Malay Pen.
Borneo
Sumatra
Java
Celebes
New Guinea
Luzon
Mindanao
Taiwan
Hainan
Korea
Honshu
Hokkaido
Kyushu
Shikoku
Sakhalin
Kamchatka Pen.
Kuril Is.
Aleutian Is.
New Siberian Is.
Severnaya Zemlya
Novaya Zemlya
Taimyr Peninsula
Kola Pen.
Scandinavia
Finland
Iceland
Greenland
Svalbard
British Isles
Alps
Carpathians
Europe
Steppe
Siberia
China
Japan
Africa
Ethiopian Highlands
Somali Pen.
Sri Lanka / Ceylon
Maldives
Lakshadweep Is.
Andaman Is.
Nicobar Is.
Chagos Arch.
Seychelles
Amirante Is.
Socotra
Cyprus
Ob
Irtysh
Yenisei
Lena
Amur
Hwang Ho
Yangtze
Si Kiang
Mekong
Irrawaddy
Salween
Brahmaputra
Ganges
Indus
Tigris
Euphrates
Nile
Volga
Don
Danube
Mt. Everest 8848
K2 8611
Communism Pk. 7495
Tropic of Cancer
Equator
Arctic Circle
Projection: Bonne
CARTOGRAPHY BY PHILIPS.COPYRIGHT REED INTERNATIONAL BOOKS LTD.
East of Greenwich
m 4000 3000 2000 1000 500 200 0
ft 12 000 9000 6000 3000 1500 600 0
200 600 / 1000 3000 / 2000 6000 / 4000 12 000 / 6000 18 000 / 8000 24 000

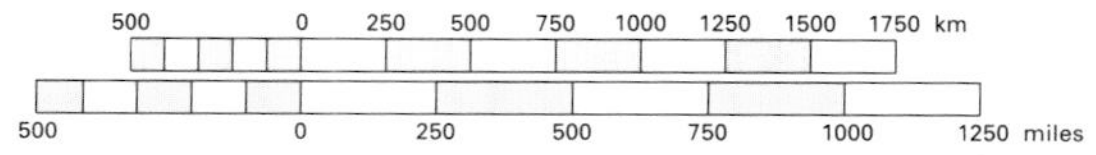
500 0 250 500 750 1000 1250 1500 1750 km
500 0 250 500 750 1000 1250 miles

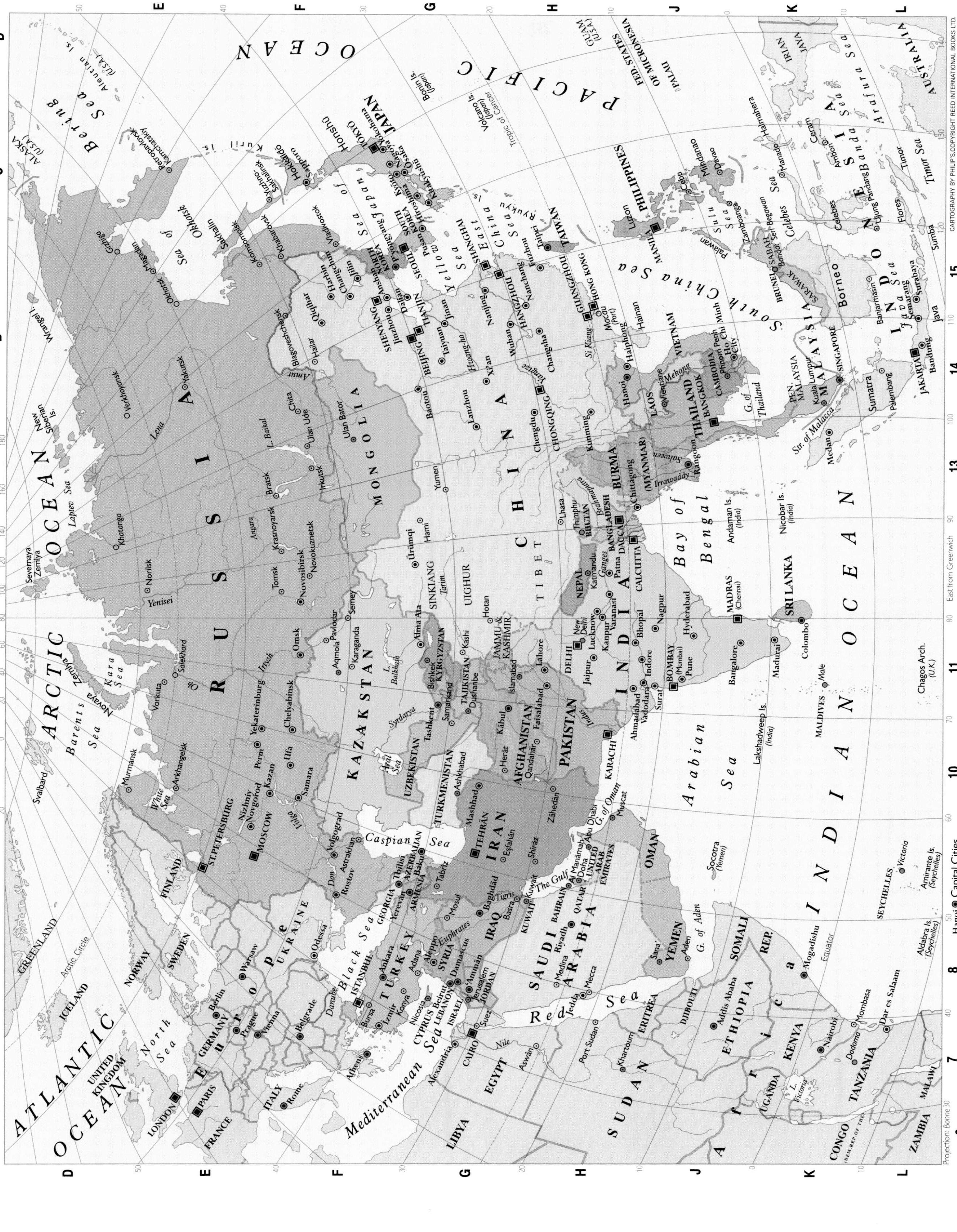
ARCTIC OCEAN
PACIFIC OCEAN
INDIAN OCEAN
ATLANTIC OCEAN
RUSSIA
KAZAKSTAN
MONGOLIA
CHINA
INDIA
PAKISTAN
AFGHANISTAN
IRAN
IRAQ
SAUDI ARABIA
TURKEY
JAPAN
INDONESIA
PHILIPPINES
THAILAND
BURMA (MYANMAR)
VIETNAM
LAOS
CAMBODIA
MALAYSIA
NEPAL
BHUTAN
BANGLADESH
SRI LANKA
OMAN
YEMEN
UZBEKISTAN
TURKMENISTAN
TAJIKISTAN
KYRGYZSTAN
Bay of Bengal
Arabian Sea
South China Sea
East China Sea
Yellow Sea
Sea of Japan
Sea of Okhotsk
Bering Sea
Caspian Sea
Black Sea
Red Sea
Mediterranean Sea
Barents Sea
Kara Sea
Laptev Sea
Arctic Circle
Tropic of Cancer
Equator
East from Greenwich
Hanoi ◉ Capital Cities
Projection: Bonne 30
CARTOGRAPHY BY PHILIPS.COPYRIGHT REED INTERNATIONAL BOOKS LTD.

JAPAN 1:4 400 000

SOUTH KOREA
Pohang
Ullung Do
Tok Do
Tsushima
Iki
Oki-Shotō
Gotō-Rettō
FUKUOKA
KITAKYŪSHŪ
Shimonoseki
Nagasaki
Kumamoto
Kagoshima
Miyazaki
Ōita
Beppu
KYŪSHŪ
Ōsumi-Kaikyō
Ōsumi-Shotō
Tane-ga-Shima
Yaku-Shima
Tokara-Rettō
Satsunan-Shotō
Amakusa-Shotō
Koshiki-Rettō
Hiroshima
Okayama
Matsue
Tottori
Izumo
CHŪGOKU
Matsuyama
Kōchi
Tokushima
Takamatsu
SHIKOKU
Tosa-Wan
Bungo-Suidō
Kii-Suidō
KŌBE
ŌSAKA
KYŌTO
Nara
Wakayama
KINKI
Wakasa-Wan
Fukui
Kanazawa
Toyama
Toyama-wan
Nagano
NAGOYA
Shizuoka
Hamamatsu
Suruga-Wan
TŌKYŌ
YOKOHAMA
KAWASAKI
Chiba
Mito
Utsunomiya
Iwaki
Chōshi
KANTŌ
Izu-Shotō
Nanpō-Shotō
PACIFIC OCEAN
RYUKYU ISLANDS
on same scale
Amami-Ō-Shima
Tokuno-Shima
Okinawa-Jima
Naha
Miyako-Jima
Ishigaki-Shima
Iriomote-Jima
Nansei-Shotō
Sakishima-Guntō
Senkaku-Shotō
Okinawa-Guntō
Amami-Guntō
Projection: Conical with two standard parallels
East from Greenwich
m
ft
© COPYRIGHT GEORGE PHILIP & SON LTD

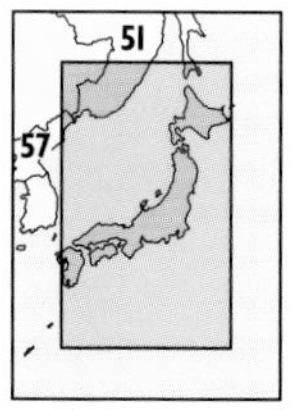

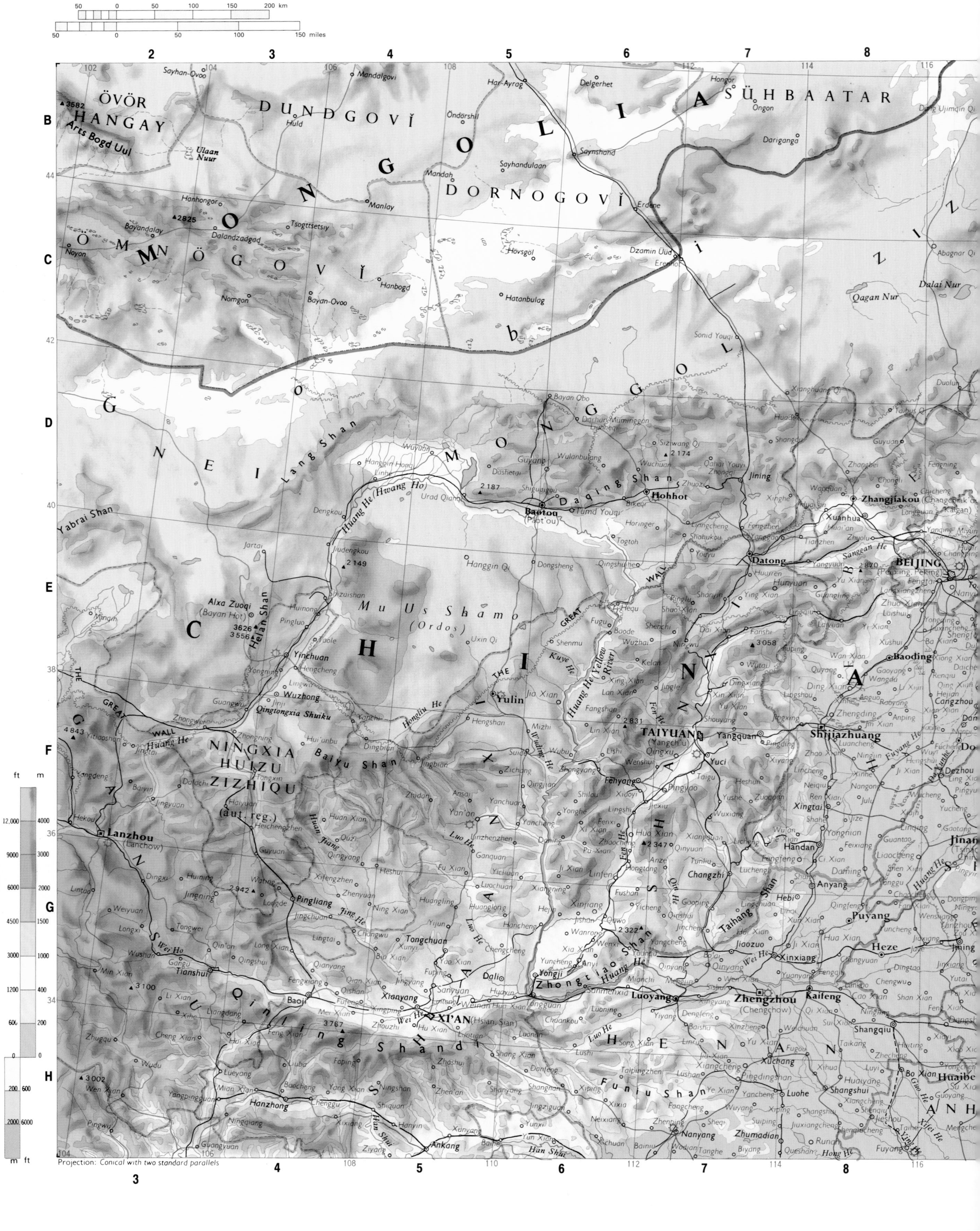

Projection: Conical with two standard parallels

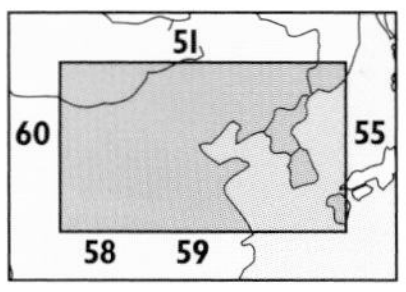
51
60
55
58
59

HARBIN
(Haerhpin)
HEILONGJIANG
RUSSIA
Ozero Khanka
Mudanjiang
Ussuriysk
(Voroshilov)
Vladivostok
Changchun
Jilin
Shuangliao
Siping
Liaoyuan
Fushun
SHENYANG
(Mukden)
Anshan
Benxi
Liaoyang
Jinzhou
Fuxin
Tieling
Dandong
Yingkou
Chifeng
Tongliao
Liaodong Wan
Liaodong Bandao
DALIAN
(Luda)
Lüshun
TIANJIN
Tangshan
Qinhuangdao
Bo Hai
(Gulf of Chihli)
Korea Bay
NORTH KOREA
P'YŎNGYANG
Hamhŭng
Hŭngnam
Chongjin
Kimchaek
(Songjin)
Wŏnsan
Tongjosŏn Man
Sinŭiju
Kaesŏng
SOUTH KOREA
SŎUL
INCH'ŎN
Suwŏn
Chunchŏn
Taejŏn
TAEGU
Kwangju
PUSAN
Ulsan
Mokpo
Chŏnju
Cheju-do
Cease Fire Line
SEA OF JAPAN
Ullung-do
Korea Strait
Tsushima
Tsushima-kaikyō
JAPAN
Sasebo
Nagasaki
Shandong Bandao
Yantai
Weihai
Weifang
Zibo
QINGDAO
(Ch'ingtao)
Laizhou Wan
HUANG HAI
(Yellow Sea)
Lianyungang
Linyi
Xuzhou
JIANGSU
Yancheng
Bengbu
Paektu-san
Changbai Shan
Yalu Jiang
East from Greenwich
COPYRIGHT GEORGE PHILIP & SON LTD

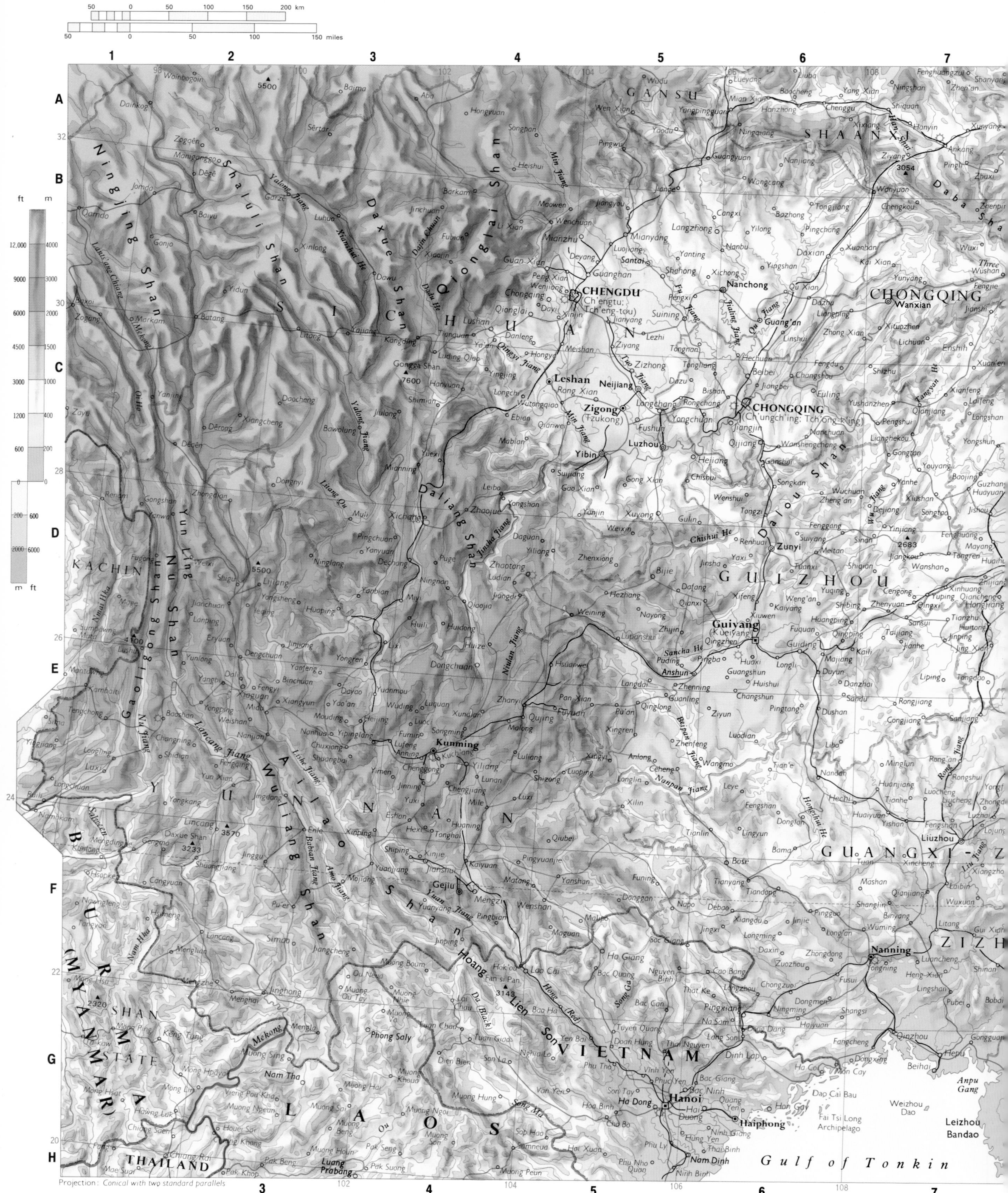

Projection: Conical with two standard parallels

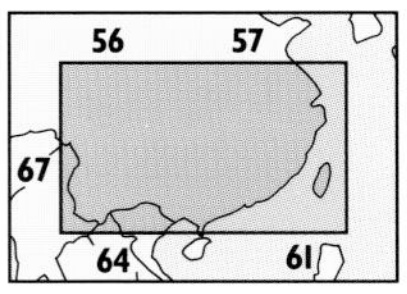
56
57
67
64
61

8
9
10
11
12
13
14
A
B
C
D
E
F
G
H
HENAN
HUBEI
ANHUI
JIANGSU
ZHEJIANG
JIANGXI
HUNAN
FUJIAN
GUANGDONG
GUANGZU
TAIWAN
HONG KONG
SHANGHAI
(Changhai)
NANJING
(Nanking; Nanching)
WUHAN
(Wou-han)
GUANGZHOU
(Kuangchou; Canton)
T'AIPEI
Nanyang
Xiangfan
Xinyang
Yichang
(Ich'ang)
Shashi
Hankou
Huangshi
Jiujiang
Changde
Changsha
Xiangtan
Zhuzhou
Hengyang
Shaoyang
Guilin
Wuzhou
Zhaoqing
Foshan
Jiangmen
Shenzhen
Kowloon
Macau
(Macao)
(Port.)
Zhanjiang
Shaoguan
Ganzhou
Ji'an
Nanchang
Jingdezhen
Linchuan
Anqing
Hefei
Huainan
Bengbu
Wuhu
Zhenjiang
(Chenchiang)
Yangzhou
Changzhou
(Ch'angchou)
Wuxi
(Wuhsi)
Suzhou
(Suchou)
Nantong
Changshu
Jiading
Songjiang
Jiaxing
Wuxing
Hangzhou
(Hangchou; Hangchow)
Shaoxing
Ningbo
(Ningpo)
Jinhua
Linhai
Wenzhou
(Wenchow)
Tunxi
Shangrao
Nanping
Sanming
Fuzhou
(Foochow; Fuchou)
Quanzhou
(Ch'uanchou)
Zhangzhou
Xiamen
(Hsiamen; Amoy)
Chao'an
Shantou
(Swatow)
Chilung
Hsinchu
T'aichung
Changhua
Chiai
T'ainan
Kaohsiung
P'ingtung
Hualien
Macheng
Dabie Shan
Mufu Shan
Jiuling Shan
Wuyi Shan
Wugong Shan
Nanling
Dahong Shan
Jing Shan
Xuefeng Shan
Chungyang Shanmo
Chang Jiang
(Yangtze)
Han Shui
Huai He
Gan Jiang
Xiang Jiang
Yuan Jiang
Zi Shui
Li Shui
Xi Jiang
Bei Jiang
Dong Jiang
Min Jiang
Fuchun Jiang
Dongting Hu
Poyang Hu
Chao Hu
Hongze Hu
Tai Hu
Hangzhou Wan
Chongming Dao
Zhoushan Dao
Dai Shan
Daqu Shan
Taizhou Liedao
Yuhuan Dao
Nanji Shan
Fuying Dao
Matsu Tao
Xinghua Wan
Nanri Dao
Chinmen Tao
Dongshan
Tropic of Cancer
Honghai Wan
Dangan Liedao
Gaolan Dao
Shangchuan Dao
Xiachuan Dao
Hailing Dao
Donghai Dao
Naozhou Dao
Leizhou Wan
Formosa Strait
Luzon Strait
SOUTH CHINA SEA
Tungsha Tao
P'enghu
Hungt'ou Hsu
Lü Tao
Maopi T'ou
Oluanpi
1834
1810
1725
2120
1629
2164
1703
2393
3931
3997
112
114
116
118
120
122
32
30
28
26
24
22
20
East from Greenwich
COPYRIGHT. GEORGE PHILIP & SON. LTD.

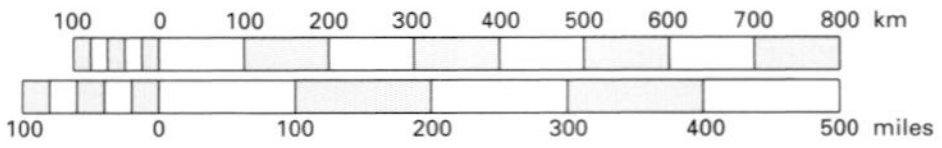
100 0 100 200 300 400 500 600 700 800 km
100 0 100 200 300 400 500 miles

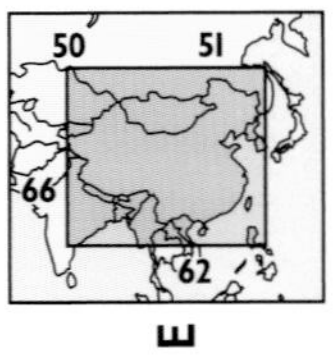
50
51
66
62

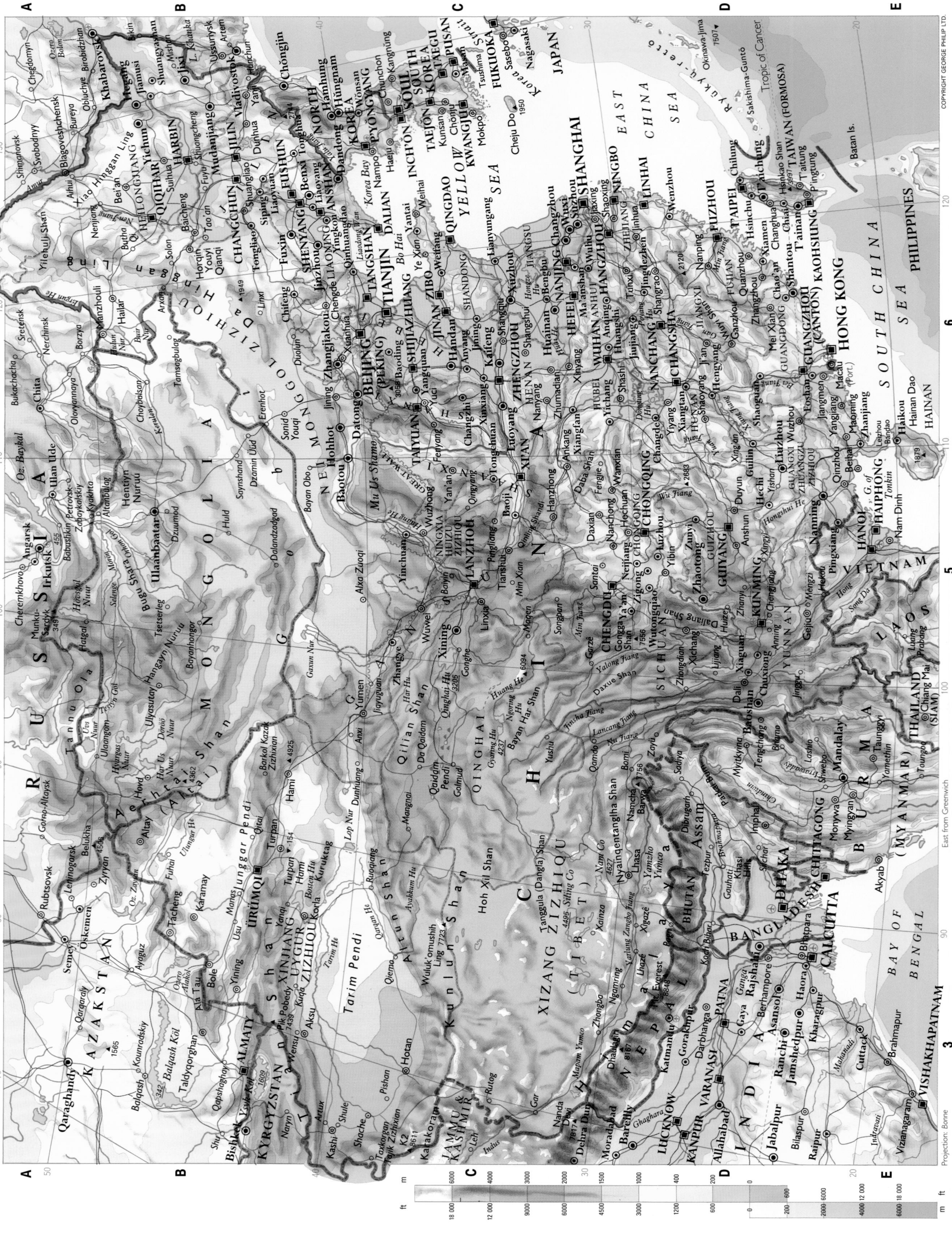
RUSSIA
MONGOLIA
KAZAKSTAN
KYRGYZSTAN
CHINA
NEPAL
BHUTAN
BANGLADESH
INDIA
BURMA (MYANMAR)
THAILAND (SIAM)
LAOS
VIETNAM
NORTH KOREA
SOUTH KOREA
JAPAN
PHILIPPINES
TAIWAN (FORMOSA)
HONG KONG
YELLOW SEA
EAST CHINA SEA
SOUTH CHINA SEA
BAY OF BENGAL
BEIJING (PEKING)
SHANGHAI
TIANJIN
CHONGQING
CHENGDU
WUHAN
GUANGZHOU (CANTON)
XI'AN
LANZHOU
ÜRÜMQI
LHASA
KUNMING
HARBIN
SHENYANG
ULAANBAATAR
PYONGYANG
SOUL
CALCUTTA
DHAKA
HANOI
Tarim Pendi
Kunlun Shan
Tian Shan
XIZANG ZIZHIQU (TIBET)
QINGHAI
NEI MONGGOL ZIZHIQU
XINJIANG UYGUR ZIZHIQU
Everest 8848
Tropic of Cancer
Projection: Bonne
East from Greenwich
m ft
6000 18 000
4000 12 000
3000 9000
2000 6000
1500 4500
1000 3000
400 1200
200 600
0
200 600
2000 6000
4000 12 000
6000 18 000
COPYRIGHT GEORGE PHILIP LTD.

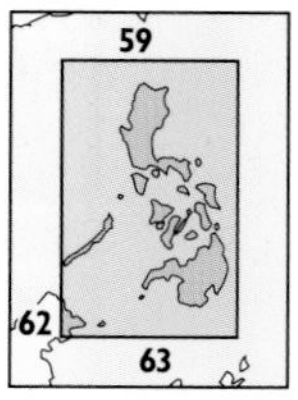
59
62
63

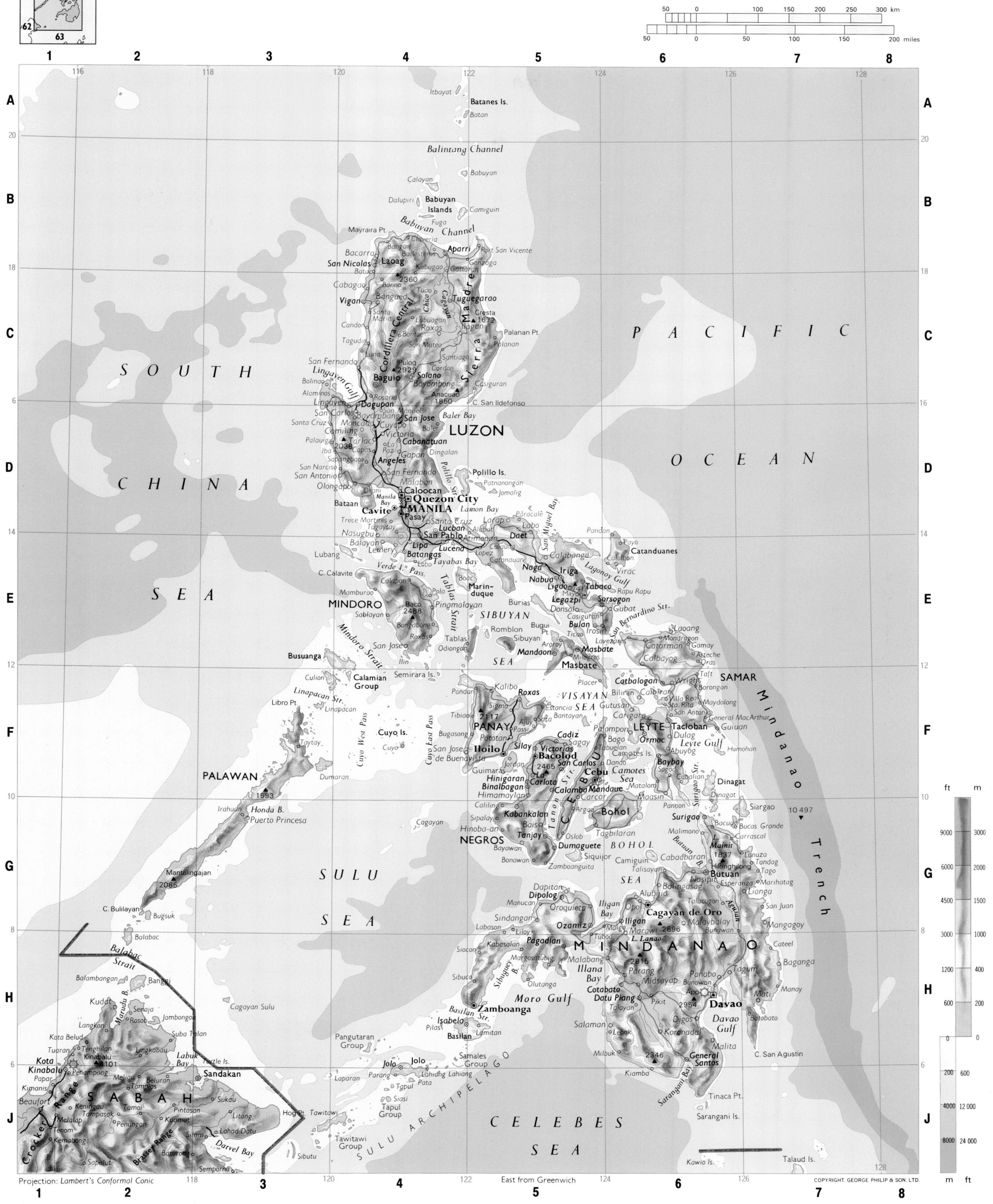
SOUTH
CHINA
SEA
PACIFIC
OCEAN
SULU
SEA
CELEBES
SEA
LUZON
MINDORO
PALAWAN
PANAY
NEGROS
MINDANAO
SAMAR
LEYTE
Bohol
Cebu
SABAH
SIBUYAN SEA
VISAYAN SEA
BOHOL SEA
CAMOTES SEA
SULU ARCHIPELAGO
Mindanao Trench
Batanes Is.
Batan
Itbayat
Balintang Channel
Babuyan
Calayan
Babuyan Islands
Camiguin
Dalupiri
Babuyan Channel
Fuga
Mayraira Pt.
Aparri
Laoag
Bacarra
San Nicolas
Vigan
Tuguegarao
Cordillera Central
Sierra Madre
Lingayen Gulf
San Fernando
Baguio
Pulog
2929
Dagupan
Cabanatuan
San Jose
Baler Bay
C. San Ildefonso
Angeles
Olongapo
Bataan
Polillo Is.
Caloocan
Quezon City
MANILA
Manila Bay
Cavite
Pasay
Lamon Bay
Batangas
Lucena
San Pablo
Lipa
Lubang
C. Calavite
Verde I. Pass.
Tayabas Bay
Marinduque
Tablas Strait
Mindoro Strait
Baco
2488
Calapan
San Jose
Busuanga
Calamian Group
Culion
Linapacan Str.
Semirara Is.
Daet
Naga
Iriga
Legazpi
Sorsogon
Catanduanes
Lagonoy Gulf
San Bernardino Str.
Masbate
Romblon
Sibuyan
Tablas
Burias
Calbayog
Catarman
Catbalogan
Tacloban
Ormoc
Leyte Gulf
Guiuan
Dinagat
Siargao
10 497
Surigao
Butuan
Cagayan de Oro
Iligan
Iligan Bay
L. Lanao
Mt. Apo
2954
Davao
Davao Gulf
General Santos
Cotabato
Illana Bay
Moro Gulf
Zamboanga
Basilan
Basilan Str.
Jolo
Tawitawi Group
Sarangani Is.
Talaud Is.
C. San Agustin
Dipolog
Ozamiz
Pagadian
Dumaguete
Siquijor
Iloilo
Roxas
Kalibo
Bacolod
Cuyo Is.
Cuyo West Pass
Cuyo East Pass
Dumaran
Puerto Princesa
Honda B.
1593
Mantalingajan
2085
C. Bulilayan
Balabac
Balabac Strait
Banggi
Cagayan Sulu
Kota Kinabalu
Kinabalu
4101
Sandakan
Crocker Range
Brassey Range
Labuk Bay
Darvel Bay
Lahad Datu
Semporna
Tawau
Projection: Lambert's Conformal Conic
East from Greenwich
COPYRIGHT. GEORGE PHILIP & SON. LTD.
50 0 100 150 200 250 300 km
50 0 50 100 150 200 miles
ft m
9000 3000
6000 2000
4500 1500
3000 1000
1200 400
600 200
0 0
200 600
4000 12 000
8000 24 000
m ft

100 0 100 200 300 400 500 km
100 0 50 100 150 200 250 300 350 miles
1 2 3 4 5
A B C D E F
BURMA (MYANMAR)
RANGOON (YANGON)
G. of Martaban
THAILAND
BANGKOK
LAOS
VIETNAM
CAMBODIA
Phnom Penh (Phnum Penh)
PHANH BHO HO CHI MINH
Gulf of Thailand
ANDAMAN SEA
SOUTH CHINA SEA
Paracel Is.
Spratly Is.
MALAYSIA
PENINSULAR MALAYSIA
KUALA LUMPUR
SINGAPORE
Johor Baharu
BRUNEI
Bandar Seri Begawan
SARAWAK
SABAH
Kota Kinabalu
Borneo
KALIMANTAN
Strait of Malacca
Sumatera
MEDAN
PALEMBANG
Padang
Jambi
Pekanbaru
Bangka
Belitung
Selat Karimata
INDONESIA
Greater Sunda Islands
JAVA SEA
Jawa (Java)
JAKARTA
BANDUNG
SEMARANG
SURABAYA
Yogyakarta
Malang
Madura
BALI
Denpasar
Lombok
Mataram
NUSA TENGGARA BARAT
Pontianak
Kuching
Banjarmasin
Balikpapan
Samarinda
Kepulauan Riau
Kepulauan Natuna
Kepulauan Anambas
Kepulauan Mentawai
Siberut
Nias
Simeulue
Banda Aceh
INDIAN OCEAN
Java Trench
Projection: Mercator
East from Greenwich

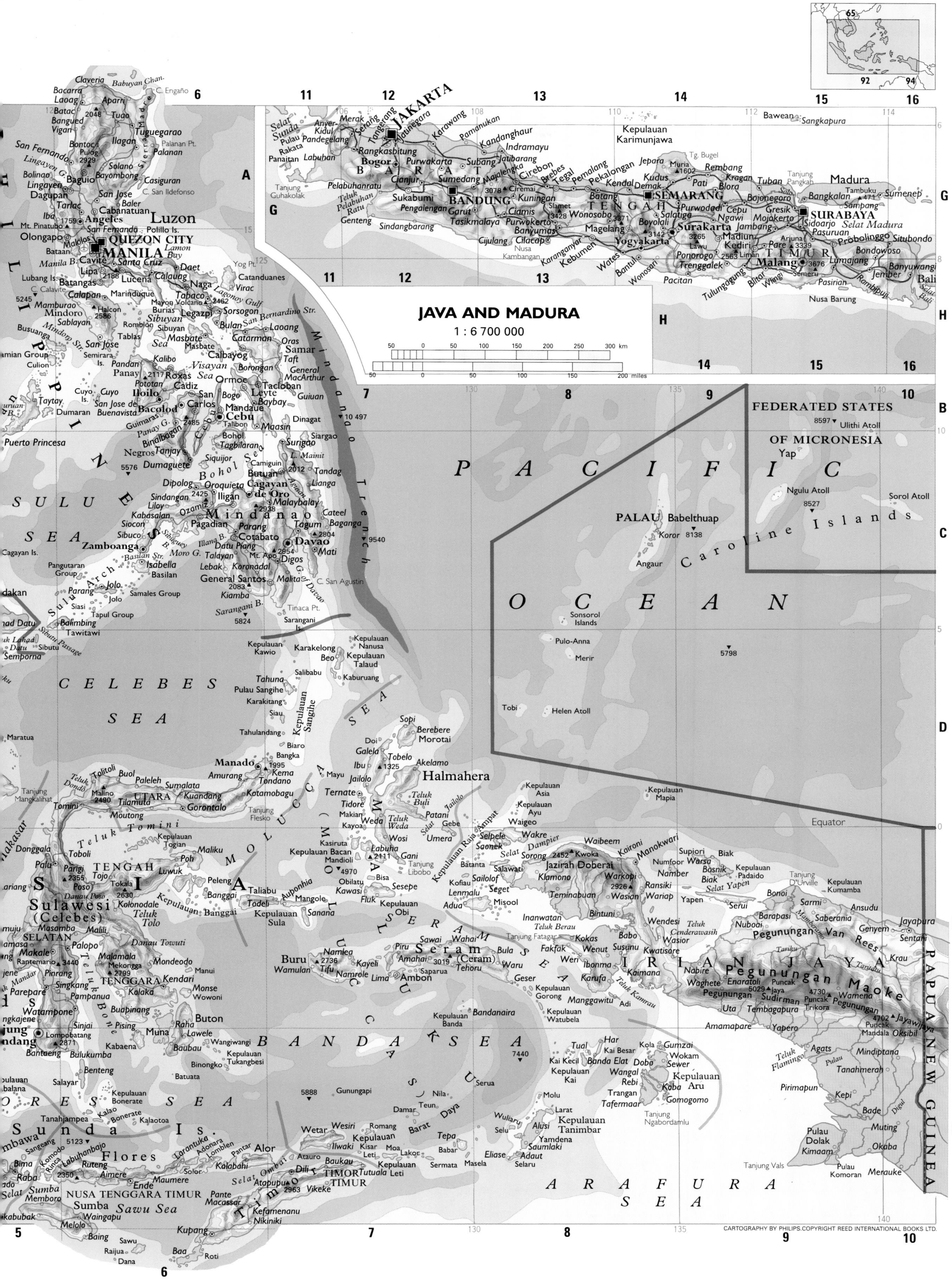
JAVA AND MADURA
1 : 6 700 000
50 0 50 100 150 200 250 300 km
50 0 50 100 150 200 miles
JAKARTA
Bogor
BANDUNG
SEMARANG
Yogyakarta
SuraKarta
SURABAYA
Madura
Malang
Kepulauan Karimunjawa
Bawean
Selat Sunda
Selat Madura
Bali
Nusa Barung
Luzon
QUEZON CITY
MANILA
Mindoro
Samar
Panay
Negros
Cebu
Bohol
Leyte
Mindanao
Zamboanga
Davao
General Santos
Puerto Princesa
SULU SEA
CELEBES SEA
Mindanao Trench
PACIFIC OCEAN
FEDERATED STATES OF MICRONESIA
Yap
Ulithi Atoll
Ngulu Atoll
Sorol Atoll
Caroline Islands
PALAU
Babelthuap
Koror
Angaur
Sonsorol Islands
Pulo-Anna
Merir
Tobi
Helen Atoll
Kepulauan Talaud
Kepulauan Sangihe
Manado
Halmahera
Morotai
Ternate
Tidore
MOLUCCA SEA
Sulawesi (Celebes)
Teluk Tomini
Teluk Bone
Kepulauan Banggai
Kepulauan Sula
Buru
Seram (Ceram)
Ambon
BANDA SEA
Kepulauan Aru
Kepulauan Kai
Kepulauan Tanimbar
IRIAN JAYA
Jazirah Doberai
Pegunungan Maoke
Puncak Jaya
Jayapura
Merauke
PAPUA NEW GUINEA
Equator
FLORES SEA
Sunda Is.
Flores
Sumba
Sawu Sea
NUSA TENGGARA TIMUR
Timor
Kupang
Dili
ARAFURA SEA
CARTOGRAPHY BY PHILIPS.COPYRIGHT REED INTERNATIONAL BOOKS LTD.

50 0 50 100 150 200 km
50 0 50 100 150 miles
A
B
C
D
E
F
1
2
3
4
5
6
7
8
HAINAN
G. of Tonkin
HANOI
Haiphong
Vientiane
BANGKOK
RANGOON
Mandalay
Da Nang
Hue
Moulmein
YUNNAN
GUANGXI ZHUANGZU ZIZHIQU
GUANGDONG
BURMA (MYANMAR)
SHAN
KAYAH
KAWTHULE
TENASSERIM
LAOS
THAILAND
VIETNAM
CAMBODIA
Mekong
Khorat
Cao Nguyen Khorat
Phnom Dangrek
Tonle Sap
ANGKOR
Chao Phraya
Salween
Sittang Myit
Mae Khlong
Hoang Lien Son
Tanen Tong Dan
Bilauk Taung
G. of Martaban
Moscos Islands
Qiongzhou Haixia
Leizhou Bandao
Dao Bach Long Vi
Cao Nguyen Boloven
Tran Ninh

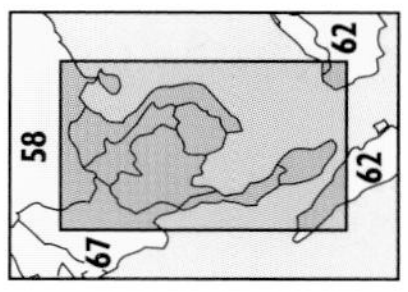
58
62
62
67

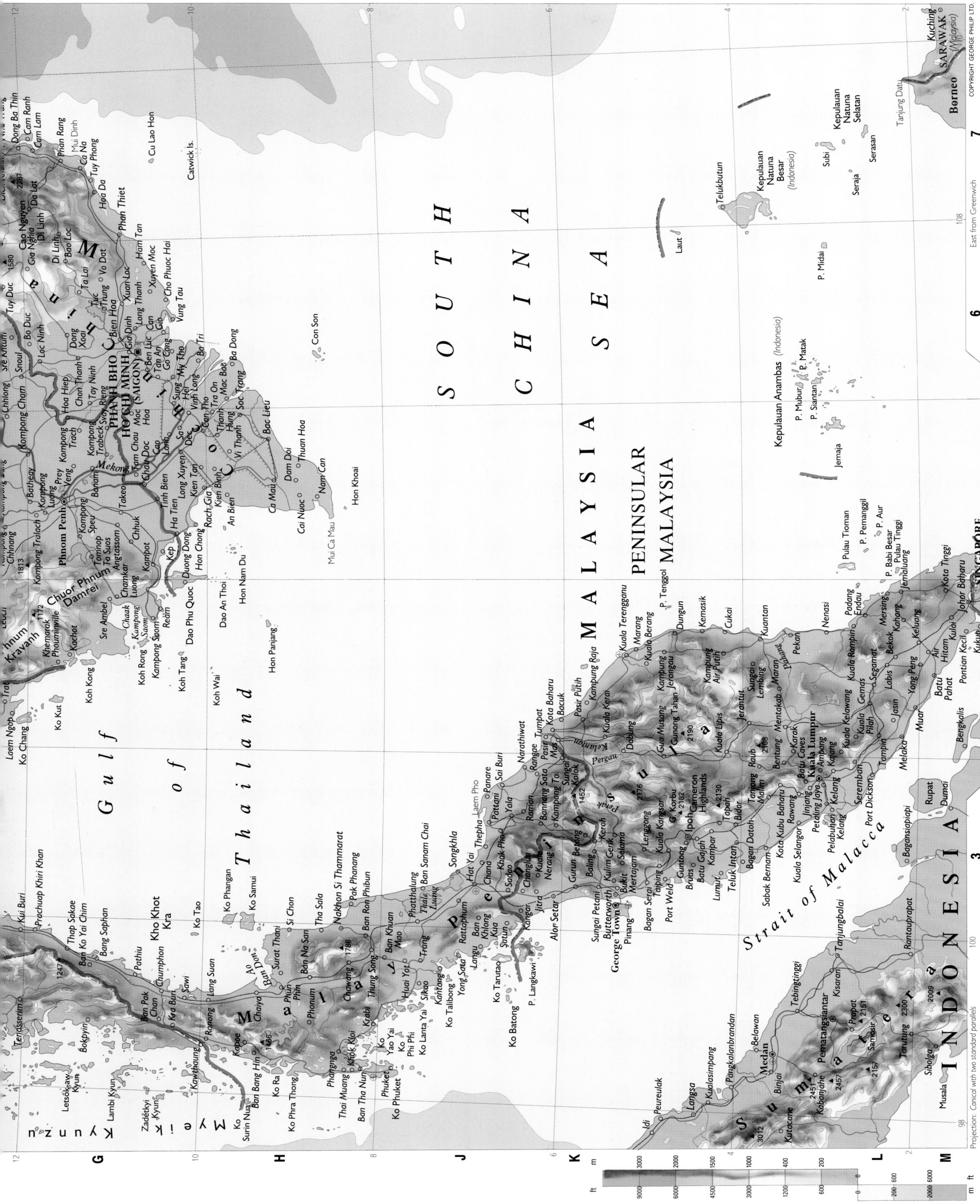
SOUTH CHINA SEA
Gulf of Thailand
Strait of Malacca
MALAYSIA
PENINSULAR MALAYSIA
INDONESIA
Sumatera
SINGAPORE
Kuala Lumpur
Phnom Penh
PHANH BHO HO CHI MINH (SAIGON)
Medan
George Town
Ipoh
Kuching
SARAWAK (Malaysia)
Borneo
Kepulauan Anambas (Indonesia)
Kepulauan Natuna Besar (Indonesia)
Kepulauan Natuna Selatan
Dao Phu Quoc
Con Son
Mui Ca Mau
Cameron Highlands
Mekong
East from Greenwich
Projection: Conical with two standard parallels
COPYRIGHT GEORGE PHILIP LTD.

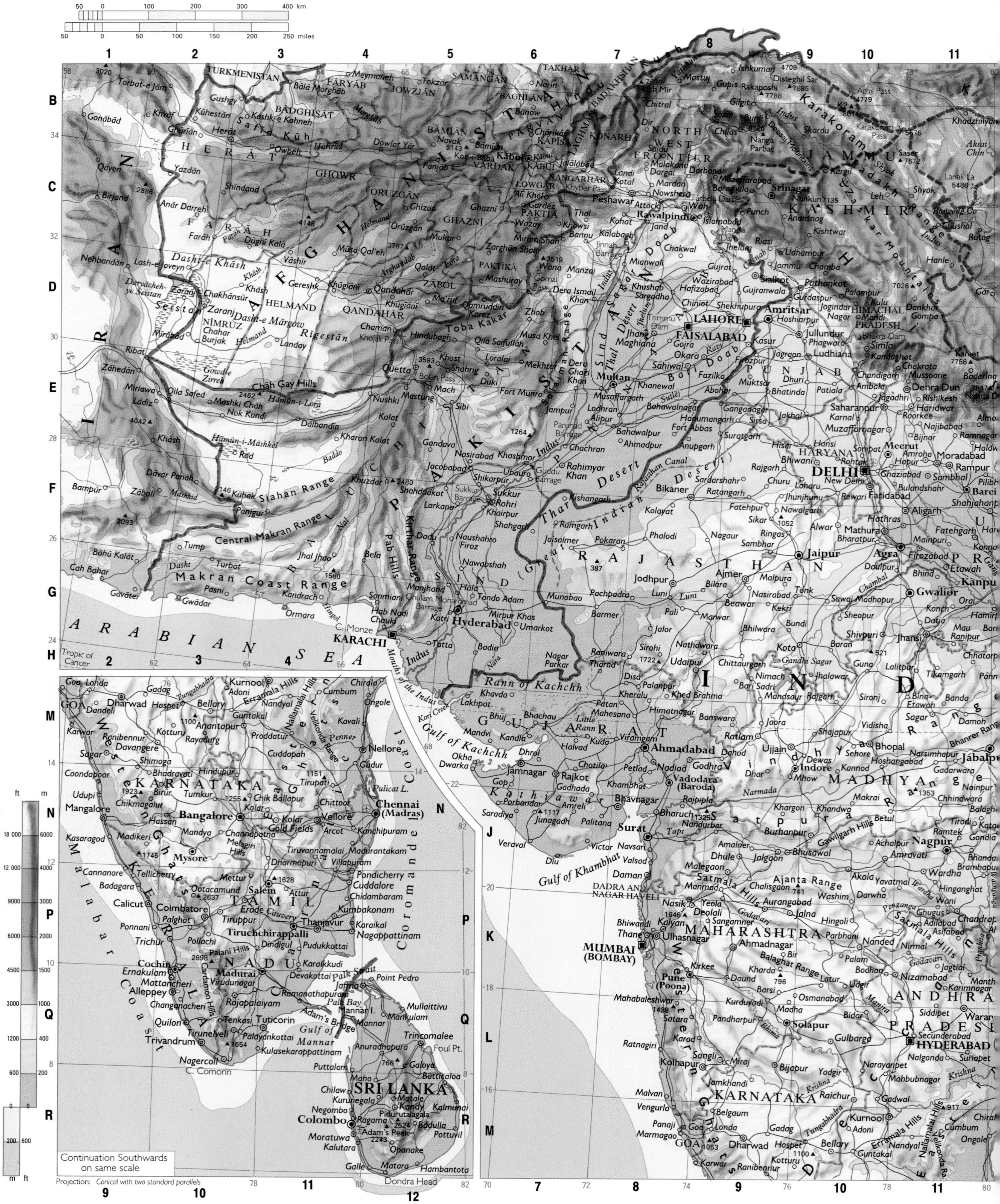

Projection: Conical with two standard parallels

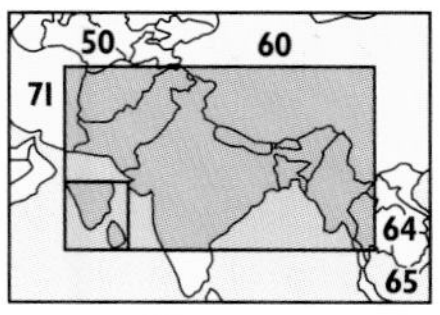
50
60
71
64
65

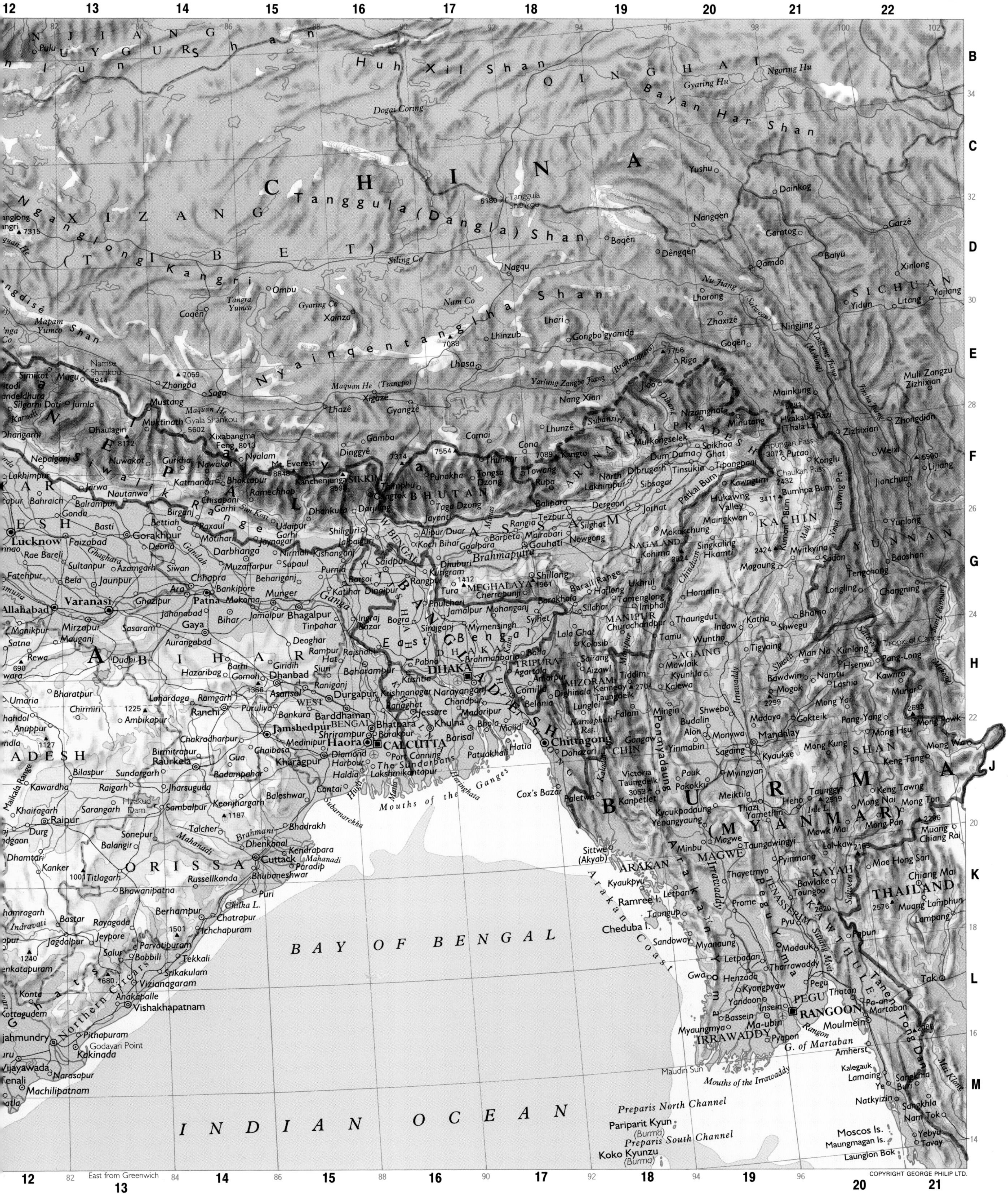
CHINA
XIZANG (TIBET)
QINGHAI
SICHUAN
YUNNAN
Huh Xil Shan
Bayan Har Shan
Tanggula (Dangla) Shan
Nyainqentanglha Shan
Nganglong Kangri
Uygur Shan
Dogai Coring
Gyaring Hu
Ngoring Hu
Yushu
Dainkog
Nangqen
Garzê
Baqên
Dêngqên
Gamtog
Qamdo
Baiyü
Xinlong
Nagqu
Siling Co
Nam Co
Gyaring Co
Xainza
Ombu
Tangra Yumco
Coqên
Mapam Yumco
Lhorong
Zhaxizê
Ningjing
Yidun
Litang
Yajiang
Lhari
Gongbo'gyamda
Lhünzub
Goqên
Riga
Lhasa
Xigazê
Gyangzê
Lhazê
Nang Xian
Yarlung Zangbo Jiang
Maquan He (Tsangpo)
Nu Jiang
Salween
Lancang Jiang (Mekong)
Jinsha Jiang
Muli Zangzu Zizhixian
Zhongdian
Zizhixian
Weixi
Lijiang
Jianchuan
Yunlong
Baoshan
Tengchong
Longling
Changning
Tropic of Cancer
Pang-Long
Kawthro
Mong Hsu
NEPAL
BHUTAN
SIKKIM
BANGLADESH
INDIA
BURMA (MYANMAR)
THAILAND
Mt. Everest 8848
Kanchenjunga 8598
Dhaulagiri 8172
Xixabangma Feng 8013
Siwalik Range
Kathmandu
Nepalganj
Pokhara
Lucknow
Faizabad
Gorakhpur
Varanasi
Allahabad
Patna
Gaya
Bhagalpur
Darbhanga
Muzaffarpur
Purnia
Kishanganj
Siliguri
Darjiling
Jalpaiguri
Thimphu
Gangtok
Punakha
Tongsa Dzong
Taga Dzong
ARUNACHAL PRADESH
ASSAM
MEGHALAYA
NAGALAND
MANIPUR
MIZORAM
TRIPURA
WEST BENGAL
BIHAR
ORISSA
MADHYA PRADESH
Brahmaputra
Ganga
Gauhati
Shillong
Cherrapunji
Dibrugarh
Tinsukia
Jorhat
Sibsagar
North Lakhimpur
Tezpur
Imphal
Kohima
Silchar
Aizawl
Agartala
Sylhet
Mymensingh
Rangpur
Dinajpur
Bogra
Rajshahi
Pabna
DHAKA
Narayanganj
Comilla
Chandpur
Barisal
Khulna
Jessore
Chittagong
Cox's Bazar
Dhanbad
Asansol
Durgapur
Ranchi
Jamshedpur
Haora
CALCUTTA
Kharagpur
Haldia
The Sundarbans
Mouths of the Ganges
Cuttack
Bhubaneshwar
Puri
Chilka L.
Berhampur
Raipur
Bilaspur
Sambalpur
Raurkela
Vishakhapatnam
Vizianagaram
Srikakulam
Rajahmundry
Kakinada
Vijayawada
Machilipatnam
Northern Circars
Eastern Ghats
BAY OF BENGAL
INDIAN OCEAN
KACHIN
SAGAING
CHIN
MAGWE
MANDALAY
SHAN
KAYAH
ARAKAN
PEGU
IRRAWADDY
TENASSERIM
KAWTHULE
Myitkyina
Putao
Bhamo
Katha
Mogaung
Homalin
Kalewa
Tiddim
Falam
Haka
Monywa
Mandalay
Sagaing
Shwebo
Meiktila
Pakokku
Magwe
Minbu
Yenangyaung
Taunggyi
Inle L.
Lashio
Hsenwi
Sittwe (Akyab)
Kyaukpyu
Ramree I.
Cheduba I.
Sandoway
Thayetmyo
Prome
Pyu
Pyinmana
Toungoo
Henzada
Bassein
Myaungmya
Yandoon
RANGOON
Pegu
Thaton
Moulmein
Martaban
Amherst
G. of Martaban
Mouths of the Irrawaddy
Chindwin
Irrawaddy
Sittang Myit
Arakan Yoma
Pegu Yoma
Arakan Coast
Preparis North Channel
Preparis South Channel
Pariparit Kyun (Burma)
Koko Kyunzu (Burma)
Moscos Is.
Maungmagan Is.
Launglon Bok
Tavoy
Yebyu
Ye
Lamaing
Kalegauk
Mae Hong Son
Chiang Mai
Chiang Rai
Lamphun
Lampang
Tak
Tanen Tong Dan
Maudin Sun
Godavari Point
East from Greenwich
COPYRIGHT GEORGE PHILIP LTD.

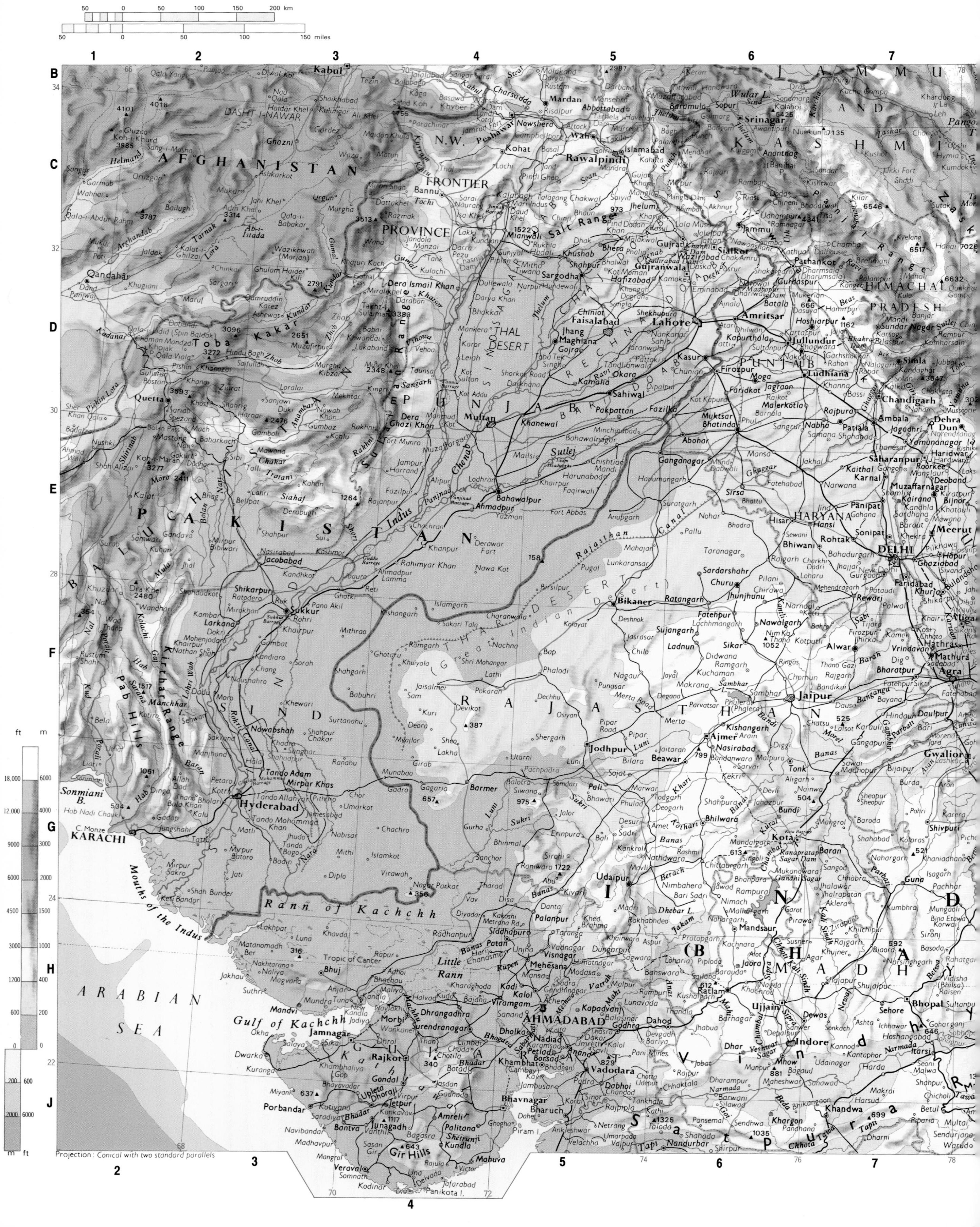

50 0 50 100 150 200 km
50 0 50 100 150 miles
1 2 3 4 5 6 7
B C D E F G H J
AFGHANISTAN
N.W. FRONTIER PROVINCE
JAMMU AND KASHMIR
HIMACHAL PRADESH
PUNJAB
HARYANA
BALUCHISTAN
PAKISTAN
SIND
RAJASTHAN
THAR DESERT
(Great Indian Desert)
THAL DESERT
INDIA
MADHYA PRADESH
GUJARAT
Rann of Kachchh
Little Rann
Gulf of Kachchh
ARABIAN SEA
Mouths of the Indus
Tropic of Cancer
Kabul
Peshawar
Islamabad
Rawalpindi
Srinagar
Jammu
Lahore
Amritsar
Faisalabad
Multan
Quetta
Bahawalpur
Sukkur
Hyderabad
KARACHI
Chandigarh
Simla
DELHI
New Delhi
Meerut
Agra
Jaipur
Jodhpur
Bikaner
Ajmer
Udaipur
Kota
Gwalior
Indore
Ujjain
Bhopal
AHMADABAD
Vadodara
Rajkot
Bhavnagar
Jamnagar
Porbandar
Salt Range
Toba Kakar Range
Kirthar Range
Pab Hills
Gir Hills
Vindhya Range
Satpura Range
Indus
Sutlej
Chenab
Jhelum
Ravi
Beas
Narmada
Tapti
Chambal
Luni
Projection: Conical with two standard parallels
ft m
18,000 6000
12,000 4000
9000 3000
6000 2000
4500 1500
3000 1000
1200 400
600 200
0 0
200 600
2000 6000
m ft

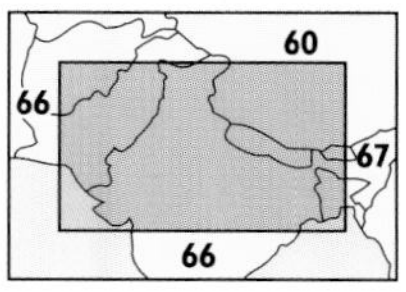
60
66
67
66

JAMMU AND KASHMIR
On same scale as Main Map
CHINA
Karakoram Range
Kunlun Shan
SODA PLAINS
N.W. FRONTIER PROVINCE
Gilgit
Deosai Mountains
JAMMU AND KASHMIR
Zaskar Mountains
Ladakh Range
Srinagar
Leh
Islamabad
Rawalpindi
PUNJAB
Jammu
Sialkot
Wazirabad
HIMACHAL PRADESH
Nganglong Kangri
CHINA
Gangdisê Shan
Mapam Yumco
XIZANG (TIBET)
Yarlung Zangbo Jiang (Brahmaputra)
Mt. Everest 8848
Annapurna 8078
Dhaulagiri 8172
NEPAL
Katmandu
Mahabharat Lekh
Siwalik Range
SIKKIM
Gangtok
BHUTAN
ASSAM
Darjiling
Garo Hills
Brahmaputra
UTTAR PRADESH
Lucknow
KANPUR
Allahabad
Varanasi
Gorakhpur
Patna
Munger
Bhagalpur
Gaya
BIHAR
Rajmahal Hills
Kaimur Hills
MADHYA PRADESH
Jabalpur
Bilaspur
Maikala Range
Ranchi
Jamshedpur
Asansol
WEST BENGAL
CALCUTTA
Haora
Kharagpur
BANGLADESH
DHAKA
Jessore
Khulna
Rajshahi
Sundarbans
Mouths of the Ganga
The Sandheads
East from Greenwich

THE MIDDLE EAST 1:6 200 000

50 0 50 100 150 200 250 300 km
50 0 50 100 150 200 miles

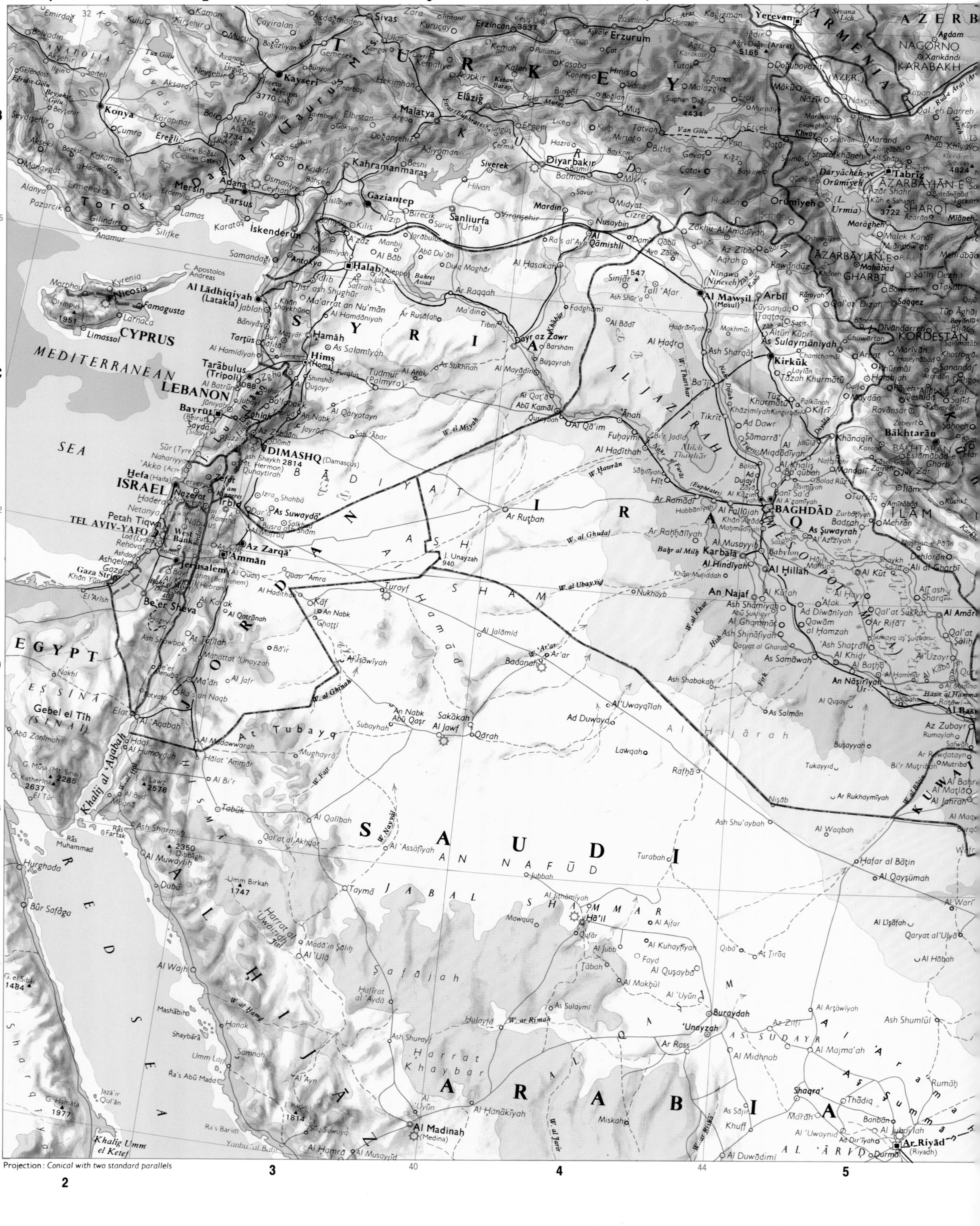

Projection: *Conical with two standard parallels*

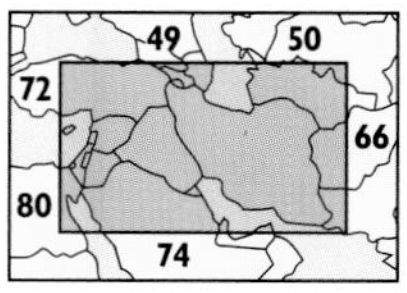
49
50
72
66
80
74

6
7
8
9
10
B
C
D
E
F
TURKMENISTAN
KARA KUM
Köppeh Dagh
CASPIAN SEA
Türkmenbashi
Ashgabat
Mary
Chärjew
Amudarya
BAKI (Baku)
Astara
Ardabil
Rasht
Bandar-e Anzali
GILAN
MAZANDARAN
Reshteh-ye Kūhhā-ye Alborz
Qazvin
Karaj
Tajrīsh 5604
TEHRĀN
Eslāmshahr
Rey
Damāvand
SEMNĀN
Semnān
Gorgān
Mashhad (Meshed)
Neyshābūr
Kūh-e Bīnālūd 3314
KHORĀSĀN
Kūh-e Sorkh 3020
Sabzevār
Torbat-e Heydarīyeh
Torbat-e Jām
MARKAZĪ
Qom
Kāshān
Arāk
DASHT-E-KAVĪR
Daryācheh-ye Namak
IRAN
Eşfahān
ESFAHĀN
Khomeynī Shahr
Najafābād
Ardestān
Nā'īn
Yazd
YAZD
DASHT-E-LUT
Ṭabas
Bīrjand
Qāyen
Gonābād
CHAHĀR MAHĀLL VA BAKHTĪĀRĪ
KHŪZESTĀN
Ahvāz
Dezfūl
Khorramshahr
Ābādān
Shatt al Arab
KOHKĪLŪYEH VA BŪYER AHMADĪ
Kūh-e Dīnār 4431
Zāgros
Shīrāz
FĀRS
Kermān
KERMĀN
Kūh-e Hazārān 4419
Kūh-e Jebāl Barez 3962
Bam
Zāhedān (Duzdab)
SĪSTĀN VA BALŪCHESTĀN
Hāmūn-e Jaz Mūrīān
Daryācheh-ye Seistan
Seistan
HORMOZGĀN
Bandar-e 'Abbās
Qeshm
Str. of Hormuz
Kūhhā-ye Bashākerd
Būshehr (Bushire)
BŪSHEHR
Kharg
Bandar-e Rīg
Kuwayt (Kuwait)
AL HASA
Ad Dammām
Al Manāmah
BAHRAIN
QATAR
Ad Dawḥah (Doha)
Al Hufūf
THE GULF
OMAN
Ra's al Khaymah
Ash Shāriqah (Sharjah)
Dubayy (Dubai)
Abū Ẓaby (Abu Dhabi)
UNITED ARAB EMIRATES
Al Fujayrah
Gulf of Oman
Jāsk
Chāh Bahār
Gavāter
AFGHANISTAN
Herāt
HERĀT
FARĀH
Farāh
NĪMRŪZ
Dasht-e Mārgow
Shīndand
BĀDGHĪSAT
Safīd Kūh
PAKISTAN
Mīrjāveh
Hamun-i-Mashkel
East from Greenwich

TURKEY AND TRANSCAUCASIA 1:4 400 000

Projection: *Conical with two standard parallels*

Division between Greeks and Turks in Cyprus; Turks to the North.

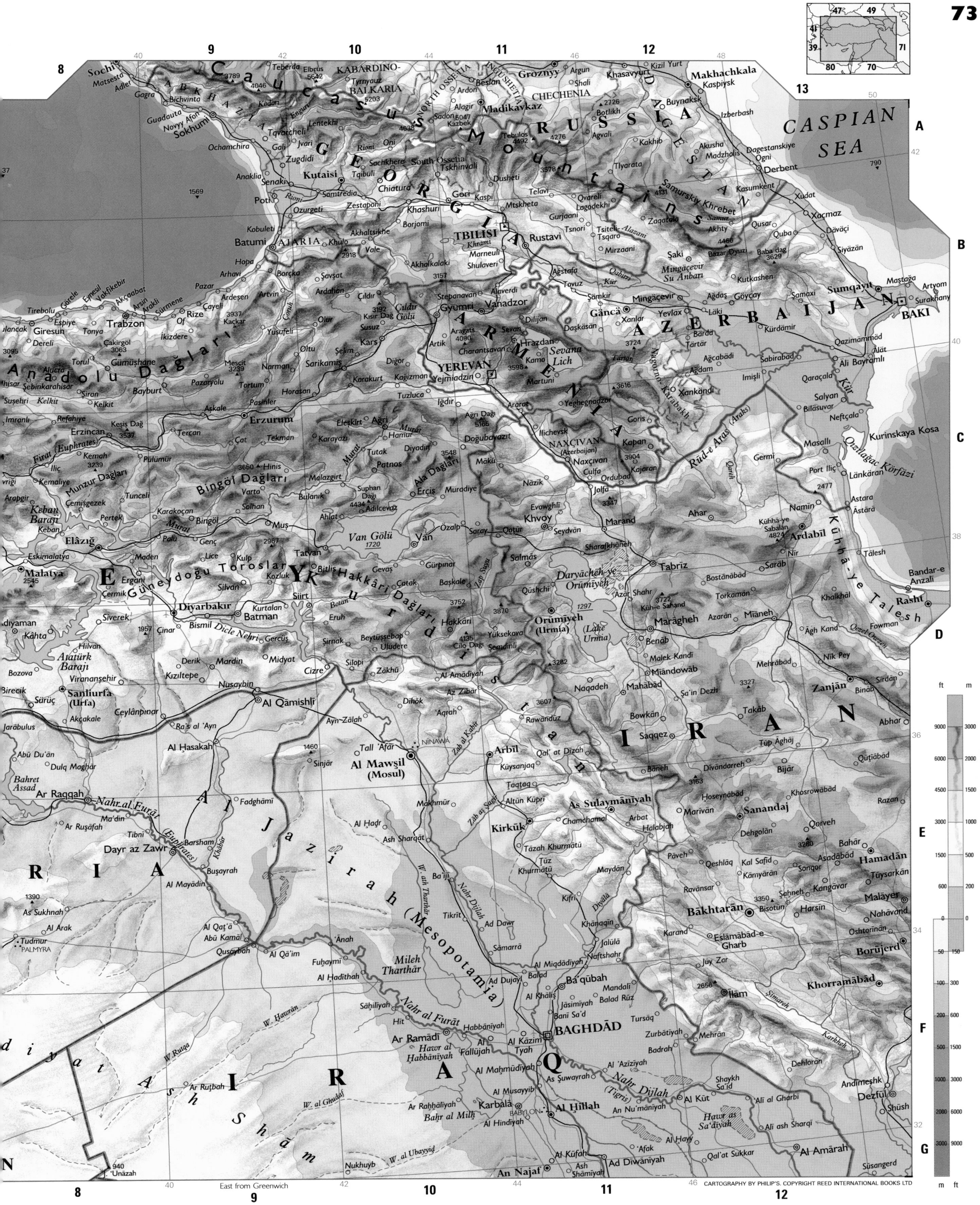
Caucasus Mountains
GEORGIA
RUSSIA
DAGESTAN
CHECHENIA
INGUSHETIA
NORTH OSSETIA
KABARDINO-BALKARIA
ABKHAZIA
AJARIA
South Ossetia
ARMENIA
AZERBAIJAN
NAXÇIVAN (Azerbaijan)
Nagorno-Karabakh
CASPIAN SEA
Anadolu Dağları
Güneydoğu Toroslar
Hakkâri Dağları
Kurdistan
Bingöl Dağları
Munzur Dağları
IRAN
IRAQ
TURKEY
SYRIA
Al Jazirah (Mesopotamia)
Bādiyat ash Shām
Sochi
Sokhumi
Kutaisi
Batumi
Poti
TBILISI
Rustavi
Gori
Vladikavkaz
Groznyy
Makhachkala
Kaspiysk
Buynaksk
Derbent
Gyumri
Vanadzor
YEREVAN
Gäncä
Mingäçevir
Sumqayıt
BAKI
Trabzon
Rize
Giresun
Erzurum
Erzincan
Kars
Ağrı
Van
Van Gölü
Muş
Bitlis
Elâzığ
Malatya
Diyarbakır
Batman
Siirt
Mardin
Şanlıurfa (Urfa)
Atatürk Barajı
Keban Barajı
Firat (Euphrates)
Al Qāmishlī
Al Ḩasakah
Ar Raqqah
Dayr az Zawr
Tudmur
PALMYRA
Al Mawşil (Mosul)
NINAWĀ
Arbīl
Kirkūk
As Sulaymānīyah
Sāmarrā
Tikrīt
Ba'qūbah
BAGHDĀD
Ar Ramādī
Al Fallūjah
Karbalā
BABYLON
Al Ḩillah
An Najaf
Al Kūt
Al 'Amārah
Ad Dīwānīyah
Nahr al Furāt
Nahr Dijlah (Tigris)
Buḩayrat ath Tharthār
Hawr al Ḩabbānīyah
Tabrīz
Daryācheh-ye Orūmīyeh (Lake Urmia)
Orūmīyeh (Urmia)
Ardabīl
Rasht
Bandar-e Anzalī
Zanjān
Hamadān
Sanandaj
Bākhtarān
Khorramābād
Borūjerd
Īlām
Dezfūl
Kūhhā-ye Ṭalesh
Kūr
Rūd-e Aras (Araks)
Qızılağac Körfäzi
Kurinskaya Kosa
Elbrus 5642
Kazbek 5047
Ağrı Dağı 5165
Aragats 4090
Sevana Lich
East from Greenwich
CARTOGRAPHY BY PHILIP'S. COPYRIGHT REED INTERNATIONAL BOOKS LTD
ft
m
9000
6000
4500
3000
1500
600
0
3000
2000
1500
1000
500
200
0
50
100
200
500
1000
2000
3000
150
300
600
1500
3000
6000
9000
47
49
41
71
39
80
70

ARABIA AND THE HORN OF AFRICA 1:13 300 000

100 0 100 200 300 400 500 600 km
100 0 100 200 300 400 miles

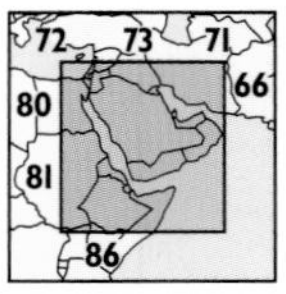

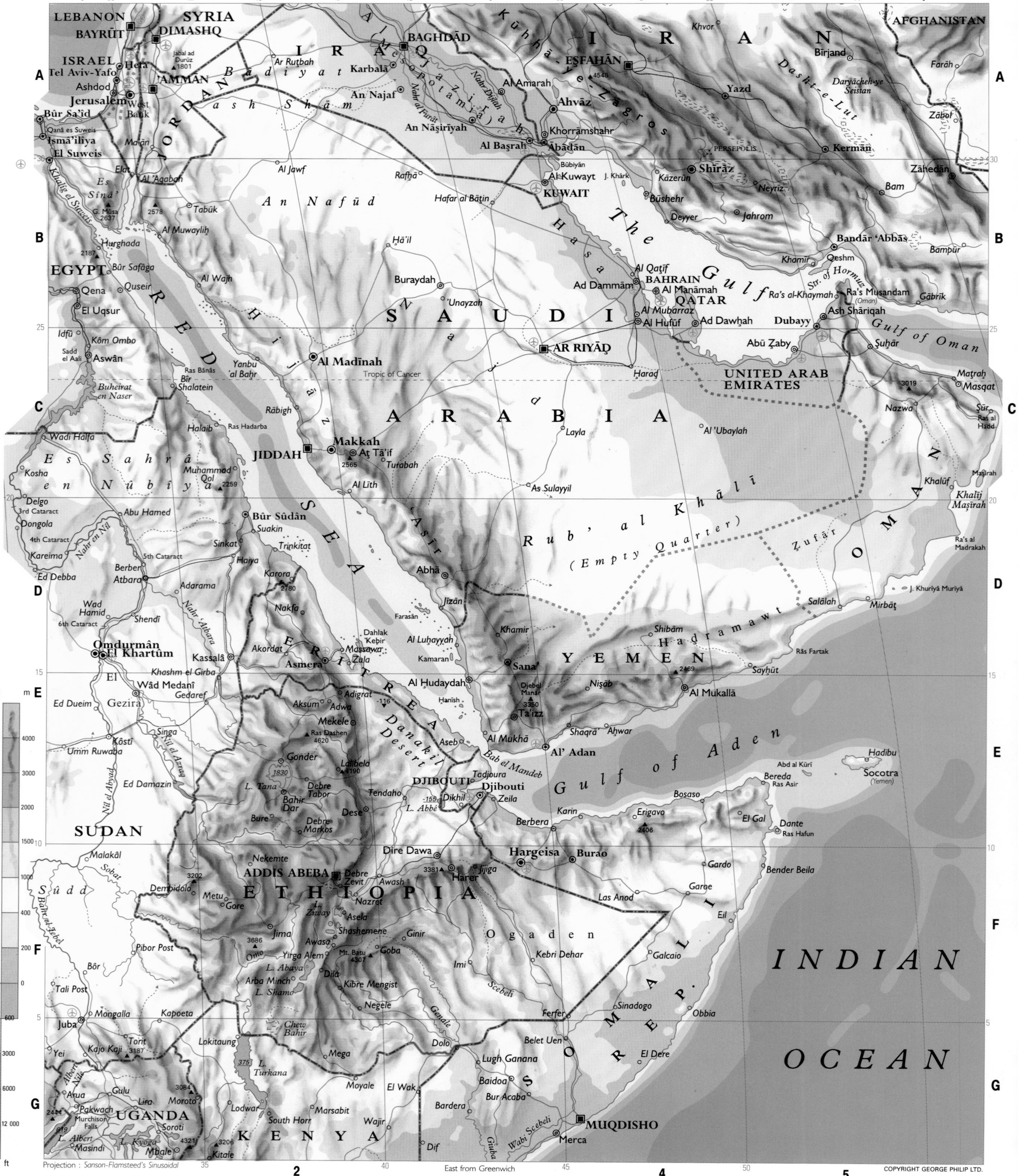

10 0 10 20 30 40 50 60 70 80 100 km

10 0 10 20 30 40 50 60 miles

1 2 3 4 5 6

A B C D E F

MEDITERRANEAN SEA

CYPRUS
Paphos
Episkopi
Episkopi Bay
Limassol
Akrotiri Bay
C. Gata

LEBANON
Al Ḥamīdiyah
Tall Kalakh
Ḥalbā
Al Mīnā'
Tarābulus (Tripoli)
Zghartā
Qurnat as Sawdā' 3088
Bsharri
Al Hirmil
Al Batrūn
Jubayl
Qartabā
Ibrāhīm
Jūniyah
Bikfayyā
2628 Sannīn
BAYRŪT (Beirut)
'Alayh
Ash Shuwayfāt
Ad Dāmūr
Zaḥlah
Jabal Lubnān
Al Biqā' (Bequa Valley)
Ba'labakk
2616
Sayda (Sidon)
Jazzīn
1942 J. al Bārūk
Lītānī
An Nabaṭīyah at Taḥtā
Ṣūr (Tyre)
Al Janūb
Marj 'Uyūn
Al Khiyām
J. ash Shaykh (Mt. Hermon) 2814

SYRIA
Ḥimṣ (Homs)
Shinshār
Furqlus
Al Quṣayr
Ḥimṣ
Al Burayj
2464
Al Labwah
Al Qaryatayn
Bi'r Ghadīr
An Nabk
Yabrūd
Sirghāyā
Al Quṭayfah
Jabal ash Sharqī
Az Zabadānī
Hawsh Mūssá
Dumayr
Khān Abū Shāmat
Baradá
Dimashq
Dūmā
DIMASHQ (Damascus)
Dārayyā
Qaṭanā
Al Kiswah
A'waj
Al Ḥājānah
Burāq
Bādiyat ash Shām
Aş Şafā
Al Qunayṭirah
Golan Heights
1197
As Sanamayn
Ar Rafid
Dar'ā
Izra
Shahbā'
W. Al Harīr
Shaykh Miskīn
Saḥam al Jawlān
Dar'ā
As Suwaydā'
Jabal ad Durūz
1800
Ṣalah
Aţ Ramthā
Buṣrá ash Shām
Şalkhad

ISRAEL
Qiryat Shemona
Nahariyya
Me'ona
'Akko (Acre)
Hagalil
Zefat
Mifraz Hefa
Karmi'el
Qiryat Yam
Hefa (Haifa)
Teverya (Tiberias)
Yam Kinneret
-210
Fiq
Qiryat Ata
Daliyat el Karmel
Nazerat (Nazareth)
Hefa
Hazafon
Yarmūk
Kinneret
Tel Megiddo
Afula
Tayiba
Umm el Fahm
Caesarea
Pardes Hanna-Karkur
Hadera
Jenin
Bet She'an
Shomron
Netanya
Tulkarm
Tubas
Samaria
Hamerkaz
Herzliyya
Nablus
Kefar Sava
Bene Beraq
Petah Tiqwa
Shilo
Tel Aviv-Yafo
Ramat Gan
West Bank
Bat Yam
Rishon le Ziyyon
Lod
Ramla
Rehovot
Yavne
Ram Allah
El Ariha (Jericho)
-289
Ashdod
Jerusalem (Yerushalayim) (Al Quds)
Qiryat Mal'akhi
Bet Shemesh
Ashqelon
Qiryat Gat
Tel Lakhish
Bayt Lahm (Bethlehem)
Gaza
Gaza Strip
N. Shiqma
Har Yehuda
Al Khalil (Hebron)
Sederot
Aẓ Ẓāhirīyah
Khān Yūnis
Rafah
N. Besor
Midbar Yehuda
Dead Sea
-403
Arad
Be'er Sheva (Beersheba)
Bor Mashash
Sedom
Dimona
Hadarom
-333
-121
Qezi'ot
Birein
Sede Boqer
Mizpe Ramon
Hanegev
N. Paran
N. Hiyyon
Ha 'Arava
Yotvata
'En 'Avrona
Elat

JORDAN
J. Umm ad Daraj
1247
Irbid
Ailūn
Jarash
Al-Mafraq
Umm al Qiţţayn
Irbid
Nahr az Zarqā'
Al Balqā'
As Salţ
Az Zarqā'
'AMMĀN
Wādī as Sīr
Karama
Nā'ūr
Azraq ash Shīshān
At Tunayb
'Ammān
Ma'dabā
W. al Haydān
Dhībān
W. Al Mawjib
Al Qaţrānah
W. Al Ghadaf
Al Hadīthah
W. Al Mahbūq
Al Karak
1305
Al Mazār
W. al Hasā
Al Karak
W. Bā'ir
Aţ Ţafīlah
Bā'ir
J. ash Shawmarī
1072
Nijil
Bi'r ad Dabbāghāt
Mahattat 'Unayzah
Ruim Tal'at al Jamālah
1736
Petra
W. Abu Şafāţ
Qa'el Jafr
Al Jafr
Ma'ān
Bi'r al Mārī
Ra's an Naqb
Ma'ān
Mahattat ash Shīdīyah
Ra's an Naqb 1435
Bi'r al Qaţţār
Bi'r al Butayyihāţ
1592
Baţn al Ghūl
Al 'Aqabah
Gulf of Aqaba
W. an Nuwayb'i
Haql
Al Mudawwarah

SAUDI ARABIA
At Tubayq

EGYPT
Bûr Sa'îd (Port Said)
Bûr Fu'ad
Qanâ es Suweis (Suez Canal)
Râs Burûn
Khalîg El Tîna
Sabkhet el Bardawîl
El 'Arîsh
El Daheir
Români
Bîr el 'Abd
Bîr el Garârât
Bîr Lahfân
W. el 'Arîsh
Bîr Qatia
Bîr el Duweidar
Bîr Kaseiba
El Qantara
Bîr el Jafir
Wâhid
Bîr Madkûr
Sînî
Ismâ'ilîya
Talâta
Bîr el Mâlhi
892
Muweilih
El Quseima
Khamsa
El Buheirat el Murrat el Kubra (Great Bitter L.)
Bîr Hasana
G. Yi'Allaq 1094
Bîr Beida
Gineifa
Bîr el Thamâda
W. el Brûk
W. Qiraiya
El 'Agrûd
Mamarr Mitla
Bîr Gebeil Hisn
W. Mahasham
El Suweis (Suez)
Bûr Taufiq
Es Sina (Sinai)
Adabiya
Uyûn Mûsa
Nakhl
W. el Sabeira
W. El 'Agaba
W. El Tamarâni
El Kuntilla
W. Ruâg
W. Girâfi
Ain Sudr
Bîr Abu Muhammad
Bîr Bad'
948 G. el Kabrît
El Thamad
Gebel el Tîh
Khalîg el Suweis
Ghubbet el Bûs
El Wabeira
Bîr el Biarât
Bîr Tâba
Shibh Jazîrat Sînâ'
Râs Matarma
Bîr Abu Sandûq
1272
W. Abu Ga'da
W. Abu el Gain
Bîr el Heisi
EL SUWEIS
Bîr Wuseit
1165

34 35 36 37 33 32 31 30

ft m
9000 3000
6000 2000
4500 1500
3000 1000
1200 400
600 200
0 0
200 600
2000 6000
m ft

1974 Cease Fire Lines

Projection: Polyconic

East from Greenwich

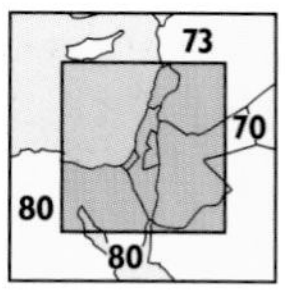

AFRICA : Physical 1:37 300 000

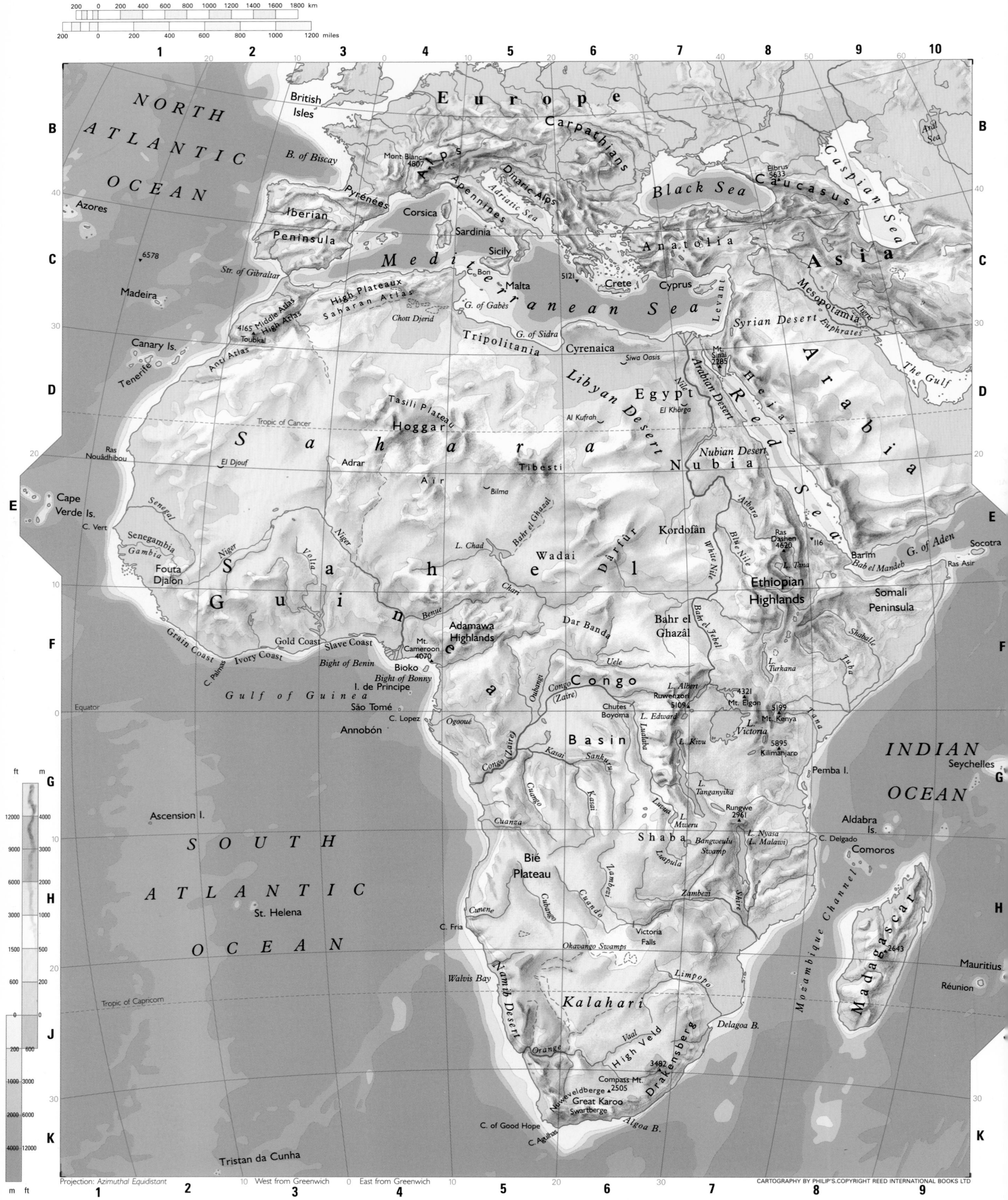

NORTH ATLANTIC OCEAN
Europe
British Isles
B. of Biscay
Carpathians
Alps
Mont Blanc 4807
Dinaric Alps
Apennines
Adriatic Sea
Black Sea
Caucasus
Elbrus 5633
Caspian Sea
Aral Sea
Azores
Iberian Peninsula
Pyrénées
Corsica
Sardinia
Sicily
Anatolia
Asia
Mediterranean Sea
Str. of Gibraltar
Madeira
High Plateaux
Saharan Atlas
Middle Atlas
High Atlas
Toubkal
Chott Djerid
C. Bon
Malta
G. of Gabès
Crete
Cyprus
Levant
Mesopotamia
Tigris
Euphrates
Syrian Desert
Canary Is.
Anti Atlas
Tenerife
G. of Sidra
Tripolitania
Cyrenaica
Siwa Oasis
Mt. Sinai 2285
Arabia
The Gulf
Libyan Desert
Egypt
Nile
Arabian Desert
Hejaz
Red Sea
El Kharga
Al Kufrah
Tasili Plateau
Hoggar
Tropic of Cancer
Sahara
Ras Nouâdhibou
El Djouf
Adrar
Tibesti
Nubian Desert
Nubia
Aïr
Bilma
Cape Verde Is.
C. Vert
Senegal
Senegambia
Gambia
Fouta Djalon
Niger
Volta
Sahel
L. Chad
Bahr el Ghazal
Wadai
Darfûr
Kordofân
Atbara
White Nile
Blue Nile
Ras Dashen 4620
L. Tana
Barim
Bab el Mandeb
G. of Aden
Socotra
Ras Asir
Ethiopian Highlands
Somali Peninsula
Guinea
Chari
Benue
Dar Banda
Bahr el Ghazâl
Bahr el Jebel
Shaballe
Juba
Grain Coast
Gold Coast
Slave Coast
Ivory Coast
C. Palmas
Bight of Benin
Mt. Cameroon 4070
Adamawa Highlands
Bioko
Bight of Bonny
I. de Principe
Gulf of Guinea
São Tomé
C. Lopez
Annobón
Equator
Uele
Congo
Oubangi
Congo (Zaïre)
L. Albert
Ruwenzori 5109
L. Turkana
Mt. Elgon 4321
Mt. Kenya 5199
Tana
Chutes Boyoma
L. Edward
L. Victoria
Lualaba
L. Kivu
Basin
Kilimanjaro 5895
Ogooué
Kasai
Sankuru
INDIAN OCEAN
Seychelles
Pemba I.
Cuango
L. Tanganyika
Rungwe 2961
Ascension I.
Cuanza
Luvua
L. Mweru
Shaba
Bangweulu Swamp
L. Nyasa (L. Malawi)
C. Delgado
Aldabra Is.
Comoros
SOUTH ATLANTIC OCEAN
Bié Plateau
Luapula
Zambezi
Shire
Mozambique Channel
Madagascar
2643
St. Helena
Cunene
Cubango
Cuando
C. Fria
Victoria Falls
Okavango Swamps
Limpopo
Namib Desert
Walvis Bay
Mauritius
Réunion
Tropic of Capricorn
Kalahari
Delagoa B.
Orange
Vaal
High Veld
Drakensberg
3482
Compass Mt. 2505
Nuweveldberge
Great Karoo
Swartberge
Algoa B.
C. of Good Hope
C. Agulhas
Tristan da Cunha
Projection: Azimuthal Equidistant
West from Greenwich
East from Greenwich
CARTOGRAPHY BY PHILIP'S.COPYRIGHT REED INTERNATIONAL BOOKS LTD

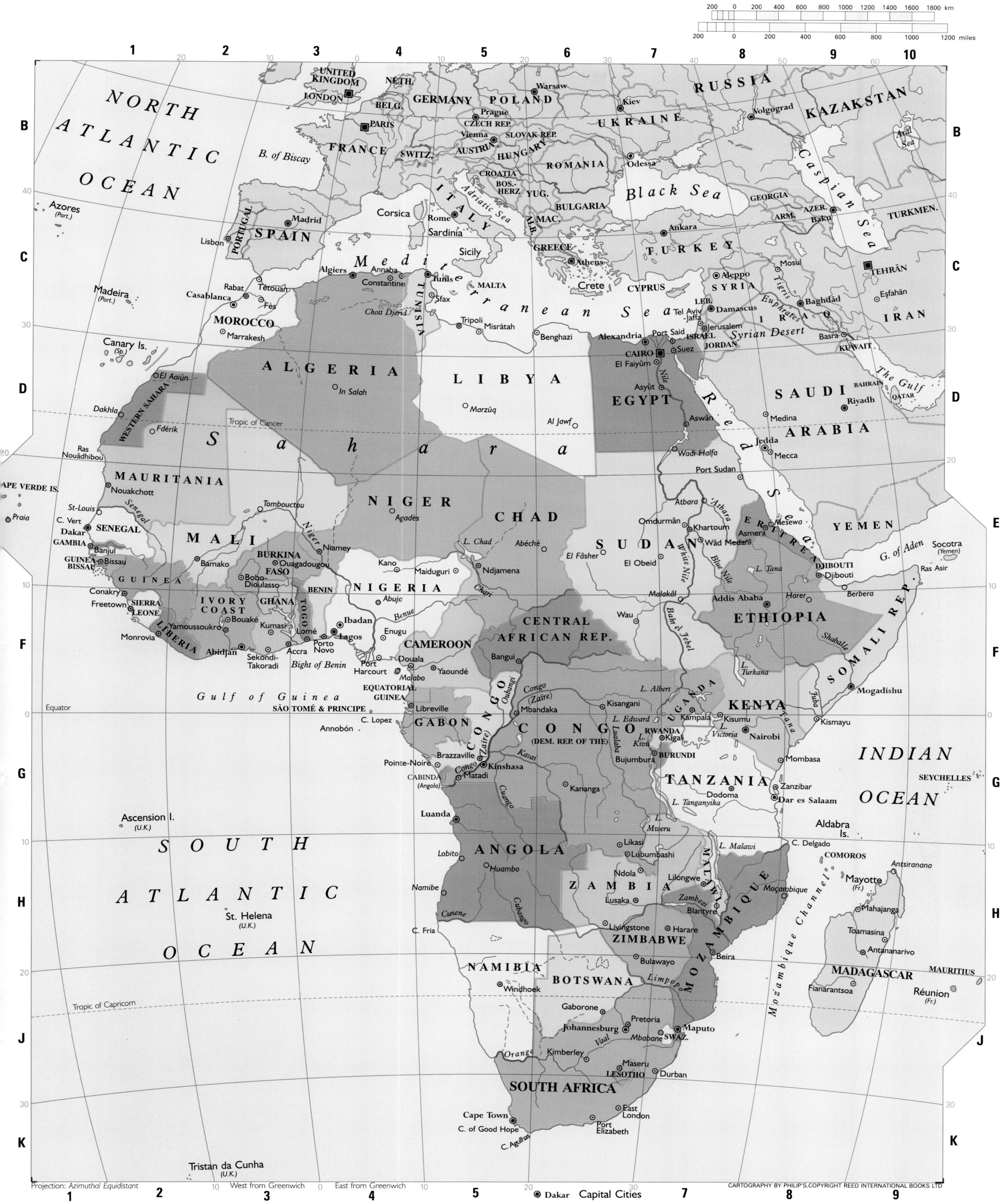
200 0 200 400 600 800 1000 1200 1400 1600 1800 km
200 0 200 400 600 800 1000 1200 miles
NORTH ATLANTIC OCEAN
Azores (Port.)
Madeira (Port.)
Canary Is. (Sp.)
CAPE VERDE IS.
Praia
UNITED KINGDOM
LONDON
NETH.
BELG.
GERMANY
POLAND
Warsaw
RUSSIA
KAZAKSTAN
PARIS
FRANCE
Prague
CZECH REP.
SLOVAK REP.
Vienna
AUSTRIA
SWITZ.
HUNGARY
UKRAINE
Kiev
Volgograd
Odessa
ROMANIA
CROATIA
BOS.-HERZ.
YUG.
BULGARIA
ITALY
Adriatic Sea
Rome
Corsica
Sardinia
Sicily
ALB.
MAC.
GREECE
Athens
Black Sea
GEORGIA
AZER.
ARM.
Baku
Caspian Sea
Aral Sea
TURKMEN.
Ankara
TURKEY
B. of Biscay
Madrid
SPAIN
PORTUGAL
Lisbon
Mediterranean Sea
MALTA
Crete
CYPRUS
Algiers
Annaba
Constantine
Tunis
Sfax
TUNISIA
Chott Djerid
Tripoli
Misrātah
Benghazi
Rabat
Casablanca
Tétouan
Fès
MOROCCO
Marrakesh
Aleppo
SYRIA
Mosul
Tigris
Euphrates
Baghdād
IRAQ
Tehrān
Esfahān
IRAN
LEB.
Damascus
Tel Aviv-Jaffa
Jerusalem
ISRAEL
JORDAN
Syrian Desert
Basra
KUWAIT
The Gulf
BAHRAIN
QATAR
Riyadh
SAUDI ARABIA
Medina
Jedda
Mecca
Alexandria
Port Said
Suez
CAIRO
El Faiyûm
Asyût
Nile
EGYPT
Aswân
Red Sea
ALGERIA
In Salah
LIBYA
Marzūq
Al Jawf
El Aaiún
WESTERN SAHARA
Dakhla
Fdérik
Tropic of Cancer
Sahara
Ras Nouâdhibou
MAURITANIA
Nouakchott
Senegal
St-Louis
C. Vert
Dakar
SENEGAL
GAMBIA
Banjul
GUINEA-BISSAU
Bissau
GUINEA
Conakry
Freetown
SIERRA LEONE
Monrovia
LIBERIA
Tombouctou
MALI
Bamako
Niger
Niamey
NIGER
Agadès
BURKINA FASO
Ouagadougou
Bobo-Dioulasso
IVORY COAST
Yamoussoukro
Bouaké
Abidjan
GHANA
Kumasi
Sekondi-Takoradi
Accra
TOGO
Lomé
BENIN
Porto Novo
NIGERIA
Kano
Maiduguri
Abuja
Ibadan
Lagos
Benue
Enugu
Port Harcourt
Bight of Benin
Gulf of Guinea
CHAD
L. Chad
Ndjamena
Abéché
Chari
Wadi Halfa
Port Sudan
Atbara
Omdurmân
Khartoum
Wad Medani
SUDAN
El Fâsher
El Obeid
White Nile
Blue Nile
Malakâl
Wau
Bahr el Jebel
Mesewa
Asmera
ERITREA
L. Tana
Addis Ababa
ETHIOPIA
Harer
Shaballe
YEMEN
Socotra (Yemen)
G. of Aden
DJIBOUTI
Djibouti
Berbera
Ras Asir
SOMALI REP.
Mogadishu
Kismayu
Juba
CENTRAL AFRICAN REP.
Bangui
CAMEROON
Douala
Yaoundé
Malabo
EQUATORIAL GUINEA
SÃO TOMÉ & PRINCIPE
Libreville
C. Lopez
Annobón
GABON
CONGO
Oubangi
Congo (Zaïre)
Mbandaka
CONGO (DEM. REP. OF THE)
Kisangani
L. Albert
UGANDA
Kampala
L. Edward
Lualaba
L. Kivu
RWANDA
Kigali
BURUNDI
Bujumbura
L. Turkana
KENYA
Kisumu
L. Victoria
Nairobi
Tana
Mombasa
Equator
Pointe-Noire
Brazzaville
Kinshasa
Kasai
CABINDA (Angola)
Matadi
Cuango
Kananga
TANZANIA
Dodoma
Zanzibar
Dar es Salaam
L. Tanganyika
INDIAN OCEAN
SEYCHELLES
Ascension I. (U.K.)
SOUTH ATLANTIC OCEAN
St. Helena (U.K.)
Luanda
Lobito
ANGOLA
Huambo
Namibe
Cunene
Cubango
C. Fria
L. Mweru
Likasi
Lubumbashi
Ndola
ZAMBIA
Lusaka
L. Malawi
MALAWI
Lilongwe
Zambezi
Blantyre
C. Delgado
COMOROS
Aldabra Is.
Antsiranana
Mayotte (Fr.)
Moçambique
MOZAMBIQUE
Mozambique Channel
Mahajanga
Toamasina
Antananarivo
MADAGASCAR
Fianarantsoa
MAURITIUS
Réunion (Fr.)
Livingstone
Harare
ZIMBABWE
Bulawayo
Beira
Limpopo
NAMIBIA
Windhoek
BOTSWANA
Gaborone
Tropic of Capricorn
Pretoria
Johannesburg
Maputo
Mbabane
SWAZ.
Vaal
Orange
Kimberley
Maseru
LESOTHO
Durban
SOUTH AFRICA
East London
Port Elizabeth
Cape Town
C. of Good Hope
C. Agulhas
Tristan da Cunha (U.K.)
Projection: Azimuthal Equidistant
West from Greenwich
East from Greenwich
Dakar Capital Cities
CARTOGRAPHY BY PHILIP'S.COPYRIGHT REED INTERNATIONAL BOOKS LTD

NORTHERN AFRICA 1:13 300 000

100 0 100 200 300 400 500 600 km

100 0 100 200 300 400 miles

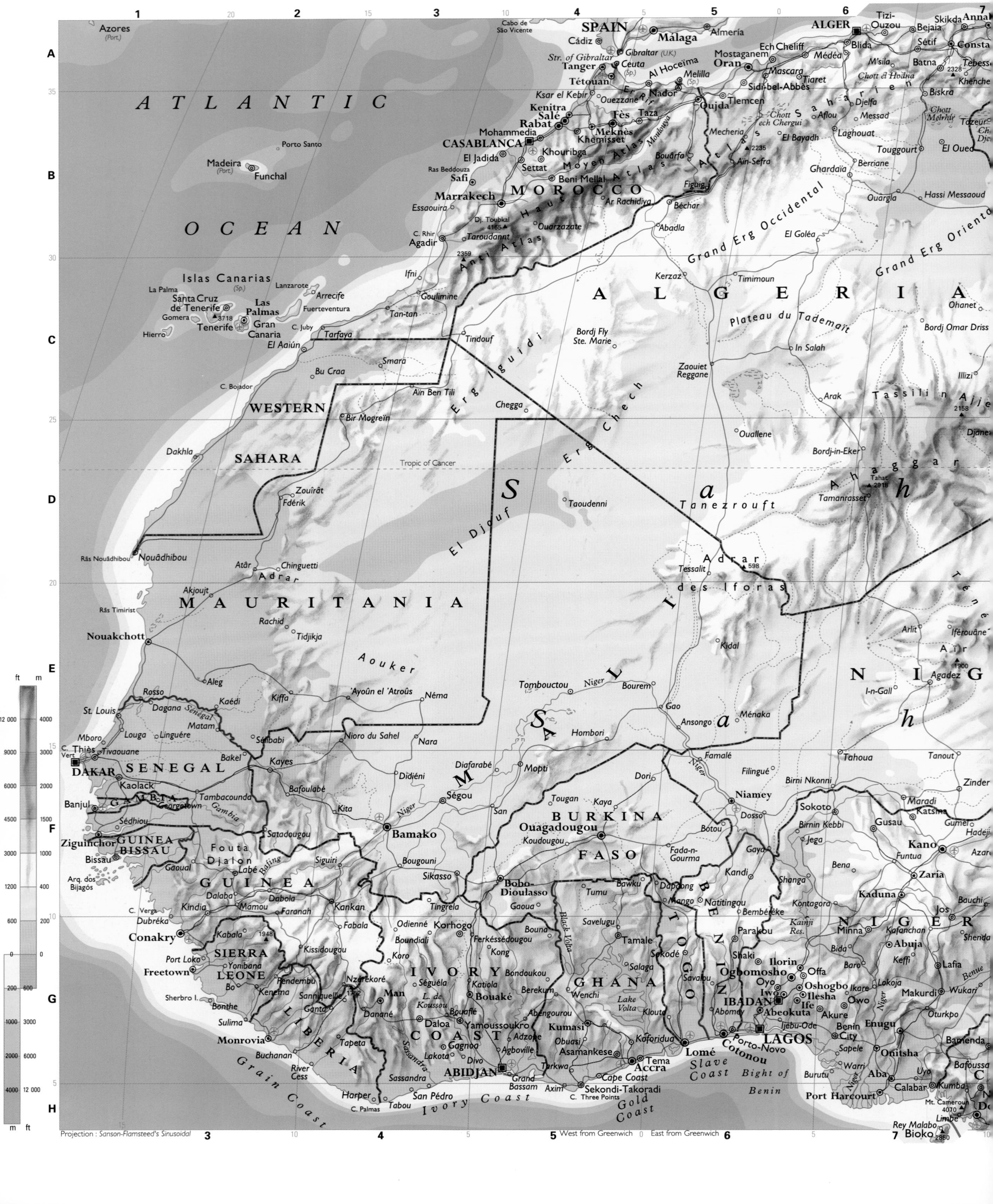

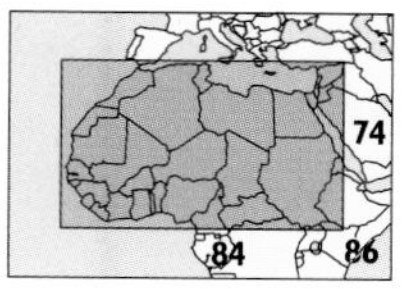
74
84
86

MEDITERRANEAN SEA
RED SEA
LIBYA
EGYPT
SUDAN
CHAD
CENTRAL AFRICAN REPUBLIC
ETHIOPIA
ERITREA
SAUDI ARABIA
SYRIA
IRAQ
JORDAN
ISRAEL
LEBANON
CYPRUS
TURKEY
GREECE
MALTA
Sicilia
Valletta
Kríti
Iráklion
Ródhos
Antalya
ADANA
Antakya
HALAB
Nahr al Furāt
Al Lādhiqīyah
Nicosia
Tarābulus
Hims
BAYRŪT
DIMASHQ
Hefa
Tel Aviv-Yafo
Ashdod
Jerusalem
West Bank
'AMMĀN
Jabal ad Durūz
1801
Ar Rutbah
Bādiyat ash Shām
Ma'ān
Al Jawf
Elat
Al 'Aqabah
Tabūk
2578
Al Muwaylih
Al Wajh
Yanbu 'al Bahr
Rābigh
Hijaz
Bizerte
Ariana
TUNIS
Béja
Nabeul
Sousse
Kairouan
Mahdia
Sfax
Golfe de Gabès
Gabès
Île de Djerba
Médenine
Zarzis
Tataouine
Dehibat
Zuwārah
Az Zāwiyah
Tarābulus
Al Khums
Misrātah
Gharyān
968
Mizdah
Tripolitania
Daraj
Ghudāmis
Surt
Khalīj Surt
Banghāzī
Zāwiyat al Baydā
Al Marj
Darnah
Tubruq
Bardīyah
Salūm
Suluq
Ajdābiyah
Cyrenaica
Al Jaghbūb
Awjilah
Hūn
Zillah
Idehan Awbārī
Brach
Sabhah
Awbārī
1200
Marzūq
Fezzan
Wāw al Kabīr
Ghat
Al Qatrūn
Sahrâ' Rebiana
Al Kufrah
Al Jawf
Sahrâ' Lîbîya
Marsá Matrûh
El Alamein
Munkhafed el Qattâra
-133
Sîwa
Qasr Farâfra
El Wâhât el-Dakhla
Mût
El Wâhât el-Khârga
El Khârga
EL ISKANDARÎYA
Damanhûr
El Mahalla el Kubra
Tanta
Zagâzig
El Mansûra
Dumyât
Bûr Sa'îd
Isma'ilîya
Qanâ es Suweis
EL GÎZA
EL QÂHIRA
Helwân
El Faiyûm
Beni Suef
Maghâgha
El Minyâ
Mallawi
Manfalût
Asyût
Tahta
Sohâg
Girga
Qena
THEBES
KARNAK
El Uqsur
Idfû
Kom Ombo
Aswân
Sadd el Aali
Buheirat en Naser
ABU SIMBEL
Nahr en Nîl
El Suweis
Khalîg el Suweis
Es Sînâ'
G. Mûsa 2637
Es Sahrâ Esh Sharqîya
Hurghada
2187
Bûr Safâga
Quseir
Ras Bânâs
Bîr Shalatein
Halaib
Ras Hadarba
J. Uweinat 1893
1082
Ma'tan as Sarra
Sahara
Toummo
Madama
Chirfa
Bardai
Aozou
Pic Toussidé 3265
Tarso Emissi 3150
Tibesti
Zouar
Emi Koussi 3415
Borkou
Bilma
Grand Erg du Bilma
Fachi
Faya-Largeau
Ounianga Sérir
Dépression du Mourdi
Fada
Ennedi
1310
Erg du Djourab
Zagaoua
Oum Chalouba
Zigey
Bahr el Ghazal
Mao
Lac Tchad
Bosso
Nguigmi
Moussoro
Biltine
Abéché
Ati
Oum Hadjer
Massakory
Ndjamena
Bokoro
Mongo
Goz Beïda
Abou-Deïa
Am-Timan
Chari
Bongor
Kousseri
Maiduguri
Potiskum
Bajoga
Bama
Maroua
Biu
Mubi
Guider
Kumo
Numan
Yola
Garoua
Logone
Laï
Pala
Moundou
Doba
Koumra
Sarh
Gashua
Geidam
Biltoum
Wad Halfa
El Wâhât el Selîma
Kosha
Es Sahrâ en Nûbîya
Delgo
3rd Cataract
Dongola
Abu Hamed
Muhammad Qol
2259
Bûr Sûdân
Suakin
Trinkitat
Sinkat
Haiya
4th Cataract
5th Cataract
Kareima
Bir 'Atrun
Ed Debba
Nahr en Nîl
Berber
Atbara
Adarama
Nahr Atbara
Karora
2780
Nakfa
Akordat
Wad Hamid
Shendî
6th Cataract
Omdurmân
El Khartûm
Kassalâ
Khashm el Girba
Gedaref
El Wuz
Sodiri
Malha
1954
Kutum
Al Junaynah
Dârfûr
Djebel Mara 3088
El Fâsher
Zalingei
Nyâlâ
Umm Keddada
Kordofân
El Gezira
Wâd Medanî
Ed Dueim
El Obeid
Kôstî
Umm Ruwaba
Er Rahad
En Nahud
El Odaiya
Abû Zabad
1325
Kâdugli
Singa
Nîl el Azraq
Nîl el Abyad
Ed Damazin
Gonder
1830
L. Tana
Bahir Dar
Bure
Debre Markos
Nekemte
Birao
Songo
Bahr el Arab
Sa'id Bundas
Bahr el Ghazâl
Raga
Jur
Bahr el Ghazâl
Sudd
Malakâl
Sobat
Gogriâl
Wâw
Tonj
Bahr el Jebel
Rumbêk
Toinya
Amadi
Tali Post
Bôr
Pibor Post
Dembidolo
3202
Metu
Gore
Jima
3686
Omo
L. Abaya
Arba Minch
L. Shamo
Chew Bahir
L. Turkana
Lokitaung
375
Kapoeta
Mongalla
Juba
Torit
3187
Kajo Kaji
Yei
Yambio
El Istiwa'iya
Faradje
Dungu
Uele
Ango
Obo
Bondo
Bomu
Bangassou
Mobaye
Mobayi
Oubangi
Zongo
Bosobolo
Libenge
Bangui
Mbaïki
Berbérati
Carnot
Bossembélé
Bouar
Bozoum
Bossangoa
Paoua
Batouri
Bertoua
Nanga-Eboko
Abong-Mbang
Yaoundé
Yoko
Bétaré Oya
Ngaoundéré
Banyo
Gashaka
Baibokoum
Kaga Bandoro
Ndélé
1276
Sibut
Bambari
Ippy
Bakouma
Yalinga
CAMEROON
Adamaoua
NIGERIA
NIGER
TUNISIA
CARTOGRAPHY BY PHILIP'S COPYRIGHT REED INTERNATIONAL BOOKS LTD
8
9
10
11
12
13
14
A
B
C
D
E
F
G
H
15
20
25
30
35
40

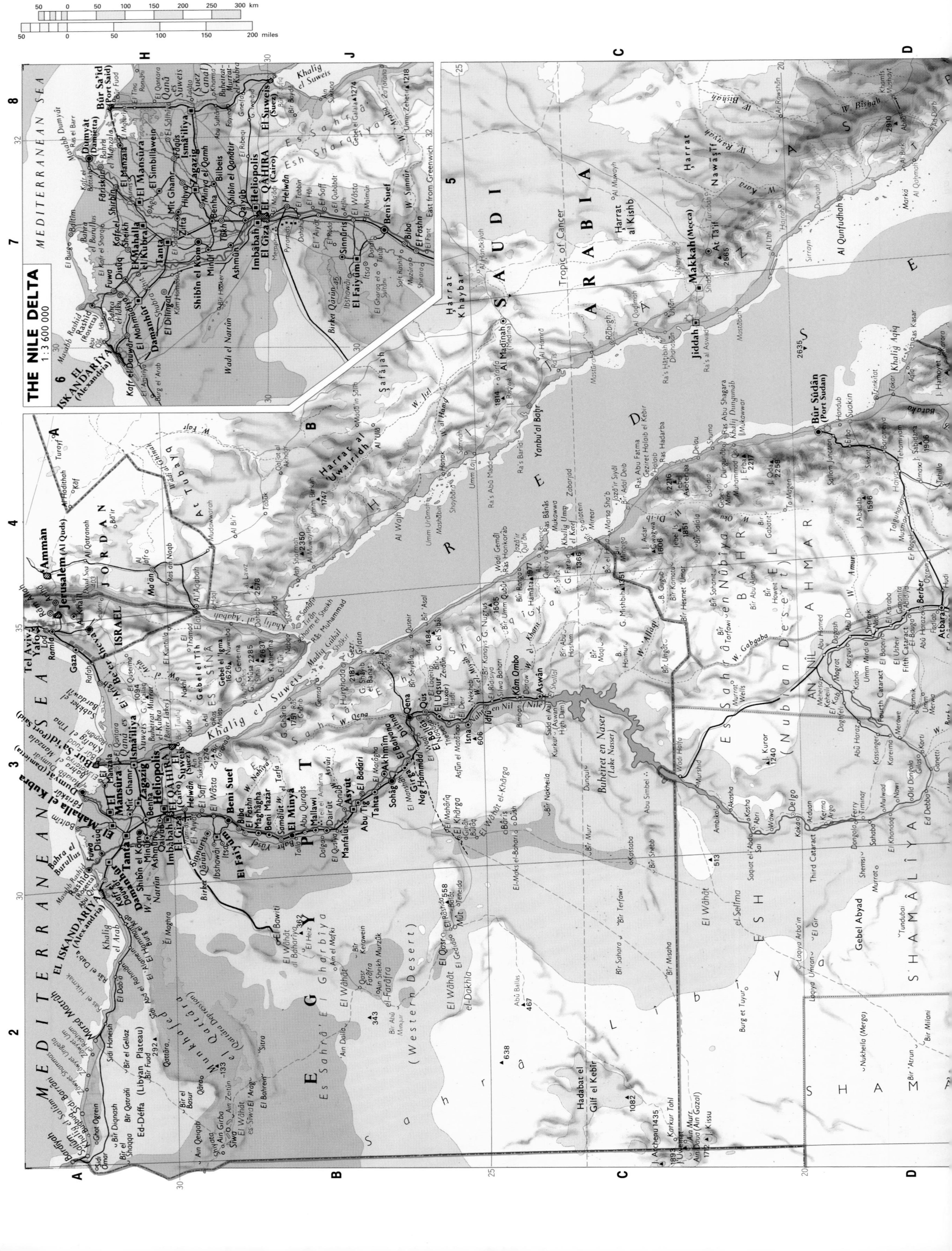
50 0 50 100 150 200 250 300 km
50 0 50 100 150 200 miles
THE NILE DELTA
1:3 600 000
MEDITERRANEAN SEA
EL ISKANDARIYA (Alexandria)
Rashid (Rosetta)
Dumyât (Damietta)
Bûr Sa'îd (Port Said)
El Mansûra
Tanta
Zagazig
Ismâ'îliya
Suez Canal
El Suweis (Suez)
EL QÂHIRA (Cairo)
Heliopolis
El Giza
Imbâbah
Helwân
El Faiyûm
Birket Qârûn
Beni Suef
East from Greenwich
EGYPT
SAUDI ARABIA
JORDAN
ISRAEL
Jerusalem (Al Quds)
'Ammân
Tel Aviv-Yafo
Gaza
SÎNÂ
Khalig el Suweis
Khalij al 'Aqabah
El Minya
Asyût
Sohâg
Qena
El Uqsur (Luxor)
Isna
Idfu
Kôm Ombo
Aswân
Buheiret en Naser (Lake Nasser)
El Wâhât el-Khârga
El Wâhât el-Dâkhla
El Wâhât el-Farâfra
El Wâhât el Bahariya
Siwa
Mersâ Matrûh
Es Sahrâ' El Gharbîya (Western Desert)
Munkhafad el Qattâra (Qattara Depression)
Ed-Déffa (Libyan Plateau)
Hadabat el Gilf el Kebîr
Sahra en Nûbiya (Nubian Desert)
Bûr Sûdân (Port Sudan)
Atbara
Berber
Dongola
Third Cataract
Fourth Cataract
Fifth Cataract
Al Madînah (Medina)
Makkah (Mecca)
Jiddah
At Tâ'if
Yanbu' al Bahr
Tropic of Cancer
Harrat Khaybar
Harrat al 'Uwairidh
RED SEA
Gebel Abyad
Wadi Halfa

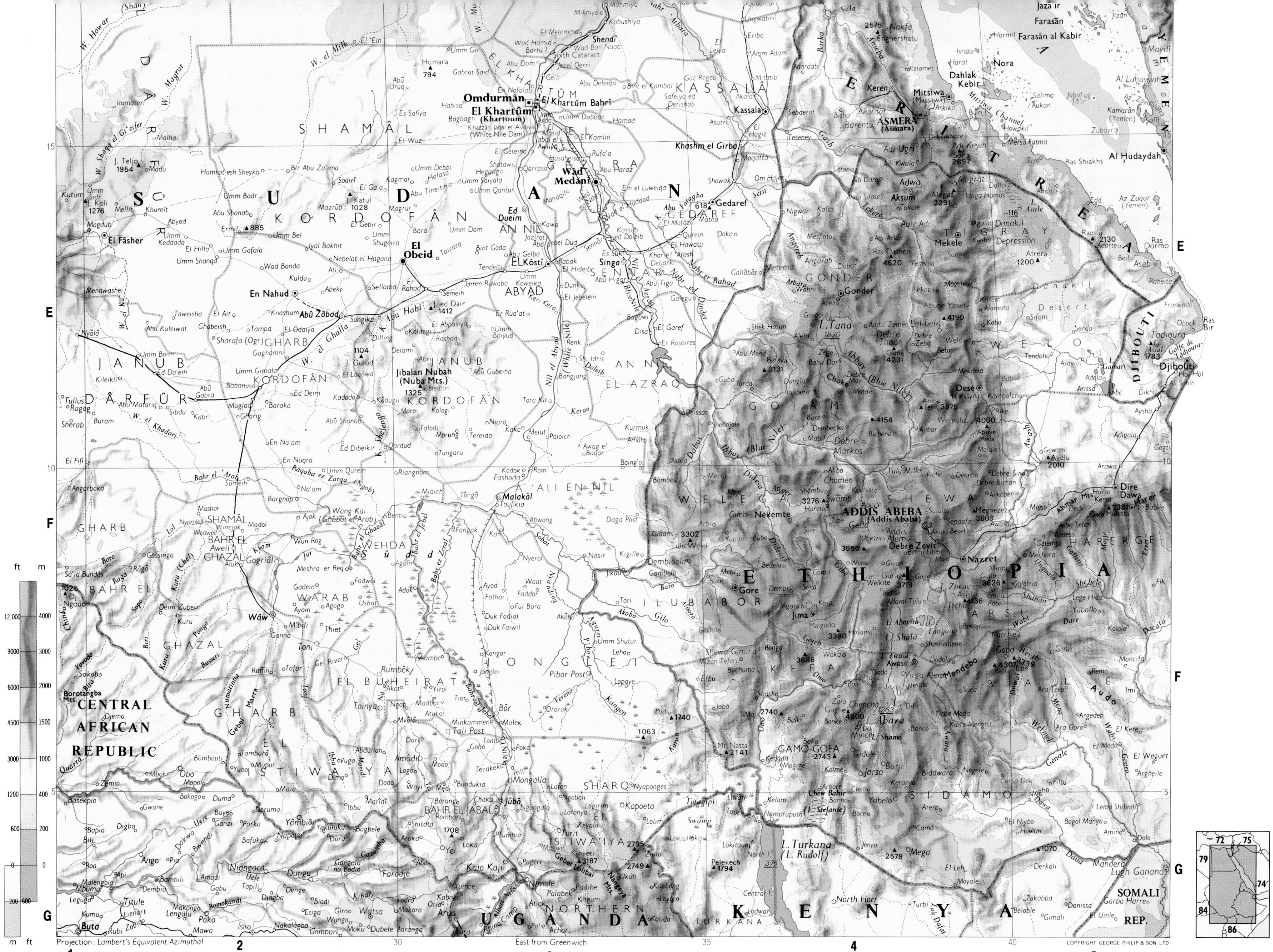
SUDAN
ETHIOPIA
ERITREA
DJIBOUTI
KENYA
UGANDA
CENTRAL AFRICAN REPUBLIC
SOMALI REP.
YEMEN
El Khartûm (Khartoum)
Omdurmân
El Khartûm Bahri
Wad Medanî
Kassala
Gedaref
El Obeid
En Nahud
El Fâsher
Malakâl
Wâw
Jûbâ
ADDIS ABEBA (Addis Ababa)
ASMERA (Asmara)
Gonder
Dese
Nazret
Dire Dawa
Djibouti
Harer
Mekele
Aksum
L. Tana
L. Turkana (L. Rudolf)
Chew Bahir (L. Stefanie)
Projection: Lambert's Equivalent Azimuthal
East from Greenwich
COPYRIGHT GEORGE PHILIP & SON LTD
ft
m
12,000
9000
6000
4500
3000
1200
600
0
200
600
4000
3000
2000
1500
1000
400
200
0
72
75
79
74
84
86

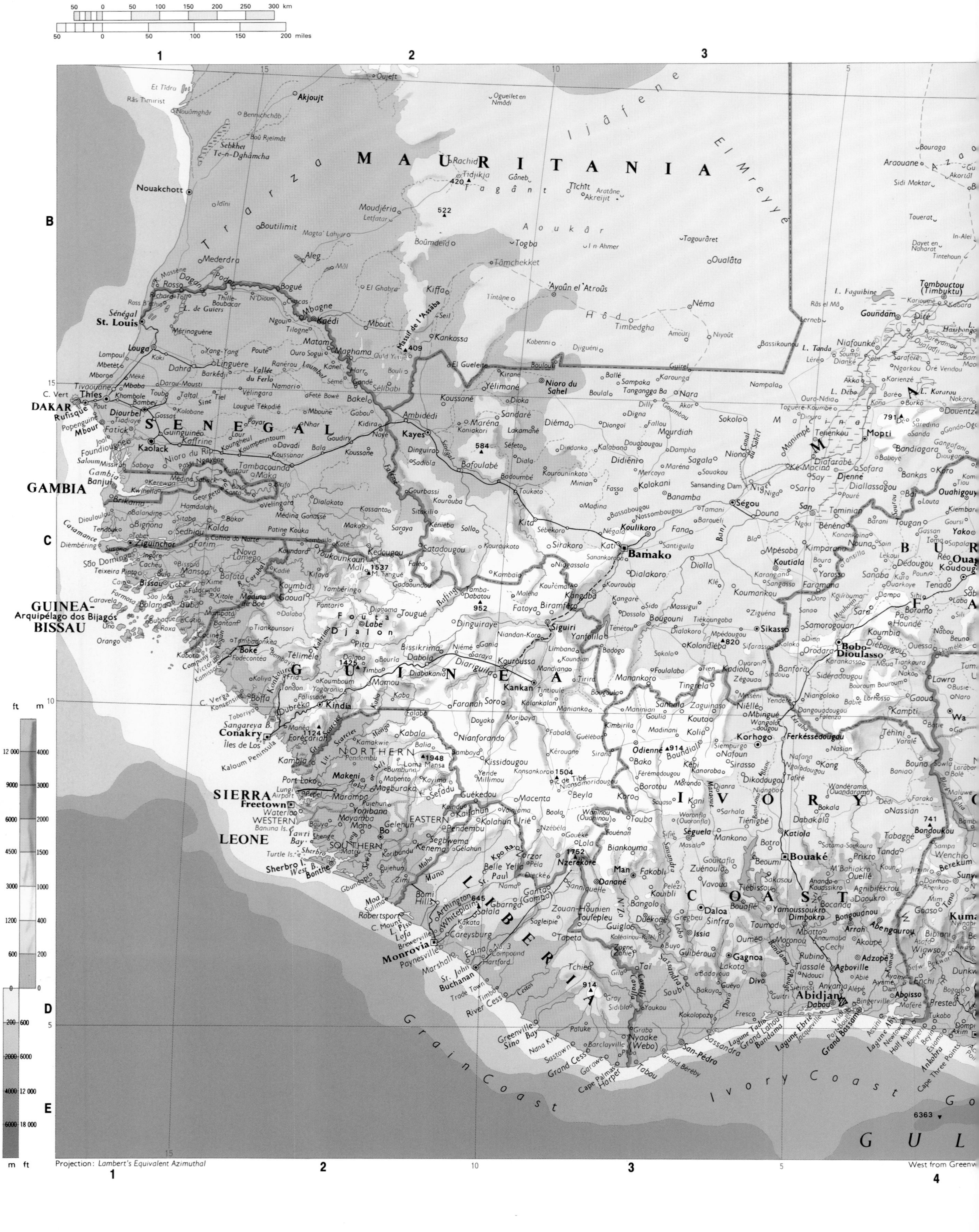
50 0 50 100 150 200 250 300 km
50 0 50 100 150 200 miles
MAURITANIA
Trarza
Ijâfene
El Mreyyé
Tagânt
Aoukâr
Hôdh
Nouakchott
Akjoujt
Tidjikja
Tîchît
Moudjéria
Boutilimit
Aleg
Kiffa
'Ayoûn el 'Atroûs
Néma
Oualâta
Timbedgha
Kaédi
Sélibabi
Rosso
St. Louis
Sénégal
Louga
SENEGAL
DAKAR
Thies
Rufisque
Mbour
Diourbel
Kaolack
Fatick
Tambacounda
Kolda
Ziguinchor
Casamance
GAMBIA
Banjul
GUINEA-BISSAU
Bissau
Bolama
Arquipélago dos Bijagós
GUINEA
Conakry
Kindia
Labe
Fouta Djalon
Boké
Mamou
Dabola
Faranah
Kankan
Siguiri
Kouroussa
Kissidougou
Guékédou
Macenta
Nzérékoré
SIERRA LEONE
Freetown
Makeni
Bo
Kenema
Bonthe
Sherbro I.
LIBERIA
Monrovia
Buchanan
Greenville
Harper
Gbarnga
Robertsport
Cape Palmas
MALI
Bamako
Koulikoro
Ségou
Kayes
Kita
Bafoulabé
Nioro du Sahel
Sikasso
Koutiala
Mopti
Djenne
San
Tombouctou (Timbuktu)
Goundam
Niafounké
Nara
Kolokani
Bougouni
IVORY COAST
Abidjan
Bouaké
Yamoussoukro
Korhogo
Odienné
Man
Daloa
Gagnoa
San-Pédro
Séguéla
Katiola
Ferkéssédougou
Dimbokro
Agboville
Grand Bassam
Bondoukou
BURKINA FASO
Bobo-Dioulasso
Ouagadougou
Koudougou
Banfora
Dédougou
Grain Coast
Ivory Coast
GULF
Projection: Lambert's Equivalent Azimuthal
West from Greenwich
ft m
12 000 4000
9000 3000
6000 2000
4500 1500
3000 1000
1200 400
600 200
0 0
200 600
2000 6000
4000 12 000
6000 18 000
m ft

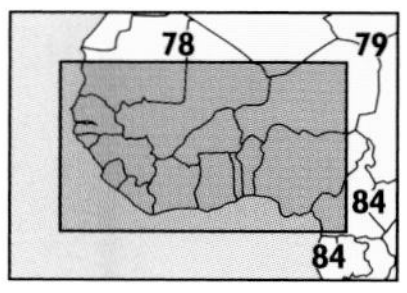
78
79
84
84

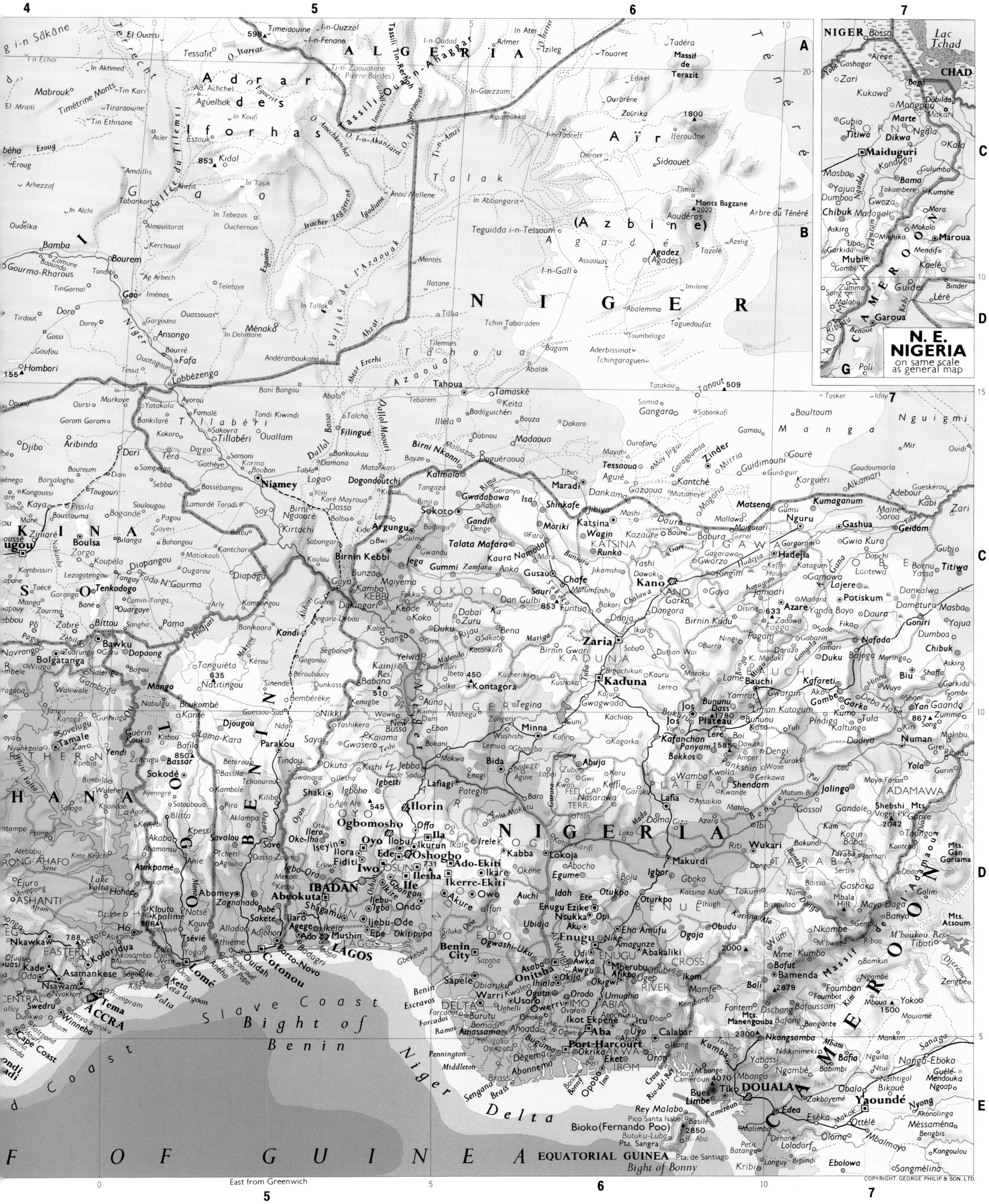
A L G E R I A
N I G E R
N I G E R I A
B E N I N
T O G O
G H A N A
C A M E R O O N
CHAD
EQUATORIAL GUINEA
Adrar des Iforhas
Aïr
(Azbine)
Ténéré
Talak
Manga
Tahoua
Niamey
Gao
Kidal
Agadez (Agadès)
Zinder
Maradi
Sokoto
Kano
Kaduna
Zaria
Jos
Bauchi
Maiduguri
Abuja
Minna
Ilorin
Ibadan
Oshogbo
Abeokuta
LAGOS
Porto-Novo
Cotonou
Lomé
ACCRA
Tema
Benin City
Enugu
Onitsha
Port-Harcourt
Calabar
Aba
Makurdi
Yola
DOUALA
Yaoundé
Garoua
Maroua
Lac Tchad
Bight of Benin
Slave Coast
Niger Delta
Bight of Bonny
Bioko (Fernando Poo)
Rey Malabo
F OF GUINEA
N. E. NIGERIA
on same scale as general map
East from Greenwich
COPYRIGHT. GEORGE PHILIP & SON. LTD.

100 0 100 200 300 400 500 600 km
100 0 100 200 300 400 miles
SUDAN
ETHIOPIA
KENYA
UGANDA
TANZANIA
CHAD
NIGERIA
CAMEROON
CENTRAL AFRICAN REPUBLIC
GABON
CONGO
CONGO (DEM. REP. OF THE)
RWANDA
BURUNDI
EQUATORIAL GUINEA
DJIBOUTI
NIGER
ERITREA
ADDIS ABEBA
NAIROBI
KINSHASA
LUANDA
DAR ES SALAAM

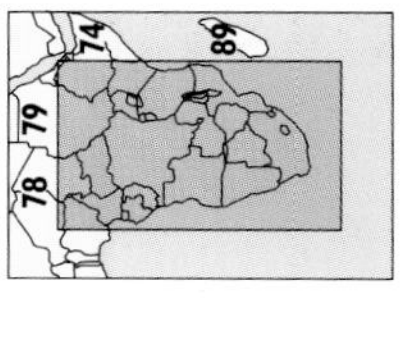

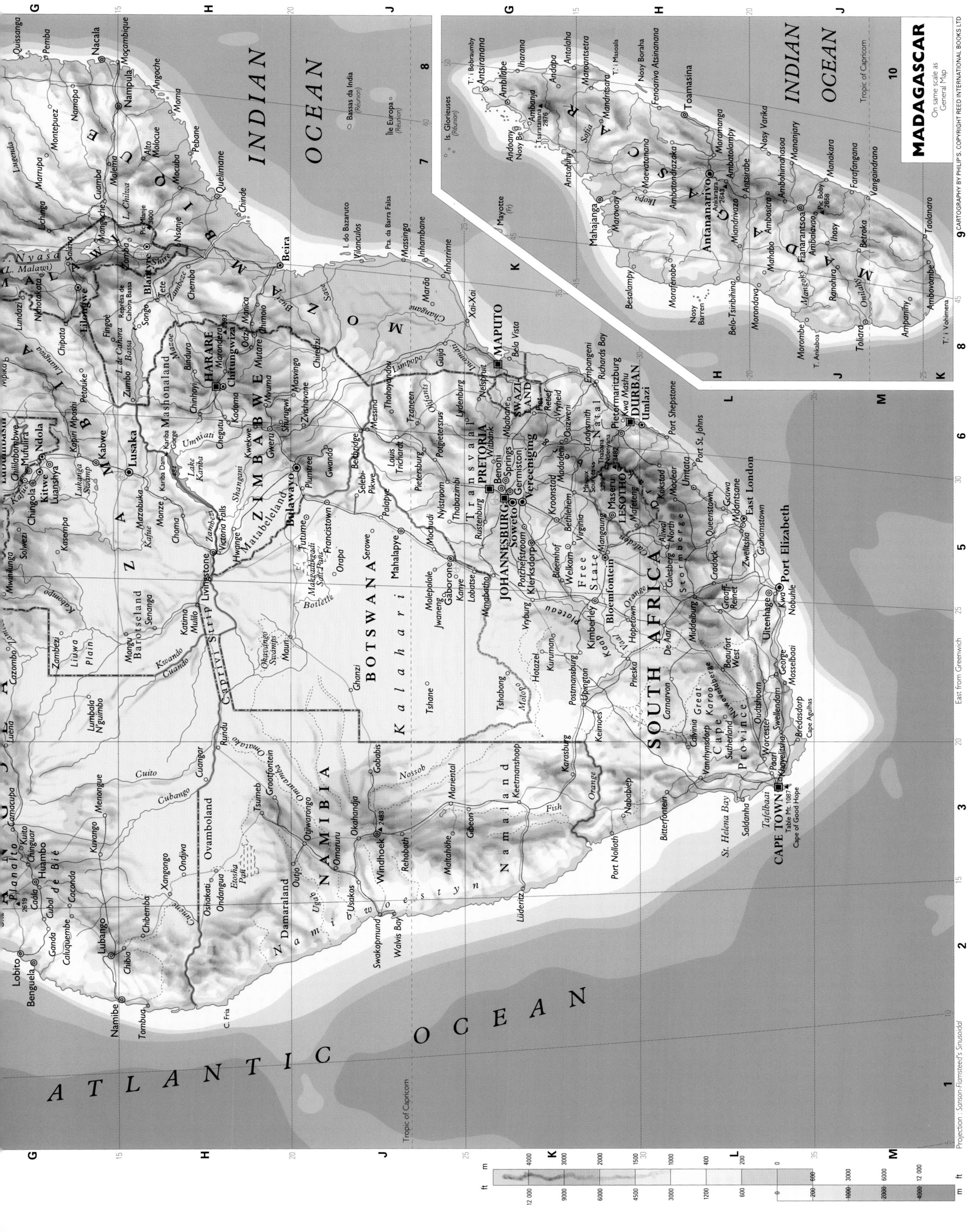
MADAGASCAR
On same scale as General Map
INDIAN OCEAN
ATLANTIC OCEAN
SOUTH AFRICA
NAMIBIA
BOTSWANA
ZIMBABWE
LESOTHO
SWAZILAND
Kalahari
Transvaal
Natal
Namaland
Damaraland
Ovamboland
Great Karoo
Cape Province
Free State
JOHANNESBURG
PRETORIA
MAPUTO
HARARE
CAPE TOWN
DURBAN
Port Elizabeth
East London
Bloemfontein
Kimberley
Windhoek
Gaborone
Bulawayo
Lusaka
Beira
Antananarivo
Toamasina
Tropic of Capricorn
East from Greenwich
Projection: Sanson-Flamsteed's Sinusoidal
CARTOGRAPHY BY PHILIP'S. COPYRIGHT REED INTERNATIONAL BOOKS LTD

50 0 50 100 150 200 250 300 km
50 0 50 100 150 200 miles
SOMALI REP.
ETHIOPIA
KENYA
UGANDA
TANZANIA
RWANDA
BURUNDI
SUDAN
CENTRAL AFRICAN REPUBLIC
Lake Victoria
NAIROBI
MOMBASA
DAR ES SALAAM
Zanzibar
Pemba I.
Mafia I.
Kampala
Kisangani
L. Turkana (L. Rudolf)
L. Tanganyika

INDIAN OCEAN
ZAMBIA
MALAWI
MOZAMBIQUE
ZIMBABWE
BOTSWANA
SOUTH AFRICA
ANGOLA
Zambezi
Lusaka
HARARE
Bulawayo
Blantyre
Lilongwe
Beira
Lubumbashi
Ndola
Kitwe
Livingstone
Mtwara-Mikindani
Lindi
Moçambique
Angoche
Chinde
Projection: Lambert's Equivalent Azimuthal
East from Greenwich
COPYRIGHT GEORGE PHILIP & SON LTD

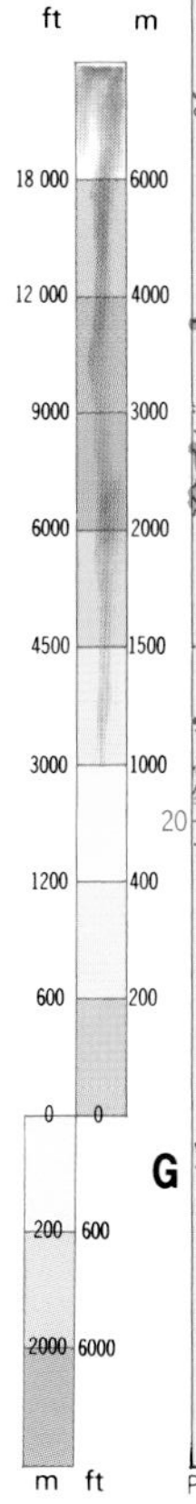

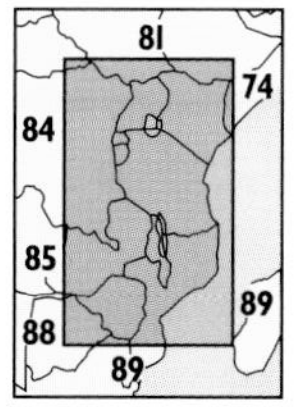
81
74
84
85
88
89
89

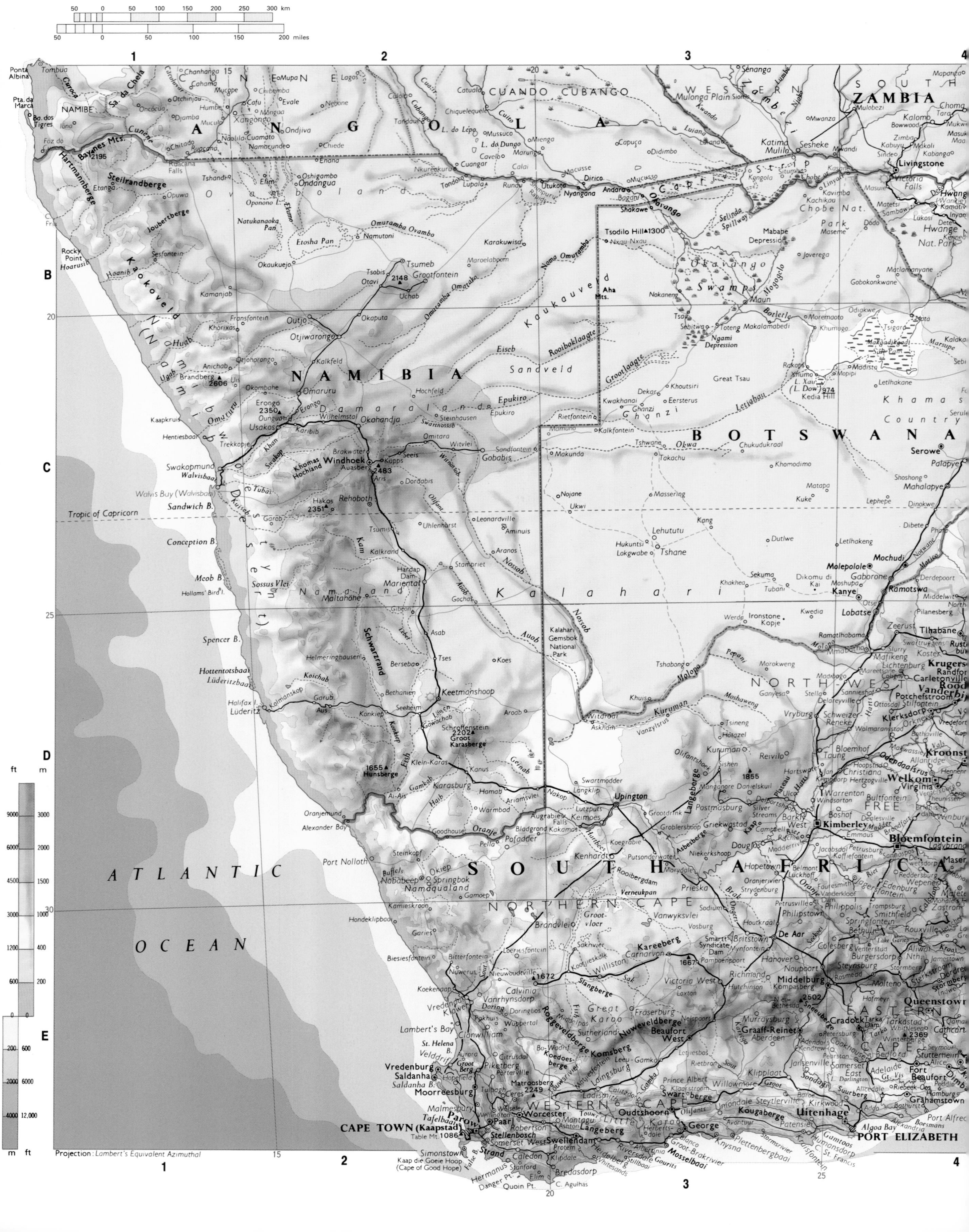

50 0 50 100 150 200 250 300 km
50 0 50 100 150 200 miles
ANGOLA
ZAMBIA
NAMIBIA
BOTSWANA
SOUTH AFRICA
ATLANTIC OCEAN
Tropic of Capricorn
CUANDO CUBANGO
NAMIBE
WESTERN
NORTH-WEST
NORTHERN CAPE
WESTERN CAPE
EASTERN CAPE
FREE
Kalahari
Okavango Swamp
Etosha Pan
Damaraland
Namaland
Namib Desert
Kaokoveld
Sandveld
Ghanzi
Khama's Country
Windhoek
Walvis Bay (Walvisbaai)
Swakopmund
Lüderitz
Keetmanshoop
Upington
Kimberley
Bloemfontein
Welkom
Gaborone
Serowe
Livingstone
Maun
Tsumeb
Oranjemund
CAPE TOWN (Kaapstad)
PORT ELIZABETH
Uitenhage
George
Oudtshoorn
Worcester
Paarl
Stellenbosch
Kaap die Goeie Hoop (Cape of Good Hope)
C. Agulhas
Table Mt. 1086
Algoa Bay
Projection: Lambert's Equivalent Azimuthal
ft m
9000 3000
6000 2000
4500 1500
3000 1000
1200 400
600 200
0 0
200 600
2000 6000
4000 12,000
m ft

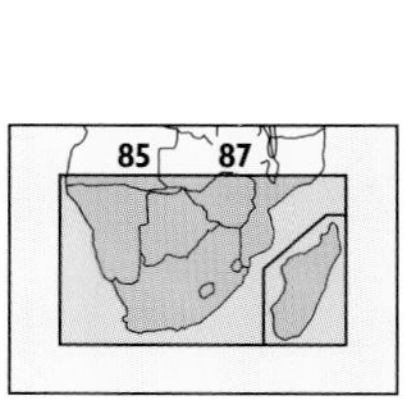
85
87

ZIMBABWE
MOZAMBIQUE
MALAWI
ZAMBÉZIA
TETE
MASHONALAND CENTRAL
MASHONALAND WEST
MASHONALAND EAST
MATABELELAND SOUTH
MASVINGO
MANICA
SOFALA
INHAMBANE
GAZA
MAPUTO
NORTHERN
MPUMALANGA
GAUTENG
SWAZILAND
KWAZULU NATAL
LESOTHO
EAST CAPE
MADAGASCAR
ANTANANARIVO
FIANARANTSOA
ANTSIRANANA
MAHAJANGA
TOLIARA
TOAMASINA
MOZAMBIQUE CHANNEL
INDIAN OCEAN
HARARE
Chitungwiza
Bulawayo
Gweru
Kwekwe
Kadoma
Masvingo
Mutare
Beira
Quelimane
Chinde
Angoche
Maputo
Xai-Xai
Inhambane
PRETORIA
JOHANNESBURG
Soweto
Benoni
Springs
Germiston
Vereeniging
Nelspruit
Mbabane
Manzini
Newcastle
Ladysmith
Empangeni
Richards Bay
Pietermaritzburg
DURBAN
Umlazi
KwaMashu
Port Shepstone
Umtata
East London
Antsiranana
Mahajanga
Toamasina
Antsirabe
Fianarantsoa
Toliara
Morondava
Taolanaro
Ile de Juan de Nova (Réunion)
Iles Glorieuses (Réunion)
I. do Bazaruto
I. Benguérua
Tropic of Capricorn
Lake Kariba
Limpopo
Zambeze
Save
Drakensberg
Lake St. Lucia
East from Greenwich
MADAGASCAR
On same scale as General Map
COPYRIGHT. GEORGE PHILIP & SON. LTD

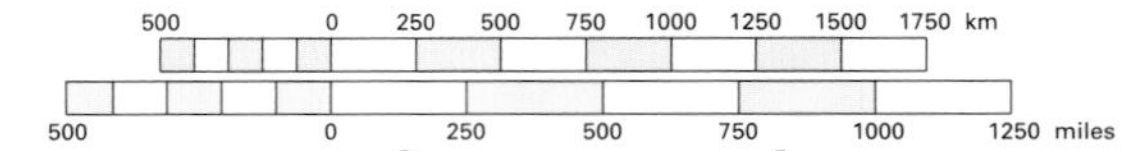
500 0 250 500 750 1000 1250 1500 1750 km
500 0 250 500 750 1000 1250 miles

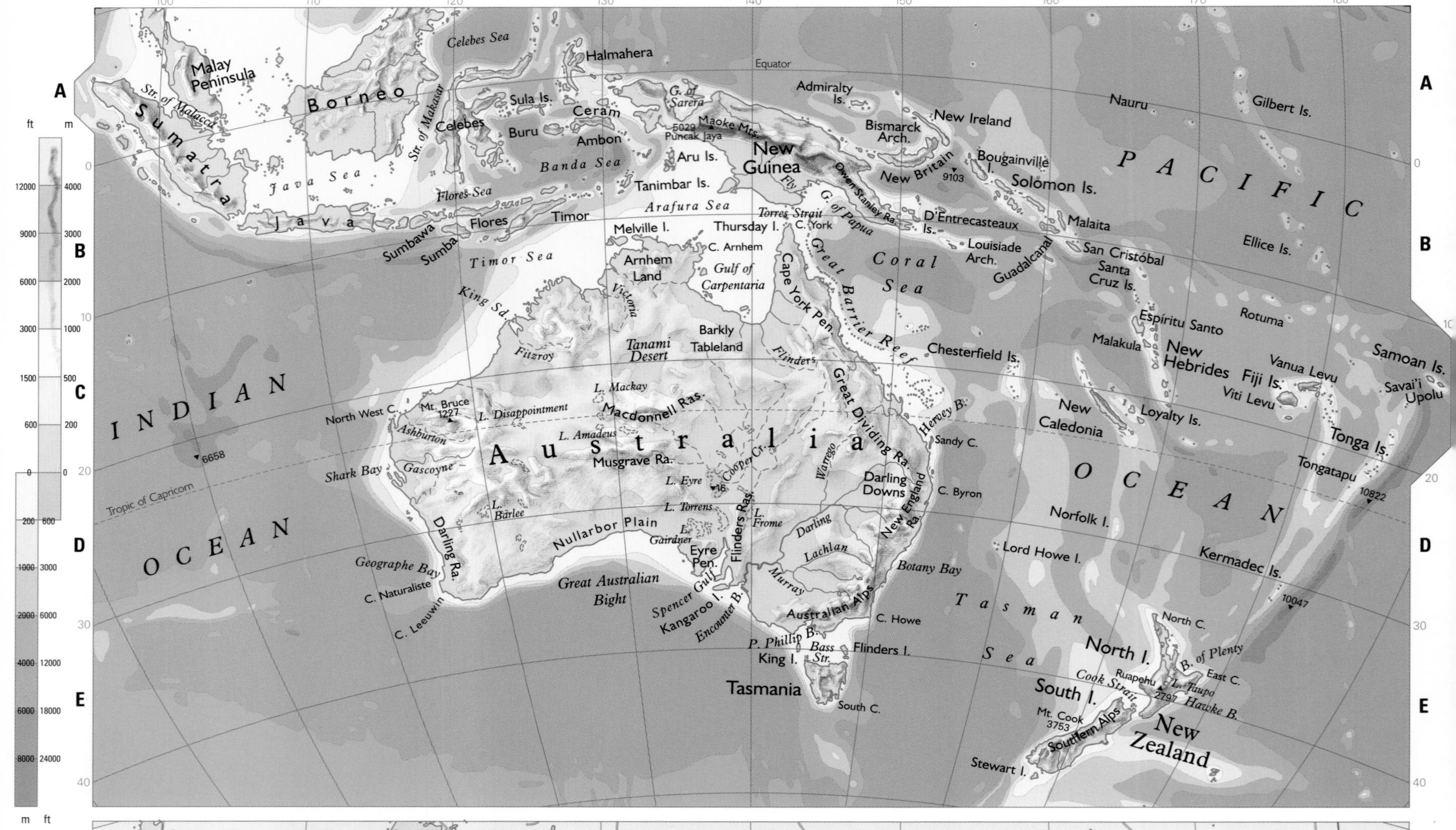
ft m
12000 4000
9000 3000
6000 2000
3000 1000
1500 500
600 200
0 0
200 600
1000 3000
2000 6000
4000 12000
6000 18000
8000 24000
m ft
Malay Peninsula
Str. of Malacca
Sumatra
Borneo
Celebes Sea
Halmahera
Str. of Makasar
Celebes
Sula Is.
Ceram
Buru
Ambon
Banda Sea
Java Sea
Flores Sea
Java
Sumbawa
Sumba
Flores
Timor
Timor Sea
G. of Sarera
Maoke Mts.
5029 Puncak Jaya
Aru Is.
Tanimbar Is.
Arafura Sea
Equator
Admiralty Is.
Bismarck Arch.
New Ireland
New Britain
9103
New Guinea
Fly
Owen Stanley Ra.
G. of Papua
Torres Strait
Thursday I.
C. York
Melville I.
C. Arnhem
Arnhem Land
Gulf of Carpentaria
Cape York Pen.
Great Barrier Reef
Coral Sea
Bougainville I.
Solomon Is.
D'Entrecasteaux Is.
Louisiade Arch.
Guadalcanal
Malaita
San Cristóbal
Santa Cruz Is.
Nauru
Gilbert Is.
PACIFIC
Ellice Is.
Rotuma
Espíritu Santo
Malakula
New Hebrides
Fiji Is.
Vanua Levu
Viti Levu
Samoan Is.
Savai'i
Upolu
Tonga Is.
Tongatapu
10822
King Sd.
Victoria
Barkly Tableland
Tanami Desert
Fitzroy
Flinders
Chesterfield Is.
Great Dividing Ra.
L. Mackay
Macdonnell Ras.
Mt. Bruce 1227
L. Disappointment
North West C.
Ashburton
L. Amadeus
Musgrave Ra.
Australia
Cooper Cr.
Warrego
Hervey B.
Sandy C.
New Caledonia
Loyalty Is.
INDIAN
6658
Shark Bay
Gascoyne
L. Eyre
-16
Darling Downs
C. Byron
OCEAN
Tropic of Capricorn
L. Barlee
L. Torrens
Flinders Ras.
L. Frome
New England Ra.
Norfolk I.
Nullarbor Plain
L. Gairdner
Darling
Darling Ra.
Eyre Pen.
Lachlan
Lord Howe I.
Kermadec Is.
Geographe Bay
Botany Bay
C. Naturaliste
Great Australian Bight
Spencer Gulf
Murray
10047
C. Leeuwin
Kangaroo I.
Encounter B.
Australian Alps
C. Howe
Tasman Sea
North C.
P. Phillip B.
Bass Str.
Flinders I.
North I.
B. of Plenty
King I.
Ruapehu 2797
L. Taupo
East C.
Cook Strait
Hawke B.
Tasmania
South I.
South C.
Mt. Cook 3753
Southern Alps
New Zealand
Stewart I.

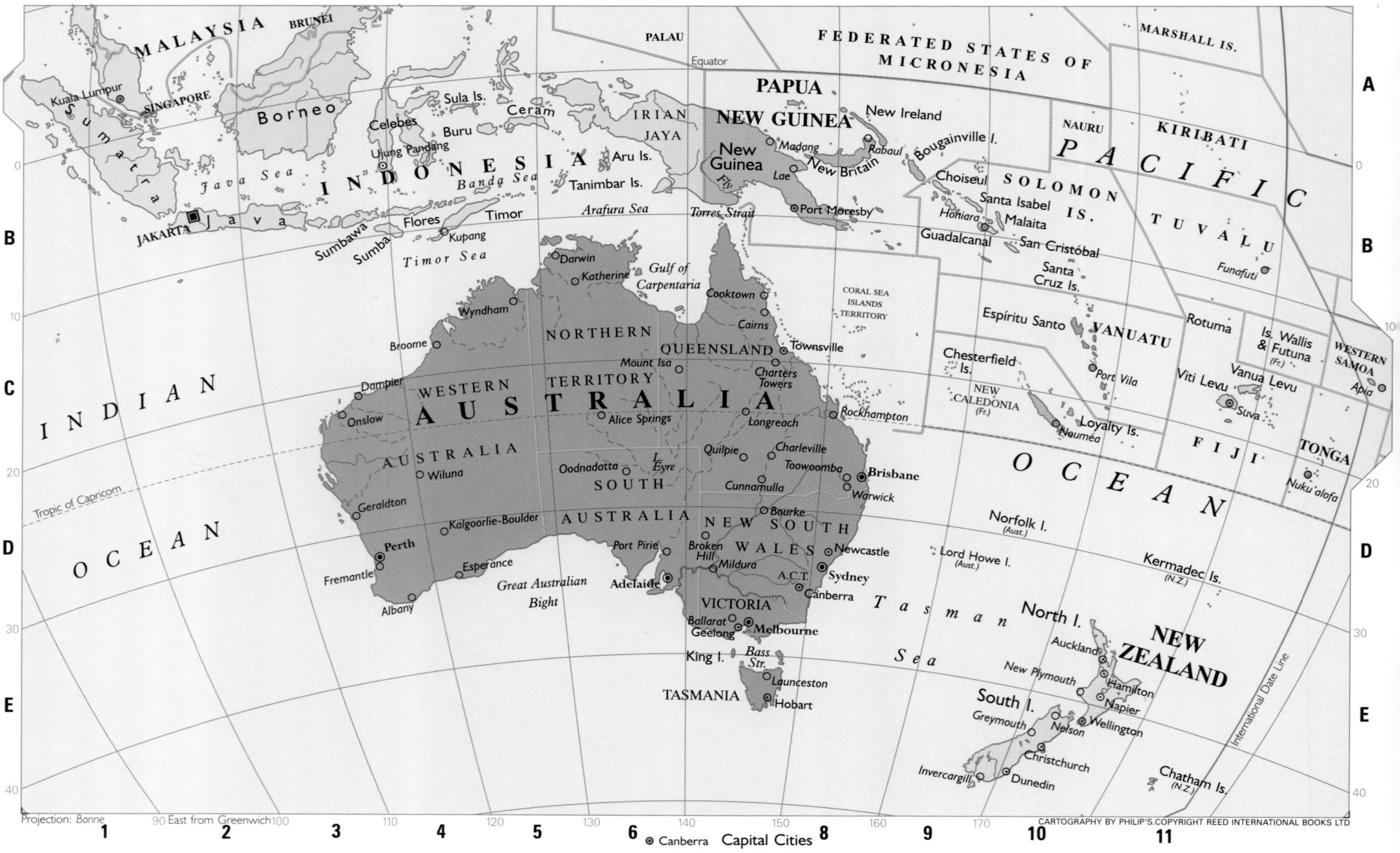
MALAYSIA
BRUNEI
PALAU
FEDERATED STATES OF MICRONESIA
MARSHALL IS.
Equator
Kuala Lumpur
SINGAPORE
Borneo
Sumatra
Celebes
Sula Is.
Ceram
Buru
Ujung Pandang
IRIAN JAYA
PAPUA NEW GUINEA
New Ireland
Madang
Rabaul
New Britain
Bougainville I.
NAURU
KIRIBATI
Java Sea
INDONESIA
Banda Sea
Aru Is.
Tanimbar Is.
New Guinea
Lae
Fly
Choiseul
SOLOMON IS.
Santa Isabel
Honiara
Malaita
Guadalcanal
San Cristóbal
PACIFIC
TUVALU
Funafuti
JAKARTA
Java
Sumbawa
Sumba
Flores
Kupang
Timor
Timor Sea
Arafura Sea
Torres Strait
Port Moresby
Santa Cruz Is.
Darwin
Katherine
Gulf of Carpentaria
Cooktown
Cairns
CORAL SEA ISLANDS TERRITORY
Wyndham
Broome
NORTHERN TERRITORY
QUEENSLAND
Townsville
Mount Isa
Charters Towers
Espíritu Santo
VANUATU
Rotuma
Is. Wallis & Futuna (Fr.)
WESTERN SAMOA
Apia
Chesterfield Is.
NEW CALEDONIA (Fr.)
Port Vila
Viti Levu
Vanua Levu
Suva
Dampier
WESTERN AUSTRALIA
AUSTRALIA
Onslow
Alice Springs
Longreach
Rockhampton
Loyalty Is.
Nouméa
INDIAN
FIJI
TONGA
Wiluna
Oodnadatta
L. Eyre
SOUTH AUSTRALIA
Quilpie
Charleville
Toowoomba
Brisbane
Cunnamulla
Warwick
OCEAN
Nuku'alofa
Tropic of Capricorn
Geraldton
Kalgoorlie-Boulder
Bourke
NEW SOUTH WALES
Norfolk I. (Aust.)
Perth
Port Pirie
Broken Hill
Mildura
Newcastle
Lord Howe I. (Aust.)
Kermadec Is. (N.Z.)
Fremantle
Esperance
Great Australian Bight
Adelaide
A.C.T.
Sydney
Canberra
Albany
VICTORIA
Ballarat
Geelong
Melbourne
Tasman Sea
North I.
NEW ZEALAND
Auckland
King I.
Bass Str.
Launceston
New Plymouth
Hamilton
TASMANIA
Hobart
South I.
Napier
Greymouth
Nelson
Wellington
International Date Line
Christchurch
Invercargill
Dunedin
Chatham Is. (N.Z.)
Projection: Bonne
East from Greenwich
Canberra Capital Cities
CARTOGRAPHY BY PHILIP'S.COPYRIGHT REED INTERNATIONAL BOOKS LTD

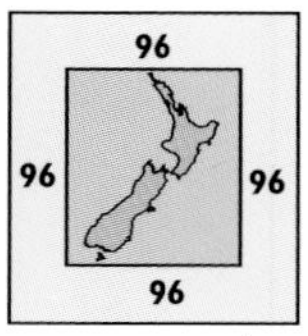
96
96
96
96

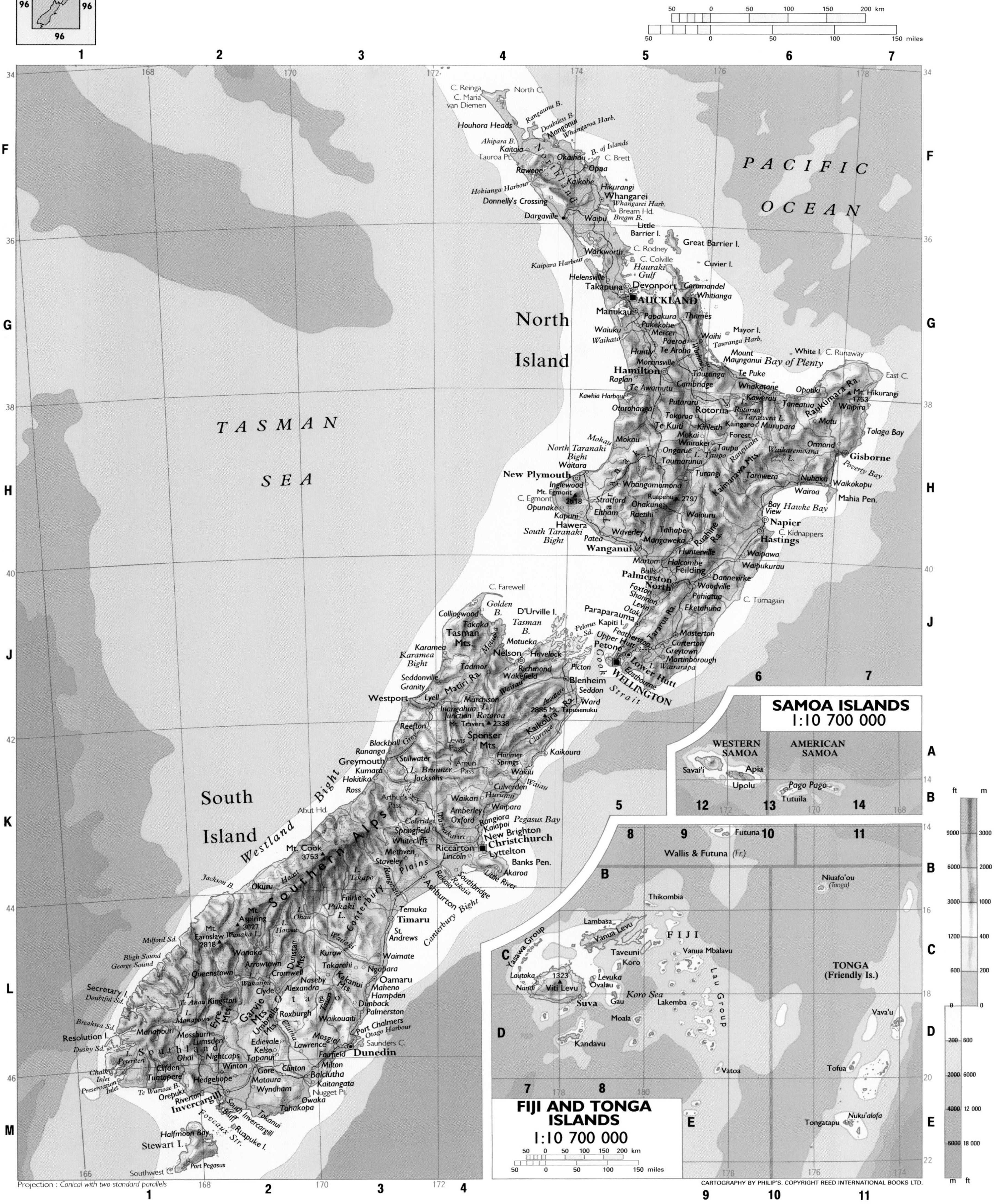
50 0 50 100 150 200 km
50 0 50 100 150 miles
PACIFIC OCEAN
TASMAN SEA
North Island
South Island
C. Reinga
North C.
C. Maria van Diemen
Houhora Heads
Rangaunu B.
Doubtless B.
Mangonui
Whangaroa Harb.
Ahipara B.
Kaitaia
Tauroa Pt.
B. of Islands
C. Brett
Okaihau
Opua
Rawene
Kaikohe
Northland
Hokianga Harbour
Hikurangi
Whangarei
Whangarei Harb.
Bream Hd.
Bream B.
Donnelly's Crossing
Dargaville
Waipu
Little Barrier I.
Great Barrier I.
Kaipara Harbour
Warkworth
C. Rodney
C. Colville
Cuvier I.
Hauraki Gulf
Helensville
Takapuna
Devonport
Coromandel
Whitianga
AUCKLAND
Manukau
Papakura
Thames
Pukekohe
Mercer
Waiuku
Waikato
Waihi
Mayor I.
Tauranga Harb.
Paeroa
Te Aroha
Huntly
Mount Maunganui
Bay of Plenty
White I.
C. Runaway
Morrinsville
Hamilton
Raglan
Tauranga
Te Puke
East C.
Cambridge
Whakatane
Opotiki
Te Awamutu
Kawhia Harbour
Kawerau
Raukumara Ra.
Mt. Hikurangi 1753
Otorohanga
Putaruru
Rotorua
Rotorua
Tarawera L.
Waipiro
Tokoroa
Te Kuiti
Kinleith
Kaingaroa Forest
Murupara
Motu
Tolaga Bay
Mokau
Mokau
Mokai
Wairakei
Ormond
North Taranaki Bight
Waitara
Ongarue
Taupo
L. Taupo
Waikaremoana L.
Gisborne
Taumarunui
Poverty Bay
New Plymouth
Inglewood
Whangamomona
Turangi
Kaimanawa Mts.
Tarawera
Nuhaka
Waikokopu
Mt. Egmont 2518
C. Egmont
Opunake
Stratford
Ruapehu 2797
Ohakune
Wairoa
Mahia Pen.
Eltham
Raetihi
Waiouru
Bay View
Hawke Bay
Kapuni
Hawera
Napier
South Taranaki Bight
Taihape
C. Kidnappers
Patea
Waverley
Mangaweka
Ruahine Ra.
Hastings
Wanganui
Hunterville
Waipawa
Marton
Halcombe
Waipukurau
Bulls
Feilding
Palmerston North
Dannevirke
Foxton
Woodville
Shannon
C. Turnagain
Levin
Pahiatua
Otaki
Eketahuna
Paraparaumu
Kapiti I.
Tararua Ra.
Featherston
Masterton
Upper Hutt
Carterton
Greytown
Martinborough
Petone
Lower Hutt
Wararapa
WELLINGTON
Eastbourne
Cook Strait
C. Farewell
Golden B.
D'Urville I.
Collingwood
Tasman B.
Takaka
Tasman Mts.
Motueka
Pelorus Sd.
Karamea
Karamea Bight
Nelson
Havelock
Tadmor
Richmond
Wakefield
Picton
Seddonville
Granity
Matiri Ra.
Blenheim
Seddon
Westport
Lyell
Murchison
Ward
Inangahua Junction
Rotoroa
Awatere
2885 Mt. Tapuaenuku
Mt. Travers 2338
Reefton
Spenser Mts.
Kaikoura Ra.
Clarence
Blackball
Grey
Lewis Pass
Kaikoura
Runanga
Stillwater
Greymouth
Hanmer Springs
Amuri Pass
Kumara
L. Brunner
Waiau
Hokitika
Jacksons
Ross
Culverden
Arthur's Pass
Waikari
Hurunui
Amberley
Waipara
Abut Hd.
Coleridge
Oxford
Rangiora
Pegasus Bay
Springfield
Kaiapoi
Whitecliffs
Waimakariri
New Brighton
Christchurch
Methven
Riccarton
Lyttelton
Westland Bight
Mt. Cook 3753
Southern Alps
Staveley
Lincoln
Banks Pen.
Plains
Akaroa
Jackson B.
Haast
Okuru
L. Tekapo
Rakaia
Little River
Ashburton
Southbridge
Canterbury Bight
Fairlie
Pukaki L.
Canterbury
Rangitata
Mt. Aspiring 3027
L. Ohau
Temuka
Timaru
Mt. Earnslaw 2818
L. Wanaka
L. Hawea
St. Andrews
Milford Sd.
Waitaki
Wanaka
Dunstan Mts.
Kurow
Waimate
Bligh Sound
George Sound
Arrowtown
Tokarahi
Cromwell
Ngapara
Queenstown
Kakanui Mts.
Oamaru
Secretary I.
Doubtful Sd.
L. Wakatipu
Naseby
Maheno
Clyde
Alexandra
Hampden
L. Te Anau
Kingston
Otago
Dunback
Eyre Mts.
Garvie Mts.
Roxburgh
Palmerston
Breaksea Sd.
Umbrella Mts.
Waikouaiti
L. Manapouri
Mossburn
Clutha
Port Chalmers
Otago Harbour
Resolution I.
Lumsden
Edievale
Mosgiel
Saunders C.
Dusky Sd.
Southland
Lawrence
Ohai
Nightcaps
Tapanui
Dunedin
L. Poteriteri
Fairfield
Chalky Inlet
Clifden
Winton
Clinton
Milton
Tuatapere
Gore
Balclutha
Preservation Inlet
Hedgehope
Mataura
Kaitangata
Te Waewae B.
Orepuki
Riverton
Wyndham
Nugget Pt.
Invercargill
Owaka
Bluff
South Invercargill
Tahakopa
Foveaux Str.
Tokanui
Halfmoon Bay
Ruapuke I.
Stewart I.
Port Pegasus
Southwest C.
Projection : Conical with two standard parallels
SAMOA ISLANDS
1:10 700 000
WESTERN SAMOA
AMERICAN SAMOA
Savai'i
Apia
Upolu
Pago Pago
Tutuila
Futuna
Wallis & Futuna (Fr.)
Niuafo'ou (Tonga)
Thikombia
Lambasa
Vanua Levu
FIJI
Yasawa Group
Taveuni
Vanua Mbalavu
Koro
Lau Group
Lautoka
1323
Levuka
Ovalau
Nandi
Viti Levu
Koro Sea
Suva
Gau
Lakemba
TONGA (Friendly Is.)
Moala
Vava'u
Kandavu
Vatoa
Tofua
FIJI AND TONGA ISLANDS
1:10 700 000
50 0 50 100 150 200 km
50 0 50 100 150 miles
Nuku'alofa
Tongatapu
CARTOGRAPHY BY PHILIP'S. COPYRIGHT REED INTERNATIONAL BOOKS LTD.
ft m
9000 3000
6000 2000
3000 1000
1200 400
600 200
0 0
200 600
2000 6000
4000 12 000
6000 18 000
m ft

WESTERN AUSTRALIA 1:7 100 000

50 0 50 100 150 200 250 300 km
50 0 50 100 150 200 miles
B
C
D
INDONESIA
TIMOR SEA
INDIAN OCEAN
NORTHERN TERRITORY
Bali
Lombok
Sumbawa
Sumba
Sawu
Roti
Semau
Timor
Dana
Raijua
Darwin
Melville I.
Bathurst I.
Cobourg Pen.
Croker I.
Katherine
Tanami Desert
Great Sandy Desert
Gibson Desert
Bonaparte Archipelago
Joseph Bonaparte Gulf
Cambridge Gulf
King Leopold Ranges
Durack Range
Cockburn Ra.
Carr Boyd Ra.
Mt. Hann 776
Mt. Ord 1007
Mt. Greenwood 152
Fitzroy Crossing
Derby
Broome
Roebuck B.
King Sound
Buccaneer Archipelago
Lacepede Is.
Adele I.
Browse I.
Cartier I.
Ashmore Reef
Hibernia Reef
Scott Reef
Seringapatam Reef
Lynher Reef
Mermaid Reef
Clerke Reef
Imperieuse Reef
Rowley Shoals
Eighty Mile Beach
C. Keraudren
Port Hedland
Karratha
Roebourne
Dampier
Dampier Archipelago
Legendre I.
Delambre I.
Enderby I.
Monte Bello Is.
Barrow I.
Pasco I.
Exmouth
Exmouth Gulf
North West C.
Hamersley Range
Mt. Bruce 1235
Mt. Meharry 1251
Newman
Ophthalmia Ra.
Chichester Ra.
Paraburdoo
Tom Price
Lake Mackay
Lake Disappointment
L. Hopkins
L. Macdonald
Gregory Lake
Tropic of Capricorn
Macdonnell Ranges
Mt. Zeil 1510
Mt. Liebig 1524
Mt. Singleton 808
Mt. Leisler 901
Reynolds Ra.
Kintore Ra.
Horden Hills
Lewis Ra.
Kimberley Downs
Halls Creek
Wyndham
Kununurra
Turkey Creek
L. Argyle
Tanami

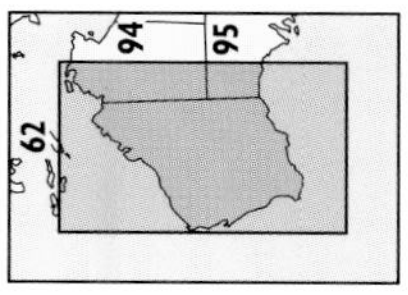
62
94
95

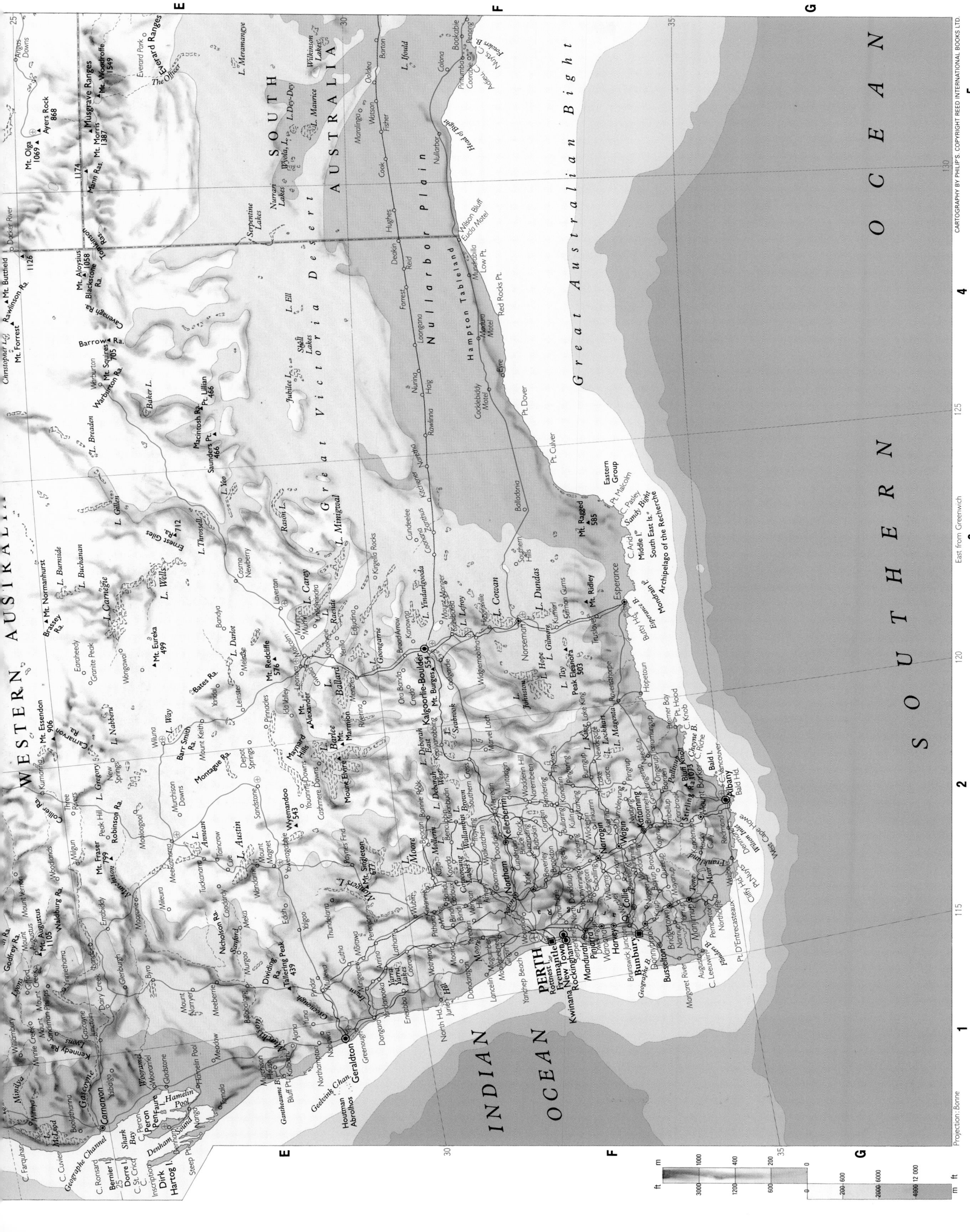
WESTERN AUSTRALIA
SOUTH AUSTRALIA
INDIAN OCEAN
SOUTHERN OCEAN
Great Australian Bight
Great Victoria Desert
Nullarbor Plain
Hampton Tableland
PERTH
Fremantle
Rockingham
Kwinana New Town
Mandurah
Bunbury
Busselton
Albany
Geraldton
Carnarvon
Kalgoorlie-Boulder
Esperance
Norseman
Northam
Narrogin
Katanning
Collie
Wagin
Merredin
Denham
Archipelago of the Recherche
Shark Bay
Houtman Abrolhos
L. Carnegie
L. Wells
L. Carey
L. Barlee
L. Moore
L. Cowan
L. Dundas
L. Lefroy
L. Austin
L. Way
Mt. Woodroffe 1549
Musgrave Ranges
Everard Ranges
Ayers Rock 868
Mt. Olga 1069
Eucla Motel
Nullarbor
Cook
Head of Bight
East from Greenwich
Projection: Bonne
CARTOGRAPHY BY PHILIP'S. COPYRIGHT REED INTERNATIONAL BOOKS LTD.
m
ft
3000
1000
1200
400
600
200
0
0
200
600
2000
6000
4000
12 000

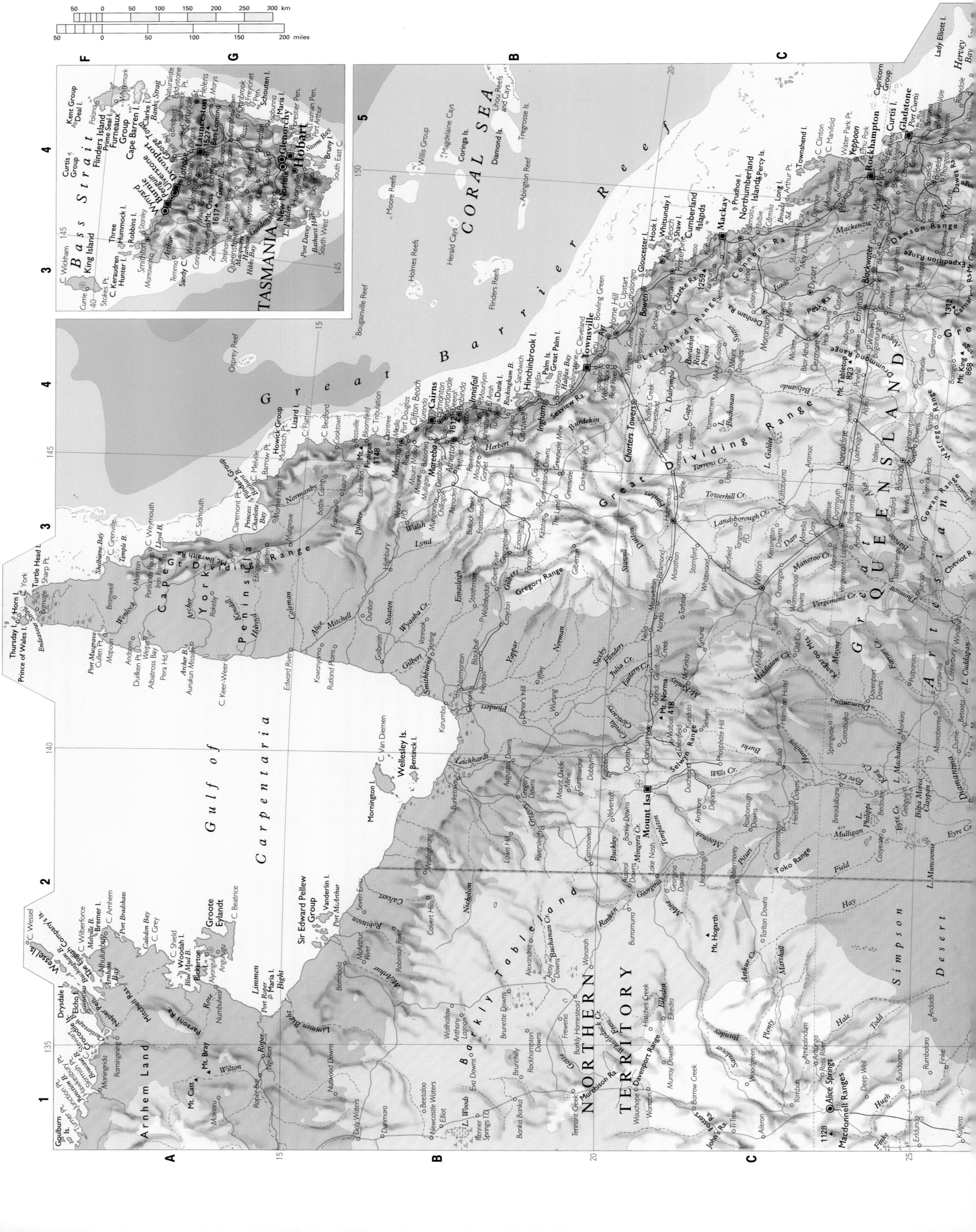
50 0 50 100 150 200 250 300 km
50 0 50 100 150 200 miles
TASMANIA
Bass Strait
King Island
Flinders Island
Furneaux Group
Cape Barren I.
Launceston
Devonport
Burnie
Hobart
Glenorchy
New Norfolk
Queenstown
Mt. Ossa 1617
Ben Lomond 1527
CORAL SEA
Great Barrier Reef
Gulf of Carpentaria
Cape York Peninsula
Great Dividing Range
QUEENSLAND
NORTHERN TERRITORY
Barkly Tableland
Great Artesian Basin
Simpson Desert
Arnhem Land
Groote Eylandt
Sir Edward Pellew Group
Wellesley Is.
Mornington I.
Thursday I.
Prince of Wales I.
Horn I.
C. York
Cairns
Townsville
Mackay
Rockhampton
Gladstone
Mount Isa
Cloncurry
Charters Towers
Alice Springs
Tennant Creek
Mareeba
Innisfail
Ingham
Bowen
Emerald
Longreach
Winton
Hughenden
Normanton
Karumba
Burketown
Cooktown
Weipa
Nhulunbuy
Tarlton Downs
Macdonnell Ranges
Mt. Bartle Frere 1612
Mt. Finnigan 1148
Dawson Range
Selwyn Range
Gregory Range
Toko Range
Davenport Range
Lake Eyre
Whitsunday I.
Cumberland Islands
Northumberland Islands
Hinchinbrook I.
Capricorn Group
Willis Group
Coringa Is.
Magdelaine Cays
Lihou Reefs and Cays
Flinders Reefs
Holmes Reefs
Osprey Reef
Bougainville Reef
Mitchell
Gilbert
Flinders
Leichhardt
Georgina
Diamantina
Burdekin
Fitzroy
Mackenzie
Herbert
Roper
Wilton
Limmen Bight
Mt. Hogarth
Mt. Tabletop 823
Mt. Norma 418
1128
A B C
1 2 3 4 5
F G
135 140 145 150 15 20 25

SOUTH AUSTRALIA
NEW SOUTH WALES
TASMAN SEA
SOUTHERN OCEAN
Bass Strait
BRISBANE
SYDNEY
CANBERRA
MELBOURNE
ADELAIDE
Port Augusta
Whyalla
Port Pirie
Port Lincoln
Kangaroo I.
King Island
Flinders Island
Broken Hill
Mildura
Wagga Wagga
Albury
Newcastle
Wollongong
Toowoomba
Lake Eyre (North)
Lake Torrens
Lake Frome
Spencer Gulf
Projection: Bonne
East from Greenwich
CARTOGRAPHY BY PHILIP'S. COPYRIGHT REED INTERNATIONAL BOOKS LTD.

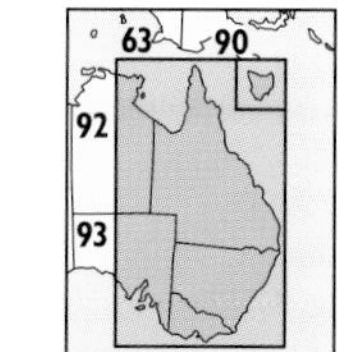
63
90
92
93

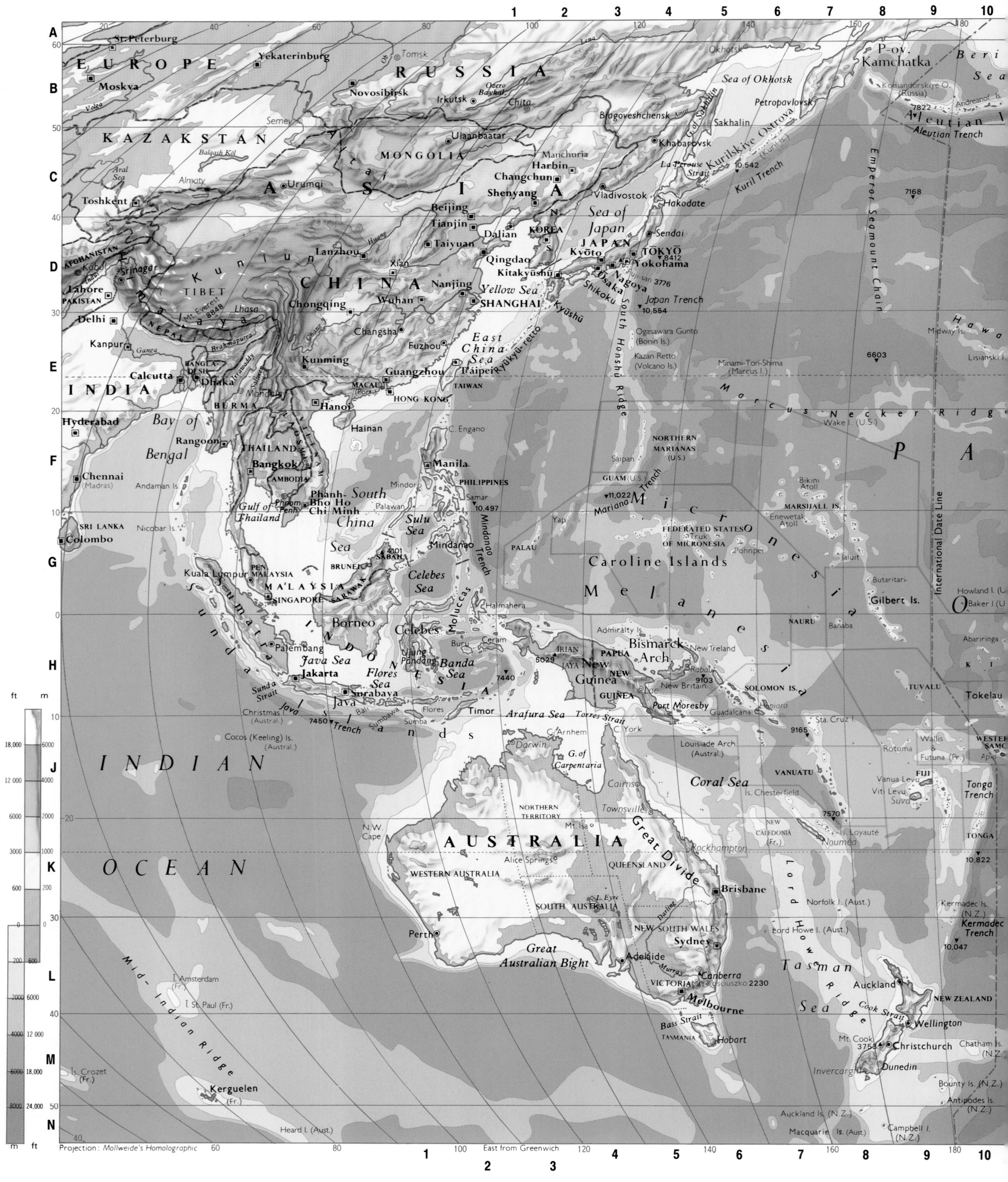

1 2 3 4 5 6 7 8 9 10
A B C D E F G H J K L M N
E U R O P E
St. Peterburg
Moskva
Yekaterinburg
R U S S I A
Novosibirsk
Tomsk
Irkutsk
Ozero Baykal
Chita
Semey
K A Z A K S T A N
Balqash Köl
Aral Sea
Almaty
Toshkent
Urumqi
A S I A
Altai
Ulaanbaatar
M O N G O L I A
Manchuria
Harbin
Changchun
Shenyang
Beijing
Tianjin
Dalian
Taiyuan
Lanzhou
Xian
Qingdao
Nanjing
C H I N A
Wuhan
SHANGHAI
Yellow Sea
Chongqing
Changsha
Fuzhou
Kunming
Guangzhou
MACAU (Port.)
HONG KONG
Taipei
TAIWAN
East China Sea
K u n l u n
TIBET
Lhasa
Mt. Everest 8848
H i m a l a y a
NEPAL
Brahmaputra
Srinagar
AFGHANISTAN
Kabul
Lahore
PAKISTAN
Delhi
Kanpur
Ganga
I N D I A
Calcutta
BANGLADESH
Dhaka
Mandalay
BURMA
Rangoon
Bay of Bengal
Hyderabad
Chennai (Madras)
Andaman Is.
Nicobar Is.
SRI LANKA
Colombo
THAILAND
Bangkok
CAMBODIA
Gulf of Thailand
Phnom Penh
Phan-Bho Ho Chi Minh
Hanoi
Hainan
South China Sea
Sea of Okhotsk
Okhotsk
P-ov. Kamchatka
Petropavlovsk
Sakhalin
Blagoveshchensk
Amur
Khabarovsk
Vladivostok
La Pérouse Strait
Kuril'skiye Ostrova (Kuril Is.)
Kuril Trench
10,542
Hakodate
Sea of Japan
KOREA
J A P A N
Sendai
TOKYO
Yokohama
8412
Kyōto
Nagoya
Ōsaka
Shikoku
Kitakyūshū
Kyūshū
Fuji-san 3776
Japan Trench
10,554
Ryūkyū-rettō
South Honshū Ridge
Ogasawara Gunto (Bonin Is.)
Kazan Retto (Volcano Is.)
Minami-Tori-Shima (Marcus I.)
Marcus Necker Ridge
Wake I. (U.S.)
Emperor Seamount Chain
7168
Komandorskiye O. (Russia)
7822
Andreanof Is.
Aleutian Trench
Beri
Midway Is.
Hawa
Lisianski I.
6603
C. Engano
Manila
PHILIPPINES
Mindoro
Samar
10,497
Palawan
Mindanao
Mindanao Trench
Sulu Sea
SABAH
4101
BRUNEI
Celebes Sea
NORTHERN MARIANAS (U.S.)
Saipan
GUAM (U.S.)
11,022
Mariana Trench
Yap
PALAU
FEDERATED STATES OF MICRONESIA
Truk
Pohnpei
Caroline Islands
M i c r o n e s i a
Bikini Atoll
MARSHALL IS.
Enewetak Atoll
Jaluit
Butaritari
Gilbert Is.
NAURU
Banaba
Howland I. (U.
Baker I. (U
Abariringa
International Date Line
P A
Kuala Lumpur
PEN. MALAYSIA
M A L A Y S I A
SINGAPORE
SARAWAK
Borneo
Sumatra
Palembang
Java Sea
Jakarta
Sunda Strait
Surabaya
Java
Bali
Java Trench
7450
Christmas I. (Austral.)
Cocos (Keeling) Is. (Austral.)
I N D O N E S I A
Sunda Islands
Celebes
Ujung Pandang
Flores Sea
Flores
Sumbawa
Sumba
Timor
Banda Sea
Buru
Ceram
Moluccas
Halmahera
IRIAN JAYA
5029
7440
PAPUA NEW GUINEA
New Guinea
Admiralty Is.
Bismarck Arch.
New Ireland
Rabaul
New Britain
9103
Port Moresby
SOLOMON IS.
Honiara
Guadalcanal
M e l a n e s i a
Arafura Sea
Torres Strait
C. York
C. Arnhem
Darwin
G. of Carpentaria
Sta. Cruz I.
9165
TUVALU
Tokelau
Louisiade Arch. (Austral.)
Coral Sea
Is. Chesterfield
VANUATU
Rotuma
Wallis & Futuna (Fr.)
Apia
WESTERN SAMOA
FIJI
Vanua Levu
Viti Levu
Suva
Tonga Trench
7570
NEW CALEDONIA (Fr.)
Is. Loyauté
Nouméa
TONGA
10,822
Cairns
Townsville
NORTHERN TERRITORY
Mt. Isa
N.W. Cape
A U S T R A L I A
Great Dividing Range
Rockhampton
Alice Springs
QUEENSLAND
WESTERN AUSTRALIA
L. Eyre
SOUTH AUSTRALIA
Brisbane
Darling
Lord Howe Rise
Norfolk I. (Aust.)
Kermadec Is. (N.Z.)
Kermadec Trench
10,047
Perth
NEW SOUTH WALES
Lord Howe I. (Aust.)
Sydney
Great Australian Bight
Adelaide
Murray
Canberra
Mt. Kosciuszko 2230
VICTORIA
Melbourne
Bass Strait
TASMANIA
Hobart
Tasman Sea
Auckland
NEW ZEALAND
Cook Strait
Wellington
Mt. Cook 3753
Christchurch
Chatham Is. (N.Z.)
Invercargill
Dunedin
Bounty Is. (N.Z.)
Antipodes Is. (N.Z.)
Auckland Is. (N.Z.)
Macquarie Is. (Aust.)
Campbell I. (N.Z.)
I N D I A N O C E A N
Mid-Indian Ridge
Î. Amsterdam (Fr.)
Î. St. Paul (Fr.)
Îs. Crozet (Fr.)
Kerguelen (Fr.)
Heard I. (Aust.)
ft m
18,000 6000
12 000 4000
6000 2000
3000 1000
600 200
0 0
200 600
2000 6000
4000 12 000
6000 18,000
8000 24,000
m ft
Projection: Mollweide's Homolographic
East from Greenwich
20 40 60 80 100 120 140 160 180

ALASKA (U.S.)
Bristol Bay
Gulf of Alaska
Juneau
Prince of Wales I.
Prince Rupert
Kitimat
Queen Charlotte Is.
CANADA
Edmonton
Hudson Bay
L. Winnipeg
GREENLAND
C. Farewell
Labrador
NORTH AMERICA
Rocky Mountains
Calgary
Regina
Winnipeg
Vancouver
Vancouver I.
Victoria
Seattle
Portland
Boise
Snake
L. Superior
St. Lawrence
Quebec
Montréal
Ottawa
Toronto
L. Huron
L. Ontario
Michigan
Pr. Edward I.
Saint John
Newfoundland
C. Sable
Boston
Buffalo
Pittsburgh
NEW YORK
Philadelphia
Baltimore
Washington
Minneapolis
Missouri
CHICAGO
Detroit
L. Erie
Cincinnati
Salt Lake City
Colorado
Denver
Kansas City
St. Louis
C. Mendocino
San Francisco
4418
UNITED STATES
Memphis
Appalachian Mts.
Oklahoma
Mississippi
Atlanta
C. Hatteras
ATLANTIC
6741
Los Angeles
San Diego
Dallas
Ciudad Juarez
Jacksonville
Bermuda (U.K.)
Houston
New Orleans
San Antonio
6225
I. Guadalupe (Mexico)
Sierra Madre
MEXICO
Gulf of California
Monterrey
Gulf of Mexico
Miami
Florida Strait
OCEAN
BAHAMAS
Hawaiian Is. (U.S.)
Tropic of Cancer
Oahu
Honolulu
4205
Hawaii
La Habana
CUBA
Yucatan Channel
Mérida
West Indies
Hispaniola
9200
Is. Revilla Gigedo (Mexico)
México
Guadalajara
Puebla
5700
7680
JAMAICA
HAITI
DOM. REP.
Kingston
PUERTO RICO (U.S.)
Leeward Is.
Acapulco
BELIZE
PACIFIC
HONDURAS
Caribbean Sea
GUATEMALA
Guatemala
San Salvador
EL SALVADOR
NICARAGUA
Managua
Windward Is.
BARBADOS
TRINIDAD & TOBAGO
I. Clipperton (Fr.)
CENTRAL AMERICA
Barranquilla
San José
Maracaibo
COSTA RICA
PANAMA
Colón
Panama
Canal
Caracas
Orinoco
Christmas Island Ridge
Palmyra Is. (U.S.)
VENEZUELA
I. del Coco (Costa Rica)
Medellín
Teraina
Tabuaeran
Bogota
Kiritimati
I. de Malpelo (Colombia)
Cali
COLOMBIA
OCEAN
Jarvis I. (U.S.)
Equator
Galápagos (Ecuador)
Quito
ECUADOR
Guayaquil
Manaus
Amazonas
Iquitos
Malden I.
Starbuck I.
C. Pariñas
BRAZIL
Îs. Marquises
Tongareva
Penrhyn Is.
Caroline I.
Trujillo
SOUTH
Manihiki
Vostok I.
Flint I.
East Pacific Ridge
PERU
Lima
6369
Suwarrow Is.
AMERICA
Cook Islands (N.Z.)
Îs. de la Société
Tuamotu Ridge
Îs. Tuamotu
Cuzco
L. Titicaca
Illampu & Ancohuma 6550
Arequipa
La Paz
Tahiti
Manuae
BOLIVIA
Austral Seamount Chain
6866
Peru-Chile Trench
FRENCH POLYNESIA
Iquique
Rarotonga
Pitcairn I. (U.K.)
Tropic of Capricorn
PARAGUAY
Ducie I. (U.K.)
8050
Antofagasta
Îs. Tubuai (Îs. Australes)
Sala-y-Gomez (Chile)
San Félix (Chile)
Asunción
Rapa
I. de Pascua (Easter I.) (Chile)
San Ambrosio (Chile)
Tucumán
ANDES
Pto. Alegre
Córdoba
Arch. de Juan Fernández (Chile)
6960
Rosario
URUGUAY
Valparaíso
Santiago
Buenos Aires
Montevideo
Pacific-Antarctic Ridge
Chile Rise
Río de la Plata
Concepción
ARGENTINA
Patagonia
SOUTH ATLANTIC OCEAN
6212
Punta Arenas
Str. of Magellan
Falkland Is. (U.K.)
Tierra del Fuego
South Georgia (U.K.)
C. Horn
West from Greenwich
COPYRIGHT, GEORGE PHILIP & SON, LTD.

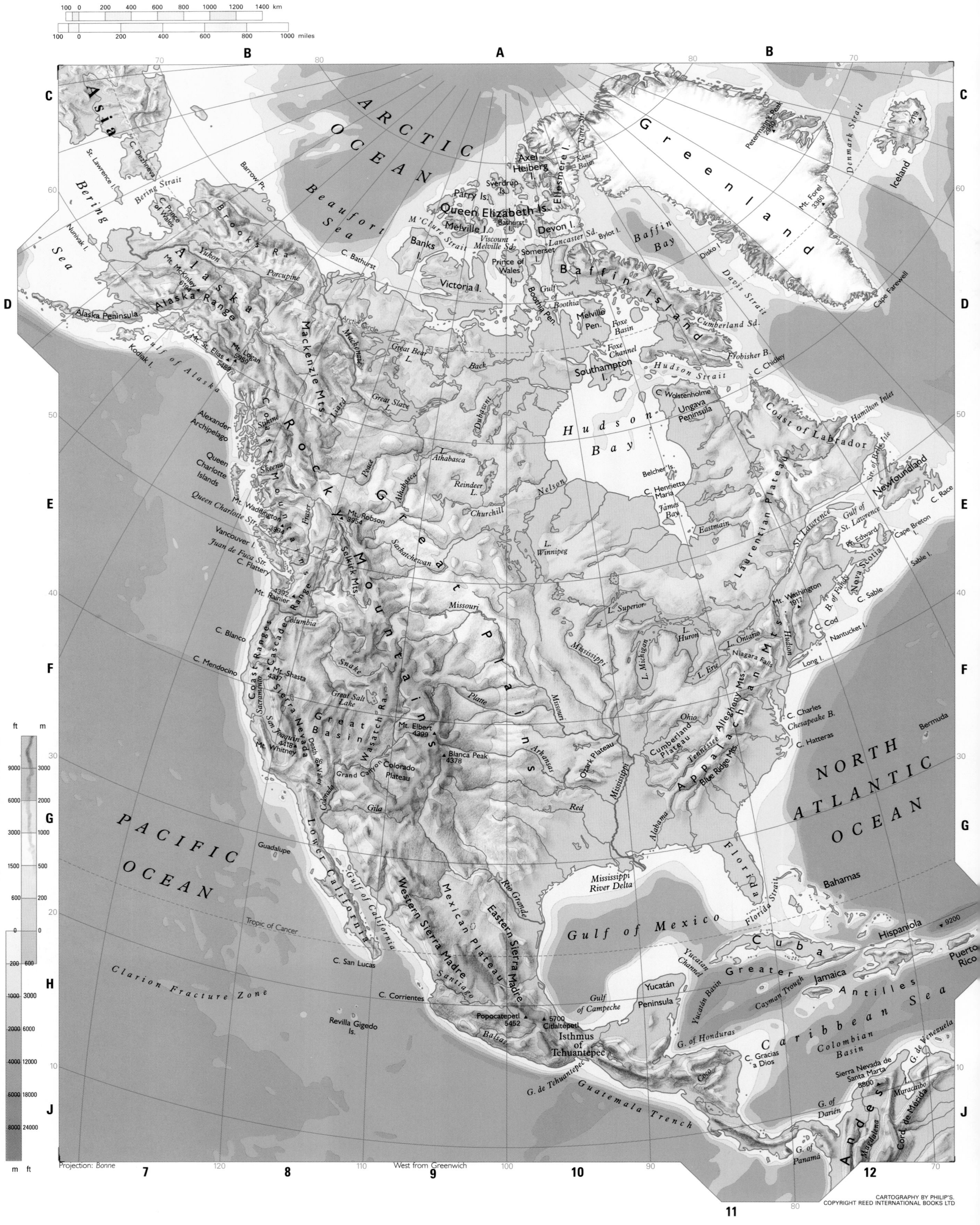
100 0 200 400 600 800 1000 1200 1400 km
100 0 200 400 600 800 1000 miles
ARCTIC OCEAN
Beaufort Sea
Asia
C. Dezhneva
St. Lawrence I.
Bering Strait
Bering Sea
Nunivak I.
C. Prince of Wales
Barrow Pt.
Brooks Ra.
Yukon
Porcupine
Alaska
Mt. McKinley 6194
Alaska Range
Alaska Peninsula
Kodiak I.
Gulf of Alaska
Mt. St. Elias 5489
Mt. Logan 5959
Mackenzie Mts.
Mackenzie
Arctic Circle
C. Bathurst
Banks I.
M'Clure Strait
Melville I.
Parry Is.
Queen Elizabeth Is.
Sverdrup Is.
Axel Heiberg I.
Ellesmere I.
Nares Str.
Kane Basin
Bathurst I.
Devon I.
Viscount Melville Sd.
Lancaster Sd.
Bylot I.
Somerset I.
Prince of Wales I.
Victoria I.
Gulf of Boothia
Boothia Pen.
Baffin Island
Baffin Bay
Disko I.
Davis Strait
Cumberland Sd.
Melville Pen.
Foxe Basin
Foxe Channel
Southampton I.
Frobisher B.
Hudson Strait
C. Chidley
C. Wolstenholme
Ungava Peninsula
Greenland
Petermann's Peak 2940
Mt. Forel 3360
Denmark Strait
Iceland
2119
Cape Farewell
Great Bear L.
Back
Great Slave L.
Dubawnt
Liard
Hudson Bay
Coast of Labrador
Hamilton Inlet
Str. of Belle Isle
Newfoundland
C. Race
Alexander Archipelago
Stikine
Coast Mountains
Rocky Mountains
Queen Charlotte Islands
Skeena
Queen Charlotte Str.
Mt. Waddington 3994
Fraser
Mt. Robson 3954
Peace
L. Athabasca
Athabasca
Reindeer L.
Churchill
Nelson
Belcher Is.
C. Henrietta Maria
James Bay
Eastmain
Laurentian Plateau
Gulf of St. Lawrence
St. Lawrence
Pt. Edward
Cape Breton I.
Nova Scotia
B. of Fundy
Sable I.
C. Sable
Vancouver I.
Juan de Fuca Str.
C. Flattery
Selkirk Mts.
Saskatchewan
Great Plains
L. Winnipeg
Mt. Rainier 4392
Cascade Range
Columbia
Missouri
L. Superior
L. Huron
L. Michigan
L. Ontario
L. Erie
Niagara Falls
Mt. Washington 1917
C. Cod
Nantucket I.
Long I.
Hudson
Appalachian Mts.
Allegheny Mts.
C. Blanco
C. Mendocino
Mt. Shasta 4317
Coast Ranges
Sacramento
Sierra Nevada
Snake
Great Salt Lake
Great Basin
Wasatch Ra.
Platte
Mississippi
Missouri
Ohio
Cumberland Plateau
Tennessee
C. Charles
Chesapeake B.
C. Hatteras
Bermuda
San Joaquin
Mt. Whitney 4418
Death Valley -86
Mt. Elbert 4399
Blanca Peak 4378
Arkansas
Ozark Plateau
Blue Ridge Mts.
NORTH ATLANTIC OCEAN
Grand Canyon
Colorado Plateau
Colorado
Gila
Red
Alabama
Florida
Florida Strait
Bahamas
PACIFIC OCEAN
Guadalupe
Lower California
Gulf of California
Rio Grande
Mississippi River Delta
Gulf of Mexico
Tropic of Cancer
Western Sierra Madre
Mexican Plateau
Eastern Sierra Madre
C. San Lucas
Cuba
Hispaniola
9200
Puerto Rico
Yucatan Channel
Yucatán Peninsula
Yucatán Basin
Greater Antilles
Cayman Trough
Jamaica
Clarion Fracture Zone
C. Corrientes
Santiago
Gulf of Campeche
Popocatepetl 5452
5700 Citlaltepetl
Revilla Gigedo Is.
Balsas
Isthmus of Tehuantepec
G. of Honduras
Caribbean Sea
Colombian Basin
C. Gracias a Dios
Coco
G. de Tehuantepec
Guatemala Trench
Sierra Nevada de Santa Marta 5800
G. de Venezuela
L. Maracaibo
G. of Darién
G. of Panamá
Andes
Magdalena
Cord. de Mérida
ft m
9000 3000
6000 2000
3000 1000
1500 500
600 200
0 0
200 600
1000 3000
2000 6000
4000 12000
6000 18000
8000 24000
m ft
Projection: Bonne
West from Greenwich
70 80 80 70 60 50 40 30 20 10 120 110 100 90 80 70
A B C D E F G H J 7 8 9 10 11 12

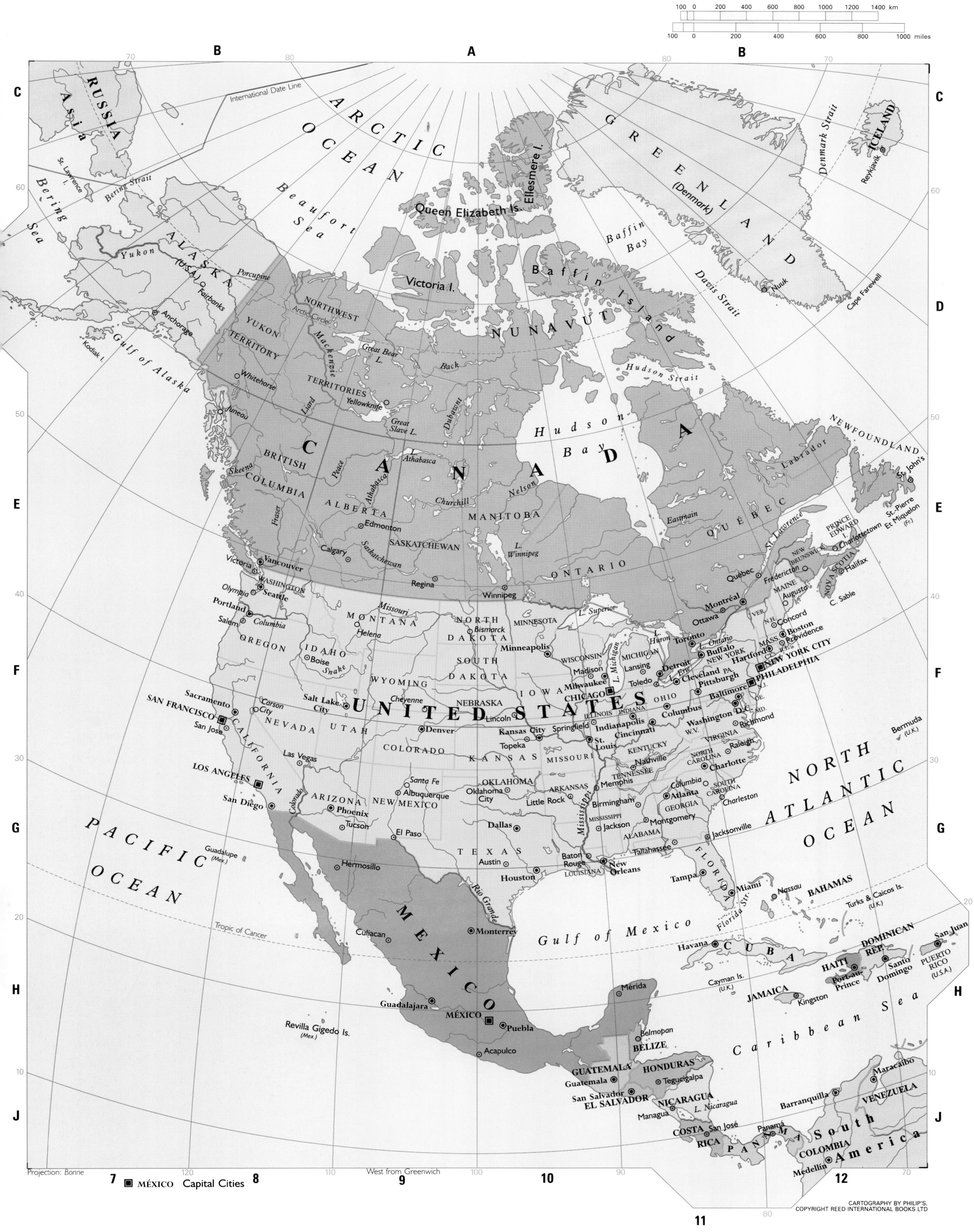
ARCTIC OCEAN
GREENLAND (Denmark)
CANADA
UNITED STATES
MEXICO
PACIFIC OCEAN
NORTH ATLANTIC OCEAN
Gulf of Mexico
Caribbean Sea
Hudson Bay
Baffin Bay
Beaufort Sea
Bering Sea
Gulf of Alaska
ALASKA (U.S.A.)
RUSSIA Asia
ICELAND
CUBA
BAHAMAS
HAITI
DOMINICAN REP.
JAMAICA
PUERTO RICO (U.S.A.)
BELIZE
GUATEMALA
HONDURAS
EL SALVADOR
NICARAGUA
COSTA RICA
PANAMA
COLOMBIA
VENEZUELA
South America
Projection: Bonne
West from Greenwich
■ MÉXICO Capital Cities
CARTOGRAPHY BY PHILIP'S.
COPYRIGHT REED INTERNATIONAL BOOKS LTD

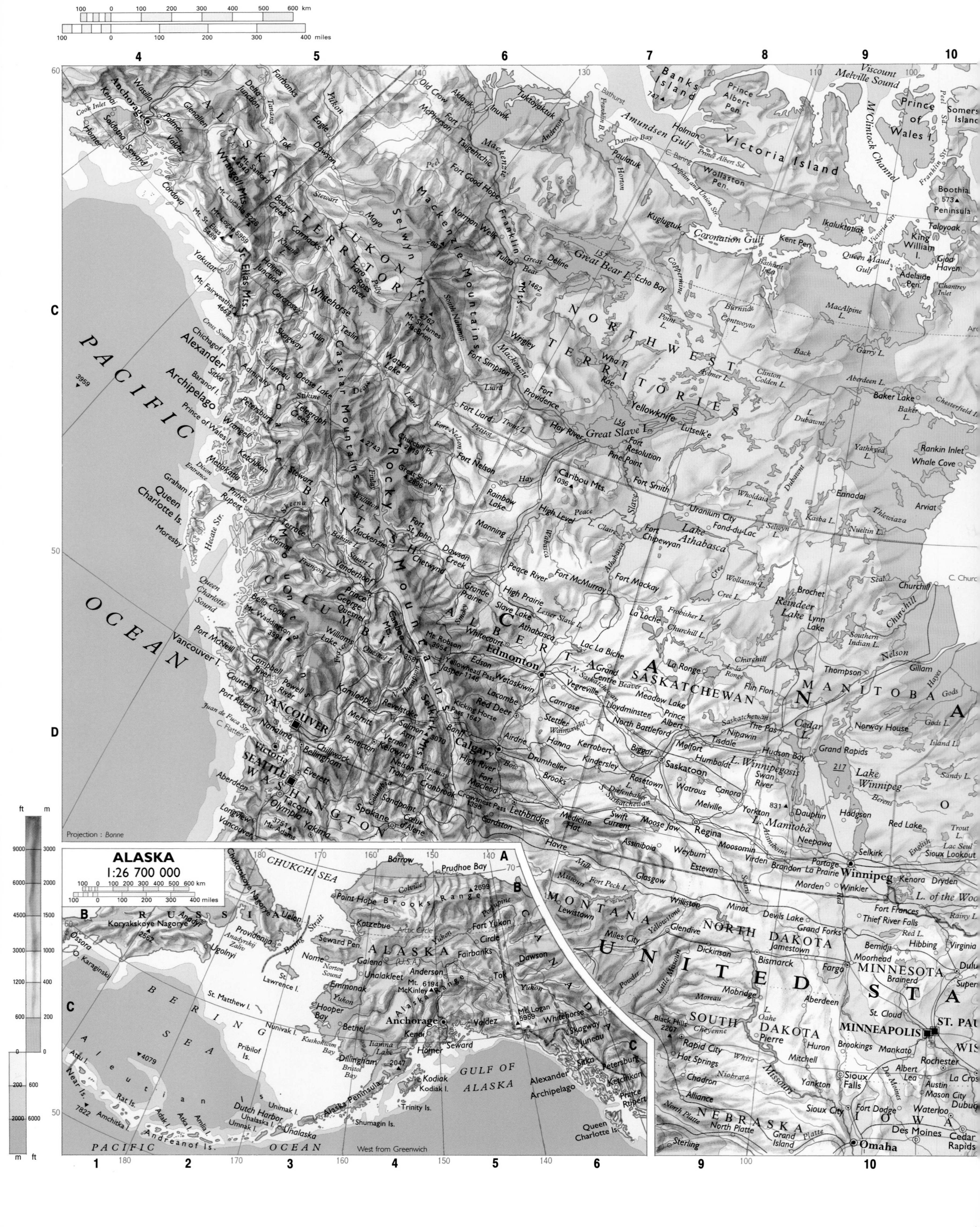
km 100 0 100 200 300 400 500 600
miles 100 0 100 200 300 400
4 5 6 7 8 9 10
C
D
PACIFIC OCEAN
ALASKA
YUKON TERRITORY
NORTHWEST TERRITORIES
BRITISH COLUMBIA
ALBERTA
SASKATCHEWAN
MANITOBA
CANADA
WASHINGTON
MONTANA
NORTH DAKOTA
SOUTH DAKOTA
NEBRASKA
IOWA
MINNESOTA
UNITED STATES
Anchorage
Fairbanks
Whitehorse
Dawson
Inuvik
Tuktoyaktuk
Yellowknife
Great Bear L.
Great Slave L.
Lake Athabasca
Victoria Island
Banks Island
Amundsen Gulf
Coronation Gulf
Viscount Melville Sound
Prince of Wales I.
Boothia Peninsula
King William I.
Mackenzie Mountains
Selwyn Mts.
Cassiar Mountains
Rocky Mountains
Coast Mountains
Columbia Mountains
Selkirk Mts.
St. Elias Mts.
Mt. Logan 5959
Mt. St. Elias 5489
Mt. Fairweather 4663
Mt. Robson 3954
Mt. Waddington 3994
Alexander Archipelago
Queen Charlotte Is.
Vancouver I.
Queen Charlotte Sound
Prince Rupert
Fort Nelson
Fort St. John
Dawson Creek
Prince George
Kamloops
VANCOUVER
Victoria
SEATTLE
Tacoma
Spokane
Edmonton
Calgary
Red Deer
Lethbridge
Medicine Hat
Saskatoon
Regina
Moose Jaw
Prince Albert
Lake Winnipeg
L. Winnipegosis
L. Manitoba
Winnipeg
Brandon
Reindeer Lake
Churchill
Rankin Inlet
Baker Lake
Fort McMurray
Fort Smith
Uranium City
Fort Chipewyan
Peace River
Grande Prairie
Fort Simpson
Hay River
Fort Providence
Norman Wells
Fort Good Hope
Bismarck
Fargo
MINNEAPOLIS
ST. PAUL
Omaha
Des Moines
Sioux Falls
Pierre
Minot
Projection : Bonne
ALASKA
1:26 700 000
km 100 0 100 200 300 400 500 600
miles 100 0 100 200 300 400
CHUKCHI SEA
BERING SEA
GULF OF ALASKA
PACIFIC OCEAN
RUSSIA
Brooks Range
Alaska Range
Barrow
Prudhoe Bay
Point Hope
Kotzebue
Nome
Fairbanks
Anchorage
Mt. McKinley 6194
Kodiak I.
Alaska Peninsula
Aleutian Is.
Unimak I.
Dutch Harbor
Pribilof Is.
St. Lawrence I.
Nunivak I.
St. Matthew I.
Juneau
Sitka
Ketchikan
Mt. Logan 5959
West from Greenwich
1 2 3 4 5 6 9 10
ft m
9000 3000
6000 2000
4500 1500
3000 1000
1200 400
600 200
0 0
200 600
2000 6000
m ft

11 12 13 14 15 16

B C D E

Devon I.
Lancaster Sound
Baffin Bay
2136
1890
Bylot I.
Arctic Bay
Borden Pen.
Eclipse Sd.
Pond Inlet
Brodeur Peninsula
C. Adair
Clyde River
C. Raper
Baffin Island
Home B.
Fury and Hecla Str.
Igloolik
Simpson Pen.
Pelly Bay
Committee B.
Sanirajak
Melville Peninsula
Foxe Basin
Prince Charles I.
Air Force I.
2591
Cumberland Peninsula
Broughton Island
C. Dyer
Pangnirtung
Hoare B.
Mercy C.
Cumberland Sd.
Nettilling L.
Rae Isthmus
Repulse Bay
NUNAVUT
C. Dorchester
Amadjuak L.
Foxe Pen.
Foxe Channel
Wager B.
Roes Welcome Sd.
Southampton I.
Sallig
Bell Pen.
Cape Dorset
Meta Incognita Peninsula
Iqaluit
Hall Peninsula
Kimmirut
Frobisher Bay
Resolution I.
Salisbury I.
Nottingham I.
Hudson Strait
Coats I.
Mansel I.
Ivujivik
Salluit
Kangiqsujuaq
Quaqtaq
Akpatok I.
C. Chidley
Péninsule d'Ungava
Puvirnituq
L. Payne
Arnaud
Kangirsuk
Ungava Bay
1652
Kangiqsualujjuaq
Hebron
Hudson Bay
Ottawa Is.
257
Kuujjuaq
Feuilles
Koksoak
George
Baleine
Nain
Inukjuak
Mélèzes
Caniapiscau
L. Minto
Sleeper Is.
King George Is.
Baker's Dozen Is.
Belcher Is.
L. à l'Eau Claire
Grande Baleine
Kuujjuarapik
L. Bienville
Schefferville
Petitsikapau L.
Smallwood Res.
Labrador
North West River
Happy Valley-Goose Bay
Churchill Falls
Churchill
Esker
Rés. de Caniapiscau
Kanaaupscow
La Grande
Labrador City
Fermont
L. Ashuanipi
Hopedale
C. Harrison
Rigolet
Cartwright
Port Hope Simpson
Belle Isle
C. Bauld
St. Anthony
Str. of Belle Isle
NEWFOUNDLAND
St-Augustin
Natashquan
Romaine
Moisie
QUÉBEC
Gagnon
1135
Rés. Manicouagan
Havre-St-Pierre
Sept-Îles
Port-Cartier
Î. d'Anticosti
Notre Dame B.
Baie Verte
Lewisporte
Gander
Bonavista
Deer Lake
Grand Falls
Trinity B.
Carbonear
St. John's
814
Corner Brook
Newfoundland
Stephenville
Channel-Port aux Basques
Marystown
Placentia B.
Placentia
C. Race
C. Henrietta Maria
Pte. Louis XIV
Peawanuck
Winisk
Severn
Chisasibi
James Bay
Big Trout L.
Attawapiskat
Akimiski I.
Wemindji
Eastmain
Charlton I.
Waskaganish
Rupert
L. Mistassini
L. Albanel
Péribonca
Manicouagan
Baie Comeau
Gulf of St. Lawrence
Cabot Str.
Fort Albany
Albany
ONTARIO
Moosonee
Nottaway
Harricana
Missinaibi
L. St. Joseph
Chibougamau
Matane
Gaspé
Pen. de Gaspé
Îs. de la Madeleine
ST.-PIERRE ET MIQUELON (Fr.)
North C.
Cape Breton I.
Glace Bay
Sydney
Port Hawkesbury
Rimouski
Campbellton
Bathurst
Chatham
PR. EDWARD I.
Summerside
Charlottetown
Northumberland Str.
Antigonish
New Glasgow
Truro
NOVA SCOTIA
Dartmouth
Halifax
Sable I. (Nova Scotia)
Bridgewater
Liverpool
Yarmouth
C. Sable
Digby
Kentville
Amherst
Moncton
Saint John
B. of Fundy
Fredericton
NEW BRUNSWICK
Edmundston
Rivière-du-Loup
Grand Falls
Woodstock
Bangor
MAINE
Augusta
Lewiston
Portland
Nakina
Kenogami
Matagami
L. Matagami
Dolbeau
L. St-Jean
Chicoutimi
Roberval
Jonquière
1190
Québec
Lévis
Thetford Mines
Hearst
Cochrane
Abitibi L.
Amos
Rés. Gouin
L. Nipigon
Geraldton
Kapuskasing
Oba
Mattagami
Timmins
Kirkland Lake
Rouyn-Noranda
Val-d'Or
La Tuque
Nipigon
Marathon
Thunder Bay
Chapleau
New Liskeard
Wawa
Lake Superior
Rés. Cabonga
Mont-Laurier
Shawinigan
Trois-Rivières
Joliette
St-Hyacinthe
Sherbrooke
Houghton
183
Sault Ste. Marie
Elliot Lake
Sudbury
Outaouais
MONTRÉAL
Granby
L. Champlain
Marquette
Ironwood
MICHIGAN
L. Nipissing
Parry Sound
North Bay
Pembroke
Hull
Ottawa
Cornwall
Montpelier
Burlington
VERMONT
NEW HAMPSHIRE
Concord
Manchester
Manistique
Manitoulin I.
Georgian Bay
Huntsville
Kingston
Escanaba
Menominee
Rhinelander
Petoskey
Traverse City
Lake Huron
Owen Sound
Barrie
Peterborough
Belleville
Oshawa
Wausau
WISCONSIN
Green Bay
Cadillac
Appleton
Sheboygan
TORONTO
Kitchener
Hamilton
L. Ontario
Syracuse
Rochester
Albany
Springfield
MASS.
BOSTON
C. Cod
Providence
R.I.
Lake Michigan
Saginaw
Grand Rapids
Flint
London
Niagara Falls
BUFFALO
NEW YORK
HARTFORD
CONN.
MILWAUKEE
Madison
Racine
Kenosha
Lansing
Sarnia
DETROIT
Windsor
174
L. Erie
Erie
Jamestown
Elmira
Binghamton
Scranton
Bridgeport
New Haven
NEW YORK
Rockford
CHICAGO
Gary
South Bend
Toledo
CLEVELAND
OHIO
INDIANA
ILLINOIS
PENNSYLVANIA
Newark
N.J.
Allentown
Trenton
GREENLAND (KALAALLIT NUNAAT) (Denmark)
Nunavik
Uummannaq
Ilulissat
Qasigiannguit
Qeqertarsuaq
Qeqertarsuaq
Kangerlussuaq
Sisimiut
Maniitsoq
2850
Nuuk
Kong Frederik VI's Kyst
Ammassalik
Qeqertarsuatsiaat
Paamiut
Arsuk
Qaqortoq
Alluitsup Paa
Nanortalik
Uummannarsuaq
Davis Strait
Labrador Sea
3809
ATLANTIC OCEAN
6309

90 80 70 60 50 40 30

West from Greenwich

11 12 13 14

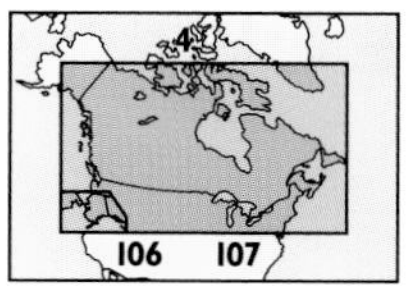

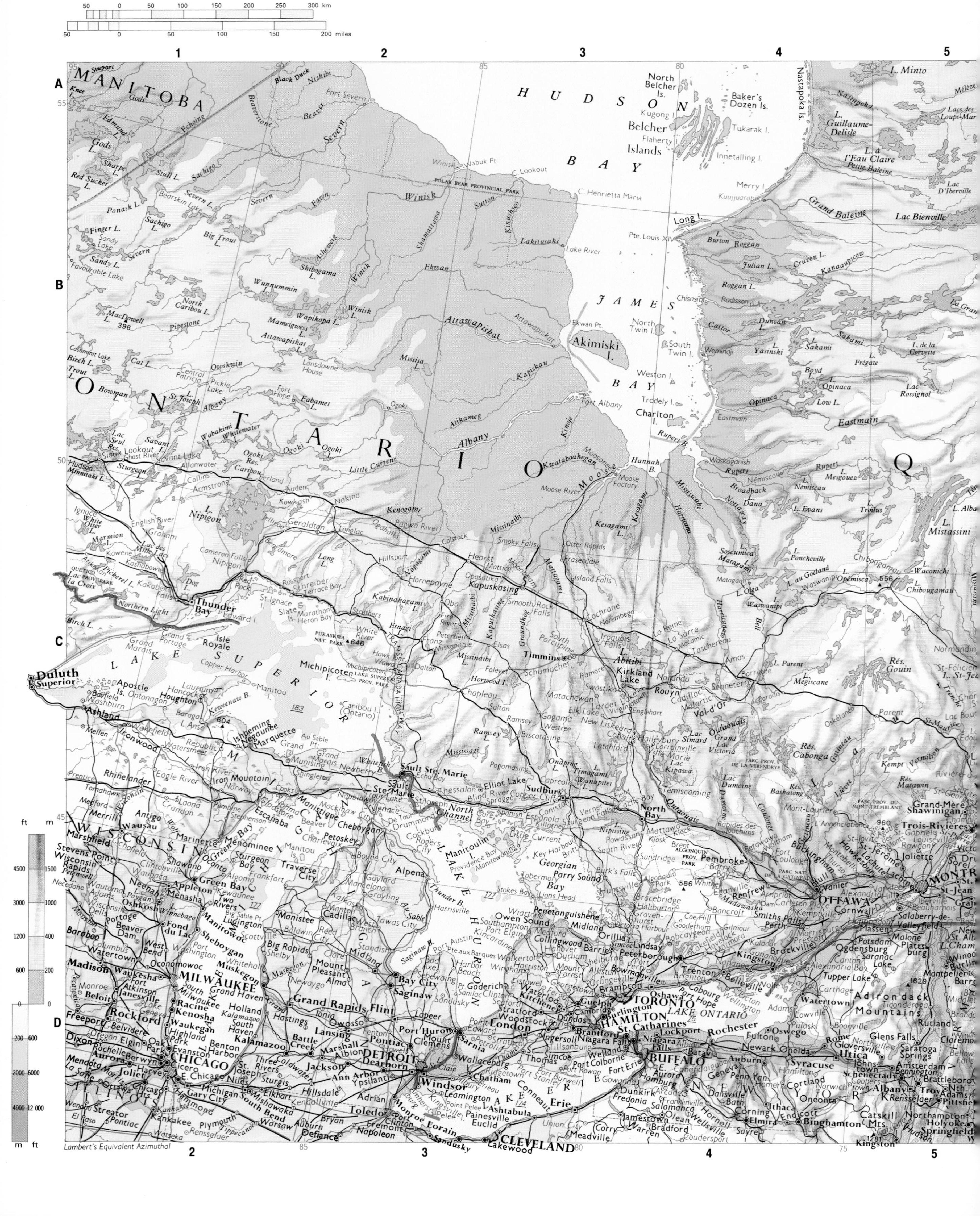

50 0 50 100 150 200 250 300 km
50 0 50 100 150 200 miles
1 2 3 4 5
A B C D
MANITOBA
ONTARIO
WISCONSIN
MICHIGAN
ILLINOIS
NEW YORK
HUDSON BAY
JAMES BAY
Belcher Islands
Akimiski I.
LAKE SUPERIOR
LAKE MICHIGAN
LAKE HURON
LAKE ERIE
LAKE ONTARIO
Fort Severn
Big Trout L.
Attawapiskat
Fort Albany
Moosonee
Kapuskasing
Timmins
Kirkland Lake
Rouyn
Val-d'Or
Chibougamau
Thunder Bay
Duluth
Superior
Sault Ste. Marie
Sudbury
North Bay
Elliot Lake
Marquette
Green Bay
Appleton
MILWAUKEE
CHICAGO
Madison
Rockford
Grand Rapids
Flint
Saginaw
Bay City
Lansing
Kalamazoo
DETROIT
Windsor
Toledo
CLEVELAND
London
Kitchener
Guelph
HAMILTON
TORONTO
St. Catharines
Niagara Falls
BUFFALO
Rochester
Syracuse
Utica
Albany
Binghamton
Erie
Kingston
OTTAWA
Peterborough
Barrie
Owen Sound
Pembroke
Trois-Rivières
Shawinigan
Joliette
Cornwall
Watertown
Adirondack Mountains
Lac Mistassini
Lac Bienville
Lambert's Equivalent Azimuthal
ft m
4500 1500
3000 1000
1200 400
600 200
0 0
200 600
2000 6000
4000 12 000
m ft

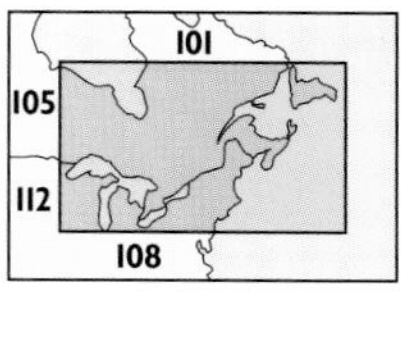

101
105
112
108

6
7
8
9
A
B
C
D
70
65
60
55
50
45
West from Greenwich
N E W F O U N D L A N D
Q U E B E C
Labrador
Labrador City
Wabush
Schefferville
Churchill Falls
Smallwood Res.
Happy Valley-Goose Bay
North-West River
Goose
L. Melville
Mealy Mts.
1128
Hamilton Inlet
Rigolet
Cartwright
Sandwich B.
Table B.
Island of Ponds
Square Islands
Alexis
St. Lewis
Mary's Harbour
Battle Harbour
Red Bay
Belle I.
Str. of Belle Isle
Hopedale
Nain
Paul I.
South Aulatsivik I.
High I.
Voiseys B.
Tunungayualok I.
Davis Inlet
Nunaksaluk I.
Kaipokok B.
Makkovik
Aillik
Adlavik Is.
C. Harrison
Holton
Indian Harbour
Groswater B.
Big Bay
Harp L.
Kogaluk
Mistastin L.
Fraser
Whale
George
Erlandson L.
Fort McKenzie
L. Nachicapau
Chakonipau L.
Otelnuk L.
Kaniapiskau
Wheeler
L. Champdoré
L. Tudor
610
Sérigny
Sandy
L. Wakuach
Whitegull L.
L. de la Hutte Sauvage
Attikamagen L.
Petitsikapau L.
Menihek Lakes
Woods L.
Kanairiktok
Naskaupi
Seal L.
Nipishish L.
Grand L.
Kaniapiskau Lake
L. Neret
L. Bermen
Nitchequon
Shabogamo L.
Opiskotish L.
Opiscoteo L.
L. Naococane
Lac Joseph
Ossokmanuan L.
Winokapau L.
Atikonak L.
Churchill
Minipi L.
Little Mecatina
Eagle
Paradise
St. Paul
Burnt L.
1128
Ashuanipi L.
Petit Lac Manicouagan
Moisie
Gagnon
Rés. Manicouagan
Ste-Marguerite
L. Plétipi
Péribonca
Nipissis
West Magpie
Magpie L.
St-Jean
Romaine
Natashquan
Nabisipi
Aguanus
Olomane
L. Musquaro
1048
L. Manitou
Lac Allard
Havre-St-Pierre
Sheldrake
Mingan
Aguanish
Natashquan
Kegaska
Gethsémani
Étamamu
Harrington Harbour
I. du Petit-Mécatina
St-Augustin
St-Augustin-Saguenay
Bradore Bay
Lourdes-de-Blanc-Sablon
L'Anse-au-Loup
Forteau
Outer I.
Port Saunders
Daniel's Harbour
L. Manouane
Outardes
Manicouagan
Betsiamites
L. Péribonca
Manouane
Rés. Pipmuacan
Walker L.
Clarke City
Sept-Îles
Port-Cartier
Rivière-Pentecôte
Godbout
Baie-Trinité
Pte. des Monts
Baie-Comeau
Hauterive
Betsiamites
Forestville
Moisie
Dét. de Jacques-Cartier
Î. d'Anticosti
Jupiter
Pte. Ouest
Port-Menier
Heath Pt.
Dét. d'Honguedo
Pte. Sud
Sud Ouest
Grande-Vallée
Petit-Cap
Rivière-au-Renard
C. de Gaspé
Gaspé
Douglastown
Mont-Louis
Ste-Anne-des-Monts
Cap-Chat
1268
Mt. Jacques-Cartier
PARC PROV. DE LA GASPÉSIE
Mts. Chic-Chocs
Pén. de Gaspé
Matane
Mont-Joli
Sayabec
Amqui
Causapscal
Matapédia
Bonaventure
Chandler
Percé
Grande-Rivière
Paspébiac
Miscou I.
Lamèque
Shippegan
Tracadie
GULF OF ST. LAWRENCE
572
St. Lawrence
Rimouski
Bic
Trois-Pistoles
Rivière-du-Loup
Cabano
Dalhousie
Campbellton
Chaleur Bay
Belledune
Atholville
Bathurst
Kedgwick
St. Arthur
Heath Steele
Neguac
Miramichi B.
Edmundston
St. Leonard
Grand Falls
819
Ft. Kent
Van Buren
Plaster Rock
NEW BRUNSWICK
Newcastle
Chatham
Collette
Richibucto
Caribou
Presque Isle
Houlton
Hartland
Stanley
Woodstock
Fredericton
Moncton
Shediac
Buctouche
Notre Dame
Chipman
Minto
Grand L.
Havelock
Petitcodiac
Sussex
Saint John
Bay of Fundy
St. Martins
Oromocto
Gagetown
St. George
St. Stephen
Calais
Eastport
Grand Manan I.
PRINCE EDWARD ISLAND
Summerside
Kensington
Charlottetown
Alberton
Tignish
North Pt.
East Pt.
Souris
Georgetown
Murray Hr.
Montague
Borden
Cape Tormentine
Northumberland Str.
Îs. de la Madeleine (Quebec)
Fatima
Cap-aux-Meules
Grande-Entrée
Havre-Aubert
Î. Brion
Cabot Strait
St. Paul I.
C. North
Pleasant Bay
Chéticamp
CAPE BRETON NAT. PARK
532
Ingonish
St. Anns B.
Sydney Mines
New Waterford
Glace Bay
N. Sydney
Sydney
Cape Breton Island
Louisbourg
Bras d'Or L.
Fourchu
St. Peters
Inverness
Port Hood
Hawkesbury
Antigonish
Pictou
New Glasgow
Stellarton
Amherst
Springhill
Parrsboro
Minas Basin
Truro
Stewiacke
Chignecto B.
Windsor
Kentville
Middleton
Bridgetown
Annapolis Royal
Digby
Weymouth
Dartmouth
Halifax
Upper Musquodoboit
Musquodoboit Hr.
Sheet Hr.
Sherbrooke
Guysborough
Canso
Chedabucto B.
L. Madame
Mahone Bay
Lunenburg
Bridgewater
Liverpool
Port Mouton
Rossignol L.
Shelburne
Lockeport
Yarmouth
Wedgeport
Clark's Harbour
C. Sable
St. Mary's B.
NOVA SCOTIA
Sable I. (Nova Scotia)
ATLANTIC OCEAN
NEWFOUNDLAND
Long Range Mts.
GROS MORNE NAT. PARK
Trout River
Deer Lake
Bay of Islands
Corner Brook
814
Cox's Cove
Howley
Grand L.
Red Indian L.
Buchans
Badger
Grand Falls
Bishop's Falls
Windsor
Botwood
Lewisporte
Gander
Glenwood
Glovertown
Dark Cove
Gambo
Springdale
South Brook
Baie Verte
La Scie
Notre Dame B.
Twillingate
Fogo
Fogo I.
Carmanville
C. Freels
Wesleyville
Bonavista B.
C. Bonavista
Bonavista
Catalina
Trinity
Trinity B.
Port Blandford
Clarenville
381
Heart's Content
Carbonear
Harbour Grace
Spaniard's Bay
Conception B.
Wabana
Torbay
St. John's
Mt. Pearl
Bay Bulls
Holyrood
Avalon Peninsula
Ferryland
C. Race
Trepassey
C. Pine
St. Mary's B.
St. Bride's
Argentia
Placentia
Placentia B.
St. Lawrence
Burin
Marystown
Fortune B.
Grand Bank
Harbour Breton
Belleoram
Terrenceville
St. Alban's
Grey Res.
Salmon Res.
Victoria Res.
White Bear Res.
Grey
Burgeo
Ramea
François
Rose Blanche
Isle aux Morts
Channel-Port aux Basques
C. Ray
St. Andrew's
South Branch
Long Range Mts.
St. David's
St. George's B.
St. George's
C. St. George
Stephenville
Port au Port B.
Long Pt.
Miquelon
Langlade
St. Pierre
SAINT-PIERRE ET MIQUELON (Fr.)
Seal Cove
Sop's Arm
Deep
Great Harbour Deep
White B.
Horse Is.
C. St. John
Roddickton
Englee
Conche
Bell I.
Groais I.
Hare B.
St. Anthony
Flower's Cove
St. Lunaire-Griquet
Alma
Arvida
Chicoutimi
Jonquière
Saguenay
Port Alfred
Grande Baie
Tadoussac
Bergeronnes
Grandes-Bergeronnes
Petit-Saguenay
St-Siméon
La Malbaie
Baie-St-Paul
PARC PROV. DES LAURENTIDES
1190
Ste-Anne-de-Beaupré
Île d'Orléans
St-Pacôme
St-Pascal
St-Jean-Port-Joli
Montmagny
Lauzon
Lévis
Armagh
Pamphile
St-Joseph
Dégelis
Notre-Dame-du-Lac
Allagash
St. John
Ashland
Eagle L.
Island Falls
Chesuncook L.
Patten
1606
Millinocket
Moosehead L.
Mattawamkeag
Greenville
Lincoln
Danforth
Guilford
Dover-Foxcroft
Bingham
Skowhegan
Old Town
Brewer
Bangor
Ellsworth
Machias
Jonesport
Bar Harbor
Mt. Desert I.
Belfast
Camden
Rockland
Waterville
Augusta
Mooselookmeguntic L.
Rumford
Bethel
Berlin
Auburn
Lewiston
Bath
Brunswick
Portland
Sebago L.
Saco
Biddeford
Sanford
Laconia
Conway
Rochester
Concord
Dover
Portsmouth
Manchester
Nashua
Haverhill
Lawrence
Lowell
Gloucester
C. Ann
Lynn
Waltham
BOSTON
Brockton
St. Johnsbury
1917
Mt. Washington
Island Pond
Coaticook
Magog
Sherbrooke
Lac-Mégantic
Asbestos
Thetford Mines
Plessisville
Beauceville
St-Georges
Ste-Marie
Drummondville
Victoriaville
MAINE

50 0 50 100 150 200 250 300 km
50 0 50 100 150 200 miles
1 2 3 4 5 6
A B C D
YUKON TERRITORY
NORTH WEST TERRITORIES
GREAT SLAVE LAKE
BRITISH COLUMBIA
ALBERTA
ALASKA
WASHINGTON
IDAHO
PACIFIC OCEAN
QUEEN CHARLOTTE ISLANDS
VANCOUVER ISLAND
ALEXANDER ARCH.
Rocky Mountains
Coast Mountains
Skeena Mountains
Cassiar Mountains
Cariboo Mountains
Selkirk Mountains
Birch Mountains
Whitehorse
Yellowknife
Prince Rupert
Prince George
Dawson Creek
Grande Prairie
EDMONTON
Red Deer
Calgary
Lethbridge
Kamloops
Kelowna
Penticton
VANCOUVER
Victoria
Bellingham
SEATTLE
Juneau
WOOD BUFFALO NATIONAL PARK
JASPER NATIONAL PARK
ft m
12 000 4000
9000 3000
6000 2000
4500 1500
3000 1000
1200 400
600 200
0 0
200 600
2000 6000
m ft
Projection: Lambert's Equivalent Azimuthal
135 130 125 120 115
West from Greenwich
55 50
3 4 5 6

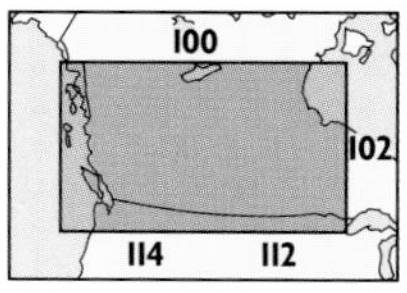
100
102
114
112

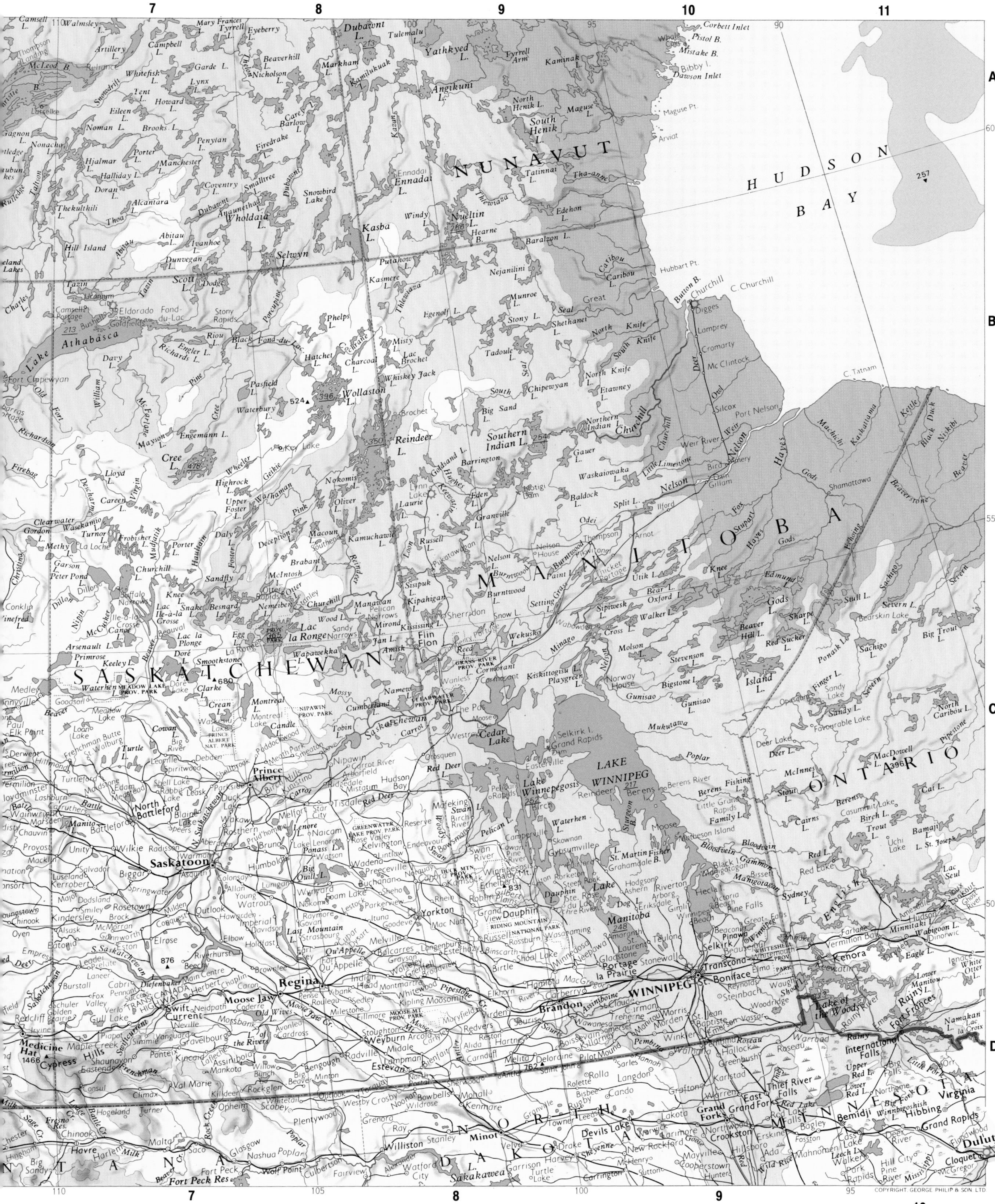
7
8
9
10
11
A
B
C
D
NUNAVUT
HUDSON BAY
MANITOBA
SASKATCHEWAN
ONTARIO
NORTH DAKOTA
MINNESOTA
Lake Athabasca
Wollaston L.
Reindeer L.
Southern Indian L.
Dubawnt L.
Nueltin L.
Yathkyed L.
Kasba L.
Lac la Ronge
Cedar Lake
Lake Winnipegosis
LAKE WINNIPEG
Lake Manitoba
Lake of the Woods
Churchill
C. Churchill
Nelson
Hayes
Saskatchewan
Flin Flon
The Pas
Thompson
Prince Albert
North Battleford
Saskatoon
Regina
Moose Jaw
Swift Current
Medicine Hat
Cypress Hills
Yorkton
Brandon
Portage la Prairie
WINNIPEG
St. Boniface
Kenora
Fort Frances
International Falls
Minot
Grand Forks
Devils Lake
Bemidji
Duluth
Weyburn
Estevan
Dauphin
Arviat
Hubbart Pt.
C. Tatnam
Port Nelson
Gillam
Gods L.
Island L.
Red Lake
Sakakawea
Fort Peck Res.
Havre
Williston
COPYRIGHT GEORGE PHILIP & SON LTD
110
105
100
95
90
60
55
50

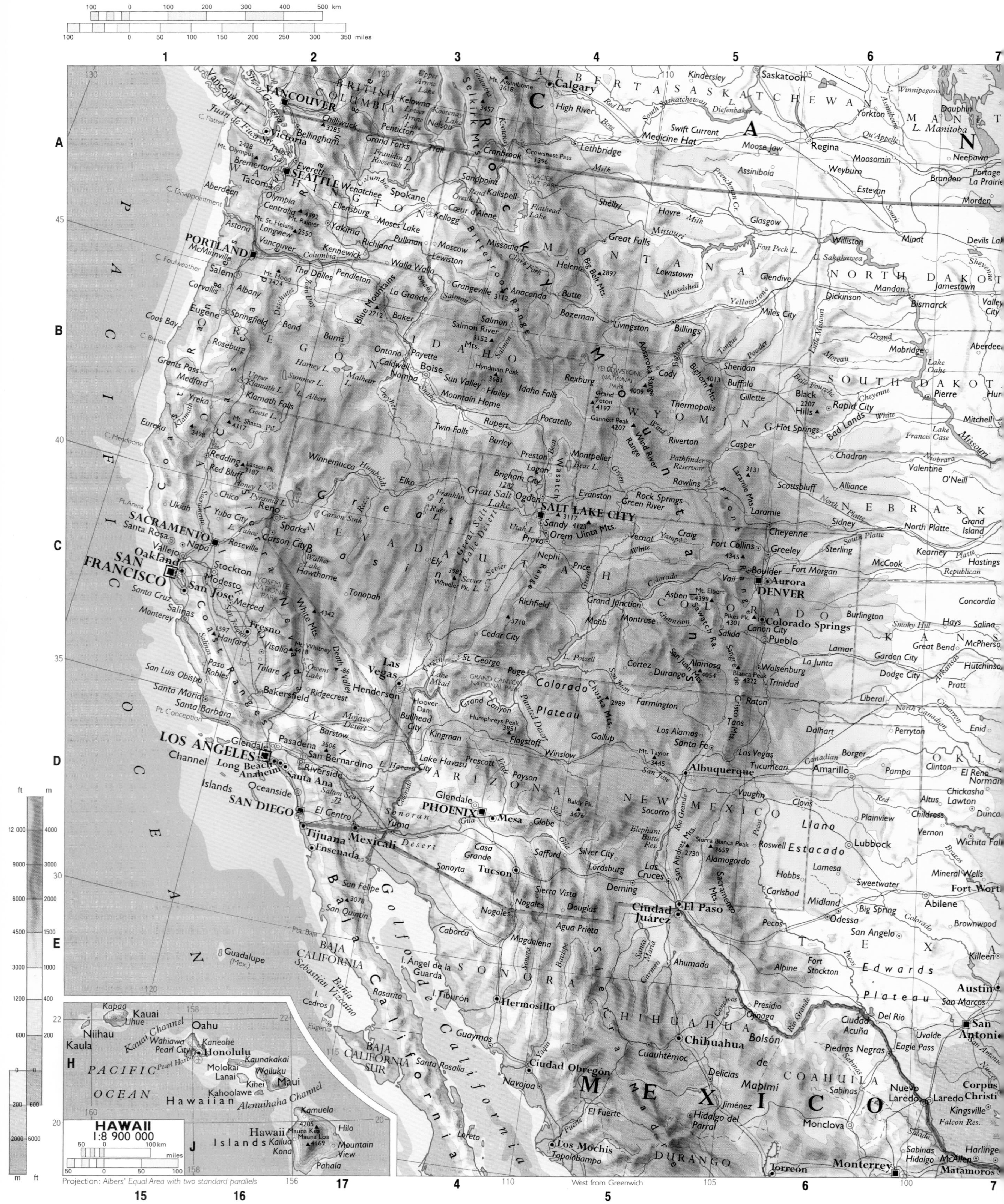

100 0 100 200 300 400 500 km
100 0 50 100 150 200 250 300 350 miles
BRITISH COLUMBIA
ALBERTA
SASKATCHEWAN
MANITOBA
CANADA
VANCOUVER
Vancouver I.
Victoria
Juan de Fuca Str.
Str. of Georgia
Chilliwack
Bellingham
Kelowna
Penticton
Nelson
Grand Forks
Trail
Calgary
High River
Red Deer
Lethbridge
Medicine Hat
Swift Current
Saskatoon
Kindersley
Moose Jaw
Regina
Yorkton
Dauphin
L. Manitoba
L. Winnipegosis
Brandon
Portage La Prairie
Moosomin
Weyburn
Estevan
Assiniboia
Morden
Neepawa
Mt. Assiniboine 3618
Crowsnest Pass 1396
Cranbrook
Selkirk Mts.
Rocky Mountains
GLACIER NAT. PARK
Mt. Olympus 2428
Bremerton
Everett
SEATTLE
Tacoma
Olympia
Centralia
Aberdeen
C. Disappointment
Mt. Rainier 4392
Mt. St. Helens 2550
Longview
Astoria
Yakima
Ellensburg
Wenatchee
Spokane
Moses Lake
Richland
Kennewick
Pullman
Walla Walla
Sandpoint
Kalispell
Coeur d'Alene
Kellogg
Moscow
Lewiston
Flathead Lake
Missoula
Bitterroot Range
Shelby
Havre
Great Falls
Glasgow
Fort Peck L.
Williston
Minot
Devils Lake
WASHINGTON
PORTLAND
McMinnville
Vancouver
The Dalles
Mt. Hood 3424
Salem
Corvallis
Albany
Eugene
Springfield
Coos Bay
Bend
Pendleton
La Grande
Baker
Blue Mountains 2712
Grangeville
Anaconda
Helena
Butte
Bozeman
Big Belt Mts. 2897
Lewistown
Glendive
MONTANA
Dickinson
Bismarck
Mandan
Jamestown
Valley City
NORTH DAKOTA
OREGON
Roseburg
Grants Pass
Medford
C. Blanco
Burns
Ontario
Caldwell
Payette
Boise
Nampa
Sun Valley
Mountain Home
Hailey
Hyndman Peak 3681
Salmon River Mts. 3152
Salmon
IDAHO
Idaho Falls
Rexburg
Livingston
Billings
Miles City
Sheridan
Buffalo
Gillette
Cody
Absaroka Range
Bighorn Mts. 4013
YELLOWSTONE NATIONAL PARK
Grand Teton 4197
Gannett Peak 4207
Wind River Range
Thermopolis
Riverton
Casper
WYOMING
Mobridge
Aberdeen
Pierre
SOUTH DAKOTA
Black Hills 2207
Rapid City
Bad Lands
Hot Springs
Mitchell
Upper Klamath L.
Klamath Falls
Goose L.
Yreka
Mt. Shasta 4317
Eureka
C. Mendocino
Redding
Lassen Pk. 3187
Red Bluff
Chico
Ukiah
Yuba City
Honey L.
Pyramid L.
Reno
Sparks
Carson City
L. Tahoe
Winnemucca
Elko
Great Basin
Great Salt Lake
Great Salt Lake Desert
Brigham City
Logan
Ogden
SALT LAKE CITY
Sandy
Orem
Provo
Uinta Mts. 4123
Pocatello
Twin Falls
Rupert
Burley
Preston
Montpelier
Bear L.
Evanston
Rock Springs
Green River
Rawlins
Pathfinder Reservoir
Laramie Mts.
Laramie
Cheyenne
Scottsbluff
Alliance
Chadron
Valentine
O'Neill
NEBRASKA
Sidney
North Platte
Grand Island
SACRAMENTO
Santa Rosa
Vallejo
Napa
Oakland
SAN FRANCISCO
Stockton
Modesto
San Jose
Santa Cruz
Monterey
Salinas
Merced
Fresno
YOSEMITE NATIONAL PARK
Hanford
Visalia
Tulare
Mt. Whitney 4418
Walker Lake
Hawthorne
Tonopah
White Mts. 4342
Ely
Wheeler Pk. 3982
Nephi
Price
Richfield
UTAH
Vernal
Craig
Fort Collins
Greeley
Boulder
Aurora
DENVER
Sterling
Fort Morgan
Grand Junction
Aspen
Mt. Elbert 4399
Vail
Montrose
Gunnison
Pikes Pk. 4301
Colorado Springs
Canon City
Pueblo
Salida
COLORADO
Moab
Cortez
Durango
San Juan Mts. 4054
Alamosa
Blanca Peak 4372
Walsenburg
Trinidad
La Junta
Lamar
Raton
Kearney
McCook
Hastings
Concordia
Burlington
Hays
Salina
Great Bend
Garden City
Dodge City
Hutchinson
Pratt
Liberal
KANSAS
San Luis Obispo
Paso Robles
Bakersfield
Santa Maria
Santa Barbara
Pt. Conception
Ridgecrest
Death Valley
Owens Lake
Las Vegas
Henderson
St. George
Cedar City
Lake Mead
Hoover Dam
Bullhead City
Kingman
Page
L. Powell
GRAND CANYON NATIONAL PARK
Colorado Plateau
Humphreys Peak 3851
Flagstaff
Painted Desert
Chuska Mts. 2989
Farmington
Gallup
Winslow
Los Alamos
Santa Fe
Taos
Las Vegas
Mt. Taylor 3445
Albuquerque
Tucumcari
Amarillo
Dalhart
Borger
Pampa
Perryton
Clinton
El Reno
Chickasha
Lawton
Norman
Mojave Desert
Barstow
Glendale
Pasadena
LOS ANGELES
Long Beach
Anaheim
Santa Ana
San Bernardino
Riverside
Oceanside
Channel Islands
SAN DIEGO
El Centro
Salton Sea -72
Lake Havasu City
Prescott
Payson
ARIZONA
Glendale
PHOENIX
Mesa
Globe
Yuma
Sonoran Desert
Tijuana
Mexicali
Ensenada
Casa Grande
Tucson
Sonoyta
Safford
Baldy Pk. 3476
Socorro
Elephant Butte Res.
NEW MEXICO
Silver City
Lordsburg
Deming
Las Cruces
San Andres Mts. 2730
Sierra Blanca Peak 3659
Alamogordo
Sacramento Mts.
Roswell
Clovis
Vaughn
Hobbs
Carlsbad
Llano Estacado
Plainview
Lubbock
Lamesa
Sweetwater
Midland
Odessa
Big Spring
Abilene
Mineral Wells
Fort Worth
Sierra Vista
Nogales
Douglas
Agua Prieta
Ciudad Juárez
El Paso
Pecos
San Angelo
Brownwood
Killeen
Fort Stockton
Alpine
Edwards Plateau
Austin
San Marcos
Del Rio
Ciudad Acuña
Uvalde
Eagle Pass
San Antonio
TEXAS
PACIFIC OCEAN
San Felipe
3078
San Quintin
Pta. Baja
BAJA CALIFORNIA
Guadalupe (Mex.)
Bahía Sebastián Vizcaíno
I. Cedros
Rosarito
I. Ángel de la Guarda
I. Tiburón
Golfo de California
Caborca
Magdalena
Hermosillo
SONORA
Guaymas
BAJA CALIFORNIA SUR
Santa Rosalía
Ciudad Obregón
Navojoa
Loreto
Los Mochis
Topolobampo
El Fuerte
Sierra Madre
CHIHUAHUA
Chihuahua
Cuauhtémoc
Delicias
Ojinaga
Presidio
Bolsón de Mapimí
Jiménez
Hidalgo del Parral
DURANGO
Torreón
COAHUILA
Sabinas
Piedras Negras
Monclova
Nuevo Laredo
Laredo
Kingsville
Corpus Christi
Falcon Res.
Monterrey
Sabinas Hidalgo
McAllen
Harlingen
Matamoros
MEXICO
HAWAII 1:8 900 000
50 0 100 km
50 0 50 100 miles
Kauai
Kapaa
Lihue
Niihau
Kaula
Kauai Channel
Oahu
Wahiawa
Kaneohe
Pearl City
Honolulu
Pearl Harbor
Molokai
Kaunakakai
Lanai
Wailuku
Kihei
Maui
Kahoolawe
Alenuihaha Channel
Hawaiian Islands
Kamuela
Hawaii
Mauna Kea 4205
Mauna Loa 4169
Hilo
Kailua Kona
Mountain View
Pahala
PACIFIC OCEAN
ft m
12 000 4000
9000 3000
6000 2000
4500 1500
3000 1000
1200 400
600 200
0 0
200 600
2000 6000
m ft
Projection: Albers' Equal Area with two standard parallels
West from Greenwich

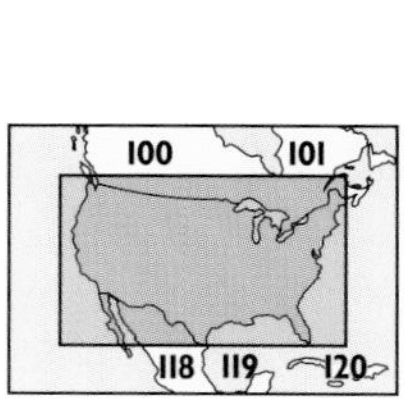

100
101
118
119
120

8
9
10
11
12
13
A
B
C
D
E
F
C A N A D A
O N T A R I O
Q U E B E C
Lake Winnipeg
Winnipeg
Berens
Albany
Trout L.
L. St. Joseph
English
L. Seul
Sioux Lookout
Nakina
Kenogami
Missinaibi
Moosonee
Moose
Abitibi
Mattagami
Hearst
Geraldton
Lake Nipigon
Nipigon
Marathon
Kenora
Dryden
Lake of the Woods
Rainy L.
Fort Frances
International Falls
Thunder Bay
I. Royale
I. St. Ignace
Michipicoten I.
Wawa
Lake Superior
Whitefish Bay
Keweenaw Bay
Apostle Is.
Thief River Falls
Grand Forks
Red Lake
Bemidji
Hibbing
Virginia
Ely
Two Harbors
Houghton
Leech L.
Duluth
Superior
Moorhead
Fargo
MINNESOTA
Ishpeming
Marquette
Sault Ste. Marie
Ashland
Ironwood
Iron Mountain
Manistique
Escanaba
Brainerd
Mille Lacs L.
Fergus Falls
Mississippi
Rice Lake
Rhinelander
St. Cloud
Big Stone Lake
Coon Rapids
MINNEAPOLIS
ST. PAUL
Willmar
Watertown
Merrill
Wausau
Menominee
Stevens Point
Eau Claire
Red Wing
Green Bay
Appleton
Manitowoc
Oshkosh
Sheboygan
Winona
WISCONSIN
La Crosse
Brookings
Minnesota
Owatonna
Mankato
Rochester
Austin
Madison
Portage
Sioux Falls
Worthington
Albert Lea
Mason City
Des Moines
Cedar
Charles City
MILWAUKEE
Janesville
Racine
Kenosha
Spencer
Cherokee
Fort Dodge
Waterloo
Dubuque
Cedar Rapids
Sioux City
Big Sioux
IOWA
Rockford
Clinton
Elgin
CHICAGO
Norfolk
Ames
Iowa City
Aurora
Joliet
Gary
Davenport
Rock Island
Galesburg
Kankakee
Columbus
Omaha
Lincoln
Council Bluffs
Ottumwa
Red Oak
Creston
Burlington
Peoria
Bloomington
Champaign
Springfield
Illinois
Decatur
Maryville
Kirksville
Quincy
Hannibal
Beatrice
St. Joseph
Chillicothe
ILLINOIS
INDIANA
Manhattan
Leavenworth
Topeka
Kansas
KANSAS CITY
Lawrence
Jefferson City
Missouri
Columbia
ST. LOUIS
East St. Louis
Alton
Effingham
Mattoon
Sedalia
MISSOURI
L. of the Ozarks
Rolla
Emporia
Newton
Wichita
Fort Scott
Nevada
Lebanon
Pittsburg
Springfield
Parsons
Arkansas City
Joplin
Bartlesville
Ponca City
Tulsa
Ozark Plateau
West Plains
Poplar Bluff
Cape Girardeau
Carbondale
Paragould
White
Fayetteville
Boston Mts.
Muskogee
Jonesboro
Blytheville
Dyersburg
Newport
Russellville
Conway
Oklahoma City
Shawnee
Fort Smith
McAlester
ARKANSAS
Ouachita Mts.
Little Rock
Arkansas
Stuttgart
Hot Springs
Ardmore
Durant
Paris
Hope
Pine Bluff
Clarksdale
Cleveland
Greenwood
Greenville
Sherman
Texarkana
Camden
El Dorado
Ouachita
Denton
DALLAS
Arlington
Marshall
Longview
Tyler
Shreveport
Monroe
Vicksburg
Jackson
Yazoo City
MISSISSIPPI
Yazoo
Waco
Corsicana
Palestine
Toledo Bend Res.
Nacogdoches
Natchez
Natchitoches
Sabine
Red
Alexandria
Lufkin
Trinity
De Ridder
Temple
Huntsville
LOUISIANA
McComb
Bogalusa
Bryan
Brazos
Lake Charles
Baton Rouge
Beaumont
Lafayette
New Iberia
Port Arthur
HOUSTON
Pasadena
Galveston
Houma
Morgan City
Atchafalaya B.
Marsh I.
NEW ORLEANS
Breton Sd.
Mississippi River Delta
L. Pontchartrain
Gulfport
Biloxi
Mobile
Hattiesburg
Laurel
Meridian
Victoria
Freeport
Port Lavaca
Matagorda I.
Aransas Pass
Padre I.
Laguna Madre
Brownsville
Rio Grande
GULF OF MEXICO
95
90
85
80
Memphis
Jackson
Corinth
Tupelo
Florence
Huntsville
Decatur
Columbus
Tuscaloosa
Birmingham
Gadsden
Anniston
ALABAMA
Demopolis
Selma
Montgomery
Auburn
Tombigbee
Alabama
Greenville
Troy
Andalusia
Dothan
Pensacola
Panama City
C. San Blas
Apalachicola
Apalachee B.
Chattahoochee
Tallahassee
Thomasville
Flint
Albany
Tifton
Valdosta
Lake City
Waycross
Douglas
Cordele
Dublin
Columbus
Macon
La Grange
GEORGIA
Statesboro
Savannah
Altamaha
Brunswick
St. Johns
Jacksonville
St. Augustine
Gainesville
Ocala
L. George
Daytona Beach
Deltona
C. Canaveral
Orlando
Lakeland
Melbourne
Palm Bay
Fort Pierce
TAMPA
Clearwater
St. Petersburg
Tampa B.
Sarasota
L. Okeechobee
West Palm Beach
Fort Lauderdale
Fort Myers
Charlotte Harbor
Cape Coral
Naples
The Everglades
MIAMI
C. Sable
Florida Bay
Florida Keys
Key West
Straits of Florida
FLORIDA
Grand Bahama I.
Freeport
Little Abaco I.
Great Abaco I.
N.E. Providence Channel
N.W. Providence Channel
BAHAMAS
Nassau
New Providence I.
Eleuthera I.
Cat I.
Exuma Sound
Andros I.
Great Exuma I.
Long I.
ATLANTIC OCEAN
ATLANTA
Athens
Roswell
Gainesville
Rome
Augusta
Savannah
Charleston
Georgetown
C. Romain
Orangeburg
SOUTH CAROLINA
Columbia
Sumter
Florence
Myrtle Beach
Long Bay
Anderson
Greenville
Spartanburg
Rock Hill
CHARLOTTE
NORTH CAROLINA
Fayetteville
Cape Fear
C. Fear
Wilmington
Onslow Bay
Jacksonville
New Bern
Goldsboro
Raleigh
Durham
Greensboro
Winston-Salem
Rocky Mount
Greenville
Pamlico Sd.
Albemarle Sd.
C. Hatteras
Hickory
Asheville
Knoxville
Chattanooga
Athens
Nashville
Murfreesboro
Clarksville
TENNESSEE
Cumberland Plateau
Appalachian Mts.
Kingsport
Johnson City
Oak Ridge
Middlesboro
Paducah
Mayfield
Hopkinsville
Bowling Green
Owensboro
Evansville
Henderson
Mount Vernon
Marion
KENTUCKY
Louisville
Frankfort
Lexington
Richmond
Danville
Somerset
Hazard
Bluefield
Beckley
Charleston
Huntington
Portsmouth
Parkersburg
WEST VIRGINIA
Clarksburg
Morgantown
Elkins
Harrisonburg
Charlottesville
Lynchburg
Roanoke
Radford
Pulaski
Danville
Richmond
Petersburg
Norfolk
Virginia Beach
Newport News
C. Charles
Elizabeth City
Chesapeake Bay
Potomac
WASHINGTON D.C.
Annapolis
BALTIMORE
Wilmington
Dover
Salisbury
Delaware B.
C. May
Atlantic City
PHILADELPHIA
Trenton
NEW JERSEY
Lancaster
Reading
Allentown
Harrisburg
Altoona
Johnstown
PITTSBURGH
Cumberland
Frederick
Wheeling
Zanesville
Canton
Akron
Youngstown
CLEVELAND
Mansfield
Marion
Lima
Findlay
Fort Wayne
Sandusky
Toledo
COLUMBUS
Dayton
Richmond
Muncie
Kokomo
Marion
Lafayette
Danville
INDIANAPOLIS
Terre Haute
Bloomington
Columbus
Vincennes
Maysville
CINCINNATI
OHIO
South Bend
Elkhart
Kalamazoo
Jackson
Ann Arbor
Battle Creek
Grand Rapids
Lansing
Muskegon
Saginaw
Midland
Bay City
Flint
Port Huron
DETROIT
Windsor
Lake Erie
Erie
Ashtabula
Lake Michigan
MICHIGAN
Manistee
Ludington
Cadillac
Traverse City
Petoskey
Alpena
Lake Huron
Saginaw Bay
Georgian Bay
Manitoulin I.
North Channel
Parry Sound
Owen Sound
Barrie
London
Kitchener
TORONTO
Hamilton
Niagara Falls
BUFFALO
Rochester
Lake Ontario
Oshawa
Peterborough
Kingston
Picton
Orillia
Huntsville
Sudbury
L. Nipissing
North Bay
Pembroke
Ottawa
Hull
Cornwall
MONTRÉAL
Ogdensburg
Watertown
Oswego
Syracuse
Utica
Schenectady
Albany
Troy
Ithaca
Binghamton
Elmira
Jamestown
Bradford
Warren
Oil City
Williamsport
Scranton
Wilkes-Barre
PENNSYLVANIA
Catskill Mts.
Poughkeepsie
Newark
Jersey City
NEW YORK
Paterson
Yonkers
Bridgeport
New Haven
Long I.
HARTFORD
CONN.
Springfield
Worcester
Providence
R.I.
Fall River
New Bedford
Martha's Vineyard
Nantucket I.
BOSTON
MASS.
Lowell
Lawrence
Nashua
Manchester
Concord
Glens Falls
Rutland
Adirondack Mts.
Burlington
Montpelier
VERMONT
Plattsburgh
L. Champlain
NEW HAMPSHIRE
White Mts.
Connecticut
Portland
Lewiston
Brunswick
Augusta
Berlin
Farmington
Waterville
Belfast
Penobscot Bay
Bangor
MAINE
Moosehead L.
Millinocket
Houlton
Presque Isle
Caribou
Fort Kent
Calais
Saint John
NEW BRUNSWICK
Edmundston
Rivière-du-Loup
Rimouski
Matane
St. Lawrence
Baie-Comeau
Chicoutimi
Jonquière
Alma
L. St-Jean
Roberval
La Tuque
St-Maurice
Québec
Drummondville
Sherbrooke
Granby
Trois-Rivières
Joliette
Shawinigan
Rés. Baskatong
Mont-Laurier
Outaouais
Rés. Cabonga
Rés. Gouin
L. Kempt
Chibougamau
L. Chibougamau
L. au Goéland
L. Matagami
Nottaway
Bell
Amos
L. Abitibi
Rouyn-Noranda
L. Témiscamingue
Kirkland Lake
Timmins
Cochrane
Atlantic
45
40
35
30
25
75
70
65

50 0 50 100 150 200 km
50 0 50 100 150 miles
ONTARIO
QUEBEC
MICHIGAN
OHIO
INDIANA
ILLINOIS
KENTUCKY
WEST VIRGINIA
VIRGINIA
PENNSYLVANIA
NEW YORK
MARYLAND
NEW JERSEY
NEW HAMPSHIRE
LAKE SUPERIOR
LAKE HURON
LAKE ERIE
LAKE ONTARIO
Georgian Bay
Chesapeake Bay
CHICAGO
DETROIT
MILWAUKEE
TORONTO
MONTREAL
Ottawa
BOSTON
NEW YORK
PHILADELPHIA
BALTIMORE
WASHINGTON D.C.
PITTSBURGH
CLEVELAND
COLUMBUS
INDIANAPOLIS
Cincinnati
Louisville
Buffalo
Québec
Richmond
Norfolk

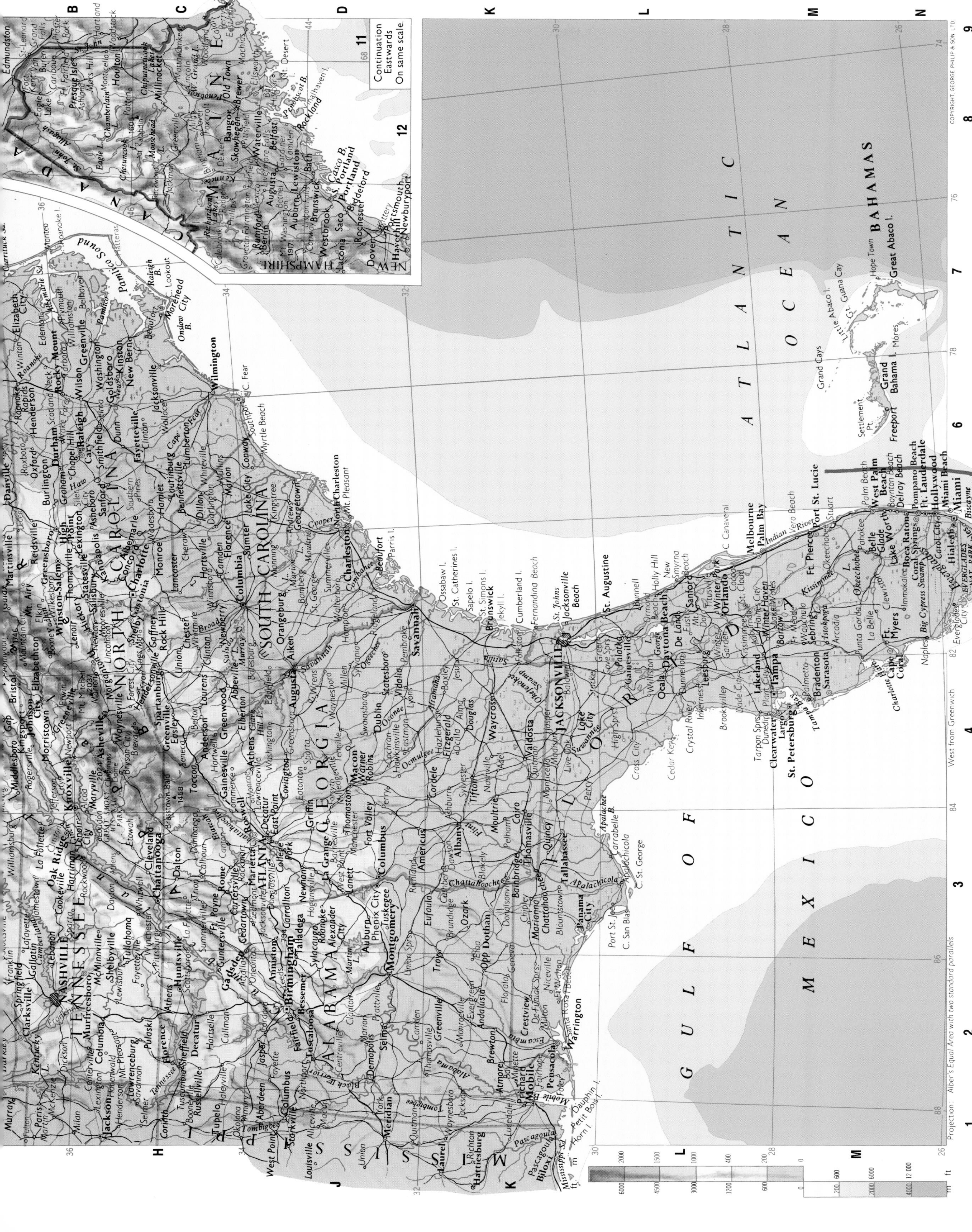
TENNESSEE
NORTH CAROLINA
SOUTH CAROLINA
GEORGIA
ALABAMA
FLORIDA
MAINE
NEW HAMPSHIRE
CANADA
ATLANTIC OCEAN
GULF OF MEXICO
BAHAMAS
Great Abaco I.
Grand Bahama I.
Freeport
Little Abaco I.
NASHVILLE
Knoxville
Chattanooga
Huntsville
Birmingham
Montgomery
Mobile
Pensacola
Tallahassee
Panama City
ATLANTA
Columbus
Macon
Augusta
Savannah
Columbia
Charleston
Charlotte
Raleigh
Durham
Wilmington
JACKSONVILLE
Orlando
Tampa
St. Petersburg
Miami
Ft. Lauderdale
West Palm Beach
Continuation Eastwards On same scale.
Augusta
Bangor
Portland
West from Greenwich
Projection: Alber's Equal Area with two standard parallels
COPYRIGHT GEORGE PHILIP & SON, LTD.

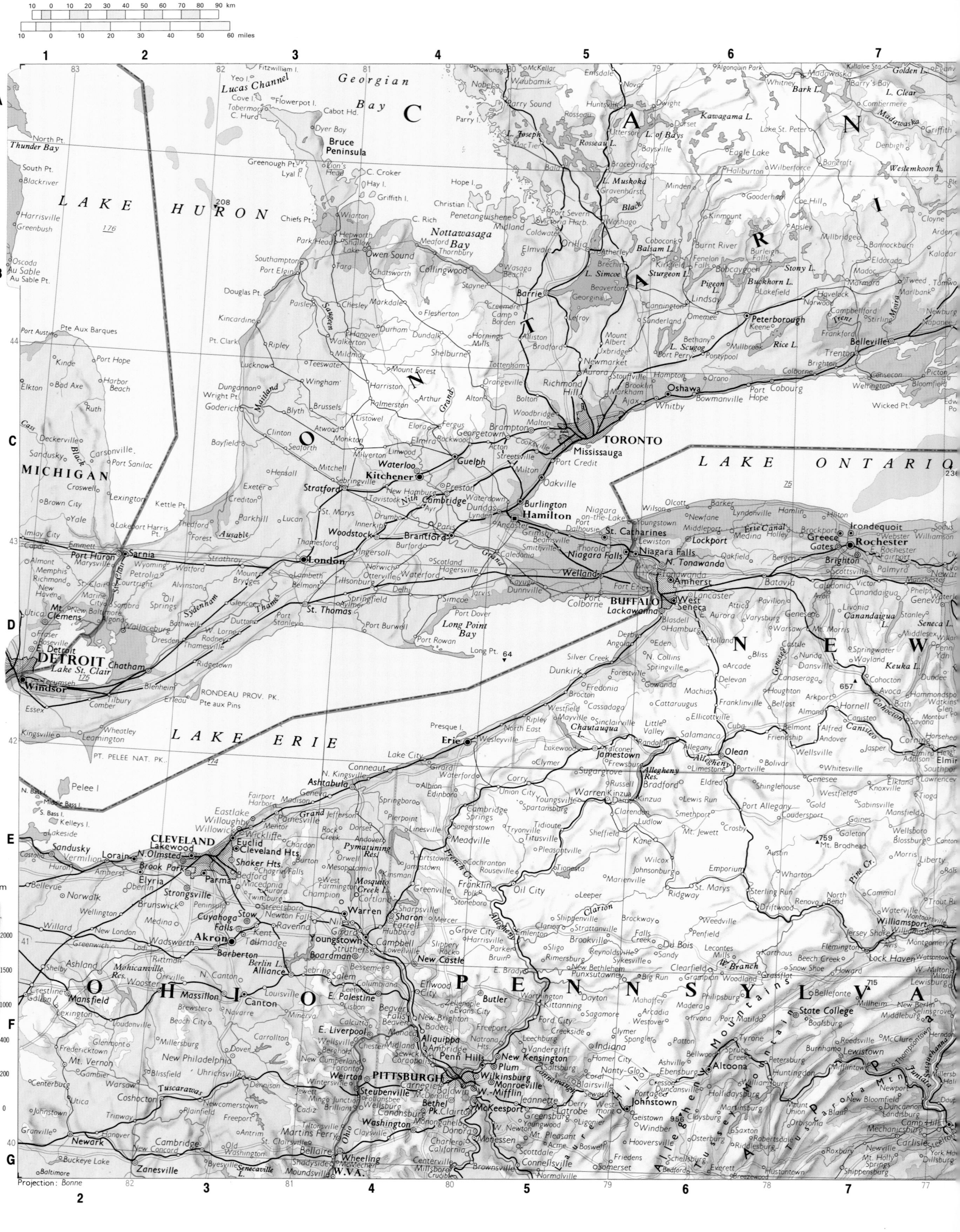

Georgian Bay
Bruce Peninsula
LAKE HURON
Nottawasaga Bay
C A N A D A
O N T A R I O
LAKE ONTARIO
TORONTO
Mississauga
Hamilton
Kitchener
Waterloo
Guelph
London
St. Catharines
Niagara Falls
BUFFALO
Rochester
MICHIGAN
DETROIT
Windsor
Lake St. Clair
LAKE ERIE
Long Point Bay
CLEVELAND
Akron
Youngstown
Canton
Erie
O H I O
P E N N S Y L V A N I A
N E W
PITTSBURGH
Allegheny Mountains
Projection: Bonne

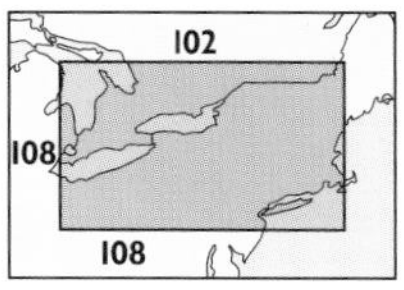
102
108
108

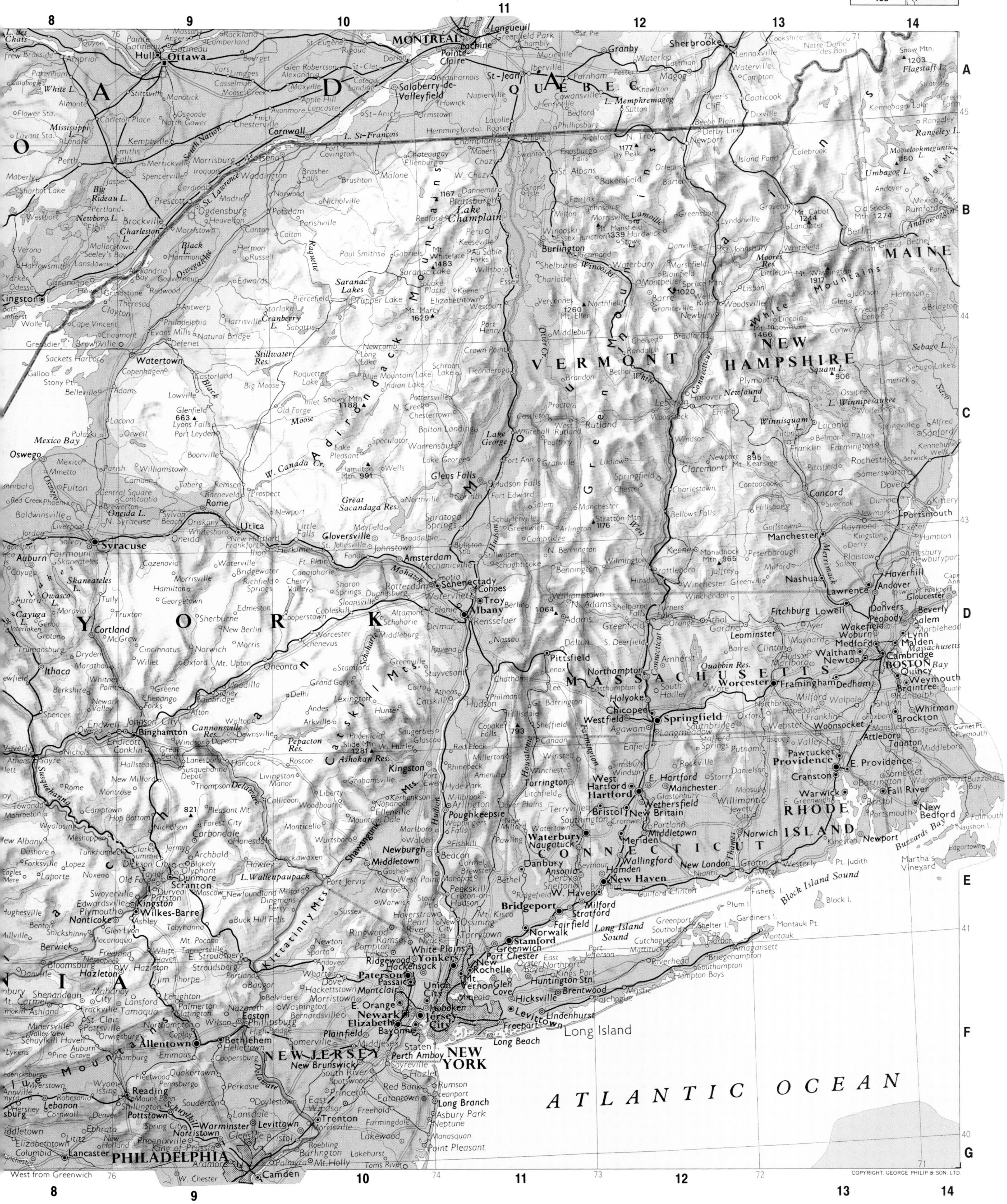
8
9
10
11
12
13
14
A
B
C
D
E
F
G
MONTREAL
Ottawa
Hull
Sherbrooke
Granby
St-Jean
Cornwall
Kingston
Q U E B E C
Lake Champlain
Plattsburgh
Burlington
Montpelier
Mt. Washington 1917
White Mountains
Mt. Marcy 1629
Saranac Lakes
Adirondack Mountains
Green Mountains
VERMONT
NEW HAMPSHIRE
MAINE
Portland
Lake George
Glens Falls
Saratoga Springs
Schenectady
Troy
Albany
Amsterdam
Utica
Rome
Syracuse
Oswego
Watertown
Ithaca
Binghamton
Cortland
Y O R K
Catskill Mts.
Kingston
Poughkeepsie
Newburgh
Middletown
Scranton
Wilkes-Barre
Hazleton
Allentown
Bethlehem
Reading
Lancaster
PHILADELPHIA
Camden
Trenton
NEW JERSEY
Paterson
Newark
Elizabeth
Jersey City
NEW YORK
Yonkers
White Plains
Stamford
Bridgeport
New Haven
Waterbury
Hartford
New London
CONNECTICUT
Springfield
Worcester
Pittsfield
MASSACHUSETTS
BOSTON
Cambridge
Lowell
Lawrence
Manchester
Concord
Nashua
Portsmouth
Providence
Pawtucket
RHODE ISLAND
Newport
Fall River
New Bedford
Long Island
Long Island Sound
Block Island Sound
Buzzards Bay
Martha's Vineyard
Long Branch
ATLANTIC OCEAN
West from Greenwich
COPYRIGHT. GEORGE PHILIP & SON. LTD

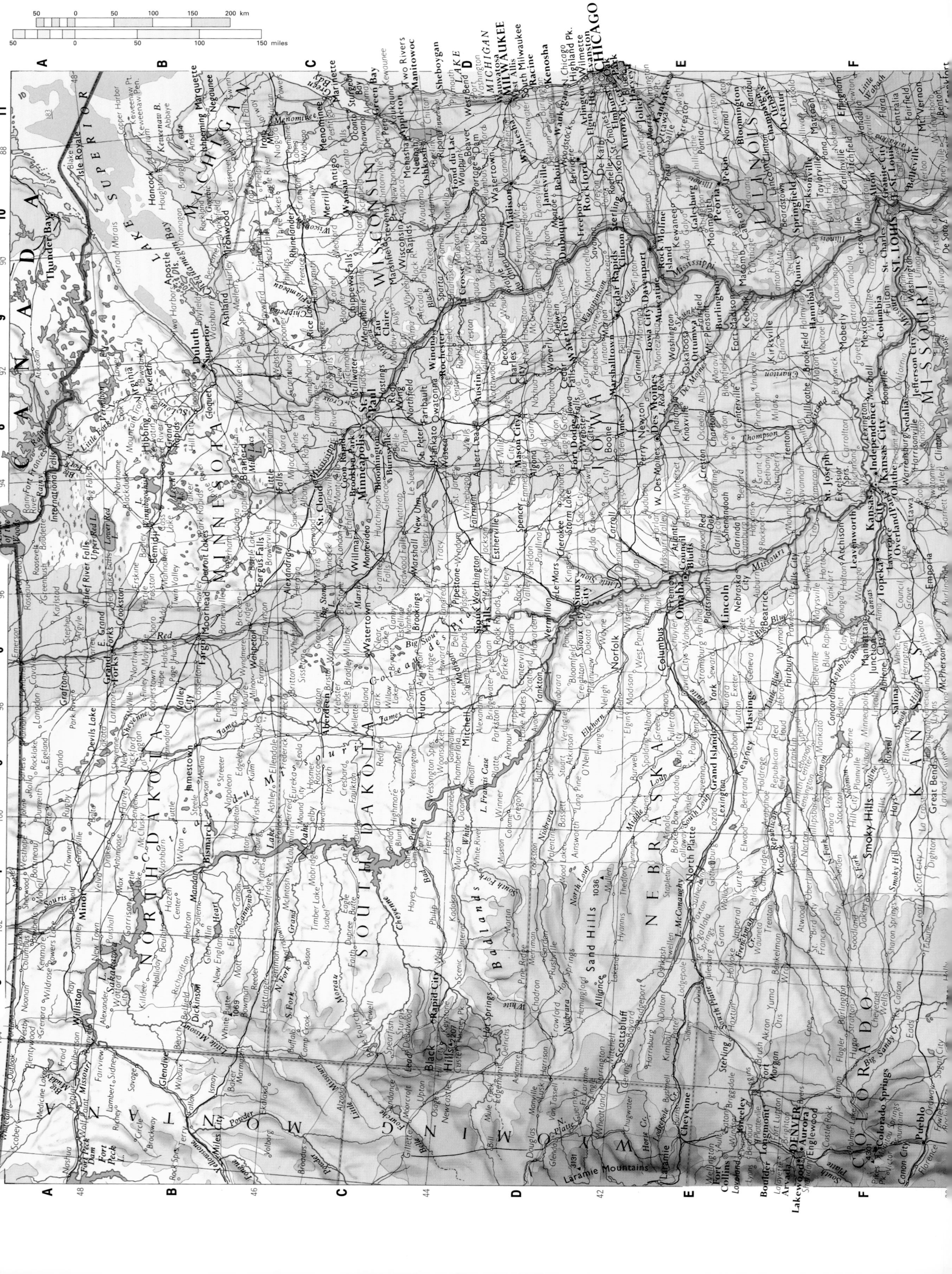
50 0 50 100 150 200 km
50 0 50 100 150 miles
C A N A D A
LAKE SUPERIOR
LAKE MICHIGAN
NORTH DAKOTA
SOUTH DAKOTA
MINNESOTA
WISCONSIN
IOWA
ILLINOIS
NEBRASKA
KANSAS
MISSOURI
MONTANA
WYOMING
COLORADO
MICHIGAN
MILWAUKEE
CHICAGO
ST. LOUIS
DENVER
Minneapolis
St. Paul
Des Moines
Omaha
Kansas City
Duluth
Bismarck
Pierre
Lincoln
Topeka
Madison
Springfield
Cheyenne
Sand Hills
Badlands
Black Hills
Laramie Mountains

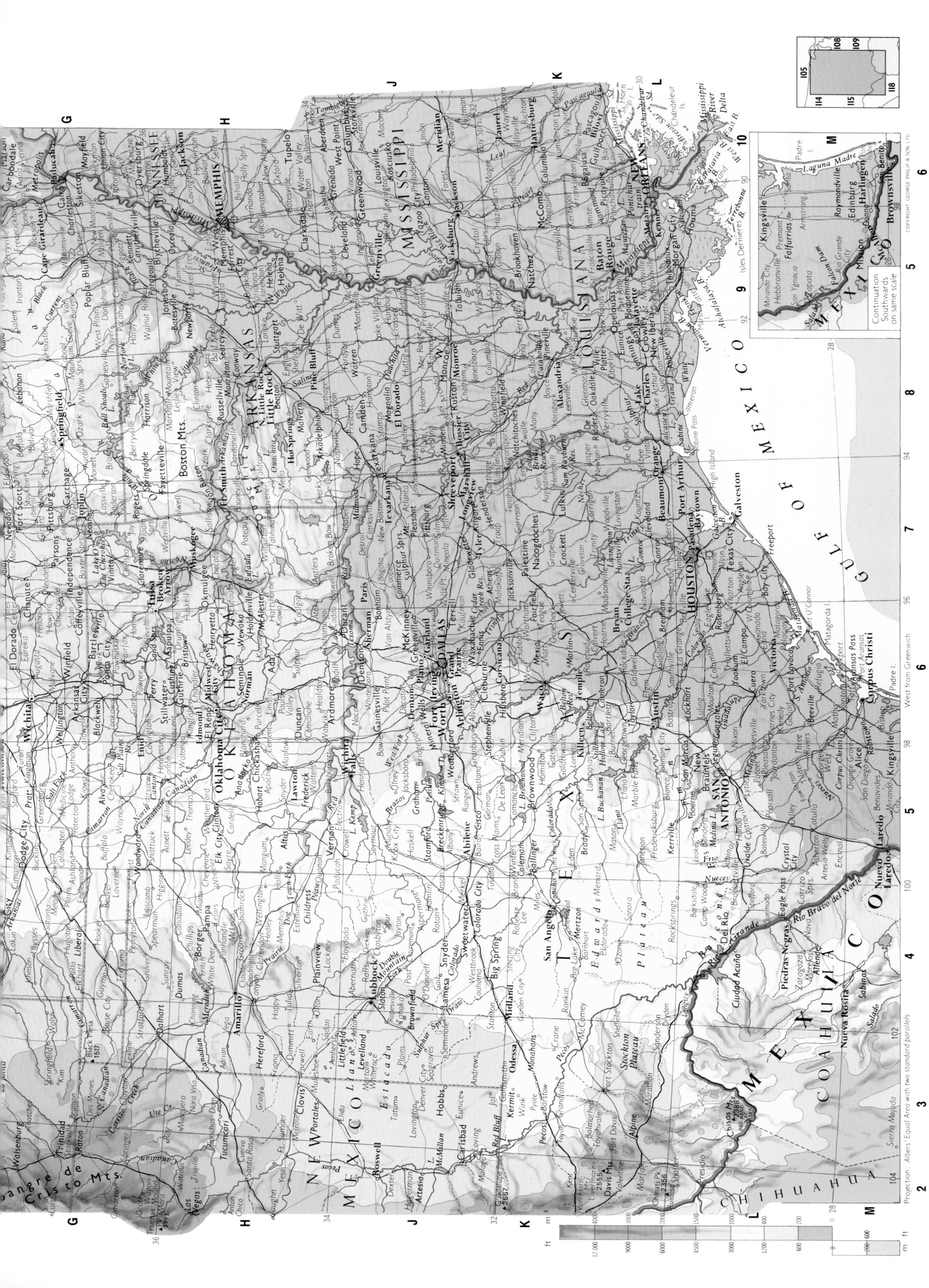
OKLAHOMA
ARKANSAS
MISSISSIPPI
LOUISIANA
TEXAS
NEW MEXICO
MEXICO
COAHUILA
CHIHUAHUA
GULF OF MEXICO
Continuation Southwards on same scale
Projection: Albers' Equal Area with two standard parallels
West from Greenwich
COPYRIGHT GEORGE PHILIP & SON, LTD.

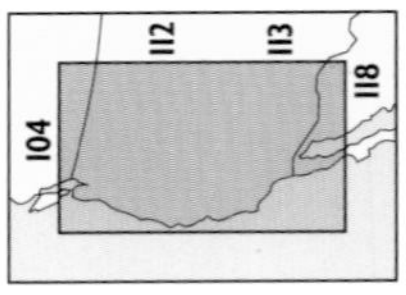
104
112
113
118

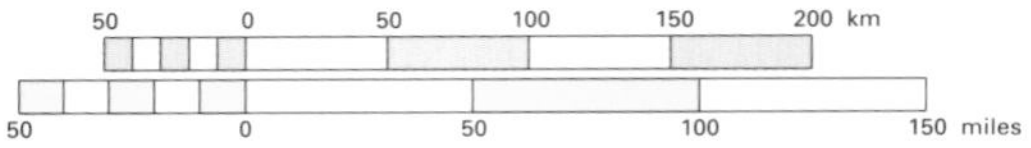
50 0 50 100 150 200 km
50 0 50 100 150 miles

WASHINGTON
OREGON
IDAHO
MONTANA
WYOMING
NEVADA
UTAH
CALIFORNIA
BRITISH COLUMBIA
ALBERTA
SASKATCHEWAN
CANADA
SEATTLE
VANCOUVER
Victoria
Tacoma
Olympia
Portland
Salem
Eugene
Spokane
Boise
Salt Lake City
Ogden
Provo
Pocatello
Idaho Falls
Twin Falls
Helena
Butte
Missoula
Great Falls
Billings
Bozeman
Casper
Rock Springs
Reno
Sacramento
Redding
Medford
Klamath Falls
Bend
Yakima
Walla Walla
Lewiston
Kalispell
Lethbridge
Medicine Hat
Bighorn Mountains
Little Belt Mts.
Big Belt Mts.
Crazy Mts.
Lewis Range
Bitterroot Range
Lemhi Range
Salmon River Mountains
Clearwater Mountains
Cabinet Mountains
Blue Mountains
Wallowa Mts.
Olympic Mts.
Klamath Mts.
Wind River Range
Uinta Mountains
Medicine Bow Mts.
Independence Mts.
Shoshone Mountains
Toiyabe Ra.
Stillwater Ra.
Trinity Mts.
Ruby Mts.
Sawtooth Ra.
Great Sandy Desert
Great Salt Lake Desert
GREAT SALT LAKE
Harney Basin
Snake River Plain
Owyhee
Yellowstone
Columbia
Snake
Missouri
Juan de Fuca Strait
Cascade Range
Sierra Nevada
Coast Ranges

COLORADO
NEW MEXICO
ARIZONA
CALIFORNIA
NEVADA
TEXAS
CHIHUAHUA
SONORA
MEXICO
BAJA CALIFORNIA
PACIFIC OCEAN
Golfo de California
Desierto de Altar
Gran Desierto
Sonora Desert
Colorado Plateau
Painted Desert
Grand Canyon
San Juan Mts.
Sangre de Cristo Mts.
Sacramento Mts.
San Andres Mts.
Uncompahgre Plat.
White Mts.
Spring Mts.
Chocolate Mts.
Santa Lucia Range
Sierra de Juarez
LOS ANGELES
SAN DIEGO
PHOENIX
Tucson
Albuquerque
Santa Fe
EL PASO
CIUDAD JUAREZ
Chihuahua
Hermosillo
Las Vegas
Bakersfield
Fresno
Santa Barbara
Long Beach
Mexicali
Tijuana
Yuma
Nogales
I. de Guadalupe (Mexico)
Bahia Sebastian Vizcaino
Projection: Albers' Equal Area with two standard parallels
West from Greenwich
COPYRIGHT GEORGE PHILIP & SON, LTD
m ft
4000 12 000
3000 9000
2000 6000
1500 4500
1000 3000
400 1200
200 600
0 0
200 600
2000 6000
4000 12 000

CENTRAL AND SOUTHERN CALIFORNIA AND WESTERN WASHINGTON 1:2 200 000

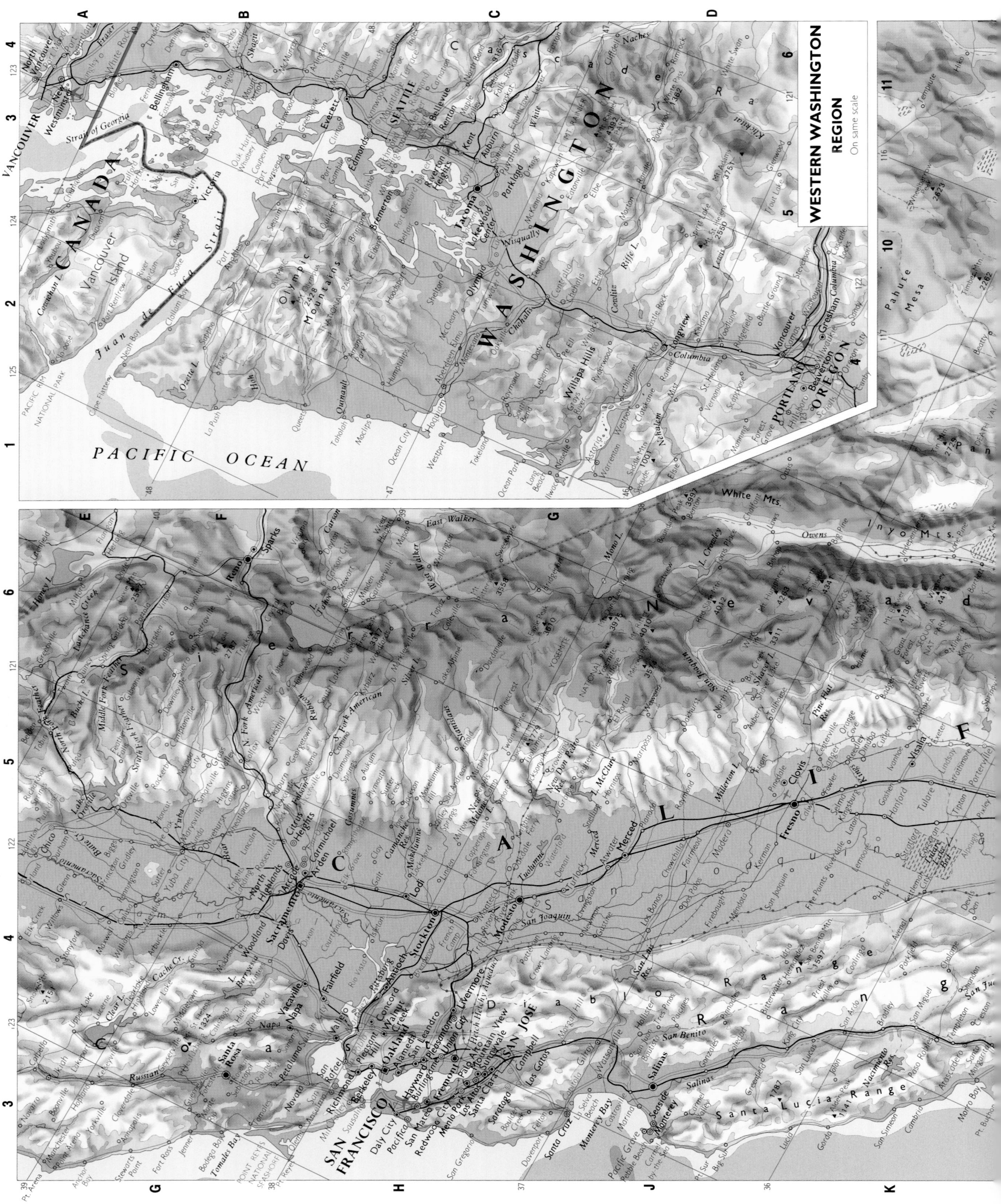

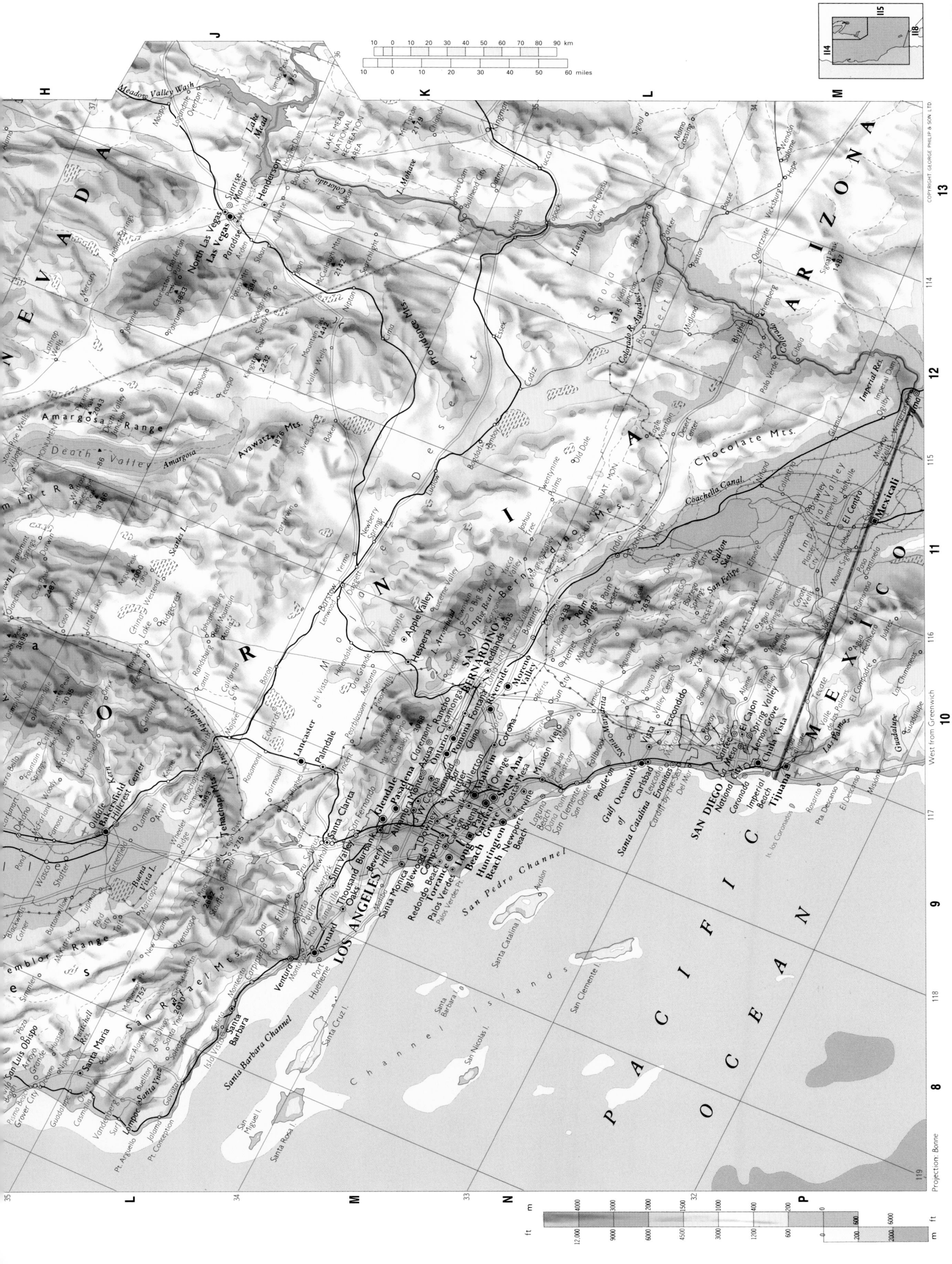
NEVADA
ARIZONA
CALIFORNIA
MEXICO
PACIFIC OCEAN
LOS ANGELES
SAN DIEGO
SAN BERNARDINO
Las Vegas
North Las Vegas
Henderson
Lake Mead
L. Mohave
L. Havasu
Death Valley
Amargosa Range
Mojave Desert
Sonora Desert
Chocolate Mts.
Salton Sea
Mexicali
Tijuana
Chula Vista
Santa Barbara
Santa Barbara Channel
Channel Islands
San Pedro Channel
Gulf of Santa Catalina
Bakersfield
Lancaster
Palmdale
Riverside
Anaheim
Santa Ana
Long Beach
Pasadena
Glendale
Oxnard
Ventura
Santa Maria
Lompoc
San Luis Obispo
Oceanside
Escondido
Palm Springs
Indio
Barstow
Hesperia
Apple Valley
Victorville
Needles
Blythe
Yuma
El Centro
Kingman
km
miles
Projection: Bonne
West from Greenwich
COPYRIGHT GEORGE PHILIP & SON LTD

50 0 50 100 150 200 250 300 km
50 0 50 100 150 200 miles
1
2
3
4
A
B
C
D
TIJUANA
MEXICALI
Ensenada
Yuma
San Luis Rio Colorado
Globe
Gila Bend
A R I Z O N A
TUCSON
Nogales
Bisbee
Douglas
Agua Prieta
Cananea
Caborca
Magdalena
Santa Ana
Hermosillo
Guaymas
Empalme
Ciudad Obregón
Navojoa
Los Mochis
Guasave
Guamúchil
Culiacán
Mazatlán
Rosario
Escuinapa
Acaponeta
Tecuala
Santiago Ixcuintla
Tepic
Compostela
Puerto Vallarta
Manzanillo
COLIMA
Colima
Tecomán
Ciudad Guzmán
Autlán
GUADALAJARA
Tlaquepaque
Ocotlán
Sayula
Zamora
La Piedad
Uruapan
Apatzingán
Zacapu
Morelia
Zitácuaro
Irapuato
Celaya
Acámbaro
Guanajuato
LEÓN
Lagos de Moreno
Aguascalientes
Zacatecas
Fresnillo
San Luis Potosí
Matehuala
Victoria de Durango
Gómez Palacio
TORREÓN
Lerdo
Saltillo
MONTERREY
Parras
Monclova
Sabinas
Nueva Rosita
Piedras Negras
Acuña
Del Rio
Eagle Pass
Hidalgo del Parral
Santa Bárbara
Jiménez
Ciudad Camargo
Delicias
CHIHUAHUA
Cuauhtémoc
Nuevo Casas Grandes
CIUDAD JUÁREZ
EL PASO
Las Cruces
Deming
Lordsburg
Roswell
Hobbs
Carlsbad
Lubbock
Big Spring
Sweetwater
San Angelo
Van Horn
N E W M E X I C O
U N I T
S O N O R A
C H I H U A H U A
C O A H U I L A
D U R A N G O
BAJA CALIFORNIA
BAJA CALIFORNIA SUR
Santa Rosalía
Loreto
La Paz
Todos Santos
San José del Cabo
C. San Lucas
Golfo de California
P A C I F I C
O C E A N
Is. de Revillagigedo (Mexico)
San Benedicto
Roca Partida
Socorro
Islas Tres Marías
I. Cedros
I. Ángel de la Guarda
I. Tiburón
I. Carmen
I. San José
I. Espíritu Santo
I. Cerralvo
I. Santa Margarita
I. Santa Magdalena
Desierto de Vizcaíno
Sierra Madre Occidental
Tropic of Cancer
30
25
20
115
110
105
100
ft m
12,000 4000
9000 3000
6000 2000
4500 1500
3000 1000
1200 400
600 200
0 0
200 600
2000 6000
4000 12,000
m ft
REFERENCE TO NUMBERS
1 Federal District
2 Aguascalientes
3 Guanajuato
4 Hidalgo
5 México
6 Morelos
7 Querétaro
8 Tlaxcala
Projection: Bi-polar oblique Conical Orthomorphic
West from Greenwich

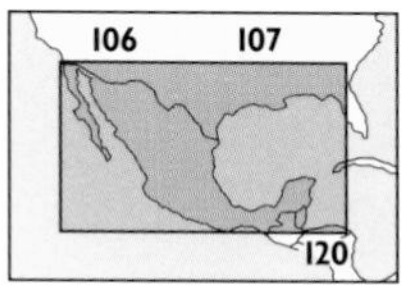
106
107
120

GULF OF MEXICO
Golfo de Campeche
UNITED STATES
ARKANSAS
MISSISSIPPI
ALABAMA
GEORGIA
LOUISIANA
FLORIDA
TEXAS
TAMAULIPAS
YUCATAN
CAMPECHE
QUINTANA ROO
TABASCO
CHIAPAS
OAXACA
PUEBLA
BELIZE
GUATEMALA
HONDURAS
CUBA
Canal de Yucatán
Tropic of Cancer
Wichita Falls
Denison
Sherman
Paris
Texarkana
Camden
El Dorado
Greenville
Tuscaloosa
Opelika
Columbus
Denton
Greenville
Selma
Phenix City
FORT WORTH
DALLAS
Marshall
Monroe
Vicksburg
Meridian
Montgomery
Americus
Cordele
Albany
Tifton
McRae
Longview
Tyler
Shreveport
Tallulah
Jackson
Troy
Waycross
Cleburne
Hillsboro
Corsicana
Natchez
Laurel
Dothan
Valdosta
Palestine
Nacogdoches
Hattiesburg
Brownwood
Waco
Lufkin
Alexandria
McComb
Tallahassee
Temple
Baton Rouge
Hammond
Bogalusa
Biloxi
MOBILE
Pensacola
Panama City
Lake City
Huntsville
Bryan
Gulfport
NEW ORLEANS
Austin
Lake Charles
Lafayette
Beaumont
HOUSTON
Port Arthur
Rosenberg
Galveston
SAN ANTONIO
Victoria
Dilley
Alice
Corpus Christi
Laredo
Kingsville
Nuevo Laredo
Zapata
Camargo
Mc Allen
Harlingen
Brownsville
Reynosa
Matamoros
Valle Hermoso
Montemorelos
Laguna Madre
Linares
Ciudad Victoria
Soto la Marina
Ciudad Mante
Ciudad Madero
Tampico
Ciudad de Valles
Laguna de Tamiahua
Tuxpan
Poza Rica
Papantla
Pachuca
Tulancingo
Jalapa Enriquez
MEXICO
Puebla
Orizaba
Córdoba
Veracruz Llave
Alvarado
Cuernavaca
Tehuacán
San Andrés Tuxtla
Coatzacoalcos
Minatitlán
Acayucan
Iguala
Chilpancingo
Oaxaca
Acapulco
Juchitán
Tehuantepec
Salina Cruz
Golfo de Tehuantepec
Tuxtla Gutiérrez
San Cristóbal de las Casas
Comitán
Tapachula
Villahermosa
Cárdenas
Frontera
Ciudad del Carmen
Laguna de Términos
Champotón
Campeche
Progreso
Mérida
Motul
Izamal
Tizimín
Valladolid
Ticul
Tekax
Peto
Felipe Carrillo Puerto
Chetumal
Cozumel
Isla Cozumel
Cancun
C. Catoche
Ambergris Cay
Belize City
Belmopan
Turneffe Is.
Golfo de Honduras
Islas de la Bahía
Puerto Barrios
Puerto Cortés
Tela
La Ceiba
San Pedro Sula
Tegucigalpa
Cobán
Huehuetenango
Quezaltenango
Totonicapán
Chiquimula
Zacapa
Jalapa
GUATEMALA
Antigua
Flores
L. Petén Itzá
Isla Desterrada
Isla Pérez
C. San Antonio
Clearwater
Apalachee Bay
Mississippi Delta
Breton Sound
Atchafalaya Bay
C. San Blas

1:7 100 000

Projection: Bi-polar oblique Conical Orthomorphic

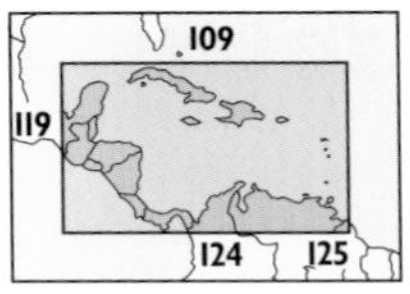
109
119
124
125

50 0 50 100 150 200 250 300 km
50 0 50 100 150 200 miles
5
6
7
8
A
B
C
D
E
ATLANTIC OCEAN
Tropic of Cancer
Puerto Rico Trench
Milwaukee Deep 9220
BEAN SEA
HISPANIOLA
ANTILLES
LESSER ANTILLES
LEEWARD ISLANDS
WINDWARD ISLANDS
MAS
Cat I.
The Bight
San Salvador (Watling I., Guanahani)
Conception I.
Rum Cay
Long I.
Clarence Town
Atwood or Samana Cay
Crooked I. Passage
Crooked I.
Plana Cays
Albert Town
Snug Corner
Mayaguana I.
Acklins I.
Mira por vos Cay
Cay Verde
Caicos Passage
Caicos Islands (Br.)
Turks I. Passage
Turks Islands (Br.)
Hogsty Reef
Little Inagua I.
Lake Rose
Great Inagua I.
Matthew Town
Moa
Baracoa
Pta de Maisi
Maisi
Guantánamo
Paso de los Vientos (Windward Passage)
Î. de la Tortue
Port-de-Paix
Cap-Haïtien
Fort-Liberté
Monte Cristi
La Isabela
Puerto Plata
C. Frances Viejo
San Francisco de Macoris
Jean-Rabel
Cap-à-Foux
Golfe de la Gonâve
Gonaïves
Hinche
Santiago de los Caballeros
La Vega
Nagua
Sánchez
Sabana de La Mar
Cord. Central
3176
St.-Marc
HAITI
DOMINICAN REP.
Hato Mayor
Jérémie
Î. de la Gonâve
PORT-AU-PRINCE
San Juan
San Pedro de Macoris
Higüey
C. Engano
La Romana
B. de Yuma
I. Saona
Navassa I. (U.S.A.)
Dame Marie
Massif de la Hotte
2280
Enriquillo
Les Cayes
Aquin
Jacmel
Barahona
Azua de Compostela
Bani
San Cristobal
SANTO DOMINGO
Pointe-à-Gravois
Î.-à-Vache
Pedernales
I. Beata
C. Beata
Canal de la Mona
Aguadilla
Arecibo
Bayamón
SAN JUAN
Carolina
1338
Ponce
Mayagüez
Isla Mona (U.S.A.)
PUERTO RICO (U.S.A.)
Caguas
Guayama
Fajardo
St. Thomas
Virgin Gorda
Tortola
Road Town
Anegada
Virgin Is. (Br.)
Anegada Passage
Sombrero (Anguilla)
Anguilla (Br.)
St.-Martin (Guad.)
St.-Barthélemy (Fr.)
St. Maarten (Neth.)
Virgin Is. (U.S.A.)
Charlotte Amalie
Frederiksted
Christiansted
St. Croix
Saba (Neth.)
St. Eustatius (Neth.)
Basseterre
ST. KITTS & NEVIS
Nevis
Barbuda
ANTIGUA & BARBUDA
St. Johns
Antigua
Redonda
Montserrat
Guadeloupe Passage
Moule
Désirade
Ste-Rose
GUADELOUPE (Fr.)
Pointe-a-Pitre
Basse-Terre
Marie-Galante (Fr.)
Grand-Bourge
I. des Saintes (Guad.)
Dominica Passage
Portsmouth
DOMINICA
Roseau
I. de Aves (Bird I.) (Venezuela)
Martinique Passage
Mt. Pelée 1397
Ste-Marie
François
Fort-de-France
Rivière-Pilc
MARTINIQUE (Fr.)
St. Lucia Channel
Castries
ST. LUCIA
Soufrière
St. Vincent Passage
Soufrière 1234
ST. VINCENT
Kingstown
Speightstown
Bridgetown
BARBADOS
& THE GRENADINES
The Grenadines
Hillsborough
GRENADINES
St. George's
GRENADA
Aruba (Neth.)
Curaçao
Bonaire
Willemstad
NETH. ANTILLES
Pta. Gallinas
C. San Román
Pen. de la Guajira
Pta. Espada
Pen. de Paraguaná
Is. de Aves (Ven.)
Is. Los Roques (Ven.)
I. Orchila (Ven.)
I. Blanquilla (Ven.)
I. Los Hermanos (Ven.)
Is. Los Testigos (Ven.)
Tobago
Scarborough
Punto Fijo
Puerto Cumarebo
Punta Cardón
Golfo de Venezuela
Ríohacha
Uribia
C. San Juan de Guía
GUAJIRA
Coro
La Vela de Coro
FALCÓN
Tucacas
Santa Marta
BARRANQUILLA
Ciénaga
San Rafael
Sa. Nevada de Santa Marta 5800
MARACAIBO
Altagracia
Mene de Mauroa
Tocuyo
Puerto Cabello
Maracay
Maiquetía
La Guaira
CARACAS
DISTRITO FEDERAL
I. La Tortuga (Ven.)
I. Margarita
La Asunción
Porlamar
NUEVA ESPARTA
Pen. de Paria
Pta. Mejillones
Dragon's Mouth
Port of Spain
Galera Pt.
Arima
Trinidad
Soledad
Sabanalarga
La Concepción
Santa Rita
Cabimas
Baragua
San Felipe
YARACUY
CARABOBO
ARAGUA
MIRANDA
Guatire
C. Codera
Higuerote
Rio Chico
Puerto La Cruz
Cumaná
Carúpano
Río Caribe
Cariaco
Güiria
Golfo de Paria
Rio Claro
San Fernando
TRINIDAD & TOBAGO
Serpent's Mouth
SUCRE
Caripito
Fundación
Valledupar
Villa del Rosario
Ciudad Ojeda
Mene Grande
Carora
LARA
BARQUISIMETO
Valencia
Yaritagua de los Morros
Villa de Cura
S. Juan de los Morros
Altagracia de Orituco
Ocumare del Tuy
Los Teques
Barcelona
Caicara
Maturín
Calamar
MAGDALENA
Agustín Codazzi
Plato
Zambrano
Machiques
Lago de Maracaibo
El Tocuyo
San Carlos
COJEDES
Aragua de Barcelona
Anaco
MONAGAS
DELTA
Tucupita
Cesar
ZULIA
La Ceiba
TRUJILLO
Acarigua
El Sombrero
Valle de la Pascua
Unare
Cantaura
El Tigre
Tigre
AMACURO
Magangué
Mompós
Corozal
Sincé
Catatumbo
Betijoque
Valera
Trujillo
PORTUGUESA
El Baúl
Calabozo
GUÁRICO
Manapire
Santa María de Ipire
Pariaguan
ANZOÁTEGUI
Ciudad Guayana
El Banco
Encontrados
San Carlos del Zulia
Guanare
Portuguesa
Sahagún
San Marcos
Planeta Rica
Majagual
NORTE DE SANTANDER
MÉRIDA
Barinas
Cord. de Mérida
Ocaña
BARINAS
Ciudad Bolivia
Libertad
Guarico
San Fernando de Apure
Apure
Orinoco
Mapire
Soledad
El Pao
Sierra Imataca
Upata
Ciudad Bolívar
Caroní
Guasipati
El Callao
Tumeremo
Emb. de Guri
Cauca
Ayapel
BOLÍVAR
Simití
Caucasia
SANTANDER
Cúcuta
TACHIRA
Santa Bárbara
Bruzual
Pto. de Nutrias
Achaguas
Caicara
VENEZUELA
West from Greenwich
75
70
65
60
25
20
15
10
ft m
12,000 4000
9000 3000
6000 2000
4500 1500
3000 1000
1200 400
600 200
0 0
200 600
2000 6000
4000 12,000
6000 18,000
8000 24,000
m ft

100 0 200 400 600 800 1000 1200 1400 km
100 0 200 400 600 800 1000 miles
Tropic of Cancer
Gulf of Campeche
Yucatan Channel
Yucatán Peninsula
Isthmus of Tehuantepec
G. de Honduras
Guatemala Trench
Cuba
Greater Antilles
Jamaica
Turks & Caicos Is.
Hispaniola
9200
Puerto Rico
Lesser Antilles
Guadeloupe
Dominica
Martinique
St. Lucia
St. Vincent
Barbados
Grenada
Tobago
Trinidad
I. Margarita
C. Gracias a Dios
Caribbean Sea
Coco
L. Nicaragua
Panama Canal
G. of Darién
Gulf of Panamá
C. de la Aguja
5800
Sierra Nevada de Santa Marta
L. Maracaibo
Cord. de Merida
Magdalena
Cordillera Occidental
Cordillera Central
Cordillera Oriental
Llanos
Orinoco
Meta
Guaviare
Guiana Highlands
Mt. Roraima
2810
Sierra Pacaraima
Essequibo
Courantyne
Serra Tumucumaque
Branco
C. Orange
NORTH ATLANTIC OCEAN
C. de San Francisco
Caquetá
Negro
Equator
Marajó I.
Amazon
Cotopaxi 5897
Chimborazo 6267
Galapagos Is.
Putumayo
Japurá
Napo
G. of Guayaquil
Pta. Pariñas
Pta. Negra
Marañón
Ucayali
Juruá
Selvas
Purus
Madeira
Aripuanã
Roosevelt
Tapajós
Teles Pires
Xingu
Tocantins
Parnaíba
C. de São Roque
Plat. of Borborema
São Francisco
Huascarán 6768
Madre de Dios
Guaporé
Arinos
Araguaia
Mamoré
Plateau of Mato Grosso
Brazilian Highlands
Chincha Alta
L. Titicaca
Nevada Ancohuma 6550
L. de Poopó
Bolivian Plateau
Chile Peru Trench
PACIFIC OCEAN
Abrolhos Bank
Gran Chaco
Paraguay
Pilcomayo
Paraná
Serra da Mantiqueira
2890
Pico da Bandeira
C. Frio
Atacama Desert
8050
Tropic of Capricorn
Cerro Ojos del Salado 6863
San Félix
San Ambrosio
Iguaçu Falls
Uruguay
Serra do Mar
Salado
Salinas Grandes
Entre Rios
Sierra de Córdoba
L. Mar Chiquita
L. dos Patos
Andes
Mt. Aconcagua 6960
Arch. de Juan Fernández
Pampas
Río de la Plata
Colorado
Bahía Blanca
Negro
SOUTH ATLANTIC OCEAN
Chile Rise
Chiloé I.
G. San Matías
40
Valdés Peninsula
Chubut
Chonos Archipelago
Mte. San Valentin 4058
Taitao Peninsula
Gulf of Penas
Gulf of San Jorge
Argentine Basin
Patagonia
6212
Wellington I.
Madre de Dios I.
West Falkland
Falkland Is.
East Falkland
Magellan's Str.
Santa Inés I.
Tierra del Fuego
Canal Cockburn
Canal Beagle
Staten I.
C. Horn
South Georgia
Projection: Lambert's Azimuthal Equal Area
West from Greenwich
ft m
12000 4000
9000 3000
6000 2000
3000 1000
1500 500
600 200
0 0
200 600
1000 3000
2000 6000
4000 12000
6000 18000
8000 24000
m ft

100 0 200 400 600 800 1000 1200 1400 km
100 0 200 400 600 800 1000 miles
Tropic of Cancer
NORTH ATLANTIC OCEAN
Havana
CUBA
BAHAMAS
Turks & Caicos Is. (U.K.)
DOMINICAN REP.
HAITI
Port-au-Prince
JAMAICA
Kingston
San Juan
PUERTO RICO (U.S.A.)
Virgin Is. (U.K.)
ST. KITTS & NEVIS
ANTIGUA & BARBUDA
Basse-Terre
GUADELOUPE (Fr.)
DOMINICA
Fort-de-France
MARTINIQUE (Fr.)
Castries
ST. LUCIA
ST. VINCENT
Kingstown
BARBADOS
Bridgetown
GRENADA
St. George's
Port of Spain
TRINIDAD & TOBAGO
MEXICO
BELIZE
GUATEMALA
Guatemala
HONDURAS
Tegucigalpa
San Salvador
EL SALVADOR
NICARAGUA
Managua
COSTA RICA
San José
Panamá
PANAMA
Caribbean Sea
Aruba
Curaçao
C. de la Aguja
Barranquilla
Cartagena
G. of Darién
Maracaibo
Barquisimeto
Caracas
Valencia
Cúcuta
San Cristóbal
Orinoco
Ciudad Guayana
Medellín
Bucaramanga
VENEZUELA
Georgetown
GUYANA
Paramaribo
SURINAM
Cayenne
C. Orange
FRENCH GUIANA
Gulf of Panamá
Magdalena
Bogotá
Cali
COLOMBIA
RORAIMA
Essequibo
Branco
AMAPÁ
Galapagos Is. (Ecuador)
Quito
ECUADOR
Guayaquil
G. of Guayaquil
Putumayo
Japurá
Napo
Iquitos
Amazon
Manaus
Marajó I.
Belém
Santarém
Equator
São Luís
Marañón
AMAZONAS
Madeira
Tapajós
PARÁ
Xingu
Tocantins
Fortaleza
MARANHÃO
Teresina
C. de São Roque
CEARÁ
RIO G. DO NORTE
Natal
PARAÍBA
Chiclayo
Juruá
Purus
Parnaíba
Trujillo
Ucayali
ACRE
Pôrto Velho
PIAUÍ
Campina Grande
Chimbote
Araguaia
PERNAMBUCO
Recife
PERU
RONDÔNIA
TOCANTINS
ALAGOAS
Maceió
Callao
LIMA
Madre de Dios
BRAZIL
SERGIPE
Aracaju
Cuzco
Mamoré
MATO GROSSO
BAHIA
Salvador
L. Titicaca
GOIÁS
São Francisco
Arequipa
La Paz
BOLIVIA
Cuiabá
DIS. FED.
Brasília
Cochabamba
Santa Cruz
Goiânia
PACIFIC OCEAN
Paraguay
MINAS GERAIS
Sucre
MATO GROSSO DO SUL
Belo Horizonte
Iquique
ESPIRITO SANTO
Ribeirão Prêto
Juiz de Fora
Vitória
Paraná
SÃO PAULO
Campinas
R. DE J.
Campos
PARAGUAY
SÃO PAULO
Niterói
RIO DE JANEIRO
Antofagasta
Pilcomayo
PARANÁ
Salta
Tropic of Capricorn
Asunción
Curitiba
San Félix (Chile)
San Ambrosio (Chile)
San Miguel de Tucumán
Resistencia
Corrientes
SANTA CATARINA
Uruguay
Salado
RIO GRANDE DO SUL
Porto Alegre
Córdoba
Santa Fe
Paraná
Pelotas
San Juan
Viña del Mar
Valparaíso
Mendoza
Rosario
URUGUAY
SANTIAGO
Arch. de Juan Fernández (Chile)
BUENOS AIRES
Montevideo
La Plata
Rio de la Plata
Talca
CHILE
ARGENTINA
Concepción
Bahía Blanca
Mar del Plata
SOUTH ATLANTIC OCEAN
Colorado
Valdivia
Negro
Viedma
Puerto Montt
Chubut
Comodoro Rivadavia
Gulf of San Jorge
Gulf of Penas
West Falkland
FALKLAND IS. (U.K.)
Stanley
East Falkland
Magellan's Str.
Punta Arenas
Tierra del Fuego
South Georgia (U.K.)
C. Horn
West from Greenwich
Projection: Lambert's Azimuthal Equal Area
LIMA Capital Cities

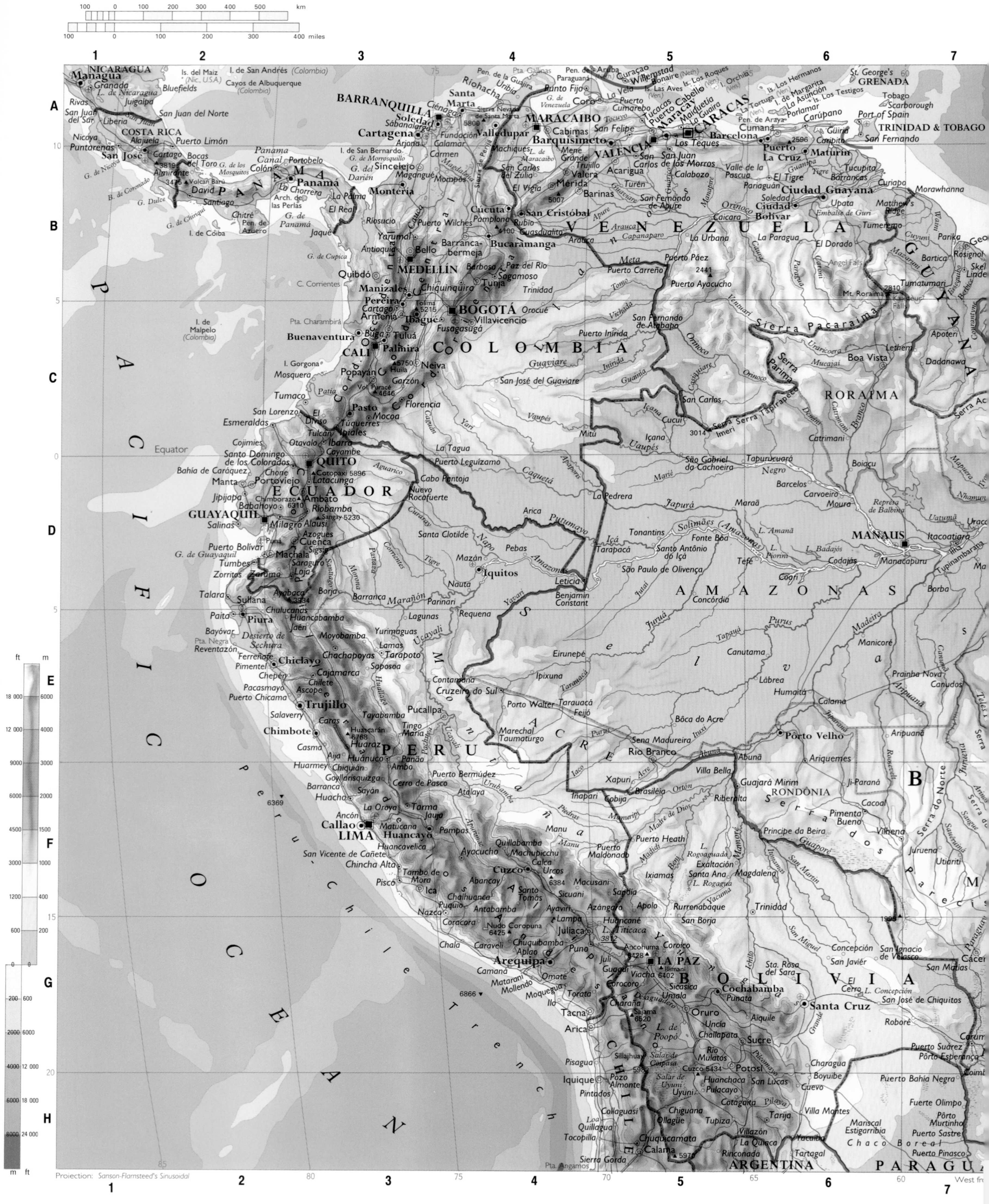

100 0 100 200 300 400 500 km
100 0 100 200 300 400 miles
NICARAGUA
Managua
COSTA RICA
San José
PANAMA
Panama
BARRANQUILLA
Cartagena
MARACAIBO
CARACAS
VALENCIA
Barquisimeto
Ciudad Guayana
TRINIDAD & TOBAGO
Port of Spain
St. George's
GRENADA
V E N E Z U E L A
GUYANA
Georgetown
MEDELLÍN
BOGOTÁ
CALI
C O L O M B I A
QUITO
GUAYAQUIL
ECUADOR
Iquitos
MANAUS
A M A Z O N A S
RORAIMA
Boa Vista
RONDÔNIA
Porto Velho
ACRE
Rio Branco
P E R U
Trujillo
Chimbote
Callao
LIMA
Huancayo
Cuzco
Arequipa
L. Titicaca
LA PAZ
B O L I V I A
Cochabamba
Santa Cruz
Sucre
Potosí
Oruro
Arica
Iquique
CHILE
ARGENTINA
PARAGUAY
P A C I F I C O C E A N
Peru-Chile Trench
Equator
Projection: Sanson-Flamsteed's Sinusoidal
ft m
18 000 6000
12 000 4000
9000 3000
6000 2000
4500 1500
3000 1000
1200 400
600 200
0 0
200 600
2000 6000
4000 12 000
6000 18 000
8000 24 000
m ft

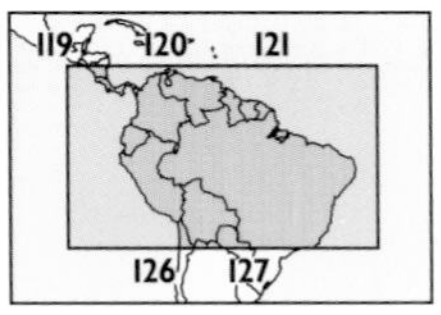
119
120
121
126
127

8
9
10
11
12
13
A
B
C
D
E
F
G
H
A T L A N T I C
O C E A N
Equator
São Paulo
(Braz.)
Rocas
Fernando de Noronha
(Braz.)
Trindade
(Braz.)
6059
Nickerie
Paramaribo
Nieuw Amsterdam
Moengo
St-Laurent
Iracoubo
Sinnamary
Kourou
Cayenne
Albina
Prof. Van Blommestein-meer
Kaw
C. Orange
St-Georges
Oiapoque
RINAM
FRENCH GUIANA
Camopi
Serra Tumucumaque
Amapá
I. de Maracá
AMAPÁ
Araguari
Merirumã
Serra do Navio
Macapá
I. Caviana
I. Mexiana
C. Maguarinho
Mazagão
Chaves
Soure
Afuá
I. de Marajó
I. Grande de Gurupá
Curuçá
Salinópolis
Vigia
Bragança
BELÉM
Castanhal
Viseu
Turiaçu
Almeirim
Gurupá
Breves
Prainha
Monte Alegre
Óbidos
Pôrto de Móz
Curralinho
Abaetetuba
Cametá
Amazonas (Amazon)
Xingu
Alenquer
Juruti
Santarém
Belterra
Aveiro
Brasília Legal
Altamira
Baião
P A R Á
Tucuruí
Represa de Tucuruí
Itaituba
Iriri
Cururupu
B. de São Marcos
Alcântara
São Luís
Barreirinhas
Tutóia
Luís Correia
Camocim
Pinheiro
Rosário
Itapecuru-Mirim
Viana
Santa Inês
Bacabal
Parnaíba
Brejo
Coroatá
Codó
Caxias
Piracuruca
Piripiri
Campo Maior
Granja
Itapipoca
Caucaia
FORTALEZA
Sobral
Maranguape
Cascavel
Baturité
Aracati
Russas
Quixadá
Ipu
Açailândia
Pedreiras
Marabá
Tocantins
MARANHÃO
Imperatriz
São João do Araguaia
Barra do Corda
Teresina
Crateús
CEARÁ
Senador Pompeu
Mossoró
Macau
Areia Branca
Ceará Mirim
C. de São Roque
Natal
RIO GRANDE DO NORTE
Caraúbas
Caicó
Currais Novos
Canguaretama
Mamanguape
Alagoa Grande
Cabedelo
João Pessoa
PARAÍBA
Campina Grande
Olinda
RECIFE
Jaboatão
Caruaru
Sousa
Patos
Cajàzeiras
Juàzeiro do Norte
Crato
Iguatu
Cedro
Amarante
Valença do Piauí
Floriano
Oeiras
Picos
PIAUÍ
Carajás
Serra dos Carajás
Tocantinópolis
Pôrto Franco
Estreito
Carolina
Colinas
Loreto
Nova Iorque
Uruçuí
Chapada do Araripe
Ouricuri
Salgueiro
Paulistana
PERNAMBUCO
Pesqueira
Garanhuns
Palmares
Vitória de Santo Antão
Maceió
Rio Largo
Arapiraca
ALAGOAS
Penedo
Aracaju
SERGIPE
São Cristóvão
Estância
Araguaína
Riachão
Conceição do Araguaia
Araguacema
Pedro Afonso
Serra do Estrondo
Santa Filomena
São João do Piauí
Caracol
Novo Remanso
Sa. Dois Irmãos
Petrolina
Juàzeiro
São Francisco
Paulo Afonso
Petrolândia
Palmeira dos Índios
Propriá
Capela
Nova Casa Nova
Represa de Sobradinho
Senhor-do-Bonfim
Jacobina
Queimadas
Serrinha
Alagoinhas
Feira de Santana
Santo Amaro
Cachoeira
Itaberaba
SALVADOR
B. de Todos os Santos
Nazaré
Valença
Jequié
Castro Alves
Serra do Sincorá
Bom Jesus da Lapa
Ibotirama
Xique-Xique
Mundo Novo
Barra
BAHIA
Parnaguá
Chapada das Mangabeiras
Serra da Tabatinga
Palmas
Pôrto Nacional
TOCANTINS
Gurupi
Peixe
Taguatinga
Barreiras
Paranã
Campos Belos
São Domingos
Santa Maria da Vitória
Serra Geral de Goiás
Posse
Carinhanha
Caetité
Brumado
Vitória da Conquista
Itabuna
Ilhéus
Ubaitaba
Canavieiras
Belmonte
Pôrto Seguro
Jequitinhonha
Itamaraju
Prado
Caravelas
Nanuque
Mucuri
Conceição da Barra
São Mateus
Linhares
Serra do Cachimbo
R A Z I L
Xingu
Santa Isabel do Morro
I. do Bananal
Serra Formosa
Serra do Roncador
O GROSSO
Planalto do Mato Grosso
Santo Antônio
Barra do Garças
Rondonópolis
Niquelândia
1678
Uruaçu
Aruanã
Serra Dourada
DIST. FED.
Formosa
BRASÍLIA
Taguatinga
Luziânia
Goiás
Anápolis
Goiânia
GOIÁS
Vianópolis
Morrinhos
Alto Araguaia
Jataí
Rio Verde
Itumbiara
Quirinópolis
Ipameri
Catalão
Paracatu
Patos de Minas
Araguari
MATO GROSSO DO SUL
Coxim
Uberlândia
Ituiutaba
Uberaba
Araxá
Patrocínio
Ibiá
MINAS GERAIS
Montes Claros
Janaúba
Januária
São Francisco
Monte Azul
Pedra Azul
Salinas
Araçuaí
Teófilo Otoni
Pirapora
Corinto
Curvelo
Diamantina
Sete Lagoas
Governador Valadares
Nova Venécia
Colatina
Ipatinga
Itabira
Caratinga
Serra do Espinhaço
ESPÍRITO SANTO
BELO HORIZONTE
Sabará
Nova Lima
Ouro Prêto
Conselheiro Lafaiete
Divinópolis
Ponte Nova
Cariacica
Vitória
Vila Velha
Cachoeiro de Itapemirim
Campo Grande
Miranda
Aquidauana
Paranaíba
Santa Fé do Sul
Águá Clara
São José do Barretos
Rio Prêto
Ribas do Rio Pardo
Três Lagoas
Andradina
Araçatuba
Panorama
Presidente Epitácio
Penápolis
Catanduva
Lins
SÃO PAULO
Araraquara
Poços de Caldas
Ribeirão Prêto
Franca
Passos
São João del Rei
Barbacena
Ubá
Itaperuna
Juiz de Fora
Três Rios
Campos
Nova Friburgo
Petrópolis
Dourados
Presidente Prudente
Marília
Bauru
Jaú
São Carlos
Piracicaba
Limeira
Campinas
Assis
Botucatu
Ponta Porã
Pedro Juan Caballero
Volta Redonda
RIO DE JANEIRO
Niterói
Cabo Frio
Mogi-Mirim
São Lourenço
2787
2890
1840
Greenwich
55
50
45
40
35
30
10
5
0
15
20

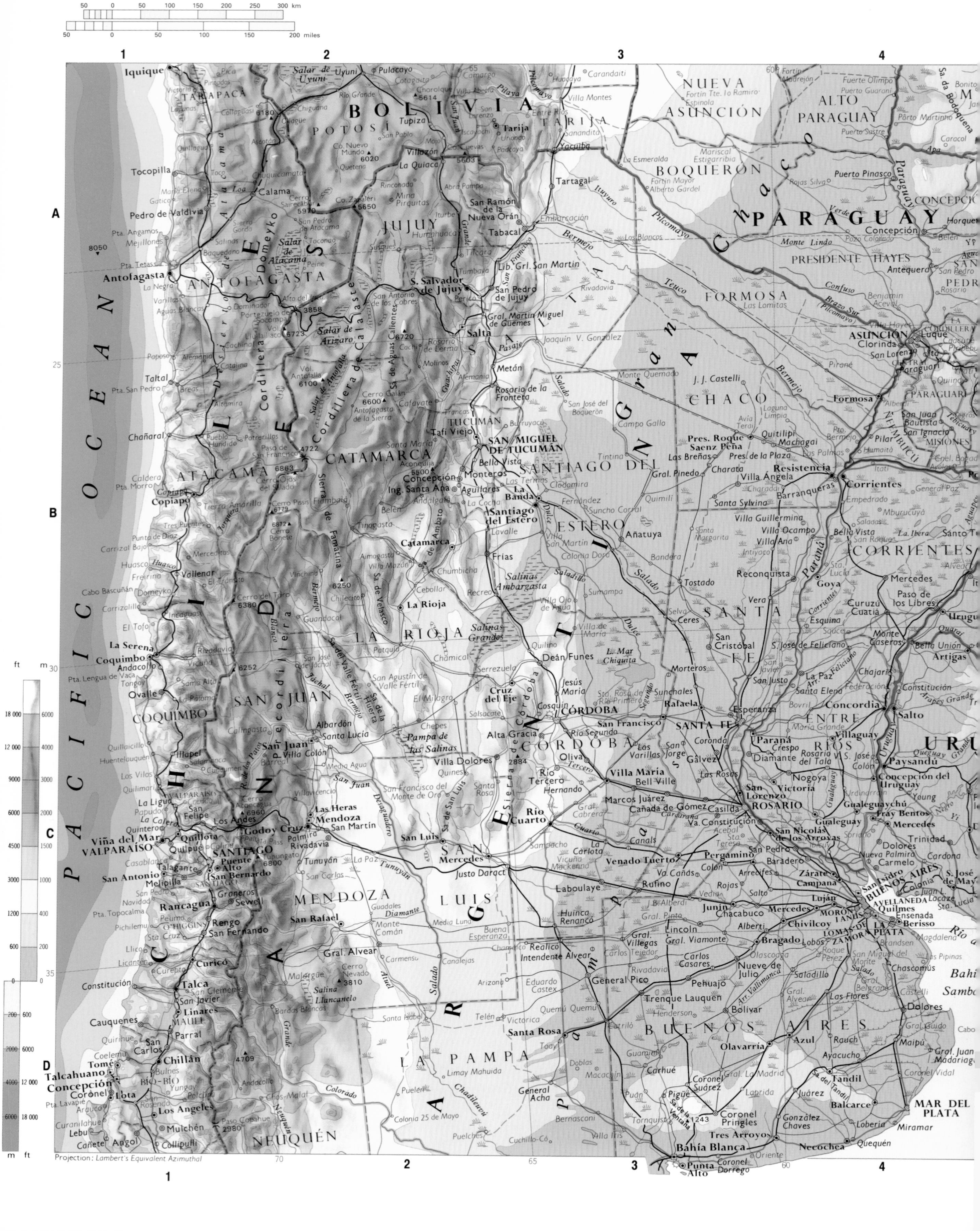

50 0 50 100 150 200 250 300 km
50 0 50 100 150 200 miles
PACIFIC OCEAN
BOLIVIA
POTOSÍ
TARIJA
PARAGUAY
NUEVA ASUNCIÓN
ALTO PARAGUAY
BOQUERÓN
PRESIDENTE HAYES
ARGENTINA
CHILE
ANDES
Gran Chaco
TARAPACÁ
ANTOFAGASTA
ATACAMA
COQUIMBO
JUJUY
SALTA
FORMOSA
CHACO
CATAMARCA
TUCUMÁN
SANTIAGO DEL ESTERO
LA RIOJA
SAN JUAN
CÓRDOBA
SANTA FE
CORRIENTES
MISIONES
ENTRE RÍOS
MENDOZA
SAN LUIS
LA PAMPA
BUENOS AIRES
NEUQUÉN
URU
Iquique
Tocopilla
Antofagasta
Taltal
Copiapó
Vallenar
La Serena
Coquimbo
Ovalle
Viña del Mar
VALPARAÍSO
SANTIAGO
San Antonio
Rancagua
San Fernando
Curicó
Talca
Linares
Chillán
Concepción
Talcahuano
Los Angeles
Calama
Salar de Uyuni
Uyuni
Tupiza
Tarija
Villazón
La Quiaca
San Salvador de Jujuy
Salta
SAN MIGUEL DE TUCUMÁN
Santiago del Estero
Catamarca
La Rioja
San Juan
Mendoza
San Luis
San Rafael
CÓRDOBA
Río Cuarto
Villa María
Santa Rosa
Bahía Blanca
ROSARIO
SANTA FE
Paraná
Resistencia
Corrientes
Formosa
ASUNCIÓN
Concepción
BUENOS AIRES
LA PLATA
MAR DEL PLATA
Tandil
Azul
Olavarría
Junín
Pergamino
Concordia
Salto
Paysandú
Projection: Lambert's Equivalent Azimuthal

124
125
128
5
6
7
A
B
C
D
25
30
35
55
50
45
40
West from Greenwich
BELO HORIZONTE
Lima
Itabirito
Vitória
Itaquari
Vila Velha
Guarapari
Castelo
Cachoeiro de Itapemirim
Três Lagoas
Andradina
Mirassol
S. José do Rio Prêto
Olímpia
Passos
Batatais
Congonhas
Cons. Lafaiete
Ouro Prêto
Ponte Nova
Araçatuba
Birigui
Catanduva
Bebedouro
Ribeirão Prêto
São Seb. do Paraíso
Oliveira
Campo Belo
Represa de Furnas
São João del Rei
Ubá
Muriaé
Carangola
Alegre
Três Pontas
Guaxupé
Barbacena
Cataguases
Itaperuna
Adamantina
Tupã
Lins
Novo Horizonte
Jaboticabal
Mococa
Casa Branca
Alfenas
Varginha
Santos Dumont
Leopoldina
Guarus
CAMPOS
MATO GROSSO DO SUL
SÃO PAULO
Presidente Prudente
Pres. Epitácio
Santo Anastácio
Rancharia
Martinópolis
Marília
Paraguaçu Paulista
Garça
Bauru
Jaú
São Carlos
Araraquara
São João da Boa Vista
Araras
Pinhal
Poços de Caldas
Pouso Alegre
Três Corações
São Lourenço
Juiz de Fora
Três Rios
Além Paraíba
RIO DE JANEIRO
Cabo de São Tomé
Ponta Porã
Pedro Juan Caballero
Amambay
Porecatu
Assis
Santa Cruz do Rio Pardo
Rio Claro
Limeira
Piracicaba
Americana
Mogi-Mirim
Ouro Fino
Itajubá
Volta Redonda
Barra do Piraí
Petrópolis
Nova Friburgo
Macaé
Paranavaí
Nova Esperança
Londrina
Rolândia
Cambará
Ourinhos
Botucatu
CAMPINAS
Cruzeiro
Guaratinguetá
Bragança Paulista
Barra Mansa
Nova Iguaçu
DUQUE DE CAXIAS
SÃO GONÇALO
NITERÓI
RIO DE JANEIRO
Cabo Frio
La. de Araruama
Umuarama
Cianorte
Maringá
Mandaguari
Arapongas
Apucarana
Cornélio Procópio
Jacarèzinho
Avaré
Tatuí
Itu
Sorocaba
Jundiaí
Taubaté
S. J. dos Campos
Jacareí
Mogi das Cruzes
Angra dos Reis
Ilha Grande
Baía da Ilha Grande
Tropic of Capricorn
Cruzeiro do Oeste
Goio Erê
Itapetininga
SÃO PAULO
SANTO ANDRÉ
São Bernardo do Campo
São Vicente
SANTOS
Guarujá
Ilha de São Sebastião
Pta. do Boi
Itanhaém
CANINDEYÚ
Guaíra
PARANÁ
BRAZIL
Itapeva
Itararé
Jaguariaíva
Paranapiacaba
Castro
Ponta Grossa
Serra do Mar
Iguape
Ilha Comprida
Ilha do Cardoso
ALTO PARANÁ
Foz do Iguaçu
Guarapuava
Ciudad del Este
Represa de Itaipu
CURITIBA
Antonina
Paranaguá
Palmeira
Irati
Lapa
Guaratuba
União da Vitória
Rio Negro
Mafra
São Francisco do Sul
Joinville
ITAPUÁ
Pto. União
Caçador
Blumenau
Itajaí
Brusque
MISIONES
Encarnación
Oberá
SANTA CATARINA
Campos Novos
Joaçaba
Rio do Sul
Ilha de Santa Catarina
Florianópolis
Erechim
Lajes
Santa Rosa
Carazinho
Passo Fundo
Santo Ângelo
Cruz Alta
Vacaria
Tubarão
Laguna
Cabo Santa Marta Grande
Criciúma
Araranguá
São Luís Gonzaga
Santiago
RIO GRANDE DO SUL
Bento Gonçalves
Caxias do Sul
Nôvo Hamburgo
Taquara
Santa Maria
Santa Cruz do Sul
Montenegro
São Leopoldo
Canoas
Alegrete
Cachoeira do Sul
Rio Pardo
Viamão
PÔRTO ALEGRE
Osorio
Santana do Livramento
Rivera
São Gabriel
Dom Pedrito
Camaquã
Lagoa dos Patos
Mostardas
Bagé
Canguçu
Pelotas
Tacuarembó
URUGUAY
Rio Grande
Melo
Jaguarão
Lagoa Mirim
San Gregorio
Rio Branco
Sta. Clara de Olimar
Sarandí del Yi
Treinta y Tres
Lagoa Mangueira
Santa Vitória do Palmar
José Batlle y Ordóñez
Lascano
Aigua
Castillos
Minas
Rocha
San Carlos
Maldonado
ATLANTIC OCEAN
5304

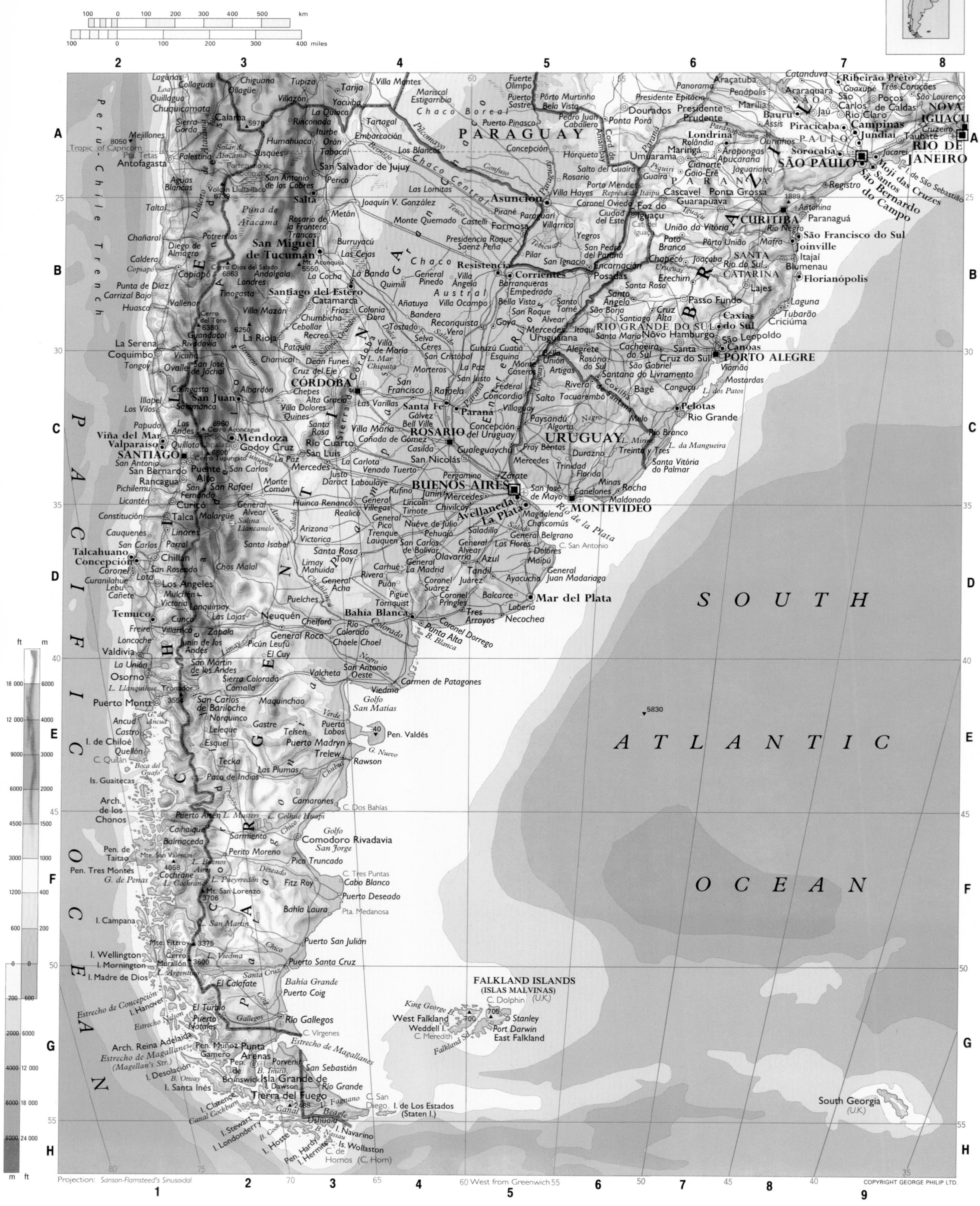

PARAGUAY
URUGUAY
SOUTH ATLANTIC OCEAN
PACIFIC OCEAN
Peru-Chile Trench
Chaco Boreal
Chaco Central
Chaco Austral
Tropic of Capricorn
Asunción
Buenos Aires
Montevideo
Santiago
São Paulo
Rio de Janeiro
Porto Alegre
Curitiba
Córdoba
Rosario
Mendoza
San Miguel de Tucumán
Salta
Antofagasta
Valparaíso
Viña del Mar
Concepción
Talcahuano
Temuco
Valdivia
Osorno
Puerto Montt
La Plata
Mar del Plata
Bahía Blanca
Neuquén
Comodoro Rivadavia
Río Gallegos
Punta Arenas
Ushuaia
Isla Grande de Tierra del Fuego
Estrecho de Magallanes (Magellan's Str.)
C. de Hornos (C. Hom)
FALKLAND ISLANDS (ISLAS MALVINAS) (U.K.)
West Falkland
East Falkland
Stanley
South Georgia (U.K.)
Pen. Valdés
Golfo San Matías
Golfo San Jorge
Río de la Plata
Mt. Aconcagua 6960
Projection: Sanson-Flamsteed's Sinusoidal
60 West from Greenwich
COPYRIGHT GEORGE PHILIP LTD.

INDEX

The index contains the names of all the principal places and features shown on the World Maps. Each name is followed by an additional entry in italics giving the country or region within which it is located. The alphabetical order of names composed of two or more words is governed primarily by the first word and then by the second. This is an example of the rule:

Mīr Kūh, *Iran*	**71**	**E8**
Mīr Shahdād, *Iran*	**71**	**E8**
Mira, *Italy*	**29**	**C9**
Mira por vos Cay, *Bahamas* . .	**121**	**B5**
Miraj, *India*	**66**	**L9**

Physical features composed of a proper name (Erie) and a description (Lake) are positioned alphabetically by the proper name. The description is positioned after the proper name and is usually abbreviated:

Erie, L., *N. Amer.* **110** **D4**

Where a description forms part of a settlement or administrative name however, it is always written in full and put in its true alphabetic position:

Mount Morris, *U.S.A.* **110** **D7**

Names beginning with M' and Mc are indexed as if they were spelled Mac. Names beginning St. are alphabetised under Saint, but Sankt, Sint, Sant', Santa and San are all spelt in full and are alphabetised accordingly. If the same place name occurs two or more times in the index and all are in the same country, each is followed by the name of the administrative subdivision in which it is located. The names are placed in the alphabetical order of the subdivisions. For example:

Jackson, *Ky., U.S.A.*	**108**	**G4**
Jackson, *Mich., U.S.A.*	**108**	**D3**
Jackson, *Minn., U.S.A.*	**112**	**D7**

The number in bold type which follows each name in the index refers to the number of the map page where that feature or place will be found. This is usually the largest scale at which the place or feature appears.

The letter and figure which are in bold type immediately after the page number give the grid square on the map page, within which the feature is situated. The letter represents the latitude and the figure the longitude.

In some cases the feature itself may fall within the specified square, while the name is outside. This is usually the case only with features which are larger than a grid square.

Rivers are indexed to their mouths or confluences, and carry the symbol → after their names. A solid square ■ follows the name of a country, while an open square □ refers to a first order administrative area.

ABBREVIATIONS USED IN THE INDEX

A.C.T. – Australian Capital Territory
Afghan. – Afghanistan
Ala. – Alabama
Alta. – Alberta
Amer. – America(n)
Arch. – Archipelago
Ariz. – Arizona
Ark. – Arkansas
Atl. Oc. – Atlantic Ocean
B. – Baie, Bahía, Bay, Bucht, Bugt
B.C. – British Columbia
Bangla. – Bangladesh
Barr. – Barrage
Bos.-H. – Bosnia-Herzegovina
C. – Cabo, Cap, Cape, Coast
C.A.R. – Central African Republic
C. Prov. – Cape Province
Calif. – California
Cent. – Central
Chan. – Channel
Colo. – Colorado
Conn. – Connecticut
Cord. – Cordillera
Cr. – Creek
Czech. – Czech Republic
D.C. – District of Columbia
Del. – Delaware
Dep. – Dependency
Des. – Desert
Dist. – District
Dj. – Djebel
Domin. – Dominica
Dom. Rep. – Dominican Republic
E. – East
E. Salv. – El Salvador
Eq. Guin. – Equatorial Guinea
Fla. – Florida
Falk. Is. – Falkland Is.
G. – Golfe, Golfo, Gulf, Guba, Gebel
Ga. – Georgia
Gt. – Great, Greater
Guinea-Biss. – Guinea-Bissau
H.K. – Hong Kong
H.P. – Himachal Pradesh
Hants. – Hampshire
Harb. – Harbor, Harbour
Hd. – Head
Hts. – Heights
I.(s). – Île, Ilha, Insel, Isla, Island, Isle
Ill. – Illinois
Ind. – Indiana
Ind. Oc. – Indian Ocean
Ivory C. – Ivory Coast
J. – Jabal, Jebel, Jazira
Junc. – Junction
K. – Kap, Kapp
Kans. – Kansas
Kep. – Kepulauan
Ky. – Kentucky
L. – Lac, Lacul, Lago, Lagoa, Lake, Limni, Loch, Lough
La. – Louisiana
Liech. – Liechtenstein
Lux. – Luxembourg
Mad. P. – Madhya Pradesh
Madag. – Madagascar
Man. – Manitoba
Mass. – Massachusetts
Md. – Maryland
Me. – Maine
Medit. S. – Mediterranean Sea
Mich. – Michigan
Minn. – Minnesota
Miss. – Mississippi
Mo. – Missouri
Mont. – Montana
Mozam. – Mozambique
Mt.(e) – Mont, Monte, Monti, Montaña, Mountain
N. – Nord, Norte, North, Northern, Nouveau
N.B. – New Brunswick
N.C. – North Carolina
N. Cal. – New Caledonia
N. Dak. – North Dakota
N.H. – New Hampshire
N.I. – North Island
N.J. – New Jersey
N. Mex. – New Mexico
N.S. – Nova Scotia
N.S.W. – New South Wales
N.W.T. – North West Territory
N.Y. – New York
N.Z. – New Zealand
Nebr. – Nebraska
Neths. – Netherlands
Nev. – Nevada
Nfld. – Newfoundland
Nic. – Nicaragua
O. – Oued, Ouadi
Occ. – Occidentale
Okla. – Oklahoma
Ont. – Ontario
Or. – Orientale
Oreg. – Oregon
Os. – Ostrov
Oz. – Ozero
P. – Pass, Passo, Pasul, Pulau
P.E.I. – Prince Edward Island
Pa. – Pennsylvania
Pac. Oc. – Pacific Ocean
Papua N.G. – Papua New Guinea
Pass. – Passage
Pen. – Peninsula, Péninsule
Phil. – Philippines
Pk. – Park, Peak
Plat. – Plateau
Prov. – Province, Provincial
Pt. – Point
Pta. – Ponta, Punta
Pte. – Pointe
Qué. – Québec
Queens. – Queensland
R. – Rio, River
R.I. – Rhode Island
Ra.(s). – Range(s)
Raj. – Rajasthan
Reg. – Region
Rep. – Republic
Res. – Reserve, Reservoir
S. – San, South, Sea
Si. Arabia – Saudi Arabia
S.C. – South Carolina
S. Dak. – South Dakota
S.I. – South Island
S. Leone – Sierra Leone
Sa. – Serra, Sierra
Sask. – Saskatchewan
Scot. – Scotland
Sd. – Sound
Sev. – Severnaya
Sib. – Siberia
Sprs. – Springs
St. – Saint
Sta. – Santa, Station
Ste. – Sainte
Sto. – Santo
Str. – Strait, Stretto
Switz. – Switzerland
Tas. – Tasmania
Tenn. – Tennessee
Tex. – Texas
Tg. – Tanjung
Trin. & Tob. – Trinidad & Tobago
U.A.E. – United Arab Emirates
U.K. – United Kingdom
U.S.A. – United States of America
Ut. P. – Uttar Pradesh
Va. – Virginia
Vdkhr. – Vodokhranilishche
Vf. – Vîrful
Vic. – Victoria
Vol. – Volcano
Vt. – Vermont
W. – Wadi, West
W. Va. – West Virginia
Wash. – Washington
Wis. – Wisconsin
Wlkp. – Wielkopolski
Wyo. – Wyoming
Yorks. – Yorkshire
Yug. – Yugoslavia

A

A Baña, *Spain* 34 C2
A Cañiza, *Spain* 34 C2
A Coruña, *Spain* 34 B2
A Estrada, *Spain* 34 C2
A Fonsagrada, *Spain* 34 B3
A Guarda, *Spain* 34 D2
A Gudiña, *Spain* 34 C3
A Rúa, *Spain* 34 C3
Aachen, *Germany* 24 E2
Aalborg = Ålborg, *Denmark* 11 G3
Aalen, *Germany* 25 G6
A'âli en Nîl □, *Sudan* 81 F3
Aalst, *Belgium* 17 D4
Aalten, *Neths.* 17 C6
Aalter, *Belgium* 17 C3
Äänekoski, *Finland* 9 E21
Aarau, *Switz.* 25 H4
Aarberg, *Switz.* 25 H3
Aare →, *Switz.* 25 H4
Aargau □, *Switz.* 25 H4
Aarhus = Århus, *Denmark* 11 H4
Aarschot, *Belgium* 17 D4
Aba, *China* 58 A3
Aba, *Dem. Rep. of the Congo* 86 B3
Aba, *Nigeria* 83 D6
Âbâ, Jazîrat, *Sudan* 81 E3
Ābādān, *Iran* 71 D6
Abade, *Ethiopia* 81 F4
Ābādeh, *Iran* 71 D7
Abadin, *Spain* 34 B3
Abadla, *Algeria* 78 B5
Abaetetuba, *Brazil* 125 D9
Abagnar Qi, *China* 56 C9
Abai, *Paraguay* 127 B4
Abak, *Nigeria* 83 E6
Abakaliki, *Nigeria* 83 D6
Abakan, *Russia* 51 D10
Abalemma, *Niger* 83 B6
Abana, *Turkey* 72 B6
Abancay, *Peru* 124 F4
Abano Terme, *Italy* 29 C8
Abarán, *Spain* 33 G3
Abariringa, *Kiribati* 96 H10
Abarqū, *Iran* 71 D7
Abashiri, *Japan* 54 C12
Abashiri-Wan, *Japan* 54 C12
Abaújszántó, *Hungary* 42 B6
Abava →, *Latvia* 44 A8
Abay, *Kazakstan* 50 E8
Abaya, L., *Ethiopia* 81 F4
Abaza, *Russia* 50 D10
Abbadia San Salvatore, *Italy* 29 F8
'Abbāsābād, *Iran* 71 C8
Abbay = Nîl el Azraq →, *Sudan* 81 D3
Abbaye, Pt., *U.S.A.* 108 B1
Abbé, L., *Ethiopia* 81 E5
Abbeville, *France* 19 B8
Abbeville, *La., U.S.A.* 113 L8
Abbeville, *S.C., U.S.A.* 109 H4
Abbiategrasso, *Italy* 28 C5
Abbieglassie, *Australia* 95 D4
Abbot Ice Shelf, *Antarctica* 5 D16
Abbotsford, *Canada* 104 D4
Abbotsford, *U.S.A.* 112 C9
Abbottabad, *Pakistan* 68 B5
Abd al Kūrī, *Ind. Oc.* 74 E5
Ābdar, *Iran* 71 D7
'Abdolābād, *Iran* 71 C8
Abéché, *Chad* 79 F10
Abejar, *Spain* 32 D2
Abekr, *Sudan* 81 E2
Abengourou, *Ivory C.* 82 D4
Abenójar, *Spain* 35 G6
Åbenrå, *Denmark* 11 J3
Abensberg, *Germany* 25 G7
Abeokuta, *Nigeria* 83 D5
Aber, *Uganda* 86 B3
Aberaeron, *U.K.* 13 E3
Aberayron = Aberaeron, *U.K.* 13 E3
Aberchirder, *U.K.* 14 D6
Abercorn = Mbala, *Zambia* 87 D3
Abercorn, *Australia* 95 D5
Aberdare, *U.K.* 13 F4
Aberdare Ra., *Kenya* 86 C4
Aberdeen, *Australia* 95 E5
Aberdeen, *Canada* 105 C7
Aberdeen, *S. Africa* 88 E3
Aberdeen, *U.K.* 14 D6
Aberdeen, *Ala., U.S.A.* 109 J1
Aberdeen, *Idaho, U.S.A.* 114 E7
Aberdeen, *S. Dak., U.S.A.* 112 C5
Aberdeen, *Wash., U.S.A.* 116 D3
Aberdeen, City of □, *U.K.* 14 D6
Aberdeenshire □, *U.K.* 14 D6
Aberdovey = Aberdyfi, *U.K.* 13 E3
Aberdyfi, *U.K.* 13 E3
Aberfeldy, *U.K.* 14 E5
Abergavenny, *U.K.* 13 F4
Abergele, *U.K.* 12 D4
Abernathy, *U.S.A.* 113 J4
Abert, L., *U.S.A.* 114 E3
Aberystwyth, *U.K.* 13 E3
Abha, *Si. Arabia* 80 D5
Abhar, *Iran* 71 B6
Abhayapuri, *India* 69 F14
Abia □, *Nigeria* 83 D6
Abide, *Turkey* 39 C11
Abidiya, *Sudan* 80 D3
Abidjan, *Ivory C.* 82 D4
Abilene, *Kans., U.S.A.* 112 F6
Abilene, *Tex., U.S.A.* 113 J5
Abingdon, *U.K.* 13 F6
Abingdon, *Ill., U.S.A.* 112 E9
Abingdon, *Va., U.S.A.* 109 G5
Abington Reef, *Australia* 94 B4
Abitau →, *Canada* 105 B7
Abitau L., *Canada* 105 A7
Abitibi L., *Canada* 102 C4
Abiy Adi, *Ethiopia* 81 E4
Abkhaz Republic □ = Abkhazia □, *Georgia* 49 J5
Abkhazia □, *Georgia* 49 J5
Abminga, *Australia* 95 D1
Abnûb, *Egypt* 80 B3
Åbo = Turku, *Finland* 9 F20
Abocho, *Nigeria* 83 D6
Abohar, *India* 68 D6
Aboisso, *Ivory C.* 82 D4
Abomey, *Benin* 83 D5
Abong-Mbang, *Cameroon* 84 D2
Abonnema, *Nigeria* 83 E6
Abony, *Hungary* 42 C5
Aboso, *Ghana* 82 D4
Abou-Deïa, *Chad* 79 F9
Aboyne, *U.K.* 14 D6
Abra Pampa, *Argentina* 126 A2
Abrantes, *Portugal* 35 F2
Abreojos, Pta., *Mexico* 118 B2
Abri, *Esh Shamâliya, Sudan* 80 C3
Abri, *Janub Kordofân, Sudan* 81 E3
Abrud, *Romania* 42 D8
Abruzzo □, *Italy* 29 F10
Absaroka Range, *U.S.A.* 114 D9
Abtenau, *Austria* 26 D6
Abū al Khaşīb, *Iraq* 71 D6
Abū 'Alī, *Si. Arabia* 71 E6
Abū 'Alī →, *Lebanon* 75 A4
Abû Ballas, *Egypt* 80 C2
Abu Deleiq, *Sudan* 81 D3
Abu Dhabi = Abū Ẓāby, *U.A.E.* 71 E7
Abû Dis, *Sudan* 80 D3
Abû Dom, *Sudan* 81 D3
Abū Du'ān, *Syria* 70 B3
Abu el Gairi, W. →, *Egypt* 75 F2
Abû Gabra, *Sudan* 81 E2
Abu Ga'da, W. →, *Egypt* 75 F1
Abû Gubeiha, *Sudan* 81 E3
Abu Habl, Khawr →, *Sudan* 81 E3
Abū Ḥadrīyah, *Si. Arabia* 71 E6
Abu Hamed, *Sudan* 80 D3
Abu Haraz, *An Nîl el Azraq, Sudan* 81 E3
Abû Haraz, *Esh Shamâliya, Sudan* 80 D3
Abû Higar, *Sudan* 81 E3
Abū Kamāl, *Syria* 70 C4
Abū Madd, Ra's, *Si. Arabia* 70 E3
Abu Matariq, *Sudan* 81 E2
Abu Qir, *Egypt* 80 H7
Abu Qireiya, *Egypt* 80 C4
Abu Qurqâs, *Egypt* 80 J7
Abu Şafāt, W. →, *Jordan* 75 E5
Abû Simbel, *Egypt* 80 C3
Abū Şukhayr, *Iraq* 70 D5
Abu Tig, *Egypt* 80 B3
Abu Tiga, *Sudan* 81 E3
Abû Zabad, *Sudan* 81 E2
Abū Ẓāby, *U.A.E.* 71 E7
Abū Zeydābād, *Iran* 71 C6
Abuja, *Nigeria* 83 D6
Abukuma-Gawa →, *Japan* 54 E10
Abukuma-Sammyaku, *Japan* 54 F10
Abunã, *Brazil* 124 E5
Abunã →, *Brazil* 124 E5
Aburo, *Dem. Rep. of the Congo* 86 B3
Abut Hd., *N.Z.* 91 K3
Abwong, *Sudan* 81 F3
Åby, *Sweden* 11 F10
Aby, Lagune, *Ivory C.* 82 D4
Åbybro, *Denmark* 11 G3
Açailândia, *Brazil* 125 D9
Acajutla, *El Salv.* 120 D2
Acámbaro, *Mexico* 118 D4
Acanthus, *Greece* 40 F7
Acaponeta, *Mexico* 118 C3
Acapulco, *Mexico* 119 D5
Acarai, Serra, *Brazil* 124 C7
Acarigua, *Venezuela* 124 B5
Acatlán, *Mexico* 119 D5
Acayucan, *Mexico* 119 D6
Accéglio, *Italy* 28 D4
Accomac, *U.S.A.* 108 G8
Accous, *France* 20 E3
Accra, *Ghana* 83 D4
Accrington, *U.K.* 12 D5
Acebal, *Argentina* 126 C3
Aceh □, *Indonesia* 62 D1
Acerra, *Italy* 31 B7
Aceuchal, *Spain* 35 G4
Achalpur, *India* 66 J10
Acheng, *China* 57 B14
Achenkirch, *Austria* 26 D4
Achensee, *Austria* 26 D4
Acher, *India* 68 H5
Achern, *Germany* 25 G4
Achill Hd., *Ireland* 15 C1
Achill I., *Ireland* 15 C1
Achim, *Germany* 24 B5
Achinsk, *Russia* 51 D10
Achol, *Sudan* 81 F3
Acıgöl, *Turkey* 39 D11
Acıpayam, *Turkey* 39 D11
Acireale, *Italy* 31 E8
Ackerman, *U.S.A.* 113 J10
Acklins I., *Bahamas* 121 B5
Acme, *Canada* 104 C6
Aconcagua, Cerro, *Argentina* 126 C2
Aconquija, Mt., *Argentina* 126 B2
Açores, Is. dos = Azores, *Atl. Oc.* 76 C1
Acquapendente, *Italy* 29 F8
Acquasanta Terme, *Italy* 29 F10
Acquasparta, *Italy* 29 F9
Acquaviva delle Fonti, *Italy* 31 B9
Ácqui Terme, *Italy* 28 D5
Acraman, L., *Australia* 95 E2
Acre = 'Akko, *Israel* 75 C4
Acre □, *Brazil* 124 E4
Acre →, *Brazil* 124 E5
Acri, *Italy* 31 C9
Acs, *Hungary* 42 C3
Actium, *Greece* 38 C2
Acton, *Canada* 110 C4
Ad Dammām, *Si. Arabia* 71 E6
Ad Dawhah, *Qatar* 71 E6
Ad Dawr, *Iraq* 70 C4
Ad Dir'īyah, *Si. Arabia* 70 E5
Ad Dīwānīyah, *Iraq* 70 D5
Ad Dujayl, *Iraq* 70 C5
Ada, *Ghana* 83 D5
Ada, *Serbia, Yug.* 42 E5
Ada, *Minn., U.S.A.* 112 B6
Ada, *Okla., U.S.A.* 113 H6
Adaja →, *Spain* 34 D6
Adamaoua, Massif de l', *Cameroon* 83 D7
Adamawa □, *Nigeria* 83 D7
Adamawa Highlands = Adamaoua, Massif de l', *Cameroon* 83 D7
Adamello, Mte., *Italy* 28 B7
Adami Tulu, *Ethiopia* 81 F4
Adaminaby, *Australia* 95 F4
Adams, *Mass., U.S.A.* 111 D11
Adams, *N.Y., U.S.A.* 111 C8
Adams, *Wis., U.S.A.* 112 D10
Adam's Bridge, *Sri Lanka* 66 Q11
Adams L., *Canada* 104 C5
Adams Mt., *U.S.A.* 116 D5
Adam's Peak, *Sri Lanka* 66 R12
Adamuz, *Spain* 35 G6
Adana, *Turkey* 72 D6
Adanero, *Spain* 34 E6
Adapazarı, *Turkey* 72 B4
Adarama, *Sudan* 81 D3
Adare, C., *Antarctica* 5 D11
Adaut, *Indonesia* 63 F8
Adavale, *Australia* 95 D3
Adda →, *Italy* 28 C6
Addis Ababa = Addis Abeba, *Ethiopia* 81 F4
Addis Abeba, *Ethiopia* 81 F4
Addis Alem, *Ethiopia* 81 F4
Addison, *U.S.A.* 110 D7
Addo, *S. Africa* 88 E4
Adebour, *Niger* 83 C7
Ādeh, *Iran* 70 B5
Adel, *U.S.A.* 109 K4
Adelaide, *Australia* 95 E2
Adelaide, *Bahamas* 120 A4
Adelaide, *S. Africa* 88 E4
Adelaide I., *Antarctica* 5 C17
Adelaide Pen., *Canada* 100 B10
Adelaide River, *Australia* 92 B5
Adelanto, *U.S.A.* 117 L9
Adele I., *Australia* 92 C3
Adélie, Terre, *Antarctica* 5 C10
Adélie Land = Adélie, Terre, *Antarctica* 5 C10
Ademuz, *Spain* 32 E3
Aden = Al 'Adan, *Yemen* 74 E4
Aden, G. of, *Asia* 74 E4
Adendorp, *S. Africa* 88 E3
Adh Dhayd, *U.A.E.* 71 E7
Adhoi, *India* 68 H4
Adi, *Indonesia* 63 E8
Adi Daro, *Ethiopia* 81 E4
Adi Keyih, *Eritrea* 81 E4
Adi Kwala, *Eritrea* 81 E4
Adi Ugri, *Eritrea* 81 E4
Adieu, C., *Australia* 93 F5
Adieu Pt., *Australia* 92 C3
Adigala, *Ethiopia* 81 E5
Adige →, *Italy* 29 C9
Adigrat, *Ethiopia* 81 E4
Adıgüzel Barajı, *Turkey* 39 C11
Adilabad, *India* 66 K11
Adilcevaz, *Turkey* 73 C10
Adin, *U.S.A.* 114 F3
Adin Khel, *Afghan.* 66 C6
Adirondack Mts., *U.S.A.* 111 C10
Adıyaman, *Turkey* 73 D8
Adjohon, *Benin* 83 D5
Adjud, *Romania* 43 D12
Adjumani, *Uganda* 86 B3
Adlavik Is., *Canada* 103 A8
Adler, *Russia* 49 J4
Admiralty G., *Australia* 92 B4
Admiralty I., *U.S.A.* 100 C6
Admiralty Inlet, *U.S.A.* 114 C2
Admiralty Is., *Papua N. G.* 96 H6
Ado, *Nigeria* 83 D5
Ado-Ekiti, *Nigeria* 83 D6
Adok, *Sudan* 81 F3
Adola, *Ethiopia* 81 E5
Adonara, *Indonesia* 63 F6
Adoni, *India* 66 M10
Adony, *Hungary* 42 C3
Adour →, *France* 20 E2
Adra, *India* 69 H12
Adra, *Spain* 35 J7
Adrano, *Italy* 31 E7
Adrar, *Algeria* 76 D4
Ádria, *Italy* 29 C9
Adrian, *Mich., U.S.A.* 108 E3
Adrian, *Tex., U.S.A.* 113 H3
Adriatic Sea, *Medit. S.* 6 G9
Adua, *Indonesia* 63 E7
Adwa, *Ethiopia* 81 E4
Adygea □, *Russia* 49 H5
Adzhar Republic □ = Ajaria □, *Georgia* 49 K6
Adzopé, *Ivory C.* 82 D4
Ægean Sea, *Medit. S.* 39 C7
Aerhtai Shan, *Mongolia* 60 B4
Ærø, *Denmark* 11 K4
Ærøskøbing, *Denmark* 11 K4
Aëtós, *Greece* 38 D3
'Afak, *Iraq* 70 C5
Afándou, *Greece* 36 C10
Afghanistan ■, *Asia* 66 C4
Afikpo, *Nigeria* 83 D6
Afragóla, *Italy* 31 B7
Afrera, *Ethiopia* 81 E5
'Afrīn, *Syria* 70 B3
Afşin, *Turkey* 72 C7
Afton, *U.S.A.* 111 D9
Afuá, *Brazil* 125 D8
'Afula, *Israel* 75 C4
Afyon, *Turkey* 39 C12
Afyon □, *Turkey* 39 C12
Afyonkarahisar = Afyon, *Turkey* 39 C12
Aga, *Egypt* 80 H7
Agadès = Agadez, *Niger* 83 B6
Agadez, *Niger* 83 B6
Agadir, *Morocco* 78 B4
Agaete, *Canary Is.* 37 F4
Ağapınar, *Turkey* 39 B12
Agar, *India* 68 H7
Agaro, *Ethiopia* 81 F4
Agartala, *India* 67 H17
Agăş, *Romania* 43 D11
Agassiz, *Canada* 104 D4
Agats, *Indonesia* 63 F9
Agbélouvé, *Togo* 83 D5
Agboville, *Ivory C.* 82 D4
Ağcabädi, *Azerbaijan* 49 K8
Ağdam, *Azerbaijan* 49 L8
Ağdaş, *Azerbaijan* 49 K8
Agde, *France* 20 E7
Agde, C. d', *France* 20 E7
Agdzhabedi = Ağcabädi, *Azerbaijan* 49 K8
Agen, *France* 20 D4
Agerbæk, *Denmark* 11 J2
Agersø, *Denmark* 11 J5
Ageyevo, *Russia* 46 E9
Āgh Kand, *Iran* 71 B6
Aghireşu, *Romania* 43 D8
Aginskoye, *Russia* 51 D12
Ağlasun, *Turkey* 39 D12
Agly →, *France* 20 F7
Agnibilékrou, *Ivory C.* 82 D4
Agnita, *Romania* 43 E9
Agnone, *Italy* 29 G11
Agofie, *Ghana* 83 D5
Agogna →, *Italy* 28 C5
Agogo, *Sudan* 81 F2
Agön, *Sweden* 10 C11
Agon Coutainville, *France* 18 C5
Ágordo, *Italy* 29 B9
Agout →, *France* 20 E5
Agra, *India* 68 F7
Agrakhanskiy Poluostrov, *Russia* 49 J8
Agramunt, *Spain* 32 D6
Agreda, *Spain* 32 D3
Ağri, *Turkey* 73 C10
Agri →, *Italy* 31 B9
Ağrı Dağı, *Turkey* 73 C11
Agriá, *Greece* 38 B5
Agrigento, *Italy* 30 E6
Agrínion, *Greece* 38 C3
Agrópoli, *Italy* 31 B7
Ağstafa, *Azerbaijan* 49 K7
Agua Caliente, *Baja Calif., Mexico* 117 N10
Agua Caliente, *Sinaloa, Mexico* 118 B3
Agua Caliente Springs, *U.S.A.* 117 N10
Água Clara, *Brazil* 125 H8
Agua Hechicero, *Mexico* 117 N10
Agua Prieta, *Mexico* 118 A3
Aguadilla, *Puerto Rico* 121 C6
Aguadulce, *Panama* 120 E3
Aguanga, *U.S.A.* 117 M10
Aguanish, *Canada* 103 B7
Aguanus →, *Canada* 103 B7
Aguapey →, *Argentina* 126 B4
Aguaray Guazú →, *Paraguay* 126 A4
Aguarico →, *Ecuador* 124 D3
Aguas →, *Spain* 32 D4
Aguas Blancas, *Chile* 126 A2
Aguas Calientes, Sierra de, *Argentina* 126 B2
Aguascalientes, *Mexico* 118 C4
Aguascalientes □, *Mexico* 118 C4
Agudo, *Spain* 35 G6
Águeda, *Portugal* 34 E2
Agueda →, *Spain* 34 D4
Aguié, *Niger* 83 C6
Aguilafuente, *Spain* 34 D6
Aguilar, *Spain* 35 H6
Aguilar de Campóo, *Spain* 34 C6
Aguilares, *Argentina* 126 B2
Aguilas, *Spain* 33 H3
Agüimes, *Canary Is.* 37 G4
Aguja, C. de la, *Colombia* 122 B3
Agulaa, *Ethiopia* 81 E4
Agulhas, C., *S. Africa* 88 E3
Agulo, *Canary Is.* 37 F2
Agung, *Indonesia* 62 F5
Agur, *Uganda* 86 B3
Agusan →, *Phil.* 61 G6
Ağva, *Turkey* 41 E13
Agvali, *Russia* 49 J8
Aha Mts., *Botswana* 88 B3
Ahaggar, *Algeria* 78 D7
Ahamansu, *Ghana* 83 D5
Ahar, *Iran* 70 B5
Ahat, *Turkey* 39 C11
Ahaus, *Germany* 24 C2
Ahipara B., *N.Z.* 91 F4
Ahir Dağı, *Turkey* 39 C12
Ahiri, *India* 66 K12
Ahlat, *Turkey* 73 C10
Ahlen, *Germany* 24 D3
Ahmad Wal, *Pakistan* 68 E1
Ahmadabad, *India* 68 H5
Aḥmadābād, *Khorāsān, Iran* 71 C9
Aḥmadābād, *Khorāsān, Iran* 71 C8
Aḥmadī, *Iran* 71 E8
Ahmadnagar, *India* 66 K9
Ahmadpur, *Pakistan* 68 E4
Ahmar, *Ethiopia* 81 F5
Ahmedabad = Ahmadabad, *India* 68 H5
Ahmednagar = Ahmadnagar, *India* 66 K9
Ahmetbey, *Turkey* 41 E11
Ahmetler, *Turkey* 39 C11
Ahmetli, *Turkey* 39 C9
Ahoada, *Nigeria* 83 D6
Ahome, *Mexico* 118 B3
Ahr →, *Germany* 24 E3
Ahram, *Iran* 71 D6
Ahrax Pt., *Malta* 36 D1
Ahrensbök, *Germany* 24 A6
Ahrensburg, *Germany* 24 B6
Āhū, *Iran* 71 C6
Ahuachapán, *El Salv.* 120 D2
Ahun, *France* 19 F9
Åhus, *Sweden* 11 J8
Ahvāz, *Iran* 71 D6
Ahvenanmaa = Åland, *Finland* 9 F19
Aḥwar, *Yemen* 74 E4
Ahzar, *Mali* 83 B5
Aichach, *Germany* 25 G7
Aichi □, *Japan* 55 G8
Aigle, *Switz.* 25 J2
Aignay-le-Duc, *France* 19 E11
Aigoual, Mt., *France* 20 D7
Aigre, *France* 20 C4
Aigua, *Uruguay* 127 C5
Aigueperse, *France* 19 F10
Aigues →, *France* 21 D8
Aigues-Mortes, *France* 21 E8
Aigues-Mortes, G. d', *France* 21 E8
Aiguilles, *France* 21 D10
Aiguillon, *France* 20 D4
Aigurande, *France* 19 F8
Aihui, *China* 60 A7
Aija, *Peru* 124 E3
Aikawa, *Japan* 54 E9
Aiken, *U.S.A.* 109 J5
Ailao Shan, *China* 58 F3
Aillant-sur-Tholon, *France* 19 E10
Aillik, *Canada* 103 A8
Ailsa Craig, *U.K.* 14 F3
'Ailūn, *Jordan* 75 C4
Aim, *Russia* 51 D14
Aimere, *Indonesia* 63 F6
Aimogasta, *Argentina* 126 B2
Ain □, *France* 19 F12
Ain →, *France* 21 C9
Aïn Ben Tili, *Mauritania* 78 C4
Ain Dalla, *Egypt* 80 B2
Ain el Mafki, *Egypt* 80 B2
Ain Girba, *Egypt* 80 B2
Ain Qeiqab, *Egypt* 80 B1
Aïn-Sefra, *Algeria* 78 B5
Ain Sheikh Murzûk, *Egypt* 80 B2
'Ain Sudr, *Egypt* 75 F2
Ain Sukhna, *Egypt* 80 J8
Ain Zeitûn, *Egypt* 80 B2
Ainaži, *Latvia* 9 H21
Aínos Óros, *Greece* 38 C2
Ainsworth, *U.S.A.* 112 D5
Aiquile, *Bolivia* 124 G5
Aïr, *Niger* 83 B6
Air Hitam, *Malaysia* 65 M4
Airaines, *France* 19 C8
Airdrie, *U.K.* 14 F5
Aire →, *France* 19 C11
Aire →, *U.K.* 12 D7
Aire, I. de l', *Spain* 37 B11
Aire-sur-la-Lys, *France* 19 B9
Aire-sur-l'Adour, *France* 20 E3
Airlie Beach, *Australia* 94 C4

Airvault, *France* 18 F6
Aisch →, *Germany* 25 F6
Aisne □, *France* 19 C10
Aisne →, *France* 19 C9
Aitana, Sierra de, *Spain* 33 G4
Aitkin, *U.S.A.* 112 B8
Aitolía Kai Akarnanía □, *Greece* 38 C3
Aitolikón, *Greece* 38 C3
Aiud, *Romania* 43 D8
Aix-en-Provence, *France* 21 E9
Aix-la-Chapelle = Aachen, *Germany* 24 E2
Aix-les-Bains, *France* 21 C9
Aixe-sur-Vienne, *France* 20 C5
Aiyansh, *Canada* 104 B3
Aíyina, *Greece* 38 D5
Aiyínion, *Greece* 40 F6
Aíyion, *Greece* 38 C4
Aizawl, *India* 67 H18
Aizenay, *France* 18 F5
Aizkraukle, *Latvia* 9 H21
Aizpute, *Latvia* 9 H19
Aizuwakamatsu, *Japan* 54 F9
Ajaccio, *France* 21 G12
Ajaccio, G. d', *France* 21 G12
Ajalpan, *Mexico* 119 D5
Ajanta Ra., *India* 66 J9
Ajari Rep. = Ajaria □, *Georgia* 49 K6
Ajaria □, *Georgia* 49 K6
Ajax, *Canada* 110 C5
Ajdâbiyah, *Libya* 79 B10
Ajdovščina, *Slovenia* 29 C10
Ajibar, *Ethiopia* 81 E4
Ajka, *Hungary* 42 C2
'Ajmān, *U.A.E.* 71 E7
Ajmer, *India* 68 F6
Ajo, *U.S.A.* 115 K7
Ajo, C. de, *Spain* 34 B7
Ajok, *Sudan* 81 F2
Ajuy, *Phil.* 61 F5
Ak Dağ, *Turkey* 39 E11
Ak Dağları, *Muğla, Turkey* 39 E11
Ak Dağları, *Sivas, Turkey* 72 C7
Akaba, *Togo* 83 D5
Akabira, *Japan* 54 C11
Akaki Beseka, *Ethiopia* 81 F4
Akala, *Sudan* 81 D4
Akamas □, *Cyprus* 36 D11
Akanthou, *Cyprus* 36 D12
Akarca, *Turkey* 39 C11
Akaroa, *N.Z.* 91 K4
Akasha, *Sudan* 80 C3
Akashi, *Japan* 55 G7
Akçaabat, *Turkey* 73 B8
Akçadağ, *Turkey* 72 C7
Akçakale, *Turkey* 73 D8
Akçakoca, *Turkey* 72 B4
Akçaova, *Turkey* 41 E13
Akçay, *Turkey* 39 E11
Akçay →, *Turkey* 39 D10
Akdağ, *Turkey* 39 C8
Akdağmadeni, *Turkey* 72 C6
Akelamo, *Indonesia* 63 D7
Åkers styckebruk, *Sweden* 10 E11
Åkersberga, *Sweden* 10 E12
Aketi, *Dem. Rep. of the Congo* 84 D4
Akhaïa □, *Greece* 38 C3
Akhalkalaki, *Georgia* 49 K6
Akhaltsikhe, *Georgia* 49 K6
Akharnaí, *Greece* 38 C5
Akhelóös →, *Greece* 38 C3
Akhendriá, *Greece* 39 G7
Akhisar, *Turkey* 39 C9
Akhladhókambos, *Greece* 38 D4
Akhmîm, *Egypt* 80 B3
Akhnur, *India* 69 C6
Akhtopol, *Bulgaria* 41 D11
Akhtuba →, *Russia* 49 G8
Akhtubinsk, *Russia* 49 F8
Akhty, *Russia* 49 K8
Akhtyrka = Okhtyrka, *Ukraine* 47 G8
Aki, *Japan* 55 H6
Akimiski I., *Canada* 102 B3
Akimovka, *Ukraine* 47 J8
Åkirkeby, *Denmark* 11 J8
Akita, *Japan* 54 E10
Akita □, *Japan* 54 E10
Akjoujt, *Mauritania* 82 B2
Akkaya Tepesi, *Turkey* 39 D11
Akkeshi, *Japan* 54 C12
'Akko, *Israel* 75 C4
Akköy, *Turkey* 39 D9
Aklampa, *Benin* 83 D5
Aklavik, *Canada* 100 B6
Akmenė, *Lithuania* 44 B9
Akmenrags, *Latvia* 44 B8
Akmolinsk = Aqmola, *Kazakstan* 50 D8
Akmonte = Almonte, *Spain* 35 H4
Akō, *Japan* 55 G7
Ako, *Nigeria* 83 C7
Akobo →, *Ethiopia* 81 F3
Akola, *India* 66 J10
Akonolinga, *Cameroon* 83 E7
Akordat, *Eritrea* 81 D4
Akosombo Dam, *Ghana* 83 D5
Akot, *Sudan* 81 F3
Akpatok I., *Canada* 101 B13
Åkrahamn, *Norway* 9 G11
Akranes, *Iceland* 8 D2
Akreïjit, *Mauritania* 82 B3
Akrítas Venétiko, Ákra, *Greece* 38 E3
Akron, *Colo., U.S.A.* 112 E3
Akron, *Ohio, U.S.A.* 110 E3
Akrotiri, *Cyprus* 36 E11
Akrotíri, Ákra, *Greece* 41 F9
Akrotiri Bay, *Cyprus* 36 E12
Aksai Chin, *India* 69 B8
Aksaray, *Turkey* 72 C6
Aksay, *Kazakstan* 50 D6
Akşehir, *Turkey* 72 C4
Akşehir Gölü, *Turkey* 72 C4
Akstafa = Ağstafa, *Azerbaijan* 49 K7
Aksu, *China* 60 B3
Aksu →, *Turkey* 72 D4
Aksum, *Ethiopia* 81 E4
Aktash, *Russia* 48 C11
Aktogay, *Kazakstan* 50 E8
Aktsyabrski, *Belarus* 47 F5
Aktyubinsk = Aqtöbe, *Kazakstan* 50 D6
Aku, *Nigeria* 83 D6
Akure, *Nigeria* 83 D6
Akureyri, *Iceland* 8 D4
Akuseki-Shima, *Japan* 55 K4
Akusha, *Russia* 49 J8
Akwa-Ibom □, *Nigeria* 83 E6
Akyab = Sittwe, *Burma* 67 J18
Akyazı, *Turkey* 72 B4
Al 'Adan, *Yemen* 74 E4
Al Aḩsā, *Si. Arabia* 71 E6
Al Ajfar, *Si. Arabia* 70 E4
Al Amādīyah, *Iraq* 70 B4
Al Amārah, *Iraq* 70 D5
Al 'Aqabah, *Jordan* 75 F4
Al Arak, *Syria* 70 C3
Al 'Aramah, *Si. Arabia* 70 E5
Al Arţāwīyah, *Si. Arabia* 70 E5
Al 'Āşimah = 'Ammān □, *Jordan* 75 D5
Al 'Assāfīyah, *Si. Arabia* 70 D3
Al 'Ayn, *Oman* 71 E7
Al 'Ayn, *Si. Arabia* 70 E3
Al A'zamīyah, *Iraq* 70 C5
Al 'Azīzīyah, *Iraq* 70 C5
Al Bāb, *Syria* 70 B3
Al Bad', *Si. Arabia* 70 D2
Al Bādī, *Iraq* 70 C4
Al Baḩrah, *Kuwait* 70 D5
Al Baḩral Mayyit = Dead Sea, *Asia* 75 D4
Al Balqā' □, *Jordan* 75 C4
Al Bārūk, J., *Lebanon* 75 B4
Al Başrah, *Iraq* 70 D5
Al Baţḩā, *Iraq* 70 D5
Al Batrūn, *Lebanon* 75 A4
Al Bayḑā, *Libya* 79 B10
Al Biqā □, *Lebanon* 75 A5
Al Bi'r, *Si. Arabia* 70 D3
Al Burayj, *Syria* 75 A5
Al Fallūjah, *Iraq* 70 C4
Al Fāw, *Iraq* 71 D6
Al Fujayrah, *U.A.E.* 71 E8
Al Ghadaf, W. →, *Jordan* 75 D5
Al Ghammās, *Iraq* 70 D5
Al Ḩābah, *Si. Arabia* 70 E5
Al Ḩadīthah, *Iraq* 70 C4
Al Ḩadīthah, *Si. Arabia* 70 D3
Al Ḩaḑr, *Iraq* 73 E10
Al Ḩājānah, *Syria* 75 B5
Al Ḩāmad, *Si. Arabia* 70 D3
Al Hamdānīyah, *Syria* 70 C3
Al Ḩamīdīyah, *Syria* 75 A4
Al Ḩammār, *Iraq* 70 D5
Al Ḩarīr, W. →, *Syria* 75 C4
Al Ḩasā, W. →, *Jordan* 75 D4
Al Ḩasakah, *Syria* 70 B4
Al Haydān, W. →, *Jordan* 75 D4
Al Ḩayy, *Iraq* 70 C5
Al Ḩillah, *Iraq* 70 C5
Al Hindīyah, *Iraq* 73 F11
Al Hirmil, *Lebanon* 75 A5
Al Hoceïma, *Morocco* 78 A5
Al Ḩudaydah, *Yemen* 74 E3
Al Hufūf, *Si. Arabia* 71 E6
Al Ḩumayḑah, *Si. Arabia* 70 D2
Al Ḩunayy, *Si. Arabia* 71 E6
Al Īsāwīyah, *Si. Arabia* 70 D3
Al Jafr, *Jordan* 75 E5
Al Jaghbūb, *Libya* 79 C10
Al Jahrah, *Kuwait* 70 D5
Al Jalāmīd, *Si. Arabia* 70 D3
Al Jamalīyah, *Qatar* 71 E6
Al Janūb □, *Lebanon* 75 B4
Al Jawf, *Libya* 79 D10
Al Jawf, *Si. Arabia* 70 D3
Al Jazirah, *Iraq* 70 C5
Al Jithāmīyah, *Si. Arabia* 70 E4
Al Jubayl, *Si. Arabia* 71 E6
Al Jubaylah, *Si. Arabia* 70 E5
Al Jubb, *Si. Arabia* 70 E4
Al Junaynah, *Sudan* 79 F10
Al Kabā'ish, *Iraq* 70 D5
Al Karak, *Jordan* 75 D4
Al Karak □, *Jordan* 75 E5
Al Kāzim Tyah, *Iraq* 70 C5
Al Khalīl, *West Bank* 75 D4
Al Khāliş, *Iraq* 73 F11
Al Khawr, *Qatar* 71 E6
Al Khiḑr, *Iraq* 70 D5
Al Khiyām, *Lebanon* 75 B4
Al Kiswah, *Syria* 75 B5
Al Kūfah, *Iraq* 73 F11
Al Kufrah, *Libya* 79 D10
Al Kuhayfīyah, *Si. Arabia* 70 E4
Al Kūt, *Iraq* 70 C5
Al Kuwayt, *Kuwait* 70 D5
Al Labwah, *Lebanon* 75 A5
Al Lādhiqīyah, *Syria* 70 C2
Al Līth, *Si. Arabia* 80 C5
Al Liwā', *Oman* 71 E8
Al Luḩayyah, *Yemen* 74 D3
Al Madīnah, *Iraq* 70 D5
Al Madīnah, *Si. Arabia* 70 E3
Al Mafraq, *Jordan* 75 C5
Al Maḩmūdīyah, *Iraq* 70 C5
Al Majma'ah, *Si. Arabia* 70 E5
Al Makhruq, W. →, *Jordan* 75 D6
Al Makḩūl, *Si. Arabia* 70 E4
Al Manāmah, *Bahrain* 71 E6
Al Maqwa', *Kuwait* 70 D5
Al Marj, *Libya* 79 B10
Al Maţlā, *Kuwait* 70 D5
Al Mawjib, W. →, *Jordan* 75 D4
Al Mawşil, *Iraq* 70 B4
Al Mayādin, *Syria* 70 C4
Al Mazār, *Jordan* 75 D4
Al Midhnab, *Si. Arabia* 70 E5
Al Minā', *Lebanon* 75 A4
Al Miqdādīyah, *Iraq* 70 C5
Al Mubarraz, *Si. Arabia* 71 E6
Al Mughayrā', *U.A.E.* 71 E7
Al Muḩarraq, *Bahrain* 71 E6
Al Mukallā, *Yemen* 74 E4
Al Mukhā, *Yemen* 74 E3
Al Musayjīd, *Si. Arabia* 70 E3
Al Musayyib, *Iraq* 70 C5
Al Muwayliḩ, *Si. Arabia* 70 E2
Al Owuho = Otukpa, *Nigeria* 83 D6
Al Qā'im, *Iraq* 70 C4
Al Qalībah, *Si. Arabia* 70 D3
Al Qāmishlī, *Syria* 73 D9
Al Qaryatayn, *Syria* 75 A6
Al Qaţ'ā, *Syria* 70 C4
Al Qaţīf, *Si. Arabia* 71 E6
Al Qatrānah, *Jordan* 75 D5
Al Qaţrūn, *Libya* 79 D9
Al Qayşūmah, *Si. Arabia* 70 D5
Al Quds = Jerusalem, *Israel* 75 D4
Al Qunayţirah, *Syria* 75 C4
Al Qunfudhah, *Si. Arabia* 80 D5
Al Qurnah, *Iraq* 70 D5
Al Quşayr, *Iraq* 70 D5
Al Quşayr, *Syria* 75 A5
Al Qutayfah, *Syria* 75 B5
Al 'Uḑaylīyah, *Si. Arabia* 71 E6
Al 'Ulā, *Si. Arabia* 70 E3
Al Uqayr, *Si. Arabia* 71 E6
Al 'Uwaynid, *Si. Arabia* 70 E5
Al 'Uwayqīlah, *Si. Arabia* 70 D4
Al 'Uyūn, *Ḩijāz, Si. Arabia* 70 E3
Al 'Uyūn, *Najd, Si. Arabia* 70 E4
Al 'Uzayr, *Iraq* 70 D5
Al Wajh, *Si. Arabia* 70 E3
Al Wakrah, *Qatar* 71 E6
Al Wannān, *Si. Arabia* 71 E6
Al Waqbah, *Si. Arabia* 70 D5
Al Wari'āh, *Si. Arabia* 70 E5
Al Wusayl, *Qatar* 71 E6
Ala, *Italy* 28 C8
Ala Dağları, *Turkey* 73 C10
Alabama □, *U.S.A.* 109 J2
Alabama →, *U.S.A.* 109 K2
Alaca, *Turkey* 72 B6
Alacaatlı, *Turkey* 39 B10
Alaçam, *Turkey* 72 B6
Alaçam Dağları, *Turkey* 39 B10
Alaçatı, *Turkey* 39 C8
Alaejos, *Spain* 34 D5
Alaérma, *Greece* 36 C9
Alagir, *Russia* 49 J7
Alagna Valsésia, *Italy* 28 C4
Alagoa Grande, *Brazil* 125 E11
Alagoas □, *Brazil* 125 E11
Alagoinhas, *Brazil* 125 F11
Alagón, *Spain* 32 D3
Alagón →, *Spain* 34 F4
Alaior, *Spain* 37 B11
Alajero, *Canary Is.* 37 F2
Alajuela, *Costa Rica* 120 D3
Alakamisy, *Madag.* 89 C8
Alameda, *Calif., U.S.A.* 116 H4
Alameda, *N. Mex., U.S.A.* 115 J10
Alaminos, *Phil.* 61 C3
Alamo, *U.S.A.* 117 J11
Alamo Crossing, *U.S.A.* 117 L13
Alamogordo, *U.S.A.* 115 K11
Alamos, *Mexico* 118 B3
Alamosa, *U.S.A.* 115 H11
Åland, *Finland* 9 F19
Alandroal, *Portugal* 35 G3
Ålands hav, *Sweden* 9 F18
Alandur, *India* 66 N12
Alange, Presa de, *Spain* 35 G4
Alania = North Ossetia □, *Russia* 49 J7
Alanís, *Spain* 35 G5
Alanya, *Turkey* 72 D5
Alaotra, Farihin', *Madag.* 89 B8
Alapayevsk, *Russia* 50 D7
Alar del Rey, *Spain* 34 C6
Alaraz, *Spain* 34 E5
Alarcón, Embalse de, *Spain* 32 F2
Alaşehir, *Turkey* 39 C10
Alaska □, *U.S.A.* 100 B5
Alaska, G. of, *Pac. Oc.* 100 C5
Alaska Peninsula, *U.S.A.* 100 C4
Alaska Range, *U.S.A.* 100 B4
Alássio, *Italy* 28 E5
Älät, *Azerbaijan* 49 L9
Alataw Shankou, *China* 60 B3
Alatri, *Italy* 29 G10
Alatyr, *Russia* 48 C8
Alatyr →, *Russia* 48 C8
Alausi, *Ecuador* 124 D3
Álava □, *Spain* 32 C2
Alava, C., *U.S.A.* 114 B1
Alaverdi, *Armenia* 49 K7
Alavus, *Finland* 9 E20
Alawoona, *Australia* 95 E3
'Alayh, *Lebanon* 75 B4
Alazani →, *Azerbaijan* 49 K8
Alba, *Italy* 28 D5
Alba □, *Romania* 43 D8
Alba Adriática, *Italy* 29 F10
Alba de Tormes, *Spain* 34 E5
Alba-Iulia, *Romania* 43 D8
Albac, *Romania* 42 D7
Albacete, *Spain* 33 F3
Albacete □, *Spain* 33 G3
Albacutya, L., *Australia* 95 F3
Ålbæk, *Denmark* 11 G4
Ålbæk Bugt, *Denmark* 11 G4
Albaida, *Spain* 33 G4
Albalate de las Nogueras, *Spain* 32 E2
Albalate del Arzobispo, *Spain* 32 D4
Alban, *France* 20 E6
Albania ■, *Europe* 40 E4
Albano Laziale, *Italy* 29 G9
Albany, *Australia* 93 G2
Albany, *Ga., U.S.A.* 109 K3
Albany, *Minn., U.S.A.* 112 C7
Albany, *N.Y., U.S.A.* 111 D11
Albany, *Oreg., U.S.A.* 114 D2
Albany, *Tex., U.S.A.* 113 J5
Albany →, *Canada* 102 B3
Albardón, *Argentina* 126 C2
Albarracín, *Spain* 32 E3
Albarracín, Sierra de, *Spain* 32 E3
Albatera, *Spain* 33 G4
Albatross B., *Australia* 94 A3
Albegna →, *Italy* 29 F8
Albemarle, *U.S.A.* 109 H5
Albemarle Sd., *U.S.A.* 109 H7
Albenga, *Italy* 28 D5
Alberche →, *Spain* 34 F6
Alberdi, *Paraguay* 126 B4
Alberes, Mts., *France* 20 F6
Ålberga, *Sweden* 11 F10
Albersdorf, *Germany* 24 A5
Albert, *France* 19 C9
Albert, L., *Australia* 95 F2
Albert Canyon, *Canada* 104 C5
Albert Edward Ra., *Australia* 92 C4
Albert L., *Africa* 86 B3
Albert Lea, *U.S.A.* 112 D8
Albert Nile →, *Uganda* 86 B3
Albert Town, *Bahamas* 121 B5
Alberta □, *Canada* 104 C6
Alberti, *Argentina* 126 D3
Albertinia, *S. Africa* 88 E3
Albertirsa, *Hungary* 42 C4
Alberton, *Canada* 103 C7
Albertville = Kalemie, *Dem. Rep. of the Congo* 86 D2
Albertville, *France* 21 C10
Albi, *France* 20 E6
Albia, *U.S.A.* 112 E8
Albina, *Surinam* 125 B8
Albina, Ponta, *Angola* 88 B1
Albino, *Italy* 28 C6
Albion, *Idaho, U.S.A.* 114 E7
Albion, *Mich., U.S.A.* 108 D3
Albion, *Nebr., U.S.A.* 112 E6
Albion, *Pa., U.S.A.* 110 E4
Albocácer, *Spain* 32 E5
Albolote, *Spain* 35 H7
Alborán, *Medit. S.* 35 K7
Alborea, *Spain* 33 F3
Ålborg, *Denmark* 11 G3
Ålborg Bugt, *Denmark* 11 H4
Alborz, Reshteh-ye Kūhhā-ye, *Iran* 71 C7
Albox, *Spain* 33 H2
Albreda, *Canada* 104 C5
Albufeira, *Portugal* 35 H2
Albula →, *Switz.* 25 J5
Albuñol, *Spain* 35 J7
Albuquerque, *U.S.A.* 115 J10
Albuquerque, Cayos de, *Caribbean* 120 D3
Alburg, *U.S.A.* 111 B11
Alburno, Mte., *Italy* 31 B8
Alburquerque, *Spain* 35 F4
Albury, *Australia* 95 F4
Alcácer do Sal, *Portugal* 35 G2
Alcáçovas, *Portugal* 35 G2
Alcalá de Chivert, *Spain* 32 E5
Alcalá de Guadaira, *Spain* 35 H5
Alcalá de Henares, *Spain* 34 E7
Alcalá de los Gazules, *Spain* 35 J5
Alcalá del Júcar, *Spain* 33 F3
Alcalá del Río, *Spain* 35 H5
Alcalá del Valle, *Spain* 35 J5
Alcalá la Real, *Spain* 35 H7
Álcamo, *Italy* 30 E5
Alcanadre, *Spain* 32 C2
Alcanadre →, *Spain* 32 D4
Alcanar, *Spain* 32 E5
Alcanede, *Portugal* 35 F2
Alcanena, *Portugal* 35 F2
Alcañices, *Spain* 34 D4
Alcañiz, *Spain* 32 D4
Alcântara, *Brazil* 125 D10
Alcántara, *Spain* 34 F4
Alcántara, Embalse de, *Spain* 34 F4
Alcantara L., *Canada* 105 A7
Alcantarilla, *Spain* 33 H3
Alcaracejos, *Spain* 35 G6
Alcaraz, *Spain* 33 G2
Alcaraz, Sierra de, *Spain* 33 G2
Alcaudete, *Spain* 35 H6
Alcázar de San Juan, *Spain* 35 F7
Alchevsk, *Ukraine* 47 H10
Alcira = Alzira, *Spain* 33 F4
Alcoa, *U.S.A.* 109 H4
Alcobaça, *Portugal* 35 F2
Alcobendas, *Spain* 34 E7
Alcolea del Pinar, *Spain* 32 D2
Alcora, *Spain* 32 E4
Alcorcón, *Spain* 34 E7
Alcoutim, *Portugal* 35 H3
Alcova, *U.S.A.* 114 E10
Alcoy, *Spain* 33 G4
Alcubierre, Sierra de, *Spain* 32 D4
Alcublas, *Spain* 32 F4
Alcúdia, *Spain* 37 B10
Alcúdia, B. d', *Spain* 37 B10
Alcudia, Sierra de la, *Spain* 35 G6
Aldabra Is., *Seychelles* 77 G8
Aldama, *Mexico* 119 C5
Aldan, *Russia* 51 D13
Aldan →, *Russia* 51 C13
Aldea, Pta. de la, *Canary Is.* 37 G4
Aldeburgh, *U.K.* 13 E9
Alder, *U.S.A.* 114 D7
Alder Pk., *U.S.A.* 116 K5
Alderney, *U.K.* 13 H5
Aldershot, *U.K.* 13 F7
Åled, *Sweden* 11 H6
Aledo, *U.S.A.* 112 E9
Alefa, *Ethiopia* 81 E4
Aleg, *Mauritania* 82 B2
Alegranza, *Canary Is.* 37 E6
Alegranza, I., *Canary Is.* 37 E6
Alegre, *Brazil* 127 A7
Alegrete, *Brazil* 127 B4
Aleisk, *Russia* 50 D9
Aleksandriya = Oleksandriya, *Kirovohrad, Ukraine* 47 H7
Aleksandriya = Oleksandriya, *Rivne, Ukraine* 47 G4
Aleksandriyskaya, *Russia* 49 J8
Aleksandrov, *Russia* 46 D10
Aleksandrov Gay, *Russia* 48 E9
Aleksandrovac, *Serbia, Yug.* 40 C5
Aleksandrovac, *Serbia, Yug.* 40 B5
Aleksandrovka = Oleksandrovka, *Ukraine* 47 H7
Aleksandrovo, *Bulgaria* 41 C8
Aleksandrovsk-Sakhalinskiy, *Russia* 51 D15
Aleksandrów Kujawski, *Poland* 45 F5
Aleksandrów Łódźki, *Poland* 45 G6
Alekseyevka, *Samara, Russia* 48 D10
Alekseyevka, *Voronezh, Russia* 47 G10
Aleksin, *Russia* 46 E9
Aleksinac, *Serbia, Yug.* 40 C5
Além Paraíba, *Brazil* 127 A7
Alemania, *Argentina* 126 B2
Alemania, *Chile* 126 B2
Alençon, *France* 18 D7
Alenquer, *Brazil* 125 D8
Alenuihaha Channel, *U.S.A.* 106 H17
Aleppo = Ḩalab, *Syria* 70 B3
Aléria, *France* 21 F13
Alert Bay, *Canada* 104 C3
Alès, *France* 21 D8
Aleşd, *Romania* 42 C7
Alessándria, *Italy* 28 D5
Ålestrup, *Denmark* 11 H3
Ålesund, *Norway* 9 E12
Alet-les-Bains, *France* 20 F6
Aletschhorn, *Switz.* 25 J4
Aleutian Is., *Pac. Oc.* 100 C2
Aleutian Trench, *Pac. Oc.* 96 C10
Alexander, *U.S.A.* 112 B3
Alexander, Mt., *Australia* 93 E3
Alexander Arch., *U.S.A.* 104 B2
Alexander Bay, *S. Africa* 88 D2
Alexander City, *U.S.A.* 109 J3
Alexander I., *Antarctica* 5 C17
Alexandra, *Australia* 95 F4
Alexandra, *N.Z.* 91 L2
Alexandra Falls, *Canada* 104 A5
Alexandria = El Iskandarîya, *Egypt* 80 H7
Alexandria, *Australia* 94 B2
Alexandria, *B.C., Canada* 104 C4
Alexandria, *Ont., Canada* 102 C5
Alexandria, *Romania* 43 G10
Alexandria, *S. Africa* 88 E4
Alexandria, *U.K.* 14 F4
Alexandria, *Ind., U.S.A.* 108 E3
Alexandria, *La., U.S.A.* 113 K8
Alexandria, *Minn., U.S.A.* 112 C7
Alexandria, *S. Dak., U.S.A.* 112 D6
Alexandria, *Va., U.S.A.* 108 F7

Alexandria Bay, U.S.A. 111 B9
Alexandrina, L., Australia 95 F2
Alexandroúpolis, Greece 41 F9
Alexis →, Canada 103 B8
Alexis Creek, Canada 104 C4
Alfabia, Spain 37 B9
Alfambra, Spain 32 E3
Alfândega da Fé, Portugal 34 D4
Alfaro, Spain 32 C3
Alfatar, Bulgaria 41 C11
Alfaz del Pi, Spain 33 G4
Alfeld, Germany 24 D5
Alfenas, Brazil 127 A6
Alfiós →, Greece 38 D3
Alföld, Hungary 42 D5
Alfonsine, Italy 29 D9
Alford, Aberds., U.K. 14 D6
Alford, Lincs., U.K. 12 D8
Alfred, Maine, U.S.A. 111 C14
Alfred, N.Y., U.S.A. 110 D7
Alfreton, U.K. 12 D6
Alfta, Sweden 10 C10
Alga, Kazakstan 50 E6
Algaida, Spain 37 B9
Algar, Spain 35 J5
Ålgård, Norway 9 G11
Algarinejo, Spain 35 H6
Algarve, Portugal 35 J2
Algeciras, Spain 35 J5
Algemesí, Spain 33 F4
Alger, Algeria 78 A6
Algeria ■, Africa 78 C6
Alghero, Italy 30 B1
Älghult, Sweden 11 G9
Algiers = Alger, Algeria 78 A6
Algoa B., S. Africa 88 E4
Algodonales, Spain 35 J5
Algodor →, Spain 34 F7
Algoma, U.S.A. 108 C2
Algona, U.S.A. 112 D7
Algonac, U.S.A. 110 D2
Algorta, Uruguay 128 C5
Alhama de Almería, Spain 35 J8
Alhama de Aragón, Spain 32 D3
Alhama de Granada, Spain 35 H7
Alhama de Murcia, Spain 33 H3
Alhambra, U.S.A. 117 L8
Alhaurín el Grande, Spain 35 J6
Alhucemas = Al Hoceïma, Morocco 78 A5
'Alī al Gharbī, Iraq 70 C5
Alī ash Sharqī, Iraq 70 C5
Äli Bayramlı, Azerbaijan 49 L9
'Alī Khēl, Afghan. 68 C3
Ali Sahîh, Djibouti 81 E5
Alī Shāh, Iran 70 B5
Ália, Italy 30 E6
'Alīābād, Khorāsān, Iran 71 C8
'Alīābād, Kordestān, Iran 70 C5
'Alīābād, Yazd, Iran 71 D7
Aliaga, Spain 32 E4
Aliağa, Turkey 39 C8
Aliákmon →, Greece 40 F6
Alibo, Ethiopia 81 F4
Alibunar, Serbia, Yug. 42 E5
Alicante, Spain 33 G4
Alicante □, Spain 33 G4
Alice, S. Africa 88 E4
Alice, U.S.A. 113 M5
Alice →, Queens., Australia 94 C3
Alice →, Queens., Australia 94 B3
Alice, Punta, Italy 31 C10
Alice Arm, Canada 104 B3
Alice Downs, Australia 92 C4
Alice Springs, Australia 94 C1
Alicedale, S. Africa 88 E4
Aliceville, U.S.A. 109 J1
Alick Cr. →, Australia 94 C3
Alicudi, Italy 31 D7
Alida, Canada 105 D8
Aligarh, Raj., India 68 G7
Aligarh, Ut. P., India 68 F8
Alīgūdarz, Iran 71 C6
Alijó, Portugal 34 D3
Alimnía, Greece 36 C9
Alingsås, Sweden 11 G6
Alipur, Pakistan 68 E4
Alipur Duar, India 67 F16
Aliquippa, U.S.A. 110 F4
Aliste →, Spain 34 D5
Alitus = Alytus, Lithuania 9 J21
Alivérion, Greece 38 C6
Aliwal North, S. Africa 88 E4
Alix, Canada 104 C6
Aljezur, Portugal 35 H2
Aljustrel, Portugal 35 H2
Alkamari, Niger 83 C7
Alkmaar, Neths. 17 B4
All American Canal, U.S.A. 115 K6
Allada, Benin 83 D5
Allah Dad, Pakistan 68 G2
Allahabad, India 69 G9
Allan, Canada 105 C7
Allanche, France 20 C6
Allanmyo, Burma 67 K19
Allanridge, S. Africa 88 D4
Allanwater, Canada 102 B1
Allaqi, Wadi →, Egypt 80 C3
Allariz, Spain 34 C3
Allassac, France 20 C5
Ålleberg, Sweden 11 F7
Allegan, U.S.A. 108 D3
Allegany, U.S.A. 110 D6
Allegheny →, U.S.A. 110 F5
Allegheny Mts., U.S.A. 98 F11
Allegheny Plateau, U.S.A. 108 G6
Allegheny Reservoir, U.S.A. 110 E6
Allègre, France 20 C7
Allen, Bog of, Ireland 15 C5
Allen, L., Ireland 15 B3
Allende, Mexico 118 B4
Allentown, U.S.A. 111 F9
Allentsteig, Austria 26 C8
Alleppey, India 66 Q10
Allepuz, Spain 32 E4
Aller →, Germany 24 C5
Alliance, Nebr., U.S.A. 112 D3
Alliance, Ohio, U.S.A. 110 F3
Allier □, France 19 F9
Allier →, France 19 F10
Allinge, Denmark 11 J8
Alliston, Canada 102 D4
Alloa, U.K. 14 E5
Allones, France 18 D8
Allora, Australia 95 D5
Allos, France 21 D10
Alluitsup Paa = Sydprøven, Greenland 4 C5
Alma, Canada 103 C5
Alma, Ga., U.S.A. 109 K4
Alma, Kans., U.S.A. 112 F6
Alma, Mich., U.S.A. 108 D3
Alma, Nebr., U.S.A. 112 E5
Alma, Wis., U.S.A. 112 C9
Alma Ata = Almaty, Kazakstan 50 E8
Almacelles, Spain 32 D5
Almada, Portugal 35 G1
Almaden, Australia 94 B3
Almadén, Spain 35 G6
Almanor, L., U.S.A. 114 F3
Almansa, Spain 33 G3
Almanza, Spain 34 C5
Almanzor, Pico, Spain 34 E5
Almanzora →, Spain 33 H3
Almaş, Munţii, Romania 42 F7
Almassora, Spain 32 F4
Almaty, Kazakstan 50 E8
Almazán, Spain 32 D2
Almeirim, Brazil 125 D8
Almeirim, Portugal 35 F2
Almelo, Neths. 17 B6
Almenar de Soria, Spain 32 D2
Almenara, Spain 32 F4
Almenara, Sierra de la, Spain 33 H3
Almendra, Embalse de, Spain 34 D4
Almendralejo, Spain 35 G4
Almere-Stad, Neths. 17 B5
Almería, Spain 35 J8
Almería □, Spain 33 H2
Almería, G. de, Spain 33 J2
Almetyevsk, Russia 48 C11
Älmhult, Sweden 11 H8
Almirante, Panama 120 E3
Almiropótamos, Greece 38 C6
Almirós, Greece 38 B4
Almiroú, Kólpos, Greece 36 D6
Almodôvar, Portugal 35 H2
Almodóvar del Campo, Spain 35 G6
Almodóvar del Río, Spain 35 H5
Almont, U.S.A. 110 D1
Almonte, Canada 111 A8
Almonte, Spain 35 H4
Almora, India 69 E8
Almoradí, Spain 33 G4
Almorox, Spain 34 E6
Almoustarat, Mali 83 B5
Älmsta, Sweden 10 E12
Almudévar, Spain 32 C4
Almuñécar, Spain 35 J7
Almunge, Sweden 10 E12
Almuradiel, Spain 35 G7
Alness, U.K. 14 D4
Alnmouth, U.K. 12 B6
Alnwick, U.K. 12 B6
Aloi, Uganda 86 B3
Alon, Burma 67 H19
Alor, Indonesia 63 F6
Alor Setar, Malaysia 65 J3
Álora, Spain 35 J6
Alosno, Spain 35 H3
Aloysius, Mt., Australia 93 E4
Alpaugh, U.S.A. 116 K7
Alpedrinha, Portugal 34 E3
Alpena, U.S.A. 108 C4
Alpes-de-Haute-Provence □, France 21 D10
Alpes-Maritimes □, France 21 E11
Alpha, Australia 94 C4
Alphen aan den Rijn, Neths. 17 B4
Alpiarça, Portugal 35 F2
Alpine, Ariz., U.S.A. 115 K9
Alpine, Calif., U.S.A. 117 N10
Alpine, Tex., U.S.A. 113 K3
Alps, Europe 6 F7
Alpu, Turkey 72 C4
Alqueta, Barragem do, Portugal 35 G3
Alrø, Denmark 11 J4
Alroy Downs, Australia 94 B2
Als, Denmark 11 K3
Alsace, France 19 D14
Alsask, Canada 105 C7
Alsasua, Spain 32 C2
Alsfeld, Germany 24 E5
Alsten, Norway 8 D15
Alstermo, Sweden 11 H9
Alston, U.K. 12 C5
Alta, Norway 8 B20
Alta, Sierra, Spain 32 E3
Alta Gracia, Argentina 126 C3
Alta Lake, Canada 104 C4
Alta Sierra, U.S.A. 117 K8
Altaelva →, Norway 8 B20
Altafjorden, Norway 8 A20
Altai = Aerhtai Shan, Mongolia 60 B4
Altamaha →, U.S.A. 109 K5
Altamira, Brazil 125 D8
Altamira, Chile 126 B2
Altamira, Mexico 119 C5
Altamira, Cuevas de, Spain 34 B6
Altamont, U.S.A. 111 D10
Altamura, Italy 31 B9
Altanbulag, Mongolia 60 A5
Altar, Mexico 118 A2
Altata, Mexico 118 C3
Altavista, U.S.A. 108 G6
Altay, China 60 B3
Altdorf, Switz. 25 J4
Alte Mellum, Germany 24 B4
Altea, Spain 33 G4
Altenberg, Germany 24 E9
Altenbruch, Germany 24 B4
Altenburg, Germany 24 E8
Altenkirchen, Mecklenburg-Vorpommern, Germany 24 A9
Altenkirchen, Rhld-Pfz., Germany 24 E3
Altenmarkt, Austria 26 D7
Alter do Chão, Portugal 35 F3
Altınoluk, Turkey 39 B8
Altınova, Turkey 39 B8
Altıntaş, Turkey 39 B12
Altınyaka, Turkey 39 E12
Altınyayla, Turkey 39 D11
Altkirch, France 19 E14
Altmark, Germany 24 C7
Altmühl →, Germany 25 G7
Altmunster, Austria 26 D6
Alto Adige = Trentino-Alto Adige □, Italy 29 B8
Alto Araguaia, Brazil 125 G8
Alto Cuchumatanes = Cuchumatanes, Sierra de los, Guatemala 120 C1
Alto del Inca, Chile 126 A2
Alto Ligonha, Mozam. 87 F4
Alto Molocue, Mozam. 87 F4
Alto Paraguay □, Paraguay 126 A4
Alto Paraná □, Paraguay 127 B5
Alton, Canada 110 C4
Alton, U.K. 13 F7
Alton, U.S.A. 112 F9
Alton Downs, Australia 95 D2
Altoona, U.S.A. 110 F6
Altötting, Germany 25 G8
Altstätten, Switz. 25 H5
Altūn Kūprī, Iraq 70 C5
Altun Shan, China 60 C3
Alturas, U.S.A. 114 F3
Altus, U.S.A. 113 H5
Alubijid, Phil. 61 G6
Alucra, Turkey 73 B8
Alūksne, Latvia 9 H22
Alunda, Sweden 10 D12
Alunite, U.S.A. 117 K12
Alupka, Ukraine 47 K8
Alushta, Ukraine 47 K8
Alusi, Indonesia 63 F8
Alustante, Spain 32 E3
Alva, U.S.A. 113 G5
Alvaiázere, Portugal 34 F2
Älvängen, Sweden 11 G6
Alvarado, Mexico 119 D5
Alvarado, U.S.A. 113 J6
Alvaro Obregón, Presa, Mexico 118 B3
Älvdalen, Sweden 10 C8
Alvear, Argentina 126 B4
Alverca, Portugal 35 G1
Alvesta, Sweden 11 H8
Alvie, Australia 95 F3
Alvin, U.S.A. 113 L7
Alvinston, Canada 110 D3
Alvito, Portugal 35 G3
Älvkarleby, Sweden 10 D11
Älvros, Sweden 10 B8
Älvsborgs län □, Sweden 11 F6
Älvsbyn, Sweden 8 D19
Alwar, India 68 F7
Alxa Zuoqi, China 56 E3
Alyata = Älät, Azerbaijan 49 L9
Alyth, U.K. 14 E5
Alytus, Lithuania 9 J21
Alzada, U.S.A. 112 C2
Alzey, Germany 25 F4
Alzira, Spain 33 F4
Am-Timan, Chad 79 F10
Amadeus, L., Australia 93 D5
Amadi, Dem. Rep. of the Congo 86 B2
Amâdi, Sudan 81 F3
Amadjuak L., Canada 101 B12
Amadora, Portugal 35 G1
Amagasaki, Japan 55 G7
Amager, Denmark 11 J6
Amakusa-Shotō, Japan 55 H5
Åmål, Sweden 10 E6
Amalfi, Italy 31 B7
Amaliás, Greece 38 D3
Amalner, India 66 J9
Amambaí, Brazil 127 A4
Amambaí →, Brazil 127 A5
Amambay □, Paraguay 127 A4
Amambay, Cordillera de, S. Amer. 127 A4
Amami-Guntō, Japan 55 L4
Amami-Ō-Shima, Japan 55 L4
Amaná, L., Brazil 124 D6
Amanda Park, U.S.A. 116 C3
Amangeldy, Kazakstan 50 D7
Amantea, Italy 31 C9
Amapá, Brazil 125 C8
Amapá □, Brazil 125 C8
Amara, Sudan 81 E3
Amarante, Brazil 125 E10
Amarante, Portugal 34 D2
Amaranth, Canada 105 C9
Amareleja, Portugal 35 G3
Amargosa →, U.S.A. 117 J10
Amargosa Range, U.S.A. 117 J10
Amári, Greece 36 D6
Amarillo, U.S.A. 113 H4
Amaro, Mte., Italy 29 F11
Amarpur, India 69 G12
Amasra, Turkey 72 B5
Amassama, Nigeria 83 D6
Amasya, Turkey 72 B6
Amatikulu, S. Africa 89 D5
Amatitlán, Guatemala 120 D1
Amatrice, Italy 29 F10
Amay, Belgium 17 D5
Amazon = Amazonas →, S. Amer. 122 D5
Amazonas □, Brazil 124 E6
Amazonas →, S. Amer. 122 D5
Ambahakily, Madag. 89 C7
Ambala, India 68 D7
Ambalavao, Madag. 89 C8
Ambalindum, Australia 94 C2
Ambanja, Madag. 89 A8
Ambarchik, Russia 51 C17
Ambarijeby, Madag. 89 A8
Ambaro, Helodranon', Madag. 89 A8
Ambato, Ecuador 124 D3
Ambato, Sierra de, Argentina 126 B2
Ambato Boeny, Madag. 89 B8
Ambatofinandrahana, Madag. 89 C8
Ambatolampy, Madag. 89 B8
Ambatondrazaka, Madag. 89 B8
Ambatosoratra, Madag. 89 B8
Ambelón, Greece 38 B4
Ambenja, Madag. 89 B8
Amberg, Germany 25 F7
Ambergris Cay, Belize 119 D7
Ambérieu-en-Bugey, France 21 C9
Amberley, N.Z. 91 K4
Ambert, France 20 C7
Ambidédi, Mali 82 C2
Ambikapur, India 69 H10
Ambikol, Sudan 80 C3
Ambilobé, Madag. 89 A8
Ambinanindrano, Madag. 89 C8
Amble, U.K. 12 B6
Ambleside, U.K. 12 C5
Ambo, Ethiopia 81 E4
Ambo, Peru 124 F3
Ambodifototra, Madag. 89 B8
Ambodilazana, Madag. 89 B8
Ambohimahasoa, Madag. 89 C8
Ambohimanga, Madag. 89 C8
Ambohitra, Madag. 89 A8
Amboise, France 18 E8
Amboseli, L., Kenya 86 C4
Ambositra, Madag. 89 C8
Ambovombe, Madag. 89 D8
Amboy, U.S.A. 117 L11
Amboyna Cay, S. China Sea 62 C4
Ambridge, U.S.A. 110 F4
Ambriz, Angola 84 F2
Amby, Australia 95 D4
Amchitka I., U.S.A. 100 C1
Amderma, Russia 50 C7
Ameca, Mexico 118 C4
Ameca →, Mexico 118 C3
Amecameca, Mexico 119 D5
Ameland, Neths. 17 A5
Amélia, Italy 29 F9
Amendolara, Italy 31 C9
American Falls, U.S.A. 114 E7
American Falls Reservoir, U.S.A. 114 E7
American Highland, Antarctica 5 D6
American Samoa ■, Pac. Oc. 91 B13
Americana, Brazil 127 A6
Americus, U.S.A. 109 K3
Amersfoort, Neths. 17 B5
Amersfoort, S. Africa 89 D4
Amery, Australia 93 F2
Amery, Canada 105 B10
Amery Ice Shelf, Antarctica 5 C6
Ames, Spain 34 C2
Ames, U.S.A. 112 E8
Amesbury, U.S.A. 111 D14
Amfíklia, Greece 38 C4
Amfilokhía, Greece 38 C3
Amfípolis, Greece 40 F7
Ámfissa, Greece 38 C4
Amga, Russia 51 C14
Amga →, Russia 51 C14
Amgu, Russia 54 B8
Amgun →, Russia 51 D14
Amherst, Burma 67 L20
Amherst, Canada 103 C7
Amherst, Mass., U.S.A. 111 D12
Amherst, N.Y., U.S.A. 110 D6
Amherst, Ohio, U.S.A. 110 E2
Amherst, Tex., U.S.A. 113 J3
Amherst I., Canada 111 B8
Amherstburg, Canada 102 D3
Amiata, Mte., Italy 29 F8
Amiens, France 19 C9
Amindaion, Greece 40 F5
Åminne, Sweden 11 G7
Amīrābād, Iran 70 C5
Amirante Is., Seychelles 52 K9
Amisk L., Canada 105 C8
Amistad, Presa de la, Mexico 118 B4
Amite, U.S.A. 113 K9
Amlwch, U.K. 12 D3
Amm Adam, Sudan 81 D4
'Ammān, Jordan 75 D4
'Ammān □, Jordan 75 D5
Ammanford, U.K. 13 F4
Ammassalik = Angmagssalik, Greenland 4 C6
Ammerån →, Sweden 10 A10
Ammersee, Germany 25 G7
Amnat Charoen, Thailand 64 E5
Amo Jiang →, China 58 F3
Āmol, Iran 71 B7
Amorgós, Greece 39 E7
Amory, U.S.A. 109 J1
Amos, Canada 102 C4
Åmot, Norway 9 G13
Åmotfors, Sweden 10 E6
Amoy = Xiamen, China 59 E12
Ampang, Malaysia 65 L3
Ampanihy, Madag. 89 C7
Ampasindava, Helodranon', Madag. 89 A8
Ampasindava, Saikanosy, Madag. 89 A8
Ampenan, Indonesia 62 F5
Amper, Nigeria 83 D6
Amper →, Germany 25 G7
Ampezzo, Italy 29 B9
Amposta, Spain 32 E5
Ampotaka, Madag. 89 D7
Ampoza, Madag. 89 C7
Amqui, Canada 103 C6
Amravati, India 66 J10
Amreli, India 68 J4
Amritsar, India 68 D6
Amroha, India 69 E8
Amrum, Germany 24 A4
Amsterdam, Neths. 17 B4
Amsterdam, U.S.A. 111 D10
Amsterdam, I., Ind. Oc. 3 F13
Amstetten, Austria 26 C7
Amudarya →, Uzbekistan 50 E6
Amundsen Gulf, Canada 100 A7
Amundsen Sea, Antarctica 5 D15
Amungen, Sweden 10 C9
Amuntai, Indonesia 62 E5
Amur →, Russia 51 D15
Amurang, Indonesia 63 D6
Amuri Pass, N.Z. 91 K4
Amurrio, Spain 32 B1
Amursk, Russia 51 D14
Amusco, Spain 34 C6
Amvrakikós Kólpos, Greece 38 C2
Amvrosiyivka, Ukraine 47 J10
Amyderya = Amudarya →, Uzbekistan 50 E6
An Bien, Vietnam 65 H5
An Hoa, Vietnam 64 E7
An Nabatīyah at Tahta, Lebanon 75 B4
An Nabk, Si. Arabia 70 D3
An Nabk, Syria 75 A5
An Nabk Abū Qaṣr, Si. Arabia 70 D3
An Nafūd, Si. Arabia 70 D4
An Najaf, Iraq 70 C5
An Nāṣirīyah, Iraq 70 D5
An Nhon, Vietnam 64 F7
An Nîl □, Sudan 80 D3
An Nîl el Abyad □, Sudan 81 E3
An Nîl el Azraq □, Sudan 81 E3
An Nu'ayrīyah, Si. Arabia 71 E6
An Nu'mānīyah, Iraq 73 F11
An Nuwayb'ī, W. →, Si. Arabia 75 F3
An Thoi, Dao, Vietnam 65 H5
An Uaimh, Ireland 15 C5
Anabar →, Russia 51 B12
'Anabtā, West Bank 75 C4
Anaconda, U.S.A. 114 C7
Anacortes, U.S.A. 116 B4
Anacuao, Mt., Phil. 61 C4
Anadarko, U.S.A. 113 H5
Anadia, Portugal 34 E2
Anadolu, Turkey 72 C5
Anadyr, Russia 51 C18
Anadyr →, Russia 51 C18
Anadyrskiy Zaliv, Russia 51 C19
Anáfi, Greece 39 E7
Anafópoulo, Greece 39 E7
Anaga, Pta. de, Canary Is. 37 F3
Anagni, Italy 29 G10
'Ānah, Iraq 70 C4
Anaheim, U.S.A. 117 M9
Anahim Lake, Canada 104 C3
Anáhuac, Mexico 118 B4
Anakapalle, India 67 L13

Anakie, *Australia* 94 C4
Anaklia, *Georgia* 49 J5
Analalava, *Madag.* 89 A8
Análipsis, *Greece* 36 A3
Anambar →, *Pakistan* 68 D3
Anambas, Kepulauan, *Indonesia* 65 L6
Anambas Is. = Anambas, Kepulauan, *Indonesia* 65 L6
Anambra □, *Nigeria* 83 D6
Anamoose, *U.S.A.* 112 B4
Anamosa, *U.S.A.* 112 D9
Anamur, *Turkey* 72 D5
Anamur Burnu, *Turkey* 72 D5
Anan, *Japan* 55 H7
Anand, *India* 68 H5
Anánes, *Greece* 38 E6
Anantnag, *India* 69 C6
Ananyiv, *Ukraine* 47 J5
Anapa, *Russia* 47 K9
Anapodháris →, *Greece* 36 E7
Anápolis, *Brazil* 125 G9
Anapu →, *Brazil* 125 D8
Anār, *Iran* 71 D7
Anārak, *Iran* 71 C7
Anarisfjällen, *Sweden* 10 A7
Anatolia = Anadolu, *Turkey* 72 C5
Anatone, *U.S.A.* 114 C5
Anatsogno, *Madag.* 89 C7
Añatuya, *Argentina* 126 B3
Anaunethad L., *Canada* 105 A8
Anbyŏn, *N. Korea* 57 E14
Ancares, Sierra de, *Spain* 34 C4
Ancenis, *France* 18 E5
Anchor Bay, *U.S.A.* 116 G3
Anchorage, *U.S.A.* 100 B5
Anci, *China* 56 E9
Ancohuma, Nevada, *Bolivia* 122 E4
Ancón, *Peru* 124 F3
Ancona, *Italy* 29 E10
Ancud, *Chile* 128 E2
Ancud, G. de, *Chile* 128 E2
Ancy-le-Franc, *France* 19 E11
Andacollo, *Argentina* 126 D1
Andacollo, *Chile* 126 C1
Andado, *Australia* 94 D2
Andalgalá, *Argentina* 126 B2
Åndalsnes, *Norway* 9 E12
Andalucía □, *Spain* 35 H6
Andalusia, *U.S.A.* 109 K2
Andalusia □ = Andalucía □, *Spain* 35 H6
Andaman Is., *Ind. Oc.* 52 H13
Andaman Sea, *Ind. Oc.* 62 B1
Andara, *Namibia* 88 B3
Andelot-Blancheville, *France* 19 D12
Andenes, *Norway* 8 B17
Andenne, *Belgium* 17 D5
Andéranboukane, *Mali* 83 B5
Andermatt, *Switz.* 25 J4
Andernach, *Germany* 24 E3
Andernos-les-Bains, *France* 20 D2
Anderslöv, *Sweden* 11 J7
Anderson, *Calif., U.S.A.* 114 F2
Anderson, *Ind., U.S.A.* 108 E3
Anderson, *Mo., U.S.A.* 113 G7
Anderson, *S.C., U.S.A.* 109 H4
Anderson →, *Canada* 100 B7
Anderstorp, *Sweden* 11 G7
Andes, Cord. de los, *S. Amer.* 122 F4
Andfjorden, *Norway* 8 B17
Andhra Pradesh □, *India* 66 L11
Andijon, *Uzbekistan* 50 E8
Andikíthira, *Greece* 38 F5
Andīmeshk, *Iran* 71 C6
Andímilos, *Greece* 38 E6
Andíparos, *Greece* 39 D7
Andípaxoi, *Greece* 38 B2
Andípsara, *Greece* 39 C7
Andírrion, *Greece* 38 C3
Andizhan = Andijon, *Uzbekistan* 50 E8
Andoain, *Spain* 32 B2
Andoany, *Madag.* 89 A8
Andong, *S. Korea* 57 F15
Andongwei, *China* 57 G10
Andorra, *Spain* 32 E4
Andorra ■, *Europe* 20 F5
Andorra La Vella, *Andorra* 20 F5
Andover, *U.K.* 13 F6
Andover, *Mass., U.S.A.* 111 D13
Andover, *N.Y., U.S.A.* 110 D7
Andover, *Ohio, U.S.A.* 110 E4
Andøya, *Norway* 8 B16
Andradina, *Brazil* 125 H8
Andrahary, Mt., *Madag.* 89 A8
Andramasina, *Madag.* 89 B8
Andranopasy, *Madag.* 89 C7
Andratx, *Spain* 37 B9
Andreanof Is., *U.S.A.* 100 C2
Andreapol, *Russia* 46 D7
Andrewilla, *Australia* 95 D2
Andrews, *S.C., U.S.A.* 109 J6
Andrews, *Tex., U.S.A.* 113 J3
Andreyevka, *Russia* 48 D10
Ándria, *Italy* 31 A9
Andriba, *Madag.* 89 B8
Andrijevica, *Montenegro, Yug.* 40 D3
Andrítsaina, *Greece* 38 D3
Androka, *Madag.* 89 C7
Andropov = Rybinsk, *Russia* 46 C10
Ándros, *Greece* 38 D6
Andros I., *Bahamas* 120 B4
Andros Town, *Bahamas* 120 B4
Andrychów, *Poland* 45 J6
Andselv, *Norway* 8 B18
Andújar, *Spain* 35 G6
Andulo, *Angola* 84 G3
Aneby, *Sweden* 11 G8
Anegada I., *Virgin Is.* 121 C7
Anegada Passage, *W. Indies* 121 C7
Anécho, *Togo* 83 D5
Anenni-Noi, *Moldova* 43 D14
Aneto, Pico de, *Spain* 32 C5
Anfu, *China* 59 D10
Ang Thong, *Thailand* 64 E3
Angamos, Punta, *Chile* 126 A1
Ang'angxi, *China* 60 B7
Angara →, *Russia* 51 D10
Angarab, *Ethiopia* 81 E4
Angarsk, *Russia* 51 D11
Angas Downs, *Australia* 93 E5
Angas Hills, *Australia* 92 D4
Angaston, *Australia* 95 E2
Ånge, *Sweden* 10 B9
Ángel, Salto = Angel Falls, *Venezuela* 124 B6
Ángel de la Guarda, I., *Mexico* 118 B2
Angel Falls, *Venezuela* 124 B6
Angeles, *Phil.* 61 D4
Ängelholm, *Sweden* 11 H6
Angellala, *Australia* 95 D4
Angels Camp, *U.S.A.* 116 G6
Ängelsberg, *Sweden* 10 E10
Anger →, *Ethiopia* 81 F4
Angereb →, *Ethiopia* 81 E4
Ångermanälven →, *Sweden* 10 B11
Ångermanland, *Sweden* 8 E18
Angermünde, *Germany* 24 B9
Angers, *Canada* 111 A9
Angers, *France* 18 E6
Angerville, *France* 19 D9
Ängesån →, *Sweden* 8 C20
Angikuni L., *Canada* 105 A9
Angkor, *Cambodia* 64 F4
Anglès, *Spain* 32 D7
Anglesey, *U.K.* 12 D3
Anglesey, Isle of □, *U.K.* 12 D3
Anglet, *France* 20 E2
Angleton, *U.S.A.* 113 L7
Anglin →, *France* 20 B4
Anglisidhes, *Cyprus* 36 E12
Anglure, *France* 19 D10
Angmagssalik, *Greenland* 4 C6
Ango, *Dem. Rep. of the Congo* 86 B2
Angoche, *Mozam.* 87 F4
Angoche, I., *Mozam.* 87 F4
Angol, *Chile* 126 D1
Angola, *Ind., U.S.A.* 108 E3
Angola, *N.Y., U.S.A.* 110 D5
Angola ■, *Africa* 85 G3
Angoon, *U.S.A.* 104 B2
Angoulême, *France* 20 C4
Angoumois, *France* 20 C4
Angra dos Reis, *Brazil* 127 A7
Angren, *Uzbekistan* 50 E8
Angtassom, *Cambodia* 65 G5
Angu, *Dem. Rep. of the Congo* 86 B1
Anguang, *China* 57 B12
Anguilla ■, *W. Indies* 121 C7
Anguo, *China* 56 E8
Angurugu, *Australia* 94 A2
Angus □, *U.K.* 14 E6
Anhanduí →, *Brazil* 127 A5
Anholt, *Denmark* 11 H5
Anhua, *China* 59 C8
Anhui □, *China* 59 B11
Anhwei □ = Anhui □, *China* 59 B11
Anichab, *Namibia* 88 C1
Ánidhros, *Greece* 39 E7
Anié, *Togo* 83 D5
Animas, *U.S.A.* 115 L9
Anina, *Romania* 42 E6
Aninoasa, *Romania* 43 F9
Anivorano, *Madag.* 89 B8
Anjalankoski, *Finland* 9 F22
Anjar, *India* 68 H4
Anjidiv I., *India* 66 M9
Anjou, *France* 18 E6
Anjozorobe, *Madag.* 89 B8
Anju, *N. Korea* 57 E13
Anka, *Nigeria* 83 C6
Ankaboa, Tanjona, *Madag.* 89 C7
Ankang, *China* 56 H5
Ankara, *Turkey* 72 C5
Ankaramena, *Madag.* 89 C8
Ankarsrum, *Sweden* 11 G10
Ankazoabo, *Madag.* 89 C7
Ankazobe, *Madag.* 89 B8
Ankisabe, *Madag.* 89 B8
Anklam, *Germany* 24 B9
Ankober, *Ethiopia* 81 F4
Ankoro, *Dem. Rep. of the Congo* 86 D2
Anlong, *China* 58 E5
Anlu, *China* 59 B9
Anmyŏn-do, *S. Korea* 57 F14
Ånn, *Sweden* 10 A6
Ann, C., *U.S.A.* 111 D14
Ann Arbor, *U.S.A.* 108 D4
Anna, *Russia* 48 E5
Anna, *U.S.A.* 113 G10
Anna Plains, *Australia* 92 C3
Annaba, *Algeria* 78 A7
Annaberg-Buchholz, *Germany* 24 E9
Annalee →, *Ireland* 15 B4
Annam, *Vietnam* 64 E7
Annamitique, Chaîne, *Asia* 64 D6
Annan, *U.K.* 14 G5
Annan →, *U.K.* 14 G5
Annapolis, *U.S.A.* 108 F7
Annapolis Royal, *Canada* 103 D6
Annapurna, *Nepal* 69 E10
Annean, L., *Australia* 93 E2
Anneberg, *Sweden* 11 G8
Annecy, *France* 21 C10
Annecy, L. d', *France* 21 C10
Annemasse, *France* 19 F13
Annenskiy Most, *Russia* 46 B9
Anning, *China* 58 E4
Anningie, *Australia* 92 D5
Anniston, *U.S.A.* 109 J3
Annobón, *Atl. Oc.* 77 G4
Annonay, *France* 21 C8
Annot, *France* 21 E10
Annotto Bay, *Jamaica* 120 C4
Ånnsjön, *Sweden* 10 A6
Annuello, *Australia* 95 E3
Annville, *U.S.A.* 111 F8
Annweiler, *Germany* 25 F3
Áno Arkhánai, *Greece* 39 F7
Áno Porróia, *Greece* 40 E7
Áno Síros, *Greece* 38 D6
Áno Viánnos, *Greece* 36 D7
Anorotsangana, *Madag.* 89 A8
Anóyia, *Greece* 36 D6
Anping, *Hebei, China* 56 E8
Anping, *Liaoning, China* 57 D12
Anpu Gang, *China* 58 G7
Anqing, *China* 59 B11
Anqiu, *China* 57 F10
Anren, *China* 59 D9
Ansager, *Denmark* 11 J2
Ansai, *China* 56 F5
Ansbach, *Germany* 25 F6
Anseba →, *Eritrea* 81 D4
Ansfelden, *Austria* 26 C7
Anshan, *China* 57 D12
Anshun, *China* 58 D5
Ansião, *Portugal* 34 F2
Ansley, *U.S.A.* 112 E5
Ansó, *Spain* 32 C4
Ansoain, *Spain* 32 C3
Anson, *U.S.A.* 113 J5
Anson B., *Australia* 92 B5
Ansongo, *Mali* 83 B5
Ansonia, *U.S.A.* 111 E11
Anstruther, *U.K.* 14 E6
Ansudu, *Indonesia* 63 E9
Antabamba, *Peru* 124 F4
Antakya, *Turkey* 72 D7
Antalaha, *Madag.* 89 A9
Antalya, *Turkey* 72 D4
Antalya □, *Turkey* 39 E12
Antalya Körfezi, *Turkey* 72 D4
Antananarivo, *Madag.* 89 B8
Antananarivo □, *Madag.* 89 B8
Antanimbaribe, *Madag.* 89 C7
Antarctic Pen., *Antarctica* 5 C18
Antarctica 5 E3
Antelope, *Zimbabwe* 87 G2
Antequera, *Paraguay* 126 A4
Antequera, *Spain* 35 H6
Antero, Mt., *U.S.A.* 115 G10
Anthemoús, *Greece* 40 F7
Anthony, *Kans., U.S.A.* 113 G5
Anthony, *N. Mex., U.S.A.* 115 K10
Anthony Lagoon, *Australia* 94 B2
Anti Atlas, *Morocco* 78 C4
Anti-Lebanon = Ash Sharqi, Al Jabal, *Lebanon* 75 B5
Antibes, *France* 21 E11
Antibes, C. d', *France* 21 E11
Anticosti, Î. d', *Canada* 103 C7
Antifer, C. d', *France* 18 C7
Antigo, *U.S.A.* 112 C10
Antigonish, *Canada* 103 C7
Antigua, *Canary Is.* 37 F5
Antigua, *W. Indies* 121 C7
Antigua & Barbuda ■, *W. Indies* 121 C7
Antigua Guatemala, *Guatemala* 120 D1
Antilla, *Cuba* 120 B4
Antimony, *U.S.A.* 115 G8
Antioch, *U.S.A.* 116 G5
Antioche, Pertuis d', *France* 20 B2
Antioquia, *Colombia* 124 B3
Antipodes Is., *Pac. Oc.* 96 M9
Antler, *U.S.A.* 112 A4
Antler →, *Canada* 105 D8
Antlers, *U.S.A.* 113 H7
Antofagasta, *Chile* 126 A1
Antofagasta □, *Chile* 126 A2
Antofagasta de la Sierra, *Argentina* 126 B2
Antofalla, *Argentina* 126 B2
Antofalla, Salar de, *Argentina* 126 B2
Anton, *U.S.A.* 113 J3
Anton Chico, *U.S.A.* 115 J11
Antongila, Helodrano, *Madag.* 89 B8
Antonibé, *Madag.* 89 B8
Antonibé, Presqu'île d', *Madag.* 89 A8
Antonina, *Brazil* 127 B6
Antonito, *U.S.A.* 115 H10
Antrain, *France* 18 D5
Antrim, *U.K.* 15 B5
Antrim □, *U.K.* 15 B5
Antrim, Mts. of, *U.K.* 15 A5
Antrim Plateau, *Australia* 92 C4
Antrodoco, *Italy* 29 F10
Antropovo, *Russia* 48 A6
Antsalova, *Madag.* 89 B7
Antsirabe, *Madag.* 89 B8
Antsiranana, *Madag.* 89 A8
Antsohihy, *Madag.* 89 A8
Antsohimbondrona Seranana, *Madag.* 89 A8
Antu, *China* 57 C15
Antwerp = Antwerpen, *Belgium* 17 C4
Antwerp, *U.S.A.* 111 B9
Antwerpen, *Belgium* 17 C4
Antwerpen □, *Belgium* 17 C4
Anupgarh, *India* 68 E5
Anuradhapura, *Sri Lanka* 66 Q12
Anveh, *Iran* 71 E7
Anvers = Antwerpen, *Belgium* 17 C4
Anvers I., *Antarctica* 5 C17
Anxi, *Fujian, China* 59 E12
Anxi, *Gansu, China* 60 B4
Anxiang, *China* 59 C9
Anxious B., *Australia* 95 E1
Anyama, *Ivory C.* 82 D4
Anyang, *China* 56 F8
Anyi, *Jiangxi, China* 59 C10
Anyi, *Shanxi, China* 56 G6
Anyuan, *China* 59 E10
Anza, *U.S.A.* 117 M10
Anze, *China* 56 F7
Anzhero-Sudzhensk, *Russia* 50 D9
Ánzio, *Italy* 30 A5
Aoga-Shima, *Japan* 55 H9
Aoiz, *Spain* 32 C3
Aomori, *Japan* 54 D10
Aomori □, *Japan* 54 D10
Aonla, *India* 69 E8
Aosta, *Italy* 28 C4
Aoudéras, *Niger* 83 B6
Aouker, *Mauritania* 82 B3
Apa →, *S. Amer.* 126 A4
Apache, *U.S.A.* 113 H5
Apalachee B., *U.S.A.* 109 L4
Apalachicola, *U.S.A.* 109 L3
Apalachicola →, *U.S.A.* 109 L3
Apapa, *Nigeria* 83 D5
Apaporis →, *Colombia* 124 D5
Aparri, *Phil.* 61 B4
Apateu, *Romania* 42 D6
Apatin, *Serbia, Yug.* 42 E4
Apatzingán, *Mexico* 118 D4
Apeldoorn, *Neths.* 17 B5
Apen, *Germany* 24 B3
Apennines = Appennini, *Italy* 28 E7
Aphrodisias, *Turkey* 39 D10
Apia, *W. Samoa* 91 A13
Apiacás, Serra dos, *Brazil* 124 E7
Apizaco, *Mexico* 119 D5
Aplao, *Peru* 124 G4
Apo, Mt., *Phil.* 63 C7
Apolakkiá, *Greece* 36 C9
Apolakkiá, Órmos, *Greece* 36 C9
Apolda, *Germany* 24 D7
Apollonia, *Greece* 38 E6
Apolo, *Bolivia* 124 F5
Aporé →, *Brazil* 125 G8
Apostle Is., *U.S.A.* 112 B9
Apóstoles, *Argentina* 127 B4
Apostolos Andreas, C., *Cyprus* 36 D13
Apostolovo, *Ukraine* 47 J7
Apoteri, *Guyana* 124 C7
Appalachian Mts., *U.S.A.* 108 G6
Äppelbo, *Sweden* 10 D8
Appennini, *Italy* 28 E7
Appennino Ligure, *Italy* 28 D6
Appenzell-Ausser Rhoden □, *Switz.* 25 H5
Appenzell-Inner Rhoden □, *Switz.* 25 H5
Appiano, *Italy* 29 B8
Apple Hill, *Canada* 111 A10
Apple Valley, *U.S.A.* 117 L9
Appleby-in-Westmorland, *U.K.* 12 C5
Appleton, *U.S.A.* 108 C1
Approuague →, *Fr. Guiana* 125 C8
Apricena, *Italy* 29 G12
Aprília, *Italy* 30 A5
Apsheronsk, *Russia* 49 H4
Apt, *France* 21 E9
Apuane, Alpi, *Italy* 28 D7
Apucarana, *Brazil* 127 A5
Apulia = Púglia □, *Italy* 31 A9
Apure →, *Venezuela* 124 B5
Apurimac →, *Peru* 124 F4
Apuseni, Munţii, *Romania* 42 D7
Aqaba = Al 'Aqabah, *Jordan* 75 F4
Aqaba, G. of, *Red Sea* 70 D2
'Aqabah, Khalīj al = Aqaba, G. of, *Red Sea* 70 D2
'Aqdā, *Iran* 71 C7
Aqīq, *Sudan* 80 D4
Aqīq, Khalīg, *Sudan* 80 D4
Aqmola, *Kazakstan* 50 D8
Aqrah, *Iraq* 70 B4
Aqtöbe, *Kazakstan* 50 D6
Aquidauana, *Brazil* 125 H7
Aquiles Serdán, *Mexico* 118 B3
Aquin, *Haiti* 121 C5
Aquitaine □, *France* 20 D3
Ar Rachidiya, *Morocco* 78 B5
Ar Rafīd, *Syria* 75 C4
Ar Raḥḥālīyah, *Iraq* 70 C4
Ar Ramādī, *Iraq* 70 C4
Ar Ramthā, *Jordan* 75 C5
Ar Raqqah, *Syria* 70 C3
Ar Rass, *Si. Arabia* 70 E4
Ar Rifā'ī, *Iraq* 70 D5
Ar Riyāḍ, *Si. Arabia* 70 E5
Ar Ru'ays, *Qatar* 71 E6
Ar Rukhaymīyah, *Iraq* 70 D5
Ar Ruqayyidah, *Si. Arabia* 71 E6
Ar Ruṣāfah, *Syria* 70 C3
Ar Ruṭbah, *Iraq* 70 C4
Ara, *India* 69 G11
'Arab, Bahr el →, *Sudan* 81 F2
Arab, Khalîg el, *Egypt* 80 H6
'Arabābād, *Iran* 71 C8
Araban, *Turkey* 72 D7
Arabatskaya Strelka, *Ukraine* 47 K8
Arabba, *Italy* 29 B8
Arabia, *Asia* 52 G8
Arabian Desert = Es Sahrâ' Esh Sharqîya, *Egypt* 80 B3
Arabian Gulf = Gulf, The, *Asia* 71 E6
Arabian Sea, *Ind. Oc.* 52 H10
Araç, *Turkey* 72 B5
Aracaju, *Brazil* 125 F11
Aracati, *Brazil* 125 D11
Araçatuba, *Brazil* 127 A5
Aracena, *Spain* 35 H4
Aracena, Sierra de, *Spain* 35 H4
Aračinovo, *Macedonia* 40 D5
Araçuaí, *Brazil* 125 G10
'Arad, *Israel* 75 D4
Arad, *Romania* 42 D6
Arad □, *Romania* 42 D6
Aradhippou, *Cyprus* 36 E12
Arafura Sea, *E. Indies* 63 F9
Aragats, *Armenia* 49 K7
Aragón □, *Spain* 32 D4
Aragón →, *Spain* 32 C3
Aragona, *Italy* 30 E6
Araguacema, *Brazil* 125 E9
Araguaia →, *Brazil* 122 D6
Araguaína, *Brazil* 125 E9
Araguari, *Brazil* 125 G9
Araguari →, *Brazil* 125 C9
Arak, *Algeria* 78 C6
Arāk, *Iran* 71 C6
Arakan Coast, *Burma* 67 K19
Arakan Yoma, *Burma* 67 K19
Arákhova, *Greece* 38 C4
Arakli, *Turkey* 73 B8
Araks = Aras, Rūd-e →, *Azerbaijan* 70 B5
Aral, *Kazakstan* 50 E7
Aral Sea, *Asia* 50 E7
Aral Tengizi = Aral Sea, *Asia* 50 E7
Aralsk = Aral, *Kazakstan* 50 E7
Aralskoye More = Aral Sea, *Asia* 50 E7
Aralsor, Ozero, *Kazakstan* 49 F9
Aramac, *Australia* 94 C4
Arambag, *India* 69 H12
Aran I., *Ireland* 15 A3
Aran Is., *Ireland* 15 C2
Aranda de Duero, *Spain* 34 D7
Arandān, *Iran* 70 C5
Aranđelovac, *Serbia, Yug.* 40 B4
Aranjuez, *Spain* 34 E7
Aranos, *Namibia* 88 C2
Aransas Pass, *U.S.A.* 113 M6
Aranyaprathet, *Thailand* 64 F4
Araouane, *Mali* 82 B4
Arapahoe, *U.S.A.* 112 E5
Arapey Grande →, *Uruguay* 126 C4
Arapgir, *Turkey* 73 C8
Arapiraca, *Brazil* 125 E11
Arapongas, *Brazil* 127 A5
Ar'ar, *Si. Arabia* 70 D4
Araranguá, *Brazil* 127 B6
Araraquara, *Brazil* 125 H9
Ararás, Serra das, *Brazil* 127 B5
Ararat, *Armenia* 73 C11
Ararat, *Australia* 95 F3
Ararat, Mt. = Ağrı Dağı, *Turkey* 73 C11
Araria, *India* 69 F12
Araripe, Chapada do, *Brazil* 125 E11
Araruama, L. de, *Brazil* 127 A7
Aras, Rūd-e →, *Azerbaijan* 70 B5
Arauca, *Colombia* 124 B4
Arauca →, *Venezuela* 124 B5
Arauco, *Chile* 126 D1
Arauco □, *Chile* 126 D1
Arawa, *Ethiopia* 81 F5
Araxá, *Brazil* 125 G9
Araya, Pen. de, *Venezuela* 124 A6
Arba Minch, *Ethiopia* 81 F4
Arbat, *Iraq* 70 C5
Árbatax, *Italy* 30 C2
Arbīl, *Iraq* 70 B5
Arboga, *Sweden* 10 E9
Arbois, *France* 19 F12

Arbore, *Ethiopia* 81 F4
Arboréa, *Italy* 30 C1
Arborfield, *Canada* 105 C8
Arborg, *Canada* 105 C9
Arbroath, *U.K.* 14 E6
Arbuckle, *U.S.A.* 116 F4
Arbus, *Italy* 30 C1
Arc →, *France* 21 C10
Arc-lès-Gray, *France* 19 E12
Arcachon, *France* 20 D2
Arcachon, Bassin d', *France* 20 D2
Arcade, *U.S.A.* 110 D6
Arcadia, *Fla., U.S.A.* 109 M5
Arcadia, *La., U.S.A.* 113 J8
Arcadia, *Nebr., U.S.A.* 112 E5
Arcadia, *Pa., U.S.A.* 110 F6
Arcadia, *Wis., U.S.A.* 112 C9
Arcata, *U.S.A.* 114 F1
Arcévia, *Italy* 29 E9
Archangel = Arkhangelsk, *Russia* 50 C5
Archar, *Bulgaria* 40 C6
Archbald, *U.S.A.* 111 E9
Archena, *Spain* 33 G3
Archer →, *Australia* 94 A3
Archer B., *Australia* 94 A3
Archers Post, *Kenya* 86 B4
Archidona, *Spain* 35 H6
Arci, Mte., *Italy* 30 C1
Arcidosso, *Italy* 29 F8
Arcis-sur-Aube, *France* 19 D11
Arckaringa, *Australia* 95 D1
Arckaringa Cr. →, *Australia* 95 D2
Arco, *Italy* 28 C7
Arco, *U.S.A.* 114 E7
Arcola, *Canada* 105 D8
Arcos = Arcos de Jalón, *Spain* 32 D2
Arcos de Jalón, *Spain* 32 D2
Arcos de la Frontera, *Spain* 35 J5
Arcos de Valdevez, *Portugal* 34 D2
Arcot, *India* 66 N11
Arcozelo, *Portugal* 34 E3
Arctic Bay, *Canada* 101 A11
Arctic Ocean, *Arctic* 4 B18
Arda →, *Bulgaria* 41 E10
Arda →, *Italy* 28 C7
Ardabīl, *Iran* 71 B6
Ardahan, *Turkey* 73 B10
Ardakān = Sepīdān, *Iran* 71 D7
Ardala, *Sweden* 11 F7
Ardales, *Spain* 35 J6
Ardèche □, *France* 21 D8
Ardèche →, *France* 21 D8
Ardee, *Ireland* 15 C5
Arden, *Canada* 110 B8
Arden, *Denmark* 11 H3
Arden, *Calif., U.S.A.* 116 G5
Arden, *Nev., U.S.A.* 117 J11
Ardenne, *Belgium* 6 F7
Ardennes = Ardenne, *Belgium* 6 F7
Ardennes □, *France* 19 C11
Ardentes, *France* 19 F8
Arderin, *Ireland* 15 C4
Ardeşen, *Turkey* 73 B9
Ardestān, *Iran* 71 C7
Árdhas →, *Greece* 41 E10
Ardhéa, *Greece* 40 F6
Ardila →, *Portugal* 35 G3
Ardino, *Bulgaria* 41 E9
Ardivachar Pt., *U.K.* 14 D1
Ardlethan, *Australia* 95 E4
Ardmore, *Australia* 94 C2
Ardmore, *Okla., U.S.A.* 113 H6
Ardmore, *Pa., U.S.A.* 111 G9
Ardmore, *S. Dak., U.S.A.* 112 D3
Ardnamurchan, Pt. of, *U.K.* 14 E2
Ardnave Pt., *U.K.* 14 F2
Ardon, *Russia* 49 J7
Ardore, *Italy* 31 D9
Ardres, *France* 19 B8
Ardrossan, *Australia* 95 E2
Ardrossan, *U.K.* 14 F4
Ards Pen., *U.K.* 15 B6
Ardud, *Romania* 42 C7
Åre, *Sweden* 10 A7
Arecibo, *Puerto Rico* 121 C6
Areia Branca, *Brazil* 125 E11
Arena, Pt., *U.S.A.* 116 G3
Arenas = Las Arenas, *Spain* 34 B6
Arenas de San Pedro, *Spain* 34 E5
Arendal, *Norway* 9 G13
Arendsee, *Germany* 24 C7
Arenys de Mar, *Spain* 32 D7
Arenzano, *Italy* 28 D5
Areópolis, *Greece* 38 E4
Arequipa, *Peru* 124 G4
Arero, *Ethiopia* 81 G4
Arès, *France* 20 D2
Arévalo, *Spain* 34 D6
Arezzo, *Italy* 29 E8
Arga →, *Spain* 32 C3
Argalastí, *Greece* 38 B5
Argamasilla de Alba, *Spain* 35 F7
Argamasilla de Calatrava, *Spain* 35 G6
Arganda, *Spain* 34 E7
Arganil, *Portugal* 34 E2
Argelès-Gazost, *France* 20 E3
Argelès-sur-Mer, *France* 20 F7
Argens →, *France* 21 E10
Argent-sur-Sauldre, *France* 19 E9
Argenta, *Italy* 29 D8
Argentan, *France* 18 D6
Argentário, Mte., *Italy* 29 F8
Argentat, *France* 20 C5
Argentera, *Italy* 28 D4
Argenteuil, *France* 19 D9
Argentia, *Canada* 103 C9
Argentiera, C. dell', *Italy* 30 B1
Argentina ■, *S. Amer.* 128 D3
Argentina Is., *Antarctica* 5 C17
Argentino, L., *Argentina* 128 G2
Argenton-Château, *France* 18 F6
Argenton-sur-Creuse, *France* 19 F8
Argeş □, *Romania* 43 F9
Argeş →, *Romania* 43 F11
Arghandab →, *Afghan.* 68 D1
Argo, *Sudan* 80 D3
Argolikós Kólpos, *Greece* 38 D4
Argolís □, *Greece* 38 D4
Argonne, *France* 19 C12
Árgos, *Greece* 38 D4
Árgos Orestikón, *Greece* 40 F5
Argostólion, *Greece* 38 C2
Arguedas, *Spain* 32 C3
Arguello, Pt., *U.S.A.* 117 L6
Arguineguín, *Canary Is.* 37 G4
Argun, *Russia* 49 J7
Argun →, *Russia* 51 D13
Argungu, *Nigeria* 83 C5
Argus Pk., *U.S.A.* 117 K9
Argyle, *U.S.A.* 112 A6
Argyle, L., *Australia* 92 C4
Argyll & Bute □, *U.K.* 14 E3
Arhavi, *Turkey* 73 B9
Århus, *Denmark* 11 H4
Århus Amtskommune □, *Denmark* 11 H4
Ariadnoye, *Russia* 54 B7
Ariamsvlei, *Namibia* 88 D2
Ariano Irpino, *Italy* 31 A8
Aribinda, *Burkina Faso* 83 C4
Arica, *Chile* 124 G4
Arica, *Colombia* 124 D4
Arico, *Canary Is.* 37 F3
Arid, C., *Australia* 93 F3
Arida, *Japan* 55 G7
Ariège □, *France* 20 F5
Ariège →, *France* 20 E5
Arieş →, *Romania* 43 D8
Arilje, *Serbia, Yug.* 40 C4
Arílla, Ákra, *Greece* 36 A3
Arima, *Trin. & Tob.* 121 D7
Arinos →, *Brazil* 122 E5
Ario de Rosales, *Mexico* 118 D4
Ariogala, *Lithuania* 44 C10
Aripuanã, *Brazil* 124 E6
Aripuanã →, *Brazil* 122 D4
Ariquemes, *Brazil* 124 E6
Arisaig, *U.K.* 14 E3
Arîsh, W. el →, *Egypt* 80 H8
Arissa, *Ethiopia* 81 E5
Aristazabal I., *Canada* 104 C3
Arivaca, *U.S.A.* 115 L8
Arivonimamo, *Madag.* 89 B8
Ariza, *Spain* 32 D2
Arizaro, Salar de, *Argentina* 126 A2
Arizona, *Argentina* 126 D2
Arizona □, *U.S.A.* 115 J8
Arizpe, *Mexico* 118 A2
Årjäng, *Sweden* 10 E6
Arjeplog, *Sweden* 8 D18
Arjona, *Colombia* 124 A3
Arjona, *Spain* 35 H6
Arjuna, *Indonesia* 63 G15
Arka, *Russia* 51 C15
Arkadak, *Russia* 48 E6
Arkadelphia, *U.S.A.* 113 H8
Arkadhía □, *Greece* 38 D4
Arkaig, L., *U.K.* 14 E3
Arkalyk = Arqalyk, *Kazakstan* 50 D7
Arkansas □, *U.S.A.* 113 H8
Arkansas →, *U.S.A.* 113 J9
Arkansas City, *U.S.A.* 113 G6
Árkathos →, *Greece* 38 B3
Arkhángelos, *Greece* 36 C10
Arkhangelsk, *Russia* 50 C5
Arkhangelskoye, *Russia* 48 E5
Arkiko, *Eritrea* 81 D4
Arklow, *Ireland* 15 D5
Árkoi, *Greece* 39 D8
Arkona, Kap, *Germany* 24 A9
Arkösund, *Sweden* 11 F10
Arkoúdhi, *Greece* 38 C2
Arkticheskiy, Mys, *Russia* 51 A10
Arkul, *Russia* 48 B10
Årla, *Sweden* 10 E10
Arlanza →, *Spain* 34 C6
Arlanzón →, *Spain* 34 C6
Arlbergpass, *Austria* 26 D3
Arlee, *U.S.A.* 114 C6
Arles, *France* 21 E8
Arlington, *S. Africa* 89 D4
Arlington, *Oreg., U.S.A.* 114 D3
Arlington, *S. Dak., U.S.A.* 112 C6
Arlington, *Va., U.S.A.* 108 F7
Arlington, *Wash., U.S.A.* 116 B4
Arlington Heights, *U.S.A.* 108 D2
Arlon, *Belgium* 17 E5
Arly, *Burkina Faso* 83 C5
Armagh, *U.K.* 15 B5
Armagh □, *U.K.* 15 B5
Armagnac, *France* 20 E4
Armançon →, *France* 19 E10
Armavir, *Russia* 49 H5
Armenia, *Colombia* 124 C3
Armenia ■, *Asia* 49 K7
Armeniş, *Romania* 42 E7
Armenistís, Ákra, *Greece* 36 C9
Armentières, *France* 19 B9
Armidale, *Australia* 95 E5
Armilla, *Spain* 35 H7
Armour, *U.S.A.* 112 D5
Armstrong, *B.C., Canada* 104 C5
Armstrong, *Ont., Canada* 102 B2
Armstrong, *U.S.A.* 113 M6
Armstrong →, *Australia* 92 C5
Armutlu, *Bursa, Turkey* 41 F12
Armutlu, *İzmir, Turkey* 39 C9
Arnaía, *Greece* 40 F7
Arnarfjörður, *Iceland* 8 D2
Arnaud →, *Canada* 101 C13
Arnauti, C., *Cyprus* 36 D11
Arnay-le-Duc, *France* 19 E11
Arnedillo, *Spain* 32 C2
Arnedo, *Spain* 32 C2
Arnett, *U.S.A.* 113 G5
Arnhem, *Neths.* 17 C5
Arnhem, C., *Australia* 94 A2
Arnhem B., *Australia* 94 A2
Arnhem Land, *Australia* 94 A1
Árnissa, *Greece* 40 F5
Arno →, *Italy* 28 E7
Arno Bay, *Australia* 95 E2
Arnold, *U.K.* 12 D6
Arnold, *Calif., U.S.A.* 116 G6
Arnold, *Nebr., U.S.A.* 112 E4
Arnoldstein, *Austria* 26 E6
Arnon →, *France* 19 E9
Arnot, *Canada* 105 B9
Arnøy, *Norway* 8 A19
Arnprior, *Canada* 102 C4
Arnsberg, *Germany* 24 D4
Arnstadt, *Germany* 24 E6
Aroab, *Namibia* 88 D2
Aroánia Óri, *Greece* 38 D4
Aroche, *Spain* 35 H4
Arolsen, *Germany* 24 D5
Aron →, *France* 19 F10
Arona, *Italy* 28 C5
Aroroy, *Phil.* 61 E5
Arosa, Ría de, *Spain* 34 C2
Arpajon, *France* 19 D9
Arpajon-sur-Cère, *France* 20 D6
Arpaşu de Jos, *Romania* 43 E9
Arqalyk, *Kazakstan* 50 D7
Arrabury, *Australia* 95 D3
Arrah = Ara, *India* 69 G11
Arraiolos, *Portugal* 35 G3
Arran, *U.K.* 14 F3
Arrandale, *Canada* 104 C3
Arras, *France* 19 B9
Arrasate, *Spain* 32 B2
Arrats →, *France* 20 D4
Arreau, *France* 20 F4
Arrecife, *Canary Is.* 37 F6
Arrecifes, *Argentina* 126 C3
Arrée, Mts. d', *France* 18 D3
Arresø, *Denmark* 11 J6
Arriaga, *Chiapas, Mexico* 119 D6
Arriaga, *San Luis Potosí, Mexico* 118 C4
Arrilalah P.O., *Australia* 94 C3
Arrino, *Australia* 93 E2
Arriondas, *Spain* 34 B5
Arromanches-les-Bains, *France* 18 C6
Arronches, *Portugal* 35 F3
Arros →, *France* 20 E3
Arrow, L., *Ireland* 15 B3
Arrow Rock Res., *U.S.A.* 114 E6
Arrowhead, *Canada* 104 C5
Arrowhead, L., *U.S.A.* 117 L9
Arrowtown, *N.Z.* 91 L2
Arroyo de la Luz, *Spain* 35 F4
Arroyo Grande, *U.S.A.* 117 K6
Års, *Denmark* 11 H3
Ars, *Iran* 70 B5
Ars-sur-Moselle, *France* 19 C13
Arsenault L., *Canada* 105 B7
Arsenev, *Russia* 54 B6
Arsi □, *Ethiopia* 81 F4
Arsiero, *Italy* 29 C8
Arsin, *Turkey* 73 B8
Arsk, *Russia* 48 B9
Årsunda, *Sweden* 10 D10
Árta, *Greece* 38 B3
Artà, *Spain* 37 B10
Árta □, *Greece* 38 B3
Arteaga, *Mexico* 118 D4
Arteche, *Phil.* 61 E6
Arteijo = Arteixo, *Spain* 34 B2
Arteixo, *Spain* 34 B2
Artem = Artyom, *Azerbaijan* 49 K10
Artem, *Russia* 54 C6
Artemovsk, *Russia* 51 D10
Artemovsk, *Ukraine* 47 H9
Artemovskiy, *Russia* 49 G5
Artenay, *France* 19 D8
Artern, *Germany* 24 D7
Artesa de Segre, *Spain* 32 D6
Artesia = Mosomane, *Botswana* 88 C4
Artesia, *U.S.A.* 113 J2
Artesia Wells, *U.S.A.* 113 L5
Artesian, *U.S.A.* 112 C6
Arthington, *Liberia* 82 D2
Arthur →, *Australia* 94 G3
Arthur Cr. →, *Australia* 94 C2
Arthur Pt., *Australia* 94 C5
Arthur's Pass, *N.Z.* 91 K3
Arthur's Town, *Bahamas* 121 B4
Artigas, *Uruguay* 126 C4
Artik, *Armenia* 49 K6
Artillery L., *Canada* 105 A7
Artois, *France* 19 B9
Artotína, *Greece* 38 C4
Artrutx, C. de, *Spain* 37 B10
Artsyz, *Ukraine* 47 J5
Artvin, *Turkey* 73 B9
Artyom, *Azerbaijan* 49 K10
Aru, Kepulauan, *Indonesia* 63 F8
Aru Is. = Aru, Kepulauan, *Indonesia* 63 F8
Aru Meru □, *Tanzania* 86 C4
Arua, *Uganda* 86 B3
Aruanã, *Brazil* 125 F8
Aruba ■, *W. Indies* 121 D6
Arucas, *Canary Is.* 37 F4
Arudy, *France* 20 E3
Arumpo, *Australia* 95 E3
Arun →, *Nepal* 69 F12
Arun →, *U.K.* 13 G7
Arunachal Pradesh □, *India* 67 F19
Arusha, *Tanzania* 86 C4
Arusha □, *Tanzania* 86 C4
Arusha Chini, *Tanzania* 86 C4
Aruwimi →, *Dem. Rep. of the Congo* 86 B1
Arvada, *U.S.A.* 114 D10
Arvayheer, *Mongolia* 60 B5
Arve →, *France* 19 F13
Árvi, *Greece* 36 E7
Arvida, *Canada* 103 C5
Arvidsjaur, *Sweden* 8 D18
Arvika, *Sweden* 10 E6
Arvin, *U.S.A.* 117 K8
Arxan, *China* 60 B6
Åryd, *Sweden* 11 H8
Aryirádhes, *Greece* 36 B3
Aryiroúpolis, *Greece* 36 D6
Arys, *Kazakstan* 50 E7
Arzachena, *Italy* 30 A2
Arzamas, *Russia* 48 C6
Arzgir, *Russia* 49 H7
Arzignano, *Italy* 29 C8
Arzúa, *Spain* 34 C2
Aš, *Czech Rep.* 26 A5
Ås, *Sweden* 10 A8
As Pontes de García Rodríquez, *Spain* 34 B3
Aş Şadr, *U.A.E.* 71 E7
Aş Şafā, *Syria* 75 B6
'As Saffānīyah, *Si. Arabia* 71 D6
Aş Şafīrah, *Syria* 70 B3
Aş Şahm, *Oman* 71 E8
As Sājir, *Si. Arabia* 70 E5
As Salamīyah, *Syria* 70 C3
As Salţ, *Jordan* 75 C4
As Sal'w'a, *Qatar* 71 E6
As Samāwah, *Iraq* 70 D5
As Sanamayn, *Syria* 75 B5
As Sohar = Şuḩār, *Oman* 71 E8
As Sukhnah, *Syria* 70 C3
As Sulaymānīyah, *Iraq* 70 C5
As Sulaymī, *Si. Arabia* 70 E4
As Summān, *Si. Arabia* 70 E5
As Suwaydā', *Syria* 75 C5
As Suwaydā' □, *Syria* 75 C5
As Şuwayrah, *Iraq* 70 C5
Åsa, *Sweden* 11 G6
Asab, *Namibia* 88 D2
Asaba, *Nigeria* 83 D6
Asadābād, *Iran* 73 E13
Asafo, *Ghana* 82 D4
Asahi-Gawa →, *Japan* 55 G6
Asahigawa, *Japan* 54 C11
Asale, L., *Ethiopia* 81 E5
Asamankese, *Ghana* 83 D4
Asansol, *India* 69 H12
Åsarna, *Sweden* 10 B8
Asbe Teferi, *Ethiopia* 81 F5
Asbesberge, *S. Africa* 88 D3
Asbestos, *Canada* 103 C5
Asbury Park, *U.S.A.* 111 F10
Ascea, *Italy* 31 B8
Ascensión, *Mexico* 118 A3
Ascensión, B. de la, *Mexico* 119 D7
Ascension I., *Atl. Oc.* 77 G2
Aschach an der Donau, *Austria* 26 C7
Aschaffenburg, *Germany* 25 F5
Aschendorf, *Germany* 24 B3
Aschersleben, *Germany* 24 D7
Asciano, *Italy* 29 E8
Áscoli Piceno, *Italy* 29 F10
Áscoli Satriano, *Italy* 31 A8
Ascope, *Peru* 124 E3
Ascotán, *Chile* 126 A2
Aseb, *Eritrea* 81 E5
Åseda, *Sweden* 11 G9
Asela, *Ethiopia* 81 F4
Åsen, *Sweden* 10 C7
Asenovgrad, *Bulgaria* 41 D8
Asfeld, *France* 19 C11
Asfûn el Matâ'na, *Egypt* 80 B3
Asgata, *Cyprus* 36 E12
Ash Fork, *U.S.A.* 115 J7
Ash Grove, *U.S.A.* 113 G8
Ash Shām, Bādiyat, *Asia* 52 F7
Ash Shamāl □, *Lebanon* 75 A5
Ash Shāmīyah, *Iraq* 70 D5
Ash Shāriqah, *U.A.E.* 71 E7
Ash Sharmah, *Si. Arabia* 70 D2
Ash Sharqāt, *Iraq* 70 C4
Ash Sharqi, Al Jabal, *Lebanon* 75 B5
Ash Shaţrah, *Iraq* 70 D5
Ash Shawbak, *Jordan* 70 D2
Ash Shawmari, J., *Jordan* 75 E5
Ash Shaykh, J., *Lebanon* 75 B4
Ash Shināfīyah, *Iraq* 70 D5
Ash Shu'aybah, *Si. Arabia* 70 E5
Ash Shumlūl, *Si. Arabia* 70 E5
Ash Shūr'a, *Iraq* 70 C4
Ash Shurayf, *Si. Arabia* 70 E3
Ash Shuwayfāt, *Lebanon* 75 B4
Ashanti □, *Ghana* 83 D4
Ashau, *Vietnam* 64 D6
Ashbourne, *U.K.* 12 D6
Ashburn, *U.S.A.* 109 K4
Ashburton, *N.Z.* 91 K3
Ashburton →, *Australia* 92 D1
Ashburton Downs, *Australia* 92 D2
Ashcroft, *Canada* 104 C4
Ashdod, *Israel* 75 D3
Asheboro, *U.S.A.* 109 H6
Asherton, *U.S.A.* 113 L5
Asheville, *U.S.A.* 109 H4
Asheweig →, *Canada* 102 B2
Ashford, *Australia* 95 D5
Ashford, *U.K.* 13 F8
Ashford, *U.S.A.* 114 C2
Ashgabat, *Turkmenistan* 50 F6
Ashibetsu, *Japan* 54 C11
Ashikaga, *Japan* 55 F9
Ashington, *U.K.* 12 B6
Ashizuri-Zaki, *Japan* 55 H6
Ashkarkot, *Afghan.* 68 C2
Ashkhabad = Ashgabat, *Turkmenistan* 50 F6
Ashland, *Kans., U.S.A.* 113 G5
Ashland, *Ky., U.S.A.* 108 F4
Ashland, *Maine, U.S.A.* 103 C6
Ashland, *Mont., U.S.A.* 114 D10
Ashland, *Nebr., U.S.A.* 112 E6
Ashland, *Ohio, U.S.A.* 110 F2
Ashland, *Oreg., U.S.A.* 114 E2
Ashland, *Pa., U.S.A.* 111 F8
Ashland, *Va., U.S.A.* 108 G7
Ashland, *Wis., U.S.A.* 112 B9
Ashley, *N. Dak., U.S.A.* 112 B5
Ashley, *Pa., U.S.A.* 111 E9
Ashmont, *Canada* 104 C6
Ashmore Reef, *Australia* 92 B3
Ashmûn, *Egypt* 80 H7
Ashmyany, *Belarus* 9 J21
Ashqelon, *Israel* 75 D3
Ashtabula, *U.S.A.* 110 E4
Ashton, *S. Africa* 88 E3
Ashton, *U.S.A.* 114 D8
Ashuanipi, L., *Canada* 103 B6
'Āṣī →, *Asia* 72 D6
Asia, Kepulauan, *Indonesia* 63 D8
Āsīā Bak, *Iran* 71 C6
Asiago, *Italy* 29 C8
Asifabad, *India* 66 K11
Asinara, *Italy* 30 A1
Asinara, G. dell', *Italy* 30 A1
Asino, *Russia* 50 D9
Asipovichy, *Belarus* 46 F5
'Asīr □, *Si. Arabia* 74 D3
Asir, Ras, *Somali Rep.* 74 E5
Aşkale, *Turkey* 73 C9
Askersund, *Sweden* 11 F8
Askham, *S. Africa* 88 D3
Askim, *Norway* 9 G14
Askja, *Iceland* 8 D5
Askøy, *Norway* 9 F11
Asl, *Egypt* 80 J8
Aslan Burnu, *Turkey* 39 C8
Aslanapa, *Turkey* 39 B11
Asmara = Asmera, *Eritrea* 81 D4
Asmera, *Eritrea* 81 D4
Asnæs, *Denmark* 11 J4
Åsnen, *Sweden* 11 H8
Asola, *Italy* 28 C7
Asoteriba, Jebel, *Sudan* 80 C4
Asotin, *U.S.A.* 114 C5
Aspe, *Spain* 33 G4
Aspen, *U.S.A.* 115 G10
Aspendos, *Turkey* 72 D4
Aspermont, *U.S.A.* 113 J4
Aspet, *France* 20 E4
Aspiring, Mt., *N.Z.* 91 L2
Aspres-sur-Buëch, *France* 21 D9
Asprókavos, Ákra, *Greece* 36 B4
Aspromonte, *Italy* 31 D9
Aspur, *India* 68 H6
Asquith, *Canada* 105 C7
Assâba, *Mauritania* 82 B2
Assad, Bahret, *Syria* 70 C3
Assam □, *India* 67 G18
Assamakka, *Niger* 83 B6
Asse, *Belgium* 17 D4
Assémini, *Italy* 30 C1
Assen, *Neths.* 17 A6
Assens, *Denmark* 11 J3
Assini, *Ivory C.* 82 D4
Assiniboia, *Canada* 105 D7
Assiniboine →, *Canada* 105 D9
Assis, *Brazil* 127 A5
Assisi, *Italy* 29 E9
Ássos, *Greece* 38 C2
Assynt, L., *U.K.* 14 C3
Astaffort, *France* 20 D4
Astakidha, *Greece* 39 F8
Astakós, *Greece* 38 C3
Astana = Aqmola, *Kazakstan* 50 D8

Astara, *Azerbaijan* 73 C13
Āstārā, *Iran* 73 C13
Asteroúsia, *Greece* 36 E7
Asti, *Italy* 28 D5
Astipálaia, *Greece* 39 E8
Astorga, *Spain* 34 C4
Astoria, *U.S.A.* 116 D3
Åstorp, *Sweden* 11 H6
Astrakhan, *Russia* 49 G9
Astudillo, *Spain* 34 C6
Asturias □, *Spain* 34 B5
Asunción, *Paraguay* 126 B4
Asunción Nochixtlán, *Mexico* 119 D5
Åsunden, *Sweden* 11 F9
Asutri, *Sudan* 81 D4
Aswa →, *Uganda* 86 B3
Aswad, Ras al, *Si. Arabia* 80 C4
Aswân, *Egypt* 80 C3
Aswân High Dam = Sadd el Aali, *Egypt* 80 C3
Asyût, *Egypt* 80 B3
Asyûti, Wadi →, *Egypt* 80 B3
Aszód, *Hungary* 42 C4
At Ţafīlah, *Jordan* 75 E4
Aţ Tā'if, *Si. Arabia* 80 C5
Aţ Ţirāq, *Si. Arabia* 70 E5
Atabey, *Turkey* 39 D12
Atacama □, *Chile* 126 B2
Atacama, Desierto de, *Chile* 126 A2
Atacama, Salar de, *Chile* 126 A2
Atakpamé, *Togo* 83 D5
Atalándi, *Greece* 38 C4
Atalaya, *Peru* 124 F4
Atalaya de Femes, *Canary Is.* 37 F6
Atami, *Japan* 55 G9
Atapupu, *Indonesia* 63 F6
Atâr, *Mauritania* 78 D3
Atarfe, *Spain* 35 H7
Atascadero, *U.S.A.* 116 K6
Atasu, *Kazakstan* 50 E8
Atatürk Barajı, *Turkey* 73 D8
Atauro, *Indonesia* 63 F7
Atbara, *Sudan* 80 D3
'Atbara →, *Sudan* 80 D3
Atbasar, *Kazakstan* 50 D7
Atça, *Turkey* 39 D10
Atchafalaya B., *U.S.A.* 113 L9
Atchison, *U.S.A.* 112 F7
Atebubu, *Ghana* 83 D4
Ateca, *Spain* 32 D3
Aterno →, *Italy* 29 F10
Atesine, Alpi, *Italy* 29 B8
Atessa, *Italy* 29 F11
Ath, *Belgium* 17 D3
Athabasca, *Canada* 104 C6
Athabasca →, *Canada* 105 B6
Athabasca, L., *Canada* 105 B7
Athboy, *Ireland* 15 C5
Athenry, *Ireland* 15 C3
Athens = Athínai, *Greece* 38 D5
Athens, *Ala., U.S.A.* 109 H2
Athens, *Ga., U.S.A.* 109 J4
Athens, *N.Y., U.S.A.* 111 D11
Athens, *Ohio, U.S.A.* 108 F4
Athens, *Pa., U.S.A.* 111 E8
Athens, *Tenn., U.S.A.* 109 H3
Athens, *Tex., U.S.A.* 113 J7
Atherley, *Canada* 110 B5
Atherton, *Australia* 94 B4
Athiéme, *Benin* 83 D5
Athienou, *Cyprus* 36 D12
Athínai, *Greece* 38 D5
Athlone, *Ireland* 15 C4
Athna, *Cyprus* 36 D12
Atholl, Forest of, *U.K.* 14 E5
Atholville, *Canada* 103 C6
Áthos, *Greece* 41 F8
Athy, *Ireland* 15 C5
Ati, *Chad* 79 F9
Ati, *Sudan* 81 E2
Atiak, *Uganda* 86 B3
Atienza, *Spain* 32 D2
Atikokan, *Canada* 102 C1
Atikonak L., *Canada* 103 B7
Atimonan, *Phil.* 61 E4
Atka, *Russia* 51 C16
Atkarsk, *Russia* 48 E7
Atkinson, *U.S.A.* 112 D5
Atlanta, *Ga., U.S.A.* 109 J3
Atlanta, *Tex., U.S.A.* 113 J7
Atlantic, *U.S.A.* 112 E7
Atlantic City, *U.S.A.* 108 F8
Atlantic Ocean 2 E9
Atlas Mts. = Haut Atlas, *Morocco* 78 B4
Atlin, *Canada* 104 B2
Atlin, L., *Canada* 104 B2
Atmore, *U.S.A.* 109 K2
Atoka, *U.S.A.* 113 H6
Átokos, *Greece* 38 C2
Atolia, *U.S.A.* 117 K9
Atoyac →, *Mexico* 119 D5
Atrak → = Atrek →, *Turkmenistan* 71 B8
Ätran, *Sweden* 11 G6
Ätran →, *Sweden* 11 H6
Atrauli, *India* 68 E8
Atrek →, *Turkmenistan* 71 B8
Atri, *Italy* 29 F10
Atsbi, *Ethiopia* 81 E4
Atsikí, *Greece* 39 B7
Atsoum, Mts., *Cameroon* 83 D7
Atsuta, *Japan* 54 C10
Attalla, *U.S.A.* 109 H2
Attapu, *Laos* 64 E6
Attáviros, *Greece* 36 C9
Attawapiskat, *Canada* 102 B3
Attawapiskat →, *Canada* 102 B3
Attawapiskat, L., *Canada* 102 B2
Attersee, *Austria* 26 D6
Attica, *U.S.A.* 108 E2
Attichy, *France* 19 C10
Attigny, *France* 19 C11
Attikamagen L., *Canada* 103 B6
Attikí □, *Greece* 38 D5
Attleboro, *U.S.A.* 111 E13
Attock, *Pakistan* 68 C5
Attopeu = Attapu, *Laos* 64 E6
Attur, *India* 66 P11
Atuel →, *Argentina* 126 D2
Åtvidaberg, *Sweden* 11 F10
Atwater, *U.S.A.* 116 H6
Atwood, *Canada* 110 C3
Atwood, *U.S.A.* 112 F4
Atyraū, *Kazakstan* 50 E6
Au Sable →, *U.S.A.* 108 C4
Au Sable Pt., *U.S.A.* 102 C2
Aubagne, *France* 21 E9
Aubarca, C. d', *Spain* 37 B7
Aube □, *France* 19 D11
Aube →, *France* 19 D10
Aubenas, *France* 21 D8
Aubenton, *France* 19 C11
Auberry, *U.S.A.* 116 H7
Aubigny-sur-Nère, *France* 19 E9
Aubin, *France* 20 D6
Aubrac, Mts. d', *France* 20 D7
Auburn, *Ala., U.S.A.* 109 J3
Auburn, *Calif., U.S.A.* 116 G5
Auburn, *Ind., U.S.A.* 108 E3
Auburn, *N.Y., U.S.A.* 111 D8
Auburn, *Nebr., U.S.A.* 112 E7
Auburn, *Wash., U.S.A.* 116 C4
Auburn Ra., *Australia* 95 D5
Auburndale, *U.S.A.* 109 L5
Aubusson, *France* 20 C6
Auce, *Latvia* 44 B9
Auch, *France* 20 E4
Auchi, *Nigeria* 83 D6
Auckland, *N.Z.* 91 G5
Auckland Is., *Pac. Oc.* 96 N8
Aude □, *France* 20 E6
Aude →, *France* 20 E7
Auden, *Canada* 102 B2
Auderville, *France* 18 C5
Audierne, *France* 18 D2
Audincourt, *France* 19 E13
Audo, *Ethiopia* 81 F5
Audubon, *U.S.A.* 112 E7
Aue, *Germany* 24 E8
Auerbach, *Germany* 24 E8
Augathella, *Australia* 95 D4
Aughnacloy, *U.K.* 15 B5
Augrabies Falls, *S. Africa* 88 D3
Augsburg, *Germany* 25 G6
Augusta, *Italy* 31 E8
Augusta, *Ark., U.S.A.* 113 H9
Augusta, *Ga., U.S.A.* 109 J5
Augusta, *Kans., U.S.A.* 113 G6
Augusta, *Maine, U.S.A.* 103 D6
Augusta, *Mont., U.S.A.* 114 C7
Augusta, *Wis., U.S.A.* 112 C9
Augustenborg, *Denmark* 11 K3
Augustów, *Poland* 44 E9
Augustus, Mt., *Australia* 92 D2
Augustus Downs, *Australia* 94 B2
Augustus I., *Australia* 92 C3
Aukan, *Eritrea* 81 D5
Aukum, *U.S.A.* 116 G6
Auld, L., *Australia* 92 D3
Aulla, *Italy* 28 D6
Aulnay, *France* 20 B3
Aulne →, *France* 18 D2
Aulnoye-Aymeries, *France* 19 B10
Ault, *France* 18 B8
Ault, *U.S.A.* 112 E2
Aulus-les-Bains, *France* 20 F5
Aumale, *France* 19 C8
Aumont-Aubrac, *France* 20 D7
Auna, *Nigeria* 83 C5
Auning, *Denmark* 11 H4
Aunis, *France* 20 B3
Auponhia, *Indonesia* 63 E7
Aups, *France* 21 E10
Aur, Pulau, *Malaysia* 65 L5
Auraiya, *India* 69 F8
Aurangabad, *Bihar, India* 69 G11
Aurangabad, *Maharashtra, India* 66 K9
Auray, *France* 18 E4
Aurich, *Germany* 24 B3
Aurillac, *France* 20 D6
Auronzo di Cadore, *Italy* 29 B9
Aurora, *Canada* 110 C5
Aurora, *S. Africa* 88 E2
Aurora, *Colo., U.S.A.* 112 F2
Aurora, *Ill., U.S.A.* 108 E1
Aurora, *Mo., U.S.A.* 113 G8
Aurora, *Nebr., U.S.A.* 112 E6
Aurora, *Ohio, U.S.A.* 110 E3
Aurukun Mission, *Australia* 94 A3
Aus, *Namibia* 88 D2
Auschwitz = Oświęcim, *Poland* 45 H6
Austerlitz = Slavkov u Brna, *Czech Rep.* 27 B9
Austin, *Minn., U.S.A.* 112 D8
Austin, *Nev., U.S.A.* 114 G5
Austin, *Pa., U.S.A.* 110 E6
Austin, *Tex., U.S.A.* 113 K6
Austin, L., *Australia* 93 E2
Austra, *Norway* 8 D14
Austral Downs, *Australia* 94 C2
Austral Is. = Tubuai Is., *Pac. Oc.* 97 K13
Austral Seamount Chain, *Pac. Oc.* 97 K13
Australia ■, *Oceania* 96 K5
Australian Alps, *Australia* 95 F4
Australian Capital Territory □, *Australia* 95 F4
Austria ■, *Europe* 26 E7
Austvågøy, *Norway* 8 B16
Auterive, *France* 20 E5
Authie →, *France* 19 B8
Authon-du-Perche, *France* 18 D7
Autlán, *Mexico* 118 D4
Autun, *France* 19 F11
Auvergne, *Australia* 92 C5
Auvergne, *France* 20 C7
Auvergne, Mts. d', *France* 20 C6
Auvézère →, *France* 20 C4
Auxerre, *France* 19 E10
Auxi-le-Château, *France* 19 B9
Auxonne, *France* 19 E12
Auzances, *France* 19 F9
Avallon, *France* 19 E10
Avalon, *U.S.A.* 117 M8
Avalon Pen., *Canada* 103 C9
Avaré, *Brazil* 127 A6
Ávas, *Greece* 41 F9
Avawatz Mts., *U.S.A.* 117 K10
Avdan Daği, *Turkey* 41 F13
Aveiro, *Brazil* 125 D7
Aveiro, *Portugal* 34 E2
Aveiro □, *Portugal* 34 E2
Āvej, *Iran* 71 C6
Avellaneda, *Argentina* 126 C4
Avellino, *Italy* 31 B7
Avenal, *U.S.A.* 116 K6
Aversa, *Italy* 31 B7
Avery, *U.S.A.* 114 C6
Aves, I. de, *W. Indies* 121 C7
Aves, Is. de, *Venezuela* 121 D6
Avesnes-sur-Helpe, *France* 19 B10
Avesta, *Sweden* 10 D10
Aveyron □, *France* 20 D6
Aveyron →, *France* 20 D5
Avezzano, *Italy* 29 F10
Avgó, *Greece* 39 F7
Aviá Terai, *Argentina* 126 B3
Aviano, *Italy* 29 B9
Aviemore, *U.K.* 14 D5
Avigliana, *Italy* 28 C4
Avigliano, *Italy* 31 B8
Avignon, *France* 21 E8
Ávila, *Spain* 34 E6
Ávila □, *Spain* 34 E6
Ávila, Sierra de, *Spain* 34 E5
Avila Beach, *U.S.A.* 117 K6
Avilés, *Spain* 34 B5
Avintes, *Portugal* 34 D2
Avionárion, *Greece* 38 C6
Avis, *Portugal* 35 F3
Avísio →, *Italy* 28 B8
Aviz = Avis, *Portugal* 35 F3
Avize, *France* 19 D11
Avlum, *Denmark* 11 H2
Avoca, *U.S.A.* 110 D7
Avoca →, *Australia* 95 F3
Avoca →, *Ireland* 15 D5
Avola, *Canada* 104 C5
Avola, *Italy* 31 F8
Avon, *N.Y., U.S.A.* 110 D7
Avon, *S. Dak., U.S.A.* 112 D5
Avon →, *Australia* 93 F2
Avon →, *Bristol, U.K.* 13 F5
Avon →, *Dorset, U.K.* 13 G6
Avon →, *Warks., U.K.* 13 E5
Avondale, *Zimbabwe* 87 F3
Avonlea, *Canada* 105 D8
Avonmore, *Canada* 111 A10
Avramov, *Bulgaria* 41 D10
Avranches, *France* 18 D5
Avre →, *France* 18 D8
Avrig, *Romania* 43 E9
Avrillé, *France* 18 E6
Avtovac, *Bos.-H.* 40 C2
Awag el Baqar, *Sudan* 81 E3
A'waj →, *Syria* 75 B5
Awaji-Shima, *Japan* 55 G7
'Awālī, *Bahrain* 71 E6
Awantipur, *India* 69 C6
Awasa, L., *Ethiopia* 81 F4
Awash, *Ethiopia* 81 F5
Awash →, *Ethiopia* 81 E5
Awaso, *Ghana* 82 D4
Awatere →, *N.Z.* 91 J5
Awbārī, *Libya* 79 C8
Awe, L., *U.K.* 14 E3
Aweil, *Sudan* 81 F2
Awgu, *Nigeria* 83 D6
Awjilah, *Libya* 79 C10
Ax-les-Thermes, *France* 20 F5
Axat, *France* 20 F6
Axe →, *U.K.* 13 F5
Axel Heiberg I., *Canada* 4 B3
Axim, *Ghana* 82 E4
Axintele, *Romania* 43 F11
Axiós →, *Greece* 40 F6
Axminster, *U.K.* 13 G4
Axvall, *Sweden* 11 F7
Ay, *France* 19 C11
Ayabaca, *Peru* 124 D3
Ayabe, *Japan* 55 G7
Ayacucho, *Argentina* 126 D4
Ayacucho, *Peru* 124 F4
Ayaguz, *Kazakstan* 50 E9
Ayamonte, *Spain* 35 H3
Ayan, *Russia* 51 D14
Ayancık, *Turkey* 72 B6
Ayas, *Turkey* 72 B5
Ayaviri, *Peru* 124 F4
Aybastı, *Turkey* 72 B7
Aydın, *Turkey* 72 D2
Aydin □, *Turkey* 39 D9
Aydin Dağları, *Turkey* 39 D10
Ayenngré, *Togo* 83 D5
Ayerbe, *Spain* 32 C4
Ayer's Cliff, *Canada* 111 A12
Ayers Rock, *Australia* 93 E5
Ayiá, *Greece* 38 B4
Ayia Aikateríni, Ákra, *Greece* 36 A3
Ayía Ánna, *Greece* 38 C5
Ayia Dhéka, *Greece* 36 D6
Ayia Gálini, *Greece* 36 D6
Ayía Marína, *Kásos, Greece* 39 F8
Ayía Marína, *Léros, Greece* 39 D8
Ayia Napa, *Cyprus* 36 E13
Ayía Paraskeví, *Greece* 39 B8
Ayia Phyla, *Cyprus* 36 E12
Ayía Rouméli, *Greece* 38 F5
Ayia Varvára, *Greece* 36 D7
Ayiássos, *Greece* 39 B8
Áyioi Theódhoroi, *Greece* 38 D5
Áyion Óros □, *Greece* 41 F8
Áyios Amvrósios, *Cyprus* 36 D12
Áyios Andréas, *Greece* 38 D4
Áyios Evstrátios, *Greece* 38 B6
Áyios Ioánnis, Ákra, *Greece* 36 D7
Áyios Isidhoros, *Greece* 36 C9
Áyios Kiríkos, *Greece* 39 D8
Áyios Matthaíos, *Greece* 36 B3
Áyios Mírono, *Greece* 39 F7
Áyios Nikólaos, *Greece* 36 D7
Áyios Pétros, *Greece* 38 C2
Áyios Seryios, *Cyprus* 36 D12
Áyios Theodhoros, *Cyprus* 36 D13
Áyios Yeóryios, *Greece* 38 D5
Aykathonisi, *Greece* 39 D8
Aykirikçi, *Turkey* 39 B12
Aylesbury, *U.K.* 13 F7
Aylmer, *Canada* 110 D4
Aylmer, L., *Canada* 100 B8
Ayn Zālah, *Iraq* 73 D10
Ayna, *Spain* 33 G2
Ayolas, *Paraguay* 126 B4
Ayom, *Sudan* 81 F2
Ayon, Ostrov, *Russia* 51 C17
Ayora, *Spain* 33 F3
Ayr, *Australia* 94 B4
Ayr, *U.K.* 14 F4
Ayr →, *U.K.* 14 F4
Ayrancı, *Turkey* 72 D5
Ayrancılar, *Turkey* 39 C9
Ayre, Pt. of, *U.K.* 12 C3
Aysha, *Ethiopia* 81 E5
Aytos, *Bulgaria* 41 D11
Aytoska Planina, *Bulgaria* 41 D11
Ayu, Kepulauan, *Indonesia* 63 D8
Ayutla, *Guatemala* 120 D1
Ayutla, *Mexico* 119 D5
Ayvacık, *Turkey* 72 C2
Ayvalık, *Turkey* 39 B8
Az Zabadānī, *Syria* 75 B5
Az Ẓāhirīyah, *West Bank* 75 D3
Az Ẓahrān, *Si. Arabia* 71 E6
Az Zarqā, *Jordan* 75 C5
Az Zībār, *Iraq* 70 B5
Az-Zilfī, *Si. Arabia* 70 E5
Az Zubayr, *Iraq* 70 D5
Azambuja, *Portugal* 35 F2
Azamgarh, *India* 69 F10
Azangaro, *Peru* 124 F4
Azaouak, Vallée de l', *Mali* 83 B5
Āzār Shahr, *Iran* 70 B5
Azarān, *Iran* 73 D12
Azärbayjan = Azerbaijan ■, *Asia* 49 K9
Āzarbāyjān-e Gharbī □, *Iran* 70 B5
Āzarbāyjān-e Sharqī □, *Iran* 70 B5
Azare, *Nigeria* 83 C7
Azay-le-Rideau, *France* 18 E7
A'zāz, *Syria* 70 B3
Azbine = Aïr, *Niger* 83 B6
Azerbaijan ■, *Asia* 49 K9
Azerbaijchan = Azerbaijan ■, *Asia* 49 K9
Azezo, *Ethiopia* 81 E4
Azimganj, *India* 69 G13
Aznalcóllar, *Spain* 35 H4
Azogues, *Ecuador* 124 D3
Azores, *Atl. Oc.* 76 C1
Azov, *Russia* 47 J10
Azov, Sea of, *Europe* 47 J9
Azovskoye More = Azov, Sea of, *Europe* 47 J9
Azpeitia, *Spain* 32 B2
Aztec, *U.S.A.* 115 H10
Azúa, *Dom. Rep.* 121 C5
Azuaga, *Spain* 35 G5
Azuara, *Spain* 32 D4
Azuer →, *Spain* 35 F7
Azuero, Pen. de, *Panama* 120 E3
Azuga, *Romania* 43 E10
Azul, *Argentina* 126 D4
Azusa, *U.S.A.* 117 L9
Azzano Décimo, *Italy* 29 C9

B

Ba Don, *Vietnam* 64 D6
Ba Dong, *Vietnam* 65 H6
Ba Ngoi = Cam Lam, *Vietnam* 65 G7
Ba Tri, *Vietnam* 65 G6
Ba Xian, *China* 56 E9
Baa, *Indonesia* 63 F6
Baamonde, *Spain* 34 B3
Baarle-Nassau, *Belgium* 17 C4
Bab el Mandeb, *Red Sea* 74 E3
Baba, *Bulgaria* 40 D7
Baba Burnu, *Turkey* 39 B8
Baba dag, *Azerbaijan* 49 K9
Bābā Kalū, *Iran* 71 D6
Babadag, *Romania* 43 F13
Babadağ, *Turkey* 39 D10
Babadayhan, *Turkmenistan* 50 F7
Babaeski, *Turkey* 41 E11
Babahoyo, *Ecuador* 124 D3
Babakin, *Australia* 93 F2
Babana, *Nigeria* 83 C5
Babar, *Indonesia* 63 F7
Babar, *Pakistan* 68 D3
Babarkach, *Pakistan* 68 E3
Babayevo, *Russia* 46 C8
Babb, *U.S.A.* 114 B7
Babenhausen, *Germany* 25 F4
Băbeni, *Romania* 43 F9
Babi Besar, Pulau, *Malaysia* 65 L4
Babia Gora, *Europe* 45 J6
Babian Jiang →, *China* 58 F3
Babile, *Ethiopia* 81 F5
Babimost, *Poland* 45 F2
Babinda, *Australia* 94 B4
Babine, *Canada* 104 B3
Babine →, *Canada* 104 B3
Babine L., *Canada* 104 C3
Babo, *Indonesia* 63 E8
Babócsa, *Hungary* 42 D2
Bābol, *Iran* 71 B7
Bābol Sar, *Iran* 71 B7
Baborów, *Poland* 45 H5
Babruysk, *Belarus* 47 F5
Babuna, *Macedonia* 40 E5
Babura, *Nigeria* 83 C6
Babusar Pass, *Pakistan* 69 B5
Babušnica, *Serbia, Yug.* 40 C6
Babuyan Chan., *Phil.* 61 B4
Babuyan Is., *Phil.* 61 B4
Babylon, *Iraq* 70 C5
Bač, *Serbia, Yug.* 42 E4
Bâc →, *Moldova* 43 D14
Bac Can, *Vietnam* 64 A5
Bac Giang, *Vietnam* 64 B6
Bac Ninh, *Vietnam* 64 B6
Bac Phan, *Vietnam* 64 B5
Bac Quang, *Vietnam* 64 A5
Bacabal, *Brazil* 125 D10
Bacalar, *Mexico* 119 D7
Bacan, Kepulauan, *Indonesia* 63 E7
Bacarra, *Phil.* 61 B4
Bacău, *Romania* 43 D11
Bacău □, *Romania* 43 D11
Baccarat, *France* 19 D13
Bacerac, *Mexico* 118 A3
Băceşti, *Romania* 43 D12
Bach Long Vi, Dao, *Vietnam* 64 B6
Bacharach, *Germany* 25 E3
Bachelina, *Russia* 50 D7
Bachuma, *Ethiopia* 81 F4
Bačina, *Serbia, Yug.* 40 C5
Back →, *Canada* 100 B9
Bačka Palanka, *Serbia, Yug.* 42 E4
Bačka Topola, *Serbia, Yug.* 42 E4
Bäckebo, *Sweden* 11 H10
Bäckefors, *Sweden* 11 F6
Bäckhammar, *Sweden* 10 E8
Bački Petrovac, *Serbia, Yug.* 42 E4
Backnang, *Germany* 25 G5
Backstairs Passage, *Australia* 95 F2
Baco, Mt., *Phil.* 61 E4
Bacolod, *Phil.* 61 F5
Bacqueville-en-Caux, *France* 18 C8
Bács-Kiskun □, *Hungary* 42 D4
Bácsalmás, *Hungary* 42 D4
Bacuag, *Phil.* 61 G6
Bacuk, *Malaysia* 65 J4
Bād, *Iran* 71 C7
Bad →, *U.S.A.* 112 C4
Bad Aussee, *Austria* 26 D6
Bad Axe, *U.S.A.* 110 C2
Bad Bergzabern, *Germany* 25 F3
Bad Berleburg, *Germany* 24 D4
Bad Bevensen, *Germany* 24 B6
Bad Bramstedt, *Germany* 24 B5
Bad Brückenau, *Germany* 25 E5
Bad Doberan, *Germany* 24 A7
Bad Driburg, *Germany* 24 D5
Bad Ems, *Germany* 25 E3
Bad Frankenhausen, *Germany* 24 D7
Bad Freienwalde, *Germany* 24 C10
Bad Goisern, *Austria* 26 D6
Bad Harzburg, *Germany* 24 D6
Bad Hersfeld, *Germany* 24 E5
Bad Hofgastein, *Austria* 26 D6
Bad Homburg, *Germany* 25 E4

Bad Honnef, *Germany* 24 E3
Bad Iburg, *Germany* 24 C4
Bad Ischl, *Austria* 26 D6
Bad Kissingen, *Germany* 25 E6
Bad Königshofen, *Germany* 25 E6
Bad Kreuznach, *Germany* 25 F3
Bad Krozingen, *Germany* 25 H3
Bad Laasphe, *Germany* 24 E4
Bad Lands, *U.S.A.* 112 D3
Bad Langensalza, *Germany* 24 D6
Bad Lauterberg, *Germany* 24 D6
Bad Leonfelden, *Austria* 26 C7
Bad Liebenwerda, *Germany* 24 D9
Bad Mergentheim, *Germany* 25 F5
Bad Münstereifel, *Germany* 24 E2
Bad Nauheim, *Germany* 25 E4
Bad Neuenahr-Ahrweiler, *Germany* 24 E3
Bad Neustadt, *Germany* 25 E6
Bad Oeynhausen, *Germany* 24 C4
Bad Oldesloe, *Germany* 24 B6
Bad Orb, *Germany* 25 E5
Bad Pyrmont, *Germany* 24 D5
Bad Reichenhall, *Germany* 25 H8
Bad Säckingen, *Germany* 25 H3
Bad Salzuflen, *Germany* 24 C4
Bad Salzungen, *Germany* 24 E6
Bad Schwartau, *Germany* 24 B6
Bad Segeberg, *Germany* 24 B6
Bad St. Leonhard, *Austria* 26 E7
Bad Tölz, *Germany* 25 H7
Bad Urach, *Germany* 25 G5
Bad Vöslau, *Austria* 27 D9
Bad Waldsee, *Germany* 25 H5
Bad Wildungen, *Germany* 24 D5
Bad Wimpfen, *Germany* 25 F5
Bad Windsheim, *Germany* 25 F6
Bad Zwischenahn, *Germany* 24 B4
Badagara, *India* 66 P9
Badagri, *Nigeria* 83 D5
Badajós, L., *Brazil* 124 D6
Badajoz, *Spain* 35 G4
Badajoz □, *Spain* 35 G4
Badalona, *Spain* 32 D7
Badalzai, *Afghan.* 68 E1
Badampahar, *India* 67 H15
Badanah, *Si. Arabia* 70 D4
Badarinath, *India* 69 D8
Badas, Kepulauan, *Indonesia* 62 D3
Baddo →, *Pakistan* 66 F4
Bade, *Indonesia* 63 F9
Baden, *Austria* 27 C9
Baden, *Switz.* 25 H4
Baden-Baden, *Germany* 25 G4
Baden-Württemberg □, *Germany* 25 G4
Badgastein, *Austria* 26 D6
Badger, *Canada* 103 C8
Badger, *U.S.A.* 116 J7
Bādghīsāt □, *Afghan.* 66 B3
Badgom, *India* 69 B6
Badia Polésine, *Italy* 29 C8
Badin, *Pakistan* 68 G3
Badogo, *Mali* 82 C3
Badong, *China* 59 B8
Badrah, *Iraq* 73 F11
Badulla, *Sri Lanka* 66 R12
Baena, *Spain* 35 H6
Baeza, *Spain* 35 H7
Bafang, *Cameroon* 83 D7
Bafatá, *Guinea-Biss.* 82 C2
Baffin B., *Canada* 4 B4
Baffin I., *Canada* 101 B12
Bafia, *Cameroon* 83 E7
Bafilo, *Togo* 83 D5
Bafing →, *Mali* 82 C2
Bafliyūn, *Syria* 70 B3
Bafoulabé, *Mali* 82 C2
Bafoussam, *Cameroon* 83 D7
Bāfq, *Iran* 71 D7
Bafra, *Turkey* 72 B6
Bafra Burnu, *Turkey* 72 B7
Bāft, *Iran* 71 D8
Bafut, *Cameroon* 83 D7
Bafwasende, *Dem. Rep. of the Congo* 86 B2
Bagamoyo, *Tanzania* 86 D4
Bagamoyo □, *Tanzania* 86 D4
Bagan Datoh, *Malaysia* 65 L3
Bagan Serai, *Malaysia* 65 K3
Baganga, *Phil.* 61 H7
Bagani, *Namibia* 88 B3
Bagansiapiapi, *Indonesia* 62 D2
Bagasra, *India* 68 J4
Bagawi, *Sudan* 81 E3
Bagdad, *U.S.A.* 117 L11
Bagdarin, *Russia* 51 D12
Bagé, *Brazil* 127 C5
Bagenalstown = Muine Bheag, *Ireland* 15 D5
Baggs, *U.S.A.* 114 F10
Bagh, *Pakistan* 69 C5
Baghdād, *Iraq* 70 C5
Bagheria, *Italy* 30 D6
Baghlān, *Afghan.* 66 A6
Bagley, *U.S.A.* 112 B7
Bagnara Cálabra, *Italy* 31 D8
Bagnasco, *Italy* 28 D5
Bagnères-de-Bigorre, *France* 20 E4
Bagnères-de-Luchon, *France* 20 F4
Bagni di Lucca, *Italy* 28 D7
Bagno di Romagna, *Italy* 29 E8
Bagnoles-de-l'Orne, *France* 18 D6
Bagnols-sur-Cèze, *France* 21 D8
Bagnorégio, *Italy* 29 F9
Bagotville, *Canada* 103 C5
Bagrationovsk, *Russia* 9 J19
Bagrdan, *Serbia, Yug.* 40 B5
Baguio, *Phil.* 61 C4
Bağyurdu, *Turkey* 39 C9
Bahabón de Esgueva, *Spain* 34 D7
Bahadurgarh, *India* 68 E7
Bahama, Canal Viejo de, *W. Indies* 120 B4
Bahamas ■, *N. Amer.* 121 B5
Bahār, *Iran* 73 E13
Baharampur, *India* 69 G13
Baharîya, El Wâhât al, *Egypt* 80 J6
Bahawalnagar, *Pakistan* 68 E5
Bahawalpur, *Pakistan* 68 E4
Bahçe, *Turkey* 72 D7
Bahçecik, *Turkey* 41 F13
Baheri, *India* 69 E8
Bahi, *Tanzania* 86 D4
Bahi Swamp, *Tanzania* 86 D4
Bahía = Salvador, *Brazil* 125 F11
Bahía □, *Brazil* 125 F10
Bahía, Is. de la, *Honduras* 120 C2
Bahía Blanca, *Argentina* 126 D3
Bahía de Caráquez, *Ecuador* 124 D2
Bahía Honda, *Cuba* 120 B3
Bahía Laura, *Argentina* 128 F3
Bahía Negra, *Paraguay* 124 H7
Bahir Dar, *Ethiopia* 81 E4
Bahmanzād, *Iran* 71 D6
Bahr el Ahmar □, *Sudan* 80 D4
Bahr el Ghazâl □, *Sudan* 81 F2
Bahr Yûsef →, *Egypt* 80 J7
Bahra el Burullus, *Egypt* 80 H7
Bahraich, *India* 69 F9
Bahrain ■, *Asia* 71 E6
Bahror, *India* 68 F7
Bāhū Kalāt, *Iran* 71 E9
Bai, *Mali* 82 C4
Bai Bung, Mui = Ca Mau, Mui, *Vietnam* 65 H5
Bai Duc, *Vietnam* 64 C5
Bai Thuong, *Vietnam* 64 C5
Baia de Aramă, *Romania* 42 E7
Baia Mare, *Romania* 43 C8
Baia-Sprie, *Romania* 43 C8
Baião, *Brazil* 125 D9
Baïbokoum, *Chad* 79 G9
Baicheng, *China* 57 B12
Băicoi, *Romania* 43 E10
Baidoa, *Somali Rep.* 74 G3
Baie Comeau, *Canada* 103 C6
Baie-St-Paul, *Canada* 103 C5
Baie Trinité, *Canada* 103 C6
Baie Verte, *Canada* 103 C8
Baignes-Ste-Radegonde, *France* 20 C3
Baigneux-les-Juifs, *France* 19 E11
Baihe, *China* 56 H6
Ba'ījī, *Iraq* 70 C4
Baikal, L. = Baykal, Oz., *Russia* 51 D11
Baile Atha Cliath = Dublin, *Ireland* 15 C5
Băile Govora, *Romania* 43 E9
Băile Herculane, *Romania* 42 F7
Băile Olăneşti, *Romania* 43 E9
Băile Tuşnad, *Romania* 43 D10
Bailei, *Ethiopia* 81 F5
Bailén, *Spain* 35 G7
Băileşti, *Romania* 43 F8
Baima, *China* 58 A3
Bain-de-Bretagne, *France* 18 E5
Bainbridge, *Ga., U.S.A.* 109 K3
Bainbridge, *N.Y., U.S.A.* 111 D9
Baing, *Indonesia* 63 F6
Bainiu, *China* 56 H7
Bainville, *U.S.A.* 112 A2
Baiona, *Spain* 34 C2
Bā'ir, *Jordan* 75 E5
Baird, *U.S.A.* 113 J5
Bairin Youqi, *China* 57 C10
Bairin Zuoqi, *China* 57 C10
Bairnsdale, *Australia* 95 F4
Bais, *Phil.* 61 G5
Baisha, *China* 56 G7
Baissa, *Nigeria* 83 D7
Baitadi, *Nepal* 69 E9
Baiyin, *China* 56 F3
Baiyü, *China* 58 B2
Baiyu Shan, *China* 56 F4
Baiyuda, *Sudan* 80 D3
Baj Baj, *India* 69 H13
Baja, *Hungary* 42 D3
Baja, Pta., *Mexico* 118 B1
Baja California, *Mexico* 118 A1
Baja California □, *Mexico* 118 B2
Baja California Sur □, *Mexico* 118 B2
Bajamar, *Canary Is.* 37 F3
Bajana, *India* 68 H4
Bājgīrān, *Iran* 71 B8
Bajimba, Mt., *Australia* 95 D5
Bajina Bašta, *Serbia, Yug.* 40 C3
Bajmok, *Serbia, Yug.* 42 E4
Bajo Nuevo, *Caribbean* 120 C4
Bajoga, *Nigeria* 83 C7
Bajool, *Australia* 94 C5
Bak, *Hungary* 42 D1
Bakar, *Croatia* 29 C11
Bakel, *Senegal* 82 C2
Baker, *Calif., U.S.A.* 117 K10
Baker, *Mont., U.S.A.* 112 B2
Baker, *Oreg., U.S.A.* 114 D5
Baker, L., *Canada* 100 B10
Baker I., *Pac. Oc.* 96 G10
Baker L., *Australia* 93 E4
Baker Lake, *Canada* 100 B10
Baker Mt., *U.S.A.* 114 B3
Bakers Creek, *Australia* 94 C4
Baker's Dozen Is., *Canada* 102 A4
Bakersfield, *Calif., U.S.A.* 117 K8
Bakersfield, *Vt., U.S.A.* 111 B12
Bakhchysaray, *Ukraine* 47 K7
Bakhmach, *Ukraine* 47 G7
Bākhtarān, *Iran* 70 C5
Bākhtarān □, *Iran* 70 C5
Bakı, *Azerbaijan* 49 K9
Bakır →, *Turkey* 39 C9
Bakırdağı, *Turkey* 72 C6
Bakkafjörður, *Iceland* 8 C6
Baklan, *Turkey* 39 C11
Bakony, *Hungary* 42 C2
Bakony Forest = Bakony, *Hungary* 42 C2
Bakori, *Nigeria* 83 C6
Bakouma, *C.A.R.* 84 C4
Baksan, *Russia* 49 J6
Baku = Bakı, *Azerbaijan* 49 K9
Bakutis Coast, *Antarctica* 5 D15
Baky = Bakı, *Azerbaijan* 49 K9
Bala, *Canada* 110 A5
Bâlâ, *Turkey* 72 C5
Bala, *U.K.* 12 E4
Bala, L., *U.K.* 12 E4
Balabac I., *Phil.* 61 H2
Balabac Str., *E. Indies* 62 C5
Balabagh, *Afghan.* 68 B4
Ba'labakk, *Lebanon* 75 B5
Balabalangan, Kepulauan, *Indonesia* 62 E5
Bălăciţa, *Romania* 43 F8
Balad, *Iraq* 70 C5
Balad Rūz, *Iraq* 70 C5
Bālādeh, *Fārs, Iran* 71 D6
Bālādeh, *Māzandaran, Iran* 71 B6
Balaghat, *India* 66 J12
Balaghat Ra., *India* 66 K10
Balaguer, *Spain* 32 D5
Balakhna, *Russia* 48 B6
Balaklava, *Australia* 95 E2
Balaklava, *Ukraine* 47 K7
Balakliya, *Ukraine* 47 H9
Balakovo, *Russia* 48 D8
Bălan, *Romania* 43 D10
Balancán, *Mexico* 119 D6
Balashov, *Russia* 48 E6
Balasinor, *India* 68 H5
Balasore = Baleshwar, *India* 67 J15
Balassagyarmat, *Hungary* 42 B4
Balât, *Egypt* 80 B2
Balaton, *Hungary* 42 D2
Balatonboglár, *Hungary* 42 D2
Balatonfüred, *Hungary* 42 D2
Balatonszentgyörgy, *Hungary* 42 D2
Balayan, *Phil.* 61 E4
Balazote, *Spain* 33 G2
Balbieriškis, *Lithuania* 44 D10
Balbigny, *France* 21 C8
Balbina, Reprêsa de, *Brazil* 124 D7
Balboa, *Panama* 120 E4
Balbriggan, *Ireland* 15 C5
Balcarce, *Argentina* 126 D4
Balcarres, *Canada* 105 C8
Bălceşti, *Romania* 43 F8
Balchik, *Bulgaria* 41 C12
Balclutha, *N.Z.* 91 M2
Balçova, *Turkey* 39 C9
Bald Hd., *Australia* 93 G2
Bald I., *Australia* 93 F2
Bald Knob, *U.S.A.* 113 H9
Baldock L., *Canada* 105 B9
Baldwin, *Fla., U.S.A.* 109 K4
Baldwin, *Mich., U.S.A.* 108 D3
Baldwinsville, *U.S.A.* 111 C8
Baldy Peak, *U.S.A.* 115 K9
Bale, *Croatia* 29 C10
Bale □, *Ethiopia* 81 F5
Baleares, Is., *Spain* 37 B10
Balearic Is. = Baleares, Is., *Spain* 37 B10
Baleine = Whale →, *Canada* 103 A6
Băleni, *Romania* 43 E12
Baler, *Phil.* 61 D4
Baler Bay, *Phil.* 61 D4
Baleshare, *U.K.* 14 D1
Baleshwar, *India* 67 J15
Balezino, *Russia* 48 B11
Balfate, *Honduras* 120 C2
Balfe's Creek, *Australia* 94 C4
Bali, *Cameroon* 83 D7
Balí, *Greece* 36 D6
Bali □, *Indonesia* 62 F5
Bali, Selat, *Indonesia* 63 H16
Baligród, *Poland* 45 J9
Balikeşir, *Turkey* 39 B9
Balıkeşir □, *Turkey* 39 B9
Balıklıçeşme, *Turkey* 41 F11
Balikpapan, *Indonesia* 62 E5
Balimbing, *Phil.* 63 C5
Baling, *Malaysia* 65 K3
Balingen, *Germany* 25 G4
Balinţ, *Romania* 42 E6
Balintang Channel, *Phil.* 61 B4
Balipara, *India* 67 F18
Balkan Mts. = Stara Planina, *Bulgaria* 40 C7
Balkhash = Balqash, *Kazakstan* 50 E8
Balkhash, Ozero = Balqash Köl, *Kazakstan* 50 E8
Balla, *Bangla.* 67 G17
Ballachulish, *U.K.* 14 E3
Balladonia, *Australia* 93 F3
Ballaghaderreen, *Ireland* 15 C3
Ballarat, *Australia* 95 F3
Ballard, L., *Australia* 93 E3
Ballater, *U.K.* 14 D5
Ballenas, Canal de, *Mexico* 118 B2
Balleny Is., *Antarctica* 5 C11
Balleroy, *France* 18 C6
Ballerup, *Denmark* 11 J6
Ballesteros, *Phil.* 61 B4
Ballı, *Turkey* 41 F11
Ballia, *India* 69 G11
Ballidu, *Australia* 93 F2
Ballina, *Australia* 95 D5
Ballina, *Ireland* 15 B2
Ballinasloe, *Ireland* 15 C3
Ballinger, *U.S.A.* 113 K5
Ballinrobe, *Ireland* 15 C2
Ballinskelligs B., *Ireland* 15 E1
Ballon, *France* 18 D7
Ballsh, *Albania* 40 F3
Ballycastle, *U.K.* 15 A5
Ballyclare, *U.K.* 15 B5
Ballyhaunis, *Ireland* 15 C3
Ballymena, *U.K.* 15 B5
Ballymoney, *U.K.* 15 A5
Ballymote, *Ireland* 15 B3
Ballynahinch, *U.K.* 15 B6
Ballyquintin Pt., *U.K.* 15 B6
Ballyshannon, *Ireland* 15 B3
Balmaceda, *Chile* 128 F2
Balmaseda, *Spain* 32 B1
Balmazújváros, *Hungary* 42 C6
Balmoral, *Australia* 95 F3
Balmorhea, *U.S.A.* 113 K3
Balonne →, *Australia* 95 D4
Balqash, *Kazakstan* 50 E8
Balqash Köl, *Kazakstan* 50 E8
Balrampur, *India* 69 F10
Balranald, *Australia* 95 E3
Balş, *Romania* 43 F9
Balsas, *Mexico* 119 D5
Balsas →, *Brazil* 125 E9
Balsas →, *Mexico* 118 D4
Bålsta, *Sweden* 10 E11
Balston Spa, *U.S.A.* 111 D11
Balta, *Romania* 42 F7
Balta, *Ukraine* 47 H5
Balta, *U.S.A.* 112 A4
Baltanás, *Spain* 34 D6
Bălţi, *Moldova* 43 C12
Baltic Sea, *Europe* 9 H18
Baltîm, *Egypt* 80 H7
Baltimore, *Ireland* 15 E2
Baltimore, *U.S.A.* 108 F7
Baltit, *Pakistan* 69 A6
Baltiysk, *Russia* 9 J18
Baltrum, *Germany* 24 B3
Baluchistan □, *Pakistan* 66 F4
Balurghat, *India* 69 G13
Balvi, *Latvia* 9 H22
Balya, *Turkey* 39 B9
Bam, *Iran* 71 D8
Bama, *China* 58 E6
Bama, *Nigeria* 83 C7
Bamako, *Mali* 82 C3
Bamba, *Mali* 83 B4
Bambari, *C.A.R.* 84 C4
Bambaroo, *Australia* 94 B4
Bamberg, *Germany* 25 F6
Bamberg, *U.S.A.* 109 J5
Bambesi, *Ethiopia* 81 F3
Bambey, *Senegal* 82 C1
Bambili, *Dem. Rep. of the Congo* 86 B2
Bamenda, *Cameroon* 83 D7
Bamfield, *Canada* 104 D3
Bāmīān □, *Afghan.* 66 B5
Bamiancheng, *China* 57 C13
Bamkin, *Cameroon* 83 D7
Bampūr, *Iran* 71 E9
Ban Ban, *Laos* 64 C4
Ban Bang Hin, *Thailand* 65 H2
Ban Chiang Klang, *Thailand* 64 C3
Ban Chik, *Laos* 64 D4
Ban Choho, *Thailand* 64 E4
Ban Dan Lan Hoi, *Thailand* 64 D2
Ban Don = Surat Thani, *Thailand* 65 H2
Ban Don, *Vietnam* 64 F6
Ban Don, Ao →, *Thailand* 65 H2
Ban Dong, *Thailand* 64 C3
Ban Hong, *Thailand* 64 C2
Ban Kaeng, *Thailand* 64 D3
Ban Kantang, *Thailand* 65 J2
Ban Keun, *Laos* 64 C4
Ban Khai, *Thailand* 64 F3
Ban Kheun, *Laos* 64 B3
Ban Khlong Kua, *Thailand* 65 J3
Ban Khuan Mao, *Thailand* 65 J2
Ban Ko Yai Chim, *Thailand* 65 G2
Ban Kok, *Thailand* 64 D4
Ban Laem, *Thailand* 64 F2
Ban Lao Ngam, *Laos* 64 E6
Ban Le Kathe, *Thailand* 64 E2
Ban Mae Chedi, *Thailand* 64 C2
Ban Mae Laeng, *Thailand* 64 B2
Ban Mae Sariang, *Thailand* 64 C1
Ban Mê Thuôt = Buon Ma Thuot, *Vietnam* 64 F7
Ban Mi, *Thailand* 64 E3
Ban Muong Mo, *Laos* 64 C4
Ban Na Mo, *Laos* 64 D5
Ban Na San, *Thailand* 65 H2
Ban Na Tong, *Laos* 64 B3
Ban Nam Bac, *Laos* 64 B4
Ban Nam Ma, *Laos* 64 A3
Ban Ngang, *Laos* 64 E6
Ban Nong Bok, *Laos* 64 D5
Ban Nong Boua, *Laos* 64 E6
Ban Nong Pling, *Thailand* 64 E3
Ban Pak Chan, *Thailand* 65 G2
Ban Phai, *Thailand* 64 D4
Ban Pong, *Thailand* 64 F2
Ban Ron Phibun, *Thailand* 65 H2
Ban Sanam Chai, *Thailand* 65 J3
Ban Sangkha, *Thailand* 64 E4
Ban Tak, *Thailand* 64 D2
Ban Tako, *Thailand* 64 E4
Ban Tha Dua, *Thailand* 64 D2
Ban Tha Li, *Thailand* 64 D3
Ban Tha Nun, *Thailand* 65 H2
Ban Thahine, *Laos* 64 E5
Ban Xien Kok, *Laos* 64 B3
Ban Yen Nhan, *Vietnam* 64 B6
Banaba, *Kiribati* 96 H8
Banalia, *Dem. Rep. of the Congo* 86 B2
Banam, *Cambodia* 65 G5
Banamba, *Mali* 82 C3
Banana, *Australia* 94 C5
Bananal, I. do, *Brazil* 125 F8
Banaras = Varanasi, *India* 69 G10
Banas →, *Gujarat, India* 68 H4
Banas →, *Mad. P., India* 69 G9
Bânâs, Ras, *Egypt* 80 C4
Banaz, *Turkey* 39 C11
Banaz →, *Turkey* 39 C11
Banbān, *Si. Arabia* 70 E5
Banbridge, *U.K.* 15 B5
Banbury, *U.K.* 13 E6
Banchory, *U.K.* 14 D6
Bancroft, *Canada* 102 C4
Band, *Romania* 43 D9
Band Bonī, *Iran* 71 E8
Band Qīr, *Iran* 71 D6
Banda, *India* 69 G9
Banda, Kepulauan, *Indonesia* 63 E7
Banda Aceh, *Indonesia* 62 C1
Banda Banda, Mt., *Australia* 95 E5
Banda Elat, *Indonesia* 63 F8
Banda Is. = Banda, Kepulauan, *Indonesia* 63 E7
Banda Sea, *Indonesia* 63 F8
Bandai-San, *Japan* 54 F10
Bandama →, *Ivory C.* 82 D3
Bandān, *Iran* 71 D9
Bandanaira, *Indonesia* 63 E7
Bandanwara, *India* 68 F6
Bandar = Machilipatnam, *India* 67 L12
Bandār 'Abbās, *Iran* 71 E8
Bandar-e Anzalī, *Iran* 71 B6
Bandar-e Bushehr = Būshehr, *Iran* 71 D6
Bandar-e Chārak, *Iran* 71 E7
Bandar-e Deylam, *Iran* 71 D6
Bandar-e Khomeynı, *Iran* 71 D6
Bandar-e Lengeh, *Iran* 71 E7
Bandar-e Maqām, *Iran* 71 E7
Bandar-e Ma'shur, *Iran* 71 D6
Bandar-e Nakhīlū, *Iran* 71 E7
Bandar-e Rīg, *Iran* 71 D6
Bandar-e Torkeman, *Iran* 71 B7
Bandar Maharani = Muar, *Malaysia* 65 L4
Bandar Penggaram = Batu Pahat, *Malaysia* 65 M4
Bandar Seri Begawan, *Brunei* 62 D5
Bandar Sri Aman, *Malaysia* 62 D4
Bandawe, *Malawi* 87 E3
Bande, *Spain* 34 C3
Bandeira, Pico da, *Brazil* 127 A7
Bandera, *Argentina* 126 B3
Bandera, *U.S.A.* 113 L5
Banderas, B. de, *Mexico* 118 C3
Bandiagara, *Mali* 82 C4
Bandırma, *Turkey* 41 F11
Bandol, *France* 21 E9
Bandon, *Ireland* 15 E3
Bandon →, *Ireland* 15 E3
Bandula, *Mozam.* 87 F3
Bandundu, *Dem. Rep. of the Congo* 84 E3
Bandung, *Indonesia* 63 G12
Bandya, *Australia* 93 E3
Băneasa, *Romania* 43 E12
Bāneh, *Iran* 70 C5
Bañeres, *Spain* 33 G4
Banes, *Cuba* 121 B4
Banff, *Canada* 104 C5
Banff, *U.K.* 14 D6
Banff Nat. Park, *Canada* 104 C5
Banfora, *Burkina Faso* 82 C4
Bang Fai →, *Laos* 64 D5
Bang Hieng →, *Laos* 64 D5
Bang Krathum, *Thailand* 64 D3
Bang Lamung, *Thailand* 64 F3
Bang Mun Nak, *Thailand* 64 D3
Bang Pa In, *Thailand* 64 E3

Bang Rakam, *Thailand* 64 D3
Bang Saphan, *Thailand* 65 G2
Bangala Dam, *Zimbabwe* 87 G3
Bangalore, *India* 66 N10
Bangangté, *Cameroon* 83 D7
Bangaon, *India* 69 H13
Bangassou, *C.A.R.* 84 D4
Banggai, Kepulauan, *Indonesia* 63 E6
Banggai Arch. = Banggai, Kepulauan, *Indonesia* 63 E6
Banggi, *Malaysia* 62 C5
Banghāzī, *Libya* 79 B10
Bangjang, *Sudan* 81 E3
Bangka, *Sulawesi, Indonesia* 63 D7
Bangka, *Sumatera, Indonesia* 62 E3
Bangka, Selat, *Indonesia* 62 E3
Bangkalan, *Indonesia* 63 G15
Bangkinang, *Indonesia* 62 D2
Bangko, *Indonesia* 62 E2
Bangkok, *Thailand* 64 F3
Bangladesh ■, *Asia* 67 H17
Bangolo, *Ivory C.* 82 D3
Bangong Co, *India* 69 B8
Bangor, *Down, U.K.* 15 B6
Bangor, *Gwynedd, U.K.* 12 D3
Bangor, *Maine, U.S.A.* 103 D6
Bangor, *Pa., U.S.A.* 111 F9
Bangued, *Phil.* 61 C4
Bangui, *C.A.R.* 84 D3
Bangui, *Phil.* 61 B4
Banguru, *Dem. Rep. of the Congo* 86 B2
Bangweulu, L., *Zambia* 87 E3
Bangweulu Swamp, *Zambia* 87 E3
Bani, *Dom. Rep.* 121 C5
Bani →, *Mali* 82 C4
Bani Bangou, *Niger* 83 B5
Banī Sa'd, *Iraq* 70 C5
Bania, *Ivory C.* 82 D4
Banihal Pass, *India* 69 C6
Bāniyās, *Syria* 70 C3
Banja Luka, *Bos.-H.* 42 F2
Banjarmasin, *Indonesia* 62 E4
Banjul, *Gambia* 82 C1
Banka Banka, *Australia* 94 B1
Bankeryd, *Sweden* 11 G8
Banket, *Zimbabwe* 87 F3
Bankilaré, *Niger* 83 C5
Bankipore, *India* 69 G11
Banks I., *B.C., Canada* 104 C3
Banks I., *N.W.T., Canada* 4 B1
Banks Pen., *N.Z.* 91 K4
Banks Str., *Australia* 94 G4
Bankura, *India* 69 H12
Bankya, *Bulgaria* 40 D7
Bann →, *Arm., U.K.* 15 B5
Bann →, *L'derry., U.K.* 15 A5
Banna, *Phil.* 61 C4
Bannalec, *France* 18 E3
Bannang Sata, *Thailand* 65 J3
Banning, *U.S.A.* 117 M10
Banningville = Bandundu, *Dem. Rep. of the Congo* 84 E3
Bannockburn, *Canada* 110 B7
Bannockburn, *U.K.* 14 E5
Bannockburn, *Zimbabwe* 87 G2
Bannu, *Pakistan* 66 C7
Bañolas = Banyoles, *Spain* 32 C7
Banon, *France* 21 D9
Baños de la Encina, *Spain* 35 G7
Baños de Molgas, *Spain* 34 C3
Bánovce nad Bebravou, *Slovak Rep.* 27 C11
Banovići, *Bos.-H.* 42 F3
Banská Bystrica, *Slovak Rep.* 27 C12
Banská Štiavnica, *Slovak Rep.* 27 C11
Bansko, *Bulgaria* 40 E7
Banskobystrický □, *Slovak Rep.* 27 C12
Banswara, *India* 68 H6
Bantayan, *Phil.* 61 F5
Bantry, *Ireland* 15 E2
Bantry B., *Ireland* 15 E2
Bantul, *Indonesia* 63 G14
Bantva, *India* 68 J4
Banu, *Afghan.* 66 B6
Banya, *Bulgaria* 41 D8
Banyak, Kepulauan, *Indonesia* 62 D1
Banyalbufar, *Spain* 37 B9
Banyo, *Cameroon* 83 D7
Banyoles, *Spain* 32 C7
Banyuls-sur-Mer, *France* 20 F7
Banyumas, *Indonesia* 63 G13
Banyuwangi, *Indonesia* 63 H16
Banzare Coast, *Antarctica* 5 C9
Banzyville = Mobayi, *Dem. Rep. of the Congo* 84 D4
Bao Ha, *Vietnam* 64 A5
Bao Lac, *Vietnam* 64 A5
Bao Loc, *Vietnam* 65 G6
Bao'an = Shenzhen, *China* 59 F10
Baocheng, *China* 56 H4
Baode, *China* 56 E6
Baodi, *China* 57 E9
Baoding, *China* 56 E8
Baoji, *China* 56 G4
Baojing, *China* 58 C7
Baokang, *China* 59 B8
Baoshan, *Shanghai, China* 59 B13
Baoshan, *Yunnan, China* 58 E2
Baotou, *China* 56 D6
Baoying, *China* 57 H10
Bap, *India* 68 F5
Bapatla, *India* 67 M12
Bapaume, *France* 19 B9
Bāqerābād, *Iran* 71 C6
Ba'qūbah, *Iraq* 70 C5
Baquedano, *Chile* 126 A2
Bar, *Montenegro, Yug.* 40 D3
Bar, *Ukraine* 47 H4
Bar Bigha, *India* 69 G11
Bar Harbor, *U.S.A.* 103 D6
Bar-le-Duc, *France* 19 D12
Bar-sur-Aube, *France* 19 D11
Bar-sur-Seine, *France* 19 D11
Băra, *Romania* 43 C12
Barabai, *Indonesia* 62 E5
Baraboo, *U.S.A.* 112 D10
Baracoa, *Cuba* 121 B5
Baradā →, *Syria* 75 B5
Baradero, *Argentina* 126 C4
Baraga, *U.S.A.* 112 B10
Bărăganul, *Romania* 43 F12
Barahona, *Dom. Rep.* 121 C5
Barahona, *Spain* 32 D2
Barail Range, *India* 67 G18
Baraka →, *Sudan* 80 D4
Barakaldo, *Spain* 32 B2
Barakhola, *India* 67 G18
Barakot, *India* 69 J11
Barakpur, *India* 69 H13
Barakula, *Australia* 95 D5
Baralaba, *Australia* 94 C4
Baralla, *Spain* 34 C3
Baralzon L., *Canada* 105 B9
Barameiya, *Sudan* 80 D4
Baramula, *India* 69 B6
Baran, *India* 68 G7
Barañain, *Spain* 32 C3
Baranavichy, *Belarus* 47 F4
Baranof I., *U.S.A.* 104 B1
Baranów Sandomierski, *Poland* 45 H8
Baranya □, *Hungary* 42 E3
Baraolt, *Romania* 43 D10
Barapasi, *Indonesia* 63 E9
Barasat, *India* 69 H13
Barat Daya, Kepulauan, *Indonesia* 63 F7
Barataria B., *U.S.A.* 113 L10
Baraut, *India* 68 E7
Barbacena, *Brazil* 127 A7
Barbados ■, *W. Indies* 121 D8
Barban, *Croatia* 29 C11
Barbària, C. de, *Spain* 37 C7
Barbaros, *Turkey* 41 F11
Barbastro, *Spain* 32 C5
Barbate = Barbate de Franco, *Spain* 35 J5
Barbate de Franco, *Spain* 35 J5
Barberino di Mugello, *Italy* 29 E8
Barberton, *S. Africa* 89 D5
Barberton, *U.S.A.* 110 E3
Barbezieux-St-Hilaire, *France* 20 C3
Barbosa, *Colombia* 124 B4
Barbourville, *U.S.A.* 109 G4
Barbuda, *W. Indies* 121 C7
Bârca, *Romania* 43 G8
Barcaldine, *Australia* 94 C4
Barcarrota, *Spain* 35 G4
Barcellona Pozzo di Gotto, *Italy* 31 D8
Barcelona, *Spain* 32 D7
Barcelona, *Venezuela* 124 A6
Barcelona □, *Spain* 32 D7
Barcelonette, *France* 21 D10
Barcelos, *Brazil* 124 D6
Barcin, *Poland* 45 F4
Barcoo →, *Australia* 94 D3
Barcs, *Hungary* 42 E2
Barczewo, *Poland* 44 E7
Bärdä, *Azerbaijan* 49 K8
Bardaï, *Chad* 79 D9
Bardas Blancas, *Argentina* 126 D2
Barddhaman, *India* 69 H12
Bardejov, *Slovak Rep.* 27 B14
Bardera, *Somali Rep.* 74 G3
Bardi, *Italy* 28 D6
Bardīyah, *Libya* 79 B10
Bardolino, *Italy* 28 C7
Bardonécchia, *Italy* 28 C3
Bardsey I., *U.K.* 12 E3
Bardstown, *U.S.A.* 108 G3
Bareilly, *India* 69 E8
Barentin, *France* 18 C7
Barenton, *France* 18 D6
Barents Sea, *Arctic* 4 B9
Barentu, *Eritrea* 81 D4
Barfleur, *France* 18 C5
Barfleur, Pte. de, *France* 18 C5
Barga, *China* 60 C3
Barga, *Italy* 28 D7
Bargara, *Australia* 94 C5
Bargas, *Spain* 34 F6
Bârgăului Bistriţa, *Romania* 43 C9
Barge, *Italy* 28 D4
Bargnop, *Sudan* 81 F2
Bargteheide, *Germany* 24 B6
Barguzin, *Russia* 51 D11
Barh, *India* 69 G11
Barhaj, *India* 69 F10
Barhi, *India* 69 G11
Bari, *India* 68 F7
Bari, *Italy* 31 A9
Bari Doab, *Pakistan* 68 D5
Bari Sardo, *Italy* 30 C2
Bariadi □, *Tanzania* 86 C3
Barīm, *Yemen* 76 E8
Barinas, *Venezuela* 124 B4
Baring, C., *Canada* 100 B8
Baringo, *Kenya* 86 B4
Baringo □, *Kenya* 86 B4
Baringo, L., *Kenya* 86 B4
Bârîs, *Egypt* 80 C3
Barisal, *Bangla.* 67 H17
Barisan, Bukit, *Indonesia* 62 E2
Barito →, *Indonesia* 62 E4
Barjac, *France* 21 D8
Barjols, *France* 21 E10
Bark L., *Canada* 110 A7
Barka = Baraka →, *Sudan* 80 D4
Barkam, *China* 58 B4
Barker, *U.S.A.* 110 C6
Barkley Sound, *Canada* 104 D3
Barkly Downs, *Australia* 94 C2
Barkly East, *S. Africa* 88 E4
Barkly Tableland, *Australia* 94 B2
Barkly West, *S. Africa* 88 D3
Barkol, Wadi →, *Sudan* 80 D3
Barksdale, *U.S.A.* 113 L4
Barla Dağı, *Turkey* 39 C12
Bârlad, *Romania* 43 D12
Bârlad →, *Romania* 43 E12
Barlee, L., *Australia* 93 E2
Barlee, Mt., *Australia* 93 D4
Barletta, *Italy* 31 A9
Barlinek, *Poland* 45 F2
Barlovento, *Canary Is.* 37 F2
Barlow L., *Canada* 105 A8
Barmedman, *Australia* 95 E4
Barmer, *India* 68 G4
Barmera, *Australia* 95 E3
Barmouth, *U.K.* 12 E3
Barmstedt, *Germany* 24 B5
Barnagar, *India* 68 H6
Barnard Castle, *U.K.* 12 C6
Barnato, *Australia* 95 E4
Barnaul, *Russia* 50 D9
Barnesville, *U.S.A.* 109 J3
Barnet, *U.K.* 13 F7
Barneveld, *Neths.* 17 B5
Barneveld, *U.S.A.* 111 C9
Barneville-Cartevert, *France* 18 C5
Barngo, *Australia* 94 D4
Barnhart, *U.S.A.* 113 K4
Barnsley, *U.K.* 12 D6
Barnstaple, *U.K.* 13 F3
Barnstaple Bay = Bideford Bay, *U.K.* 13 F3
Barnsville, *U.S.A.* 112 B6
Baro, *Nigeria* 83 D6
Baro →, *Ethiopia* 81 F3
Baroda = Vadodara, *India* 68 H5
Baroda, *India* 68 G7
Baroe, *S. Africa* 88 E3
Baron Ra., *Australia* 92 D4
Barpeta, *India* 67 F17
Barques, Pt. Aux, *U.S.A.* 108 C4
Barquísimeto, *Venezuela* 124 A5
Barra, *Brazil* 125 F10
Barra, *U.K.* 14 E1
Barra, Sd. of, *U.K.* 14 D1
Barra de Navidad, *Mexico* 118 D4
Barra do Corda, *Brazil* 125 E9
Barra do Piraí, *Brazil* 127 A7
Barra Falsa, Pta. da, *Mozam.* 89 C6
Barra Hd., *U.K.* 14 E1
Barra Mansa, *Brazil* 127 A7
Barraba, *Australia* 95 E5
Barrackpur = Barakpur, *India* 69 H13
Barrafranca, *Italy* 31 E7
Barraigh = Barra, *U.K.* 14 E1
Barranca, *Lima, Peru* 124 F3
Barranca, *Loreto, Peru* 124 D3
Barrancabermeja, *Colombia* 124 B4
Barrancas, *Venezuela* 124 B6
Barrancos, *Portugal* 35 G4
Barranqueras, *Argentina* 126 B4
Barranquilla, *Colombia* 124 A4
Barraute, *Canada* 102 C4
Barre, *Mass., U.S.A.* 111 D12
Barre, *Vt., U.S.A.* 111 B12
Barreal, *Argentina* 126 C2
Barreiras, *Brazil* 125 F10
Barreirinhas, *Brazil* 125 D10
Barreiro, *Portugal* 35 G1
Barrême, *France* 21 E10
Barren, Nosy, *Madag.* 89 B7
Barretos, *Brazil* 125 H9
Barrhead, *Canada* 104 C6
Barrie, *Canada* 102 D4
Barrier Ra., *Australia* 95 E3
Barrière, *Canada* 104 C4
Barrington, *U.S.A.* 111 E13
Barrington L., *Canada* 105 B8
Barrington Tops, *Australia* 95 E5
Barringun, *Australia* 95 D4
Barro do Garças, *Brazil* 125 G8
Barron, *U.S.A.* 112 C9
Barrow, *U.S.A.* 100 A4
Barrow →, *Ireland* 15 D5
Barrow Creek, *Australia* 94 C1
Barrow I., *Australia* 92 D2
Barrow-in-Furness, *U.K.* 12 C4
Barrow Pt., *Australia* 94 A3
Barrow Pt., *U.S.A.* 98 B4
Barrow Ra., *Australia* 93 E4
Barrow Str., *Canada* 4 B3
Barruecopardo, *Spain* 34 D4
Barruelo de Santullán, *Spain* 34 C6
Barry, *U.K.* 13 F4
Barry's Bay, *Canada* 102 C4
Barsalogho, *Burkina Faso* 83 C4
Barsat, *Pakistan* 69 A5
Barsham, *Syria* 70 C4
Barsi, *India* 66 K9
Barsinghausen, *Germany* 24 C5
Barsoi, *India* 67 G15
Barstow, *Calif., U.S.A.* 117 L9
Barstow, *Tex., U.S.A.* 113 K3
Barth, *Germany* 24 A8
Barthélemy, Col, *Vietnam* 64 C5
Bartica, *Guyana* 124 B7
Bartin, *Turkey* 72 B5
Bartlesville, *U.S.A.* 113 G7
Bartlett, *Calif., U.S.A.* 116 J8
Bartlett, *Tex., U.S.A.* 113 K6
Bartlett, L., *Canada* 104 A5
Bartolomeu Dias, *Mozam.* 87 G4
Barton, *Australia* 93 F5
Barton upon Humber, *U.K.* 12 D7
Bartoszyce, *Poland* 44 D7
Bartow, *U.S.A.* 109 M5
Barú, Volcan, *Panama* 120 E3
Barumba, *Dem. Rep. of the Congo* 86 B1
Baruth, *Germany* 24 C9
Barvinkove, *Ukraine* 47 H9
Barwani, *India* 68 H6
Barwice, *Poland* 44 E3
Barycz →, *Poland* 45 G3
Barysaw, *Belarus* 46 E5
Barysh, *Russia* 48 D8
Barzān, *Iraq* 70 B5
Bârzava, *Romania* 42 D6
Bas-Rhin □, *France* 19 D14
Bašaid, *Serbia, Yug.* 42 E5
Bāsa'idū, *Iran* 71 E7
Basal, *Pakistan* 68 C5
Basankusa, *Dem. Rep. of the Congo* 84 D3
Basarabeasca, *Moldova* 43 D13
Basarabi, *Romania* 43 F13
Basauri, *Spain* 32 B2
Basawa, *Afghan.* 68 B4
Bascuñán, C., *Chile* 126 B1
Basel, *Switz.* 25 H3
Baselland □, *Switz.* 25 H3
Basento →, *Italy* 31 B9
Bāshī, *Iran* 71 D6
Bashi Channel, *Phil.* 60 D7
Bashkir Republic = Bashkortostan □, *Russia* 50 D6
Bashkortostan □, *Russia* 50 D6
Basilan, *Phil.* 61 H5
Basilan Str., *Phil.* 61 H5
Basildon, *U.K.* 13 F8
Basilicata □, *Italy* 31 B9
Basim = Washim, *India* 66 J10
Basin, *U.S.A.* 114 D9
Basingstoke, *U.K.* 13 F6
Baška, *Croatia* 29 D11
Başkale, *Turkey* 73 C10
Baskatong, Rés., *Canada* 102 C4
Basle = Basel, *Switz.* 25 H3
Başmakçı, *Turkey* 39 D12
Basoda, *India* 68 H7
Basoka, *Dem. Rep. of the Congo* 86 B1
Basque, Pays, *France* 20 E2
Basque Provinces = País Vasco □, *Spain* 32 C2
Basra = Al Başrah, *Iraq* 70 D5
Bass Str., *Australia* 94 F4
Bassano, *Canada* 104 C6
Bassano del Grappa, *Italy* 29 C8
Bassar, *Togo* 83 D5
Bassas da India, *Ind. Oc.* 85 J7
Basse-Normandie □, *France* 18 D6
Basse Santa-Su, *Gambia* 82 C2
Basse-Terre, *Guadeloupe* 121 C7
Bassein, *Burma* 67 L19
Basseterre, *St. Kitts & Nevis* 121 C7
Bassett, *Nebr., U.S.A.* 112 D5
Bassett, *Va., U.S.A.* 109 G6
Bassi, *India* 68 D7
Bassigny, *France* 19 E12
Bassikounou, *Mauritania* 82 B3
Bassum, *Germany* 24 C4
Båstad, *Sweden* 11 H6
Bastak, *Iran* 71 E7
Baştām, *Iran* 71 B7
Bastar, *India* 67 K12
Bastelica, *France* 21 F13
Basti, *India* 69 F10
Bastia, *France* 21 F13
Bastogne, *Belgium* 17 D5
Bastrop, *U.S.A.* 113 K6
Bat Yam, *Israel* 75 C3
Bata, *Eq. Guin.* 84 D1
Bata, *Romania* 42 D7
Bataan, *Phil.* 61 D4
Batabanó, *Cuba* 120 B3
Batabanó, G. de, *Cuba* 120 B3
Batac, *Phil.* 61 B4
Batagai, *Russia* 51 C14
Batajnica, *Serbia, Yug.* 40 B4
Batak, *Bulgaria* 41 E8
Batalha, *Portugal* 34 F2
Batama, *Dem. Rep. of the Congo* 86 B2
Batamay, *Russia* 51 C13
Batan I., *Phil.* 61 A4
Batanes Is., *Phil.* 61 A4
Batang, *China* 58 B2
Batang, *Indonesia* 63 G13
Batangas, *Phil.* 61 E4
Batanta, *Indonesia* 63 E8
Batatais, *Brazil* 127 A6
Batavia, *U.S.A.* 110 D6
Bataysk, *Russia* 47 J10
Batchelor, *Australia* 92 B5
Batdambang, *Cambodia* 64 F4
Bateman's B., *Australia* 95 F5
Batemans Bay, *Australia* 95 F5
Bates Ra., *Australia* 93 E3
Batesburg, *U.S.A.* 109 J5
Batesville, *Ark., U.S.A.* 113 H9
Batesville, *Miss., U.S.A.* 113 H10
Batesville, *Tex., U.S.A.* 113 L5
Bath, *U.K.* 13 F5
Bath, *Maine, U.S.A.* 103 D6
Bath, *N.Y., U.S.A.* 110 D7
Bath & North East Somerset □, *U.K.* 13 F5
Batheay, *Cambodia* 65 G5
Bathurst = Banjul, *Gambia* 82 C1
Bathurst, *Australia* 95 E4
Bathurst, *Canada* 103 C6
Bathurst, *S. Africa* 88 E4
Bathurst, C., *Canada* 4 B1
Bathurst B., *Australia* 94 A3
Bathurst Harb., *Australia* 94 G4
Bathurst I., *Australia* 92 B5
Bathurst I., *Canada* 4 B2
Bathurst Inlet, *Canada* 100 B9
Batie, *Burkina Faso* 82 D4
Batlow, *Australia* 95 F4
Batman, *Turkey* 73 D9
Batna, *Algeria* 78 A7
Batobato, *Phil.* 61 H7
Batočina, *Serbia, Yug.* 40 B5
Batoka, *Zambia* 87 F2
Baton Rouge, *U.S.A.* 113 K9
Batong, Ko, *Thailand* 65 J2
Bátonyterenye, *Hungary* 42 C4
Batopilas, *Mexico* 118 B3
Batouri, *Cameroon* 84 D2
Båtsfjord, *Norway* 8 A23
Battambang = Batdambang, *Cambodia* 64 F4
Batticaloa, *Sri Lanka* 66 R12
Battipáglia, *Italy* 31 B7
Battle, *U.K.* 13 G8
Battle →, *Canada* 105 C7
Battle Camp, *Australia* 94 B3
Battle Creek, *U.S.A.* 108 D3
Battle Ground, *U.S.A.* 116 E4
Battle Harbour, *Canada* 103 B8
Battle Lake, *U.S.A.* 112 B7
Battle Mountain, *U.S.A.* 114 F5
Battlefields, *Zimbabwe* 87 F2
Battleford, *Canada* 105 C7
Battonya, *Hungary* 42 D6
Batu, Kepulauan, *Indonesia* 62 E1
Batu, Mt., *Ethiopia* 81 F4
Batu Caves, *Malaysia* 65 L3
Batu Gajah, *Malaysia* 65 K3
Batu Is. = Batu, Kepulauan, *Indonesia* 62 E1
Batu Pahat, *Malaysia* 65 M4
Batuata, *Indonesia* 63 F6
Batumi, *Georgia* 49 K5
Baturaja, *Indonesia* 62 E2
Baturité, *Brazil* 125 D11
Bau, *Malaysia* 62 D4
Baubau, *Indonesia* 63 F6
Bauchi, *Nigeria* 83 C6
Bauchi □, *Nigeria* 83 C7
Baud, *France* 18 E3
Baudette, *U.S.A.* 112 A7
Bauer, C., *Australia* 95 E1
Bauhinia Downs, *Australia* 94 C4
Baukau, *Indonesia* 63 F7
Baume-les-Dames, *France* 19 E13
Baunatal, *Germany* 24 D5
Baunei, *Italy* 30 B2
Bauru, *Brazil* 127 A6
Bauska, *Latvia* 9 H21
Bautino, *Kazakstan* 49 H10
Bautzen, *Germany* 24 D10
Bavānāt, *Iran* 71 D7
Bavanište, *Serbia, Yug.* 42 F5
Bavaria = Bayern □, *Germany* 25 G7
Båven, *Sweden* 10 E10
Bavi Sadri, *India* 68 G6
Bavispe →, *Mexico* 118 B3
Bawdwin, *Burma* 67 H20
Bawean, *Indonesia* 62 F4
Bawku, *Ghana* 83 C4
Bawlake, *Burma* 67 K20
Bawolung, *China* 58 C3
Baxley, *U.S.A.* 109 K4
Baxoi, *China* 58 B1
Baxter Springs, *U.S.A.* 113 G7
Bay Bulls, *Canada* 103 C9
Bay City, *Mich., U.S.A.* 108 D4
Bay City, *Oreg., U.S.A.* 114 D2
Bay City, *Tex., U.S.A.* 113 L7
Bay de Verde, *Canada* 103 C9
Bay Minette, *U.S.A.* 109 K2
Bay St. Louis, *U.S.A.* 113 K10
Bay Springs, *U.S.A.* 113 K10
Bay View, *N.Z.* 91 H6
Baya, *Dem. Rep. of the Congo* 87 E2
Bayamo, *Cuba* 120 B4
Bayamón, *Puerto Rico* 121 C6
Bayan Har Shan, *China* 60 C4
Bayan Hot = Alxa Zuoqi, *China* 56 E3
Bayan Obo, *China* 56 D5

Bayan-Ovoo, *Mongolia* 56 C4
Bayana, *India* 68 F7
Bayanaŭyl, *Kazakstan* 50 D8
Bayandalay, *Mongolia* 56 C2
Bayanhongor, *Mongolia* 60 B5
Bayard, *U.S.A.* 112 E3
Bayawan, *Phil.* 61 G5
Baybay, *Phil.* 61 F6
Bayburt, *Turkey* 73 B9
Bayerische Alpen, *Germany* 25 H7
Bayerischer Wald, *Germany* 25 G8
Bayern □, *Germany* 25 G7
Bayeux, *France* 18 C6
Bayfield, *Canada* 110 C3
Bayfield, *U.S.A.* 112 B9
Bayındır, *Turkey* 39 C9
Baykal, Oz., *Russia* 51 D11
Baykonur = Bayqongyr, *Kazakstan* 50 E7
Baynes Mts., *Namibia* 88 B1
Bayombong, *Phil.* 61 C4
Bayon, *France* 19 D13
Bayona = Baiona, *Spain* 34 C2
Bayonne, *France* 20 E2
Bayonne, *U.S.A.* 111 F10
Bayovar, *Peru* 124 E2
Bayqongyr, *Kazakstan* 50 E7
Bayram-Ali = Bayramaly, *Turkmenistan* 50 F7
Bayramaly, *Turkmenistan* 50 F7
Bayramiç, *Turkey* 39 B8
Bayreuth, *Germany* 25 F7
Bayrischzell, *Germany* 25 H8
Bayrūt, *Lebanon* 75 B4
Bayt Lahm, *West Bank* 75 D4
Baytown, *U.S.A.* 113 L7
Bayzo, *Niger* 83 C5
Baza, *Spain* 35 H8
Bazar Dyuzi, *Russia* 49 K8
Bazardüzü = Bazar Dyuzi, *Russia* 49 K8
Bazarny Karabulak, *Russia* 48 D8
Bazarnyy Syzgan, *Russia* 48 D8
Bazaruto, I. do, *Mozam.* 89 C6
Bazas, *France* 20 D3
Bazhong, *China* 58 B6
Bazmān, Kūh-e, *Iran* 71 D9
Beach, *U.S.A.* 112 B3
Beach City, *U.S.A.* 110 F3
Beachport, *Australia* 95 F3
Beachy Hd., *U.K.* 13 G8
Beacon, *Australia* 93 F2
Beacon, *U.S.A.* 111 E11
Beaconia, *Canada* 105 C9
Beagle, Canal, *S. Amer.* 122 J4
Beagle Bay, *Australia* 92 C3
Bealanana, *Madag.* 89 A8
Beamsville, *Canada* 110 C5
Bear →, *U.S.A.* 116 G5
Béar, C., *France* 20 F7
Bear I., *Ireland* 15 E2
Bear L., *B.C., Canada* 104 B3
Bear L., *Man., Canada* 105 B9
Bear L., *U.S.A.* 114 F8
Bearcreek, *U.S.A.* 114 D9
Beardmore, *Canada* 102 C2
Beardmore Glacier, *Antarctica* 5 E11
Beardstown, *U.S.A.* 112 F9
Béarn, *France* 20 E3
Bearpaw Mts., *U.S.A.* 114 B9
Bearskin Lake, *Canada* 102 B1
Beas de Segura, *Spain* 35 G8
Beasain, *Spain* 32 B2
Beata, C., *Dom. Rep.* 121 C5
Beata, I., *Dom. Rep.* 121 C5
Beatrice, *U.S.A.* 112 E6
Beatrice, *Zimbabwe* 87 F3
Beatrice, C., *Australia* 94 A2
Beatton →, *Canada* 104 B4
Beatton River, *Canada* 104 B4
Beatty, *U.S.A.* 116 J10
Beaucaire, *France* 21 E8
Beauce, Plaine de la, *France* 19 D8
Beauceville, *Canada* 103 C5
Beaudesert, *Australia* 95 D5
Beaufort, *France* 21 C10
Beaufort, *Malaysia* 62 C5
Beaufort, *N.C., U.S.A.* 109 H7
Beaufort, *S.C., U.S.A.* 109 J5
Beaufort Sea, *Arctic* 4 B1
Beaufort West, *S. Africa* 88 E3
Beaugency, *France* 19 E8
Beauharnois, *Canada* 102 C5
Beaujeu, *France* 19 F11
Beaujolais, *France* 19 F11
Beaulieu →, *Canada* 104 A6
Beaulieu-sur-Dordogne, *France* 20 D5
Beaulieu-sur-Mer, *France* 21 E11
Beauly, *U.K.* 14 D4
Beauly →, *U.K.* 14 D4
Beaumaris, *U.K.* 12 D3
Beaumont, *Belgium* 17 D4
Beaumont, *France* 20 D4
Beaumont, *U.S.A.* 113 K7
Beaumont-de-Lomagne, *France* 20 E5
Beaumont-le-Roger, *France* 18 C7
Beaumont-sur-Sarthe, *France* 18 D7
Beaune, *France* 19 E11
Beaune-la-Rolande, *France* 19 D9
Beaupréau, *France* 18 E6
Beauraing, *Belgium* 17 D4
Beaurepaire, *France* 21 C9
Beauséjour, *Canada* 105 C9
Beauvais, *France* 19 C9
Beauval, *Canada* 105 B7
Beauvoir-sur-Mer, *France* 18 F4
Beauvoir-sur-Niort, *France* 20 B3
Beaver, *Okla., U.S.A.* 113 G4
Beaver, *Pa., U.S.A.* 110 F4
Beaver, *Utah, U.S.A.* 115 G7
Beaver →, *B.C., Canada* 104 B4
Beaver →, *Ont., Canada* 102 A2
Beaver →, *Sask., Canada* 105 B7
Beaver City, *U.S.A.* 112 E5
Beaver Dam, *U.S.A.* 112 D10
Beaver Falls, *U.S.A.* 110 F4
Beaver Hill L., *Canada* 105 C10
Beaver I., *U.S.A.* 108 C3
Beaverhill L., *Alta., Canada* 104 C6
Beaverhill L., *N.W.T., Canada* 105 A8
Beaverlodge, *Canada* 104 B5
Beavermouth, *Canada* 104 C5
Beaverstone →, *Canada* 102 B2
Beaverton, *Canada* 110 B5
Beaverton, *U.S.A.* 116 E4
Beawar, *India* 68 F6
Bebedouro, *Brazil* 127 A6
Beboa, *Madag.* 89 B7
Bebra, *Germany* 24 E5
Beccles, *U.K.* 13 E9
Bečej, *Serbia, Yug.* 42 E5
Beceni, *Romania* 43 E11
Becerreá, *Spain* 34 C3
Béchar, *Algeria* 78 B5
Bechyně, *Czech Rep.* 26 B7
Beckley, *U.S.A.* 108 G5
Beckum, *Germany* 24 D4
Beclean, *Romania* 43 C9
Bečov nad Teplou, *Czech Rep.* 26 A5
Bečva →, *Czech Rep.* 27 B10
Bédar, *Spain* 33 H3
Bédarieux, *France* 20 E7
Bedele, *Ethiopia* 81 F4
Bederkesa, *Germany* 24 B4
Bedeso, *Ethiopia* 81 F5
Bedford, *Canada* 102 C5
Bedford, *S. Africa* 88 E4
Bedford, *U.K.* 13 E7
Bedford, *Ind., U.S.A.* 108 F2
Bedford, *Iowa, U.S.A.* 112 E7
Bedford, *Ohio, U.S.A.* 110 E3
Bedford, *Pa., U.S.A.* 110 F6
Bedford, *Va., U.S.A.* 108 G6
Bedford, C., *Australia* 94 B4
Bedford Downs, *Australia* 92 C4
Bedfordshire □, *U.K.* 13 E7
Będków, *Poland* 45 G6
Bednja →, *Croatia* 29 B13
Bednodemyanovsk, *Russia* 48 D6
Bedónia, *Italy* 28 D6
Bedourie, *Australia* 94 C2
Bedum, *Neths.* 17 A6
Będzin, *Poland* 45 H6
Beech Grove, *U.S.A.* 108 F2
Beechy, *Canada* 105 C7
Beelitz, *Germany* 24 C8
Beenleigh, *Australia* 95 D5
Be'er Menuha, *Israel* 70 D2
Be'er Sheva, *Israel* 75 D3
Beersheba = Be'er Sheva, *Israel* 75 D3
Beeskow, *Germany* 24 C10
Beeston, *U.K.* 12 E6
Beetaloo, *Australia* 94 B1
Beetzendorf, *Germany* 24 C7
Beeville, *U.S.A.* 113 L6
Befale, *Dem. Rep. of the Congo* 84 D4
Befandriana, *Madag.* 89 C7
Befotaka, *Madag.* 89 C8
Bega, *Australia* 95 F4
Bega, Canalul, *Romania* 42 E5
Bégard, *France* 18 D3
Beğendik, *Turkey* 41 F10
Begusarai, *India* 69 G12
Behābād, *Iran* 71 C8
Behara, *Madag.* 89 C8
Behbehān, *Iran* 71 D6
Behshahr, *Iran* 71 B7
Bei Jiang →, *China* 59 F9
Bei'an, *China* 60 B7
Beibei, *China* 60 D5
Beihai, *China* 58 G7
Beijing, *China* 56 E9
Beijing □, *China* 56 E9
Beilen, *Neths.* 17 B6
Beiliu, *China* 59 F8
Beilngries, *Germany* 25 F7
Beilpajah, *Australia* 95 E3
Beilul, *Eritrea* 81 E5
Beinn na Faoghla = Benbecula, *U.K.* 14 D1
Beipiao, *China* 57 D11
Beira, *Mozam.* 87 F3
Beirut = Bayrūt, *Lebanon* 75 B4
Beitaolaizhao, *China* 57 B13
Beitbridge, *Zimbabwe* 87 G3
Beiuş, *Romania* 42 D7
Beizhen, *Liaoning, China* 57 D11
Beizhen, *Shandong, China* 57 F10
Beizhengzhen, *China* 57 B12
Beja, *Portugal* 35 G3
Béja, *Tunisia* 79 A7
Beja □, *Portugal* 35 H3
Bejaia, *Algeria* 78 A7
Béjar, *Spain* 34 E5
Bejestān, *Iran* 71 C8
Bekçiler, *Turkey* 39 E11
Békés, *Hungary* 42 D6
Békés □, *Hungary* 42 D6
Békéscsaba, *Hungary* 42 D6
Bekilli, *Turkey* 39 C11
Bekily, *Madag.* 89 C8
Bekoji, *Ethiopia* 81 F4
Bekok, *Malaysia* 65 L4
Bekwai, *Ghana* 83 D4
Bela, *India* 69 G10
Bela, *Pakistan* 68 F2
Bela Crkva, *Serbia, Yug.* 42 F6
Bela Palanka, *Serbia, Yug.* 40 C6
Bela Vista, *Brazil* 126 A4
Bela Vista, *Mozam.* 89 D5
Bélâbre, *France* 20 B5
Belalcázar, *Spain* 35 G5
Belanovica, *Serbia, Yug.* 40 B4
Belarus ■, *Europe* 46 F4
Belau = Palau ■, *Pac. Oc.* 96 G5
Belavenona, *Madag.* 89 C8
Belawan, *Indonesia* 62 D1
Belaya, *Ethiopia* 81 E4
Belaya Glina, *Russia* 49 G5
Belaya Kalitva, *Russia* 49 F5
Belaya Tserkov = Bila Tserkva, *Ukraine* 47 H6
Belceşti, *Romania* 43 C12
Bełchatów, *Poland* 45 G6
Belcher Is., *Canada* 101 C12
Belchite, *Spain* 32 D4
Belden, *U.S.A.* 116 E5
Belém, *Brazil* 125 D9
Belén, *Argentina* 126 B2
Belén, *Paraguay* 126 A4
Belen, *U.S.A.* 115 J10
Belene, *Bulgaria* 41 C9
Beleni, *Turkey* 72 D7
Bélesta, *France* 20 F5
Belet Uen, *Somali Rep.* 74 G4
Belev, *Russia* 46 F9
Belevi, *Turkey* 39 C9
Belfair, *U.S.A.* 116 C4
Belfast, *S. Africa* 89 D5
Belfast, *U.K.* 15 B6
Belfast, *Maine, U.S.A.* 103 D6
Belfast, *N.Y., U.S.A.* 110 D6
Belfast L., *U.K.* 15 B6
Belfield, *U.S.A.* 112 B3
Belfort, *France* 19 E13
Belfort, Territoire de □, *France* 19 E13
Belfry, *U.S.A.* 114 D9
Belgaum, *India* 66 M9
Belgioioso, *Italy* 28 C6
Belgium ■, *Europe* 17 D4
Belgodère, *France* 21 F13
Belgorod, *Russia* 47 G9
Belgorod-Dnestrovskiy = Bilhorod-Dnistrovskyy, *Ukraine* 47 J6
Belgrade = Beograd, *Serbia, Yug.* 40 B4
Belgrade, *U.S.A.* 114 D8
Belhaven, *U.S.A.* 109 H7
Beli Drim →, *Europe* 40 D4
Beli Manastir, *Croatia* 42 E3
Beli Timok →, *Serbia, Yug.* 40 C6
Bélice →, *Italy* 30 E5
Belinskiy, *Russia* 48 D6
Belinyu, *Indonesia* 62 E3
Beliton Is. = Belitung, *Indonesia* 62 E3
Belitung, *Indonesia* 62 E3
Beliu, *Romania* 42 D6
Belize ■, *Cent. Amer.* 119 D7
Belize City, *Belize* 119 D7
Beljakovci, *Macedonia* 40 D5
Beljanica, *Serbia, Yug.* 40 B5
Belkovskiy, Ostrov, *Russia* 51 B14
Bell →, *Canada* 102 C4
Bell Bay, *Australia* 94 G4
Bell I., *Canada* 103 B8
Bell-Irving →, *Canada* 104 B3
Bell Peninsula, *Canada* 101 B11
Bell Ville, *Argentina* 126 C3
Bella, *Italy* 31 B8
Bella Bella, *Canada* 104 C3
Bella Coola, *Canada* 104 C3
Bella Unión, *Uruguay* 126 C4
Bella Vista, *Corrientes, Argentina* 126 B4
Bella Vista, *Tucuman, Argentina* 126 B2
Bellac, *France* 20 B5
Bellágio, *Italy* 28 C6
Bellaire, *U.S.A.* 110 F4
Bellária, *Italy* 29 D9
Bellary, *India* 66 M10
Bellata, *Australia* 95 D4
Belle Fourche, *U.S.A.* 112 C3
Belle Fourche →, *U.S.A.* 112 C3
Belle Glade, *U.S.A.* 109 M5
Belle-Île, *France* 18 E3
Belle Isle, *Canada* 103 B8
Belle Isle, Str. of, *Canada* 103 B8
Belle Plaine, *Iowa, U.S.A.* 112 E8
Belle Plaine, *Minn., U.S.A.* 112 C8
Belle Yella, *Liberia* 82 D3
Belledonne, *France* 21 C10
Belledune, *Canada* 103 C6
Bellefontaine, *U.S.A.* 108 E4
Bellefonte, *U.S.A.* 110 F7
Bellegarde, *France* 19 E9
Bellegarde-en-Marche, *France* 20 C6
Bellegarde-sur-Valserine, *France* 19 F12
Bellême, *France* 18 D7
Belleoram, *Canada* 103 C8
Belleville, *Canada* 102 D4
Belleville, *France* 19 F11
Belleville, *Ill., U.S.A.* 112 F10
Belleville, *Kans., U.S.A.* 112 F6
Belleville, *N.Y., U.S.A.* 111 C8
Belleville-sur-Vie, *France* 18 F5
Bellevue, *Canada* 104 D6
Bellevue, *Idaho, U.S.A.* 114 E6
Bellevue, *Ohio, U.S.A.* 110 E2
Bellevue, *Wash., U.S.A.* 116 C4
Belley, *France* 21 C9
Bellin = Kangirsuk, *Canada* 101 C13
Bellinge, *Denmark* 11 J4
Bellingen, *Australia* 95 E5
Bellingham, *U.S.A.* 116 B4
Bellingshausen Sea, *Antarctica* 5 C17
Bellinzona, *Switz.* 25 J5
Bello, *Colombia* 124 B3
Bellows Falls, *U.S.A.* 111 C12
Bellpat, *Pakistan* 68 E3
Bellpuig d'Urgell, *Spain* 32 D6
Belluno, *Italy* 29 B9
Bellville, *U.S.A.* 113 L6
Bellwood, *U.S.A.* 110 F6
Bélmez, *Spain* 35 G5
Belmont, *Australia* 95 E5
Belmont, *Canada* 110 D3
Belmont, *S. Africa* 88 D3
Belmont, *U.S.A.* 110 D6
Belmonte, *Brazil* 125 G11
Belmonte, *Portugal* 34 E3
Belmonte, *Spain* 33 F2
Belmopan, *Belize* 119 D7
Belmullet, *Ireland* 15 B2
Belo Horizonte, *Brazil* 125 G10
Belo-sur-Mer, *Madag.* 89 C7
Belo-Tsiribihina, *Madag.* 89 B7
Belogorsk = Bilohirsk, *Ukraine* 47 K8
Belogorsk, *Russia* 51 D13
Belogradchik, *Bulgaria* 40 C6
Belogradets, *Bulgaria* 41 C11
Beloha, *Madag.* 89 D8
Beloit, *Kans., U.S.A.* 112 F5
Beloit, *Wis., U.S.A.* 112 D10
Belokorovichi, *Ukraine* 47 G5
Belomorsk, *Russia* 50 C4
Belonia, *India* 67 H17
Belopolye = Bilopillya, *Ukraine* 47 G8
Belorechensk, *Russia* 49 H4
Belorussia = Belarus ■, *Europe* 46 F4
Beloslav, *Bulgaria* 41 C11
Belovo, *Bulgaria* 41 D8
Belovo, *Russia* 50 D9
Belovodsk, *Ukraine* 47 H10
Beloye, Ozero, *Russia* 46 B9
Beloye More, *Russia* 50 C4
Belozem, *Bulgaria* 41 D9
Belozersk, *Russia* 46 B9
Belpasso, *Italy* 31 E7
Beltana, *Australia* 95 E2
Belterra, *Brazil* 125 D8
Beltinci, *Slovenia* 29 B13
Belton, *S.C., U.S.A.* 109 H4
Belton, *Tex., U.S.A.* 113 K6
Belton Res., *U.S.A.* 113 K6
Beltsy = Bălţi, *Moldova* 43 C12
Belturbet, *Ireland* 15 B4
Belukha, *Russia* 50 E9
Beluran, *Malaysia* 62 C5
Beluša, *Slovak Rep.* 27 B11
Belušić, *Serbia, Yug.* 40 C5
Belvedere Maríttimo, *Italy* 31 C8
Belvès, *France* 20 D5
Belvidere, *Ill., U.S.A.* 112 D10
Belvidere, *N.J., U.S.A.* 111 F9
Belvis de la Jara, *Spain* 34 F6
Belyando →, *Australia* 94 C4
Belyy, *Russia* 46 E7
Belyy, Ostrov, *Russia* 50 B8
Belyy Yar, *Russia* 50 D9
Bełżec, *Poland* 45 H10
Belzig, *Germany* 24 C8
Belzoni, *U.S.A.* 113 J9
Bełżyce, *Poland* 45 G9
Bemaraha, Lembalemban' i, *Madag.* 89 B7
Bemarivo, *Madag.* 89 C7
Bemarivo →, *Madag.* 89 B8
Bemavo, *Madag.* 89 C8
Bembéréke, *Benin* 83 C5
Bembesi, *Zimbabwe* 87 G2
Bembesi →, *Zimbabwe* 87 F2
Bembézar →, *Spain* 35 H5
Bembibre, *Spain* 34 C4
Bemidji, *U.S.A.* 112 B7
Ben, *Iran* 71 C6
Ben Cruachan, *U.K.* 14 E3
Ben Dearg, *U.K.* 14 D4
Ben Hope, *U.K.* 14 C4
Ben Lawers, *U.K.* 14 E4
Ben Lomond, *N.S.W., Australia* 95 E5
Ben Lomond, *Tas., Australia* 94 G4
Ben Lomond, *U.K.* 14 E4
Ben Luc, *Vietnam* 65 G6
Ben Macdhui, *U.K.* 14 D5
Ben Mhor, *U.K.* 14 D1
Ben More, *Arg. & Bute, U.K.* 14 E2
Ben More, *Stirl., U.K.* 14 E4
Ben More Assynt, *U.K.* 14 C4
Ben Nevis, *U.K.* 14 E3
Ben Quang, *Vietnam* 64 D6
Ben Vorlich, *U.K.* 14 E4
Ben Wyvis, *U.K.* 14 D4
Bena, *Nigeria* 83 C6
Benāb, *Iran* 73 D12
Benagerie, *Australia* 95 E3
Benalla, *Australia* 95 F4
Benalmádena, *Spain* 35 J6
Benambra, Mt., *Australia* 95 F4
Benares = Varanasi, *India* 69 G10
Bénat, C., *France* 21 E10
Benavente, *Portugal* 35 G2
Benavente, *Spain* 34 C5
Benavides, *U.S.A.* 113 M5
Benavides de Órbigo, *Spain* 34 C5
Benbecula, *U.K.* 14 D1
Benbonyathe, *Australia* 95 E2
Bencubbin, *Australia* 93 F2
Bend, *U.S.A.* 114 D3
Bender Beila, *Somali Rep.* 74 F5
Bendering, *Australia* 93 F2
Bendery = Tighina, *Moldova* 43 D14
Bendigo, *Australia* 95 F3
Bendorf, *Germany* 24 E3
Benē Beraq, *Israel* 75 C3
Bénéna, *Mali* 82 C4
Benenitra, *Madag.* 89 C8
Benešov, *Czech Rep.* 26 B7
Benevento, *Italy* 31 A7
Benfeld, *France* 19 D14
Benga, *Mozam.* 87 F3
Bengal, Bay of, *Ind. Oc.* 67 M17
Bengbu, *China* 57 H9
Benghazi = Banghāzī, *Libya* 79 B10
Bengkalis, *Indonesia* 62 D2
Bengkulu, *Indonesia* 62 E2
Bengkulu □, *Indonesia* 62 E2
Bengough, *Canada* 105 D7
Bengtsfors, *Sweden* 10 E6
Benguela, *Angola* 85 G2
Benguérua, I., *Mozam.* 89 C6
Benha, *Egypt* 80 H7
Beni, *Dem. Rep. of the Congo* 86 B2
Beni →, *Bolivia* 124 F5
Beni Mazâr, *Egypt* 80 J7
Beni Mellal, *Morocco* 78 B4
Beni Suef, *Egypt* 80 J7
Beniah L., *Canada* 104 A6
Benicarló, *Spain* 32 E5
Benicássim, *Spain* 32 E5
Benicia, *U.S.A.* 116 G4
Benidorm, *Spain* 33 G4
Benin ■, *Africa* 83 D5
Benin, Bight of, *W. Afr.* 83 E5
Benin City, *Nigeria* 83 D6
Benisa, *Spain* 33 G5
Benitses, *Greece* 36 A3
Benjamin Aceval, *Paraguay* 126 A4
Benjamin Constant, *Brazil* 124 D4
Benjamin Hill, *Mexico* 118 A2
Benkelman, *U.S.A.* 112 E4
Benkovac, *Croatia* 29 D12
Benlidi, *Australia* 94 C3
Bennett, *Canada* 104 B2
Bennett, L., *Australia* 92 D5
Bennetta, Ostrov, *Russia* 51 B15
Bennettsville, *U.S.A.* 109 H6
Bennington, *U.S.A.* 111 D11
Bénodet, *France* 18 E2
Benoni, *S. Africa* 89 D4
Benque Viejo, *Belize* 119 D7
Bensheim, *Germany* 25 F4
Benson, *U.S.A.* 115 L8
Bent, *Iran* 71 E8
Benteng, *Indonesia* 63 F6
Bentinck I., *Australia* 94 B2
Bentiu, *Sudan* 81 F2
Bento Gonçalves, *Brazil* 127 B5
Benton, *Ark., U.S.A.* 113 H8
Benton, *Calif., U.S.A.* 116 H8
Benton, *Ill., U.S.A.* 112 G10
Benton Harbor, *U.S.A.* 108 D2
Bentu Liben, *Ethiopia* 81 F4
Bentung, *Malaysia* 65 L3
Benue □, *Nigeria* 83 D6
Benue →, *Nigeria* 83 D6
Benxi, *China* 57 D12
Beo, *Indonesia* 63 D7
Beograd, *Serbia, Yug.* 40 B4
Beowawe, *U.S.A.* 114 F5
Bepan Jiang →, *China* 58 E6
Beppu, *Japan* 55 H5
Beqaa Valley = Al Biqā □, *Lebanon* 75 A5
Berane, *Montenegro, Yug.* 40 D3
Berati, *Albania* 40 F3
Berau, Teluk, *Indonesia* 63 E8
Berber, *Sudan* 80 D3
Berbera, *Somali Rep.* 74 E4
Berbérati, *C.A.R.* 84 D3
Berbice →, *Guyana* 124 B7
Berceto, *Italy* 28 D6
Berchidda, *Italy* 30 B2
Berchtesgaden, *Germany* 25 H8
Berck, *France* 19 B8

Berdichev = Berdychiv, *Ukraine* 47 H5
Berdsk, *Russia* 50 D9
Berdyansk, *Ukraine* 47 J9
Berdychiv, *Ukraine* 47 H5
Berea, *U.S.A.* 108 G3
Berebere, *Indonesia* 63 D7
Bereda, *Somali Rep.* 74 E5
Berehove, *Ukraine* 47 H2
Berekum, *Ghana* 82 D4
Berenice, *Egypt* 80 C4
Berens →, *Canada* 105 C9
Berens I., *Canada* 105 C9
Berens River, *Canada* 105 C9
Berestechko, *Ukraine* 47 G3
Bereşti, *Romania* 43 D12
Beretău →, *Romania* 42 C6
Berettyó →, *Hungary* 42 D6
Berettyóújfalu, *Hungary* 42 C6
Berevo, *Mahajanga, Madag.* 89 B7
Berevo, *Toliara, Madag.* 89 B7
Bereza, *Belarus* 47 F3
Berezhany, *Ukraine* 47 H3
Berezina = Byarezina →, *Belarus* 47 F6
Berezivka, *Ukraine* 47 J6
Berezna, *Ukraine* 47 G6
Berezniki, *Russia* 50 D6
Berezovo, *Russia* 50 C7
Berga, *Spain* 32 C6
Berga, *Sweden* 11 G10
Bergama, *Turkey* 39 B9
Bérgamo, *Italy* 28 C6
Bergara, *Spain* 32 B2
Bergby, *Sweden* 10 D11
Bergedorf, *Germany* 24 B6
Bergeforsen, *Sweden* 10 B11
Bergen, *Mecklenburg-Vorpommern, Germany* 24 A9
Bergen, *Niedersachsen, Germany* 24 C5
Bergen, *Neths.* 17 B4
Bergen, *Norway* 9 F11
Bergen, *U.S.A.* 110 C7
Bergen op Zoom, *Neths.* 17 C4
Bergerac, *France* 20 D4
Bergheim, *Germany* 24 E2
Bergisch Gladbach, *Germany* 24 E3
Bergkamen, *Germany* 24 D3
Bergkvara, *Sweden* 11 H10
Bergshamra, *Sweden* 10 E12
Bergsjö, *Sweden* 10 C11
Bergues, *France* 19 B9
Bergviken, *Sweden* 10 C10
Bergville, *S. Africa* 89 D4
Berhala, Selat, *Indonesia* 62 E2
Berhampore = Baharampur, *India* 69 G13
Berhampur = Brahmapur, *India* 67 K14
Berheci →, *Romania* 43 E12
Bering Sea, *Pac. Oc.* 100 C1
Bering Strait, *Pac. Oc.* 4 C17
Beringovskiy, *Russia* 51 C18
Berisso, *Argentina* 126 C4
Berja, *Spain* 35 J8
Berkeley, *U.S.A.* 116 H4
Berkeley Springs, *U.S.A.* 108 F6
Berkner I., *Antarctica* 5 D18
Berkovitsa, *Bulgaria* 40 C7
Berkshire Downs, *U.K.* 13 F6
Berland →, *Canada* 104 C5
Berlanga, *Spain* 35 G5
Berlenga, I., *Portugal* 35 F1
Berlin, *Germany* 24 C9
Berlin, *Md., U.S.A.* 108 F8
Berlin, *N.H., U.S.A.* 111 B13
Berlin, *Wis., U.S.A.* 108 D1
Berlin □, *Germany* 24 C9
Bermeja, Sierra, *Spain* 35 J5
Bermejo →, *Formosa, Argentina* 126 B4
Bermejo →, *San Juan, Argentina* 126 C2
Bermeo, *Spain* 32 B2
Bermillo de Sayago, *Spain* 34 D4
Bermuda ■, *Atl. Oc.* 98 F13
Bern, *Switz.* 25 J3
Bern □, *Switz.* 25 J3
Bernado, *U.S.A.* 115 J10
Bernalda, *Italy* 31 B9
Bernalillo, *U.S.A.* 115 J10
Bernardo de Irigoyen, *Argentina* 127 B5
Bernardo O'Higgins □, *Chile* 126 C1
Bernasconi, *Argentina* 126 D3
Bernau, *Bayern, Germany* 25 H8
Bernau, *Brandenburg, Germany* 24 C9
Bernay, *France* 18 C7
Bernburg, *Germany* 24 D7
Berndorf, *Austria* 26 D9
Berne = Bern, *Switz.* 25 J3
Berne = Bern □, *Switz.* 25 J3
Berner Alpen, *Switz.* 25 J3
Berneray, *U.K.* 14 D1
Bernier I., *Australia* 93 D1
Bernina, Piz, *Switz.* 25 J5
Bernkastel-Kues, *Germany* 25 F3
Beroroha, *Madag.* 89 C8
Béroubouay, *Benin* 83 C5
Beroun, *Czech Rep.* 26 B7
Berounka →, *Czech Rep.* 26 B7
Berovo, *Macedonia* 40 E6
Berre, Étang de, *France* 21 E9
Berre-l'Étang, *France* 21 E9
Berri, *Australia* 95 E3
Berry, *Australia* 95 E5
Berry, *France* 19 F8
Berry Is., *Bahamas* 120 A4
Berryessa L., *U.S.A.* 116 G4
Berryville, *U.S.A.* 113 G8
Bersenbrück, *Germany* 24 C3
Bershad, *Ukraine* 47 H5
Berthold, *U.S.A.* 112 A4
Berthoud, *U.S.A.* 112 E2
Bertincourt, *France* 19 B9
Bertoua, *Cameroon* 84 D2
Bertraghboy B., *Ireland* 15 C2
Bertrand, *U.S.A.* 112 E5
Berwick, *U.S.A.* 111 E8
Berwick-upon-Tweed, *U.K.* 12 B6
Berwyn Mts., *U.K.* 12 E4
Beryslav, *Ukraine* 47 J7
Berzasca, *Romania* 42 F6
Berzence, *Hungary* 42 D2
Besal, *Pakistan* 69 B5
Besalampy, *Madag.* 89 B7
Besançon, *France* 19 E13
Besar, *Indonesia* 62 E5
Beshenkovichi, *Belarus* 46 E5
Beška, *Serbia, Yug.* 42 E5
Beslan, *Russia* 49 J7
Besna Kobila, *Serbia, Yug.* 40 D6
Besnard L., *Canada* 105 B7
Besni, *Turkey* 72 D7
Besor, N. →, *Egypt* 75 D3
Bessarabiya, *Moldova* 47 J5
Bessarabka = Basarabeasca, *Moldova* 43 D13
Bessèges, *France* 21 D8
Bessemer, *Ala., U.S.A.* 109 J2
Bessemer, *Mich., U.S.A.* 112 B9
Bessin, *France* 18 C6
Bessines-sur-Gartempe, *France* 20 B5
Bet She'an, *Israel* 75 C4
Bet Shemesh, *Israel* 75 D4
Betafo, *Madag.* 89 B8
Betancuria, *Canary Is.* 37 F5
Betanzos, *Spain* 34 B2
Bétaré Oya, *Cameroon* 84 C2
Bétera, *Spain* 33 F4
Bethal, *S. Africa* 89 D4
Bethanien, *Namibia* 88 D2
Bethany, *U.S.A.* 112 E7
Bethel, *Alaska, U.S.A.* 100 B3
Bethel, *Vt., U.S.A.* 111 C12
Bethel Park, *U.S.A.* 110 F4
Béthenville, *France* 19 C11
Bethlehem = Bayt Lahm, *West Bank* 75 D4
Bethlehem, *S. Africa* 89 D4
Bethlehem, *U.S.A.* 111 F9
Bethulie, *S. Africa* 88 E4
Béthune, *France* 19 B9
Béthune →, *France* 18 C8
Bethungra, *Australia* 95 E4
Betioky, *Madag.* 89 C7
Betong, *Thailand* 65 K3
Betoota, *Australia* 94 D3
Betroka, *Madag.* 89 C8
Betsiamites, *Canada* 103 C6
Betsiamites →, *Canada* 103 C6
Betsiboka →, *Madag.* 89 B8
Bettiah, *India* 69 F11
Bettna, *Sweden* 11 F10
Béttola, *Italy* 28 D6
Betul, *India* 66 J10
Betung, *Malaysia* 62 D4
Betws-y-Coed, *U.K.* 12 D4
Betxi, *Spain* 32 F4
Betzdorf, *Germany* 24 E3
Beuil, *France* 21 D10
Beulah, *U.S.A.* 112 B4
Beuvron →, *France* 18 E8
Beveren, *Belgium* 17 C4
Beverley, *Australia* 93 F2
Beverley, *U.K.* 12 D7
Beverly, *Mass., U.S.A.* 111 D14
Beverly, *Wash., U.S.A.* 114 C4
Beverly Hills, *U.S.A.* 117 L8
Beverungen, *Germany* 24 D5
Bex, *Switz.* 25 J3
Bexhill, *U.K.* 13 G8
Bey Dağları, *Turkey* 39 E12
Beyānlū, *Iran* 70 C5
Beyazköy, *Turkey* 41 E11
Beycayırı, *Turkey* 41 F10
Beydağ, *Turkey* 39 C10
Beyeğaç, *Turkey* 39 D10
Beyin, *Ghana* 82 D4
Beykoz, *Turkey* 41 E13
Beyla, *Guinea* 82 D3
Beynat, *France* 20 C5
Beyneu, *Kazakstan* 50 E6
Beyoba, *Turkey* 39 C9
Beyoğlu, *Turkey* 41 E12
Beypazarı, *Turkey* 72 B4
Beyşehir, *Turkey* 72 D4
Beyşehir Gölü, *Turkey* 72 D4
Beytüşşebap, *Turkey* 73 D10
Bezdan, *Serbia, Yug.* 42 E3
Bezhetsk, *Russia* 46 D9
Béziers, *France* 20 E7
Bezwada = Vijayawada, *India* 67 L12
Bhachau, *India* 66 H7
Bhadarwah, *India* 69 C6
Bhadrakh, *India* 67 J15
Bhadravati, *India* 66 N9
Bhagalpur, *India* 69 G12
Bhakkar, *Pakistan* 68 D4
Bhakra Dam, *India* 68 D7
Bhamo, *Burma* 67 G20
Bhandara, *India* 66 J11
Bhanrer Ra., *India* 68 H8
Bharat = India ■, *Asia* 66 K11
Bharatpur, *India* 68 F7
Bhatinda, *India* 68 D6
Bhatpara, *India* 69 H13
Bhaun, *Pakistan* 68 C5
Bhaunagar = Bhavnagar, *India* 68 J5
Bhavnagar, *India* 68 J5
Bhawanipatna, *India* 67 K12
Bhera, *Pakistan* 68 C5
Bhilsa = Vidisha, *India* 68 H7
Bhilwara, *India* 68 G6
Bhima →, *India* 66 L10
Bhimavaram, *India* 67 L12
Bhimbar, *Pakistan* 69 C6
Bhind, *India* 69 F8
Bhiwandi, *India* 66 K8
Bhiwani, *India* 68 E7
Bhola, *Bangla.* 67 H17
Bhopal, *India* 68 H7
Bhubaneshwar, *India* 67 J14
Bhuj, *India* 68 H3
Bhusaval, *India* 66 J9
Bhutan ■, *Asia* 67 F17
Biafra, B. of = Bonny, Bight of, *Africa* 83 E6
Biak, *Indonesia* 63 E9
Biała, *Poland* 45 H4
Biała →, *Poland* 45 H7
Biała Piska, *Poland* 44 E9
Biała Podlaska, *Poland* 45 F10
Biała Podlaska □, *Poland* 45 G10
Biała Rawska, *Poland* 45 G7
Białobrzegi, *Poland* 45 G7
Białogard, *Poland* 44 D2
Białowieża, *Poland* 45 F10
Biały Bór, *Poland* 44 E3
Białystok, *Poland* 45 E10
Białystok □, *Poland* 45 E10
Biancavilla, *Italy* 31 E7
Bianco, *Italy* 31 D9
Bīārjmand, *Iran* 71 B7
Biaro, *Indonesia* 63 D7
Biarritz, *France* 20 E2
Biasca, *Switz.* 25 J4
Biba, *Egypt* 80 J7
Bibai, *Japan* 54 C10
Bibbiena, *Italy* 29 E8
Bibby I., *Canada* 105 A10
Bibel →, *Spain* 34 C3
Biberach, *Germany* 25 G5
Bibiani, *Ghana* 82 D4
Biboohra, *Australia* 94 B4
Bibungwa, *Dem. Rep. of the Congo* 86 C2
Bic, *Canada* 103 C6
Bicaj, *Albania* 40 E4
Bicaz, *Romania* 43 D11
Bicazu Ardelean, *Romania* 43 D10
Bíccari, *Italy* 31 A8
Bicester, *U.K.* 13 F6
Bichena, *Ethiopia* 81 E4
Bichvinta, *Georgia* 49 J5
Bickerton I., *Australia* 94 A2
Bicknell, *Ind., U.S.A.* 108 F2
Bicknell, *Utah, U.S.A.* 115 G8
Bicske, *Hungary* 42 C3
Bida, *Nigeria* 83 D6
Bidar, *India* 66 L10
Biddeford, *U.S.A.* 103 D5
Biddwara, *Ethiopia* 81 F4
Bideford, *U.K.* 13 F3
Bideford Bay, *U.K.* 13 F3
Bidor, *Malaysia* 65 K3
Bie, *Sweden* 10 E10
Bié, Planalto de, *Angola* 85 G3
Bieber, *U.S.A.* 114 F3
Biebrza →, *Poland* 45 E9
Biecz, *Poland* 45 J8
Biel, *Switz.* 25 H3
Bielawa, *Poland* 45 H3
Bielefeld, *Germany* 24 C4
Bielersee, *Switz.* 25 H3
Biella, *Italy* 28 C5
Bielsk Podlaski, *Poland* 45 F10
Bielsko-Biała, *Poland* 45 J6
Bielsko-Biała □, *Poland* 45 J6
Bien Hoa, *Vietnam* 65 G6
Bienfait, *Canada* 105 D8
Bienne = Biel, *Switz.* 25 H3
Bienvenida, *Spain* 35 G4
Bienville, L., *Canada* 102 A5
Bierné, *France* 18 E6
Bierun, *Poland* 45 H6
Bierutów, *Poland* 45 G4
Biescas, *Spain* 32 C4
Biese →, *Germany* 24 C7
Biesiesfontein, *S. Africa* 88 E2
Bietigheim-Bissingen, *Germany* 25 G5
Bieżuń, *Poland* 45 F6
Biferno →, *Italy* 29 G12
Big →, *Canada* 103 B8
Big B., *Canada* 103 A7
Big Bear City, *U.S.A.* 117 L10
Big Bear Lake, *U.S.A.* 117 L10
Big Beaver, *Canada* 105 D7
Big Belt Mts., *U.S.A.* 114 C8
Big Bend, *Swaziland* 89 D5
Big Bend National Park, *U.S.A.* 113 L3
Big Black →, *U.S.A.* 113 K9
Big Blue →, *U.S.A.* 112 F6
Big Cr. →, *Canada* 104 C4
Big Creek, *U.S.A.* 116 H7
Big Cypress Swamp, *U.S.A.* 109 M5
Big Falls, *U.S.A.* 112 A8
Big Fork →, *U.S.A.* 112 A8
Big Horn Mts. = Bighorn Mts., *U.S.A.* 114 D10
Big Lake, *U.S.A.* 113 K4
Big Moose, *U.S.A.* 111 C10
Big Muddy Cr. →, *U.S.A.* 112 A2
Big Pine, *U.S.A.* 116 H8
Big Piney, *U.S.A.* 114 E8
Big Quill L., *Canada* 105 C8
Big Rapids, *U.S.A.* 108 D3
Big River, *Canada* 105 C7
Big Run, *U.S.A.* 110 F6
Big Sable Pt., *U.S.A.* 108 C2
Big Sand L., *Canada* 105 B9
Big Sandy, *U.S.A.* 114 B8
Big Sandy Cr. →, *U.S.A.* 112 F3
Big Sioux →, *U.S.A.* 112 D6
Big Spring, *U.S.A.* 113 J4
Big Springs, *U.S.A.* 112 E3
Big Stone City, *U.S.A.* 112 C6
Big Stone Gap, *U.S.A.* 109 G4
Big Stone L., *U.S.A.* 112 C6
Big Sur, *U.S.A.* 116 J5
Big Timber, *U.S.A.* 114 D9
Big Trout L., *Canada* 102 B2
Biğa, *Turkey* 41 F11
Biga →, *Turkey* 41 F11
Bigadiç, *Turkey* 39 B10
Biganos, *France* 20 D3
Bigfork, *U.S.A.* 114 B6
Biggar, *Canada* 105 C7
Biggar, *U.K.* 14 F5
Bigge I., *Australia* 92 B4
Biggenden, *Australia* 95 D5
Biggleswade, *U.K.* 13 E7
Biggs, *U.S.A.* 116 F5
Bighorn, *U.S.A.* 114 C10
Bighorn →, *U.S.A.* 114 C10
Bighorn Mts., *U.S.A.* 114 D10
Bignona, *Senegal* 82 C1
Bigorre, *France* 20 E4
Bigstone L., *Canada* 105 C9
Biguglia, Étang de, *France* 21 F13
Bigwa, *Tanzania* 86 D4
Bihać, *Bos.-H.* 29 D12
Bihar, *India* 69 G11
Bihar □, *India* 69 G12
Biharamulo, *Tanzania* 86 C3
Biharamulo □, *Tanzania* 86 C3
Biharkeresztes, *Hungary* 42 C6
Bihor □, *Romania* 42 D7
Bihor, Munţii, *Romania* 42 D7
Bijagós, Arquipélago dos, *Guinea-Biss.* 82 C1
Bijaipur, *India* 68 F7
Bijapur, *Karnataka, India* 66 L9
Bijapur, *Mad. P., India* 67 K12
Bījār, *Iran* 70 C5
Bijeljina, *Bos.-H.* 42 F4
Bijelo Polje, *Montenegro, Yug.* 40 C3
Bijie, *China* 58 D5
Bijnor, *India* 68 E8
Bikaner, *India* 68 E5
Bikapur, *India* 69 F10
Bikeqi, *China* 56 D6
Bikfayyā, *Lebanon* 75 B4
Bikin, *Russia* 51 E14
Bikin →, *Russia* 54 A7
Bikini Atoll, *Pac. Oc.* 96 F8
Bikoué, *Cameroon* 83 E7
Bila Tserkva, *Ukraine* 47 H6
Bilara, *India* 68 F5
Bilaspur, *Mad. P., India* 69 H10
Bilaspur, *Punjab, India* 68 D7
Biläsuvar, *Azerbaijan* 73 C13
Bilauk Taungdan, *Thailand* 64 F2
Bilbao, *Spain* 32 B2
Bilbeis, *Egypt* 80 H7
Bilbo = Bilbao, *Spain* 32 B2
Bilbor, *Romania* 43 C10
Bilciureşti, *Romania* 43 F10
Bíldudalur, *Iceland* 8 D2
Bílé Karpaty, *Europe* 27 B11
Bileća, *Bos.-H.* 40 D2
Bilecik, *Turkey* 72 B4
Biłgoraj, *Poland* 45 H9
Bilhorod-Dnistrovskyy, *Ukraine* 47 J6
Bilibino, *Russia* 51 C17
Bilibiza, *Mozam.* 87 E5
Biliran I., *Phil.* 61 F6
Bilishti, *Albania* 40 F5
Bill, *U.S.A.* 112 D2
Billabalong, *Australia* 93 E2
Billdal, *Sweden* 11 G5
Billiluna, *Australia* 92 C4
Billings, *U.S.A.* 114 D9
Billiton Is. = Belitung, *Indonesia* 62 E3
Billsta, *Sweden* 10 A12
Billund, *Denmark* 11 J3
Bilma, *Niger* 79 E8
Bilo Gora, *Croatia* 42 E2
Biloela, *Australia* 94 C5
Bilohirsk, *Ukraine* 47 K8
Bilopillya, *Ukraine* 47 G8
Biloxi, *U.S.A.* 113 K10
Bilpa Morea Claypan, *Australia* 94 D3
Biltine, *Chad* 79 F10
Bilyana, *Australia* 94 B4
Bilyarsk, *Russia* 48 C10
Bima, *Indonesia* 63 F5
Bimban, *Egypt* 80 C3
Bimbila, *Ghana* 83 D5
Bimini Is., *Bahamas* 120 A4
Bin Xian, *Heilongjiang, China* 57 B14
Bin Xian, *Shaanxi, China* 56 G5
Bina-Etawah, *India* 68 G8
Bīnāb, *Iran* 71 B6
Binalbagan, *Phil.* 61 F5
Binalong, *Australia* 95 E4
Bīnālūd, Kūh-e, *Iran* 71 B8
Binatang = Bintangor, *Malaysia* 62 D4
Binbee, *Australia* 94 C4
Binche, *Belgium* 17 D4
Binchuan, *China* 58 E3
Binda, *Australia* 95 D4
Bindle, *Australia* 95 D4
Bindslev, *Denmark* 11 G4
Bindura, *Zimbabwe* 87 F3
Binefar, *Spain* 32 D5
Bingara, *N.S.W., Australia* 95 D5
Bingara, *Queens., Australia* 95 D3
Bingen, *Germany* 25 F3
Bingerville, *Ivory C.* 82 D4
Bingham, *U.S.A.* 103 C6
Bingham Canyon, *U.S.A.* 114 F7
Binghamton, *U.S.A.* 111 D9
Bingöl, *Turkey* 73 C9
Bingöl Dağları, *Turkey* 73 C9
Bingsjö, *Sweden* 10 C9
Binh Dinh = An Nhon, *Vietnam* 64 F7
Binh Khe, *Vietnam* 64 F7
Binh Son, *Vietnam* 64 E7
Binhai, *China* 57 G10
Binic, *France* 18 D4
Binisatua, *Spain* 37 B11
Binjai, *Indonesia* 62 D1
Binnaway, *Australia* 95 E4
Binongko, *Indonesia* 63 F6
Binscarth, *Canada* 105 C8
Bintan, *Indonesia* 62 D2
Bintangor, *Malaysia* 62 D4
Bintulu, *Malaysia* 62 D4
Bintuni, *Indonesia* 63 E8
Binyang, *China* 58 F7
Binz, *Germany* 24 A9
Binzert = Bizerte, *Tunisia* 79 A7
Bío Bío □, *Chile* 126 D1
Biograd na Moru, *Croatia* 29 E12
Bioko, *Eq. Guin.* 83 E6
Biokovo, *Croatia* 29 E14
Bir, *India* 66 K9
Bir, Ras, *Djibouti* 81 E5
Bîr Abu Hashim, *Egypt* 80 C3
Bîr Abu M'nqar, *Egypt* 80 B2
Bîr Abu Muḥammad, *Egypt* 75 F3
Bi'r ad Dabbāghāt, *Jordan* 75 E4
Bîr Adal Deib, *Sudan* 80 C4
Bi'r al Butayyihāt, *Jordan* 75 F4
Bi'r al Mārī, *Jordan* 75 E4
Bi'r al Qattār, *Jordan* 75 F4
Bîr 'Asal, *Egypt* 80 B3
Bîr Autrun, *Sudan* 80 D2
Bîr Beiḍa, *Egypt* 75 E3
Bîr Diqnash, *Egypt* 80 A2
Bîr el 'Abd, *Egypt* 75 D2
Bîr el Basur, *Egypt* 80 B2
Bîr el Biarât, *Egypt* 75 F3
Bîr el Duweidar, *Egypt* 75 E1
Bîr el Garârât, *Egypt* 75 D2
Bîr el Gellaz, *Egypt* 80 A2
Bîr el Heisi, *Egypt* 75 F3
Bîr el Jafir, *Egypt* 75 E1
Bîr el Mâlḥi, *Egypt* 75 E2
Bîr el Shaqqa, *Egypt* 80 A2
Bîr el Thamâda, *Egypt* 75 E2
Bîr Fuad, *Egypt* 80 A2
Bîr Gebeil Ḥiṣn, *Egypt* 75 E2
Bi'r Ghadīr, *Syria* 75 A6
Bîr Haimur, *Egypt* 80 C3
Bîr Ḥasana, *Egypt* 75 E2
Bi'r Jadīd, *Iraq* 70 C4
Bîr Kanayis, *Egypt* 80 C3
Bîr Kaseiba, *Egypt* 75 E2
Bîr Kerawein, *Egypt* 80 B2
Bîr Lahfân, *Egypt* 75 E2
Bîr Madkûr, *Egypt* 75 E1
Bîr Maql, *Egypt* 80 C3
Bîr Misaha, *Egypt* 80 C2
Bîr Mogreïn, *Mauritania* 78 C3
Bîr Murr, *Egypt* 80 C3
Bi'r Muṭribah, *Kuwait* 70 D5
Bîr Nakheila, *Egypt* 80 C3
Bîr Qaṭia, *Egypt* 75 E1
Bîr Qatrani, *Egypt* 80 A2
Bîr Ranga, *Egypt* 80 C4
Bîr Sahara, *Egypt* 80 C2
Bîr Seiyâla, *Egypt* 80 B3
Bîr Shalatein, *Egypt* 80 C4
Bîr Shebb, *Egypt* 80 C2
Bîr Shût, *Egypt* 80 C4
Bîr Terfawi, *Egypt* 80 C2
Bîr Umm Qubûr, *Egypt* 80 C3
Bîr Ungât, *Egypt* 80 C3
Bîr Za'farâna, *Egypt* 80 J8
Bîr Zeidûn, *Egypt* 80 B3
Biramféro, *Guinea* 82 C3
Biratnagar, *Nepal* 69 F12

Birawa,
Dem. Rep. of the Congo 86 C2
Birch Hills, *Canada* 105 C7
Birch I., *Canada* 105 C9
Birch L., *N.W.T., Canada* 104 A5
Birch L., *Ont., Canada* 102 B1
Birch L., *U.S.A.* 102 C1
Birch Mts., *Canada* 104 B6
Birch River, *Canada* 105 C8
Birchip, *Australia* 95 F3
Birchiş, *Romania* 42 E7
Bird, *Canada* 105 B10
Bird City, *U.S.A.* 112 F4
Bird I. = Aves, I. de,
W. Indies 121 C7
Birdsville, *Australia* 94 D2
Birdum, *Australia* 92 C5
Birecik, *Turkey* 73 D8
Birein, *Israel* 75 E3
Bireuen, *Indonesia* 62 C1
Birifo, *Gambia* 82 C2
Birigui, *Brazil* 127 A5
Birkenfeld, *Germany* 25 F3
Birkenhead, *U.K.* 12 D4
Birkerød, *Denmark* 11 J6
Birket Qârûn, *Egypt* 80 J7
Birkfeld, *Austria* 26 D8
Bîrlad = Bârlad, *Romania* 43 D12
Birmingham, *U.K.* 13 E6
Birmingham, *U.S.A.* 109 J2
Birmitrapur, *India* 67 H14
Birni Ngaouré, *Niger* 83 C5
Birni Nkonni, *Niger* 83 C6
Birnin Gwari, *Nigeria* 83 C6
Birnin Kebbi, *Nigeria* 83 C5
Birnin Kudu, *Nigeria* 83 C6
Birobidzhan, *Russia* 51 E14
Birr, *Ireland* 15 C4
Birrie →, *Australia* 95 D4
Birsilpur, *India* 68 E5
Birsk, *Russia* 50 D6
Birštonas, *Lithuania* 44 D11
Birtle, *Canada* 105 C8
Birur, *India* 66 N9
Biryuchiy, *Ukraine* 47 J8
Biržai, *Lithuania* 9 H21
Birzebbugga, *Malta* 36 D2
Bisa, *Indonesia* 63 E7
Bisáccia, *Italy* 31 A8
Bisacquino, *Italy* 30 E6
Bisalpur, *India* 69 E8
Bisbee, *U.S.A.* 115 L9
Biscarosse, *France* 20 D2
Biscarrosse et de Parentis,
Étang de, *France* 20 D2
Biscay, B. of, *Atl. Oc.* 6 F5
Biscayne B., *U.S.A.* 109 N5
Biscéglie, *Italy* 31 A9
Bischheim, *France* 19 D14
Bischofshofen, *Austria* 26 D6
Bischofswerda, *Germany* 24 D10
Bischwiller, *France* 19 D14
Biscoe Bay, *Antarctica* 5 D13
Biscoe Is., *Antarctica* 5 C17
Biscostasing, *Canada* 102 C3
Biševo, *Croatia* 29 F13
Bisha, *Eritrea* 81 D4
Bishah, W. →, *Si. Arabia* 80 C5
Bishan, *China* 58 C6
Bishkek, *Kyrgyzstan* 50 E8
Bishnupur, *India* 69 H12
Bisho, *S. Africa* 89 E4
Bishop, *Calif., U.S.A.* 116 H8
Bishop, *Tex., U.S.A.* 113 M6
Bishop Auckland, *U.K.* 12 C6
Bishop's Falls, *Canada* 103 C8
Bishop's Stortford, *U.K.* 13 F8
Bisignano, *Italy* 31 C9
Bisina, L., *Uganda* 86 B3
Biskra, *Algeria* 78 B7
Biskupiec, *Poland* 44 E7
Bismarck, *U.S.A.* 112 B4
Bismarck Arch.,
Papua N. G. 96 H7
Bismark, *Germany* 24 C7
Bismil, *Turkey* 73 D9
Biso, *Uganda* 86 B3
Bison, *U.S.A.* 112 C3
Bīsotūn, *Iran* 70 C5
Bispgården, *Sweden* 10 A10
Bissagos = Bijagós,
Arquipélago dos,
Guinea-Biss. 82 C1
Bissau, *Guinea-Biss.* 82 C1
Bissett, *Canada* 105 C9
Bissikrima, *Guinea* 82 C2
Bistcho L., *Canada* 104 B5
Bistreţ, *Romania* 43 G8
Bistrica = Ilirska-Bistrica,
Slovenia 29 C11
Bistriţa, *Romania* 43 C9
Bistriţa →, *Romania* 43 D11
Bistriţa Năsăud □,
Romania 43 C9
Bistriţei, Munţii, *Romania* 43 C10
Biswan, *India* 69 F9
Bisztynek, *Poland* 44 D7
Bitburg, *Germany* 25 F2
Bitche, *France* 19 C14
Bithynia, *Turkey* 72 B4
Bitlis, *Turkey* 73 C10
Bitola, *Macedonia* 40 E5
Bitolj = Bitola, *Macedonia* 40 E5
Bitonto, *Italy* 31 A9
Bitter Creek, *U.S.A.* 114 F9
Bitter L. = Buheirat-
Murrat-el-Kubra, *Egypt* 80 H8
Bitterfeld, *Germany* 24 D8
Bitterfontein, *S. Africa* 88 E2
Bitterroot →, *U.S.A.* 114 C6
Bitterroot Range, *U.S.A.* 114 D6
Bitterwater, *U.S.A.* 116 J6
Bitti, *Italy* 30 B2
Bittou, *Burkina Faso* 83 C4
Biu, *Nigeria* 83 C7
Bivolari, *Romania* 43 C12
Bivolu, Vf., *Romania* 43 C10
Biwa-Ko, *Japan* 55 G8
Biwabik, *U.S.A.* 112 B8
Bixad, *Romania* 43 C8
Biyang, *China* 56 H7
Biysk, *Russia* 50 D9
Bizana, *S. Africa* 89 E4
Bizen, *Japan* 55 G7
Bizerte, *Tunisia* 79 A7
Bjargtangar, *Iceland* 8 D1
Bjärnum, *Sweden* 11 H7
Bjästa, *Sweden* 10 A12
Bjelasica,
Montenegro, Yug. 40 D3
Bjelašnica, *Bos.-H.* 42 G3
Bjelovar, *Croatia* 29 C13
Bjerringbro, *Denmark* 11 H3
Björbo, *Sweden* 10 D8
Björklinge, *Sweden* 10 D11
Björneborg, *Sweden* 10 E8
Bjørnevatn, *Norway* 8 B23
Bjørnøya, *Arctic* 4 B8
Bjursås, *Sweden* 10 D9
Bjuv, *Sweden* 11 H6
Blace, *Serbia, Yug.* 40 C5
Blachownia, *Poland* 45 H5
Black = Da →, *Vietnam* 64 B5
Black →, *Canada* 110 B5
Black →, *Ark., U.S.A.* 113 H9
Black →, *N.Y., U.S.A.* 111 C8
Black →, *Wis., U.S.A.* 112 D9
Black Diamond, *Canada* 104 C6
Black Forest =
Schwarzwald, *Germany* 25 G4
Black Hd., *Ireland* 15 C2
Black Hills, *U.S.A.* 112 D3
Black I., *Canada* 105 C9
Black L., *Canada* 105 B7
Black L., *U.S.A.* 108 C3
Black Mesa, *U.S.A.* 113 G3
Black Mt. = Mynydd Du,
U.K. 13 F4
Black Mts., *U.K.* 13 F4
Black Range, *U.S.A.* 115 K10
Black River, *Jamaica* 120 C4
Black River Falls, *U.S.A.* 112 C9
Black Sea, *Eurasia* 6 G12
Black Volta →, *Africa* 82 D4
Black Warrior →, *U.S.A.* 109 J2
Blackall, *Australia* 94 C4
Blackball, *N.Z.* 91 K3
Blackbull, *Australia* 94 B3
Blackburn, *U.K.* 12 D5
Blackburn with Darwen □,
U.K. 12 D5
Blackduck, *U.S.A.* 112 B7
Blackfoot, *U.S.A.* 114 E7
Blackfoot →, *U.S.A.* 114 C7
Blackfoot River Reservoir,
U.S.A. 114 E8
Blackie, *Canada* 104 C6
Blackpool, *U.K.* 12 D4
Blackpool □, *U.K.* 12 D4
Blackriver, *U.S.A.* 110 B1
Blacks Harbour, *Canada* 103 C6
Blacksburg, *U.S.A.* 108 G5
Blacksod B., *Ireland* 15 B1
Blackstone, *U.S.A.* 108 G7
Blackstone →, *Canada* 104 A4
Blackstone Ra., *Australia* 93 E4
Blackville, *Canada* 103 C6
Blackwater, *Australia* 94 C4
Blackwater →, *Meath,*
Ireland 15 C4
Blackwater →, *Waterford,*
Ireland 15 D4
Blackwater →, *U.K.* 15 B5
Blackwater Cr. →,
Australia 95 D3
Blackwell, *U.S.A.* 113 G6
Blackwells Corner, *U.S.A.* 117 K7
Blaenau Ffestiniog, *U.K.* 12 E4
Blaenau Gwent □, *U.K.* 13 F4
Blagaj, *Bos.-H.* 40 C1
Blagnac, *France* 20 E5
Blagodarnyy, *Russia* 49 H6
Blagoevgrad, *Bulgaria* 40 D7
Blagoveshchensk, *Russia* 51 D13
Blain, *France* 18 E5
Blaine, *U.S.A.* 116 B4
Blaine Lake, *Canada* 105 C7
Blair, *U.S.A.* 112 E6
Blair Athol, *Australia* 94 C4
Blair Atholl, *U.K.* 14 E5
Blairgowrie, *U.K.* 14 E5
Blairmore, *Canada* 104 D6
Blairsden, *U.S.A.* 116 F6
Blairsville, *U.S.A.* 110 F5
Blaj, *Romania* 43 D8
Blake Pt., *U.S.A.* 112 A10
Blakely, *U.S.A.* 109 K3
Blâmont, *France* 19 D13
Blanc, C., *Spain* 37 B9
Blanc, Mont, *Alps* 21 C10
Blanca, B., *Argentina* 122 G4
Blanca Peak, *U.S.A.* 115 H11
Blanchard, *U.S.A.* 113 H6
Blanche, C., *Australia* 95 E1
Blanche, L., *S. Austral.,*
Australia 95 D2
Blanche, L., *W. Austral.,*
Australia 92 D3
Blanco, *S. Africa* 88 E3
Blanco, *U.S.A.* 113 K5
Blanco →, *Argentina* 126 C2
Blanco, C., *Costa Rica* 120 E2
Blanco, C., *U.S.A.* 114 E1
Blanda →, *Iceland* 8 D3
Blandford Forum, *U.K.* 13 G5
Blanding, *U.S.A.* 115 H9
Blanes, *Spain* 32 D7
Blangy-sur-Bresle, *France* 19 C8
Blanice →, *Czech Rep.* 26 B7
Blankaholm, *Sweden* 11 G10
Blankenberge, *Belgium* 17 C3
Blankenburg, *Germany* 24 D6
Blanquefort, *France* 20 D3
Blanquillo, *Uruguay* 127 C4
Blansko, *Czech Rep.* 27 B9
Blantyre, *Malawi* 87 F4
Blarney, *Ireland* 15 E3
Błaszki, *Poland* 45 G5
Blatná, *Czech Rep.* 26 B6
Blato, *Croatia* 29 F13
Blaubeuren, *Germany* 25 G5
Blaustein, *Germany* 25 G5
Blåvands Huk, *Denmark* 11 J2
Blaydon, *U.K.* 12 C6
Blaye, *France* 20 C3
Blaye-les-Mines, *France* 20 D6
Blayney, *Australia* 95 E4
Blaze, Pt., *Australia* 92 B5
Błażowa, *Poland* 45 J9
Bleckede, *Germany* 24 B6
Bled, *Slovenia* 29 B11
Bleiburg, *Austria* 26 E7
Blejeşti, *Romania* 43 F10
Blekinge, *Sweden* 9 H16
Blekinge län □, *Sweden* 11 H9
Blenheim, *Canada* 110 D3
Blenheim, *N.Z.* 91 J4
Bléone →, *France* 21 D10
Blérancourt, *France* 19 C10
Bletchley, *U.K.* 13 F7
Blida, *Algeria* 78 A6
Blidö, *Sweden* 10 E12
Blidsberg, *Sweden* 11 G7
Blieskastel, *Germany* 25 F3
Bligh Sound, *N.Z.* 91 L1
Blind River, *Canada* 102 C3
Blinishti, *Albania* 40 E3
Blitar, *Indonesia* 63 H15
Blitta, *Togo* 83 D5
Block I., *U.S.A.* 111 E13
Block Island Sd., *U.S.A.* 111 E13
Blodgett Iceberg Tongue,
Antarctica 5 C9
Bloemfontein, *S. Africa* 88 D4
Bloemhof, *S. Africa* 88 D4
Blois, *France* 18 E8
Blomskog, *Sweden* 10 E6
Blomstermåla, *Sweden* 11 H10
Blönduós, *Iceland* 8 D3
Błonie, *Poland* 45 F7
Bloodvein →, *Canada* 105 C9
Bloody Foreland, *Ireland* 15 A3
Bloomer, *U.S.A.* 112 C9
Bloomfield, *Australia* 94 B4
Bloomfield, *Canada* 110 C7
Bloomfield, *Iowa, U.S.A.* 112 E8
Bloomfield, *N. Mex.,*
U.S.A. 115 H10
Bloomfield, *Nebr., U.S.A.* 112 D6
Bloomington, *Ill., U.S.A.* 112 E10
Bloomington, *Ind., U.S.A.* 108 F2
Bloomington, *Minn.,*
U.S.A. 112 C8
Bloomsburg, *U.S.A.* 111 F8
Blora, *Indonesia* 63 G14
Blossburg, *U.S.A.* 110 E7
Blouberg, *S. Africa* 89 C4
Blountstown, *U.S.A.* 109 K3
Bludenz, *Austria* 26 D2
Blue Island, *U.S.A.* 108 E2
Blue Lake, *U.S.A.* 114 F2
Blue Mesa Reservoir,
U.S.A. 115 G10
Blue Mts., *Oreg., U.S.A.* 114 D4
Blue Mts., *Pa., U.S.A.* 111 F8
Blue Mud B., *Australia* 94 A2
Blue Nile = Nîl el
Azraq →, *Sudan* 81 D3
Blue Rapids, *U.S.A.* 112 F6
Blue Ridge Mts., *U.S.A.* 109 G5
Blueberry →, *Canada* 104 B4
Bluefield, *U.S.A.* 108 G5
Bluefields, *Nic.* 120 D3
Bluff, *Australia* 94 C4
Bluff, *N.Z.* 91 M2
Bluff, *U.S.A.* 115 H9
Bluff Knoll, *Australia* 93 F2
Bluff Pt., *Australia* 93 E1
Bluffton, *U.S.A.* 108 E3
Blumenau, *Brazil* 127 B6
Blunt, *U.S.A.* 112 C5
Bly, *U.S.A.* 114 E3
Blyth, *Canada* 110 C3
Blyth, *U.K.* 12 B6
Blythe, *U.S.A.* 117 M12
Bo, *S. Leone* 82 D2
Bo Duc, *Vietnam* 65 G6
Bo Hai, *China* 57 E10
Bo Xian, *China* 56 H8
Boa Vista, *Brazil* 124 C6
Boac, *Phil.* 61 E4
Boaco, *Nic.* 120 D2
Bo'ai, *China* 56 G7
Boal, *Spain* 34 B4
Boardman, *U.S.A.* 110 E4
Boatman, *Australia* 95 D4
Bobadah, *Australia* 95 E4
Bobai, *China* 58 F7
Bobbili, *India* 67 K13
Bóbbio, *Italy* 28 D6
Bobcaygeon, *Canada* 102 D4
Böblingen, *Germany* 25 G5
Bobo-Dioulasso,
Burkina Faso 82 C4
Bobolice, *Poland* 44 E3
Boboshevo, *Bulgaria* 40 D7
Bobov Dol, *Bulgaria* 40 D6
Bóbr →, *Poland* 45 F2
Bobraomby, Tanjon' i,
Madag. 89 A8
Bobrinets, *Ukraine* 47 H7
Bobrov, *Russia* 48 E5
Bobrovitsa, *Ukraine* 47 G6
Bobruysk = Babruysk,
Belarus 47 F5
Bôca do Acre, *Brazil* 124 E5
Boca Raton, *U.S.A.* 109 M5
Bocanda, *Ivory C.* 82 D4
Bocas del Toro, *Panama* 120 E3
Boceguillas, *Spain* 34 D7
Bochnia, *Poland* 45 J7
Bocholt, *Germany* 24 D2
Bochum, *Germany* 24 D3
Bockenem, *Germany* 24 C6
Boćki, *Poland* 45 F10
Bocognano, *France* 21 F13
Bocoyna, *Mexico* 118 B3
Bocşa, *Romania* 42 E6
Böda, *Sweden* 11 G11
Boda, *Kopparberg, Sweden* 10 C9
Boda, *Västernorrland,*
Sweden 10 B10
Bodafors, *Sweden* 11 G8
Bodaybo, *Russia* 51 D12
Boddam, *U.K.* 14 B7
Boddington, *Australia* 93 F2
Bodega Bay, *U.S.A.* 116 G3
Boden, *Sweden* 8 D19
Bodensee, *Europe* 25 H5
Bodenteich, *Germany* 24 C6
Bodhan, *India* 66 K10
Bodinga, *Nigeria* 83 C6
Bodmin, *U.K.* 13 G3
Bodmin Moor, *U.K.* 13 G3
Bodø, *Norway* 8 C16
Bodrog →, *Hungary* 42 B6
Bodrum, *Turkey* 39 D9
Bódva →, *Hungary* 42 B5
Boën, *France* 21 C8
Boende,
Dem. Rep. of the Congo 84 E4
Boerne, *U.S.A.* 113 L5
Boffa, *Guinea* 82 C2
Bogalusa, *U.S.A.* 113 K10
Bogan Gate, *Australia* 95 E4
Bogantungan, *Australia* 94 C4
Bogata, *U.S.A.* 113 J7
Bogatić, *Serbia, Yug.* 40 B3
Boğazkale, *Turkey* 72 B6
Boğazlıyan, *Turkey* 72 C6
Bogen, *Sweden* 10 D6
Bogense, *Denmark* 11 J4
Bogetići, *Montenegro, Yug.* 40 D2
Boggabilla, *Australia* 95 D5
Boggabri, *Australia* 95 E5
Boggeragh Mts., *Ireland* 15 D3
Bognor Regis, *U.K.* 13 G7
Bogo, *Phil.* 61 F6
Bogodukhov =
Bohodukhiv, *Ukraine* 47 G8
Bogong, Mt., *Australia* 95 F4
Bogor, *Indonesia* 63 G12
Bogoroditsk, *Russia* 46 F10
Bogorodsk, *Russia* 48 B6
Bogoso, *Ghana* 82 D4
Bogotá, *Colombia* 124 C4
Bogotol, *Russia* 50 D9
Bogra, *Bangla.* 67 G16
Boguchany, *Russia* 51 D10
Boguchar, *Russia* 48 F5
Bogué, *Mauritania* 82 B2
Boguslav, *Ukraine* 47 H6
Boguszów-Gorce, *Poland* 45 H3
Bohain-en-Vermandois,
France 19 C10
Bohemia Downs, *Australia* 92 C4
Bohemian Forest =
Böhmerwald, *Germany* 25 F9
Bohena Cr. →, *Australia* 95 E4
Bohinjska Bistrica, *Slovenia* 29 B11
Böhmerwald, *Germany* 25 F9
Bohmte, *Germany* 24 C4
Bohodukhiv, *Ukraine* 47 G8
Bohol, *Phil.* 61 G6
Bohol Sea, *Phil.* 63 C6
Böhönye, *Hungary* 42 D2
Bohuslän, *Sweden* 11 F5
Boi, *Nigeria* 83 D6
Boi, Pta. de, *Brazil* 127 A6
Boiaçu, *Brazil* 124 D6
Boileau, C., *Australia* 92 C3
Boiro, *Spain* 34 C2
Boise, *U.S.A.* 114 E5
Boise City, *U.S.A.* 113 G3
Boissevain, *Canada* 105 D8
Bòite →, *Italy* 29 B9
Boitzenburg, *Germany* 24 B9
Boizenburg, *Germany* 24 B6
Bojador C., *W. Sahara* 78 C3
Bojana →, *Albania* 40 E3
Bojano, *Italy* 31 A7
Bojanowo, *Poland* 45 G3
Bøjden, *Denmark* 11 J4
Bojnūrd, *Iran* 71 B8
Bojonegoro, *Indonesia* 63 G14
Boju, *Nigeria* 83 D6
Boka, *Serbia, Yug.* 42 E5
Boka Kotorska,
Montenegro, Yug. 40 D2
Bokala, *Ivory C.* 82 D4
Boké, *Guinea* 82 C2
Bokhara →, *Australia* 95 D4
Bokkos, *Nigeria* 83 D6
Boknafjorden, *Norway* 9 G11
Bokoro, *Chad* 79 F9
Bokpyin, *Burma* 65 G2
Boksitogorsk, *Russia* 46 C7
Bol, *Croatia* 29 E13
Bolama, *Guinea-Biss.* 82 C1
Bolan Pass, *Pakistan* 66 E5
Bolaños →, *Mexico* 118 C4
Bolaños de Calatrava,
Spain 35 G7
Bolayır, *Turkey* 41 F10
Bolbec, *France* 18 C7
Boldājī, *Iran* 71 D6
Boldeşti-Scăeni, *Romania* 43 E11
Bole, *China* 60 B3
Bole, *Ethiopia* 81 F4
Bolekhiv, *Ukraine* 47 H2
Bolesławiec, *Poland* 45 G2
Bolgatanga, *Ghana* 83 C4
Bolgrad = Bolhrad,
Ukraine 47 K5
Bolhrad, *Ukraine* 47 K5
Boli, *Sudan* 81 F2
Bolinao, *Phil.* 61 C3
Bolintin-Vale, *Romania* 43 F10
Bolívar, *Argentina* 126 D3
Bolivar, *Mo., U.S.A.* 113 G8
Bolivar, *Tenn., U.S.A.* 113 H10
Bolivia ■, *S. Amer.* 124 G6
Bolivian Plateau, *S. Amer.* 122 E4
Boljevac, *Serbia, Yug.* 40 C5
Bolkhov, *Russia* 46 F9
Bolków, *Poland* 45 H3
Bollebygd, *Sweden* 11 G6
Bollène, *France* 21 D8
Bollnäs, *Sweden* 10 C10
Bollon, *Australia* 95 D4
Bollstabruk, *Sweden* 10 B11
Bolmen, *Sweden* 11 H7
Bolobo,
Dem. Rep. of the Congo 84 E3
Bologna, *Italy* 29 D8
Bologoye, *Russia* 46 D8
Bolonchenticul, *Mexico* 119 D7
Bolótana, *Italy* 30 B1
Boloven, Cao Nguyen,
Laos 64 E6
Bolpur, *India* 69 H12
Bolsena, *Italy* 29 F8
Bolsena, L. di, *Italy* 29 F8
Bolshaya Chernigovka,
Russia 48 D10
Bolshaya Glushitsa, *Russia* 48 D10
Bolshaya Martynovka,
Russia 49 G5
Bolshaya Vradiyevka,
Ukraine 47 J6
Bolshevik, Ostrov, *Russia* 51 B11
Bolshoi Kavkas = Caucasus
Mountains, *Eurasia* 49 J7
Bolshoy Anyuy →, *Russia* 51 C17
Bolshoy Begichev, Ostrov,
Russia 51 B12
Bolshoy Lyakhovskiy,
Ostrov, *Russia* 51 B15
Bolshoy Tokmak =
Tokmak, *Ukraine* 47 J8
Bolshoy Tyuters, Ostrov,
Russia 9 G22
Bolsward, *Neths.* 17 A5
Bolt Head, *U.K.* 13 G4
Boltaña, *Spain* 32 C5
Boltigen, *Switz.* 25 J3
Bolton, *Canada* 110 C5
Bolton, *U.K.* 12 D5
Bolu, *Turkey* 72 B4
Bolungavík, *Iceland* 8 C2
Boluo, *China* 59 F10
Bolvadin, *Turkey* 72 C4
Bolzano, *Italy* 29 B8
Bom Jesus da Lapa, *Brazil* 125 F10
Boma,
Dem. Rep. of the Congo 84 F2
Bomaderry, *Australia* 95 E5
Bombala, *Australia* 95 F4
Bombarral, *Portugal* 35 F1
Bombay = Mumbai, *India* 66 K8
Bomboma,
Dem. Rep. of the Congo 84 D3
Bombombwa,
Dem. Rep. of the Congo 86 B2
Bomi Hills, *Liberia* 82 D2
Bomili,
Dem. Rep. of the Congo 86 B2
Bømlo, *Norway* 9 G11
Bomokandi →,
Dem. Rep. of the Congo 86 B2
Bomu →, *C.A.R.* 84 D4
Bon, C., *Tunisia* 76 C5
Bon Sar Pa, *Vietnam* 64 F6
Bonaire, *Neth. Ant.* 121 D6
Bonang, *Australia* 95 F4

Bonanza, Nic. 120 D3
Bonaparte Arch., Australia 92 B3
Boñar, Spain 34 C5
Bonaventure, Canada 103 C6
Bonavista, Canada 103 C9
Bonavista, C., Canada 103 C9
Bonawan, Phil. 61 G5
Bondeno, Italy 29 D8
Bondo, Dem. Rep. of the Congo 86 B1
Bondoukou, Ivory C. 82 D4
Bondowoso, Indonesia 63 G15
Bone, Teluk, Indonesia 63 E6
Bonerate, Indonesia 63 F6
Bonerate, Kepulauan, Indonesia 63 F6
Bo'ness, U.K. 14 E5
Bonete, Cerro, Argentina 126 B2
Bong Son = Hoai Nhon, Vietnam 64 E7
Bongabong, Phil. 61 E4
Bongor, Chad 79 F9
Bongouanou, Ivory C. 82 D4
Bonham, U.S.A. 113 J6
Bonifacio, France 21 G13
Bonifacio, Bouches de, Medit. S. 30 A2
Bonin Is. = Ogasawara Gunto, Pac. Oc. 96 E6
Bonke, Ethiopia 81 F4
Bonn, Germany 24 E3
Bonnat, France 19 F8
Bonne Terre, U.S.A. 113 G9
Bonners Ferry, U.S.A. 114 B5
Bonnétable, France 18 D7
Bonneval, Eure-et-Loir, France 18 D8
Bonneval, Savoie, France 21 C11
Bonneville, France 19 F13
Bonney, L., Australia 95 F3
Bonnie Downs, Australia 94 C3
Bonnie Rock, Australia 93 F2
Bonny, Nigeria 83 E6
Bonny →, Nigeria 83 E6
Bonny, Bight of, Africa 83 E6
Bonny-sur-Loire, France 19 E9
Bonnyrigg, U.K. 14 F5
Bonnyville, Canada 105 C6
Bono, Italy 30 B2
Bonoi, Indonesia 63 E9
Bonorva, Italy 30 B1
Bonsall, U.S.A. 117 M9
Bontang, Indonesia 62 D5
Bonthe, S. Leone 82 D2
Bontoc, Phil. 61 C4
Bonyeri, Ghana 82 D4
Bonyhád, Hungary 42 D3
Bonython Ra., Australia 92 D4
Bookabie, Australia 93 F5
Booker, U.S.A. 113 G4
Boolaboolka L., Australia 95 E3
Booligal, Australia 95 E3
Boonah, Australia 95 D5
Boone, Iowa, U.S.A. 112 D8
Boone, N.C., U.S.A. 109 G5
Booneville, Ark., U.S.A. 113 H8
Booneville, Miss., U.S.A. 109 H1
Boonville, Calif., U.S.A. 116 F3
Boonville, Ind., U.S.A. 108 F2
Boonville, Mo., U.S.A. 112 F8
Boonville, N.Y., U.S.A. 111 C9
Boorindal, Australia 95 E4
Boorowa, Australia 95 E4
Boothia, Gulf of, Canada 4 B3
Boothia Pen., Canada 100 A10
Bootle, U.K. 12 D4
Booué, Gabon 84 E2
Boppard, Germany 25 E3
Boquete, Panama 120 E3
Boquilla, Presa de la, Mexico 118 B3
Boquillas del Carmen, Mexico 118 B4
Bor, Czech Rep. 26 B5
Bor, Russia 48 B7
Bor, Serbia, Yug. 40 B6
Bôr, Sudan 81 F3
Bor, Sweden 11 G8
Bor, Turkey 72 D6
Bor Mashash, Israel 75 D3
Borah Peak, U.S.A. 114 D7
Borang, Sudan 81 G3
Borås, Sweden 11 G6
Borāzjān, Iran 71 D6
Borba, Brazil 124 D7
Borba, Portugal 35 G3
Borborema, Planalto da, Brazil 122 D7
Borcea, Romania 43 F12
Borçka, Turkey 73 B9
Bord Khūn-e Now, Iran 71 D6
Borda, C., Australia 95 F2
Bordeaux, France 20 D3
Borden, Australia 93 F2
Borden, Canada 103 C7
Borden I., Canada 4 B2
Bordertown, Australia 95 F3
Borðeyri, Iceland 8 D3
Bordighera, Italy 28 E4
Bordj Fly Ste. Marie, Algeria 78 C5
Bordj-in-Eker, Algeria 78 D7
Bordj Omar Driss, Algeria 78 C7
Borehamwood, U.K. 13 F7
Borek Wielkopolski, Poland 45 G4
Borensberg, Sweden 11 F9
Borgå = Porvoo, Finland 9 F21
Borgarfjörður, Iceland 8 D7
Borgarnes, Iceland 8 D3
Børgefjellet, Norway 8 D15
Borger, Neths. 17 B6
Borger, U.S.A. 113 H4
Borgholm, Sweden 11 H10
Bórgia, Italy 31 D9
Borgo San Dalmazzo, Italy 28 D4
Borgo San Lorenzo, Italy 29 E8
Borgo Val di Taro, Italy 28 D6
Borgo Valsugana, Italy 29 B8
Borgomanero, Italy 28 C5
Borgorose, Italy 29 F10
Borgosésia, Italy 28 C5
Borikhane, Laos 64 C4
Borisoglebsk, Russia 48 E6
Borisov = Barysaw, Belarus 46 E5
Borisovka, Russia 47 G9
Borja, Peru 124 D3
Borja, Spain 32 D3
Borjas Blancas = Les Borges Blanques, Spain 32 D5
Borjomi, Georgia 49 K6
Borken, Germany 24 D9
Børkop, Denmark 11 J3
Borkou, Chad 79 E9
Borkum, Germany 24 B2
Borlänge, Sweden 10 D9
Borley, C., Antarctica 5 C5
Borlu, Turkey 39 C10
Bormida →, Italy 28 D5
Bórmio, Italy 28 B7
Borna, Germany 24 D8
Borne Sulinowo, Poland 44 E3
Borneo, E. Indies 62 D5
Bornholm, Denmark 11 J8
Bornholms Amtskommune □, Denmark 11 J8
Bornholmsgattet, Europe 11 J8
Borno □, Nigeria 83 C7
Bornos, Spain 35 J5
Bornova, Turkey 39 C9
Bornu Yassa, Nigeria 83 C7
Borodino, Russia 46 E8
Borogontsy, Russia 51 C14
Boromo, Burkina Faso 82 C4
Boron, U.S.A. 117 L9
Borongan, Phil. 61 F6
Bororen, Australia 94 C5
Borotangba Mts., C.A.R. 81 F2
Borovan, Bulgaria 40 C7
Borovichi, Russia 46 C7
Borovsk, Russia 46 E9
Borrby, Sweden 11 J8
Borrego Springs, U.S.A. 117 M10
Borriol, Spain 32 E4
Borroloola, Australia 94 B2
Borşa, Cluj, Romania 43 D8
Borşa, Maramureş, Romania 43 C9
Borsec, Romania 43 D10
Borsod-Abaúj-Zemplén □, Hungary 42 B6
Bort-les-Orgues, France 20 C6
Borth, U.K. 13 E3
Börtnan, Sweden 10 B7
Borūjerd, Iran 71 C6
Boryslav, Ukraine 47 H2
Boryspil, Ukraine 47 G6
Borzhomi = Borjomi, Georgia 49 K6
Borzna, Ukraine 47 G7
Borzya, Russia 51 D12
Bosa, Italy 30 B1
Bosanska Dubica, Bos.-H. 29 C13
Bosanska Gradiška, Bos.-H. 42 E2
Bosanska Kostajnica, Bos.-H. 29 C13
Bosanska Krupa, Bos.-H. 29 D13
Bosanski Brod, Bos.-H. 42 E2
Bosanski Novi, Bos.-H. 29 C13
Bosanski Petrovac, Bos.-H. 29 D13
Bosanski Šamac, Bos.-H. 42 E3
Bosansko Grahovo, Bos.-H. 29 D13
Bosaso, Somali Rep. 74 E4
Boscastle, U.K. 13 G3
Bose, China 58 F6
Boshan, China 57 F9
Boshof, S. Africa 88 D4
Boshrūyeh, Iran 71 C8
Bosilegrad, Serbia, Yug. 40 D6
Boskovice, Czech Rep. 27 B9
Bosna →, Bos.-H. 42 E3
Bosna i Hercegovina = Bosnia-Herzegovina ■, Europe 42 G2
Bosnia-Herzegovina ■, Europe 42 G2
Bosnik, Indonesia 63 E9
Bosobolo, Dem. Rep. of the Congo 84 D3
Bosporus = İstanbul Boğazı, Turkey 41 E13
Bossangoa, C.A.R. 84 C3
Bossier City, U.S.A. 113 J8
Bosso, Niger 83 C7
Bostānābād, Iran 70 B5
Bosten Hu, China 60 B3
Boston, U.K. 12 E7
Boston, U.S.A. 111 D13
Boston Bar, Canada 104 D4
Bosut →, Croatia 42 E3
Boswell, Canada 104 D5
Boswell, Okla., U.S.A. 113 H7
Boswell, Pa., U.S.A. 110 F5
Botad, India 68 H4
Botan →, Turkey 73 D10
Botany B., Australia 95 E5
Botene, Laos 64 D3
Botev, Bulgaria 41 D8
Botevgrad, Bulgaria 40 D7
Bothaville, S. Africa 88 D4
Bothnia, G. of, Europe 8 E19
Bothwell, Australia 94 G4
Bothwell, Canada 110 D3
Boticas, Portugal 34 D3
Botletle →, Botswana 88 C3
Botlikh, Russia 49 J8
Botna →, Moldova 43 D14
Botoroaga, Romania 43 F10
Botoşani, Romania 43 C11
Botoşani □, Romania 43 C11
Botricello, Italy 31 D9
Botro, Ivory C. 82 D3
Botswana ■, Africa 88 C3
Bottineau, U.S.A. 112 A4
Bottnaryd, Sweden 11 G7
Bottrop, Germany 24 D2
Botucatu, Brazil 127 A6
Botwood, Canada 103 C8
Bou Djébéha, Mali 82 B4
Bouaflé, Ivory C. 82 D3
Bouaké, Ivory C. 82 D3
Bouar, C.A.R. 84 C3
Bouârfa, Morocco 78 B5
Boucaut B., Australia 94 A1
Bouches-du-Rhône □, France 21 E9
Bougainville, C., Australia 92 B4
Bougainville Reef, Australia 94 B4
Bougie = Bejaia, Algeria 78 A7
Bougouni, Mali 82 C3
Bouillon, Belgium 17 E5
Boulazac, France 20 C4
Boulder, Colo., U.S.A. 112 E2
Boulder, Mont., U.S.A. 114 C7
Boulder City, U.S.A. 117 K12
Boulder Creek, U.S.A. 116 H4
Boulder Dam = Hoover Dam, U.S.A. 117 K12
Bouli, Mauritania 82 B2
Boulia, Australia 94 C2
Bouligny, France 19 C12
Boulogne →, France 18 E5
Boulogne-sur-Gesse, France 20 E4
Boulogne-sur-Mer, France 19 B8
Bouloire, France 18 E7
Boulsa, Burkina Faso 83 C4
Boultoum, Niger 83 C7
Boun Neua, Laos 64 B3
Boun Tai, Laos 64 B3
Bouna, Ivory C. 82 D4
Boundary Peak, U.S.A. 116 H8
Boundiali, Ivory C. 82 D3
Bountiful, U.S.A. 114 F8
Bounty Is., Pac. Oc. 96 M9
Bourbon-Lancy, France 19 F10
Bourbon-l'Archambault, France 19 F10
Bourbonnais, France 19 F10
Bourbonne-les-Bains, France 19 E12
Bourbourg, France 19 B9
Bourem, Mali 83 B4
Bourg, France 20 C3
Bourg-Argental, France 21 C8
Bourg-de-Péage, France 21 C9
Bourg-en-Bresse, France 19 F12
Bourg-Lastic, France 20 C6
Bourg-Madame, France 20 F5
Bourg-St-Andéol, France 21 D8
Bourg-St-Maurice, France 21 C10
Bourganeuf, France 20 C5
Bourges, France 19 E9
Bourget, Canada 111 A9
Bourget, L. du, France 21 C9
Bourgneuf, B. de, France 18 E4
Bourgneuf-en-Retz, France 18 E5
Bourgogne, France 19 F11
Bourgoin-Jallieu, France 21 C9
Bourgueil, France 18 E7
Bourke, Australia 95 E4
Bourne, U.K. 12 E7
Bournemouth, U.K. 13 G6
Bournemouth □, U.K. 13 G6
Bouse, U.S.A. 117 M13
Boussac, France 19 F9
Boussé, Burkina Faso 83 C4
Boutilimit, Mauritania 82 B2
Boutonne →, France 20 C3
Bouvet I. = Bouvetøya, Antarctica 3 G10
Bouvetøya, Antarctica 3 G10
Bouxwiller, France 19 D14
Bouzonville, France 19 C13
Bova Marina, Italy 31 E8
Bovalino Marina, Italy 31 D9
Bovec, Slovenia 29 B10
Bovill, U.S.A. 114 C5
Bovino, Italy 31 A8
Bow Island, Canada 104 D6
Bowbells, U.S.A. 112 A3
Bowdle, U.S.A. 112 C5
Bowelling, Australia 93 F2
Bowen, Australia 94 C4
Bowen Mts., Australia 95 F4
Bowie, Ariz., U.S.A. 115 K9
Bowie, Tex., U.S.A. 113 J6
Bowkān, Iran 70 B5
Bowland, Forest of, U.K. 12 D5
Bowling Green, Ky., U.S.A. 108 G2
Bowling Green, Ohio, U.S.A. 108 E4
Bowling Green, C., Australia 94 B4
Bowman, U.S.A. 112 B3
Bowman I., Antarctica 5 C8
Bowmans, Australia 95 E2
Bowmanville, Canada 102 D4
Bowmore, U.K. 14 F2
Bowral, Australia 95 E5
Bowraville, Australia 95 E5
Bowron →, Canada 104 C4
Bowser L., Canada 104 B3
Bowsman, Canada 105 C8
Bowwood, Zambia 87 F2
Boxholm, Sweden 11 F9
Boxmeer, Neths. 17 C5
Boxtel, Neths. 17 C5
Boyabat, Turkey 72 B6
Boyalıca, Turkey 41 F13
Boyce, U.S.A. 113 K8
Boyer →, Canada 104 B5
Boyle, Ireland 15 C3
Boyne →, Ireland 15 C5
Boyne City, U.S.A. 108 C3
Boynitsa, Bulgaria 40 C6
Boynton Beach, U.S.A. 109 M5
Boyoma, Chutes, Dem. Rep. of the Congo 86 B2
Boyuibe, Bolivia 124 G6
Boyup Brook, Australia 93 F2
Boz Burun, Turkey 41 F12
Boz Dağ, Turkey 39 D11
Boz Dağları, Turkey 39 C10
Bozburun, Turkey 39 E10
Bozcaada, Turkey 39 B8
Bozdoğan, Turkey 39 D10
Bozeman, U.S.A. 114 D8
Bozen = Bolzano, Italy 29 B8
Boževac, Serbia, Yug. 40 B5
Bozkır, Turkey 72 D5
Bozkurt, Turkey 39 D11
Bozouls, France 20 D6
Bozoum, C.A.R. 84 C3
Bozova, Antalya, Turkey 39 D12
Bozova, Sanliurfa, Turkey 73 D8
Bozovici, Romania 42 F7
Bozüyük, Turkey 39 B12
Bra, Italy 28 D4
Braås, Sweden 11 G9
Brabant □, Belgium 17 D4
Brabant L., Canada 105 B8
Brabrand, Denmark 11 H4
Brač, Croatia 29 E13
Bracadale, L., U.K. 14 D2
Bracciano, Italy 29 F9
Bracciano, L. di, Italy 29 F9
Bracebridge, Canada 102 C4
Brach, Libya 79 C8
Bracieux, France 18 E8
Bräcke, Sweden 10 B9
Brackettville, U.S.A. 113 L4
Brački Kanal, Croatia 29 E13
Bracknell, U.K. 13 F7
Bracknell Forest □, U.K. 13 F7
Brad, Romania 42 D7
Brádano →, Italy 31 B9
Bradenton, U.S.A. 109 M4
Bradford, Canada 110 B5
Bradford, U.K. 12 D6
Bradford, Pa., U.S.A. 110 E6
Bradford, Vt., U.S.A. 111 C12
Bradley, Ark., U.S.A. 113 J8
Bradley, Calif., U.S.A. 116 K6
Bradley, S. Dak., U.S.A. 112 C6
Bradley Institute, Zimbabwe 87 F3
Bradore Bay, Canada 103 B8
Bradshaw, Australia 92 C5
Brady, U.S.A. 113 K5
Brædstrup, Denmark 11 J3
Braemar, Australia 95 E2
Braemar, U.K. 14 D5
Braeside, Canada 111 A8
Braga, Portugal 34 D2
Braga □, Portugal 34 D2
Bragadiru, Romania 43 G10
Bragado, Argentina 126 D3
Bragança, Brazil 125 D9
Bragança, Portugal 34 D4
Bragança □, Portugal 34 D4
Bragança Paulista, Brazil 127 A6
Brahmanbaria, Bangla. 67 H17
Brahmani →, India 67 J15
Brahmapur, India 67 K14
Brahmaputra →, India 69 H13
Braich-y-pwll, U.K. 12 E3
Braidwood, Australia 95 F4
Brăila, Romania 43 E12
Brăila □, Romania 43 E12
Brainerd, U.S.A. 112 B7
Braintree, U.K. 13 F8
Braintree, U.S.A. 111 D14
Brak →, S. Africa 88 D3
Brake, Germany 24 B4
Brakel, Germany 24 D5
Bräkne-Hoby, Sweden 11 H9
Brakwater, Namibia 88 C2
Brålanda, Sweden 11 F6
Bralorne, Canada 104 C4
Bramberg, Germany 25 E6
Bramdrupdam, Denmark 11 J3
Bramming, Denmark 11 J2
Brämön, Sweden 10 B11
Brampton, Canada 102 D4
Brampton, U.K. 12 C5
Bramsche, Germany 24 C3
Bramwell, Australia 94 A3
Branco →, Brazil 122 D4
Brande, Denmark 11 J3
Brandenburg = Neubrandenburg, Germany 24 B9
Brandenburg, Germany 24 C8
Brandenburg □, Germany 24 C9
Brandfort, S. Africa 88 D4
Brando, France 21 F13
Brandon, Canada 105 D9
Brandon, U.S.A. 111 C11
Brandon B., Ireland 15 D1
Brandon Mt., Ireland 15 D1
Brandsen, Argentina 126 D4
Brandvlei, S. Africa 88 E3
Brandýs nad Labem, Czech Rep. 26 A7
Brăneşti, Romania 43 F11
Branford, U.S.A. 111 E12
Braniewo, Poland 44 D6
Bransfield Str., Antarctica 5 C18
Brańsk, Poland 45 F9
Branson, Colo., U.S.A. 113 G3
Branson, Mo., U.S.A. 113 G8
Brantford, Canada 102 D3
Brantôme, France 20 C4
Branxholme, Australia 95 F3
Branzi, Italy 28 B6
Bras d'Or, L., Canada 103 C7
Brasil, Planalto, Brazil 122 E6
Brasiléia, Brazil 124 F5
Brasília, Brazil 125 G9
Brasília Legal, Brazil 125 D7
Braslaw, Belarus 9 J22
Braslovče, Slovenia 29 B12
Braşov, Romania 43 E10
Braşov □, Romania 43 E10
Brass, Nigeria 83 E6
Brass →, Nigeria 83 E6
Brassac-les-Mines, France 20 C7
Brasschaat, Belgium 17 C4
Brassey, Banjaran, Malaysia 62 D5
Brassey Ra., Australia 93 E3
Brasstown Bald, U.S.A. 109 H4
Brastad, Sweden 11 F5
Brastavătu, Romania 43 G9
Bratan = Morozov, Bulgaria 41 D9
Brateş, Romania 43 E11
Bratislava, Slovak Rep. 27 C10
Bratislavský □, Slovak Rep. 27 C10
Bratsigovo, Bulgaria 41 D8
Bratsk, Russia 51 D11
Brattleboro, U.S.A. 111 D12
Bratunac, Bos.-H. 42 F4
Braunau, Austria 26 C6
Braunschweig, Germany 24 C6
Braunton, U.K. 13 F3
Bravicea, Moldova 43 C13
Bråviken, Sweden 11 F10
Bravo del Norte →, Mexico 118 B5
Bravo del Norte, Rio → = Grande, Rio →, U.S.A. 113 N6
Brawley, U.S.A. 117 N11
Bray, Ireland 15 C5
Bray, Mt., Australia 94 A1
Bray-sur-Seine, France 19 D10
Brazeau →, Canada 104 C5
Brazil, U.S.A. 108 F2
Brazil ■, S. Amer. 125 F9
Brazilian Highlands = Brasil, Planalto, Brazil 122 E6
Brazo Sur →, S. Amer. 126 B4
Brazos →, U.S.A. 113 L7
Brazzaville, Congo 84 E3
Brčko, Bos.-H. 42 F3
Brda →, Poland 45 E5
Brdy, Czech Rep. 26 B6
Breadalbane, Australia 94 C2
Breaden, L., Australia 93 E4
Breaksea Sd., N.Z. 91 L1
Bream B., N.Z. 91 F5
Bream Hd., N.Z. 91 F5
Breas, Chile 126 B1
Breaza, Romania 43 E10
Brebes, Indonesia 63 G13
Brechin, Canada 110 B5
Brechin, U.K. 14 E6
Brecht, Belgium 17 C4
Breckenridge, Colo., U.S.A. 114 G10
Breckenridge, Minn., U.S.A. 112 B6
Breckenridge, Tex., U.S.A. 113 J5
Breckland, U.K. 13 E8
Břeclav, Czech Rep. 27 C9
Brecon, U.K. 13 F4
Brecon Beacons, U.K. 13 F4
Breda, Neths. 17 C4
Bredaryd, Sweden 11 G7
Bredasdorp, S. Africa 88 E3
Bredbo, Australia 95 F4
Bredebro, Denmark 11 J2
Bredstedt, Germany 24 A4
Bree, Belgium 17 C5
Bregalnica →, Macedonia 40 E6
Bregenz, Austria 26 D2
Bregovo, Bulgaria 40 B6
Bréhal, France 18 D5
Bréhat, Î. de, France 18 D4
Breiðafjörður, Iceland 8 D2

Breil-sur-Roya, *France* 21 E11
Breisach, *Germany* 25 G3
Brejo, *Brazil* 125 D10
Bremen, *Germany* 24 B4
Bremen □, *Germany* 24 B4
Bremer I., *Australia* 94 A2
Bremerhaven, *Germany* 24 B4
Bremerton, *U.S.A.* 116 C4
Bremervörde, *Germany* 24 B5
Brenes, *Spain* 35 H5
Brenham, *U.S.A.* 113 K6
Brenne, *France* 20 B5
Brennerpass, *Austria* 26 D4
Breno, *Italy* 28 C7
Brent, *Canada* 102 C4
Brenta →, *Italy* 29 C9
Brentwood, *U.K.* 13 F8
Brentwood, *U.S.A.* 111 F11
Bréscia, *Italy* 28 C7
Breskens, *Neths.* 17 C3
Breslau = Wrocław, *Poland* 45 G4
Bresle →, *France* 18 B8
Bressanone, *Italy* 29 B8
Bressay, *U.K.* 14 A7
Bresse, *France* 19 F12
Bressuire, *France* 18 F6
Brest, *Belarus* 47 F2
Brest, *France* 18 D2
Brest-Litovsk = Brest, *Belarus* 47 F2
Bretagne, *France* 18 D3
Bretçu, *Romania* 43 D11
Bretenoux, *France* 20 D5
Breteuil, *Eure, France* 18 D7
Breteuil, *Oise, France* 19 C9
Breton, *Canada* 104 C6
Breton, Pertuis, *France* 20 B2
Breton Sd., *U.S.A.* 113 L10
Brett, C., *N.Z.* 91 F5
Bretten, *Germany* 25 F4
Breuil-Cervínia, *Italy* 28 C4
Brevard, *U.S.A.* 109 H4
Breves, *Brazil* 125 D8
Brewarrina, *Australia* 95 E4
Brewer, *U.S.A.* 103 D6
Brewer, Mt., *U.S.A.* 116 J8
Brewster, *N.Y., U.S.A.* 111 E11
Brewster, *Wash., U.S.A.* 114 B4
Brewster, Kap, *Greenland* 4 B6
Brewton, *U.S.A.* 109 K2
Breyten, *S. Africa* 89 D5
Breza, *Bos.-H.* 42 F3
Brezhnev = Naberezhnyye Chelny, *Russia* 48 C11
Brežice, *Slovenia* 29 C12
Březnice, *Czech Rep.* 26 B6
Breznik, *Bulgaria* 40 D6
Brezno, *Slovak Rep.* 27 C12
Brezoi, *Romania* 43 E9
Brezovo, *Bulgaria* 41 D9
Briançon, *France* 21 D10
Briare, *France* 19 E9
Briático, *Italy* 31 D9
Bribie I., *Australia* 95 D5
Briceni, *Moldova* 43 B12
Bricquebec, *France* 18 C5
Bridgehampton, *U.S.A.* 111 F12
Bridgend, *U.K.* 13 F4
Bridgend □, *U.K.* 13 F4
Bridgeport, *Calif., U.S.A.* 116 G7
Bridgeport, *Conn., U.S.A.* 111 E11
Bridgeport, *Nebr., U.S.A.* 112 E3
Bridgeport, *Tex., U.S.A.* 113 J6
Bridger, *U.S.A.* 114 D9
Bridgeton, *U.S.A.* 108 F8
Bridgetown, *Australia* 93 F2
Bridgetown, *Barbados* 121 D8
Bridgetown, *Canada* 103 D6
Bridgewater, *Canada* 103 D7
Bridgewater, *Mass., U.S.A.* 111 E14
Bridgewater, *S. Dak., U.S.A.* 112 D6
Bridgewater, C., *Australia* 95 F3
Bridgnorth, *U.K.* 13 E5
Bridgton, *U.S.A.* 111 B14
Bridgwater, *U.K.* 13 F5
Bridgwater B., *U.K.* 13 F4
Bridlington, *U.K.* 12 C7
Bridlington B., *U.K.* 12 C7
Bridport, *Australia* 94 G4
Bridport, *U.K.* 13 G5
Briec, *France* 18 D2
Brienne-le-Château, *France* 19 D11
Brienon-sur-Armançon, *France* 19 E10
Brienz, *Switz.* 25 J4
Brienzersee, *Switz.* 25 J3
Brig, *Switz.* 25 J3
Brigg, *U.K.* 12 D7
Briggsdale, *U.S.A.* 112 E2
Brigham City, *U.S.A.* 114 F7
Bright, *Australia* 95 F4
Brighton, *Australia* 95 F2
Brighton, *Canada* 102 D4
Brighton, *U.K.* 13 G7
Brighton, *U.S.A.* 112 F2
Brignogan-Plage, *France* 18 D2
Brignoles, *France* 21 E10
Brihuega, *Spain* 32 E2
Brikama, *Gambia* 82 C1
Brilliant, *Canada* 104 D5
Brilliant, *U.S.A.* 110 F4
Brilon, *Germany* 24 D4
Bríndisi, *Italy* 31 B10
Brinje, *Croatia* 29 D12
Brinkley, *U.S.A.* 113 H9
Brinkworth, *Australia* 95 E2
Brinnon, *U.S.A.* 116 C4
Brion, I., *Canada* 103 C7
Brionne, *France* 18 C7
Brionski, *Croatia* 29 D10
Brioude, *France* 20 C7
Briouze, *France* 18 D6
Brisbane, *Australia* 95 D5
Brisbane →, *Australia* 95 D5
Brisighella, *Italy* 29 D8
Bristol, *U.K.* 13 F5
Bristol, *Conn., U.S.A.* 111 E12
Bristol, *Pa., U.S.A.* 111 F10
Bristol, *R.I., U.S.A.* 111 E13
Bristol, *S. Dak., U.S.A.* 112 C6
Bristol, *Tenn., U.S.A.* 109 G4
Bristol, City of □, *U.K.* 13 F5
Bristol B., *U.S.A.* 100 C4
Bristol Channel, *U.K.* 13 F3
Bristol I., *Antarctica* 5 B1
Bristol L., *U.S.A.* 115 J5
Bristow, *U.S.A.* 113 H6
British Columbia □, *Canada* 104 C3
British Isles, *Europe* 6 E5
Brits, *S. Africa* 89 D4
Britstown, *S. Africa* 88 E3
Britt, *Canada* 102 C3
Brittany = Bretagne, *France* 18 D3
Britton, *U.S.A.* 112 C6
Brive-la-Gaillarde, *France* 20 C5
Briviesca, *Spain* 34 C7
Brixen = Bressanone, *Italy* 29 B8
Brixham, *U.K.* 13 G4
Brixton, *Australia* 94 C3
Brnaze, *Croatia* 29 E13
Brno, *Czech Rep.* 27 B9
Broad →, *U.S.A.* 109 J5
Broad Arrow, *Australia* 93 F3
Broad B., *U.K.* 14 C2
Broad Haven, *Ireland* 15 B2
Broad Law, *U.K.* 14 F5
Broad Sd., *Australia* 94 C4
Broadhurst Ra., *Australia* 92 D3
Broads, The, *U.K.* 12 E9
Broadus, *U.S.A.* 112 C2
Broadview, *Canada* 105 C8
Broager, *Denmark* 11 K3
Broby, *Sweden* 11 H8
Broceni, *Latvia* 44 B9
Brochet, *Canada* 105 B8
Brochet, L., *Canada* 105 B8
Brock, *Canada* 105 C7
Brocken, *Germany* 24 D6
Brockport, *U.S.A.* 110 C7
Brockton, *U.S.A.* 111 D13
Brockville, *Canada* 102 D4
Brockway, *Mont., U.S.A.* 112 B2
Brockway, *Pa., U.S.A.* 110 E6
Brocton, *U.S.A.* 110 D5
Brod, *Macedonia* 40 E5
Brodarevo, *Serbia, Yug.* 40 C3
Brodeur Pen., *Canada* 101 A11
Brodick, *U.K.* 14 F3
Brodnica, *Poland* 45 E6
Brody, *Ukraine* 47 G3
Brogan, *U.S.A.* 114 D5
Broglie, *France* 18 C7
Brok, *Poland* 45 F8
Broken Arrow, *U.S.A.* 113 G7
Broken Bow, *Nebr., U.S.A.* 112 E5
Broken Bow, *Okla., U.S.A.* 113 H7
Broken Hill = Kabwe, *Zambia* 87 E2
Broken Hill, *Australia* 95 E3
Brokind, *Sweden* 11 F9
Bromley, *U.K.* 13 F8
Bromölla, *Sweden* 11 H8
Bromsgrove, *U.K.* 13 E5
Brønderslev, *Denmark* 11 G3
Brong-Ahafo □, *Ghana* 82 D4
Broni, *Italy* 28 C6
Bronkhorstspruit, *S. Africa* 89 D4
Brønnøysund, *Norway* 8 D15
Bronte, *Italy* 31 E7
Bronte, *U.S.A.* 113 K4
Bronte Park, *Australia* 94 G4
Brook Park, *U.S.A.* 110 E4
Brookfield, *U.S.A.* 112 F8
Brookhaven, *U.S.A.* 113 K9
Brookings, *Oreg., U.S.A.* 114 E1
Brookings, *S. Dak., U.S.A.* 112 C6
Brooklin, *Canada* 110 C6
Brooklyn Park, *U.S.A.* 112 C8
Brookmere, *Canada* 104 D4
Brooks, *Canada* 104 C6
Brooks B., *Canada* 104 C3
Brooks L., *Canada* 105 A7
Brooks Range, *U.S.A.* 100 B5
Brooksville, *U.S.A.* 109 L4
Brookville, *U.S.A.* 108 F3
Brooloo, *Australia* 95 D5
Broom, L., *U.K.* 14 D3
Broome, *Australia* 92 C3
Broomehill, *Australia* 93 F2
Broons, *France* 18 D4
Brora, *U.K.* 14 C5
Brora →, *U.K.* 14 C5
Brørup, *Denmark* 11 J2
Brösarp, *Sweden* 11 J8
Brosna →, *Ireland* 15 C4
Broşteni, *Mehedinţi, Romania* 42 F7
Broşteni, *Suceava, Romania* 43 C10
Brothers, *U.S.A.* 114 E3
Brou, *France* 18 D8
Brouage, *France* 20 C2
Brough, *U.K.* 12 C5
Brough Hd., *U.K.* 14 B5
Broughton Island, *Canada* 101 B13
Broumov, *Czech Rep.* 27 A9
Brovary, *Ukraine* 47 G6
Brovst, *Denmark* 11 G3
Browerville, *U.S.A.* 112 B7
Brown, Pt., *Australia* 95 E1
Brown Willy, *U.K.* 13 G3
Brownfield, *U.S.A.* 113 J3
Browning, *U.S.A.* 114 B7
Brownlee, *Canada* 105 C7
Brownsville, *Oreg., U.S.A.* 114 D2
Brownsville, *Tenn., U.S.A.* 113 H10
Brownsville, *Tex., U.S.A.* 113 N6
Brownwood, *U.S.A.* 113 K5
Brownwood, L., *U.S.A.* 113 K5
Browse I., *Australia* 92 B3
Bruas, *Malaysia* 65 K3
Bruay-la-Buissière, *France* 19 B9
Bruce, Mt., *Australia* 92 D2
Bruce Pen., *Canada* 110 B3
Bruce Rock, *Australia* 93 F2
Bruche →, *France* 19 D14
Bruchsal, *Germany* 25 F4
Bruck an der Leitha, *Austria* 27 C9
Bruck an der Mur, *Austria* 26 D8
Brue →, *U.K.* 13 F5
Bruges = Brugge, *Belgium* 17 C3
Brugg, *Switz.* 25 H4
Brugge, *Belgium* 17 C3
Brûlé, *Canada* 104 C5
Brûlon, *France* 18 E6
Brumado, *Brazil* 125 F10
Brumath, *France* 19 D14
Brumunddal, *Norway* 9 F14
Brunchilly, *Australia* 94 B1
Brundidge, *U.S.A.* 109 K3
Bruneau, *U.S.A.* 114 E6
Bruneau →, *U.S.A.* 114 E6
Bruneck = Brunico, *Italy* 29 B8
Brunei = Bandar Seri Begawan, *Brunei* 62 D5
Brunei ■, *Asia* 62 D5
Brunette Downs, *Australia* 94 B2
Brunflo, *Sweden* 10 A8
Brunico, *Italy* 29 B8
Brunna, *Sweden* 10 E11
Brunnen, *Switz.* 25 J4
Brunner, L., *N.Z.* 91 K3
Bruno, *Canada* 105 C7
Brunsbüttel, *Germany* 24 B5
Brunssum, *Neths.* 17 D5
Brunswick = Braunschweig, *Germany* 24 C6
Brunswick, *Ga., U.S.A.* 109 K5
Brunswick, *Maine, U.S.A.* 103 D6
Brunswick, *Md., U.S.A.* 108 F7
Brunswick, *Mo., U.S.A.* 112 F8
Brunswick, *Ohio, U.S.A.* 110 E3
Brunswick, Pen. de, *Chile* 128 G2
Brunswick B., *Australia* 92 C3
Brunswick Junction, *Australia* 93 F2
Bruntál, *Czech Rep.* 27 B10
Bruny I., *Australia* 94 G4
Brus Laguna, *Honduras* 120 C3
Brusartsi, *Bulgaria* 40 C7
Brush, *U.S.A.* 112 E3
Brushton, *U.S.A.* 111 B10
Brusio, *Switz.* 25 J6
Brusque, *Brazil* 127 B6
Brussel, *Belgium* 17 D4
Brussels = Brussel, *Belgium* 17 D4
Brussels, *Canada* 110 C3
Brusy, *Poland* 44 E4
Bruthen, *Australia* 95 F4
Bruxelles = Brussel, *Belgium* 17 D4
Bruyères, *France* 19 D13
Bruz, *France* 18 D5
Brwinów, *Poland* 45 F7
Bryagovo, *Bulgaria* 41 E9
Bryan, *Ohio, U.S.A.* 108 E3
Bryan, *Tex., U.S.A.* 113 K6
Bryan, Mt., *Australia* 95 E2
Bryanka, *Ukraine* 47 H10
Bryansk, *Bryansk, Russia* 47 F8
Bryansk, *Dagestan, Russia* 49 H8
Bryanskoye = Bryansk, *Russia* 49 H8
Bryant, *U.S.A.* 112 C6
Bryne, *Norway* 9 G11
Bryson City, *U.S.A.* 109 H4
Bryukhovetskaya, *Russia* 47 K10
Brza Palanka, *Serbia, Yug.* 40 B6
Brzeg, *Poland* 45 H4
Brzeg Dolny, *Poland* 45 G3
Brześć Kujawski, *Poland* 45 F5
Brzesko, *Poland* 45 J7
Brzeziny, *Poland* 45 G6
Brzozów, *Poland* 45 J9
Bsharri, *Lebanon* 75 A5
Bū Baqarah, *U.A.E.* 71 E8
Bu Craa, *W. Sahara* 78 C3
Bū Ḩasā, *U.A.E.* 71 F7
Bua, *Sweden* 11 G6
Bua Yai, *Thailand* 64 E4
Buapinang, *Indonesia* 63 E6
Buba, *Guinea-Biss.* 82 C2
Bubanza, *Burundi* 86 C2
Būbiyān, *Kuwait* 71 D6
Buca, *Turkey* 39 C9
Bucak, *Turkey* 39 D12
Bucaramanga, *Colombia* 124 B4
Bucas Grande I., *Phil.* 61 G6
Buccaneer Arch., *Australia* 92 C3
Buccino, *Italy* 31 B8
Bucecea, *Romania* 43 C11
Buchach, *Ukraine* 47 H3
Buchan, *U.K.* 14 D6
Buchan Ness, *U.K.* 14 D7
Buchanan, *Canada* 105 C8
Buchanan, *Liberia* 82 D2
Buchanan, L., *Queens., Australia* 94 C4
Buchanan, L., *W. Austral., Australia* 93 E3
Buchanan, L., *U.S.A.* 113 K5
Buchanan Cr. →, *Australia* 94 B2
Buchans, *Canada* 103 C8
Bucharest = Bucureşti, *Romania* 43 F11
Buchen, *Germany* 25 F5
Buchholz, *Germany* 24 B5
Buchloe, *Germany* 25 G6
Buchon, Pt., *U.S.A.* 116 K6
Buciumi, *Romania* 42 C8
Bückeburg, *Germany* 24 C5
Buckeye, *U.S.A.* 115 K7
Buckhannon, *U.S.A.* 108 F5
Buckhaven, *U.K.* 14 E5
Buckie, *U.K.* 14 D6
Buckingham, *Canada* 102 C4
Buckingham, *U.K.* 13 F7
Buckingham B., *Australia* 94 A2
Buckinghamshire □, *U.K.* 13 F7
Buckle Hd., *Australia* 92 B4
Buckleboo, *Australia* 95 E2
Buckley, *U.K.* 12 D4
Buckley, *U.S.A.* 114 C2
Buckley →, *Australia* 94 C2
Bucklin, *U.S.A.* 113 G5
Bucks L., *U.S.A.* 116 F5
Bucquoy, *France* 19 B9
Buctouche, *Canada* 103 C7
Bucureşti, *Romania* 43 F11
Bucyrus, *U.S.A.* 108 E4
Budacu, Vf., *Romania* 43 C10
Budalin, *Burma* 67 H19
Budaörs, *Hungary* 42 C3
Budapest, *Hungary* 42 C4
Budapest □, *Hungary* 42 C4
Budaun, *India* 69 E8
Budd Coast, *Antarctica* 5 C8
Buddusò, *Italy* 30 B2
Bude, *U.K.* 13 G3
Budennovsk, *Russia* 49 H7
Budeşti, *Romania* 43 F11
Budge Budge = Baj Baj, *India* 69 H13
Budgewoi, *Australia* 95 E5
Budia, *Spain* 32 E2
Büdingen, *Germany* 25 E5
Budjala, *Dem. Rep. of the Congo* 84 D3
Budoni, *Italy* 30 B2
Búdrio, *Italy* 29 D8
Budva, *Montenegro, Yug.* 40 D2
Budzyń, *Poland* 45 F3
Buea, *Cameroon* 83 E6
Buellton, *U.S.A.* 117 L6
Buena Park, *U.S.A.* 117 M9
Buena Vista, *Colo., U.S.A.* 115 G10
Buena Vista, *Va., U.S.A.* 108 G6
Buena Vista L., *U.S.A.* 117 K7
Buenaventura, *Colombia* 124 C3
Buenaventura, *Mexico* 118 B3
Buendía, Embalse de, *Spain* 32 E2
Buenos Aires, *Argentina* 126 C4
Buenos Aires, *Costa Rica* 120 E3
Buenos Aires □, *Argentina* 126 D4
Buenos Aires, L., *Chile* 128 F2
Buffalo, *Mo., U.S.A.* 113 G8
Buffalo, *N.Y., U.S.A.* 110 D6
Buffalo, *Okla., U.S.A.* 113 G5
Buffalo, *S. Dak., U.S.A.* 112 C3
Buffalo, *Wyo., U.S.A.* 114 D10
Buffalo →, *Canada* 104 A5
Buffalo Head Hills, *Canada* 104 B5
Buffalo L., *Canada* 104 C6
Buffalo Narrows, *Canada* 105 B7
Buffels →, *S. Africa* 88 D2
Buford, *U.S.A.* 109 H4
Bug → = Buh →, *Ukraine* 47 J6
Bug →, *Poland* 45 F8
Buga, *Colombia* 124 C3
Buganda, *Uganda* 86 C3
Buganga, *Uganda* 86 C3
Bugasong, *Phil.* 61 F5
Bugeat, *France* 20 C5
Bugel, Tanjung, *Indonesia* 63 G14
Bugibba, *Malta* 36 D1
Bugojno, *Bos.-H.* 42 F2
Bugsuk, *Phil.* 61 G2
Buguma, *Nigeria* 83 E6
Bugun Shara, *Mongolia* 60 B5
Buguruslan, *Russia* 50 D6
Buh →, *Ukraine* 47 J6
Buharkent, *Turkey* 39 D10
Buheirat-Murrat-el-Kubra, *Egypt* 80 H8
Bühl, *Germany* 25 G4
Buhl, *Idaho, U.S.A.* 114 E6
Buhl, *Minn., U.S.A.* 112 B8
Buhuşi, *Romania* 43 D11
Buick, *U.S.A.* 113 G9
Builth Wells, *U.K.* 13 E4
Buinsk, *Russia* 48 C9
Buir Nur, *Mongolia* 60 B6
Buis-les-Baronnies, *France* 21 D9
Buitrago = Buitrago del Lozoya, *Spain* 34 E7
Buitrago del Lozoya, *Spain* 34 E7
Bujalance, *Spain* 35 H6
Bujanovac, *Serbia, Yug.* 40 D5
Bujaraloz, *Spain* 32 D4
Buje, *Croatia* 29 C10
Bujumbura, *Burundi* 86 C2
Bük, *Hungary* 42 C1
Buk, *Poland* 45 F3
Bukachacha, *Russia* 51 D12
Bukama, *Dem. Rep. of the Congo* 87 D2
Bukavu, *Dem. Rep. of the Congo* 86 C2
Bukene, *Tanzania* 86 C3
Bukhara = Bukhoro, *Uzbekistan* 50 F7
Bukhoro, *Uzbekistan* 50 F7
Bukima, *Tanzania* 86 C3
Bukit Mertajam, *Malaysia* 65 K3
Bukittinggi, *Indonesia* 62 E2
Bükk, *Hungary* 42 B5
Bukoba, *Tanzania* 86 C3
Bukoba □, *Tanzania* 86 C3
Bukuru, *Nigeria* 83 D6
Bukuya, *Uganda* 86 B3
Bula, *Guinea-Biss.* 82 C1
Bula, *Indonesia* 63 E8
Bülach, *Switz.* 25 H4
Bulahdelah, *Australia* 95 E5
Bulan, *Phil.* 61 E5
Bulancak, *Turkey* 73 B8
Bulandshahr, *India* 68 E7
Bulanık, *Turkey* 73 C10
Bûlâq, *Egypt* 80 B3
Bulawayo, *Zimbabwe* 87 G2
Buldan, *Turkey* 39 C10
Bulgan, *Mongolia* 60 B5
Bulgar, *Russia* 48 C9
Bulgaria ■, *Europe* 41 D9
Bulgheria, Monte, *Italy* 31 B8
Bulgroo, *Australia* 95 D3
Bulgunnia, *Australia* 95 E1
Bulgurca, *Turkey* 39 C9
Buli, Teluk, *Indonesia* 63 D7
Buliluyan, C., *Phil.* 61 G2
Bulki, *Ethiopia* 81 F4
Bulkley →, *Canada* 104 B3
Bull Shoals L., *U.S.A.* 113 G8
Bullaque →, *Spain* 35 G6
Bullara, *Australia* 92 D1
Bullaring, *Australia* 93 F2
Bullas, *Spain* 33 G3
Bulle, *Switz.* 25 J3
Bulli, *Australia* 95 E5
Büllingen, *Belgium* 17 D6
Bullock Creek, *Australia* 94 B3
Bulloo →, *Australia* 95 D3
Bulloo Downs, *Queens., Australia* 95 D3
Bulloo Downs, *W. Austral., Australia* 92 D2
Bulloo L., *Australia* 95 D3
Bulls, *N.Z.* 91 J5
Bully-les-Mines, *France* 19 B9
Bulnes, *Chile* 126 D1
Bulqiza, *Albania* 40 E4
Bulsar = Valsad, *India* 66 J8
Bultfontein, *S. Africa* 88 D4
Bulukumba, *Indonesia* 63 F6
Bulun, *Russia* 51 B13
Bumba, *Dem. Rep. of the Congo* 84 D4
Bumbeşti-Jiu, *Romania* 43 E8
Bumbiri I., *Tanzania* 86 C3
Bumhpa Bum, *Burma* 67 F20
Bumi →, *Zimbabwe* 87 F2
Buna, *Kenya* 86 B4
Bunawan, *Agusan del S., Phil.* 61 G6
Bunawan, *Davao del S., Phil.* 61 H6
Bunazi, *Tanzania* 86 C3
Bunbury, *Australia* 93 F2
Bunclody, *Ireland* 15 D5
Buncrana, *Ireland* 15 A4
Bundaberg, *Australia* 95 C5
Bünde, *Germany* 24 C4
Bundey →, *Australia* 94 C2
Bundi, *India* 68 G6
Bundooma, *Australia* 94 C1
Bundoran, *Ireland* 15 B3
Bundukia, *Sudan* 81 F3
Bung Kan, *Thailand* 64 C4
Bungatakada, *Japan* 55 H5
Bungay, *U.K.* 13 E9
Bungil Cr. →, *Australia* 94 D4
Bungo-Suidō, *Japan* 55 H6
Bungoma, *Kenya* 86 B3
Bungu, *Tanzania* 86 D4
Bunia, *Dem. Rep. of the Congo* 86 B3
Bunji, *Pakistan* 69 B6
Bunkie, *U.S.A.* 113 K8
Bunnell, *U.S.A.* 109 L5
Buñol, *Spain* 33 F4
Buntok, *Indonesia* 62 E4
Bununu, *Nigeria* 83 D6
Bununu Dass, *Nigeria* 83 C6
Bünyan, *Turkey* 72 C6
Bunyu, *Indonesia* 62 D5
Bunza, *Nigeria* 83 C5
Buol, *Indonesia* 63 D6

Buon Brieng, *Vietnam* 64 F7
Buon Ma Thuot, *Vietnam* 64 F7
Buong Long, *Cambodia* 64 F6
Buorkhaya, Mys, *Russia* 51 B14
Buqayq, *Si. Arabia* 71 E6
Buqbuq, *Egypt* 80 A2
Bur Acaba, *Somali Rep.* 74 G3
Bûr Fuad, *Egypt* 80 H8
Bûr Safâga, *Egypt* 80 B3
Bûr Sa'îd, *Egypt* 80 H8
Bûr Sûdân, *Sudan* 80 D4
Bûr Taufiq, *Egypt* 80 J8
Bura, *Kenya* 86 C4
Burao, *Somali Rep.* 74 F4
Burāq, *Syria* 75 B5
Buras, *U.S.A.* 113 L10
Buraydah, *Si. Arabia* 70 E5
Burbank, *U.S.A.* 117 L8
Burcher, *Australia* 95 E4
Burdekin →, *Australia* 94 B4
Burdett, *Canada* 104 D6
Burdur, *Turkey* 39 D12
Burdur □, *Turkey* 39 D12
Burdur Gölü, *Turkey* 39 D12
Burdwan = Barddhaman, *India* 69 H12
Bure, *Ethiopia* 81 E4
Bure →, *U.K.* 12 E9
Büren, *Germany* 24 D4
Bureya →, *Russia* 51 E13
Burford, *Canada* 110 C4
Burg, *Germany* 24 C7
Burg auf Fehmarn, *Germany* 24 A7
Burg el Arab, *Egypt* 80 H6
Burg et Tuyur, *Sudan* 80 C2
Burg Stargard, *Germany* 24 B9
Burgas, *Bulgaria* 41 D11
Burgas □, *Bulgaria* 41 D10
Burgaski Zaliv, *Bulgaria* 41 D11
Burgdorf, *Germany* 24 C6
Burgdorf, *Switz.* 25 H3
Burgenland □, *Austria* 27 D9
Burgeo, *Canada* 103 C8
Burgersdorp, *S. Africa* 88 E4
Burges, Mt., *Australia* 93 F3
Burghausen, *Germany* 25 G8
Búrgio, *Italy* 30 E6
Burglengenfeld, *Germany* 25 F8
Burgohondo, *Spain* 34 E6
Burgos, *Spain* 34 C7
Burgos □, *Spain* 34 C7
Burgstädt, *Germany* 24 E8
Burgsvik, *Sweden* 11 G12
Burguillos del Cerro, *Spain* 35 G4
Burgundy = Bourgogne, *France* 19 F11
Burhaniye, *Turkey* 39 B8
Burhanpur, *India* 66 J10
Buri Pen., *Eritrea* 81 D4
Burias, *Phil.* 61 E5
Burica, Pta., *Costa Rica* 120 E3
Burigi, L., *Tanzania* 86 C3
Burin, *Canada* 103 C8
Buriram, *Thailand* 64 E4
Burj Sāfitā, *Syria* 70 C3
Burji, *Ethiopia* 81 F4
Burkburnett, *U.S.A.* 113 H5
Burke, *U.S.A.* 114 C6
Burke →, *Australia* 94 C2
Burketown, *Australia* 94 B2
Burkina Faso ■, *Africa* 82 C4
Burk's Falls, *Canada* 102 C4
Burlada, *Spain* 32 C3
Burley, *U.S.A.* 114 E7
Burlingame, *U.S.A.* 116 H4
Burlington, *Canada* 110 C5
Burlington, *Colo., U.S.A.* 112 F3
Burlington, *Iowa, U.S.A.* 112 E9
Burlington, *Kans., U.S.A.* 112 F7
Burlington, *N.C., U.S.A.* 109 G6
Burlington, *N.J., U.S.A.* 111 F10
Burlington, *Vt., U.S.A.* 111 B11
Burlington, *Wash., U.S.A.* 116 B4
Burlington, *Wis., U.S.A.* 108 D1
Burlyu-Tyube, *Kazakstan* 50 E8
Burma ■, *Asia* 67 J20
Burnaby I., *Canada* 104 C2
Burnet, *U.S.A.* 113 K5
Burney, *U.S.A.* 114 F3
Burngup, *Australia* 93 F2
Burnham, *U.S.A.* 110 F7
Burnham-on-Sea, *U.K.* 13 F5
Burnie, *Australia* 94 G4
Burnley, *U.K.* 12 D5
Burns, *Oreg., U.S.A.* 114 E4
Burns, *Wyo., U.S.A.* 112 E2
Burns Lake, *Canada* 104 C3
Burnside →, *Canada* 100 B9
Burnside, L., *Australia* 93 E3
Burnsville, *U.S.A.* 112 C8
Burnt River, *Canada* 110 B6
Burntwood →, *Canada* 105 B9
Burntwood L., *Canada* 105 B8
Burqān, *Kuwait* 70 D5
Burqin, *China* 60 B3
Burra, *Australia* 95 E2
Burramurra, *Australia* 94 C2
Burray, *U.K.* 14 C6
Burreli, *Albania* 40 E4
Burren Junction, *Australia* 95 E4
Burrendong Dam, *Australia* 95 E4
Burriana, *Spain* 32 F4
Burrinjuck Res., *Australia* 95 F4
Burro, Serranías del, *Mexico* 118 B4
Burrow Hd., *U.K.* 14 G4
Burruyacú, *Argentina* 126 B3
Burry Port, *U.K.* 13 F3
Bursa, *Turkey* 41 F13
Burseryd, *Sweden* 11 G7
Burstall, *Canada* 105 C7
Burton L., *Canada* 102 B4
Burton upon Trent, *U.K.* 12 E6
Burtundy, *Australia* 95 E3
Buru, *Indonesia* 63 E7
Burullus, Bahra el, *Egypt* 80 H7
Burûn, Râs, *Egypt* 75 D2
Burundi ■, *Africa* 86 C3
Bururi, *Burundi* 86 C2
Burutu, *Nigeria* 83 D6
Burwell, *U.S.A.* 112 E5
Burwick, *U.K.* 14 C5
Bury, *U.K.* 12 D5
Bury St. Edmunds, *U.K.* 13 E8
Buryatia □, *Russia* 51 D12
Buryn, *Ukraine* 47 G7
Burzenin, *Poland* 45 G5
Busalla, *Italy* 28 D5
Busango Swamp, *Zambia* 87 E2
Buşayrah, *Syria* 70 C4
Buşayyah, *Iraq* 70 D5
Busca, *Italy* 28 D4
Bushati, *Albania* 40 E3
Būshehr, *Iran* 71 D6
Būshehr □, *Iran* 71 D6
Bushell, *Canada* 105 B7
Bushenyi, *Uganda* 86 C3
Bushire = Būshehr, *Iran* 71 D6
Bushnell, *Ill., U.S.A.* 112 E9
Bushnell, *Nebr., U.S.A.* 112 E3
Busia □, *Kenya* 86 B3
Busie, *Ghana* 82 C4
Businga, *Dem. Rep. of the Congo* 84 D4
Busko-Zdrój, *Poland* 45 H7
Busovača, *Bos.-H.* 42 F2
Buşra ash Shām, *Syria* 75 C5
Busselton, *Australia* 93 F2
Busseto, *Italy* 28 D7
Bussière-Badil, *France* 20 C4
Bussolengo, *Italy* 28 C7
Bussum, *Neths.* 17 B5
Buşteni, *Romania* 43 E10
Busto, C., *Spain* 34 B4
Busto Arsízio, *Italy* 28 C5
Busu-Djanoa, *Dem. Rep. of the Congo* 84 D4
Büsum, *Germany* 24 A4
Buta, *Dem. Rep. of the Congo* 86 B1
Butare, *Rwanda* 86 C2
Butaritari, *Kiribati* 96 G9
Bute, *U.K.* 14 F3
Bute Inlet, *Canada* 104 C4
Butemba, *Uganda* 86 B3
Butembo, *Dem. Rep. of the Congo* 86 B2
Buteni, *Romania* 42 D7
Butera, *Italy* 31 E7
Butha Qi, *China* 60 B7
Butiaba, *Uganda* 86 B3
Butler, *Mo., U.S.A.* 112 F7
Butler, *Pa., U.S.A.* 110 F5
Buton, *Indonesia* 63 F6
Butte, *Mont., U.S.A.* 114 C7
Butte, *Nebr., U.S.A.* 112 D5
Butte Creek →, *U.S.A.* 116 F5
Butterworth = Gcuwa, *S. Africa* 89 E4
Butterworth, *Malaysia* 65 K3
Buttevant, *Ireland* 15 D3
Buttfield, Mt., *Australia* 93 D4
Button B., *Canada* 105 B10
Buttonwillow, *U.S.A.* 117 K7
Butty Hd., *Australia* 93 F3
Butuan, *Phil.* 61 G6
Butuku-Luba, *Eq. Guin.* 83 E6
Butung = Buton, *Indonesia* 63 F6
Buturlinovka, *Russia* 48 E5
Butzbach, *Germany* 25 E4
Bützow, *Germany* 24 B7
Buxar, *India* 69 G10
Buxtehude, *Germany* 24 B5
Buxton, *U.K.* 12 D6
Buxy, *France* 19 F11
Buy, *Russia* 48 A5
Buynaksk, *Russia* 49 J8
Büyük Menderes →, *Turkey* 39 D9
Büyükçekmece, *Turkey* 41 E12
Büyükkarıştıran, *Turkey* 41 E11
Büyükkemikli Burnu, *Turkey* 41 F10
Büyükorhan, *Turkey* 39 B10
Büyükyoncalı, *Turkey* 41 E11
Buzançais, *France* 18 F8
Buzău, *Romania* 43 E11
Buzău □, *Romania* 43 E11
Buzău →, *Romania* 43 E12
Buzău, Pasul, *Romania* 43 E11
Buzen, *Japan* 55 H5
Buzet, *Croatia* 29 C10
Buzi →, *Mozam.* 87 F3
Buziaş, *Romania* 42 E6
Buzuluk, *Russia* 50 D6
Buzuluk →, *Russia* 48 E6
Buzzards Bay, *U.S.A.* 111 E14
Bwana Mkubwe, *Dem. Rep. of the Congo* 87 E2
Byala, *Ruse, Bulgaria* 41 C9
Byala, *Varna, Bulgaria* 41 D11
Byala Slatina, *Bulgaria* 40 C7
Byarezina →, *Belarus* 47 F6
Bychawa, *Poland* 45 G9
Byczyna, *Poland* 45 G5
Bydgoszcz, *Poland* 45 E5
Bydgoszcz □, *Poland* 45 E4
Byelarus = Belarus ■, *Europe* 46 F4
Byelorussia = Belarus ■, *Europe* 46 F4
Byers, *U.S.A.* 112 F2
Byesville, *U.S.A.* 110 G3
Byhalia, *U.S.A.* 113 H10
Bykhaw, *Belarus* 46 F6
Bykhov = Bykhaw, *Belarus* 46 F6
Bykovo, *Russia* 48 F7
Bylas, *U.S.A.* 115 K8
Bylot I., *Canada* 101 A12
Byrd, C., *Antarctica* 5 C17
Byro, *Australia* 93 E2
Byrock, *Australia* 95 E4
Byron Bay, *Australia* 95 D5
Byrranga, Gory, *Russia* 51 B11
Byrranga Mts. = Byrranga, Gory, *Russia* 51 B11
Byrum, *Denmark* 11 G5
Byske, *Sweden* 8 D19
Byske älv →, *Sweden* 8 D19
Bystrzyca →, *Lublin, Poland* 45 G9
Bystrzyca →, *Wrocław, Poland* 45 G3
Bystrzyca Kłodzka, *Poland* 45 H3
Bytča, *Slovak Rep.* 27 B11
Bytom, *Poland* 45 H5
Bytom Odrzański, *Poland* 45 G2
Bytów, *Poland* 44 D4
Byumba, *Rwanda* 86 C3
Bzenec, *Czech Rep.* 27 C10
Bzura →, *Poland* 45 F7

C

Ca →, *Vietnam* 64 C5
Ca Mau, *Vietnam* 65 H5
Ca Mau, Mui, *Vietnam* 65 H5
Ca Na, *Vietnam* 65 G7
Caacupé, *Paraguay* 126 B4
Caála, *Angola* 85 G3
Caamano Sd., *Canada* 104 C3
Caazapá, *Paraguay* 126 B4
Caazapá □, *Paraguay* 127 B4
Cabadbaran, *Phil.* 61 G6
Cabalian, *Phil.* 61 F6
Cabana, *Spain* 34 B2
Cabañaquinta, *Spain* 34 B5
Cabanatuan, *Phil.* 61 D4
Cabanes, *Spain* 32 E5
Cabano, *Canada* 103 C6
Čabar, *Croatia* 29 C11
Cabazon, *U.S.A.* 117 M10
Cabedelo, *Brazil* 125 E12
Cabeza del Buey, *Spain* 35 G5
Cabezón de la Sal, *Spain* 34 B6
Cabildo, *Chile* 126 C1
Cabimas, *Venezuela* 124 A4
Cabinda, *Angola* 84 F2
Cabinda □, *Angola* 84 F2
Cabinet Mts., *U.S.A.* 114 C6
Cabo Blanco, *Argentina* 128 F3
Cabo Frio, *Brazil* 127 A7
Cabo Pantoja, *Peru* 124 D3
Cabonga, Réservoir, *Canada* 102 C4
Cabool, *U.S.A.* 113 G8
Caboolture, *Australia* 95 D5
Cabora Bassa Dam = Cahora Bassa, Reprêsa de, *Mozam.* 87 F3
Caborca, *Mexico* 118 A2
Cabot, Mt., *U.S.A.* 111 B13
Cabot Str., *Canada* 103 C8
Cabra, *Spain* 35 H6
Cabra del Santo Cristo, *Spain* 35 H7
Cábras, *Italy* 30 C1
Cabrera, *Spain* 37 B9
Cabrera, Sierra, *Spain* 34 C4
Cabri, *Canada* 105 C7
Cabriel →, *Spain* 33 F3
Cabugao, *Phil.* 61 C4
Cacabelos, *Spain* 34 C4
Čačak, *Serbia, Yug.* 40 C4
Cáccamo, *Italy* 30 E6
Cacém, *Portugal* 35 G1
Cáceres, *Brazil* 124 G7
Cáceres, *Spain* 35 F4
Cáceres □, *Spain* 34 F5
Cache Bay, *Canada* 102 C4
Cache Cr. →, *U.S.A.* 116 G5
Cacheu, *Guinea-Biss.* 82 C1
Cachi, *Argentina* 126 B2
Cachimbo, Serra do, *Brazil* 125 E7
Cachoeira, *Brazil* 125 F11
Cachoeira de Itapemirim, *Brazil* 127 A7
Cachoeira do Sul, *Brazil* 127 C5
Cachopo, *Portugal* 35 H3
Cacoal, *Brazil* 124 F6
Cacólo, *Angola* 84 G3
Caconda, *Angola* 85 G3
Čadca, *Slovak Rep.* 27 B11
Caddo, *U.S.A.* 113 H6
Cadell Cr. →, *Australia* 94 C3
Cader Idris, *U.K.* 13 E4
Cadí, Sierra del, *Spain* 32 C6
Cadibarrawirracanna, L., *Australia* 95 D2
Cadillac, *Canada* 102 C4
Cadillac, *France* 20 D3
Cadillac, *U.S.A.* 108 C3
Cadiz, *Phil.* 61 F5
Cádiz, *Spain* 35 J4
Cadiz, *U.S.A.* 110 F4
Cádiz □, *Spain* 35 J5
Cádiz, G. de, *Spain* 35 J3
Cadney Park, *Australia* 95 D1
Cadomin, *Canada* 104 C5
Cadotte →, *Canada* 104 B5
Cadours, *France* 20 E5
Cadoux, *Australia* 93 F2
Caen, *France* 18 C6
Caernarfon, *U.K.* 12 D3
Caernarfon B., *U.K.* 12 D3
Caernarvon = Caernarfon, *U.K.* 12 D3
Caerphilly, *U.K.* 13 F4
Caerphilly □, *U.K.* 13 F4
Caesarea, *Israel* 75 C3
Caetité, *Brazil* 125 F10
Cafayate, *Argentina* 126 B2
Cafu, *Angola* 88 B2
Cagayan →, *Phil.* 61 B4
Cagayan de Oro, *Phil.* 61 G6
Cagayan Is., *Phil.* 61 G4
Cagayan Sulu I., *Phil.* 61 H3
Cagli, *Italy* 29 E9
Cágliari, *Italy* 30 C2
Cágliari, G. di, *Italy* 30 C2
Cagnano Varano, *Italy* 29 G12
Cagnes-sur-Mer, *France* 21 E11
Caguán →, *Colombia* 124 D4
Caguas, *Puerto Rico* 121 C6
Caha Mts., *Ireland* 15 E2
Cahama, *Angola* 88 B1
Caher, *Ireland* 15 D4
Caherciveen, *Ireland* 15 E1
Cahora Bassa, Reprêsa de, *Mozam.* 87 F3
Cahore Pt., *Ireland* 15 D5
Cahors, *France* 20 D5
Cahul, *Moldova* 43 E13
Cai Bau, Dao, *Vietnam* 64 B6
Cai Nuoc, *Vietnam* 65 H5
Caia, *Mozam.* 87 F4
Caianda, *Angola* 87 E1
Caibarién, *Cuba* 120 B4
Caibiran, *Phil.* 61 F6
Caicara, *Venezuela* 124 B5
Caicó, *Brazil* 125 E11
Caicos Is., *W. Indies* 121 B5
Caicos Passage, *W. Indies* 121 B5
Căinari, *Moldova* 43 D14
Caird Coast, *Antarctica* 5 D1
Cairn Gorm, *U.K.* 14 D5
Cairngorm Mts., *U.K.* 14 D5
Cairnryan, *U.K.* 14 G3
Cairns, *Australia* 94 B4
Cairo = El Qâhira, *Egypt* 80 H7
Cairo, *Ga., U.S.A.* 109 K3
Cairo, *Ill., U.S.A.* 113 G10
Cairo Montenotte, *Italy* 28 D5
Caithness, Ord of, *U.K.* 14 C5
Cajamarca, *Peru* 124 E3
Cajarc, *France* 20 D5
Cajàzeiras, *Brazil* 125 E11
Čajetina, *Serbia, Yug.* 40 C3
Çakirgol, *Turkey* 73 B8
Çakırlar, *Turkey* 39 E12
Čakovec, *Croatia* 29 B13
Çal, *Turkey* 39 C11
Cala, *Spain* 35 H4
Cala →, *Spain* 35 H4
Cala Cadolar, Punta de = Rotja, Pta., *Spain* 33 G6
Cala d'Or, *Spain* 37 B10
Cala en Porter, *Spain* 37 B11
Cala Figuera, C. de, *Spain* 37 B9
Cala Forcat, *Spain* 37 B10
Cala Major, *Spain* 37 B9
Cala Mezquida = Sa Mesquida, *Spain* 37 B11
Cala Millor, *Spain* 37 B10
Cala Ratjada, *Spain* 37 B10
Cala Santa Galdana, *Spain* 37 B10
Calabanga, *Phil.* 61 E5
Calabar, *Nigeria* 83 E6
Calabozo, *Venezuela* 124 B5
Calábria □, *Italy* 31 C9
Calaburras, Pta. de, *Spain* 35 J6
Calaceite, *Spain* 32 D5
Calacuccia, *France* 21 F13
Calafat, *Romania* 42 G7
Calafate, *Argentina* 128 G2
Calafell, *Spain* 32 D6
Calahorra, *Spain* 32 C3
Calais, *France* 19 B8
Calais, *U.S.A.* 103 C6
Calalaste, Cord. de, *Argentina* 126 B2
Calama, *Brazil* 124 E6
Calama, *Chile* 126 A2
Calamar, *Colombia* 124 A4
Calamba, *Phil.* 61 F5
Calamian Group, *Phil.* 61 F3
Calamocha, *Spain* 32 E3
Calamonte, *Spain* 35 G4
Călan, *Romania* 42 E7
Calañas, *Spain* 35 H4
Calanda, *Spain* 32 E4
Calang, *Indonesia* 62 D1
Calangiánus, *Italy* 30 B2
Calapan, *Phil.* 61 E4
Călărasi, *Moldova* 43 C13
Călăraşi, *Romania* 43 F12
Călăraşi □, *Romania* 43 F12
Calasparra, *Spain* 33 G3
Calatafimi, *Italy* 30 E5
Calatayud, *Spain* 32 D3
Călăţele, *Romania* 42 D8
Calato = Kálathos, *Greece* 39 E10
Calauag, *Phil.* 61 E5
Calavà, C., *Italy* 31 D7
Calavite, C., *Phil.* 61 E4
Calayan, *Phil.* 61 B4
Calbayog, *Phil.* 61 E6
Calca, *Peru* 124 F4
Calcasieu L., *U.S.A.* 113 L8
Calcutta, *India* 69 H13
Caldaro, *Italy* 29 B8
Caldas da Rainha, *Portugal* 35 F1
Caldas de Reis, *Spain* 34 C2
Calder →, *U.K.* 12 D6
Caldera, *Chile* 126 B1
Caldwell, *Idaho, U.S.A.* 114 E5
Caldwell, *Kans., U.S.A.* 113 G6
Caldwell, *Tex., U.S.A.* 113 K6
Caledon, *S. Africa* 88 E2
Caledon →, *S. Africa* 88 E4
Caledon B., *Australia* 94 A2
Caledonia, *Canada* 110 C5
Caledonia, *U.S.A.* 110 D7
Calella, *Spain* 32 D7
Calemba, *Angola* 88 B2
Calenzana, *France* 21 F12
Calexico, *U.S.A.* 117 N11
Calf of Man, *U.K.* 12 C3
Calgary, *Canada* 104 C6
Calheta, *Madeira* 37 D2
Calhoun, *U.S.A.* 109 H3
Cali, *Colombia* 124 C3
Calicut, *India* 66 P9
Caliente, *U.S.A.* 115 H6
California, *Mo., U.S.A.* 112 F8
California, *Pa., U.S.A.* 110 F5
California □, *U.S.A.* 116 H4
California, Baja, *Mexico* 118 A1
California, Baja, T.N. □ = Baja California □, *Mexico* 118 B2
California, Baja, T.S. □ = Baja California Sur □, *Mexico* 118 B2
California, G. de, *Mexico* 118 B2
California City, *U.S.A.* 117 K9
California Hot Springs, *U.S.A.* 117 K8
Călimăneşti, *Romania* 43 E9
Călimani, Munţii, *Romania* 43 C10
Calingasta, *Argentina* 126 C2
Calipatria, *U.S.A.* 117 M11
Calistoga, *U.S.A.* 116 G4
Calitri, *Italy* 31 B8
Calitzdorp, *S. Africa* 88 E3
Callabonna, L., *Australia* 95 D3
Callac, *France* 18 D3
Callan, *Ireland* 15 D4
Callander, *U.K.* 14 E4
Callao, *Peru* 124 F3
Callaway, *U.S.A.* 112 E5
Calles, *Mexico* 119 C5
Callide, *Australia* 94 C5
Calling Lake, *Canada* 104 B6
Calliope, *Australia* 94 C5
Callosa de Ensarriá, *Spain* 33 G4
Callosa de Segura, *Spain* 33 G4
Calne, *U.K.* 13 F6
Calola, *Angola* 88 B2
Calolbon, *Phil.* 61 E6
Calonge, *Spain* 32 D8
Caloocan, *Phil.* 61 D4
Calore →, *Italy* 31 A7
Caloundra, *Australia* 95 D5
Calpe, *Spain* 33 G5
Calpella, *U.S.A.* 116 F3
Calpine, *U.S.A.* 116 F6
Calstock, *Canada* 102 C3
Caltabellotta, *Italy* 30 E6
Caltagirone, *Italy* 31 E7
Caltanissetta, *Italy* 31 E7
Çaltılıbük, *Turkey* 41 G12
Caluire-et-Cuire, *France* 19 G11
Calulo, *Angola* 84 G2
Calumet, *U.S.A.* 108 B1
Caluso, *Italy* 28 C4
Calvados □, *France* 18 C6
Calvert, *U.S.A.* 113 K6
Calvert →, *Australia* 94 B2
Calvert Hills, *Australia* 94 B2
Calvert I., *Canada* 104 C3
Calvert Ra., *Australia* 92 D3
Calvi, *France* 21 F12
Calviá, *Spain* 33 F7
Calvillo, *Mexico* 118 C4
Calvinia, *S. Africa* 88 E2
Calvo = Calvo, Mte., *Italy* 29 G12
Calvo, Mte., *Italy* 29 G12
Calwa, *U.S.A.* 116 J7
Calzada Almuradiel = Almuradiel, *Spain* 35 G7
Calzada de Calatrava, *Spain* 35 G7
Cam →, *U.K.* 13 E8
Cam Lam, *Vietnam* 65 G7
Cam Pha, *Vietnam* 64 B6
Cam Ranh, *Vietnam* 65 G7
Cam Xuyen, *Vietnam* 64 C6
Camabatela, *Angola* 84 F3
Camacha, *Madeira* 37 D3
Camacho, *Mexico* 118 C4

Camacupa, *Angola* 85 G3
Camagüey, *Cuba* 120 B4
Camaiore, *Italy* 28 E7
Camaná, *Peru* 124 G4
Camanche Reservoir, *U.S.A.* 116 G6
Camaquã →, *Brazil* 127 C5
Câmara de Lobos, *Madeira* 37 D3
Camarat, C., *France* 21 E10
Camarès, *France* 20 E6
Camaret-sur-Mer, *France* 18 D2
Camargue, *France* 21 E8
Camarillo, *U.S.A.* 117 L7
Camariñas, *Spain* 34 B1
Camarón, C., *Honduras* 120 C2
Camarones, *Argentina* 128 E3
Camas, *Spain* 35 H4
Camas, *U.S.A.* 116 E4
Camas Valley, *U.S.A.* 114 E2
Cambará, *Brazil* 127 A5
Cambay = Khambhat, *India* 68 H5
Cambay, G. of = Khambhat, G. of, *India* 68 J5
Cambil, *Spain* 35 H7
Cambo-les-Bains, *France* 20 E2
Cambodia ■, *Asia* 64 F5
Camborne, *U.K.* 13 G2
Cambrai, *France* 19 B10
Cambre, *Spain* 34 B2
Cambria, *U.S.A.* 116 K5
Cambrian Mts., *U.K.* 13 E4
Cambridge, *Canada* 102 D3
Cambridge, *Jamaica* 120 C4
Cambridge, *N.Z.* 91 G5
Cambridge, *U.K.* 13 E8
Cambridge, *Idaho, U.S.A.* 114 D5
Cambridge, *Mass., U.S.A.* 111 D13
Cambridge, *Md., U.S.A.* 108 F7
Cambridge, *Minn., U.S.A.* 112 C8
Cambridge, *N.Y., U.S.A.* 111 C11
Cambridge, *Nebr., U.S.A.* 112 E4
Cambridge, *Ohio, U.S.A.* 110 F3
Cambridge G., *Australia* 92 B4
Cambridge Springs, *U.S.A.* 110 E4
Cambridgeshire □, *U.K.* 13 E7
Cambrils, *Spain* 32 D6
Cambuci, *Brazil* 127 A7
Cambundi-Catembo, *Angola* 84 G3
Camden, *Ala., U.S.A.* 109 K2
Camden, *Ark., U.S.A.* 113 J8
Camden, *Maine, U.S.A.* 103 D6
Camden, *N.J., U.S.A.* 111 G9
Camden, *S.C., U.S.A.* 109 H5
Camden Sd., *Australia* 92 C3
Camdenton, *U.S.A.* 113 F8
Çameli, *Turkey* 39 D11
Camenca, *Moldova* 43 B13
Camerino, *Italy* 29 E10
Cameron, *Ariz., U.S.A.* 115 J8
Cameron, *La., U.S.A.* 113 L8
Cameron, *Mo., U.S.A.* 112 F7
Cameron, *Tex., U.S.A.* 113 K6
Cameron Falls, *Canada* 102 C2
Cameron Highlands, *Malaysia* 65 K3
Cameron Hills, *Canada* 104 B5
Cameroon ■, *Africa* 84 C2
Camerota, *Italy* 31 B8
Cameroun →, *Cameroon* 83 E6
Cameroun, Mt., *Cameroon* 83 E6
Cametá, *Brazil* 125 D9
Çamiçi Gölü, *Turkey* 39 D9
Camiguin □, *Phil.* 61 G6
Camiguin I., *Phil.* 61 B4
Camiling, *Phil.* 61 D4
Caminha, *Portugal* 34 D2
Camino, *U.S.A.* 116 G6
Camira Creek, *Australia* 95 D5
Cammal, *U.S.A.* 110 E7
Cammarata, *Italy* 30 E6
Camocim, *Brazil* 125 D10
Camooweal, *Australia* 94 B2
Camopi, *Fr. Guiana* 125 C8
Camotes Is., *Phil.* 61 F6
Camotes Sea, *Phil.* 61 F6
Camp Crook, *U.S.A.* 112 C3
Camp Nelson, *U.S.A.* 117 J8
Camp Wood, *U.S.A.* 113 L5
Campagna, *Italy* 31 B8
Campana, *Argentina* 126 C4
Campana, I., *Chile* 128 F1
Campanário, *Madeira* 37 D2
Campanario, *Spain* 35 G5
Campània □, *Italy* 31 B7
Campbell, *S. Africa* 88 D3
Campbell, *Calif., U.S.A.* 116 H5
Campbell, *Ohio, U.S.A.* 110 E4
Campbell I., *Pac. Oc.* 96 N8
Campbell L., *Canada* 105 A7
Campbell River, *Canada* 104 C3
Campbell Town, *Australia* 94 G4
Campbellford, *Canada* 110 B7
Campbellpur, *Pakistan* 68 C5
Campbellsville, *U.S.A.* 108 G3
Campbellton, *Canada* 103 C6
Campbelltown, *Australia* 95 E5
Campbeltown, *U.K.* 14 F3
Campeche, *Mexico* 119 D6
Campeche □, *Mexico* 119 D6
Campeche, B. de, *Mexico* 119 D6
Campello, *Spain* 33 G4
Câmpeni, *Romania* 42 D8
Camperdown, *Australia* 95 F3
Camperville, *Canada* 105 C8
Campi Salentina, *Italy* 31 B11
Câmpia Turzii, *Romania* 43 D8
Campidano, *Italy* 30 C1
Campíglia Maríttima, *Italy* 28 E7
Campillo de Altobuey, *Spain* 33 F3
Campillos, *Spain* 35 H6
Câmpina, *Romania* 43 E10
Campina Grande, *Brazil* 125 E11
Campinas, *Brazil* 127 A6
Campli, *Italy* 29 F10
Campo, *Spain* 32 C5
Campo de Criptana, *Spain* 35 F7
Campo de Gibraltar, *Spain* 35 J5
Campo Grande, *Brazil* 125 H8
Campo Maíor, *Brazil* 125 D10
Campo Maior, *Portugal* 35 F3
Campo Mourão, *Brazil* 127 A5
Campo Túres, *Italy* 29 B8
Campobasso, *Italy* 31 A7
Campobello di Licata, *Italy* 30 E6
Campobello di Mazara, *Italy* 30 E5
Campofelice di Roccella, *Italy* 30 E6
Campomarino, *Italy* 29 G12
Camporeale, *Italy* 30 E6
Camporrobles, *Spain* 32 F3
Campos, *Brazil* 127 A7
Campos Belos, *Brazil* 125 F9
Campos del Puerto, *Spain* 37 B10
Campos Novos, *Brazil* 127 B5
Camprodón, *Spain* 32 C7
Camptonville, *U.S.A.* 116 F5
Câmpulung, *Argeş, Romania* 43 E10
Câmpulung, *Suceava, Romania* 43 C10
Câmpuri, *Romania* 43 D11
Camrose, *Canada* 104 C6
Camsell Portage, *Canada* 105 B7
Çamyuva, *Turkey* 39 E12
Çan, *Turkey* 41 F11
Can Clavo, *Spain* 37 C7
Can Creu, *Spain* 37 C7
Can Gio, *Vietnam* 65 G6
Can Tho, *Vietnam* 65 G5
Canaan, *U.S.A.* 111 D11
Canada ■, *N. Amer.* 100 C10
Cañada de Gómez, *Argentina* 126 C3
Canadian, *U.S.A.* 113 H4
Canadian →, *U.S.A.* 113 H7
Çanakkale, *Turkey* 41 F10
Çanakkale □, *Turkey* 41 F10
Çanakkale Boğazı, *Turkey* 41 F10
Canal Flats, *Canada* 104 C5
Canalejas, *Argentina* 126 D2
Canals, *Argentina* 126 C3
Canals, *Spain* 33 G4
Canandaigua, *U.S.A.* 110 D7
Cananea, *Mexico* 118 A2
Canarias, Is., *Atl. Oc.* 37 F4
Canarreos, Arch. de los, *Cuba* 120 B3
Canary Is. = Canarias, Is., *Atl. Oc.* 37 F4
Canatlán, *Mexico* 118 C4
Canaveral, C., *U.S.A.* 109 L5
Cañaveruelas, *Spain* 32 E2
Canavieiras, *Brazil* 125 G11
Canbelego, *Australia* 95 E4
Canberra, *Australia* 95 F4
Canby, *Calif., U.S.A.* 114 F3
Canby, *Minn., U.S.A.* 112 C6
Canby, *Oreg., U.S.A.* 116 E4
Cancale, *France* 18 D5
Canche →, *France* 19 B8
Cancún, *Mexico* 119 C7
Candanchu, *Spain* 32 C4
Çandarlı, *Turkey* 39 C8
Çandarlı Körfezi, *Turkey* 39 C8
Candas, *Spain* 34 B5
Candé, *France* 18 E5
Candela, *Italy* 31 A8
Candelaria, *Argentina* 127 B4
Candelaria, *Canary Is.* 37 F3
Candeleda, *Spain* 34 E5
Candelo, *Australia* 95 F4
Candia = Iráklion, *Greece* 36 D7
Candia, Sea of = Crete, Sea of, *Greece* 39 E7
Candle L., *Canada* 105 C7
Candlemas I., *Antarctica* 5 B1
Cando, *U.S.A.* 112 A5
Candon, *Phil.* 61 C4
Canea = Khaniá, *Greece* 36 D6
Canelli, *Italy* 28 D5
Canelones, *Uruguay* 127 C4
Canet-Plage, *France* 20 F7
Cañete, *Chile* 126 D1
Cañete, *Peru* 124 F3
Cañete, *Spain* 32 E3
Cañete de las Torres, *Spain* 35 H6
Cangas, *Spain* 34 C2
Cangas de Narcea, *Spain* 34 B4
Cangas de Onís, *Spain* 34 B5
Canguaretama, *Brazil* 125 E11
Canguçu, *Brazil* 127 C5
Cangxi, *China* 58 B5
Cangyuan, *China* 58 F2
Cangzhou, *China* 56 E9
Caniapiscau = Kaniapiskau →, *Canada* 103 A6
Caniapiscau, L. = Kaniapiskau L., *Canada* 103 B6
Canicatti, *Italy* 30 E6
Canicattì Bagni, *Italy* 31 E8
Caniles, *Spain* 35 H8
Canim Lake, *Canada* 104 C4
Canindeyu □, *Paraguay* 127 A5
Canino, *Italy* 29 F8
Canisteo, *U.S.A.* 110 D7
Canisteo →, *U.S.A.* 110 D7
Cañitas, *Mexico* 118 C4
Cañizal, *Spain* 34 D5
Canjáyar, *Spain* 35 H8
Çankırı, *Turkey* 72 B5
Cankuzo, *Burundi* 86 C3
Canmore, *Canada* 104 C5
Cann River, *Australia* 95 F4
Canna, *U.K.* 14 D2
Cannanore, *India* 66 P9
Cannes, *France* 21 E11
Canning Town = Port Canning, *India* 69 H13
Cannington, *Canada* 110 B5
Cannóbio, *Italy* 28 B5
Cannock, *U.K.* 13 E5
Cannon Ball →, *U.S.A.* 112 B4
Cannondale Mt., *Australia* 94 D4
Canoas, *Brazil* 127 B5
Canoe L., *Canada* 105 B7
Canon City, *U.S.A.* 112 F2
Canora, *Canada* 105 C8
Canosa di Púglia, *Italy* 31 A9
Canowindra, *Australia* 95 E4
Canso, *Canada* 103 C7
Cantabria □, *Spain* 34 B7
Cantabria, Sierra de, *Spain* 32 C2
Cantabrian Mts. = Cantábrica, Cordillera, *Spain* 34 C5
Cantábrica, Cordillera, *Spain* 34 C5
Cantal □, *France* 20 C6
Cantal, Plomb du, *France* 20 C6
Cantanhede, *Portugal* 34 E2
Cantavieja, *Spain* 32 E4
Čantavir, *Serbia, Yug.* 42 E4
Cantemir, *Moldova* 43 D13
Canterbury, *Australia* 94 D3
Canterbury, *U.K.* 13 F9
Canterbury □, *N.Z.* 91 K3
Canterbury Bight, *N.Z.* 91 L3
Canterbury Plains, *N.Z.* 91 K3
Cantil, *U.S.A.* 117 K9
Cantillana, *Spain* 35 H5
Canton = Guangzhou, *China* 59 F9
Canton, *Ga., U.S.A.* 109 H3
Canton, *Ill., U.S.A.* 112 E9
Canton, *Miss., U.S.A.* 113 J9
Canton, *Mo., U.S.A.* 112 E9
Canton, *N.Y., U.S.A.* 111 B9
Canton, *Ohio, U.S.A.* 110 F3
Canton, *Okla., U.S.A.* 113 G5
Canton, *S. Dak., U.S.A.* 112 D6
Canton L., *U.S.A.* 113 G5
Cantù, *Italy* 28 C6
Canudos, *Brazil* 124 E7
Canumã →, *Brazil* 124 D7
Canutama, *Brazil* 124 E6
Canutillo, *U.S.A.* 115 L10
Canvey, *U.K.* 13 F8
Canyon, *Tex., U.S.A.* 113 H4
Canyon, *Wyo., U.S.A.* 114 D8
Canyonlands National Park, *U.S.A.* 115 G9
Canyonville, *U.S.A.* 114 E2
Cao Bang, *Vietnam* 64 A6
Cao He →, *China* 57 D13
Cao Lanh, *Vietnam* 65 G5
Cao Xian, *China* 56 G8
Cáorle, *Italy* 29 C9
Cap-aux-Meules, *Canada* 103 C7
Cap-Chat, *Canada* 103 C6
Cap-de-la-Madeleine, *Canada* 102 C5
Cap-Haïtien, *Haiti* 121 C5
Capáccio, *Italy* 31 B8
Capaci, *Italy* 30 D6
Capanaparo →, *Venezuela* 124 B5
Capànnori, *Italy* 28 E7
Capbreton, *France* 20 E2
Capdenac, *France* 20 D6
Capdepera, *Spain* 32 F8
Cape →, *Australia* 94 C4
Cape Barren I., *Australia* 94 G4
Cape Breton Highlands Nat. Park, *Canada* 103 C7
Cape Breton I., *Canada* 103 C7
Cape Charles, *U.S.A.* 108 G8
Cape Coast, *Ghana* 83 D4
Cape Coral, *U.S.A.* 109 M5
Cape Dorset, *Canada* 101 B12
Cape Fear →, *U.S.A.* 109 H6
Cape Girardeau, *U.S.A.* 113 G10
Cape Jervis, *Australia* 95 F2
Cape May, *U.S.A.* 108 F8
Cape May Point, *U.S.A.* 107 C12
Cape Palmas, *Liberia* 82 E3
Cape Tormentine, *Canada* 103 C7
Cape Town, *S. Africa* 88 E2
Cape Verde Is. ■, *Atl. Oc.* 77 E1
Cape Vincent, *U.S.A.* 111 B8
Cape York Peninsula, *Australia* 94 A3
Capela, *Brazil* 125 F11
Capella, *Australia* 94 C4
Capendu, *France* 20 E6
Capestang, *France* 20 E7
Capim →, *Brazil* 125 D9
Capistrello, *Italy* 29 G10
Capitan, *U.S.A.* 115 K11
Capitola, *U.S.A.* 116 J5
Capizzi, *Italy* 31 E7
Capoche →, *Mozam.* 87 F3
Capoterra, *Italy* 30 C1
Cappadocia, *Turkey* 72 C6
Capraia, *Italy* 28 E6
Caprara, Pta., *Italy* 30 A1
Caprarola, *Italy* 29 F9
Capreol, *Canada* 102 C3
Caprera, *Italy* 30 A2
Capri, *Italy* 31 B7
Capricorn Group, *Australia* 94 C5
Capricorn Ra., *Australia* 92 D2
Caprino Veronese, *Italy* 28 C7
Caprivi Strip, *Namibia* 88 B3
Captainganj, *India* 69 F10
Captain's Flat, *Australia* 95 F4
Captieux, *France* 20 D3
Caquetá →, *Colombia* 122 D4
Caracal, *Romania* 43 F9
Caracas, *Venezuela* 124 A5
Caracol, *Brazil* 125 E10
Caradoc, *Australia* 95 E3
Caráglio, *Italy* 28 D4
Carajas, *Brazil* 125 E8
Carajás, Serra dos, *Brazil* 125 E8
Carangola, *Brazil* 127 A7
Carani, *Australia* 93 F2
Caransebeş, *Romania* 42 E7
Carantec, *France* 18 D3
Caras, *Peru* 124 E3
Caraş Severin □, *Romania* 42 E7
Caraşova, *Romania* 42 E6
Caratasca, L., *Honduras* 120 C3
Caratinga, *Brazil* 125 G10
Caraúbas, *Brazil* 125 E11
Caravaca = Caravaca de la Cruz, *Spain* 33 G3
Caravaca de la Cruz, *Spain* 33 G3
Caravággio, *Italy* 28 C6
Caravelas, *Brazil* 125 G11
Caraveli, *Peru* 124 G4
Caràzinho, *Brazil* 127 B5
Carballino = O Carballiño, *Spain* 34 C2
Carballo, *Spain* 34 B2
Carberry, *Canada* 105 D9
Carbó, *Mexico* 118 B2
Carbon, *Canada* 104 C6
Carbonara, C., *Italy* 30 C2
Carbondale, *Colo., U.S.A.* 114 G10
Carbondale, *Ill., U.S.A.* 113 G10
Carbondale, *Pa., U.S.A.* 111 E9
Carbonear, *Canada* 103 C9
Carboneras, *Spain* 33 J3
Carboneras de Guadazaón, *Spain* 32 F3
Carbónia, *Italy* 30 C1
Carcabuey, *Spain* 35 H6
Carcagente = Carcaixent, *Spain* 33 F4
Carcaixent, *Spain* 33 F4
Carcajou, *Canada* 104 B5
Carcar, *Phil.* 61 F5
Carcasse, C., *Haiti* 121 C5
Carcassonne, *France* 20 E6
Carcross, *Canada* 100 B6
Cardabia, *Australia* 92 D1
Çardak, *Çanakkale, Turkey* 41 F10
Çardak, *Denizli, Turkey* 39 D11
Cardamon Hills, *India* 66 Q10
Cardeña, *Spain* 35 G6
Cárdenas, *Cuba* 120 B3
Cárdenas, *San Luis Potosí, Mexico* 119 C5
Cárdenas, *Tabasco, Mexico* 119 D6
Cardenete, *Spain* 32 F3
Cardiff, *U.K.* 13 F4
Cardiff □, *U.K.* 13 F4
Cardiff-by-the-Sea, *U.S.A.* 117 M9
Cardigan, *U.K.* 13 E3
Cardigan B., *U.K.* 13 E3
Cardinal, *Canada* 111 B9
Cardona, *Spain* 32 D6
Cardona, *Uruguay* 126 C4
Cardoner →, *Spain* 32 D6
Cardross, *Canada* 105 D7
Cardston, *Canada* 104 D6
Cardwell, *Australia* 94 B4
Careen L., *Canada* 105 B7
Carei, *Romania* 42 C7
Careme = Ciremai, *Indonesia* 63 G13
Carentan, *France* 18 C5
Carey, *Idaho, U.S.A.* 114 E7
Carey, *Ohio, U.S.A.* 108 E4
Carey, L., *Australia* 93 E3
Carey L., *Canada* 105 A8
Careysburg, *Liberia* 82 D2
Cargèse, *France* 21 F12
Carhaix-Plouguer, *France* 18 D3
Carhué, *Argentina* 126 D3
Caria, *Turkey* 39 D10
Cariacica, *Brazil* 125 H10
Cariati, *Italy* 31 C9
Caribbean Sea, *W. Indies* 121 D5
Cariboo Mts., *Canada* 104 C4
Caribou, *U.S.A.* 103 C6
Caribou →, *Man., Canada* 105 B10
Caribou →, *N.W.T., Canada* 104 A3
Caribou I., *Canada* 102 C2
Caribou Is., *Canada* 104 A6
Caribou L., *Man., Canada* 105 B9
Caribou L., *Ont., Canada* 102 B2
Caribou Mts., *Canada* 104 B5
Carichic, *Mexico* 118 B3
Carigara, *Phil.* 61 F6
Carignan, *France* 19 C12
Carignano, *Italy* 28 D4
Carillo, *Mexico* 118 B4
Carinda, *Australia* 95 E4
Cariñena, *Spain* 32 D3
Carinhanha, *Brazil* 125 F10
Carinhanha →, *Brazil* 125 F10
Carini, *Italy* 30 D6
Cariño, *Spain* 34 B3
Carínola, *Italy* 30 A6
Carinthia □ = Kärnten □, *Austria* 26 E6
Caripito, *Venezuela* 124 A6
Carlbrod = Dimitrovgrad, *Serbia, Yug.* 40 C6
Carlet, *Spain* 33 F4
Carleton Place, *Canada* 102 C4
Carletonville, *S. Africa* 88 D4
Cârlibaba, *Romania* 43 C10
Carlin, *U.S.A.* 114 F5
Carlingford L., *U.K.* 15 B5
Carlinville, *U.S.A.* 112 F10
Carlisle, *U.K.* 12 C5
Carlisle, *U.S.A.* 110 F7
Carlit, Pic, *France* 20 F5
Carloforte, *Italy* 30 C1
Carlos Casares, *Argentina* 126 D3
Carlos Tejedor, *Argentina* 126 D3
Carlow, *Ireland* 15 D5
Carlow □, *Ireland* 15 D5
Carlsbad, *Calif., U.S.A.* 117 M9
Carlsbad, *N. Mex., U.S.A.* 113 J2
Carluke, *U.K.* 14 F5
Carlyle, *Canada* 105 D8
Carlyle, *U.S.A.* 112 F10
Carmacks, *Canada* 100 B6
Carmagnola, *Italy* 28 D4
Carman, *Canada* 105 D9
Carmangay, *Canada* 104 C6
Carmanville, *Canada* 103 C9
Carmarthen, *U.K.* 13 F3
Carmarthen B., *U.K.* 13 F3
Carmarthenshire □, *U.K.* 13 F3
Carmaux, *France* 20 D6
Carmel, *U.S.A.* 111 E11
Carmel-by-the-Sea, *U.S.A.* 116 J5
Carmel Valley, *U.S.A.* 116 J5
Carmelo, *Uruguay* 126 C4
Carmen, *Colombia* 124 B3
Carmen, *Paraguay* 127 B4
Carmen →, *Mexico* 118 A3
Carmen, I., *Mexico* 118 B2
Carmen de Patagones, *Argentina* 128 E4
Cármenes, *Spain* 34 C5
Carmensa, *Argentina* 126 D2
Carmi, *U.S.A.* 108 F1
Carmichael, *U.S.A.* 116 G5
Carmila, *Australia* 94 C4
Carmona, *Spain* 35 H5
Carn Ban, *U.K.* 14 D4
Carn Eige, *U.K.* 14 D3
Carnarvon, *Queens., Australia* 94 C4
Carnarvon, *W. Austral., Australia* 93 D1
Carnarvon, *S. Africa* 88 E3
Carnarvon Ra., *Queens., Australia* 94 D4
Carnarvon Ra., *W. Austral., Australia* 93 E3
Carnation, *U.S.A.* 116 C5
Carndonagh, *Ireland* 15 A4
Carnduff, *Canada* 105 D8
Carnegie, *U.S.A.* 110 F4
Carnegie, L., *Australia* 93 E3
Carnic Alps = Karnische Alpen, *Europe* 26 E6
Carniche Alpi = Karnische Alpen, *Europe* 26 E6
Carnot, *C.A.R.* 84 D3
Carnot, C., *Australia* 95 E2
Carnot B., *Australia* 92 C3
Carnoustie, *U.K.* 14 E6
Carnsore Pt., *Ireland* 15 D5
Caro, *U.S.A.* 108 D4
Carol City, *U.S.A.* 109 N5
Carolina, *Brazil* 125 E9
Carolina, *Puerto Rico* 121 C6
Carolina, *S. Africa* 89 D5
Caroline I., *Kiribati* 97 H12
Caroline Is., *Pac. Oc.* 96 G7
Caron, *Canada* 105 C7
Caroni →, *Venezuela* 124 B6
Caroníe = Nébrodi, Monti, *Italy* 31 E7
Caroona, *Australia* 95 E5
Carpathians, *Europe* 6 F10
Carpaţii Meridionali, *Romania* 43 E9
Carpentaria, G. of, *Australia* 94 A2
Carpentaria Downs, *Australia* 94 B3
Carpentras, *France* 21 D9
Carpi, *Italy* 28 D7
Cărpineni, *Moldova* 43 D13
Carpinteria, *U.S.A.* 117 L7
Carpio, *Spain* 34 D5
Carpolac = Morea, *Australia* 95 F3
Carr Boyd Ra., *Australia* 92 C4
Carrabelle, *U.S.A.* 109 L3
Carral, *Spain* 34 B2
Carranya, *Australia* 92 C4
Carrara, *Italy* 28 D7

Carrascal, *Phil.* 61 G6
Carrascosa del Campo, *Spain* 32 E2
Carrauntoohill, *Ireland* 15 D2
Carrick-on-Shannon, *Ireland* 15 C3
Carrick-on-Suir, *Ireland* 15 D4
Carrickfergus, *U.K.* 15 B6
Carrickmacross, *Ireland* 15 C5
Carrieton, *Australia* 95 E2
Carrington, *U.S.A.* 112 B5
Carrión →, *Spain* 34 D6
Carrión de los Condes, *Spain* 34 C6
Carrizal Bajo, *Chile* 126 B1
Carrizalillo, *Chile* 126 B1
Carrizo Cr. →, *U.S.A.* 113 G3
Carrizo Springs, *U.S.A.* 113 L5
Carrizozo, *U.S.A.* 115 K11
Carroll, *U.S.A.* 112 D7
Carrollton, *Ga., U.S.A.* 109 J3
Carrollton, *Ill., U.S.A.* 112 F9
Carrollton, *Ky., U.S.A.* 108 F3
Carrollton, *Mo., U.S.A.* 112 F8
Carrollton, *Ohio, U.S.A.* 110 F3
Carron →, *U.K.* 14 D4
Carron, L., *U.K.* 14 D3
Carrot →, *Canada* 105 C8
Carrot River, *Canada* 105 C8
Carrouges, *France* 18 D6
Carrù, *Italy* 28 D4
Carruthers, *Canada* 105 C7
Çarşamba, *Turkey* 72 B7
Carsóli, *Italy* 29 F10
Carson, *Calif., U.S.A.* 117 M8
Carson, *N. Dak., U.S.A.* 112 B4
Carson →, *U.S.A.* 116 F8
Carson City, *U.S.A.* 116 F7
Carson Sink, *U.S.A.* 114 G4
Cartagena, *Colombia* 124 A3
Cartagena, *Spain* 33 H4
Cartago, *Colombia* 124 C3
Cartago, *Costa Rica* 120 E3
Cártama, *Spain* 35 J6
Cartaxo, *Portugal* 35 F2
Cartaya, *Spain* 35 H3
Cartersville, *U.S.A.* 109 H3
Carterton, *N.Z.* 91 J5
Carthage, *Ark., U.S.A.* 113 H8
Carthage, *Ill., U.S.A.* 112 E9
Carthage, *Mo., U.S.A.* 113 G7
Carthage, *S. Dak., U.S.A.* 112 C6
Carthage, *Tex., U.S.A.* 113 J7
Cartier I., *Australia* 92 B3
Cartwright, *Canada* 103 B8
Caruaru, *Brazil* 125 E11
Carúpano, *Venezuela* 124 A6
Caruthersville, *U.S.A.* 113 G10
Carvin, *France* 19 B9
Carvoeiro, *Brazil* 124 D6
Carvoeiro, C., *Portugal* 35 F1
Cary, *U.S.A.* 109 H6
Casa Branca, *Portugal* 35 G2
Casa Grande, *U.S.A.* 115 K8
Casablanca, *Chile* 126 C1
Casablanca, *Morocco* 78 B4
Casacalenda, *Italy* 29 G11
Casalbordino, *Italy* 29 F11
Casale Monferrato, *Italy* 28 C5
Casalmaggiore, *Italy* 28 D7
Casalpusterlengo, *Italy* 28 C6
Casamance →, *Senegal* 82 C1
Casarano, *Italy* 31 B11
Casares, *Spain* 35 J5
Casas Grandes, *Mexico* 118 A3
Casas Ibáñez, *Spain* 33 F3
Casasimarro, *Spain* 33 F2
Casatejada, *Spain* 34 F5
Casavieja, *Spain* 34 E6
Cascade, *Idaho, U.S.A.* 114 D5
Cascade, *Mont., U.S.A.* 114 C8
Cascade Locks, *U.S.A.* 116 E5
Cascade Ra., *U.S.A.* 116 D5
Cascais, *Portugal* 35 G1
Cascavel, *Brazil* 127 A5
Cáscina, *Italy* 28 E7
Caselle Torinese, *Italy* 28 C4
Caserta, *Italy* 31 A7
Cashel, *Ireland* 15 D4
Cashmere, *U.S.A.* 114 C3
Cashmere Downs, *Australia* 93 E2
Casiguran, *Phil.* 61 C5
Casilda, *Argentina* 126 C3
Casimcea, *Romania* 43 F13
Casino, *Australia* 95 D5
Casiquiare →, *Venezuela* 124 C5
Caslan, *Canada* 104 C6
Čáslav, *Czech Rep.* 26 B8
Casma, *Peru* 124 E3
Casmalia, *U.S.A.* 117 L6
Cásola Valsénio, *Italy* 29 D8
Cásoli, *Italy* 29 F11
Caspe, *Spain* 32 D4
Casper, *U.S.A.* 114 E10
Caspian Depression, *Eurasia* 49 G9
Caspian Sea, *Eurasia* 50 E6
Cass City, *U.S.A.* 108 D4
Cass Lake, *U.S.A.* 112 B7
Cassà de la Selva, *Spain* 32 D7
Cassano allo Iónio, *Italy* 31 C9
Casse, Grande, *France* 21 C10
Cassel, *France* 19 B9
Casselman, *Canada* 111 A9
Casselton, *U.S.A.* 112 B6
Cassiar, *Canada* 104 B3
Cassiar Mts., *Canada* 104 B2
Cassino, *Italy* 30 A6
Cassis, *France* 21 E9
Cassville, *U.S.A.* 113 G8
Castagneto Carducci, *Italy* 28 E7
Castaic, *U.S.A.* 117 L8
Castanhal, *Brazil* 125 D9
Castéggio, *Italy* 28 C6
Castejón de Monegros, *Spain* 32 D4
Castèl di Sangro, *Italy* 29 G11
Castèl San Giovanni, *Italy* 28 C6
Castèl San Pietro Terme, *Italy* 29 D8
Castelbuono, *Italy* 31 E7
Castelfidardo, *Italy* 29 E10
Castelfiorentino, *Italy* 28 E7
Castelfranco Emília, *Italy* 28 D8
Castelfranco Véneto, *Italy* 29 C8
Casteljaloux, *France* 20 D4
Castellabate, *Italy* 31 B7
Castellammare, G. di, *Italy* 30 D5
Castellammare del Golfo, *Italy* 30 D5
Castellammare di Stábia, *Italy* 31 B7
Castellamonte, *Italy* 28 C4
Castellane, *France* 21 E10
Castellaneta, *Italy* 31 B9
Castelli, *Argentina* 126 D4
Castelló de la Plana, *Spain* 32 F4
Castellón de la Plana □, *Spain* 32 E4
Castellote, *Spain* 32 E4
Castelmáuro, *Italy* 29 G11
Castelnau-de-Médoc, *France* 20 C3
Castelnau-Magnoac, *France* 20 E4
Castelnaudary, *France* 20 E5
Castelnovo ne' Monti, *Italy* 28 D7
Castelnuovo di Val di Cécina, *Italy* 28 E7
Castelo, *Brazil* 127 A7
Castelo Branco, *Portugal* 34 F3
Castelo Branco □, *Portugal* 34 F3
Castelo de Paiva, *Portugal* 34 D2
Castelo de Vide, *Portugal* 35 F3
Castelsardo, *Italy* 30 B1
Castelsarrasin, *France* 20 D5
Casteltérmini, *Italy* 30 E6
Castelvetrano, *Italy* 30 E5
Casterton, *Australia* 95 F3
Castets, *France* 20 E2
Castiglion Fiorentino, *Italy* 29 E8
Castiglione del Lago, *Italy* 29 E9
Castiglione della Pescáia, *Italy* 28 F7
Castiglione delle Stiviere, *Italy* 28 C7
Castilblanco, *Spain* 35 F5
Castilla, Playa de, *Spain* 35 J4
Castilla-La Mancha □, *Spain* 6 H5
Castilla y Leon □, *Spain* 34 D6
Castillo de Locubín, *Spain* 35 H7
Castillon-en-Couserans, *France* 20 F5
Castillonès, *France* 20 D4
Castillos, *Uruguay* 127 C5
Castle Dale, *U.S.A.* 114 G8
Castle Douglas, *U.K.* 14 G5
Castle Rock, *Colo., U.S.A.* 112 F2
Castle Rock, *Wash., U.S.A.* 116 D4
Castlebar, *Ireland* 15 C2
Castleblaney, *Ireland* 15 B5
Castlederg, *U.K.* 15 B4
Castleford, *U.K.* 12 D6
Castlegar, *Canada* 104 D5
Castlemaine, *Australia* 95 F3
Castlepollard, *Ireland* 15 C4
Castlerea, *Ireland* 15 C3
Castlereagh →, *Australia* 95 E4
Castlereagh B., *Australia* 94 A2
Castletown, *U.K.* 12 C3
Castletown Bearhaven, *Ireland* 15 E2
Castlevale, *Australia* 94 C4
Castor, *Canada* 104 C6
Castres, *France* 20 E6
Castricum, *Neths.* 17 B4
Castries, *St. Lucia* 121 D7
Castril, *Spain* 35 H8
Castro, *Brazil* 127 A6
Castro, *Chile* 128 E2
Castro Alves, *Brazil* 125 F11
Castro del Río, *Spain* 35 H6
Castro-Urdiales, *Spain* 34 B7
Castro Verde, *Portugal* 35 H2
Castrojeriz, *Spain* 34 C6
Castropol, *Spain* 34 B4
Castroreale, *Italy* 31 D8
Castrovíllari, *Italy* 31 C9
Castroville, *Calif., U.S.A.* 116 J5
Castroville, *Tex., U.S.A.* 113 L5
Castuera, *Spain* 35 G5
Casummit Lake, *Canada* 102 B1
Çat, *Turkey* 73 C9
Cat Ba, Dao, *Vietnam* 64 B6
Cat I., *Bahamas* 121 B4
Cat I., *U.S.A.* 113 K10
Cat L., *Canada* 102 B1
Čata, *Slovak Rep.* 27 D11
Catacamas, *Honduras* 120 D2
Cataguases, *Brazil* 127 A7
Catahoula L., *U.S.A.* 113 K8
Çatak, *Turkey* 73 C10
Catalão, *Brazil* 125 G9
Çatalca, *Turkey* 41 E12
Catalina, *Canada* 103 C9
Catalonia = Cataluña □, *Spain* 32 D6
Cataluña □, *Spain* 32 D6
Çatalzeytin, *Turkey* 72 B6
Catamarca, *Argentina* 126 B2
Catamarca □, *Argentina* 126 B2
Catanauan, *Phil.* 61 E5
Catanduanes, *Phil.* 61 E6
Catanduva, *Brazil* 127 A6
Catánia, *Italy* 31 E8
Catánia, G. di, *Italy* 31 E8
Catanzaro, *Italy* 31 D9
Catarman, *Phil.* 61 E6
Catbalogan, *Phil.* 61 F6
Cateel, *Phil.* 61 H7
Caterham, *U.K.* 13 F7
Cathcart, *S. Africa* 88 E4
Cathlamet, *U.S.A.* 116 D3
Catio, *Guinea-Biss.* 82 C1
Catlettsburg, *U.S.A.* 108 F4
Çatma Dağı, *Turkey* 39 C11
Catoche, C., *Mexico* 119 C7
Cátria, Mte., *Italy* 29 E9
Catrimani, *Brazil* 124 C6
Catrimani →, *Brazil* 124 C6
Catskill, *U.S.A.* 111 D11
Catskill Mts., *U.S.A.* 111 D10
Catt, Mt., *Australia* 94 A1
Cattaraugus, *U.S.A.* 110 D6
Cattólica, *Italy* 29 E9
Cattólica Eraclea, *Italy* 30 E6
Catuala, *Angola* 88 B2
Catur, *Mozam.* 87 E4
Catwick Is., *Vietnam* 65 H7
Cauca →, *Colombia* 124 B4
Caucaia, *Brazil* 125 D11
Caucasus Mountains, *Eurasia* 49 J7
Caudete, *Spain* 33 G3
Caudry, *France* 19 B10
Caulnes, *France* 18 D4
Caulónia, *Italy* 31 D9
Caungula, *Angola* 84 F3
Cauquenes, *Chile* 126 D1
Caura →, *Venezuela* 124 B6
Cauresi →, *Mozam.* 87 F3
Căuşani, *Moldova* 43 D14
Causapscal, *Canada* 103 C6
Caussade, *France* 20 D5
Causse-Méjean, *France* 20 D7
Cauterets, *France* 20 F3
Cauvery →, *India* 66 P11
Caux, Pays de, *France* 18 C7
Cava de' Tirreni, *Italy* 31 B7
Cávado →, *Portugal* 34 D2
Cavaillon, *France* 21 E9
Cavalaire-sur-Mer, *France* 21 E10
Cavalese, *Italy* 29 B8
Cavalier, *U.S.A.* 112 A6
Cavalla = Cavally →, *Africa* 82 E3
Cavalleria, C. de, *Spain* 37 A11
Cavallo, I. de, *France* 21 G13
Cavally →, *Africa* 82 E3
Cavan, *Ireland* 15 B4
Cavan □, *Ireland* 15 C4
Cavárzere, *Italy* 29 C9
Çavdarhisar, *Turkey* 39 B11
Çavdır, *Turkey* 39 D11
Cave City, *U.S.A.* 108 G3
Cavenagh Ra., *Australia* 93 E4
Cavendish, *Australia* 95 F3
Caviana, I., *Brazil* 125 C8
Cavite, *Phil.* 61 D4
Cavnic, *Romania* 43 C8
Cavour, *Italy* 28 D4
Cavtat, *Croatia* 40 D2
Cawndilla L., *Australia* 95 E3
Cawnpore = Kanpur, *India* 69 F9
Caxias, *Brazil* 125 D10
Caxias do Sul, *Brazil* 127 B5
Çay, *Turkey* 72 C4
Cay Sal Bank, *Bahamas* 120 B4
Cayambe, *Ecuador* 124 C3
Çaycuma, *Turkey* 72 B5
Çayeli, *Turkey* 73 B9
Cayenne, *Fr. Guiana* 125 B8
Caygören Barajı, *Turkey* 39 B10
Çayiralan, *Turkey* 72 C6
Caylus, *France* 20 D5
Cayman Brac, *Cayman Is.* 120 C4
Cayman Is. ■, *W. Indies* 120 C3
Cayo Romano, *Cuba* 121 B4
Cayres, *France* 20 D7
Cayuga, *Canada* 110 D5
Cayuga, *U.S.A.* 111 D8
Cayuga L., *U.S.A.* 111 D8
Cazalla de la Sierra, *Spain* 35 H5
Căzăneşti, *Romania* 43 F12
Cazaubon, *France* 20 E3
Cazaux et de Sanguinet, Étang de, *France* 20 D2
Cazères, *France* 20 E5
Cazin, *Bos.-H.* 29 D12
Čazma, *Croatia* 29 C13
Cazombo, *Angola* 85 G4
Cazorla, *Spain* 35 H7
Cazorla, Sierra de, *Spain* 35 G8
Cea →, *Spain* 34 C5
Ceamurlia de Jos, *Romania* 43 F13
Ceanannus Mor, *Ireland* 15 C5
Ceará = Fortaleza, *Brazil* 125 D11
Ceará □, *Brazil* 125 E11
Ceará Mirim, *Brazil* 125 E11
Ceauru, L., *Romania* 43 F8
Cebaco, I. de, *Panama* 120 E3
Cebollar, *Argentina* 126 B2
Cebollera, Sierra de, *Spain* 32 D2
Cebreros, *Spain* 34 E6
Cebu, *Phil.* 61 F5
Čečava, *Bos.-H.* 42 F2
Ceccano, *Italy* 30 A6
Cece, *Hungary* 42 D3
Cechi, *Ivory C.* 82 D4
Cecil Plains, *Australia* 95 D5
Cécina, *Italy* 28 E7
Cécina →, *Italy* 28 E7
Ceclavín, *Spain* 34 F4
Cedar →, *U.S.A.* 112 E9
Cedar City, *U.S.A.* 115 H7
Cedar Creek Reservoir, *U.S.A.* 113 J6
Cedar Falls, *Iowa, U.S.A.* 112 D8
Cedar Falls, *Wash., U.S.A.* 116 C5
Cedar Key, *U.S.A.* 109 L4
Cedar L., *Canada* 105 C9
Cedar Rapids, *U.S.A.* 112 E9
Cedartown, *U.S.A.* 109 H3
Cedarvale, *Canada* 104 B3
Cedarville, *S. Africa* 89 E4
Cedarville, *U.S.A.* 114 F3
Cedeira, *Spain* 34 B2
Cedral, *Mexico* 118 C4
Cedrino →, *Italy* 30 B2
Cedro, *Brazil* 125 E11
Cedros, I. de, *Mexico* 118 B1
Ceduna, *Australia* 95 E1
Cedynia, *Poland* 45 F1
Cée, *Spain* 34 C1
Cefalù, *Italy* 31 D7
Cega →, *Spain* 34 D6
Cegléd, *Hungary* 42 C4
Céglie Messápico, *Italy* 31 B10
Cehegín, *Spain* 33 G3
Ceheng, *China* 58 E5
Cehu-Silvaniei, *Romania* 43 C8
Ceica, *Romania* 42 D7
Ceira →, *Portugal* 34 E2
Čelákovice, *Czech Rep.* 26 A7
Celano, *Italy* 29 F10
Celanova, *Spain* 34 C3
Celaya, *Mexico* 118 C4
Celebes = Sulawesi □, *Indonesia* 63 E6
Celebes Sea, *Indonesia* 63 D6
Čelić, *Bos.-H.* 42 F3
Celina, *U.S.A.* 108 E3
Celinac, *Bos.-H.* 42 F2
Celje, *Slovenia* 29 B12
Celldömölk, *Hungary* 42 C2
Celle, *Germany* 24 C6
Celorico da Beira, *Portugal* 34 E3
Çeltikçi, *Turkey* 39 D12
Cement, *U.S.A.* 113 H5
Çemişgezek, *Turkey* 73 C8
Cengong, *China* 58 D7
Ceno →, *Italy* 28 D7
Centallo, *Italy* 28 D4
Centelles, *Spain* 32 D7
Center, *N. Dak., U.S.A.* 112 B4
Center, *Tex., U.S.A.* 113 K7
Centerfield, *U.S.A.* 115 G8
Centerville, *Calif., U.S.A.* 116 J7
Centerville, *Iowa, U.S.A.* 112 E8
Centerville, *Pa., U.S.A.* 110 F5
Centerville, *S. Dak., U.S.A.* 112 D6
Centerville, *Tenn., U.S.A.* 109 H2
Centerville, *Tex., U.S.A.* 113 K7
Cento, *Italy* 29 D8
Central, *U.S.A.* 115 K9
Central □, *Kenya* 86 C4
Central □, *Malawi* 87 E3
Central □, *Zambia* 87 E2
Central, Cordillera, *Colombia* 122 C3
Central, Cordillera, *Costa Rica* 120 D3
Central, Cordillera, *Dom. Rep.* 121 C5
Central, Cordillera, *Phil.* 61 C4
Central African Rep. ■, *Africa* 84 C4
Central City, *Ky., U.S.A.* 108 G2
Central City, *Nebr., U.S.A.* 112 E6
Central I., *Kenya* 86 B4
Central Makran Range, *Pakistan* 66 F4
Central Patricia, *Canada* 102 B1
Central Russian Uplands, *Europe* 6 E13
Central Siberian Plateau, *Russia* 52 C14
Centralia, *Ill., U.S.A.* 112 F10
Centralia, *Mo., U.S.A.* 112 F8
Centralia, *Wash., U.S.A.* 116 D4
Centreville, *Ala., U.S.A.* 109 J2
Centreville, *Miss., U.S.A.* 113 K9
Ćeotina →, *Bos.-H.* 40 C2
Cephalonia = Kefallinía, *Greece* 38 C2
Čepin, *Croatia* 42 E3
Ceprano, *Italy* 30 A6
Ceptura, *Romania* 43 E11
Cepu, *Indonesia* 63 G14
Ceram = Seram, *Indonesia* 63 E7
Ceram Sea = Seram Sea, *Indonesia* 63 E7
Cerbère, *France* 20 F7
Cerbicales, Is., *France* 21 G13
Cercal, *Portugal* 35 H2
Cerdaña, *Spain* 32 C6
Cère →, *France* 20 D5
Cerea, *Italy* 29 C8
Ceredigion □, *U.K.* 13 E3
Ceres, *Argentina* 126 B3
Ceres, *S. Africa* 88 E2
Ceres, *U.S.A.* 116 H6
Céret, *France* 20 F6
Cergy, *France* 19 C9
Cerignola, *Italy* 31 A8
Cerigo = Kíthira, *Greece* 38 E5
Cérilly, *France* 19 F9
Cerisiers, *France* 19 D10
Cerizay, *France* 18 F6
Çerkeş, *Turkey* 72 B5
Çerkezköy, *Turkey* 41 E12
Cerknica, *Slovenia* 29 C11
Cerkovica, *Bulgaria* 41 C8
Cermerno, *Serbia, Yug.* 40 C4
Çermik, *Turkey* 73 C8
Cerna, *Romania* 43 E13
Cerna →, *Romania* 43 F8
Cernavodă, *Romania* 43 F13
Cernay, *France* 19 E14
Cernik, *Croatia* 42 E2
Cerralvo, I., *Mexico* 118 C3
Cërrik, *Albania* 40 E3
Cerritos, *Mexico* 118 C4
Certaldo, *Italy* 28 E8
Cervaro →, *Italy* 31 A8
Cervati, Monte, *Italy* 31 B8
Cervera, *Spain* 32 D6
Cervera de Pisuerga, *Spain* 34 C6
Cervera del Río Alhama, *Spain* 32 C3
Cervéteri, *Italy* 29 F9
Cérvia, *Italy* 29 D9
Cervignano del Friuli, *Italy* 29 C10
Cervinara, *Italy* 31 A7
Cervione, *France* 21 F13
Cervo, *Spain* 34 B3
Cesarò, *Italy* 31 E7
Cesena, *Italy* 29 D9
Cesenático, *Italy* 29 D9
Cēsis, *Latvia* 9 H21
Česká Lípa, *Czech Rep.* 26 A7
Česká Třebová, *Czech Rep.* 27 B9
České Budějovice, *Czech Rep.* 26 C7
České Velenice, *Czech Rep.* 26 C7
Českomoravská Vrchovina, *Czech Rep.* 26 B8
Český Brod, *Czech Rep.* 26 A7
Český Krumlov, *Czech Rep.* 26 C7
Český Těšín, *Czech Rep.* 27 B11
Česma →, *Croatia* 29 C13
Çeşme, *Turkey* 39 C8
Cessnock, *Australia* 95 E5
Cesson-Sévigné, *France* 18 D5
Cestas, *France* 20 D3
Cestos →, *Liberia* 82 D3
Cetate, *Romania* 42 F8
Cetin Grad, *Croatia* 29 C12
Cetina →, *Croatia* 29 E13
Cetinje, *Montenegro, Yug.* 40 D2
Cetraro, *Italy* 31 C8
Ceuta, *N. Afr.* 78 A4
Ceva, *Italy* 28 D5
Cévennes, *France* 20 D7
Ceyhan, *Turkey* 72 D6
Ceyhan →, *Turkey* 72 D6
Ceylânpınar, *Turkey* 73 D9
Ceylon = Sri Lanka ■, *Asia* 66 R12
Cèze →, *France* 21 D8
Cha-am, *Thailand* 64 F2
Cha Pa, *Vietnam* 64 A4
Chabanais, *France* 20 C4
Chabeuil, *France* 21 D9
Chablais, *France* 19 F13
Chablis, *France* 19 E10
Chacabuco, *Argentina* 126 C3
Chachapoyas, *Peru* 124 E3
Chachoengsao, *Thailand* 64 F3
Chachran, *Pakistan* 66 E7
Chachro, *Pakistan* 68 G4
Chaco □, *Argentina* 126 B3
Chaco □, *Paraguay* 126 B4
Chaco Austral, *S. Amer.* 128 B4
Chaco Boreal, *S. Amer.* 128 A4
Chaco Central, *S. Amer.* 128 A4
Chad ■, *Africa* 79 F8
Chad, L. = Tchad, L., *Chad* 79 F8
Chadan, *Russia* 51 D10
Chadileuvú →, *Argentina* 126 D2
Chadiza, *Zambia* 87 E3
Chadron, *U.S.A.* 112 D3
Chadyr-Lunga = Ciadâr-Lunga, *Moldova* 43 D13
Chae Hom, *Thailand* 64 C2
Chaem →, *Thailand* 64 C2
Chaeryŏng, *N. Korea* 57 E13
Chagai Hills, *Afghan.* 66 E3
Chagda, *Russia* 51 D14
Chagny, *France* 19 F11
Chagoda, *Russia* 46 C8
Chagos Arch., *Ind. Oc.* 52 K11
Chāh Ākhvor, *Iran* 71 C8
Chāh Bahār, *Iran* 71 E9
Chāh-e-Malek, *Iran* 71 D8
Chāh Kavīr, *Iran* 71 D7
Chahar Burjak, *Afghan.* 66 D3
Chaibasa, *India* 67 H14
Chaillé-les-Marais, *France* 20 B2
Chainat, *Thailand* 64 E3

Chaiya, *Thailand* 65 H2
Chaj Doab, *Pakistan* 68 C5
Chajari, *Argentina* 126 C4
Chake Chake, *Tanzania* 86 D4
Chakhānsūr, *Afghan.* 66 D3
Chakonipau, L., *Canada* 103 A6
Chakradharpur, *India* 69 H11
Chakwal, *Pakistan* 68 C5
Chala, *Peru* 124 G4
Chalais, *France* 20 C4
Chalchihuites, *Mexico* 118 C4
Chalcis = Khalkís, *Greece* 38 C5
Châlette-sur-Loing, *France* 19 D9
Chaleur B., *Canada* 103 C6
Chalfant, *U.S.A.* 116 H8
Chalhuanca, *Peru* 124 F4
Chalindrey, *France* 19 E12
Chaling, *China* 59 D9
Chalisgaon, *India* 66 J9
Chalky Inlet, *N.Z.* 91 M1
Challans, *France* 18 F5
Challapata, *Bolivia* 124 G5
Challis, *U.S.A.* 114 D6
Chalna, *India* 69 H13
Chalon-sur-Saône, *France* 19 F11
Chalonnes-sur-Loire, *France* 18 E6
Châlons-en-Champagne, *France* 19 D11
Châlus, *France* 20 C4
Chalyaphum, *Thailand* 64 E4
Cham, *Germany* 25 F8
Cham, Cu Lao, *Vietnam* 64 E7
Chama, *U.S.A.* 115 H10
Chaman, *Pakistan* 66 D5
Chamba, *India* 68 C7
Chamba, *Tanzania* 87 E4
Chambal →, *India* 69 F8
Chamberlain, *U.S.A.* 112 D5
Chamberlain →, *Australia* 92 C4
Chambers, *U.S.A.* 115 J9
Chambersburg, *U.S.A.* 108 F7
Chambéry, *France* 21 C9
Chambly, *Canada* 111 A11
Chambord, *Canada* 103 C5
Chamboulive, *France* 20 C5
Chamchamal, *Iraq* 70 C5
Chamela, *Mexico* 118 D3
Chamical, *Argentina* 126 C2
Chamkar Luong, *Cambodia* 65 G4
Chamonix-Mont Blanc, *France* 21 C10
Champa, *India* 69 H10
Champagne, *Canada* 104 A1
Champagne, *France* 19 D11
Champagnole, *France* 19 F12
Champaign, *U.S.A.* 108 E1
Champassak, *Laos* 64 E5
Champaubert, *France* 19 D10
Champdeniers-St-Denis, *France* 20 B3
Champeix, *France* 20 C7
Champlain, *Canada* 108 B9
Champlain, *U.S.A.* 111 B11
Champlain, L., *U.S.A.* 111 B11
Champlitte, *France* 19 E12
Champotón, *Mexico* 119 D6
Chamusca, *Portugal* 35 F2
Chana, *Thailand* 65 J3
Chañaral, *Chile* 126 B1
Chanārān, *Iran* 71 B8
Chanasma, *India* 68 H5
Chandannagar, *India* 69 H13
Chandausi, *India* 69 E8
Chandeleur Is., *U.S.A.* 113 L10
Chandeleur Sd., *U.S.A.* 113 L10
Chandigarh, *India* 68 D7
Chandler, *Australia* 95 D1
Chandler, *Canada* 103 C7
Chandler, *Ariz., U.S.A.* 115 K8
Chandler, *Okla., U.S.A.* 113 H6
Chandmani, *Mongolia* 60 B4
Chandpur, *Bangla.* 67 H17
Chandpur, *India* 68 E8
Chandrapur, *India* 66 K11
Chānf, *Iran* 71 E9
Chang, *Pakistan* 68 F3
Chang, Ko, *Thailand* 65 G4
Ch'ang Chiang = Chang Jiang →, *China* 59 B13
Chang Jiang →, *China* 59 B13
Changa, *India* 69 C7
Changanacheri, *India* 66 Q10
Changane →, *Mozam.* 89 C5
Changbai, *China* 57 D15
Changbai Shan, *China* 57 C15
Changchiak'ou = Zhangjiakou, *China* 56 D8
Ch'angchou = Changzhou, *China* 59 B12
Changchun, *China* 57 C13
Changchunling, *China* 57 B13
Changde, *China* 59 C8
Changdo-ri, *N. Korea* 57 E14
Changfeng, *China* 59 A11
Changhai = Shanghai, *China* 59 B13
Changhua, *China* 59 B12
Changhua, *Taiwan* 59 E13
Changhŭng, *S. Korea* 57 G14
Changhŭngni, *N. Korea* 57 D15
Changjiang, *China* 60 E5
Changjin, *N. Korea* 57 D14
Changjin-chŏsuji, *N. Korea* 57 D14
Changle, *China* 59 E12
Changli, *China* 57 E10
Changling, *China* 57 B12
Changlun, *Malaysia* 65 J3
Changning, *Hunan, China* 59 D9
Changning, *Yunnan, China* 58 E2
Changping, *China* 56 D9
Changsha, *China* 59 C9
Changshan, *China* 59 C12
Changshou, *China* 58 C6
Changshu, *China* 59 B13
Changshun, *China* 58 D6
Changtai, *China* 59 E11
Changting, *China* 59 E11
Changwu, *China* 56 G4
Changxing, *China* 59 B12
Changyang, *China* 59 B8
Changyi, *China* 57 F10
Changyŏn, *N. Korea* 57 E13
Changyuan, *China* 56 G8
Changzhi, *China* 56 F7
Changzhou, *China* 59 B12
Chanhanga, *Angola* 88 B1
Chanlar = Xanlar, *Azerbaijan* 49 K8
Channapatna, *India* 66 N10
Channel Is., *U.K.* 13 H5
Channel Is., *U.S.A.* 117 M7
Channel-Port aux Basques, *Canada* 103 C8
Channing, *Mich., U.S.A.* 108 B1
Channing, *Tex., U.S.A.* 113 H3
Chantada, *Spain* 34 C3
Chanthaburi, *Thailand* 64 F4
Chantilly, *France* 19 C9
Chantonnay, *France* 18 F5
Chantrey Inlet, *Canada* 100 B10
Chanute, *U.S.A.* 113 G7
Chanza →, *Spain* 35 H3
Chao Hu, *China* 59 B11
Chao Phraya →, *Thailand* 64 F3
Chao Phraya Lowlands, *Thailand* 64 E3
Chao Xian, *China* 59 B11
Chao'an, *China* 59 F11
Chaocheng, *China* 56 F8
Chaoyang, *Guangdong, China* 59 F11
Chaoyang, *Liaoning, China* 57 D11
Chapala, *Mozam.* 87 F4
Chapala, L. de, *Mexico* 118 C4
Chapayev, *Kazakstan* 48 E10
Chapayevsk, *Russia* 48 D9
Chapecó, *Brazil* 127 B5
Chapel Hill, *U.S.A.* 109 H6
Chapleau, *Canada* 102 C3
Chaplin, *Canada* 105 C7
Chaplino, *Ukraine* 47 H9
Chaplygin, *Russia* 46 F11
Chapra = Chhapra, *India* 69 G11
Chara, *Russia* 51 D12
Charadai, *Argentina* 126 B4
Charagua, *Bolivia* 124 G6
Charambirá, Punta, *Colombia* 124 C3
Charaña, *Bolivia* 124 G5
Charantsavan, *Armenia* 49 K7
Charata, *Argentina* 126 B3
Charcas, *Mexico* 118 C4
Charcoal L., *Canada* 105 B8
Chard, *U.K.* 13 G5
Chardon, *U.S.A.* 110 E3
Chardzhou = Chärjew, *Turkmenistan* 50 F7
Charente □, *France* 20 C4
Charente →, *France* 20 C2
Charente-Maritime □, *France* 20 C3
Charenton-du-Cher, *France* 19 F9
Chari →, *Chad* 79 F8
Chārīkār, *Afghan.* 66 B6
Chariton →, *U.S.A.* 112 F8
Chärjew, *Turkmenistan* 50 F7
Charkhari, *India* 69 G8
Charkhi Dadri, *India* 68 E7
Charleroi, *Belgium* 17 D4
Charleroi, *U.S.A.* 110 F5
Charles, C., *U.S.A.* 108 G8
Charles City, *U.S.A.* 112 D8
Charles L., *Canada* 105 B6
Charles Town, *U.S.A.* 108 F7
Charleston, *Ill., U.S.A.* 108 F1
Charleston, *Miss., U.S.A.* 113 H9
Charleston, *Mo., U.S.A.* 113 G10
Charleston, *S.C., U.S.A.* 109 J6
Charleston, *W. Va., U.S.A.* 108 F5
Charleston Peak, *U.S.A.* 117 J11
Charlestown, *Ireland* 15 C3
Charlestown, *S. Africa* 89 D4
Charlestown, *U.S.A.* 108 F3
Charleville = Rath Luirc, *Ireland* 15 D3
Charleville, *Australia* 95 D4
Charleville-Mézières, *France* 19 C11
Charlevoix, *U.S.A.* 108 C3
Charlieu, *France* 19 F11
Charlotte, *Mich., U.S.A.* 108 D3
Charlotte, *N.C., U.S.A.* 109 H5
Charlotte Amalie, *Virgin Is.* 121 C7
Charlotte Harbor, *U.S.A.* 109 M4
Charlottenberg, *Sweden* 10 E6
Charlottesville, *U.S.A.* 108 F6
Charlottetown, *Canada* 103 C7
Charlton, *Australia* 95 F3
Charlton, *U.S.A.* 112 E8
Charlton I., *Canada* 102 B4
Charmes, *France* 19 D13
Charny, *Canada* 103 C5
Charolles, *France* 19 F11
Chârost, *France* 19 F9
Charre, *Mozam.* 87 F4
Charroux, *France* 20 B4
Charsadda, *Pakistan* 68 B4
Charters Towers, *Australia* 94 C4
Chartres, *France* 18 D8
Chascomús, *Argentina* 126 D4
Chasefu, *Zambia* 87 E3
Chasseneuil-sur-Bonnieure, *France* 20 C4
Chāt, *Iran* 71 B7
Chatal Balkan = Udvoy Balkan, *Bulgaria* 41 D10
Château-Arnoux, *France* 21 D10
Château-Chinon, *France* 19 E10
Château-d'Olonne, *France* 20 B2
Château-du-Loir, *France* 18 E7
Château-Gontier, *France* 18 E6
Château-la-Vallière, *France* 18 E7
Château-Landon, *France* 19 D9
Château-Renault, *France* 18 E7
Château-Salins, *France* 19 D13
Château-Thierry, *France* 19 C10
Châteaubourg, *France* 18 D5
Châteaubriant, *France* 18 E5
Châteaudun, *France* 18 D8
Châteaugiron, *France* 18 D5
Châteaulin, *France* 18 D2
Châteaumeillant, *France* 19 F9
Châteauneuf-du-Faou, *France* 18 D3
Châteauneuf-sur-Charente, *France* 20 C3
Châteauneuf-sur-Cher, *France* 19 F9
Châteauneuf-sur-Loire, *France* 19 E9
Châteaurenard, *Bouches-du-Rhône, France* 21 E8
Châteaurenard, *Loiret, France* 19 E9
Châteauroux, *France* 19 F8
Châteauvillain, *France* 19 D11
Châtelaillon-Plage, *France* 20 B2
Châtelguyon, *France* 20 C7
Châtellerault, *France* 18 F7
Châtelus-Malvaleix, *France* 19 F9
Chatfield, *U.S.A.* 112 D9
Chatham, *N.B., Canada* 103 C6
Chatham, *Ont., Canada* 102 D3
Chatham, *U.K.* 13 F8
Chatham, *La., U.S.A.* 113 J8
Chatham, *N.Y., U.S.A.* 111 D11
Chatham Is., *Pac. Oc.* 96 M10
Chatham Str., *U.S.A.* 104 B2
Châtillon, *Italy* 28 C4
Châtillon-Coligny, *France* 19 E9
Châtillon-en-Diois, *France* 21 D9
Châtillon-sur-Indre, *France* 18 F8
Châtillon-sur-Loire, *France* 19 E9
Châtillon-sur-Seine, *France* 19 E11
Chatmohar, *Bangla.* 69 G13
Chatra, *India* 69 G11
Chatrapur, *India* 67 K14
Chats, L. des, *Canada* 111 A8
Chatsworth, *Canada* 110 B4
Chatsworth, *Zimbabwe* 87 F3
Chattahoochee →, *U.S.A.* 109 K3
Chattanooga, *U.S.A.* 109 H3
Chatteris, *U.K.* 13 E8
Chaturat, *Thailand* 64 E3
Chau Doc, *Vietnam* 65 G5
Chaudes-Aigues, *France* 20 D7
Chauffailles, *France* 19 F11
Chauk, *Burma* 67 J19
Chaukan La, *Burma* 67 F20
Chaumont, *France* 19 D12
Chaumont, *U.S.A.* 111 B8
Chaumont-en-Vexin, *France* 19 C8
Chaumont-sur-Loire, *France* 18 E8
Chaunay, *France* 20 B4
Chauny, *France* 19 C10
Chausey, Îs., *France* 18 D5
Chaussin, *France* 19 F12
Chautauqua L., *U.S.A.* 110 D5
Chauvigny, *France* 18 F7
Chauvin, *Canada* 105 C6
Chavanges, *France* 19 D11
Chaves, *Brazil* 125 D9
Chaves, *Portugal* 34 D3
Chawang, *Thailand* 65 H2
Chazelles-sur-Lyon, *France* 21 C8
Chazy, *U.S.A.* 111 B11
Cheb, *Czech Rep.* 26 A5
Cheboksarskoye Vdkhr., *Russia* 48 B8
Cheboksary, *Russia* 48 B8
Cheboygan, *U.S.A.* 108 C3
Chebsara, *Russia* 46 C10
Chech, Erg, *Africa* 78 D5
Chechen, Ostrov, *Russia* 49 H8
Chechenia □, *Russia* 49 J7
Checheno-Ingush Republic = Chechenia □, *Russia* 49 J7
Chechnya = Chechenia □, *Russia* 49 J7
Chechon, *S. Korea* 57 F15
Chęciny, *Poland* 45 H7
Checleset B., *Canada* 104 C3
Checotah, *U.S.A.* 113 H7
Chedabucto B., *Canada* 103 C7
Cheduba I., *Burma* 67 K18
Cheepie, *Australia* 95 D4
Chef-Boutonne, *France* 20 B3
Chegdomyn, *Russia* 51 D14
Chegga, *Mauritania* 78 C4
Chegutu, *Zimbabwe* 87 F3
Chehalis, *U.S.A.* 116 D4
Cheiron, Mt., *France* 21 E10
Cheju Do, *S. Korea* 57 H14
Chekalin, *Russia* 46 E9
Chekiang = Zhejiang □, *China* 59 C13
Chel = Kuru, Bahr el →, *Sudan* 81 F2
Chela, Sa. da, *Angola* 88 B1
Chelan, *U.S.A.* 114 C4
Chelan, L., *U.S.A.* 114 B3
Cheleken, *Turkmenistan* 50 F6
Chelforó, *Argentina* 128 D3
Chelkar = Shalqar, *Kazakstan* 50 E6
Chelkar Tengiz, Solonchak, *Kazakstan* 50 E7
Chelles, *France* 19 D9
Chełm, *Poland* 45 G10
Chełm □, *Poland* 45 G10
Chełmno, *Poland* 45 E5
Chelmsford, *U.K.* 13 F8
Chełmża, *Poland* 45 E5
Chelsea, *Okla., U.S.A.* 113 G7
Chelsea, *Vt., U.S.A.* 111 C12
Cheltenham, *U.K.* 13 F5
Chelva, *Spain* 32 F4
Chelyabinsk, *Russia* 50 D7
Chelyuskin, C., *Russia* 52 B14
Chemainus, *Canada* 104 D4
Chembar = Belinskiy, *Russia* 48 D6
Chemillé, *France* 18 E6
Chemnitz, *Germany* 24 E8
Chemult, *U.S.A.* 114 E3
Chen, Gora, *Russia* 51 C15
Chen Xian, *China* 59 E9
Chenab →, *Pakistan* 68 D4
Chenango Forks, *U.S.A.* 111 D9
Chencha, *Ethiopia* 81 F4
Chenchiang = Zhenjiang, *China* 59 A12
Cheney, *U.S.A.* 114 C5
Cheng Xian, *China* 56 H3
Chengbu, *China* 59 D8
Chengcheng, *China* 56 G5
Chengchou = Zhengzhou, *China* 56 G7
Chengde, *China* 57 D9
Chengdong Hu, *China* 59 A11
Chengdu, *China* 58 B5
Chenggong, *China* 58 E4
Chenggu, *China* 56 H4
Chengjiang, *China* 58 E4
Chengkou, *China* 58 B7
Ch'engtu = Chengdu, *China* 58 B5
Chengwu, *China* 56 G8
Chengxi Hu, *China* 59 A11
Chengyang, *China* 57 F11
Chenjiagang, *China* 57 G10
Chenkán, *Mexico* 119 D6
Chennai, *India* 66 N12
Chenôve, *France* 19 E12
Chenxi, *China* 59 C8
Cheom Ksan, *Cambodia* 64 E5
Chepelare, *Bulgaria* 41 E8
Chepén, *Peru* 124 E3
Chepes, *Argentina* 126 C2
Chepo, *Panama* 120 E4
Chepstow, *U.K.* 13 F5
Cheptulil, Mt., *Kenya* 86 B4
Chequamegon B., *U.S.A.* 112 B9
Cher □, *France* 19 E9
Cher →, *France* 18 E7
Chéradi, *Italy* 31 B10
Cherasco, *Italy* 28 D4
Cheraw, *U.S.A.* 109 H6
Cherbourg, *France* 18 C5
Cherdakly, *Russia* 48 C9
Cherdyn, *Russia* 50 C6
Cheremkhovo, *Russia* 51 D11
Cherepanovo, *Russia* 50 D9
Cherepovets, *Russia* 46 C9
Chergui, Chott ech, *Algeria* 78 B6
Cherikov = Cherykaw, *Belarus* 46 F6
Cherkasy, *Ukraine* 47 H7
Cherkessk, *Russia* 49 H6
Cherlak, *Russia* 50 D8
Chernaya, *Russia* 51 B9
Cherni, *Bulgaria* 40 D7
Chernigov = Chernihiv, *Ukraine* 47 G6
Chernihiv, *Ukraine* 47 G6
Chernivtsi, *Ukraine* 47 H3
Chernobyl = Chornobyl, *Ukraine* 47 G6
Chernogorsk, *Russia* 51 D10
Chernomorskoye = Chornomorske, *Ukraine* 47 K7
Chernovtsy = Chernivtsi, *Ukraine* 47 H3
Chernyakhovsk, *Russia* 9 J19
Chernyanka, *Russia* 47 G9
Chernyshevskiy, *Russia* 51 C12
Chernyye Zemli, *Russia* 49 H8
Cherokee, *Iowa, U.S.A.* 112 D7
Cherokee, *Okla., U.S.A.* 113 G5
Cherokees, Lake O' The, *U.S.A.* 113 G7
Cherrapunji, *India* 67 G17
Cherry Creek, *U.S.A.* 114 G6
Cherry Valley, *U.S.A.* 117 M10
Cherryvale, *U.S.A.* 113 G7
Cherskiy, *Russia* 51 C17
Cherskogo Khrebet, *Russia* 51 C15
Chertkovo, *Russia* 47 H11
Cherven, *Belarus* 46 F5
Cherven-Bryag, *Bulgaria* 41 C8
Chervonohrad, *Ukraine* 47 G3
Cherwell →, *U.K.* 13 F6
Cherykaw, *Belarus* 46 F6
Chesapeake, *U.S.A.* 108 G7
Chesapeake B., *U.S.A.* 108 G7
Cheshire □, *U.K.* 12 D5
Cheshskaya Guba, *Russia* 50 C5
Cheshunt, *U.K.* 13 F7
Chesil Beach, *U.K.* 13 G5
Cheslatta L., *Canada* 104 C3
Chesley, *Canada* 110 B3
Cheste, *Spain* 33 F4
Chester, *U.K.* 12 D5
Chester, *Calif., U.S.A.* 114 F3
Chester, *Ill., U.S.A.* 113 G10
Chester, *Mont., U.S.A.* 114 B8
Chester, *Pa., U.S.A.* 108 F8
Chester, *S.C., U.S.A.* 109 H5
Chester-le-Street, *U.K.* 12 C6
Chesterfield, *U.K.* 12 D6
Chesterfield, Is., *N. Cal.* 96 J7
Chesterfield Inlet, *Canada* 100 B10
Chesterton Ra., *Australia* 95 D4
Chesterville, *Canada* 111 A9
Chesuncook L., *U.S.A.* 103 C6
Chéticamp, *Canada* 103 C7
Chetrosu, *Moldova* 43 B12
Chetumal, B. de, *Mexico* 119 D7
Chetwynd, *Canada* 104 B4
Chevanceaux, *France* 20 C3
Cheviot, The, *U.K.* 12 B5
Cheviot Hills, *U.K.* 12 B5
Cheviot Ra., *Australia* 94 D3
Chew Bahir, *Ethiopia* 81 G4
Chewelah, *U.S.A.* 114 B5
Cheyenne, *Okla., U.S.A.* 113 H5
Cheyenne, *Wyo., U.S.A.* 112 E2
Cheyenne →, *U.S.A.* 112 C4
Cheyenne Wells, *U.S.A.* 112 F3
Cheyne B., *Australia* 93 F2
Chhabra, *India* 68 G7
Chhapra, *India* 69 G11
Chhata, *India* 68 F7
Chhatarpur, *India* 69 G8
Chhep, *Cambodia* 64 F5
Chhindwara, *India* 69 H8
Chhlong, *Cambodia* 65 F5
Chhuk, *Cambodia* 65 G5
Chi →, *Thailand* 64 E5
Chiai, *Taiwan* 59 F13
Chiali, *Taiwan* 59 F13
Chiamussu = Jiamusi, *China* 60 B8
Chianciano Terme, *Italy* 29 E8
Chiang Dao, *Thailand* 64 C2
Chiang Kham, *Thailand* 64 C3
Chiang Khan, *Thailand* 64 D3
Chiang Khong, *Thailand* 64 B3
Chiang Mai, *Thailand* 64 C2
Chiang Saen, *Thailand* 64 B3
Chiapa →, *Mexico* 119 D6
Chiapa de Corzo, *Mexico* 119 D6
Chiapas □, *Mexico* 119 D6
Chiaramonte Gulfi, *Italy* 31 E7
Chiaravalle, *Italy* 29 E10
Chiaravalle Centrale, *Italy* 31 D9
Chiari, *Italy* 28 C6
Chiatura, *Georgia* 49 J6
Chiautla, *Mexico* 119 D5
Chiávari, *Italy* 28 D6
Chiavenna, *Italy* 28 B6
Chiba, *Japan* 55 G10
Chibabava, *Mozam.* 89 C5
Chibemba, *Cunene, Angola* 85 H2
Chibemba, *Huila, Angola* 88 B2
Chibia, *Angola* 85 H2
Chibougamau, *Canada* 102 C5
Chibougamau L., *Canada* 102 C5
Chibuk, *Nigeria* 83 C7
Chic-Chocs, Mts., *Canada* 103 C6
Chicacole = Srikakulam, *India* 67 K13
Chicago, *U.S.A.* 108 E2
Chicago Heights, *U.S.A.* 108 E2
Chichagof I., *U.S.A.* 104 B1
Chicheng, *China* 56 D8
Chichester, *U.K.* 13 G7
Chichibu, *Japan* 55 F9
Ch'ich'ihaerh = Qiqihar, *China* 60 B7
Chickasha, *U.S.A.* 113 H6
Chiclana de la Frontera, *Spain* 35 J4
Chiclayo, *Peru* 124 E3
Chico, *U.S.A.* 116 F5
Chico →, *Chubut, Argentina* 128 E3
Chico →, *Santa Cruz, Argentina* 128 G3
Chicomo, *Mozam.* 89 C5
Chicontepec, *Mexico* 119 C5
Chicopee, *U.S.A.* 111 D12
Chicoutimi, *Canada* 103 C5
Chicualacuala, *Mozam.* 89 C5
Chidambaram, *India* 66 P11
Chidenguele, *Mozam.* 89 C5
Chidley, C., *Canada* 4 C4
Chiede, *Angola* 88 B2
Chiefs Pt., *Canada* 110 B3

Chiem Hoa, *Vietnam* 64 A5
Chiemsee, *Germany* 25 H8
Chiengi, *Zambia* 87 D2
Chiengmai = Chiang Mai, *Thailand* 64 C2
Chienti →, *Italy* 29 E10
Chieri, *Italy* 28 C4
Chiers →, *France* 19 C11
Chiesa in Valmalenco, *Italy* 28 B6
Chiese →, *Italy* 28 C7
Chieti, *Italy* 29 F11
Chifeng, *China* 57 C10
Chigirin, *Ukraine* 47 H7
Chignecto B., *Canada* 103 C7
Chiguana, *Bolivia* 126 A2
Chigwell, *U.K.* 13 F8
Chiha-ri, *N. Korea* 57 E14
Chihli, G. of = Bo Hai, *China* 57 E10
Chihuahua, *Mexico* 118 B3
Chihuahua □, *Mexico* 118 B3
Chiili, *Kazakstan* 50 E7
Chik Bollapur, *India* 66 N10
Chikmagalur, *India* 66 N9
Chikwawa, *Malawi* 87 F3
Chilac, *Mexico* 119 D5
Chilako →, *Canada* 104 C4
Chilam Chavki, *Pakistan* 69 B6
Chilanga, *Zambia* 87 F2
Chilapa, *Mexico* 119 D5
Chilas, *Pakistan* 69 B6
Chilaw, *Sri Lanka* 66 R11
Chilcotin →, *Canada* 104 C4
Childers, *Australia* 95 D5
Childress, *U.S.A.* 113 H4
Chile ■, *S. Amer.* 128 D2
Chile Rise, *Pac. Oc.* 97 L18
Chilecito, *Argentina* 126 B2
Chilete, *Peru* 124 E3
Chilia, Braţul →, *Romania* 43 E14
Chililabombwe, *Zambia* 87 E2
Chilin = Jilin, *China* 57 C14
Chilka L., *India* 67 K14
Chilko →, *Canada* 104 C4
Chilko, L., *Canada* 104 C4
Chillagoe, *Australia* 94 B3
Chillán, *Chile* 126 D1
Chillicothe, *Ill., U.S.A.* 112 E10
Chillicothe, *Mo., U.S.A.* 112 F8
Chillicothe, *Ohio, U.S.A.* 108 F4
Chilliwack, *Canada* 104 D4
Chilo, *India* 68 F5
Chiloane, I., *Mozam.* 89 C5
Chiloé, I. de, *Chile* 122 H3
Chilpancingo, *Mexico* 119 D5
Chiltern Hills, *U.K.* 13 F7
Chilton, *U.S.A.* 108 C1
Chilubi, *Zambia* 87 E2
Chilubula, *Zambia* 87 E3
Chilumba, *Malawi* 87 E3
Chilung, *Taiwan* 59 E13
Chilwa, L., *Malawi* 87 F4
Chimaltitán, *Mexico* 118 C4
Chimán, *Panama* 120 E4
Chimay, *Belgium* 17 D4
Chimbay, *Uzbekistan* 50 E6
Chimborazo, *Ecuador* 122 D3
Chimbote, *Peru* 124 E3
Chimkent = Shymkent, *Kazakstan* 50 E7
Chimoio, *Mozam.* 87 F3
Chimpembe, *Zambia* 87 D2
Chin □, *Burma* 67 J18
Chin Ling Shan = Qinling Shandi, *China* 56 H5
China, *Mexico* 119 B5
China ■, *Asia* 56 E3
China Lake, *U.S.A.* 117 K9
Chinan = Jinan, *China* 56 F9
Chinandega, *Nic.* 120 D2
Chinati Peak, *U.S.A.* 113 L2
Chincha Alta, *Peru* 122 E3
Chinchilla, *Australia* 95 D5
Chinchilla de Monte Aragón, *Spain* 33 G3
Chinchorro, Banco, *Mexico* 119 D7
Chinchou = Jinzhou, *China* 57 D11
Chincoteague, *U.S.A.* 108 G8
Chinde, *Mozam.* 87 F4
Chindo, *S. Korea* 57 G14
Chindwin →, *Burma* 67 J19
Chineni, *India* 69 C6
Chinga, *Mozam.* 87 F4
Chingola, *Zambia* 87 E2
Chingole, *Malawi* 87 E3
Ch'ingtao = Qingdao, *China* 57 F11
Chinguetti, *Mauritania* 78 D3
Chingune, *Mozam.* 89 C5
Chinhae, *S. Korea* 57 G15
Chinhanguanine, *Mozam.* 89 D5
Chinhoyi, *Zimbabwe* 87 F3
Chiniot, *Pakistan* 68 D5
Chínipas, *Mexico* 118 B3
Chinju, *S. Korea* 57 G15
Chinle, *U.S.A.* 115 H9
Chinmen, *Taiwan* 59 E13
Chinmen Tao, *Taiwan* 59 E13
Chinnampo = Nampo, *N. Korea* 57 E13
Chino, *Japan* 55 G9
Chino, *U.S.A.* 117 L9
Chino Valley, *U.S.A.* 115 J7
Chinon, *France* 18 E7
Chinook, *Canada* 105 C6
Chinook, *U.S.A.* 114 B9
Chinsali, *Zambia* 87 E3
Chióggia, *Italy* 29 C9
Chipata, *Zambia* 87 E3
Chiperceni, *Moldova* 43 C13
Chipewyan L., *Canada* 105 B9
Chipinge, *Zimbabwe* 87 G3
Chipiona, *Spain* 35 J4
Chipley, *U.S.A.* 109 K3
Chipman, *Canada* 103 C6
Chipoka, *Malawi* 87 E3
Chippenham, *U.K.* 13 F5
Chippewa →, *U.S.A.* 112 C8
Chippewa Falls, *U.S.A.* 112 C9
Chipping Norton, *U.K.* 13 F6
Chiprovtsi, *Bulgaria* 40 C6
Chiquián, *Peru* 124 F3
Chiquimula, *Guatemala* 120 D2
Chiquinquira, *Colombia* 124 B4
Chir →, *Russia* 49 F6
Chirala, *India* 66 M12
Chiramba, *Mozam.* 87 F3
Chirawa, *India* 68 E6
Chirchiq, *Uzbekistan* 50 E7
Chiredzi, *Zimbabwe* 89 C5
Chiricahua Peak, *U.S.A.* 115 L9
Chiriquí, G. de, *Panama* 120 E3
Chiriquí, L. de, *Panama* 120 E3
Chirivira Falls, *Zimbabwe* 87 G3
Chirmiri, *India* 67 H13
Chirnogi, *Romania* 43 F11
Chirpan, *Bulgaria* 41 D9
Chirripó Grande, Cerro, *Costa Rica* 120 E3
Chisamba, *Zambia* 87 E2
Chisapani Garhi, *Nepal* 67 F14
Chisasibi, *Canada* 102 B4
Ch'ishan, *Taiwan* 59 F13
Chisholm, *Canada* 104 C6
Chishtian Mandi, *Pakistan* 68 E5
Chishui, *China* 58 C5
Chishui He →, *China* 58 C5
Chisimaio, *Somali Rep.* 77 G8
Chisimba Falls, *Zambia* 87 E3
Chişinău, *Moldova* 43 C13
Chişineu Criş, *Romania* 42 D6
Chisone →, *Italy* 28 D4
Chisos Mts., *U.S.A.* 113 L3
Chistopol, *Russia* 48 C10
Chita, *Russia* 51 D12
Chitipa, *Malawi* 87 D3
Chitose, *Japan* 54 C10
Chitral, *Pakistan* 66 B7
Chitré, *Panama* 120 E3
Chittagong, *Bangla.* 67 H17
Chittagong □, *Bangla.* 67 G17
Chittaurgarh, *India* 68 G6
Chittoor, *India* 66 N11
Chitungwiza, *Zimbabwe* 87 F3
Chiusi, *Italy* 29 E8
Chiva, *Spain* 33 F4
Chivasso, *Italy* 28 C4
Chivhu, *Zimbabwe* 87 F3
Chivilcoy, *Argentina* 126 C4
Chiwanda, *Tanzania* 87 E3
Chixi, *China* 59 G9
Chizera, *Zambia* 87 E2
Chkalov = Orenburg, *Russia* 50 D6
Chkolovsk, *Russia* 48 B6
Chloride, *U.S.A.* 117 K12
Chlumec nad Cidlinou, *Czech Rep.* 26 A8
Chmielnik, *Poland* 45 H7
Cho Bo, *Vietnam* 64 B5
Cho-do, *N. Korea* 57 E13
Cho Phuoc Hai, *Vietnam* 65 G6
Choba, *Kenya* 86 B4
Chobe National Park, *Botswana* 88 B4
Chochiwŏn, *S. Korea* 57 F14
Chocianów, *Poland* 45 G2
Chociwel, *Poland* 44 E2
Choctawhatchee B., *U.S.A.* 107 D9
Chodecz, *Poland* 45 F6
Chodov, *Czech Rep.* 26 A5
Chodziez, *Poland* 45 F3
Choele Choel, *Argentina* 128 D3
Choix, *Mexico* 118 B3
Chojna, *Poland* 45 F1
Chojnice, *Poland* 44 E4
Chojnów, *Poland* 45 G2
Chōkai-San, *Japan* 54 E10
Choke, *Ethiopia* 81 E4
Chokurdakh, *Russia* 51 B15
Cholame, *U.S.A.* 116 K6
Cholet, *France* 18 E6
Choluteca, *Honduras* 120 D2
Choluteca →, *Honduras* 120 D2
Chom Bung, *Thailand* 64 F2
Chom Thong, *Thailand* 64 C2
Choma, *Zambia* 87 F2
Chomen Swamp, *Ethiopia* 81 F4
Chomun, *India* 68 F6
Chomutov, *Czech Rep.* 26 A6
Chon Buri, *Thailand* 64 F3
Chon Thanh, *Vietnam* 65 G6
Chonan, *S. Korea* 57 F14
Chone, *Ecuador* 124 D3
Chong Kai, *Cambodia* 64 F4
Chong Mek, *Thailand* 64 E5
Chong'an, *China* 59 D12
Chongde, *China* 59 B13
Chŏngdo, *S. Korea* 57 G15
Chŏngha, *S. Korea* 57 F15
Chŏngjin, *N. Korea* 57 D15
Chŏngju, *N. Korea* 57 E13
Chŏngju, *S. Korea* 57 F14
Chongli, *China* 56 D8
Chongming, *China* 59 B13
Chongming Dao, *China* 59 B13
Chongqing, *Chongqing, China* 58 C6
Chongqing, *Sichuan, China* 58 B4
Chongqing □, *China* 58 B7
Chongren, *China* 59 D11
Chŏngŭp, *S. Korea* 57 G14
Chongzuo, *China* 58 F6
Chŏnju, *S. Korea* 57 G14
Chonos, Arch. de los, *Chile* 122 H3
Chop, *Ukraine* 47 H2
Chopim →, *Brazil* 127 B5
Chorbat La, *India* 69 B7
Chorley, *U.K.* 12 D5
Chornobyl, *Ukraine* 47 G6
Chornomorske, *Ukraine* 47 K7
Chorolque, Cerro, *Bolivia* 126 A2
Choroszcz, *Poland* 45 E9
Chorregon, *Australia* 94 C3
Chortkiv, *Ukraine* 47 H3
Chŏrwŏn, *S. Korea* 57 E14
Chorzele, *Poland* 45 E7
Chorzów, *Poland* 45 H5
Chos-Malal, *Argentina* 126 D1
Chosan, *N. Korea* 57 D13
Choszczno, *Poland* 45 E2
Choteau, *U.S.A.* 114 C7
Chotěboř, *Czech Rep.* 26 B8
Chotila, *India* 68 H4
Chowchilla, *U.S.A.* 116 H6
Choybalsan, *Mongolia* 60 B6
Christchurch, *N.Z.* 91 K4
Christchurch, *U.K.* 13 G6
Christian I., *Canada* 110 B4
Christiana, *S. Africa* 88 D4
Christiansfeld, *Denmark* 11 J3
Christiansted, *Virgin Is.* 121 C7
Christie B., *Canada* 105 A6
Christina →, *Canada* 105 B6
Christmas Cr. →, *Australia* 92 C4
Christmas Creek, *Australia* 92 C4
Christmas I. = Kiritimati, *Kiribati* 97 G12
Christmas I., *Ind. Oc.* 96 J2
Christopher L., *Australia* 93 D4
Chrudim, *Czech Rep.* 26 B8
Chrzanów, *Poland* 45 H6
Chtimba, *Malawi* 87 E3
Chu = Shu, *Kazakstan* 50 E8
Chu → = Shu →, *Kazakstan* 52 E10
Chu →, *Vietnam* 64 C5
Chu Chua, *Canada* 104 C4
Chu Lai, *Vietnam* 64 E7
Chu Xian, *China* 59 A12
Ch'uanchou = Quanzhou, *China* 59 E12
Chuankou, *China* 56 G6
Chūbu □, *Japan* 55 F8
Chubut →, *Argentina* 122 H4
Chuchi L., *Canada* 104 B4
Chudovo, *Russia* 46 C6
Chudskoye, Oz., *Russia* 9 G22
Chūgoku □, *Japan* 55 G6
Chūgoku-Sanchi, *Japan* 55 G6
Chuguyev = Chuhuyiv, *Ukraine* 47 H9
Chugwater, *U.S.A.* 112 E2
Chuhuyiv, *Ukraine* 47 H9
Chukchi Sea, *Russia* 51 C19
Chukotskoye Nagorye, *Russia* 51 C18
Chula Vista, *U.S.A.* 117 N9
Chulucanas, *Peru* 124 E2
Chulym →, *Russia* 50 D9
Chum Phae, *Thailand* 64 D4
Chum Saeng, *Thailand* 64 E3
Chumar, *India* 69 C8
Chumbicha, *Argentina* 126 B2
Chumerna, *Bulgaria* 41 D9
Chumikan, *Russia* 51 D14
Chumphon, *Thailand* 65 G2
Chumuare, *Mozam.* 87 E3
Chumunjin, *S. Korea* 57 F15
Chuna →, *Russia* 51 D10
Chun'an, *China* 59 C12
Chunchŏn, *S. Korea* 57 F14
Chunchura, *India* 69 H13
Chunga, *Zambia* 87 F2
Chunggang-ŭp, *N. Korea* 57 D14
Chunghwa, *N. Korea* 57 E13
Chungju, *S. Korea* 57 F14
Chungking = Chongqing, *China* 58 C6
Chungli, *Taiwan* 59 E13
Chungmu, *S. Korea* 57 G15
Chungt'iaoshan = Zhongtiao Shan, *China* 56 G6
Chungyang Shanmo, *Taiwan* 59 F13
Chunian, *Pakistan* 68 D6
Chunya, *Tanzania* 87 D3
Chunya □, *Tanzania* 86 D3
Chunyang, *China* 57 C15
Chuquibamba, *Peru* 124 G4
Chuquicamata, *Chile* 126 A2
Chur, *Switz.* 25 J5
Churachandpur, *India* 67 G18
Churchill, *Canada* 105 B10
Churchill →, *Man., Canada* 105 B10
Churchill →, *Nfld., Canada* 103 B7
Churchill, C., *Canada* 105 B10
Churchill Falls, *Canada* 103 B7
Churchill L., *Canada* 105 B7
Churchill Pk., *Canada* 104 B3
Churu, *India* 68 E6
Churún Merú = Angel Falls, *Venezuela* 124 B6
Chushal, *India* 69 C8
Chusovoy, *Russia* 50 D6
Chuuronjang, *N. Korea* 57 D15
Chuvash Republic □ = Chuvashia □, *Russia* 48 C8
Chuvashia □, *Russia* 48 C8
Chuwārtah, *Iraq* 70 C5
Chuxiong, *China* 58 E3
Ci Xian, *China* 56 F8
Ciacova, *Romania* 42 E6
Ciadâr-Lunga, *Moldova* 43 D13
Ciamis, *Indonesia* 63 G13
Cianjur, *Indonesia* 63 G12
Cianorte, *Brazil* 128 B6
Cibola, *U.S.A.* 117 M12
Cicero, *U.S.A.* 108 E2
Cidacos →, *Spain* 32 C3
Cide, *Turkey* 72 B5
Ciechanów, *Poland* 45 F7
Ciechanów □, *Poland* 45 E7
Ciechanowiec, *Poland* 45 F9
Ciechocinek, *Poland* 45 F5
Ciego de Avila, *Cuba* 120 B4
Ciénaga, *Colombia* 124 A4
Cienfuegos, *Cuba* 120 B3
Cierp, *France* 20 F4
Cíes, Is., *Spain* 34 C2
Cieszanów, *Poland* 45 H10
Cieszyn, *Poland* 45 J5
Cieza, *Spain* 33 G3
Çifteler, *Turkey* 72 C4
Cifuentes, *Spain* 32 E2
Cihanbeyli, *Turkey* 72 C5
Cihuatlán, *Mexico* 118 D4
Cijara, Embalse de, *Spain* 35 F6
Cijulang, *Indonesia* 63 G13
Cilacap, *Indonesia* 63 G13
Çıldır, *Turkey* 73 B10
Çıldır Gölü, *Turkey* 73 B10
Cili, *China* 59 C8
Cilibia, *Romania* 43 E12
Cilicia, *Turkey* 72 D5
Cill Chainnigh = Kilkenny, *Ireland* 15 D4
Cilo Dağı, *Turkey* 73 D10
Cima, *U.S.A.* 117 K11
Cimarron, *Kans., U.S.A.* 113 G4
Cimarron, *N. Mex., U.S.A.* 113 G2
Cimarron →, *U.S.A.* 113 G6
Cimişlia, *Moldova* 43 D13
Cimone, Mte., *Italy* 28 D7
Çinar, *Turkey* 73 D9
Çınarcık, *Turkey* 41 F13
Cinca →, *Spain* 32 D5
Cincar, *Bos.-H.* 42 G2
Cincinnati, *U.S.A.* 108 F3
Çine, *Turkey* 39 D10
Ciney, *Belgium* 17 D5
Cíngoli, *Italy* 29 E10
Cinigiano, *Italy* 29 F8
Cinto, Mte., *France* 21 F12
Cintruénigo, *Spain* 32 C3
Ciocile, *Romania* 43 F12
Ciolăneşti din Deal, *Romania* 43 F10
Ciorani, *Romania* 43 F11
Čiovo, *Croatia* 29 E13
Circeo, Mte., *Italy* 30 A6
Çirçir, *Turkey* 72 C7
Circle, *Alaska, U.S.A.* 100 B5
Circle, *Mont., U.S.A.* 112 B2
Circleville, *Ohio, U.S.A.* 108 F4
Circleville, *Utah, U.S.A.* 115 G7
Cirebon, *Indonesia* 63 G13
Ciremai, *Indonesia* 63 G13
Cirencester, *U.K.* 13 F6
Cireşu, *Romania* 42 F7
Cirey-sur-Vezouze, *France* 19 D13
Ciriè, *Italy* 28 C4
Cirium, *Cyprus* 36 E11
Cirò, *Italy* 31 C10
Cirò Marina, *Italy* 31 C10
Ciron →, *France* 20 D3
Cisco, *U.S.A.* 113 J5
Cislău, *Romania* 43 E11
Cisna, *Poland* 45 J9
Cisnădie, *Romania* 43 E9
Cisterna di Latina, *Italy* 30 A5
Cisternino, *Italy* 31 B10
Cistierna, *Spain* 34 C5
Citeli-Ckaro = Tsiteli-Tsqaro, *Georgia* 49 K8
Citlaltépetl, *Mexico* 119 D5
Citrus Heights, *U.S.A.* 116 G5
Citrusdal, *S. Africa* 88 E2
Città della Pieve, *Italy* 29 F9
Città di Castello, *Italy* 29 E9
Città Sant' Angelo, *Italy* 29 F11
Cittadella, *Italy* 29 C8
Cittaducale, *Italy* 29 F9
Cittanova, *Italy* 31 D9
City of Edinburgh □, *U.K.* 14 F5
City of Glasgow □, *U.K.* 14 F4
Ciuc, Munţii, *Romania* 43 D11
Ciucaş, Vf., *Romania* 43 E10
Ciucea, *Romania* 42 D7
Ciuciulea, *Moldova* 43 C12
Ciuciuleni, *Moldova* 43 C13
Ciudad Altamirano, *Mexico* 118 D4
Ciudad Bolívar, *Venezuela* 124 B6
Ciudad Camargo, *Mexico* 118 B3
Ciudad Chetumal, *Mexico* 119 D7
Ciudad de Valles, *Mexico* 119 C5
Ciudad del Carmen, *Mexico* 119 D6
Ciudad del Este, *Paraguay* 127 B5
Ciudad Delicias = Delicias, *Mexico* 118 B3
Ciudad Guayana, *Venezuela* 124 B6
Ciudad Guerrero, *Mexico* 118 B3
Ciudad Guzmán, *Mexico* 118 D4
Ciudad Juárez, *Mexico* 118 A3
Ciudad Madero, *Mexico* 119 C5
Ciudad Mante, *Mexico* 119 C5
Ciudad Obregón, *Mexico* 118 B3
Ciudad Real, *Spain* 35 G7
Ciudad Real □, *Spain* 35 G7
Ciudad Rodrigo, *Spain* 34 E4
Ciudad Trujillo = Santo Domingo, *Dom. Rep.* 121 C6
Ciudad Victoria, *Mexico* 119 C5
Ciudadela, *Spain* 37 B10
Ciulniţa, *Romania* 43 F12
Ciumeghiu, *Romania* 42 D6
Ciuperceni, *Romania* 42 F8
Civa Burnu, *Turkey* 72 B7
Cividale del Friuli, *Italy* 29 B10
Cívita Castellana, *Italy* 29 F9
Civitanova Marche, *Italy* 29 E10
Civitavécchia, *Italy* 29 F8
Civray, *France* 20 B4
Çivril, *Turkey* 39 C11
Cixerri →, *Italy* 30 C1
Cizre, *Turkey* 73 D10
Cizur Mayor, *Spain* 32 C3
Clackmannanshire □, *U.K.* 14 E5
Clacton-on-Sea, *U.K.* 13 F9
Clain →, *France* 18 F7
Claire, L., *Canada* 104 B6
Clairemont, *U.S.A.* 113 J4
Clairton, *U.S.A.* 110 F5
Clairvaux-les-Lacs, *France* 19 F12
Claise →, *France* 20 B5
Clallam Bay, *U.S.A.* 116 B2
Clamecy, *France* 19 E10
Clanton, *U.S.A.* 109 J2
Clanwilliam, *S. Africa* 88 E2
Clara, *Ireland* 15 C4
Clara →, *Australia* 94 B3
Claraville, *U.S.A.* 117 K8
Clare, *Australia* 95 E2
Clare, *U.S.A.* 108 D3
Clare □, *Ireland* 15 D3
Clare →, *Ireland* 15 C2
Clare I., *Ireland* 15 C1
Claremont, *Calif., U.S.A.* 117 L9
Claremont, *N.H., U.S.A.* 111 C12
Claremont Pt., *Australia* 94 A3
Claremore, *U.S.A.* 113 G7
Claremorris, *Ireland* 15 C3
Clarence →, *Australia* 95 D5
Clarence →, *N.Z.* 91 K4
Clarence, I., *Chile* 128 G2
Clarence I., *Antarctica* 5 C18
Clarence Str., *Australia* 92 B5
Clarence Str., *U.S.A.* 104 B2
Clarence Town, *Bahamas* 121 B5
Clarendon, *Ark., U.S.A.* 113 H9
Clarendon, *Tex., U.S.A.* 113 H4
Clarenville, *Canada* 103 C9
Claresholm, *Canada* 104 D6
Clarie Coast, *Antarctica* 5 C9
Clarinda, *U.S.A.* 112 E7
Clarion, *Iowa, U.S.A.* 112 D8
Clarion, *Pa., U.S.A.* 110 E5
Clarion →, *U.S.A.* 110 E5
Clark, *U.S.A.* 112 C6
Clark, Pt., *Canada* 110 B3
Clark Fork, *U.S.A.* 114 B5
Clark Fork →, *U.S.A.* 114 B5
Clark Hill L., *U.S.A.* 109 J4
Clarkdale, *U.S.A.* 115 J7
Clarke City, *Canada* 103 B6
Clarke I., *Australia* 94 G4
Clarke L., *Canada* 105 C7
Clarke Ra., *Australia* 94 C4
Clark's Fork →, *U.S.A.* 114 D9
Clark's Harbour, *Canada* 103 D6
Clarks Summit, *U.S.A.* 111 E9
Clarksburg, *U.S.A.* 108 F5
Clarksdale, *U.S.A.* 113 H9
Clarkston, *U.S.A.* 114 C5
Clarksville, *Ark., U.S.A.* 113 H8
Clarksville, *Tenn., U.S.A.* 109 G2
Clarksville, *Tex., U.S.A.* 113 J7
Clatskanie, *U.S.A.* 116 D3
Claude, *U.S.A.* 113 H4
Claveria, *Phil.* 61 B4
Clay, *U.S.A.* 116 G5
Clay Center, *U.S.A.* 112 F6
Claypool, *U.S.A.* 115 K8
Claysville, *U.S.A.* 110 F4
Clayton, *Idaho, U.S.A.* 114 D6
Clayton, *N. Mex., U.S.A.* 113 G3
Cle Elum, *U.S.A.* 114 C3
Clear, C., *Ireland* 15 E2
Clear I., *Ireland* 15 E2
Clear L., *U.S.A.* 116 F4
Clear Lake, *S. Dak., U.S.A.* 112 C6
Clear Lake, *Wash., U.S.A.* 114 B2
Clear Lake Reservoir, *U.S.A.* 114 F3
Clearfield, *Pa., U.S.A.* 108 E6
Clearfield, *Utah, U.S.A.* 114 F8
Clearlake Highlands, *U.S.A.* 116 G4
Clearmont, *U.S.A.* 114 D10
Clearwater, *Canada* 104 C4
Clearwater, *U.S.A.* 109 M4

Clearwater →, Alta., Canada 104 C6
Clearwater →, Alta., Canada 105 B6
Clearwater Cr. →, Canada 104 A3
Clearwater Mts., U.S.A. 114 C6
Clearwater Prov. Park, Canada 105 C8
Cleburne, U.S.A. 113 J6
Clee Hills, U.K. 13 E5
Cleethorpes, U.K. 12 D7
Cleeve Cloud, U.K. 13 F6
Clelles, France 21 D9
Clerke Reef, Australia 92 C2
Clermont, Australia 94 C4
Clermont, France 19 C9
Clermont-en-Argonne, France 19 C12
Clermont-Ferrand, France 20 C7
Clermont-l'Hérault, France 20 E7
Clerval, France 19 E13
Clervaux, Lux. 17 D6
Cles, Italy 28 B8
Clevedon, U.K. 13 F5
Cleveland, Australia 95 D5
Cleveland, Miss., U.S.A. 113 J9
Cleveland, Ohio, U.S.A. 110 E3
Cleveland, Okla., U.S.A. 113 G6
Cleveland, Tenn., U.S.A. 109 H3
Cleveland, Tex., U.S.A. 113 K7
Cleveland, C., Australia 94 B4
Cleveland Heights, U.S.A. 110 E3
Clevelândia, Brazil 127 B5
Clew B., Ireland 15 C2
Clewiston, U.S.A. 109 M5
Clifden, Ireland 15 C1
Clifden, N.Z. 91 M1
Cliffdell, U.S.A. 116 D5
Clifton, Australia 95 D5
Clifton, Ariz., U.S.A. 115 K9
Clifton, Tex., U.S.A. 113 K6
Clifton Beach, Australia 94 B4
Clifton Forge, U.S.A. 108 G6
Clifton Hills, Australia 95 D2
Climax, Canada 105 D7
Clinch →, U.S.A. 109 H3
Clingmans Dome, U.S.A. 109 H4
Clint, U.S.A. 115 L10
Clinton, B.C., Canada 104 C4
Clinton, Ont., Canada 102 D3
Clinton, N.Z. 91 M2
Clinton, Ark., U.S.A. 113 H8
Clinton, Ill., U.S.A. 112 E10
Clinton, Ind., U.S.A. 108 F2
Clinton, Iowa, U.S.A. 112 E9
Clinton, Mass., U.S.A. 111 D13
Clinton, Mo., U.S.A. 112 F8
Clinton, N.C., U.S.A. 109 H6
Clinton, Okla., U.S.A. 113 H5
Clinton, S.C., U.S.A. 109 H5
Clinton, Tenn., U.S.A. 109 G3
Clinton, Wash., U.S.A. 116 C4
Clinton C., Australia 94 C5
Clinton Colden L., Canada 100 B9
Clintonville, U.S.A. 112 C10
Clipperton, I., Pac. Oc. 97 F17
Clisham, U.K. 14 D2
Clisson, France 18 E5
Clitheroe, U.K. 12 D5
Clive L., Canada 104 A5
Cloates, Pt., Australia 92 D1
Clocolan, S. Africa 89 D4
Clodomira, Argentina 126 B3
Clogher Hd., Ireland 15 C5
Clonakilty, Ireland 15 E3
Clonakilty B., Ireland 15 E3
Cloncurry, Australia 94 C3
Cloncurry →, Australia 94 B3
Clondalkin, Ireland 15 C5
Clones, Ireland 15 B4
Clonmel, Ireland 15 D4
Cloppenburg, Germany 24 C4
Cloquet, U.S.A. 112 B8
Clorinda, Argentina 126 B4
Cloud Peak, U.S.A. 114 D10
Cloudcroft, U.S.A. 115 K11
Cloverdale, U.S.A. 116 G4
Clovis, Calif., U.S.A. 116 J7
Clovis, N. Mex., U.S.A. 113 H3
Cloyes-sur-le-Loir, France 18 E8
Cluj □, Romania 43 D8
Cluj-Napoca, Romania 43 D8
Clunes, Australia 95 F3
Cluny, France 19 F11
Cluses, France 19 F13
Clusone, Italy 28 C6
Clutha →, N.Z. 91 M2
Clwyd →, U.K. 12 D4
Clyde, N.Z. 91 L2
Clyde, U.S.A. 110 C8
Clyde →, U.K. 14 F4
Clyde, Firth of, U.K. 14 F3
Clyde River, Canada 101 A13
Clydebank, U.K. 14 F4
Clymer, U.S.A. 110 D5
Ćmielów, Poland 45 H8
Côa →, Portugal 34 D3
Coachella, U.S.A. 117 M10
Coachella Canal, U.S.A. 117 N12
Coahoma, U.S.A. 113 J4
Coahuayana →, Mexico 118 D4
Coahuayutla, Mexico 118 D4
Coahuila □, Mexico 118 B4
Coal →, Canada 104 B3
Coalane, Mozam. 87 F4
Coalcomán, Mexico 118 D4
Coaldale, Canada 104 D6
Coalgate, U.S.A. 113 H6
Coalinga, U.S.A. 116 J6
Coalisland, U.K. 15 B5
Coalville, U.K. 12 E6
Coalville, U.S.A. 114 F8
Coari, Brazil 124 D6
Coast □, Kenya 86 C4
Coast Mts., Canada 104 C3
Coast Ranges, U.S.A. 116 G4
Coatbridge, U.K. 14 F4
Coatepec, Mexico 119 D5
Coatepeque, Guatemala 120 D1
Coatesville, U.S.A. 108 F8
Coaticook, Canada 103 C5
Coats I., Canada 101 B11
Coats Land, Antarctica 5 D1
Coatzacoalcos, Mexico 119 D6
Cobadin, Romania 43 F13
Cobalt, Canada 102 C4
Cobán, Guatemala 120 C1
Çobanlar, Turkey 39 C12
Cobar, Australia 95 E4
Cóbh, Ireland 15 E3
Cobham, Australia 95 E3
Cobija, Bolivia 124 F5
Cobleskill, U.S.A. 111 D10
Coboconk, Canada 110 B6
Cobourg, Canada 102 D4
Cobourg Pen., Australia 92 B5
Cobram, Australia 95 F4
Cobre, U.S.A. 114 F6
Cóbué, Mozam. 87 E3
Coburg, Germany 25 E6
Coca, Spain 34 D6
Cocanada = Kakinada, India 67 L13
Cocentaina, Spain 33 G4
Cochabamba, Bolivia 124 G5
Cochem, Germany 25 E3
Cochemane, Mozam. 87 F3
Cochin, India 66 Q10
Cochin China, Vietnam 65 G6
Cochise, U.S.A. 115 K9
Cochran, U.S.A. 109 J4
Cochrane, Alta., Canada 104 C6
Cochrane, Ont., Canada 102 C3
Cochrane, Chile 128 F2
Cochrane →, Canada 105 B8
Cochrane, L., Chile 128 F2
Cockburn, Australia 95 E3
Cockburn, Canal, Chile 122 J3
Cockburn I., Canada 102 C3
Cockburn Ra., Australia 92 C4
Cockermouth, U.K. 12 C4
Cocklebiddy Motel, Australia 93 F4
Coco →, Cent. Amer. 120 D3
Cocoa, U.S.A. 109 L5
Cocobeach, Gabon 84 D1
Cocora, Romania 43 F12
Cocos, I. del, Pac. Oc. 97 G19
Cocos Is., Ind. Oc. 96 J1
Cod, C., U.S.A. 107 B12
Codajás, Brazil 124 D6
Coderre, Canada 105 C7
Codigoro, Italy 29 D9
Codlea, Romania 43 E10
Codó, Brazil 125 D10
Codogno, Italy 28 C6
Codróipo, Italy 29 C10
Codru, Munţii, Romania 42 D7
Cody, U.S.A. 114 D9
Coe Hill, Canada 102 D4
Coelemu, Chile 126 D1
Coen, Australia 94 A3
Coesfeld, Germany 24 D3
Cœur d'Alene, U.S.A. 114 C5
Cœur d'Alene L., U.S.A. 114 C5
Coevorden, Neths. 17 B6
Cofete, Canary Is. 37 F5
Coffeyville, U.S.A. 113 G7
Coffin B., Australia 95 E2
Coffin Bay Peninsula, Australia 95 E2
Coffs Harbour, Australia 95 E5
Cofrentes, Spain 33 F3
Cogalnic →, Moldova 43 E14
Cogealac, Romania 43 F13
Coghinas →, Italy 30 B1
Coghinas, L. del, Italy 30 B2
Cognac, France 20 C3
Cogne, Italy 28 C4
Cogolin, France 21 E10
Cogolludo, Spain 32 E1
Cohagen, U.S.A. 114 C10
Cohoes, U.S.A. 111 D11
Cohuna, Australia 95 F3
Coiba, I., Panama 120 E3
Coig →, Argentina 128 G3
Coigeach, Rubha, U.K. 14 C3
Coihaique, Chile 128 F2
Coimbatore, India 66 P10
Coimbra, Brazil 124 G7
Coimbra, Portugal 34 E2
Coimbra □, Portugal 34 E2
Coín, Spain 35 J6
Coipasa, Salar de, Bolivia 124 G5
Cojimies, Ecuador 124 C3
Cojocna, Romania 43 D8
Cojutepequé, El Salv. 120 D2
Čoka, Serbia, Yug. 42 E5
Cokeville, U.S.A. 114 E8
Colac, Australia 95 F3
Colatina, Brazil 125 G10
Colbeck, C., Antarctica 5 D13
Colbinabbin, Australia 95 F3
Colborne, Canada 110 C7
Colby, U.S.A. 112 F4
Colchagua □, Chile 126 C1
Colchester, U.K. 13 F8
Coldstream, U.K. 14 F6
Coldwater, Canada 110 B5
Coldwater, U.S.A. 113 G5
Colebrook, Australia 94 G4
Colebrook, U.S.A. 111 B13
Coleman, Canada 104 D6
Coleman, U.S.A. 113 K5
Coleman →, Australia 94 B3
Colenso, S. Africa 89 D4
Coleraine, Australia 95 F3
Coleraine, U.K. 15 A5
Coleridge, L., N.Z. 91 K3
Colesberg, S. Africa 88 E4
Coleville, U.S.A. 116 G7
Colfax, Calif., U.S.A. 116 F6
Colfax, La., U.S.A. 113 K8
Colfax, Wash., U.S.A. 114 C5
Colhué Huapi, L., Argentina 128 F3
Colibaşi, Moldova 43 E13
Colibaşi, Romania 43 F9
Cólico, Italy 28 B6
Coligny, France 19 F12
Coligny, S. Africa 89 D4
Colima, Mexico 118 D4
Colima □, Mexico 118 D4
Colima, Nevado de, Mexico 118 D4
Colina, Chile 126 C1
Colina do Norte, Guinea-Biss. 82 C2
Colinas, Brazil 125 E10
Colindres, Spain 34 B7
Coll, U.K. 14 E2
Collaguasi, Chile 126 A2
Collarada, Peña, Spain 32 C4
Collarenebri, Australia 95 D4
Collbran, U.S.A. 115 G10
Colle di Val d'Elsa, Italy 28 E8
Collécchio, Italy 28 D7
Colleen Bawn, Zimbabwe 87 G2
College Park, U.S.A. 109 J3
College Station, U.S.A. 113 K6
Collesalvetti, Italy 28 E7
Collette, Canada 103 C6
Collie, Australia 93 F2
Collier B., Australia 92 C3
Collier Ra., Australia 92 D2
Collina, Passo di, Italy 28 D7
Collingwood, Canada 102 D3
Collingwood, N.Z. 91 J4
Collins, Canada 102 B2
Collinsville, Australia 94 C4
Collipulli, Chile 126 D1
Collooney, Ireland 15 B3
Colmar, France 19 D14
Colmars, France 21 D10
Colmenar, Spain 35 J6
Colmenar de Oreja, Spain 34 E7
Colmenar Viejo, Spain 34 E7
Colo →, Australia 95 E5
Cologne = Köln, Germany 24 E2
Colom, I. d'en, Spain 37 B11
Coloma, U.S.A. 116 G6
Colomb-Béchar = Béchar, Algeria 78 B5
Colombey-les-Belles, France 19 D12
Colombey-les-Deux-Églises, France 19 D11
Colombia ■, S. Amer. 124 C4
Colombian Basin, S. Amer. 98 H12
Colombo, Sri Lanka 66 R11
Colome, U.S.A. 112 D5
Colomiers, France 20 E5
Colón, Argentina 126 C4
Colón, Cuba 120 B3
Colón, Panama 120 E4
Colona, Australia 93 F5
Colonia de Sant Jordi, Spain 37 B9
Colonia del Sacramento, Uruguay 126 C4
Colonia Dora, Argentina 126 B3
Colonial Heights, U.S.A. 108 G7
Colonna, C., Italy 31 C10
Colonsay, Canada 105 C7
Colonsay, U.K. 14 E2
Colorado □, U.S.A. 115 G10
Colorado →, Argentina 128 D4
Colorado →, N. Amer. 115 L6
Colorado →, U.S.A. 113 L7
Colorado City, U.S.A. 113 J4
Colorado Desert, U.S.A. 106 D3
Colorado Plateau, U.S.A. 115 H8
Colorado River Aqueduct, U.S.A. 117 L12
Colorado Springs, U.S.A. 112 F2
Colorno, Italy 28 D7
Colotlán, Mexico 118 C4
Colton, N.Y., U.S.A. 111 B10
Colton, Wash., U.S.A. 114 C5
Columbia, La., U.S.A. 113 J8
Columbia, Miss., U.S.A. 113 K10
Columbia, Mo., U.S.A. 112 F8
Columbia, Pa., U.S.A. 111 F8
Columbia, S.C., U.S.A. 109 J5
Columbia, Tenn., U.S.A. 109 H2
Columbia →, U.S.A. 114 C1
Columbia, C., Canada 4 A4
Columbia, District of □, U.S.A. 108 F7
Columbia, Mt., Canada 104 C5
Columbia Basin, U.S.A. 114 C4
Columbia Falls, U.S.A. 114 B6
Columbia Heights, U.S.A. 112 C8
Columbiana, U.S.A. 110 F4
Columbretes, Is., Spain 32 F5
Columbus, Ga., U.S.A. 109 J3
Columbus, Ind., U.S.A. 108 F3
Columbus, Kans., U.S.A. 113 G7
Columbus, Miss., U.S.A. 109 J1
Columbus, Mont., U.S.A. 114 D9
Columbus, N. Dak., U.S.A. 112 A3
Columbus, N. Mex., U.S.A. 115 L10
Columbus, Nebr., U.S.A. 112 E6
Columbus, Ohio, U.S.A. 108 F4
Columbus, Tex., U.S.A. 113 L6
Columbus, Wis., U.S.A. 112 D10
Colunga, Spain 34 B5
Colusa, U.S.A. 116 F4
Colville, U.S.A. 114 B5
Colville →, U.S.A. 100 A4
Colville, C., N.Z. 91 G5
Colwyn Bay, U.K. 12 D4
Coma, Ethiopia 81 F4
Comácchio, Italy 29 D9
Comalcalco, Mexico 119 D6
Comallo, Argentina 128 E2
Comana, Romania 43 F11
Comanche, Okla., U.S.A. 113 H6
Comanche, Tex., U.S.A. 113 K5
Comăneşti, Romania 43 D11
Comarnic, Romania 43 E10
Comayagua, Honduras 120 D2
Combahee →, U.S.A. 109 J5
Combeaufontaine, France 19 E12
Comber, Canada 110 D2
Comber, U.K. 15 B6
Comblain-au-Pont, Belgium 17 D5
Combourg, France 18 D5
Combrailles, France 19 F9
Combronde, France 20 C7
Comeragh Mts., Ireland 15 D4
Comet, Australia 94 C4
Comilla, Bangla. 67 H17
Comino, Malta 36 C1
Comino, C., Italy 30 B2
Cómiso, Italy 31 F7
Comitán, Mexico 119 D6
Commentry, France 19 F9
Commerce, Ga., U.S.A. 109 H4
Commerce, Tex., U.S.A. 113 J7
Commercy, France 19 D12
Committee B., Canada 101 B11
Commonwealth B., Antarctica 5 C10
Commoron Cr. →, Australia 95 D5
Communism Pk. = Kommunizma, Pik, Tajikistan 50 F8
Como, Italy 28 C6
Como, L. di, Italy 28 B6
Comodoro Rivadavia, Argentina 128 F3
Comorâşte, Romania 42 E6
Comorin, C., India 66 Q10
Comoro Is. = Comoros ■, Ind. Oc. 77 H8
Comoros ■, Ind. Oc. 77 H8
Comox, Canada 104 D4
Compiègne, France 19 C9
Comporta, Portugal 35 G2
Compostela, Mexico 118 C4
Comprida, I., Brazil 127 A6
Compton, U.S.A. 117 M8
Compton Downs, Australia 95 E4
Comrat, Moldova 43 D13
Con Cuong, Vietnam 64 C5
Con Son, Vietnam 65 H6
Conakry, Guinea 82 D2
Conara Junction, Australia 94 G4
Concarneau, France 18 E3
Conceição, Mozam. 87 F4
Conceição da Barra, Brazil 125 G11
Conceição do Araguaia, Brazil 125 E9
Concepción, Argentina 126 B2
Concepción, Bolivia 124 G6
Concepción, Chile 126 D1
Concepción, Mexico 119 D6
Concepción, Paraguay 126 A4
Concepción □, Chile 126 D1
Concepción →, Mexico 118 A2
Concepción, Est. de, Chile 128 G2
Concepción, L., Bolivia 124 G6
Concepción, Punta, Mexico 118 B2
Concepción del Oro, Mexico 118 C4
Concepción del Uruguay, Argentina 126 C4
Conception, Pt., U.S.A. 117 L6
Conception B., Namibia 88 C1
Conception I., Bahamas 121 B4
Concession, Zimbabwe 87 F3
Conchas Dam, U.S.A. 113 H2
Conche, Canada 103 B8
Conches-en-Ouche, France 18 D7
Concho, U.S.A. 115 J9
Concho →, U.S.A. 113 K5
Conchos →, Chihuahua, Mexico 118 B4
Conchos →, Tamaulipas, Mexico 119 B5
Concord, Calif., U.S.A. 116 H4
Concord, N.C., U.S.A. 109 H5
Concord, N.H., U.S.A. 111 C13
Concordia, Argentina 126 C4
Concórdia, Brazil 124 D5
Concordia, Mexico 118 C3
Concordia, U.S.A. 112 F6
Concrete, U.S.A. 114 B3
Condamine, Australia 95 D5
Condat, France 20 C6
Conde, U.S.A. 112 C5
Condé-sur-Noireau, France 18 D6
Condeúba, Brazil 125 F10
Condobolin, Australia 95 E4
Condom, France 20 E4
Condon, U.S.A. 114 D3
Conegliano, Italy 29 C9
Conejera, I. = Conills, I. des, Spain 37 B9
Conejos, Mexico 118 B4
Confolens, France 20 B4
Confuso →, Paraguay 126 B4
Congaz, Moldova 43 D13
Congjiang, China 58 E7
Congleton, U.K. 12 D5
Congo (Kinshasa) = Congo, Dem. Rep. of the ■, Africa 84 E4
Congo ■, Africa 84 E3
Congo →, Africa 84 F2
Congo, Dem. Rep. of the ■, Africa 84 E4
Congo Basin, Africa 76 G6
Congonhas, Brazil 127 A7
Congress, U.S.A. 115 J7
Conil = Conil de la Frontera, Spain 35 J4
Conil de la Frontera, Spain 35 J4
Conills, I. des, Spain 37 B9
Coniston, Canada 102 C3
Conjeeveram = Kanchipuram, India 66 N11
Conjuboy, Australia 94 B3
Conklin, Canada 105 B6
Conlea, Australia 95 E3
Conn, L., Ireland 15 B2
Connacht □, Ireland 15 C2
Conneaut, U.S.A. 110 E4
Connecticut □, U.S.A. 111 E12
Connecticut →, U.S.A. 111 E12
Connell, U.S.A. 114 C4
Connellsville, U.S.A. 110 F5
Connemara, Ireland 15 C2
Connemaugh →, U.S.A. 110 F5
Connerré, France 18 D7
Connersville, U.S.A. 108 F3
Connors Ra., Australia 94 C4
Conoble, Australia 95 E3
Conques, France 20 D6
Conquest, Canada 105 C7
Conrad, U.S.A. 114 B8
Conran, C., Australia 95 F4
Conroe, U.S.A. 113 K7
Conselheiro Lafaiete, Brazil 127 A7
Conselve, Italy 29 C8
Consett, U.K. 12 C6
Consort, Canada 105 C6
Constance = Konstanz, Germany 25 H5
Constance, L. = Bodensee, Europe 25 H5
Constanţa, Romania 43 F13
Constanţa □, Romania 43 F13
Constantina, Spain 35 H5
Constantine, Algeria 78 A7
Constitución, Chile 126 D1
Constitución, Uruguay 126 C4
Consuegra, Spain 35 F7
Consul, Canada 105 D7
Contact, U.S.A. 114 F6
Contai, India 69 J12
Contamana, Peru 124 E4
Contarina, Italy 29 C9
Contas →, Brazil 125 F11
Contes, France 21 E11
Contoocook, U.S.A. 111 C13
Contra Costa, Mozam. 89 D5
Contres, France 18 E8
Contrexéville, France 19 D12
Conversano, Italy 31 B10
Conway = Conwy, U.K. 12 D4
Conway = Conwy →, U.K. 12 D4
Conway, Ark., U.S.A. 113 H8
Conway, N.H., U.S.A. 111 C13
Conway, S.C., U.S.A. 109 J6
Conway, L., Australia 95 D2
Conwy, U.K. 12 D4
Conwy □, U.K. 12 D4
Conwy →, U.K. 12 D4
Coober Pedy, Australia 95 D1
Cooch Behar = Koch Bihar, India 67 F16
Coodardy, Australia 93 E2
Cook, Australia 93 F5
Cook, U.S.A. 112 B8
Cook, B., Chile 128 H3
Cook, Mt., N.Z. 91 K3
Cook Inlet, U.S.A. 100 C4
Cook Is., Pac. Oc. 97 J12
Cook Strait, N.Z. 91 J5
Cookeville, U.S.A. 109 G3
Cookhouse, S. Africa 88 E4
Cookshire, Canada 111 A13
Cookstown, U.K. 15 B5
Cooksville, Canada 110 C5
Cooktown, Australia 94 B4
Coolabah, Australia 95 E4
Cooladdi, Australia 95 D4
Coolah, Australia 95 E4
Coolamon, Australia 95 E4

Coolangatta, *Australia* 95 D5
Coolgardie, *Australia* 93 F3
Coolibah, *Australia* 92 C5
Coolidge, *U.S.A.* 115 K8
Coolidge Dam, *U.S.A.* 115 K8
Cooma, *Australia* 95 F4
Coon Rapids, *U.S.A.* 112 C8
Coonabarabran, *Australia* 95 E4
Coonamble, *Australia* 95 E4
Coonana, *Australia* 93 F3
Coondapoor, *India* 66 N9
Coongie, *Australia* 95 D3
Coongoola, *Australia* 95 D4
Cooninie, L., *Australia* 95 D2
Cooper, *U.S.A.* 113 J7
Cooper →, *U.S.A.* 109 J6
Cooper Cr. →, *Australia* 95 D2
Cooperstown, *N. Dak., U.S.A.* 112 B5
Cooperstown, *N.Y., U.S.A.* 111 D10
Coorabie, *Australia* 93 F5
Coorabulka, *Australia* 94 C3
Coorow, *Australia* 93 E2
Cooroy, *Australia* 95 D5
Coos Bay, *U.S.A.* 114 E1
Cootamundra, *Australia* 95 E4
Cootehill, *Ireland* 15 B4
Cooyar, *Australia* 95 D5
Cooyeana, *Australia* 94 C2
Copahue Paso, *Argentina* 126 D1
Copainalá, *Mexico* 119 D6
Copalnic Mănăştur, *Romania* 43 C8
Copán, *Honduras* 120 D2
Cope, *U.S.A.* 112 F3
Cope, C., *Spain* 33 H3
Copenhagen = København, *Denmark* 11 J6
Copertino, *Italy* 31 B11
Copiapó, *Chile* 126 B1
Copiapó →, *Chile* 126 B1
Copley, *Australia* 95 E2
Copp L., *Canada* 104 A6
Copparo, *Italy* 29 D8
Coppename →, *Surinam* 125 B7
Copper Cliff, *Canada* 102 C3
Copper Harbor, *U.S.A.* 108 B2
Copper Queen, *Zimbabwe* 87 F2
Copperbelt □, *Zambia* 87 E2
Coppermine = Kugluktuk, *Canada* 100 B8
Coppermine →, *Canada* 100 B8
Copperopolis, *U.S.A.* 116 H6
Copşa Mică, *Romania* 43 D9
Coquet →, *U.K.* 12 B6
Coquilhatville = Mbandaka, *Dem. Rep. of the Congo* 84 D3
Coquille, *U.S.A.* 114 E1
Coquimbo, *Chile* 126 C1
Coquimbo □, *Chile* 126 C1
Corabia, *Romania* 43 G9
Coracora, *Peru* 124 G4
Coral Gables, *U.S.A.* 109 N5
Coral Sea, *Pac. Oc.* 96 J7
Coral Springs, *U.S.A.* 109 M5
Coraopolis, *U.S.A.* 110 F4
Corato, *Italy* 31 A9
Corbeil-Essonnes, *France* 19 D9
Corbie, *France* 19 C9
Corbières, *France* 20 F6
Corbigny, *France* 19 E10
Corbin, *U.S.A.* 108 G3
Corbones →, *Spain* 35 H5
Corbu, *Romania* 43 F13
Corby, *U.K.* 13 E7
Corcaigh = Cork, *Ireland* 15 E3
Corcoran, *U.S.A.* 116 J7
Cordele, *U.S.A.* 109 K4
Cordell, *U.S.A.* 113 H5
Cordenòns, *Italy* 29 C9
Cordes, *France* 20 D5
Córdoba, *Argentina* 126 C3
Córdoba, *Mexico* 119 D5
Córdoba, *Spain* 35 H6
Córdoba □, *Argentina* 126 C3
Córdoba □, *Spain* 35 G6
Córdoba, Sierra de, *Argentina* 126 C3
Cordon, *Phil.* 61 C4
Cordova, *Ala., U.S.A.* 109 J2
Cordova, *Alaska, U.S.A.* 100 B5
Corella, *Spain* 32 C3
Corella →, *Australia* 94 B3
Corfield, *Australia* 94 C3
Corfu, Str. of, *Greece* 36 A4
Corgo = O Corgo, *Spain* 34 C3
Cori, *Italy* 30 A5
Coria, *Spain* 34 F4
Coria del Río, *Spain* 35 H4
Corigliano Cálabro, *Italy* 31 C9
Coringa Is., *Australia* 94 B4
Corinna, *Australia* 94 G4
Corinth = Kórinthos, *Greece* 38 D4
Corinth, *Miss., U.S.A.* 109 H1
Corinth, *N.Y., U.S.A.* 111 C11
Corinth, G. of = Korinthiakós Kólpos, *Greece* 38 C4
Corinth Canal, *Greece* 38 D4
Corinto, *Brazil* 125 G10
Corinto, *Nic.* 120 D2
Cork, *Ireland* 15 E3
Cork □, *Ireland* 15 E3
Cork Harbour, *Ireland* 15 E3
Corlay, *France* 18 D3
Corleone, *Italy* 30 E6
Corleto Perticara, *Italy* 31 B9
Çorlu, *Turkey* 41 E11
Cormack L., *Canada* 104 A4
Cormòns, *Italy* 29 C10
Cormorant, *Canada* 105 C8
Cormorant L., *Canada* 105 C8
Corn Is. = Maíz, Is. del, *Nic.* 120 D3
Cornélio Procópio, *Brazil* 127 A5
Cornell, *U.S.A.* 112 C9
Corner Brook, *Canada* 103 C8
Corneşti, *Moldova* 43 C13
Corníglio, *Italy* 28 D7
Corning, *Ark., U.S.A.* 113 G9
Corning, *Calif., U.S.A.* 114 G2
Corning, *Iowa, U.S.A.* 112 E7
Corning, *N.Y., U.S.A.* 110 D7
Corno Grande, *Italy* 29 F10
Cornwall, *Canada* 102 C5
Cornwall □, *U.K.* 13 G3
Corny Pt., *Australia* 95 E2
Coro, *Venezuela* 124 A5
Coroatá, *Brazil* 125 D10
Corocoro, *Bolivia* 124 G5
Coroico, *Bolivia* 124 G5
Coromandel, *N.Z.* 91 G5
Coromandel Coast, *India* 66 N12
Corona, *Australia* 95 E3
Corona, *Calif., U.S.A.* 117 M9
Corona, *N. Mex., U.S.A.* 115 J11
Coronado, *U.S.A.* 117 N9
Coronado, B. de, *Costa Rica* 120 E3
Coronados, Is. los, *U.S.A.* 117 N9
Coronation, *Canada* 104 C6
Coronation Gulf, *Canada* 100 B9
Coronation I., *Antarctica* 5 C18
Coronation I., *U.S.A.* 104 B2
Coronation Is., *Australia* 92 B3
Coronda, *Argentina* 126 C3
Coronel, *Chile* 126 D1
Coronel Bogado, *Paraguay* 126 B4
Coronel Dorrego, *Argentina* 126 D3
Coronel Oviedo, *Paraguay* 126 B4
Coronel Pringles, *Argentina* 126 D3
Coronel Suárez, *Argentina* 126 D3
Coronel Vidal, *Argentina* 126 D4
Coropuna, Nevado, *Peru* 124 G4
Çorovoda, *Albania* 40 F4
Corowa, *Australia* 95 F4
Corozal, *Belize* 119 D7
Corps, *France* 21 D9
Corpus, *Argentina* 127 B4
Corpus Christi, *U.S.A.* 113 M6
Corpus Christi, L., *U.S.A.* 113 L6
Corral de Almaguer, *Spain* 34 F7
Corralejo, *Canary Is.* 37 F6
Corraun Pen., *Ireland* 15 C2
Corréggio, *Italy* 28 D7
Correntes, C. das, *Mozam.* 89 C6
Corrèze □, *France* 20 C5
Corrèze →, *France* 20 C5
Corrib, L., *Ireland* 15 C2
Corridónia, *Italy* 29 E10
Corrientes, *Argentina* 126 B4
Corrientes □, *Argentina* 126 B4
Corrientes →, *Argentina* 126 C4
Corrientes →, *Peru* 124 D4
Corrientes, C., *Colombia* 124 B3
Corrientes, C., *Cuba* 120 B3
Corrientes, C., *Mexico* 118 C3
Corrigan, *U.S.A.* 113 K7
Corrigin, *Australia* 93 F2
Corry, *U.S.A.* 110 E5
Corse, *France* 21 G13
Corse, C., *France* 21 E13
Corse-du-Sud □, *France* 21 G13
Corsica = Corse, *France* 21 G13
Corsicana, *U.S.A.* 113 J6
Corte, *France* 21 F13
Corte Pinto, *Portugal* 35 H3
Cortegana, *Spain* 35 H4
Cortez, *U.S.A.* 115 H9
Cortina d'Ampezzo, *Italy* 29 B9
Cortland, *U.S.A.* 111 D8
Cortona, *Italy* 29 E8
Coruche, *Portugal* 35 G2
Çoruh →, *Turkey* 49 K5
Çorum, *Turkey* 72 B6
Corumbá, *Brazil* 124 G7
Corund, *Romania* 43 D10
Corunna = A Coruña, *Spain* 34 B2
Corvallis, *U.S.A.* 114 D2
Corvette, L. de la, *Canada* 102 B5
Corydon, *U.S.A.* 112 E8
Cosalá, *Mexico* 118 C3
Cosamaloapan, *Mexico* 119 D5
Cosenza, *Italy* 31 C9
Coşereni, *Romania* 43 F11
Coshocton, *U.S.A.* 110 F3
Cosmo Newberry, *Australia* 93 E3
Cosne-Cours-sur-Loire, *France* 19 E9
Coso Junction, *U.S.A.* 117 J9
Coso Pk., *U.S.A.* 117 J9
Cospeito, *Spain* 34 B3
Cosquín, *Argentina* 126 C3
Cossato, *Italy* 28 C5
Cossé-le-Vivien, *France* 18 E6
Cosson →, *France* 18 E8
Costa Blanca, *Spain* 33 G4
Costa Brava, *Spain* 32 D8
Costa del Sol, *Spain* 35 J6
Costa Dorada, *Spain* 32 D6
Costa Mesa, *U.S.A.* 117 M9
Costa Rica ■, *Cent. Amer.* 120 E3
Costa Smeralda, *Italy* 30 A2
Costeşti, *Romania* 43 F9
Costigliole d'Asti, *Italy* 28 D5
Costilla, *U.S.A.* 115 H11
Cosumnes →, *U.S.A.* 116 G5
Coswig, *Sachsen, Germany* 24 D9
Coswig, *Sachsen-Anhalt, Germany* 24 D8
Cotabato, *Phil.* 61 H6
Cotagaita, *Bolivia* 126 A2
Côte d'Azur, *France* 21 E11
Côte-d'Ivoire = Ivory Coast ■, *Africa* 82 D4
Côte d'Or, *France* 19 E11
Côte-d'Or □, *France* 19 E11
Coteau des Prairies, *U.S.A.* 112 C6
Coteau du Missouri, *U.S.A.* 112 B4
Coteau Landing, *Canada* 111 A10
Cotentin, *France* 18 C5
Côtes-d'Armor □, *France* 18 D4
Côtes de Meuse, *France* 19 C12
Côtes-du-Nord = Côtes-d'Armor □, *France* 18 D4
Cotiella, *Spain* 32 C5
Cotillo, *Canary Is.* 37 F5
Cotiujeni, *Moldova* 43 C13
Cotonou, *Benin* 83 D5
Cotopaxi, *Ecuador* 122 D3
Cotronei, *Italy* 31 C9
Cotswold Hills, *U.K.* 13 F5
Cottage Grove, *U.S.A.* 114 E2
Cottbus, *Germany* 24 D10
Cottonwood, *U.S.A.* 115 J7
Cotulla, *U.S.A.* 113 L5
Coubre, Pte. de la, *France* 20 C2
Couches, *France* 19 F11
Couço, *Portugal* 35 G2
Coudersport, *U.S.A.* 110 E6
Couedic, C. du, *Australia* 95 F2
Couëron, *France* 18 E5
Couesnon →, *France* 18 D5
Couhé, *France* 20 B4
Coulanges-sur-Yonne, *France* 19 E10
Coulee City, *U.S.A.* 114 C4
Coulman I., *Antarctica* 5 D11
Coulommiers, *France* 19 D10
Coulon →, *France* 21 E9
Coulonge →, *Canada* 102 C4
Coulonges-sur-l'Autize, *France* 20 B3
Coulounieix-Chamiers, *France* 20 C4
Coulterville, *U.S.A.* 116 H6
Council, *U.S.A.* 114 D5
Council Bluffs, *U.S.A.* 112 E7
Council Grove, *U.S.A.* 112 F6
Coupeville, *U.S.A.* 116 B4
Courantyne →, *S. Amer.* 122 C5
Courcelles, *Belgium* 17 D4
Courçon, *France* 20 B3
Courmayeur, *Italy* 28 C3
Couronne, C., *France* 21 E9
Cours-la-Ville, *France* 19 F11
Coursan, *France* 20 E7
Courseulles-sur-Mer, *France* 18 C6
Courtenay, *Canada* 104 D4
Courtenay, *France* 19 D10
Courtland, *U.S.A.* 116 G5
Courtrai = Kortrijk, *Belgium* 17 D3
Courtright, *Canada* 110 D2
Coushatta, *U.S.A.* 113 J8
Coutances, *France* 18 C5
Coutras, *France* 20 C3
Coutts, *Canada* 104 D6
Couvin, *Belgium* 17 D4
Covarrubias, *Spain* 34 C7
Covasna, *Romania* 43 E11
Covasna □, *Romania* 43 E10
Coventry, *U.K.* 13 E6
Coventry L., *Canada* 105 A7
Covilhã, *Portugal* 34 E3
Covington, *Ga., U.S.A.* 109 J4
Covington, *Ky., U.S.A.* 108 F3
Covington, *Okla., U.S.A.* 113 G6
Covington, *Tenn., U.S.A.* 113 H10
Cowal, L., *Australia* 95 E4
Cowan, *Canada* 105 C8
Cowan, L., *Australia* 93 F3
Cowan L., *Canada* 105 C7
Cowangie, *Australia* 95 F3
Cowansville, *Canada* 111 A12
Cowarie, *Australia* 95 D2
Cowcowing Lakes, *Australia* 93 F2
Cowdenbeath, *U.K.* 14 E5
Cowell, *Australia* 95 E2
Cowes, *U.K.* 13 G6
Cowlitz →, *U.S.A.* 116 D4
Cowra, *Australia* 95 E4
Cox, *Spain* 33 G4
Coxilha Grande, *Brazil* 127 B5
Coxim, *Brazil* 125 G8
Cox's Bazar, *Bangla.* 67 J17
Cox's Cove, *Canada* 103 C8
Coyame, *Mexico* 118 B3
Coyote Wells, *U.S.A.* 117 N11
Coyuca de Benítez, *Mexico* 119 D4
Coyuca de Catalan, *Mexico* 118 D4
Cozad, *U.S.A.* 112 E5
Cozes, *France* 20 C3
Cozumel, *Mexico* 119 C7
Cozumel, I. de, *Mexico* 119 C7
Craboon, *Australia* 95 E4
Cracow = Kraków, *Poland* 45 H6
Cracow, *Australia* 95 D5
Cradock, *S. Africa* 88 E4
Craig, *Alaska, U.S.A.* 104 B2
Craig, *Colo., U.S.A.* 114 F10
Craigavon, *U.K.* 15 B5
Craigmore, *Zimbabwe* 87 G3
Crailsheim, *Germany* 25 F6
Craiova, *Romania* 43 F8
Cramsie, *Australia* 94 C3
Cranberry Portage, *Canada* 105 C8
Cranbrook, *Tas., Australia* 94 G4
Cranbrook, *W. Austral., Australia* 93 F2
Cranbrook, *Canada* 104 D5
Crandon, *U.S.A.* 112 C10
Crane, *Oreg., U.S.A.* 114 E4
Crane, *Tex., U.S.A.* 113 K3
Cranston, *U.S.A.* 111 E13
Craon, *France* 18 E6
Craonne, *France* 19 C10
Craponne-sur-Arzon, *France* 20 C7
Crasna, *Romania* 43 D12
Crasna →, *Romania* 42 C7
Crasnei, Munţii, *Romania* 43 C8
Crater L., *U.S.A.* 114 E2
Crateús, *Brazil* 125 E10
Crati →, *Italy* 31 C9
Crato, *Brazil* 125 E11
Crato, *Portugal* 35 F3
Crawford, *U.S.A.* 112 D3
Crawfordsville, *U.S.A.* 108 E2
Crawley, *U.K.* 13 F7
Crazy Mts., *U.S.A.* 114 C8
Crean L., *Canada* 105 C7
Crécy-en-Ponthieu, *France* 19 B8
Crediton, *Canada* 110 C3
Credo, *Australia* 93 F3
Cree →, *Canada* 105 B7
Cree →, *U.K.* 14 G4
Cree L., *Canada* 105 B7
Creede, *U.S.A.* 115 H10
Creel, *Mexico* 118 B3
Creighton, *U.S.A.* 112 D6
Creil, *France* 19 C9
Crema, *Italy* 28 C6
Cremona, *Italy* 28 C7
Crepaja, *Serbia, Yug.* 42 E5
Crépy, *France* 19 C10
Crépy-en-Valois, *France* 19 C9
Cres, *Croatia* 29 D11
Cresbard, *U.S.A.* 112 C5
Crescent, *Okla., U.S.A.* 113 H6
Crescent, *Oreg., U.S.A.* 114 E3
Crescent City, *U.S.A.* 114 F1
Crescentino, *Italy* 28 C5
Crespo, *Argentina* 126 C3
Cressy, *Australia* 95 F3
Crest, *France* 21 D9
Cresta, Mt., *Phil.* 61 C5
Crested Butte, *U.S.A.* 115 G10
Crestline, *Calif., U.S.A.* 117 L9
Crestline, *Ohio, U.S.A.* 110 F2
Creston, *Canada* 104 D5
Creston, *Calif., U.S.A.* 116 K6
Creston, *Iowa, U.S.A.* 112 E7
Creston, *Wash., U.S.A.* 114 C4
Crestview, *Calif., U.S.A.* 116 H8
Crestview, *Fla., U.S.A.* 109 K2
Crêt de la Neige, *France* 19 F12
Crete = Kríti, *Greece* 36 D7
Crete, *U.S.A.* 112 E6
Crete, Sea of, *Greece* 39 E7
Créteil, *France* 19 D9
Creus, C. de, *Spain* 32 C8
Creuse □, *France* 19 F9
Creuse →, *France* 20 B4
Creutzwald, *France* 19 C13
Creuzburg, *Germany* 24 D6
Crèvecœur-le-Grand, *France* 19 C9
Crevillente, *Spain* 33 G4
Crewe, *U.K.* 12 D5
Crewkerne, *U.K.* 13 G5
Criciúma, *Brazil* 127 B6
Cricova, *Moldova* 43 C13
Crieff, *U.K.* 14 E5
Crikvenica, *Croatia* 29 C11
Crimea □, *Ukraine* 47 K8
Crimean Pen. = Krymskyy Pivostriv, *Ukraine* 47 K8
Crimmitschau, *Germany* 24 E8
Cristuru Secuiesc, *Romania* 43 D10
Crişul Alb →, *Romania* 42 D6
Crişul Negru →, *Romania* 42 D6
Crişul Repede →, *Romania* 42 D5
Criuleni, *Moldova* 43 C14
Crivitz, *Germany* 24 B7
Crna →, *Macedonia* 40 E5
Crna Gora = Montenegro □, *Yugoslavia* 40 D3
Crna Gora, *Macedonia* 40 D5
Crna Reka = Crna →, *Macedonia* 40 E5
Crna Trava, *Serbia, Yug.* 40 D6
Crni Drim →, *Macedonia* 40 E4
Crni Timok →, *Serbia, Yug.* 40 C6
Crnoljeva Planina, *Serbia, Yug.* 40 D5
Črnomelj, *Slovenia* 29 C12
Croagh Patrick, *Ireland* 15 C2
Croatia ■, *Europe* 29 C13
Crocker, Banjaran, *Malaysia* 62 C5
Crockett, *U.S.A.* 113 K7
Crocodile = Krokodil →, *Mozam.* 89 D5
Crocodile Is., *Australia* 94 A1
Crocq, *France* 20 C6
Crodo, *Italy* 28 B5
Crohy Hd., *Ireland* 15 B3
Croisette, C., *France* 21 E9
Croisic, Pte. du, *France* 18 E4
Croix, L. La, *Canada* 102 C1
Croker, C., *Australia* 92 B5
Croker I., *Australia* 92 B5
Cromarty, *Canada* 105 B10
Cromarty, *U.K.* 14 D4
Cromer, *U.K.* 12 E9
Cromwell, *N.Z.* 91 L2
Cronat, *France* 19 F10
Cronulla, *Australia* 95 E5
Crook, *U.K.* 12 C6
Crooked →, *Canada* 104 C4
Crooked →, *U.S.A.* 114 D3
Crooked I., *Bahamas* 121 B5
Crooked Island Passage, *Bahamas* 121 B5
Crookston, *Minn., U.S.A.* 112 B6
Crookston, *Nebr., U.S.A.* 112 D4
Crooksville, *U.S.A.* 108 F4
Crookwell, *Australia* 95 E4
Crosby, *U.K.* 12 D4
Crosby, *Minn., U.S.A.* 112 B8
Crosby, *N. Dak., U.S.A.* 105 D8
Crosby, *Pa., U.S.A.* 110 E6
Crosbyton, *U.S.A.* 113 J4
Crosía, *Italy* 31 C9
Cross →, *Nigeria* 83 E6
Cross City, *U.S.A.* 109 L4
Cross Fell, *U.K.* 12 C5
Cross L., *Canada* 105 C9
Cross Plains, *U.S.A.* 113 J5
Cross River □, *Nigeria* 83 D6
Cross Sound, *U.S.A.* 100 C6
Crossett, *U.S.A.* 113 J9
Crossfield, *Canada* 104 C6
Crosshaven, *Ireland* 15 E3
Croton-on-Hudson, *U.S.A.* 111 E11
Crotone, *Italy* 31 C10
Crow →, *Canada* 104 B4
Crow Agency, *U.S.A.* 114 D10
Crow Hd., *Ireland* 15 E1
Crowell, *U.S.A.* 113 J5
Crowley, *U.S.A.* 113 K8
Crowley, L., *U.S.A.* 116 H8
Crown Point, *U.S.A.* 108 E2
Crows Landing, *U.S.A.* 116 H5
Crows Nest, *Australia* 95 D5
Crowsnest Pass, *Canada* 104 D6
Croydon, *Australia* 94 B3
Croydon, *U.K.* 13 F7
Crozet Is., *Ind. Oc.* 3 G12
Crozon, *France* 18 D2
Cruz, C., *Cuba* 120 C4
Cruz Alta, *Brazil* 127 B5
Cruz de Incio, *Spain* 34 C3
Cruz del Eje, *Argentina* 126 C3
Cruzeiro, *Brazil* 127 A7
Cruzeiro do Oeste, *Brazil* 127 A5
Cruzeiro do Sul, *Brazil* 124 E4
Cry L., *Canada* 104 B3
Crystal Bay, *U.S.A.* 116 F7
Crystal Brook, *Australia* 95 E2
Crystal City, *Mo., U.S.A.* 112 F9
Crystal City, *Tex., U.S.A.* 113 L5
Crystal Falls, *U.S.A.* 108 B1
Crystal River, *U.S.A.* 109 L4
Crystal Springs, *U.S.A.* 113 K9
Csenger, *Hungary* 42 C7
Csongrád, *Hungary* 42 D5
Csongrád □, *Hungary* 42 D5
Csorna, *Hungary* 42 C2
Csurgo, *Hungary* 42 D2
Cu Lao Hon, *Vietnam* 65 G7
Cua Rao, *Vietnam* 64 C5
Cuácua →, *Mozam.* 87 F4
Cuamato, *Angola* 88 B2
Cuamba, *Mozam.* 87 E4
Cuando →, *Angola* 85 H4
Cuando Cubango □, *Angola* 88 B3
Cuangar, *Angola* 88 B2
Cuanza →, *Angola* 76 G5
Cuarto →, *Argentina* 126 C3
Cuatrociénegas, *Mexico* 118 B4
Cuauhtémoc, *Mexico* 118 B3
Cuba, *Portugal* 35 G3
Cuba, *N. Mex., U.S.A.* 115 J10
Cuba, *N.Y., U.S.A.* 110 D6
Cuba ■, *W. Indies* 120 B4
Cuballing, *Australia* 93 F2
Cubango →, *Africa* 88 B3
Çubuk, *Turkey* 72 B5
Cuchumatanes, Sierra de los, *Guatemala* 120 C1
Cuckfield, *U.K.* 13 F7
Cucuí, *Brazil* 124 C5
Cucurpe, *Mexico* 118 A2
Cúcuta, *Colombia* 124 B4
Cudalbi, *Romania* 43 E12
Cuddalore, *India* 66 P11
Cuddapah, *India* 66 M11
Cuddapan, L., *Australia* 94 D3
Cudgewa, *Australia* 95 F4
Cudillero, *Spain* 34 B4
Cue, *Australia* 93 E2
Cuéllar, *Spain* 34 D6
Cuenca, *Ecuador* 124 D3

Cuenca, *Spain* 32 E2
Cuenca □, *Spain* 32 F3
Cuenca, Serranía de, *Spain* 32 F3
Cuerdo del Pozo, Embalse de la, *Spain* 32 D2
Cuernavaca, *Mexico* 119 D5
Cuero, *U.S.A.* 113 L6
Cuers, *France* 21 E10
Cuervo, *U.S.A.* 113 H2
Cuevas del Almanzora, *Spain* 33 H3
Cuevo, *Bolivia* 124 H6
Cugir, *Romania* 43 E8
Cugnaux, *France* 20 E5
Cuhai-Bakony →, *Hungary* 42 C2
Cuiabá, *Brazil* 125 G7
Cuiabá →, *Brazil* 125 G7
Cuijk, *Neths.* 17 C5
Cuilco, *Guatemala* 120 C1
Cuillin Hills, *U.K.* 14 D2
Cuillin Sd., *U.K.* 14 D2
Cuiseaux, *France* 19 F12
Cuito →, *Angola* 88 B3
Cuitzeo, L. de, *Mexico* 118 D4
Cujmir, *Romania* 42 F7
Cukai, *Malaysia* 65 K4
Culbertson, *U.S.A.* 112 A2
Culcairn, *Australia* 95 F4
Culebra, Sierra de la, *Spain* 34 D4
Culfa, *Azerbaijan* 73 C11
Culgoa →, *Australia* 95 D4
Culiacán, *Mexico* 118 C3
Culiacán →, *Mexico* 118 C3
Culion, *Phil.* 61 F4
Cúllar, *Spain* 35 H8
Cullarin Ra., *Australia* 95 E4
Cullen, *U.K.* 14 D6
Cullen Pt., *Australia* 94 A3
Cullera, *Spain* 33 F4
Cullman, *U.S.A.* 109 H2
Culoz, *France* 21 C9
Culpeper, *U.S.A.* 108 F7
Culuene →, *Brazil* 125 F8
Culver, Pt., *Australia* 93 F3
Culverden, *N.Z.* 91 K4
Cumaná, *Venezuela* 124 A6
Cumaovası, *Turkey* 39 C9
Cumberland, *Canada* 104 D4
Cumberland, *Md., U.S.A.* 108 F6
Cumberland, *Wis., U.S.A.* 112 C8
Cumberland →, *U.S.A.* 109 G2
Cumberland I., *U.S.A.* 109 K5
Cumberland Is., *Australia* 94 C4
Cumberland L., *Canada* 105 C8
Cumberland Pen., *Canada* 101 B13
Cumberland Plateau, *U.S.A.* 109 H3
Cumberland Sd., *Canada* 101 B13
Cumbernauld, *U.K.* 14 F5
Cumborah, *Australia* 95 D4
Cumbres Mayores, *Spain* 35 G4
Cumbria □, *U.K.* 12 C5
Cumbrian Mts., *U.K.* 12 C5
Cumbum, *India* 66 M11
Cuminá →, *Brazil* 125 D7
Cummings Mt., *U.S.A.* 117 K8
Cummins, *Australia* 95 E2
Cumnock, *Australia* 95 E4
Cumnock, *U.K.* 14 F4
Cumpas, *Mexico* 118 B3
Cumplida, Pta., *Canary Is.* 37 F2
Çumra, *Turkey* 72 D5
Cunco, *Chile* 128 D2
Cuncumén, *Chile* 126 C1
Cundeelee, *Australia* 93 F3
Cunderdin, *Australia* 93 F2
Cunene →, *Angola* 88 B1
Cúneo, *Italy* 28 D4
Cunillera, I. = Sa Conillera, *Spain* 37 C7
Cunlhat, *France* 20 C7
Cunnamulla, *Australia* 95 D4
Cuorgnè, *Italy* 28 C4
Cupar, *Canada* 105 C8
Cupar, *U.K.* 14 E5
Cupcini, *Moldova* 43 B12
Cupica, G. de, *Colombia* 124 B3
Ćuprija, *Serbia, Yug.* 40 C5
Curaçao, *Neth. Ant.* 121 D6
Curanilahue, *Chile* 126 D1
Curaray →, *Peru* 124 D4
Cure →, *France* 19 E10
Curepto, *Chile* 126 D1
Curiapo, *Venezuela* 124 B6
Curicó, *Chile* 126 C1
Curicó □, *Chile* 126 C1
Curinga, *Italy* 31 D9
Curitiba, *Brazil* 127 B6
Currabubula, *Australia* 95 E5
Currais Novos, *Brazil* 125 E11
Curralinho, *Brazil* 125 D9
Currant, *U.S.A.* 114 G6
Curraweena, *Australia* 95 E4
Currawilla, *Australia* 94 D3
Current →, *U.S.A.* 113 G9
Currie, *Australia* 94 F3
Currie, *U.S.A.* 114 F6
Currituck Sd., *U.S.A.* 109 G8
Curtea de Argeş, *Romania* 43 E9
Curtici, *Romania* 42 D6
Curtis, *U.S.A.* 112 E4
Curtis Group, *Australia* 94 F4
Curtis I., *Australia* 94 C5
Curuápanema →, *Brazil* 125 D7
Curuçá, *Brazil* 125 D9
Curuguaty, *Paraguay* 127 A4
Curup, *Indonesia* 62 E2
Cururupu, *Brazil* 125 D10
Curuzú Cuatiá, *Argentina* 126 B4
Curvelo, *Brazil* 125 G10
Cushing, *U.S.A.* 113 H6
Cushing, Mt., *Canada* 104 B3
Cusihuiriáchic, *Mexico* 118 B3
Cusna, Mte., *Italy* 28 D7
Cusset, *France* 19 F10
Custer, *U.S.A.* 112 D3
Cut Bank, *U.S.A.* 114 B7
Cuthbert, *U.S.A.* 109 K3
Cutler, *U.S.A.* 116 J7
Cutro, *Italy* 31 C9
Cuttaburra →, *Australia* 95 D3
Cuttack, *India* 67 J14
Cuvier, C., *Australia* 93 D1
Cuvier I., *N.Z.* 91 G5
Cuxhaven, *Germany* 24 B4
Cuyahoga Falls, *U.S.A.* 110 E3
Cuyapo, *Phil.* 61 D4
Cuyo, *Phil.* 61 F4
Cuyo East Pass, *Phil.* 61 F4
Cuyo West Pass, *Phil.* 61 F4
Cuyuni →, *Guyana* 124 B7
Cuzco, *Bolivia* 124 H5
Cuzco, *Peru* 124 F4
Čvrsnica, *Bos.-H.* 42 G2
Cwmbran, *U.K.* 13 F4
Cyangugu, *Rwanda* 86 C2
Cybinka, *Poland* 45 F1
Cyclades = Kikládhes, *Greece* 38 E6
Cygnet, *Australia* 94 G4
Cynthiana, *U.S.A.* 108 F3
Cypress Hills, *Canada* 105 D7
Cyprus ■, *Asia* 36 E12
Cyrenaica, *Libya* 79 C10
Czaplinek, *Poland* 44 E3
Czar, *Canada* 105 C6
Czarna →, *Piotrkow Trybunalski, Poland* 45 G6
Czarna →, *Tarnobrzeg, Poland* 45 H8
Czarna Białostocka, *Poland* 45 E10
Czarna Woda, *Poland* 44 E5
Czarne, *Poland* 44 E3
Czarnków, *Poland* 45 F3
Czech Rep. ■, *Europe* 26 B8
Czechowice-Dziedzice, *Poland* 45 J5
Czempiń, *Poland* 45 F3
Czeremcha, *Poland* 45 F10
Czerniejewo, *Poland* 45 F4
Czersk, *Poland* 44 E4
Czerwieńsk, *Poland* 45 F2
Czerwionka-Leszczyny, *Poland* 45 H5
Częstochowa, *Poland* 45 H6
Częstochowa □, *Poland* 45 H6
Człopa, *Poland* 45 E3
Człuchów, *Poland* 44 E4
Czyżew-Osada, *Poland* 45 F9

D

Da →, *Vietnam* 64 B5
Da Hinggan Ling, *China* 60 B7
Da Lat, *Vietnam* 65 G7
Da Nang, *Vietnam* 64 D7
Da Qaidam, *China* 60 C4
Da Yunhe →, *China* 57 G11
Da'an, *China* 57 B13
Dab'a, Râs el, *Egypt* 80 H6
Daba Shan, *China* 58 B7
Dabai, *Nigeria* 83 C6
Dabakala, *Ivory C.* 82 D4
Dabas, *Hungary* 42 C4
Dabhoi, *India* 68 H5
Dąbie, *Poland* 45 F5
Dabie Shan, *China* 59 B10
Dabo = Pasirkuning, *Indonesia* 62 E2
Dabola, *Guinea* 82 C2
Dabou, *Ivory C.* 82 D4
Daboya, *Ghana* 83 D4
Dąbrowa Białostocka, *Poland* 44 E10
Dąbrowa Górnicza, *Poland* 45 H6
Dąbrowa Tarnowska, *Poland* 45 H7
Dabu, *China* 59 E11
Dabung, *Malaysia* 65 K4
Dabus →, *Ethiopia* 81 E4
Dacato →, *Ethiopia* 81 F5
Dacca = Dhaka, *Bangla.* 69 H14
Dacca = Dhaka □, *Bangla.* 69 G14
Dachau, *Germany* 25 G7
Dachstein, Hoher, *Austria* 26 D6
Dačice, *Czech Rep.* 26 B8
Dadanawa, *Guyana* 124 C7
Daday, *Turkey* 72 B5
Dade City, *U.S.A.* 109 L4
Dadiya, *Nigeria* 83 D7
Dadra & Nagar Haveli □, *India* 66 J8
Dadri = Charkhi Dadri, *India* 68 E7
Dadu, *Pakistan* 68 F2
Dadu He →, *China* 58 C4
Daet, *Phil.* 61 D5
Dafang, *China* 58 D5
Dağ, *Turkey* 39 D12
Dagana, *Senegal* 82 B1
Dagash, *Sudan* 80 D3
Dagestan □, *Russia* 49 J8
Dagestanskiye Ogni, *Russia* 49 J9
Daggett, *U.S.A.* 117 L10
Daghestan Republic = Dagestan □, *Russia* 49 J8
Daghfeli, *Sudan* 80 D3
Dağlıq Qarabağ = Nagorno-Karabakh, *Azerbaijan* 73 C12
Dagö = Hiiumaa, *Estonia* 9 G20
Dagu, *China* 57 E9
Daguan, *China* 58 D4
Dagupan, *Phil.* 61 C4
Dahab, *Egypt* 80 B3
Dahlak Kebir, *Eritrea* 81 D5
Dahlenburg, *Germany* 24 B6
Dahlonega, *U.S.A.* 109 H4
Dahme, *Germany* 24 D9
Dahod, *India* 68 H6
Dahomey = Benin ■, *Africa* 83 D5
Dahong Shan, *China* 59 B9
Dahra, *Senegal* 82 B1
Dai Hao, *Vietnam* 64 C6
Dai-Sen, *Japan* 55 G6
Dai Shan, *China* 59 B14
Dai Xian, *China* 56 E7
Daicheng, *China* 56 E9
Daimiel, *Spain* 35 F7
Daingean, *Ireland* 15 C4
Dainkog, *China* 58 A1
Daintree, *Australia* 94 B4
Daiō-Misaki, *Japan* 55 G8
Dairût, *Egypt* 80 B3
Daisetsu-Zan, *Japan* 54 C11
Dajarra, *Australia* 94 C2
Dajin Chuan →, *China* 58 B3
Dak Dam, *Cambodia* 64 F6
Dak Nhe, *Vietnam* 64 E6
Dak Pek, *Vietnam* 64 E6
Dak Song, *Vietnam* 65 F6
Dak Sui, *Vietnam* 64 E6
Dakar, *Senegal* 82 C1
Dakhla, *W. Sahara* 78 D2
Dakhla, El Wâhât el-, *Egypt* 80 B2
Dakingari, *Nigeria* 83 C5
Dakor, *India* 68 H5
Dakoro, *Niger* 83 C6
Dakota City, *U.S.A.* 112 D6
Đakovica, *Serbia, Yug.* 40 D4
Đakovo, *Croatia* 42 E3
Dalaba, *Guinea* 82 C2
Dalachi, *China* 56 F3
Dalai Nur, *China* 56 C9
Dālakī, *Iran* 71 D6
Dalälven, *Sweden* 10 D10
Dalaman, *Turkey* 39 E10
Dalaman →, *Turkey* 39 E10
Dalandzadgad, *Mongolia* 56 C3
Dalarna, *Sweden* 10 D8
Dālbandīn, *Pakistan* 66 E4
Dalbeattie, *U.K.* 14 G5
Dalbosjön, *Sweden* 11 F6
Dalby, *Australia* 95 D5
Dalby, *Sweden* 11 J7
Dalga, *Egypt* 80 B3
Dalgān, *Iran* 71 E8
Dalhart, *U.S.A.* 113 G3
Dalhousie, *Canada* 103 C6
Dalhousie, *India* 68 C6
Dali, *Shaanxi, China* 56 G5
Dali, *Yunnan, China* 58 E3
Dalian, *China* 57 E11
Daliang Shan, *China* 58 D4
Daling He →, *China* 57 D11
Dāliyat el Karmel, *Israel* 75 C4
Dalj, *Croatia* 42 E3
Dalkeith, *U.K.* 14 F5
Dall I., *U.S.A.* 104 C2
Dallarnil, *Australia* 95 D5
Dallas, *Oreg., U.S.A.* 114 D2
Dallas, *Tex., U.S.A.* 113 J6
Dallol, *Ethiopia* 81 E5
Dalmacija, *Croatia* 29 E13
Dalmatia = Dalmacija, *Croatia* 29 E13
Dalmellington, *U.K.* 14 F4
Dalnegorsk, *Russia* 54 B7
Dalnerechensk, *Russia* 54 B6
Daloa, *Ivory C.* 82 D3
Dalou Shan, *China* 58 C6
Dalry, *U.K.* 14 F4
Dals Långed, *Sweden* 11 F6
Dalsjöfors, *Sweden* 11 G7
Dalsland, *Sweden* 11 F6
Daltenganj, *India* 69 H11
Dalton, *Canada* 102 C3
Dalton, *Ga., U.S.A.* 109 H3
Dalton, *Mass., U.S.A.* 111 D11
Dalton, *Nebr., U.S.A.* 112 E3
Dalton Iceberg Tongue, *Antarctica* 5 C9
Dalton-in-Furness, *U.K.* 12 C4
Dalupiri I., *Phil.* 61 B4
Dalvík, *Iceland* 8 D4
Daly →, *Australia* 92 B5
Daly City, *U.S.A.* 116 H4
Daly L., *Canada* 105 B7
Daly Waters, *Australia* 94 B1
Dalyan, *Turkey* 39 E10
Dam Doi, *Vietnam* 65 H5
Dam Ha, *Vietnam* 64 B6
Daman, *India* 66 J8
Dāmaneh, *Iran* 71 C6
Damanhûr, *Egypt* 80 H7
Damanzhuang, *China* 56 E9
Damar, *Indonesia* 63 F7
Damaraland, *Namibia* 88 C2
Damascus = Dimashq, *Syria* 75 B5
Damaturu, *Nigeria* 83 C7
Damāvand, *Iran* 71 C7
Damāvand, Qolleh-ye, *Iran* 71 C7
Damba, *Angola* 84 F3
Dâmboviţa □, *Romania* 43 F10
Dâmboviţa →, *Romania* 43 F11
Dâmbovnic →, *Romania* 43 F10
Dame Marie, *Haiti* 121 C5
Dāmghān, *Iran* 71 B7
Dămienesti, *Romania* 43 D11
Damietta = Dumyât, *Egypt* 80 H7
Daming, *China* 56 F8
Damīr Qābū, *Syria* 70 B4
Dammam = Ad Dammām, *Si. Arabia* 71 E6
Dammarie-les-Lys, *France* 19 D9
Dammartin-en-Goële, *France* 19 C9
Damme, *Germany* 24 C4
Damodar →, *India* 69 H12
Damoh, *India* 69 H8
Dampier, *Australia* 92 D2
Dampier, Selat, *Indonesia* 63 E8
Dampier Arch., *Australia* 92 D2
Damrei, Chuor Phnum, *Cambodia* 65 G4
Damvillers, *France* 19 C12
Dan-Gulbi, *Nigeria* 83 C6
Dan Xian, *China* 64 C7
Dana, *Indonesia* 63 F6
Dana, L., *Canada* 102 B4
Dana, Mt., *U.S.A.* 116 H7
Danakil Depression, *Ethiopia* 81 E5
Danao, *Phil.* 61 F6
Danbury, *U.S.A.* 111 E11
Danby L., *U.S.A.* 115 J6
Dand, *Afghan.* 68 D1
Dandaragan, *Australia* 93 F2
Dandeldhura, *Nepal* 69 E9
Dandeli, *India* 66 M9
Dandenong, *Australia* 95 F4
Dandong, *China* 57 D13
Danfeng, *China* 56 H6
Danforth, *U.S.A.* 103 C6
Dangan Liedao, *China* 59 F10
Dangé-St-Roman, *France* 20 B4
Dângeni, *Romania* 43 C11
Danger Is. = Pukapuka, *Cook Is.* 97 J11
Danger Pt., *S. Africa* 88 E2
Dangla, *Ethiopia* 81 E4
Dangla Shan = Tanggula Shan, *China* 60 C4
Dangora, *Nigeria* 83 C6
Dangrek, Phnom, *Thailand* 64 E5
Dangriga, *Belize* 119 D7
Dangshan, *China* 56 G9
Dangtu, *China* 59 B12
Dangyang, *China* 59 B8
Daniel, *U.S.A.* 114 E8
Daniel's Harbour, *Canada* 103 B8
Danielskuil, *S. Africa* 88 D3
Danielson, *U.S.A.* 111 E13
Danilov, *Russia* 46 C11
Danilovgrad, *Montenegro, Yug.* 40 D3
Danilovka, *Russia* 48 E7
Daning, *China* 56 F6
Danissa, *Kenya* 86 B5
Danja, *Nigeria* 83 C6
Dankalwa, *Nigeria* 83 C7
Dankama, *Nigeria* 83 C6
Dankhar Gompa, *India* 66 C11
Dankov, *Russia* 46 F10
Danleng, *China* 58 B4
Danlí, *Honduras* 120 D2
Dannemora, *U.S.A.* 111 B11
Dannenberg, *Germany* 24 B7
Dannevirke, *N.Z.* 91 J6
Dannhauser, *S. Africa* 89 D5
Dansville, *U.S.A.* 110 D7
Dantan, *India* 69 J12
Dante, *Somali Rep.* 74 E5
Danube = Dunărea →, *Europe* 43 E14
Danvers, *U.S.A.* 111 D14
Danville, *Ill., U.S.A.* 108 E2
Danville, *Ky., U.S.A.* 108 G3
Danville, *Va., U.S.A.* 109 G6
Danyang, *China* 59 B12
Danzhai, *China* 58 D6
Danzig = Gdańsk, *Poland* 44 D5
Dão →, *Portugal* 34 E2
Dao Xian, *China* 59 E8
Daocheng, *China* 58 C3
Dapaong, *Togo* 83 C5
Dapitan, *Phil.* 61 G5
Daqing Shan, *China* 56 D6
Daqu Shan, *China* 59 B14
Dar Banda, *Africa* 76 F6
Dar el Beida = Casablanca, *Morocco* 78 B4
Dar es Salaam, *Tanzania* 86 D4
Dar Mazār, *Iran* 71 D8
Dar'ā, *Syria* 75 C5
Dar'ā □, *Syria* 75 C5
Dārāb, *Iran* 71 D7
Darabani, *Romania* 43 B11
Daraj, *Libya* 79 B8
Dārān, *Iran* 71 C6
Daravica, *Serbia, Yug.* 40 D4
Daraw, *Egypt* 80 C3
Dārayyā, *Syria* 75 B5
Darazo, *Nigeria* 83 C7
Darband, *Pakistan* 68 B5
Darband, Kūh-e, *Iran* 71 D8
Darbhanga, *India* 69 F11
Darby, *U.S.A.* 114 C6
Darda, *Croatia* 42 E3
Dardanelle, *Ark., U.S.A.* 113 H8
Dardanelle, *Calif., U.S.A.* 116 G7
Dardanelles = Çanakkale Boğazı, *Turkey* 41 F10
Darende, *Turkey* 72 C7
Dārestān, *Iran* 71 D8
Darfo, *Italy* 28 C7
Dârfûr, *Sudan* 79 F10
Dargai, *Pakistan* 68 B4
Dargan Ata, *Uzbekistan* 50 E7
Dargaville, *N.Z.* 91 F4
Darhan Muminggan Lianheqi, *China* 56 D6
Dari, *Sudan* 81 F3
Darıca, *Turkey* 72 B3
Darién, G. del, *Colombia* 122 C3
Dariganga, *Mongolia* 56 B7
Darinskoye, *Kazakstan* 48 E10
Darjeeling = Darjiling, *India* 69 F13
Darjiling, *India* 69 F13
Dark Cove, *Canada* 103 C9
Darkan, *Australia* 93 F2
Darkhazīneh, *Iran* 71 D6
Darkot Pass, *Pakistan* 69 A5
Darling →, *Australia* 95 E3
Darling Downs, *Australia* 95 D5
Darling Ra., *Australia* 93 F2
Darlington, *U.K.* 12 C6
Darlington, *S.C., U.S.A.* 109 H6
Darlington, *Wis., U.S.A.* 112 D9
Darlington □, *U.K.* 12 C6
Darlington, L., *S. Africa* 88 E4
Darlot, L., *Australia* 93 E3
Darłowo, *Poland* 44 D3
Dărmăneşti, *Bacău, Romania* 43 D11
Dărmăneşti, *Suceava, Romania* 43 C11
Darmstadt, *Germany* 25 F4
Darnah, *Libya* 79 B10
Darnall, *S. Africa* 89 D5
Darney, *France* 19 D13
Darnley, C., *Antarctica* 5 C6
Darnley B., *Canada* 100 B7
Daroca, *Spain* 32 D3
Darr, *Australia* 94 C3
Darr →, *Australia* 94 C3
Darrington, *U.S.A.* 114 B3
Darsser Ort, *Germany* 24 A8
Dart →, *U.K.* 13 G4
Dart, C., *Antarctica* 5 D14
Dartford, *U.K.* 13 F8
Dartmoor, *U.K.* 13 G4
Dartmouth, *Australia* 94 C3
Dartmouth, *Canada* 103 D7
Dartmouth, *U.K.* 13 G4
Dartmouth, L., *Australia* 95 D4
Dartuch, C. = Artrutx, C. de, *Spain* 37 B10
Daruvar, *Croatia* 42 E2
Darvaza, *Turkmenistan* 50 E6
Darvel, Teluk = Lahad Datu, Teluk, *Malaysia* 63 D5
Darwen, *U.K.* 12 D5
Darwha, *India* 66 J10
Darwin, *Australia* 92 B5
Darwin, *U.S.A.* 117 J9
Darwin River, *Australia* 92 B5
Daryoi Amu = Amudarya →, *Uzbekistan* 50 E6
Dās, *U.A.E.* 71 E7
Dashetai, *China* 56 D5
Dashhowuz, *Turkmenistan* 50 E6
Dashkesan = Daşkäsän, *Azerbaijan* 49 K7
Dasht, *Iran* 71 B8
Dasht →, *Pakistan* 66 G2
Dasht-e Mārgow, *Afghan.* 66 D3
Dasht-i-Nawar, *Afghan.* 68 C3
Daska, *Pakistan* 68 C6
Daşkäsän, *Azerbaijan* 49 K7
Dassa, *Benin* 83 D5
Datça, *Turkey* 39 E9
Datia, *India* 69 G8
Datian, *China* 59 E11
Datong, *Anhui, China* 59 B11
Datong, *Shanxi, China* 56 D7
Datteln, *Germany* 24 D3
Datu, Tanjung, *Indonesia* 62 D3
Datu Piang, *Phil.* 61 H6
Daugava →, *Latvia* 9 H21
Daugavpils, *Latvia* 9 J22
Daulpur, *India* 68 F7
Daun, *Germany* 25 E2
Dauphin, *Canada* 105 C8
Dauphin I., *U.S.A.* 109 K1
Dauphin L., *Canada* 105 C9
Dauphiné, *France* 21 C9
Daura, *Borno, Nigeria* 83 C7
Daura, *Kaduna, Nigeria* 83 C6
Dausa, *India* 68 F7
Däväçi, *Azerbaijan* 49 K9
Davangere, *India* 66 M9
Davao, *Phil.* 61 H6
Davao, G. of, *Phil.* 61 H6
Dāvar Panāh, *Iran* 71 E9
Davenport, *Calif., U.S.A.* 116 H4

Davenport, *Iowa, U.S.A.* 112 E9
Davenport, *Wash., U.S.A.* 114 C4
Davenport Downs, *Australia* 94 C3
Davenport Ra., *Australia* 94 C1
Daventry, *U.K.* 13 E6
David, *Panama* 120 E3
David City, *U.S.A.* 112 E6
David Gorodok = Davyd Haradok, *Belarus* 47 F4
Davidson, *Canada* 105 C7
Davis, *U.S.A.* 116 G5
Davis Dam, *U.S.A.* 117 K12
Davis Inlet, *Canada* 103 A7
Davis Mts., *U.S.A.* 113 K2
Davis Sea, *Antarctica* 5 C7
Davis Str., *N. Amer.* 101 B14
Davos, *Switz.* 25 J5
Davutlar, *Turkey* 39 D9
Davy L., *Canada* 105 B7
Davyd Haradok, *Belarus* 47 F4
Dawa →, *Ethiopia* 81 G5
Dawaki, *Bauchi, Nigeria* 83 D6
Dawaki, *Kano, Nigeria* 83 C6
Dawei, *Burma* 64 E2
Dawes Ra., *Australia* 94 C5
Dawlish, *U.K.* 13 G4
Dawros Hd., *Ireland* 15 B3
Dawson, *Canada* 100 B6
Dawson, *Ga., U.S.A.* 109 K3
Dawson, *N. Dak., U.S.A.* 112 B5
Dawson, I., *Chile* 128 G2
Dawson Creek, *Canada* 104 B4
Dawson Inlet, *Canada* 105 A10
Dawson Ra., *Australia* 94 C4
Dawu, *China* 58 B3
Dax, *France* 20 E2
Daxian, *China* 58 B6
Daxin, *China* 58 F6
Daxindian, *China* 57 F11
Daxinggou, *China* 57 C15
Daxue Shan, *Sichuan, China* 58 B3
Daxue Shan, *Yunnan, China* 58 F2
Dayao, *China* 58 E3
Daye, *China* 59 B10
Dayi, *China* 58 B4
Daylesford, *Australia* 95 F3
Dayong, *China* 59 C8
Dayr az Zawr, *Syria* 70 C4
Daysland, *Canada* 104 C6
Dayton, *Nev., U.S.A.* 116 F7
Dayton, *Ohio, U.S.A.* 108 F3
Dayton, *Pa., U.S.A.* 110 F5
Dayton, *Tenn., U.S.A.* 109 H3
Dayton, *Wash., U.S.A.* 114 C4
Daytona Beach, *U.S.A.* 109 L5
Dayu, *China* 59 E10
Dayville, *U.S.A.* 114 D4
Dazhu, *China* 58 B6
Dazkırı, *Turkey* 39 D11
Dazu, *China* 58 C5
De Aar, *S. Africa* 88 E3
De Funiak Springs, *U.S.A.* 109 K2
De Grey, *Australia* 92 D2
De Grey →, *Australia* 92 D2
De Haan, *Belgium* 17 C3
De Kalb, *U.S.A.* 112 E10
De Land, *U.S.A.* 109 L5
De Leon, *U.S.A.* 113 J5
De Panne, *Belgium* 17 C2
De Pere, *U.S.A.* 108 C1
De Queen, *U.S.A.* 113 H7
De Quincy, *U.S.A.* 113 K8
De Ridder, *U.S.A.* 113 K8
De Smet, *U.S.A.* 112 C6
De Soto, *U.S.A.* 112 F9
De Tour Village, *U.S.A.* 108 C4
De Witt, *U.S.A.* 113 H9
Dead Sea, *Asia* 75 D4
Deadwood, *U.S.A.* 112 C3
Deadwood L., *Canada* 104 B3
Deakin, *Australia* 93 F4
Deal, *U.K.* 13 F9
Deal I., *Australia* 94 F4
Dealesville, *S. Africa* 88 D4
De'an, *China* 59 C10
Dean, Forest of, *U.K.* 13 F5
Deán Funes, *Argentina* 126 C3
Dearborn, *U.S.A.* 102 D3
Dease →, *Canada* 104 B3
Dease L., *Canada* 104 B2
Dease Lake, *Canada* 104 B2
Death Valley, *U.S.A.* 117 J10
Death Valley Junction, *U.S.A.* 117 J10
Death Valley National Monument, *U.S.A.* 117 J10
Deauville, *France* 18 C7
Deba, *Spain* 32 B2
Deba Habe, *Nigeria* 83 C7
Debaltsevo, *Ukraine* 47 H10
Debao, *China* 58 F6
Debar, *Macedonia* 40 E4
Debden, *Canada* 105 C7
Dębica, *Poland* 45 H8
Dęblin, *Poland* 45 G8
Dębno, *Poland* 45 F1
Débo, L., *Mali* 82 B4
Debolt, *Canada* 104 B5
Deborah East, L., *Australia* 93 F2
Deborah West, L., *Australia* 93 F2
Debrc, *Serbia, Yug.* 40 B3
Debre Birhan, *Ethiopia* 81 F4
Debre Markos, *Ethiopia* 81 E4
Debre May, *Ethiopia* 81 E4
Debre Sina, *Ethiopia* 81 F4
Debre Tabor, *Ethiopia* 81 E4
Debre Zebit, *Ethiopia* 81 E4
Debrecen, *Hungary* 42 C6
Debrzno, *Poland* 44 E4
Dečani, *Serbia, Yug.* 40 D4
Decatur, *Ala., U.S.A.* 109 H2
Decatur, *Ga., U.S.A.* 109 J3
Decatur, *Ill., U.S.A.* 112 F10
Decatur, *Ind., U.S.A.* 108 E3
Decatur, *Tex., U.S.A.* 113 J6
Decazeville, *France* 20 D6
Deccan, *India* 66 L11
Deception L., *Canada* 105 B8
Dechang, *China* 58 D4
Děčín, *Czech Rep.* 26 A7
Decize, *France* 19 F10
Deckerville, *U.S.A.* 110 C2
Decollatura, *Italy* 31 C9
Decorah, *U.S.A.* 112 D9
Deda, *Romania* 43 D9
Dedéagach = Alexandroúpolis, *Greece* 41 F9
Dedham, *U.S.A.* 111 D13
Dédougou, *Burkina Faso* 82 C4
Dedovichi, *Russia* 46 D5
Dedza, *Malawi* 87 E3
Dee →, *Aberds., U.K.* 14 D6
Dee →, *Dumf. & Gall., U.K.* 14 G4
Dee →, *Wales, U.K.* 12 D4
Deep B., *Canada* 104 A5
Deep Well, *Australia* 94 C1
Deepwater, *Australia* 95 D5
Deer →, *Canada* 105 B10
Deer Lake, *Nfld., Canada* 103 C8
Deer Lake, *Ont., Canada* 105 C10
Deer Lodge, *U.S.A.* 114 C7
Deer Park, *U.S.A.* 114 C5
Deer River, *U.S.A.* 112 B8
Deeral, *Australia* 94 B4
Deerdepoort, *S. Africa* 88 C4
Deferiet, *U.S.A.* 111 B9
Defiance, *U.S.A.* 108 E3
Dêgê, *China* 58 B2
Degebe →, *Portugal* 35 G3
Degeberga, *Sweden* 11 J8
Degema, *Nigeria* 83 E6
Degerfors, *Sweden* 10 E8
Degerhamn, *Sweden* 11 H10
Deggendorf, *Germany* 25 G8
Değirmendere, *Turkey* 41 F13
Deh Bīd, *Iran* 71 D7
Deh-e Shīr, *Iran* 71 D7
Dehaj, *Iran* 71 D7
Dehdez, *Iran* 71 D6
Dehestān, *Iran* 71 D7
Dehgolān, *Iran* 70 C5
Dehi Titan, *Afghan.* 66 C3
Dehibat, *Tunisia* 79 B8
Dehlorān, *Iran* 70 C5
Dehnow-e Kūhestān, *Iran* 71 E8
Dehra Dun, *India* 68 D8
Dehri, *India* 69 G11
Dehua, *China* 59 E12
Dehui, *China* 57 B13
Deinze, *Belgium* 17 D3
Dej, *Romania* 43 C8
Deje, *Sweden* 10 E7
Dejiang, *China* 58 C7
Dekemhare, *Eritrea* 81 D4
Dekese, *Dem. Rep. of the Congo* 84 E4
Del Mar, *U.S.A.* 117 N9
Del Norte, *U.S.A.* 115 H10
Del Rio, *U.S.A.* 113 L4
Delai, *Sudan* 80 D4
Delano, *U.S.A.* 117 K7
Delareyville, *S. Africa* 88 D4
Delavan, *U.S.A.* 112 D10
Delaware, *U.S.A.* 108 E4
Delaware □, *U.S.A.* 108 F8
Delaware →, *U.S.A.* 108 F8
Delaware B., *U.S.A.* 107 C12
Delbrück, *Germany* 24 D4
Delčevo, *Macedonia* 40 E6
Delegate, *Australia* 95 F4
Delémont, *Switz.* 25 H3
Delft, *Neths.* 17 B4
Delfzijl, *Neths.* 17 A6
Delgado, C., *Mozam.* 87 E5
Delgerhet, *Mongolia* 56 B6
Delgo, *Sudan* 80 C3
Delhi, *Canada* 110 D4
Delhi, *India* 68 E7
Delhi, *U.S.A.* 111 D10
Deli Jovan, *Serbia, Yug.* 40 B6
Delia, *Canada* 104 C6
Delice, *Turkey* 72 C6
Delicias, *Mexico* 118 B3
Delījān, *Iran* 71 C6
Déline, *Canada* 100 B7
Delitzsch, *Germany* 24 D8
Dell City, *U.S.A.* 115 L11
Dell Rapids, *U.S.A.* 112 D6
Delle, *France* 19 E14
Delmar, *U.S.A.* 111 D11
Delmenhorst, *Germany* 24 B4
Delnice, *Croatia* 29 C11
Delong, Ostrova, *Russia* 51 B15
Deloraine, *Australia* 94 G4
Deloraine, *Canada* 105 D8
Delphi, *Greece* 38 C4
Delphi, *U.S.A.* 108 E2
Delphos, *U.S.A.* 108 E3
Delportshoop, *S. Africa* 88 D3
Delray Beach, *U.S.A.* 109 M5
Delsbo, *Sweden* 10 C10
Delta, *Colo., U.S.A.* 115 G9
Delta, *Utah, U.S.A.* 114 G7
Delta □, *Nigeria* 83 D6
Delungra, *Australia* 95 D5
Delvinákion, *Greece* 38 B2
Delvinë, *Albania* 40 G4
Demanda, Sierra de la, *Spain* 32 C2
Demavand = Damāvand, *Iran* 71 C7
Dembecha, *Ethiopia* 81 E4
Dembi, *Ethiopia* 81 F4
Dembia, *Dem. Rep. of the Congo* 86 B2
Dembidolo, *Ethiopia* 81 F3
Demer →, *Belgium* 17 D4
Demetrias, *Greece* 38 B5
Demidov, *Russia* 46 E6
Deming, *N. Mex., U.S.A.* 115 K10
Deming, *Wash., U.S.A.* 116 B4
Demini →, *Brazil* 124 D6
Demirci, *Turkey* 39 B10
Demirköprü Barajı, *Turkey* 39 C10
Demirköy, *Turkey* 41 E11
Demmin, *Germany* 24 B9
Demonte, *Italy* 28 D4
Demopolis, *U.S.A.* 109 J2
Demyansk, *Russia* 46 D7
Den Burg, *Neths.* 17 A4
Den Chai, *Thailand* 64 D3
Den Haag = 's-Gravenhage, *Neths.* 17 B4
Den Helder, *Neths.* 17 B4
Den Oever, *Neths.* 17 B5
Denain, *France* 19 B10
Denair, *U.S.A.* 116 H6
Denau, *Uzbekistan* 50 F7
Denbigh, *U.K.* 12 D4
Denbighshire □, *U.K.* 12 D4
Dendang, *Indonesia* 62 E3
Dendermonde, *Belgium* 17 C4
Deneba, *Ethiopia* 81 F4
Deng Xian, *China* 59 A9
Dengchuan, *China* 58 E3
Denge, *Nigeria* 83 C6
Dengfeng, *China* 56 G7
Dengi, *Nigeria* 83 D6
Dengkou, *China* 56 D4
Denham, *Australia* 93 E1
Denham Ra., *Australia* 94 C4
Denham Sd., *Australia* 93 E1
Denia, *Spain* 33 G5
Denial B., *Australia* 95 E1
Deniliquin, *Australia* 95 F3
Denison, *Iowa, U.S.A.* 112 E7
Denison, *Tex., U.S.A.* 113 J6
Denison Plains, *Australia* 92 C4
Denizli, *Turkey* 39 D11
Denizli □, *Turkey* 39 D11
Denman Glacier, *Antarctica* 5 C7
Denmark, *Australia* 93 F2
Denmark ■, *Europe* 11 J3
Denmark Str., *Atl. Oc.* 4 C6
Dennison, *U.S.A.* 110 F3
Denny, *U.K.* 14 E5
Denpasar, *Indonesia* 62 F5
Denton, *Mont., U.S.A.* 114 C9
Denton, *Tex., U.S.A.* 113 J6
D'Entrecasteaux, Pt., *Australia* 93 F2
Denu, *Ghana* 83 D5
Denver, *U.S.A.* 112 F2
Denver City, *U.S.A.* 113 J3
Deoband, *India* 68 E7
Deoghar, *India* 69 G12
Deolali, *India* 66 K8
Deoli = Devli, *India* 68 G6
Déols, *France* 19 F8
Deoria, *India* 69 F10
Deosai Mts., *Pakistan* 69 B6
Deping, *China* 57 F9
Deposit, *U.S.A.* 111 D9
Depot Springs, *Australia* 93 E3
Deputatskiy, *Russia* 51 C14
Dêqên, *China* 58 C2
Deqing, *China* 59 F8
Dera Ghazi Khan, *Pakistan* 68 D4
Dera Ismail Khan, *Pakistan* 68 D4
Derbent, *Russia* 49 J9
Derbent, *Turkey* 39 C10
Derby, *Australia* 92 C3
Derby, *U.K.* 12 E6
Derby, *Conn., U.S.A.* 111 E11
Derby, *N.Y., U.S.A.* 110 D6
Derby City □, *U.K.* 12 E6
Derbyshire □, *U.K.* 12 D6
Derecske, *Hungary* 42 C6
Dereköy, *Turkey* 41 E11
Dereli, *Turkey* 73 B8
Derg →, *U.K.* 15 B4
Derg, L., *Ireland* 15 D3
Dergachi = Derhaci, *Ukraine* 47 G9
Dergaon, *India* 67 F19
Derhaci, *Ukraine* 47 G9
Derik, *Turkey* 73 D9
Derinkuyu, *Turkey* 72 C6
Dermantsi, *Bulgaria* 41 C8
Dernieres, Isles, *U.S.A.* 113 L9
Dêrong, *China* 58 C2
Derry = Londonderry, *U.K.* 15 B4
Derry = Londonderry □, *U.K.* 15 B4
Derryveagh Mts., *Ireland* 15 B3
Derudub, *Sudan* 80 D4
Derval, *France* 18 E5
Dervéni, *Greece* 38 C4
Derventa, *Bos.-H.* 42 F2
Derwent, *Canada* 105 C6
Derwent →, *Cumb., U.K.* 12 C4
Derwent →, *Derby, U.K.* 12 E6
Derwent →, *N. Yorks., U.K.* 12 D7
Derwent Water, *U.K.* 12 C4
Des Moines, *Iowa, U.S.A.* 112 E8
Des Moines, *N. Mex., U.S.A.* 113 G3
Des Moines →, *U.S.A.* 112 E9
Desa, *Romania* 42 G8
Desaguadero →, *Argentina* 126 C2
Desaguadero →, *Bolivia* 124 G5
Descanso, Pta., *Mexico* 117 N9
Descartes, *France* 20 B4
Deschaillons, *Canada* 103 C5
Descharme →, *Canada* 105 B7
Deschutes →, *U.S.A.* 114 D3
Dese, *Ethiopia* 81 E4
Deseado →, *Argentina* 128 F3
Desenzano del Garda, *Italy* 28 C7
Desert Center, *U.S.A.* 117 M11
Desert Hot Springs, *U.S.A.* 117 M10
Désirade, I., *Guadeloupe* 121 C7
Deskenatlata L., *Canada* 104 A6
Desna →, *Ukraine* 47 G6
Desnătui →, *Romania* 43 G8
Desolación, I., *Chile* 128 G2
Despeñaperros, Paso, *Spain* 35 G7
Despotovac, *Serbia, Yug.* 40 B5
Dessau, *Germany* 24 D8
Dessye = Dese, *Ethiopia* 81 E4
D'Estrees B., *Australia* 95 F2
Desuri, *India* 68 G5
Desvres, *France* 19 B8
Det Udom, *Thailand* 64 E5
Deta, *Romania* 42 E6
Dete, *Zimbabwe* 87 F2
Đetinja →, *Serbia, Yug.* 40 C4
Detmold, *Germany* 24 D4
Detour, Pt., *U.S.A.* 108 C2
Detroit, *Mich., U.S.A.* 102 D3
Detroit, *Tex., U.S.A.* 113 J7
Detroit Lakes, *U.S.A.* 112 B7
Detva, *Slovak Rep.* 27 C12
Deurne, *Neths.* 17 C5
Deutsche Bucht, *Germany* 24 A4
Deutschlandsberg, *Austria* 26 E8
Deux-Sèvres □, *France* 18 F6
Deva, *Romania* 42 E7
Devakottai, *India* 66 Q11
Devaprayag, *India* 69 D8
Dévaványa, *Hungary* 42 C5
Deveci Dağları, *Turkey* 72 B7
Devecikonağı, *Turkey* 41 G12
Devecser, *Hungary* 42 C2
Develi, *Turkey* 72 C6
Deventer, *Neths.* 17 B6
Deveron →, *U.K.* 14 D6
Devesel, *Romania* 42 F7
Devgadh Bariya, *India* 68 H5
Devils Den, *U.S.A.* 116 K7
Devils Lake, *U.S.A.* 112 A5
Devils Paw, *Canada* 104 B2
Devin, *Bulgaria* 41 E8
Devizes, *U.K.* 13 F6
Devli, *India* 68 G6
Devnya, *Bulgaria* 41 C11
Devolii →, *Albania* 40 F4
Devon, *Canada* 104 C6
Devon □, *U.K.* 13 G4
Devon I., *Canada* 4 B3
Devonport, *Australia* 94 G4
Devonport, *N.Z.* 91 G5
Devrek, *Turkey* 72 B4
Devrekâni, *Turkey* 72 B5
Devrez →, *Turkey* 72 B6
Dewas, *India* 68 H7
Dewetsdorp, *S. Africa* 88 D4
Dexing, *China* 59 C11
Dexter, *Mo., U.S.A.* 113 G10
Dexter, *N. Mex., U.S.A.* 113 J2
Dey-Dey, L., *Australia* 93 E5
Deyang, *China* 58 B5
Deyhūk, *Iran* 71 C8
Deyyer, *Iran* 71 E6
Dezadeash L., *Canada* 104 A1
Dezfūl, *Iran* 71 C6
Dezhneva, Mys, *Russia* 51 C19
Dezhou, *China* 56 F9
Dháfni, *Kríti, Greece* 36 D7
Dháfni, *Pelóponnisos, Greece* 38 D4
Dhahaban, *Si. Arabia* 80 C4
Dhahiriya = Aẓ Ẓāhirīyah, *West Bank* 75 D3
Dhahran = Aẓ Ẓahrān, *Si. Arabia* 71 E6
Dhaka, *Bangla.* 69 H14
Dhaka □, *Bangla.* 69 G14
Dhali, *Cyprus* 36 D12
Dhamási, *Greece* 38 B4
Dhampur, *India* 69 E8
Dhamtari, *India* 67 J12
Dhanbad, *India* 69 H12
Dhangarhi, *Nepal* 67 E12
Dhankuta, *Nepal* 69 F12
Dhar, *India* 68 H6
Dharampur, *India* 68 H6
Dharamsala = Dharmsala, *India* 68 C7
Dharmapuri, *India* 66 N11
Dharmsala, *India* 68 C7
Dharwad, *India* 66 M9
Dhaulagiri, *Nepal* 69 E10
Dhebar, L., *India* 68 G6
Dheftera, *Cyprus* 36 D12
Dhenkanal, *India* 67 J14
Dhenoúsa, *Greece* 39 D7
Dherinia, *Cyprus* 36 D12
Dheskáti, *Greece* 40 G5
Dhespotikó, *Greece* 38 E6
Dhestina, *Greece* 38 C4
Dhiarrizos →, *Cyprus* 36 E11
Dhībān, *Jordan* 75 D4
Dhidhimótikhon, *Greece* 41 E10
Dhíkti Óros, *Greece* 36 D7
Dhilianáta, *Greece* 38 C2
Dhílos, *Greece* 39 D7
Dhimitsána, *Greece* 38 D4
Dhírfis = Dhírfis Óros, *Greece* 38 C5
Dhírfis Óros, *Greece* 38 C5
Dhodhekánisos, *Greece* 39 E8
Dhodhekánisos □, *Greece* 39 E8
Dhokós, *Greece* 38 D5
Dholiana, *Greece* 38 B2
Dholka, *India* 68 H5
Dhomokós, *Greece* 38 B4
Dhoraji, *India* 68 J4
Dhoxáton, *Greece* 41 E8
Dhragonísi, *Greece* 39 D7
Dhráhstis, Ákra, *Greece* 36 A3
Dhrangadhra, *India* 68 H4
Dhrápanon, Ákra, *Greece* 36 D6
Dhriopís, *Greece* 38 D6
Dhrol, *India* 68 H4
Dhuburi, *India* 67 F16
Dhule, *India* 66 J9
Di Linh, *Vietnam* 65 G7
Di Linh, Cao Nguyen, *Vietnam* 65 G7
Día, *Greece* 36 D7
Diablo, Mt., *U.S.A.* 116 H5
Diablo Range, *U.S.A.* 116 J5
Diafarabé, *Mali* 82 C4
Diala, *Mali* 82 C3
Dialakoro, *Mali* 82 C3
Diallassagou, *Mali* 82 C4
Diamante, *Argentina* 126 C3
Diamante, *Italy* 31 C8
Diamante →, *Argentina* 126 C2
Diamantina, *Brazil* 125 G10
Diamantina →, *Australia* 95 D2
Diamantino, *Brazil* 125 F7
Diamond Bar, *U.S.A.* 117 L9
Diamond Harbour, *India* 69 H13
Diamond Is., *Australia* 94 B5
Diamond Mts., *U.S.A.* 114 G6
Diamond Springs, *U.S.A.* 116 G6
Diamondville, *U.S.A.* 114 F8
Dianalund, *Denmark* 11 J5
Dianbai, *China* 59 G8
Diancheng, *China* 59 G8
Diano Marina, *Italy* 28 E5
Dianra, *Ivory C.* 82 D3
Diapaga, *Burkina Faso* 83 C5
Diapangou, *Burkina Faso* 83 C5
Diariguila, *Guinea* 82 C2
Dībā, *Oman* 71 E8
Dibaya-Lubue, *Dem. Rep. of the Congo* 84 E3
Dibbi, *Ethiopia* 81 G5
Dibete, *Botswana* 88 C4
Dibrugarh, *India* 67 F19
Dickinson, *U.S.A.* 112 B3
Dickson = Dikson, *Russia* 50 B9
Dickson, *U.S.A.* 109 G2
Dickson City, *U.S.A.* 111 E9
Dicle Nehri →, *Turkey* 73 D9
Dicomano, *Italy* 29 E8
Didesa, W. →, *Ethiopia* 81 E4
Didiéni, *Mali* 82 C3
Didsbury, *Canada* 104 C6
Didwana, *India* 68 F6
Die, *France* 21 D9
Diébougou, *Burkina Faso* 82 C4
Diefenbaker L., *Canada* 105 C7
Diego de Almagro, *Chile* 128 B2
Diego Garcia, *Ind. Oc.* 3 E13
Diekirch, *Lux.* 17 E6
Diéma, *Mali* 82 C3
Diembéring, *Senegal* 82 C1
Dien Ban, *Vietnam* 64 E7
Dien Bien, *Vietnam* 64 B4
Dien Khanh, *Vietnam* 65 F7
Diepholz, *Germany* 24 C4
Dieppe, *France* 18 C8
Dierks, *U.S.A.* 113 H8
Diest, *Belgium* 17 D5
Dietikon, *Switz.* 25 H4
Dieulefit, *France* 21 D9
Dieuze, *France* 19 D13
Differdange, *Lux.* 17 E5
Dig, *India* 68 F7
Digba, *Dem. Rep. of the Congo* 86 B2
Digby, *Canada* 103 D6
Digges, *Canada* 105 B10
Dighinala, *Bangla.* 67 H18
Dighton, *U.S.A.* 112 F4
Digne-les-Bains, *France* 21 D10
Digoin, *France* 19 F11
Digor, *Turkey* 73 B10
Digos, *Phil.* 61 H6
Digranes, *Iceland* 8 C6
Digul →, *Indonesia* 63 F9
Dihang →, *India* 67 F19
Dīhōk, *Iraq* 70 B3
Dijlah, Nahr →, *Asia* 70 D5

Dijon, *France* 19 E12
Dikala, *Sudan* 81 G3
Dikili, *Turkey* 39 B8
Dikkil, *Djibouti* 81 E5
Dikomu di Kai, *Botswana* 88 C3
Diksmuide, *Belgium* 17 C2
Dikson, *Russia* 50 B9
Dikwa, *Nigeria* 83 C7
Dila, *Ethiopia* 81 F4
Dili, *Indonesia* 63 F7
Dilijan, *Armenia* 49 K7
Dilizhan = Dilijan, *Armenia* 49 K7
Dilj, *Croatia* 42 E3
Dillenburg, *Germany* 24 E4
Dilley, *U.S.A.* 113 L5
Dilling, *Sudan* 81 E2
Dillingen, *Bayern, Germany* 25 G6
Dillingen, *Saarland, Germany* 25 F2
Dillingham, *U.S.A.* 100 C4
Dillon, *Canada* 105 B7
Dillon, *Mont., U.S.A.* 114 D7
Dillon, *S.C., U.S.A.* 109 H6
Dillon →, *Canada* 105 B7
Dilolo, *Dem. Rep. of the Congo* 84 G4
Dilston, *Australia* 94 G4
Dimas, *Mexico* 118 C3
Dimashq, *Syria* 75 B5
Dimashq □, *Syria* 75 B5
Dimbaza, *S. Africa* 89 E4
Dimbokro, *Ivory C.* 82 D4
Dimboola, *Australia* 95 F3
Dîmboviţa = Dâmboviţa →, *Romania* 43 F11
Dimbulah, *Australia* 94 B4
Dimitrovgrad, *Bulgaria* 41 D9
Dimitrovgrad, *Russia* 48 C9
Dimitrovgrad, *Serbia, Yug.* 40 C6
Dimitrovo = Pernik, *Bulgaria* 40 D7
Dimmitt, *U.S.A.* 113 H3
Dimo, *Sudan* 81 F2
Dimona, *Israel* 75 D4
Dimovo, *Bulgaria* 40 C6
Dinagat, *Phil.* 61 F6
Dinajpur, *Bangla.* 67 G16
Dinan, *France* 18 D4
Dīnān Āb, *Iran* 71 C8
Dinant, *Belgium* 17 D4
Dinapur, *India* 69 G11
Dinar, *Turkey* 39 C12
Dīnār, Kūh-e, *Iran* 71 D6
Dinara Planina, *Croatia* 29 D13
Dinard, *France* 18 D4
Dinaric Alps = Dinara Planina, *Croatia* 29 D13
Dinder, Nahr ed →, *Sudan* 81 E3
Dindigul, *India* 66 P11
Ding Xian, *China* 56 E8
Dingalan, *Phil.* 61 D4
Dingbian, *China* 56 F4
Dingelstädt, *Germany* 24 D6
Dinghai, *China* 59 B14
Dingle, *Ireland* 15 D1
Dingle, *Sweden* 11 F5
Dingle B., *Ireland* 15 D1
Dingmans Ferry, *U.S.A.* 111 E10
Dingnan, *China* 59 E10
Dingo, *Australia* 94 C4
Dingolfing, *Germany* 25 G8
Dingtao, *China* 56 G8
Dinguiraye, *Guinea* 82 C2
Dingwall, *U.K.* 14 D4
Dingxi, *China* 56 G3
Dingxiang, *China* 56 E7
Dingyuan, *China* 59 A11
Dinh, Mui, *Vietnam* 65 G7
Dinh Lap, *Vietnam* 64 B6
Dinokwe, *Botswana* 88 C4
Dinosaur National Monument, *U.S.A.* 114 F9
Dinuba, *U.S.A.* 116 J7
Diö, *Sweden* 11 H8
Diósgyör, *Hungary* 42 B5
Diosig, *Romania* 42 C7
Diourbel, *Senegal* 82 C1
Diplo, *Pakistan* 68 G3
Dipolog, *Phil.* 61 G5
Dir, *Pakistan* 66 B7
Diré, *Mali* 82 B4
Dire Dawa, *Ethiopia* 81 F5
Diriamba, *Nic.* 120 D2
Dirk Hartog I., *Australia* 93 E1
Dirranbandi, *Australia* 95 D4
Disa, *India* 68 G5
Disa, *Sudan* 81 E3
Disappointment, C., *U.S.A.* 114 C2
Disappointment, L., *Australia* 92 D3
Disaster B., *Australia* 95 F4
Discovery B., *Australia* 95 F3
Disentis, *Switz.* 25 J4
Dishna, *Egypt* 80 B3
Disina, *Nigeria* 83 C6
Disko, *Greenland* 4 C5
Disko Bugt, *Greenland* 4 C5
Disna = Dzisna →, *Belarus* 46 E5
Diss, *U.K.* 13 E9
Disteghil Sar, *Pakistan* 69 A6
Distrito Federal □, *Brazil* 125 G9
Disūq, *Egypt* 80 H7
Diu, *India* 68 J4
Dīvāndarreh, *Iran* 70 C5
Dives →, *France* 18 C6
Dives-sur-Mer, *France* 18 C6
Divichi = Däväçi, *Azerbaijan* 49 K9
Divide, *U.S.A.* 114 D7
Dividing Ra., *Australia* 93 E2
Divinópolis, *Brazil* 125 H10
Divjake, *Albania* 40 F3
Divnoye, *Russia* 49 H6
Divo, *Ivory C.* 82 D3
Divriği, *Turkey* 73 C8
Dīwāl Kol, *Afghan.* 68 B2
Dixie Mt., *U.S.A.* 116 F6
Dixon, *Calif., U.S.A.* 116 G5
Dixon, *Ill., U.S.A.* 112 E10
Dixon, *Mont., U.S.A.* 114 C6
Dixon, *N. Mex., U.S.A.* 115 H11
Dixon Entrance, *U.S.A.* 104 C2
Dixonville, *Canada* 104 B5
Diyadin, *Turkey* 73 C10
Diyālā →, *Iraq* 73 F11
Diyarbakır, *Turkey* 73 D9
Djakarta = Jakarta, *Indonesia* 63 G12
Djamba, *Angola* 88 B1
Djambala, *Congo* 84 E2
Djanet, *Algeria* 78 D7
Djawa = Jawa, *Indonesia* 63 G14
Djelfa, *Algeria* 78 B6
Djema, *C.A.R.* 86 A2
Djenné, *Mali* 82 C4
Djerba, I. de, *Tunisia* 79 B8
Djerid, Chott, *Tunisia* 78 B7
Djibo, *Burkina Faso* 83 C4
Djibouti, *Djibouti* 81 E5
Djibouti ■, *Africa* 81 E5
Djolu, *Dem. Rep. of the Congo* 84 D4
Djougou, *Benin* 83 D5
Djoum, *Cameroon* 84 D2
Djourab, Erg du, *Chad* 79 E9
Djugu, *Dem. Rep. of the Congo* 86 B3
Djúpivogur, *Iceland* 8 D6
Djurås, *Sweden* 10 D9
Djursland, *Denmark* 11 H4
Dmitriya Lapteva, Proliv, *Russia* 51 B15
Dmitriyev Lgovskiy, *Russia* 47 F8
Dmitrov, *Russia* 46 D9
Dmitrovsk-Orlovskiy, *Russia* 47 F8
Dnepr → = Dnipro →, *Ukraine* 47 J7
Dneprodzerzhinsk = Dniprodzerzhynsk, *Ukraine* 47 H8
Dneprodzerzhinskoye Vdkhr. = Dniprodzerzhynske Vdskh., *Ukraine* 47 H8
Dnepropetrovsk = Dnipropetrovsk, *Ukraine* 47 H8
Dneprorudnoye = Dniprorudne, *Ukraine* 47 J8
Dnestr → = Dnister →, *Europe* 47 J6
Dnestrovski = Belgorod, *Russia* 47 G9
Dnieper = Dnipro →, *Ukraine* 47 J7
Dniester = Dnister →, *Europe* 47 J6
Dnipro →, *Ukraine* 47 J7
Dniprodzerzhynsk, *Ukraine* 47 H8
Dniprodzerzhynske Vdskh., *Ukraine* 47 H8
Dnipropetrovsk, *Ukraine* 47 H8
Dniprorudne, *Ukraine* 47 J8
Dnister →, *Europe* 47 J6
Dnistrovskyy Lyman, *Ukraine* 47 J6
Dno, *Russia* 46 D5
Dnyapro = Dnipro →, *Ukraine* 47 J7
Doan Hung, *Vietnam* 64 B5
Doba, *Chad* 79 G9
Dobbiaco, *Italy* 29 B9
Dobbyn, *Australia* 94 B3
Dobczyce, *Poland* 45 J7
Dobele, *Latvia* 9 H20
Dobele □, *Latvia* 44 B10
Döbeln, *Germany* 24 D9
Doberai, Jazirah, *Indonesia* 63 E8
Dobiegniew, *Poland* 45 F2
Doblas, *Argentina* 126 D3
Dobo, *Indonesia* 63 F8
Doboj, *Bos.-H.* 42 F3
Dobra, *Konin, Poland* 45 G5
Dobra, *Szczecin, Poland* 44 E2
Dobra, *Dîmbovita, Romania* 43 F10
Dobra, *Hunedoara, Romania* 42 E7
Dobre Miasto, *Poland* 44 E7
Dobreşti, *Romania* 42 D7
Dobreta-Turnu Severin, *Romania* 42 F7
Dobrich, *Bulgaria* 41 C11
Dobrinishta, *Bulgaria* 40 E7
Dobříš, *Czech Rep.* 26 B7
Dobrodzień, *Poland* 45 H5
Dobropole, *Ukraine* 47 H9
Dobruja, *Europe* 43 F13
Dobrush, *Belarus* 47 F6
Dobrzany, *Poland* 44 E2
Dobrzyń nad Wisłą, *Poland* 45 F6
Dobtong, *Sudan* 81 F3
Doc, Mui, *Vietnam* 64 D6
Dockska, *Sweden* 10 A12
Doda, *India* 69 C6
Dodecanese = Dhodhekánisos, *Greece* 39 E8
Dodge Center, *U.S.A.* 112 C8
Dodge City, *U.S.A.* 113 G5
Dodge L., *Canada* 105 B7
Dodgeville, *U.S.A.* 112 D9
Dodo, *Sudan* 81 F2
Dodola, *Ethiopia* 81 F4
Dodoma, *Tanzania* 86 D4
Dodoma □, *Tanzania* 86 D4
Dodona, *Greece* 38 B2
Dodsland, *Canada* 105 C7
Dodson, *U.S.A.* 114 B9
Dodurga, *Turkey* 39 B11
Doesburg, *Neths.* 17 B6
Doetinchem, *Neths.* 17 C6
Dog Creek, *Canada* 104 C4
Dog L., *Man., Canada* 105 C9
Dog L., *Ont., Canada* 102 C2
Doğanşehir, *Turkey* 72 C7
Dogi, *Afghan.* 66 C3
Dogliani, *Italy* 28 D4
Dogondoutchi, *Niger* 83 C5
Dogran, *Pakistan* 68 D5
Doğubayazıt, *Turkey* 73 C11
Doguéraoua, *Niger* 83 C6
Doha = Ad Dawhah, *Qatar* 71 E6
Dohazari, *Bangla.* 67 H18
Doi, *Indonesia* 63 D7
Doi Luang, *Thailand* 64 C3
Doi Saket, *Thailand* 64 C2
Doig →, *Canada* 104 B4
Dois Irmãos, Sa., *Brazil* 125 E10
Dojransko Jezero, *Macedonia* 40 E6
Dokkum, *Neths.* 17 A5
Dokri, *Pakistan* 68 F3
Dokuchayevsk, *Ukraine* 47 J9
Dol-de-Bretagne, *France* 18 D5
Dolak, Pulau, *Indonesia* 63 F9
Doland, *U.S.A.* 112 C5
Dolbeau, *Canada* 103 C5
Dole, *France* 19 E12
Doleib, Wadi →, *Sudan* 81 E3
Dolenji Logatec, *Slovenia* 29 C11
Dolgellau, *U.K.* 12 E4
Dolgelley = Dolgellau, *U.K.* 12 E4
Dolhasca, *Romania* 43 C11
Dolianova, *Italy* 30 C2
Dolinskaya = Dolynska, *Ukraine* 47 H7
Dolj □, *Romania* 43 F8
Dollard, *Neths.* 17 A7
Dolna Banya, *Bulgaria* 40 D7
Dolni Chiflik, *Bulgaria* 41 D11
Dolni Dŭbnik, *Bulgaria* 41 C8
Dolný Kubín, *Slovak Rep.* 27 B12
Dolo, *Ethiopia* 81 G5
Dolo, *Italy* 29 C9
Dolomites = Dolomiti, *Italy* 29 B8
Dolomiti, *Italy* 29 B8
Dolores, *Argentina* 126 D4
Dolores, *Uruguay* 126 C4
Dolores, *U.S.A.* 115 H9
Dolores →, *U.S.A.* 115 G9
Dolovo, *Serbia, Yug.* 42 F5
Dolphin, C., *Falk. Is.* 128 G5
Dolphin and Union Str., *Canada* 100 B8
Dolsk, *Poland* 45 G4
Dolynska, *Ukraine* 47 H7
Dolzhanskaya, *Russia* 47 J9
Dom Pedrito, *Brazil* 127 C5
Doma, *Nigeria* 83 D6
Domaniç, *Turkey* 39 B11
Domasi, *Malawi* 87 F4
Domažlice, *Czech Rep.* 26 B5
Dombarovskiy, *Russia* 50 D6
Dombås, *Norway* 9 E13
Dombasle-sur-Meurthe, *France* 19 D13
Dombes, *France* 21 C9
Dombóvár, *Hungary* 42 D3
Dombrád, *Hungary* 42 B6
Domel I. = Letsôk-aw Kyun, *Burma* 65 G2
Domérat, *France* 19 F9
Domeyko, *Chile* 126 B1
Domeyko, Cordillera, *Chile* 126 A2
Domfront, *France* 18 D6
Dominador, *Chile* 126 A2
Dominica ■, *W. Indies* 121 C7
Dominica Passage, *W. Indies* 121 C7
Dominican Rep. ■, *W. Indies* 121 C5
Dömitz, *Germany* 24 B7
Domme, *France* 20 D5
Domneşti, *Romania* 43 E9
Domodóssola, *Italy* 28 B5
Dompaire, *France* 19 D13
Dompierre-sur-Besbre, *France* 19 F10
Dompim, *Ghana* 82 D4
Domrémy-la-Pucelle, *France* 19 D12
Domville, Mt., *Australia* 95 D5
Domvraína, *Greece* 38 C4
Domžale, *Slovenia* 29 B11
Don →, *Russia* 47 J10
Don →, *Aberds., U.K.* 14 D6
Don →, *S. Yorks., U.K.* 12 D7
Don, C., *Australia* 92 B5
Don Benito, *Spain* 35 G5
Don Martín, Presa de, *Mexico* 118 B4
Dona Ana = Nhamaabué, *Mozam.* 87 F4
Doña Mencía, *Spain* 35 H6
Donaghadee, *U.K.* 15 B6
Donald, *Australia* 95 F3
Donalda, *Canada* 104 C6
Donaldsonville, *U.S.A.* 113 K9
Donalsonville, *U.S.A.* 109 K3
Donau = Dunărea →, *Europe* 43 E14
Donau →, *Austria* 27 C10
Donaueschingen, *Germany* 25 H4
Donauwörth, *Germany* 25 G6
Doncaster, *U.K.* 12 D6
Dondo, *Mozam.* 87 F3
Dondo, Teluk, *Indonesia* 63 D6
Dondra Head, *Sri Lanka* 66 S12
Donduşeni, *Moldova* 43 B12
Donegal, *Ireland* 15 B3
Donegal □, *Ireland* 15 B4
Donegal B., *Ireland* 15 B3
Donets →, *Russia* 49 G5
Donetsk, *Ukraine* 47 J9
Dong Ba Thin, *Vietnam* 65 F7
Dong Dang, *Vietnam* 64 B6
Dong Giam, *Vietnam* 64 C5
Dong Ha, *Vietnam* 64 D6
Dong Hene, *Laos* 64 D5
Dong Hoi, *Vietnam* 64 D6
Dong Jiang →, *China* 59 F10
Dong Khe, *Vietnam* 64 A6
Dong Ujimqin Qi, *China* 56 B9
Dong Van, *Vietnam* 64 A5
Dong Xoai, *Vietnam* 65 G6
Donga, *Nigeria* 83 D7
Dong'an, *China* 59 D8
Dongara, *Australia* 93 E1
Dongbei, *China* 57 D13
Dongchuan, *China* 58 D4
Donges, *France* 18 E4
Dongfang, *China* 64 C7
Dongfeng, *China* 57 C13
Donggala, *Indonesia* 63 E5
Donggan, *China* 58 F5
Donggou, *China* 57 E13
Dongguan, *China* 59 F9
Dongguang, *China* 56 F9
Donghai Dao, *China* 59 G8
Dongjingcheng, *China* 57 B15
Donglan, *China* 58 E6
Dongliu, *China* 59 B11
Dongmen, *China* 58 F6
Dongning, *China* 57 B16
Dongnyi, *China* 58 C3
Dongola, *Sudan* 80 D3
Dongping, *China* 56 G9
Dongshan, *China* 59 F11
Dongsheng, *China* 56 E6
Dongtai, *China* 57 H11
Dongting Hu, *China* 59 C9
Dongxiang, *China* 59 C11
Dongxing, *China* 58 G7
Dongyang, *China* 59 C13
Dongzhi, *China* 59 B11
Donington, C., *Australia* 95 E2
Doniphan, *U.S.A.* 113 G9
Donja Stubica, *Croatia* 29 C12
Donji Dušnik, *Serbia, Yug.* 40 C6
Donji Miholjac, *Croatia* 42 E3
Donji Milanovac, *Serbia, Yug.* 40 B6
Donji Vakuf, *Bos.-H.* 42 F2
Dønna, *Norway* 8 C15
Donna, *U.S.A.* 113 M5
Donnaconna, *Canada* 103 C5
Donnelly's Crossing, *N.Z.* 91 F4
Donnybrook, *Australia* 93 F2
Donnybrook, *S. Africa* 89 D4
Donora, *U.S.A.* 110 F5
Donor's Hill, *Australia* 94 B3
Donostia = Donostia-San Sebastián, *Spain* 32 B3
Donostia-San Sebastián, *Spain* 32 B3
Donskoy, *Russia* 46 F10
Donsol, *Phil.* 61 E5
Donzère, *France* 21 D8
Donzy, *France* 19 E10
Doon →, *U.K.* 14 F4
Dora, L., *Australia* 92 D3
Dora Báltea →, *Italy* 28 C5
Dora Ripária →, *Italy* 28 C4
Doran L., *Canada* 105 A7
Dorchester, *U.K.* 13 G5
Dorchester, C., *Canada* 101 B12
Dordogne □, *France* 20 C4
Dordogne →, *France* 20 C3
Dordrecht, *Neths.* 17 C4
Dordrecht, *S. Africa* 88 E4
Dore →, *France* 20 C7
Dore, Mts., *France* 20 C6
Doré L., *Canada* 105 C7
Doré Lake, *Canada* 105 C7
Dorfen, *Germany* 25 G8
Dorgali, *Italy* 30 B2
Dori, *Burkina Faso* 83 C4
Doring →, *S. Africa* 88 E2
Doringbos, *S. Africa* 88 E2
Dorion, *Canada* 102 C5
Dormaa-Ahenkro, *Ghana* 82 D4
Dormans, *France* 19 C10
Dormo, Ras, *Eritrea* 81 E5
Dornbirn, *Austria* 26 D2
Dornes, *France* 19 F10
Dorneşti, *Romania* 43 C11
Dornie, *U.K.* 14 D3
Dornoch, *U.K.* 14 D4
Dornoch Firth, *U.K.* 14 D4
Dornogovĭ □, *Mongolia* 56 C6
Doro, *Mali* 83 B4
Dorog, *Hungary* 42 C3
Dorogobuzh, *Russia* 46 E7
Dorohoi, *Romania* 43 C11
Döröö Nuur, *Mongolia* 60 B4
Dorr, *Iran* 71 C6
Dorre I., *Australia* 93 E1
Dorrigo, *Australia* 95 E5
Dorris, *U.S.A.* 114 F3
Dorset, *Canada* 110 A6
Dorset, *U.S.A.* 110 E4
Dorset □, *U.K.* 13 G5
Dorsten, *Germany* 24 D2
Dortmund, *Germany* 24 D3
Dortmund-Ems-Kanal →, *Germany* 24 D3
Dörtyol, *Turkey* 72 D7
Dorum, *Germany* 24 B4
Doruma, *Dem. Rep. of the Congo* 86 B2
Dorūneh, *Iran* 71 C8
Dos Bahías, C., *Argentina* 128 E3
Dos Hermanas, *Spain* 35 H5
Dos Palos, *U.S.A.* 116 J6
Döşemealtı, *Turkey* 39 D12
Dosso, *Niger* 83 C5
Dothan, *U.S.A.* 109 K3
Doty, *U.S.A.* 116 D3
Douai, *France* 19 B10
Douala, *Cameroon* 83 E6
Douarnenez, *France* 18 D2
Double Island Pt., *Australia* 95 D5
Doubrava →, *Czech Rep.* 26 A8
Doubs □, *France* 19 E13
Doubs →, *France* 19 F12
Doubtful Sd., *N.Z.* 91 L1
Doubtless B., *N.Z.* 91 F4
Doudeville, *France* 18 C7
Doué-la-Fontaine, *France* 18 E6
Douentza, *Mali* 82 C4
Douglas, *S. Africa* 88 D3
Douglas, *U.K.* 12 C3
Douglas, *Alaska, U.S.A.* 104 B2
Douglas, *Ariz., U.S.A.* 115 L9
Douglas, *Ga., U.S.A.* 109 K4
Douglas, *Wyo., U.S.A.* 112 D2
Douglastown, *Canada* 103 C7
Douglasville, *U.S.A.* 109 J3
Doukáton, Ákra, *Greece* 38 C2
Doulevant-le-Château, *France* 19 D11
Doullens, *France* 19 B9
Douna, *Mali* 82 C3
Dounreay, *U.K.* 14 C5
Dourada, Serra, *Brazil* 125 F9
Dourados, *Brazil* 127 A5
Dourados →, *Brazil* 127 A5
Dourdan, *France* 19 D9
Douro →, *Europe* 34 D2
Douvaine, *France* 19 F13
Douvres-la-Délivrande, *France* 18 C6
Douze →, *France* 20 E3
Dove →, *U.K.* 12 E6
Dove Creek, *U.S.A.* 115 H9
Dover, *Australia* 94 G4
Dover, *U.K.* 13 F9
Dover, *Del., U.S.A.* 108 F8
Dover, *N.H., U.S.A.* 111 C14
Dover, *N.J., U.S.A.* 111 F10
Dover, *Ohio, U.S.A.* 110 F3
Dover, Pt., *Australia* 93 F4
Dover, Str. of, *Europe* 13 G9
Dover-Foxcroft, *U.S.A.* 103 C6
Dover Plains, *U.S.A.* 111 E11
Dovey = Dyfi →, *U.K.* 13 E3
Dovrefjell, *Norway* 9 E13
Dow Rūd, *Iran* 71 C6
Dowa, *Malawi* 87 E3
Dowagiac, *U.S.A.* 108 E2
Dowgha'i, *Iran* 71 B8
Dowlatābād, *Iran* 71 D8
Down □, *U.K.* 15 B5
Downey, *Calif., U.S.A.* 117 M8
Downey, *Idaho, U.S.A.* 114 E7
Downham Market, *U.K.* 13 E8
Downieville, *U.S.A.* 116 F6
Downpatrick, *U.K.* 15 B6
Downpatrick Hd., *Ireland* 15 B2
Dowsārī, *Iran* 71 D8
Doyle, *U.S.A.* 116 E6
Doylestown, *U.S.A.* 111 F9
Drac →, *France* 21 C9
Dračevo, *Macedonia* 40 E5
Drachten, *Neths.* 17 A6
Drăgăneşti, *Moldova* 43 C13
Drăgăneşti-Olt, *Romania* 43 F9
Drăgăneşti-Vlaşca, *Romania* 43 F10
Dragaš, *Serbia, Yug.* 40 D4
Drăgăşani, *Romania* 43 F9
Dragichyn, *Belarus* 47 F3
Dragocvet, *Serbia, Yug.* 40 C5
Dragovishtitsa, *Bulgaria* 40 D6
Draguignan, *France* 21 E10
Drain, *U.S.A.* 114 E2
Drake, *Australia* 95 E5
Drake, *U.S.A.* 112 B4
Drake Passage, *S. Ocean* 5 B17

Drakensberg, S. Africa 89 E4
Dráma, Greece 41 E8
Dráma □, Greece 41 E8
Drammen, Norway 9 G14
Drangajökull, Iceland 8 C2
Dranov, Ostrov, Romania 43 F14
Dras, India 69 B6
Drau = Drava →, Croatia 42 E3
Drava →, Croatia 42 E3
Dravograd, Slovenia 29 B12
Drawa →, Poland 45 F2
Drawno, Poland 45 E2
Drawsko Pomorskie, Poland 44 E2
Drayton Valley, Canada 104 C6
Dreieich, Germany 25 E4
Dren, Serbia, Yug. 40 C4
Drenthe □, Neths. 17 B6
Drepanum, C., Cyprus 36 E11
Dresden, Canada 110 D2
Dresden, Germany 24 D9
Dreux, France 18 D8
Drezdenko, Poland 45 F2
Driffield, U.K. 12 C7
Driftwood, U.S.A. 110 E6
Driggs, U.S.A. 114 E8
Drin i Zi →, Albania 40 E4
Drina →, Bos.-H. 40 B3
Drincea →, Romania 42 F7
Drini →, Albania 40 D3
Drinjača →, Bos.-H. 42 F4
Drissa = Vyerkhnyadzvinsk, Belarus 46 E4
Drniš, Croatia 29 E13
Drøbak, Norway 9 G14
Drobin, Poland 45 F6
Drochia, Moldova 43 B12
Drogheda, Ireland 15 C5
Drogichin = Dragichyn, Belarus 47 F3
Drogobych = Drohobych, Ukraine 47 H2
Drohiczyn, Poland 45 F9
Drohobych, Ukraine 47 H2
Droichead Atha = Drogheda, Ireland 15 C5
Droichead Nua, Ireland 15 C5
Droitwich, U.K. 13 E5
Drôme □, France 21 D9
Drôme →, France 21 D8
Dromedary, C., Australia 95 F5
Dromore, U.K. 15 B4
Dromore West, Ireland 15 B3
Dronero, Italy 28 D4
Dronfield, Australia 94 C3
Dronfield, U.K. 12 D6
Dronne →, France 20 C3
Dronninglund, Denmark 11 G4
Dronten, Neths. 17 B5
Dropt →, France 20 D3
Drosendorf, Austria 26 C8
Droué, France 18 D8
Drumbo, Canada 110 C4
Drumheller, Canada 104 C6
Drummond, U.S.A. 114 C7
Drummond I., U.S.A. 102 C3
Drummond Pt., Australia 95 E2
Drummond Ra., Australia 94 C4
Drummondville, Canada 102 C5
Drumright, U.S.A. 113 H6
Druskininkai, Lithuania 9 J20
Drut →, Belarus 47 F6
Druya, Belarus 46 E4
Druzhba, Bulgaria 41 C12
Druzhina, Russia 51 C15
Drvar, Bos.-H. 29 D13
Drvenik, Croatia 29 E13
Drwęca →, Poland 45 E5
Dry Tortugas, U.S.A. 120 B3
Dryanovo, Bulgaria 41 D9
Dryden, Canada 105 D10
Dryden, U.S.A. 113 K3
Drygalski I., Antarctica 5 C7
Drysdale →, Australia 92 B4
Drysdale I., Australia 94 A2
Drzewica, Poland 45 G7
Drzewiczka →, Poland 45 G7
Dschang, Cameroon 83 D7
Du Bois, U.S.A. 110 E6
Du Quoin, U.S.A. 112 G10
Duanesburg, U.S.A. 111 D10
Duaringa, Australia 94 C4
Ḍubā, Si. Arabia 70 E2
Dubai = Dubayy, U.A.E. 71 E7
Dubăsari, Moldova 43 C14
Dubăsari Vdkhr., Moldova 43 C13
Dubawnt →, Canada 105 A8
Dubawnt, L., Canada 105 A8
Dubayy, U.A.E. 71 E7
Dubbo, Australia 95 E4
Dubele, Dem. Rep. of the Congo 86 B2
Dübendorf, Switz. 25 H4
Dubica, Croatia 29 C13
Dublin, Ireland 15 C5
Dublin, Ga., U.S.A. 109 J4
Dublin, Tex., U.S.A. 113 J5
Dublin □, Ireland 15 C5
Dubna, Russia 46 D9
Dubnica nad Váhom, Slovak Rep. 27 C11
Dubno, Ukraine 47 G3
Dubois, U.S.A. 114 D7
Dubossary = Dubăsari, Moldova 43 C14
Dubossary Vdkhr. = Dubăsari Vdkhr., Moldova 43 C13
Dubovka, Russia 49 F7
Dubovskoye, Russia 49 G6
Dubrajpur, India 69 H12
Dubréka, Guinea 82 D2
Dubrovitsa = Dubrovytsya, Ukraine 47 G4
Dubrovnik, Croatia 40 D2
Dubrovytsya, Ukraine 47 G4
Dubuque, U.S.A. 112 D9
Dubysa →, Lithuania 44 C10
Duchang, China 59 C11
Duchesne, U.S.A. 114 F8
Duchess, Australia 94 C2
Ducie I., Pac. Oc. 97 K15
Duck Cr. →, Australia 92 D2
Duck Lake, Canada 105 C7
Duck Mountain Prov. Park, Canada 105 C8
Duckwall, Mt., U.S.A. 116 H6
Duderstadt, Germany 24 D6
Dudhi, India 67 G13
Dudinka, Russia 51 C9
Dudley, U.K. 13 E5
Dueñas, Spain 34 D6
Duero = Douro →, Europe 34 D2
Dufftown, U.K. 14 D5
Dufourspitz, Switz. 25 K3
Dugi Otok, Croatia 29 D11
Dugo Selo, Croatia 29 C13
Duifken Pt., Australia 94 A3
Duisburg, Germany 24 D2
Duiwelskloof, S. Africa 89 C5
Dukati, Albania 40 F3
Dūkdamīn, Iran 71 C8
Duke I., U.S.A. 104 C2
Dukelský Průsmyk, Slovak Rep. 27 B14
Dukhān, Qatar 71 E6
Dukhovshchina, Russia 46 E7
Duki, Pakistan 66 D6
Dukla, Poland 45 J8
Duku, Bauchi, Nigeria 83 C7
Duku, Sokoto, Nigeria 83 C5
Dulag, Phil. 61 F6
Dulce →, Argentina 126 C3
Dulce, G., Costa Rica 120 E3
Dulf, Iraq 70 C5
Dŭlgopol, Bulgaria 41 C11
Dulit, Banjaran, Malaysia 62 D4
Duliu, China 56 E9
Dullewala, Pakistan 68 D4
Dülmen, Germany 24 D3
Dulovo, Bulgaria 41 C11
Dulq Maghār, Syria 70 B3
Dululu, Australia 94 C5
Duluth, U.S.A. 112 B8
Dum Dum, India 69 H13
Dum Duma, India 67 F19
Dūmā, Syria 75 B5
Dumaguete, Phil. 61 G5
Dumai, Indonesia 62 D2
Dumaran, Phil. 61 F3
Dumas, Ark., U.S.A. 113 J9
Dumas, Tex., U.S.A. 113 H4
Dumbarton, U.K. 14 F4
Ďumbier, Slovak Rep. 27 C12
Dumbleyung, Australia 93 F2
Dumbrăveni, Romania 43 D9
Dumfries, U.K. 14 F5
Dumfries & Galloway □, U.K. 14 F5
Dumitreşti, Romania 43 E11
Dumka, India 69 G12
Dumlupınar, Turkey 39 C12
Dümmer, Germany 24 C4
Dumoine →, Canada 102 C4
Dumoine L., Canada 102 C4
Dumraon, India 69 G11
Dumyât, Egypt 80 H7
Dumyât, Masabb, Egypt 80 H7
Dún Dealgan = Dundalk, Ireland 15 B5
Dun Laoghaire, Ireland 15 C5
Dun-le-Palestel, France 19 F8
Dun-sur-Auron, France 19 F9
Dun-sur-Meuse, France 19 C12
Duna = Dunărea →, Europe 43 E14
Duna →, Hungary 42 E3
Duna-völgyi-főcsatorna, Hungary 42 D4
Dunaföldvár, Hungary 42 D3
Dunaj = Dunărea →, Europe 43 E14
Dunaj →, Slovak Rep. 27 D11
Dunajec →, Poland 45 H7
Dunajská Streda, Slovak Rep. 27 C10
Dunakeszi, Hungary 42 C4
Dunapataj, Hungary 42 D4
Dunărea →, Europe 43 E14
Dunaszekcső, Hungary 42 D3
Dunaújváros, Hungary 42 D3
Dunav = Dunărea →, Europe 43 E14
Dunavaţu de Jos, Romania 43 F14
Dunavtsi, Bulgaria 40 C6
Dunay, Russia 54 C6
Dunback, N.Z. 91 L3
Dunbar, Australia 94 B3
Dunbar, U.K. 14 E6
Dunblane, U.K. 14 E5
Duncan, Canada 104 D4
Duncan, Ariz., U.S.A. 115 K9
Duncan, Okla., U.S.A. 113 H6
Duncan, L., Canada 102 B4
Duncan L., Canada 104 A6
Duncan Town, Bahamas 120 B4
Duncannon, U.S.A. 110 F7
Duncansby Head, U.K. 14 C5
Dundaga, Latvia 44 A9
Dundalk, Canada 110 B4
Dundalk, Ireland 15 B5
Dundalk Bay, Ireland 15 C5
Dundas, Canada 102 D4
Dundas, L., Australia 93 F3
Dundas I., Canada 104 C2
Dundas Str., Australia 92 B5
Dundee, S. Africa 89 D5
Dundee, U.K. 14 E6
Dundee City □, U.K. 14 E6
Dundgovĭ □, Mongolia 56 B4
Dundoo, Australia 95 D3
Dundrum, U.K. 15 B6
Dundrum B., U.K. 15 B6
Dundwara, India 69 F8
Dunedin, N.Z. 91 L3
Dunedin, U.S.A. 109 L4
Dunedin →, Canada 104 B4
Dunfermline, U.K. 14 E5
Dungannon, Canada 110 C3
Dungannon, U.K. 15 B5
Dungarpur, India 68 H5
Dungarvan, Ireland 15 D4
Dungarvan Harbour, Ireland 15 D4
Dungeness, U.K. 13 G8
Dungo, L. do, Angola 88 B2
Dungog, Australia 95 E5
Dungu, Dem. Rep. of the Congo 86 B2
Dungun, Malaysia 65 K4
Dungunâb, Sudan 80 C4
Dungunâb, Khalij, Sudan 80 C4
Dunhua, China 57 C15
Dunhuang, China 60 B4
Dunk I., Australia 94 B4
Dunkeld, U.K. 14 E5
Dunkerque, France 19 A9
Dunkery Beacon, U.K. 13 F4
Dunkirk = Dunkerque, France 19 A9
Dunkirk, U.S.A. 110 D5
Dunkuj, Sudan 81 E3
Dunkwa, Central, Ghana 82 D4
Dunkwa, Central, Ghana 83 D4
Dunlap, U.S.A. 112 E7
Dúnleary = Dun Laoghaire, Ireland 15 C5
Dunleer, Ireland 15 C5
Dunmanus B., Ireland 15 E2
Dunmanway, Ireland 15 E2
Dunmara, Australia 94 B1
Dunmore, U.S.A. 111 E9
Dunmore Hd., Ireland 15 D1
Dunmore Town, Bahamas 120 A4
Dunn, U.S.A. 109 H6
Dunnellon, U.S.A. 109 L4
Dunnet Hd., U.K. 14 C5
Dunning, U.S.A. 112 E4
Dunnville, Canada 110 D5
Dunolly, Australia 95 F3
Dunoon, U.K. 14 F4
Dunqul, Egypt 80 C3
Duns, U.K. 14 F6
Dunseith, U.S.A. 112 A4
Dunsmuir, U.S.A. 114 F2
Dunstable, U.K. 13 F7
Dunstan Mts., N.Z. 91 L2
Dunster, Canada 104 C5
Dunvegan L., Canada 105 A7
Duolun, China 56 C9
Duong Dong, Vietnam 65 G4
Dupree, U.S.A. 112 C4
Dupuyer, U.S.A. 114 B7
Duque de Caxias, Brazil 127 A7
Durack →, Australia 92 C4
Durack Ra., Australia 92 C4
Durağan, Turkey 72 B6
Durak, Turkey 39 B10
Durance →, France 21 E8
Durand, U.S.A. 108 D4
Durango, Mexico 118 C4
Durango, U.S.A. 115 H10
Durango □, Mexico 118 C4
Duranillin, Australia 93 F2
Durankulak, Bulgaria 41 C12
Durant, U.S.A. 113 J6
Duratón →, Spain 34 D6
Durazno, Uruguay 126 C4
Durazzo = Durrësi, Albania 40 E3
Durban, France 20 F6
Durban, S. Africa 89 D5
Durbuy, Belgium 17 D5
Dúrcal, Spain 35 J7
Đurđevac, Croatia 42 D2
Düren, Germany 24 E2
Durg, India 67 J12
Durgapur, India 69 H12
Durham, Canada 102 D3
Durham, U.K. 12 C6
Durham, Calif., U.S.A. 116 F5
Durham, N.C., U.S.A. 109 H6
Durham □, U.K. 12 C6
Durham Downs, Australia 95 D4
Durleşti, Moldova 43 C13
Durmitor, Montenegro, Yug. 40 C2
Durness, U.K. 14 C4
Durrësi, Albania 40 E3
Durrie, Australia 94 D3
Durrow, Ireland 15 D4
Dursey I., Ireland 15 E1
Dursunbey, Turkey 39 B10
Durtal, France 18 E6
Duru, Dem. Rep. of the Congo 86 B2
Duru Gölü, Turkey 41 E12
Durusu, Turkey 41 E12
Durūz, Jabal ad, Jordan 75 C5
D'Urville, Tanjung, Indonesia 63 E9
D'Urville I., N.Z. 91 J4
Duryea, U.S.A. 111 E9
Dûsh, Egypt 80 C3
Dushak, Turkmenistan 50 F7
Dushan, China 58 E6
Dushanbe, Tajikistan 50 F7
Dusheti, Georgia 49 J7
Dusky Sd., N.Z. 91 L1
Dussejour, C., Australia 92 B4
Düsseldorf, Germany 24 D2
Duszniki-Zdrój, Poland 45 H3
Dutch Harbor, U.S.A. 100 C3
Dutlwe, Botswana 88 C3
Dutsan Wai, Nigeria 83 C6
Dutton, Canada 110 D3
Dutton →, Australia 94 C3
Duved, Sweden 10 A6
Düvertepe, Turkey 39 B10
Duyun, China 58 D6
Düzağac, Turkey 39 C12
Düzce, Turkey 72 B4
Duzdab = Zāhedān, Iran 71 D9
Dve Mogili, Bulgaria 41 C9
Dvina, Severnaya →, Russia 50 C5
Dvinsk = Daugavpils, Latvia 9 J22
Dvor, Croatia 29 C13
Dvůr Králové nad Labem, Czech Rep. 26 A8
Dwarka, India 68 H3
Dwellingup, Australia 93 F2
Dwight, Canada 110 A5
Dwight, U.S.A. 108 E1
Dyatkovo, Russia 46 F8
Dyatlovo = Dzyatlava, Belarus 46 F3
Dyce, U.K. 14 D6
Dyer, C., Canada 101 B13
Dyer Plateau, Antarctica 5 D17
Dyersburg, U.S.A. 113 G10
Dyfi →, U.K. 13 E3
Dyje →, Czech Rep. 27 C9
Dymer, Ukraine 47 G6
Dynevor Downs, Australia 95 D3
Dynów, Poland 45 J9
Dysart, Canada 105 C8
Dzamin Üüd, Mongolia 56 C6
Dzerzhinsk, Russia 48 B6
Dzhalinda, Russia 51 D13
Dzhambul = Zhambyl, Kazakstan 50 E8
Dzhankoy, Ukraine 47 K8
Dzhanybek, Kazakstan 48 F8
Dzharylhach, Ostriv, Ukraine 47 J7
Dzhezkazgan = Zhezqazghan, Kazakstan 50 E7
Dzhizak = Jizzakh, Uzbekistan 50 E7
Dzhugdzur, Khrebet, Russia 51 D14
Dzhvari = Jvari, Georgia 49 J6
Działdowo, Poland 45 E7
Działoszyce, Poland 45 H7
Działoszyn, Poland 45 G5
Dzierzgoń, Poland 44 E6
Dzierżoniów, Poland 45 H3
Dzilam de Bravo, Mexico 119 C7
Dzisna, Belarus 46 E5
Dzisna →, Belarus 46 E5
Dziwnów, Poland 44 D1
Dzungaria = Junggar Pendi, China 60 B3
Dzungarian Gate = Alataw Shankou, China 60 B3
Dzuumod, Mongolia 60 B5
Dzyarzhynsk, Belarus 46 F4
Dzyatlava, Belarus 46 F3

E

Eabamet, L., Canada 102 B2
Eads, U.S.A. 112 F3
Eagle, U.S.A. 114 G10
Eagle →, Canada 103 B8
Eagle Butte, U.S.A. 112 C4
Eagle Grove, U.S.A. 112 D8
Eagle L., Calif., U.S.A. 114 F3
Eagle L., Maine, U.S.A. 103 C6
Eagle Lake, U.S.A. 113 L6
Eagle Mountain, U.S.A. 117 M11
Eagle Nest, U.S.A. 115 H11
Eagle Pass, U.S.A. 113 L4
Eagle Pk., U.S.A. 116 G7
Eagle Pt., Australia 92 C3
Eagle River, U.S.A. 112 C10
Ealing, U.K. 13 F7
Earaheedy, Australia 93 E3
Earl Grey, Canada 105 C8
Earle, U.S.A. 113 H9
Earlimart, U.S.A. 117 K7
Earn →, U.K. 14 E5
Earn, L., U.K. 14 E4
Earnslaw, Mt., N.Z. 91 L2
Earth, U.S.A. 113 H3
Easley, U.S.A. 109 H4
East Angus, Canada 103 C5
East Aurora, U.S.A. 110 D6
East Ayrshire □, U.K. 14 F4
East B., U.S.A. 113 L10
East Bengal, Bangla. 67 H17
East Beskids = Vychodné Beskydy, Europe 27 B15
East Brady, U.S.A. 110 F5
East C., N.Z. 91 G7
East Chicago, U.S.A. 108 E2
East China Sea, Asia 60 C7
East Coulee, Canada 104 C6
East Dereham, U.K. 13 E8
East Dunbartonshire □, U.K. 14 F4
East Falkland, Falk. Is. 122 J5
East Grand Forks, U.S.A. 112 B6
East Greenwich, U.S.A. 111 E13
East Grinstead, U.K. 13 F8
East Hartford, U.S.A. 111 E12
East Helena, U.S.A. 114 C8
East Indies, Asia 52 K15
East Jordan, U.S.A. 108 C3
East Kilbride, U.K. 14 F4
East Lansing, U.S.A. 108 D3
East Liverpool, U.S.A. 110 F4
East London, S. Africa 89 E4
East Lothian □, U.K. 14 F6
East Main = Eastmain, Canada 102 B4
East Orange, U.S.A. 111 F10
East Pacific Ridge, Pac. Oc. 97 J17
East Palestine, U.S.A. 110 F4
East Pine, Canada 104 B4
East Point, U.S.A. 109 J3
East Providence, U.S.A. 111 E13
East Pt., Canada 103 C7
East Renfrewshire □, U.K. 14 F4
East Retford = Retford, U.K. 12 D7
East Riding of Yorkshire □, U.K. 12 D7
East St. Louis, U.S.A. 112 F9
East Schelde → = Oosterschelde, Neths. 17 C4
East Siberian Sea, Russia 51 B17
East Stroudsburg, U.S.A. 111 E9
East Sussex □, U.K. 13 G8
East Tawas, U.S.A. 108 C4
East Toorale, Australia 95 E4
East Walker →, U.S.A. 116 G7
Eastbourne, N.Z. 91 J5
Eastbourne, U.K. 13 G8
Eastend, Canada 105 D7
Easter Islands = Pascua, I. de, Pac. Oc. 97 K17
Eastern □, Kenya 86 C4
Eastern □, Uganda 86 B3
Eastern Cape □, S. Africa 88 E4
Eastern Cr. →, Australia 94 C3
Eastern Ghats, India 66 N11
Eastern Group = Lau Group, Fiji 91 C9
Eastern Group, Australia 93 F3
Eastern Province □, S. Leone 82 D2
Eastern Transvaal = Mpumalanga □, S. Africa 89 B5
Easterville, Canada 105 C9
Easthampton, U.S.A. 111 D12
Eastland, U.S.A. 113 J5
Eastleigh, U.K. 13 G6
Eastmain, Canada 102 B4
Eastmain →, Canada 102 B4
Eastman, Canada 111 A12
Eastman, U.S.A. 109 J4
Easton, Md., U.S.A. 108 F7
Easton, Pa., U.S.A. 111 F9
Easton, Wash., U.S.A. 116 C5
Eastport, U.S.A. 103 D6
Eastsound, U.S.A. 116 B4
Eaton, U.S.A. 112 E2
Eatonia, Canada 105 C7
Eatonton, U.S.A. 109 J4
Eatontown, U.S.A. 111 F10
Eatonville, U.S.A. 116 D4
Eau Claire, U.S.A. 112 C9
Eauze, France 20 E4
Ebagoola, Australia 94 A3
Eban, Nigeria 83 D5
Ebbw Vale, U.K. 13 F4
Ebeltoft, Denmark 11 H4
Ebeltoft Vig, Denmark 11 H4
Ebensburg, U.S.A. 110 F6
Ebensee, Austria 26 D6
Eber Gölü, Turkey 72 C4
Eberbach, Germany 25 F4
Eberswalde-Finow, Germany 24 C9
Ebetsu, Japan 54 C10
Ebian, China 58 C4
Ebingen, Germany 25 G5
Éboli, Italy 31 B8
Ebolowa, Cameroon 83 E7
Ebrach, Germany 25 F6
Ébrié, Lagune, Ivory C. 82 D4
Ebro →, Spain 32 E5
Ebro, Embalse del, Spain 34 C7
Ebstorf, Germany 24 B6
Eceabat, Turkey 41 F10

Ech Cheliff, *Algeria* 78 A6
Echeng, *China* 59 B10
Echigo-Sammyaku, *Japan* 55 F9
Échirolles, *France* 21 C9
Echizen-Misaki, *Japan* 55 G7
Echmiadzin = Yejmiadzin, *Armenia* 49 K7
Echo Bay, *N.W.T., Canada* 100 B8
Echo Bay, *Ont., Canada* 102 C3
Echoing →, *Canada* 105 B10
Echternach, *Lux.* 17 E6
Echuca, *Australia* 95 F3
Ecija, *Spain* 35 H5
Eckental, *Germany* 25 F7
Eckernförde, *Germany* 24 A5
Eclipse Is., *Australia* 92 B4
Écommoy, *France* 18 E7
Écouché, *France* 18 D6
Ecuador ■, *S. Amer.* 124 D3
Écueillé, *France* 18 E8
Ed, *Sweden* 11 F5
Ed Dabbura, *Sudan* 80 D3
Ed Dâmer, *Sudan* 80 D3
Ed Debba, *Sudan* 80 D3
Ed-Déffa, *Egypt* 80 A2
Ed Deim, *Sudan* 81 E2
Ed Dueim, *Sudan* 81 E3
Edah, *Australia* 93 E2
Edam, *Canada* 105 C7
Edam, *Neths.* 17 B5
Edane, *Sweden* 10 E6
Eday, *U.K.* 14 B6
Edd, *Eritrea* 81 E5
Eddrachillis B., *U.K.* 14 C3
Eddystone Pt., *Australia* 94 G4
Ede, *Neths.* 17 B5
Ede, *Nigeria* 83 D5
Edéa, *Cameroon* 83 E7
Edebäck, *Sweden* 10 D7
Edehon L., *Canada* 105 A9
Edelény, *Hungary* 42 B5
Eden, *Australia* 95 F4
Eden, *N.C., U.S.A.* 109 G6
Eden, *N.Y., U.S.A.* 110 D6
Eden, *Tex., U.S.A.* 113 K5
Eden, *Wyo., U.S.A.* 114 E9
Eden →, *U.K.* 12 C4
Eden L., *Canada* 105 B8
Edenburg, *S. Africa* 88 D4
Edendale, *S. Africa* 89 D5
Edenderry, *Ireland* 15 C4
Edenton, *U.S.A.* 109 G7
Edenville, *S. Africa* 89 D4
Eder →, *Germany* 24 D5
Eder-Stausee, *Germany* 24 D4
Edewecht, *Germany* 24 B3
Edgar, *U.S.A.* 112 E6
Edgartown, *U.S.A.* 111 E14
Edge Hill, *U.K.* 13 E6
Edgefield, *U.S.A.* 109 J5
Edgeley, *U.S.A.* 112 B5
Edgemont, *U.S.A.* 112 D3
Edgeøya, *Svalbard* 4 B9
Édhessa, *Greece* 40 F6
Edievale, *N.Z.* 91 L2
Edina, *Liberia* 82 D2
Edina, *U.S.A.* 112 E8
Edinburg, *U.S.A.* 113 M5
Edinburgh, *U.K.* 14 F5
Edineţ, *Moldova* 43 B12
Edirne, *Turkey* 41 E10
Edirne □, *Turkey* 41 E10
Edison, *U.S.A.* 116 B4
Edithburgh, *Australia* 95 F2
Edjudina, *Australia* 93 E3
Edmeston, *U.S.A.* 111 D9
Edmond, *U.S.A.* 113 H6
Edmonds, *U.S.A.* 116 C4
Edmonton, *Australia* 94 B4
Edmonton, *Canada* 104 C6
Edmund L., *Canada* 105 C10
Edmundston, *Canada* 103 C6
Edna, *U.S.A.* 113 L6
Edna Bay, *U.S.A.* 104 B2
Edo □, *Nigeria* 83 D6
Edolo, *Italy* 28 B7
Edremit, *Turkey* 39 B9
Edremit Körfezi, *Turkey* 39 B8
Edsbro, *Sweden* 10 E12
Edsbyn, *Sweden* 10 C9
Edson, *Canada* 104 C5
Eduardo Castex, *Argentina* 126 D3
Edward →, *Australia* 95 F3
Edward, L., *Africa* 86 C2
Edward I., *Canada* 102 C2
Edward River, *Australia* 94 A3
Edward VII Land, *Antarctica* 5 E13
Edwards, *U.S.A.* 117 L9
Edwards Plateau, *U.S.A.* 113 K4
Edwardsville, *U.S.A.* 111 E9
Edzo, *Canada* 104 A5
Eeklo, *Belgium* 17 C3
Eferding, *Austria* 26 C7
Effingham, *U.S.A.* 108 F1
Eforie, *Romania* 43 F13
Ega →, *Spain* 32 C3
Égadi, Ísole, *Italy* 30 E5
Eganville, *Canada* 102 C4
Egeland, *U.S.A.* 112 A5
Egenolf L., *Canada* 105 B9
Eger = Cheb, *Czech Rep.* 26 A5
Eger, *Hungary* 42 C5
Eger →, *Hungary* 42 C5
Egersund, *Norway* 9 G12
Egg L., *Canada* 105 B7
Eggenburg, *Austria* 26 C8
Eggenfelden, *Germany* 25 G8
Éghezée, *Belgium* 17 D4
Eginbah, *Australia* 92 D2
Égletons, *France* 20 C6
Egmont, C., *N.Z.* 91 H4
Egmont, Mt., *N.Z.* 91 H5
Eğridir, *Turkey* 72 D4
Eğridir Gölü, *Turkey* 72 D4
Egtved, *Denmark* 11 J3
Egume, *Nigeria* 83 D6
Éguzon-Chantôme, *France* 19 F8
Egvekinot, *Russia* 51 C19
Egyek, *Hungary* 42 C5
Egypt ■, *Africa* 80 J7
Eha Amufu, *Nigeria* 83 D6
Ehime □, *Japan* 55 H6
Ehingen, *Germany* 25 G5
Ehrenberg, *U.S.A.* 117 M12
Ehrwald, *Austria* 26 D3
Eibar, *Spain* 32 B2
Eichstätt, *Germany* 25 G7
Eider →, *Germany* 24 A4
Eidsvold, *Australia* 95 D5
Eidsvoll, *Norway* 9 F14
Eifel, *Germany* 25 E2
Eiffel Flats, *Zimbabwe* 87 F3
Eiger, *Switz.* 28 B5
Eigg, *U.K.* 14 E2
Eighty Mile Beach, *Australia* 92 C3
Eil, *Somali Rep.* 74 F4
Eil, L., *U.K.* 14 E3
Eildon, L., *Australia* 95 F4
Eileen L., *Canada* 105 A7
Eilenburg, *Germany* 24 D8
Ein el Luweiqa, *Sudan* 81 E3
Einasleigh, *Australia* 94 B3
Einasleigh →, *Australia* 94 B3
Einbeck, *Germany* 24 D5
Eindhoven, *Neths.* 17 C5
Einsiedeln, *Switz.* 25 H4
Eire = Ireland ■, *Europe* 15 C4
Eiríksjökull, *Iceland* 8 D3
Eirunepé, *Brazil* 124 E5
Eisenach, *Germany* 24 E6
Eisenberg, *Germany* 24 E7
Eisenerz, *Austria* 26 D7
Eisenhüttenstadt, *Germany* 24 C10
Eisenkappel, *Austria* 26 E7
Eisenstadt, *Austria* 27 D9
Eisfeld, *Germany* 25 E6
Eisleben, *Germany* 24 D7
Eislingen, *Germany* 25 G5
Eivissa, *Spain* 37 C7
Eixe, Serra do, *Spain* 34 C4
Ejea de los Caballeros, *Spain* 32 C3
Ejutla, *Mexico* 119 D5
Ekalaka, *U.S.A.* 112 C2
Ekenässjön, *Sweden* 11 G9
Ekerö, *Sweden* 10 E11
Eket, *Nigeria* 83 E6
Eketahuna, *N.Z.* 91 J5
Ekhínos, *Greece* 41 E9
Ekibastuz, *Kazakstan* 50 D8
Ekoli, *Dem. Rep. of the Congo* 86 C1
Ekoln, *Sweden* 10 E11
Ekshärad, *Sweden* 10 D7
Eksjö, *Sweden* 11 G8
Ekwan →, *Canada* 102 B3
Ekwan Pt., *Canada* 102 B3
El Aaiún, *W. Sahara* 78 C3
El 'Agrûd, *Egypt* 75 E3
El 'Aiyat, *Egypt* 80 J7
El Alamein, *Egypt* 80 H6
El 'Aqaba, W. →, *Egypt* 75 E2
El 'Arag, *Egypt* 80 B2
El Arahal, *Spain* 35 H5
El Arîḥā, *West Bank* 75 D4
El Arish, *Australia* 94 B4
El 'Arîsh, *Egypt* 75 D2
El 'Arîsh, W. →, *Egypt* 75 D2
El Asnam = Ech Cheliff, *Algeria* 78 A6
El Astillero, *Spain* 34 B7
El Badâri, *Egypt* 80 B3
El Bahrein, *Egypt* 80 B2
El Ballâs, *Egypt* 80 B3
El Balyana, *Egypt* 80 B3
El Baqeir, *Sudan* 80 D3
El Barco de Ávila, *Spain* 34 E5
El Barco de Valdeorras = O Barco, *Spain* 34 C4
El Bauga, *Sudan* 80 D3
El Bawiti, *Egypt* 80 J6
El Bayadh, *Algeria* 78 B6
El Bierzo, *Spain* 34 C4
El Bluff, *Nic.* 120 D3
El Bonillo, *Spain* 33 G2
El Brûk, W. →, *Egypt* 75 E2
El Buheirat □, *Sudan* 81 F3
El Burgo de Osma, *Spain* 32 D1
El Cajon, *U.S.A.* 117 N10
El Campo, *U.S.A.* 113 L6
El Centro, *U.S.A.* 117 N11
El Cerro, *Bolivia* 124 G6
El Cerro de Andévalo, *Spain* 35 H4
El Compadre, *Mexico* 117 N10
El Coronil, *Spain* 35 H5
El Cuy, *Argentina* 128 D3
El Cuyo, *Mexico* 119 C7
El Dab'a, *Egypt* 80 H6
El Daheir, *Egypt* 75 D3
El Deir, *Egypt* 80 B3
El Dere, *Somali Rep.* 74 G4
El Descanso, *Mexico* 117 N10
El Desemboque, *Mexico* 118 A2
El Dilingat, *Egypt* 80 H7
El Diviso, *Colombia* 124 C3
El Djouf, *Mauritania* 76 D3
El Dorado, *Ark., U.S.A.* 113 J8
El Dorado, *Kans., U.S.A.* 113 G6
El Dorado, *Venezuela* 124 B6
El Ejido, *Spain* 35 J8
El Escorial, *Spain* 34 E6
El Espinar, *Spain* 34 D6
El Faiyûm, *Egypt* 80 J7
El Fâsher, *Sudan* 81 E2
El Fashn, *Egypt* 80 J7
El Ferrol = Ferrol, *Spain* 34 B2
El Fifi, *Sudan* 81 E2
El Fuerte, *Mexico* 118 B3
El Gal, *Somali Rep.* 74 E5
El Gebir, *Sudan* 81 E2
El Gedida, *Egypt* 80 B2
El Geneina = Al Junaynah, *Sudan* 79 F10
El Geteina, *Sudan* 81 E3
El Gezira □, *Sudan* 81 E3
El Gîza, *Egypt* 80 J7
El Grau, *Spain* 33 G4
El Hagiz, *Sudan* 81 D4
El Hammam, *Egypt* 80 H6
El Hawata, *Sudan* 81 E3
El Heiz, *Egypt* 80 B2
El 'Idisât, *Egypt* 80 B3
El Iskandarîya, *Egypt* 80 H7
El Jadida, *Morocco* 78 B4
El Jebelein, *Sudan* 81 E3
El Kab, *Sudan* 80 D3
El Kabrît, G., *Egypt* 75 F2
El Kamlin, *Sudan* 81 D3
El Karaba, *Sudan* 80 D3
El Khandaq, *Sudan* 80 D3
El Khârga, *Egypt* 80 B3
El Khartûm, *Sudan* 81 D3
El Khartûm □, *Sudan* 81 D3
El Khartûm Bahrî, *Sudan* 81 D3
El Kuntilla, *Egypt* 75 E3
El Laqâwa, *Sudan* 81 E2
El Laqeita, *Egypt* 80 B3
El Leiya, *Sudan* 81 D4
El Maestrazgo, *Spain* 32 E4
El Mafâza, *Sudan* 81 E3
El Mahalla el Kubra, *Egypt* 80 H7
El Mahârîq, *Egypt* 80 B3
El Mahmûdîya, *Egypt* 80 H7
El Maks el-Bahari, *Egypt* 80 C3
El Manshâh, *Egypt* 80 B3
El Mansûra, *Egypt* 80 H7
El Manzala, *Egypt* 80 H7
El Marâgha, *Egypt* 80 B3
El Masid, *Sudan* 81 D3
El Masnou, *Spain* 32 D7
El Matariya, *Egypt* 80 H8
El Medano, *Canary Is.* 37 F3
El Metemma, *Sudan* 81 D3
El Milagro, *Argentina* 126 C2
El Minyâ, *Egypt* 80 J7
El Monte, *U.S.A.* 117 L8
El Montseny, *Spain* 32 D7
El Mreyye, *Mauritania* 82 B3
El Obeid, *Sudan* 81 E3
El Odaiya, *Sudan* 81 E2
El Oro, *Mexico* 119 D4
El Oued, *Algeria* 78 B7
El Palmito, Presa, *Mexico* 118 B3
El Paso, *U.S.A.* 115 L10
El Paso Robles, *U.S.A.* 116 K6
El Pedernoso, *Spain* 33 F2
El Pedroso, *Spain* 35 H5
El Pobo de Dueñas, *Spain* 32 E3
El Portal, *U.S.A.* 116 H7
El Porvenir, *Mexico* 118 A3
El Prat de Llobregat, *Spain* 32 D7
El Progreso, *Honduras* 120 C2
El Pueblito, *Mexico* 118 B3
El Pueblo, *Canary Is.* 37 F2
El Puente del Arzobispo, *Spain* 34 F5
El Puerto de Santa María, *Spain* 35 J4
El Qâhira, *Egypt* 80 H7
El Qantara, *Egypt* 75 E1
El Qasr, *Egypt* 80 B2
El Quseima, *Egypt* 75 E3
El Qusîya, *Egypt* 80 B3
El Râshda, *Egypt* 80 B2
El Real, *Panama* 124 B3
El Reno, *U.S.A.* 113 H6
El Rîdisiya, *Egypt* 80 C3
El Rio, *U.S.A.* 117 L7
El Ronquillo, *Spain* 35 H4
El Roque, Pta., *Canary Is.* 37 F4
El Rosarito, *Mexico* 118 B2
El Rubio, *Spain* 35 H5
El Saff, *Egypt* 80 J7
El Saheira, W. →, *Egypt* 75 E2
El Salto, *Mexico* 118 C3
El Salvador ■, *Cent. Amer.* 120 D2
El Sauce, *Nic.* 120 D2
El Saucejo, *Spain* 35 H5
El Shallal, *Egypt* 80 C3
El Simbillawein, *Egypt* 80 H7
El Suweis, *Egypt* 80 J8
El Tamarâni, W. →, *Egypt* 75 E3
El Thamad, *Egypt* 75 F3
El Tigre, *Venezuela* 124 B6
El Tîh, G., *Egypt* 75 F2
El Tîna, Khalîg, *Egypt* 75 D1
El Tofo, *Chile* 126 B1
El Tránsito, *Chile* 126 B1
El Tûr, *Egypt* 80 J8
El Turbio, *Argentina* 128 G2
El Uqsur, *Egypt* 80 B3
El Venado, *Mexico* 118 C4
El Vendrell, *Spain* 32 D6
El Vigía, *Venezuela* 124 B4
El Viso del Alcor, *Spain* 35 H5
El Wabeira, *Egypt* 75 F2
El Wak, *Kenya* 86 B5
El Waqf, *Egypt* 80 B3
El Wâsta, *Egypt* 80 J7
El Weguet, *Ethiopia* 81 F5
El Wuz, *Sudan* 81 D3
Elafónisos, *Greece* 38 E4
Élancourt, *France* 19 D8
Élassa, *Greece* 39 F8
Elassón, *Greece* 38 B4
Elat, *Israel* 75 F3
Eláthia, *Greece* 38 C4
Elâzığ, *Turkey* 73 C8
Elba, *Italy* 28 F7
Elba, *U.S.A.* 109 K2
Elbasani, *Albania* 40 E4
Elbe, *U.S.A.* 116 D4
Elbe →, *Europe* 24 B4
Elbe-Seitenkanal, *Germany* 24 C6
Elbert, Mt., *U.S.A.* 115 G10
Elberta, *U.S.A.* 108 C2
Elberton, *U.S.A.* 109 H4
Elbeuf, *France* 18 C8
Elbing = Elbląg, *Poland* 44 D6
Elbistan, *Turkey* 72 C7
Elbląg, *Poland* 44 D6
Elbląg □, *Poland* 44 D6
Elbow, *Canada* 105 C7
Elbrus, *Asia* 49 J6
Elburz Mts. = Alborz, Reshteh-ye Kūhhā-ye, *Iran* 71 C7
Elche, *Spain* 33 G4
Elche de la Sierra, *Spain* 33 G2
Elcho I., *Australia* 94 A2
Elda, *Spain* 33 G4
Elde →, *Germany* 24 B7
Eldon, *Mo., U.S.A.* 112 F8
Eldon, *Wash., U.S.A.* 116 C3
Eldora, *U.S.A.* 112 D8
Eldorado, *Argentina* 127 B5
Eldorado, *Canada* 105 B7
Eldorado, *Mexico* 118 C3
Eldorado, *Ill., U.S.A.* 108 G1
Eldorado, *Tex., U.S.A.* 113 K4
Eldorado Springs, *U.S.A.* 113 G8
Eldoret, *Kenya* 86 B4
Eldred, *U.S.A.* 110 E6
Elea, C., *Cyprus* 36 D13
Electra, *U.S.A.* 113 H5
Elefantes →, *Mozam.* 89 C5
Elektrogorsk, *Russia* 46 E10
Elektrostal, *Russia* 46 E10
Elele, *Nigeria* 83 D6
Elena, *Bulgaria* 41 D9
Elephant Butte Reservoir, *U.S.A.* 115 K10
Elephant I., *Antarctica* 5 C18
Eleshnitsa, *Bulgaria* 40 E7
Eleşkirt, *Turkey* 73 C10
Eleuthera, *Bahamas* 120 B4
Elevsís, *Greece* 38 C5
Elevtheroúpolis, *Greece* 41 F8
Elgeyo-Marakwet □, *Kenya* 86 B4
Elgin, *N.B., Canada* 103 C6
Elgin, *Ont., Canada* 111 B8
Elgin, *U.K.* 14 D5
Elgin, *Ill., U.S.A.* 108 D1
Elgin, *N. Dak., U.S.A.* 112 B4
Elgin, *Nebr., U.S.A.* 112 E5
Elgin, *Nev., U.S.A.* 115 H6
Elgin, *Oreg., U.S.A.* 114 D5
Elgin, *Tex., U.S.A.* 113 K6
Elgoibar, *Spain* 32 B2
Elgon, Mt., *Africa* 86 B3
Eliase, *Indonesia* 63 F8
Elida, *U.S.A.* 113 J3
Elikón, *Greece* 38 C4
Elim, *S. Africa* 88 E2
Elin Pelin, *Bulgaria* 40 D7
Elisabethville = Lubumbashi, *Dem. Rep. of the Congo* 87 E2
Elista, *Russia* 49 G7
Elizabeth, *Australia* 95 E2
Elizabeth, *U.S.A.* 111 F10
Elizabeth City, *U.S.A.* 109 G7
Elizabethton, *U.S.A.* 109 G4
Elizabethtown, *Ky., U.S.A.* 108 G3
Elizabethtown, *N.Y., U.S.A.* 111 B11
Elizabethtown, *Pa., U.S.A.* 111 F8
Elizondo, *Spain* 32 B3
Ełk, *Poland* 44 E9
Ełk →, *Poland* 44 E9
Elk City, *U.S.A.* 113 H5
Elk Creek, *U.S.A.* 116 F4
Elk Grove, *U.S.A.* 116 G5
Elk Island Nat. Park, *Canada* 104 C6
Elk Lake, *Canada* 102 C3
Elk Point, *Canada* 105 C6
Elk River, *Idaho, U.S.A.* 114 C5
Elk River, *Minn., U.S.A.* 112 C8
Elkedra, *Australia* 94 C2
Elkedra →, *Australia* 94 C2
Elkhart, *Ind., U.S.A.* 108 E3
Elkhart, *Kans., U.S.A.* 113 G4
Elkhorn, *Canada* 105 D8
Elkhorn →, *U.S.A.* 112 E6
Elkhovo, *Bulgaria* 41 D10
Elkin, *U.S.A.* 109 G5
Elkins, *U.S.A.* 108 F6
Elko, *Canada* 104 D5
Elko, *U.S.A.* 114 F6
Ell, L., *Australia* 93 E4
Ellef Ringnes I., *Canada* 4 B2
Ellendale, *Australia* 92 C3
Ellendale, *U.S.A.* 112 B5
Ellensburg, *U.S.A.* 114 C3
Ellenville, *U.S.A.* 111 E10
Ellery, Mt., *Australia* 95 F4
Ellesmere, L., *N.Z.* 91 M4
Ellesmere I., *Canada* 4 B4
Ellesmere Port, *U.K.* 12 D5
Ellice Is. = Tuvalu ■, *Pac. Oc.* 96 H9
Ellinwood, *U.S.A.* 112 F5
Elliot, *Australia* 94 B1
Elliot, *S. Africa* 89 E4
Elliot Lake, *Canada* 102 C3
Elliotdale = Xhora, *S. Africa* 89 E4
Ellis, *U.S.A.* 112 F5
Elliston, *Australia* 95 E1
Ellisville, *U.S.A.* 113 K10
Ellon, *U.K.* 14 D6
Ellore = Eluru, *India* 67 L12
Ells →, *Canada* 104 B6
Ellsworth, *U.S.A.* 112 F5
Ellsworth Land, *Antarctica* 5 D16
Ellsworth Mts., *Antarctica* 5 D16
Ellwangen, *Germany* 25 G6
Ellwood City, *U.S.A.* 110 F4
Elm, *Switz.* 25 J5
Elma, *Canada* 105 D9
Elma, *U.S.A.* 116 D3
Elmadağ, *Turkey* 72 C5
Elmalı, *Turkey* 39 E11
Elmhurst, *U.S.A.* 108 E2
Elmina, *Ghana* 83 D4
Elmira, *Canada* 110 C4
Elmira, *U.S.A.* 110 D8
Elmore, *Australia* 95 F3
Elmore, *U.S.A.* 117 M11
Elmshorn, *Germany* 24 B5
Elmvale, *Canada* 110 B5
Elne, *France* 20 F6
Elora, *Canada* 110 C4
Elos, *Greece* 38 E4
Eloúnda, *Greece* 36 D7
Eloy, *U.S.A.* 115 K8
Éloyes, *France* 19 D13
Elrose, *Canada* 105 C7
Elsas, *Canada* 102 C3
Elsdorf, *Germany* 24 E2
Elsie, *U.S.A.* 116 E3
Elsinore = Helsingør, *Denmark* 11 H6
Elsinore, *U.S.A.* 115 G7
Elster →, *Germany* 24 D7
Elsterwerda, *Germany* 24 D9
Eltham, *N.Z.* 91 H5
Elton, *Russia* 49 F8
Elton, Ozero, *Russia* 49 F8
Eltville, *Germany* 25 E4
Eluru, *India* 67 L12
Elvas, *Portugal* 35 G3
Elven, *France* 18 E4
Elverum, *Norway* 9 F14
Elvire →, *Australia* 92 C4
Elvo →, *Italy* 28 C5
Elwood, *Ind., U.S.A.* 108 E3
Elwood, *Nebr., U.S.A.* 112 E5
Elx = Elche, *Spain* 33 G4
Ely, *U.K.* 13 E8
Ely, *Minn., U.S.A.* 112 B9
Ely, *Nev., U.S.A.* 114 G6
Elyria, *U.S.A.* 110 E2
Elyrus, *Greece* 38 F5
Elz →, *Germany* 25 G3
Emådalen, *Sweden* 10 C8
Emāmrūd, *Iran* 71 B7
Emån →, *Sweden* 11 G10
Emba, *Kazakstan* 50 E6
Emba →, *Kazakstan* 50 E6
Embarcación, *Argentina* 126 A3
Embarras Portage, *Canada* 105 B6
Embetsu, *Japan* 54 B10
Embi = Emba, *Kazakstan* 50 E6
Embi → = Emba →, *Kazakstan* 50 E6
Embóna, *Greece* 36 C9
Embrun, *France* 21 D10
Embu, *Kenya* 86 C4
Embu □, *Kenya* 86 C4
Emden, *Germany* 24 B3
Emecik, *Turkey* 39 E9
Emerald, *Australia* 94 C4
Emerson, *Canada* 105 D9
Emery, *U.S.A.* 115 G8
Emet, *Turkey* 39 B11
Emi Koussi, *Chad* 79 E9
Emília-Romagna □, *Italy* 28 D8
Emilius, Mte., *Italy* 28 C4
Eminabad, *Pakistan* 68 C6
Emine, Nos, *Bulgaria* 41 D11
Emirdağ, *Turkey* 72 C4
Emlenton, *U.S.A.* 110 E5
Emlichheim, *Germany* 24 C2
Emmaboda, *Sweden* 11 H9
Emme →, *Switz.* 25 H3
Emmeloord, *Neths.* 17 B5
Emmen, *Neths.* 17 B6
Emmen, *Switz.* 25 H4
Emmendingen, *Germany* 25 G3
Emmental, *Switz.* 25 J3

Emmerich, *Germany* 24 D2
Emmet, *Australia* 94 C3
Emmetsburg, *U.S.A.* 112 D7
Emmett, *U.S.A.* 114 E5
Emőd, *Hungary* 42 C5
Emona, *Bulgaria* 41 D11
Empalme, *Mexico* 118 B2
Empangeni, *S. Africa* 89 D5
Empedrado, *Argentina* 126 B4
Emperor Seamount Chain, *Pac. Oc.* 96 D9
Empoli, *Italy* 28 E7
Emporia, *Kans., U.S.A.* 112 F6
Emporia, *Va., U.S.A.* 109 G7
Emporium, *U.S.A.* 110 E6
Empress, *Canada* 105 C7
Empty Quarter = Rub' al Khālī, *Si. Arabia* 74 D4
Ems →, *Germany* 24 B3
Emsdale, *Canada* 110 A5
Emsdetten, *Germany* 24 C3
Emu, *China* 57 C15
Emu Park, *Australia* 94 C5
'En 'Avrona, *Israel* 75 F4
En Nahud, *Sudan* 81 E2
Ena, *Japan* 55 G8
Enana, *Namibia* 88 B2
Enånger, *Sweden* 10 C11
Enaratoli, *Indonesia* 63 E9
Enard B., *U.K.* 14 C3
Enare = Inarijärvi, *Finland* 8 B22
Encantadas, Serra, *Brazil* 127 C5
Encarnación, *Paraguay* 127 B4
Encarnación de Diaz, *Mexico* 118 C4
Enchi, *Ghana* 82 D4
Encinal, *U.S.A.* 113 L5
Encinitas, *U.S.A.* 117 M9
Encino, *U.S.A.* 115 J11
Encounter B., *Australia* 95 F2
Encs, *Hungary* 42 B6
Ende, *Indonesia* 63 F6
Endeavour, *Canada* 105 C8
Endeavour Str., *Australia* 94 A3
Endelave, *Denmark* 11 J4
Enderbury I., *Kiribati* 96 H10
Enderby, *Canada* 104 C5
Enderby I., *Australia* 92 D2
Enderby Land, *Antarctica* 5 C5
Enderlin, *U.S.A.* 112 B6
Endicott, *N.Y., U.S.A.* 111 D8
Endicott, *Wash., U.S.A.* 114 C5
Endyalgout I., *Australia* 92 B5
Enewetak Atoll, *Pac. Oc.* 96 F8
Enez, *Turkey* 41 F10
Engadin, *Switz.* 25 J6
Engaño, C., *Dom. Rep.* 121 C6
Engaño, C., *Phil.* 63 A6
Engcobo, *S. Africa* 89 E4
Engelberg, *Switz.* 25 J4
Engels, *Russia* 48 E8
Engemann L., *Canada* 105 B7
Enggano, *Indonesia* 62 F2
England, *U.S.A.* 113 H9
England □, *U.K.* 12 D7
Englee, *Canada* 103 B8
Englehart, *Canada* 102 C4
Engler L., *Canada* 105 B7
Englewood, *Colo., U.S.A.* 112 F2
Englewood, *Kans., U.S.A.* 113 G5
English →, *Canada* 105 C10
English Bazar = Ingraj Bazar, *India* 69 G13
English Channel, *Europe* 13 G6
English River, *Canada* 102 C1
Engures ezers, *Latvia* 44 A10
Enguri →, *Georgia* 49 J5
Enid, *U.S.A.* 113 G6
Enipévs →, *Greece* 38 B4
Enkhuizen, *Neths.* 17 B5
Enköping, *Sweden* 10 E11
Enle, *China* 58 F3
Enna, *Italy* 31 E7
Ennadai, *Canada* 105 A8
Ennadai L., *Canada* 105 A8
Ennedi, *Chad* 79 E10
Enngonia, *Australia* 95 D4
Ennigerloh, *Germany* 24 D4
Ennis, *Ireland* 15 D3
Ennis, *Mont., U.S.A.* 114 D8
Ennis, *Tex., U.S.A.* 113 J6
Enniscorthy, *Ireland* 15 D5
Enniskillen, *U.K.* 15 B4
Ennistimon, *Ireland* 15 D2
Enns, *Austria* 26 C7
Enns →, *Austria* 26 C7
Enontekiö, *Finland* 8 B20
Enping, *China* 59 F9
Enriquillo, L., *Dom. Rep.* 121 C5
Enschede, *Neths.* 17 B6
Ensenada, *Argentina* 126 C4
Ensenada, *Mexico* 118 A1
Enshi, *China* 58 B7
Ensiola, Pta. de n', *Spain* 37 B9
Ensisheim, *France* 19 E14
Entebbe, *Uganda* 86 B3
Enterprise, *Canada* 104 A5
Enterprise, *Oreg., U.S.A.* 114 D5
Enterprise, *Utah, U.S.A.* 115 H7
Entraygues-sur-Truyère, *France* 20 D6
Entre Ríos, *Bolivia* 126 A3
Entre Ríos □, *Argentina* 126 C4
Entrepeñas, Embalse de, *Spain* 32 E2
Entroncamento, *Portugal* 35 F2
Enugu, *Nigeria* 83 D6
Enugu □, *Nigeria* 83 D6
Enugu Ezike, *Nigeria* 83 D6
Enumclaw, *U.S.A.* 116 C5
Envermeu, *France* 18 C8
Enviken, *Sweden* 10 D9
Enying, *Hungary* 42 D3
Enza →, *Italy* 28 D7
Eólie, Ís., *Italy* 31 D7
Epanomí, *Greece* 40 F6
Epe, *Neths.* 17 B5
Epe, *Nigeria* 83 D5
Épernay, *France* 19 C10
Épernon, *France* 19 D8
Ephesus, *Turkey* 39 D9
Ephraim, *U.S.A.* 114 G8
Ephrata, *U.S.A.* 114 C4
Epidaurus Limera, *Greece* 38 E5
Épila, *Spain* 32 D3
Épinac, *France* 19 F11
Épinal, *France* 19 D13
Episkopi, *Cyprus* 36 E11
Episkopí, *Greece* 36 D6
Episkopi Bay, *Cyprus* 36 E11
Epitálion, *Greece* 38 D3
Eppan = Appiano, *Italy* 29 B8
Eppingen, *Germany* 25 F4
Epsom, *U.K.* 13 F7
Epukiro, *Namibia* 88 C2
Equatorial Guinea ■, *Africa* 84 D1
Er Rahad, *Sudan* 81 E3
Er Rif, *Morocco* 78 A5
Er Roseires, *Sudan* 81 E3
Eraclea, *Italy* 29 C9
Erāwadī Myit = Irrawaddy →, *Burma* 67 M19
Erba, *Italy* 28 C6
Erba, *Sudan* 80 D4
Erbaa, *Turkey* 72 B7
Erbeskopf, *Germany* 25 F3
Erbil = Arbīl, *Iraq* 70 B5
Erçiş, *Turkey* 73 C10
Érd, *Hungary* 42 C3
Erdao Jiang →, *China* 57 C14
Erdek, *Turkey* 41 F11
Erdemli, *Turkey* 72 D6
Erdene, *Mongolia* 56 B6
Erding, *Germany* 25 G7
Erdre →, *France* 18 E5
Erebus, Mt., *Antarctica* 5 D11
Erechim, *Brazil* 127 B5
Ereğli, *Konya, Turkey* 72 D6
Ereğli, *Zonguldak, Turkey* 72 B4
Erei, Monti, *Italy* 31 E7
Erenhot, *China* 56 C7
Eresma →, *Spain* 34 D6
Eressós, *Greece* 39 B7
Erewadi Myitwanya, *Burma* 67 M19
Erfenisdam, *S. Africa* 88 D4
Erftstadt, *Germany* 24 E2
Erft →, *Germany* 24 D2
Erfurt, *Germany* 24 E7
Ergani, *Turkey* 73 C8
Ergene →, *Turkey* 41 E10
Ergeni Vozvyshennost, *Russia* 49 G7
Ērgli, *Latvia* 9 H21
Erhlin, *Taiwan* 59 F13
Eria →, *Spain* 34 C5
Eriba, *Sudan* 81 D4
Eriboll, L., *U.K.* 14 C4
Érice, *Italy* 30 D5
Erie, *U.S.A.* 110 D4
Erie, L., *N. Amer.* 110 D4
Erie Canal, *U.S.A.* 110 C7
Erieau, *Canada* 110 D3
Erigavo, *Somali Rep.* 74 E4
Erikoúsa, *Greece* 36 A3
Eriksdale, *Canada* 105 C9
Erímanthos, *Greece* 38 D3
Erimo-misaki, *Japan* 54 D11
Eriskay, *U.K.* 14 D1
Erithraí, *Greece* 38 C5
Eritrea ■, *Africa* 81 E4
Erjas →, *Portugal* 34 F3
Erkelenz, *Germany* 24 D2
Erkner, *Germany* 24 C9
Erlangen, *Germany* 25 F6
Erldunda, *Australia* 94 D1
Ermelo, *Neths.* 17 B5
Ermelo, *S. Africa* 89 D4
Ermenek, *Turkey* 72 D5
Ermióni, *Greece* 38 D5
Ermones, *Greece* 36 A3
Ernakulam = Cochin, *India* 66 Q10
Erne →, *Ireland* 15 B3
Erne, Lower L., *U.K.* 15 B4
Erne, Upper L., *U.K.* 15 B4
Ernée, *France* 18 D6
Ernest Giles Ra., *Australia* 93 E3
Ernstberg, *Germany* 25 E2
Erode, *India* 66 P10
Eromanga, *Australia* 95 D3
Erongo, *Namibia* 88 C2
Erquy, *France* 18 D4
Errabiddy, *Australia* 93 E2
Erramala Hills, *India* 66 M11
Errer →, *Ethiopia* 81 F5
Errigal, *Ireland* 15 A3
Erris Hd., *Ireland* 15 B1
Erseka, *Albania* 40 F4
Erskine, *U.S.A.* 112 B7
Erstein, *France* 19 D14
Ertholmene, *Denmark* 11 J9
Ertil, *Russia* 48 E5
Ertis → = Irtysh →, *Russia* 50 C7
Eruh, *Turkey* 73 D10
Eruwa, *Nigeria* 83 D5
Ervy-le-Châtel, *France* 19 D10
Erwin, *U.S.A.* 109 G4
Eryuan, *China* 58 D2
Erzgebirge, *Germany* 24 E8
Erzin, *Russia* 51 D10
Erzincan, *Turkey* 73 C8
Erzurum, *Turkey* 73 C9
Es Caló, *Spain* 37 C8
Es Canar, *Spain* 37 B8
Es Mercadal, *Spain* 37 B11
Es Migjorn Gran, *Spain* 37 B11
Es Sahrâ' Esh Sharqîya, *Egypt* 80 B3
Es Sînâ', *Egypt* 80 J8
Es Sûkî, *Sudan* 81 E3
Es Vedrà, *Spain* 37 C7
Esambo, *Dem. Rep. of the Congo* 86 C1
Esan-Misaki, *Japan* 54 D10
Esashi, *Hokkaidō, Japan* 54 B11
Esashi, *Hokkaidō, Japan* 54 D10
Esbjerg, *Denmark* 11 J2
Escalante, *U.S.A.* 115 H8
Escalante →, *U.S.A.* 115 H8
Escalón, *Mexico* 118 B4
Escambia →, *U.S.A.* 109 K2
Escanaba, *U.S.A.* 108 C2
Esch-sur-Alzette, *Lux.* 17 E6
Eschede, *Germany* 24 C6
Eschwege, *Germany* 24 D6
Eschweiler, *Germany* 24 E2
Escondido, *U.S.A.* 117 M9
Escuinapa, *Mexico* 118 C3
Escuintla, *Guatemala* 120 D1
Eséka, *Cameroon* 83 E7
Eşen →, *Turkey* 39 E11
Esenguly, *Turkmenistan* 50 F6
Esens, *Germany* 24 B3
Esenyurt, *Turkey* 41 E12
Esera →, *Spain* 32 C5
Eşfahān, *Iran* 71 C6
Esfīdeh, *Iran* 71 C8
Esgueva →, *Spain* 34 D6
Esh Sham = Dimashq, *Syria* 75 B5
Esh Shamâlîya □, *Sudan* 80 D2
Esha Ness, *U.K.* 14 A7
Eshan, *China* 58 E4
Esher, *U.K.* 13 F7
Eshowe, *S. Africa* 89 D5
Esiama, *Ghana* 82 E4
Esil → = Ishim →, *Russia* 50 D8
Esino →, *Italy* 29 E10
Esk →, *Cumb., U.K.* 14 G5
Esk →, *N. Yorks., U.K.* 12 C7
Eskifjörður, *Iceland* 8 D7
Eskilsäter, *Sweden* 11 F7
Eskilstuna, *Sweden* 10 E10
Eskimalatya, *Turkey* 73 C8
Eskimo Pt., *Canada* 105 A10
Eskişehir, *Turkey* 39 B12
Eskişehir □, *Turkey* 39 B12
Esla →, *Spain* 34 D4
Eslāmābād-e Gharb, *Iran* 70 C5
Eslöv, *Sweden* 11 J7
Eşme, *Turkey* 39 C10
Esmeraldas, *Ecuador* 124 C3
Espalion, *France* 20 D6
Espanola, *Canada* 102 C3
Esparreguera, *Spain* 32 D6
Esparta, *Costa Rica* 120 E3
Espelkamp, *Germany* 24 C4
Esperance, *Australia* 93 F3
Esperance B., *Australia* 93 F3
Esperanza, *Argentina* 126 C3
Esperanza, *Phil.* 61 G6
Espéraza, *France* 20 F6
Espichel, C., *Portugal* 35 G1
Espiel, *Spain* 35 G5
Espigão, Serra do, *Brazil* 127 B5
Espinazo, Sierra del = Espinhaço, Serra do, *Brazil* 125 G10
Espinhaço, Serra do, *Brazil* 125 G10
Espinho, *Portugal* 34 D2
Espinilho, Serra do, *Brazil* 127 B5
Espinosa de los Monteros, *Spain* 34 B7
Espírito Santo □, *Brazil* 125 H10
Espíritu Santo, B. del, *Mexico* 119 D7
Espíritu Santo, I., *Mexico* 118 C2
Espita, *Mexico* 119 C7
Espiye, *Turkey* 73 B8
Espluga de Francolí, *Spain* 32 D6
Espoo, *Finland* 9 F21
Espuña, Sierra de, *Spain* 33 H3
Espungabera, *Mozam.* 89 C5
Esquel, *Argentina* 128 E2
Esquina, *Argentina* 126 C4
Essaouira, *Morocco* 78 B4
Essebie, *Dem. Rep. of the Congo* 86 B3
Essen, *Belgium* 17 C4
Essen, *Germany* 24 D3
Essendon, Mt., *Australia* 93 E3
Essequibo →, *Guyana* 122 C5
Essex, *Canada* 110 D2
Essex, *Calif., U.S.A.* 117 L11
Essex, *N.Y., U.S.A.* 111 B11
Essex □, *U.K.* 13 F8
Esslingen, *Germany* 25 G5
Essonne □, *France* 19 D9
Estaca de Bares, C. de, *Spain* 34 B3
Estadilla, *Spain* 32 C5
Estados, I. de Los, *Argentina* 122 J4
Estagel, *France* 20 F6
Eşţahbānāt, *Iran* 71 D7
Estância, *Brazil* 125 F11
Estancia, *U.S.A.* 115 J10
Estārm, *Iran* 71 D8
Estarreja, *Portugal* 34 E2
Estats, Pic d', *Spain* 32 C6
Estcourt, *S. Africa* 89 D4
Este, *Italy* 29 C8
Estelí, *Nic.* 120 D2
Estella, *Spain* 32 C2
Estellencs, *Spain* 37 B9
Estelline, *S. Dak., U.S.A.* 112 C6
Estelline, *Tex., U.S.A.* 113 H4
Estena →, *Spain* 35 F6
Estepa, *Spain* 35 H6
Estepona, *Spain* 35 J5
Esterhazy, *Canada* 105 C8
Esternay, *France* 19 D10
Esterri d'Aneu, *Spain* 32 C6
Estevan, *Canada* 105 D8
Estevan Group, *Canada* 104 C3
Estherville, *U.S.A.* 112 D7
Estissac, *France* 19 D10
Eston, *Canada* 105 C7
Estonia ■, *Europe* 9 G21
Estoril, *Portugal* 35 G1
Estouk, *Mali* 83 B5
Estreito, *Brazil* 125 E9
Estrela, Serra da, *Portugal* 34 E3
Estrella, *Spain* 35 G7
Estremoz, *Portugal* 35 G3
Estrondo, Serra do, *Brazil* 125 E9
Esztergom, *Hungary* 42 C3
Et Tîdra, *Mauritania* 82 B1
Etadunna, *Australia* 95 D2
Etah, *India* 69 F8
Étain, *France* 19 C12
Etamamu, *Canada* 103 B8
Étampes, *France* 19 D9
Etanga, *Namibia* 88 B1
Étaples, *France* 19 B8
Etawah, *India* 69 F8
Etawah →, *U.S.A.* 109 H3
Etawney L., *Canada* 105 B9
Ete, *Nigeria* 83 D6
Ethel, *U.S.A.* 116 D4
Ethel Creek, *Australia* 92 D3
Ethelbert, *Canada* 105 C8
Ethiopia ■, *Africa* 74 F3
Ethiopian Highlands, *Ethiopia* 52 J7
Etili, *Turkey* 41 G10
Etive, L., *U.K.* 14 E3
Etna, *Italy* 31 E7
Etoile, *Dem. Rep. of the Congo* 87 E2
Etolin I., *U.S.A.* 104 B2
Etosha Pan, *Namibia* 88 B2
Etowah, *U.S.A.* 109 H3
Étréchy, *France* 19 D9
Étrépagny, *France* 19 C8
Étretat, *France* 18 C7
Etropole, *Bulgaria* 41 D8
Ettelbruck, *Lux.* 17 E6
Ettlingen, *Germany* 25 G4
Ettrick Water →, *U.K.* 14 F6
Etuku, *Dem. Rep. of the Congo* 86 C2
Etulia, *Moldova* 43 E13
Etzatlán, *Mexico* 118 C4
Eu, *France* 18 B8
Euboea = Évvoia, *Greece* 38 C6
Eucla Motel, *Australia* 93 F4
Euclid, *U.S.A.* 110 E3
Eucumbene, L., *Australia* 95 F4
Eudora, *U.S.A.* 113 J9
Eufaula, *Ala., U.S.A.* 109 K3
Eufaula, *Okla., U.S.A.* 113 H7
Eufaula L., *U.S.A.* 113 H7
Eugene, *U.S.A.* 114 E2
Eugowra, *Australia* 95 E4
Eulo, *Australia* 95 D4
Eunice, *La., U.S.A.* 113 K8
Eunice, *N. Mex., U.S.A.* 113 J3
Eupen, *Belgium* 17 D6
Euphrates = Furāt, Nahr al →, *Asia* 70 D5
Eure □, *France* 18 C8
Eure →, *France* 18 C8
Eure-et-Loir □, *France* 18 D8
Eureka, *Canada* 4 B3
Eureka, *Calif., U.S.A.* 114 F1
Eureka, *Kans., U.S.A.* 113 G6
Eureka, *Mont., U.S.A.* 114 B6
Eureka, *Nev., U.S.A.* 114 G5
Eureka, *S. Dak., U.S.A.* 112 C5
Eureka, *Utah, U.S.A.* 114 G7
Eureka, Mt., *Australia* 93 E3
Euroa, *Australia* 95 F4
Europa, Île, *Ind. Oc.* 85 J8
Europa, Picos de, *Spain* 34 B6
Europa, Pta. de, *Gib.* 35 J5
Europoort, *Neths.* 17 C4
Euskirchen, *Germany* 24 E2
Eustis, *U.S.A.* 109 L5
Eutin, *Germany* 24 A6
Eutsuk L., *Canada* 104 C3
Eva Downs, *Australia* 94 B1
Evale, *Angola* 88 B2
Evans, *U.S.A.* 112 E2
Evans Head, *Australia* 95 D5
Evans L., *Canada* 102 B4
Evans Mills, *U.S.A.* 111 B9
Evanston, *Ill., U.S.A.* 108 E2
Evanston, *Wyo., U.S.A.* 114 F8
Evansville, *Ind., U.S.A.* 108 G2
Evansville, *Wis., U.S.A.* 112 D10
Évaux-les-Bains, *France* 19 F9
Evaz, *Iran* 71 E7
Evciler, *Afyon, Turkey* 39 C11
Evciler, *Çanakkale, Turkey* 39 B8
Eveleth, *U.S.A.* 112 B8
Evensk, *Russia* 51 C16
Everard, L., *Australia* 95 E2
Everard Park, *Australia* 93 E5
Everard Ranges, *Australia* 93 E5
Everest, Mt., *Nepal* 69 E12
Everett, *Pa., U.S.A.* 110 F6
Everett, *Wash., U.S.A.* 116 C4
Everglades, The, *U.S.A.* 109 N5
Everglades City, *U.S.A.* 109 N5
Everglades National Park, *U.S.A.* 109 N5
Evergreen, *U.S.A.* 109 K2
Everöd, *Sweden* 11 J8
Everson, *U.S.A.* 114 B2
Evertsberg, *Sweden* 10 C7
Evesham, *U.K.* 13 E6
Évian-les-Bains, *France* 19 F13
Évinos →, *Greece* 38 C3
Évisa, *France* 21 F12
Evje, *Norway* 9 G12
Évora, *Portugal* 35 G3
Évora □, *Portugal* 35 G3
Evowghlī, *Iran* 70 B5
Évreux, *France* 18 C8
Evritanía □, *Greece* 38 B3
Évron, *France* 18 D6
Évros □, *Greece* 41 E10
Évros →, *Bulgaria* 72 B2
Evrótas →, *Greece* 38 E4
Évry, *France* 19 D9
Évvoia, *Greece* 38 C6
Évvoia □, *Greece* 38 C5
Evxinoúpolis, *Greece* 38 B4
Ewe, L., *U.K.* 14 D3
Ewing, *U.S.A.* 112 D5
Ewo, *Congo* 84 E2
Exaltación, *Bolivia* 124 F5
Excelsior Springs, *U.S.A.* 112 F7
Excideuil, *France* 20 C5
Exe →, *U.K.* 13 G4
Exeter, *Canada* 110 C3
Exeter, *U.K.* 13 G4
Exeter, *Calif., U.S.A.* 116 J7
Exeter, *N.H., U.S.A.* 111 D14
Exeter, *Nebr., U.S.A.* 112 E6
Exmoor, *U.K.* 13 F4
Exmouth, *Australia* 92 D1
Exmouth, *U.K.* 13 G4
Exmouth G., *Australia* 92 D1
Expedition Ra., *Australia* 94 C4
Extremadura □, *Spain* 35 F4
Exuma Sound, *Bahamas* 120 B4
Eyasi, L., *Tanzania* 86 C4
Eye Pen., *U.K.* 14 C2
Eyeberry L., *Canada* 105 A8
Eyemouth, *U.K.* 14 F6
Eygurande, *France* 19 G9
Eyjafjörður, *Iceland* 8 C4
Eymet, *France* 20 D4
Eymoutiers, *France* 20 C5
Eynesil, *Turkey* 73 B8
Eyre, *Australia* 93 F4
Eyre (North), L., *Australia* 95 D2
Eyre (South), L., *Australia* 95 D2
Eyre Cr. →, *Australia* 95 D2
Eyre Mts., *N.Z.* 91 L2
Eyre Pen., *Australia* 95 E2
Eysturoy, *Færoe Is.* 8 E9
Eyvānkī, *Iran* 71 C6
Ez Zeidab, *Sudan* 80 D3
Ezcaray, *Spain* 32 C1
Ežerėlis, *Lithuania* 44 D10
Ezine, *Turkey* 39 B8
Ezouza →, *Cyprus* 36 E11

F

F.Y.R.O.M. = Macedonia ■, *Europe* 40 E5
Fabens, *U.S.A.* 115 L10
Fabero, *Spain* 34 C4
Fåborg, *Denmark* 11 J4
Fabriano, *Italy* 29 E9
Făcăeni, *Romania* 43 F12
Fachi, *Niger* 79 E8
Fada, *Chad* 79 E10
Fada-n-Gourma, *Burkina Faso* 83 C5
Fadd, *Hungary* 42 D3
Faddeyevskiy, Ostrov, *Russia* 51 B15
Fadghāmī, *Syria* 70 C4
Fadlab, *Sudan* 80 D3
Faenza, *Italy* 29 D8
Færoe Is. = Føroyar, *Atl. Oc.* 8 F9
Fafa, *Mali* 83 B5
Fafe, *Portugal* 34 D2
Fagam, *Nigeria* 83 C7
Făgăras, *Romania* 43 E9
Făgăras, Munții, *Romania* 43 E9
Fågelmara, *Sweden* 11 H9
Fagerhult, *Sweden* 11 G9
Fagersta, *Sweden* 10 D9
Făget, *Romania* 42 E7

Făget, Munţii, *Romania* .. 43 C8
Fagnano, L., *Argentina* ... 128 G3
Fagnières, *France* 19 D11
Fahlīān, *Iran* 71 D6
Fahraj, *Kermān, Iran* 71 D8
Fahraj, *Yazd, Iran* 71 D7
Faial, *Madeira* 37 D3
Fair Hd., *U.K.* 15 A5
Fair Oaks, *U.S.A.* 116 G5
Fairbank, *U.S.A.* 115 L8
Fairbanks, *U.S.A.* 100 B5
Fairbury, *U.S.A.* 112 E6
Fairfax, *U.S.A.* 113 G6
Fairfield, *Ala., U.S.A.* ... 109 J2
Fairfield, *Calif., U.S.A.* .. 116 G4
Fairfield, *Conn., U.S.A.* .. 111 E11
Fairfield, *Idaho, U.S.A.* .. 114 E6
Fairfield, *Ill., U.S.A.* 108 F1
Fairfield, *Iowa, U.S.A.* ... 112 E9
Fairfield, *Mont., U.S.A.* .. 114 C8
Fairfield, *Tex., U.S.A.* ... 113 K7
Fairford, *Canada* 105 C9
Fairhope, *U.S.A.* 109 K2
Fairlie, *N.Z.* 91 L3
Fairmead, *U.S.A.* 116 H6
Fairmont, *Minn., U.S.A.* . 112 D7
Fairmont, *W. Va., U.S.A.* 108 F5
Fairmount, *U.S.A.* 117 L8
Fairplay, *U.S.A.* 115 G11
Fairport, *U.S.A.* 110 C7
Fairport Harbor, *U.S.A.* .. 110 E3
Fairview, *Australia* 94 B3
Fairview, *Canada* 104 B5
Fairview, *Mont., U.S.A.* .. 112 B2
Fairview, *Okla., U.S.A.* ... 113 G5
Fairview, *Utah, U.S.A.* ... 114 G8
Fairweather, Mt., *U.S.A.* . 100 C6
Faisalabad, *Pakistan* 68 D5
Faith, *U.S.A.* 112 C3
Faizabad, *India* 69 F10
Fajardo, *Puerto Rico* 121 C6
Fakenham, *U.K.* 12 E8
Fåker, *Sweden* 10 A8
Fakfak, *Indonesia* 63 E8
Fakiya, *Bulgaria* 41 D11
Fakobli, *Ivory C.* 82 D3
Fakse, *Denmark* 11 J6
Fakse Bugt, *Denmark* 11 J6
Fakse Ladeplads, *Denmark* 11 J6
Faku, *China* 57 C12
Falaise, *France* 18 D6
Falaise, Mui, *Vietnam* 64 C5
Falakrón Óros, *Greece* ... 40 E7
Falam, *Burma* 67 H18
Falces, *Spain* 32 C3
Fălciu, *Romania* 43 D13
Falcó, C. des, *Spain* 37 C7
Falcon Dam, *U.S.A.* 113 M5
Falconara Maríttima, *Italy* 29 E10
Falcone, C. del, *Italy* 30 B1
Falconer, *U.S.A.* 110 D5
Faléa, *Mali* 82 C2
Falerum, *Sweden* 11 F10
Faleshty = Făleşti,
Moldova 43 C12
Făleşti, *Moldova* 43 C12
Falfurrias, *U.S.A.* 113 M5
Falher, *Canada* 104 B5
Falirakí, *Greece* 36 C10
Falkenberg, *Germany* 24 D9
Falkenberg, *Sweden* 11 H6
Falkensee, *Germany* 24 C9
Falkirk, *U.K.* 14 F5
Falkirk □, *U.K.* 14 F5
Falkland, *U.K.* 14 E5
Falkland Is. □, *Atl. Oc.* .. 128 G5
Falkland Sd., *Falk. Is.* 128 G5
Falkonéra, *Greece* 38 E5
Falköping, *Sweden* 11 F7
Fall River, *U.S.A.* 111 E13
Fall River Mills, *U.S.A.* .. 114 F3
Fallbrook, *U.S.A.* 115 K5
Fallbrook, *Calif., U.S.A.* .. 117 M9
Fallon, *Mont., U.S.A.* 112 B2
Fallon, *Nev., U.S.A.* 114 G4
Falls City, *Nebr., U.S.A.* .. 112 E7
Falls City, *Oreg., U.S.A.* .. 114 D2
Falls Creek, *U.S.A.* 110 E6
Falmouth, *Jamaica* 120 C4
Falmouth, *U.K.* 13 G2
Falmouth, *U.S.A.* 108 F3
False B., *S. Africa* 88 E2
Falso, C., *Honduras* 120 C3
Falster, *Denmark* 11 K5
Falsterbo, *Sweden* 9 J15
Fălticeni, *Romania* 43 C11
Falun, *Sweden* 10 D9
Famagusta, *Cyprus* 36 D12
Famagusta Bay, *Cyprus* .. 36 D13
Famatina, Sierra de,
Argentina 126 B2
Family L., *Canada* 105 C9
Famoso, *U.S.A.* 117 K7
Fan Xian, *China* 56 G8
Fana, *Mali* 82 C3
Fanad Hd., *Ireland* 15 A4
Fanárion, *Greece* 38 B3
Fandriana, *Madag.* 89 C8
Fang, *Thailand* 64 C2
Fang Xian, *China* 59 A8
Fangchang, *China* 59 B12
Fangcheng,
Guangxi Zhuangzu,
China 58 G7
Fangcheng, *Henan, China* 56 H7
Fangliao, *Taiwan* 59 F13
Fangshan, *China* 56 E6
Fangzi, *China* 57 F10
Fani i Madh →, *Albania* . 40 E4
Fanjiatun, *China* 57 C13
Fannich, L., *U.K.* 14 D4
Fannūj, *Iran* 71 E8
Fanny Bay, *Canada* 104 D4
Fanø, *Denmark* 11 J2
Fano, *Italy* 29 E10
Fanshaw, *U.S.A.* 104 B2
Fanshi, *China* 56 E7
Fao = Al Fāw, *Iraq* 71 D6
Faqirwali, *Pakistan* 68 E5
Fara in Sabina, *Italy* 29 F9
Faradje,
Dem. Rep. of the Congo 86 B2
Farafangana, *Madag.* 89 C8
Farâfra, El Wâhât el-,
Egypt 80 B2
Farāh, *Afghan.* 66 C3
Farāh □, *Afghan.* 66 C3
Farahalana, *Madag.* 89 A9
Faraid, Gebel, *Egypt* 80 C4
Faramana, *Burkina Faso* .. 82 C4
Faranah, *Guinea* 82 C2
Farasān, Jazā'ir, *Si. Arabia* 74 D3
Farasan Is. = Farasān,
Jazā'ir, *Si. Arabia* 74 D3
Faratsiho, *Madag.* 89 B8
Fardes →, *Spain* 35 H7
Fareham, *U.K.* 13 G6
Farewell, C., *N.Z.* 91 J4
Farewell C. = Farvel, Kap,
Greenland 4 D5
Färgelanda, *Sweden* 11 F5
Farghona, *Uzbekistan* 50 E8
Fargo, *U.S.A.* 112 B6
Fār'iah, W. al →,
West Bank 75 C4
Faribault, *U.S.A.* 112 C8
Faridkot, *India* 68 D6
Faridpur, *Bangla.* 69 H13
Färila, *Sweden* 10 C9
Farim, *Guinea-Biss.* 82 C1
Farīmān, *Iran* 71 C8
Farina, *Australia* 95 E2
Fariones, Pta., *Canary Is.* . 37 E6
Fâriskûr, *Egypt* 80 H7
Färjestaden, *Sweden* 11 H10
Farkadhón, *Greece* 38 B4
Farmakonisi, *Greece* 39 D9
Farmerville, *U.S.A.* 113 J8
Farmington, *Calif., U.S.A.* 116 H6
Farmington, *N.H., U.S.A.* 111 C13
Farmington, *N. Mex.,*
U.S.A. 115 H9
Farmington, *Utah, U.S.A.* 114 F8
Farmington →, *U.S.A.* .. 111 E12
Farmville, *U.S.A.* 108 G6
Färnäs, *Sweden* 10 D8
Farne Is., *U.K.* 12 B6
Farnham, *Canada* 111 A12
Faro, *Brazil* 125 D7
Faro, *Portugal* 35 H3
Fårö, *Sweden* 9 H18
Faro □, *Portugal* 35 H2
Fårösund, *Sweden* 11 G13
Farquhar, C., *Australia* ... 93 D1
Farrars Cr. →, *Australia* . 94 D3
Farrāshband, *Iran* 71 D7
Farrell, *U.S.A.* 110 E4
Farrell Flat, *Australia* 95 E2
Farrokhī, *Iran* 71 C8
Farruch, C. = Ferrutx, C.,
Spain 37 B10
Farrukhabad-cum-
Fatehgarh, *India* 69 F8
Fārs □, *Iran* 71 D7
Fársala, *Greece* 38 B4
Farsø, *Denmark* 11 H3
Farsund, *Norway* 9 G12
Fartak, Râs, *Si. Arabia* ... 70 D2
Fârţăneşti, *Romania* 43 E12
Fartura, Serra da, *Brazil* .. 127 B5
Faru, *Nigeria* 83 C6
Fārūj, *Iran* 71 B8
Fårup, *Denmark* 11 H3
Farvel, Kap, *Greenland* ... 4 D5
Farwell, *U.S.A.* 113 H3
Fasā, *Iran* 71 D7
Fasano, *Italy* 31 B10
Fashoda, *Sudan* 81 F3
Fastiv, *Ukraine* 47 G5
Fastov = Fastiv, *Ukraine* . 47 G5
Fatagar, Tanjung, *Indonesia* 63 E8
Fatehgarh, *India* 69 F8
Fatehpur, *Raj., India* 68 F6
Fatehpur, *Ut. P., India* ... 69 G9
Fatesh, *Russia* 47 F8
Fatick, *Senegal* 82 C1
Fatima, *Canada* 103 C7
Fátima, *Portugal* 35 F2
Fatoya, *Guinea* 82 C3
Fatsa, *Turkey* 72 B7
Faucille, Col de la, *France* 19 F13
Faulkton, *U.S.A.* 112 C5
Faulquemont, *France* 19 C13
Faure I., *Australia* 93 E1
Făurei, *Romania* 43 E12
Fauresmith, *S. Africa* 88 D4
Fauske, *Norway* 8 C16
Favara, *Italy* 30 E6
Favàritx, C. de, *Spain* 37 B11
Faverges, *France* 21 C10
Favignana, *Italy* 30 E5
Favignana, I., *Italy* 30 E5
Favourable Lake, *Canada* . 102 B1
Fawn →, *Canada* 102 A2
Fawnskin, *U.S.A.* 117 L10
Faxaflói, *Iceland* 8 D2
Faxälven →, *Sweden* 10 A10
Faya-Largeau, *Chad* 79 E9
Fayd, *Si. Arabia* 70 E4
Fayence, *France* 21 E10
Fayette, *Ala., U.S.A.* 109 J2
Fayette, *Mo., U.S.A.* 112 F8
Fayetteville, *Ark., U.S.A.* 113 G7
Fayetteville, *N.C., U.S.A.* 109 H6
Fayetteville, *Tenn., U.S.A.* 109 H2
Fayón, *Spain* 32 D5
Fazilka, *India* 68 D6
Fazilpur, *Pakistan* 68 E4
Fdérik, *Mauritania* 78 D3
Feale →, *Ireland* 15 D2
Fear, C., *U.S.A.* 109 J7
Feather →, *U.S.A.* 114 G3
Feather Falls, *U.S.A.* 116 F5
Featherston, *N.Z.* 91 J5
Featherstone, *Zimbabwe* .. 87 F3
Fécamp, *France* 18 C7
Federación, *Argentina* 126 C4
Féderal, *Argentina* 128 C5
Fedeshkūh, *Iran* 71 D7
Fehérgyarmat, *Hungary* .. 42 C7
Fehmarn, *Germany* 24 A7
Fehmarn Bælt, *Europe* ... 11 K5
Fehmarn Belt = Fehmarn
Bælt, *Europe* 11 K5
Fei Xian, *China* 57 G9
Feijó, *Brazil* 124 E4
Feilding, *N.Z.* 91 J5
Feira de Santana, *Brazil* .. 125 F11
Feixiang, *China* 56 F8
Fejér □, *Hungary* 42 C3
Fejø, *Denmark* 11 K5
Feke, *Turkey* 72 D6
Fekete →, *Hungary* 42 E3
Felanitx, *Spain* 37 B10
Feldbach, *Austria* 26 E8
Feldberg, *Baden-W.,*
Germany 25 H3
Feldberg,
Mecklenburg-Vorpommern,
Germany 24 B9
Feldkirch, *Austria* 26 D2
Feldkirchen, *Austria* 26 E7
Felipe Carrillo Puerto,
Mexico 119 D7
Felixstowe, *U.K.* 13 F9
Felletin, *France* 20 C6
Fellingsbro, *Sweden* 10 E9
Felton, *U.S.A.* 116 H4
Feltre, *Italy* 29 B8
Femer Bælt = Fehmarn
Bælt, *Europe* 11 K5
Femø, *Denmark* 11 K5
Femunden, *Norway* 9 E14
Fen He →, *China* 56 G6
Fene, *Spain* 34 B2
Fenelon Falls, *Canada* 110 B6
Fener Burnu, *Turkey* 39 E9
Feneroa, *Ethiopia* 81 E4
Feng Xian, *Jiangsu, China* 56 G9
Feng Xian, *Shaanxi, China* 56 H4
Fengári, *Greece* 41 F9
Fengcheng, *Jiangxi, China* 59 C10
Fengcheng, *Liaoning,*
China 57 D13
Fengdu, *China* 58 C6
Fengfeng, *China* 56 F8
Fenggang, *China* 58 D6
Fenghua, *China* 59 C13
Fenghuang, *China* 58 D7
Fenghuangzui, *China* 58 A7
Fengjie, *China* 58 B7
Fengkai, *China* 59 F8
Fengle, *China* 59 B9
Fengning, *China* 56 D9
Fengqing, *China* 58 E2
Fengqiu, *China* 56 G8
Fengrun, *China* 57 E10
Fengshan,
Guangxi Zhuangzu,
China 58 E7
Fengshan,
Guangxi Zhuangzu,
China 58 E6
Fengtai, *Anhui, China* 59 A11
Fengtai, *Beijing, China* ... 56 E9
Fengxian, *China* 59 B13
Fengxiang, *China* 56 G4
Fengxin, *China* 59 C10
Fengyang, *China* 57 H9
Fengyi, *China* 58 E3
Fengzhen, *China* 56 D7
Fennimore, *U.S.A.* 112 D9
Feno, C. de, *France* 21 G12
Fenoarivo Afovoany,
Madag. 89 B8
Fenoarivo Atsinanana,
Madag. 89 B8
Fens, The, *U.K.* 12 E7
Fensmark, *Denmark* 11 J5
Fenton, *U.S.A.* 108 D4
Fenxi, *China* 56 F6
Fenyang, *China* 56 F6
Fenyi, *China* 59 D10
Feodosiya, *Ukraine* 47 K8
Ferdows, *Iran* 71 C8
Fère-Champenoise, *France* 19 D10
Fère-en-Tardenois, *France* 19 C10
Ferentino, *Italy* 29 G10
Ferfer, *Somali Rep.* 74 F4
Fergana = Farghona,
Uzbekistan 50 E8
Fergus, *Canada* 102 D3
Fergus Falls, *U.S.A.* 112 B6
Feričanci, *Croatia* 42 E2
Ferkéssédougou, *Ivory C.* . 82 D3
Ferlach, *Austria* 26 E7
Ferland, *Canada* 102 B2
Ferlo, Vallée du, *Senegal* . 82 B2
Fermanagh □, *U.K.* 15 B4
Fermo, *Italy* 29 E10
Fermoselle, *Spain* 34 D4
Fermoy, *Ireland* 15 D3
Fernán Nuñéz, *Spain* 35 H6
Fernández, *Argentina* 126 B3
Fernandina Beach, *U.S.A.* 109 K5
Fernando de Noronha,
Brazil 125 D12
Fernando Póo = Bioko,
Eq. Guin. 83 E6
Ferndale, *Calif., U.S.A.* .. 114 F1
Ferndale, *Wash., U.S.A.* . 116 B4
Fernie, *Canada* 104 D5
Fernlees, *Australia* 94 C4
Fernley, *U.S.A.* 114 G4
Ferozepore = Firozpur,
India 68 D6
Férrai, *Greece* 41 F10
Ferrandina, *Italy* 31 B9
Ferrara, *Italy* 29 D8
Ferrato, C., *Italy* 30 C2
Ferreira do Alentejo,
Portugal 35 G2
Ferreñafe, *Peru* 124 E3
Ferrerías, *Spain* 37 B11
Ferret, C., *France* 20 D2
Ferrette, *France* 19 E14
Ferriday, *U.S.A.* 113 K9
Ferriere, *Italy* 28 D6
Ferrières, *France* 19 D9
Ferro, Capo, *Italy* 30 A2
Ferrol, *Spain* 34 B2
Ferron, *U.S.A.* 115 G8
Ferrutx, C., *Spain* 37 B10
Ferryland, *Canada* 103 C9
Fertile, *U.S.A.* 112 B6
Fertőszentmiklós, *Hungary* 42 C1
Fès, *Morocco* 78 B5
Fessenden, *U.S.A.* 112 B5
Feteşti, *Romania* 43 F12
Fethiye, *Turkey* 39 E11
Fethiye Körfezi, *Turkey* .. 39 E10
Fetlar, *U.K.* 14 A8
Feuilles →, *Canada* 101 C12
Feurs, *France* 21 C8
Fezzan, *Libya* 79 C8
Fiambalá, *Argentina* 126 B2
Fianarantsoa, *Madag.* 89 C8
Fianarantsoa □, *Madag.* .. 89 B8
Fichtelgebirge, *Germany* .. 25 E7
Ficksburg, *S. Africa* 89 D4
Fidenza, *Italy* 28 D7
Fiditi, *Nigeria* 83 D5
Field, *Canada* 102 C3
Field →, *Australia* 94 C2
Field I., *Australia* 92 B5
Fieni, *Romania* 43 E10
Fieri, *Albania* 40 F3
Fierzë, *Albania* 40 D4
Fife □, *U.K.* 14 E5
Fife Ness, *U.K.* 14 E6
Fifth Cataract, *Sudan* 80 D3
Figari, *France* 21 G13
Figeac, *France* 20 D6
Figeholm, *Sweden* 11 G10
Figline Valdarno, *Italy* ... 29 E8
Figtree, *Zimbabwe* 87 G2
Figueira Castelo Rodrigo,
Portugal 34 E4
Figueira da Foz, *Portugal* . 34 E2
Figueiró dos Vinhos,
Portugal 34 F2
Figueres, *Spain* 32 C7
Figuig, *Morocco* 78 B5
Fihaonana, *Madag.* 89 B8
Fiherenana, *Madag.* 89 B8
Fiherenana →, *Madag.* .. 89 C7
Fiji ■, *Pac. Oc.* 91 C8
Fika, *Nigeria* 83 C7
Filabres, Sierra de los,
Spain 35 H8
Filadélfia, *Italy* 31 D9
Fil'akovo, *Slovak Rep.* ... 27 C12
Filer, *U.S.A.* 114 E6
Filey, *U.K.* 12 C7
Filey B., *U.K.* 12 C7
Filfla, *Malta* 36 D1
Filiaşi, *Romania* 43 F8
Filiátes, *Greece* 38 B2
Filiatrá, *Greece* 38 D3
Filicudi, *Italy* 31 D7
Filingué, *Niger* 83 C5
Filiourí →, *Greece* 41 E9
Filipstad, *Sweden* 10 E8
Filisur, *Switz.* 25 J5
Fillmore, *Canada* 105 D8
Fillmore, *Calif., U.S.A.* .. 117 L8
Fillmore, *Utah, U.S.A.* ... 115 G7
Filótion, *Greece* 39 D7
Filottrano, *Italy* 29 E10
Finale Emília, *Italy* 29 D8
Finale Lígure, *Italy* 28 D5
Fiñana, *Spain* 35 H8
Finch, *Canada* 111 A9
Findhorn →, *U.K.* 14 D5
Findlay, *U.S.A.* 108 E4
Finger L., *Canada* 105 C10
Fíngoè, *Mozam.* 87 E3
Finike, *Turkey* 39 E12
Finike Körfezi, *Turkey* ... 39 E12
Finiq, *Albania* 40 G4
Finistère □, *France* 18 D3
Finisterre = Fisterra, *Spain* 34 C1
Finisterre, C. = Fisterra,
C., *Spain* 34 C1
Finke, *Australia* 94 D1
Finke →, *Australia* 95 D2
Finland ■, *Europe* 8 E22
Finland, G. of, *Europe* ... 9 G21
Finlay →, *Canada* 104 B3
Finley, *Australia* 95 F4
Finley, *U.S.A.* 112 B6
Finn →, *Ireland* 15 B4
Finnerödja, *Sweden* 11 F8
Finnigan, Mt., *Australia* .. 94 B4
Finniss, C., *Australia* 95 E1
Finnmark, *Norway* 8 B20
Finnsnes, *Norway* 8 B18
Finspång, *Sweden* 11 F9
Finsteraarhorn, *Switz.* 25 J4
Finsterwalde, *Germany* ... 24 D9
Fiora →, *Italy* 29 F8
Fiorenzuola d'Arda, *Italy* . 28 D6
Fīq, *Syria* 75 C4
Firat = Furāt, Nahr al →,
Asia 70 D5
Fire River, *Canada* 102 C3
Firebag →, *Canada* 105 B6
Firebaugh, *U.S.A.* 116 J6
Firedrake L., *Canada* 105 A8
Firenze, *Italy* 29 E8
Firenzuola, *Italy* 29 D8
Firk →, *Iraq* 70 D5
Firmi, *France* 20 D6
Firminy, *France* 21 C8
Firozabad, *India* 69 F8
Firozpur, *India* 68 D6
Fīrūzābād, *Iran* 71 D7
Fīrūzkūh, *Iran* 71 C7
Firvale, *Canada* 104 C3
Fish →, *Namibia* 88 D2
Fish →, *S. Africa* 88 E3
Fisher, *Australia* 93 F5
Fisher B., *Canada* 105 C9
Fishguard, *U.K.* 13 E3
Fishing L., *Canada* 105 C9
Fismes, *France* 19 C10
Fisterra, *Spain* 34 C1
Fisterra, C., *Spain* 34 C1
Fitchburg, *U.S.A.* 111 D13
Fitz Roy, *Argentina* 128 F3
Fitzgerald, *Canada* 104 B6
Fitzgerald, *U.S.A.* 109 K4
Fitzmaurice →, *Australia* 92 B5
Fitzroy →, *Queens.,*
Australia 94 C5
Fitzroy →, *W. Austral.,*
Australia 92 C3
Fitzroy, Mte., *Argentina* .. 128 F2
Fitzroy Crossing, *Australia* 92 C4
Fitzwilliam I., *Canada* 110 A3
Fiuggi, *Italy* 29 G10
Fiume = Rijeka, *Croatia* . 29 C11
Five Points, *U.S.A.* 116 J6
Fivizzano, *Italy* 28 D7
Fizi,
Dem. Rep. of the Congo 86 C2
Fjällbacka, *Sweden* 11 F5
Fjärdhundra, *Sweden* 10 E10
Fjellerup, *Denmark* 11 H4
Fjerritslev, *Denmark* 11 G3
Fjugesta, *Sweden* 10 E8
Flagler, *U.S.A.* 112 F3
Flagstaff, *U.S.A.* 115 J8
Flaherty I., *Canada* 102 A4
Flåm, *Norway* 9 F12
Flambeau →, *U.S.A.* 112 C9
Flamborough Hd., *U.K.* .. 12 C7
Fläming, *Germany* 24 C8
Flaming Gorge Dam,
U.S.A. 114 F9
Flaming Gorge Reservoir,
U.S.A. 114 F9
Flamingo, Teluk, *Indonesia* 63 F9
Flanders = Flandre,
Europe 19 B9
Flandre, *Europe* 19 B9
Flandre Occidentale =
West-Vlaanderen □,
Belgium 17 D2
Flandre Orientale = Oost-
Vlaanderen □, *Belgium* 17 C3
Flandreau, *U.S.A.* 112 C6
Flanigan, *U.S.A.* 116 E7
Flannan Is., *U.K.* 14 C1
Flåsjön, *Sweden* 8 D16
Flat →, *Canada* 104 A3
Flat River, *U.S.A.* 113 G9
Flathead L., *U.S.A.* 114 C7
Flattery, C., *Australia* 94 A4
Flattery, C., *U.S.A.* 116 B2
Flaxton, *U.S.A.* 112 A3
Fleetwood, *U.K.* 12 D4
Flekkefjord, *Norway* 9 G12
Flemington, *U.S.A.* 110 E7
Flen, *Sweden* 10 E10
Flensburg, *Germany* 24 A5
Flers, *France* 18 D6
Flesherton, *Canada* 110 B4
Flesko, Tanjung, *Indonesia* 63 D6
Fleurance, *France* 20 E4
Fleurier, *Switz.* 25 J2
Flevoland □, *Neths.* 17 B5
Flin Flon, *Canada* 105 C8
Flinders →, *Australia* 94 B3
Flinders B., *Australia* 93 F2

Flinders Group, *Australia* 94 A3
Flinders I., *Australia* 94 G4
Flinders Ranges, *Australia* 95 E2
Flinders Reefs, *Australia* 94 B4
Flint, *U.K.* 12 D4
Flint, *U.S.A.* 108 D4
Flint →, *U.S.A.* 109 K3
Flint I., *Kiribati* 97 J12
Flinton, *Australia* 95 D4
Flintshire □, *U.K.* 12 D4
Fliseryd, *Sweden* 11 G10
Flix, *Spain* 32 D5
Flixecourt, *France* 19 B9
Floby, *Sweden* 11 F7
Floda, *Sweden* 11 G6
Flodden, *U.K.* 12 B5
Flogny-la-Chapelle, *France* 19 E10
Floodwood, *U.S.A.* 112 B8
Flora, *U.S.A.* 108 F1
Florac, *France* 20 D7
Florala, *U.S.A.* 109 K2
Florence = Firenze, *Italy* 29 E8
Florence, *Ala., U.S.A.* 109 H2
Florence, *Ariz., U.S.A.* 115 K8
Florence, *Colo., U.S.A.* 112 F2
Florence, *Oreg., U.S.A.* 114 E1
Florence, *S.C., U.S.A.* 109 H6
Florence, L., *Australia* 95 D2
Florencia, *Colombia* 124
Florennes, *Belgium* 17 D4
Florensac, *France* 20 E7
Florenville, *Belgium* 17 E5
Flores, *Guatemala* 120 C2
Flores, *Indonesia* 63 F6
Flores I., *Canada* 104 D3
Flores Sea, *Indonesia* 63 F6
Floreşti, *Moldova* 43 C13
Floresville, *U.S.A.* 113 L5
Floriano, *Brazil* 125 E10
Florianópolis, *Brazil* 127 B6
Florida, *Cuba* 120 B4
Florida, *Uruguay* 127 C4
Florida □, *U.S.A.* 109 L5
Florida, Straits of, *U.S.A.* 120 B4
Florida B., *U.S.A.* 120 B3
Florida Keys, *U.S.A.* 107 F10
Florídia, *Italy* 31 E8
Flórina, *Greece* 40 F5
Flórina □, *Greece* 40 F5
Florø, *Norway* 9 F11
Flower Station, *Canada* 111 A8
Flower's Cove, *Canada* 103 B8
Floydada, *U.S.A.* 113 J4
Fluk, *Indonesia* 63 E7
Flúmen →, *Spain* 32 D4
Flumendosa →, *Italy* 30 C2
Fluminimaggiore, *Italy* 30 C1
Flushing = Vlissingen, *Neths.* 17 C3
Fluviá →, *Spain* 32 C8
Flying Fish, C., *Antarctica* 5 D15
Foam Lake, *Canada* 105 C8
Foča, *Bos.-H.* 40 C2
Foça, *Turkey* 39 C8
Focşani, *Romania* 43 E12
Fogang, *China* 59 F9
Fóggia, *Italy* 31 A8
Foggo, *Nigeria* 83 C6
Foglia →, *Italy* 29 E9
Fogo, *Canada* 103 C9
Fogo I., *Canada* 103 C9
Fohnsdorf, *Austria* 26 D7
Föhr, *Germany* 24 A4
Foia, *Portugal* 35 H2
Foix, *France* 20 E5
Fojnica, *Bos.-H.* 42 G2
Fokino, *Russia* 46 F8
Fokís □, *Greece* 38 C4
Folda, *Nord-Trøndelag, Norway* 8 D14
Folda, *Nordland, Norway* 8 C16
Főldeák, *Hungary* 42 D5
Folégandros, *Greece* 38 E6
Foleyet, *Canada* 102 C3
Folgefonni, *Norway* 9 F12
Foligno, *Italy* 29 F9
Folkestone, *U.K.* 13 F9
Folkston, *U.S.A.* 109 K5
Follett, *U.S.A.* 113 G4
Follónica, *Italy* 28 F7
Follónica, G. di, *Italy* 28 F7
Folsom Res., *U.S.A.* 116 G5
Folteşti, *Romania* 43 E13
Fond-du-Lac, *Canada* 105 B7
Fond du Lac, *U.S.A.* 112 D10
Fond-du-Lac →, *Canada* 105 B7
Fonda, *U.S.A.* 111 D10
Fondi, *Italy* 30 A6
Fonfría, *Spain* 34 D4
Fonni, *Italy* 30 B2
Fonsagrada = A Fonsagrada, *Spain* 34 B3
Fonseca, G. de, *Cent. Amer.* 120 D2
Font-Romeu, *France* 20 F5
Fontaine-Française, *France* 19 E12
Fontainebleau, *France* 19 D9
Fontana, *U.S.A.* 117 L9
Fontas →, *Canada* 104 B4
Fonte Boa, *Brazil* 124 D5
Fontem, *Cameroon* 83 D6
Fontenay-le-Comte, *France* 20 B3
Fontur, *Iceland* 8 C6
Fonyód, *Hungary* 42 D2
Foochow = Fuzhou, *China* 59 D12
Foping, *China* 56 H5
Forbach, *France* 19 C13
Forbes, *Australia* 95 E4
Forbesganj, *India* 69 F12
Forcados, *Nigeria* 83 D6
Forcados →, *Nigeria* 83 D6
Forcalquier, *France* 21 E9
Forchheim, *Germany* 25 F7
Ford City, *Calif., U.S.A.* 117 K7
Ford City, *Pa., U.S.A.* 110 F5
Førde, *Norway* 9 F11
Ford's Bridge, *Australia* 95 D4
Fordyce, *U.S.A.* 113 J8
Forécariah, *Guinea* 82 D2
Forel, Mt., *Greenland* 4 C6
Foremost, *Canada* 104 D6
Forest, *Canada* 110 C3
Forest, *U.S.A.* 113 J10
Forest City, *Iowa, U.S.A.* 112 D8
Forest City, *N.C., U.S.A.* 109 H5
Forest City, *Pa., U.S.A.* 111 E9
Forest Grove, *U.S.A.* 116 E3
Forestburg, *Canada* 104 C6
Foresthill, *U.S.A.* 116 F6
Forestier Pen., *Australia* 94 G4
Forestville, *Canada* 103 C6
Forestville, *Calif., U.S.A.* 116 G4
Forestville, *Wis., U.S.A.* 108 C2
Forez, Mts. du, *France* 20 C7
Forfar, *U.K.* 14 E6
Forks, *U.S.A.* 116 C2
Forlì, *Italy* 29 D9
Forman, *U.S.A.* 112 B6
Formazza, *Italy* 28 B5
Formby Pt., *U.K.* 12 D4
Formentera, *Spain* 37 C7
Formentor, C. de, *Spain* 37 B10
Former Yugoslav Republic of Macedonia = Macedonia ■, *Europe* 40 E5
Fórmia, *Italy* 30 A6
Formígine, *Italy* 28 D7
Formosa = Taiwan ■, *Asia* 59 F13
Formosa, *Argentina* 126 B4
Formosa, *Brazil* 125 G9
Formosa □, *Argentina* 126 B4
Formosa, Serra, *Brazil* 125 F8
Formosa Bay, *Kenya* 86 C5
Formosa Strait, *Asia* 59 E12
Fornells, *Spain* 37 A11
Fornos de Algodres, *Portugal* 34 E3
Fornovo di Taro, *Italy* 28 D7
Føroyar, *Atl. Oc.* 8 F9
Forres, *U.K.* 14 D5
Forrest, *Vic., Australia* 95 F3
Forrest, *W. Austral., Australia* 93 F4
Forrest, Mt., *Australia* 93 D4
Forrest City, *U.S.A.* 113 H9
Fors, *Sweden* 10 D10
Forsayth, *Australia* 94 B3
Forshaga, *Sweden* 10 E7
Förslöv, *Sweden* 11 H6
Forsmo, *Sweden* 10 A11
Forssa, *Finland* 9 F20
Forst, *Germany* 24 D10
Forster, *Australia* 95 E5
Forsvik, *Sweden* 11 F8
Forsyth, *Ga., U.S.A.* 109 J4
Forsyth, *Mont., U.S.A.* 114 C10
Fort Albany, *Canada* 102 B3
Fort Apache, *U.S.A.* 115 K9
Fort Assiniboine, *Canada* 104 C6
Fort Augustus, *U.K.* 14 D4
Fort Beaufort, *S. Africa* 88 E4
Fort Benton, *U.S.A.* 114 C8
Fort Bragg, *U.S.A.* 114 G2
Fort Bridger, *U.S.A.* 114 F8
Fort Chipewyan, *Canada* 105 B6
Fort Collins, *U.S.A.* 112 E2
Fort-Coulonge, *Canada* 102 C4
Fort Davis, *U.S.A.* 113 K3
Fort-de-France, *Martinique* 121 D7
Fort Defiance, *U.S.A.* 115 J9
Fort Dodge, *U.S.A.* 112 D7
Fort Edward, *U.S.A.* 111 C11
Fort Frances, *Canada* 105 D10
Fort Garland, *U.S.A.* 115 H11
Fort George = Chisasibi, *Canada* 102 B4
Fort Good-Hope, *Canada* 100 B7
Fort Hancock, *U.S.A.* 115 L11
Fort Hertz = Putao, *Burma* 67 F20
Fort Hope, *Canada* 102 B2
Fort Irwin, *U.S.A.* 117 K10
Fort Jameson = Chipata, *Zambia* 87 E3
Fort Kent, *U.S.A.* 103 C6
Fort Klamath, *U.S.A.* 114 E3
Fort-Lamy = Ndjamena, *Chad* 79 F8
Fort Laramie, *U.S.A.* 112 D2
Fort Lauderdale, *U.S.A.* 109 M5
Fort Liard, *Canada* 104 A4
Fort Liberté, *Haiti* 121 C5
Fort Lupton, *U.S.A.* 112 E2
Fort Mackay, *Canada* 104 B6
Fort McKenzie, *Canada* 103 A6
Fort Macleod, *Canada* 104 D6
Fort McMurray, *Canada* 104 B6
Fort McPherson, *Canada* 100 B6
Fort Madison, *U.S.A.* 112 E9
Fort Meade, *U.S.A.* 109 M5
Fort Morgan, *U.S.A.* 112 E3
Fort Myers, *U.S.A.* 109 M5
Fort Nelson, *Canada* 104 B4
Fort Nelson →, *Canada* 104 B4
Fort Norman = Tulita, *Canada* 100 B7
Fort Payne, *U.S.A.* 109 H3
Fort Peck, *U.S.A.* 114 B10
Fort Peck Dam, *U.S.A.* 114 C10
Fort Peck L., *U.S.A.* 114 C10
Fort Pierce, *U.S.A.* 109 M5
Fort Pierre, *U.S.A.* 112 C4
Fort Plain, *U.S.A.* 111 D10
Fort Portal, *Uganda* 86 B3
Fort Providence, *Canada* 104 A5
Fort Qu'Appelle, *Canada* 105 C8
Fort Resolution, *Canada* 104 A6
Fort Rixon, *Zimbabwe* 87 G2
Fort Rosebery = Mansa, *Zambia* 87 E2
Fort Ross, *U.S.A.* 116 G3
Fort Rupert = Waskaganish, *Canada* 102 B4
Fort St. James, *Canada* 104 C4
Fort St. John, *Canada* 104 B4
Fort Sandeman = Zhob, *Pakistan* 68 D3
Fort Saskatchewan, *Canada* 104 C6
Fort Scott, *U.S.A.* 113 G7
Fort Severn, *Canada* 102 A2
Fort Shevchenko, *Kazakstan* 49 H10
Fort Simpson, *Canada* 104 A4
Fort Smith, *Canada* 104 B6
Fort Smith, *U.S.A.* 113 H7
Fort Stanton, *U.S.A.* 115 K11
Fort Stockton, *U.S.A.* 113 K3
Fort Sumner, *U.S.A.* 113 H2
Fort Trinquet = Bir Mogreïn, *Mauritania* 78 C3
Fort Valley, *U.S.A.* 109 J4
Fort Vermilion, *Canada* 104 B5
Fort Walton Beach, *U.S.A.* 109 K2
Fort Wayne, *U.S.A.* 108 E3
Fort William, *U.K.* 14 E3
Fort Worth, *U.S.A.* 113 J6
Fort Yates, *U.S.A.* 112 B4
Fort Yukon, *U.S.A.* 100 B5
Fortaleza, *Brazil* 125 D11
Forteau, *Canada* 103 B8
Forth →, *U.K.* 14 E5
Forth, Firth of, *U.K.* 14 E6
Fortore →, *Italy* 29 G12
Fortrose, *U.K.* 14 D4
Fortuna, *Spain* 33 G3
Fortuna, *Calif., U.S.A.* 114 F1
Fortuna, *N. Dak., U.S.A.* 112 A3
Fortune B., *Canada* 103 C8
Fos-sur-Mer, *France* 21 E8
Foshan, *China* 59 F9
Fosna, *Norway* 8 E14
Fosnavåg, *Norway* 9 E11
Fossano, *Italy* 28 D4
Fossil, *U.S.A.* 114 D3
Fossilbrook, *Australia* 94 B3
Fossombrone, *Italy* 29 E9
Fosston, *U.S.A.* 112 B7
Foster, *Canada* 111 A12
Foster →, *Canada* 105 B7
Fosters Ra., *Australia* 94 C1
Fostoria, *U.S.A.* 108 E4
Fouesnant, *France* 18 E2
Fougères, *France* 18 D5
Foul Pt., *Sri Lanka* 66 Q12
Foula, *U.K.* 14 A6
Foulness I., *U.K.* 13 F8
Foulpointe, *Madag.* 89 B8
Foumban, *Cameroon* 83 D7
Foundiougne, *Senegal* 82 C1
Fountain, *Colo., U.S.A.* 112 F2
Fountain, *Utah, U.S.A.* 114 G8
Fountain Springs, *U.S.A.* 117 K8
Fourchambault, *France* 19 E10
Fourchu, *Canada* 103 C7
Fouriesburg, *S. Africa* 88 D4
Fourmies, *France* 19 B11
Fournás, *Greece* 38 B3
Foúrnoi, *Greece* 39 D8
Fours, *France* 19 F10
Fouta Djalon, *Guinea* 82 C2
Foux, Cap-à-, *Haiti* 121 C5
Foveaux Str., *N.Z.* 91 M2
Fowey, *U.K.* 13 G3
Fowler, *Calif., U.S.A.* 116 J7
Fowler, *Colo., U.S.A.* 112 F3
Fowler, *Kans., U.S.A.* 113 G4
Fowlers B., *Australia* 93 F5
Fowlerton, *U.S.A.* 113 L5
Fowman, *Iran* 73 D13
Fox →, *Canada* 105 B10
Fox Valley, *Canada* 105 C7
Foxe Basin, *Canada* 4 C4
Foxe Chan., *Canada* 101 B12
Foxe Pen., *Canada* 101 B12
Foxen, *Sweden* 10 E5
Foxpark, *U.S.A.* 114 F10
Foxton, *N.Z.* 91 J5
Foyle, Lough, *U.K.* 15 A4
Foynes, *Ireland* 15 D2
Foz, *Spain* 34 B3
Fóz do Cunene, *Angola* 88 B1
Foz do Iguaçu, *Brazil* 127 B5
Frackville, *U.S.A.* 111 F8
Fraga, *Spain* 32 D5
Framingham, *U.S.A.* 111 D13
Frampol, *Poland* 45 H9
Franca, *Brazil* 125 H9
Francavilla al Mare, *Italy* 29 F11
Francavilla Fontana, *Italy* 31 B10
France ■, *Europe* 7 F6
Frances, *Australia* 95 F3
Frances →, *Canada* 104 A3
Frances L., *Canada* 104 A3
Francés Viejo, C., *Dom. Rep.* 121 C6
Franceville, *Gabon* 84 E2
Franche-Comté, *France* 19 F12
Francisco I. Madero, *Coahuila, Mexico* 118 B4
Francisco I. Madero, *Durango, Mexico* 118 C4
Francistown, *Botswana* 89 C4
Francofonte, *Italy* 31 E7
François, *Canada* 103 C8
François L., *Canada* 104 C3
Franeker, *Neths.* 17 A5
Frankado, *Djibouti* 81 E5
Frankenberg, *Germany* 24 D4
Frankenwald, *Germany* 25 E7
Frankfort, *S. Africa* 89 D4
Frankfort, *Ind., U.S.A.* 108 E2
Frankfort, *Kans., U.S.A.* 112 F6
Frankfort, *Ky., U.S.A.* 108 F3
Frankfort, *Mich., U.S.A.* 108 C2
Frankfurt, *Brandenburg, Germany* 24 C10
Frankfurt, *Hessen, Germany* 25 E4
Fränkische Alb, *Germany* 25 F7
Fränkische Rezat →, *Germany* 25 F7
Fränkische Saale →, *Germany* 25 E5
Fränkische Schweiz, *Germany* 25 F7
Frankland →, *Australia* 93 G2
Franklin, *Ky., U.S.A.* 109 G2
Franklin, *La., U.S.A.* 113 L9
Franklin, *Mass., U.S.A.* 111 D13
Franklin, *N.H., U.S.A.* 111 C13
Franklin, *Nebr., U.S.A.* 112 E5
Franklin, *Pa., U.S.A.* 110 E5
Franklin, *Tenn., U.S.A.* 109 H2
Franklin, *Va., U.S.A.* 109 G7
Franklin, *W. Va., U.S.A.* 108 F6
Franklin B., *Canada* 100 B7
Franklin D. Roosevelt L., *U.S.A.* 114 B4
Franklin I., *Antarctica* 5 D11
Franklin L., *U.S.A.* 114 F6
Franklin Mts., *Canada* 100 B7
Franklin Str., *Canada* 100 A10
Franklinton, *U.S.A.* 113 K9
Franklinville, *U.S.A.* 110 D6
Franks Pk., *U.S.A.* 114 E9
Frankston, *Australia* 95 F4
Frånö, *Sweden* 10 B11
Fränsta, *Sweden* 10 B10
Frantsa Iosifa, Zemlya, *Russia* 4 A10
Franz, *Canada* 102 C3
Franz Josef Land = Frantsa Iosifa, Zemlya, *Russia* 4 A10
Franzburg, *Germany* 24 A8
Frascati, *Italy* 29 G9
Fraser →, *B.C., Canada* 104 D4
Fraser →, *Nfld., Canada* 103 A7
Fraser, Mt., *Australia* 93 E2
Fraser I., *Australia* 95 D5
Fraser Lake, *Canada* 104 C4
Fraserburg, *S. Africa* 88 E3
Fraserburgh, *U.K.* 14 D6
Fraserdale, *Canada* 102 C3
Frashëri, *Albania* 40 F4
Frasne, *France* 19 F13
Frăteşti, *Romania* 43 G10
Frauenfeld, *Switz.* 25 H4
Fray Bentos, *Uruguay* 126 C4
Frazier Downs, *Australia* 92 C3
Frechilla, *Spain* 34 C6
Fredericia, *Denmark* 11 J3
Frederick, *Md., U.S.A.* 108 F7
Frederick, *Okla., U.S.A.* 113 H5
Frederick, *S. Dak., U.S.A.* 112 C5
Frederick Sd., *U.S.A.* 104 B2
Fredericksburg, *Tex., U.S.A.* 113 K5
Fredericksburg, *Va., U.S.A.* 108 F7
Fredericktown, *U.S.A.* 113 G9
Frederico I. Madero, Presa, *Mexico* 118 B3
Fredericton, *Canada* 103 C6
Fredericton Junc., *Canada* 103 C6
Frederiksborg Amtskommune □, *Denmark* 11 J6
Frederikshåb, *Greenland* 4 C5
Frederikshavn, *Denmark* 11 G4
Frederikssund, *Denmark* 11 J6
Frederiksted, *Virgin Is.* 121 C7
Frederiksværk, *Denmark* 11 J6
Fredonia, *Ariz., U.S.A.* 115 H7
Fredonia, *Kans., U.S.A.* 113 G7
Fredonia, *N.Y., U.S.A.* 110 D5
Fredriksberg, *Sweden* 10 D8
Fredrikstad, *Norway* 9 G14
Free State □, *S. Africa* 88 D4
Freehold, *U.S.A.* 111 F10
Freel Peak, *U.S.A.* 116 G7
Freeland, *U.S.A.* 111 E9
Freels, C., *Canada* 103 C9
Freeman, *Calif., U.S.A.* 117 K9
Freeman, *S. Dak., U.S.A.* 112 D6
Freeport, *Bahamas* 120 A4
Freeport, *Canada* 103 D6
Freeport, *Ill., U.S.A.* 112 D10
Freeport, *N.Y., U.S.A.* 111 F11
Freeport, *Tex., U.S.A.* 113 L7
Freetown, *S. Leone* 82 D2
Frégate, L., *Canada* 102 B5
Fregenal de la Sierra, *Spain* 35 G4
Fregene, *Italy* 29 G9
Fréhel, C., *France* 18 D4
Freiberg, *Germany* 24 E9
Freibourg = Fribourg, *Switz.* 25 J3
Freiburg, *Baden-W., Germany* 25 H3
Freiburg, *Niedersachsen, Germany* 24 B5
Freilassing, *Germany* 25 H8
Freire, *Chile* 128 D2
Freirina, *Chile* 126 B1
Freising, *Germany* 25 G7
Freistadt, *Austria* 26 C7
Freital, *Germany* 24 D9
Fréjus, *France* 21 E10
Fremantle, *Australia* 93 F2
Fremont, *Calif., U.S.A.* 116 H4
Fremont, *Mich., U.S.A.* 108 D3
Fremont, *Nebr., U.S.A.* 112 E6
Fremont, *Ohio, U.S.A.* 108 E4
Fremont →, *U.S.A.* 115 G8
Fremont L., *U.S.A.* 114 E9
French Camp, *U.S.A.* 116 H5
French Creek →, *U.S.A.* 110 E5
French Guiana ■, *S. Amer.* 125 C8
French Pass, *N.Z.* 91 J4
French Polynesia ■, *Pac. Oc.* 97 K13
Frenchglen, *U.S.A.* 114 E4
Frenchman Butte, *Canada* 105 C7
Frenchman Cr. →, *Mont., U.S.A.* 114 B10
Frenchman Cr. →, *Nebr., U.S.A.* 112 E4
Frenšt´t pod Radhoštěm, *Czech Rep.* 27 B11
Fresco →, *Brazil* 125 E8
Freshfield, C., *Antarctica* 5 C10
Fresnay-sur-Sarthe, *France* 18 D7
Fresnillo, *Mexico* 118 C4
Fresno, *U.S.A.* 116 J7
Fresno Alhandiga, *Spain* 34 E5
Fresno Reservoir, *U.S.A.* 114 B9
Freudenstadt, *Germany* 25 G4
Frévent, *France* 19 B9
Frew →, *Australia* 94 C2
Frewena, *Australia* 94 B2
Freycinet Pen., *Australia* 94 G4
Freyming-Merlebach, *France* 19 C13
Freyung, *Germany* 25 G9
Fria, *Guinea* 82 C2
Fria, C., *Namibia* 88 B1
Friant, *U.S.A.* 116 J7
Frías, *Argentina* 126 B2
Fribourg, *Switz.* 25 J3
Fribourg □, *Switz.* 25 J3
Fridafors, *Sweden* 11 H8
Friday Harbor, *U.S.A.* 116 B3
Friedberg, *Bayern, Germany* 25 G6
Friedberg, *Hessen, Germany* 25 E4
Friedland, *Germany* 24 B9
Friedrichshafen, *Germany* 25 H5
Friedrichskoog, *Germany* 24 A4
Friedrichstadt, *Germany* 24 A5
Friendly Is. = Tonga ■, *Pac. Oc.* 91 D11
Friesach, *Austria* 26 E7
Friesack, *Germany* 24 C8
Friesland □, *Neths.* 17 A5
Friesoythe, *Germany* 24 B3
Friggesund, *Sweden* 10 C10
Frillesås, *Sweden* 11 G6
Frinnaryd, *Sweden* 11 G8
Frio →, *U.S.A.* 113 L5
Frio, C., *Brazil* 122 F6
Friol, *Spain* 34 B3
Friona, *U.S.A.* 113 H3
Fristad, *Sweden* 11 G6
Fritch, *U.S.A.* 113 H4
Fritsla, *Sweden* 11 G6
Fritzlar, *Germany* 24 D5
Friuli-Venézia Giulia □, *Italy* 29 B9
Frobisher B., *Canada* 101 B13
Frobisher Bay = Iqaluit, *Canada* 101 B13
Frobisher L., *Canada* 105 B7
Frohavet, *Norway* 8 E13
Frohnleiten, *Austria* 26 D8
Froid, *U.S.A.* 112 A2
Frolovo, *Russia* 48 F6
Fromberg, *U.S.A.* 114 D9
Frombork, *Poland* 44 D6
Frome, *U.K.* 13 F5
Frome →, *U.K.* 13 G5
Frome, L., *Australia* 95 E2
Frome Downs, *Australia* 95 E2
Frómista, *Spain* 34 C6
Front Range, *U.S.A.* 114 G11
Front Royal, *U.S.A.* 108 F6
Fronteira, *Portugal* 35 F3
Frontera, *Canary Is.* 37 G2
Frontera, *Mexico* 119 D6
Frontignan, *France* 20 E7
Frosinone, *Italy* 30 A6
Frostburg, *U.S.A.* 108 F6
Frostisen, *Norway* 8 B17
Frouard, *France* 19 D13
Frövi, *Sweden* 10 E9

Frøya, *Norway* 8 E13
Frumoasa, *Romania* 43 D10
Frunze = Bishkek, *Kyrgyzstan* 50 E8
Fruška Gora, *Serbia, Yug.* 42 E4
Frutal, *Brazil* 125 H9
Frutigen, *Switz.* 25 J3
Frýdek-Místek, *Czech Rep.* 27 B11
Frýdlant, *Czech Rep.* 26 A8
Fryvaldov = Jeseník, *Czech Rep.* 27 A10
Fthiótis □, *Greece* 38 C4
Fu Jiang →, *China* 58 C6
Fu Xian, *Liaoning, China* 57 E11
Fu Xian, *Shaanxi, China* 56 G5
Fu'an, *China* 59 D12
Fubian, *China* 58 B4
Fucécchio, *Italy* 28 E7
Fucheng, *China* 56 F9
Fuchou = Fuzhou, *China* 59 D12
Fuchū, *Japan* 55 G6
Fuchuan, *China* 59 E8
Fuchun Jiang →, *China* 59 B13
Fúcino, Piana del, *Italy* 29 F10
Fuding, *China* 59 D13
Fuencaliente, *Canary Is.* 37 F2
Fuencaliente, *Spain* 35 G6
Fuencaliente, Pta., *Canary Is.* 37 F2
Fuengirola, *Spain* 35 J6
Fuenlabrada, *Spain* 34 E7
Fuensalida, *Spain* 34 E6
Fuente-Alamo, *Spain* 33 G3
Fuente-Álamo de Murcia, *Spain* 33 H3
Fuente de Cantos, *Spain* 35 G4
Fuente del Maestre, *Spain* 35 G4
Fuente el Fresno, *Spain* 35 F7
Fuente Obejuna, *Spain* 35 G5
Fuente Palmera, *Spain* 35 H5
Fuentes de Andalucía, *Spain* 35 H5
Fuentes de Ebro, *Spain* 32 D4
Fuentes de León, *Spain* 35 G4
Fuentes de Oñoro, *Spain* 34 E4
Fuentesaúco, *Spain* 34 D5
Fuerte →, *Mexico* 118 B3
Fuerte Olimpo, *Paraguay* 126 A4
Fuerteventura, *Canary Is.* 37 F6
Fufeng, *China* 56 G5
Fuga I., *Phil.* 61 B4
Fugong, *China* 58 D2
Fugou, *China* 56 G8
Fugu, *China* 56 E6
Fuhai, *China* 60 B3
Fuḥaymī, *Iraq* 70 C4
Fuji, *Japan* 55 G9
Fuji-San, *Japan* 55 G9
Fuji-yoshida, *Japan* 55 G9
Fujian □, *China* 59 E12
Fujinomiya, *Japan* 55 G9
Fujisawa, *Japan* 55 G9
Fukien = Fujian □, *China* 59 E12
Fukuchiyama, *Japan* 55 G7
Fukue-Shima, *Japan* 55 H4
Fukui, *Japan* 55 F8
Fukui □, *Japan* 55 G8
Fukuoka, *Japan* 55 H5
Fukuoka □, *Japan* 55 H5
Fukushima, *Japan* 54 F10
Fukushima □, *Japan* 54 F10
Fukuyama, *Japan* 55 G6
Fulda, *Germany* 24 E5
Fulda →, *Germany* 24 D5
Fuling, *China* 58 C6
Fullerton, *Calif., U.S.A.* 117 M9
Fullerton, *Nebr., U.S.A.* 112 E6
Fulongquan, *China* 57 B13
Fülöpszállás, *Hungary* 42 D4
Fulton, *Mo., U.S.A.* 112 F9
Fulton, *N.Y., U.S.A.* 111 C8
Fulton, *Tenn., U.S.A.* 109 G1
Fuluälven →, *Sweden* 10 C7
Fulufjället, *Sweden* 10 C6
Fumay, *France* 19 C11
Fumel, *France* 20 D4
Fumin, *China* 58 E4
Funabashi, *Japan* 55 G10
Funäsdalen, *Sweden* 10 B6
Funchal, *Madeira* 37 D3
Fundación, *Colombia* 124 A4
Fundão, *Portugal* 34 E3
Fundu Moldovei, *Romania* 43 C10
Fundulea, *Romania* 43 F11
Fundy, B. of, *Canada* 103 D6
Funing, *Hebei, China* 57 E10
Funing, *Jiangsu, China* 57 H10
Funing, *Yunnan, China* 58 F5
Funiu Shan, *China* 56 H7
Funsi, *Ghana* 82 C4
Funtua, *Nigeria* 83 C6
Fuping, *Hebei, China* 56 E8
Fuping, *Shaanxi, China* 56 G5
Fuqing, *China* 59 E12
Fuquan, *China* 58 D6
Furano, *Japan* 54 C11
Furāt, Nahr al →, *Asia* 70 D5
Fūrg, *Iran* 71 D7
Furmanov, *Russia* 48 B5
Furmanovo, *Kazakstan* 48 F9
Furnás, *Spain* 37 B8
Furnas, Reprêsa de, *Brazil* 127 A6
Furneaux Group, *Australia* 94 G4
Furqlus, *Syria* 75 A6
Fürstenau, *Germany* 24 C3
Fürstenberg, *Germany* 24 B9
Fürstenfeld, *Austria* 26 D9
Fürstenfeldbruck, *Germany* 25 G7
Fürstenwalde, *Germany* 24 C10
Fürth, *Germany* 25 F6
Furth im Wald, *Germany* 25 F8
Furtwangen, *Germany* 25 G4
Furudal, *Sweden* 10 C9
Furukawa, *Japan* 54 E10
Furulund, *Sweden* 11 J7
Fury and Hecla Str., *Canada* 101 B11
Fusagasuga, *Colombia* 124 C4
Fuscaldo, *Italy* 31 C9
Fushan, *Shandong, China* 57 F11
Fushan, *Shanxi, China* 56 G6
Fushë Arrëzi, *Albania* 40 D4
Fushë-Krujë, *Albania* 40 E3
Fushun, *Liaoning, China* 57 D12
Fushun, *Sichuan, China* 58 C5
Fusong, *China* 57 C14
Füssen, *Germany* 25 H6
Fusui, *China* 58 F6
Futog, *Yugoslavia* 42 E4
Futuna, *Wall. & F. Is.* 91 B8
Fuwa, *Egypt* 80 H7
Fuxin, *China* 57 C11
Fuyang, *Anhui, China* 56 H8
Fuyang, *Zhejiang, China* 59 B12
Fuyang He →, *China* 56 E9
Fuying Dao, *China* 59 D13
Fuyu, *China* 57 B13
Fuyuan, *Heilongjiang, China* 60 B8
Fuyuan, *Yunnan, China* 58 E5
Füzesgyarmat, *Hungary* 42 C6
Fuzhou, *China* 59 D12
Fylde, *U.K.* 12 D5
Fyn, *Denmark* 11 J4
Fyne, L., *U.K.* 14 F3
Fyns Amtskommune □, *Denmark* 11 J4
Fynshav, *Denmark* 11 K3

G

Gaanda, *Nigeria* 83 C7
Gabarin, *Nigeria* 83 C7
Gabas →, *France* 20 E3
Gabela, *Angola* 84 G2
Gabès, *Tunisia* 79 B8
Gabès, G. de, *Tunisia* 79 B8
Gabgaba, W. →, *Egypt* 80 C3
Gąbin, *Poland* 45 F6
Gabon ■, *Africa* 84 E2
Gaborone, *Botswana* 88 C4
Gabriels, *U.S.A.* 111 B10
Gābrīk, *Iran* 71 E8
Gabrovo, *Bulgaria* 41 D9
Gacé, *France* 18 D7
Gāch Sār, *Iran* 71 B6
Gachsārān, *Iran* 71 D6
Gacko, *Bos.-H.* 40 C2
Gadag, *India* 66 M9
Gadamai, *Sudan* 81 D4
Gadap, *Pakistan* 68 G2
Gadarwara, *India* 69 H8
Gadebusch, *Germany* 24 B7
Gadein, *Sudan* 81 F2
Gadhada, *India* 68 J4
Gádor, Sierra de, *Spain* 35 J8
Gadsden, *Ala., U.S.A.* 109 H3
Gadsden, *Ariz., U.S.A.* 115 K6
Gadwal, *India* 66 L10
Gadyach = Hadyach, *Ukraine* 47 G8
Găeşti, *Romania* 43 F10
Gaeta, *Italy* 30 A6
Gaeta, G. di, *Italy* 30 A6
Gaffney, *U.S.A.* 109 H5
Gafsa, *Tunisia* 78 B7
Gagarin, *Russia* 46 E8
Gagetown, *Canada* 103 C6
Gaggenau, *Germany* 25 G4
Gagino, *Russia* 48 C7
Gagliano del Capo, *Italy* 31 C11
Gagnef, *Sweden* 10 D9
Gagnoa, *Ivory C.* 82 D3
Gagnon, *Canada* 103 B6
Gagnon, L., *Canada* 105 A6
Gagra, *Georgia* 49 J5
Gahini, *Rwanda* 86 C3
Gahmar, *India* 69 G10
Gai Xian, *China* 57 D12
Gaïdhouronísi, *Greece* 36 E7
Gail, *U.S.A.* 113 J4
Gail →, *Austria* 26 E6
Gaillac, *France* 20 E5
Gaillimh = Galway, *Ireland* 15 C2
Gaillon, *France* 18 C8
Gaines, *U.S.A.* 110 E7
Gainesville, *Fla., U.S.A.* 109 L4
Gainesville, *Ga., U.S.A.* 109 H4
Gainesville, *Mo., U.S.A.* 113 G8
Gainesville, *Tex., U.S.A.* 113 J6
Gainsborough, *U.K.* 12 D7
Gairdner, L., *Australia* 95 E2
Gairloch, L., *U.K.* 14 D3
Gaj, *Croatia* 42 E2
Gakuch, *Pakistan* 69 A5
Galán, Cerro, *Argentina* 126 B2
Galana →, *Kenya* 86 C5
Galanta, *Slovak Rep.* 27 C10
Galapagar, *Spain* 34 E7
Galápagos, *Pac. Oc.* 122 D1
Galashiels, *U.K.* 14 F6
Galatás, *Greece* 38 D5
Galaţi, *Romania* 43 E13
Galaţi □, *Romania* 43 E12
Galatia, *Turkey* 72 C5
Galatina, *Italy* 31 B11
Galátone, *Italy* 31 B11
Galax, *U.S.A.* 109 G5
Galaxídhion, *Greece* 38 C4
Galbraith, *Australia* 94 B3
Galcaio, *Somali Rep.* 74 F4
Galdhøpiggen, *Norway* 9 F12
Galeana, *Mexico* 118 C4
Galela, *Indonesia* 63 D7
Galera, *Spain* 33 H2
Galera Point, *Trin. & Tob.* 121 D7
Galesburg, *U.S.A.* 112 E9
Galeton, *U.S.A.* 110 E7
Gali, *Georgia* 49 J5
Galicea Mare, *Romania* 43 F8
Galich, *Russia* 48 A6
Galiche, *Bulgaria* 40 C7
Galicia □, *Spain* 34 C3
Galilee = Hagalil, *Israel* 75 C4
Galilee, L., *Australia* 94 C4
Galilee, Sea of = Yam Kinneret, *Israel* 75 C4
Galinoporni, *Cyprus* 36 D13
Galion, *U.S.A.* 110 F2
Galiuro Mts., *U.S.A.* 115 K8
Gallabat, *Sudan* 81 E4
Gallan Hd., *U.K.* 14 C1
Gallarate, *Italy* 28 C5
Gallatin, *U.S.A.* 109 G2
Galle, *Sri Lanka* 66 R12
Gállego →, *Spain* 32 D4
Gallegos →, *Argentina* 128 G3
Galley Hd., *Ireland* 15 E3
Galliate, *Italy* 28 C5
Gallinas, Pta., *Colombia* 124 A4
Gallipoli = Gelibolu, *Turkey* 41 F10
Gallípoli, *Italy* 31 B10
Gallipolis, *U.S.A.* 108 F4
Gällivare, *Sweden* 8 C19
Gallneukirchen, *Austria* 26 C7
Gällö, *Sweden* 10 B9
Gallo, C., *Italy* 30 D6
Gallocanta, L. de, *Spain* 32 E3
Galloway, *U.K.* 14 F4
Galloway, Mull of, *U.K.* 14 G4
Gallup, *U.S.A.* 115 J9
Gallur, *Spain* 32 D3
Galong, *Australia* 95 E4
Galoya, *Sri Lanka* 66 Q12
Galt, *U.S.A.* 116 G5
Galten, *Denmark* 11 H3
Galtür, *Austria* 26 E3
Galty Mts., *Ireland* 15 D3
Galtymore, *Ireland* 15 D3
Galva, *U.S.A.* 112 E9
Galve de Sorbe, *Spain* 32 D1
Galveston, *U.S.A.* 113 L7
Galveston B., *U.S.A.* 113 L7
Gálvez, *Argentina* 126 C3
Galway, *Ireland* 15 C2
Galway □, *Ireland* 15 C2
Galway B., *Ireland* 15 C2
Gam →, *Vietnam* 64 B5
Gamagori, *Japan* 55 G8
Gamari, L., *Ethiopia* 81 E5
Gamawa, *Nigeria* 83 C7
Gamay, *Phil.* 61 E6
Gambaga, *Ghana* 83 C4
Gambat, *Pakistan* 68 F3
Gambela, *Ethiopia* 81 F3
Gambia ■, *W. Afr.* 82 C1
Gambia →, *W. Afr.* 82 C1
Gambier, C., *Australia* 92 B5
Gambier Is., *Australia* 95 F2
Gamboli, *Pakistan* 68 E3
Gamboma, *Congo* 84 E3
Gamerco, *U.S.A.* 115 J9
Gamla Uppsala, *Sweden* 10 E11
Gamlakarleby = Kokkola, *Finland* 8 E20
Gamleby, *Sweden* 11 G10
Gammon →, *Canada* 105 C9
Gamu-Gofa □, *Ethiopia* 81 F4
Gan, *France* 20 E3
Gan Goriama, Mts., *Cameroon* 83 D7
Gan Jiang →, *China* 59 C11
Ganado, *Ariz., U.S.A.* 115 J9
Ganado, *Tex., U.S.A.* 113 L6
Gananoque, *Canada* 102 D4
Ganāveh, *Iran* 71 D6
Gäncä, *Azerbaijan* 49 K8
Gancheng, *China* 64 C7
Gand = Gent, *Belgium* 17 C3
Ganda, *Angola* 85 G2
Gandak →, *India* 69 G11
Gandava, *Pakistan* 68 E2
Gander, *Canada* 103 C9
Gander L., *Canada* 103 C9
Ganderkesee, *Germany* 24 B4
Ganderowe Falls, *Zimbabwe* 87 F2
Gandesa, *Spain* 32 D5
Gandhi Sagar, *India* 68 G6
Gandi, *Nigeria* 83 C6
Gandía, *Spain* 33 G4
Gandino, *Italy* 28 C6
Gando, Pta., *Canary Is.* 37 G4
Gandole, *Nigeria* 83 D7
Ganedidalem = Gani, *Indonesia* 63 E7
Ganetti, *Sudan* 80 D3
Ganga →, *India* 69 H14
Ganganagar, *India* 68 E5
Gangapur, *India* 68 F7
Gangara, *Niger* 83 C6
Gangaw, *Burma* 67 H19
Gangdisê Shan, *China* 67 D12
Ganges = Ganga →, *India* 69 H14
Ganges, *France* 20 E7
Ganges, Mouths of the, *India* 69 J14
Gånghester, *Sweden* 11 G7
Gangi, *Italy* 31 E7
Gângiova, *Romania* 43 G8
Gangoh, *India* 68 E7
Gangtok, *India* 67 F16
Gangu, *China* 56 G3
Gangyao, *China* 57 B14
Gani, *Indonesia* 63 E7
Ganj, *India* 69 F8
Gannat, *France* 19 F10
Gannett Peak, *U.S.A.* 114 E9
Gannvalley, *U.S.A.* 112 C5
Ganquan, *China* 56 F5
Gänserdorf, *Austria* 27 C9
Ganshui, *China* 58 C6
Gansu □, *China* 56 G3
Ganta, *Liberia* 82 D3
Gantheaume, C., *Australia* 95 F2
Gantheaume B., *Australia* 93 E1
Gantsevichi = Hantsavichy, *Belarus* 47 F4
Ganyem = Genyem, *Indonesia* 63 E10
Ganyu, *China* 57 G10
Ganyushkino, *Kazakstan* 49 G9
Ganzhou, *China* 59 E10
Gao, *Mali* 83 B5
Gao Xian, *China* 58 C5
Gao'an, *China* 59 C10
Gaohe, *China* 59 F9
Gaohebu, *China* 59 B11
Gaokeng, *China* 59 D9
Gaolan Dao, *China* 59 G9
Gaoligong Shan, *China* 58 E2
Gaomi, *China* 57 F10
Gaoping, *China* 56 G7
Gaotang, *China* 56 F9
Gaoua, *Burkina Faso* 82 C4
Gaoual, *Guinea* 82 C2
Gaoxiong = Kaohsiung, *Taiwan* 59 F13
Gaoyang, *China* 56 E8
Gaoyou, *China* 59 A12
Gaoyou Hu, *China* 57 H10
Gaoyuan, *China* 57 F9
Gaozhou, *China* 59 G8
Gap, *France* 21 D10
Gapan, *Phil.* 61 D4
Gar, *China* 60 C2
Garabogazköl Aylagy, *Turkmenistan* 50 E6
Garachico, *Canary Is.* 37 F3
Garachiné, *Panama* 120 E4
Garafia, *Canary Is.* 37 F2
Garajonay, *Canary Is.* 37 F2
Garanhuns, *Brazil* 125 E11
Garawe, *Liberia* 82 E3
Garba Tula, *Kenya* 86 B4
Garber, *U.S.A.* 113 G6
Garberville, *U.S.A.* 114 F2
Garbsen, *Germany* 24 C5
Gard □, *France* 21 D8
Gard →, *France* 21 E8
Garda, L. di, *Italy* 28 C7
Gardanne, *France* 21 E9
Gårdby, *Sweden* 11 H10
Garde L., *Canada* 105 A7
Gardelegen, *Germany* 24 C7
Garden City, *Kans., U.S.A.* 113 G4
Garden City, *Tex., U.S.A.* 113 K4
Garden Grove, *U.S.A.* 117 M9
Gardēz, *Afghan.* 68 C3
Gardhíki, *Greece* 38 C3
Gardiner, *U.S.A.* 114 D8
Gardiners I., *U.S.A.* 111 E12
Gardner, *U.S.A.* 111 D13
Gardner Canal, *Canada* 104 C3
Gardnerville, *U.S.A.* 116 G7
Gardno, Jezioro, *Poland* 44 D4
Gardo, *Somali Rep.* 74 F4
Gardone Val Trómpia, *Italy* 28 C7
Gárdony, *Hungary* 42 C3
Garešnica, *Croatia* 29 C13
Garéssio, *Italy* 28 D5
Garey, *U.S.A.* 117 L6
Garfield, *U.S.A.* 114 C5
Garforth, *U.K.* 12 D6
Gargaliánoi, *Greece* 38 D3
Gargan, Mt., *France* 20 C5
Gargouna, *Mali* 83 B5
Gargždai, *Lithuania* 44 C8
Garhshankar, *India* 68 D7
Garibaldi Prov. Park, *Canada* 104 D4
Garies, *S. Africa* 88 E2
Garigliano →, *Italy* 30 A6
Garissa, *Kenya* 86 C4
Garissa □, *Kenya* 86 C5
Garkida, *Nigeria* 83 C7
Garko, *Nigeria* 83 C6
Garland, *Tex., U.S.A.* 113 J6
Garland, *Utah, U.S.A.* 114 F7
Garlasco, *Italy* 28 C5
Garliava, *Lithuania* 44 D10
Garlin, *France* 20 E3
Garm, *Tajikistan* 50 F8
Garmāb, *Iran* 71 C8
Garmisch-Partenkirchen, *Germany* 25 H7
Garmsār, *Iran* 71 C7
Garner, *U.S.A.* 112 D8
Garnett, *U.S.A.* 112 F7
Garo Hills, *India* 69 G14
Garoe, *Somali Rep.* 74 F4
Garonne →, *France* 20 C3
Garonne, Canal Latéral à la, *France* 20 D4
Garoua, *Cameroon* 83 D7
Garpenberg, *Sweden* 10 D10
Garphyttan, *Sweden* 10 E8
Garrel, *Germany* 24 C4
Garrigue = Garrigues, *France* 20 E7
Garrigues, *France* 20 E7
Garrison, *Mont., U.S.A.* 114 C7
Garrison, *N. Dak., U.S.A.* 112 B4
Garrison, *Tex., U.S.A.* 113 K7
Garrison Res. = Sakakawea, L., *U.S.A.* 112 B4
Garron Pt., *U.K.* 15 A6
Garrovillas, *Spain* 35 F4
Garrucha, *Spain* 33 H3
Garry →, *U.K.* 14 E5
Garry, L., *Canada* 100 B9
Garsen, *Kenya* 86 C5
Gärsnäs, *Sweden* 11 J8
Garson L., *Canada* 105 B6
Gartempe →, *France* 20 B4
Gartz, *Germany* 24 B10
Garu, *Ghana* 83 C4
Garub, *Namibia* 88 D2
Garut, *Indonesia* 63 G12
Garvão, *Portugal* 35 H2
Garvie Mts., *N.Z.* 91 L2
Garwa = Garoua, *Cameroon* 83 D7
Garwa, *India* 69 G10
Garwolin, *Poland* 45 G8
Gary, *U.S.A.* 108 E2
Garz, *Germany* 24 A9
Garzê, *China* 58 B3
Garzón, *Colombia* 124 C3
Gas-San, *Japan* 54 E10
Gasan Kuli = Esenguly, *Turkmenistan* 50 F6
Gascogne, *France* 20 E4
Gascogne, G. de, *Europe* 20 E2
Gascony = Gascogne, *France* 20 E4
Gascoyne →, *Australia* 93 D1
Gascoyne Junc. T.O., *Australia* 93 E2
Gascueña, *Spain* 32 E2
Gash, Wadi →, *Ethiopia* 81 D4
Gashaka, *Nigeria* 83 D7
Gasherbrum, *Pakistan* 69 B7
Gashua, *Nigeria* 83 C7
Gaspé, *Canada* 103 C7
Gaspé, C. de, *Canada* 103 C7
Gaspé, Pén. de, *Canada* 103 C6
Gaspésie, Parc Prov. de la, *Canada* 103 C6
Gassaway, *U.S.A.* 108 F5
Gassol, *Nigeria* 83 D7
Gasteiz = Vitoria-Gasteiz, *Spain* 32 C2
Gastonia, *U.S.A.* 109 H5
Gastoúni, *Greece* 38 D3
Gastoúri, *Greece* 38 B1
Gastre, *Argentina* 128 E3
Gästrikland, *Sweden* 10 D10
Gata, C., *Cyprus* 36 E12
Gata, C. de, *Spain* 33 J2
Gata, Sierra de, *Spain* 34 E4
Gataga →, *Canada* 104 B3
Gătaia, *Romania* 42 E6
Gatchina, *Russia* 46 C6
Gatehouse of Fleet, *U.K.* 14 G4
Gates, *U.S.A.* 110 C7
Gateshead, *U.K.* 12 C6
Gatesville, *U.S.A.* 113 K6
Gaths, *Zimbabwe* 87 G3
Gatico, *Chile* 126 A1
Gâtinais, *France* 19 D9
Gâtine, Hauteurs de, *France* 20 B3
Gatineau, *Canada* 102 C4
Gatineau →, *Canada* 102 C4
Gatineau, Parc de la, *Canada* 102 C4
Gattaran, *Phil.* 61 B4
Gattinara, *Italy* 28 C5
Gatun, L., *Panama* 120 E4
Gatyana, *S. Africa* 89 E4
Gau, *Fiji* 91 D8
Gaucín, *Spain* 35 J5
Gauer L., *Canada* 105 B9
Gauhati, *India* 69 F14
Gauja →, *Latvia* 9 H21
Gaula →, *Norway* 8 E14
Gausta, *Norway* 9 G13
Gauteng □, *S. Africa* 89 D4
Gāv Koshī, *Iran* 71 D8
Gāvakān, *Iran* 71 D7
Gavarnie, *France* 20 F3
Gavāter, *Iran* 71 E9
Gāvbandī, *Iran* 71 E7
Gavdhopoúla, *Greece* 36 E6
Gávdhos, *Greece* 36 E6
Gavi, *Italy* 28 D5
Gavião, *Portugal* 35 F3
Gaviota, *U.S.A.* 117 L6
Gävle, *Sweden* 10 D11
Gävleborgs län □, *Sweden* 10 C10
Gävlebukten, *Sweden* 10 D11

Gavorrano, *Italy* 28 F7
Gavray, *France* 18 D5
Gavrilov Yam, *Russia* 46 D10
Gávrion, *Greece* 38 D6
Gawachab, *Namibia* 88 D2
Gawilgarh Hills, *India* 66 J10
Gawler, *Australia* 95 E2
Gaxun Nur, *China* 60 B5
Gaya, *India* 69 G11
Gaya, *Niger* 83 C5
Gaya, *Nigeria* 83 C6
Gaylord, *U.S.A.* 108 C3
Gayndah, *Australia* 95 D5
Gaysin = Haysyn, *Ukraine* 47 H5
Gayvoron = Hayvoron, *Ukraine* 47 H5
Gaza, *Gaza Strip* 75 D3
Gaza □, *Mozam.* 89 C5
Gaza Strip □, *Asia* 75 D3
Gazaoua, *Niger* 83 C6
Gāzbor, *Iran* 71 D8
Gazi, *Dem. Rep. of the Congo* 86 B1
Gaziantep, *Turkey* 72 D7
Gazipaşa, *Turkey* 72 D5
Gbarnga, *Liberia* 82 D3
Gbekebo, *Nigeria* 83 D5
Gboko, *Nigeria* 83 D6
Gbongan, *Nigeria* 83 D5
Gcuwa, *S. Africa* 89 E4
Gdańsk, *Poland* 44 D5
Gdańsk □, *Poland* 44 D5
Gdańska, Zatoka, *Poland* 44 D6
Gdov, *Russia* 9 G22
Gdynia, *Poland* 44 D5
Gebe, *Indonesia* 63 D7
Gebeciler, *Turkey* 39 C12
Gebeit Mine, *Sudan* 80 C4
Gebze, *Turkey* 41 F13
Gecha, *Ethiopia* 81 F4
Gedaref, *Sudan* 81 E4
Gediz, *Turkey* 39 B11
Gediz →, *Turkey* 39 C8
Gedo, *Ethiopia* 81 F4
Gèdre, *France* 20 F4
Gedser, *Denmark* 11 K5
Geegully Cr. →, *Australia* 92 C3
Geel, *Belgium* 17 C4
Geelong, *Australia* 95 F3
Geelvink Chan., *Australia* 93 E1
Geesthacht, *Germany* 24 B6
Geidam, *Nigeria* 83 C7
Geikie →, *Canada* 105 B8
Geilenkirchen, *Germany* 24 E2
Geili, *Sudan* 81 D3
Geisingen, *Germany* 25 H4
Geislingen, *Germany* 25 G5
Geita, *Tanzania* 86 C3
Geita □, *Tanzania* 86 C3
Gejiu, *China* 58 F4
Gel →, *Sudan* 81 F2
Gel River, *Sudan* 81 F2
Gela, *Italy* 31 E7
Gela, G. di, *Italy* 31 F7
Gelderland □, *Neths.* 17 B6
Geldern, *Germany* 24 D2
Geldrop, *Neths.* 17 C5
Geleen, *Neths.* 17 D5
Gelehun, *S. Leone* 82 D2
Gelembe, *Turkey* 39 B9
Gelendost, *Turkey* 72 C4
Gelendzhik, *Russia* 47 K10
Gelibolu, *Turkey* 41 F10
Gelibolu Yarımadası, *Turkey* 41 F10
Gelidonya Burnu, *Turkey* 72 D4
Gelnhausen, *Germany* 25 E5
Gelnica, *Slovak Rep.* 27 C13
Gelsenkirchen, *Germany* 24 D3
Gelting, *Germany* 24 A5
Gemas, *Malaysia* 65 L4
Gembloux, *Belgium* 17 D4
Gemena, *Dem. Rep. of the Congo* 84 D3
Gemerek, *Turkey* 72 C7
Gemla, *Sweden* 11 H8
Gemlik, *Turkey* 41 F13
Gemlik Körfezi, *Turkey* 41 F12
Gemona del Friuli, *Italy* 29 B10
Gemsa, *Egypt* 80 B3
Gemünden, *Germany* 25 E5
Genale, *Ethiopia* 81 F4
Genç, *Turkey* 73 C9
Gençay, *France* 20 B4
Geneina, Gebel, *Egypt* 80 J8
General Acha, *Argentina* 126 D3
General Alvear, *Buenos Aires, Argentina* 126 D4
General Alvear, *Mendoza, Argentina* 126 D2
General Artigas, *Paraguay* 126 B4
General Belgrano, *Argentina* 126 D4
General Cabrera, *Argentina* 126 C3
General Cepeda, *Mexico* 118 B4
General Guido, *Argentina* 126 D4
General Juan Madariaga, *Argentina* 126 D4
General La Madrid, *Argentina* 126 D3
General MacArthur, *Phil.* 61 F6
General Martin Miguel de Güemes, *Argentina* 126 A3
General Paz, *Argentina* 126 B4
General Pico, *Argentina* 126 D3
General Pinedo, *Argentina* 126 B3
General Pinto, *Argentina* 126 C3
General Roca, *Argentina* 128 D3
General Santos, *Phil.* 61 H6
General Toshevo, *Bulgaria* 41 C12
General Trevino, *Mexico* 119 B5
General Trías, *Mexico* 118 B3
General Viamonte, *Argentina* 126 D3
General Villegas, *Argentina* 126 D3
Genesee, *Idaho, U.S.A.* 114 C5
Genesee, *Pa., U.S.A.* 110 E7
Genesee →, *U.S.A.* 110 C7
Geneseo, *Ill., U.S.A.* 112 E9
Geneseo, *Kans., U.S.A.* 112 F5
Geneseo, *N.Y., U.S.A.* 110 D7
Geneva = Genève, *Switz.* 25 J2
Geneva, *Ala., U.S.A.* 109 K3
Geneva, *N.Y., U.S.A.* 110 D8
Geneva, *Nebr., U.S.A.* 112 E6
Geneva, *Ohio, U.S.A.* 110 E4
Geneva, L. = Léman, L., *Europe* 19 F13
Geneva, L., *U.S.A.* 108 D1
Genève, *Switz.* 25 J2
Gengenbach, *Germany* 25 G4
Gengma, *China* 58 F2
Genichesk = Henichesk, *Ukraine* 47 J8
Genil →, *Spain* 35 H5
Genk, *Belgium* 17 D5
Genlis, *France* 19 E12
Gennargentu, Mti. del, *Italy* 30 B2
Gennes, *France* 18 E6
Genoa = Génova, *Italy* 28 D5
Genoa, *Australia* 95 F4
Genoa, *N.Y., U.S.A.* 111 D8
Genoa, *Nebr., U.S.A.* 112 E6
Genoa, *Nev., U.S.A.* 116 F7
Génova, *Italy* 28 D5
Génova, G. di, *Italy* 28 E6
Genriyetty, Ostrov, *Russia* 51 B16
Gent, *Belgium* 17 C3
Genthin, *Germany* 24 C8
Genyem, *Indonesia* 63 E10
Genzano di Lucánia, *Italy* 31 B9
Genzano di Roma, *Italy* 29 G9
Geoagiu, *Romania* 43 E8
Geographe B., *Australia* 93 F2
Geographe Chan., *Australia* 93 D1
Geokchay = Göyçay, *Azerbaijan* 49 K8
Georga, Zemlya, *Russia* 50 A5
George, *S. Africa* 88 E3
George →, *Canada* 103 A6
George, L., *N.S.W., Australia* 95 F4
George, L., *S. Austral., Australia* 95 F3
George, L., *W. Austral., Australia* 92 D3
George, L., *Uganda* 86 B3
George, L., *Fla., U.S.A.* 109 L5
George, L., *N.Y., U.S.A.* 111 C11
George Gill Ra., *Australia* 92 D5
George River = Kangiqsualujjuaq, *Canada* 101 C13
George Sound, *N.Z.* 91 L1
George Town, *Bahamas* 120 B4
George Town, *Malaysia* 65 K3
George V Land, *Antarctica* 5 C10
George VI Sound, *Antarctica* 5 D17
George West, *U.S.A.* 113 L5
Georgetown, *Australia* 94 B3
Georgetown, *Ont., Canada* 102 D4
Georgetown, *P.E.I., Canada* 103 C7
Georgetown, *Cayman Is.* 120 C3
Georgetown, *Gambia* 82 C2
Georgetown, *Guyana* 124 B7
Georgetown, *Calif., U.S.A.* 116 G6
Georgetown, *Colo., U.S.A.* 114 G11
Georgetown, *Ky., U.S.A.* 108 F3
Georgetown, *S.C., U.S.A.* 109 J6
Georgetown, *Tex., U.S.A.* 113 K6
Georgia □, *U.S.A.* 109 K5
Georgia ■, *Asia* 49 J6
Georgia, Str. of, *Canada* 104 D4
Georgian B., *Canada* 102 C3
Georgina →, *Australia* 94 C2
Georgina Downs, *Australia* 94 C2
Georgiu-Dezh = Liski, *Russia* 47 G10
Georgiyevsk, *Russia* 49 H6
Georgsmarienhütte, *Germany* 24 C4
Gera, *Germany* 24 E8
Geraardsbergen, *Belgium* 17 D3
Geral, Serra, *Brazil* 127 B6
Geral de Goiás, Serra, *Brazil* 125 F9
Geraldine, *U.S.A.* 114 C8
Geraldton, *Australia* 93 E1
Geraldton, *Canada* 102 C2
Gérardmer, *France* 19 D13
Gercüş, *Turkey* 73 D9
Gerede, *Turkey* 72 B5
Gerês, Sierra do, *Portugal* 34 D3
Gereshk, *Afghan.* 66 D4
Geretsried, *Germany* 25 H7
Gérgal, *Spain* 33 H2
Gerik, *Malaysia* 65 K3
Gering, *U.S.A.* 112 E3
Gerlach, *U.S.A.* 114 F4
Gerlachovský štit, *Slovak Rep.* 27 B13
German Planina, *Macedonia* 40 D6
Germansen Landing, *Canada* 104 B4
Germany ■, *Europe* 24 E6
Germencik, *Turkey* 39 D9
Germering, *Germany* 25 G7
Germersheim, *Germany* 25 F4
Germī, *Iran* 73 C13
Germiston, *S. Africa* 89 D4
Gernika-Lumo, *Spain* 32 B2
Gernsheim, *Germany* 25 F4
Gero, *Japan* 55 G8
Gerolzhofen, *Germany* 25 F6
Gerona = Girona, *Spain* 32 D7
Gerrard, *Canada* 104 C5
Gers □, *France* 20 E4
Gers →, *France* 20 D4
Gersfeld, *Germany* 24 E5
Gersthofen, *Germany* 25 G6
Gerzat, *France* 20 C7
Gerze, *Turkey* 72 B6
Geseke, *Germany* 24 D4
Geser, *Indonesia* 63 E8
Gesso →, *Italy* 28 D4
Gestro, Wabi →, *Ethiopia* 81 G5
Getafe, *Spain* 34 E7
Gethsémani, *Canada* 103 B7
Getinge, *Sweden* 11 H6
Gettysburg, *Pa., U.S.A.* 108 F7
Gettysburg, *S. Dak., U.S.A.* 112 C5
Getxo, *Spain* 32 B2
Getz Ice Shelf, *Antarctica* 5 D14
Gevaş, *Turkey* 73 C10
Gévaudan, *France* 20 D7
Gevgelija, *Macedonia* 40 E6
Gévora →, *Spain* 35 G4
Gex, *France* 19 F13
Geyikli, *Turkey* 39 B8
Geyser, *U.S.A.* 114 C8
Geyserville, *U.S.A.* 116 G4
Geyve, *Turkey* 72 B4
Ghâbat el Arab = Wang Kai, *Sudan* 81 F2
Ghaghara →, *India* 69 G11
Ghalla, Wadi el →, *Sudan* 81 E2
Ghana ■, *W. Afr.* 83 D4
Ghansor, *India* 69 H9
Ghanzi, *Botswana* 88 C3
Ghanzi □, *Botswana* 88 C3
Gharb el Istiwa'iya □, *Sudan* 81 G3
Gharbîya, Es Sahrâ el, *Egypt* 80 B2
Ghard Abû Muharik, *Egypt* 80 B3
Ghardaïa, *Algeria* 78 B6
Ghârib, G., *Egypt* 80 J8
Gharyān, *Libya* 79 B8
Ghat, *Libya* 79 D8
Ghatal, *India* 69 H12
Ghatampur, *India* 69 F9
Ghaṭṭī, *Si. Arabia* 70 D3
Ghawdex = Gozo, *Malta* 36 C1
Ghazal, Bahr el →, *Chad* 79 F9
Ghazâl, Bahr el →, *Sudan* 81 F3
Ghaziabad, *India* 68 E7
Ghazipur, *India* 69 G10
Ghaznī, *Afghan.* 68 C3
Ghaznī □, *Afghan.* 66 C6
Ghedi, *Italy* 28 C7
Ghelari, *Romania* 42 E7
Ghent = Gent, *Belgium* 17 C3
Gheorghe Gheorghiu-Dej = Oneşti, *Romania* 43 D11
Gheorgheni, *Romania* 43 D10
Gherla, *Romania* 43 C8
Ghidigeni, *Romania* 43 D12
Ghilarza, *Italy* 30 B1
Ghimeş-Făget, *Romania* 43 D11
Ghisonaccia, *France* 21 F13
Ghisoni, *France* 21 F13
Ghizao, *Afghan.* 68 C1
Ghizar →, *Pakistan* 69 A5
Ghogha, *India* 68 J5
Ghot Ogrein, *Egypt* 80 A2
Ghotaru, *India* 68 F4
Ghotki, *Pakistan* 68 E3
Ghowr □, *Afghan.* 66 C4
Ghudaf, W. al →, *Iraq* 70 C4
Ghudāmis, *Libya* 77 C4
Ghughri, *India* 69 H9
Ghugus, *India* 66 K11
Ghulam Mohammad Barrage, *Pakistan* 68 G3
Ghūrīān, *Afghan.* 66 B2
Gia Dinh, *Vietnam* 65 G6
Gia Lai = Plei Ku, *Vietnam* 64 F7
Gia Nghia, *Vietnam* 65 G6
Gia Ngoc, *Vietnam* 64 E7
Gia Vuc, *Vietnam* 64 E7
Giannutri, *Italy* 28 F8
Giant Forest, *U.S.A.* 116 J8
Giant Mts. = Krkonoše, *Czech Rep.* 26 A8
Giants Causeway, *U.K.* 15 A5
Giarabub = Al Jaghbūb, *Libya* 79 C10
Giarre, *Italy* 31 E8
Giaveno, *Italy* 28 C4
Gibara, *Cuba* 120 B4
Gibb River, *Australia* 92 C4
Gibbon, *U.S.A.* 112 E5
Gibe →, *Ethiopia* 81 F4
Gibellina Nuova, *Italy* 30 E5
Gibraleón, *Spain* 35 H4
Gibraltar ■, *Europe* 35 J5
Gibraltar, Str. of, *Medit. S.* 35 K5
Gibson Desert, *Australia* 92 D4
Gibsons, *Canada* 104 D4
Gibsonville, *U.S.A.* 116 F6
Giddings, *U.S.A.* 113 K6
Gidole, *Ethiopia* 81 F4
Gien, *France* 19 E9
Giengen, *Germany* 25 G6
Giessen, *Germany* 24 E4
Gīfān, *Iran* 71 B8
Gifatin, Geziret, *Egypt* 80 B3
Gifford Creek, *Australia* 92 D2
Gifhorn, *Germany* 24 C6
Gifu, *Japan* 55 G8
Gifu □, *Japan* 55 G8
Gigant, *Russia* 49 G5
Giganta, Sa. de la, *Mexico* 118 B2
Gigen, *Bulgaria* 41 C8
Gigha, *U.K.* 14 F3
Gíglio, *Italy* 28 F7
Gignac, *France* 20 E7
Gigüela →, *Spain* 35 F7
Gijón, *Spain* 34 B5
Gil I., *Canada* 104 C3
Gila →, *U.S.A.* 115 K6
Gila Bend, *U.S.A.* 115 K7
Gila Bend Mts., *U.S.A.* 115 K7
Gīlān □, *Iran* 71 B6
Gilău, *Romania* 43 D8
Gilbert →, *Australia* 94 B3
Gilbert Is., *Kiribati* 96 G9
Gilbert Plains, *Canada* 105 C8
Gilbert River, *Australia* 94 B3
Gilberton, *Australia* 94 B3
Gilf el Kebîr, Hadabat el, *Egypt* 80 C2
Gilford I., *Canada* 104 C3
Gilgandra, *Australia* 95 E4
Gilgil, *Kenya* 86 C4
Gilgit, *India* 69 B6
Gilgit →, *Pakistan* 69 B6
Giljeva Planina, *Serbia, Yug.* 40 C3
Gillam, *Canada* 105 B10
Gilleleje, *Denmark* 11 H6
Gillen, L., *Australia* 93 E3
Gilles, L., *Australia* 95 E2
Gillette, *U.S.A.* 112 C2
Gilliat, *Australia* 94 C3
Gillingham, *U.K.* 13 F8
Gilmer, *U.S.A.* 113 J7
Gilmore, *Australia* 95 F4
Gilmore, L., *Australia* 93 F3
Gilmour, *Canada* 102 D4
Gilo →, *Ethiopia* 81 F3
Gilort →, *Romania* 43 F8
Gilroy, *U.S.A.* 116 H5
Gimbi, *Ethiopia* 81 F4
Gimli, *Canada* 105 C9
Gimo, *Sweden* 10 D12
Gimone →, *France* 20 E5
Gimont, *France* 20 E4
Gin Gin, *Australia* 95 D5
Ginâh, *Egypt* 80 B3
Gindie, *Australia* 94 C4
Gingin, *Australia* 93 F2
Ginir, *Ethiopia* 81 F5
Ginosa, *Italy* 31 B9
Ginzo de Limia = Xinzo de Limia, *Spain* 34 C3
Gióia, G. di, *Italy* 31 D8
Gióia del Colle, *Italy* 31 B9
Gióia Táuro, *Italy* 31 D8
Gioiosa Iónica, *Italy* 31 D9
Gioiosa Marea, *Italy* 31 D7
Gióna, Óros, *Greece* 38 C4
Giovi, Passo dei, *Italy* 28 D5
Giovinazzo, *Italy* 31 A9
Gir Hills, *India* 68 J4
Girab, *India* 68 F4
Girâfi, W. →, *Egypt* 75 F3
Giraltovce, *Slovak Rep.* 27 B14
Girard, *Kans., U.S.A.* 113 G7
Girard, *Ohio, U.S.A.* 110 E4
Girard, *Pa., U.S.A.* 110 D4
Girdle Ness, *U.K.* 14 D6
Giresun, *Turkey* 73 B8
Girga, *Egypt* 80 B3
Giridih, *India* 69 G12
Girifalco, *Italy* 31 D9
Girilambone, *Australia* 95 E4
Girne = Kyrenia, *Cyprus* 36 D12
Giro, *Nigeria* 83 C5
Giromagny, *France* 19 E13
Girona, *Spain* 32 D7
Girona □, *Spain* 32 C7
Gironde □, *France* 20 D3
Gironde →, *France* 20 C2
Gironella, *Spain* 32 C6
Giru, *Australia* 94 B4
Girvan, *U.K.* 14 F4
Gisborne, *N.Z.* 91 H7
Gisenyi, *Rwanda* 86 C2
Gislaved, *Sweden* 11 G7
Gisors, *France* 19 C8
Gitega, *Burundi* 86 C2
Giuba →, *Somali Rep.* 74 G3
Giugliano in Campania, *Italy* 31 B7
Giulianova, *Italy* 29 F10
Giurgeni, *Romania* 43 F12
Giurgiu, *Romania* 43 G10
Giurgiu □, *Romania* 43 F10
Giurgiuleşti, *Moldova* 43 E13
Give, *Denmark* 11 J3
Givet, *France* 19 B11
Givors, *France* 21 C8
Givry, *France* 19 F11
Giyon, *Ethiopia* 81 F4
Giza = El Gîza, *Egypt* 80 J7
Gizhiga, *Russia* 51 C17
Gizhiginskaya Guba, *Russia* 51 C16
Giżycko, *Poland* 44 D8
Gizzeria, *Italy* 31 D9
Gjalicës e Lumës, Mal, *Albania* 40 D4
Gjegjani, *Albania* 40 E4
Gjirokastra, *Albania* 40 F4
Gjoa Haven, *Canada* 100 B10
Gjøvik, *Norway* 9 F14
Gjuhës, Kep i, *Albania* 40 F3
Glace Bay, *Canada* 103 C8
Glacier Bay, *U.S.A.* 104 B1
Glacier Nat. Park, *Canada* 104 C5
Glacier Park, *U.S.A.* 114 B7
Glacier Peak, *U.S.A.* 114 B3
Gladewater, *U.S.A.* 113 J7
Gladstone, *Queens., Australia* 94 C5
Gladstone, *S. Austral., Australia* 95 E2
Gladstone, *W. Austral., Australia* 93 E1
Gladstone, *Canada* 105 C9
Gladstone, *U.S.A.* 108 C2
Gladwin, *U.S.A.* 108 D3
Gladys L., *Canada* 104 B2
Glafsfjorden, *Sweden* 10 E6
Głagów Małapolski, *Poland* 45 H8
Glåma = Glomma →, *Norway* 9 G14
Gláma, *Iceland* 8 D2
Glamis, *U.S.A.* 117 N11
Glamoč, *Bos.-H.* 29 D13
Glamsbjerg, *Denmark* 11 J4
Glarus, *Switz.* 25 H5
Glarus □, *Switz.* 25 J5
Glasco, *Kans., U.S.A.* 112 F6
Glasco, *N.Y., U.S.A.* 111 D11
Glasgow, *U.K.* 14 F4
Glasgow, *Ky., U.S.A.* 108 G3
Glasgow, *Mont., U.S.A.* 114 B10
Glastonbury, *U.K.* 13 F5
Glastonbury, *U.S.A.* 111 E12
Glauchau, *Germany* 24 E8
Glava, *Sweden* 10 E6
Glavice, *Croatia* 29 E13
Glazov, *Russia* 48 A11
Gleisdorf, *Austria* 26 D8
Gleiwitz = Gliwice, *Poland* 45 H5
Glen, *U.S.A.* 111 B13
Glen Affric, *U.K.* 14 D3
Glen Canyon Dam, *U.S.A.* 115 H8
Glen Canyon National Recreation Area, *U.S.A.* 115 H8
Glen Coe, *U.K.* 14 E3
Glen Cove, *U.S.A.* 111 F11
Glen Garry, *U.K.* 14 D3
Glen Innes, *Australia* 95 D5
Glen Lyon, *U.S.A.* 111 E8
Glen Mor, *U.K.* 14 D4
Glen Moriston, *U.K.* 14 D4
Glen Spean, *U.K.* 14 E4
Glen Ullin, *U.S.A.* 112 B4
Glénan, Îs. de, *France* 18 E3
Glenburgh, *Australia* 93 E2
Glencoe, *Canada* 110 D3
Glencoe, *S. Africa* 89 D5
Glencoe, *U.S.A.* 112 C7
Glendale, *Ariz., U.S.A.* 115 K7
Glendale, *Calif., U.S.A.* 117 L8
Glendale, *Oreg., U.S.A.* 114 E2
Glendale, *Zimbabwe* 87 F3
Glendive, *U.S.A.* 112 B2
Glendo, *U.S.A.* 112 D2
Glenelg, *Australia* 95 E2
Glenelg →, *Australia* 95 F3
Glenflorrie, *Australia* 92 D2
Glengarriff, *Ireland* 15 E2
Glengyle, *Australia* 94 C2
Glenmora, *U.S.A.* 113 K8
Glenmorgan, *Australia* 95 D4
Glenn, *U.S.A.* 116 F4
Glennamaddy, *Ireland* 15 C3
Glenns Ferry, *U.S.A.* 114 E6
Glenorchy, *Australia* 94 G4
Glenore, *Australia* 94 B3
Glenormiston, *Australia* 94 C2
Glenreagh, *Australia* 95 E5
Glenrock, *U.S.A.* 114 E11
Glenrothes, *U.K.* 14 E5
Glens Falls, *U.S.A.* 111 C11
Glenties, *Ireland* 15 B3
Glenville, *U.S.A.* 108 F5
Glenwood, *Alta., Canada* 104 D6
Glenwood, *Nfld., Canada* 103 C9
Glenwood, *Ark., U.S.A.* 113 H8
Glenwood, *Hawaii, U.S.A.* 106 J17
Glenwood, *Iowa, U.S.A.* 112 E7
Glenwood, *Minn., U.S.A.* 112 C7
Glenwood, *Wash., U.S.A.* 116 D5
Glenwood Springs, *U.S.A.* 114 G10
Glettinganes, *Iceland* 8 D7
Glifádha, *Greece* 38 D5
Glimåkra, *Sweden* 11 H8
Glina, *Croatia* 29 C13
Glinojeck, *Poland* 45 F7
Gliwice, *Poland* 45 H5
Globe, *U.S.A.* 115 K8

Glodeanu Siliştea, *Romania* 43 F11
Glodeni, *Moldova* 43 C12
Glödnitz, *Austria* 26 E7
Gloggnitz, *Austria* 26 D8
Głogów, *Poland* 45 G3
Głogówek, *Poland* 45 H4
Glomma →, *Norway* 9 G14
Glorieuses, Is., *Ind. Oc.* 89 A8
Glóssa, *Greece* 38 B5
Glossop, *U.K.* 12 D6
Gloucester, *Australia* 95 E5
Gloucester, *U.K.* 13 F5
Gloucester, *U.S.A.* 111 D14
Gloucester I., *Australia* 94 C4
Gloucestershire □, *U.K.* 13 F5
Gloversville, *U.S.A.* 111 C10
Glovertown, *Canada* 103 C9
Głowno, *Poland* 45 G6
Głubczyce, *Poland* 45 H4
Glubokiy, *Russia* 49 F5
Glubokoye = Hlybokaye, *Belarus* 46 E4
Głuchołazy, *Poland* 45 H4
Glücksburg, *Germany* 24 A5
Glückstadt, *Germany* 24 B5
Glukhov = Hlukhiv, *Ukraine* 47 G7
Glusk, *Belarus* 47 F5
Głuszyca, *Poland* 45 H3
Glyngøre, *Denmark* 11 H2
Gmünd, *Kärnten, Austria* 26 E6
Gmünd, *Niederösterreich, Austria* 26 C8
Gmunden, *Austria* 26 D6
Gnarp, *Sweden* 10 B11
Gnesta, *Sweden* 10 E11
Gniew, *Poland* 44 E5
Gniewkowo, *Poland* 45 F5
Gniezno, *Poland* 45 F4
Gnjilane, *Serbia, Yug.* 40 D5
Gnoien, *Germany* 24 B8
Gnosjö, *Sweden* 11 G7
Gnowangerup, *Australia* 93 F2
Go Cong, *Vietnam* 65 G6
Gō-no-ura, *Japan* 55 H4
Goa, *India* 66 M8
Goa □, *India* 66 M8
Goalen Hd., *Australia* 95 F5
Goalpara, *India* 67 F17
Goalundo Ghat, *Bangla.* 69 H13
Goaso, *Ghana* 82 D4
Goat Fell, *U.K.* 14 F3
Goba, *Ethiopia* 81 F4
Goba, *Mozam.* 89 D5
Gobabis, *Namibia* 88 C2
Göbel, *Turkey* 41 F12
Gobi, *Asia* 56 C6
Gobō, *Japan* 55 H7
Gobo, *Sudan* 81 F3
Göçbeyli, *Turkey* 39 B9
Goch, *Germany* 24 D2
Gochas, *Namibia* 88 C2
Godavari →, *India* 67 L13
Godavari Point, *India* 67 L13
Godbout, *Canada* 103 C6
Godda, *India* 69 G12
Godech, *Bulgaria* 40 C7
Goderich, *Canada* 102 D3
Goderville, *France* 18 C7
Godhavn, *Greenland* 4 C5
Godhra, *India* 68 H5
Gödöllő, *Hungary* 42 C4
Godoy Cruz, *Argentina* 126 C2
Gods →, *Canada* 105 B10
Gods L., *Canada* 105 C10
Godthåb = Nuuk, *Greenland* 4 C5
Godwin Austen = K2, *Pakistan* 69 B7
Goeie Hoop, Kaap die = Good Hope, C. of, *S. Africa* 88 E2
Goéland, L. au, *Canada* 102 C4
Goeree, *Neths.* 17 C3
Goes, *Neths.* 17 C3
Gogama, *Canada* 102 C3
Gogango, *Australia* 94 C5
Gogebic, L., *U.S.A.* 112 B10
Gogolin, *Poland* 45 H5
Gogra = Ghaghara →, *India* 69 G11
Gogriâl, *Sudan* 81 F2
Goiânia, *Brazil* 125 G9
Goiás, *Brazil* 125 G8
Goiás □, *Brazil* 125 F9
Goio-Ere, *Brazil* 127 A5
Góis, *Portugal* 34 E2
Gojam □, *Ethiopia* 81 E4
Gojeb, Wabi →, *Ethiopia* 81 F4
Gojō, *Japan* 55 G7
Gojra, *Pakistan* 68 D5
Gokarannath, *India* 69 F9
Gökçeada, *Turkey* 41 F9
Gökçedağ, *Turkey* 39 B10
Gökçen, *Turkey* 39 C9
Gökçeören, *Turkey* 39 C10
Gökçeyazı, *Turkey* 39 B9
Gökırmak →, *Turkey* 72 B6
Gökova, *Turkey* 39 D10
Gökova Körfezi, *Turkey* 39 E9
Göksu →, *Turkey* 72 D6
Göksun, *Turkey* 72 C7
Gokteik, *Burma* 67 H20
Göktepe, *Turkey* 39 D10
Gokurt, *Pakistan* 68 E2
Gola, *India* 69 E9
Golakganj, *India* 69 F13
Golan Heights = Hagolan, *Syria* 75 C4
Gołańcz, *Poland* 45 F4
Golāshkerd, *Iran* 71 E8
Golaya Pristen = Hola Pristan, *Ukraine* 47 J7
Gölbaşı, *Adiyaman, Turkey* 72 D7
Gölbaşı, *Ankara, Turkey* 72 C5
Golchikha, *Russia* 4 B12
Golconda, *U.S.A.* 114 F5
Gölcük, *Kocaeli, Turkey* 41 F13
Gölcük, *Niğde, Turkey* 72 C6
Gold Beach, *U.S.A.* 114 E1
Gold Coast, *Australia* 95 D5
Gold Coast, *W. Afr.* 83 E4
Gold Hill, *U.S.A.* 114 E2
Gołdap, *Poland* 44 D9
Goldberg, *Germany* 24 B8
Golden, *Canada* 104 C5
Golden, *U.S.A.* 112 F2
Golden B., *N.Z.* 91 J4
Golden Gate, *U.S.A.* 114 H2
Golden Hinde, *Canada* 104 D3
Golden Lake, *Canada* 110 A7
Golden Prairie, *Canada* 105 C7
Golden Vale, *Ireland* 15 D3
Goldendale, *U.S.A.* 114 D3
Goldfield, *U.S.A.* 115 H5
Goldfields, *Canada* 105 B7
Goldsand L., *Canada* 105 B8
Goldsboro, *U.S.A.* 109 H7
Goldsmith, *U.S.A.* 113 K3
Goldsworthy, *Australia* 92 D2
Goldthwaite, *U.S.A.* 113 K5
Golegã, *Portugal* 35 F2
Goleniów, *Poland* 44 E1
Golestānak, *Iran* 71 D7
Goleta, *U.S.A.* 117 L7
Golfito, *Costa Rica* 120 E3
Golfo Aranci, *Italy* 30 B2
Gölgeli Dağları, *Turkey* 39 D10
Gölhisar, *Turkey* 39 D11
Goliad, *U.S.A.* 113 L6
Golija, *Montenegro, Yug.* 40 C2
Golija, *Serbia, Yug.* 40 C4
Golina, *Poland* 45 F5
Gölköy, *Turkey* 72 B7
Göllersdorf, *Austria* 26 C9
Gölmarmara, *Turkey* 39 C9
Golo →, *France* 21 F13
Gölova, *Turkey* 39 E12
Golpāyegān, *Iran* 71 C6
Gölpazarı, *Turkey* 72 B4
Golra, *Pakistan* 68 C5
Golspie, *U.K.* 14 D5
Golub-Dobrzyń, *Poland* 45 E6
Golubac, *Serbia, Yug.* 40 B5
Golyam Perelik, *Bulgaria* 41 E8
Golyama Kamchiya →, *Bulgaria* 41 C11
Goma, *Dem. Rep. of the Congo* 86 C2
Gomati →, *India* 69 G10
Gombari, *Dem. Rep. of the Congo* 86 B2
Gombe, *Nigeria* 83 C7
Gömbe, *Turkey* 39 E11
Gombe →, *Tanzania* 86 C3
Gombi, *Nigeria* 83 C7
Gomel = Homyel, *Belarus* 47 F6
Gomera, *Canary Is.* 37 F2
Gómez Palacio, *Mexico* 118 B4
Gomīshān, *Iran* 71 B7
Gommern, *Germany* 24 C7
Gomogomo, *Indonesia* 63 F8
Gomoh, *India* 67 H15
Gomotartsi, *Bulgaria* 40 B6
Gompa = Ganta, *Liberia* 82 D3
Gomphi, *Greece* 38 B3
Gonābād, *Iran* 71 C8
Gonaïves, *Haiti* 121 C5
Gonâve, G. de la, *Haiti* 121 C5
Gonâve, I. de la, *Haiti* 121 C5
Gonbad-e Kāvūs, *Iran* 71 B7
Gönc, *Hungary* 42 B6
Gonda, *India* 69 F9
Gondal, *India* 68 J4
Gonder, *Ethiopia* 81 E4
Gonder □, *Ethiopia* 81 E4
Gondia, *India* 66 J12
Gondola, *Mozam.* 87 F3
Gondomar, *Portugal* 34 D2
Gondrecourt-le-Château, *France* 19 D12
Gönen, *Balıkesir, Turkey* 41 F11
Gönen, *Isparta, Turkey* 39 D12
Gönen →, *Turkey* 41 F11
Gong Xian, *China* 58 C5
Gong'an, *China* 59 B9
Gongcheng, *China* 59 E8
Gongga Shan, *China* 58 C3
Gongguan, *China* 58 G7
Gonghe, *China* 60 C5
Gongola →, *Nigeria* 83 D7
Gongolgon, *Australia* 95 E4
Gongshan, *China* 58 D2
Gongtan, *China* 58 C7
Goniadz, *Poland* 44 E9
Goniri, *Nigeria* 83 C7
Gonjo, *China* 58 B2
Gonnesa, *Italy* 30 C1
Gónnos, *Greece* 38 B4
Gonnosfanádiga, *Italy* 30 C1
Gonzaga, *Phil.* 61 B5
Gonzales, *Calif., U.S.A.* 116 J5
Gonzales, *Tex., U.S.A.* 113 L6
González Chaves, *Argentina* 126 D3
Good Hope, C. of, *S. Africa* 88 E2
Gooderham, *Canada* 102 D4
Goodeve, *Canada* 105 C8
Gooding, *U.S.A.* 114 E6
Goodland, *U.S.A.* 112 F4
Goodnight, *U.S.A.* 113 H4
Goodooga, *Australia* 95 D4
Goodsoil, *Canada* 105 C7
Goodsprings, *U.S.A.* 115 J6
Goole, *U.K.* 12 D7
Goolgowi, *Australia* 95 E4
Goomalling, *Australia* 93 F2
Goombalie, *Australia* 95 D4
Goonda, *Mozam.* 87 F3
Goondiwindi, *Australia* 95 D5
Goongarrie, L., *Australia* 93 F3
Goonyella, *Australia* 94 C4
Gooray, *Australia* 95 D5
Goose →, *Canada* 103 B7
Goose L., *U.S.A.* 114 F3
Gop, *India* 66 H6
Gopalganj, *India* 69 F11
Göppingen, *Germany* 25 G5
Gor, *Spain* 35 H8
Góra, *Leszno, Poland* 45 G3
Góra, *Płock, Poland* 45 F7
Góra Kalwaria, *Poland* 45 G8
Gorakhpur, *India* 69 F10
Goražde, *Bos.-H.* 42 G3
Gorbatov, *Russia* 48 B6
Gorbea, Peña, *Spain* 32 B2
Gorda, *U.S.A.* 116 K5
Gorda, Pta., *Canary Is.* 37 F2
Gorda, Pta., *Nic.* 120 D3
Gordan B., *Australia* 92 B5
Gördes, *Turkey* 39 C10
Gordon, *U.S.A.* 112 D3
Gordon →, *Australia* 94 G4
Gordon Downs, *Australia* 92 C4
Gordon L., *Alta., Canada* 105 B6
Gordon L., *N.W.T., Canada* 104 A6
Gordonvale, *Australia* 94 B4
Gore, *Australia* 95 D5
Gore, *Ethiopia* 81 F4
Gore, *N.Z.* 91 M2
Gore Bay, *Canada* 102 C3
Görele, *Turkey* 73 B8
Goreme, *Turkey* 72 C6
Gorey, *Ireland* 15 D5
Gorg, *Iran* 71 D8
Gorgān, *Iran* 71 B7
Gorgona, *Italy* 28 E6
Gorgona, I., *Colombia* 124 C3
Gorgora, *Ethiopia* 81 E4
Gorham, *U.S.A.* 111 B13
Gori, *Georgia* 49 J7
Gorinchem, *Neths.* 17 C4
Goris, *Armenia* 73 C12
Goritsy, *Russia* 46 D9
Gorízia, *Italy* 29 C10
Gorj □, *Romania* 43 E8
Gorki = Horki, *Belarus* 46 E6
Gorki = Nizhniy Novgorod, *Russia* 48 B7
Gorkiy = Nizhniy Novgorod, *Russia* 48 B7
Gorkovskoye Vdkhr., *Russia* 48 B6
Gorlice, *Poland* 45 J8
Görlitz, *Germany* 24 D10
Gorlovka = Horlivka, *Ukraine* 47 H10
Gorman, *Calif., U.S.A.* 117 L8
Gorman, *Tex., U.S.A.* 113 J5
Gorna Dzhumayo = Blagoevgrad, *Bulgaria* 40 D7
Gorna Oryakhovitsa, *Bulgaria* 41 C9
Gornja Radgona, *Slovenia* 29 B13
Gornja Tuzla, *Bos.-H.* 42 F3
Gornji Grad, *Slovenia* 29 B11
Gornji Milanovac, *Serbia, Yug.* 40 B4
Gornji Vakuf, *Bos.-H.* 42 G2
Gorno Ablanovo, *Bulgaria* 41 C9
Gorno-Altay □, *Russia* 50 D9
Gorno-Altaysk, *Russia* 50 D9
Gornyatskiy, *Russia* 49 F5
Gornyi, *Russia* 54 B6
Gornyy, *Russia* 48 E9
Gorodenka = Horodenka, *Ukraine* 47 H3
Gorodets, *Russia* 48 B6
Gorodishche = Horodyshche, *Ukraine* 47 H6
Gorodishche, *Russia* 48 D7
Gorodnya = Horodnya, *Ukraine* 47 G6
Gorodok = Haradok, *Belarus* 46 E6
Gorodok = Horodok, *Ukraine* 47 H2
Gorodovikovsk, *Russia* 49 G5
Gorokhov = Horokhiv, *Ukraine* 47 G3
Gorokhovets, *Russia* 48 B6
Gorom Gorom, *Burkina Faso* 83 C4
Goromonzi, *Zimbabwe* 87 F3
Gorongose →, *Mozam.* 89 C5
Gorongoza, *Mozam.* 87 F3
Gorongoza, Sa. da, *Mozam.* 87 F3
Gorontalo, *Indonesia* 63 D6
Goronyo, *Nigeria* 83 C6
Górowo Iławeckie, *Poland* 44 D7
Gorron, *France* 18 D6
Gorshechnoye, *Russia* 47 G10
Gort, *Ireland* 15 C3
Gortis, *Greece* 36 D6
Góry Bystrzyckie, *Poland* 45 H3
Goryachiy Klyuch, *Russia* 49 H4
Gorzkowice, *Poland* 45 G6
Górzno, *Poland* 45 E6
Gorzów Śląski, *Poland* 45 G5
Gorzów Wielkopolski, *Poland* 45 F2
Gorzów Wielkopolski □, *Poland* 45 F2
Gosford, *Australia* 95 E5
Goshen, *Calif., U.S.A.* 116 J7
Goshen, *Ind., U.S.A.* 108 E3
Goshen, *N.Y., U.S.A.* 111 E10
Goshogawara, *Japan* 54 D10
Goslar, *Germany* 24 D6
Gospič, *Croatia* 29 D12
Gosport, *U.K.* 13 G6
Gosse →, *Australia* 94 B1
Gostivar, *Macedonia* 40 E4
Gostyń, *Poland* 45 G4
Gostynin, *Poland* 45 F6
Göta älv →, *Sweden* 11 G5
Göta kanal, *Sweden* 11 F9
Götaland, *Sweden* 11 G8
Göteborg, *Sweden* 11 G5
Göteborgs och Bohus län □, *Sweden* 11 F5
Götene, *Sweden* 11 F7
Goteşti, *Moldova* 43 D13
Gotha, *Germany* 24 E6
Gothenburg = Göteborg, *Sweden* 11 G5
Gothenburg, *U.S.A.* 112 E4
Gotland, *Sweden* 11 G12
Gotlands län □, *Sweden* 11 G12
Gotse Delchev, *Bulgaria* 40 E7
Gotska Sandön, *Sweden* 9 G18
Gōtsu, *Japan* 55 G6
Góttero, Monte, *Italy* 28 D6
Göttingen, *Germany* 24 D5
Gottwald = Zmiyev, *Ukraine* 47 H9
Gottwaldov = Zlín, *Czech Rep.* 27 B10
Goubangzi, *China* 57 D11
Gouda, *Neths.* 17 B4
Goúdhoura, Ákra, *Greece* 36 E8
Goudiry, *Senegal* 82 C2
Gough I., *Atl. Oc.* 2 G9
Gouin, Rés., *Canada* 102 C5
Gouitafla, *Ivory C.* 82 D3
Goulburn, *Australia* 95 E4
Goulburn Is., *Australia* 94 A1
Goulia, *Ivory C.* 82 C3
Gouménissa, *Greece* 40 F6
Goúra, *Greece* 38 D4
Gourdon, *France* 20 D5
Gouré, *Niger* 83 C7
Gourin, *France* 18 D3
Gourits →, *S. Africa* 88 E3
Gourma Rharous, *Mali* 83 B4
Goúrnais, *Greece* 36 D7
Gournay-en-Bray, *France* 19 C8
Gourock Ra., *Australia* 95 F4
Goursi, *Burkina Faso* 82 C4
Gouverneur, *U.S.A.* 111 B9
Gouviá, *Greece* 36 A3
Gouzon, *France* 19 F9
Govan, *Canada* 105 C8
Governador Valadares, *Brazil* 125 G10
Governor's Harbour, *Bahamas* 120 A4
Gowan Ra., *Australia* 94 D4
Gowanda, *U.S.A.* 110 D6
Gowd-e Zirreh, *Afghan.* 66 E3
Gower, *U.K.* 13 F3
Gowna, L., *Ireland* 15 C4
Goya, *Argentina* 126 B4
Göyçay, *Azerbaijan* 49 K8
Goyder Lagoon, *Australia* 95 D2
Goyllarisquisga, *Peru* 124 F3
Göynük, *Antalya, Turkey* 39 E12
Göynük, *Bolu, Turkey* 72 B4
Goz Beïda, *Chad* 79 F10
Goz Regeb, *Sudan* 81 D4
Gozdnica, *Poland* 45 G2
Gozo, *Malta* 36 C1
Graaff-Reinet, *S. Africa* 88 E3
Grabow, *Germany* 24 B7
Grabów nad Prosną, *Poland* 45 G5
Gračac, *Croatia* 29 D12
Gračanica, *Bos.-H.* 42 F3
Graçay, *France* 19 E8
Grace, *U.S.A.* 114 E8
Graceville, *U.S.A.* 112 C6
Gracias a Dios, C., *Honduras* 120 D3
Graciosa, I., *Canary Is.* 37 E6
Grad Sofiya □, *Bulgaria* 40 D7
Gradac, *Montenegro, Yug.* 40 C3
Gradačac, *Bos.-H.* 42 F3
Gradeška Planina, *Macedonia* 40 E6
Gradets, *Bulgaria* 41 D10
Gradišče, *Slovenia* 29 B12
Grădiştea de Munte, *Romania* 43 E8
Grado, *Italy* 29 C10
Grado, *Spain* 34 B4
Gradule, *Australia* 95 D4
Grady, *U.S.A.* 113 H3
Graeca, Lacul, *Romania* 43 F11
Grafenau, *Germany* 25 G9
Gräfenberg, *Germany* 25 F7
Grafham Water, *U.K.* 13 E7
Grafton, *Australia* 95 D5
Grafton, *U.S.A.* 112 A6
Graham, *Canada* 102 C1
Graham, *N.C., U.S.A.* 109 G6
Graham, *Tex., U.S.A.* 113 J5
Graham →, *Canada* 104 B4
Graham, Mt., *U.S.A.* 115 K9
Graham Bell, Ostrov = Greem-Bell, Ostrov, *Russia* 50 A7
Graham I., *Canada* 104 C2
Graham Land, *Antarctica* 5 C17
Grahamdale, *Canada* 105 C9
Grahamstown, *S. Africa* 88 E4
Grahovo, *Montenegro, Yug.* 40 D2
Graie, Alpi, *Europe* 21 C11
Grain Coast, *W. Afr.* 82 E3
Grajaú, *Brazil* 125 E9
Grajaú →, *Brazil* 125 D10
Grajewo, *Poland* 44 E9
Gramada, *Bulgaria* 40 C6
Gramat, *France* 20 D5
Grammichele, *Italy* 31 E7
Grámmos, Óros, *Greece* 40 F4
Grampian Highlands = Grampian Mts., *U.K.* 14 E5
Grampian Mts., *U.K.* 14 E5
Gramsh, *Albania* 40 F4
Gran Canaria, *Canary Is.* 37 G4
Gran Chaco, *S. Amer.* 126 B3
Gran Paradiso, *Italy* 28 C4
Gran Sasso d'Itália, *Italy* 29 F10
Granada, *Nic.* 120 D2
Granada, *Spain* 35 H7
Granada, *U.S.A.* 113 F3
Granada □, *Spain* 35 H7
Granadilla de Abona, *Canary Is.* 37 F3
Granard, *Ireland* 15 C4
Granbury, *U.S.A.* 113 J6
Granby, *Canada* 102 C5
Grand →, *Mo., U.S.A.* 112 F8
Grand →, *S. Dak., U.S.A.* 112 C4
Grand Bahama, *Bahamas* 120 A4
Grand Bank, *Canada* 103 C8
Grand Bassam, *Ivory C.* 82 D4
Grand Bérébry, *Ivory C.* 82 E3
Grand-Bourg, *Guadeloupe* 121 C7
Grand Canal = Yun Ho →, *China* 57 E9
Grand Canyon, *U.S.A.* 115 H7
Grand Canyon National Park, *U.S.A.* 115 H7
Grand Cayman, *Cayman Is.* 120 C3
Grand Cess, *Liberia* 82 E3
Grand Coulee, *U.S.A.* 114 C4
Grand Coulee Dam, *U.S.A.* 114 C4
Grand Falls, *Canada* 103 C8
Grand Forks, *Canada* 104 D5
Grand Forks, *U.S.A.* 112 B6
Grand Haven, *U.S.A.* 108 D2
Grand I., *U.S.A.* 108 B2
Grand Island, *U.S.A.* 112 E5
Grand Isle, *U.S.A.* 113 L10
Grand Junction, *U.S.A.* 115 G9
Grand L., *N.B., Canada* 103 C6
Grand L., *Nfld., Canada* 103 C8
Grand L., *Nfld., Canada* 103 B7
Grand L., *U.S.A.* 113 L8
Grand Lac Victoria, *Canada* 102 C4
Grand Lahou, *Ivory C.* 82 D3
Grand Lake, *U.S.A.* 114 F11
Grand-Lieu, L. de, *France* 18 E5
Grand Manan I., *Canada* 103 D6
Grand Marais, *Canada* 112 B9
Grand Marais, *U.S.A.* 108 B3
Grand-Mère, *Canada* 102 C5
Grand Popo, *Benin* 83 D5
Grand Portage, *U.S.A.* 102 C2
Grand Prairie, *U.S.A.* 113 J6
Grand Rapids, *Canada* 105 C9
Grand Rapids, *Mich., U.S.A.* 108 D2
Grand Rapids, *Minn., U.S.A.* 112 B8
Grand St-Bernard, Col du, *Europe* 25 K3
Grand Teton, *U.S.A.* 114 E8
Grand Union Canal, *U.K.* 13 E7
Grand Valley, *U.S.A.* 114 G9
Grand View, *Canada* 105 C8
Grandas de Salime, *Spain* 34 B4
Grande →, *Jujuy, Argentina* 126 A2
Grande →, *Mendoza, Argentina* 126 D2
Grande →, *Bolivia* 124 G6
Grande →, *Bahia, Brazil* 125 F10
Grande →, *Minas Gerais, Brazil* 125 H8
Grande, B., *Argentina* 128 G3
Grande, Rio →, *U.S.A.* 113 N6
Grande Baie, *Canada* 103 C5

Grande Baleine, R. de la →, *Canada* 102 A4
Grande Cache, *Canada* 104 C5
Grande de Santiago →, *Mexico* 118 C3
Grande-Entrée, *Canada* 103 C7
Grande Prairie, *Canada* 104 B5
Grande-Rivière, *Canada* 103 C7
Grande-Vallée, *Canada* 103 C6
Grandes-Bergeronnes, *Canada* 103 C6
Grandfalls, *U.S.A.* 113 K3
Grandoe Mines, *Canada* 104 B3
Grândola, *Portugal* 35 G2
Grandpré, *France* 19 C11
Grandview, *U.S.A.* 114 C4
Grandvilliers, *France* 19 C8
Graneros, *Chile* 126 C1
Grangemouth, *U.K.* 14 E5
Granger, *Wash., U.S.A.* 114 C3
Granger, *Wyo., U.S.A.* 114 F9
Grängesberg, *Sweden* 10 D9
Grangeville, *U.S.A.* 114 D5
Granite City, *U.S.A.* 112 F9
Granite Falls, *U.S.A.* 112 C7
Granite Mt., *U.S.A.* 117 M10
Granite Peak, *Australia* 93 E3
Granite Peak, *U.S.A.* 114 D9
Granitola, C., *Italy* 30 E5
Granity, *N.Z.* 91 J3
Granja, *Brazil* 125 D10
Granja de Moreruela, *Spain* 34 D5
Granja de Torrehermosa, *Spain* 35 G5
Gränna, *Sweden* 11 F8
Granollers, *Spain* 32 D7
Gransee, *Germany* 24 B9
Grant, *U.S.A.* 112 E4
Grant, Mt., *U.S.A.* 114 G4
Grant City, *U.S.A.* 112 E7
Grant I., *Australia* 92 B5
Grant Range, *U.S.A.* 115 G6
Grantham, *U.K.* 12 E7
Grantown-on-Spey, *U.K.* 14 D5
Grants, *U.S.A.* 115 J10
Grants Pass, *U.S.A.* 114 E2
Grantsburg, *U.S.A.* 112 C8
Grantsville, *U.S.A.* 114 F7
Granville, *France* 18 D5
Granville, *N. Dak., U.S.A.* 112 A4
Granville, *N.Y., U.S.A.* 108 D9
Granville L., *Canada* 105 B8
Grapeland, *U.S.A.* 113 K7
Graskop, *S. Africa* 89 C5
Gräsö, *Sweden* 10 D12
Grass →, *Canada* 105 B9
Grass Range, *U.S.A.* 114 C9
Grass River Prov. Park, *Canada* 105 C8
Grass Valley, *Calif., U.S.A.* 116 F6
Grass Valley, *Oreg., U.S.A.* 114 D3
Grassano, *Italy* 31 B9
Grasse, *France* 21 E10
Grassmere, *Australia* 95 E3
Gråsten, *Denmark* 11 K3
Grästorp, *Sweden* 11 F6
Gratkorn, *Austria* 26 D8
Graubünden □, *Switz.* 25 J5
Graulhet, *France* 20 E5
Graus, *Spain* 32 C5
Grave, Pte. de, *France* 20 C2
Gravelbourg, *Canada* 105 D7
Gravelines, *France* 19 A9
's-Gravenhage, *Neths.* 17 B4
Gravenhurst, *Canada* 110 B5
Gravesend, *Australia* 95 D5
Gravesend, *U.K.* 13 F8
Gravina in Púglia, *Italy* 31 B9
Gravois, Pointe-à-, *Haiti* 121 C5
Gravone →, *France* 21 G12
Gray, *France* 19 E12
Grayling, *U.S.A.* 108 C3
Grayling →, *Canada* 104 B4
Grays Harbor, *U.S.A.* 114 C1
Grays L., *U.S.A.* 114 E8
Grays River, *U.S.A.* 116 D3
Grayson, *Canada* 105 C8
Grayvoron, *Russia* 47 G8
Graz, *Austria* 26 D8
Grdelica, *Serbia, Yug.* 40 D6
Greasy L., *Canada* 104 A4
Great Abaco I., *Bahamas* 120 A4
Great Artesian Basin, *Australia* 94 C3
Great Australian Bight, *Australia* 93 F5
Great Bahama Bank, *Bahamas* 120 B4
Great Barrier I., *N.Z.* 91 G5
Great Barrier Reef, *Australia* 94 B4
Great Barrington, *U.S.A.* 111 D11
Great Basin, *U.S.A.* 114 G5
Great Bear →, *Canada* 100 B7
Great Bear L., *Canada* 100 B8
Great Belt = Store Bælt, *Denmark* 11 J4
Great Bend, *Kans., U.S.A.* 112 F5
Great Bend, *Pa., U.S.A.* 111 E9
Great Blasket I., *Ireland* 15 D1
Great Britain, *Europe* 6 E5
Great Central, *Canada* 104 D3
Great Dividing Ra., *Australia* 94 C4
Great Driffield = Driffield, *U.K.* 12 C7
Great Exuma I., *Bahamas* 120 B4
Great Falls, *Canada* 105 C9
Great Falls, *U.S.A.* 114 C8
Great Fish = Groot Vis →, *S. Africa* 88 E4
Great Guana Cay, *Bahamas* 120 B4
Great Harbour Deep, *Canada* 103 B8
Great I., *Canada* 105 B9
Great Inagua I., *Bahamas* 121 B5
Great Indian Desert = Thar Desert, *India* 68 F5
Great Karoo, *S. Africa* 88 E3
Great Lake, *Australia* 94 G4
Great Malvern, *U.K.* 13 E5
Great Ormes Head, *U.K.* 12 D4
Great Ouse →, *U.K.* 12 E8
Great Palm I., *Australia* 94 B4
Great Plains, *N. Amer.* 106 A6
Great Ruaha →, *Tanzania* 86 D4
Great Saint Bernard Pass = Grand St-Bernard, Col du, *Europe* 25 K3
Great Salt L., *U.S.A.* 114 F7
Great Salt Lake Desert, *U.S.A.* 114 F7
Great Salt Plains L., *U.S.A.* 113 G5
Great Sandy Desert, *Australia* 92 D3
Great Sangi = Sangihe, Pulau, *Indonesia* 63 D7
Great Scarcies →, *S. Leone* 82 D2
Great Skellig, *Ireland* 15 E1
Great Slave L., *Canada* 104 A5
Great Smoky Mts. Nat. Park, *U.S.A.* 109 H4
Great Stour = Stour →, *U.K.* 13 F9
Great Victoria Desert, *Australia* 93 E4
Great Wall, *China* 56 E5
Great Whernside, *U.K.* 12 C6
Great Yarmouth, *U.K.* 13 E9
Greater Antilles, *W. Indies* 121 C5
Greater London □, *U.K.* 13 F7
Greater Manchester □, *U.K.* 12 D5
Greater Sunda Is., *Indonesia* 62 F4
Grebbestad, *Sweden* 11 F5
Grebenka = Hrebenka, *Ukraine* 47 G7
Greco, C., *Cyprus* 36 E13
Greco, Mte., *Italy* 29 G10
Gredos, Sierra de, *Spain* 34 E6
Greece, *U.S.A.* 110 C7
Greece ■, *Europe* 38 B3
Greeley, *Colo., U.S.A.* 112 E2
Greeley, *Nebr., U.S.A.* 112 E5
Greem-Bell, Ostrov, *Russia* 50 A7
Green →, *Ky., U.S.A.* 108 G2
Green →, *Utah, U.S.A.* 115 G9
Green B., *U.S.A.* 108 C2
Green Bay, *U.S.A.* 108 C2
Green C., *Australia* 95 F5
Green Cove Springs, *U.S.A.* 109 L5
Green River, *U.S.A.* 115 G8
Greenbank, *U.S.A.* 116 B4
Greenbush, *Mich., U.S.A.* 110 B1
Greenbush, *Minn., U.S.A.* 112 A6
Greencastle, *U.S.A.* 108 F2
Greene, *U.S.A.* 111 D9
Greenfield, *Calif., U.S.A.* 116 J5
Greenfield, *Calif., U.S.A.* 117 K8
Greenfield, *Ind., U.S.A.* 108 F3
Greenfield, *Iowa, U.S.A.* 112 E7
Greenfield, *Mass., U.S.A.* 111 D12
Greenfield, *Mo., U.S.A.* 113 G8
Greenfield Park, *Canada* 111 A11
Greenland ■, *N. Amer.* 4 C5
Greenland Sea, *Arctic* 4 B7
Greenock, *U.K.* 14 F4
Greenore, *Ireland* 15 B5
Greenore Pt., *Ireland* 15 D5
Greenough →, *Australia* 93 E1
Greenport, *U.S.A.* 111 E12
Greensboro, *Ga., U.S.A.* 109 J4
Greensboro, *N.C., U.S.A.* 109 G6
Greensburg, *Ind., U.S.A.* 108 F3
Greensburg, *Kans., U.S.A.* 113 G5
Greensburg, *Pa., U.S.A.* 110 F5
Greenstone Pt., *U.K.* 14 D3
Greenville, *Liberia* 82 D3
Greenville, *Ala., U.S.A.* 109 K2
Greenville, *Calif., U.S.A.* 116 E6
Greenville, *Ill., U.S.A.* 112 F10
Greenville, *Maine, U.S.A.* 103 C6
Greenville, *Mich., U.S.A.* 108 D3
Greenville, *Miss., U.S.A.* 113 J9
Greenville, *N.C., U.S.A.* 109 H7
Greenville, *Ohio, U.S.A.* 108 E3
Greenville, *Pa., U.S.A.* 110 E4
Greenville, *S.C., U.S.A.* 109 H4
Greenville, *Tenn., U.S.A.* 109 G4
Greenville, *Tex., U.S.A.* 113 J6
Greenwater Lake Prov. Park, *Canada* 105 C8
Greenwich, *U.K.* 13 F8
Greenwich, *Conn., U.S.A.* 111 E11
Greenwich, *N.Y., U.S.A.* 111 C11
Greenwich, *Ohio, U.S.A.* 110 E2
Greenwood, *Canada* 104 D5
Greenwood, *Miss., U.S.A.* 113 J9
Greenwood, *S.C., U.S.A.* 109 H4
Greenwood, Mt., *Australia* 92 B5
Gregory, *U.S.A.* 112 D5
Gregory →, *Australia* 94 B2
Gregory, L., *S. Austral., Australia* 95 D2
Gregory, L., *W. Austral., Australia* 93 E2
Gregory Downs, *Australia* 94 B2
Gregory L., *Australia* 92 D4
Gregory Ra., *Queens., Australia* 94 B3
Gregory Ra., *W. Austral., Australia* 92 D3
Greiffenberg, *Germany* 24 B9
Greifswald, *Germany* 24 A9
Greifswalder Bodden, *Germany* 24 A9
Grein, *Austria* 26 C7
Greiz, *Germany* 24 E8
Gremikha, *Russia* 50 C4
Grenå, *Denmark* 11 H4
Grenada, *U.S.A.* 113 J10
Grenada ■, *W. Indies* 121 D7
Grenade, *France* 20 E5
Grenadines, *W. Indies* 121 D7
Grenchen, *Switz.* 25 H3
Grenen, *Denmark* 11 G4
Grenfell, *Australia* 95 E4
Grenfell, *Canada* 105 C8
Grenoble, *France* 21 C9
Grenora, *U.S.A.* 112 A3
Grenville, C., *Australia* 94 A3
Grenville Chan., *Canada* 104 C3
Gréoux-les-Bains, *France* 21 E9
Gresham, *U.S.A.* 116 E4
Gresik, *Indonesia* 63 G15
Gretna, *U.K.* 14 F5
Greven, *Germany* 24 C3
Grevená, *Greece* 40 F5
Grevená □, *Greece* 40 F5
Grevenbroich, *Germany* 24 D2
Grevenmacher, *Lux.* 17 E6
Grevesmühlen, *Germany* 24 B7
Grevestrand, *Denmark* 11 J6
Grey →, *N.Z.* 91 K3
Grey, C., *Australia* 94 A2
Grey Ra., *Australia* 95 D3
Grey Res., *Canada* 103 C8
Greybull, *U.S.A.* 114 D9
Greymouth, *N.Z.* 91 K3
Greystones, *Ireland* 15 C5
Greytown, *N.Z.* 91 J5
Greytown, *S. Africa* 89 D5
Gribanovskiy, *Russia* 48 E5
Gribbell I., *Canada* 104 C3
Gribës, Mal i, *Albania* 40 F3
Gridley, *U.S.A.* 116 F5
Griekwastad, *S. Africa* 88 D3
Griesheim, *Germany* 25 F4
Grieskirchen, *Austria* 26 C6
Griffin, *U.S.A.* 109 J3
Griffith, *Australia* 95 E4
Grignols, *France* 20 D3
Grigoriopol, *Moldova* 43 C14
Grimaylov = Hrymayliv, *Ukraine* 47 H4
Grimes, *U.S.A.* 116 F5
Grimma, *Germany* 24 D8
Grimmen, *Germany* 24 A9
Grimsay, *U.K.* 14 D1
Grimsby, *Canada* 110 C5
Grimsby, *U.K.* 12 D7
Grímsey, *Iceland* 8 C5
Grimshaw, *Canada* 104 B5
Grimslöv, *Sweden* 11 H8
Grimstad, *Norway* 9 G13
Grindelwald, *Switz.* 25 J4
Grindsted, *Denmark* 11 J2
Grindu, *Romania* 43 F11
Grinnell, *U.S.A.* 112 E8
Grintavec, *Slovenia* 29 B11
Gris-Nez, C., *France* 19 B8
Grisolles, *France* 20 E5
Grisons = Graubünden □, *Switz.* 25 J5
Grisslehamn, *Sweden* 10 D12
Grmeč Planina, *Bos.-H.* 29 D13
Groais I., *Canada* 103 B8
Grobiņa, *Latvia* 44 B8
Groblersdal, *S. Africa* 89 D4
Grobming, *Austria* 26 D6
Grocka, *Serbia, Yug.* 40 B4
Gródek, *Poland* 45 E10
Grodków, *Poland* 45 H4
Grodno = Hrodna, *Belarus* 46 F2
Grodzisk Mazowiecki, *Poland* 45 F7
Grodzisk Wielkopolski, *Poland* 45 F3
Grodzyanka = Hrodzyanka, *Belarus* 46 F5
Groesbeck, *U.S.A.* 113 K6
Groix, *France* 18 E3
Groix, Î. de, *France* 18 E3
Grójec, *Poland* 45 G7
Gronau, *Niedersachsen, Germany* 24 C5
Gronau, *Nordrhein-Westfalen, Germany* 24 C3
Grong, *Norway* 8 D15
Grönhögen, *Sweden* 11 H10
Groningen, *Neths.* 17 A6
Groningen □, *Neths.* 17 A6
Groom, *U.S.A.* 113 H4
Groot →, *S. Africa* 88 E3
Groot Berg →, *S. Africa* 88 E2
Groot-Brakrivier, *S. Africa* 88 E3
Groot-Kei →, *S. Africa* 89 E4
Groot Vis →, *S. Africa* 88 E4
Groote Eylandt, *Australia* 94 A2
Grootfontein, *Namibia* 88 B2
Grootlaagte →, *Africa* 88 C3
Grootvloer, *S. Africa* 88 E3
Gros C., *Canada* 104 A6
Grósio, *Italy* 28 B7
Grosne →, *France* 19 F11
Grossa, Pta., *Spain* 37 B8
Grossenbrode, *Germany* 24 A7
Grossenhain, *Germany* 24 D9
Grosser Arber, *Germany* 25 F9
Grosser Plöner See, *Germany* 24 A6
Grosseto, *Italy* 29 F8
Grossgerungs, *Austria* 26 C7
Grossglockner, *Austria* 26 D5
Groswater B., *Canada* 103 B8
Groton, *Conn., U.S.A.* 111 E12
Groton, *S. Dak., U.S.A.* 112 C5
Grottáglie, *Italy* 31 B10
Grottaminarda, *Italy* 31 A8
Grottammare, *Italy* 29 F10
Grouard Mission, *Canada* 104 B5
Grouin, Pte. du, *France* 18 D5
Groundhog →, *Canada* 102 C3
Grouse Creek, *U.S.A.* 114 F7
Grouw, *Neths.* 17 A5
Grove City, *U.S.A.* 110 E4
Groveland, *U.S.A.* 116 H6
Grover City, *U.S.A.* 117 K6
Groveton, *N.H., U.S.A.* 111 B13
Groveton, *Tex., U.S.A.* 113 K7
Grožnjan, *Croatia* 29 C10
Groznyy, *Russia* 49 J7
Grubišno Polje, *Croatia* 42 E2
Grudovo, *Bulgaria* 41 D11
Grudusk, *Poland* 45 E7
Grudziądz, *Poland* 44 E5
Gruinard B., *U.K.* 14 D3
Gruissan, *France* 20 E7
Grumo Áppula, *Italy* 31 A9
Grums, *Sweden* 10 E7
Grünberg, *Germany* 24 E4
Gründau, *Germany* 25 E5
Grundy Center, *U.S.A.* 112 D8
Grünstadt, *Germany* 25 F4
Gruvberget, *Sweden* 10 C10
Gruver, *U.S.A.* 113 G4
Gruyères, *Switz.* 25 J3
Gruža, *Serbia, Yug.* 40 C4
Gryazi, *Russia* 47 F10
Gryazovets, *Russia* 46 C11
Grybów, *Poland* 45 J7
Grycksbo, *Sweden* 10 D9
Gryfice, *Poland* 44 E2
Gryfino, *Poland* 45 E1
Gryfów Śląski, *Poland* 45 G2
Grythyttan, *Sweden* 10 E8
Gstaad, *Switz.* 25 J3
Gua, *India* 67 H14
Gua Musang, *Malaysia* 65 K3
Guacanayabo, G. de, *Cuba* 120 B4
Guachípas →, *Argentina* 126 B2
Guadajoz →, *Spain* 35 H6
Guadalajara, *Mexico* 118 C4
Guadalajara, *Spain* 32 E1
Guadalajara □, *Spain* 32 E2
Guadalcanal, *Solomon Is.* 96 H8
Guadalcanal, *Spain* 35 G5
Guadalén →, *Spain* 35 G7
Guadales, *Argentina* 126 C2
Guadalete →, *Spain* 35 J4
Guadalimar →, *Spain* 35 G7
Guadalmena →, *Spain* 35 G8
Guadalmez →, *Spain* 35 G5
Guadalope →, *Spain* 32 D4
Guadalquivir →, *Spain* 35 J4
Guadalupe = Guadeloupe ■, *W. Indies* 121 C7
Guadalupe, *Mexico* 117 N10
Guadalupe, *Spain* 35 F5
Guadalupe, *U.S.A.* 117 L6
Guadalupe →, *Mexico* 117 N10
Guadalupe →, *U.S.A.* 113 L6
Guadalupe, Sierra de, *Spain* 35 F5
Guadalupe Bravos, *Mexico* 118 A3
Guadalupe I., *Pac. Oc.* 98 G8
Guadalupe Peak, *U.S.A.* 115 L11
Guadalupe y Calvo, *Mexico* 118 B3
Guadarrama, Sierra de, *Spain* 34 E7
Guadauta, *Georgia* 49 J5
Guadeloupe ■, *W. Indies* 121 C7
Guadeloupe Passage, *W. Indies* 121 C7
Guadiamar →, *Spain* 35 J4
Guadiana →, *Portugal* 35 H3
Guadiana Menor →, *Spain* 35 H7
Guadiaro →, *Spain* 35 J5
Guadiato →, *Spain* 35 H5
Guadiela →, *Spain* 32 E2
Guadix, *Spain* 35 H7
Guafo, Boca del, *Chile* 128 E2
Guainía →, *Colombia* 124 C5
Guaíra, *Brazil* 127 A5
Guaitecas, Is., *Chile* 128 E2
Guajará-Mirim, *Brazil* 124 F5
Guajira, Pen. de la, *Colombia* 124 A4
Gualán, *Guatemala* 120 C2
Gualdo Tadino, *Italy* 29 E9
Gualeguay, *Argentina* 126 C4
Gualeguaychú, *Argentina* 126 C4
Guam ■, *Pac. Oc.* 96 F6
Guaminí, *Argentina* 126 D3
Guamúchil, *Mexico* 118 B3
Guan Xian, *China* 58 B4
Guanabacoa, *Cuba* 120 B3
Guanacaste, Cordillera del, *Costa Rica* 120 D2
Guanaceví, *Mexico* 118 B3
Guanahani = San Salvador, *Bahamas* 121 B5
Guanajay, *Cuba* 120 B3
Guanajuato, *Mexico* 118 C4
Guanajuato □, *Mexico* 118 C4
Guandacol, *Argentina* 126 B2
Guane, *Cuba* 120 B3
Guang'an, *China* 58 B6
Guangchang, *China* 59 D11
Guangde, *China* 59 B12
Guangdong □, *China* 59 F9
Guangfeng, *China* 59 C12
Guanghan, *China* 58 B5
Guanghua, *China* 59 A8
Guangji, *China* 59 C10
Guangling, *China* 56 E8
Guangning, *China* 59 F9
Guangrao, *China* 57 F10
Guangshun, *China* 58 D6
Guangwu, *China* 56 F3
Guangxi Zhuangzu Zizhiqu □, *China* 58 F7
Guangyuan, *China* 58 A5
Guangze, *China* 59 D11
Guangzhou, *China* 59 F9
Guanipa →, *Venezuela* 124 B6
Guanling, *China* 58 E5
Guannan, *China* 57 G10
Guantánamo, *Cuba* 121 B4
Guantao, *China* 56 F8
Guanyang, *China* 59 E8
Guanyun, *China* 57 G10
Guápiles, *Costa Rica* 120 D3
Guaporé →, *Brazil* 122 E4
Guaqui, *Bolivia* 124 G5
Guara, Sierra de, *Spain* 32 C4
Guarapari, *Brazil* 127 A7
Guarapuava, *Brazil* 127 B5
Guaratinguetá, *Brazil* 127 A6
Guaratuba, *Brazil* 127 B6
Guarda, *Portugal* 34 E3
Guarda □, *Portugal* 34 E3
Guardafui, C. = Asir, Ras, *Somali Rep.* 74 E5
Guardamar del Segura, *Spain* 33 G4
Guardavalle, *Italy* 31 D9
Guárdia Sanframondi, *Italy* 31 A7
Guardiagrele, *Italy* 29 F11
Guardo, *Spain* 34 C6
Guareña, *Spain* 35 G4
Guareña →, *Spain* 34 D5
Guaria □, *Paraguay* 126 B4
Guárico □, *Venezuela* 124 B5
Guarujá, *Brazil* 127 A6
Guarus, *Brazil* 127 A7
Guasave, *Mexico* 118 B3
Guasdualito, *Venezuela* 124 B4
Guastalla, *Italy* 28 D7
Guatemala, *Guatemala* 120 D1
Guatemala ■, *Cent. Amer.* 120 C1
Guaviare →, *Colombia* 122 C4
Guaxupé, *Brazil* 127 A6
Guayama, *Puerto Rico* 121 C6
Guayaquil, *Ecuador* 124 D3
Guayaquil, G. de, *Ecuador* 122 D2
Guaymas, *Mexico* 118 B2
Guazhou, *China* 59 A12
Guba, *Dem. Rep. of the Congo* 87 E2
Gûbâl, Madîq, *Egypt* 80 B3
Gubat, *Phil.* 61 E6
Gúbbio, *Italy* 29 E9
Guben, *Germany* 24 D10
Gubin, *Poland* 45 G1
Gubio, *Nigeria* 83 C7
Gubkin, *Russia* 47 G9
Guča, *Serbia, Yug.* 40 C4
Gudata = Guadauta, *Georgia* 49 J5
Gudbrandsdalen, *Norway* 9 F14
Guddu Barrage, *Pakistan* 66 E6
Gudenå →, *Denmark* 11 H4
Gudermes, *Russia* 49 J8
Gudhjem, *Denmark* 11 J8
Gudivada, *India* 67 L12
Gudur, *India* 66 M11
Guebwiller, *France* 19 E14
Guecho = Getxo, *Spain* 32 B2
Guékédou, *Guinea* 82 D2
Guelph, *Canada* 102 D3
Guéméné-Penfao, *France* 18 E5
Guéméné-sur-Scorff, *France* 18 D3
Guéné, *Benin* 83 C5
Guer, *France* 18 E4
Guérande, *France* 18 E4
Guéret, *France* 19 F8
Guérigny, *France* 19 E10
Guerneville, *U.S.A.* 116 G4
Guernica = Gernika-Lumo, *Spain* 32 B2
Guernsey, *U.K.* 13 H5

Guernsey, *U.S.A.* 112 D2
Guerrero □, *Mexico* 119 D5
Gueugnon, *France* 19 F11
Gueydan, *U.S.A.* 113 K8
Gūgher, *Iran* 71 D8
Guglionesi, *Italy* 29 G11
Gui Jiang →, *China* 59 F8
Gui Xian, *China* 58 F7
Guia, *Canary Is.* 37 F4
Guia de Isora, *Canary Is.* 37 F3
Guia Lopes da Laguna, *Brazil* 127 A4
Guiana, *S. Amer.* 122 C4
Guichi, *China* 59 B11
Guider, *Cameroon* 83 D7
Guidimouni, *Niger* 83 C6
Guiding, *China* 58 D6
Guidong, *China* 59 D9
Guidónia-Montecélio, *Italy* 29 F9
Guiglo, *Ivory C.* 82 D3
Guijá, *Mozam.* 89 C5
Guijuelo, *Spain* 34 E5
Guildford, *U.K.* 13 F7
Guilford, *U.S.A.* 103 C6
Guilin, *China* 59 E8
Guillaumes, *France* 21 D10
Guillestre, *France* 21 D10
Guilvinec, *France* 18 E2
Güimar, *Canary Is.* 37 F3
Guimarães, *Portugal* 34 D2
Guimaras, *Phil.* 61 F5
Guinda, *U.S.A.* 116 G4
Guinea, *Africa* 76 F4
Guinea ■, *W. Afr.* 82 C2
Guinea, Gulf of, *Atl. Oc.* 83 E5
Guinea-Bissau ■, *Africa* 82 C2
Güines, *Cuba* 120 B3
Guingamp, *France* 18 D3
Guipavas, *France* 18 D2
Guiping, *China* 59 F8
Guipúzcoa □, *Spain* 32 B2
Güiria, *Venezuela* 124 A6
Guiscard, *France* 19 C10
Guise, *France* 19 C10
Guitiriz, *Spain* 34 B3
Guiuan, *Phil.* 61 F6
Guixi, *China* 59 C11
Guiyang, *Guizhou, China* 58 D6
Guiyang, *Hunan, China* 59 E9
Guizhou □, *China* 58 D6
Gujan-Mestras, *France* 20 D2
Gujarat □, *India* 68 H4
Gujiang, *China* 59 D10
Gujranwala, *Pakistan* 68 C6
Gujrat, *Pakistan* 68 C6
Gukovo, *Russia* 49 F5
Gulbarga, *India* 66 L10
Gulbene, *Latvia* 9 H22
Gulf, The, *Asia* 71 E6
Gulfport, *U.S.A.* 113 K10
Gulgong, *Australia* 95 E4
Gulin, *China* 58 C5
Gulistan, *Pakistan* 68 D2
Gull Lake, *Canada* 105 C7
Gullbrandstorp, *Sweden* 11 H6
Gullspång, *Sweden* 11 F8
Güllük, *Turkey* 39 D9
Güllük Korfezi, *Turkey* 39 D9
Gulma, *Nigeria* 83 C5
Gulmarg, *India* 69 B6
Gülnar, *Turkey* 72 D5
Gülpınar, *Turkey* 39 B8
Gülşehir, *Turkey* 72 C6
Gulshad, *Kazakstan* 50 E8
Gulu, *Uganda* 86 B3
Gŭlŭbovo, *Bulgaria* 41 D9
Gulwe, *Tanzania* 86 D4
Gulyaypole = Hulyaypole, *Ukraine* 47 J9
Gum Lake, *Australia* 95 E3
Gumal →, *Pakistan* 68 D4
Gumbaz, *Pakistan* 68 D3
Gumel, *Nigeria* 83 C6
Gumiel de Hizán, *Spain* 34 D7
Gumlu, *Australia* 94 B4
Gumma □, *Japan* 55 F9
Gummersbach, *Germany* 24 D3
Gummi, *Nigeria* 83 C6
Gümüldür, *Turkey* 39 C9
Gümüşçay, *Turkey* 41 F11
Gümüşhaciköy, *Turkey* 72 B6
Gümüşhane, *Turkey* 73 B8
Gümüşsu, *Turkey* 39 C11
Gumzai, *Indonesia* 63 F8
Guna, *Ethiopia* 81 E4
Guna, *India* 68 G7
Gundagai, *Australia* 95 F4
Gundelfingen, *Germany* 25 G6
Güney, *Burdur, Turkey* 39 D11
Güney, *Denizli, Turkey* 39 C11
Güneydoğu Toroslar, *Turkey* 73 C9
Gunisao →, *Canada* 105 C9
Gunisao L., *Canada* 105 C9
Günlüce, *Turkey* 39 E10
Gunnarskog, *Sweden* 10 E6
Gunnbjørn Fjeld, *Greenland* 4 C6
Gunnebo, *Sweden* 11 G10
Gunnedah, *Australia* 95 E5
Gunningbar Cr. →, *Australia* 95 E4
Gunnison, *Colo., U.S.A.* 115 G10
Gunnison, *Utah, U.S.A.* 114 G8
Gunnison →, *U.S.A.* 115 G9
Gunpowder, *Australia* 94 B2
Guntakal, *India* 66 M10
Guntersville, *U.S.A.* 109 H2
Guntong, *Malaysia* 65 K3
Guntur, *India* 67 L12
Gunungapi, *Indonesia* 63 F7
Gunungsitoli, *Indonesia* 62 D1
Günz →, *Germany* 25 G6
Gunza, *Angola* 84 G2
Günzburg, *Germany* 25 G6
Gunzenhausen, *Germany* 25 F6
Guo He →, *China* 57 H9
Guoyang, *China* 56 H9
Gupis, *Pakistan* 69 A5
Gura Humorului, *Romania* 43 C10
Gura-Teghii, *Romania* 43 E11
Gurag, *Ethiopia* 81 F4
Gurahonţ, *Romania* 42 D7
Gurdaspur, *India* 68 C6
Gurdon, *U.S.A.* 113 J8
Güre, *Balıkesir, Turkey* 39 B8
Güre, *Uşak, Turkey* 39 C11
Gurgaon, *India* 68 E7
Gürgentepe, *Turkey* 72 B7
Gurghiu, Munţii, *Romania* 43 D10
Gurgueia →, *Brazil* 125 E10
Gurha, *India* 68 G4
Guri, Embalse de, *Venezuela* 124 B6
Gurjaani, *Georgia* 49 K7
Gurk →, *Austria* 26 E7
Gurkha, *Nepal* 69 E11
Gurley, *Australia* 95 D4
Gürpınar, *İst., Turkey* 41 F12
Gürpınar, *Van, Turkey* 73 C10
Gürsu, *Turkey* 41 F13
Gurué, *Mozam.* 87 F4
Gurun, *Malaysia* 65 K3
Gürün, *Turkey* 72 C7
Gurupá, *Brazil* 125 D8
Gurupá, I. Grande de, *Brazil* 125 D8
Gurupi, *Brazil* 125 F9
Gurupi →, *Brazil* 125 D9
Guryev = Atyraū, *Kazakstan* 50 E6
Gus-Khrustalnyy, *Russia* 48 C5
Gusau, *Nigeria* 83 C6
Gusev, *Russia* 9 J20
Gushan, *China* 57 E12
Gushgy, *Turkmenistan* 50 F7
Gushi, *China* 59 A10
Gushiago, *Ghana* 83 D4
Gusinje, *Montenegro, Yug.* 40 D3
Gusinoozersk, *Russia* 51 D11
Gúspini, *Italy* 30 C1
Güssing, *Austria* 27 D9
Gustavsberg, *Sweden* 10 E12
Gustine, *U.S.A.* 116 H6
Güstrow, *Germany* 24 B8
Gusum, *Sweden* 11 F10
Guta = Kolárovo, *Slovak Rep.* 27 D10
Gütersloh, *Germany* 24 D4
Gutha, *Australia* 93 E2
Guthalongra, *Australia* 94 B4
Guthrie, *U.S.A.* 113 H6
Gutian, *China* 59 D12
Guttenberg, *U.S.A.* 112 D9
Guyana ■, *S. Amer.* 124 C7
Guyane française = French Guiana ■, *S. Amer.* 125 C8
Guyang, *China* 56 D6
Guyenne, *France* 20 D4
Guymon, *U.S.A.* 113 G4
Guyra, *Australia* 95 E5
Guyuan, *Hebei, China* 56 D8
Guyuan, *Ningxia Huizu, China* 56 G4
Güzelbahçe, *Turkey* 39 C8
Guzhang, *China* 58 C7
Guzhen, *China* 57 H9
Guzmán, L. de, *Mexico* 118 A3
Gvardeysk, *Russia* 9 J19
Gvardeyskoye, *Ukraine* 47 K8
Gwa, *Burma* 67 L19
Gwaai, *Zimbabwe* 87 F2
Gwabegar, *Australia* 95 E4
Gwadabawa, *Nigeria* 83 C6
Gwādar, *Pakistan* 66 G3
Gwagwada, *Nigeria* 83 C6
Gwalia, *Australia* 93 E3
Gwalior, *India* 68 F8
Gwanda, *Zimbabwe* 87 G2
Gwandu, *Nigeria* 83 C5
Gwane, *Dem. Rep. of the Congo* 86 B2
Gwaram, *Nigeria* 83 C7
Gwarzo, *Nigeria* 83 C6
Gwda →, *Poland* 45 E3
Gweebarra B., *Ireland* 15 B3
Gweedore, *Ireland* 15 A3
Gweru, *Zimbabwe* 87 F2
Gwi, *Nigeria* 83 D6
Gwinn, *U.S.A.* 108 B2
Gwio Kura, *Nigeria* 83 C7
Gwol, *Ghana* 82 C4
Gwoza, *Nigeria* 83 C7
Gwydir →, *Australia* 95 D4
Gwynedd □, *U.K.* 12 E3
Gyandzha = Gäncä, *Azerbaijan* 49 K8
Gyaring Hu, *China* 60 C4
Gydanskiy Poluostrov, *Russia* 50 C8
Gympie, *Australia* 95 D5
Gyomaendrőd, *Hungary* 42 D5
Gyöngyös, *Hungary* 42 C4
Győr, *Hungary* 42 C2
Győr-Moson-Sopron □, *Hungary* 42 C2
Gypsum Pt., *Canada* 104 A6
Gypsumville, *Canada* 105 C9
Gyueshevo, *Bulgaria* 40 D6
Gyula, *Hungary* 42 D6
Gyumri, *Armenia* 49 K6
Gyzylarbat, *Turkmenistan* 50 F6
Gzhatsk = Gagarin, *Russia* 46 E8

H

Ha 'Arava →, *Israel* 75 E4
Ha Coi, *Vietnam* 64 B6
Ha Dong, *Vietnam* 64 B5
Ha Giang, *Vietnam* 64 A5
Ha Tien, *Vietnam* 65 G5
Ha Tinh, *Vietnam* 64 C5
Ha Trung, *Vietnam* 64 C5
Haaksbergen, *Neths.* 17 B6
Haapsalu, *Estonia* 9 G20
Haarlem, *Neths.* 17 B4
Haast →, *N.Z.* 91 K2
Haast Bluff, *Australia* 92 D5
Hab Nadi Chauki, *Pakistan* 68 G2
Habaswein, *Kenya* 86 B4
Habay, *Canada* 104 B5
Ḩabbānīyah, *Iraq* 70 C4
Ḩabbānīyah, Hawr al, *Iraq* 73 F10
Habo, *Sweden* 11 G8
Haboro, *Japan* 54 B10
Hachenburg, *Germany* 24 E3
Hachijō-Jima, *Japan* 55 H9
Hachinohe, *Japan* 54 D10
Hachiōji, *Japan* 55 G9
Hachŏn, *N. Korea* 57 D15
Hacıbektaş, *Turkey* 72 C6
Hacılar, *Turkey* 72 C6
Hackås, *Sweden* 10 B8
Hackensack, *U.S.A.* 111 F10
Hadali, *Pakistan* 68 C5
Hadarba, Ras, *Sudan* 80 C4
Hadarom □, *Israel* 75 E4
Hadejia, *Nigeria* 83 C7
Hadejia →, *Nigeria* 83 C7
Haden, *Australia* 95 D5
H̱adera, *Israel* 75 C3
H̱adera, N. →, *Israel* 75 C3
Haderslev, *Denmark* 11 J3
Hadhramaut = Ḩadramawt, *Yemen* 74 D4
Hadım, *Turkey* 72 D5
Hadong, *S. Korea* 57 G14
Ḩadramawt, *Yemen* 74 D4
Ḩadrānīyah, *Iraq* 70 C4
Hadrian's Wall, *U.K.* 12 B5
Hadsten, *Denmark* 11 H4
Hadsund, *Denmark* 11 H4
Hadyach, *Ukraine* 47 G8
Haeju, *N. Korea* 57 E13
Haenam, *S. Korea* 57 G14
Haerhpin = Harbin, *China* 57 B14
Hafar al Bāţin, *Si. Arabia* 70 D5
Hafik, *Turkey* 72 C7
Ḩafīrat al 'Aydā, *Si. Arabia* 70 E3
Hafizabad, *Pakistan* 68 C5
Haflong, *India* 67 G18
Hafnarfjörður, *Iceland* 8 D3
Hafun, Ras, *Somali Rep.* 74 E5
Hagalil, *Israel* 75 C4
Hagby, *Sweden* 11 H10
Hagen, *Germany* 24 D3
Hagenow, *Germany* 24 B7
Hagerman, *U.S.A.* 113 J2
Hagerstown, *U.S.A.* 108 F7
Hagetmau, *France* 20 E3
Hagfors, *Sweden* 10 D7
Hagi, *Japan* 55 G5
Hagolan, *Syria* 75 C4
Hagondange, *France* 19 C13
Hags Hd., *Ireland* 15 D2
Hague, C. de la, *France* 18 C5
Hague, The = 's-Gravenhage, *Neths.* 17 B4
Haguenau, *France* 19 D14
Hai □, *Tanzania* 86 C4
Hai Duong, *Vietnam* 64 B6
Hai'an, *Guangdong, China* 59 G8
Hai'an, *Jiangsu, China* 59 A13
Haicheng, *Fujian, China* 59 E11
Haicheng, *Liaoning, China* 57 D12
Haidar Khel, *Afghan.* 68 C3
Haifa = H̱efa, *Israel* 75 C4
Haifeng, *China* 59 F10
Haig, *Australia* 93 F4
Haiger, *Germany* 24 E4
Haikang, *China* 59 G8
Haikou, *China* 60 D6
Ḩā'il, *Si. Arabia* 70 E4
Hailar, *China* 60 B6
Hailey, *U.S.A.* 114 E6
Haileybury, *Canada* 102 C4
Hailin, *China* 57 B15
Hailing Dao, *China* 59 G8
Hailong, *China* 57 C13
Hailun, *China* 60 B7
Hailuoto, *Finland* 8 D21
Haimen, *Guangdong, China* 59 F11
Haimen, *Jiangsu, China* 59 B13
Haimen, *Zhejiang, China* 59 C13
Hainan □, *China* 60 E5
Hainaut □, *Belgium* 17 D4
Hainburg, *Austria* 27 C9
Haines, *U.S.A.* 114 D5
Haines City, *U.S.A.* 109 L5
Haines Junction, *Canada* 104 A1
Hainfeld, *Austria* 26 C8
Haining, *China* 59 B13
Haiphong, *Vietnam* 60 D5
Haiti ■, *W. Indies* 121 C5
Haiya, *Sudan* 80 D4
Haiyan, *China* 59 B13
Haiyang, *China* 57 F11
Haiyuan, *Guangxi Zhuangzu, China* 58 F6
Haiyuan, *Ningxia Huizu, China* 56 F3
Haizhou, *China* 57 G10
Haizhou Wan, *China* 57 G10
Hajdú-Bihar □, *Hungary* 42 C6
Hajdúböszörmény, *Hungary* 42 C6
Hajdúdurog, *Hungary* 42 C6
Hajdúhadház, *Hungary* 42 C6
Hajdúnánás, *Hungary* 42 C6
Hajdúsámson, *Hungary* 42 C6
Hajdúszoboszló, *Hungary* 42 C6
Hajipur, *India* 69 G11
Ḩājjī Muḩsin, *Iraq* 70 C5
Ḩājjīābād, *Eşfahan, Iran* 71 C7
Ḩājjīābād, *Hormozgān, Iran* 71 D7
Hajnówka, *Poland* 45 F10
Hakansson, Mts., *Dem. Rep. of the Congo* 87 D2
Hakkâri, *Turkey* 73 D10
Hakkâri Dağları, *Turkey* 73 C10
Hakken-Zan, *Japan* 55 G7
Hakodate, *Japan* 54 D10
Håksberg, *Sweden* 10 D9
Haku-San, *Japan* 55 F8
Hakui, *Japan* 55 F8
Hala, *Pakistan* 66 G6
Ḩalab, *Syria* 70 B3
Ḩalabjah, *Iraq* 70 C5
Halaib, *Sudan* 80 C4
Hālat 'Ammār, *Si. Arabia* 70 D3
Halbā, *Lebanon* 75 A5
Halberstadt, *Germany* 24 D7
Halcombe, *N.Z.* 91 J5
Halcon, *Phil.* 63 B6
Halden, *Norway* 9 G14
Haldensleben, *Germany* 24 C7
Haldia, *India* 67 H16
Haldwani, *India* 69 E8
Hale →, *Australia* 94 C2
Haleakala Crater, *U.S.A.* 106 H16
Halesowen, *U.K.* 13 E5
Haleyville, *U.S.A.* 109 H2
Half Assini, *Ghana* 82 D4
Halfway →, *Canada* 104 B4
Haliburton, *Canada* 102 C4
Halifax, *Australia* 94 B4
Halifax, *Canada* 103 D7
Halifax, *U.K.* 12 D6
Halifax B., *Australia* 94 B4
Halifax I., *Namibia* 88 D2
Halīl →, *Iran* 71 E8
Halkirk, *U.K.* 14 C5
Hall in Tirol, *Austria* 26 D4
Hall Pt., *Australia* 92 C3
Hallabro, *Sweden* 11 H9
Halland, *Sweden* 9 H15
Hallands län □, *Sweden* 11 H6
Hallands Väderö, *Sweden* 11 H6
Hallandsås, *Sweden* 11 H7
Hällbybrunn, *Sweden* 10 E10
Halle, *Belgium* 17 D4
Halle, *Nordrhein-Westfalen, Germany* 24 C4
Halle, *Sachsen-Anhalt, Germany* 24 D7
Hällefors, *Sweden* 10 E8
Hälleforsnäs, *Sweden* 10 E10
Hallein, *Austria* 26 D6
Hällekis, *Sweden* 11 F7
Hallen, *Sweden* 10 A8
Hallett, *Australia* 95 E2
Hallettsville, *U.S.A.* 113 L6
Halliday, *U.S.A.* 112 B3
Halliday L., *Canada* 105 A7
Hallim, *S. Korea* 57 H14
Hallingdalselvi →, *Norway* 9 F13
Hallock, *U.S.A.* 105 D9
Halls Creek, *Australia* 92 C4
Hallsberg, *Sweden* 10 E9
Hallstahammar, *Sweden* 10 E10
Hallstatt, *Austria* 26 D6
Hallstavik, *Sweden* 10 D12
Hallstead, *U.S.A.* 111 E9
Halmahera, *Indonesia* 63 D7
Halmeu, *Romania* 42 C8
Halmstad, *Sweden* 11 H6
Hals, *Denmark* 11 H4
Hälsingborg = Helsingborg, *Sweden* 11 H6
Hälsingland, *Sweden* 10 C10
Halstad, *U.S.A.* 112 B6
Halstead, *U.K.* 13 F8
Haltern, *Germany* 24 D3
Halti, *Finland* 8 B19
Halton □, *U.K.* 12 D5
Haltwhistle, *U.K.* 12 C5
Halul, *Qatar* 71 E7
Ḩalvān, *Iran* 71 C8
Ham, *France* 19 C10
Ham Tan, *Vietnam* 65 G6
Ham Yen, *Vietnam* 64 A5
Hamab, *Namibia* 88 D2
Hamad, *Sudan* 81 D3
Hamada, *Japan* 55 G6
Hamadān, *Iran* 71 C6
Hamadān □, *Iran* 71 C6
Hamāh, *Syria* 70 C3
Hamamatsu, *Japan* 55 G8
Hamar, *Norway* 9 F14
Hamâta, Gebel, *Egypt* 80 C4
Hambantota, *Sri Lanka* 66 R12
Hamber Prov. Park, *Canada* 104 C5
Hamburg, *Germany* 24 B5
Hamburg, *Ark., U.S.A.* 113 J9
Hamburg, *Iowa, U.S.A.* 112 E7
Hamburg, *N.Y., U.S.A.* 110 D6
Hamburg, *Pa., U.S.A.* 111 F9
Hamburg □, *Germany* 24 B5
Ḩamḑ, W. al →, *Si. Arabia* 70 E3
Hamden, *U.S.A.* 111 E12
Hamdibey, *Turkey* 39 B9
Häme, *Finland* 9 F20
Hämeenlinna, *Finland* 9 F21
Hamélé, *Ghana* 82 C4
Hamelin Pool, *Australia* 93 E1
Hameln, *Germany* 24 C5
Hamer Koke, *Ethiopia* 81 F4
Hamerkaz □, *Israel* 75 C3
Hamersley Ra., *Australia* 92 D2
Hamhung, *N. Korea* 57 E14
Hami, *China* 60 B4
Hamilton, *Australia* 95 F3
Hamilton, *Canada* 102 D4
Hamilton, *N.Z.* 91 G5
Hamilton, *U.K.* 14 F4
Hamilton, *Mo., U.S.A.* 112 F8
Hamilton, *Mont., U.S.A.* 114 C6
Hamilton, *N.Y., U.S.A.* 111 D9
Hamilton, *Ohio, U.S.A.* 108 F3
Hamilton, *Tex., U.S.A.* 113 K5
Hamilton →, *Australia* 94 C2
Hamilton City, *U.S.A.* 116 F4
Hamilton Hotel, *Australia* 94 C3
Hamilton Inlet, *Canada* 103 B8
Hamina, *Finland* 9 F22
Hamiota, *Canada* 105 C8
Hamitabat, *Turkey* 41 E11
Hamlet, *U.S.A.* 109 H6
Hamley Bridge, *Australia* 95 E2
Hamlin = Hameln, *Germany* 24 C5
Hamlin, *N.Y., U.S.A.* 110 C7
Hamlin, *Tex., U.S.A.* 113 J4
Hamm, *Germany* 24 D3
Hammarstrand, *Sweden* 10 A10
Hammelburg, *Germany* 25 E5
Hammeren, *Denmark* 11 J8
Hammerfest, *Norway* 8 A20
Hammerum, *Denmark* 11 H3
Hamminkeln, *Germany* 24 D2
Hammond, *Ind., U.S.A.* 108 E2
Hammond, *La., U.S.A.* 113 K9
Hammonton, *U.S.A.* 108 F8
Hamneda, *Sweden* 11 H7
Hamoyet, Jebel, *Sudan* 80 D4
Hampden, *N.Z.* 91 L3
Hampshire □, *U.K.* 13 F6
Hampshire Downs, *U.K.* 13 F6
Hampton, *Ark., U.S.A.* 113 J8
Hampton, *Iowa, U.S.A.* 112 D8
Hampton, *N.H., U.S.A.* 111 D14
Hampton, *S.C., U.S.A.* 109 J5
Hampton, *Va., U.S.A.* 108 G7
Hampton Tableland, *Australia* 93 F4
Hamra, *Sweden* 10 C8
Hamrat esh Sheykh, *Sudan* 81 E2
Hamur, *Turkey* 73 C10
Hamyang, *S. Korea* 57 G14
Han Jiang →, *China* 59 F11
Han Shui →, *China* 59 B10
Hana, *U.S.A.* 106 H17
Hanak, *Si. Arabia* 70 E3
Hanamaki, *Japan* 54 E10
Hanang, *Tanzania* 86 C4
Hanau, *Germany* 25 E4
Hanbogd, *Mongolia* 56 C4
Hançalar, *Turkey* 39 C11
Hânceşti, *Moldova* 43 D13
Hancheng, *China* 56 G6
Hanchuan, *China* 59 B9
Hancock, *Mich., U.S.A.* 112 B10
Hancock, *Minn., U.S.A.* 112 C7
Hancock, *N.Y., U.S.A.* 111 E9
Handa, *Japan* 55 G8
Handan, *China* 56 F8
Handeni, *Tanzania* 86 D4
Handeni □, *Tanzania* 86 D4
Handlová, *Slovak Rep.* 27 C11
Handub, *Sudan* 80 D4
Handwara, *India* 69 B6
Hanegev, *Israel* 75 E4
Haney, *Canada* 104 D4
Hanford, *U.S.A.* 116 J7
Hang Chat, *Thailand* 64 C2
Hang Dong, *Thailand* 64 C2
Hangang →, *S. Korea* 57 F14
Hangayn Nuruu, *Mongolia* 60 B4
Hangchou = Hangzhou, *China* 59 B13
Hanggin Houqi, *China* 56 D4
Hanggin Qi, *China* 56 E5
Hangu, *China* 57 E9

Hangzhou, *China* 59 B13
Hangzhou Wan, *China* 59 B13
Hanhongor, *Mongolia* 56 C3
Ḩanīdh, *Si. Arabia* 71 E6
Ḩanīsh, *Yemen* 74 E3
Haniska, *Slovak Rep.* 27 C14
Hanjiang, *China* 59 E12
Hankinson, *U.S.A.* 112 B6
Hanko, *Finland* 9 G20
Hankou, *China* 59 B10
Hanksville, *U.S.A.* 115 G8
Hanle, *India* 69 C8
Hanmer Springs, *N.Z.* 91 K4
Hann →, *Australia* 92 C4
Hann, Mt., *Australia* 92 C4
Hanna, *Canada* 104 C6
Hannaford, *U.S.A.* 112 B5
Hannah, *U.S.A.* 112 A5
Hannah B., *Canada* 102 B4
Hannibal, *U.S.A.* 112 F9
Hannik, *Sudan* 80 D3
Hannover, *Germany* 24 C5
Hanö, *Sweden* 11 H8
Hanöbukten, *Sweden* 11 J8
Hanoi, *Vietnam* 60 D5
Hanover = Hannover, *Germany* 24 C5
Hanover, *Canada* 110 B3
Hanover, *S. Africa* 88 E3
Hanover, *N.H., U.S.A.* 111 C12
Hanover, *Ohio, U.S.A.* 110 F2
Hanover, *Pa., U.S.A.* 108 F7
Hanover, I., *Chile* 128 G2
Hanshou, *China* 59 C8
Hansi, *India* 68 E6
Hanson, L., *Australia* 95 E2
Hanstholm, *Denmark* 11 G2
Hantsavichy, *Belarus* 47 F4
Hanyang, *China* 59 B10
Hanyin, *China* 58 A7
Hanyuan, *China* 58 C4
Hanzhong, *China* 56 H4
Hanzhuang, *China* 57 G9
Haora, *India* 69 H13
Haoxue, *China* 59 B9
Haparanda, *Sweden* 8 D21
Happy, *U.S.A.* 113 H4
Happy Camp, *U.S.A.* 114 F2
Happy Valley-Goose Bay, *Canada* 103 B7
Hapsu, *N. Korea* 57 D15
Hapur, *India* 68 E7
Ḩaql, *Si. Arabia* 75 F3
Har, *Indonesia* 63 F8
Har-Ayrag, *Mongolia* 56 B5
Har Hu, *China* 60 C4
Har Us Nuur, *Mongolia* 60 B4
Har Yehuda, *Israel* 75 D3
Ḩaraḑ, *Si. Arabia* 74 C4
Haradok, *Belarus* 46 E6
Häradsbäck, *Sweden* 11 H8
Haranomachi, *Japan* 54 F10
Harare, *Zimbabwe* 87 F3
Harat, *Eritrea* 81 D4
Harbin, *China* 57 B14
Harbiye, *Turkey* 72 D7
Harbo, *Sweden* 10 D11
Harboør, *Denmark* 11 H2
Harbor Beach, *U.S.A.* 108 D4
Harbor Springs, *U.S.A.* 108 C3
Harbour Breton, *Canada* 103 C8
Harbour Grace, *Canada* 103 C9
Harburg, *Germany* 24 B5
Hårby, *Denmark* 11 J4
Harda, *India* 68 H7
Hardangerfjorden, *Norway* 9 F12
Hardangervidda, *Norway* 9 F12
Hardap Dam, *Namibia* 88 C2
Hardenberg, *Neths.* 17 B6
Harderwijk, *Neths.* 17 B5
Hardey →, *Australia* 92 D2
Hardin, *U.S.A.* 114 D10
Harding, *S. Africa* 89 E4
Harding Ra., *Australia* 92 C3
Hardisty, *Canada* 104 C6
Hardman, *U.S.A.* 114 D4
Hardoi, *India* 69 F9
Hardwar = Haridwar, *India* 68 E8
Hardwick, *U.S.A.* 111 B12
Hardy, *U.S.A.* 113 G9
Hardy, Pen., *Chile* 128 H3
Hare B., *Canada* 103 B8
Hareid, *Norway* 9 E12
Haren, *Germany* 24 C3
Harer, *Ethiopia* 81 F5
Harerge □, *Ethiopia* 81 F5
Hareto, *Ethiopia* 81 F4
Harfleur, *France* 18 C7
Hargeisa, *Somali Rep.* 74 F3
Harghita □, *Romania* 43 D10
Harghita, Munţii, *Romania* 43 D10
Hargshamn, *Sweden* 10 D12
Hari →, *Indonesia* 62 E2
Haria, *Canary Is.* 37 E6
Haridwar, *India* 68 E8
Haringhata →, *Bangla.* 67 J16
Harīrūd →, *Asia* 66 A2
Härjedalen, *Sweden* 10 B7
Harlan, *Iowa, U.S.A.* 112 E7
Harlan, *Ky., U.S.A.* 109 G4
Hârlău, *Romania* 43 C11
Harlech, *U.K.* 12 E3
Harlem, *U.S.A.* 114 B9
Hårlev, *Denmark* 11 J6
Harlingen, *Neths.* 17 A5
Harlingen, *U.S.A.* 113 M6
Harlow, *U.K.* 13 F8
Harlowton, *U.S.A.* 114 C9
Harmancık, *Turkey* 39 B11
Harmånger, *Sweden* 10 C11
Harmil, *Eritrea* 81 D5
Harney Basin, *U.S.A.* 114 E4
Harney L., *U.S.A.* 114 E4
Harney Peak, *U.S.A.* 112 D3
Härnön, *Sweden* 10 B12
Härnösand, *Sweden* 10 B11
Haro, *Spain* 32 C2
Haroldswick, *U.K.* 14 A8
Harp L., *Canada* 103 A7
Harper, *Liberia* 82 E3
Harplinge, *Sweden* 11 H6
Harrand, *Pakistan* 68 E4
Harriman, *U.S.A.* 109 H3
Harrington Harbour, *Canada* 103 B8
Harris, *U.K.* 14 D2
Harris, Sd. of, *U.K.* 14 D1
Harris L., *Australia* 95 E2
Harrisburg, *Ill., U.S.A.* 113 G10
Harrisburg, *Nebr., U.S.A.* 112 E3
Harrisburg, *Oreg., U.S.A.* 114 D2
Harrisburg, *Pa., U.S.A.* 110 F8
Harrismith, *S. Africa* 89 D4
Harrison, *Ark., U.S.A.* 113 G8
Harrison, *Idaho, U.S.A.* 114 C5
Harrison, *Nebr., U.S.A.* 112 D3
Harrison, C., *Canada* 103 B8
Harrison L., *Canada* 104 D4
Harrisonburg, *U.S.A.* 108 F6
Harrisonville, *U.S.A.* 112 F7
Harriston, *Canada* 102 D3
Harrisville, *U.S.A.* 110 B1
Harrogate, *U.K.* 12 C6
Harrow, *U.K.* 13 F7
Harsefeld, *Germany* 24 B5
Harsewinkel, *Germany* 24 D4
Harsīn, *Iran* 70 C5
Hârşova, *Romania* 43 F12
Harstad, *Norway* 8 B17
Hart, *U.S.A.* 108 D2
Hart, L., *Australia* 95 E2
Hartbees →, *S. Africa* 88 D3
Hartberg, *Austria* 26 D8
Hartford, *Conn., U.S.A.* 111 E12
Hartford, *Ky., U.S.A.* 108 G2
Hartford, *S. Dak., U.S.A.* 112 D6
Hartford, *Wis., U.S.A.* 112 D10
Hartford City, *U.S.A.* 108 E3
Hartland, *Canada* 103 C6
Hartland Pt., *U.K.* 13 F3
Hartlepool, *U.K.* 12 C6
Hartlepool □, *U.K.* 12 C6
Hartley Bay, *Canada* 104 C3
Hartmannberge, *Namibia* 88 B1
Hartney, *Canada* 105 D8
Hârtop, *Moldova* 43 D13
Harts →, *S. Africa* 88 D3
Hartselle, *U.S.A.* 109 H2
Hartshorne, *U.S.A.* 113 H7
Hartsville, *U.S.A.* 109 H5
Hartwell, *U.S.A.* 109 H4
Harunabad, *Pakistan* 68 E5
Harvand, *Iran* 71 D7
Harvey, *Australia* 93 F2
Harvey, *Ill., U.S.A.* 108 E2
Harvey, *N. Dak., U.S.A.* 112 B5
Harwich, *U.K.* 13 F9
Haryana □, *India* 68 E7
Haryn →, *Belarus* 47 F4
Harz, *Germany* 24 D6
Harzgerode, *Germany* 24 D7
Hasaheisa, *Sudan* 81 E3
Hasan Kīādeh, *Iran* 71 B6
Ḩasanābād, *Iran* 71 C7
Hasanpur, *India* 68 E8
Haselünne, *Germany* 24 C3
Hashimoto, *Japan* 55 G7
Hashtjerd, *Iran* 71 C6
Haskell, *Okla., U.S.A.* 113 H7
Haskell, *Tex., U.S.A.* 113 J5
Hasköy, *Turkey* 41 E10
Haslach, *Germany* 25 G4
Hasle, *Denmark* 11 J8
Haslemere, *U.K.* 13 F7
Haslev, *Denmark* 11 J5
Hasparren, *France* 20 E2
Hassa, *Turkey* 72 D7
Hassela, *Sweden* 10 B10
Hasselt, *Belgium* 17 D5
Hassfurt, *Germany* 25 E6
Hassi Messaoud, *Algeria* 78 B7
Hässleholm, *Sweden* 11 H7
Hassloch, *Germany* 25 F4
Hästholmen, *Sweden* 11 F8
Hastings, *N.Z.* 91 H6
Hastings, *U.K.* 13 G8
Hastings, *Mich., U.S.A.* 108 D3
Hastings, *Minn., U.S.A.* 112 C8
Hastings, *Nebr., U.S.A.* 112 E5
Hastings Ra., *Australia* 95 E5
Hästveda, *Sweden* 11 H7
Hat Yai, *Thailand* 65 J3
Hatanbulag, *Mongolia* 56 C5
Hatay = Antalya, *Turkey* 72 D4
Hatch, *U.S.A.* 115 K10
Hatches Creek, *Australia* 94 C2
Hatchet L., *Canada* 105 B8
Haţeg, *Romania* 42 E7
Hateruma-Shima, *Japan* 55 M1
Hatfield P.O., *Australia* 95 E3
Hatgal, *Mongolia* 60 A5
Hathras, *India* 68 F8
Hatia, *Bangla.* 67 H17
Hato Mayor, *Dom. Rep.* 121 C6
Hattah, *Australia* 95 E3
Hatteras, C., *U.S.A.* 109 H8
Hattiesburg, *U.S.A.* 113 K10
Hatvan, *Hungary* 42 C4
Hau Duc, *Vietnam* 64 E7
Haugesund, *Norway* 9 G11
Haukipudas, *Finland* 8 D21
Haultain →, *Canada* 105 B7
Hauraki G., *N.Z.* 91 G5
Hausruck, *Austria* 26 C6
Haut Atlas, *Morocco* 78 B4
Haut-Rhin □, *France* 19 E14
Haut-Zaïre □, *Dem. Rep. of the Congo* 86 B2
Haute-Corse □, *France* 21 F13
Haute-Garonne □, *France* 20 E5
Haute-Loire □, *France* 20 C7
Haute-Marne □, *France* 19 D12
Haute-Normandie □, *France* 18 C7
Haute-Saône □, *France* 19 E13
Haute-Savoie □, *France* 21 C10
Haute-Vienne □, *France* 20 C5
Hauterive, *Canada* 103 C6
Hautes-Alpes □, *France* 21 D10
Hautes Fagnes = Hohe Venn, *Belgium* 17 D6
Hautes-Pyrénées □, *France* 20 F4
Hauteville-Lompnès, *France* 21 C9
Hautmont, *France* 19 B10
Hauts-de-Seine □, *France* 19 D9
Hauts Plateaux, *Algeria* 76 C4
Hauzenberg, *Germany* 25 G9
Havana = La Habana, *Cuba* 120 B3
Havana, *U.S.A.* 112 E9
Havant, *U.K.* 13 G7
Havârna, *Romania* 43 B11
Havasu, L., *U.S.A.* 117 L12
Havdhem, *Sweden* 11 G12
Havel →, *Germany* 24 C8
Havelian, *Pakistan* 68 B5
Havelock, *N.B., Canada* 103 C6
Havelock, *Ont., Canada* 102 D4
Havelock, *N.Z.* 91 J4
Haverfordwest, *U.K.* 13 F3
Haverhill, *U.S.A.* 111 D13
Haverstraw, *U.S.A.* 111 E11
Håverud, *Sweden* 11 F6
Havířov, *Czech.* 27 B11
Havlíčkův Brod, *Czech Rep.* 26 B8
Havneby, *Denmark* 11 J2
Havran, *Turkey* 39 B9
Havre, *U.S.A.* 114 B9
Havre-Aubert, *Canada* 103 C7
Havre-St.-Pierre, *Canada* 103 B7
Havsa, *Turkey* 41 E10
Havza, *Turkey* 72 B6
Haw →, *U.S.A.* 109 H6
Hawaii □, *U.S.A.* 106 H16
Hawaii I., *Pac. Oc.* 106 J17
Hawaiian Is., *Pac. Oc.* 106 H17
Hawaiian Ridge, *Pac. Oc.* 97 E11
Hawarden, *Canada* 105 C7
Hawarden, *U.S.A.* 112 D6
Hawea, L., *N.Z.* 91 L2
Hawera, *N.Z.* 91 H5
Hawick, *U.K.* 14 F6
Hawk Junction, *Canada* 102 C3
Hawke B., *N.Z.* 91 H6
Hawker, *Australia* 95 E2
Hawkesbury, *Canada* 102 C5
Hawkesbury I., *Canada* 104 C3
Hawkesbury Pt., *Australia* 94 A1
Hawkinsville, *U.S.A.* 109 J4
Hawkwood, *Australia* 95 D5
Hawley, *U.S.A.* 112 B6
Hawrān, *Syria* 70 C3
Ḩawrān, W. →, *Iraq* 73 F10
Hawsh Mūssá, *Lebanon* 75 B4
Hawthorne, *U.S.A.* 114 G4
Hawzen, *Ethiopia* 81 E4
Haxtun, *U.S.A.* 112 E3
Hay, *Australia* 95 E3
Hay →, *Australia* 94 C2
Hay →, *Canada* 104 A5
Hay, C., *Australia* 92 B4
Hay L., *Canada* 104 B5
Hay Lakes, *Canada* 104 C6
Hay-on-Wye, *U.K.* 13 E4
Hay River, *Canada* 104 A5
Hay Springs, *U.S.A.* 112 D3
Haya = Tehoru, *Indonesia* 63 E7
Hayachine-San, *Japan* 54 E10
Hayange, *France* 19 C13
Haydarlı, *Turkey* 39 C12
Hayden, *Ariz., U.S.A.* 115 K8
Hayden, *Colo., U.S.A.* 114 F10
Haydon, *Australia* 94 B3
Hayes, *U.S.A.* 112 C4
Hayes →, *Canada* 105 B10
Hayle, *U.K.* 13 G2
Hayling I., *U.K.* 13 G7
Haymana, *Turkey* 72 C5
Haynesville, *U.S.A.* 113 J8
Hayrabolu, *Turkey* 41 E11
Hays, *Canada* 104 C6
Hays, *U.S.A.* 112 F5
Haysyn, *Ukraine* 47 H5
Hayvoron, *Ukraine* 47 H5
Hayward, *Calif., U.S.A.* 116 H4
Hayward, *Wis., U.S.A.* 112 B9
Haywards Heath, *U.K.* 13 G7
Hazafon □, *Israel* 75 C4
Hazarām, Kūh-e, *Iran* 71 D8
Hazard, *U.S.A.* 108 G4
Hazaribag, *India* 69 H11
Hazaribag Road, *India* 69 G11
Hazebrouck, *France* 19 B9
Hazelton, *Canada* 104 B3
Hazelton, *U.S.A.* 112 B4
Hazen, *N. Dak., U.S.A.* 112 B4
Hazen, *Nev., U.S.A.* 114 G4
Hazlehurst, *Ga., U.S.A.* 109 K4
Hazlehurst, *Miss., U.S.A.* 113 K9
Hazleton, *U.S.A.* 111 F9
Hazlett, L., *Australia* 92 D4
He Xian, *Anhui, China* 59 B12
He Xian, *Guangxi Zhuangzu, China* 59 E8
Head of Bight, *Australia* 93 F5
Headlands, *Zimbabwe* 87 F3
Healdsburg, *U.S.A.* 116 G4
Healdton, *U.S.A.* 113 H6
Healesville, *Australia* 95 F4
Heard I., *Ind. Oc.* 3 G13
Hearne, *U.S.A.* 113 K6
Hearne B., *Canada* 105 A9
Hearne L., *Canada* 104 A6
Hearst, *Canada* 102 C3
Heart →, *U.S.A.* 112 B4
Heart's Content, *Canada* 103 C9
Heath Pt., *Canada* 103 C7
Heath Steele, *Canada* 103 C6
Heavener, *U.S.A.* 113 H7
Hebbronville, *U.S.A.* 113 M5
Hebei □, *China* 56 E9
Hebel, *Australia* 95 D4
Heber, *U.S.A.* 117 N11
Heber Springs, *U.S.A.* 113 H9
Hebert, *Canada* 105 C7
Hebgen L., *U.S.A.* 114 D8
Hebi, *China* 56 G8
Hebrides, *U.K.* 6 D4
Hebron = Al Khalīl, *West Bank* 75 D4
Hebron, *Canada* 101 C13
Hebron, *N. Dak., U.S.A.* 112 B3
Hebron, *Nebr., U.S.A.* 112 E6
Heby, *Sweden* 10 E10
Hecate Str., *Canada* 104 C2
Hechi, *China* 58 E7
Hechingen, *Germany* 25 G4
Hechuan, *China* 58 B6
Hecla, *U.S.A.* 112 C5
Hecla I., *Canada* 105 C9
Hédé, *France* 18 D5
Hede, *Sweden* 10 B7
Hedemora, *Sweden* 10 D9
Hedensted, *Denmark* 11 J3
Hedesunda, *Sweden* 10 D10
Hedley, *U.S.A.* 113 H4
Heerde, *Neths.* 17 B6
Heerenveen, *Neths.* 17 B5
Heerhugowaard, *Neths.* 17 B4
Heerlen, *Neths.* 17 D5
Ḩefa, *Israel* 75 C4
Ḩefa □, *Israel* 75 C4
Hefei, *China* 59 B11
Hegang, *China* 60 B8
Heichengzhen, *China* 56 F4
Heide, *Germany* 24 A5
Heidelberg, *Germany* 25 F4
Heidelberg, *S. Africa* 88 E3
Heidenau, *Germany* 24 E9
Heidenheim, *Germany* 25 G6
Heijing, *China* 58 E3
Heilbad Heiligenstadt, *Germany* 24 D6
Heilbron, *S. Africa* 89 D4
Heilbronn, *Germany* 25 F5
Heiligenblut, *Austria* 26 D5
Heiligenhafen, *Germany* 24 A6
Heilongjiang □, *China* 57 A14
Heilunkiang = Heilongjiang □, *China* 57 A14
Heimaey, *Iceland* 8 E3
Heinola, *Finland* 9 F22
Heinsberg, *Germany* 24 D2
Heinze Is., *Burma* 67 M20
Heishan, *China* 57 D12
Heishui, *Liaoning, China* 57 C10
Heishui, *Sichuan, China* 58 A4
Hejaz = Ḩijāz □, *Si. Arabia* 80 C5
Hejian, *China* 56 E9
Hejiang, *China* 58 C5
Hejin, *China* 56 G6
Hekımhan, *Turkey* 72 C7
Hekla, *Iceland* 8 E4
Hekou, *Gansu, China* 56 F2
Hekou, *Guangdong, China* 59 F9
Hekou, *Yunnan, China* 60 D5
Hel, *Poland* 44 D5
Helagsfjället, *Sweden* 10 B6
Helan Shan, *China* 56 E3
Helechosa, *Spain* 35 F6
Helena, *Ark., U.S.A.* 113 H9
Helena, *Mont., U.S.A.* 114 C7
Helendale, *U.S.A.* 117 L9
Helensburgh, *U.K.* 14 E4
Helensville, *N.Z.* 91 G5
Helgasjön, *Sweden* 11 H8
Helgeland, *Norway* 8 C15
Helgoland, *Germany* 24 A3
Heligoland = Helgoland, *Germany* 24 A3
Heligoland B. = Deutsche Bucht, *Germany* 24 A4
Heliopolis, *Egypt* 80 H7
Hella, *Iceland* 8 E3
Hellevoetsluis, *Neths.* 17 C4
Hellín, *Spain* 33 G3
Helmand □, *Afghan.* 66 D4
Helmand →, *Afghan.* 66 D2
Helme →, *Germany* 24 D7
Helmond, *Neths.* 17 C5
Helmsdale, *U.K.* 14 C5
Helmsdale →, *U.K.* 14 C5
Helmstedt, *Germany* 24 C7
Helong, *China* 57 C15
Helper, *U.S.A.* 114 G8
Helsingborg, *Sweden* 11 H6
Helsinge, *Denmark* 11 H6
Helsingfors = Helsinki, *Finland* 9 F21
Helsingør, *Denmark* 11 H6
Helsinki, *Finland* 9 F21
Helska, Mierzeja, *Poland* 44 D5
Helston, *U.K.* 13 G2
Helvellyn, *U.K.* 12 C4
Helwân, *Egypt* 80 J7
Hemel Hempstead, *U.K.* 13 F7
Hemet, *U.S.A.* 117 M10
Hemingford, *U.S.A.* 112 D3
Hemphill, *U.S.A.* 113 K8
Hempstead, *U.S.A.* 113 K6
Hemse, *Sweden* 11 G12
Hemsön, *Sweden* 10 B12
Henån, *Sweden* 11 F5
Henan □, *China* 56 H8
Henares →, *Spain* 34 E7
Henashi-Misaki, *Japan* 54 D9
Hendaye, *France* 20 E2
Hendek, *Turkey* 72 B4
Henderson, *Argentina* 126 D3
Henderson, *Ky., U.S.A.* 108 G2
Henderson, *N.C., U.S.A.* 109 G6
Henderson, *Nev., U.S.A.* 117 J12
Henderson, *Tenn., U.S.A.* 109 H1
Henderson, *Tex., U.S.A.* 113 J7
Hendersonville, *U.S.A.* 109 H4
Hendījān, *Iran* 71 D6
Hendon, *Australia* 95 D5
Heng Xian, *China* 58 F7
Hengcheng, *China* 56 E4
Hengdaohezi, *China* 57 B15
Hengelo, *Neths.* 17 B6
Hengfeng, *China* 59 C10
Hengshan, *Hunan, China* 59 D9
Hengshan, *Shaanxi, China* 56 F5
Hengshui, *China* 56 F8
Hengyang, *Hunan, China* 59 D9
Hengyang, *Hunan, China* 59 D9
Henichesk, *Ukraine* 47 J8
Hénin-Beaumont, *France* 19 B9
Henlopen, C., *U.S.A.* 108 F8
Hennan, *Sweden* 10 B9
Hennebont, *France* 18 E3
Hennenman, *S. Africa* 88 D4
Hennessey, *U.S.A.* 113 G6
Hennigsdorf, *Germany* 24 C9
Henrietta, *U.S.A.* 113 J5
Henrietta, Ostrov = Genriyetty, Ostrov, *Russia* 51 B16
Henrietta Maria, C., *Canada* 102 A3
Henry, *U.S.A.* 112 E10
Henryetta, *U.S.A.* 113 H7
Hensall, *Canada* 110 C3
Henstedt-Ulzburg, *Germany* 24 B6
Hentiyn Nuruu, *Mongolia* 60 B5
Henty, *Australia* 95 F4
Henzada, *Burma* 67 L19
Hephaestia, *Greece* 39 B7
Heping, *China* 59 E10
Heppner, *U.S.A.* 114 D4
Hepu, *China* 58 G7
Hepworth, *Canada* 110 B3
Heqing, *China* 58 D3
Hequ, *China* 56 E6
Héraðsflói, *Iceland* 8 D6
Héraðsvötn →, *Iceland* 8 D4
Herald Cays, *Australia* 94 B4
Herāt, *Afghan.* 66 B3
Herāt □, *Afghan.* 66 B3
Hérault □, *France* 20 E7
Hérault →, *France* 20 E7
Herbault, *France* 18 E8
Herbert →, *Australia* 94 B4
Herbert Downs, *Australia* 94 C2
Herberton, *Australia* 94 B4
Herbignac, *France* 18 E4
Herborn, *Germany* 24 E4
Herby, *Poland* 45 H5
Herceg-Novi, *Montenegro, Yug.* 40 D2
Herðubreið, *Iceland* 8 D5
Hereford, *U.K.* 13 E5
Hereford, *U.S.A.* 113 H3
Herefordshire □, *U.K.* 13 E5
Hereke, *Turkey* 41 F13
Herencia, *Spain* 35 F7
Herentals, *Belgium* 17 C4
Herford, *Germany* 24 C4
Héricourt, *France* 19 E13
Herington, *U.S.A.* 112 F6
Herisau, *Switz.* 25 H5
Hérisson, *France* 19 F9
Herkimer, *U.S.A.* 111 D10
Herlong, *U.S.A.* 116 E6
Herm, *U.K.* 13 H5
Herman, *U.S.A.* 112 C6
Hermann, *U.S.A.* 112 F9
Hermannsburg, *Germany* 24 C6

Hermannsburg Mission, *Australia* 92 D5
Hermanus, *S. Africa* 88 E2
Herment, *France* 20 C6
Hermidale, *Australia* 95 E4
Hermiston, *U.S.A.* 114 D4
Hermitage, *N.Z.* 91 K3
Hermite, I., *Chile* 128 H3
Hermon, Mt. = Ash Shaykh, J., *Lebanon* 75 B4
Hermosillo, *Mexico* 118 B2
Hernád →, *Hungary* 42 C6
Hernandarias, *Paraguay* 127 B5
Hernandez, *U.S.A.* 116 J6
Hernando, *Argentina* 126 C3
Hernando, *U.S.A.* 113 H10
Hernani, *Spain* 32 B3
Herne, *Germany* 24 D3
Herne Bay, *U.K.* 13 F9
Herning, *Denmark* 11 H2
Heroica = Caborca, *Mexico* 118 A2
Heroica Nogales = Nogales, *Mexico* 118 A2
Heron Bay, *Canada* 102 C2
Herradura, Pta. de la, *Canary Is.* 37 F5
Herreid, *U.S.A.* 112 C4
Herrenberg, *Germany* 25 G4
Herrera, *Spain* 35 H6
Herrera de Alcántara, *Spain* 35 F3
Herrera de Pisuerga, *Spain* 34 C6
Herrera del Duque, *Spain* 35 F5
Herrestad, *Sweden* 11 F5
Herrick, *Australia* 94 G4
Herrin, *U.S.A.* 113 G10
Herrljunga, *Sweden* 11 F7
Hersbruck, *Germany* 25 F7
Hersonissos, *Greece* 36 D7
Herstal, *Belgium* 17 D5
Hertford, *U.K.* 13 F7
Hertfordshire □, *U.K.* 13 F7
's-Hertogenbosch, *Neths.* 17 C5
Hertzogville, *S. Africa* 88 D4
Hervás, *Spain* 34 E5
Herzberg, *Brandenburg, Germany* 24 D9
Herzberg, *Niedersachsen, Germany* 24 D6
Herzliyya, *Israel* 75 C3
Herzogenburg, *Austria* 26 C8
Ḩeşār, *Fārs, Iran* 71 D6
Ḩeşār, *Markazī, Iran* 71 C6
Hesdin, *France* 19 B9
Heshui, *China* 56 G5
Heshun, *China* 56 F7
Hesperia, *U.S.A.* 117 L9
Hesse = Hessen □, *Germany* 24 E4
Hessen □, *Germany* 24 E4
Hestra, *Sweden* 11 G7
Hetch Hetchy Aqueduct, *U.S.A.* 116 H5
Hettinger, *U.S.A.* 112 C3
Hettstedt, *Germany* 24 D7
Heves, *Hungary* 42 C5
Heves □, *Hungary* 42 C5
Hexham, *U.K.* 12 C5
Hexi, *Yunnan, China* 58 E4
Hexi, *Zhejiang, China* 59 D12
Hexigten Qi, *China* 57 C9
Ḩeydarābād, *Iran* 71 D7
Heyfield, *Australia* 95 F4
Heysham, *U.K.* 12 C5
Heyuan, *China* 59 F10
Heywood, *Australia* 95 F3
Heze, *China* 56 G8
Hezhang, *China* 58 D5
Hi Vista, *U.S.A.* 117 L9
Hialeah, *U.S.A.* 109 N5
Hiawatha, *Kans., U.S.A.* 112 F7
Hiawatha, *Utah, U.S.A.* 114 G8
Hibbing, *U.S.A.* 112 B8
Hibbs B., *Australia* 94 G4
Hibernia Reef, *Australia* 92 B3
Hickory, *U.S.A.* 109 H5
Hicks, Pt., *Australia* 95 F4
Hicksville, *U.S.A.* 111 F11
Hida, *Romania* 43 C8
Hida-Gawa →, *Japan* 55 G8
Hida-Sammyaku, *Japan* 55 F8
Hidaka-Sammyaku, *Japan* 54 C11
Hidalgo, *Mexico* 119 C5
Hidalgo □, *Mexico* 119 C5
Hidalgo, Presa M., *Mexico* 118 B3
Hidalgo, Pta. del, *Canary Is.* 37 F3
Hidalgo del Parral, *Mexico* 118 B3
Hiddensee, *Germany* 24 A9
Hieflau, *Austria* 26 D7
Hiendelaencina, *Spain* 32 D2
Hierro, *Canary Is.* 37 G1
Higashiajima-San, *Japan* 54 F10
Higashiōsaka, *Japan* 55 G7
Higgins, *U.S.A.* 113 G4
Higgins Corner, *U.S.A.* 116 F5
Higginsville, *Australia* 93 F3
High Atlas = Haut Atlas, *Morocco* 78 B4
High I., *Canada* 103 A7
High Island, *U.S.A.* 113 L7
High Level, *Canada* 104 B5
High Point, *U.S.A.* 109 H6
High Prairie, *Canada* 104 B5
High River, *Canada* 104 C6
High Springs, *U.S.A.* 109 L4
High Tatra = Tatry, *Slovak Rep.* 27 B13
High Veld, *Africa* 76 J6
High Wycombe, *U.K.* 13 F7
Highbury, *Australia* 94 B3
Highland □, *U.K.* 14 D4
Highland Park, *U.S.A.* 108 D2
Highmore, *U.S.A.* 112 C5
Highrock L., *Canada* 105 B7
Higüey, *Dom. Rep.* 121 C6
Hihya, *Egypt* 80 H7
Hiiumaa, *Estonia* 9 G20
Híjar, *Spain* 32 D4
Ḩijāz □, *Si. Arabia* 80 C5
Hijo = Tagum, *Phil.* 61 H6
Hikari, *Japan* 55 H5
Hiko, *U.S.A.* 116 H11
Hikone, *Japan* 55 G8
Hikurangi, *N.Z.* 91 F5
Hikurangi, Mt., *N.Z.* 91 H6
Hildburghausen, *Germany* 24 E6
Hildesheim, *Germany* 24 C5
Hill →, *Australia* 93 F2
Hill City, *Idaho, U.S.A.* 114 E6
Hill City, *Kans., U.S.A.* 112 F5
Hill City, *Minn., U.S.A.* 112 B8
Hill City, *S. Dak., U.S.A.* 112 D3
Hill Island L., *Canada* 105 A7
Hillared, *Sweden* 11 G7
Hillcrest Center, *U.S.A.* 117 K8
Hillegom, *Neths.* 17 B4
Hillerød, *Denmark* 11 J6
Hillerstorp, *Sweden* 11 G7
Hillman, *U.S.A.* 108 C4
Hillmond, *Canada* 105 C7
Hillsboro, *Kans., U.S.A.* 112 F6
Hillsboro, *N. Dak., U.S.A.* 112 B6
Hillsboro, *N.H., U.S.A.* 111 C13
Hillsboro, *N. Mex., U.S.A.* 115 K10
Hillsboro, *Oreg., U.S.A.* 116 E4
Hillsboro, *Tex., U.S.A.* 113 J6
Hillsborough, *Grenada* 121 D7
Hillsdale, *Mich., U.S.A.* 108 E3
Hillsdale, *N.Y., U.S.A.* 111 D11
Hillside, *Australia* 92 D2
Hillsport, *Canada* 102 C2
Hillston, *Australia* 95 E4
Hilo, *U.S.A.* 106 J17
Hilton, *U.S.A.* 110 C7
Hilvan, *Turkey* 73 D8
Hilversum, *Neths.* 17 B5
Himachal Pradesh □, *India* 68 D7
Himalaya, *Asia* 69 E11
Himamaylan, *Phil.* 61 F5
Himara, *Albania* 40 F3
Himatnagar, *India* 66 H8
Himeji, *Japan* 55 G7
Himi, *Japan* 55 F8
Himmerland, *Denmark* 11 H3
Ḩimş, *Syria* 75 A5
Ḩimş □, *Syria* 75 A6
Hinche, *Haiti* 121 C5
Hinchinbrook I., *Australia* 94 B4
Hinckley, *U.K.* 13 E6
Hinckley, *U.S.A.* 114 G7
Hindaun, *India* 68 F7
Hindmarsh, L., *Australia* 95 F3
Hindsholm, *Denmark* 11 J4
Hindu Bagh, *Pakistan* 68 D2
Hindu Kush, *Asia* 66 B7
Hindubagh, *Pakistan* 66 D5
Hindupur, *India* 66 N10
Hines Creek, *Canada* 104 B5
Hinganghat, *India* 66 J11
Hingham, *U.S.A.* 114 B8
Hingoli, *India* 66 K10
Hinigaran, *Phil.* 61 F5
Hinis, *Turkey* 73 C9
Hinna = Imi, *Ethiopia* 81 F5
Hinna, *Nigeria* 83 C7
Hinnerup, *Denmark* 11 H4
Hinnøya, *Norway* 8 B16
Hinojosa del Duque, *Spain* 35 G5
Hinsdale, *U.S.A.* 114 B10
Hinterrhein →, *Switz.* 25 J5
Hinton, *Canada* 104 C5
Hinton, *U.S.A.* 108 G5
Hınzır Burnu, *Turkey* 72 D6
Hirado, *Japan* 55 H4
Hirakud Dam, *India* 67 J13
Hiratsuka, *Japan* 55 G9
Hirfanlı Barajı, *Turkey* 72 C5
Hiroo, *Japan* 54 C11
Hirosaki, *Japan* 54 D10
Hiroshima, *Japan* 55 G6
Hiroshima □, *Japan* 55 G6
Hirson, *France* 19 C11
Hirtshals, *Denmark* 11 G3
Hisar, *India* 68 E6
Hisarcık, *Turkey* 39 B11
Hisaria, *Bulgaria* 41 D8
Hisb →, *Iraq* 70 D5
Ḩismá, *Si. Arabia* 70 D3
Hispaniola, *W. Indies* 121 C5
Hīt, *Iraq* 70 C4
Hita, *Japan* 55 H5
Hitachi, *Japan* 55 F10
Hitchin, *U.K.* 13 F7
Hitoyoshi, *Japan* 55 H5
Hitra, *Norway* 8 E13
Hitzacker, *Germany* 24 B7
Hiyyon, N. →, *Israel* 75 E4
Hjalmar L., *Canada* 105 A7
Hjälmaren, *Sweden* 10 E9
Hjältevad, *Sweden* 11 G9
Hjo, *Sweden* 11 F8
Hjørring, *Denmark* 11 G3
Hjortkvarn, *Sweden* 11 F9
Hlinsko, *Czech Rep.* 26 B8
Hlohovec, *Slovak Rep.* 27 C10
Hlučín, *Czech Rep.* 27 B11
Hluhluwe, *S. Africa* 89 D5
Hlukhiv, *Ukraine* 47 G7
Hlyboka, *Ukraine* 47 H3
Hlybokaye, *Belarus* 46 E4
Hnúšťa, *Slovak Rep.* 27 C12
Ho, *Ghana* 83 D5
Ho Chi Minh City = Phanh Bho Ho Chi Minh, *Vietnam* 65 G6
Ho Thuong, *Vietnam* 64 C5
Hoa Binh, *Vietnam* 64 B5
Hoa Da, *Vietnam* 65 G7
Hoa Hiep, *Vietnam* 65 G5
Hoai Nhon, *Vietnam* 64 E7
Hoang Lien Son, *Vietnam* 64 A4
Hobart, *Australia* 94 G4
Hobart, *U.S.A.* 113 H5
Hobbs, *U.S.A.* 113 J3
Hobbs Coast, *Antarctica* 5 D14
Hoboken, *U.S.A.* 111 F10
Hobro, *Denmark* 11 H3
Hoburgen, *Sweden* 11 H12
Hocalar, *Turkey* 39 C11
Hochschwab, *Austria* 26 D8
Höchstadt, *Germany* 25 F6
Hockenheim, *Germany* 25 F4
Hodaka-Dake, *Japan* 55 F8
Hodgson, *Canada* 105 C9
Hódmezővásárhely, *Hungary* 42 D5
Hodna, Chott el, *Algeria* 78 A6
Hodonín, *Czech Rep.* 27 C10
Hoeamdong, *N. Korea* 57 C16
Hœdic, Î. de, *France* 18 E4
Hoek van Holland, *Neths.* 17 C4
Hoengsŏng, *S. Korea* 57 F14
Hoeryong, *N. Korea* 57 C15
Hoeyang, *N. Korea* 57 E14
Hof, *Germany* 25 E7
Hofgeismar, *Germany* 24 D5
Hofheim, *Germany* 25 E4
Hofmeyr, *S. Africa* 88 E4
Höfn, *Iceland* 8 D6
Hofors, *Sweden* 10 D10
Hofsjökull, *Iceland* 8 D4
Hōfu, *Japan* 55 G5
Hogan Group, *Australia* 94 F4
Höganäs, *Sweden* 11 H6
Hogansville, *U.S.A.* 109 J3
Hogeland, *U.S.A.* 114 B9
Hoggar = Ahaggar, *Algeria* 78 D7
Högsäter, *Sweden* 11 F6
Högsby, *Sweden* 11 G10
Högsjö, *Sweden* 10 E9
Hogsty Reef, *Bahamas* 121 B5
Hoh →, *U.S.A.* 116 C2
Hoh Xil Shan, *China* 60 C3
Hohe Acht, *Germany* 25 E3
Hohe Tauern, *Austria* 26 D5
Hohe Venn, *Belgium* 17 D6
Hohenau, *Austria* 27 C9
Hohenems, *Austria* 26 D2
Hohenloher Ebene, *Germany* 25 F5
Hohenwald, *U.S.A.* 109 H2
Hohenwestedt, *Germany* 24 A5
Hohhot, *China* 56 D6
Hóhlakas, *Greece* 36 D9
Hohoe, *Ghana* 83 D5
Hoi An, *Vietnam* 64 E7
Hoi Xuan, *Vietnam* 64 B5
Hoisington, *U.S.A.* 112 F5
Højer, *Denmark* 11 K2
Hōjō, *Japan* 55 H6
Hok, *Sweden* 11 G8
Hökensås, *Sweden* 11 G8
Hökerum, *Sweden* 11 G7
Hokianga Harbour, *N.Z.* 91 F4
Hokitika, *N.Z.* 91 K3
Hokkaidō □, *Japan* 54 C11
Hol-Hol, *Djibouti* 81 E5
Hola Pristan, *Ukraine* 47 J7
Holbæk, *Denmark* 11 J5
Holbrook, *Australia* 95 F4
Holbrook, *U.S.A.* 115 J8
Holden, *Canada* 104 C6
Holden, *U.S.A.* 114 G7
Holdenville, *U.S.A.* 113 H6
Holdfast, *Canada* 105 C7
Holdrege, *U.S.A.* 112 E5
Holešov, *Czech Rep.* 27 B10
Holguín, *Cuba* 120 B4
Holíč, *Slovak Rep.* 27 C10
Holice, *Czech Rep.* 26 A8
Höljes, *Sweden* 10 D6
Hollabrunn, *Austria* 26 C9
Hollams Bird I., *Namibia* 88 C1
Holland, *U.S.A.* 108 D2
Hollandia = Jayapura, *Indonesia* 63 E10
Hollfeld, *Germany* 25 F7
Hollidaysburg, *U.S.A.* 110 F6
Hollis, *U.S.A.* 113 H5
Hollister, *Calif., U.S.A.* 116 J5
Hollister, *Idaho, U.S.A.* 114 E6
Höllviken, *Sweden* 11 J6
Holly, *U.S.A.* 112 F3
Holly Hill, *U.S.A.* 109 L5
Holly Springs, *U.S.A.* 113 H10
Hollywood, *Calif., U.S.A.* 115 J4
Hollywood, *Fla., U.S.A.* 109 N5
Holman, *Canada* 100 A8
Hólmavík, *Iceland* 8 D3
Holmes Reefs, *Australia* 94 B4
Holmsjö, *Sweden* 11 H9
Holmsjön, *Västernorrland, Sweden* 10 B10
Holmsjön, *Västernorrland, Sweden* 10 B9
Holmsland Klit, *Denmark* 11 J2
Holmsund, *Sweden* 8 E19
Holod, *Romania* 42 D7
Holroyd →, *Australia* 94 A3
Holstebro, *Denmark* 11 H2
Holsworthy, *U.K.* 13 G3
Holton, *Canada* 103 B8
Holton, *U.S.A.* 112 F7
Holtville, *U.S.A.* 117 N11
Holwerd, *Neths.* 17 A5
Holy I., *Angl., U.K.* 12 D3
Holy I., *Northumb., U.K.* 12 B6
Holyhead, *U.K.* 12 D3
Holyoke, *Colo., U.S.A.* 112 E3
Holyoke, *Mass., U.S.A.* 111 D12
Holyrood, *Canada* 103 C9
Holzkirchen, *Germany* 25 H7
Holzminden, *Germany* 24 D5
Homa Bay, *Kenya* 86 C3
Homa Bay □, *Kenya* 86 C3
Homalin, *Burma* 67 G19
Homand, *Iran* 71 C8
Homberg, *Germany* 24 D5
Hombori, *Mali* 83 B4
Homburg, *Germany* 25 F3
Home B., *Canada* 101 B13
Home Hill, *Australia* 94 B4
Homedale, *U.S.A.* 114 E5
Homer, *Alaska, U.S.A.* 100 C4
Homer, *La., U.S.A.* 113 J8
Homestead, *Australia* 94 C4
Homestead, *Fla., U.S.A.* 109 N5
Homestead, *Oreg., U.S.A.* 114 D5
Homewood, *U.S.A.* 116 F6
Hominy, *U.S.A.* 113 G6
Homoine, *Mozam.* 89 C6
Homoljske Planina, *Serbia, Yug.* 40 B5
Homorod, *Romania* 43 D10
Homs = Ḩimş, *Syria* 75 A5
Homyel, *Belarus* 47 F6
Hon Chong, *Vietnam* 65 G5
Hon Me, *Vietnam* 64 C5
Honan = Henan □, *China* 56 H8
Honaz, *Turkey* 39 D11
Honbetsu, *Japan* 54 C11
Honcut, *U.S.A.* 116 F5
Honda Bay, *Phil.* 61 G3
Hondarribia, *Spain* 32 B3
Hondeklipbaai, *S. Africa* 88 E2
Hondo, *Japan* 55 H5
Hondo, *U.S.A.* 113 L5
Hondo →, *Belize* 119 D7
Honduras ■, *Cent. Amer.* 120 D2
Honduras, G. de, *Caribbean* 120 C2
Hønefoss, *Norway* 9 F14
Honesdale, *U.S.A.* 111 E9
Honey L., *U.S.A.* 116 E6
Honfleur, *France* 18 C7
Høng, *Denmark* 11 J5
Hong Gai, *Vietnam* 64 B6
Hong He →, *China* 56 H8
Hong Kong, *China* 59 F10
Hong'an, *China* 59 B10
Hongchŏn, *S. Korea* 57 F14
Honghai Wan, *China* 59 F10
Honghu, *China* 59 C9
Hongjiang, *China* 58 D7
Hongliu He →, *China* 56 F5
Hongor, *Mongolia* 56 B7
Hongsa, *Laos* 64 C3
Hongshui He →, *China* 58 F7
Hongsŏng, *S. Korea* 57 F14
Hongtong, *China* 56 F6
Honguedo, Détroit d', *Canada* 103 C7
Hongwon, *N. Korea* 57 E14
Hongya, *China* 58 C4
Hongyuan, *China* 58 A4
Hongze Hu, *China* 57 H10
Honiara, *Solomon Is.* 96 H7
Honiton, *U.K.* 13 G4
Honjō, *Japan* 54 E10
Honkorâb, Ras, *Egypt* 80 C4
Honningsvåg, *Norway* 8 A21
Hönö, *Sweden* 11 G5
Honolulu, *U.S.A.* 106 H16
Honshū, *Japan* 55 G9
Hontoria del Pinar, *Spain* 32 D1
Hood, Mt., *U.S.A.* 114 D3
Hood, Pt., *Australia* 93 F2
Hood River, *U.S.A.* 114 D3
Hoodsport, *U.S.A.* 116 C3
Hooge, *Germany* 24 A4
Hoogeveen, *Neths.* 17 B6
Hoogezand-Sappemeer, *Neths.* 17 A6
Hooghly → = Hugli →, *India* 69 J13
Hooghly-Chinsura = Chunchura, *India* 69 H13
Hook Hd., *Ireland* 15 D5
Hook I., *Australia* 94 C4
Hook of Holland = Hoek van Holland, *Neths.* 17 C4
Hooker, *U.S.A.* 113 G4
Hooker Creek, *Australia* 92 C5
Hoopeston, *U.S.A.* 108 E2
Hoopstad, *S. Africa* 88 D4
Höör, *Sweden* 11 J7
Hoorn, *Neths.* 17 B5
Hoover Dam, *U.S.A.* 117 K12
Hooversville, *U.S.A.* 110 F6
Hop Bottom, *U.S.A.* 111 E9
Hopa, *Turkey* 73 B9
Hope, *Canada* 104 D4
Hope, *Ariz., U.S.A.* 117 M13
Hope, *Ark., U.S.A.* 113 J8
Hope, *N. Dak., U.S.A.* 112 B6
Hope, L., *Australia* 95 D2
Hope Town, *Bahamas* 120 A4
Hopedale, *Canada* 103 A7
Hopefield, *S. Africa* 88 E2
Hopei = Hebei □, *China* 56 E9
Hopelchén, *Mexico* 119 D7
Hopetoun, *Vic., Australia* 95 F3
Hopetoun, *W. Austral., Australia* 93 F3
Hopetown, *S. Africa* 88 D3
Hopfgarten, *Austria* 26 D5
Hopkins, *U.S.A.* 112 E7
Hopkins, L., *Australia* 92 D4
Hopkinsville, *U.S.A.* 109 G2
Hopland, *U.S.A.* 116 G3
Hoquiam, *U.S.A.* 116 D3
Horasan, *Turkey* 73 B10
Horažďovice, *Czech Rep.* 26 B6
Horb, *Germany* 25 G4
Hörby, *Sweden* 11 J7
Horcajo de Santiago, *Spain* 32 F1
Horden Hills, *Australia* 92 D5
Horezu, *Romania* 43 E8
Horgen, *Switz.* 25 H4
Horgoš, *Serbia, Yug.* 42 D4
Hořice, *Czech Rep.* 26 A8
Horinger, *China* 56 D6
Horki, *Belarus* 46 E6
Horlick Mts., *Antarctica* 5 E15
Horlivka, *Ukraine* 47 H10
Hormoz, *Iran* 71 E7
Hormoz, Jaz. ye, *Iran* 71 E8
Hormuz, Str. of, *The Gulf* 71 E8
Horn, *Austria* 26 C8
Horn, *Iceland* 8 C2
Horn, *Sweden* 11 G9
Horn →, *Canada* 104 A5
Horn, Cape = Hornos, C. de, *Chile* 122 J4
Horn Head, *Ireland* 15 A3
Horn I., *Australia* 94 A3
Horn I., *U.S.A.* 109 K1
Horn Mts., *Canada* 104 A5
Hornachuelos, *Spain* 35 H5
Hornavan, *Sweden* 8 C17
Hornbeck, *U.S.A.* 113 K8
Hornbrook, *U.S.A.* 114 F2
Hornburg, *Germany* 24 C6
Horncastle, *U.K.* 12 D7
Horndal, *Sweden* 10 D10
Hornell, *U.S.A.* 110 D7
Hornell L., *Canada* 104 A5
Hornepayne, *Canada* 102 C3
Horní Planá, *Czech Rep.* 26 C7
Hornitos, *U.S.A.* 116 H6
Hornos, C. de, *Chile* 122 J4
Hornoy-le-Bourg, *France* 19 C8
Hornsby, *Australia* 95 E5
Hornsea, *U.K.* 12 D7
Hornslandet, *Sweden* 10 C11
Hörnum, *Germany* 24 A4
Horobetsu, *Japan* 54 C10
Horodenka, *Ukraine* 47 H3
Horodnya, *Ukraine* 47 G6
Horodok, *Khmelnytskyy, Ukraine* 47 H4
Horodok, *Lviv, Ukraine* 47 H2
Horodyshche, *Ukraine* 47 H6
Horokhiv, *Ukraine* 47 G3
Horovice, *Czech Rep.* 26 B6
Horqin Youyi Qianqi, *China* 57 A12
Horqueta, *Paraguay* 126 A4
Horred, *Sweden* 11 G6
Horse Creek, *U.S.A.* 112 E3
Horse Is., *Canada* 103 B8
Horsefly L., *Canada* 104 C4
Horsens, *Denmark* 11 J3
Horsham, *Australia* 95 F3
Horsham, *U.K.* 13 F7
Horšovský Týn, *Czech Rep.* 26 B5
Horten, *Norway* 9 G14
Hortobágy →, *Hungary* 42 C6
Horton, *U.S.A.* 112 F7
Horton →, *Canada* 100 B7
Horwood, L., *Canada* 102 C3
Hosaina, *Ethiopia* 81 F4
Hose, Gunung-Gunung, *Malaysia* 62 D4
Ḩoseynābād, *Khuzestān, Iran* 71 C6
Ḩoseynābād, *Kordestān, Iran* 70 C5
Hoshangabad, *India* 68 H7
Hoshiarpur, *India* 68 D6
Hosmer, *U.S.A.* 112 C5
Hospet, *India* 66 M10
Hoste, I., *Chile* 128 H3
Hostens, *France* 20 D3
Hot, *Thailand* 64 C2
Hot Creek Range, *U.S.A.* 114 G6
Hot Springs, *Ark., U.S.A.* 113 H8
Hot Springs, *S. Dak., U.S.A.* 112 D3
Hotagen, *Sweden* 8 E16
Hotan, *China* 60 C2
Hotazel, *S. Africa* 88 D3
Hotchkiss, *U.S.A.* 115 G10

Hotham, C., Australia 92 B5
Hoting, Sweden 8 D17
Hotolishti, Albania 40 E4
Hotte, Massif de la, Haiti 121 C5
Hottentotsbaai, Namibia 88 D1
Houat, Î. de, France 18 E4
Houck, U.S.A. 115 J9
Houdan, France 19 D8
Houei Sai, Laos 64 B3
Houeillès, France 20 D4
Houffalize, Belgium 17 D5
Houghton, U.S.A. 112 B10
Houghton L., U.S.A. 108 C3
Houhora Heads, N.Z. 91 F4
Houlton, U.S.A. 103 C6
Houma, U.S.A. 113 L9
Houndé, Burkina Faso 82 C4
Hourtin, France 20 C2
Hourtin-Carcans, Étang d', France 20 C2
Houston, Canada 104 C3
Houston, Mo., U.S.A. 113 G9
Houston, Tex., U.S.A. 113 L7
Houtman Abrolhos, Australia 93 E1
Hovd, Mongolia 60 B4
Hove, U.K. 13 G7
Hoveyzeh, Iran 71 D6
Hovmantorp, Sweden 11 H9
Hövsgöl, Mongolia 56 C5
Hövsgöl Nuur, Mongolia 60 A5
Hovsta, Sweden 10 E9
Howakil, Eritrea 81 D5
Howar, Wadi →, Sudan 81 D2
Howard, Australia 95 D5
Howard, Kans., U.S.A. 113 G6
Howard, Pa., U.S.A. 110 F7
Howard, S. Dak., U.S.A. 112 C6
Howard I., Australia 94 A2
Howard L., Canada 105 A7
Howe, U.S.A. 114 E7
Howe, C., Australia 95 F5
Howell, U.S.A. 108 D4
Howick, Canada 111 A11
Howick, S. Africa 89 D5
Howick Group, Australia 94 A4
Howitt, L., Australia 95 D2
Howland I., Pac. Oc. 96 G10
Howley, Canada 103 C8
Howrah = Haora, India 69 H13
Howth Hd., Ireland 15 C5
Höxter, Germany 24 D5
Hoy, U.K. 14 C5
Hoya, Germany 24 C5
Høyanger, Norway 9 F12
Hoyerswerda, Germany 24 D10
Hoylake, U.K. 12 D4
Hoyos, Spain 34 E4
Hpungan Pass, Burma 67 F20
Hradec Králové, Czech Rep. 26 A8
Hrádek, Czech Rep. 27 C9
Hranice, Czech Rep. 27 B10
Hrazdan, Armenia 49 K7
Hrebenka, Ukraine 47 G7
Hrodna, Belarus 46 F2
Hrodzyanka, Belarus 46 F5
Hron →, Slovak Rep. 27 D11
Hrubieszów, Poland 45 H10
Hrubý Jeseník, Czech Rep. 27 A10
Hrvatska = Croatia ■, Europe 29 C13
Hrymayliv, Ukraine 47 H4
Hsenwi, Burma 67 H20
Hsiamen = Xiamen, China 59 E12
Hsian = Xi'an, China 56 G5
Hsinchu, Taiwan 59 E13
Hsinhailien = Lianyungang, China 57 G10
Hsüchou = Xuzhou, China 57 G9
Hu Xian, China 56 G5
Hua Hin, Thailand 64 F2
Hua Xian, Henan, China 56 G8
Hua Xian, Shaanxi, China 56 G5
Hua'an, China 59 E11
Huacheng, China 59 E10
Huachinera, Mexico 118 A3
Huacho, Peru 124 F3
Huade, China 56 D7
Huadian, China 57 C14
Huai He →, China 59 A12
Huai Yot, Thailand 65 J2
Huai'an, Hebei, China 56 D8
Huai'an, Jiangsu, China 57 H10
Huaibei, China 56 G9
Huaide, China 57 C13
Huaidezhen, China 57 C13
Huaihua, China 58 D7
Huaiji, China 59 F9
Huainan, China 59 A11
Huaining, China 59 B11
Huairen, China 56 E7
Huairou, China 56 D9
Huaiyang, China 56 H8
Huaiyuan, Anhui, China 57 H9
Huaiyuan, Guangxi Zhuangzu, China 58 E7
Huajianzi, China 57 D13
Huajuapan de Leon, Mexico 119 D5
Hualapai Peak, U.S.A. 115 J7
Hualien, Taiwan 59 E13
Huallaga →, Peru 124 E3
Huambo, Angola 85 G3
Huan Jiang →, China 56 G5
Huan Xian, China 56 F4
Huancabamba, Peru 124 E3
Huancane, Peru 124 G5
Huancavelica, Peru 124 F3
Huancayo, Peru 124 F3
Huanchaca, Bolivia 124 H5
Huang Hai = Yellow Sea, China 57 G12
Huang He →, China 57 F10
Huang Xian, China 57 F11
Huangchuan, China 59 A10
Huanggang, China 59 B10
Huangling, China 56 G5
Huangliu, China 60 E5
Huanglong, China 56 G5
Huanglongtan, China 59 A8
Huangmei, China 59 B10
Huangpi, China 59 B10
Huangping, China 58 D6
Huangshi, China 59 B10
Huangsongdian, China 57 C14
Huangyan, China 59 C13
Huangyangsi, China 59 D8
Huaning, China 58 E4
Huanjiang, China 58 E7
Huantai, China 57 F9
Huánuco, Peru 124 E3
Huaping, China 58 D3
Huaraz, Peru 124 E3
Huarmey, Peru 124 F3
Huarong, China 59 C9
Huascarán, Peru 122 D3
Huasco, Chile 126 B1
Huasco →, Chile 126 B1
Huasna, U.S.A. 117 K6
Huatabampo, Mexico 118 B3
Huauchinango, Mexico 119 C5
Huautla de Jiménez, Mexico 119 D5
Huaxi, China 58 D6
Huay Namota, Mexico 118 C4
Huayin, China 56 G6
Huayuan, China 58 C7
Huazhou, China 59 G8
Hubbard, U.S.A. 113 K6
Hubbart Pt., Canada 105 B10
Hubei □, China 59 B9
Hubli-Dharwad = Dharwad, India 66 M9
Huchang, N. Korea 57 D14
Hucknall, U.K. 12 D6
Huddersfield, U.K. 12 D6
Hude, Germany 24 B4
Hudi, Sudan 80 D3
Hudiksvall, Sweden 10 C11
Hudson, Canada 105 C10
Hudson, Mass., U.S.A. 111 D13
Hudson, Mich., U.S.A. 108 E3
Hudson, N.Y., U.S.A. 111 D11
Hudson, Wis., U.S.A. 112 C8
Hudson, Wyo., U.S.A. 114 E9
Hudson →, U.S.A. 111 F10
Hudson Bay, N.W.T., Canada 101 C11
Hudson Bay, Sask., Canada 105 C8
Hudson Falls, U.S.A. 111 C11
Hudson Mts., Antarctica 5 D16
Hudson Str., Canada 101 B13
Hudson's Hope, Canada 104 B4
Hue, Vietnam 64 D6
Huebra →, Spain 34 D4
Huedin, Romania 42 D8
Huehuetenango, Guatemala 120 C1
Huejúcar, Mexico 118 C4
Huélamo, Spain 32 E3
Huelgoat, France 18 D3
Huelma, Spain 35 H7
Huelva, Spain 35 H4
Huelva □, Spain 35 H4
Huelva →, Spain 35 H5
Huentelauquén, Chile 126 C1
Huércal-Overa, Spain 33 H3
Huerta, Sa. de la, Argentina 126 C2
Huertas, C. de las, Spain 33 G4
Huerva →, Spain 32 D4
Huesca, Spain 32 C4
Huesca □, Spain 32 C5
Huéscar, Spain 33 H2
Huetamo, Mexico 118 D4
Huete, Spain 32 E2
Hugh →, Australia 94 D1
Hughenden, Australia 94 C3
Hughes, Australia 93 F4
Hugli →, India 69 J13
Hugo, U.S.A. 112 F3
Hugoton, U.S.A. 113 G4
Hui Xian, Gansu, China 56 H4
Hui Xian, Henan, China 56 G7
Hui'an, China 59 E12
Hui'anbu, China 56 F4
Huichang, China 59 E10
Huichapán, Mexico 119 C5
Huidong, China 58 D4
Huifa He →, China 57 C14
Huila, Nevado del, Colombia 124 C3
Huilai, China 59 F11
Huili, China 58 D4
Huimin, China 57 F9
Huinan, China 57 C14
Huinca Renancó, Argentina 126 C3
Huining, China 56 G3
Huinong, China 56 E4
Huishui, China 58 D6
Huisne →, France 18 E7
Huiting, China 56 G9
Huitong, China 58 D7
Huixtla, Mexico 119 D6
Huize, China 58 D4
Huizhou, China 59 F10
Hukawng Valley, Burma 67 F20
Hukou, China 59 C11
Hukuntsi, Botswana 88 C3
Hula, Ethiopia 81 F4
Hulan, China 60 B7
Ḩulayfā', Si. Arabia 70 E4
Huld, Mongolia 56 B3
Hulin He →, China 57 B12
Hull = Kingston upon Hull, U.K. 12 D7
Hull, Canada 102 C4
Hull →, U.K. 12 D7
Hulst, Neths. 17 C4
Hultsfred, Sweden 11 G9
Hulun Nur, China 60 B6
Hulyaypole, Ukraine 47 J9
Humahuaca, Argentina 126 A2
Humaitá, Brazil 124 E6
Humaitá, Paraguay 126 B4
Humansdorp, S. Africa 88 E3
Humbe, Angola 88 B1
Humber →, U.K. 12 D7
Humbert River, Australia 92 C5
Humble, U.S.A. 113 L8
Humboldt, Canada 105 C7
Humboldt, Iowa, U.S.A. 112 D7
Humboldt, Tenn., U.S.A. 113 H10
Humboldt →, U.S.A. 114 F4
Humboldt Gletscher, Greenland 4 B4
Hume, U.S.A. 116 J8
Hume, L., Australia 95 F4
Humenné, Slovak Rep. 27 C14
Hummelsta, Sweden 10 E10
Humphreys, Mt., U.S.A. 116 H8
Humphreys Peak, U.S.A. 115 J8
Humpolec, Czech Rep. 26 B8
Humptulips, U.S.A. 116 C3
Hūn, Libya 79 C9
Hun Jiang →, China 57 D13
Húnaflói, Iceland 8 D3
Hunan □, China 59 D9
Hunchun, China 57 C16
Hundested, Denmark 11 J5
Hundred Mile House, Canada 104 C4
Hunedoara, Romania 42 E7
Hunedoara □, Romania 42 E7
Hünfeld, Germany 24 E5
Hung Yen, Vietnam 64 B6
Hungary ■, Europe 27 D12
Hungary, Plain of, Europe 6 F10
Hungerford, Australia 95 D3
Hŭngnam, N. Korea 57 E14
Huni Valley, Ghana 82 D4
Hunneberg, Sweden 11 F6
Hunnebostrand, Sweden 11 F5
Hunsberge, Namibia 88 D2
Hunsrück, Germany 25 F3
Hunstanton, U.K. 12 E8
Hunte →, Germany 24 B4
Hunter, N. Dak., U.S.A. 112 B6
Hunter, N.Y., U.S.A. 111 D10
Hunter I., Australia 94 G3
Hunter I., Canada 104 C3
Hunter Ra., Australia 95 E5
Hunters Road, Zimbabwe 87 F2
Hunterville, N.Z. 91 H5
Huntingburg, U.S.A. 108 F2
Huntingdon, Canada 102 C5
Huntingdon, U.K. 13 E7
Huntingdon, U.S.A. 110 F6
Huntington, Ind., U.S.A. 108 E3
Huntington, N.Y., U.S.A. 111 F11
Huntington, Oreg., U.S.A. 114 D5
Huntington, Utah, U.S.A. 114 G8
Huntington, W. Va., U.S.A. 108 F4
Huntington Beach, U.S.A. 117 M9
Huntington Park, U.S.A. 115 K4
Huntly, N.Z. 91 G5
Huntly, U.K. 14 D6
Huntsville, Canada 102 C4
Huntsville, Ala., U.S.A. 109 H2
Huntsville, Tex., U.S.A. 113 K7
Hunyani →, Zimbabwe 87 F3
Hunyuan, China 56 E7
Hunza →, India 69 B6
Huo Xian, China 56 F6
Huong Hoa, Vietnam 64 D6
Huong Khe, Vietnam 64 C5
Huonville, Australia 94 G4
Huoqiu, China 59 A11
Huoshan, Anhui, China 59 A12
Huoshan, Anhui, China 59 B11
Hupeh = Hubei □, China 59 B9
Ḩūr, Iran 71 D8
Hurbanovo, Slovak Rep. 27 D11
Hure Qi, China 57 C11
Hurezani, Romania 43 F8
Hurghada, Egypt 80 B3
Hurley, N. Mex., U.S.A. 115 K9
Hurley, Wis., U.S.A. 112 B9
Huron, Calif., U.S.A. 116 J6
Huron, Ohio, U.S.A. 110 E2
Huron, S. Dak., U.S.A. 112 C5
Huron, L., U.S.A. 110 B2
Hurricane, U.S.A. 115 H7
Hurso, Ethiopia 81 F5
Hurunui →, N.Z. 91 K4
Hurup, Denmark 11 H2
Húsavík, Iceland 8 C5
Huşi, Romania 43 D13
Huskvarna, Sweden 11 G8
Hussar, Canada 104 C6
Hustadvika, Norway 8 E12
Hustopeče, Czech Rep. 27 C9
Husum, Germany 24 A5
Husum, Sweden 10 A13
Hutchinson, Kans., U.S.A. 113 F6
Hutchinson, Minn., U.S.A. 112 C7
Hüttenberg, Austria 26 E7
Huttig, U.S.A. 113 J8
Hutton, Mt., Australia 95 D4
Huwun, Ethiopia 81 G5
Huy, Belgium 17 D5
Hvalpsund, Denmark 11 H3
Hvammstangi, Iceland 8 D3
Hvar, Croatia 29 E13
Hvarski Kanal, Croatia 29 E13
Hvítá →, Iceland 8 D3
Hwachon-chosuji, S. Korea 57 E14
Hwang Ho = Huang He →, China 57 F10
Hwange, Zimbabwe 87 F2
Hwange Nat. Park, Zimbabwe 88 B4
Hyannis, U.S.A. 112 E4
Hyargas Nuur, Mongolia 60 B4
Hybo, Sweden 10 C10
Hyden, Australia 93 F2
Hyderabad, India 66 L11
Hyderabad, Pakistan 68 G3
Hyères, France 21 E10
Hyères, Îs. d', France 21 F10
Hyesan, N. Korea 57 D15
Hyland →, Canada 104 B3
Hyltebruk, Sweden 11 H7
Hymia, India 69 C8
Hyndman Peak, U.S.A. 114 E6
Hyōgo □, Japan 55 G7
Hyrum, U.S.A. 114 F8
Hysham, U.S.A. 114 C10
Hythe, U.K. 13 F9
Hyūga, Japan 55 H5
Hyvinge = Hyvinkää, Finland 9 F21
Hyvinkää, Finland 9 F21

I

I-n-Gall, Niger 83 B6
Iablaniţa, Romania 42 F7
Iaco →, Brazil 124 E5
Iacobeni, Romania 43 C10
Iakora, Madag. 89 C8
Ialomiţa □, Romania 43 F12
Ialomiţa →, Romania 43 F12
Ialoveni, Moldova 43 D13
Ialpug →, Moldova 43 E13
Ianca, Romania 43 E12
Iara, Romania 43 D8
Iargara, Moldova 43 D13
Iaşi, Romania 43 C12
Iaşi □, Romania 43 C12
Íasmos, Greece 41 E9
Iba, Phil. 61 D4
Ibadan, Nigeria 83 D5
Ibagué, Colombia 124 C3
Iballja, Albania 40 D4
Ibăneşti, Botoşani, Romania 43 B11
Ibăneşti, Mureş, Romania 43 D9
Ibar →, Serbia, Yug. 40 C4
Ibaraki □, Japan 55 F10
Ibarra, Ecuador 124 C3
Ibba, Sudan 81 G2
Ibba, Bahr el →, Sudan 81 F2
Ibbenbüren, Germany 24 C3
Ibembo, Dem. Rep. of the Congo 86 B1
Ibera, L., Argentina 126 B4
Iberian Peninsula, Europe 6 H5
Iberville, Canada 102 C5
Iberville, Lac d', Canada 102 A5
Ibi, Nigeria 83 D6
Ibi, Spain 33 G4
Ibiá, Brazil 125 G9
Ibicuy, Argentina 126 C4
Ibioapaba, Sa. da, Brazil 125 D10
Ibiza = Eivissa, Spain 37 C7
Íblei, Monti, Italy 31 E7
Ibo, Mozam. 87 E5
Ibonma, Indonesia 63 E8
Ibotirama, Brazil 125 F10
Ibrāhīm →, Lebanon 75 A4
Ibriktepe, Turkey 41 E10
Ibshawâi, Egypt 80 J7
Ibu, Indonesia 63 D7
Ibusuki, Japan 55 J5
Ica, Peru 124 F3
Iça →, Brazil 124 D5
Içana, Brazil 124 C5
Içana →, Brazil 124 C5
Içel = Mersin, Turkey 72 D6
Iceland ■, Europe 8 D4
Ich'ang = Yichang, China 59 B8
Ichchapuram, India 67 K14
Ichihara, Japan 55 G10
Ichikawa, Japan 55 G9
Ichilo →, Bolivia 124 G6
Ichinohe, Japan 54 D10
Ichinomiya, Japan 55 G8
Ichinoseki, Japan 54 E10
Ichnya, Ukraine 47 G7
Ichŏn, S. Korea 57 F14
Icod, Canary Is. 37 F3
Icy Str., U.S.A. 104 B1
Ida Grove, U.S.A. 112 D7
Ida Valley, Australia 93 E3
Idabel, U.S.A. 113 J7
Idaga Hamus, Ethiopia 81 E4
Idah, Nigeria 83 D6
Idaho □, U.S.A. 114 D7
Idaho City, U.S.A. 114 E6
Idaho Falls, U.S.A. 114 E7
Idaho Springs, U.S.A. 114 G11
Idanha-a-Nova, Portugal 34 F3
Idar-Oberstein, Germany 25 F3
Idfû, Egypt 80 C3
Ídhi Óros, Greece 36 D6
Ídhra, Greece 38 D5
Idi, Indonesia 62 C1
Idiofa, Dem. Rep. of the Congo 84 E3
Idkerberget, Sweden 10 D9
Idku, Bahra el, Egypt 80 H7
Idlib, Syria 70 C3
Idre, Sweden 10 C6
Idria, U.S.A. 116 J6
Idrija, Slovenia 29 C11
Idritsa, Russia 46 D5
Idutywa, S. Africa 89 E4
Ieper, Belgium 17 D2
Ierápetra, Greece 36 E7
Ierissós, Greece 40 F7
Ierissóu Kólpos, Greece 40 F7
Iernut, Romania 43 D9
Iesi, Italy 29 E10
Iésolo, Italy 29 C9
Ifach, Peñón de, Spain 33 G5
'Ifāl, W. al →, Si. Arabia 70 D2
Ifanadiana, Madag. 89 C8
Ife, Nigeria 83 D5
Iférouâne, Niger 83 B6
Iffley, Australia 94 B3
Ifni, Morocco 78 C3
Ifon, Nigeria 83 D6
Iforas, Adrar des, Mali 83 B5
Ifould, L., Australia 93 F5
Iganga, Uganda 86 B3
Igarapava, Brazil 125 H9
Igarka, Russia 50 C9
Igatimi, Paraguay 127 A4
Igbetti, Nigeria 83 D5
Igbo-Ora, Nigeria 83 D5
Igboho, Nigeria 83 D5
Iğdır, Turkey 73 C11
Igelfors, Sweden 11 F9
Iggesund, Sweden 10 C11
Iglésias, Italy 30 C1
Igloolik, Canada 101 B11
Igma, Gebel el, Egypt 80 J8
Ignace, Canada 102 C1
İğneada, Turkey 41 E11
İğneada Burnu, Turkey 41 E12
Igoumenítsa, Greece 38 B2
Igra, Russia 48 B11
Iguaçu →, Brazil 127 B5
Iguaçu, Cat. del, Brazil 127 B5
Iguaçu Falls = Iguaçu, Cat. del, Brazil 127 B5
Iguala, Mexico 119 D5
Igualada, Spain 32 D6
Iguassu = Iguaçu →, Brazil 127 B5
Iguatu, Brazil 125 E11
Igunga □, Tanzania 86 C3
Iharana, Madag. 89 A9
Iheya-Shima, Japan 55 L3
Ihiala, Nigeria 83 D6
Ihosy, Madag. 89 C8
Ihotry, L., Madag. 89 C7
Ii, Finland 8 D21
Ii-Shima, Japan 55 L3
Iida, Japan 55 G8
Iijoki →, Finland 8 D21
Iisalmi, Finland 8 E22
Iiyama, Japan 55 F9
Iizuka, Japan 55 H5
Ijebu-Igbo, Nigeria 83 D5
Ijebu-Ode, Nigeria 83 D5
IJmuiden, Neths. 17 B4
IJssel →, Neths. 17 B5
IJsselmeer, Neths. 17 B5
Ijuí →, Brazil 127 B4
Ikale, Nigeria 83 D6
Ikare, Nigeria 83 D6
Ikaría, Greece 39 D8
Ikast, Denmark 11 H3
Ikeda, Japan 55 G6
Ikeja, Nigeria 83 D5
Ikela, Dem. Rep. of the Congo 84 E4
Ikerre-Ekiti, Nigeria 83 D6
Ikhtiman, Bulgaria 40 D7
Iki, Japan 55 H4
Ikimba L., Tanzania 86 C3
Ikire, Nigeria 83 D5
İkizdere, Turkey 73 B9
Ikom, Nigeria 83 D6
Ikopa →, Madag. 89 B8
Ikot Ekpene, Nigeria 83 D6
Ikungu, Tanzania 86 C3
Ikurun, Nigeria 83 D5
Ila, Nigeria 83 D5
Ilagan, Phil. 61 C4
Īlām, Iran 70 C5
Ilam, Nepal 69 F12
Ilan, Taiwan 59 E13
Ilanskiy, Russia 51 D10
Ilaro, Nigeria 83 D5
Iława, Poland 44 E6
Ilbilbie, Australia 94 C4
Ile-à-la-Crosse, Canada 105 B7

Ile-à-la-Crosse, Lac, *Canada* 105 B7
Île-de-France □, *France* 19 D9
Ileanda, *Romania* 43 C8
Ilebo, *Dem. Rep. of the Congo* 84 E4
Ileje □, *Tanzania* 87 D3
Ilek, *Russia* 50 D6
Ilero, *Nigeria* 83 D5
Ilesha, *Kwara, Nigeria* 83 D5
Ilesha, *Oyo, Nigeria* 83 D5
Ilford, *Canada* 105 B9
Ilfracombe, *Australia* 94 C3
Ilfracombe, *U.K.* 13 F3
Ilgaz, *Turkey* 72 B5
Ilgaz Dağları, *Turkey* 72 B5
Ilgın, *Turkey* 72 C4
Ílhavo, *Portugal* 34 E2
Ilhéus, *Brazil* 125 F11
Ili →, *Kazakstan* 50 E8
Ilia, *Romania* 42 E7
Ilia □, *Greece* 38 D3
Iliç, *Turkey* 73 C8
Ilıca, *Turkey* 39 B9
Ilichevsk, *Azerbaijan* 73 C11
Iliff, *U.S.A.* 112 E3
Iligan, *Phil.* 61 G6
Iligan Bay, *Phil.* 61 G6
Ilíkí, L., *Greece* 38 C5
Ilin I., *Phil.* 61 E4
Iliodhrómia, *Greece* 38 B5
Ilion, *U.S.A.* 111 D9
Ilirska-Bistrica, *Slovenia* 29 C11
Ilkeston, *U.K.* 12 E6
Ilkley, *U.K.* 12 D6
Illampu = Ancohuma, Nevada, *Bolivia* 122 E4
Illana B., *Phil.* 61 H5
Illapel, *Chile* 126 C1
Ille-et-Vilaine □, *France* 18 D5
Ille-sur-Têt, *France* 20 F6
Iller →, *Germany* 25 G5
Illertissen, *Germany* 25 G6
Illescas, *Spain* 34 E7
Illetas, *Spain* 37 B9
Illichivsk, *Ukraine* 47 J6
Illiers-Combray, *France* 18 D8
Illimani, *Bolivia* 124 G5
Illinois □, *U.S.A.* 107 B9
Illinois →, *U.S.A.* 107 C8
Illium = Troy, *Turkey* 39 B8
Illkirch-Graffenstaden, *France* 19 D14
Íllora, *Spain* 35 H7
Ilm →, *Germany* 24 D7
Ilmajoki, *Finland* 9 E20
Ilmen, Ozero, *Russia* 46 C6
Ilmenau, *Germany* 24 E6
Ilo, *Peru* 124 G4
Ilobu, *Nigeria* 83 D5
Iloilo, *Phil.* 61 F5
Ilora, *Nigeria* 83 D5
Ilorin, *Nigeria* 83 D5
Ilovatka, *Russia* 48 E7
Ilovlya, *Russia* 49 F7
Ilovlya →, *Russia* 49 F7
Iłowa, *Poland* 45 G2
Ilubabor □, *Ethiopia* 81 F4
Ilva Mică, *Romania* 43 C9
Ilwaco, *U.S.A.* 116 D2
Ilwaki, *Indonesia* 63 F7
Ilyichevsk = Illichivsk, *Ukraine* 47 J6
Iłża, *Poland* 45 G8
Iłżanka →, *Poland* 45 G8
Imabari, *Japan* 55 G6
Imaloto →, *Madag.* 89 C8
İmamoğlu, *Turkey* 72 D6
Imandra, Ozero, *Russia* 50 C4
Imari, *Japan* 55 H4
Imasa, *Sudan* 80 D4
Imathía □, *Greece* 40 F6
Imatra, *Finland* 46 B5
Imbâbah, *Egypt* 80 H7
Imbler, *U.S.A.* 114 D5
imeni 26 Bakinskikh Komissarov = Neftçala, *Azerbaijan* 73 C13
Imeri, Serra, *Brazil* 124 C5
Imerimandroso, *Madag.* 89 B8
Imi, *Ethiopia* 81 F5
Imishly = Imişli, *Azerbaijan* 49 L9
Imişli, *Azerbaijan* 49 L9
Imlay, *U.S.A.* 114 F4
Imlay City, *U.S.A.* 110 D1
Immenstadt, *Germany* 25 H6
Immingham, *U.K.* 12 D7
Immokalee, *U.S.A.* 109 M5
Imo □, *Nigeria* 83 D6
Ímola, *Italy* 29 D8
Imotski, *Croatia* 29 E14
Imperatriz, *Brazil* 125 E9
Impéria, *Italy* 28 E5
Imperial, *Canada* 105 C7
Imperial, *Calif., U.S.A.* 117 N11
Imperial, *Nebr., U.S.A.* 112 E4
Imperial Beach, *U.S.A.* 117 N9
Imperial Dam, *U.S.A.* 117 N12
Imperial Reservoir, *U.S.A.* 117 N12
Imperial Valley, *U.S.A.* 117 N11
Imperieuse Reef, *Australia* 92 C2
Impfondo, *Congo* 84 D3
Imphal, *India* 67 G18
Imphy, *France* 19 F10
İmranlı, *Turkey* 73 C8
İmroz = Gökçeada, *Turkey* 41 F9
İmroz, *Turkey* 41 F9
Imst, *Austria* 26 D3
Imuruan B., *Phil.* 63 B5
In Delimane, *Mali* 83 B5
In Salah, *Algeria* 78 C6
In Tallak, *Mali* 83 B5
Ina, *Japan* 55 G8
Inangahua Junction, *N.Z.* 91 J3
Inanwatan, *Indonesia* 63 E8
Iñapari, *Peru* 124 F5
Inari, *Finland* 8 B22
Inarijärvi, *Finland* 8 B22
Inawashiro-Ko, *Japan* 54 F10
Inca, *Spain* 37 B9
Incaguasi, *Chile* 126 B1
İnce Burun, *Turkey* 72 A6
Incekum Burnu, *Turkey* 72 D5
Inch'ŏn, *S. Korea* 57 F14
Incio = Cruz de Incio, *Spain* 34 C3
İncirliova, *Turkey* 39 D9
Incomáti →, *Mozam.* 89 D5
Inda Silase, *Ethiopia* 81 E4
Indal, *Sweden* 10 B11
Indalsälven →, *Sweden* 10 B11
Indaw, *Burma* 67 G20
Indbir, *Ethiopia* 81 F4
Independence, *Calif., U.S.A.* 116 J8
Independence, *Iowa, U.S.A.* 112 D9
Independence, *Kans., U.S.A.* 113 G7
Independence, *Mo., U.S.A.* 112 F7
Independence, *Oreg., U.S.A.* 114 D2
Independence Fjord, *Greenland* 4 A6
Independence Mts., *U.S.A.* 114 F5
Independenţa, *Romania* 43 E12
Index, *U.S.A.* 116 C5
India ■, *Asia* 66 K11
Indian →, *U.S.A.* 109 M5
Indian Cabins, *Canada* 104 B5
Indian Harbour, *Canada* 103 B8
Indian Head, *Canada* 105 C8
Indian Ocean 52 K11
Indian Springs, *U.S.A.* 117 J11
Indiana, *U.S.A.* 110 F5
Indiana □, *U.S.A.* 108 F3
Indianapolis, *U.S.A.* 108 F2
Indianola, *Iowa, U.S.A.* 112 E8
Indianola, *Miss., U.S.A.* 113 J9
Indigirka →, *Russia* 51 B15
Inđija, *Serbia, Yug.* 42 E5
Indio, *U.S.A.* 117 M10
Indonesia ■, *Asia* 62 F5
Indore, *India* 68 H6
Indramayu, *Indonesia* 63 G13
Indravati →, *India* 67 K12
Indre □, *France* 19 F8
Indre →, *France* 18 E7
Indre-et-Loire □, *France* 18 E7
Indus →, *Pakistan* 68 G2
Indus, Mouth of the, *Pakistan* 68 H3
İnebolu, *Turkey* 72 B5
İnecik, *Turkey* 41 F11
İnegöl, *Turkey* 41 F13
Ineu, *Romania* 42 D6
Infantes = Villanueva de los Infantes, *Spain* 35 G7
Infiernillo, Presa del, *Mexico* 118 D4
Infiesto, *Spain* 34 B5
Ingelstad, *Sweden* 11 H8
Ingenio, *Canary Is.* 37 G4
Ingenio Santa Ana, *Argentina* 126 B2
Ingersoll, *Canada* 110 C4
Ingham, *Australia* 94 B4
Ingleborough, *U.K.* 12 C5
Inglewood, *Queens., Australia* 95 D5
Inglewood, *Vic., Australia* 95 F3
Inglewood, *N.Z.* 91 H5
Inglewood, *U.S.A.* 117 M8
Ingólfshöfði, *Iceland* 8 E5
Ingolstadt, *Germany* 25 G7
Ingomar, *U.S.A.* 114 C10
Ingonish, *Canada* 103 C7
Ingore, *Guinea-Biss.* 82 C1
Ingraj Bazar, *India* 69 G13
Ingrid Christensen Coast, *Antarctica* 5 C6
Ingul → = Inhul →, *Ukraine* 47 J7
Ingulec = Inhulec, *Ukraine* 47 J7
Ingulets → = Inhulets →, *Ukraine* 47 J7
Inguri → = Enguri →, *Georgia* 49 J5
Ingushetia □, *Russia* 49 J7
Ingwavuma, *S. Africa* 89 D5
Inhaca, I., *Mozam.* 89 D5
Inhafenga, *Mozam.* 89 C5
Inhambane, *Mozam.* 89 C6
Inhambane □, *Mozam.* 89 C5
Inhaminga, *Mozam.* 87 F4
Inharrime, *Mozam.* 89 C6
Inharrime →, *Mozam.* 89 C6
Inhisar, *Turkey* 39 A12
Inhul →, *Ukraine* 47 J7
Inhulec, *Ukraine* 47 J7
Inhulets →, *Ukraine* 47 J7
Iniesta, *Spain* 33 F3
Ining = Yining, *China* 60 B3
Inírida →, *Colombia* 124 C5
Inishbofin, *Ireland* 15 C1
Inisheer, *Ireland* 15 C2
Inishfree B., *Ireland* 15 A3
Inishkea North, *Ireland* 15 B1
Inishkea South, *Ireland* 15 B1
Inishmaan, *Ireland* 15 C2
Inishmore, *Ireland* 15 C2
Inishowen Pen., *Ireland* 15 A4
Inishshark, *Ireland* 15 C1
Inishturk, *Ireland* 15 C1
Inishvickillane, *Ireland* 15 D1
Injune, *Australia* 95 D4
Inklin, *Canada* 104 B2
Inklin →, *Canada* 104 B2
Inkom, *U.S.A.* 114 E7
Inle L., *Burma* 67 J20
Inn →, *Austria* 26 C6
Innamincka, *Australia* 95 D3
Inner Hebrides, *U.K.* 14 E2
Inner Mongolia = Nei Monggol Zizhiqu □, *China* 56 D7
Inner Sound, *U.K.* 14 D3
Innerkip, *Canada* 110 C4
Innetalling I., *Canada* 102 A4
Innisfail, *Australia* 94 B4
Innisfail, *Canada* 104 C6
In'no-shima, *Japan* 55 G6
Innsbruck, *Austria* 26 D4
Innviertel, *Austria* 26 C6
Inny →, *Ireland* 15 C4
Inongo, *Dem. Rep. of the Congo* 84 E3
İnönü, *Turkey* 39 B12
Inoucdjouac = Inukjuak, *Canada* 101 C12
Inowrocław, *Poland* 45 F5
Inpundong, *N. Korea* 57 D14
Inscription, C., *Australia* 93 E1
Insein, *Burma* 67 L20
Insjön, *Sweden* 10 D9
Ińsko, *Poland* 44 E2
Însurăţei, *Romania* 43 F12
Intendente Alvear, *Argentina* 126 D3
İntepe, *Turkey* 39 A8
Interior, *U.S.A.* 112 D4
Interlaken, *Switz.* 25 J3
International Falls, *U.S.A.* 112 A8
Intiyaco, *Argentina* 126 B3
Întorsura Buzăului, *Romania* 43 E11
Inukjuak, *Canada* 101 C12
Inútil, B., *Chile* 128 G2
Inuvik, *Canada* 100 B6
Inveraray, *U.K.* 14 E3
Inverbervie, *U.K.* 14 E6
Invercargill, *N.Z.* 91 M2
Inverclyde □, *U.K.* 14 F4
Inverell, *Australia* 95 D5
Invergordon, *U.K.* 14 D4
Invermere, *Canada* 104 C5
Inverness, *Canada* 103 C7
Inverness, *U.K.* 14 D4
Inverness, *U.S.A.* 109 L4
Inverurie, *U.K.* 14 D6
Inverway, *Australia* 92 C4
Investigator Group, *Australia* 95 E1
Investigator Str., *Australia* 95 F2
Inya, *Russia* 50 D9
Inyanga, *Zimbabwe* 87 F3
Inyangani, *Zimbabwe* 87 F3
Inyantue, *Zimbabwe* 87 F2
Inyo Mts., *U.S.A.* 115 H5
Inyokern, *U.S.A.* 117 K9
Inza, *Russia* 48 D8
Inzhavino, *Russia* 48 D6
Iō-Jima, *Japan* 55 J5
Ioánnina, *Greece* 38 B2
Ioánnina □, *Greece* 38 B2
Iola, *U.S.A.* 113 G7
Ion Corvin, *Romania* 43 F12
Iona, *U.K.* 14 E2
Ione, *Calif., U.S.A.* 116 G6
Ione, *Wash., U.S.A.* 114 B5
Ionia, *U.S.A.* 108 D3
Ionian Sea, *Medit. S.* 6 H9
Iónioi Nísoi □, *Greece* 38 C2
Íos, *Greece* 39 E7
Iowa □, *U.S.A.* 112 D8
Iowa City, *U.S.A.* 112 E9
Iowa Falls, *U.S.A.* 112 D8
Ipala, *Tanzania* 86 C3
Ipameri, *Brazil* 125 G9
Ipáti, *Greece* 38 C4
Ipatinga, *Brazil* 125 G10
Ipatovo, *Russia* 49 H6
Ipel' →, *Europe* 27 D11
Ipiales, *Colombia* 124 C3
Ipin = Yibin, *China* 58 C5
Ípiros □, *Greece* 38 B2
Ipixuna, *Brazil* 124 E4
Ipoh, *Malaysia* 65 K3
Ippy, *C.A.R.* 84 C4
Ipsala, *Turkey* 41 F10
Ipsário, Óros, *Greece* 41 F8
Ipswich, *Australia* 95 D5
Ipswich, *U.K.* 13 E9
Ipswich, *Mass., U.S.A.* 111 D14
Ipswich, *S. Dak., U.S.A.* 112 C5
Ipu, *Brazil* 125 D10
Iqaluit, *Canada* 101 B13
Iquique, *Chile* 124 H4
Iquitos, *Peru* 124 D4
Irabu-Jima, *Japan* 55 M2
Iracoubo, *Fr. Guiana* 125 B8
Īrafshān, *Iran* 71 E9
Irahuan, *Phil.* 61 G3
Iráklia, *Kikládhes, Greece* 39 E7
Iráklia, *Sérrai, Greece* 40 E7
Iráklion, *Greece* 36 D7
Iráklion □, *Greece* 36 D7
Irala, *Paraguay* 127 B5
Iramba □, *Tanzania* 86 C3
Iran ■, *Asia* 71 C7
Iran, Gunung-Gunung, *Malaysia* 62 D4
Iran, Plateau of, *Asia* 52 F9
Iran Ra. = Iran, Gunung-Gunung, *Malaysia* 62 D4
Īrānshahr, *Iran* 71 E9
Irapuato, *Mexico* 118 C4
Iraq ■, *Asia* 70 C5
Irati, *Brazil* 127 B5
Irbes saurums, *Latvia* 44 A9
Irbid, *Jordan* 75 C4
Irbid □, *Jordan* 75 C5
Iregua →, *Spain* 32 C7
Ireland ■, *Europe* 15 C4
Irele, *Nigeria* 83 D6
Irgiz, Bolshaya →, *Russia* 48 D9
Irhyangdong, *N. Korea* 57 D15
Iri, *S. Korea* 57 G14
Irian Jaya □, *Indonesia* 63 E9
Irié, *Guinea* 82 D3
Iriga, *Phil.* 61 E5
Iringa, *Tanzania* 86 D4
Iringa □, *Tanzania* 86 D4
Iriomote-Jima, *Japan* 55 M1
Iriona, *Honduras* 120 C2
Iriri →, *Brazil* 125 D8
Irish Republic ■, *Europe* 15 C3
Irish Sea, *U.K.* 12 D3
Irkutsk, *Russia* 51 D11
Irlığanlı, *Turkey* 39 D11
Irma, *Canada* 105 C6
Irō-Zaki, *Japan* 55 G9
Iroise, Mer d', *France* 18 D2
Iron Baron, *Australia* 95 E2
Iron Gate = Portile de Fier, *Europe* 42 F7
Iron Knob, *Australia* 95 E2
Iron Mountain, *U.S.A.* 108 C1
Iron Ra., *Australia* 94 A3
Iron River, *U.S.A.* 112 B10
Irondequoit, *U.S.A.* 110 C7
Ironstone Kopje, *Botswana* 88 D3
Ironton, *Mo., U.S.A.* 113 G9
Ironton, *Ohio, U.S.A.* 108 F4
Ironwood, *U.S.A.* 112 B9
Iroquois Falls, *Canada* 102 C3
Irosin, *Phil.* 61 E6
Irpin, *Ukraine* 47 G6
Irrara Cr. →, *Australia* 95 D4
Irrawaddy □, *Burma* 67 L19
Irrawaddy →, *Burma* 67 M19
Irsina, *Italy* 31 B9
Irtysh →, *Russia* 50 C7
Irumu, *Dem. Rep. of the Congo* 86 B2
Irún, *Spain* 32 B3
Irunea = Pamplona, *Spain* 32 C3
Irurzun, *Spain* 32 C3
Irvine, *Canada* 105 D6
Irvine, *U.K.* 14 F4
Irvine, *Calif., U.S.A.* 117 M9
Irvine, *Ky., U.S.A.* 108 G4
Irvinestown, *U.K.* 15 B4
Irving, *U.S.A.* 113 J6
Irvona, *U.S.A.* 110 F6
Irwin →, *Australia* 93 E1
Irymple, *Australia* 95 E3
Is-sur-Tille, *France* 19 E12
Isa, *Nigeria* 83 C6
Isaac →, *Australia* 94 C4
Isabel, *U.S.A.* 112 C4
Isabela, I., *Mexico* 118 C3
Isabelia, Cord., *Nic.* 120 D2
Isabella, *Phil.* 61 H5
Isabella Ra., *Australia* 92 D3
Isaccea, *Romania* 43 E13
Ísafjarðardjúp, *Iceland* 8 C2
Ísafjörður, *Iceland* 8 C2
Isagarh, *India* 68 G7
Isahaya, *Japan* 55 H5
Isaka, *Tanzania* 86 C3
Isakly, *Russia* 48 C10
Işalniţa, *Romania* 43 F8
Isana = Içana →, *Brazil* 124 C5
Isar →, *Germany* 25 G8
Isarco →, *Italy* 29 B8
Ísari, *Greece* 38 D3
Íscar, *Spain* 34 D6
Iscehisar, *Turkey* 39 C12
Íschia, *Italy* 30 B6
Isdell →, *Australia* 92 C3
Ise, *Japan* 55 G8
Ise-Wan, *Japan* 55 G8
Isefjord, *Denmark* 11 J5
Isel →, *Austria* 26 E5
Iseo, *Italy* 28 C7
Iseo, L. d', *Italy* 28 C7
Iseramagazi, *Tanzania* 86 C3
Isère □, *France* 21 C9
Isère →, *France* 21 D8
Iserlohn, *Germany* 24 D3
Isérnia, *Italy* 31 A7
Iseyin, *Nigeria* 83 D5
Ishigaki-Shima, *Japan* 55 M2
Ishikari-Gawa →, *Japan* 54 C10
Ishikari-Sammyaku, *Japan* 54 C11
Ishikari-Wan, *Japan* 54 C10
Ishikawa □, *Japan* 55 F8
Ishim, *Russia* 50 D7
Ishim →, *Russia* 50 D8
Ishinomaki, *Japan* 54 E10
Ishioka, *Japan* 55 F10
Ishkuman, *Pakistan* 69 A5
Ishmi, *Albania* 40 E3
Ishpeming, *U.S.A.* 108 B2
Isigny-sur-Mer, *France* 18 C5
Isıklar Dağı, *Turkey* 41 F11
Işıklı, *Turkey* 39 C11
Isil Kul, *Russia* 50 D8
Ísili, *Italy* 30 C2
Isiolo, *Kenya* 86 B4
Isiolo □, *Kenya* 86 B4
Isiro, *Dem. Rep. of the Congo* 86 B2
Isisford, *Australia* 94 C3
İskenderun, *Turkey* 72 D7
İskenderun Körfezi, *Turkey* 72 D6
İskilip, *Turkey* 72 B6
Iskŭr →, *Bulgaria* 41 C8
Iskŭr, Yazovir, *Bulgaria* 40 D7
Iskut →, *Canada* 104 B2
Isla →, *U.K.* 14 E5
Isla Cristina, *Spain* 35 H3
Isla Vista, *U.S.A.* 117 L7
İslâhiye, *Turkey* 72 D7
Islamabad, *Pakistan* 68 C5
Islamkot, *Pakistan* 68 G4
Island →, *Canada* 104 A4
Island Falls, *Canada* 102 C3
Island Falls, *U.S.A.* 103 C6
Island L., *Canada* 105 C10
Island Lagoon, *Australia* 95 E2
Island Pond, *U.S.A.* 111 B13
Islands, B. of, *Canada* 103 C8
Islay, *U.K.* 14 F2
Isle →, *France* 20 D3
Isle aux Morts, *Canada* 103 C8
Isle of Wight □, *U.K.* 13 G6
Isle Royale, *U.S.A.* 112 B10
Isleta, *U.S.A.* 115 J10
Isleton, *U.S.A.* 116 G5
Ismail = Izmayil, *Ukraine* 47 K5
Ismâ'ilîya, *Egypt* 80 H8
Ismaning, *Germany* 25 G7
Ismay, *U.S.A.* 112 B2
Isna, *Egypt* 80 B3
Isogstalo, *India* 69 B8
Ísola del Liri, *Italy* 29 G10
Ísola della Scala, *Italy* 28 C7
Ísola di Capo Rizzuto, *Italy* 31 D10
Isparta, *Turkey* 39 D12
Isperikh, *Bulgaria* 41 C10
Íspica, *Italy* 31 F7
Israel ■, *Asia* 75 D3
Issia, *Ivory C.* 82 D3
Issoire, *France* 20 C7
Issoudun, *France* 19 F8
Issyk-Kul = Ysyk-Köl, *Kyrgyzstan* 52 E11
Issyk-Kul, Ozero = Ysyk-Köl, Ozero, *Kyrgyzstan* 50 E8
Ist, *Croatia* 29 D11
Istaihah, *U.A.E.* 71 F7
Istállós-kő, *Hungary* 42 B5
İstanbul, *Turkey* 41 E12
İstanbul □, *Turkey* 41 E12
İstanbul Boğazı, *Turkey* 41 E13
Istiaía, *Greece* 38 C5
Istok, *Serbia, Yug.* 40 D4
Istokpoga, L., *U.S.A.* 109 M5
Istra, *Croatia* 29 C10
Istres, *France* 21 E8
Istria = Istra, *Croatia* 29 C10
Itá, *Paraguay* 126 B4
Itaberaba, *Brazil* 125 F10
Itabira, *Brazil* 125 G10
Itabirito, *Brazil* 127 A7
Itabuna, *Brazil* 125 F11
Itacaunas →, *Brazil* 125 E9
Itacoatiara, *Brazil* 124 D7
Itaipú, Represa de, *Brazil* 127 B5
Itaituba, *Brazil* 125 D7
Itajaí, *Brazil* 127 B6
Itajubá, *Brazil* 127 A6
Itaka, *Tanzania* 87 D3
Italy ■, *Europe* 7 G8
Itamaraju, *Brazil* 125 G11
Itampolo, *Madag.* 89 C7
Itapecuru-Mirim, *Brazil* 125 D10
Itaperuna, *Brazil* 127 A7
Itapetininga, *Brazil* 127 A6
Itapeva, *Brazil* 127 A6
Itapicuru →, *Bahia, Brazil* 125 F11
Itapicuru →, *Maranhão, Brazil* 125 D10
Itapipoca, *Brazil* 125 D11
Itapuá □, *Paraguay* 127 B4
Itaquari, *Brazil* 127 A7
Itaquí, *Brazil* 126 B4
Itararé, *Brazil* 127 A6
Itarsi, *India* 68 H7
Itatí, *Argentina* 126 B4
Itbayat, *Phil.* 61 A4
Itchen →, *U.K.* 13 G6
Itéa, *Greece* 38 C4
Itezhi Tezhi, L., *Zambia* 87 F2
Ithaca = Itháki, *Greece* 38 C2
Ithaca, *U.S.A.* 111 D8
Itháki, *Greece* 38 C2
Itiquira →, *Brazil* 125 G7
Ito, *Japan* 55 G9
Itoigawa, *Japan* 55 F8
Iton →, *France* 18 C8
Itonamas →, *Bolivia* 124 F6

Itri, *Italy* 30 A6
Itsa, *Egypt* 80 J7
Íttiri, *Italy* 30 B1
Ittoqqortoormiit = Scoresbysund, *Greenland* 4 B6
Itu, *Brazil* 127 A6
Itu, *Nigeria* 83 D6
Ituiutaba, *Brazil* 125 G9
Itumbiara, *Brazil* 125 G9
Ituna, *Canada* 105 C8
Itunge Port, *Tanzania* 87 D3
Iturbe, *Argentina* 126 A2
Ituri →, *Dem. Rep. of the Congo* 86 B2
Iturup, Ostrov, *Russia* 51 E15
Ituxi →, *Brazil* 124 E6
Ituyuro →, *Argentina* 126 A3
Itzehoe, *Germany* 24 B5
Ivaí →, *Brazil* 127 A5
Ivalo, *Finland* 8 B22
Ivalojoki →, *Finland* 8 B22
Ivanava, *Belarus* 47 F3
Ivančice, *Czech Rep.* 27 B9
Ivănești, *Romania* 43 D12
Ivangorod, *Russia* 46 C5
Ivanhoe, *N.S.W., Australia* 95 E3
Ivanhoe, *W. Austral., Australia* 92 C4
Ivanhoe, *U.S.A.* 116 J7
Ivanhoe L., *Canada* 105 A7
Ivanić Grad, *Croatia* 29 C13
Ivanjica, *Serbia, Yug.* 40 C4
Ivanjska, *Bos.-H.* 42 F2
Ivankoyskoye Vdkhr., *Russia* 46 D9
Ivano-Frankivsk, *Ukraine* 47 H3
Ivano-Frankovsk = Ivano-Frankivsk, *Ukraine* 47 H3
Ivanovo = Ivanava, *Belarus* 47 F3
Ivanovo, *Russia* 46 D11
Ivanšćica, *Croatia* 29 B13
Ivato, *Madag.* 89 C8
Ivatsevichy, *Belarus* 47 F3
Ivaylovgrad, *Bulgaria* 41 E10
Ivinheima →, *Brazil* 127 A5
Ivohibe, *Madag.* 89 C8
Ivory Coast ■, *Africa* 82 D4
Ivösjön, *Sweden* 11 H8
Ivrea, *Italy* 28 C4
İvrindi, *Turkey* 39 B9
Ivujivik, *Canada* 101 B12
Ivybridge, *U.K.* 13 G4
Iwaizumi, *Japan* 54 E10
Iwaki, *Japan* 55 F10
Iwakuni, *Japan* 55 G6
Iwamizawa, *Japan* 54 C10
Iwanai, *Japan* 54 C10
Iwata, *Japan* 55 G8
Iwate □, *Japan* 54 E10
Iwate-San, *Japan* 54 E10
Iwo, *Nigeria* 83 D5
Iwonicz-Zdrój, *Poland* 45 J8
Ixiamas, *Bolivia* 124 F5
Ixopo, *S. Africa* 89 E5
Ixtepec, *Mexico* 119 D5
Ixtlán del Río, *Mexico* 118 C4
Iyo, *Japan* 55 H6
Izabal, L. de, *Guatemala* 120 C2
Izamal, *Mexico* 119 C7
Izberbash, *Russia* 49 J8
Izbica, *Poland* 45 H10
Izbica Kujawska, *Poland* 45 F5
Izbiceni, *Romania* 43 G9
Izena-Shima, *Japan* 55 L3
Izgrev, *Bulgaria* 41 C10
Izhevsk, *Russia* 50 D6
Izmayil, *Ukraine* 47 K5
İzmir, *Turkey* 39 C9
İzmir □, *Turkey* 39 C9
İzmir Körfezi, *Turkey* 39 C8
İzmit = Kocaeli, *Turkey* 41 F13
Iznájar, *Spain* 35 H6
Iznalloz, *Spain* 35 H7
İznik, *Turkey* 72 B3
İznik Gölü, *Turkey* 41 F13
Izobil'nyy, *Russia* 49 H5
Izola, *Slovenia* 29 C10
Izra, *Syria* 75 C5
Iztochni Rodopi, *Bulgaria* 41 E9
Izu-Shotō, *Japan* 55 G10
Izumi-sano, *Japan* 55 G7
Izumo, *Japan* 55 G6
Izyaslav, *Ukraine* 47 G4
Izyum, *Ukraine* 47 H9

J

Jaba, *Ethiopia* 81 F4
Jabal el Awlîya, *Sudan* 81 D3
Jabalón →, *Spain* 35 G6
Jabalpur, *India* 69 H8
Jabbūl, *Syria* 70 B3
Jablah, *Syria* 70 C3
Jablanac, *Croatia* 29 D11
Jablanica, *Bos.-H.* 42 G2
Jablonec nad Nisou, *Czech Rep.* 26 A8
Jablonica, *Slovak Rep.* 27 C10
Jabłonowo Pomorskie, *Poland* 44 E6
Jablunkov, *Czech Rep.* 27 B11
Jaboatão, *Brazil* 125 E11
Jaboticabal, *Brazil* 127 A6
Jabukovac, *Serbia, Yug.* 40 B6
Jaca, *Spain* 32 C4
Jacareí, *Brazil* 127 A6
Jacarèzinho, *Brazil* 127 A6
Jackman, *U.S.A.* 103 C5
Jacksboro, *U.S.A.* 113 J5
Jackson, *Australia* 95 D4
Jackson, *Ala., U.S.A.* 109 K2
Jackson, *Calif., U.S.A.* 116 G6
Jackson, *Ky., U.S.A.* 108 G4
Jackson, *Mich., U.S.A.* 108 D3
Jackson, *Minn., U.S.A.* 112 D7
Jackson, *Miss., U.S.A.* 113 J9
Jackson, *Mo., U.S.A.* 113 G10
Jackson, *Ohio, U.S.A.* 108 F4
Jackson, *Tenn., U.S.A.* 109 H1
Jackson, *Wyo., U.S.A.* 114 E8
Jackson B., *N.Z.* 91 K2
Jackson L., *U.S.A.* 114 E8
Jacksons, *N.Z.* 91 K3
Jacksonville, *Ala., U.S.A.* 109 J3
Jacksonville, *Calif., U.S.A.* 116 H6
Jacksonville, *Fla., U.S.A.* 109 K5
Jacksonville, *Ill., U.S.A.* 112 F9
Jacksonville, *N.C., U.S.A.* 109 H7
Jacksonville, *Oreg., U.S.A.* 114 E2
Jacksonville, *Tex., U.S.A.* 113 K7
Jacksonville Beach, *U.S.A.* 109 K5
Jacmel, *Haiti* 121 C5
Jacob Lake, *U.S.A.* 115 H7
Jacobabad, *Pakistan* 68 E3
Jacobina, *Brazil* 125 F10
Jacques-Cartier, Mt., *Canada* 103 C6
Jacqueville, *Ivory C.* 82 D4
Jacuí →, *Brazil* 127 C5
Jacumba, *U.S.A.* 117 N10
Jacundá →, *Brazil* 125 D8
Jade, *Germany* 24 B4
Jadebusen, *Germany* 24 B4
Jadotville = Likasi, *Dem. Rep. of the Congo* 87 E2
Jadovnik, *Serbia, Yug.* 40 C3
Jadraque, *Spain* 32 E2
Jaén, *Peru* 124 E3
Jaén, *Spain* 35 H7
Jaén □, *Spain* 35 H7
Jaffa = Tel Aviv-Yafo, *Israel* 75 C3
Jaffa, C., *Australia* 95 F2
Jaffna, *Sri Lanka* 66 Q12
Jagadhri, *India* 68 D7
Jagadishpur, *India* 69 G11
Jagdalpur, *India* 67 K13
Jagersfontein, *S. Africa* 88 D4
Jagodina, *Serbia, Yug.* 40 B5
Jagraon, *India* 66 D9
Jagst →, *Germany* 25 F5
Jagtial, *India* 66 K11
Jaguariaíva, *Brazil* 127 A6
Jaguaribe →, *Brazil* 125 D11
Jagüey Grande, *Cuba* 120 B3
Jahangirabad, *India* 68 E8
Jahrom, *Iran* 71 D7
Jailolo, *Indonesia* 63 D7
Jailolo, Selat, *Indonesia* 63 D7
Jaipur, *India* 68 F6
Jājarm, *Iran* 71 B8
Jajce, *Bos.-H.* 42 F2
Jakarta, *Indonesia* 63 G12
Jakobstad = Pietarsaari, *Finland* 8 E20
Jakupica, *Macedonia* 40 E5
Jal, *U.S.A.* 113 J3
Jalalabad, *Afghan.* 68 B4
Jalalabad, *India* 69 F8
Jalalpur Jattan, *Pakistan* 68 C6
Jalama, *U.S.A.* 117 L6
Jalapa, *Guatemala* 120 D2
Jalapa Enríquez, *Mexico* 119 D5
Jalasjärvi, *Finland* 9 E20
Jalaun, *India* 69 F8
Jaleswar, *Nepal* 69 F11
Jalgaon, *Maharashtra, India* 66 J10
Jalgaon, *Maharashtra, India* 66 J9
Jalībah, *Iraq* 70 D5
Jalingo, *Nigeria* 83 D7
Jalisco □, *Mexico* 118 D4
Jalkot, *Pakistan* 69 B5
Jallas →, *Spain* 34 C1
Jalna, *India* 66 K9
Jalón →, *Spain* 32 D3
Jalpa, *Mexico* 118 C4
Jalpaiguri, *India* 67 F16
Jaluit I., *Pac. Oc.* 96 G8
Jalūlā, *Iraq* 70 C5
Jamaari, *Nigeria* 83 C6
Jamaica ■, *W. Indies* 120 C4
Jamalpur, *Bangla.* 67 G16
Jamalpur, *India* 69 G12
Jamalpurganj, *India* 69 H13
Jamanxim →, *Brazil* 125 D7
Jambi, *Indonesia* 62 E2
Jambi □, *Indonesia* 62 E2
Jambusar, *India* 68 H5
James →, *U.S.A.* 112 D6
James B., *Canada* 101 C12
James Ranges, *Australia* 92 D5
James Ross I., *Antarctica* 5 C18
Jamestown, *Australia* 95 E2
Jamestown, *S. Africa* 88 E4
Jamestown, *Ky., U.S.A.* 108 G3
Jamestown, *N. Dak., U.S.A.* 112 B5
Jamestown, *N.Y., U.S.A.* 110 D5
Jamestown, *Pa., U.S.A.* 110 E4
Jamestown, *Tenn., U.S.A.* 109 G3
Jamīlābād, *Iran* 71 C6
Jamiltepec, *Mexico* 119 D5
Jämjö, *Sweden* 11 H9
Jamkhandi, *India* 66 L9
Jammerbugt, *Denmark* 11 G3
Jammu, *India* 68 C6
Jammu & Kashmir □, *India* 69 B7
Jamnagar, *India* 68 H4
Jampur, *Pakistan* 68 E4
Jamrud, *Pakistan* 68 C4
Jämsä, *Finland* 9 F21
Jamshedpur, *India* 69 H12
Jamtara, *India* 69 H12
Jämtland, *Sweden* 8 E15
Jämtlands län □, *Sweden* 10 B7
Jan L., *Canada* 105 C8
Jan Mayen, *Arctic* 4 B7
Janakkala, *Finland* 9 F21
Janaúba, *Brazil* 125 G10
Jand, *Pakistan* 68 C5
Jandaq, *Iran* 71 C7
Jandia, *Canary Is.* 37 F5
Jandia, Pta. de, *Canary Is.* 37 F5
Jandola, *Pakistan* 68 C4
Jandowae, *Australia* 95 D5
Jándula →, *Spain* 35 G6
Janesville, *U.S.A.* 112 D10
Janga, *Ghana* 83 C4
Janikowo, *Poland* 45 F5
Janīn, *West Bank* 75 C4
Janinà = Ioánnina □, *Greece* 38 B2
Janja, *Bos.-H.* 42 F4
Janjevo, *Serbia, Yug.* 40 D5
Janjina, *Croatia* 29 F14
Janos, *Mexico* 118 A3
Jánoshalma, *Hungary* 42 D4
Jánosháza, *Hungary* 42 C2
Jánossomorja, *Hungary* 42 C2
Janów, *Poland* 45 H6
Janów Lubelski, *Poland* 45 H9
Janów Podlaski, *Poland* 45 F10
Janowiec Wielkopolski, *Poland* 45 F4
Januária, *Brazil* 125 G10
Janub Dârfûr □, *Sudan* 81 E2
Janub Kordofân □, *Sudan* 81 E3
Janubio, *Canary Is.* 37 F6
Janville, *France* 19 D8
Janzé, *France* 18 E5
Jaora, *India* 68 H6
Japan ■, *Asia* 55 G8
Japan, Sea of, *Asia* 54 E7
Japan Trench, *Pac. Oc.* 96 D6
Japen = Yapen, *Indonesia* 63 E9
Japurá →, *Brazil* 122 D4
Jaqué, *Panama* 124 B3
Jarābulus, *Syria* 70 B3
Jaraicejo, *Spain* 35 F5
Jaraíz de la Vera, *Spain* 34 E5
Jarama →, *Spain* 34 E7
Jaramānah, *Syria* 72 F7
Jarandilla, *Spain* 34 E5
Jaranwala, *Pakistan* 68 D5
Jarash, *Jordan* 75 C4
Järbo, *Sweden* 10 D10
Jardim, *Brazil* 126 A4
Jardín →, *Spain* 33 G2
Jardines de la Reina, Is., *Cuba* 120 B4
Jargalang, *China* 57 C12
Jargalant = Hovd, *Mongolia* 60 B4
Jari →, *Brazil* 125 D8
Jarīr, W. al →, *Si. Arabia* 70 E4
Järlåsa, *Sweden* 10 E11
Jarmen, *Germany* 24 B9
Järna, *Kopparberg, Sweden* 10 D8
Järna, *Stockholm, Sweden* 10 E11
Jarnac, *France* 20 C3
Jarny, *France* 19 C12
Jarocin, *Poland* 45 G4
Jaroměř, *Czech Rep.* 26 A8
Jarosław, *Poland* 45 H9
Järpås, *Sweden* 11 F6
Järpen, *Sweden* 10 A7
Jarrahdale, *Australia* 93 F2
Jarres, Plaine des, *Laos* 64 C4
Jarso, *Ethiopia* 81 F4
Jartai, *China* 56 E3
Jarud Qi, *China* 57 B11
Järvenpää, *Finland* 9 F21
Jarvis, *Canada* 110 D4
Jarvis I., *Pac. Oc.* 97 H12
Jarvorník, *Czech Rep.* 27 A10
Järvsö, *Sweden* 10 C10
Jarwa, *India* 69 F10
Jaša Tomić, *Serbia, Yug.* 42 E5
Jasień, *Poland* 45 G2
Jāsimīyah, *Iraq* 70 C5
Jasin, *Malaysia* 65 L4
Jāsk, *Iran* 71 E8
Jasło, *Poland* 45 J8
Jasmund, *Germany* 24 A9
Jasper, *Alta., Canada* 104 C5
Jasper, *Ont., Canada* 111 B9
Jasper, *Ala., U.S.A.* 109 J2
Jasper, *Fla., U.S.A.* 109 K4
Jasper, *Minn., U.S.A.* 112 D6
Jasper, *Tex., U.S.A.* 113 K8
Jasper Nat. Park, *Canada* 104 C5
Jastarnia, *Poland* 44 D5
Jastrebarsko, *Croatia* 29 C12
Jastrowie, *Poland* 44 E3
Jastrzębie Zdrój, *Poland* 45 J5
Jász-Nagykun-Szolnok □, *Hungary* 42 C5
Jászapáti, *Hungary* 42 C5
Jászárokszállás, *Hungary* 42 C4
Jászberény, *Hungary* 42 C4
Jászkisér, *Hungary* 42 C5
Jászladány, *Hungary* 42 C5
Jataí, *Brazil* 125 G8
Jati, *Pakistan* 68 G3
Jatibarang, *Indonesia* 63 G13
Jatinegara, *Indonesia* 63 G12
Játiva = Xátiva, *Spain* 33 G4
Jättendal, *Sweden* 10 C11
Jaú, *Brazil* 127 A6
Jauja, *Peru* 124 F3
Jaunpur, *India* 69 G10
Java = Jawa, *Indonesia* 63 G14
Java Sea, *Indonesia* 62 E3
Java Trench, *Ind. Oc.* 96 H2
Javalambre, Sa. de, *Spain* 32 E4
Jávea, *Spain* 33 G5
Javhlant = Ulyasutay, *Mongolia* 60 B4
Jawa, *Indonesia* 63 G14
Jawor, *Poland* 45 G3
Jaworzno, *Poland* 45 H6
Jaworzyna Śląska, *Poland* 45 H3
Jay, *U.S.A.* 113 G7
Jaya, Puncak, *Indonesia* 63 E9
Jayanti, *India* 67 F16
Jayapura, *Indonesia* 63 E10
Jayawijaya, Pegunungan, *Indonesia* 63 F9
Jaynagar, *India* 67 F15
Jayrūd, *Syria* 70 C3
Jayton, *U.S.A.* 113 J4
Jazīreh-ye Shīf, *Iran* 71 D6
Jazminal, *Mexico* 118 C4
Jazzīn, *Lebanon* 75 B4
Jean, *U.S.A.* 117 K11
Jean Marie River, *Canada* 104 A4
Jean Rabel, *Haiti* 121 C5
Jeanerette, *U.S.A.* 113 L9
Jeanette, Ostrov = Zhannetty, Ostrov, *Russia* 51 B16
Jeannette, *U.S.A.* 110 F5
Jebba, *Nigeria* 83 D5
Jebel, Bahr el →, *Sudan* 81 F3
Jebel Qerri, *Sudan* 81 D3
Jedburgh, *U.K.* 14 F6
Jedda = Jiddah, *Si. Arabia* 74 C2
Jedlicze, *Poland* 45 J8
Jędrzejów, *Poland* 45 H7
Jedwabne, *Poland* 45 E9
Jedway, *Canada* 104 C2
Jeetzel →, *Germany* 24 B7
Jefferson, *Iowa, U.S.A.* 112 D7
Jefferson, *Ohio, U.S.A.* 110 E4
Jefferson, *Tex., U.S.A.* 113 J7
Jefferson, *Wis., U.S.A.* 112 D10
Jefferson, Mt., *Nev., U.S.A.* 114 G5
Jefferson, Mt., *Oreg., U.S.A.* 114 D3
Jefferson City, *Mo., U.S.A.* 112 F8
Jefferson City, *Tenn., U.S.A.* 109 G4
Jeffersonville, *U.S.A.* 108 F3
Jega, *Nigeria* 83 C5
Jēkabpils, *Latvia* 9 H21
Jelcz-Laskowice, *Poland* 45 G4
Jelenia Góra, *Poland* 45 H2
Jelenia Góra □, *Poland* 45 G2
Jelgava, *Latvia* 9 H20
Jelgava □, *Latvia* 44 B10
Jelica, *Serbia, Yug.* 40 C4
Jelli, *Sudan* 81 F3
Jellicoe, *Canada* 102 C2
Jelšava, *Slovak Rep.* 27 C13
Jemaja, *Indonesia* 65 L5
Jemaluang, *Malaysia* 65 L4
Jember, *Indonesia* 63 H15
Jembongan, *Malaysia* 62 C5
Jena, *Germany* 24 E7
Jena, *U.S.A.* 113 K8
Jenbach, *Austria* 26 D4
Jenkins, *U.S.A.* 108 G4
Jenner, *U.S.A.* 116 G3
Jennings, *U.S.A.* 113 K8
Jennings →, *Canada* 104 B2
Jeparit, *Australia* 95 F3
Jequié, *Brazil* 125 F10
Jequitinhonha, *Brazil* 125 G10
Jequitinhonha →, *Brazil* 125 G11
Jerantut, *Malaysia* 65 L4
Jérémie, *Haiti* 121 C5
Jerez, Punta, *Mexico* 119 C5
Jerez de García Salinas, *Mexico* 118 C4
Jerez de la Frontera, *Spain* 35 J4
Jerez de los Caballeros, *Spain* 35 G4
Jericho = El Arīḥā, *West Bank* 75 D4
Jericho, *Australia* 94 C4
Jerichow, *Germany* 24 C8
Jerilderie, *Australia* 95 F4
Jermyn, *U.S.A.* 111 E9
Jerome, *U.S.A.* 115 J8
Jersey, *U.K.* 13 H5
Jersey City, *U.S.A.* 111 F10
Jersey Shore, *U.S.A.* 110 E7
Jerseyville, *U.S.A.* 112 F9
Jerusalem, *Israel* 75 D4
Jervis B., *Australia* 95 F5
Jerzu, *Italy* 30 C2
Jesenice, *Slovenia* 29 B11
Jeseník, *Czech Rep.* 27 A10
Jesenké, *Slovak Rep.* 27 C13
Jesselton = Kota Kinabalu, *Malaysia* 62 C5
Jessnitz, *Germany* 24 D8
Jessore, *Bangla.* 67 H16
Jesup, *U.S.A.* 109 K5
Jesús Carranza, *Mexico* 119 D5
Jesús María, *Argentina* 126 C3
Jetmore, *U.S.A.* 113 F5
Jetpur, *India* 68 J4
Jeumont, *France* 19 B11
Jevnaker, *Norway* 9 F14
Jewett, *Ohio, U.S.A.* 110 F3
Jewett, *Tex., U.S.A.* 113 K6
Jewett City, *U.S.A.* 111 E13
Jeyḥūnābād, *Iran* 71 C6
Jeypore, *India* 67 K13
Jeziorak, Jezioro, *Poland* 44 E6
Jeziorany, *Poland* 44 E7
Jeziorka →, *Poland* 45 F8
Jhajjar, *India* 68 E7
Jhal Jhao, *Pakistan* 66 F4
Jhalawar, *India* 68 G7
Jhang Maghiana, *Pakistan* 68 D5
Jhansi, *India* 69 G8
Jharia, *India* 69 H12
Jharsuguda, *India* 67 J14
Jhelum, *Pakistan* 68 C5
Jhelum →, *Pakistan* 68 D5
Jhunjhunu, *India* 68 E6
Ji-Paraná, *Brazil* 124 F6
Ji Xian, *Hebei, China* 56 F8
Ji Xian, *Henan, China* 56 G8
Ji Xian, *Shanxi, China* 56 F6
Jia Xian, *Henan, China* 56 H7
Jia Xian, *Shaanxi, China* 56 E6
Jiading, *China* 59 B13
Jiahe, *China* 59 E9
Jialing Jiang →, *China* 58 C6
Jiamusi, *China* 60 B8
Ji'an, *Jiangxi, China* 59 D10
Ji'an, *Jilin, China* 57 D14
Jianchang, *China* 57 D11
Jianchangying, *China* 57 D10
Jianchuan, *China* 58 D2
Jiande, *China* 59 C12
Jiangbei, *China* 58 C6
Jiangcheng, *China* 58 F3
Jiangdi, *China* 58 D4
Jiange, *China* 58 A5
Jiangjin, *China* 58 C6
Jiangkou, *China* 58 D7
Jiangle, *China* 59 D11
Jiangling, *China* 59 B9
Jiangmen, *China* 59 F9
Jiangshan, *China* 59 C12
Jiangsu □, *China* 57 H11
Jiangxi □, *China* 59 D11
Jiangyin, *China* 59 B13
Jiangyong, *China* 59 E8
Jiangyou, *China* 58 B5
Jianhe, *China* 58 D7
Jianli, *China* 59 C9
Jianning, *China* 59 D11
Jian'ou, *China* 59 D12
Jianshi, *China* 58 B7
Jianshui, *China* 58 F4
Jianyang, *Fujian, China* 59 D12
Jianyang, *Sichuan, China* 58 B5
Jiao Xian, *China* 57 F11
Jiaohe, *Hebei, China* 56 E9
Jiaohe, *Jilin, China* 57 C14
Jiaoling, *China* 59 E11
Jiaozhou Wan, *China* 57 F11
Jiaozuo, *China* 56 G7
Jiashan, *China* 59 A11
Jiawang, *China* 57 G9
Jiaxiang, *China* 56 G9
Jiaxing, *China* 59 B13
Jiayi = Chiai, *Taiwan* 59 F13
Jiayu, *China* 59 C9
Jibiya, *Nigeria* 83 C6
Jibou, *Romania* 43 C8
Jibuti = Djibouti ■, *Africa* 81 E5
Jicarón, I., *Panama* 120 E3
Jičín, *Czech Rep.* 26 A8
Jiddah, *Si. Arabia* 74 C2
Jido, *India* 67 E19
Jieshou, *China* 56 H8
Jiexiu, *China* 56 F6
Jieyang, *China* 59 F11
Jigawa □, *Nigeria* 83 C6
Jiggalong, *Australia* 92 D3
Jihlava, *Czech Rep.* 26 B8
Jihlava →, *Czech Rep.* 27 C9
Jihočeský □, *Czech Rep.* 26 B7
Jihomoravský □, *Czech Rep.* 27 B9
Jijiga, *Ethiopia* 74 F3
Jikamshi, *Nigeria* 83 C6
Jilin, *China* 57 C14
Jilin □, *China* 57 C14
Jiloca →, *Spain* 32 D3
Jilong = Chilung, *Taiwan* 59 E13
Jima, *Ethiopia* 81 F4
Jimbolia, *Romania* 42 E5
Jimena de la Frontera, *Spain* 35 J5
Jiménez, *Mexico* 118 B4
Jimo, *China* 57 F11
Jin Jiang →, *China* 59 C10
Jin Xian, *Hebei, China* 56 E8
Jin Xian, *Liaoning, China* 57 E11
Jinan, *China* 56 F9
Jincheng, *China* 56 G7
Jinchuan, *China* 58 B4
Jind, *India* 68 E7
Jindabyne, *Australia* 95 F4

Jindřichův Hradec, *Czech Rep.* 26 B8
Jing He →, *China* 56 G5
Jing Shan, *China* 59 B8
Jing Xian, *Anhui, China* 59 B12
Jing Xian, *Hunan, China* 58 D7
Jing'an, *China* 59 C10
Jingbian, *China* 56 F5
Jingchuan, *China* 56 G4
Jingde, *China* 59 B12
Jingdezhen, *China* 59 C11
Jingdong, *China* 58 E3
Jinggu, *China* 58 F3
Jinghai, *China* 56 E9
Jinghong, *China* 58 G3
Jingjiang, *China* 59 A13
Jingle, *China* 56 E6
Jingmen, *China* 59 B9
Jingning, *China* 56 G3
Jingpo Hu, *China* 57 C15
Jingshan, *China* 59 B9
Jingtai, *China* 56 F3
Jingxi, *China* 58 F6
Jingxing, *China* 56 E8
Jingyang, *China* 56 G5
Jingyu, *China* 57 C14
Jingyuan, *China* 56 F3
Jingziguan, *China* 56 H6
Jinhua, *China* 59 C12
Jining, *Nei Mongol Zizhiqu, China* 56 D7
Jining, *Shandong, China* 56 G9
Jinja, *Uganda* 86 B3
Jinjang, *Malaysia* 65 L3
Jinji, *China* 56 F4
Jinjiang, *Fujian, China* 59 E12
Jinjiang, *Yunnan, China* 58 D3
Jinjie, *China* 58 F6
Jinjini, *Ghana* 82 D4
Jinkou, *China* 59 B10
Jinmen Dao, *China* 59 E12
Jinnah Barrage, *Pakistan* 66 C7
Jinning, *China* 58 E4
Jinotega, *Nic.* 120 D2
Jinotepe, *Nic.* 120 D2
Jinping, *Guizhou, China* 58 D7
Jinping, *Yunnan, China* 58 F4
Jinsha, *China* 58 D6
Jinsha Jiang →, *China* 58 C5
Jinshan, *China* 59 B13
Jinshi, *China* 59 C8
Jintan, *China* 59 B12
Jinxi, *Jiangxi, China* 59 D11
Jinxi, *Liaoning, China* 57 D11
Jinxian, *China* 59 C11
Jinxiang, *China* 56 G9
Jinyun, *China* 59 C13
Jinzhai, *China* 59 B10
Jinzhou, *China* 57 D11
Jiparaná →, *Brazil* 124 E6
Jipijapa, *Ecuador* 124 D2
Jiquilpan, *Mexico* 118 D4
Jishan, *China* 56 G6
Jishou, *China* 58 C7
Jishui, *China* 59 D10
Jisr ash Shughūr, *Syria* 70 C3
Jitarning, *Australia* 93 F2
Jitra, *Malaysia* 65 J3
Jiu →, *Romania* 43 G8
Jiudengkou, *China* 56 E4
Jiujiang, *Guangdong, China* 59 F9
Jiujiang, *Jiangxi, China* 59 C10
Jiuling Shan, *China* 59 C10
Jiulong, *China* 58 C3
Jiuquan, *China* 60 C4
Jiutai, *China* 57 B13
Jiuxiangcheng, *China* 56 H8
Jiuxincheng, *China* 56 E8
Jiuyuhang, *China* 59 B12
Jixi, *Anhui, China* 59 B12
Jixi, *Heilongjiang, China* 57 B16
Jiyang, *China* 57 F9
Jīzān, *Si. Arabia* 74 D3
Jize, *China* 56 F8
Jizera →, *Czech Rep.* 26 A7
Jizō-Zaki, *Japan* 55 G6
Jizzakh, *Uzbekistan* 50 E7
Joaçaba, *Brazil* 127 B5
João Pessoa, *Brazil* 125 E12
Joaquín V. González, *Argentina* 126 B3
Jobourg, Nez de, *France* 18 C5
Jódar, *Spain* 35 H7
Jodhpur, *India* 68 F5
Jœuf, *France* 19 C12
Jofane, *Mozam.* 89 C5
Jõgeva, *Estonia* 9 G22
Joggins, *Canada* 103 C7
Jogjakarta = Yogyakarta, *Indonesia* 63 G14
Johannesburg, *S. Africa* 89 D4
Johannesburg, *U.S.A.* 117 K9
Johansfors, *Sweden* 11 H9
John Day, *U.S.A.* 114 D4
John Day →, *U.S.A.* 114 D3
John H. Kerr Reservoir, *U.S.A.* 109 G6
John o' Groats, *U.K.* 14 C5
Johnnie, *U.S.A.* 117 J10
John's Ra., *Australia* 94 C1
Johnson, *U.S.A.* 113 G4
Johnson City, *N.Y., U.S.A.* 111 D9
Johnson City, *Tenn., U.S.A.* 109 G4
Johnson City, *Tex., U.S.A.* 113 K5
Johnsonburg, *U.S.A.* 110 E6
Johnsondale, *U.S.A.* 117 K8
Johnson's Crossing, *Canada* 104 A2
Johnston, L., *Australia* 93 F3
Johnston Falls = Mambilima Falls, *Zambia* 87 E2
Johnston I., *Pac. Oc.* 97 F11
Johnstone Str., *Canada* 104 C3
Johnstown, *N.Y., U.S.A.* 111 C10
Johnstown, *Pa., U.S.A.* 110 F6
Johor Baharu, *Malaysia* 65 M4
Jõhvi, *Estonia* 9 G22
Joigny, *France* 19 E10
Joinville, *Brazil* 127 B6
Joinville, *France* 19 D12
Joinville I., *Antarctica* 5 C18
Jojutla, *Mexico* 119 D5
Jokkmokk, *Sweden* 8 C18
Jökulsá á Bru →, *Iceland* 8 D6
Jökulsá á Fjöllum →, *Iceland* 8 C5
Jolfā, *Āzarbājān-e Sharqī, Iran* 70 B5
Jolfā, *Eşfahan, Iran* 71 C6
Joliet, *U.S.A.* 108 E1
Joliette, *Canada* 102 C5
Jolo, *Phil.* 61 J4
Jolon, *U.S.A.* 116 K5
Jomalig, *Phil.* 61 D5
Jombang, *Indonesia* 63 G15
Jomda, *China* 58 B2
Jonava, *Lithuania* 9 J21
Jones Sound, *Canada* 4 B3
Jonesboro, *Ark., U.S.A.* 113 H9
Jonesboro, *Ill., U.S.A.* 113 G10
Jonesboro, *La., U.S.A.* 113 J8
Jonesport, *U.S.A.* 103 D6
Jonglei, *Sudan* 81 F3
Jonglei □, *Sudan* 81 F3
Joniškis, *Lithuania* 9 H20
Jönköping, *Sweden* 11 G8
Jönköpings län □, *Sweden* 11 G8
Jonquière, *Canada* 103 C5
Jonsered, *Sweden* 11 G6
Jonzac, *France* 20 C3
Joplin, *U.S.A.* 113 G7
Jordan, *U.S.A.* 114 C10
Jordan ■, *Asia* 75 E5
Jordan →, *Asia* 75 D4
Jordan Valley, *U.S.A.* 114 E5
Jordanów, *Poland* 45 J6
Jorhat, *India* 67 F19
Jörn, *Sweden* 8 D19
Jorong, *Indonesia* 62 E4
Jørpeland, *Norway* 9 G11
Jorquera →, *Chile* 126 B2
Jos, *Nigeria* 83 D6
Jošanička Banja, *Serbia, Yug.* 40 C4
José Batlle y Ordóñez, *Uruguay* 127 C4
Joseni, *Romania* 43 D10
Joseph, *U.S.A.* 114 D5
Joseph, L., *Nfld., Canada* 103 B6
Joseph, L., *Ont., Canada* 110 A5
Joseph Bonaparte G., *Australia* 92 B4
Joseph City, *U.S.A.* 115 J8
Joshua Tree, *U.S.A.* 117 L10
Joshua Tree National Monument, *U.S.A.* 117 M10
Josselin, *France* 18 E4
Jostedalsbreen, *Norway* 9 F12
Jotunheimen, *Norway* 9 F13
Joué-lès-Tours, *France* 18 E7
Jourdanton, *U.S.A.* 113 L5
Joussard, *Canada* 104 B5
Joutseno, *Finland* 46 B5
Jovellanos, *Cuba* 120 B3
Joyeuse, *France* 21 D8
Józefów, *Warszawa, Poland* 45 F8
Józefów, *Zamośc, Poland* 45 H10
Ju Xian, *China* 57 F10
Juan Aldama, *Mexico* 118 C4
Juan Bautista Alberdi, *Argentina* 126 C3
Juan de Fuca Str., *Canada* 116 B3
Juan de Nova, *Ind. Oc.* 89 B7
Juan Fernández, Arch. de, *Pac. Oc.* 122 G2
Juan José Castelli, *Argentina* 126 B3
Juan L. Lacaze, *Uruguay* 126 C4
Juankoski, *Finland* 8 E23
Juárez, *Argentina* 126 D4
Juárez, *Mexico* 117 N11
Juárez, Sierra de, *Mexico* 118 A1
Juàzeiro, *Brazil* 125 E10
Juàzeiro do Norte, *Brazil* 125 E11
Jûbâ, *Sudan* 81 G3
Jubayl, *Lebanon* 75 A4
Jubbah, *Si. Arabia* 70 D4
Jubbulpore = Jabalpur, *India* 69 H8
Jübek, *Germany* 24 A5
Jubga, *Russia* 49 H4
Jubilee L., *Australia* 93 E4
Juby, C., *Morocco* 78 C3
Júcar = Xúquer →, *Spain* 33 F4
Júcaro, *Cuba* 120 B4
Juchitán, *Mexico* 119 D5
Judaea = Har Yehuda, *Israel* 75 D3
Judenburg, *Austria* 26 D7
Judith →, *U.S.A.* 114 C9
Judith, Pt., *U.S.A.* 111 E13
Judith Gap, *U.S.A.* 114 C9
Juelsminde, *Denmark* 11 J4
Jugoslavia = Yugoslavia ■, *Europe* 40 C4
Juigalpa, *Nic.* 120 D2
Juillac, *France* 20 C5
Juist, *Germany* 24 B2
Juiz de Fora, *Brazil* 127 A7
Jujuy □, *Argentina* 126 A2
Julesburg, *U.S.A.* 112 E3
Juli, *Peru* 124 G5
Julia Cr. →, *Australia* 94 C3
Julia Creek, *Australia* 94 C3
Juliaca, *Peru* 124 G4
Julian, *U.S.A.* 117 M10
Julian Alps = Julijske Alpe, *Slovenia* 29 B11
Julianatop, *Surinam* 125 C7
Julianehåb, *Greenland* 4 C5
Jülich, *Germany* 24 E2
Julijske Alpe, *Slovenia* 29 B11
Julimes, *Mexico* 118 B3
Jullundur, *India* 68 D6
Julu, *China* 56 F8
Jumbo, *Zimbabwe* 87 F3
Jumbo Pk., *U.S.A.* 117 J12
Jumentos Cays, *Bahamas* 121 B4
Jumilla, *Spain* 33 G3
Jumla, *Nepal* 69 E10
Jumna = Yamuna →, *India* 69 G9
Junagadh, *India* 68 J4
Junction, *Tex., U.S.A.* 113 K5
Junction, *Utah, U.S.A.* 115 G7
Junction B., *Australia* 94 A1
Junction City, *Kans., U.S.A.* 112 F6
Junction City, *Oreg., U.S.A.* 114 D2
Junction Pt., *Australia* 94 A1
Jundah, *Australia* 94 C3
Jundiaí, *Brazil* 127 A6
Juneau, *U.S.A.* 100 C6
Junee, *Australia* 95 E4
Jungfrau, *Switz.* 25 J3
Junggar Pendi, *China* 60 B3
Jungshahi, *Pakistan* 68 G2
Juniata →, *U.S.A.* 110 F7
Junín, *Argentina* 126 C3
Junín de los Andes, *Argentina* 128 D2
Jūniyah, *Lebanon* 75 B4
Juntura, *U.S.A.* 114 E4
Jupiter →, *Canada* 103 C7
Jur, Nahr el →, *Sudan* 81 F2
Jura = Jura, Mts. du, *Europe* 19 F13
Jura = Schwäbische Alb, *Germany* 25 G5
Jura, *U.K.* 14 F3
Jura □, *France* 19 F12
Jura □, *Switz.* 25 H3
Jūra →, *Lithuania* 44 C9
Jura, Mts. du, *Europe* 19 F13
Jura, Sd. of, *U.K.* 14 F3
Jurbarkas, *Lithuania* 44 C9
Jurilovca, *Romania* 43 F13
Jūrmala, *Latvia* 9 H20
Jurong, *China* 59 B12
Juruá →, *Brazil* 122 D4
Juruena, *Brazil* 124 F7
Juruena →, *Brazil* 124 E7
Juruti, *Brazil* 125 D7
Jussey, *France* 19 E12
Justo Daract, *Argentina* 126 C2
Jutaí →, *Brazil* 124 D5
Jüterbog, *Germany* 24 D9
Juticalpa, *Honduras* 120 D2
Jutland = Jylland, *Denmark* 11 H3
Juventud, I. de la, *Cuba* 120 B3
Juvigny-sous-Andaine, *France* 18 D6
Juwain, *Afghan.* 66 D2
Jūy Zar, *Iran* 70 C5
Juye, *China* 56 G9
Juzennecourt, *France* 19 D11
Jvari, *Georgia* 49 J6
Jyderup, *Denmark* 11 J5
Jylland, *Denmark* 11 H3
Jyväskylä, *Finland* 9 E21

K

K2, *Pakistan* 69 B7
Kaap Plateau, *S. Africa* 88 D3
Kaapkruis, *Namibia* 88 C1
Kaapstad = Cape Town, *S. Africa* 88 E2
Kabaena, *Indonesia* 63 F6
Kabala, *S. Leone* 82 D2
Kabale, *Uganda* 86 C3
Kabalo, *Dem. Rep. of the Congo* 86 D2
Kabambare, *Dem. Rep. of the Congo* 86 C2
Kabango, *Dem. Rep. of the Congo* 87 D2
Kabanjahe, *Indonesia* 62 D1
Kabankalan, *Phil.* 61 G5
Kabara, *Mali* 82 B4
Kabardinka, *Russia* 47 K10
Kabardino-Balkar Republic = Kabardino-Balkaria □, *Russia* 49 J6
Kabardino-Balkaria □, *Russia* 49 J6
Kabarega Falls = Murchison Falls, *Uganda* 86 B3
Kabasalan, *Phil.* 61 H5
Kabba, *Nigeria* 83 D6
Kabin Buri, *Thailand* 64 F3
Kabinakagami L., *Canada* 102 C3
Kabna, *Sudan* 80 D3
Kabompo, *Zambia* 87 E1
Kabompo →, *Zambia* 85 G4
Kabondo, *Dem. Rep. of the Congo* 87 D2
Kabongo, *Dem. Rep. of the Congo* 86 D2
Kabou, *Togo* 83 D5
Kabra, *Australia* 94 C5
Kabūd Gonbad, *Iran* 71 B8
Kabugao, *Phil.* 61 B4
Kābul, *Afghan.* 68 B3
Kābul □, *Afghan.* 66 B6
Kabul →, *Pakistan* 68 C5
Kabunga, *Dem. Rep. of the Congo* 86 C2
Kaburuang, *Indonesia* 63 D7
Kabushiya, *Sudan* 81 D3
Kabwe, *Zambia* 87 E2
Kačanik, *Serbia, Yug.* 40 D5
Kačerginė, *Lithuania* 44 D10
Kachchh, Gulf of, *India* 68 H3
Kachchh, Rann of, *India* 68 H4
Kachebera, *Zambia* 87 E3
Kachin □, *Burma* 67 G20
Kachira, L., *Uganda* 86 C3
Kachiry, *Kazakstan* 50 D8
Kachisi, *Ethiopia* 81 F4
Kachot, *Cambodia* 65 G4
Kaçkar, *Turkey* 73 B9
Kadan, *Czech Rep.* 26 A6
Kadan Kyun, *Burma* 64 F2
Kadanai →, *Afghan.* 68 D1
Kadarkút, *Hungary* 42 D2
Kade, *Ghana* 83 D4
Kadi, *India* 68 H5
Kadina, *Australia* 95 E2
Kadınhanı, *Turkey* 72 C5
Kadirli, *Turkey* 72 D7
Kadiyevka = Stakhanov, *Ukraine* 47 H10
Kadoka, *U.S.A.* 112 D4
Kadom, *Russia* 48 C6
Kadoma, *Zimbabwe* 87 F2
Kâdugli, *Sudan* 81 E2
Kaduna, *Nigeria* 83 C6
Kaduna □, *Nigeria* 83 C6
Kaduy, *Russia* 46 C9
Kaédi, *Mauritania* 82 B2
Kaélé, *Cameroon* 83 C7
Kaeng Khoï, *Thailand* 64 E3
Kaesŏng, *N. Korea* 57 F14
Kāf, *Si. Arabia* 70 D3
Kafan = Kapan, *Armenia* 73 C12
Kafanchan, *Nigeria* 83 D6
Kafareti, *Nigeria* 83 C7
Kaffrine, *Senegal* 82 C1
Kafinda, *Zambia* 87 E3
Kafirévs, Ákra, *Greece* 38 C6
Kafr el Dauwâr, *Egypt* 80 H7
Kafr el Sheikh, *Egypt* 80 H7
Kafue, *Zambia* 87 F2
Kafue →, *Zambia* 85 H5
Kafue Flats, *Zambia* 87 F2
Kafue Nat. Park, *Zambia* 87 F2
Kafulwe, *Zambia* 87 D2
Kaga, *Afghan.* 68 B4
Kaga Bandoro, *C.A.R.* 84 C3
Kagan, *Uzbekistan* 50 F7
Kagawa □, *Japan* 55 G7
Kagera □, *Tanzania* 86 C3
Kagera →, *Uganda* 86 C3
Kağizman, *Turkey* 73 B10
Kagoshima, *Japan* 55 J5
Kagoshima □, *Japan* 55 J5
Kagul = Cahul, *Moldova* 43 E13
Kahak, *Iran* 71 B6
Kahama, *Tanzania* 86 C3
Kahama □, *Tanzania* 86 C3
Kahang, *Malaysia* 65 L4
Kahayan →, *Indonesia* 62 E4
Kahe, *Tanzania* 86 C4
Kahniah →, *Canada* 104 B4
Kahnūj, *Iran* 71 E8
Kahoka, *U.S.A.* 112 E9
Kahoolawe, *U.S.A.* 106 H16
Kahramanmaraş, *Turkey* 72 D7
Kâhta, *Turkey* 73 D8
Kahuta, *Pakistan* 68 C5
Kai, Kepulauan, *Indonesia* 63 F8
Kai Besar, *Indonesia* 63 F8
Kai Is. = Kai, Kepulauan, *Indonesia* 63 F8
Kai Kecil, *Indonesia* 63 F8
Kai Xian, *China* 58 B7
Kaiama, *Nigeria* 83 D5
Kaiapoi, *N.Z.* 91 K4
Kaieteur Falls, *Guyana* 124 B7
Kaifeng, *China* 56 G8
Kaihua, *China* 59 C12
Kaikohe, *N.Z.* 91 F4
Kaikoura, *N.Z.* 91 K4
Kaikoura Ra., *N.Z.* 91 J4
Kailahun, *S. Leone* 82 D2
Kaili, *China* 58 D6
Kailu, *China* 57 C11
Kailua Kona, *U.S.A.* 106 J17
Kaimana, *Indonesia* 63 E8
Kaimanawa Mts., *N.Z.* 91 H5
Kaimganj, *India* 69 F8
Kaimur Hills, *India* 69 G10
Kaingaroa Forest, *N.Z.* 91 H6
Kainji Res., *Nigeria* 83 C5
Kainuu, *Finland* 8 D23
Kaipara Harbour, *N.Z.* 91 G5
Kaiping, *China* 59 F9
Kaipokok B., *Canada* 103 B8
Kairana, *India* 68 E7
Kaironi, *Indonesia* 63 E8
Kairouan, *Tunisia* 79 A8
Kaiserslautern, *Germany* 25 F3
Kaiserstuhl, *Germany* 25 G3
Kaitaia, *N.Z.* 91 F4
Kaitangata, *N.Z.* 91 M2
Kaithal, *India* 68 E7
Kaitu →, *Pakistan* 68 C4
Kaiwi Channel, *U.S.A.* 106 H16
Kaiyang, *China* 58 D6
Kaiyuan, *Liaoning, China* 57 C13
Kaiyuan, *Yunnan, China* 58 F4
Kajaani, *Finland* 8 D22
Kajabbi, *Australia* 94 C3
Kajana = Kajaani, *Finland* 8 D22
Kajang, *Malaysia* 65 L3
Kajaran, *Armenia* 73 C12
Kajiado, *Kenya* 86 C4
Kajiado □, *Kenya* 86 C4
Kajo Kaji, *Sudan* 81 G3
Kaka, *Sudan* 81 E3
Kakabeka Falls, *Canada* 102 C2
Kakamas, *S. Africa* 88 D3
Kakamega, *Kenya* 86 B3
Kakamega □, *Kenya* 86 B3
Kakanj, *Bos.-H.* 42 F3
Kakanui Mts., *N.Z.* 91 L3
Kake, *Japan* 55 G6
Kakegawa, *Japan* 55 G9
Kakeroma-Jima, *Japan* 55 K4
Kakhib, *Russia* 49 J8
Kakhovka, *Ukraine* 47 J7
Kakhovske Vdskh., *Ukraine* 47 J7
Kakinada, *India* 67 L13
Kakisa →, *Canada* 104 A5
Kakisa L., *Canada* 104 A5
Kakogawa, *Japan* 55 G7
Kakwa →, *Canada* 104 C5
Kāl Güsheh, *Iran* 71 D8
Kal Safīd, *Iran* 70 C5
Kala, *Nigeria* 83 C7
Kalabagh, *Pakistan* 68 C4
Kalabahi, *Indonesia* 63 F6
Kalabáka, *Greece* 38 B3
Kalach, *Russia* 48 E5
Kalach na Donu, *Russia* 49 F6
Kaladan →, *Burma* 67 J18
Kaladar, *Canada* 110 B7
Kalahari, *Africa* 88 C3
Kalahari Gemsbok Nat. Park, *S. Africa* 88 D3
Kalajoki, *Finland* 8 D20
Kālak, *Iran* 71 E8
Kalakamati, *Botswana* 89 C4
Kalakan, *Russia* 51 D12
Kalakh, *Syria* 70 C3
K'alak'unlun Shank'ou, *Pakistan* 69 B7
Kalam, *Pakistan* 69 B5
Kalama, *Dem. Rep. of the Congo* 86 C2
Kalama, *U.S.A.* 116 E4
Kalámai, *Greece* 38 D4
Kalamariá, *Greece* 40 F6
Kalamata = Kalámai, *Greece* 38 D4
Kalamazoo, *U.S.A.* 108 D3
Kalamazoo →, *U.S.A.* 108 D2
Kalambo Falls, *Tanzania* 87 D3
Kálamos, *Attikí, Greece* 38 C5
Kálamos, *Iónioi Nísoi, Greece* 38 C2
Kalannie, *Australia* 93 F2
Kalāntarī, *Iran* 71 C7
Kalao, *Indonesia* 63 F6
Kalaotoa, *Indonesia* 63 F6
Kälarne, *Sweden* 10 B10
Kalasin, *Thailand* 64 D4
Kalat, *Pakistan* 66 E5
Kalāteh, *Iran* 71 B7
Kalāteh-ye-Ganj, *Iran* 71 E8
Kálathos, *Greece* 39 E10
Kalaus →, *Russia* 49 H7
Kalávrita, *Greece* 38 C4
Kalbarri, *Australia* 93 E1
Kale, *Antalya, Turkey* 39 E12
Kale, *Denizli, Turkey* 39 D10
Kalecik, *Turkey* 72 B5
Kalegauk Kyun, *Burma* 67 M20
Kalehe, *Dem. Rep. of the Congo* 86 C2
Kalema, *Tanzania* 86 C3
Kalemie, *Dem. Rep. of the Congo* 86 D2
Kalety, *Poland* 45 H5
Kalewa, *Burma* 67 H19
Kalgan = Zhangjiakou, *China* 56 D8
Kalgoorlie-Boulder, *Australia* 93 F3
Kaliakra, Nos, *Bulgaria* 41 C12
Kalianda, *Indonesia* 62 F3
Kalibo, *Phil.* 61 F5
Kaliganj, *Bangla.* 69 H13
Kalima, *Dem. Rep. of the Congo* 86 C2
Kalimantan □, *Indonesia* 62 E4

Kalimantan Barat □, *Indonesia* 62 E4
Kalimantan Selatan □, *Indonesia* 62 E5
Kalimantan Tengah □, *Indonesia* 62 E4
Kalimantan Timur □, *Indonesia* 62 D5
Kálimnos, *Greece* 39 E8
Kalimpong, *India* 69 F13
Kalinin = Tver, *Russia* 46 D8
Kaliningrad, *Russia* 9 J19
Kalininsk, *Russia* 48 E7
Kalinkavichy, *Belarus* 47 F5
Kalinkovichi = Kalinkavichy, *Belarus* 47 F5
Kalinovik, *Bos.-H.* 40 C2
Kalipetrovo, *Bulgaria* 41 B11
Kaliro, *Uganda* 86 B3
Kalirrákhi, *Greece* 41 F8
Kalispell, *U.S.A.* 114 B6
Kalisz, *Poland* 45 G5
Kalisz □, *Poland* 45 G4
Kalisz Pomorski, *Poland* 45 E2
Kaliua, *Tanzania* 86 D3
Kalívia Thorikoú, *Greece* 38 D5
Kalix, *Sweden* 8 D20
Kalix →, *Sweden* 8 D20
Kalka, *India* 68 D7
Kalkan, *Turkey* 39 E11
Kalkaska, *U.S.A.* 108 C3
Kalkfeld, *Namibia* 88 C2
Kalkfontein, *Botswana* 88 C3
Kalkım, *Turkey* 39 B9
Kalkrand, *Namibia* 88 C2
Kållandsö, *Sweden* 11 F7
Kallavesi, *Finland* 8 E22
Källby, *Sweden* 11 F7
Kållered, *Sweden* 11 G6
Kallimasiá, *Greece* 39 C8
Kallinge, *Sweden* 11 H9
Kallithéa, *Greece* 38 D5
Kallmeti, *Albania* 40 E3
Kalloní, *Greece* 39 B8
Kallonís, Kólpos, *Greece* 39 B8
Kallsjön, *Sweden* 8 E15
Kalmalo, *Nigeria* 83 C6
Kalmar, *Sweden* 11 H10
Kalmar län □, *Sweden* 11 G10
Kalmar sund, *Sweden* 11 H10
Kalmyk Republic = Kalmykia □, *Russia* 49 G8
Kalmykia □, *Russia* 49 G8
Kalmykovo, *Kazakstan* 50 E6
Kalna, *India* 69 H13
Kalocsa, *Hungary* 42 D4
Kalofer, *Bulgaria* 41 D8
Kalokhorio, *Cyprus* 36 E12
Kaloko, *Dem. Rep. of the Congo* 86 D2
Kalol, *Gujarat, India* 68 H5
Kalol, *Gujarat, India* 68 H5
Kalolímnos, *Greece* 39 D9
Kalomo, *Zambia* 87 F2
Kalonerón, *Greece* 38 D3
Kalpi, *India* 69 F8
Kaltern = Caldaro, *Italy* 29 B8
Kaltungo, *Nigeria* 83 D7
Kalu, *Pakistan* 68 G2
Kaluga, *Russia* 46 E9
Kalulushi, *Zambia* 87 E2
Kalundborg, *Denmark* 11 J5
Kalush, *Ukraine* 47 H3
Kałuszyn, *Poland* 45 F8
Kalutara, *Sri Lanka* 66 R12
Kalvarija, *Lithuania* 44 D10
Kalyazin, *Russia* 46 D9
Kama, *Dem. Rep. of the Congo* 86 C2
Kama →, *Russia* 6 D16
Kamachumu, *Tanzania* 86 C3
Kamaishi, *Japan* 54 E10
Kamalia, *Pakistan* 68 D5
Kaman, *Turkey* 72 C5
Kamapanda, *Zambia* 87 E1
Kamaran, *Yemen* 74 D3
Kamativi, *Zimbabwe* 87 F2
Kamba, *Nigeria* 83 C5
Kambalda, *Australia* 93 F3
Kambar, *Pakistan* 68 F3
Kambia, *S. Leone* 82 D2
Kambolé, *Zambia* 87 D3
Kambos, *Cyprus* 36 D11
Kambove, *Dem. Rep. of the Congo* 87 E2
Kamchatka, Poluostrov, *Russia* 51 D17
Kamchatka Pen. = Kamchatka, Poluostrov, *Russia* 51 D17
Kamchiya →, *Bulgaria* 41 C11
Kamen, *Russia* 50 D9
Kamen-Rybolov, *Russia* 54 B6
Kamenica, *Serbia, Yug.* 40 C6
Kamenica, *Serbia, Yug.* 40 B3
Kamenice nad Lipou, *Czech Rep.* 26 B8
Kamenjak, Rt., *Croatia* 29 D10
Kamenka = Kaminka, *Ukraine* 47 H7
Kamenka, *Kazakstan* 48 E10
Kamenka, *Penza, Russia* 48 D6
Kamenka, *Voronezh, Russia* 47 G10
Kamenka Bugskaya = Kamyanka-Buzka, *Ukraine* 47 G3
Kamenka Dneprovskaya = Kamyanka-Dniprovska, *Ukraine* 47 J8
Kamennomostskiy, *Russia* 49 H5
Kameno, *Bulgaria* 41 D11
Kamenolomini, *Russia* 49 G5
Kamensk-Shakhtinskiy, *Russia* 49 F5
Kamensk Uralskiy, *Russia* 50 D7
Kamenskiy, *Russia* 48 E7
Kamenskoye, *Russia* 51 C17
Kamenyak, *Bulgaria* 41 C10
Kamenz, *Germany* 24 D10
Kameoka, *Japan* 55 G7
Kami, *Albania* 40 D4
Kamiah, *U.S.A.* 114 C5
Kamień Krajeński, *Poland* 44 E4
Kamień Pomorski, *Poland* 44 E1
Kamienna →, *Poland* 45 G8
Kamienna Góra, *Poland* 45 H3
Kamieńsk, *Poland* 45 G6
Kamieskroon, *S. Africa* 88 E2
Kamilukuak, L., *Canada* 105 A8
Kamin-Kashyrskyy, *Ukraine* 47 G3
Kamina, *Dem. Rep. of the Congo* 87 D2
Kaminak L., *Canada* 105 A10
Kaminka, *Ukraine* 47 H7
Kaminoyama, *Japan* 54 E10
Kamiros, *Greece* 36 C9
Kamituga, *Dem. Rep. of the Congo* 86 C2
Kamloops, *Canada* 104 C4
Kamnik, *Slovenia* 29 B11
Kamo, *Armenia* 49 K7
Kamo, *Japan* 54 F9
Kamoke, *Pakistan* 68 C6
Kamp →, *Austria* 26 C8
Kampala, *Uganda* 86 B3
Kampang Chhnang, *Cambodia* 65 F5
Kampar, *Malaysia* 65 K3
Kampar →, *Indonesia* 62 D2
Kampen, *Neths.* 17 B5
Kamphaeng Phet, *Thailand* 64 D2
Kampolombo, L., *Zambia* 87 E2
Kampong Saom, *Cambodia* 65 G4
Kampong Saom, Chaak, *Cambodia* 65 G4
Kampong To, *Thailand* 65 J3
Kampot, *Cambodia* 65 G5
Kampti, *Burkina Faso* 82 C4
Kampuchea = Cambodia ■, *Asia* 64 F5
Kampung Air Putih, *Malaysia* 65 K4
Kampung Jerangau, *Malaysia* 65 K4
Kampung Raja, *Malaysia* 65 K4
Kampungbaru = Tolitoli, *Indonesia* 63 D6
Kamrau, Teluk, *Indonesia* 63 E8
Kamsack, *Canada* 105 C8
Kamskoye Ustye, *Russia* 48 C9
Kamuchawie L., *Canada* 105 B8
Kamui-Misaki, *Japan* 54 C10
Kamyanets-Podilskyy, *Ukraine* 47 H4
Kamyanka-Buzka, *Ukraine* 47 G3
Kamyanka-Dniprovska, *Ukraine* 47 J8
Kāmyārān, *Iran* 70 C5
Kamyshin, *Russia* 48 E7
Kamyzyak, *Russia* 49 G9
Kanaaupscow, *Canada* 102 B4
Kanaaupscow →, *Canada* 101 C12
Kanab, *U.S.A.* 115 H7
Kanab →, *U.S.A.* 115 H7
Kanagi, *Japan* 54 D10
Kanairiktok →, *Canada* 103 A7
Kanália, *Greece* 38 B4
Kananga, *Dem. Rep. of the Congo* 84 F4
Kanarraville, *U.S.A.* 115 H7
Kanash, *Russia* 48 C8
Kanaskat, *U.S.A.* 116 C5
Kanastraíon, Ákra = Palioúrion, Ákra, *Greece* 40 G7
Kanawha →, *U.S.A.* 108 F4
Kanazawa, *Japan* 55 F8
Kanchanaburi, *Thailand* 64 E2
Kanchenjunga, *Nepal* 69 F13
Kanchipuram, *India* 66 N11
Kańczuga, *Poland* 45 J9
Kandahar = Qandahār, *Afghan.* 66 D4
Kandalaksha, *Russia* 50 C4
Kandalu, *Afghan.* 66 E3
Kandangan, *Indonesia* 62 E5
Kandanos, *Greece* 36 D5
Kandava, *Latvia* 44 A9
Kandhíla, *Greece* 38 D4
Kandhkot, *Pakistan* 68 E3
Kandhla, *India* 68 E7
Kandi, *Benin* 83 C5
Kandi, *India* 69 H13
Kandıra, *Turkey* 72 B4
Kandla, *India* 68 H4
Kandos, *Australia* 95 E4
Kandy, *Sri Lanka* 66 R12
Kane, *U.S.A.* 110 E6
Kane Basin, *Greenland* 4 B4
Kanevskaya, *Russia* 49 G4
Kanfanar, *Croatia* 29 C10
Kangaba, *Mali* 82 C3
Kangal, *Turkey* 72 C7
Kangān, *Fārs, Iran* 71 E7
Kangān, *Hormozgān, Iran* 71 E8
Kangar, *Malaysia* 65 J3
Kangaroo I., *Australia* 95 F2
Kangasala, *Finland* 9 F21
Kangāvar, *Iran* 71 C6
Kangding, *China* 58 B3
Kăngdong, *N. Korea* 57 E14
Kangean, Kepulauan, *Indonesia* 62 F5
Kangean Is. = Kangean, Kepulauan, *Indonesia* 62 F5
Kanggye, *N. Korea* 57 D14
Kanggyŏng, *S. Korea* 57 F14
Kanghwa, *S. Korea* 57 F14
Kangiqsualujjuaq, *Canada* 101 C13
Kangiqsujuaq, *Canada* 101 B12
Kangirsuk, *Canada* 101 C13
Kangnŭng, *S. Korea* 57 F15
Kangping, *China* 57 C12
Kangto, *India* 67 F18
Kani, *Ivory C.* 82 D3
Kaniama, *Dem. Rep. of the Congo* 86 D1
Kaniapiskau →, *Canada* 103 A6
Kaniapiskau L., *Canada* 103 B6
Kanin, Poluostrov, *Russia* 50 C5
Kanin Nos, Mys, *Russia* 50 C5
Kanin Pen. = Kanin, Poluostrov, *Russia* 50 C5
Kanina, *Albania* 40 F3
Kaniva, *Australia* 95 F3
Kanjiža, *Serbia, Yug.* 42 D5
Kanjut Sar, *Pakistan* 69 A6
Kankaanpää, *Finland* 9 F20
Kankakee, *U.S.A.* 108 E2
Kankakee →, *U.S.A.* 108 E1
Kankan, *Guinea* 82 C3
Kankendy = Xankändi, *Azerbaijan* 73 C12
Kanker, *India* 67 J12
Kannapolis, *U.S.A.* 109 H5
Kannauj, *India* 69 F8
Kannod, *India* 66 H10
Kano, *Nigeria* 83 C6
Kano □, *Nigeria* 83 C6
Kan'onji, *Japan* 55 G6
Kanoroba, *Ivory C.* 82 D3
Kanowit, *Malaysia* 62 D4
Kanowna, *Australia* 93 F3
Kanoya, *Japan* 55 J5
Kanpetlet, *Burma* 67 J18
Kanpur, *India* 69 F9
Kansas □, *U.S.A.* 112 F6
Kansas →, *U.S.A.* 112 F7
Kansas City, *Kans., U.S.A.* 112 F7
Kansas City, *Mo., U.S.A.* 112 F7
Kansenia, *Dem. Rep. of the Congo* 87 E2
Kansk, *Russia* 51 D10
Kansŏng, *S. Korea* 57 E15
Kansu = Gansu □, *China* 56 G3
Kantché, *Niger* 83 C6
Kanté, *Togo* 83 D5
Kantemirovka, *Russia* 47 H10
Kantharalak, *Thailand* 64 E5
Kantō □, *Japan* 55 F9
Kantō-Sanchi, *Japan* 55 G9
Kanturk, *Ireland* 15 D3
Kanuma, *Japan* 55 F9
Kanus, *Namibia* 88 D2
Kanye, *Botswana* 88 C4
Kanzenze, *Dem. Rep. of the Congo* 87 E2
Kanzi, Ras, *Tanzania* 86 D4
Kaohsiung, *Taiwan* 59 F13
Kaokoveld, *Namibia* 88 B1
Kaolack, *Senegal* 82 C1
Kaoshan, *China* 57 B13
Kapadvanj, *India* 68 H5
Kapaklı, *Turkey* 41 E11
Kapan, *Armenia* 73 C12
Kapanga, *Dem. Rep. of the Congo* 84 F4
Kapchagai = Qapshaghay, *Kazakstan* 50 E8
Kapela = Velika Kapela, *Croatia* 29 C12
Kapéllo, Ákra, *Greece* 38 E5
Kapema, *Dem. Rep. of the Congo* 87 E2
Kapfenberg, *Austria* 26 D8
Kapı Dağı, *Turkey* 41 F11
Kapiri Mposhi, *Zambia* 87 E2
Kapiskau →, *Canada* 102 B3
Kapit, *Malaysia* 62 D4
Kapiti I., *N.Z.* 91 J5
Kaplice, *Czech Rep.* 26 C7
Kapoe, *Thailand* 65 H2
Kapoeta, *Sudan* 81 G3
Kápolnásnyék, *Hungary* 42 C3
Kapos →, *Hungary* 42 D3
Kaposvár, *Hungary* 42 D2
Kapowsin, *U.S.A.* 116 D4
Kappeln, *Germany* 24 A5
Kappelshamn, *Sweden* 11 G12
Kapps, *Namibia* 88 C2
Kaprije, *Croatia* 29 E12
Kapsan, *N. Korea* 57 D15
Kapsukas = Marijampolė, *Lithuania* 9 J20
Kapuas →, *Indonesia* 62 E3
Kapuas Hulu, Pegunungan, *Malaysia* 62 D4
Kapuas Hulu Ra. = Kapuas Hulu, Pegunungan, *Malaysia* 62 D4
Kapulo, *Dem. Rep. of the Congo* 87 D2
Kapunda, *Australia* 95 E2
Kapuni, *N.Z.* 91 H5
Kapurthala, *India* 68 D6
Kapuskasing, *Canada* 102 C3
Kapuskasing →, *Canada* 102 C3
Kapustin Yar, *Russia* 49 F7
Kaputar, *Australia* 95 E5
Kaputir, *Kenya* 86 B4
Kapuvár, *Hungary* 42 C2
Kara, *Russia* 50 C7
Kara Ada, *Turkey* 39 E9
Kara Bogaz Gol, Zaliv = Garabogazköl Aylagy, *Turkmenistan* 50 E6
Kara Burun, *Turkey* 39 E9
Kara Kalpak Republic □ = Karakalpakstan □, *Uzbekistan* 50 E6
Kara Kum, *Turkmenistan* 50 F7
Kara Sea, *Russia* 50 B8
Karaadilli, *Turkey* 39 C12
Karabiğa, *Turkey* 41 F11
Karabük, *Turkey* 72 B5
Karaburun, *Turkey* 39 C8
Karaburun, *Albania* 40 F3
Karabutak = Qarabutaq, *Kazakstan* 50 E7
Karacabey, *Turkey* 41 F12
Karacakılavuz, *Turkey* 41 E11
Karacaköy, *Turkey* 41 E12
Karacasu, *Turkey* 39 D10
Karachala = Qaraçala, *Azerbaijan* 49 L9
Karachayevsk, *Russia* 49 J5
Karachev, *Russia* 47 F8
Karachey-Cherkessia □, *Russia* 49 J5
Karachi, *Pakistan* 68 G2
Karad, *India* 66 L9
Karadirek, *Turkey* 39 C12
Karaga, *Ghana* 83 D4
Karaganda = Qaraghandy, *Kazakstan* 50 E8
Karagayly, *Kazakstan* 50 E8
Karaginskiy, Ostrov, *Russia* 51 D17
Karagüney Dağları, *Turkey* 72 B6
Karagwe □, *Tanzania* 86 C3
Karahallı, *Turkey* 39 C11
Karaikal, *India* 66 P11
Karaikkudi, *India* 66 P11
Karaisali, *Turkey* 72 D6
Karaj, *Iran* 71 C6
Karak, *Malaysia* 65 L4
Karakalpakstan □, *Uzbekistan* 50 E6
Karakelong, *Indonesia* 63 D7
Karakitang, *Indonesia* 63 D7
Karaklis = Vanadzor, *Armenia* 49 K7
Karakoçan, *Turkey* 73 C9
Karakoram Pass, *Pakistan* 69 B7
Karakoram Ra., *Pakistan* 69 B7
Karakurt, *Turkey* 73 B10
Karalon, *Russia* 51 D12
Karaman, *Balıkesir, Turkey* 39 B9
Karaman, *Konya, Turkey* 72 D5
Karamanlı, *Turkey* 39 D11
Karamay, *China* 60 B3
Karambu, *Indonesia* 62 E5
Karamea Bight, *N.Z.* 91 J3
Karamsad, *India* 68 H5
Karamürsel, *Turkey* 41 F13
Karand, *Iran* 70 C5
Karanganyar, *Indonesia* 63 G13
Karaova, *Turkey* 39 D9
Karapınar, *Turkey* 72 D5
Karasburg, *Namibia* 88 D2
Karasino, *Russia* 50 C9
Karasjok, *Norway* 8 B21
Karasu, *Turkey* 72 B4
Karasu →, *Turkey* 39 E12
Karasuk, *Russia* 50 D8
Karasuyama, *Japan* 55 F10
Karataş, *Adana, Turkey* 72 D6
Karataş, *Manisa, Turkey* 39 C10
Karataş Burnu, *Turkey* 72 D6
Karatau = Qaratau, *Kazakstan* 50 E8
Karatau, Khrebet, *Kazakstan* 50 E7
Karatoprak, *Turkey* 39 D9
Karauli, *India* 68 F7
Karavastasë, L. e, *Albania* 40 F3
Karávi, *Greece* 38 E5
Karavostasi, *Cyprus* 36 D11
Karawang, *Indonesia* 63 G12
Karawanken, *Europe* 26 E7
Karayazı, *Turkey* 73 C10
Karazhal, *Kazakstan* 50 E8
Karbalā, *Iraq* 70 C5
Kårböle, *Sweden* 10 C9
Karcag, *Hungary* 42 C5
Karcha →, *Pakistan* 69 B7
Karczew, *Poland* 45 F8
Kardam, *Bulgaria* 41 C12
Kardeljovo = Ploče, *Croatia* 29 E14
Kardhámila, *Greece* 39 C8
Kardhamíli, *Greece* 38 E4
Kardhítsa, *Greece* 38 B3
Kardhítsa □, *Greece* 38 B3
Kärdla, *Estonia* 9 G20
Kareeberge, *S. Africa* 88 E3
Kareima, *Sudan* 80 D3
Karelia □, *Russia* 50 C4
Karelian Republic □ = Karelia □, *Russia* 50 C4
Kārevāndar, *Iran* 71 E9
Kargasok, *Russia* 50 D9
Kargat, *Russia* 50 D9
Kargı, *Turkey* 72 B6
Kargil, *India* 69 B7
Kargopol, *Russia* 46 B10
Kargowa, *Poland* 45 F2
Karguéri, *Niger* 83 C7
Kariá, *Greece* 38 C2
Kariaí, *Greece* 41 F8
Karīān, *Iran* 71 E8
Kariba, *Zimbabwe* 87 F2
Kariba, L., *Zimbabwe* 87 F2
Kariba Dam, *Zimbabwe* 87 F2
Kariba Gorge, *Zambia* 87 F2
Karibib, *Namibia* 88 C2
Karimata, Kepulauan, *Indonesia* 62 E3
Karimata, Selat, *Indonesia* 62 E3
Karimata Is. = Karimata, Kepulauan, *Indonesia* 62 E3
Karimnagar, *India* 66 K11
Karimunjawa, Kepulauan, *Indonesia* 62 F4
Karin, *Somali Rep.* 74 E4
Káristos, *Greece* 38 C6
Karīt, *Iran* 71 C8
Kariya, *Japan* 55 G8
Karjala, *Finland* 46 A5
Karkaralinsk = Qarqaraly, *Kazakstan* 50 E8
Karkinitska Zatoka, *Ukraine* 47 K7
Karkinitskiy Zaliv = Karkinitska Zatoka, *Ukraine* 47 K7
Karkur Tohl, *Egypt* 80 C2
Karl Liebknecht, *Russia* 47 G8
Karl-Marx-Stadt = Chemnitz, *Germany* 24 E8
Karlholmsbruk, *Sweden* 10 D11
Karlino, *Poland* 44 D2
Karlivka, *Ukraine* 47 H8
Karlobag, *Croatia* 29 D12
Karlovac, *Croatia* 29 C12
Karlovka = Karlivka, *Ukraine* 47 H8
Karlovo, *Bulgaria* 41 D8
Karlovy Vary, *Czech Rep.* 26 A5
Karlsbad = Karlovy Vary, *Czech Rep.* 26 A5
Karlsborg, *Sweden* 11 F8
Karlshamn, *Sweden* 11 H8
Karlskoga, *Sweden* 10 E8
Karlskrona, *Sweden* 11 H9
Karlsruhe, *Germany* 25 F4
Karlstad, *Sweden* 10 E7
Karlstad, *U.S.A.* 112 A6
Karlstadt, *Germany* 25 F5
Karmėlava, *Lithuania* 44 D11
Karnal, *India* 68 E7
Karnali →, *Nepal* 69 E9
Karnaphuli Res., *Bangla.* 67 H18
Karnataka □, *India* 66 N10
Karnes City, *U.S.A.* 113 L6
Karnische Alpen, *Europe* 26 E6
Karnobat, *Bulgaria* 41 D10
Kärnten □, *Austria* 26 E6
Karo, *Mali* 82 C4
Karoi, *Zimbabwe* 87 F2
Karonga, *Malawi* 87 D3
Karoonda, *Australia* 95 F2
Karora, *Sudan* 80 D4
Káros, *Greece* 39 E7
Karousádhes, *Greece* 38 B1
Karpacz, *Poland* 45 H2
Karpasia □, *Cyprus* 36 D13
Kárpathos, *Greece* 39 F9
Kárpathos, Stenón, *Greece* 39 F9
Karpenísion, *Greece* 38 C3
Karpuz Burnu = Apostolos Andreas, C., *Cyprus* 36 D13
Karpuzlu, *Turkey* 39 D9
Kars, *Turkey* 73 B10
Karsakpay, *Kazakstan* 50 E7
Karsha, *Kazakstan* 48 F10
Karshi = Qarshi, *Uzbekistan* 50 F7
Karsiyang, *India* 69 F13
Karst = Kras, *Croatia* 29 C10
Kartal, *Turkey* 41 F13
Kartál Óros, *Greece* 41 E9
Kartaly, *Russia* 50 D7
Kartapur, *India* 68 D6
Karthaus, *U.S.A.* 110 E6
Kartuzy, *Poland* 44 D5
Karufa, *Indonesia* 63 E8
Karumba, *Australia* 94 B3
Karumo, *Tanzania* 86 C3
Karumwa, *Tanzania* 86 C3
Karungu, *Kenya* 86 C3
Karup, *Denmark* 11 H3
Karviná, *Czech Rep.* 27 B11
Karwar, *India* 66 M9
Karwi, *India* 69 G9
Kaş, *Turkey* 39 E11
Kasaba, *Turkey* 39 E11
Kasache, *Malawi* 87 E3
Kasai →, *Dem. Rep. of the Congo* 84 E3
Kasai Oriental □, *Dem. Rep. of the Congo* 86 D1
Kasaji, *Dem. Rep. of the Congo* 87 E1
Kasama, *Zambia* 87 E3

Kasan-dong, *N. Korea* 57 D14
Kasane, *Namibia* 88 B3
Kasanga, *Tanzania* 87 D3
Kasaragod, *India* 66 N9
Kasba L., *Canada* 105 A8
Kāseh Garān, *Iran* 70 C5
Kasempa, *Zambia* 87 E2
Kasenga, *Dem. Rep. of the Congo* 87 E2
Kasese, *Uganda* 86 B3
Kasewa, *Zambia* 87 E2
Kasganj, *India* 69 F8
Kashabowie, *Canada* 102 C1
Kāshān, *Iran* 71 C6
Kashi, *China* 60 C2
Kashimbo, *Dem. Rep. of the Congo* 87 E2
Kashin, *Russia* 46 D9
Kashipur, *India* 69 E8
Kashira, *Russia* 46 E10
Kashiwazaki, *Japan* 55 F9
Kashk-e Kohneh, *Afghan.* 66 B3
Kāshmar, *Iran* 71 C8
Kashmir, *Asia* 69 C7
Kashmor, *Pakistan* 68 E3
Kashpirovka, *Russia* 48 D9
Kashun Noerh = Gaxun Nur, *China* 60 B5
Kasimov, *Russia* 48 C5
Kasinge, *Dem. Rep. of the Congo* 86 D2
Kasiruta, *Indonesia* 63 E7
Kaskaskia →, *U.S.A.* 112 G10
Kaskattama →, *Canada* 105 B10
Kaskinen, *Finland* 9 E19
Kaslo, *Canada* 104 D5
Kasmere L., *Canada* 105 B8
Kasongo, *Dem. Rep. of the Congo* 86 C2
Kasongo Lunda, *Dem. Rep. of the Congo* 84 F3
Kásos, *Greece* 39 F8
Kásos, Stenón, *Greece* 39 F8
Kaspi, *Georgia* 49 K7
Kaspichan, *Bulgaria* 41 C11
Kaspiysk, *Russia* 49 J8
Kaspiyskiy, *Russia* 49 H8
Kassab ed Doleib, *Sudan* 81 E3
Kassaba, *Egypt* 80 C2
Kassalâ, *Sudan* 81 D4
Kassalâ □, *Sudan* 81 D4
Kassándra, *Greece* 40 F7
Kassándrinon, *Greece* 40 F7
Kassel, *Germany* 24 D5
Kassinger, *Sudan* 80 D3
Kassiópi, *Greece* 36 A3
Kastamonu, *Turkey* 72 B5
Kastav, *Croatia* 29 C11
Kastélli, *Greece* 36 D5
Kastéllion, *Greece* 36 D7
Kastellórizon = Megiste, *Greece* 39 E11
Kástellos, *Greece* 39 E9
Kastellou, Ákra, *Greece* 39 F9
Kasterlee, *Belgium* 17 C4
Kastlösa, *Sweden* 11 H10
Kastóri, *Greece* 38 D4
Kastoría, *Greece* 40 F5
Kastoría □, *Greece* 40 F5
Kastorías, Límni, *Greece* 40 F5
Kastornoye, *Russia* 47 G10
Kastós, *Greece* 38 C2
Kastrosikiá, *Greece* 38 B2
Kastsyukovichy, *Belarus* 46 F7
Kasulu, *Tanzania* 86 C3
Kasulu □, *Tanzania* 86 C3
Kasumi, *Japan* 55 G7
Kasumkent, *Russia* 49 K9
Kasungu, *Malawi* 87 E3
Kasur, *Pakistan* 68 D6
Kataba, *Zambia* 87 F2
Katako Kombe, *Dem. Rep. of the Congo* 86 C1
Katákolon, *Greece* 38 D3
Katale, *Tanzania* 86 C3
Katamatite, *Australia* 95 F4
Katanda, *Kivu, Dem. Rep. of the Congo* 86 C2
Katanda, *Shaba, Dem. Rep. of the Congo* 86 D1
Katanga = Shaba □, *Dem. Rep. of the Congo* 86 D2
Katangi, *India* 66 J11
Katastári, *Greece* 38 D2
Katavi Swamp, *Tanzania* 86 D3
Kateríni, *Greece* 40 F6
Katha, *Burma* 67 G20
Katherîna, Gebel, *Egypt* 80 J8
Katherine, *Australia* 92 B5
Kathiawar, *India* 68 H4
Kathikas, *Cyprus* 36 E11
Kati, *Mali* 82 C3
Katihar, *India* 69 G12
Katima Mulilo, *Zambia* 88 B3
Katimbira, *Malawi* 87 E3
Katingan = Mendawai →, *Indonesia* 62 E4
Katiola, *Ivory C.* 82 D3
Katlanovo, *Macedonia* 40 E5
Katmandu, *Nepal* 69 F11
Kato Akhaïa, *Greece* 38 C3
Káto Arkhánai, *Greece* 36 D7
Káto Khorió, *Greece* 36 D7
Kato Pyrgos, *Cyprus* 36 D11
Káto Stavros, *Greece* 40 F7
Katokhí, *Greece* 38 C3
Katompe, *Dem. Rep. of the Congo* 86 D2
Katonga →, *Uganda* 86 B3
Katoomba, *Australia* 95 E5
Katoúna, *Greece* 38 C3
Katowice, *Poland* 45 H6
Katowice □, *Poland* 45 H6
Katrancı Dağı, *Turkey* 39 D12
Katrine, L., *U.K.* 14 E4
Katrineholm, *Sweden* 11 E10
Katsepe, *Madag.* 89 B8
Katsina, *Nigeria* 83 C6
Katsina □, *Nigeria* 83 C6
Katsina Ala →, *Nigeria* 83 D6
Katsumoto, *Japan* 55 H4
Katsuura, *Japan* 55 G10
Katsuyama, *Japan* 55 F8
Kattaviá, *Greece* 36 D9
Kattegat, *Denmark* 11 H5
Katthammarsvik, *Sweden* 11 G12
Katumba, *Dem. Rep. of the Congo* 86 D2
Katungu, *Kenya* 86 C5
Katwa, *India* 69 H13
Katwijk, *Neths.* 17 B4
Kąty Wrocławskie, *Poland* 45 G3
Kauai, *U.S.A.* 106 H15
Kauai Channel, *U.S.A.* 106 H15
Kaub, *Germany* 25 E3
Kaufbeuren, *Germany* 25 H6
Kaufman, *U.S.A.* 113 J6
Kauhajoki, *Finland* 9 E20
Kaukauna, *U.S.A.* 108 C1
Kaukauveld, *Namibia* 88 C3
Kaunas, *Lithuania* 9 J20
Kaunos, *Turkey* 39 E10
Kaura Namoda, *Nigeria* 83 C6
Kautokeino, *Norway* 8 B20
Kavacha, *Russia* 51 C17
Kavadarci, *Macedonia* 40 E6
Kavaja, *Albania* 40 E3
Kavak, *Turkey* 72 B7
Kavak Dağı, *Turkey* 39 D10
Kavaklı, *Turkey* 41 E11
Kavaklıdere, *Turkey* 39 D10
Kavalerovo, *Russia* 54 B7
Kavali, *India* 66 M12
Kavála, *Greece* 41 F8
Kavála □, *Greece* 41 E8
Kavála Kólpos, *Greece* 41 F8
Kavār, *Iran* 71 D7
Kavarna, *Bulgaria* 41 C12
Kavkaz, *Russia* 47 K9
Kävlinge, *Sweden* 11 J7
Kavos, *Greece* 36 B4
Kavoúsi, *Greece* 39 F7
Kaw, *Fr. Guiana* 125 C8
Kawa, *Sudan* 81 E3
Kawagama L., *Canada* 110 A6
Kawagoe, *Japan* 55 G9
Kawaguchi, *Japan* 55 G9
Kawaihae, *U.S.A.* 106 H17
Kawambwa, *Zambia* 87 D2
Kawanoe, *Japan* 55 G6
Kawardha, *India* 69 J9
Kawasaki, *Japan* 55 G9
Kawasi, *Indonesia* 63 E7
Kawene, *Canada* 102 C1
Kawerau, *N.Z.* 91 H6
Kawhia Harbour, *N.Z.* 91 H5
Kawio, Kepulauan, *Indonesia* 63 D7
Kawnro, *Burma* 67 H21
Kawthaung, *Burma* 65 H2
Kawthoolei = Kawthule □, *Burma* 67 L20
Kawthule □, *Burma* 67 L20
Kaxholmen, *Sweden* 11 G8
Kaya, *Burkina Faso* 83 C4
Kayah □, *Burma* 67 K20
Kayalıköy Barajı, *Turkey* 41 E11
Kayan →, *Indonesia* 62 D5
Kaycee, *U.S.A.* 114 E10
Kayeli, *Indonesia* 63 E7
Kayenta, *U.S.A.* 115 H8
Kayes, *Mali* 82 C2
Kayı, *Turkey* 39 B12
Kayima, *S. Leone* 82 D2
Kaymakçı, *Turkey* 39 C10
Kayoa, *Indonesia* 63 D7
Kayomba, *Zambia* 87 E1
Kayoro, *Ghana* 83 C4
Kayrunnera, *Australia* 95 E3
Kaysatskoye, *Russia* 48 F8
Kayseri, *Turkey* 72 C6
Kaysville, *U.S.A.* 114 F8
Kaz Dağı, *Turkey* 39 B8
Kazachye, *Russia* 51 B14
Kazakstan ■, *Asia* 50 E8
Kazan, *Russia* 48 C9
Kazan-Rettō, *Pac. Oc.* 96 E6
Kazanlŭk, *Bulgaria* 41 D9
Kazanskaya, *Russia* 48 F5
Kazatin = Kozyatyn, *Ukraine* 47 H5
Kazbek, *Russia* 49 J7
Kāzerūn, *Iran* 71 D6
Kazi Magomed = Qazimämmäd, *Azerbaijan* 49 K9
Kazimierz Dolny, *Poland* 45 G8
Kazimierza Wielka, *Poland* 45 H7
Kazincbarcika, *Hungary* 42 B5
Kazlų Rūda, *Lithuania* 44 D10
Kaztalovka, *Kazakstan* 48 F9
Kazuno, *Japan* 54 D10
Kazym →, *Russia* 50 C7
Kcynia, *Poland* 45 F4
Ké-Macina, *Mali* 82 C3
Kéa, *Greece* 38 D6
Keady, *U.K.* 15 B5
Keams Canyon, *U.S.A.* 115 J8
Kearney, *U.S.A.* 112 E5
Keban, *Turkey* 73 C8
Keban Baraji, *Turkey* 73 C8
Kebbi □, *Nigeria* 83 C6
Kébi, *Ivory C.* 82 D3
Kebnekaise, *Sweden* 8 C18
Kebri Dehar, *Ethiopia* 74 F3
Kebumen, *Indonesia* 63 G13
Kecel, *Hungary* 42 D4
Kechika →, *Canada* 104 B3
Keçiborlu, *Turkey* 39 D12
Kecskemét, *Hungary* 42 D4
Kedada, *Ethiopia* 81 F4
Kėdainiai, *Lithuania* 9 J21
Kedgwick, *Canada* 103 C6
Kédhros Óros, *Greece* 36 D6
Kedia Hill, *Botswana* 88 C3
Kediri, *Indonesia* 63 G15
Kédougou, *Senegal* 82 C2
Kędzierzyn-Koźle, *Poland* 45 H5
Keeler, *U.S.A.* 116 J9
Keeley L., *Canada* 105 C7
Keeling Is. = Cocos Is., *Ind. Oc.* 96 J1
Keene, *Calif., U.S.A.* 117 K8
Keene, *N.H., U.S.A.* 111 D12
Keeper Hill, *Ireland* 15 D3
Keer-Weer, C., *Australia* 94 A3
Keeseville, *U.S.A.* 111 B11
Keetmanshoop, *Namibia* 88 D2
Keewatin, *U.S.A.* 112 B8
Keewatin □, *Canada* 105 A10
Keewatin →, *Canada* 105 B8
Kefa □, *Ethiopia* 81 F4
Kefallinía, *Greece* 38 C2
Kefallinía □, *Greece* 38 C2
Kéfalos, *Greece* 39 E8
Kefamenanu, *Indonesia* 63 F6
Keffi, *Nigeria* 83 D6
Keflavík, *Iceland* 8 D2
Keg River, *Canada* 104 B5
Kegaska, *Canada* 103 B7
Kehl, *Germany* 25 G3
Keighley, *U.K.* 12 D6
Keila, *Estonia* 9 G21
Keimoes, *S. Africa* 88 D3
Keita, *Niger* 83 C6
Keitele, *Finland* 8 E22
Keith, *Australia* 95 F3
Keith, *U.K.* 14 D6
Kejser Franz Joseph Fjord = Kong Franz Joseph Fd., *Greenland* 4 B6
Kekri, *India* 68 G6
Kelamet, *Eritrea* 81 D4
Kelan, *China* 56 E6
Kelang, *Malaysia* 65 L3
Kelantan →, *Malaysia* 65 J4
Këlcyra, *Albania* 40 F4
Kelekçi, *Turkey* 39 D11
Keles, *Turkey* 41 G13
Keleti-főcsatorna, *Hungary* 42 C6
Kelheim, *Germany* 25 G7
Kelkit, *Turkey* 73 B8
Kelkit →, *Turkey* 72 B7
Keller, *U.S.A.* 114 B4
Kellerberrin, *Australia* 93 F2
Kellett, C., *Canada* 4 B1
Kelleys I., *U.S.A.* 110 E2
Kellogg, *U.S.A.* 114 C5
Kells = Ceanannus Mor, *Ireland* 15 C5
Kelmė, *Lithuania* 44 C9
Kelokedhara, *Cyprus* 36 E11
Kelowna, *Canada* 104 D5
Kelsey Bay, *Canada* 104 C3
Kelseyville, *U.S.A.* 116 G4
Kelso, *N.Z.* 91 L2
Kelso, *U.K.* 14 F6
Kelso, *U.S.A.* 116 D4
Keluang, *Malaysia* 65 L4
Kelvington, *Canada* 105 C8
Kem, *Russia* 50 C4
Kema, *Indonesia* 63 D7
Kemah, *Turkey* 73 C8
Kemaliye, *Erzincan, Turkey* 73 C8
Kemaliye, *Manisa, Turkey* 39 C10
Kemalpaşa, *Turkey* 39 C9
Kemano, *Canada* 104 C3
Kemasik, *Malaysia* 65 K4
Kembolcha, *Ethiopia* 81 E4
Kemer, *Antalya, Turkey* 39 E12
Kemer, *Burdur, Turkey* 39 D12
Kemer, *Muğla, Turkey* 39 E11
Kemer Barajı, *Turkey* 39 D10
Kemerovo, *Russia* 50 D9
Kemi, *Finland* 8 D21
Kemi älv = Kemijoki →, *Finland* 8 D21
Kemijärvi, *Finland* 8 C22
Kemijoki →, *Finland* 8 D21
Kemmerer, *U.S.A.* 114 F8
Kemmuna = Comino, *Malta* 36 C1
Kemp, L., *U.S.A.* 113 J5
Kemp Land, *Antarctica* 5 C5
Kempsey, *Australia* 95 E5
Kempt, L., *Canada* 102 C5
Kempten, *Germany* 25 H6
Kemptville, *Canada* 102 D4
Kendal, *Indonesia* 63 G14
Kendal, *U.K.* 12 C5
Kendall, *Australia* 95 E5
Kendall →, *Australia* 94 A3
Kendallville, *U.S.A.* 108 E3
Kendari, *Indonesia* 63 E6
Kendawangan, *Indonesia* 62 E4
Kende, *Nigeria* 83 C5
Kendenup, *Australia* 93 F2
Kendrapara, *India* 67 J15
Këndrevicës, Maja e, *Albania* 40 F3
Kendrew, *S. Africa* 88 E3
Kendrick, *U.S.A.* 114 C5
Kene Thao, *Laos* 64 D3
Kenedy, *U.S.A.* 113 L6
Kenema, *S. Leone* 82 D2
Keng Kok, *Laos* 64 D5
Keng Tawng, *Burma* 67 J21
Keng Tung, *Burma* 67 J21
Kengeja, *Tanzania* 86 D4
Kenhardt, *S. Africa* 88 D3
Kenitra, *Morocco* 78 B4
Kenli, *China* 57 F10
Kenmare, *Ireland* 15 E2
Kenmare, *U.S.A.* 112 A3
Kenmare River, *Ireland* 15 E2
Kennebec, *U.S.A.* 112 D5
Kennedy, *Zimbabwe* 87 F2
Kennedy Ra., *Australia* 93 D2
Kennedy Taungdeik, *Burma* 67 H18
Kenner, *U.S.A.* 113 L9
Kennet →, *U.K.* 13 F7
Kenneth Ra., *Australia* 92 D2
Kennett, *U.S.A.* 113 G9
Kennewick, *U.S.A.* 114 C4
Kénogami, *Canada* 103 C5
Kenogami →, *Canada* 102 B3
Kenora, *Canada* 105 D10
Kenosha, *U.S.A.* 108 D2
Kensington, *Canada* 103 C7
Kensington, *U.S.A.* 112 F5
Kensington Downs, *Australia* 94 C3
Kent, *Ohio, U.S.A.* 110 E3
Kent, *Oreg., U.S.A.* 114 D3
Kent, *Tex., U.S.A.* 113 K2
Kent, *Wash., U.S.A.* 116 C4
Kent □, *U.K.* 13 F8
Kent Group, *Australia* 94 F4
Kent Pen., *Canada* 100 B9
Kentau, *Kazakstan* 50 E7
Kentland, *U.S.A.* 108 E2
Kenton, *U.S.A.* 108 E4
Kentucky □, *U.S.A.* 108 G3
Kentucky →, *U.S.A.* 108 F3
Kentucky L., *U.S.A.* 109 G2
Kentville, *Canada* 103 C7
Kentwood, *U.S.A.* 113 K9
Kenya ■, *Africa* 86 B4
Kenya, Mt., *Kenya* 86 C4
Keo Neua, Deo, *Vietnam* 64 C5
Keokuk, *U.S.A.* 112 E9
Kep, *Cambodia* 65 G5
Kep, *Vietnam* 64 B6
Kepez, *Turkey* 41 F10
Kepi, *Indonesia* 63 F9
Kępice, *Poland* 44 D3
Kępno, *Poland* 45 G4
Kepsut, *Turkey* 39 B10
Kerala □, *India* 66 P10
Kerama-Rettō, *Japan* 55 L3
Keran, *Pakistan* 69 B5
Kerang, *Australia* 95 F3
Keratéa, *Greece* 38 D5
Keraudren, C., *Australia* 92 C2
Kerava, *Finland* 9 F21
Kerch, *Ukraine* 47 K9
Kerchenskiy Proliv, *Black Sea* 47 K9
Kerchoual, *Mali* 83 B5
Kerempe Burnu, *Turkey* 72 A5
Keren, *Eritrea* 81 D4
Kerewan, *Gambia* 82 C1
Kerguelen, *Ind. Oc.* 3 G13
Keri, *Greece* 38 D2
Keri Kera, *Sudan* 81 E3
Kericho, *Kenya* 86 C4
Kericho □, *Kenya* 86 C4
Kerinci, *Indonesia* 62 E2
Kerki, *Turkmenistan* 50 F7
Kerkinítis, Límni, *Greece* 40 E7
Kérkira, *Greece* 38 B1
Kérkira □, *Greece* 38 B1
Kerkrade, *Neths.* 17 D6
Kerma, *Sudan* 80 D3
Kermadec Is., *Pac. Oc.* 96 L10
Kermadec Trench, *Pac. Oc.* 96 L10
Kermān, *Iran* 71 D8
Kerman, *U.S.A.* 116 J6
Kermān □, *Iran* 71 D8
Kermānshāh = Bākhtarān, *Iran* 70 C5
Kermen, *Bulgaria* 41 D10
Kermit, *U.S.A.* 113 K3
Kern →, *U.S.A.* 117 K7
Kernhof, *Austria* 26 D8
Kernville, *U.S.A.* 117 K8
Keroh, *Malaysia* 65 K3
Kerpen, *Germany* 24 E2
Kerrera, *U.K.* 14 E3
Kerrobert, *Canada* 105 C7
Kerrville, *U.S.A.* 113 K5
Kerry □, *Ireland* 15 D2
Kerry Hd., *Ireland* 15 D2
Kersa, *Ethiopia* 81 F5
Kerulen →, *Asia* 60 B6
Kerzaz, *Algeria* 78 C5
Kesagami →, *Canada* 102 B4
Kesagami L., *Canada* 102 B3
Keşan, *Turkey* 41 F10
Kesennuma, *Japan* 54 E10
Keshit, *Iran* 71 D8
Keşiş Dağ, *Turkey* 73 C8
Keskin, *Turkey* 72 C5
Kestell, *S. Africa* 89 D4
Kestenga, *Russia* 50 C4
Keswick, *U.K.* 12 C4
Keszthely, *Hungary* 42 D2
Ket →, *Russia* 50 D9
Keta, *Ghana* 83 D5
Ketapang, *Indonesia* 62 E4
Ketchikan, *U.S.A.* 100 C6
Ketchum, *U.S.A.* 114 E6
Kete Krachi, *Ghana* 83 D4
Ketef, Khalîg Umm el, *Egypt* 80 C4
Keti Bandar, *Pakistan* 68 G2
Ketri, *India* 68 E6
Kętrzyn, *Poland* 44 D8
Kettering, *U.K.* 13 E7
Kettering, *U.S.A.* 108 F3
Kettle →, *Canada* 105 B11
Kettle Falls, *U.S.A.* 114 B4
Kettleman City, *U.S.A.* 116 J7
Kęty, *Poland* 45 J6
Keuruu, *Finland* 9 E21
Kevelaer, *Germany* 24 D2
Kevin, *U.S.A.* 114 B8
Kewanee, *U.S.A.* 112 E10
Kewaunee, *U.S.A.* 108 C2
Keweenaw B., *U.S.A.* 108 B1
Keweenaw Pen., *U.S.A.* 108 B2
Keweenaw Pt., *U.S.A.* 108 B2
Key Harbour, *Canada* 102 C3
Key West, *U.S.A.* 107 F10
Keynsham, *U.K.* 13 F5
Keyser, *U.S.A.* 108 F6
Keystone, *U.S.A.* 112 D3
Kezhma, *Russia* 51 D11
Kežmarok, *Slovak Rep.* 27 B13
Khabarovsk, *Russia* 51 E14
Khabr, *Iran* 71 D8
Khābūr →, *Syria* 70 C4
Khachmas = Xaçmaz, *Azerbaijan* 49 K9
Khachrod, *India* 68 H6
Khadari, W. el →, *Sudan* 81 E2
Khadro, *Pakistan* 68 F3
Khadyzhensk, *Russia* 49 H4
Khadzhilyangar, *India* 69 B8
Khagaria, *India* 69 G12
Khaipur, *Bahawalpur, Pakistan* 68 E5
Khaipur, *Hyderabad, Pakistan* 68 F3
Khair, *India* 68 F7
Khairabad, *India* 69 F9
Khairagarh, *India* 69 J9
Khairpur, *Pakistan* 66 F6
Khakassia □, *Russia* 50 D9
Khakhea, *Botswana* 88 C3
Khalafābād, *Iran* 71 D6
Khalilabad, *India* 69 F10
Khalīlī, *Iran* 71 E7
Khalkhāl, *Iran* 71 B6
Khálki, *Dhodhekánisos, Greece* 39 E9
Khálki, *Thessalía, Greece* 38 B4
Khalkidhikí □, *Greece* 40 F7
Khalkís, *Greece* 38 C5
Khalmer-Sede = Tazovskiy, *Russia* 50 C8
Khalmer Yu, *Russia* 50 C7
Khalūf, *Oman* 74 C6
Kham Keut, *Laos* 64 C5
Khamas Country, *Botswana* 88 C4
Khambhaliya, *India* 68 H3
Khambhat, *India* 68 H5
Khambhat, G. of, *India* 68 J5
Khamilonísion, *Greece* 39 F8
Khamīr, *Iran* 71 E7
Khamir, *Yemen* 74 D3
Khamsa, *Egypt* 75 E1
Khān Abū Shāmat, *Syria* 75 B5
Khān Azād, *Iraq* 70 C5
Khān Mujiddah, *Iraq* 70 C4
Khān Shaykhūn, *Syria* 70 C3
Khān Yūnis, *Gaza Strip* 75 D3
Khānaqīn, *Iraq* 70 C5
Khānbāghī, *Iran* 71 B7
Khandrá, *Greece* 39 F8
Khandwa, *India* 66 J10
Khandyga, *Russia* 51 C14
Khāneh, *Iran* 70 B5
Khanewal, *Pakistan* 68 D4
Khanh Duong, *Vietnam* 64 F7
Khaniá, *Greece* 36 D6
Khaniá □, *Greece* 36 D6
Khaníon, Kólpos, *Greece* 36 D5
Khanka, L., *Asia* 54 B6
Khankendy = Xankändi, *Azerbaijan* 73 C12
Khanna, *India* 68 D7
Khanpur, *Pakistan* 68 E4
Khanty-Mansiysk, *Russia* 50 C7
Khapalu, *Pakistan* 69 B7
Khapcheranga, *Russia* 51 E12
Kharabali, *Russia* 49 G8
Kharagpur, *India* 69 H12
Khárakas, *Greece* 36 D7
Kharan Kalat, *Pakistan* 66 E4
Kharānaq, *Iran* 71 C7
Kharda, *India* 66 K9

Kitui, *Kenya* 86 C4
Kitui □, *Kenya* 86 C4
Kitwe, *Zambia* 87 E2
Kitzbühel, *Austria* 26 D5
Kitzbühler Alpen, *Austria* 26 D5
Kitzingen, *Germany* 25 F6
Kivarli, *India* 68 G5
Kivertsi, *Ukraine* 47 G3
Kividhes, *Cyprus* 36 E11
Kivik, *Sweden* 11 J8
Kivotós, *Greece* 40 F5
Kivu □, *Dem. Rep. of the Congo* 86 C2
Kivu, L., *Dem. Rep. of the Congo* 86 C2
Kiyev = Kyyiv, *Ukraine* 47 G6
Kiyevskoye Vdkhr. = Kyyivske Vdskh., *Ukraine* 47 G6
Kıyıköy, *Turkey* 41 E12
Kiziguru, *Rwanda* 86 C3
Kızıl Adalar, *Turkey* 41 F13
Kızıl Irmak →, *Turkey* 72 B6
Kizil Jilga, *India* 69 B8
Kizil Yurt, *Russia* 49 J8
Kızılcabölük, *Turkey* 39 D11
Kızılcadağ, *Turkey* 39 D11
Kızılcahamam, *Turkey* 72 B5
Kızılhisar, *Turkey* 72 D3
Kızılırmak, *Turkey* 72 B5
Kızılkaya, *Turkey* 39 D12
Kızılören, *Turkey* 39 C12
Kızıltepe, *Turkey* 73 D9
Kizimkazi, *Tanzania* 86 D4
Kizlyar, *Russia* 49 J8
Kizyl-Arvat = Gyzylarbat, *Turkmenistan* 50 F6
Kjellerup, *Denmark* 11 H3
Kjölur, *Iceland* 8 D4
Kladanj, *Bos.-H.* 42 F3
Kladnica, *Serbia, Yug.* 40 C4
Kladno, *Czech Rep.* 26 A7
Kladovo, *Serbia, Yug.* 40 B6
Klaeng, *Thailand* 64 F3
Klagenfurt, *Austria* 26 E7
Klaipėda, *Lithuania* 9 J19
Klaipėda □, *Lithuania* 44 C8
Klaksvík, *Færoe Is.* 8 E9
Klamath →, *U.S.A.* 114 F1
Klamath Falls, *U.S.A.* 114 E3
Klamath Mts., *U.S.A.* 114 F2
Klanjec, *Croatia* 29 B12
Klappan →, *Canada* 104 B3
Klarälven →, *Sweden* 10 E7
Klässbol, *Sweden* 10 E6
Klatovy, *Czech Rep.* 26 B6
Klawer, *S. Africa* 88 E2
Klawock, *U.S.A.* 104 B2
Klazienaveen, *Neths.* 17 B6
Kłecko, *Poland* 45 F4
Kleczew, *Poland* 45 F5
Kleena Kleene, *Canada* 104 C4
Klein, *U.S.A.* 114 C9
Klein-Karas, *Namibia* 88 D2
Klekovača, *Bos.-H.* 29 D13
Klenoec, *Macedonia* 40 E4
Klenovec, *Slovak Rep.* 27 C12
Klerksdorp, *S. Africa* 88 D4
Kleszczele, *Poland* 45 F10
Kletnya, *Russia* 46 F7
Kletsk = Klyetsk, *Belarus* 47 F4
Kletskiy, *Russia* 49 F6
Kleve, *Germany* 24 D2
Klickitat, *U.S.A.* 114 D3
Klickitat →, *U.S.A.* 116 E5
Klidhes, *Cyprus* 36 D13
Klimovichi, *Belarus* 46 F6
Klin, *Russia* 46 D9
Klinaklini →, *Canada* 104 C3
Klintehamn, *Sweden* 11 G12
Klintsy, *Russia* 47 F7
Klipdale, *S. Africa* 88 E2
Klippan, *Sweden* 11 H7
Klipplaat, *S. Africa* 88 E3
Klisura, *Bulgaria* 41 D8
Kljajićevo, *Serbia, Yug.* 42 E4
Ključ, *Bos.-H.* 29 D13
Kłobuck, *Poland* 45 H5
Klockestrand, *Sweden* 10 B11
Kłodawa, *Poland* 45 F5
Kłodzko, *Poland* 45 H3
Klosi, *Albania* 40 E4
Klosterneuburg, *Austria* 27 C9
Klosters, *Switz.* 25 J5
Klötze, *Germany* 24 C7
Klouto, *Togo* 83 D5
Kluane L., *Canada* 100 B6
Kluczbork, *Poland* 45 H5
Klyetsk, *Belarus* 47 F4
Klyuchevskaya, Gora, *Russia* 51 D17
Knäred, *Sweden* 11 H7
Knaresborough, *U.K.* 12 C6
Knee L., *Man., Canada* 105 B10
Knee L., *Sask., Canada* 105 B7
Knezha, *Bulgaria* 41 C8
Knić, *Serbia, Yug.* 40 C4
Knight Inlet, *Canada* 104 C3
Knighton, *U.K.* 13 E4
Knights Ferry, *U.S.A.* 116 H6
Knights Landing, *U.S.A.* 116 G5
Knin, *Croatia* 29 D13
Knislinge, *Sweden* 11 H8
Knittelfeld, *Austria* 26 D7
Knivsta, *Sweden* 10 E11
Knjaževac, *Serbia, Yug.* 40 C6
Knob, C., *Australia* 93 F2
Knock, *Ireland* 15 C3
Knockmealdown Mts., *Ireland* 15 D4
Knokke-Heist, *Belgium* 17 C3
Knossós, *Greece* 36 D7
Knox, *U.S.A.* 108 E2
Knox, C., *Canada* 104 C2
Knox City, *U.S.A.* 113 J5
Knox Coast, *Antarctica* 5 C8
Knoxville, *Iowa, U.S.A.* 112 E8
Knoxville, *Tenn., U.S.A.* 109 H4
Knysna, *S. Africa* 88 E3
Knyszyn, *Poland* 44 E9
Ko Kha, *Thailand* 64 C2
Koartac = Quaqtaq, *Canada* 101 B13
Koba, *Indonesia* 63 F8
Kobarid, *Slovenia* 29 B10
Kobayashi, *Japan* 55 J5
Kobdo = Hovd, *Mongolia* 60 B4
Kōbe, *Japan* 55 G7
Kobelyaky, *Ukraine* 47 H8
København, *Denmark* 11 J6
Københavns Amtskommune □, *Denmark* 11 J6
Kōbi-Sho, *Japan* 55 M1
Koblenz, *Germany* 25 E3
Kobo, *Ethiopia* 81 E4
Kobryn, *Belarus* 47 F3
Kobuleti, *Georgia* 49 K5
Kobylin, *Poland* 45 G4
Kobyłka, *Poland* 45 F8
Kobylkino, *Russia* 48 C6
Koca →, *Turkey* 41 F11
Kocabaş, *Turkey* 39 D11
Kocaeli, *Turkey* 41 F13
Kocaeli □, *Turkey* 41 F13
Kočane, *Serbia, Yug.* 40 C5
Kočani, *Macedonia* 40 E6
Koçarlı, *Turkey* 39 D9
Koceljevo, *Serbia, Yug.* 40 B3
Kočevje, *Slovenia* 29 C11
Koch Bihar, *India* 67 F16
Kochang, *S. Korea* 57 G14
Kochas, *India* 69 G10
Kocher →, *Germany* 25 F5
Kōchi, *Japan* 55 H6
Kōchi □, *Japan* 55 H6
Kochiu = Gejiu, *China* 58 F4
Kock, *Poland* 45 G9
Kode, *Sweden* 11 G5
Kodiak, *U.S.A.* 100 C4
Kodiak I., *U.S.A.* 100 C4
Kodinar, *India* 68 J4
Kodori →, *Georgia* 49 J5
Koes, *Namibia* 88 D2
Kofçaz, *Turkey* 41 E11
Koffiefontein, *S. Africa* 88 D4
Kofiau, *Indonesia* 63 E7
Köflach, *Austria* 26 D8
Koforidua, *Ghana* 83 D4
Kōfu, *Japan* 55 G9
Koga, *Japan* 55 F9
Kogaluk →, *Canada* 103 A7
Kogan, *Australia* 95 D5
Køge, *Denmark* 11 J6
Køge Bugt, *Denmark* 11 J6
Kogi □, *Nigeria* 83 D6
Kogin Baba, *Nigeria* 83 D7
Koh-i-Bābā, *Afghan.* 66 B5
Koh-i-Khurd, *Afghan.* 68 C1
Kohat, *Pakistan* 68 C4
Kohima, *India* 67 G19
Kohkīlūyeh va Būyer Aḥmadi □, *Iran* 71 D6
Kohler Ra., *Antarctica* 5 D15
Kohtla-Järve, *Estonia* 9 G22
Koillismaa, *Finland* 8 D23
Koin-dong, *N. Korea* 57 D14
Koinare, *Bulgaria* 41 C8
Kojetín, *Czech Rep.* 27 B10
Kojŏ, *N. Korea* 57 E14
Kojonup, *Australia* 93 F2
Kojūr, *Iran* 71 B6
Koka, *Sudan* 80 C3
Kokand = Qŭqon, *Uzbekistan* 50 E8
Kokanee Glacier Prov. Park, *Canada* 104 D5
Kokas, *Indonesia* 63 E8
Kokava, *Slovak Rep.* 27 C12
Kokchetav = Kökshetaū, *Kazakstan* 50 D7
Kokemäenjoki →, *Finland* 9 F19
Kokhma, *Russia* 48 B5
Kokkola, *Finland* 8 E20
Koko, *Nigeria* 83 C5
Koko Kyunzu, *Burma* 67 M18
Kokolopozo, *Ivory C.* 82 D3
Kokomo, *U.S.A.* 108 E2
Kokoro, *Niger* 83 C5
Koksan, *N. Korea* 57 E14
Kökshetaū, *Kazakstan* 50 D7
Koksoak →, *Canada* 101 C13
Kokstad, *S. Africa* 89 E4
Kokubu, *Japan* 55 J5
Kola, *Indonesia* 63 F8
Kola Pen. = Kolskiy Poluostrov, *Russia* 50 C4
Kolahoi, *India* 69 B6
Kolahun, *Liberia* 82 D2
Kolaka, *Indonesia* 63 E6
Kolar, *India* 66 N11
Kolar Gold Fields, *India* 66 N11
Kolari, *Finland* 8 C20
Kolárovo, *Slovak Rep.* 27 D10
Kolašin, *Montenegro, Yug.* 40 D3
Kolayat, *India* 66 F8
Kolbäck, *Sweden* 10 E10
Kolbäcksån →, *Sweden* 10 E10
Kolbermoor, *Germany* 25 H8
Kolbuszowa, *Poland* 45 H8
Kolchugino = Leninsk-Kuznetskiy, *Russia* 50 D9
Kolchugino, *Russia* 46 D10
Kolda, *Senegal* 82 C2
Kolding, *Denmark* 11 J3
Kolepom = Dolak, Pulau, *Indonesia* 63 F9
Kolguyev, Ostrov, *Russia* 50 C5
Kolhapur, *India* 66 L9
Kolia, *Ivory C.* 82 D3
Kolín, *Czech Rep.* 26 A8
Kolind, *Denmark* 11 H4
Kolkas rags, *Latvia* 9 H20
Kölleda, *Germany* 24 D7
Kollum, *Neths.* 17 A6
Kolmanskop, *Namibia* 88 D2
Köln, *Germany* 24 E2
Kolno, *Poland* 44 E8
Koło, *Poland* 45 F5
Kołobrzeg, *Poland* 44 D2
Kolokani, *Mali* 82 C3
Kolomna, *Russia* 46 E10
Kolomyya, *Ukraine* 47 H3
Kolondiéba, *Mali* 82 C3
Kolonodale, *Indonesia* 63 E6
Kolonowskie, *Poland* 45 H5
Kolosib, *India* 67 G18
Kolpashevo, *Russia* 50 D9
Kolpino, *Russia* 46 C6
Kolpny, *Russia* 47 F9
Kolskiy Poluostrov, *Russia* 50 C4
Kolsva, *Sweden* 10 E9
Kolubara →, *Serbia, Yug.* 40 B4
Koluszki, *Poland* 45 G6
Kolwezi, *Dem. Rep. of the Congo* 87 E2
Kolyma →, *Russia* 51 C17
Kolymskoye Nagorye, *Russia* 51 C16
Kôm Ombo, *Egypt* 80 C3
Komandorskiye Is. = Komandorskiye Ostrova, *Russia* 51 D17
Komandorskiye Ostrova, *Russia* 51 D17
Komárno, *Slovak Rep.* 27 D11
Komárom, *Hungary* 42 C3
Komárom-Esztergom □, *Hungary* 42 C3
Komatipoort, *S. Africa* 89 D5
Komatou Yialou, *Cyprus* 36 D13
Komatsu, *Japan* 55 F8
Komatsujima, *Japan* 55 H7
Kombissiri, *Burkina Faso* 83 C4
Kombori, *Burkina Faso* 82 C4
Kombóti, *Greece* 38 B3
Komen, *Slovenia* 29 C10
Komenda, *Ghana* 83 D4
Komi □, *Russia* 50 C6
Komiža, *Croatia* 29 E13
Komló, *Hungary* 42 D3
Kommunarsk = Alchevsk, *Ukraine* 47 H10
Kommunizma, Pik, *Tajikistan* 50 F8
Komodo, *Indonesia* 63 F5
Komoé, *Ivory C.* 82 D4
Komoran, Pulau, *Indonesia* 63 F9
Komoro, *Japan* 55 F9
Komotini, *Greece* 41 E9
Komovi, *Montenegro, Yug.* 40 D3
Kompasberg, *S. Africa* 88 E3
Kompong Bang, *Cambodia* 65 F5
Kompong Cham, *Cambodia* 65 G5
Kompong Chhnang = Kampang Chhnang, *Cambodia* 65 F5
Kompong Chikreng, *Cambodia* 64 F5
Kompong Kleang, *Cambodia* 64 F5
Kompong Luong, *Cambodia* 65 G5
Kompong Pranak, *Cambodia* 64 F5
Kompong Som = Kampong Saom, *Cambodia* 65 G4
Kompong Som, Chhung = Kampong Saom, Chaak, *Cambodia* 65 G4
Kompong Speu, *Cambodia* 65 G5
Kompong Sralao, *Cambodia* 64 E5
Kompong Thom, *Cambodia* 64 F5
Kompong Trabeck, *Cambodia* 64 F5
Kompong Trabeck, *Cambodia* 65 G5
Kompong Trach, *Cambodia* 65 G5
Kompong Tralach, *Cambodia* 65 G5
Komrat = Comrat, *Moldova* 43 D13
Komsberg, *S. Africa* 88 E3
Komsomolets, Ostrov, *Russia* 51 A10
Komsomolsk, *Amur, Russia* 51 D14
Komsomolsk, *Ivanovo, Russia* 46 D11
Komsomolskiy, *Russia* 48 C7
Kömür Burnu, *Turkey* 39 C8
Kon Tum, *Vietnam* 64 E7
Kon Tum, Plateau du, *Vietnam* 64 E7
Konakovo, *Russia* 46 D9
Konarhá □, *Afghan.* 66 B7
Konārī, *Iran* 71 D6
Konawa, *U.S.A.* 113 H6
Konch, *India* 69 G8
Konde, *Tanzania* 86 C4
Kondiá, *Greece* 39 B7
Kondinin, *Australia* 93 F2
Kondoa, *Tanzania* 86 C4
Kondoa □, *Tanzania* 86 D4
Kondókali, *Greece* 36 A3
Kondopaga, *Russia* 46 A8
Kondratyevo, *Russia* 51 D10
Kondrovo, *Russia* 46 E8
Konduga, *Nigeria* 83 C7
Köneürgench, *Turkmenistan* 50 E6
Konevo, *Russia* 46 A10
Kong, *Ivory C.* 82 D4
Kong → = Khong →, *Cambodia* 64 F5
Kong, Koh, *Cambodia* 65 G4
Kong Christian IX.s Land, *Greenland* 4 C6
Kong Christian X.s Land, *Greenland* 4 B6
Kong Franz Joseph Fd., *Greenland* 4 B6
Kong Frederik IX.s Land, *Greenland* 4 C5
Kong Frederik VI.s Kyst, *Greenland* 4 C5
Kong Frederik VIII.s Land, *Greenland* 4 B6
Kong Oscar Fjord, *Greenland* 4 B6
Kongeå →, *Denmark* 11 J2
Kongerslev, *Denmark* 11 H4
Kongju, *S. Korea* 57 F14
Konglu, *Burma* 67 F20
Kongolo, *Kasai Or., Dem. Rep. of the Congo* 86 D1
Kongolo, *Shaba, Dem. Rep. of the Congo* 86 D2
Kongor, *Sudan* 81 F3
Kongoussi, *Burkina Faso* 83 C4
Kongsberg, *Norway* 9 G13
Kongsvinger, *Norway* 9 F15
Kongwa, *Tanzania* 86 D4
Koni, *Dem. Rep. of the Congo* 87 E2
Koni, Mts., *Dem. Rep. of the Congo* 87 E2
Koniecpol, *Poland* 45 H6
Königs Wusterhausen, *Germany* 24 C9
Königsberg = Kaliningrad, *Russia* 9 J19
Königsbrunn, *Germany* 25 G6
Königslutter, *Germany* 24 C6
Konin, *Poland* 45 F5
Konin □, *Poland* 45 F5
Konispoli, *Albania* 40 G4
Kónitsa, *Greece* 38 A2
Konjic, *Bos.-H.* 42 G2
Konkiep, *Namibia* 88 D2
Konkouré →, *Guinea* 82 D2
Könnern, *Germany* 24 D7
Kono, *S. Leone* 82 D2
Konongo, *Ghana* 83 D4
Konosha, *Russia* 46 B11
Kōnosu, *Japan* 55 F9
Konotop, *Ukraine* 47 G7
Konqi He →, *China* 60 B4
Końskie, *Poland* 45 G7
Konstancin-Jeziorna, *Poland* 45 F8
Konstantinovka = Kostyantynivka, *Ukraine* 47 H9
Konstantinovsk, *Russia* 49 G5
Konstantynów Łódźki, *Poland* 45 G6
Konstanz, *Germany* 25 H5
Kont, *Iran* 71 E9
Kontagora, *Nigeria* 83 C6
Konya, *Turkey* 72 D5
Konya Ovası, *Turkey* 72 C5
Konz, *Germany* 25 F2
Konza, *Kenya* 86 C4
Kookynie, *Australia* 93 E3
Kooline, *Australia* 92 D2
Kooloonong, *Australia* 95 E3
Koolyanobbing, *Australia* 93 F2
Koondrook, *Australia* 95 F3
Koonibba, *Australia* 95 E1
Koorawatha, *Australia* 95 E4
Koorda, *Australia* 93 F2
Kooskia, *U.S.A.* 114 C6
Kootenai →, *Canada* 114 B5
Kootenay L., *Canada* 104 D5
Kootenay Nat. Park, *Canada* 104 C5
Kootjieskolk, *S. Africa* 88 E3
Kopanovka, *Russia* 49 G8
Kopaonik, *Serbia, Yug.* 40 C4
Kópavogur, *Iceland* 8 D3
Koper, *Slovenia* 29 C10
Kopervik, *Norway* 9 G11
Kopi, *Australia* 95 E2
Köping, *Sweden* 10 E10
Köpingsvik, *Sweden* 11 H10
Kopište, *Croatia* 29 F13
Kopliku, *Albania* 40 D3
Köpmanholmen, *Sweden* 10 A12
Kopparberg, *Sweden* 10 E9
Kopparbergs län □, *Sweden* 10 C8
Koppeh Dāgh, *Asia* 71 B8
Koppies, *S. Africa* 89 D4
Koppom, *Sweden* 10 E6
Koprivlen, *Bulgaria* 40 E7
Koprivnica, *Croatia* 29 B13
Kopřivnice, *Czech Rep.* 27 B11
Koprivshtitsa, *Bulgaria* 41 D8
Köprübaşı, *Turkey* 39 C10
Kopychyntsi, *Ukraine* 47 H3
Korab, *Macedonia* 40 E4
Korakiána, *Greece* 36 A3
Korba, *India* 69 H10
Korbach, *Germany* 24 D4
Korbu, G., *Malaysia* 65 K3
Korça, *Albania* 40 F4
Korce = Korça, *Albania* 40 F4
Korčula, *Croatia* 29 F13
Korčulanski Kanal, *Croatia* 29 E13
Kord Kūy, *Iran* 71 B7
Kord Sheykh, *Iran* 71 D7
Kordestān □, *Iran* 70 C5
Kordofân, *Sudan* 79 F11
Korea, North ■, *Asia* 57 E14
Korea, South ■, *Asia* 57 G15
Korea Bay, *Korea* 57 E13
Korea Strait, *Asia* 57 H15
Korenevo, *Russia* 47 G8
Korenovsk, *Russia* 49 H4
Korets, *Ukraine* 47 G4
Korfantów, *Poland* 45 H4
Korgan, *Turkey* 72 B7
Korgus, *Sudan* 80 D3
Korhogo, *Ivory C.* 82 D3
Koribundu, *S. Leone* 82 D2
Korinthía □, *Greece* 38 D4
Korinthiakós Kólpos, *Greece* 38 C4
Kórinthos, *Greece* 38 D4
Korioumé, *Mali* 82 B4
Koríssa, Límni, *Greece* 36 B3
Kōriyama, *Japan* 54 F10
Korkuteli, *Turkey* 39 D12
Kormakiti, C., *Cyprus* 36 D11
Körmend, *Hungary* 42 C1
Kornat, *Croatia* 29 E12
Korneshty = Corneşti, *Moldova* 43 C13
Korneuburg, *Austria* 27 C9
Kórnik, *Poland* 45 F4
Koro, *Fiji* 91 C8
Koro, *Ivory C.* 82 D3
Koro, *Mali* 82 C4
Koro Sea, *Fiji* 91 C9
Korocha, *Russia* 47 G9
Köroğlu Dağları, *Turkey* 72 B5
Korogwe, *Tanzania* 86 D4
Korogwe □, *Tanzania* 86 D4
Koroit, *Australia* 95 F3
Koronadal, *Phil.* 61 H6
Koróni, *Greece* 38 E3
Korónia, Limni, *Greece* 40 F7
Koronís, *Greece* 39 D7
Koronowo, *Poland* 45 E4
Koror, *Pac. Oc.* 63 C8
Körös →, *Hungary* 42 D5
Köröstarcsa, *Hungary* 42 D6
Korosten, *Ukraine* 47 G5
Korostyshev, *Ukraine* 47 G5
Korotoyak, *Russia* 47 G10
Korraraika, Helodranon' i, *Madag.* 89 B7
Korsakov, *Russia* 51 E15
Korsberga, *Sweden* 11 G9
Korshunovo, *Russia* 51 D12
Korsør, *Denmark* 11 J5
Korsun Shevchenkovskiy, *Ukraine* 47 H6
Korsze, *Poland* 44 D8
Korti, *Sudan* 80 D3
Kortrijk, *Belgium* 17 D3
Korucu, *Turkey* 39 B9
Korwai, *India* 68 G8
Koryakskoye Nagorye, *Russia* 51 C18
Koryŏng, *S. Korea* 57 G15
Koryukovka, *Ukraine* 47 G7
Kos, *Greece* 39 E9
Kosa, *Ethiopia* 81 F4
Kosaya Gora, *Russia* 46 E9
Kościan, *Poland* 45 F3
Kościerzyna, *Poland* 44 D4
Kosciusko, *U.S.A.* 113 J10
Kosciusko I., *U.S.A.* 104 B2
Kosciuszko, Mt., *Australia* 95 F4
Kösély →, *Hungary* 42 C6
Kosha, *Sudan* 80 C3
Koshava, *Bulgaria* 40 B7
K'oshih = Kashi, *China* 60 C2
Koshiki-Rettō, *Japan* 55 J4
Kosi, *India* 68 F7
Košice, *Slovak Rep.* 27 C14
Košický □, *Slovak Rep.* 27 C14
Kosjerić, *Serbia, Yug.* 40 B3
Koşk, *Turkey* 39 D10
Koskhinoú, *Greece* 36 C10
Kosŏng, *N. Korea* 57 E15
Kosovo □, *Serbia, Yug.* 40 D4
Kosovska Mitrovica, *Serbia, Yug.* 40 D4
Kossou, L. de, *Ivory C.* 82 D3
Kosta, *Sweden* 11 H9
Kostajnica, *Croatia* 29 C13
Kostanjevica, *Slovenia* 29 C12
Kostenets, *Bulgaria* 40 D7
Koster, *S. Africa* 88 D4

Kôstî, *Sudan* 81 E3
Kostinbrod, *Bulgaria* 40 D7
Kostolac, *Serbia, Yug.* 40 B5
Kostopil, *Ukraine* 47 G4
Kostroma, *Russia* 46 D11
Kostromskoye Vdkhr., *Russia* 46 D11
Kostrzyn, *Gorzow Wlkp., Poland* 45 F1
Kostrzyn, *Poznań, Poland* 45 F4
Kostyantynivka, *Ukraine* 47 H9
Kostyukovichi = Kastsyukovichy, *Belarus* 46 F7
Koszalin, *Poland* 44 D3
Koszalin □, *Poland* 44 E3
Kőszeg, *Hungary* 42 C1
Kot Addu, *Pakistan* 68 D4
Kot Moman, *Pakistan* 68 C5
Kota, *India* 68 G6
Kota Baharu, *Malaysia* 65 J4
Kota Belud, *Malaysia* 62 C5
Kota Kinabalu, *Malaysia* 62 C5
Kota Kubu Baharu, *Malaysia* 65 L3
Kota Tinggi, *Malaysia* 65 M4
Kotaagung, *Indonesia* 62 F2
Kotabaru, *Indonesia* 62 E5
Kotabumi, *Indonesia* 62 E2
Kotamobagu, *Indonesia* 63 D6
Kotaneelee →, *Canada* 104 A4
Kotcho L., *Canada* 104 B4
Kotel, *Bulgaria* 41 D10
Kotelnich, *Russia* 48 A9
Kotelnikovo, *Russia* 49 G6
Kotelnyy, Ostrov, *Russia* 51 B14
Köthen, *Germany* 24 D7
Kothi, *India* 69 G9
Kotiro, *Pakistan* 68 F2
Kotka, *Finland* 9 F22
Kotlas, *Russia* 50 C5
Kotlenska Planina, *Bulgaria* 41 D10
Kotli, *Pakistan* 68 C5
Kotmul, *Pakistan* 69 B6
Kotonkoro, *Nigeria* 83 C6
Kotor, *Montenegro, Yug.* 40 D2
Kotor Varoš, *Bos.-H.* 42 F2
Kotoriba, *Croatia* 29 B13
Kotovo, *Russia* 48 E7
Kotovsk, *Russia* 48 D5
Kotovsk, *Ukraine* 47 J5
Kotputli, *India* 68 F7
Kotri, *Pakistan* 68 G3
Kótronas, *Greece* 38 E4
Kötschach-Mauthen, *Austria* 26 E6
Kottayam, *India* 66 Q10
Kotturu, *India* 66 M10
Kotuy →, *Russia* 51 B11
Kotzebue, *U.S.A.* 100 B3
Koudougou, *Burkina Faso* 82 C4
Koufonísi, *Greece* 36 E8
Koufonísia, *Greece* 39 E7
Kougaberge, *S. Africa* 88 E3
Kouibli, *Ivory C.* 82 D3
Kouilou →, *Congo* 84 E2
Koula Moutou, *Gabon* 84 E2
Koulen = Kulen, *Cambodia* 64 F5
Koulikoro, *Mali* 82 C3
Kouloúra, *Greece* 36 A3
Koúm-bournoú, Ákra, *Greece* 36 C10
Koumala, *Australia* 94 C4
Koumankou, *Mali* 82 C3
Koumbia, *Burkina Faso* 82 C4
Koumbia, *Guinea* 82 C2
Koumboum, *Guinea* 82 C2
Koumpenntoum, *Senegal* 82 C2
Koumra, *Chad* 79 G9
Koundara, *Guinea* 82 C2
Kounradskiy, *Kazakstan* 50 E8
Kountze, *U.S.A.* 113 K7
Koupéla, *Burkina Faso* 83 C4
Kouris →, *Cyprus* 36 E11
Kourou, *Fr. Guiana* 125 B8
Kouroussa, *Guinea* 82 C3
Koussané, *Mali* 82 C2
Kousseri, *Cameroon* 79 F8
Koutiala, *Mali* 82 C3
Kouto, *Ivory C.* 82 D3
Kouvé, *Togo* 83 D5
Kouvola, *Finland* 9 F22
Kovačica, *Serbia, Yug.* 42 E5
Kovel, *Ukraine* 47 G3
Kovin, *Serbia, Yug.* 42 F5
Kovrov, *Russia* 48 B5
Kowal, *Poland* 45 F6
Kowalewo Pomorskie, *Poland* 45 E5
Kowanyama, *Australia* 94 B3
Kowkash, *Canada* 102 B2
Kowloon, *H.K.* 59 F10
Kowŏn, *N. Korea* 57 E14
Köyceğiz, *Turkey* 39 E10
Köyceğiz Gölü, *Turkey* 39 E10
Koyulhisar, *Turkey* 72 B7
Koyunyeri, *Turkey* 41 F10
Koza, *Japan* 55 L3
Kozak, *Turkey* 39 B9
Kozan, *Turkey* 72 D6
Kozáni, *Greece* 40 F5
Kozáni □, *Greece* 40 F5
Kozara, *Bos.-H.* 29 D14
Kozarac, *Bos.-H.* 29 D13
Kozelets, *Ukraine* 47 G6
Kozelsk, *Russia* 46 E8
Kozhikode = Calicut, *India* 66 P9
Koziegłowy, *Poland* 45 H6
Kozienice, *Poland* 45 G8
Kozje, *Slovenia* 29 B12
Kozloduy, *Bulgaria* 40 C7
Kozlovets, *Bulgaria* 41 C9
Kozlovka, *Russia* 48 C9
Kozlu, *Turkey* 72 B4
Kozluk, *Turkey* 73 C9
Koźmin, *Poland* 45 G4
Kozmodemyansk, *Russia* 48 B8
Kożuchów, *Poland* 45 G2
Kozyatyn, *Ukraine* 47 H5
Kpabia, *Ghana* 83 D4
Kpalimé, *Togo* 83 D5
Kpandae, *Ghana* 83 D4
Kpessi, *Togo* 83 D5
Kra, Isthmus of = Kra, Kho Khot, *Thailand* 65 G2
Kra, Kho Khot, *Thailand* 65 G2
Kra Buri, *Thailand* 65 G2
Krabi, *Thailand* 65 H2
Kracheh, *Cambodia* 64 F6
Kragan, *Indonesia* 63 G14
Kragerø, *Norway* 9 G13
Kragujevac, *Serbia, Yug.* 40 B4
Krajenka, *Poland* 45 E3
Krajina, *Bos.-H.* 29 D13
Krakatau = Rakata, Pulau, *Indonesia* 62 F3
Krakor, *Cambodia* 64 F5
Kraków, *Poland* 45 H6
Kraków □, *Poland* 45 H6
Kralanh, *Cambodia* 64 F4
Králíky, *Czech Rep.* 27 A9
Kraljevo, *Serbia, Yug.* 40 C4
Královský Chlmec, *Slovak Rep.* 27 C14
Kralupy nad Vltavou, *Czech Rep.* 26 A7
Kramatorsk, *Ukraine* 47 H9
Kramfors, *Sweden* 10 B11
Kraniá, *Greece* 40 G5
Kranía Elassónas, *Greece* 38 B4
Kranídhion, *Greece* 38 D5
Kranj, *Slovenia* 29 B11
Kranjska Gora, *Slovenia* 29 B10
Kranskop, *S. Africa* 89 D5
Krapina, *Croatia* 29 B12
Krapina →, *Croatia* 29 C12
Krapkowice, *Poland* 45 H4
Kras, *Croatia* 29 C10
Kraskino, *Russia* 54 C5
Krāslava, *Latvia* 46 E4
Kraslice, *Czech Rep.* 26 A5
Krasnaya Gorbatka, *Russia* 48 C5
Krasnaya Polyana, *Russia* 49 J5
Kraśnik, *Poland* 45 H9
Krasnoarmeisk, *Ukraine* 47 H9
Krasnoarmeysk, *Russia* 48 E7
Krasnoarmeyskiy, *Russia* 49 G6
Krasnobrod, *Poland* 45 H10
Krasnodar, *Russia* 49 H4
Krasnodon, *Ukraine* 47 H10
Krasnogorskiy, *Russia* 48 B9
Krasnograd = Krasnohrad, *Ukraine* 47 H8
Krasnogvardeyskoye, *Russia* 49 H5
Krasnogvardyesk, *Ukraine* 47 K8
Krasnohrad, *Ukraine* 47 H8
Krasnokutsk, *Ukraine* 47 G8
Krasnolesnyy, *Russia* 47 G10
Krasnoperekopsk, *Ukraine* 47 J7
Krasnorechenskiy, *Russia* 54 B7
Krasnoselkup, *Russia* 50 C9
Krasnoslobodsk, *Mordvinia, Russia* 48 C6
Krasnoslobodsk, *Volgograd, Russia* 49 F7
Krasnoturinsk, *Russia* 50 D7
Krasnovodsk = Türkmenbashi, *Turkmenistan* 50 F6
Krasnoyarsk, *Russia* 51 D10
Krasnoye = Krasnyy, *Russia* 46 E6
Krasnozavodsk, *Russia* 46 D10
Krasny Sulin, *Russia* 47 J11
Krasnystaw, *Poland* 45 H10
Krasnyy, *Russia* 46 E6
Krasnyy Kholm, *Russia* 46 C9
Krasnyy Kut, *Russia* 48 E8
Krasnyy Liman, *Ukraine* 47 H9
Krasnyy Luch, *Ukraine* 47 H10
Krasnyy Profintern, *Russia* 46 D11
Krasnyy Yar, *Astrakhan, Russia* 49 G9
Krasnyy Yar, *Samara, Russia* 48 D10
Krasnyy Yar, *Volgograd, Russia* 48 E7
Krasnyye Baki, *Russia* 48 B7
Krasnyyoskolske Vdskh., *Ukraine* 47 H9
Kraszna →, *Hungary* 42 B7
Kratie = Kracheh, *Cambodia* 64 F6
Kratovo, *Macedonia* 40 D6
Krau, *Indonesia* 63 E10
Kravanh, Chuor Phnum, *Cambodia* 65 G4
Krefeld, *Germany* 24 D2
Krémaston, Límni, *Greece* 38 C3
Kremen, *Croatia* 29 D12
Kremenchug = Kremenchuk, *Ukraine* 47 H7
Kremenchuk, *Ukraine* 47 H7
Kremenchuksk Vdskh., *Ukraine* 47 H7
Kremenets, *Ukraine* 47 G3
Kremennaya, *Ukraine* 47 H10
Kremges = Svitlovodsk, *Ukraine* 47 H7
Kremmen, *Germany* 24 C9
Kremmling, *U.S.A.* 114 F10
Kremnica, *Slovak Rep.* 27 C11
Krems, *Austria* 26 C8
Kremsmünster, *Austria* 26 C7
Kretinga, *Lithuania* 9 J19
Krettsy, *Russia* 46 C7
Kreuzberg, *Germany* 25 E5
Kreuztal, *Germany* 24 E4
Kría Vrísi, *Greece* 40 F6
Kribi, *Cameroon* 83 E6
Krichem, *Bulgaria* 41 D8
Krichev = Krychaw, *Belarus* 46 F6
Krim, *Slovenia* 29 C11
Kriós, Ákra, *Greece* 36 D5
Krishna →, *India* 67 M12
Krishnanagar, *India* 69 H13
Kristdala, *Sweden* 11 G10
Kristiansand, *Norway* 9 G13
Kristianstad, *Sweden* 11 H8
Kristianstads län □, *Sweden* 11 H7
Kristiansund, *Norway* 8 E12
Kristiinankaupunki, *Finland* 9 E19
Kristinehamn, *Sweden* 10 E8
Kristinestad = Kristiinankaupunki, *Finland* 9 E19
Kríti, *Greece* 36 D7
Kritsá, *Greece* 36 D7
Kriva →, *Macedonia* 40 D5
Kriva Palanka, *Macedonia* 40 D6
Krivaja →, *Bos.-H.* 42 F3
Krivelj, *Serbia, Yug.* 40 B6
Krivoy Rog = Kryvyy Rih, *Ukraine* 47 J7
Križevci, *Croatia* 29 B13
Krk, *Croatia* 29 C11
Krka →, *Slovenia* 29 C12
Krkonoše, *Czech Rep.* 26 A8
Krnov, *Czech Rep.* 27 A10
Krobia, *Poland* 45 G3
Krokeaí, *Greece* 38 E4
Krokek, *Sweden* 11 F10
Krokodil →, *Mozam.* 89 D5
Krokom, *Sweden* 10 A8
Krokowa, *Poland* 44 D5
Krolevets, *Ukraine* 47 G7
Kroměříž, *Czech Rep.* 27 B10
Krompachy, *Slovak Rep.* 27 C13
Kromy, *Russia* 47 F8
Kronach, *Germany* 25 E7
Kronobergs län □, *Sweden* 11 H8
Kronprins Olav Kyst, *Antarctica* 5 C5
Kronshtadt, *Russia* 46 C5
Kroonstad, *S. Africa* 88 D4
Kröpelin, *Germany* 24 A7
Kropotkin, *Russia* 49 H5
Kropp, *Germany* 24 A5
Krosna, *Lithuania* 44 D10
Krośniewice, *Poland* 45 F6
Krosno, *Poland* 45 J8
Krosno □, *Poland* 45 J9
Krosno Odrzańskie, *Poland* 45 F2
Krotoszyn, *Poland* 45 G4
Krotovka, *Russia* 48 D10
Kroussón, *Greece* 36 D6
Krraba, *Albania* 40 E3
Krško, *Slovenia* 29 C12
Krstača, *Serbia, Yug.* 40 D4
Kruger Nat. Park, *S. Africa* 89 C5
Krugersdorp, *S. Africa* 89 D4
Kruisfontein, *S. Africa* 88 E3
Kruja, *Albania* 40 E3
Krulevshchina = Krulyewshchyna, *Belarus* 46 E4
Krulyewshchyna, *Belarus* 46 E4
Kruma, *Albania* 40 D4
Krumbach, *Germany* 25 G6
Krumovgrad, *Bulgaria* 41 E9
Krung Thep = Bangkok, *Thailand* 64 F3
Krupanj, *Serbia, Yug.* 40 B3
Krupina, *Slovak Rep.* 27 C12
Krupinica →, *Slovak Rep.* 27 C11
Krupki, *Belarus* 46 E5
Kruševac, *Serbia, Yug.* 40 C5
Kruševo, *Macedonia* 40 E5
Kruszwica, *Poland* 45 F5
Kruzof I., *U.S.A.* 104 B1
Krychaw, *Belarus* 46 F6
Krymsk, *Russia* 47 K10
Krymskiy Poluostrov = Krymskyy Pivostriv, *Ukraine* 47 K8
Krymskyy Pivostriv, *Ukraine* 47 K8
Krynica, *Poland* 45 J7
Krynica Morska, *Poland* 44 D6
Krynki, *Poland* 45 E10
Kryvyy Rih, *Ukraine* 47 J7
Krzepice, *Poland* 45 H5
Krzeszów, *Poland* 45 H9
Krzna →, *Poland* 45 F10
Krzywiń, *Poland* 45 G3
Krzyż Wielkopolski, *Poland* 45 F2
Ksar el Kebir, *Morocco* 78 B4
Ksar es Souk = Ar Rachidiya, *Morocco* 78 B5
Ksiąz Wielkopolski, *Poland* 45 F4
Kstovo, *Russia* 48 B7
Kuala Berang, *Malaysia* 65 K4
Kuala Dungun = Dungun, *Malaysia* 65 K4
Kuala Kangsar, *Malaysia* 65 K3
Kuala Kelawang, *Malaysia* 65 L4
Kuala Kerai, *Malaysia* 65 K4
Kuala Lipis, *Malaysia* 65 K4
Kuala Lumpur, *Malaysia* 65 L3
Kuala Nerang, *Malaysia* 65 J3
Kuala Pilah, *Malaysia* 65 L4
Kuala Rompin, *Malaysia* 65 L4
Kuala Selangor, *Malaysia* 65 L3
Kuala Sepetang, *Malaysia* 65 K3
Kuala Terengganu, *Malaysia* 65 K4
Kualajelai, *Indonesia* 62 E4
Kualakapuas, *Indonesia* 62 E4
Kualakurun, *Indonesia* 62 E4
Kualapembuang, *Indonesia* 62 E4
Kualasimpang, *Indonesia* 62 D1
Kuancheng, *China* 57 D10
Kuandang, *Indonesia* 63 D6
Kuandian, *China* 57 D13
Kuangchou = Guangzhou, *China* 59 F9
Kuantan, *Malaysia* 65 L4
Kuba = Quba, *Azerbaijan* 49 K9
Kuban →, *Russia* 47 K9
Kubenskoye, Ozero, *Russia* 46 C10
Kubokawa, *Japan* 55 H6
Kubrat, *Bulgaria* 41 C10
Kučevo, *Serbia, Yug.* 40 B5
Kucha Gompa, *India* 69 B7
Kuchaman, *India* 68 F6
Kuchenspitze, *Austria* 26 D3
Kuching, *Malaysia* 62 D4
Kuchino-eruba-Jima, *Japan* 55 J5
Kuchino-Shima, *Japan* 55 K4
Kuchinotsu, *Japan* 55 H5
Kuchl, *Austria* 26 D6
Kucing = Kuching, *Malaysia* 62 D4
Kuçovë, *Albania* 40 F3
Küçükbahçe, *Turkey* 39 C8
Küçükköy, *Turkey* 39 B8
Küçükkuyu, *Turkey* 39 B8
Küçükmenderes →, *Turkey* 39 D9
Kud →, *Pakistan* 68 F2
Kuda, *India* 66 H7
Kudat, *Malaysia* 62 C5
Kudirkos Naumiestis, *Lithuania* 44 D9
Kudowa-Zdrój, *Poland* 45 H3
Kudus, *Indonesia* 63 G14
Kudymkar, *Russia* 50 D6
Kueiyang = Guiyang, *China* 58 D6
Kufra Oasis = Al Kufrah, *Libya* 79 D10
Kufstein, *Austria* 26 D5
Kugluktuk, *Canada* 100 B8
Kugong I., *Canada* 102 A4
Kūh-e-Hazārān, *Iran* 71 D8
Kūhak, *Iran* 66 F3
Kūhbonān, *Iran* 71 D8
Kūhestak, *Iran* 71 E8
Kūhīn, *Iran* 71 C6
Kūhīrī, *Iran* 71 E9
Kuhnsdorf, *Austria* 26 E7
Kūhpāyeh, *Eşfahan, Iran* 71 C7
Kūhpāyeh, *Kermān, Iran* 71 D8
Kui Buri, *Thailand* 65 F2
Kuito, *Angola* 85 G3
Kujang, *N. Korea* 57 E14
Kuji, *Japan* 54 D10
Kujū-San, *Japan* 55 H5
Kukavica, *Serbia, Yug.* 40 D5
Kukawa, *Nigeria* 83 C7
Kukerin, *Australia* 93 F2
Kukësi, *Albania* 40 D4
Kukmor, *Russia* 48 B10
Kukup, *Malaysia* 65 M4
Kukvidze, *Russia* 48 E6
Kula, *Bulgaria* 40 C6
Kula, *Serbia, Yug.* 42 E4
Kula, *Turkey* 39 C10
Kulai, *Malaysia* 65 M4
Kulal, Mt., *Kenya* 86 B4
Kulaly, Ostrov, *Kazakstan* 49 H10
Kulasekarappattinam, *India* 66 Q11
Kulautuva, *Lithuania* 44 D10
Kuldīga, *Latvia* 9 H19
Kuldīga □, *Latvia* 44 B8
Kuldja = Yining, *China* 60 B3
Kuldu, *Sudan* 81 E2
Kulebaki, *Russia* 48 C6
Kulen, *Cambodia* 64 F5
Kulen Vakuf, *Bos.-H.* 29 D13
Kulgam, *India* 69 C6
Kulim, *Malaysia* 65 K3
Kulin, *Australia* 93 F2
Kulja, *Australia* 93 F2
Kullen, *Sweden* 11 H6
Kulm, *U.S.A.* 112 B5
Kulmbach, *Germany* 25 E7
Külob, *Tajikistan* 50 F7
Kulp, *Turkey* 73 C9
Kulsary, *Kazakstan* 50 E6
Kulti, *India* 69 H12
Kulu, *Turkey* 72 C5
Kulumbura, *Australia* 92 B4
Kulunda, *Russia* 50 D8
Kulungar, *Afghan.* 68 C3
Külvand, *Iran* 71 D7
Kulwin, *Australia* 95 F3
Kulyab = Külob, *Tajikistan* 50 F7
Kuma →, *Russia* 49 H8
Kumafşarı, *Turkey* 39 D11
Kumaganum, *Nigeria* 83 C7
Kumagaya, *Japan* 55 F9
Kumai, *Indonesia* 62 E4
Kumalar Dağı, *Turkey* 39 C12
Kumamba, Kepulauan, *Indonesia* 63 E9
Kumamoto, *Japan* 55 H5
Kumamoto □, *Japan* 55 H5
Kumanovo, *Macedonia* 40 D5
Kumara, *N.Z.* 91 K3
Kumarl, *Australia* 93 F3
Kumasi, *Ghana* 82 D4
Kumayri = Gyumri, *Armenia* 49 K6
Kumba, *Cameroon* 83 E6
Kumbağ, *Turkey* 41 F11
Kumbakonam, *India* 66 P11
Kumbarilla, *Australia* 95 D5
Kumbo, *Cameroon* 83 D7
Kŭmchŏn, *N. Korea* 57 E14
Kumdok, *India* 69 C8
Kume-Shima, *Japan* 55 L3
Kumeny, *Russia* 48 A9
Kŭmhwa, *S. Korea* 57 E14
Kumi, *Uganda* 86 B3
Kumkale, *Turkey* 41 G10
Kumla, *Sweden* 10 E9
Kumluca, *Turkey* 39 E12
Kummerower See, *Germany* 24 B8
Kumo, *Nigeria* 83 C7
Kumon Bum, *Burma* 67 F20
Kumylzhenskaya, *Russia* 48 F6
Kunágota, *Hungary* 42 D6
Kunama, *Australia* 95 F4
Kunashir, Ostrov, *Russia* 51 E15
Kunda, *Estonia* 9 G22
Kundla, *India* 68 J4
Kungala, *Australia* 95 D5
Kungälv, *Sweden* 11 G5
Kunghit I., *Canada* 104 C2
Kungrad = Qŭnghirot, *Uzbekistan* 50 E6
Kungsängen, *Sweden* 10 E11
Kungsbacka, *Sweden* 11 G6
Kungsgården, *Sweden* 10 D10
Kungshamn, *Sweden* 11 F5
Kungsör, *Sweden* 10 E10
Kungur, *Russia* 50 D6
Kungurri, *Australia* 94 C4
Kunhar →, *Pakistan* 69 B5
Kunhegyes, *Hungary* 42 C5
Kuningan, *Indonesia* 63 G13
Kunlong, *Burma* 67 H21
Kunlun Shan, *Asia* 60 C3
Kunmadaras, *Hungary* 42 C5
Kunming, *China* 58 E4
Kunów, *Poland* 45 H8
Kunsan, *S. Korea* 57 G14
Kunshan, *China* 59 B13
Kunszentmárton, *Hungary* 42 D5
Kunszentmiklós, *Hungary* 42 C4
Kununurra, *Australia* 92 C4
Kunwarara, *Australia* 94 C5
Kunya-Urgench = Köneürgench, *Turkmenistan* 50 E6
Künzelsau, *Germany* 25 F5
Kuopio, *Finland* 8 E22
Kupa →, *Croatia* 29 C13
Kupang, *Indonesia* 63 F6
Kupres, *Bos.-H.* 42 G2
Kupyansk, *Ukraine* 47 H9
Kupyansk-Uzlovoi, *Ukraine* 47 H9
Kuqa, *China* 60 B3
Kür →, *Azerbaijan* 73 C13
Kura = Kür →, *Azerbaijan* 73 C13
Kuranda, *Australia* 94 B4
Kurashiki, *Japan* 55 G6
Kurayoshi, *Japan* 55 G6
Kürdämir, *Azerbaijan* 49 K9
Kurdistan, *Asia* 73 D10
Kŭrdzhali, *Bulgaria* 41 E9
Kure, *Japan* 55 G6
Küre, *Turkey* 72 B5
Küre Dağları, *Turkey* 72 B6
Kuressaare, *Estonia* 9 G20
Kurgan, *Russia* 50 D7
Kurganinsk, *Russia* 49 H5
Kurgannaya = Kurganinsk, *Russia* 49 H5
Kuria Maria Is. = Khurīyā Murīyā, Jazā 'ir, *Oman* 74 D6
Kuridala, *Australia* 94 C3
Kurigram, *Bangla.* 67 G16
Kurikka, *Finland* 9 E20
Kuril Is. = Kurilskiye Ostrova, *Russia* 51 E16
Kuril Trench, *Pac. Oc.* 96 C7
Kurilsk, *Russia* 51 E15
Kurilskiye Ostrova, *Russia* 51 E16
Kurino, *Japan* 55 J5
Kurinskaya Kosa, *Azerbaijan* 73 C13
Kurkur, *Egypt* 80 C3
Kurlovskiy, *Russia* 48 C5
Kurmuk, *Sudan* 81 E3
Kurnool, *India* 66 M11
Kuro-Shima, *Kagoshima, Japan* 55 J4
Kuro-Shima, *Okinawa, Japan* 55 M2
Kurow, *N.Z.* 91 L3

Kurów, *Poland* 45 **G9**
Kurrajong, *Australia* 95 **E5**
Kurram →, *Pakistan* 68 **C4**
Kurri Kurri, *Australia* 95 **E5**
Kursavka, *Russia* 49 **H6**
Kuršėnai, *Lithuania* 44 **B9**
Kurshskiy Zaliv, *Russia* 9 **J19**
Kursk, *Russia* 47 **G9**
Kuršumlija, *Serbia, Yug.* 40 **C5**
Kuršumlijska Banja, *Serbia, Yug.* 40 **C5**
Kurşunlu, *Bursa, Turkey* 41 **F13**
Kurşunlu, *Çankırı, Turkey* 72 **B5**
Kurtalan, *Turkey* 73 **D9**
Kurtbey, *Turkey* 41 **E10**
Kuru, Bahr el →, *Sudan* 81 **F2**
Kurucaşile, *Turkey* 72 **B5**
Kuruktag, *China* 60 **B3**
Kuruman, *S. Africa* 88 **D3**
Kuruman →, *S. Africa* 88 **D3**
Kurume, *Japan* 55 **H5**
Kurunegala, *Sri Lanka* 66 **R12**
Kus Gölü, *Turkey* 41 **F11**
Kuşadası, *Turkey* 72 **D2**
Kuşadası Körfezı, *Turkey* 39 **D8**
Kusatsu, *Japan* 55 **F9**
Kusawa L., *Canada* 104 **A1**
Kusel, *Germany* 25 **F3**
Kushchevskaya, *Russia* 49 **G4**
Kushikino, *Japan* 55 **J5**
Kushima, *Japan* 55 **J5**
Kushimoto, *Japan* 55 **H7**
Kushiro, *Japan* 54 **C12**
Kushiro →, *Japan* 54 **C12**
Kūshk, *Iran* 71 **D8**
Kushka = Gushgy, *Turkmenistan* 50 **F7**
Kūshkī, *Īlām, Iran* 70 **C5**
Kūshkī, *Khorāsān, Iran* 71 **B8**
Kūshkū, *Iran* 71 **E7**
Kushol, *India* 69 **C7**
Kushtia, *Bangla.* 67 **H16**
Kushum →, *Kazakstan* 48 **F10**
Kuskokwim B., *U.S.A.* 100 **C3**
Kussharo-Ko, *Japan* 54 **C12**
Kustanay = Qostanay, *Kazakstan* 50 **D7**
Kut, Ko, *Thailand* 65 **G4**
Kütahya, *Turkey* 39 **B12**
Kütahya □, *Turkey* 39 **B11**
Kutaisi, *Georgia* 49 **J6**
Kutaraja = Banda Aceh, *Indonesia* 62 **C1**
Kutch, Gulf of = Kachchh, Gulf of, *India* 68 **H3**
Kutch, Rann of = Kachchh, Rann of, *India* 68 **H4**
Kutina, *Croatia* 29 **C13**
Kutiyana, *India* 68 **J4**
Kutjevo, *Croatia* 42 **E2**
Kutkashen, *Azerbaijan* 49 **K8**
Kutná Hora, *Czech Rep.* 26 **B8**
Kutno, *Poland* 45 **F6**
Kuttabul, *Australia* 94 **C4**
Kutu, *Dem. Rep. of the Congo* 84 **E3**
Kutum, *Sudan* 81 **E1**
Kúty, *Slovak Rep.* 27 **C10**
Kuujjuaq, *Canada* 101 **C13**
Kuŭp-tong, *N. Korea* 57 **D14**
Kuusamo, *Finland* 8 **D23**
Kuusankoski, *Finland* 9 **F22**
Kuvshinovo, *Russia* 46 **D8**
Kuwait = Al Kuwayt, *Kuwait* 70 **D5**
Kuwait ■, *Asia* 70 **D5**
Kuwana, *Japan* 55 **G8**
Kuybyshev = Samara, *Russia* 48 **D10**
Kuybyshev, *Russia* 50 **D8**
Kuybyshevo, *Ukraine* 47 **J9**
Kuybyshevskoye Vdkhr., *Russia* 48 **C9**
Kuye He →, *China* 56 **E6**
Kūyeh, *Iran* 70 **B5**
Kūysanjaq, *Iraq* 70 **B5**
Kuyucak, *Turkey* 39 **D10**
Kuyumba, *Russia* 51 **C10**
Kuzey Anadolu Dağları, *Turkey* 72 **B7**
Kuzmin, *Serbia, Yug.* 42 **E4**
Kuznetsk, *Russia* 48 **D8**
Kvænangen, *Norway* 8 **A19**
Kværndrup, *Denmark* 11 **J4**
Kvaløy, *Norway* 8 **B18**
Kvänum, *Sweden* 11 **F7**
Kvareli = Qvareli, *Georgia* 49 **K7**
Kvarner, *Croatia* 29 **D11**
Kvarnerič, *Croatia* 29 **D11**
Kvicksund, *Sweden* 10 **E10**
Kvillsfors, *Sweden* 11 **G9**
Kvismare kanal, *Sweden* 10 **E9**
Kvissleby, *Sweden* 10 **B11**
Kwabhaca, *S. Africa* 89 **E4**
Kwadacha →, *Canada* 104 **B3**
Kwakhanai, *Botswana* 88 **C3**
Kwakoegron, *Surinam* 125 **B7**
Kwale, *Kenya* 86 **C4**
Kwale, *Nigeria* 83 **D6**
Kwale □, *Kenya* 86 **C4**
KwaMashu, *S. Africa* 89 **D5**
Kwando →, *Africa* 88 **B3**
Kwangdaeri, *N. Korea* 57 **D14**
Kwangju, *S. Korea* 57 **G14**
Kwango →, *Dem. Rep. of the Congo* 77 **G5**
Kwangsi-Chuang = Guangxi Zhuangzu Zizhiqu □, *China* 58 **F7**
Kwangtung = Guangdong □, *China* 59 **F9**
Kwara □, *Nigeria* 83 **D6**
Kwataboahegan →, *Canada* 102 **B3**
Kwatisore, *Indonesia* 63 **E8**
KwaZulu Natal □, *S. Africa* 89 **D5**
Kweichow = Guizhou □, *China* 58 **D6**
Kwekwe, *Zimbabwe* 87 **F2**
Kwidzyn, *Poland* 44 **E5**
Kwimba □, *Tanzania* 86 **C3**
Kwinana New Town, *Australia* 93 **F2**
Kwisa →, *Poland* 45 **G2**
Kwoka, *Indonesia* 63 **E8**
Kyabra Cr. →, *Australia* 95 **D3**
Kyabram, *Australia* 95 **F4**
Kyaikto, *Burma* 64 **D1**
Kyakhta, *Russia* 51 **D11**
Kyancutta, *Australia* 95 **E2**
Kyangin, *Burma* 67 **K19**
Kyaukpadaung, *Burma* 67 **J19**
Kyaukpyu, *Burma* 67 **K18**
Kyaukse, *Burma* 67 **J20**
Kybartai, *Lithuania* 44 **D9**
Kyburz, *U.S.A.* 116 **G6**
Kyenjojo, *Uganda* 86 **B3**
Kyjov, *Czech Rep.* 27 **B10**
Kyle Dam, *Zimbabwe* 87 **G3**
Kyle of Lochalsh, *U.K.* 14 **D3**
Kyll →, *Germany* 25 **F2**
Kyllburg, *Germany* 25 **E2**
Kymijoki →, *Finland* 9 **F22**
Kyneton, *Australia* 95 **F3**
Kynuna, *Australia* 94 **C3**
Kyō-ga-Saki, *Japan* 55 **G7**
Kyoga, L., *Uganda* 86 **B3**
Kyogle, *Australia* 95 **D5**
Kyongju, *S. Korea* 57 **G15**
Kyongpyaw, *Burma* 67 **L19**
Kyŏngsŏng, *N. Korea* 57 **D15**
Kyōto, *Japan* 55 **G7**
Kyōto □, *Japan* 55 **G7**
Kyparissovouno, *Cyprus* 36 **D12**
Kyperounda, *Cyprus* 36 **E11**
Kyrenia, *Cyprus* 36 **D12**
Kyrgyzstan ■, *Asia* 50 **E8**
Kyritz, *Germany* 24 **C8**
Kyrkhult, *Sweden* 11 **H8**
Kyrönjoki →, *Finland* 8 **E19**
Kystatyam, *Russia* 51 **C13**
Kysucké Nové Mesto, *Slovak Rep.* 27 **B11**
Kythréa, *Cyprus* 36 **D12**
Kyunhla, *Burma* 67 **H19**
Kyuquot, *Canada* 104 **C3**
Kyurdamir = Kürdämir, *Azerbaijan* 49 **K9**
Kyūshū, *Japan* 55 **H5**
Kyūshū □, *Japan* 55 **H5**
Kyūshū-Sanchi, *Japan* 55 **H5**
Kyustendil, *Bulgaria* 40 **D6**
Kyusyur, *Russia* 51 **B13**
Kywong, *Australia* 95 **E4**
Kyyiv, *Ukraine* 47 **G6**
Kyyivske Vdskh., *Ukraine* 47 **G6**
Kyzyl, *Russia* 51 **D10**
Kyzyl Kum, *Uzbekistan* 50 **E7**
Kyzyl-Kyya, *Kyrgyzstan* 50 **E8**
Kzyl-Orda = Qyzylorda, *Kazakstan* 50 **E7**

L

La Albuera, *Spain* 35 **G4**
La Alcarria, *Spain* 32 **E2**
La Almarcha, *Spain* 32 **F2**
La Almunia de Doña Godina, *Spain* 32 **D3**
La Asunción, *Venezuela* 124 **A6**
La Banda, *Argentina* 126 **B3**
La Bañeza, *Spain* 34 **C5**
La Barca, *Mexico* 118 **C4**
La Barge, *U.S.A.* 114 **E8**
La Bastide-Puylaurent, *France* 20 **D7**
La Baule-Escoubiac, *France* 18 **E4**
La Belle, *U.S.A.* 109 **M5**
La Biche →, *Canada* 104 **B4**
La Bisbal d'Empordà, *Spain* 32 **D8**
La Bomba, *Mexico* 118 **A1**
La Bresse, *France* 19 **D13**
La Bureba, *Spain* 34 **C7**
La Calera, *Chile* 126 **C1**
La Campiña, *Spain* 35 **H6**
La Canal = Sa Canal, *Spain* 37 **C7**
La Cañiza = A Cañiza, *Spain* 34 **C2**
La Canourgue, *France* 20 **D7**
La Capelle, *France* 19 **C10**
La Carlota, *Argentina* 126 **C3**
La Carlota, *Phil.* 61 **F5**
La Carlota, *Spain* 35 **H6**
La Carolina, *Spain* 35 **G7**
La Cavalerie, *France* 20 **D7**
La Ceiba, *Honduras* 120 **C2**
La Chaise-Dieu, *France* 20 **C7**
La Chapelle d'Angillon, *France* 19 **E9**
La Chapelle-St-Luc, *France* 19 **D11**
La Chapelle-sur-Erdre, *France* 18 **E5**
La Charité-sur-Loire, *France* 19 **E10**
La Chartre-sur-le-Loir, *France* 18 **E7**
La Châtaigneraie, *France* 20 **B3**
La Châtre, *France* 19 **F9**
La Chaux-de-Fonds, *Switz.* 25 **H2**
La Ciotat, *France* 21 **E9**
La Clayette, *France* 19 **F11**
La Cocha, *Argentina* 126 **B2**
La Concepción = Ri-Aba, *Eq. Guin.* 83 **E6**
La Concordia, *Mexico* 119 **D6**
La Conner, *U.S.A.* 114 **B2**
La Coruña = A Coruña, *Spain* 34 **B2**
La Coruña □, *Spain* 34 **B2**
La Côte-St-André, *France* 21 **C9**
La Courtine-le-Trucq, *France* 20 **C6**
La Crau, *Bouches-du-Rhône, France* 21 **E8**
La Crau, *Var, France* 21 **E10**
La Crete, *Canada* 104 **B5**
La Crosse, *Kans., U.S.A.* 112 **F5**
La Crosse, *Wis., U.S.A.* 112 **D9**
La Cruz, *Costa Rica* 120 **D2**
La Cruz, *Mexico* 118 **C3**
La Escondida, *Mexico* 118 **C5**
La Esmeralda, *Paraguay* 126 **A3**
La Esperanza, *Cuba* 120 **B3**
La Esperanza, *Honduras* 120 **D2**
La Estrada = A Estrada, *Spain* 34 **C2**
La Faouët, *France* 18 **D3**
La Fayette, *U.S.A.* 109 **H3**
La Fé, *Cuba* 120 **B3**
La Fère, *France* 19 **C10**
La Ferté-Bernard, *France* 18 **D7**
La Ferté-Gaucher, *France* 19 **D10**
La Ferté-Macé, *France* 18 **D6**
La Ferté-St-Aubin, *France* 19 **E8**
La Ferté-sous-Jouarre, *France* 19 **D10**
La Ferté-Vidame, *France* 18 **D7**
La Flèche, *France* 18 **E6**
La Follette, *U.S.A.* 109 **G3**
La Fregeneda, *Spain* 34 **E4**
La Fuente de San Esteban, *Spain* 34 **E4**
La Gacilly, *France* 18 **E4**
La Gineta, *Spain* 33 **F2**
La Grand-Combe, *France* 21 **D8**
La Grande, *U.S.A.* 114 **D4**
La Grande-Motte, *France* 21 **E8**
La Grange, *Calif., U.S.A.* 116 **H6**
La Grange, *Ga., U.S.A.* 109 **J3**
La Grange, *Ky., U.S.A.* 108 **F3**
La Grange, *Tex., U.S.A.* 113 **L6**
La Grave, *France* 21 **C10**
La Guaira, *Venezuela* 124 **A5**
La Guardia = A Guarda, *Spain* 34 **D2**
La Gudiña = A Gudiña, *Spain* 34 **C3**
La Guerche-de-Bretagne, *France* 18 **E5**
La Guerche-sur-l'Aubois, *France* 19 **F9**
La Habana, *Cuba* 120 **B3**
La Harpe, *U.S.A.* 112 **E9**
La Haye-du-Puits, *France* 18 **C5**
La Horra, *Spain* 34 **D7**
La Independencia, *Mexico* 119 **D6**
La Isabela, *Dom. Rep.* 121 **C5**
La Jara, *U.S.A.* 115 **H11**
La Jonquera, *Spain* 32 **C7**
La Junta, *U.S.A.* 113 **F3**
La Laguna, *Canary Is.* 37 **F3**
La Libertad, *Guatemala* 120 **C1**
La Libertad, *Mexico* 118 **B2**
La Ligua, *Chile* 126 **C1**
La Línea de la Concepción, *Spain* 35 **J5**
La Loche, *Canada* 105 **B7**
La Londe-les-Maures, *France* 21 **E10**
La Lora, *Spain* 34 **C7**
La Loupe, *France* 18 **D8**
La Louvière, *Belgium* 17 **D4**
La Machine, *France* 19 **F10**
La Maddalena, *Italy* 30 **A2**
La Malbaie, *Canada* 103 **C5**
La Mancha, *Spain* 33 **F2**
La Mariña, *Spain* 34 **B3**
La Mesa, *Calif., U.S.A.* 117 **N9**
La Mesa, *N. Mex., U.S.A.* 115 **K10**
La Misión, *Mexico* 118 **A1**
La Motte-Achard, *France* 18 **F5**
La Motte, *France* 21 **D10**
La Motte-Chalançon, *France* 21 **D9**
La Motte-Servolex, *France* 21 **C9**
La Moure, *U.S.A.* 112 **B5**
La Muela, *Spain* 32 **D3**
La Mure, *France* 21 **D9**
La Negra, *Chile* 126 **A1**
La Oliva, *Canary Is.* 37 **F6**
La Orotava, *Canary Is.* 37 **F3**
La Oroya, *Peru* 124
La Pacaudière, *France* 19 **F10**
La Palma, *Canary Is.* 37 **F2**
La Palma, *Panama* 120 **E4**
La Palma del Condado, *Spain* 35 **H4**
La Paloma, *Chile* 126 **C1**
La Pampa □, *Argentina* 126 **D2**
La Paragua, *Venezuela* 124 **B6**
La Paz, *Entre Ríos, Argentina* 126 **C4**
La Paz, *San Luis, Argentina* 126 **C2**
La Paz, *Bolivia* 124 **G5**
La Paz, *Honduras* 120 **D2**
La Paz, *Mexico* 118 **C2**
La Paz, *Phil.* 61 **D4**
La Paz Centro, *Nic.* 120 **D2**
La Pedrera, *Colombia* 124 **D5**
La Perouse Str., *Asia* 54 **B11**
La Pesca, *Mexico* 119 **C5**
La Piedad, *Mexico* 118 **C4**
La Pine, *U.S.A.* 114 **E3**
La Plant, *U.S.A.* 112 **C4**
La Plata, *Argentina* 126 **D4**
La Pobla de Lillet, *Spain* 32 **C6**
La Pola de Gordón, *Spain* 34 **C5**
La Porta, *France* 21 **F13**
La Porte, *U.S.A.* 108 **E2**
La Presanella, *Italy* 28 **B7**
La Puebla = Sa Pobla, *Spain* 32 **F8**
La Puebla de Cazalla, *Spain* 35 **H5**
La Puebla de los Infantes, *Spain* 35 **H5**
La Puebla de Montalbán, *Spain* 34 **F6**
La Puebla del Río, *Spain* 35 **H4**
La Puerta de Segura, *Spain* 35 **G8**
La Purísima, *Mexico* 118 **B2**
La Push, *U.S.A.* 116 **C2**
La Quiaca, *Argentina* 126 **A2**
La Reine, *Canada* 102 **C4**
La Réole, *France* 20 **D3**
La Restinga, *Canary Is.* 37 **G2**
La Rioja, *Argentina* 126 **B2**
La Rioja □, *Argentina* 126 **B2**
La Rioja □, *Spain* 32 **C2**
La Robla, *Spain* 34 **C5**
La Roche-Bernard, *France* 18 **E4**
La Roche-Canillac, *France* 20 **C5**
La Roche-en-Ardenne, *Belgium* 17 **D5**
La Roche-sur-Foron, *France* 19 **F13**
La Roche-sur-Yon, *France* 18 **F5**
La Rochefoucauld, *France* 20 **C4**
La Rochelle, *France* 20 **B2**
La Roda, *Spain* 33 **F2**
La Roda de Andalucía, *Spain* 35 **H6**
La Romana, *Dom. Rep.* 121 **C6**
La Ronge, *Canada* 105 **B7**
La Rumorosa, *Mexico* 117 **N10**
La Sabina = Sa Savina, *Spain* 37 **C7**
La Sagra, *Spain* 33 **H2**
La Salle, *U.S.A.* 112 **E10**
La Sanabria, *Spain* 34 **C4**
La Santa, *Canary Is.* 37 **E6**
La Sarre, *Canada* 102 **C4**
La Scie, *Canada* 103 **C8**
La Selva, *Spain* 32 **C7**
La Selva Beach, *U.S.A.* 116 **J5**
La Selva del Camp, *Spain* 32 **D6**
La Serena, *Chile* 126 **B1**
La Serena, *Spain* 35 **G5**
La Seu d'Urgell, *Spain* 32 **C6**
La Seyne-sur-Mer, *France* 21 **E9**
La Sila, *Italy* 31 **C9**
La Solana, *Spain* 35 **G7**
La Souterraine, *France* 19 **F8**
La Spézia, *Italy* 28 **D6**
La Suze-sur-Sarthe, *France* 18 **E7**
La Tagua, *Colombia* 124 **C4**
La Teste, *France* 20 **D2**
La Tortuga, *Venezuela* 121 **D6**
La Tour-du-Pin, *France* 21 **C9**
La Tranche-sur-Mer, *France* 18 **F5**
La Tremblade, *France* 20 **C2**
La Tuque, *Canada* 102 **C5**
La Unión, *Chile* 128 **E2**
La Unión, *El Salv.* 120 **D2**
La Unión, *Mexico* 118 **D4**
La Unión, *Spain* 33 **H4**
La Urbana, *Venezuela* 124 **B5**
La Vall d'Uixó, *Spain* 32 **F4**
La Vecilla de Curveño, *Spain* 34 **C5**
La Vega, *Dom. Rep.* 121 **C5**
La Vela, *Venezuela* 124 **A5**
La Veleta, *Spain* 35 **H7**
La Venta, *Mexico* 119 **D6**
La Ventura, *Mexico* 118 **C4**
La Voulte-sur-Rhône, *France* 21 **D8**
Laa an der Thaya, *Austria* 27 **C9**
Laaber, Grosse →, *Germany* 25 **G8**
Laage, *Germany* 24 **B8**
Laatzen, *Germany* 24 **C5**
Laba →, *Russia* 49 **H4**
Labason, *Phil.* 61 **G5**
Labastide-Murat, *France* 20 **D5**
Labastide-Rouairoux, *France* 20 **E6**
Labbézenga, *Mali* 83 **B5**
Labe = Elbe →, *Europe* 24 **B4**
Labé, *Guinea* 82 **C2**
Laberge, L., *Canada* 104 **A1**
Labin, *Croatia* 29 **C11**
Labinsk, *Russia* 49 **H5**
Labis, *Malaysia* 65 **L4**
Łabiszyn, *Poland* 45 **F4**
Labo, *Phil.* 61 **D5**
Laboe, *Germany* 24 **A6**
Laborec →, *Slovak Rep.* 27 **C14**
Labouheyre, *France* 20 **D3**
Laboulaye, *Argentina* 126 **C3**
Labrador, *Canada* 103 **B7**
Labrador City, *Canada* 103 **B6**
Lábrea, *Brazil* 124 **E6**
Labrède, *France* 20 **D3**
Labruguière, *France* 20 **E6**
Labuan, *Malaysia* 62 **C5**
Labuan, Pulau, *Malaysia* 62 **C5**
Labuha, *Indonesia* 63 **E7**
Labuhan, *Indonesia* 63 **G11**
Labuhanbajo, *Indonesia* 63 **F6**
Labuk, Telok, *Malaysia* 62 **C5**
Labyrinth, L., *Australia* 95 **E2**
Labytnangi, *Russia* 50 **C7**
Laç, *Albania* 40 **E3**
Lac Allard, *Canada* 103 **B7**
Lac Bouchette, *Canada* 103 **C5**
Lac du Flambeau, *U.S.A.* 112 **B10**
Lac Édouard, *Canada* 102 **C5**
Lac La Biche, *Canada* 104 **C6**
Lac la Martre = Wha Ti, *Canada* 100 **B8**
Lac-Mégantic, *Canada* 103 **C5**
Lac Seul, Res., *Canada* 102 **B1**
Lac Thien, *Vietnam* 64 **F7**
Lacanau, *France* 20 **D2**
Lacanau, Étang de, *France* 20 **D2**
Lacantúm →, *Mexico* 119 **D6**
Lacara →, *Spain* 35 **G4**
Lacaune, *France* 20 **E6**
Lacaune, Mts. de, *France* 20 **E6**
Laccadive Is. = Lakshadweep Is., *Ind. Oc.* 52 **H11**
Lacepede B., *Australia* 95 **F2**
Lacepede Is., *Australia* 92 **C3**
Lacerdónia, *Mozam.* 87 **F4**
Lacey, *U.S.A.* 116 **C4**
Lachhmangarh, *India* 68 **F6**
Lachi, *Pakistan* 68 **C4**
Lachine, *Canada* 102 **C5**
Lachlan →, *Australia* 95 **E3**
Lachute, *Canada* 102 **C5**
Lackawanna, *U.S.A.* 110 **D6**
Lacolle, *Canada* 111 **A11**
Lacombe, *Canada* 104 **C6**
Lacona, *U.S.A.* 111 **C8**
Láconi, *Italy* 30 **C2**
Laconia, *U.S.A.* 111 **C13**
Lacq, *France* 20 **E3**
Lacrosse, *U.S.A.* 114 **C5**
Ladakh Ra., *India* 69 **C8**
Lądek-Zdrój, *Poland* 45 **H3**
Ládhon →, *Greece* 38 **D3**
Ladik, *Turkey* 72 **B6**
Ladismith, *S. Africa* 88 **E3**
Ladíspoli, *Italy* 29 **G9**
Lādīz, *Iran* 71 **D9**
Ladnun, *India* 68 **F6**
Ladoga, L. = Ladozhskoye Ozero, *Russia* 46 **B6**
Ladozhskoye Ozero, *Russia* 46 **B6**
Lady Grey, *S. Africa* 88 **E4**
Ladybrand, *S. Africa* 88 **D4**
Ladysmith, *Canada* 104 **D4**
Ladysmith, *S. Africa* 89 **D4**
Ladysmith, *U.S.A.* 112 **C9**
Lae, *Papua N. G.* 96 **H6**
Laem Ngop, *Thailand* 65 **F4**
Laem Pho, *Thailand* 65 **J3**
Læsø, *Denmark* 11 **G5**
Læsø Rende, *Denmark* 11 **G4**
Lafayette, *Colo., U.S.A.* 112 **F2**
Lafayette, *Ind., U.S.A.* 108 **E2**
Lafayette, *La., U.S.A.* 113 **K9**
Lafayette, *Tenn., U.S.A.* 109 **G3**
Laferte →, *Canada* 104 **A5**
Lafia, *Nigeria* 83 **D6**
Lafiagi, *Nigeria* 83 **D6**
Lafleche, *Canada* 105 **D7**
Lafon, *Sudan* 81 **F3**
Lagan, *Sweden* 11 **H7**
Lagan →, *Sweden* 11 **H6**
Lagan →, *U.K.* 15 **B6**
Lagarfljót →, *Iceland* 8 **D6**
Lage, *Germany* 24 **D4**
Lågen →, *Oppland, Norway* 9 **F14**
Lågen →, *Vestfold, Norway* 9 **G14**
Lägerdorf, *Germany* 24 **B5**
Laghouat, *Algeria* 78 **B6**
Lagnieu, *France* 21 **C9**
Lagny-sur-Marne, *France* 19 **D9**
Lago, *Italy* 31 **C9**
Lagôa, *Portugal* 35 **H2**
Lagoaça, *Portugal* 34 **D4**
Lagodekhi, *Georgia* 49 **K8**
Lagónegro, *Italy* 31 **B8**
Lagonoy G., *Phil.* 61 **E5**
Lagos, *Nigeria* 83 **D5**
Lagos, *Portugal* 35 **H2**
Lagos de Moreno, *Mexico* 118 **C4**
Lagrange, *Australia* 92 **C3**
Lagrange B., *Australia* 92 **C3**
Laguardia, *Spain* 32 **C2**

Laguépie, *France* 20 D5
Laguna, *Brazil* 127 B6
Laguna, *U.S.A.* 115 J10
Laguna Beach, *U.S.A.* 117 M9
Laguna de Duera, *Spain* 34 D6
Laguna Limpia, *Argentina* 126 B4
Laguna Madre, *U.S.A.* 119 B5
Lagunas, *Chile* 126 A2
Lagunas, *Peru* 124 E3
Lahad Datu, *Malaysia* 63 D5
Lahad Datu, Teluk, *Malaysia* 63 D5
Lahan Sai, *Thailand* 64 E4
Lahanam, *Laos* 64 D5
Laharpur, *India* 69 F9
Lahat, *Indonesia* 62 E2
Lahewa, *Indonesia* 62 D1
Lahiang Lahiang, *Phil.* 61 H4
Lāhījān, *Iran* 71 B6
Lahn →, *Germany* 25 E3
Lahnstein, *Germany* 25 E3
Laholm, *Sweden* 11 H7
Laholmsbukten, *Sweden* 11 H6
Lahontan Reservoir, *U.S.A.* 114 G4
Lahore, *Pakistan* 68 D6
Lahr, *Germany* 25 G3
Lahti, *Finland* 9 F21
Lahtis = Lahti, *Finland* 9 F21
Laï, *Chad* 79 G9
Lai Chau, *Vietnam* 64 A4
Lai'an, *China* 59 A12
Laibin, *China* 58 F7
Laidley, *Australia* 95 D5
Laifeng, *China* 58 C7
L'Aigle, *France* 18 D7
Laignes, *France* 19 E11
L'Aiguillon-sur-Mer, *France* 20 B2
Laikipia □, *Kenya* 86 B4
Laingsburg, *S. Africa* 88 E3
Lainio älv →, *Sweden* 8 C20
Lairg, *U.K.* 14 C4
Laishui, *China* 56 E8
Laissac, *France* 20 D6
Láives, *Italy* 29 B8
Laiwu, *China* 57 F9
Laixi, *China* 57 F11
Laiyang, *China* 57 F11
Laiyuan, *China* 56 E8
Laizhou Wan, *China* 57 F10
Laja →, *Mexico* 118 C4
Lajere, *Nigeria* 83 C7
Lajes, *Brazil* 127 B5
Lajkovac, *Serbia, Yug.* 40 B4
Lajosmizse, *Hungary* 42 C4
Lak Sao, *Laos* 64 C5
Lakaband, *Pakistan* 68 D3
Lake Alpine, *U.S.A.* 116 G7
Lake Andes, *U.S.A.* 112 D5
Lake Anse, *U.S.A.* 108 B1
Lake Arthur, *U.S.A.* 113 K8
Lake Cargelligo, *Australia* 95 E4
Lake Charles, *U.S.A.* 113 K8
Lake City, *Colo., U.S.A.* 115 G10
Lake City, *Fla., U.S.A.* 109 K4
Lake City, *Iowa, U.S.A.* 112 D7
Lake City, *Mich., U.S.A.* 108 C3
Lake City, *Minn., U.S.A.* 112 C8
Lake City, *Pa., U.S.A.* 110 D4
Lake City, *S.C., U.S.A.* 109 J6
Lake George, *U.S.A.* 111 C11
Lake Grace, *Australia* 93 F2
Lake Harbour = Kimmirut, *Canada* 101 B13
Lake Havasu City, *U.S.A.* 117 L12
Lake Hughes, *U.S.A.* 117 L8
Lake Isabella, *U.S.A.* 117 K8
Lake King, *Australia* 93 F2
Lake Lenore, *Canada* 105 C8
Lake Louise, *Canada* 104 C5
Lake Mead National Recreation Area, *U.S.A.* 117 K12
Lake Mills, *U.S.A.* 112 D8
Lake Nash, *Australia* 94 C2
Lake Providence, *U.S.A.* 113 J9
Lake River, *Canada* 102 B3
Lake Superior Prov. Park, *Canada* 102 C3
Lake Village, *U.S.A.* 113 J9
Lake Wales, *U.S.A.* 109 M5
Lake Worth, *U.S.A.* 109 M5
Lakefield, *Canada* 102 D4
Lakeland, *Australia* 94 B3
Lakeland, *U.S.A.* 109 M5
Lakemba, *Fiji* 91 D9
Lakeport, *U.S.A.* 116 F4
Lakes Entrance, *Australia* 95 F4
Lakeside, *Ariz., U.S.A.* 115 J9
Lakeside, *Calif., U.S.A.* 117 N10
Lakeside, *Nebr., U.S.A.* 112 D3
Lakeview, *U.S.A.* 114 E3
Lakewood, *Colo., U.S.A.* 112 F2
Lakewood, *N.J., U.S.A.* 111 F10
Lakewood, *Ohio, U.S.A.* 110 E3
Lakewood Center, *U.S.A.* 116 C4
Lakhaniá, *Greece* 36 D9
Lakhonpheng, *Laos* 64 E5
Lakhpat, *India* 68 H3
Läki, *Azerbaijan* 49 K8
Lakin, *U.S.A.* 113 G4
Lakitusaki →, *Canada* 102 B3
Lákkoi, *Greece* 36 D5
Lakonía □, *Greece* 38 E4
Lakonikós Kólpos, *Greece* 38 E4
Lakor, *Indonesia* 63 F7
Lakota, *Ivory C.* 82 D3
Lakota, *U.S.A.* 112 A5
Laksefjorden, *Norway* 8 A22
Lakselv, *Norway* 8 A21
Lakshadweep Is., *Ind. Oc.* 52 H11
Lakshmikantapur, *India* 69 H13
Lala Ghat, *India* 67 G18
Lala Musa, *Pakistan* 68 C5
Lalago, *Tanzania* 86 C3
Lalapanzi, *Zimbabwe* 87 F3
Lalapaşa, *Turkey* 41 E10
Lalbenque, *France* 20 D5
L'Albufera, *Spain* 33 F4
Lalganj, *India* 69 G11
Lalibela, *Ethiopia* 81 E4
Lalin, *China* 57 B14
Lalín, *Spain* 34 C2
Lalin He →, *China* 57 B13
Lalinde, *France* 20 D4
Lalitapur = Patan, *Nepal* 67 F14
Lalitpur, *India* 69 G8
Lam, *Vietnam* 64 B6
Lam Pao Res., *Thailand* 64 D4
Lama Kara, *Togo* 83 D5
Lamaing, *Burma* 67 M20
Lamar, *Colo., U.S.A.* 112 F3
Lamar, *Mo., U.S.A.* 113 G7
Lamas, *Peru* 124 E3
Lamastre, *France* 21 D8
Lambach, *Austria* 26 C6
Lamballe, *France* 18 D4
Lambaréné, *Gabon* 84 E2
Lambasa, *Fiji* 91 C8
Lambay I., *Ireland* 15 C5
Lambert, *U.S.A.* 112 B2
Lambert Glacier, *Antarctica* 5 D6
Lamberts Bay, *S. Africa* 88 E2
Lambesc, *France* 21 E9
Lambi Kyun, *Burma* 65 G2
Lámbia, *Greece* 38 D3
Lambro →, *Italy* 28 C6
Lame, *Nigeria* 83 C6
Lame Deer, *U.S.A.* 114 D10
Lamego, *Portugal* 34 D3
Lamèque, *Canada* 103 C7
Lameroo, *Australia* 95 F3
Lamesa, *U.S.A.* 113 J4
Lamía, *Greece* 38 C4
Lamitan, *Phil.* 61 H5
Lammermuir Hills, *U.K.* 14 F6
Lammhult, *Sweden* 11 G8
Lamon B., *Phil.* 61 D5
Lamont, *Canada* 104 C6
Lamont, *U.S.A.* 117 K8
Lamotte-Beuvron, *France* 19 E9
Lampa, *Peru* 124 G4
Lampang, *Thailand* 64 C2
Lampasas, *U.S.A.* 113 K5
Lampazos de Naranjo, *Mexico* 118 B4
Lampertheim, *Germany* 25 F4
Lampeter, *U.K.* 13 E3
Lampman, *Canada* 105 D8
Lamprechtshausen, *Austria* 26 D5
Lamprey, *Canada* 105 B10
Lampung □, *Indonesia* 62 F2
Lamu, *Kenya* 86 C5
Lamu □, *Kenya* 86 C5
Lamy, *U.S.A.* 115 J11
Lan Xian, *China* 56 E6
Lanai, *U.S.A.* 106 H16
Lanak La, *India* 69 B8
Lanak'o Shank'ou = Lanak La, *India* 69 B8
Lanao, L., *Phil.* 61 H6
Lanark, *Canada* 111 A8
Lanark, *U.K.* 14 F5
Lancang, *China* 58 F2
Lancang Jiang →, *China* 58 G3
Lancashire □, *U.K.* 12 D5
Lancaster, *Canada* 111 A10
Lancaster, *U.K.* 12 C5
Lancaster, *Calif., U.S.A.* 117 L8
Lancaster, *Ky., U.S.A.* 108 G3
Lancaster, *N.H., U.S.A.* 111 B13
Lancaster, *N.Y., U.S.A.* 110 D6
Lancaster, *Pa., U.S.A.* 111 F8
Lancaster, *S.C., U.S.A.* 109 H5
Lancaster, *Wis., U.S.A.* 112 D9
Lancaster Sd., *Canada* 4 B3
Lancer, *Canada* 105 C7
Lanchow = Lanzhou, *China* 56 F2
Lanciano, *Italy* 29 F11
Lancun, *China* 57 F11
Łańcut, *Poland* 45 H9
Landau, *Bayern, Germany* 25 G8
Landau, *Rhld-Pfz., Germany* 25 F4
Landeck, *Austria* 26 D3
Lander, *U.S.A.* 114 E9
Lander →, *Australia* 92 D5
Landerneau, *France* 18 D2
Landeryd, *Sweden* 11 G7
Landes, *France* 20 D2
Landes □, *France* 20 E3
Landete, *Spain* 32 F3
Landi Kotal, *Pakistan* 68 B4
Landivisiau, *France* 18 D2
Landor, *Australia* 93 E2
Landquart, *Switz.* 25 J5
Landrecies, *France* 19 B10
Land's End, *U.K.* 13 G2
Landsberg, *Germany* 25 G6
Landsborough Cr. →, *Australia* 94 C3
Landsbro, *Sweden* 11 G8
Landshut, *Germany* 25 G8
Landskrona, *Sweden* 11 J6
Landstuhl, *Germany* 25 F3
Landvetter, *Sweden* 11 G6
Lanesboro, *U.S.A.* 111 E9
Lanester, *France* 18 E3
Lanett, *U.S.A.* 109 J3
Lang Bay, *Canada* 104 D4
Lang Qua, *Vietnam* 64 A5
Lang Shan, *China* 56 D4
Lang Son, *Vietnam* 64 B6
Lang Suan, *Thailand* 65 H2
Langå, *Denmark* 11 H3
La'nga Co, *China* 67 D12
Lángadhás, *Greece* 40 F7
Langádhia, *Greece* 38 D4
Långan →, *Sweden* 10 A8
Langar, *Iran* 71 C9
Langara I., *Canada* 104 C2
Långås, *Sweden* 11 H6
Langdai, *China* 58 D5
Langdon, *U.S.A.* 112 A5
Långe Jan = Ölands södra udde, *Sweden* 11 H10
Langeac, *France* 20 C7
Langeais, *France* 18 E7
Langeb Baraka →, *Sudan* 80 D4
Langeberg, *S. Africa* 88 E3
Langeberge, *S. Africa* 88 D3
Langeland, *Denmark* 11 K4
Langelands Bælt, *Denmark* 11 K4
Langen, *Hessen, Germany* 25 F4
Langen, *Niedersachsen, Germany* 24 B4
Langenburg, *Canada* 105 C8
Langeneß, *Germany* 24 A4
Langenlois, *Austria* 26 C8
Langeoog, *Germany* 24 B3
Langeskov, *Denmark* 11 J4
Länghem, *Sweden* 11 G7
Langhirano, *Italy* 28 D7
Langholm, *U.K.* 14 F5
Langjökull, *Iceland* 8 D3
Langkawi, Pulau, *Malaysia* 65 J2
Langklip, *S. Africa* 88 D3
Langkon, *Malaysia* 62 C5
Langlade, *St- P. & M.* 103 C8
Langlois, *U.S.A.* 114 E1
Langnau, *Switz.* 25 J3
Langogne, *France* 20 D7
Langon, *France* 20 D3
Langøya, *Norway* 8 B16
Langreo, *Spain* 34 B5
Langres, *France* 19 E12
Langres, Plateau de, *France* 19 E12
Langsa, *Indonesia* 62 D1
Långsele, *Sweden* 10 A11
Långshyttan, *Sweden* 10 D10
Langtry, *U.S.A.* 113 L4
Langu, *Thailand* 65 J2
Languedoc, *France* 20 E7
Languedoc-Roussillon □, *France* 20 E6
Langxi, *China* 59 B12
Langxiangzhen, *China* 56 E9
Langzhong, *China* 58 B5
Lanigan, *Canada* 105 C7
Lankao, *China* 56 G8
Länkäran, *Azerbaijan* 73 C13
Lanmeur, *France* 18 D3
Lannemezan, *France* 20 E4
Lannilis, *France* 18 D2
Lannion, *France* 18 D3
L'Annonciation, *Canada* 102 C5
Lanouaille, *France* 20 C5
Lanping, *China* 58 D2
Lansdale, *U.S.A.* 111 F9
Lansdowne, *Australia* 95 E5
Lansdowne, *Canada* 111 B8
Lansdowne House, *Canada* 102 B2
L'Anse, *U.S.A.* 102 C2
L'Anse au Loup, *Canada* 103 B8
Lansford, *U.S.A.* 111 F9
Lanshan, *China* 59 E9
Lansing, *U.S.A.* 108 D3
Lanslebourg-Mont-Cenis, *France* 21 C10
Lanta Yai, Ko, *Thailand* 65 J2
Lantian, *China* 56 G5
Lanus, *Argentina* 126 C4
Lanusei, *Italy* 30 C2
Lanuza, *Phil.* 61 G7
Lanxi, *China* 59 C12
Lanzarote, *Canary Is.* 37 F6
Lanzhou, *China* 56 F2
Lanzo Torinese, *Italy* 28 C4
Lao →, *Italy* 31 C8
Lao Bao, *Laos* 64 D6
Lao Cai, *Vietnam* 64 A4
Laoag, *Phil.* 61 B4
Laoang, *Phil.* 61 E6
Laoha He →, *China* 57 C11
Laois □, *Ireland* 15 D4
Laon, *France* 19 C10
Laona, *U.S.A.* 108 C1
Laos ■, *Asia* 64 D5
Lapa, *Brazil* 127 B6
Lapalisse, *France* 19 F10
Lapeer, *U.S.A.* 108 D4
Lapeyrade, *France* 20 D3
Lapithos, *Cyprus* 36 D12
Lapland = Lappland, *Europe* 8 B21
Laporte, *U.S.A.* 111 E8
Lapovo, *Serbia, Yug.* 40 B5
Lappeenranta, *Finland* 9 F23
Lappland, *Europe* 8 B21
Laprida, *Argentina* 126 D3
Lapseki, *Turkey* 72 B2
Laptev Sea, *Russia* 51 B13
Lapua, *Finland* 8 E20
Lăpuş →, *Romania* 43 C8
Lapuş, Munţii, *Romania* 43 C8
Lăpuşna, *Moldova* 43 D13
Łapy, *Poland* 45 F9
L'Áquila, *Italy* 29 F10
Lār, *Āzarbājān-e Sharqī, Iran* 70 B5
Lār, *Fārs, Iran* 71 E7
Larabanga, *Ghana* 82 D4
Laragne-Montéglin, *France* 21 D9
Laramie, *U.S.A.* 112 E2
Laramie Mts., *U.S.A.* 112 E2
Laranjeiras do Sul, *Brazil* 127 B5
Larantuka, *Indonesia* 63 F6
Larap, *Phil.* 61 D5
Larat, *Indonesia* 63 F8
L'Arbresle, *France* 21 C8
Lärbro, *Sweden* 11 G12
Larde, *Mozam.* 87 F4
Larder Lake, *Canada* 102 C4
Lardhos, Ákra = Líndhos, Ákra, *Greece* 36 C10
Lardhos, Órmos, *Greece* 36 C10
Laredo, *Spain* 34 B7
Laredo, *U.S.A.* 113 M5
Laredo Sd., *Canada* 104 C3
Largentière, *France* 21 D8
L'Argentière-la-Bessée, *France* 21 D10
Largo, *U.S.A.* 109 M4
Largs, *U.K.* 14 F4
Lari, *Italy* 28 E7
Lariang, *Indonesia* 63 E5
Larimore, *U.S.A.* 112 B6
Lārīn, *Iran* 71 C7
Larino, *Italy* 29 G11
Lárisa, *Greece* 38 B4
Lárisa □, *Greece* 38 B4
Larkana, *Pakistan* 68 F3
Larnaca, *Cyprus* 36 E12
Larnaca Bay, *Cyprus* 36 E12
Larne, *U.K.* 15 B6
Larned, *U.S.A.* 112 F5
Laroquebrou, *France* 20 D6
Larrimah, *Australia* 92 C5
Larsen Ice Shelf, *Antarctica* 5 C17
Laruns, *France* 20 F3
Larvik, *Norway* 9 G14
Larzac, Causse du, *France* 20 E7
Las Alpujarras, *Spain* 33 J1
Las Animas, *U.S.A.* 112 F3
Las Anod, *Somali Rep.* 74 F4
Las Arenas, *Spain* 34 B6
Las Brenãs, *Argentina* 126 B3
Las Cabezas de San Juan, *Spain* 35 J5
Las Cejas, *Argentina* 128 B4
Las Chimeneas, *Mexico* 117 N10
Las Cruces, *U.S.A.* 115 K10
Las Flores, *Argentina* 126 D4
Las Heras, *Argentina* 126 C2
Las Lajas, *Argentina* 128 D2
Las Lomitas, *Argentina* 126 A3
Las Marismas, *Spain* 35 H4
Las Minas, *Spain* 33 G3
Las Navas de la Concepción, *Spain* 35 H5
Las Navas del Marqués, *Spain* 34 E6
Las Palmas, *Argentina* 126 B4
Las Palmas, *Canary Is.* 37 F4
Las Palmas →, *Mexico* 117 N10
Las Pedroñas, *Spain* 33 F2
Las Piedras, *Uruguay* 127 C4
Las Pipinas, *Argentina* 126 D4
Las Plumas, *Argentina* 128 E3
Las Rosas, *Argentina* 126 C3
Las Rozas, *Spain* 34 E7
Las Tablas, *Panama* 120 E3
Las Termas, *Argentina* 126 B3
Las Truchas, *Mexico* 118 D4
Las Varillas, *Argentina* 126 C3
Las Vegas, *N. Mex., U.S.A.* 115 J11
Las Vegas, *Nev., U.S.A.* 117 J11
Lasarte, *Spain* 32 B2
Lascano, *Uruguay* 127 C5
Lashburn, *Canada* 105 C7
Lashio, *Burma* 67 H20
Lashkar, *India* 68 F8
Łasin, *Poland* 44 E6
Lasíthi, *Greece* 36 D7
Lasíthi □, *Greece* 36 D7
Lask, *Poland* 45 G6
Łaskarzew, *Poland* 45 G8
Laško, *Slovenia* 29 B12
Lassay-les-Châteaux, *France* 18 D6
Lassen Pk., *U.S.A.* 114 F3
Last Mountain L., *Canada* 105 C7
Lastchance Cr. →, *U.S.A.* 116 E5
Lastoursville, *Gabon* 84 E2
Lastovo, *Croatia* 29 F13
Lastovski Kanal, *Croatia* 29 F14
Lat Yao, *Thailand* 64 E2
Latacunga, *Ecuador* 124 D3
Latakia = Al Lādhiqīyah, *Syria* 70 C2
Latchford, *Canada* 102 C4
Laterza, *Italy* 31 B9
Latham, *Australia* 93 E2
Lathen, *Germany* 24 C3
Lathrop Wells, *U.S.A.* 117 J10
Latiano, *Italy* 31 B10
Latina, *Italy* 30 A5
Latisana, *Italy* 29 C10
Latium = Lazio □, *Italy* 29 F9
Laton, *U.S.A.* 116 J7
Latorytsya →, *Slovak Rep.* 27 C14
Latouche Treville, C., *Australia* 92 C3
Latrobe, *Australia* 94 G4
Latrobe, *U.S.A.* 110 F5
Latrónico, *Italy* 31 B9
Latvia ■, *Europe* 9 H20
Lau Group, *Fiji* 91 C9
Lauchhammer, *Germany* 24 D9
Lauda-Königshofen, *Germany* 25 F5
Lauenburg, *Germany* 24 B6
Lauf, *Germany* 25 F7
Laujar de Andarax, *Spain* 33 H2
Laukaa, *Finland* 9 E21
Launceston, *Australia* 94 G4
Launceston, *U.K.* 13 G3
Laune →, *Ireland* 15 D2
Launglon Bok, *Burma* 64 F1
Laupheim, *Germany* 25 G5
Laura, *Australia* 94 B3
Laureana di Borrello, *Italy* 31 D9
Laurel, *Miss., U.S.A.* 113 K10
Laurel, *Mont., U.S.A.* 114 D9
Laurencekirk, *U.K.* 14 E6
Laurens, *U.S.A.* 109 H4
Laurentian Plateau, *Canada* 103 B6
Laurentides, Parc Prov. des, *Canada* 103 C5
Lauria, *Italy* 31 B8
Laurie L., *Canada* 105 B8
Laurinburg, *U.S.A.* 109 H6
Laurium, *U.S.A.* 108 B1
Lausanne, *Switz.* 25 J2
Laut, *Indonesia* 65 K6
Laut Kecil, Kepulauan, *Indonesia* 62 E5
Lauterbach, *Germany* 24 E5
Lauterecken, *Germany* 25 F3
Lautoka, *Fiji* 91 C7
Lauzès, *France* 20 D5
Lauzon, *Canada* 103 C5
Lava Hot Springs, *U.S.A.* 114 E7
Lavagh More, *Ireland* 15 B3
Lavagna, *Italy* 28 D6
Laval, *France* 18 D6
Lavalle, *Argentina* 126 B2
Lávara, *Greece* 41 E10
Lavardac, *France* 20 D4
Lavaur, *France* 20 E5
Lavelanet, *France* 20 F5
Lavello, *Italy* 31 A8
Laverne, *U.S.A.* 113 G5
Laverton, *Australia* 93 E3
Lavìs, *Italy* 28 B8
Lávkos, *Greece* 38 B5
Lavos, *Portugal* 34 E2
Lavradio, *Portugal* 35 G1
Lavras, *Brazil* 127 A7
Lavre, *Portugal* 35 G2
Lávrion, *Greece* 38 D6
Lávris, *Greece* 36 D6
Lavumisa, *Swaziland* 89 D5
Lawas, *Malaysia* 62 D5
Lawele, *Indonesia* 63 F6
Lawn Hill, *Australia* 94 B2
Lawng Pit, *Burma* 67 G20
Lawqah, *Si. Arabia* 70 D4
Lawra, *Ghana* 82 C4
Lawrence, *N.Z.* 91 L2
Lawrence, *Kans., U.S.A.* 112 F7
Lawrence, *Mass., U.S.A.* 111 D13
Lawrenceburg, *Ind., U.S.A.* 108 F3
Lawrenceburg, *Tenn., U.S.A.* 109 H2
Lawrenceville, *U.S.A.* 109 J4
Laws, *U.S.A.* 116 H8
Lawton, *U.S.A.* 113 H5
Lawu, *Indonesia* 63 G14
Laxå, *Sweden* 11 F8
Laxford, L., *U.K.* 14 C3
Laxou, *France* 19 D13
Lay →, *France* 20 B2
Laylān, *Iraq* 70 C5
Layon →, *France* 18 E6
Laysan I., *Pac. Oc.* 97 E11
Laytonville, *U.S.A.* 114 G2
Lazarevac, *Serbia, Yug.* 40 B4
Lazarevskoye, *Russia* 49 J4
Lazdijai, *Lithuania* 44 D10
Lazio □, *Italy* 29 F9
Lazo, *Moldova* 43 C13
Lazo, *Russia* 54 C6
Le Beausset, *France* 21 E9
Le Blanc, *France* 20 B5
Le Bleymard, *France* 20 D7
Le Bourgneuf-la-Fôret, *France* 18 D6
Le Bugue, *France* 20 D4
Le Canourgue = La Canourgue, *France* 20 D7
Le Cateau Cambrésis, *France* 19 B10
Le Caylar, *France* 20 E7
Le Chambon-Feugerolles, *France* 21 C8
Le Châtelet, *France* 19 F9
Le Chesne, *France* 19 C11
Le Cheylard, *France* 21 D8
Le Conquet, *France* 18 D2
Le Creusot, *France* 19 F11
Le Croisic, *France* 18 E4
Le Donjon, *France* 19 F10

Le Dorat, France 20 B5
Le François, Martinique 121 D7
Le Grand-Lucé, France 18 E7
Le Grand-Pressigny, France 18 F7
Le Grand-Quevilly, France 18 C8
Le Havre, France 18 C7
Le Lavandou, France 21 E10
Le Lion-d'Angers, France 18 E6
Le Louroux-Béconnais, France 18 E6
Le Luc, France 21 E10
Le Lude, France 18 E7
Le Mans, France 18 E7
Le Mars, U.S.A. 112 D6
Le Mayet-de-Montagne, France 19 F10
Le Mêle-sur-Sarthe, France 18 D7
Le Monastier-sur-Gazeille, France 20 D7
Le Monêtier-les-Bains, France 21 D10
Le Mont-Dore, France 20 C6
Le Mont-St-Michel, France 18 D5
Le Moule, Guadeloupe 121 C7
Le Muy, France 21 E10
Le Palais, France 18 E3
Le Perthus, France 20 F6
Le Puy-en-Velay, France 20 C7
Le Roy, U.S.A. 113 F7
Le Sueur, U.S.A. 112 C8
Le Teil, France 21 D8
Le Teilleul, France 18 D6
Le Theil, France 18 D7
Le Thillot, France 19 E13
Le Thuy, Vietnam 64 D6
Le Touquet-Paris-Plage, France 19 B8
Le Tréport, France 18 B8
Le Val-d'Ajol, France 19 E13
Le Verdon-sur-Mer, France 20 C2
Le Vigan, France 20 E7
Lea →, U.K. 13 F8
Leach, Cambodia 65 F4
Lead, U.S.A. 112 C3
Leader, Canada 105 C7
Leadville, U.S.A. 115 G10
Leaf →, U.S.A. 113 K10
Leakey, U.S.A. 113 L5
Leamington, Canada 102 D3
Leamington, U.S.A. 114 G7
Leamington Spa = Royal Leamington Spa, U.K. 13 E6
Le'an, China 59 D10
Leandro Norte Alem, Argentina 127 B4
Leane, L., Ireland 15 D2
Learmonth, Australia 92 D1
Leask, Canada 105 C7
Leatherhead, U.K. 13 F7
Leavenworth, Kans., U.S.A. 112 F7
Leavenworth, Wash., U.S.A. 114 C3
Łeba, Poland 44 D4
Łeba →, Poland 44 D4
Lebach, Germany 25 F2
Lebak, Phil. 61 H6
Lebam, U.S.A. 116 D3
Lebane, Serbia, Yug. 40 D5
Lebanon, Ind., U.S.A. 108 E2
Lebanon, Kans., U.S.A. 112 F5
Lebanon, Ky., U.S.A. 108 G3
Lebanon, Mo., U.S.A. 113 G8
Lebanon, Oreg., U.S.A. 114 D2
Lebanon, Pa., U.S.A. 111 F8
Lebanon, Tenn., U.S.A. 109 G2
Lebanon ■, Asia 75 B5
Lebec, U.S.A. 117 L8
Lebedyan, Russia 47 F10
Lebedyn, Ukraine 47 G8
Lebomboberge, S. Africa 89 C5
Lębork, Poland 44 D4
Lebrija, Spain 35 J4
Łebsko, Jezioro, Poland 44 D4
Lebu, Chile 126 D1
Leca da Palmeira, Portugal 34 D2
Lecce, Italy 31 B11
Lecco, Italy 28 C6
Lecco, L. di, Italy 28 C6
Lécera, Spain 32 D4
Lech, Austria 26 D3
Lech →, Germany 25 G6
Lechang, China 59 E9
Lechtaler Alpen, Austria 26 D3
Lectoure, France 20 E4
Łęczna, Poland 45 G9
Łęczyca, Poland 45 F6
Ledesma, Spain 34 D5
Ledong, China 64 C7
Leduc, Canada 104 C6
Lee, U.S.A. 111 D11
Lee →, Ireland 15 E3
Lee Vining, U.S.A. 116 H7
Leech L., U.S.A. 112 B7
Leedey, U.S.A. 113 H5
Leeds, U.K. 12 D6
Leeds, U.S.A. 109 J2
Leek, Neths. 17 A6
Leek, U.K. 12 D5
Leer, Germany 24 B3
Leesburg, U.S.A. 109 L5
Leesville, U.S.A. 113 K8
Leeton, Australia 95 E4
Leetonia, U.S.A. 110 F4
Leeu Gamka, S. Africa 88 E3
Leeuwarden, Neths. 17 A5
Leeuwin, C., Australia 93 F2
Leeward Is., Atl. Oc. 121 C7
Lefka, Cyprus 36 D11
Lefkoniko, Cyprus 36 D12
Lefors, U.S.A. 113 H4
Lefroy, L., Australia 93 F3
Łeg →, Poland 45 H8
Legal, Canada 104 C6
Leganés, Spain 34 E7
Legazpi, Phil. 61 E5
Lège, France 20 D2
Legendre I., Australia 92 D2
Leghorn = Livorno, Italy 28 E7
Legionowo, Poland 45 F7
Legnago, Italy 29 C8
Legnano, Italy 28 C5
Legnica, Poland 45 G3
Legnica □, Poland 45 G3
Legrad, Croatia 29 B13
Legume, Australia 95 D5
Leh, India 69 B7
Lehi, U.S.A. 114 F8
Lehighton, U.S.A. 111 F9
Lehliu, Romania 43 F11
Lehrte, Germany 24 C5
Lehututu, Botswana 88 C3
Lei Shui →, China 59 D9
Leiah, Pakistan 68 D4
Leibnitz, Austria 26 E8
Leibo, China 58 C4
Leicester, U.K. 13 E6
Leicester City □, U.K. 13 E6
Leicestershire □, U.K. 13 E6
Leichhardt →, Australia 94 B2
Leichhardt Ra., Australia 94 C4
Leiden, Neths. 17 B4
Leie →, Belgium 17 C3
Leifers = Láives, Italy 29 B8
Leimen, Germany 25 F4
Leine →, Germany 24 C5
Leinefelde, Germany 24 D6
Leinster, Australia 93 E3
Leinster □, Ireland 15 C4
Leinster, Mt., Ireland 15 D5
Leipalingis, Lithuania 44 D10
Leipzig, Germany 24 D8
Leiria, Portugal 34 F2
Leiria □, Portugal 34 F2
Leirvik, Norway 9 G11
Leisler, Mt., Australia 92 D4
Leith, U.K. 14 F5
Leith Hill, U.K. 13 F7
Leitha →, Europe 27 D10
Leitrim, Ireland 15 B3
Leitrim □, Ireland 15 B4
Leitza, Spain 32 B3
Leiyang, China 59 D9
Leizhou Bandao, China 60 D6
Leizhou Wan, China 59 G8
Lek →, Neths. 17 C4
Leka, Norway 8 D14
Lekáni, Greece 41 E8
Lekbibaj, Albania 40 D3
Lekeitio, Spain 32 B2
Lekhainá, Greece 38 D3
Leksand, Sweden 10 D9
Lékva Óros, Greece 36 D6
Leland, U.S.A. 113 J9
Leland Lakes, Canada 105 B6
Lelång, Sweden 10 E6
Leleque, Argentina 128 E2
Lelystad, Neths. 17 B5
Lem, Denmark 11 H2
Lema, Nigeria 83 C5
Léman, L., Europe 19 F13
Lemera, Dem. Rep. of the Congo 86 C2
Lemery, Phil. 61 E4
Lemhi Ra., U.S.A. 114 D7
Lemmer, Neths. 17 B5
Lemmon, U.S.A. 112 C3
Lemon Grove, U.S.A. 117 N9
Lemoore, U.S.A. 116 J7
Lempdes, France 20 C7
Lemvig, Denmark 11 H2
Lena →, Russia 51 B13
Lenart, Slovenia 29 B12
Lenartovce, Slovak Rep. 27 C13
Lencloître, France 18 F7
Léndas, Greece 36 E6
Lendava, Slovenia 29 B13
Lendeh, Iran 71 D6
Lendinara, Italy 29 C8
Lengerich, Germany 24 C3
Lenggong, Malaysia 65 K3
Lenggries, Germany 25 H7
Lengua de Vaca, Pta., Chile 126 C1
Lengyeltóti, Hungary 42 D2
Lenhovda, Sweden 11 G9
Lenina, Kanal →, Russia 49 J7
Leninabad = Khudzhand, Tajikistan 50 E7
Leninakan = Gyumri, Armenia 49 K6
Leningrad = Sankt-Peterburg, Russia 46 C6
Lenino, Ukraine 47 K8
Leninogorsk, Kazakstan 50 D9
Leninsk, Russia 49 F7
Leninsk-Kuznetskiy, Russia 50 D9
Leninskoye, Russia 48 A8
Lenk, Switz. 25 J3
Lenkoran = Länkäran, Azerbaijan 73 C13
Lenmalu, Indonesia 63 E8
Lenne →, Germany 24 D3
Lennestadt, Germany 24 D4
Lennoxville, Canada 111 A13
Leno, Italy 28 C7
Lenoir, U.S.A. 109 H5
Lenoir City, U.S.A. 109 H3
Lenora, U.S.A. 112 F4
Lenore L., Canada 105 C8
Lenox, U.S.A. 111 D11
Lens, France 19 B9
Lensahn, Germany 24 A6
Lensk, Russia 51 C12
Lentekhi, Georgia 49 J6
Lenti, Hungary 42 D1
Lentini, Italy 31 E8
Lenwood, U.S.A. 117 L9
Lenzen, Germany 24 B7
Léo, Burkina Faso 82 C4
Leoben, Austria 26 D8
Leodhas = Lewis, U.K. 14 C2
Leola, U.S.A. 112 C5
Leominster, U.K. 13 E5
Leominster, U.S.A. 111 D13
Léon, France 20 E2
León, Mexico 118 C4
León, Nic. 120 D2
León, Spain 34 C5
Leon, U.S.A. 112 E8
León □, Spain 34 C5
León, Montes de, Spain 34 C4
Leonardtown, U.S.A. 108 F7
Leonberg, Germany 25 G5
Leonding, Austria 26 C7
Leonessa, Italy 29 F9
Leonforte, Italy 31 E7
Leongatha, Australia 95 F4
Leonídhion, Greece 38 D4
Leonora, Australia 93 E3
Léopold II, Lac = Mai-Ndombe, L., Dem. Rep. of the Congo 84 E3
Leopoldina, Brazil 127 A7
Leopoldsburg, Belgium 17 C5
Léopoldville = Kinshasa, Dem. Rep. of the Congo 84 E3
Leoti, U.S.A. 112 F4
Leova, Moldova 43 D13
Leoville, Canada 105 C7
Lépa, L. do, Angola 88 B2
Lepe, Spain 35 H3
Lepel = Lyepyel, Belarus 46 E5
Lepenoú, Greece 38 C3
Leping, China 59 C11
Lepontine, Alpi, Italy 28 B5
Leppävirta, Finland 9 E22
Lepsény, Hungary 42 D3
Lequeitio = Lekeitio, Spain 32 B2
Lercara Friddi, Italy 30 E6
Lerdo, Mexico 118 B4
Lere, Nigeria 83 D6
Leribe, Lesotho 89 D4
Lérici, Italy 28 D6
Lérida = Lleida, Spain 32 D5
Lérins, Îs. de, France 21 E11
Lerma, Spain 34 C7
Léros, Greece 39 D8
Lérouville, France 19 D12
Lerum, Sweden 11 G6
Lerwick, U.K. 14 A7
Leş, Romania 42 D6
Les Abrets, France 21 C9
Les Andelys, France 18 C8
Les Borges Blanques, Spain 32 D5
Les Cayes, Haiti 121 C5
Les Essarts, France 18 F5
Les Étroits, Canada 103 C6
Les Herbiers, France 18 F5
Les Minquiers, Plateau des, Chan. Is. 18 D4
Les Pieux, France 18 C5
Les Ponts-de-Cé, France 18 E6
Les Riceys, France 19 E11
Les Sables-d'Olonne, France 20 B2
Les Vans, France 21 D8
Lesbos = Lésvos, Greece 39 B8
L'Escala, Spain 32 C8
Leshan, China 58 C4
Lésina, Italy 29 G12
Lésina, L. di, Italy 29 G12
Lesjöfors, Sweden 10 E8
Lesko, Poland 45 J9
Leskov I., Antarctica 5 B1
Leskovac, Serbia, Yug. 40 C5
Leskoviku, Albania 40 F4
Leslie, U.S.A. 113 H8
Leśna, Poland 45 G2
Lesneven, France 18 D2
Leśnica, Poland 45 H5
Lešnica, Serbia, Yug. 40 B3
Lesnoye, Russia 46 C8
Lesopilnoye, Russia 54 A7
Lesotho ■, Africa 89 D4
Lesozavodsk, Russia 54 B6
Lesparre-Médoc, France 20 C3
Lessay, France 18 C5
Lesse →, Belgium 17 D4
Lessebo, Sweden 11 H9
Lesser Antilles, W. Indies 121 D7
Lesser Slave L., Canada 104 B5
Lesser Sunda Is., Indonesia 63 F6
Lessines, Belgium 17 D3
Lester, U.S.A. 116 C5
Lestock, Canada 105 C8
Lesuer I., Australia 92 B4
Lésvos, Greece 39 B8
Leszno, Poland 45 G3
Leszno □, Poland 45 G3
Letälven, Sweden 10 E8
Létavértes, Hungary 42 C6
Letchworth, U.K. 13 F7
Letea, Ostrov, Romania 43 E14
Lethbridge, Canada 104 D6
Lethem, Guyana 124 C7
Leti, Kepulauan, Indonesia 63 F7
Leti Is. = Leti, Kepulauan, Indonesia 63 F7
Letiahau →, Botswana 88 C3
Leticia, Colombia 124 D5
Leting, China 57 E10
Letjiesbos, S. Africa 88 E3
Letlhakeng, Botswana 88 C3
Letpadan, Burma 67 L19
Letpan, Burma 67 K19
Letsôk-aw Kyun, Burma 65 G2
Letterkenny, Ireland 15 B4
Leu, Romania 43 F9
Leucadia, U.S.A. 117 M9
Leucate, France 20 F7
Leucate, Étang de, France 20 F7
Leuk, Switz. 25 J3
Leuşeni, Moldova 43 D13
Leuser, G., Indonesia 62 D1
Leutkirch, Germany 25 H6
Leuven, Belgium 17 D4
Leuze-en-Hainaut, Belgium 17 D3
Lev Tolstoy, Russia 46 F10
Levádhia, Greece 38 C4
Levan, U.S.A. 114 G8
Levanger, Norway 8 E14
Levani, Albania 40 F3
Levant, Î. du, France 21 E10
Lévanto, Italy 28 D6
Lévanzo, Italy 30 D5
Levelland, U.S.A. 113 J3
Leven, U.K. 14 E6
Leven, L., U.K. 14 E5
Leven, Toraka, Madag. 89 A8
Leveque C., Australia 92 C3
Leverano, Italy 31 B10
Leverkusen, Germany 24 D3
Levice, Slovak Rep. 27 C11
Lévico Terme, Italy 29 C8
Levie, France 21 G13
Levier, France 19 F13
Levin, N.Z. 91 J5
Lévis, Canada 103 C5
Levis, L., Canada 104 A5
Levítha, Greece 39 D8
Levittown, N.Y., U.S.A. 111 F11
Levittown, Pa., U.S.A. 111 F10
Levka, Bulgaria 41 E10
Levkás, Greece 38 C2
Levkás □, Greece 38 C2
Levkímmi, Greece 36 B4
Levkímmi, Ákra, Greece 36 B4
Levkôsia = Nicosia, Cyprus 36 D12
Levoča, Slovak Rep. 27 B13
Levroux, France 19 F8
Levski, Bulgaria 41 C9
Levskigrad = Karlovo, Bulgaria 41 D8
Lewellen, U.S.A. 112 E3
Lewes, U.K. 13 G8
Lewes, U.S.A. 108 F8
Lewin Brzeski, Poland 45 H4
Lewis, U.K. 14 C2
Lewis →, U.S.A. 116 E4
Lewis, Butt of, U.K. 14 C2
Lewis Ra., Australia 92 D4
Lewis Range, U.S.A. 114 C7
Lewisburg, Pa., U.S.A. 110 F8
Lewisburg, Tenn., U.S.A. 109 H2
Lewisporte, Canada 103 C8
Lewiston, Idaho, U.S.A. 114 C5
Lewiston, Maine, U.S.A. 109 C11
Lewistown, Mont., U.S.A. 114 C9
Lewistown, Pa., U.S.A. 110 F7
Lexington, Ill., U.S.A. 112 E10
Lexington, Ky., U.S.A. 108 F3
Lexington, Miss., U.S.A. 113 J9
Lexington, Mo., U.S.A. 112 F8
Lexington, N.C., U.S.A. 109 H5
Lexington, Nebr., U.S.A. 112 E5
Lexington, Ohio, U.S.A. 110 F2
Lexington, Oreg., U.S.A. 114 D4
Lexington, Tenn., U.S.A. 109 H1
Lexington Park, U.S.A. 108 F7
Leyburn, U.K. 12 C6
Leye, China 58 E6
Leyland, U.K. 12 D5
Leyre →, France 20 D2
Leyte, Phil. 61 F6
Leyte Gulf, Phil. 61 F6
Leżajsk, Poland 45 H9
Lezay, France 20 B3
Lezha, Albania 40 E3
Lezhi, China 58 B5
Lézignan-Corbières, France 20 E6
Lezoux, France 20 C7
Lgov, Russia 47 G8
Lhasa, China 60 D4
Lhazê, China 60 D3
Lhokkruet, Indonesia 62 D1
Lhokseumawe, Indonesia 62 C1
L'Hospitalet de Llobregat, Spain 32 D7
Lhuntsi Dzong, India 67 F17
Li, Thailand 64 D2
Li Shui →, China 59 C9
Li Xian, Gansu, China 56 G3
Li Xian, Hebei, China 56 E8
Li Xian, Hunan, China 59 C8
Li Xian, Sichuan, China 58 B4
Liádhoi, Greece 39 E8
Lian Xian, China 59 E9
Liancheng, China 59 E11
Lianga, Phil. 61 G7
Liangcheng, Nei Mongol Zizhiqu, China 56 D7
Liangcheng, Shandong, China 57 G10
Liangdang, China 56 H4
Lianghekou, China 58 C7
Liangping, China 58 B6
Lianhua, China 59 D9
Lianjiang, Fujian, China 59 D12
Lianjiang, Guangdong, China 59 G8
Lianping, China 59 E10
Lianshan, China 59 E9
Lianshanguan, China 57 D12
Lianshui, China 57 H10
Lianyuan, China 59 D8
Lianyungang, China 57 G10
Liao He →, China 57 D11
Liaocheng, China 56 F8
Liaodong Bandao, China 57 E12
Liaodong Wan, China 57 D11
Liaoning □, China 57 D12
Liaoyang, China 57 D12
Liaoyuan, China 57 C13
Liaozhong, China 57 D12
Liapádhes, Greece 38 B1
Liard →, Canada 104 A4
Liari, Pakistan 68 G2
Libau = Liepāja, Latvia 9 H19
Libby, U.S.A. 114 B6
Libenge, Dem. Rep. of the Congo 84 D3
Liberal, Kans., U.S.A. 113 G4
Liberal, Mo., U.S.A. 113 G7
Liberec, Czech Rep. 26 A8
Liberia, Costa Rica 120 D2
Liberia ■, W. Afr. 82 D3
Liberty, Mo., U.S.A. 112 F7
Liberty, Tex., U.S.A. 113 K7
Libiąż, Poland 45 H6
Lîbîya, Sahrâ', Africa 79 C10
Libo, China 58 E6
Libobo, Tanjung, Indonesia 63 E7
Libode, S. Africa 89 E4
Libohava, Albania 40 F4
Libourne, France 20 D3
Libramont, Belgium 17 E5
Librazhdi, Albania 40 E4
Libreville, Gabon 84 D1
Libya ■, N. Afr. 79 C9
Libyan Desert = Lîbîya, Sahrâ', Africa 79 C10
Libyan Plateau = Ed-Déffa, Egypt 80 A2
Licantén, Chile 126 D1
Licata, Italy 30 E6
Lice, Turkey 73 C9
Licheng, China 56 F7
Lichfield, U.K. 13 E6
Lichinga, Mozam. 87 E4
Lichtenburg, S. Africa 88 D4
Lichtenfels, Germany 25 E7
Lichuan, Hubei, China 58 B7
Lichuan, Jiangxi, China 59 D11
Licosa, Punta, Italy 31 B7
Lida, Belarus 9 K21
Lida, U.S.A. 115 H5
Liden, Sweden 10 B10
Lidhoríkion, Greece 38 C4
Lidhult, Sweden 11 H7
Lidköping, Sweden 11 F7
Lido, Italy 29 C9
Lido, Niger 83 C5
Lido di Roma = Óstia, Lido di, Italy 29 G9
Lidzbark, Poland 45 E6
Lidzbark Warmiński, Poland 44 D7
Liebenwalde, Germany 24 C9
Lieberose, Germany 24 D10
Liebig, Mt., Australia 92 D5
Liebling, Romania 42 E6
Liechtenstein ■, Europe 25 H5
Liège, Belgium 17 D5
Liège □, Belgium 17 D5
Liegnitz = Legnica, Poland 45 G3
Lienart, Dem. Rep. of the Congo 86 B2
Lienyünchiangshih = Lianyungang, China 57 G10
Lienz, Austria 26 E5
Liepāja, Latvia 9 H19
Liepāja □, Latvia 44 B8
Liepājas ezers, Latvia 44 B8
Lier, Belgium 17 C4
Liernais, France 19 E11
Liești, Romania 43 E12
Liévin, France 19 B9
Lièvre →, Canada 102 C4
Liezen, Austria 26 D7
Liffey →, Ireland 15 C5
Lifford, Ireland 15 B4
Liffré, France 18 D5
Lifudzin, Russia 54 B7
Ligao, Phil. 61 E5
Lightning Ridge, Australia 95 D4
Lignano Sabbiadoro, Italy 29 C10
Ligny-en-Barrois, France 19 D12
Ligourión, Greece 38 D5
Ligueil, France 18 E7
Liguria □, Italy 28 D5
Ligurian Sea, Medit. S. 6 G7
Lihou Reefs and Cays, Australia 94 B5

Lihue, *U.S.A.* 106 H15
Lijiang, *China* 58 D3
Likasi, *Dem. Rep. of the Congo* 87 E2
Likenäs, *Sweden* 10 D8
Likhoslavl, *Russia* 46 D8
Likhovskoy, *Russia* 47 H11
Likoma I., *Malawi* 87 E3
Likumburu, *Tanzania* 87 D4
L'Île-Bouchard, *France* 18 E7
L'Île-Rousse, *France* 21 F12
Liling, *China* 59 D9
Lilla Edet, *Sweden* 11 F6
Lille, *France* 19 B10
Lille Bælt, *Denmark* 11 J3
Lillebonne, *France* 18 C7
Lillehammer, *Norway* 9 F14
Lillesand, *Norway* 9 G13
Lillhärdal, *Sweden* 10 C8
Lillian Point, Mt., *Australia* 93 E4
Lillo, *Spain* 34 F7
Lillooet →, *Canada* 104 D4
Lilongwe, *Malawi* 87 E3
Liloy, *Phil.* 63 C6
Lim →, *Bos.-H.* 40 C3
Lima, *Indonesia* 63 E7
Lima, *Peru* 124 F3
Lima, *Mont., U.S.A.* 114 D7
Lima, *Ohio, U.S.A.* 108 E3
Lima →, *Portugal* 34 D2
Limages, *Canada* 111 A9
Liman, *Russia* 49 H8
Limanowa, *Poland* 45 J7
Limassol, *Cyprus* 36 E12
Limavady, *U.K.* 15 A5
Limay →, *Argentina* 128 D3
Limay Mahuida, *Argentina* 126 D2
Limbach-Oberfrohna, *Germany* 24 E8
Limbang, *Brunei* 62 D5
Limbara, Mte., *Italy* 30 B2
Limbaži, *Latvia* 9 H21
Limbdi, *India* 68 H4
Limbe, *Cameroon* 83 E6
Limbri, *Australia* 95 E5
Limbunya, *Australia* 92 C4
Limburg, *Germany* 25 E4
Limburg □, *Belgium* 17 C5
Limburg □, *Neths.* 17 C5
Limedsforsen, *Sweden* 10 D7
Limeira, *Brazil* 127 A6
Limenária, *Greece* 41 F8
Limerick, *Ireland* 15 D3
Limerick □, *Ireland* 15 D3
Limestone, *U.S.A.* 110 D6
Limestone →, *Canada* 105 B10
Limfjorden, *Denmark* 11 H3
Limia = Lima →, *Portugal* 34 D2
Limín Khersonísou, *Greece* 39 F7
Limingen, *Norway* 8 D15
Limmared, *Sweden* 11 G7
Limmen Bight, *Australia* 94 A2
Limmen Bight →, *Australia* 94 B2
Límni, *Greece* 38 C5
Límnos, *Greece* 39 B7
Limoges, *France* 20 C5
Limón, *Costa Rica* 120 E3
Limon, *U.S.A.* 112 F3
Limone Piemonte, *Italy* 28 D4
Limousin, *France* 20 C5
Limousin, Plateaux du, *France* 20 C5
Limoux, *France* 20 E6
Limpopo →, *Africa* 89 D5
Limuru, *Kenya* 86 C4
Lin Xian, *China* 56 F6
Lin'an, *China* 59 B12
Linapacan I., *Phil.* 61 F3
Linapacan Str., *Phil.* 61 F3
Linares, *Chile* 126 D1
Linares, *Mexico* 119 C5
Linares, *Spain* 35 G7
Linares □, *Chile* 126 D1
Linaro, Capo, *Italy* 29 F8
Línas Mte., *Italy* 30 C1
Lincang, *China* 58 F3
Lincheng, *China* 56 F8
Linchuan, *China* 59 D11
Lincoln, *Argentina* 126 C3
Lincoln, *N.Z.* 91 K4
Lincoln, *U.K.* 12 D7
Lincoln, *Calif., U.S.A.* 116 G5
Lincoln, *Ill., U.S.A.* 112 E10
Lincoln, *Kans., U.S.A.* 112 F5
Lincoln, *Maine, U.S.A.* 103 C6
Lincoln, *N.H., U.S.A.* 111 B13
Lincoln, *N. Mex., U.S.A.* 115 K11
Lincoln, *Nebr., U.S.A.* 112 E6
Lincoln Hav = Lincoln Sea, *Arctic* 4 A5
Lincoln Sea, *Arctic* 4 A5
Lincolnshire □, *U.K.* 12 D7
Lincolnshire Wolds, *U.K.* 12 D7
Lincolnton, *U.S.A.* 109 H5
L'Incudine, *France* 21 G13
Lind, *U.S.A.* 114 C4
Linda, *U.S.A.* 116 F5
Lindau, *Germany* 25 H5
Linden, *Guyana* 124 B7
Linden, *Calif., U.S.A.* 116 G5
Linden, *Tex., U.S.A.* 113 J7
Lindenhurst, *U.S.A.* 111 F11
Lindesberg, *Sweden* 10 E9
Lindesnes, *Norway* 9 H12
Líndhos, *Greece* 36 C10
Líndhos, Ákra, *Greece* 36 C10
Lindi, *Tanzania* 87 D4
Lindi □, *Tanzania* 87 D4
Lindi →, *Dem. Rep. of the Congo* 86 B2
Lindö, *Sweden* 11 F10
Lindome, *Sweden* 11 G6
Lindoso, *Portugal* 34 D2
Lindow, *Germany* 24 C8
Lindsay, *Canada* 102 D4
Lindsay, *Calif., U.S.A.* 116 J7
Lindsay, *Okla., U.S.A.* 113 H6
Lindsborg, *U.S.A.* 112 F6
Lindsdal, *Sweden* 11 H10
Linfen, *China* 56 F6
Ling Xian, *Hunan, China* 59 D9
Ling Xian, *Shandong, China* 56 F9
Lingao, *China* 64 C7
Lingayen, *Phil.* 63 A6
Lingayen G., *Phil.* 61 C4
Lingbi, *China* 57 H9
Lingbo, *Sweden* 10 C10
Lingchuan, *Guangxi Zhuangzu, China* 59 E8
Lingchuan, *Shanxi, China* 56 G7
Lingen, *Germany* 24 C3
Lingga, *Indonesia* 62 E2
Lingga, Kepulauan, *Indonesia* 62 E2
Lingga Arch. = Lingga, Kepulauan, *Indonesia* 62 E2
Linghem, *Sweden* 11 F9
Lingle, *U.S.A.* 112 D2
Lingling, *China* 59 D8
Lingqiu, *China* 56 E8
Lingshan, *China* 58 F7
Lingshi, *China* 56 F6
Lingshou, *China* 56 E8
Lingshui, *China* 64 C8
Lingtai, *China* 56 G4
Linguère, *Senegal* 82 B1
Lingwu, *China* 56 E4
Lingyuan, *China* 57 D10
Lingyun, *China* 58 E6
Linhai, *China* 59 C13
Linhares, *Brazil* 125 G10
Linhe, *China* 56 D4
Linjiang, *China* 57 D14
Linköping, *Sweden* 11 F9
Linkou, *China* 57 B16
Linli, *China* 59 C8
Linnhe, L., *U.K.* 14 E3
Linqi, *China* 56 G7
Linqing, *China* 56 F8
Linqu, *China* 57 F10
Linru, *China* 56 G7
Lins, *Brazil* 127 A6
Linshui, *China* 58 B6
Lintao, *China* 56 G2
Linth →, *Switz.* 25 H5
Linthal, *Switz.* 25 J5
Lintlaw, *Canada* 105 C8
Linton, *Canada* 103 C5
Linton, *Ind., U.S.A.* 108 F2
Linton, *N. Dak., U.S.A.* 112 B4
Lintong, *China* 56 G5
Linville, *Australia* 95 D5
Linwood, *Canada* 110 C4
Linwu, *China* 59 E9
Linxi, *China* 57 C10
Linxia, *China* 60 C5
Linxiang, *China* 59 C9
Linyanti →, *Africa* 88 B4
Linyi, *China* 57 G10
Linz, *Austria* 26 C7
Linz, *Germany* 24 E3
Linzhenzhen, *China* 56 F5
Linzi, *China* 57 F10
Lion, G. du, *France* 20 E7
Lionárisso, *Cyprus* 36 D13
Lioni, *Italy* 31 B8
Lions, G. of = Lion, G. du, *France* 20 E7
Lion's Den, *Zimbabwe* 87 F3
Lion's Head, *Canada* 102 D3
Liozno = Lyozna, *Belarus* 46 E6
Lipa, *Phil.* 61 E4
Lipali, *Mozam.* 87 F4
Lipany, *Slovak Rep.* 27 B13
Lípari, *Italy* 31 D7
Lípari, Is. = Eólie, Ís., *Italy* 31 D7
Lipcani, *Moldova* 43 B11
Lipetsk, *Russia* 47 F10
Lipiany, *Poland* 45 E1
Liping, *China* 58 D7
Lipkany = Lipcani, *Moldova* 43 B11
Lipljan, *Serbia, Yug.* 40 D5
Lipník nad Bečvou, *Czech Rep.* 27 B10
Lipno, *Poland* 45 F6
Lipova, *Romania* 42 D6
Lipovcy Manzovka, *Russia* 54 B6
Lipovets, *Ukraine* 47 H5
Lippe →, *Germany* 24 D2
Lippstadt, *Germany* 24 D4
Lipscomb, *U.S.A.* 113 G4
Lipsk, *Poland* 44 E10
Lipsko, *Poland* 45 G8
Lipsói, *Greece* 39 D8
Liptovský Hrádok, *Slovak Rep.* 27 B12
Liptovský Milkuláš, *Slovak Rep.* 27 B12
Liptrap C., *Australia* 95 F4
Lipu, *China* 59 E8
Lira, *Uganda* 86 B3
Liri →, *Italy* 30 A6
Liria = Lliria, *Spain* 33 F4
Lisala, *Dem. Rep. of the Congo* 84 D4
Lisboa, *Portugal* 35 G1
Lisboa □, *Portugal* 35 F1
Lisbon = Lisboa, *Portugal* 35 G1
Lisbon, *N. Dak., U.S.A.* 112 B6
Lisbon, *N.H., U.S.A.* 111 B13
Lisbon, *Ohio, U.S.A.* 110 F4
Lisburn, *U.K.* 15 B5
Liscannor B., *Ireland* 15 D2
Liscia →, *Italy* 30 A2
Lishe Jiang →, *China* 58 E3
Lishi, *China* 56 F6
Lishu, *China* 57 C13
Lishui, *Jiangsu, China* 59 B12
Lishui, *Zhejiang, China* 59 C12
Lisianski I., *Pac. Oc.* 96 E10
Lisichansk = Lysychansk, *Ukraine* 47 H10
Lisieux, *France* 18 C7
Liski, *Russia* 47 G10
L'Isle-Jourdain, *Gers, France* 20 E5
L'Isle-Jourdain, *Vienne, France* 20 B4
L'Isle-sur-la-Sorgue, *France* 21 E9
Lisle-sur-Tarn, *France* 20 E5
Lismore, *Australia* 95 D5
Lismore, *Ireland* 15 D4
Lista, *Norway* 9 G12
Lister, Mt., *Antarctica* 5 D11
Liston, *Australia* 95 D5
Listowel, *Canada* 102 D3
Listowel, *Ireland* 15 D2
Lit, *Sweden* 10 A8
Lit-et-Mixe, *France* 20 D2
Litang, *Guangxi Zhuangzu, China* 58 F7
Litang, *Sichuan, China* 58 B3
Litang Qu →, *China* 58 C3
Litani →, *Lebanon* 75 B4
Litchfield, *Calif., U.S.A.* 116 E6
Litchfield, *Conn., U.S.A.* 111 E11
Litchfield, *Ill., U.S.A.* 112 F10
Litchfield, *Minn., U.S.A.* 112 C7
Liteni, *Romania* 43 C11
Lithgow, *Australia* 95 E5
Líthinon, Ákra, *Greece* 36 E6
Lithuania ■, *Europe* 9 J20
Litija, *Slovenia* 29 B11
Litókhoron, *Greece* 40 F6
Litoměřice, *Czech Rep.* 26 A7
Litomyšl, *Czech Rep.* 27 B9
Litschau, *Austria* 26 C8
Little Abaco I., *Bahamas* 120 A4
Little Barrier I., *N.Z.* 91 G5
Little Belt Mts., *U.S.A.* 114 C8
Little Blue →, *U.S.A.* 112 F6
Little Cadotte →, *Canada* 104 B5
Little Cayman, I., *Cayman Is.* 120 C3
Little Churchill →, *Canada* 105 B9
Little Colorado →, *U.S.A.* 115 H8
Little Current, *Canada* 102 C3
Little Current →, *Canada* 102 B3
Little Falls, *Minn., U.S.A.* 112 C7
Little Falls, *N.Y., U.S.A.* 111 C10
Little Fork →, *U.S.A.* 112 A8
Little Grand Rapids, *Canada* 105 C9
Little Humboldt →, *U.S.A.* 114 F5
Little Inagua I., *Bahamas* 121 B5
Little Karoo, *S. Africa* 88 E3
Little Lake, *U.S.A.* 117 K9
Little Laut Is. = Laut Kecil, Kepulauan, *Indonesia* 62 E5
Little Minch, *U.K.* 14 D2
Little Missouri →, *U.S.A.* 112 B3
Little Ouse →, *U.K.* 13 E9
Little Rann, *India* 68 H4
Little Red →, *U.S.A.* 113 H9
Little River, *N.Z.* 91 K4
Little Rock, *U.S.A.* 113 H8
Little Ruaha →, *Tanzania* 86 D4
Little Sable Pt., *U.S.A.* 108 D2
Little Sioux →, *U.S.A.* 112 E6
Little Smoky →, *Canada* 104 C5
Little Snake →, *U.S.A.* 114 F9
Little Valley, *U.S.A.* 110 D6
Little Wabash →, *U.S.A.* 108 G1
Littlefield, *U.S.A.* 113 J3
Littlefork, *U.S.A.* 112 A8
Littlehampton, *U.K.* 13 G7
Littleton, *U.S.A.* 111 B13
Litvinov, *Czech Rep.* 26 A6
Liu He →, *China* 57 D11
Liu Jiang →, *China* 58 F7
Liuba, *China* 56 H4
Liucheng, *China* 58 E7
Liugou, *China* 57 D10
Liuhe, *China* 57 C13
Liuheng Dao, *China* 59 C14
Liukang Tenggaja = Sabalana, Kepulauan, *Indonesia* 63 F5
Liuli, *Tanzania* 87 E3
Liuwa Plain, *Zambia* 85 G4
Liuyang, *China* 59 C9
Liuzhou, *China* 58 E7
Liuzhuang, *China* 57 H11
Livada, *Romania* 42 C8
Livadherón, *Greece* 40 F5
Livadhia, *Cyprus* 36 E12
Livádhion, *Greece* 38 A4
Livarot, *France* 18 D7
Live Oak, *Calif., U.S.A.* 116 F5
Live Oak, *Fla., U.S.A.* 109 K4
Liveras, *Cyprus* 36 D11
Liveringa, *Australia* 92 C3
Livermore, *U.S.A.* 116 H5
Livermore, Mt., *U.S.A.* 113 K2
Liverpool, *Australia* 95 E5
Liverpool, *Canada* 103 D7
Liverpool, *U.K.* 12 D4
Liverpool Bay, *U.K.* 12 D4
Liverpool Plains, *Australia* 95 E5
Liverpool Ra., *Australia* 95 E5
Livigno, *Italy* 28 B7
Livingston, *Guatemala* 120 C2
Livingston, *U.K.* 14 F5
Livingston, *Calif., U.S.A.* 116 H6
Livingston, *Mont., U.S.A.* 114 D8
Livingston, *Tex., U.S.A.* 113 K7
Livingstone, *Zambia* 87 F2
Livingstone Mts., *Tanzania* 87 D3
Livingstonia, *Malawi* 87 E3
Livno, *Bos.-H.* 42 G2
Livny, *Russia* 47 F9
Livonia, *U.S.A.* 108 D4
Livorno, *Italy* 28 E7
Livramento, *Brazil* 127 C4
Livron-sur-Drôme, *France* 21 D8
Liwale, *Tanzania* 87 D4
Liwale □, *Tanzania* 87 D4
Liwiec →, *Poland* 45 F8
Lixi, *China* 58 D3
Lixoúrion, *Greece* 38 C2
Liyang, *China* 59 B12
Lizard I., *Australia* 94 A4
Lizard Pt., *U.K.* 13 H2
Lizzano, *Italy* 31 B10
Ljig, *Serbia, Yug.* 40 B4
Ljubija, *Bos.-H.* 29 D13
Ljubinje, *Bos.-H.* 40 D2
Ljubljana, *Slovenia* 29 B11
Ljubno, *Slovenia* 29 B11
Ljubovija, *Serbia, Yug.* 40 B3
Ljugarn, *Sweden* 11 G12
Ljung, *Sweden* 11 G7
Ljungan →, *Sweden* 10 B11
Ljungaverk, *Sweden* 10 B10
Ljungby, *Sweden* 9 H15
Ljungbyholm, *Sweden* 11 H10
Ljungdalen, *Sweden* 10 B6
Ljungsbro, *Sweden* 11 F9
Ljungskile, *Sweden* 11 F5
Ljusdal, *Sweden* 10 C10
Ljusfallshammar, *Sweden* 11 F9
Ljusnan →, *Sweden* 10 C11
Ljusne, *Sweden* 10 C11
Ljutomer, *Slovenia* 29 B13
Llagostera, *Spain* 32 D7
Llancanelo, Salina, *Argentina* 126 D2
Llandeilo, *U.K.* 13 F4
Llandovery, *U.K.* 13 F4
Llandrindod Wells, *U.K.* 13 E4
Llandudno, *U.K.* 12 D4
Llanelli, *U.K.* 13 F3
Llanes, *Spain* 34 B6
Llangollen, *U.K.* 12 E4
Llanidloes, *U.K.* 13 E4
Llano, *U.S.A.* 113 K5
Llano →, *U.S.A.* 113 K5
Llano Estacado, *U.S.A.* 113 J3
Llanos, *S. Amer.* 122 C3
Llanquihue, L., *Chile* 128 E1
Llanwrtyd Wells, *U.K.* 13 E4
Llebeig, C. des, *Spain* 37 B9
Lleida, *Spain* 32 D5
Lleida □, *Spain* 32 C6
Llentrisca, C., *Spain* 37 C7
Llera, *Mexico* 119 C5
Llerena, *Spain* 35 G5
Lleyn Peninsula, *U.K.* 12 E3
Llico, *Chile* 126 C1
Lliria, *Spain* 33 F4
Llobregat →, *Spain* 32 D7
Llodio, *Spain* 32 B2
Lloret de Mar, *Spain* 32 D7
Lloyd B., *Australia* 94 A3
Lloyd L., *Canada* 105 B7
Lloydminster, *Canada* 105 C7
Llucena del Cid, *Spain* 32 E4
Llucmajor, *Spain* 37 B9
Llullaillaco, Volcán, *S. Amer.* 126 A2
Lo →, *Vietnam* 64 B5
Loa, *U.S.A.* 115 G8
Loa →, *Chile* 126 A1
Loano, *Italy* 28 D5
Lobatse, *Botswana* 88 D4
Löbau, *Germany* 24 D10
Lobenstein, *Germany* 24 E7
Lobería, *Argentina* 126 D4
Löberöd, *Sweden* 11 J7
Łobez, *Poland* 44 E2
Lobito, *Angola* 85 G2
Lobos, *Argentina* 126 D4
Lobos, I., *Mexico* 118 B2
Lobos, I. de, *Canary Is.* 37 F6
Łobżenica, *Poland* 45 E4
Loc Binh, *Vietnam* 64 B6
Loc Ninh, *Vietnam* 65 G6
Locarno, *Switz.* 25 J4
Loch Baghasdail = Lochboisdale, *U.K.* 14 D1
Loch Garman = Wexford, *Ireland* 15 D5
Loch Nam Madadh = Lochmaddy, *U.K.* 14 D1
Lochaber, *U.K.* 14 E3
Locharbriggs, *U.K.* 14 F5
Lochboisdale, *U.K.* 14 D1
Lochem, *Neths.* 17 B6
Loches, *France* 18 E7
Lochgilphead, *U.K.* 14 E3
Lochinver, *U.K.* 14 C3
Lochmaddy, *U.K.* 14 D1
Lochnagar, *Australia* 94 C4
Lochnagar, *U.K.* 14 E5
Łochów, *Poland* 45 F8
Lochy, L., *U.K.* 14 E4
Lock, *Australia* 95 E2
Lock Haven, *U.S.A.* 110 E7
Lockeford, *U.S.A.* 116 G5
Lockeport, *Canada* 103 D6
Lockerbie, *U.K.* 14 F5
Lockhart, *U.S.A.* 113 L6
Lockhart, L., *Australia* 93 F2
Lockney, *U.S.A.* 113 H4
Lockport, *U.S.A.* 110 C6
Locminé, *France* 18 E4
Locri, *Italy* 31 D9
Locronan, *France* 18 D2
Lod, *Israel* 75 D3
Lodeinoye Pole, *Russia* 46 B7
Lodève, *France* 20 E7
Lodge Grass, *U.S.A.* 114 D10
Lodgepole, *U.S.A.* 112 E3
Lodgepole Cr. →, *U.S.A.* 112 E2
Lodhran, *Pakistan* 68 E4
Lodi, *Italy* 28 C6
Lodi, *U.S.A.* 116 G5
Lodja, *Dem. Rep. of the Congo* 86 C1
Lodosa, *Spain* 32 C2
Lödöse, *Sweden* 11 F6
Lodwar, *Kenya* 86 B4
Łódź, *Poland* 45 G6
Łódź □, *Poland* 45 G6
Loei, *Thailand* 64 D3
Loengo, *Dem. Rep. of the Congo* 86 C2
Loeriesfontein, *S. Africa* 88 E2
Lofer, *Austria* 26 D5
Lofoten, *Norway* 8 B15
Lofsdalen, *Sweden* 10 B7
Lofsen →, *Sweden* 10 B7
Loftahammar, *Sweden* 11 G10
Logan, *Kans., U.S.A.* 112 F5
Logan, *Ohio, U.S.A.* 108 F4
Logan, *Utah, U.S.A.* 114 F8
Logan, *W. Va., U.S.A.* 108 G5
Logan, Mt., *Canada* 100 B5
Logan Pass, *U.S.A.* 104 D6
Logandale, *U.S.A.* 117 J12
Logansport, *Ind., U.S.A.* 108 E2
Logansport, *La., U.S.A.* 113 K8
Logo, *Sudan* 81 F3
Logone →, *Chad* 79 F9
Logroño, *Spain* 32 C2
Logrosán, *Spain* 35 F5
Løgstør, *Denmark* 11 H3
Løgumkloster, *Denmark* 11 J2
Lohals, *Denmark* 11 J4
Lohardaga, *India* 69 H11
Lohja, *Finland* 9 F21
Löhne, *Germany* 24 C4
Lohr, *Germany* 25 F5
Loi-kaw, *Burma* 67 K20
Loimaa, *Finland* 9 F20
Loir →, *France* 18 E6
Loir-et-Cher □, *France* 18 E8
Loire □, *France* 21 C8
Loire →, *France* 18 E4
Loire-Atlantique □, *France* 18 E5
Loiret □, *France* 19 E9
Loitz, *Germany* 24 B9
Loja, *Ecuador* 124 D3
Loja, *Spain* 35 H6
Loji = Kawasi, *Indonesia* 63 E7
Løjt Kirkeby, *Denmark* 11 J3
Loka, *Sudan* 81 G3
Lokandu, *Dem. Rep. of the Congo* 86 C2
Lokeren, *Belgium* 17 C3
Lokhvitsa, *Ukraine* 47 G7
Lokichokio, *Kenya* 86 B3
Lokitaung, *Kenya* 86 B4
Lokkan tekojärvi, *Finland* 8 C22
Løkken, *Denmark* 11 G3
Loknya, *Russia* 46 D6
Lokoja, *Nigeria* 83 D6
Lokot, *Russia* 47 F8
Lol →, *Sudan* 81 F2
Lola, *Guinea* 82 D3
Lola, Mt., *U.S.A.* 116 F6
Lolibai, Gebel, *Sudan* 81 G3
Lolimi, *Sudan* 81 G3
Loliondo, *Tanzania* 86 C4
Lolland, *Denmark* 11 K5
Lollar, *Germany* 24 E4
Lolo, *U.S.A.* 114 C6
Lolodorf, *Cameroon* 83 E7
Lom, *Bulgaria* 40 C7
Lom →, *Bulgaria* 40 C7
Lom Kao, *Thailand* 64 D3
Lom Sak, *Thailand* 64 D
Loma, *U.S.A.* 11
Loma Linda, *U.S.A.*
Lomami →, *Dem. Rep. of th*

Lomas de Zamóra, *Argentina* 126 C4
Lombadina, *Australia* 92 C3
Lombárdia □, *Italy* 28 C6
Lombardy = Lombárdia □, *Italy* 28 C6
Lombez, *France* 20 E4
Lomblen, *Indonesia* 63 F6
Lombok, *Indonesia* 62 F5
Lomé, *Togo* 83 D5
Lomela, *Dem. Rep. of the Congo* 84 E4
Lomela →, *Dem. Rep. of the Congo* 84 E4
Lometa, *U.S.A.* 113 K5
Lomianki, *Poland* 45 F7
Lomma, *Sweden* 11 J7
Lommel, *Belgium* 17 C5
Lomond, *Canada* 104 C6
Lomond, L., *U.K.* 14 E4
Lomphat, *Cambodia* 64 F6
Lompobatang, *Indonesia* 63 F5
Lompoc, *U.S.A.* 117 L6
Łomża, *Poland* 45 E9
Łomża □, *Poland* 45 E9
Loncoche, *Chile* 128 D2
Londa, *India* 66 M9
Londiani, *Kenya* 86 C4
Londinières, *France* 18 C8
London, *Canada* 102 D3
London, *U.K.* 13 F7
London, *Ky., U.S.A.* 108 G3
London, *Ohio, U.S.A.* 108 F4
London, Greater □, *U.K.* 13 F7
Londonderry, *U.K.* 15 B4
Londonderry □, *U.K.* 15 B4
Londonderry, C., *Australia* 92 B4
Londonderry, I., *Chile* 128 H2
Londres, *Argentina* 128 B3
Londrina, *Brazil* 127 A5
Lone Pine, *U.S.A.* 116 J8
Long Beach, *Calif., U.S.A.* 117 M8
Long Beach, *N.Y., U.S.A.* 111 F11
Long Beach, *Wash., U.S.A.* 116 D2
Long Branch, *U.S.A.* 111 F11
Long Creek, *U.S.A.* 114 D4
Long Eaton, *U.K.* 12 E6
Long I., *Australia* 94 C4
Long I., *Bahamas* 121 B4
Long I., *Ireland* 15 E2
Long I., *U.S.A.* 111 F11
Long Island Sd., *U.S.A.* 111 E12
Long L., *Canada* 102 C2
Long Lake, *U.S.A.* 111 C10
Long Pine, *U.S.A.* 112 D5
Long Point B., *Canada* 110 D4
Long Pt., *Nfld., Canada* 103 C8
Long Pt., *Ont., Canada* 110 D4
Long Range Mts., *Canada* 103 C8
Long Reef, *Australia* 92 B4
Long Str. = Longa, Proliv, *Russia* 4 C16
Long Thanh, *Vietnam* 65 G6
Long Xian, *China* 56 G4
Long Xuyen, *Vietnam* 65 G5
Longá, *Greece* 38 E3
Longa, Proliv, *Russia* 4 C16
Long'an, *China* 58 F6
Longarone, *Italy* 29 B9
Longbenton, *U.K.* 12 B6
Longchang, *China* 58 C5
Longchi, *China* 58 C4
Longchuan, *Guangdong, China* 59 E10
Longchuan, *Yunnan, China* 58 E1
Longde, *China* 56 G4
Longeau, *France* 19 E12
Longford, *Australia* 94 G4
Longford, *Ireland* 15 C4
Longford □, *Ireland* 15 C4
Longguan, *China* 56 D8
Longhua, *China* 57 D9
Longhui, *China* 59 D8
Longido, *Tanzania* 86 C4
Longiram, *Indonesia* 62 E5
Longkou, *Jiangxi, China* 59 D10
Longkou, *Shandong, China* 57 F11
Longlac, *Canada* 102 C2
Longli, *China* 58 D6
Longlin, *China* 58 E5
Longling, *China* 58 E2
Longmen, *China* 59 F10
Longming, *China* 58 F6
Longmont, *U.S.A.* 112 E2
Longnan, *China* 59 E10
Longnawan, *Indonesia* 62 D4
Longobucco, *Italy* 31 C9
Longquan, *China* 59 C12
Longreach, *Au~tralia* 94 C3
Longshan, *C…* 58 C7
Longshe… 59 E8
Lon… 94 C4
J… *…ce* 18 E6
… 19 C9
… 111 A11
19 C12
19 E12
…4 C6
… J7
D4
…12
…3
Lonoke, *U.S.A.* 113 H9
Lonquimay, *Chile* 128 D2
Lons-le-Saunier, *France* 19 F12
Lönsboda, *Sweden* 11 H8
Looe, *U.K.* 13 G3
Lookout, C., *Canada* 102 A3
Lookout, C., *U.S.A.* 109 H7
Loolmalasin, *Tanzania* 86 C4
Loon →, *Alta., Canada* 104 B5
Loon →, *Man., Canada* 105 B8
Loon Lake, *Canada* 105 C7
Loongana, *Australia* 93 F4
Loop Hd., *Ireland* 15 D2
Lop Buri, *Thailand* 64 E3
Lop Nor = Lop Nur, *China* 60 B4
Lop Nur, *China* 60 B4
Lopare, *Bos.-H.* 42 F3
Lopatin, *Russia* 49 J8
Lopatina, Gora, *Russia* 51 D15
Lopaye, *Sudan* 81 F3
Lopez, *Phil.* 61 E5
Lopez, C., *Gabon* 84 E1
Lopphavet, *Norway* 8 A19
Lora →, *Afghan.* 66 D4
Lora, Hamun-i-, *Pakistan* 66 E4
Lora Cr. →, *Australia* 95 D2
Lora del Río, *Spain* 35 H5
Lorain, *U.S.A.* 110 E2
Loralai, *Pakistan* 68 D3
Lorca, *Spain* 33 H3
Lord Howe I., *Pac. Oc.* 96 L7
Lord Howe Ridge, *Pac. Oc.* 96 L8
Lordsburg, *U.S.A.* 115 K9
Loreto, *Brazil* 125 E9
Loreto, *Italy* 29 E10
Loreto, *Mexico* 118 B2
Lorgues, *France* 21 E10
Lorient, *France* 18 E3
Lőrinci, *Hungary* 42 C4
Lorn, *U.K.* 14 E3
Lorn, Firth of, *U.K.* 14 E3
Lorne, *Australia* 95 F3
Lorovouno, *Cyprus* 36 D11
Lörrach, *Germany* 25 H3
Lorraine □, *France* 19 D13
Lorrainville, *Canada* 102 C4
Los, *Sweden* 10 C9
Los, Îles de, *Guinea* 82 D2
Los Alamos, *Calif., U.S.A.* 117 L6
Los Alamos, *N. Mex., U.S.A.* 115 J10
Los Altos, *U.S.A.* 116 H4
Los Andes, *Chile* 126 C1
Los Angeles, *Chile* 126 D1
Los Angeles, *U.S.A.* 117 M8
Los Angeles Aqueduct, *U.S.A.* 117 K9
Los Banos, *U.S.A.* 116 H6
Los Barrios, *Spain* 35 J5
Los Blancos, *Argentina* 126 A3
Los Corrales de Buelna, *Spain* 34 B6
Los Cristianos, *Canary Is.* 37 F3
Los Gallardos, *Spain* 33 H3
Los Gatos, *U.S.A.* 116 H5
Los Hermanos, *Venezuela* 121 D7
Los Islotes, *Canary Is.* 37 E6
Los Llanos de Aridane, *Canary Is.* 37 F2
Los Lunas, *U.S.A.* 115 J10
Los Mochis, *Mexico* 118 B3
Los Monegros, *Spain* 32 D4
Los Nietos, *Spain* 33 H4
Los Olivos, *U.S.A.* 117 L6
Los Palacios, *Cuba* 120 B3
Los Palacios y Villafranca, *Spain* 35 H5
Los Reyes, *Mexico* 118 D4
Los Roques, *Venezuela* 124 A5
Los Santos de Maimona, *Spain* 35 G4
Los Teques, *Venezuela* 124 A5
Los Testigos, *Venezuela* 124 A6
Los Vilos, *Chile* 126 C1
Los Yébenes, *Spain* 35 F7
Łosice, *Poland* 45 F9
Løsning, *Denmark* 11 J3
Lossiemouth, *U.K.* 14 D5
Lostwithiel, *U.K.* 13 G3
Lot □, *France* 20 D5
Lot →, *France* 20 D4
Lot-et-Garonne □, *France* 20 D4
Lota, *Chile* 126 D1
Loţfābād, *Iran* 71 B8
Lothair, *S. Africa* 89 D5
Lotorp, *Sweden* 11 F9
Lötschbergtunnel, *Switz.* 25 J3
Löttorp, *Sweden* 11 G11
Lotung, *Taiwan* 59 E13
Loubomo, *Congo* 84 E2
Loudéac, *France* 18 D4
Loudi, *China* 59 D8
Loudon, *U.S.A.* 109 H3
Loudonville, *U.S.A.* 110 F2
Loudun, *France* 18 E7
Loue →, *France* 19 E12
Louga, *Senegal* 82 B1
Loughborough, *U.K.* 12 E6
Loughrea, *Ireland* 15 C3
Loughros More B., *Ireland* 15 B3
Louhans, *France* 19 F12
Louis Trichardt, *S. Africa* 89 C4
Louis XIV, Pte., *Canada* 102 B4
Louisa, *U.S.A.* 108 F4
Louisbourg, *Canada* 103 C8
Louise I., *Canada* 104 C2
Louiseville, *Canada* 102 C5
Louisiade Arch., *Papua N. G.* 96 J7
Louisiana, *U.S.A.* 112 F9
Louisiana □, *U.S.A.* 113 K9
Louisville, *Ky., U.S.A.* 108 F3
Louisville, *Miss., U.S.A.* 113 J10
Loulay, *France* 20 B3
Loulé, *Portugal* 35 H3
Louny, *Czech Rep.* 26 A6
Loup City, *U.S.A.* 112 E5
Lourdes, *France* 20 E3
Lourdes-du-Blanc-Sablon, *Canada* 103 B8
Lourenço-Marques = Maputo, *Mozam.* 89 D5
Lourinhã, *Portugal* 35 F1
Lousã, *Portugal* 34 E2
Louth, *Australia* 95 E4
Louth, *Ireland* 15 C5
Louth, *U.K.* 12 D7
Louth □, *Ireland* 15 C5
Loutrá Aidhipsoú, *Greece* 38 C5
Loutráki, *Greece* 38 D4
Louvain = Leuven, *Belgium* 17 D4
Louviers, *France* 18 C8
Louwsburg, *S. Africa* 89 D5
Lovat →, *Russia* 46 C6
Lovćen, *Montenegro, Yug.* 40 D2
Love, *Canada* 105 C8
Lovech, *Bulgaria* 41 C8
Lovech □, *Bulgaria* 41 C8
Loveland, *U.S.A.* 112 E2
Lovell, *U.S.A.* 114 D9
Lovelock, *U.S.A.* 114 F4
Lóvere, *Italy* 28 C7
Lövestad, *Sweden* 11 J7
Loviisa, *Finland* 9 F22
Loving, *U.S.A.* 113 J2
Lovington, *U.S.A.* 113 J3
Lovisa = Loviisa, *Finland* 9 F22
Lovosice, *Czech Rep.* 26 A7
Lovran, *Croatia* 29 C11
Lovrin, *Romania* 42 E5
Lövstabruk, *Sweden* 10 D11
Lövstabukten, *Sweden* 10 D11
Low Pt., *Australia* 93 F4
Low Tatra = Nízké Tatry, *Slovak Rep.* 27 C12
Lowa, *Dem. Rep. of the Congo* 86 C2
Lowa →, *Dem. Rep. of the Congo* 86 C2
Lowell, *U.S.A.* 111 D13
Lower Arrow L., *Canada* 104 D5
Lower Austria = Niederösterreich □, *Austria* 26 C8
Lower California = Baja California, *Mexico* 118 A1
Lower Hutt, *N.Z.* 91 J5
Lower L., *U.S.A.* 114 F3
Lower Lake, *U.S.A.* 116 G4
Lower Post, *Canada* 104 B3
Lower Red L., *U.S.A.* 112 B7
Lower Saxony = Niedersachsen □, *Germany* 24 C4
Lower Tunguska = Tunguska, Nizhnyaya →, *Russia* 51 C9
Lowestoft, *U.K.* 13 E9
Łowicz, *Poland* 45 F6
Lowville, *U.S.A.* 111 C9
Loxton, *Australia* 95 E3
Loxton, *S. Africa* 88 E3
Loyalton, *U.S.A.* 116 F6
Loyalty Is. = Loyauté, Is., *N. Cal.* 96 K8
Loyang = Luoyang, *China* 56 G7
Loyauté, Is., *N. Cal.* 96 K8
Loyev = Loyew, *Belarus* 47 G6
Loyew, *Belarus* 47 G6
Loyoro, *Uganda* 86 B3
Lož, *Slovenia* 29 C11
Lozère □, *France* 20 D7
Loznica, *Serbia, Yug.* 40 B3
Lozova, *Ukraine* 47 H9
Luachimo, *Angola* 84 F4
Lualaba →, *Dem. Rep. of the Congo* 86 B2
Luampa, *Zambia* 87 F1
Lu'an, *China* 59 B11
Luan Chau, *Vietnam* 64 B4
Luan He →, *China* 57 E10
Luan Xian, *China* 57 E10
Luancheng, *Guangxi Zhuangzu, China* 58 F7
Luancheng, *Hebei, China* 56 F8
Luanco, *Spain* 34 B5
Luanda, *Angola* 84 F2
Luang, Thale, *Thailand* 65 J3
Luang Prabang, *Laos* 64 C4
Luangwa, *Zambia* 87 F3
Luangwa →, *Zambia* 87 E3
Luangwa Valley, *Zambia* 87 E3
Luanne, *China* 57 D9
Luanping, *China* 57 D9
Luanshya, *Zambia* 87 E2
Luapula □, *Zambia* 87 E2
Luapula →, *Africa* 87 D2
Luarca, *Spain* 34 B4
Luashi, *Dem. Rep. of the Congo* 87 E1
Luau, *Angola* 84 G4
Lubaczów, *Poland* 45 H10
Lubań, *Poland* 45 G2
Lubana, Ozero = Lubānas Ezers, *Latvia* 9 H22
Lubānas Ezers, *Latvia* 9 H22
Lubang, *Phil.* 61 E4
Lubang Is., *Phil.* 63 B6
Lubartów, *Poland* 45 G9
Lubawa, *Poland* 44 E6
Lübbecke, *Germany* 24 C4
Lübben, *Germany* 24 D9
Lübbenau, *Germany* 24 D9
Lubbock, *U.S.A.* 113 J4
Lübeck, *Germany* 24 B6
Lübecker Bucht, *Germany* 24 A6
Lubefu, *Dem. Rep. of the Congo* 86 C1
Lubefu →, *Dem. Rep. of the Congo* 86 C1
Lubero = Luofu, *Dem. Rep. of the Congo* 86 C2
Lubersac, *France* 20 C5
Lubicon L., *Canada* 104 B5
Lubień Kujawski, *Poland* 45 F6
Lubin, *Poland* 45 G3
Lublin, *Poland* 45 G9
Lublin □, *Poland* 45 G9
Lubliniec, *Poland* 45 H5
Lubnān, J., *Lebanon* 75 B4
Lubnān, Jabal, *Lebanon* 75 B4
Lubniewice, *Poland* 45 F2
Lubny, *Ukraine* 47 G7
Lubomierz, *Poland* 45 G2
Luboń, *Poland* 45 F3
Lubongola, *Dem. Rep. of the Congo* 86 C2
L'ubotín, *Slovak Rep.* 27 B13
Lubraniec, *Poland* 45 F5
Lubsko, *Poland* 45 G1
Lübtheen, *Germany* 24 B7
Lubuagan, *Phil.* 61 C4
Lubudi →, *Dem. Rep. of the Congo* 87 D2
Lubuklinggau, *Indonesia* 62 E2
Lubuksikaping, *Indonesia* 62 D2
Lubumbashi, *Dem. Rep. of the Congo* 87 E2
Lubunda, *Dem. Rep. of the Congo* 86 D2
Lubungu, *Zambia* 87 E2
Lubutu, *Dem. Rep. of the Congo* 86 C2
Luc An Chau, *Vietnam* 64 A5
Luc-en-Diois, *France* 21 D9
Lucan, *Canada* 110 C3
Lucban, *Phil.* 61 D4
Lucca, *Italy* 28 E7
Lucé, *France* 18 D8
Luce Bay, *U.K.* 14 G4
Lucea, *Jamaica* 120 C4
Lucedale, *U.S.A.* 109 K1
Lucena, *Phil.* 61 E4
Lucena, *Spain* 35 H6
Lučenec, *Slovak Rep.* 27 C12
Lucera, *Italy* 31 A8
Lucerne = Luzern, *Switz.* 25 H4
Lucerne, *U.S.A.* 116 F4
Lucerne Valley, *U.S.A.* 117 L10
Lucero, *Mexico* 118 A3
Luchena →, *Spain* 33 H3
Lucheng, *China* 56 F7
Lucheringo →, *Mozam.* 87 E4
Luchiang, *Taiwan* 59 E13
Lüchow, *Germany* 24 C7
Luchuan, *China* 59 F8
Luckau, *Germany* 24 D9
Luckenwalde, *Germany* 24 C9
Lucknow, *India* 69 F9
Luçon, *France* 20 B2
Lüda = Dalian, *China* 57 E11
Luda Kamchiya →, *Bulgaria* 41 C11
Ludbreg, *Croatia* 29 B13
Lüdenscheid, *Germany* 24 D3
Lüderitz, *Namibia* 88 D2
Ludewe □, *Tanzania* 87 E3
Ludhiana, *India* 68 D6
Ludian, *China* 58 D4
Luding Qiao, *China* 58 C4
Lüdinghausen, *Germany* 24 D3
Ludington, *U.S.A.* 108 D2
Ludlow, *U.K.* 13 E5
Ludlow, *Calif., U.S.A.* 117 L10
Ludlow, *Vt., U.S.A.* 111 C12
Ludus, *Romania* 43 D9
Ludvika, *Sweden* 10 D9
Ludwigsburg, *Germany* 25 G5
Ludwigsfelde, *Germany* 24 C9
Ludwigshafen, *Germany* 25 F4
Ludwigslust, *Germany* 24 B7
Ludza, *Latvia* 46 D4
Lueki, *Dem. Rep. of the Congo* 86 C2
Luena, *Dem. Rep. of the Congo* 87 D2
Luena, *Zambia* 87 E3
Lüeyang, *China* 56 H4
Lufeng, *Guangdong, China* 59 F10
Lufeng, *Yunnan, China* 58 E4
Lufira →, *Dem. Rep. of the Congo* 87 D2
Lufkin, *U.S.A.* 113 K7
Lufupa, *Dem. Rep. of the Congo* 87 E1
Luga, *Russia* 46 C5
Luga →, *Russia* 46 C5
Lugano, *Switz.* 25 J4
Lugano, L. di, *Switz.* 28 C6
Lugansk = Luhansk, *Ukraine* 47 H10
Lugard's Falls, *Kenya* 86 C4
Lugela, *Mozam.* 87 F4
Lugenda →, *Mozam.* 87 E4
Lugh Ganana, *Somali Rep.* 74 G3
Lugnaquilla, *Ireland* 15 D5
Lugo, *Italy* 29 D8
Lugo, *Spain* 34 B3
Lugo □, *Spain* 34 C3
Lugoj, *Romania* 42 E6
Lugovoy, *Kazakstan* 50 E8
Luhansk, *Ukraine* 47 H10
Luhe, *China* 59 A12
Luhe →, *Germany* 24 B6
Luhuo, *China* 58 B3
Luiana, *Angola* 88 B3
Luimneach = Limerick, *Ireland* 15 D3
Luing, *U.K.* 14 E3
Luino, *Italy* 28 C5
Luís Correia, *Brazil* 125 D10
Luitpold Coast, *Antarctica* 5 D1
Luiza, *Dem. Rep. of the Congo* 84 F4
Luizi, *Dem. Rep. of the Congo* 86 D2
Luján, *Argentina* 126 C4
Lujiang, *China* 59 B11
Lukanga Swamp, *Zambia* 87 E2
Lukavac, *Bos.-H.* 42 F3
Lukenie →, *Dem. Rep. of the Congo* 84 E3
Lukhisaral, *India* 69 G12
Lŭki, *Bulgaria* 41 E8
Lukolela, *Dem. Rep. of the Congo* 86 D1
Lukosi, *Zimbabwe* 87 F2
Lukovë, *Albania* 40 G3
Lukovit, *Bulgaria* 41 C8
Łuków, *Poland* 45 G9
Lukoyanov, *Russia* 48 C7
Lule älv →, *Sweden* 8 D19
Luleå, *Sweden* 8 D20
Lüleburgaz, *Turkey* 41 E11
Luliang, *China* 58 E4
Luling, *U.S.A.* 113 L6
Lulong, *China* 57 E10
Lulonga →, *Dem. Rep. of the Congo* 84 D3
Lulua →, *Dem. Rep. of the Congo* 84 E4
Luluabourg = Kananga, *Dem. Rep. of the Congo* 84 F4
Lumajang, *Indonesia* 63 H15
Lumbala N'guimbo, *Angola* 85 G4
Lumberton, *Miss., U.S.A.* 113 K10
Lumberton, *N.C., U.S.A.* 109 H6
Lumberton, *N. Mex., U.S.A.* 115 H10
Lumbwa, *Kenya* 86 C4
Lumsden, *N.Z.* 91 L2
Lumut, *Malaysia* 65 K3
Lumut, Tanjung, *Indonesia* 62 E3
Luna, *Phil.* 61 C4
Lunan, *China* 58 E4
Lunavada, *India* 68 H5
Lunca, *Romania* 43 C10
Lunca Corbului, *Romania* 43 F9
Lund, *Sweden* 11 J7
Lund, *U.S.A.* 114 G6
Lundazi, *Zambia* 87 E3
Lunderskov, *Denmark* 11 J3
Lundi →, *Zimbabwe* 87 G3
Lundu, *Malaysia* 62 D3
Lundy, *U.K.* 13 F3
Lune →, *U.K.* 12 C5
Lüneburg, *Germany* 24 B6
Lüneburg Heath = Lüneburger Heide, *Germany* 24 B6
Lüneburger Heide, *Germany* 24 B6
Lunel, *France* 21 E8
Lünen, *Germany* 24 D3
Lunenburg, *Canada* 103 D7
Lunéville, *France* 19 D13
Lunga →, *Zambia* 87 E2
Lungi Airport, *S. Leone* 82 D2
Lunglei, *India* 67 H18
Luni, *India* 68 G5
Luni →, *India* 68 G4
Luninets = Luninyets, *Belarus* 47 F4
Luning, *U.S.A.* 114 G4
Lunino, *Russia* 48 D7
Luninyets, *Belarus* 47 F4
Lunsemfwa →, *Zambia* 87 E3
Lunsemfwa Falls, *Zambia* 87 E2
Luo He →, *China* 56 G6
Luocheng, *China* 58 E7
Luochuan, *China* 56 G5
Luoci, *China* 58 E4
Luodian, *China* 58 E6
Luoding, *China* 59 F8
Luofu, *Dem. Rep. of the Congo* 86 C2
Luohe, *China* 56 H8
Luojiang, *China* 58 B5
Luonan, *China* 56 G6
Luoning, *China* 56 G6
Luoshan, *China* 59 A10
Luotian, *China* 59 B10
Luoyang, *China* 56 G7
Luoyuan, *China* 59 D12
Luozigou, *China* 57 C16

Lupanshui, *China* 58 D5
Lupeni, *Romania* 43 E8
Lupilichi, *Mozam.* 87 E4
Łupków, *Poland* 45 J9
Lupoing, *China* 58 E5
Luquan, *China* 58 E4
Luque, *Paraguay* 126 B4
Lúras, *Italy* 30 B2
Luray, *U.S.A.* 108 F6
Lure, *France* 19 E13
Lurgan, *U.K.* 15 B5
Lusaka, *Zambia* 87 F2
Lusambo, *Dem. Rep. of the Congo* 86 C1
Lusangaye, *Dem. Rep. of the Congo* 86 C2
Luseland, *Canada* 105 C7
Lushan, *Henan, China* 56 H7
Lushan, *Sichuan, China* 58 B4
Lushi, *China* 56 G6
Lushnja, *Albania* 40 F3
Lushoto, *Tanzania* 86 C4
Lushoto □, *Tanzania* 86 C4
Lushui, *China* 58 E2
Lüshun, *China* 57 E11
Lusignan, *France* 20 B4
Lusigny-sur-Barse, *France* 19 D11
Lusk, *U.S.A.* 112 D2
Lussac-les-Châteaux, *France* 20 B4
Lustenau, *Austria* 26 D2
Luta = Dalian, *China* 57 E11
Lutherstadt Wittenberg, *Germany* 24 D8
Luton, *U.K.* 13 F7
Luton □, *U.K.* 13 F7
Lutselke, *Canada* 105 A6
Lutsk, *Ukraine* 47 G3
Lützow Holmbukta, *Antarctica* 5 C4
Lutzputs, *S. Africa* 88 D3
Luverne, *U.S.A.* 112 D6
Luvua, *Dem. Rep. of the Congo* 87 D2
Luvua →, *Dem. Rep. of the Congo* 86 D2
Luwegu →, *Tanzania* 87 D4
Luwuk, *Indonesia* 63 E6
Luxembourg, *Lux.* 17 E6
Luxembourg □, *Belgium* 17 E5
Luxembourg ■, *Europe* 7 F7
Luxeuil-les-Bains, *France* 19 E13
Luxi, *Hunan, China* 59 C8
Luxi, *Yunnan, China* 58 E4
Luxi, *Yunnan, China* 58 E2
Luxor = El Uqsur, *Egypt* 80 B3
Luy-de-Béarn →, *France* 20 E3
Luy-de-France →, *France* 20 E3
Luyi, *China* 56 H8
Luz-St-Sauveur, *France* 20 F4
Luzern, *Switz.* 25 H4
Luzern □, *Switz.* 25 H3
Luzhai, *China* 58 E7
Luzhou, *China* 58 C5
Luziânia, *Brazil* 125 G9
Lužnice →, *Czech Rep.* 26 B7
Luzon, *Phil.* 61 D4
Luzy, *France* 19 F10
Luzzi, *Italy* 31 C9
Lviv, *Ukraine* 47 H3
Lvov = Lviv, *Ukraine* 47 H3
Lwówek, *Poland* 45 F3
Lwówek Śląski, *Poland* 45 G2
Lyakhavichy, *Belarus* 47 F4
Lyakhovskiye, Ostrova, *Russia* 51 B15
Lyaki = Läki, *Azerbaijan* 49 K8
Lyallpur = Faisalabad, *Pakistan* 68 D5
Lyaskovets, *Bulgaria* 41 C9
Lybster, *U.K.* 14 C5
Lycaonia, *Turkey* 72 D5
Lychen, *Germany* 24 B9
Lychkova, *Russia* 46 D7
Lycia, *Turkey* 39 E11
Lyckebyån →, *Sweden* 11 H9
Lycksele, *Sweden* 8 D18
Lycosura, *Greece* 38 D4
Lydda = Lod, *Israel* 75 D3
Lydenburg, *S. Africa* 89 D5
Lydia, *Turkey* 39 C10
Łydynia →, *Poland* 45 F7
Lyell, *N.Z.* 91 J4
Lyell I., *Canada* 104 C2
Lyepyel, *Belarus* 46 E5
Lygnern, *Sweden* 11 G6
Lyman, *U.S.A.* 114 F8
Lyme B., *U.K.* 13 G4
Lyme Regis, *U.K.* 13 G5
Lymington, *U.K.* 13 G6
Łyna →, *Poland* 9 J19
Lynchburg, *U.S.A.* 108 G6
Lynd →, *Australia* 94 B3
Lynd Ra., *Australia* 95 D4
Lynden, *Canada* 110 C4
Lynden, *U.S.A.* 116 B4
Lyndhurst, *Queens., Australia* 94 B3
Lyndhurst, *S. Austral., Australia* 95 E2
Lyndon →, *Australia* 93 D1
Lyndonville, *N.Y., U.S.A.* 110 C6
Lyndonville, *Vt., U.S.A.* 111 B12
Lyngen, *Norway* 8 B19
Lynher Reef, *Australia* 92 C3
Lynn, *U.S.A.* 111 D14
Lynn Canal, *U.S.A.* 104 B1
Lynn Lake, *Canada* 105 B8
Lynnwood, *U.S.A.* 116 C4
Lynton, *U.K.* 13 F4
Lyntupy, *Belarus* 9 J22
Lynx L., *Canada* 105 A7
Lyon, *France* 21 C8
Lyonnais, *France* 21 C8
Lyons = Lyon, *France* 21 C8
Lyons, *Colo., U.S.A.* 112 E2
Lyons, *Ga., U.S.A.* 109 J4
Lyons, *Kans., U.S.A.* 112 F5
Lyons, *N.Y., U.S.A.* 110 C8
Lyozna, *Belarus* 46 E6
Lys = Leie →, *Belgium* 17 C3
Lysá nad Labem, *Czech Rep.* 26 A7
Lysekil, *Sweden* 11 F5
Lyskovo, *Russia* 48 B7
Lystrup, *Denmark* 11 H4
Lysvik, *Sweden* 10 D7
Lysychansk, *Ukraine* 47 H10
Lytham St. Anne's, *U.K.* 12 D4
Lytle, *U.S.A.* 113 L5
Lyttelton, *N.Z.* 91 K4
Lytton, *Canada* 104 C4
Lyuban, *Russia* 46 C6
Lyubertsy, *Russia* 46 E9
Lyubim, *Russia* 46 C11
Lyubimets, *Bulgaria* 41 E10
Lyuboml, *Ukraine* 47 G3
Lyubotyn, *Ukraine* 47 H8
Lyubytino, *Russia* 46 C7
Lyudinovo, *Russia* 46 F8

M

Ma →, *Vietnam* 64 C5
Ma'adaba, *Jordan* 75 E4
Maamba, *Zambia* 88 B4
Ma'ān, *Jordan* 75 E4
Ma'ān □, *Jordan* 75 F5
Maanselkä, *Finland* 8 C23
Ma'anshan, *China* 59 B12
Maarianhamina, *Finland* 9 F18
Ma'arrat an Nu'mān, *Syria* 70 C3
Maas →, *Neths.* 17 C4
Maaseik, *Belgium* 17 C5
Maastricht, *Neths.* 17 D5
Maave, *Mozam.* 89 C5
Mabel L., *Canada* 104 C5
Mabenge, *Dem. Rep. of the Congo* 86 B1
Mabian, *China* 58 C4
Mablethorpe, *U.K.* 12 D8
Mably, *France* 19 F11
Maboma, *Dem. Rep. of the Congo* 86 B2
Mabrouk, *Mali* 83 B4
Mabton, *U.S.A.* 114 C3
Mac Bac, *Vietnam* 65 H6
Macachín, *Argentina* 126 D3
Macaé, *Brazil* 127 A7
Macael, *Spain* 33 H2
McAlester, *U.S.A.* 113 H7
McAllen, *U.S.A.* 113 M5
Macamic, *Canada* 102 C4
Macao = Macau ■, *Asia* 59 F9
Macão, *Portugal* 35 F3
Macapá, *Brazil* 125 C8
McArthur →, *Australia* 94 B2
McArthur, Port, *Australia* 94 B2
McArthur River, *Australia* 94 B2
Macau, *Brazil* 125 E11
Macau ■, *Asia* 59 F9
McBride, *Canada* 104 C4
McCall, *U.S.A.* 114 D5
McCamey, *U.S.A.* 113 K3
McCammon, *U.S.A.* 114 E7
McCauley I., *Canada* 104 C2
McCleary, *U.S.A.* 116 C3
Macclesfield, *U.K.* 12 D5
McClintock, *Canada* 105 B10
M'Clintock Chan., *Canada* 100 A9
McClintock Ra., *Australia* 92 C4
McCloud, *U.S.A.* 114 F2
McCluer I., *Australia* 92 B5
McClure, *U.S.A.* 110 F7
McClure, L., *U.S.A.* 116 H6
M'Clure Str., *Canada* 4 B2
McClusky, *U.S.A.* 112 B4
McComb, *U.S.A.* 113 K9
McConaughy, L., *U.S.A.* 112 E4
McCook, *U.S.A.* 112 E4
McCullough Mt., *U.S.A.* 117 K11
McCusker →, *Canada* 105 B7
McDame, *Canada* 104 B3
McDermitt, *U.S.A.* 114 F5
Macdonald, L., *Australia* 92 D4
McDonald Is., *Ind. Oc.* 3 G13
Macdonnell Ranges, *Australia* 92 D5
McDouall Peak, *Australia* 95 D1
MacDowell L., *Canada* 102 B1
Macduff, *U.K.* 14 D6
Maceda, *Spain* 34 C3
Macedonia ■, *Europe* 40 E5
Maceió, *Brazil* 125 E11
Maceira, *Portugal* 34 F2
Macenta, *Guinea* 82 D3
Macerata, *Italy* 29 E10
McFarland, *U.S.A.* 117 K7
McFarlane →, *Canada* 105 B7
Macfarlane, L., *Australia* 95 E2
McGehee, *U.S.A.* 113 J9
McGill, *U.S.A.* 114 G6
Macgillycuddy's Reeks, *Ireland* 15 E2
MacGregor, *Canada* 105 D9
McGregor, *U.S.A.* 112 D9
McGregor →, *Canada* 104 B4
McGregor Ra., *Australia* 95 D3
Mach, *Pakistan* 66 E5
Māch Kowr, *Iran* 71 E9
Machado = Jiparaná →, *Brazil* 124 E6
Machagai, *Argentina* 126 B3
Machakos, *Kenya* 86 C4
Machakos □, *Kenya* 86 C4
Machala, *Ecuador* 124 D3
Machanga, *Mozam.* 89 C6
Machattie, L., *Australia* 94 C2
Machault, *France* 19 C11
Machava, *Mozam.* 89 D5
Machece, *Mozam.* 87 F4
Machecoul, *France* 18 F5
Macheng, *China* 59 B10
Machero, *Spain* 35 F6
Machias, *U.S.A.* 103 D6
Machichi →, *Canada* 105 B10
Machico, *Madeira* 37 D3
Machilipatnam, *India* 67 L12
Machiques, *Venezuela* 124 A4
Machupicchu, *Peru* 124 F4
Machynlleth, *U.K.* 13 E4
Maciejowice, *Poland* 45 G8
McIlwraith Ra., *Australia* 94 A3
Măcin, *Romania* 43 E13
Macina, *Mali* 82 C4
McIntosh, *U.S.A.* 112 C4
McIntosh L., *Canada* 105 B8
Macintosh Ra., *Australia* 93 E4
Macintyre →, *Australia* 95 D5
Macizo Galaico, *Spain* 34 C3
Mackay, *Australia* 94 C4
Mackay, *U.S.A.* 114 E7
MacKay →, *Canada* 104 B6
Mackay, L., *Australia* 92 D4
McKay Ra., *Australia* 92 D3
McKeesport, *U.S.A.* 110 F5
McKenna, *U.S.A.* 116 D4
Mackenzie, *Canada* 104 B4
McKenzie, *U.S.A.* 109 G1
Mackenzie →, *Australia* 94 C4
Mackenzie →, *Canada* 100 B6
McKenzie →, *U.S.A.* 114 D2
Mackenzie Bay, *Canada* 4 B1
Mackenzie City = Linden, *Guyana* 124 B7
Mackenzie Highway, *Canada* 104 B5
Mackenzie Mts., *Canada* 100 B7
Mackinaw City, *U.S.A.* 108 C3
McKinlay, *Australia* 94 C3
McKinlay →, *Australia* 94 C3
McKinley, Mt., *U.S.A.* 4 C18
McKinley Sea, *Arctic* 4 A7
McKinney, *U.S.A.* 113 J6
Mackinnon Road, *Kenya* 86 C4
Macksville, *Australia* 95 E5
McLaughlin, *U.S.A.* 112 C4
Maclean, *Australia* 95 D5
McLean, *U.S.A.* 113 H4
McLeansboro, *U.S.A.* 112 F10
Maclear, *S. Africa* 89 E4
Macleay →, *Australia* 95 E5
McLennan, *Canada* 104 B5
McLeod, B., *Canada* 105 A7
McLeod, L., *Australia* 93 D1
MacLeod Lake, *Canada* 104 C4
McLoughlin, Mt., *U.S.A.* 114 E2
McLure, *Canada* 104 C4
McMechen, *U.S.A.* 110 G4
McMillan, L., *U.S.A.* 113 J2
McMinnville, *Oreg., U.S.A.* 114 D2
McMinnville, *Tenn., U.S.A.* 109 H3
McMorran, *Canada* 105 C7
McMurdo Sd., *Antarctica* 5 D11
McMurray = Fort McMurray, *Canada* 104 B6
McMurray, *U.S.A.* 116 B4
McNary, *U.S.A.* 115 J9
MacNutt, *Canada* 105 C8
Macodoene, *Mozam.* 89 C6
Macomb, *U.S.A.* 112 E9
Macomer, *Italy* 30 B1
Mâcon, *France* 19 F11
Macon, *Ga., U.S.A.* 109 J4
Macon, *Miss., U.S.A.* 109 J1
Macon, *Mo., U.S.A.* 112 F8
Macossa, *Mozam.* 87 F3
Macoun L., *Canada* 105 B8
Macovane, *Mozam.* 89 C6
McPherson, *U.S.A.* 112 F6
McPherson Pk., *U.S.A.* 117 L7
McPherson Ra., *Australia* 95 D5
Macquarie Harbour, *Australia* 94 G4
Macquarie Is., *Pac. Oc.* 96 N7
MacRobertson Land, *Antarctica* 5 D6
Macroom, *Ireland* 15 E3
Macroy, *Australia* 92 D2
MacTier, *Canada* 110 A5
Macubela, *Mozam.* 87 F4
Macugnaga, *Italy* 28 C4
Macuiza, *Mozam.* 87 F3
Macusani, *Peru* 124 F4
Macuse, *Mozam.* 87 F4
Macuspana, *Mexico* 119 D6
Macusse, *Angola* 88 B3
McVille, *U.S.A.* 112 B5
Madadeni, *S. Africa* 89 D5
Madagali, *Nigeria* 83 C7
Madagascar ■, *Africa* 89 C8
Madā'in Sālih, *Si. Arabia* 70 E3
Madama, *Niger* 79 D8
Madame I., *Canada* 103 C7
Madan, *Bulgaria* 41 E8
Madaoua, *Niger* 83 C6
Madara, *Nigeria* 83 C7
Madaripur, *Bangla.* 67 H17
Madauk, *Burma* 67 L20
Madawaska, *Canada* 110 A7
Madawaska →, *Canada* 102 C4
Madaya, *Burma* 67 H20
Madbar, *Sudan* 81 F3
Maddalena, *Italy* 30 A2
Maddaloni, *Italy* 31 A7
Madeira, *Atl. Oc.* 37 D3
Madeira →, *Brazil* 122 D5
Madeleine, Is. de la, *Canada* 103 C7
Maden, *Turkey* 73 C8
Madera, *U.S.A.* 116 J6
Madha, *India* 66 L9
Madhubani, *India* 69 F12
Madhya Pradesh □, *India* 68 J8
Madian, *China* 59 A11
Madidi →, *Bolivia* 124 F5
Madikeri, *India* 66 N9
Madill, *U.S.A.* 113 H6
Madimba, *Dem. Rep. of the Congo* 84 E3
Ma'din, *Syria* 70 C3
Madingou, *Congo* 84 E2
Madirovalo, *Madag.* 89 B8
Madison, *Calif., U.S.A.* 116 G5
Madison, *Fla., U.S.A.* 109 K4
Madison, *Ind., U.S.A.* 108 F3
Madison, *Nebr., U.S.A.* 112 E6
Madison, *Ohio, U.S.A.* 110 E3
Madison, *S. Dak., U.S.A.* 112 D6
Madison, *Wis., U.S.A.* 112 D10
Madison →, *U.S.A.* 114 D8
Madisonville, *Ky., U.S.A.* 108 G2
Madisonville, *Tex., U.S.A.* 113 K7
Madista, *Botswana* 88 C4
Madiun, *Indonesia* 63 G14
Madol, *Sudan* 81 F2
Madon →, *France* 19 D13
Madona, *Latvia* 9 H22
Madonie, *Italy* 30 E6
Madonna di Campíglio, *Italy* 28 B7
Madra Dağı, *Turkey* 39 B9
Madras = Chennai, *India* 66 N12
Madras = Tamil Nadu □, *India* 66 P10
Madras, *U.S.A.* 114 D3
Madre, L., *Mexico* 119 C5
Madre, Laguna, *U.S.A.* 113 M6
Madre, Sierra, *Phil.* 61 C5
Madre de Dios →, *Bolivia* 122 E4
Madre de Dios, I., *Chile* 122 J3
Madre del Sur, Sierra, *Mexico* 119 D5
Madre Occidental, Sierra, *Mexico* 118 B3
Madre Oriental, Sierra, *Mexico* 118 C5
Madri, *India* 68 G5
Madrid, *Spain* 34 E7
Madrid □, *Spain* 34 E7
Madridejos, *Spain* 35 F7
Madrigal de las Altas Torres, *Spain* 34 D6
Madrona, Sierra, *Spain* 35 G6
Madroñera, *Spain* 35 F5
Madu, *Sudan* 81 E2
Madura, Selat, *Indonesia* 63 G15
Madura Motel, *Australia* 93 F4
Madurai, *India* 66 Q11
Madurantakam, *India* 66 N11
Madzhalis, *Russia* 49 J8
Mae Chan, *Thailand* 64 B2
Mae Hong Son, *Thailand* 64 C2
Mae Khlong →, *Thailand* 64 F3
Mae Phrik, *Thailand* 64 D2
Mae Ramat, *Thailand* 64 D2
Mae Rim, *Thailand* 64 C2
Mae Sot, *Thailand* 64 D2
Mae Suai, *Thailand* 64 C2
Mae Tha, *Thailand* 64 C2
Maebashi, *Japan* 55 F9
Maella, *Spain* 32 D5
Maesteg, *U.K.* 13 F4
Maestra, Sierra, *Cuba* 120 B4
Maevatanana, *Madag.* 89 B8
Mafeking = Mafikeng, *S. Africa* 88 D4
Mafeking, *Canada* 105 C8
Maféré, *Ivory C.* 82 D4
Mafeteng, *Lesotho* 88 D4
Maffra, *Australia* 95 F4
Mafia I., *Tanzania* 86 D4
Mafikeng, *S. Africa* 88 D4
Mafra, *Brazil* 127 B6
Mafra, *Portugal* 35 G1
Mafungabusi Plateau, *Zimbabwe* 87 F2
Magadan, *Russia* 51 D16
Magadi, *Kenya* 86 C4
Magadi, L., *Kenya* 86 C4
Magaliesburg, *S. Africa* 89 D4
Magallanes, Estrecho de, *Chile* 122 J3
Magaluf, *Spain* 33 F7
Magangué, *Colombia* 124 B4
Magaria, *Niger* 83 C6
Magburaka, *S. Leone* 82 D2
Magdalen Is. = Madeleine, Is. de la, *Canada* 103 C7
Magdalena, *Argentina* 126 D4
Magdalena, *Bolivia* 124 F6
Magdalena, *Mexico* 118 A2
Magdalena, *U.S.A.* 115 J10
Magdalena →, *Colombia* 122 B3
Magdalena →, *Mexico* 118 A2
Magdalena, B., *Mexico* 118 C2
Magdalena, Llano de la, *Mexico* 118 C2
Magdeburg, *Germany* 24 C7
Magdelaine Cays, *Australia* 94 B5
Magdub, *Sudan* 81 E2
Magee, *U.S.A.* 113 K10
Magelang, *Indonesia* 63 G14
Magellan's Str. = Magallanes, Estrecho de, *Chile* 122 J3
Magenta, *Italy* 28 C5
Magenta, L., *Australia* 93 F2
Magerøya, *Norway* 8 A21
Maggia →, *Switz.* 25 J4
Maggiorasca, Mte., *Italy* 28 D6
Maggiore, L., *Italy* 28 C5
Maghama, *Mauritania* 82 B2
Magherafelt, *U.K.* 15 B5
Magione, *Italy* 29 E9
Magistralnyy, *Russia* 51 D11
Maglaj, *Bos.-H.* 42 F3
Magliano in Toscana, *Italy* 29 F8
Máglie, *Italy* 31 B11
Magnac-Laval, *France* 20 B5
Magnetic Pole (North) = North Magnetic Pole, *Canada* 4 B2
Magnetic Pole (South) = South Magnetic Pole, *Antarctica* 5 C9
Magnisía □, *Greece* 38 B5
Magnitogorsk, *Russia* 50 D6
Magnolia, *Ark., U.S.A.* 113 J8
Magnolia, *Miss., U.S.A.* 113 K9
Magny-en-Vexin, *France* 19 C8
Magog, *Canada* 103 C5
Magoro, *Uganda* 86 B3
Magosa = Famagusta, *Cyprus* 36 D12
Magouládhes, *Greece* 36 A3
Magoye, *Zambia* 87 F2
Magpie L., *Canada* 103 B7
Magrath, *Canada* 104 D6
Magre →, *Spain* 33 F4
Magrur, Wadi →, *Sudan* 81 D2
Magu □, *Tanzania* 86 C3
Maguan, *China* 58 F5
Maguarinho, C., *Brazil* 125 D9
Mağusa = Famagusta, *Cyprus* 36 D12
Maguse L., *Canada* 105 A9
Maguse Pt., *Canada* 105 A10
Magwe, *Burma* 67 J19
Maha Sarakham, *Thailand* 64 D4
Mahābād, *Iran* 70 B5
Mahabharat Lekh, *Nepal* 69 E10
Mahabo, *Madag.* 89 C7
Mahadeo Hills, *India* 68 H8
Mahagi, *Dem. Rep. of the Congo* 86 B3
Mahajamba →, *Madag.* 89 B8
Mahajamba, Helodranon' i, *Madag.* 89 B8
Mahajan, *India* 68 E5
Mahajanga, *Madag.* 89 B8
Mahajanga □, *Madag.* 89 B8
Mahajilo →, *Madag.* 89 B8
Mahakam →, *Indonesia* 62 E5
Mahalapye, *Botswana* 88 C4
Maḩallāt, *Iran* 71 C6
Māhān, *Iran* 71 D8
Mahanadi →, *India* 67 J15
Mahanoro, *Madag.* 89 B8
Mahanoy City, *U.S.A.* 111 F8
Maharashtra □, *India* 66 J9
Mahari Mts., *Tanzania* 86 D3
Mahasham, W. →, *Egypt* 75 E3
Mahasolo, *Madag.* 89 B8
Mahattat ash Shīdīyah, *Jordan* 75 F4
Mahattat 'Unayzah, *Jordan* 75 E4
Mahaxay, *Laos* 64 D5
Mahbubnagar, *India* 66 L10
Maḩḑah, *Oman* 71 E7
Mahdia, *Tunisia* 79 A8
Mahe, *India* 69 C8
Mahenge, *Tanzania* 87 D4
Maheno, *N.Z.* 91 L3
Mahesana, *India* 68 H5
Mahia Pen., *N.Z.* 91 H6
Mahilyow, *Belarus* 46 F6
Mahmiya, *Sudan* 81 D3
Mahmud Kot, *Pakistan* 68 D4
Mahmudia, *Romania* 43 E14
Mahmudiye, *Turkey* 39 B12
Mahmutbey, *Turkey* 41 E12
Mahnomen, *U.S.A.* 112 B7
Mahoba, *India* 69 G8
Mahón = Maó, *Spain* 37 B11
Mahone Bay, *Canada* 103 D7
Mahuta, *Nigeria* 83 C5
Mahya Dağı, *Turkey* 41 E11
Mai-Ndombe, L., *Dem. Rep. of the Congo* 84 E3
Mai-Sai, *Thailand* 64 B2

Maia, *Portugal* 34 D2
Maia, *Spain* 32 B3
Maials, *Spain* 32 D5
Maîche, *France* 19 E13
Maicurú →, *Brazil* 125 D8
Máida, *Italy* 31 D9
Maidan Khula, *Afghan.* 68 C3
Maidenhead, *U.K.* 13 F7
Maidi, *Yemen* 81 D5
Maidstone, *Canada* 105 C7
Maidstone, *U.K.* 13 F8
Maiduguri, *Nigeria* 83 C7
Măieruş, *Romania* 43 E10
Maignelay Montigny, *France* 19 C9
Maigo, *Phil.* 61 G5
Maigudo, *Ethiopia* 81 F4
Maijdi, *Bangla.* 67 H17
Maikala Ra., *India* 67 J12
Maillezais, *France* 20 B3
Mailsi, *Pakistan* 68 E5
Main →, *Germany* 25 F4
Main →, *U.K.* 15 B5
Main Centre, *Canada* 105 C7
Mainburg, *Germany* 25 G7
Maine, *France* 18 D6
Maine □, *U.S.A.* 103 C6
Maine →, *Ireland* 15 D2
Maine-et-Loire □, *France* 18 E6
Maïne-Soroa, *Niger* 83 C7
Maingkwan, *Burma* 67 F20
Mainit, L., *Phil.* 61 G6
Mainland, *Orkney, U.K.* 14 C5
Mainland, *Shet., U.K.* 14 A7
Mainpuri, *India* 69 F8
Maintal, *Germany* 25 E4
Maintenon, *France* 19 D8
Maintirano, *Madag.* 89 B7
Mainz, *Germany* 25 E4
Maipú, *Argentina* 126 D4
Maiquetía, *Venezuela* 124 A5
Máira →, *Italy* 28 D4
Mairabari, *India* 67 F18
Maisí, *Cuba* 121 B5
Maisi, Pta. de, *Cuba* 121 B5
Maitland, *N.S.W., Australia* 95 E5
Maitland, *S. Austral., Australia* 95 E2
Maitland →, *Canada* 110 C3
Maiyema, *Nigeria* 83 C5
Maiyuan, *China* 59 E11
Maiz, Is. del, *Nic.* 120 D3
Maizuru, *Japan* 55 G7
Majalengka, *Indonesia* 63 G13
Majene, *Indonesia* 63 E5
Majevica, *Bos.-H.* 42 F3
Maji, *Ethiopia* 81 F4
Majiang, *China* 58 D6
Major, *Canada* 105 C7
Majorca = Mallorca, *Spain* 37 B10
Maka, *Senegal* 82 C2
Makak, *Cameroon* 83 E7
Makale, *Indonesia* 63 E5
Makamba, *Burundi* 86 C2
Makarikari = Makgadikgadi Salt Pans, *Botswana* 88 C4
Makarovo, *Russia* 51 D11
Makarska, *Croatia* 29 E14
Makaryev, *Russia* 48 B6
Makasar = Ujung Pandang, *Indonesia* 63 F5
Makasar, Selat, *Indonesia* 63 E5
Makasar, Str. of = Makasar, Selat, *Indonesia* 63 E5
Makat, *Kazakstan* 50 E6
Makedonija = Macedonia ■, *Europe* 40 E5
Makena, *U.S.A.* 106 H16
Makeni, *S. Leone* 82 D2
Makeyevka = Makiyivka, *Ukraine* 47 H9
Makgadikgadi Salt Pans, *Botswana* 88 C4
Makhachkala, *Russia* 49 J8
Makharadze = Ozurgeti, *Georgia* 49 K5
Makhmūr, *Iraq* 70 C4
Makian, *Indonesia* 63 D7
Makindu, *Kenya* 86 C4
Makinsk, *Kazakstan* 50 D8
Makiyivka, *Ukraine* 47 H9
Makkah, *Si. Arabia* 80 C4
Makkovik, *Canada* 103 A8
Makó, *Hungary* 42 D5
Makokou, *Gabon* 84 D2
Makongo, *Dem. Rep. of the Congo* 86 B2
Makoro, *Dem. Rep. of the Congo* 86 B2
Maków Mazowiecki, *Poland* 45 F8
Maków Podhalański, *Poland* 45 J6
Makrá, *Greece* 39 E7
Makrai, *India* 66 H10
Makran Coast Range, *Pakistan* 66 G4
Makrana, *India* 68 F6
Mákri, *Greece* 41 F9
Makriyialos, *Greece* 36 D7
Mākū, *Iran* 70 B5
Makunda, *Botswana* 88 C3
Makurazaki, *Japan* 55 J5
Makurdi, *Nigeria* 83 D6
Makūyeh, *Iran* 71 D7
Makwassie, *S. Africa* 88 D4
Mal B., *Ireland* 15 D2
Mala, Pta., *Panama* 120 E3
Mala Belozërka, *Ukraine* 47 J8
Mala Kapela, *Croatia* 29 D12
Mała Panew →, *Poland* 45 H4
Mala Vyska, *Ukraine* 47 H6
Malabang, *Phil.* 61 H6
Malabar Coast, *India* 66 P9
Malabo = Rey Malabo, *Eq. Guin.* 83 E6
Malabon, *Phil.* 61 D4
Malacca, Str. of, *Indonesia* 65 L3
Malacky, *Slovak Rep.* 27 C10
Malad City, *U.S.A.* 114 E7
Maladeta, *Spain* 32 C5
Maladzyechna, *Belarus* 46 E4
Málaga, *Spain* 35 J6
Malaga, *U.S.A.* 113 J2
Málaga □, *Spain* 35 J6
Malagarasi, *Tanzania* 86 D3
Malagarasi →, *Tanzania* 86 D2
Malagón, *Spain* 35 F7
Malagón →, *Spain* 35 H3
Malahide, *Ireland* 15 C5
Malaimbandy, *Madag.* 89 C8
Malakâl, *Sudan* 81 F3
Malakand, *Pakistan* 68 B4
Malakoff, *U.S.A.* 113 J7
Malang, *Indonesia* 63 G15
Malangen, *Norway* 8 B18
Malanje, *Angola* 84 F3
Mälaren, *Sweden* 10 E11
Malargüe, *Argentina* 126 D2
Malartic, *Canada* 102 C4
Malaryta, *Belarus* 47 G3
Malatya, *Turkey* 73 C8
Malawi ■, *Africa* 87 E3
Malawi, L. = Nyasa, L., *Africa* 87 E3
Malay Pen., *Asia* 65 J3
Malaya Belozërka = Mala Belozërka, *Ukraine* 47 J8
Malaya Vishera, *Russia* 46 C7
Malaya Viska = Mala Vyska, *Ukraine* 47 H6
Malaybalay, *Phil.* 61 G6
Malāyer, *Iran* 71 C6
Malaysia ■, *Asia* 62 D4
Malazgirt, *Turkey* 73 C10
Malbon, *Australia* 94 C3
Malbooma, *Australia* 95 E1
Malbork, *Poland* 44 D6
Malcésine, *Italy* 28 C7
Malchin, *Germany* 24 B8
Malchow, *Germany* 24 B8
Malcolm, *Australia* 93 E3
Malcolm, Pt., *Australia* 93 F3
Malczyce, *Poland* 45 G3
Maldegem, *Belgium* 17 C3
Malden, *Mass., U.S.A.* 111 D13
Malden, *Mo., U.S.A.* 113 G10
Malden I., *Kiribati* 97 H12
Maldives ■, *Ind. Oc.* 52 J11
Maldonado, *Uruguay* 127 C5
Maldonado, Punta, *Mexico* 119 D5
Malè, *Italy* 28 B7
Malé Karpaty, *Slovak Rep.* 27 C10
Maléa, Ákra, *Greece* 38 E5
Malegaon, *India* 66 J9
Malei, *Mozam.* 87 F4
Malek Kandī, *Iran* 70 B5
Malela, *Dem. Rep. of the Congo* 86 C2
Malema, *Mozam.* 87 E4
Máleme, *Greece* 36 D5
Målerås, *Sweden* 11 H9
Malerkotla, *India* 68 D6
Máles, *Greece* 36 D7
Malesherbes, *France* 19 D9
Maleshevska Planina, *Europe* 40 E7
Malesína, *Greece* 38 C5
Malestroit, *France* 18 E4
Malfa, *Italy* 31 D7
Malgobek, *Russia* 49 J7
Malgomaj, *Sweden* 8 D17
Malgrat = Malgrat de Mar, *Spain* 32 D7
Malgrat de Mar, *Spain* 32 D7
Malha, *Sudan* 81 D2
Malheur →, *U.S.A.* 114 D5
Malheur L., *U.S.A.* 114 E4
Mali, *Guinea* 82 C2
Mali ■, *Africa* 82 B4
Mali →, *Burma* 67 G20
Mali Kanal, *Serbia, Yug.* 42 E4
Mali Kyun, *Burma* 64 F2
Malibu, *U.S.A.* 117 L8
Maliku, *Indonesia* 63 E6
Malili, *Indonesia* 63 E6
Målilla, *Sweden* 11 G9
Malimba, Mts., *Dem. Rep. of the Congo* 86 D2
Malin Hd., *Ireland* 15 A4
Malin Pen., *Ireland* 15 A4
Malindi, *Kenya* 86 C5
Malines = Mechelen, *Belgium* 17 C4
Malino, *Indonesia* 63 D6
Malinyi, *Tanzania* 87 D4
Malipo, *China* 58 F5
Maliqi, *Albania* 40 F4
Malita, *Phil.* 63 C7
Maljenik, *Serbia, Yug.* 40 C5
Malkara, *Turkey* 41 F10
Małkinia Górna, *Poland* 45 F9
Malko Tŭrnovo, *Bulgaria* 41 E11
Mallacoota, *Australia* 95 F4
Mallacoota Inlet, *Australia* 95 F4
Mallaig, *U.K.* 14 D3
Mallawan, *India* 69 F9
Mallawi, *Egypt* 80 B3
Mallemort, *France* 21 E9
Málles Venosta, *Italy* 28 B7
Mállia, *Greece* 36 D7
Mallión, Kólpos, *Greece* 36 D7
Mallorca, *Spain* 37 B10
Mallorytown, *Canada* 111 B9
Mallow, *Ireland* 15 D3
Malmbäck, *Sweden* 11 G8
Malmberget, *Sweden* 8 C19
Malmédy, *Belgium* 17 D6
Malmesbury, *S. Africa* 88 E2
Malmköping, *Sweden* 10 E10
Malmö, *Sweden* 11 J6
Malmöhus län □, *Sweden* 11 J7
Malmslätt, *Sweden* 11 F9
Malmyzh, *Russia* 48 B10
Malnaş, *Romania* 43 D10
Malo Konare, *Bulgaria* 41 D8
Maloarkhangelsk, *Russia* 47 F9
Malolos, *Phil.* 63 B6
Malombe L., *Malawi* 87 E4
Małomice, *Poland* 45 G2
Malomir, *Bulgaria* 41 D10
Malone, *U.S.A.* 111 B10
Malong, *China* 58 E4
Malorad, *Bulgaria* 40 C7
Måløy, *Norway* 9 F11
Maloyaroslovets, *Russia* 46 E9
Malpartida, *Spain* 35 F4
Malpaso, *Canary Is.* 37 G1
Malpelo, *Colombia* 124 C2
Malpica de Bergantiños, *Spain* 34 B2
Mals = Málles Venosta, *Italy* 28 B7
Malta, *Idaho, U.S.A.* 114 E7
Malta, *Mont., U.S.A.* 114 B10
Malta ■, *Europe* 36 D2
Maltahöhe, *Namibia* 88 C2
Maltepe, *Turkey* 41 F13
Malton, *Canada* 110 C5
Malton, *U.K.* 12 C7
Maluku, *Indonesia* 63 E7
Maluku □, *Indonesia* 63 E7
Maluku Sea = Molucca Sea, *Indonesia* 63 E6
Malumfashi, *Nigeria* 83 C6
Malung, *Sweden* 10 D7
Malungsfors, *Sweden* 10 D7
Malvan, *India* 66 L8
Malvern, *U.S.A.* 113 H8
Malvern Hills, *U.K.* 13 E5
Malvinas, Is. = Falkland Is. □, *Atl. Oc.* 128 G5
Malý Dunaj →, *Slovak Rep.* 27 D11
Malya, *Tanzania* 86 C3
Malyn, *Ukraine* 47 G5
Malyy Lyakhovskiy, Ostrov, *Russia* 51 B15
Mama, *Russia* 51 D12
Mamadysh, *Russia* 48 C10
Mamanguape, *Brazil* 125 E11
Mamasa, *Indonesia* 63 E5
Mambasa, *Dem. Rep. of the Congo* 86 B2
Mamberamo →, *Indonesia* 63 E9
Mambilima Falls, *Zambia* 87 E2
Mambirima, *Dem. Rep. of the Congo* 87 E2
Mambo, *Tanzania* 86 C4
Mambrui, *Kenya* 86 C5
Mamburao, *Phil.* 61 E4
Mameigwess L., *Canada* 102 B2
Mamers, *France* 18 D7
Mamfé, *Cameroon* 83 D6
Mammoth, *U.S.A.* 115 K8
Mamoré →, *Bolivia* 122 E4
Mamou, *Guinea* 82 C2
Mampatá, *Guinea-Biss.* 82 C2
Mampong, *Ghana* 83 D4
Mamry, Jezioro, *Poland* 44 D8
Mamuju, *Indonesia* 63 E5
Mamuras, *Albania* 40 E3
Man, *Ivory C.* 82 D3
Man, I. of, *U.K.* 12 C3
Man Na, *Burma* 67 H20
Mana →, *Fr. Guiana* 125 B8
Manaar, G. of = Mannar, G. of, *Asia* 66 Q11
Manacapuru, *Brazil* 124 D6
Manacor, *Spain* 37 B10
Manado, *Indonesia* 63 D6
Managua, *Nic.* 120 D2
Managua, L., *Nic.* 120 D2
Manakara, *Madag.* 89 C8
Manama = Al Manāmah, *Bahrain* 71 E6
Manambao →, *Madag.* 89 B7
Manambato, *Madag.* 89 A8
Manambolo →, *Madag.* 89 B7
Manambolosy, *Madag.* 89 B8
Mananara, *Madag.* 89 B8
Mananara →, *Madag.* 89 C8
Mananjary, *Madag.* 89 C8
Manantenina, *Madag.* 89 C8
Manaos = Manaus, *Brazil* 124 D7
Manapire →, *Venezuela* 124 B5
Manapouri, *N.Z.* 91 L1
Manapouri, L., *N.Z.* 91 L1
Manas, *China* 60 B3
Manas →, *India* 67 F17
Manaslu, *Nepal* 69 E11
Manasquan, *U.S.A.* 111 F10
Manassa, *U.S.A.* 115 H11
Manaung, *Burma* 67 K18
Manaus, *Brazil* 124 D7
Manavgat, *Turkey* 72 D4
Manawan L., *Canada* 105 B8
Manay, *Phil.* 61 H7
Manbij, *Syria* 70 B3
Mancelona, *U.S.A.* 108 C3
Mancha Real, *Spain* 35 H7
Manche □, *France* 18 C5
Manchester, *U.K.* 12 D5
Manchester, *Calif., U.S.A.* 116 G3
Manchester, *Conn., U.S.A.* 111 E12
Manchester, *Ga., U.S.A.* 109 J3
Manchester, *Iowa, U.S.A.* 112 D9
Manchester, *Ky., U.S.A.* 108 G4
Manchester, *N.H., U.S.A.* 111 D13
Manchester, *N.Y., U.S.A.* 110 D7
Manchester, *Vt., U.S.A.* 111 C11
Manchester L., *Canada* 105 A7
Manchuria = Dongbei, *China* 57 D13
Manchurian Plain, *China* 52 E16
Manciano, *Italy* 29 F8
Mancifa, *Ethiopia* 81 F5
Mand →, *Iran* 71 D7
Manda, *Chunya, Tanzania* 86 D3
Manda, *Ludewe, Tanzania* 87 E3
Mandabé, *Madag.* 89 C7
Mandaguari, *Brazil* 127 A5
Mandah, *Mongolia* 56 B5
Mandal, *Norway* 9 G12
Mandalay, *Burma* 67 J20
Mandale = Mandalay, *Burma* 67 J20
Mandalgovi, *Mongolia* 56 B4
Mandalī, *Iraq* 70 C5
Mandan, *U.S.A.* 112 B4
Mandaon, *Phil.* 61 E5
Mandar, Teluk, *Indonesia* 63 E5
Mándas, *Italy* 30 C2
Mandaue, *Phil.* 61 F5
Mandelieu-la-Napoule, *France* 21 E10
Mandera, *Kenya* 86 B5
Mandera □, *Kenya* 86 B5
Mandi, *India* 68 D7
Mandimba, *Mozam.* 87 E4
Mandioli, *Indonesia* 63 E7
Mandla, *India* 69 H9
Mandø, *Denmark* 11 J2
Mandoto, *Madag.* 89 B8
Mandoúdhion, *Greece* 38 C5
Mándra, *Greece* 38 C5
Mandra, *Pakistan* 68 C5
Mandrákhi, *Greece* 39 E9
Mandrare →, *Madag.* 89 D8
Mandritsara, *Madag.* 89 B8
Mandsaur, *India* 68 G6
Mandurah, *Australia* 93 F2
Mandúria, *Italy* 31 B10
Mandvi, *India* 68 H3
Mandya, *India* 66 N10
Mandzai, *Pakistan* 68 D2
Mané, *Burkina Faso* 83 C4
Maneh, *Iran* 71 B8
Manengouba, Mts., *Cameroon* 83 E6
Manérbio, *Italy* 28 C7
Maneroo, *Australia* 94 C3
Maneroo Cr. →, *Australia* 94 C3
Manfalût, *Egypt* 80 B3
Manfred, *Australia* 95 E3
Manfredónia, *Italy* 29 G12
Manfredónia, G. di, *Italy* 29 G13
Manga, *Burkina Faso* 83 C4
Manga, *Niger* 83 C7
Mangabeiras, Chapada das, *Brazil* 125 F9
Mangalia, *Romania* 43 G13
Mangalore, *India* 66 N9
Mangaweka, *N.Z.* 91 H5
Manggar, *Indonesia* 62 E3
Manggawitu, *Indonesia* 63 E8
Mangkalihat, Tanjung, *Indonesia* 63 D5
Mangla Dam, *Pakistan* 69 C5
Manglaur, *India* 68 E7
Mangnai, *China* 60 C4
Mango, *Togo* 83 C5
Mangoche, *Malawi* 87 E4
Mangoky →, *Madag.* 89 C7
Mangole, *Indonesia* 63 E7
Mangombe, *Dem. Rep. of the Congo* 86 C2
Mangonui, *N.Z.* 91 F4
Mangualde, *Portugal* 34 E3
Mangueira, L. da, *Brazil* 127 C5
Mangum, *U.S.A.* 113 H5
Mangyshlak Poluostrov, *Kazakstan* 50 E6
Manhattan, *U.S.A.* 112 F6
Manhiça, *Mozam.* 89 D5
Mania →, *Madag.* 89 B8
Maniago, *Italy* 29 B9
Manica, *Mozam.* 89 B5
Manica e Sofala □, *Mozam.* 89 B5
Manicaland □, *Zimbabwe* 87 F3
Manicoré, *Brazil* 124 E6
Manicouagan →, *Canada* 103 C6
Manīfah, *Si. Arabia* 71 E6
Manifold, *Australia* 94 C5
Manifold, C., *Australia* 94 C5
Maniganggo, *China* 58 B2
Manigotagan, *Canada* 105 C9
Manihiki, *Cook Is.* 97 J11
Manika, Plateau de la, *Dem. Rep. of the Congo* 87 E2
Manila, *Phil.* 61 D4
Manila, *U.S.A.* 114 F9
Manila B., *Phil.* 61 D4
Manilla, *Australia* 95 E5
Manimpé, *Mali* 82 C3
Maningrida, *Australia* 94 A1
Manipur □, *India* 67 G19
Manipur →, *Burma* 67 H19
Manisa, *Turkey* 39 C9
Manisa □, *Turkey* 39 C9
Manistee, *U.S.A.* 108 C2
Manistee →, *U.S.A.* 108 C2
Manistique, *U.S.A.* 108 C2
Manito L., *Canada* 105 C7
Manitoba □, *Canada* 105 B9
Manitoba, L., *Canada* 105 C9
Manitou, *Canada* 105 D9
Manitou I., *U.S.A.* 102 C2
Manitou Is., *U.S.A.* 108 C3
Manitou L., *Canada* 103 B6
Manitou Springs, *U.S.A.* 112 F2
Manitoulin I., *Canada* 102 C3
Manitowaning, *Canada* 102 C3
Manitowoc, *U.S.A.* 108 C2
Manizales, *Colombia* 124 B3
Manja, *Madag.* 89 C7
Manjacaze, *Mozam.* 89 C5
Manjakandriana, *Madag.* 89 B8
Manjhand, *Pakistan* 68 G3
Manjil, *Iran* 71 B6
Manjimup, *Australia* 93 F2
Manjra →, *India* 66 K10
Mankato, *Kans., U.S.A.* 112 F5
Mankato, *Minn., U.S.A.* 112 C8
Mankayane, *Swaziland* 89 D5
Mankono, *Ivory C.* 82 D3
Mankota, *Canada* 105 D7
Manlay, *Mongolia* 56 B4
Manlleu, *Spain* 32 C7
Manly, *Australia* 95 E5
Manmad, *India* 66 J9
Mann Ranges, *Australia* 93 E5
Manna, *Indonesia* 62 E2
Mannahill, *Australia* 95 E3
Mannar, *Sri Lanka* 66 Q11
Mannar, G. of, *Asia* 66 Q11
Mannar I., *Sri Lanka* 66 Q11
Mannheim, *Germany* 25 F4
Manning, *Canada* 104 B5
Manning, *Oreg., U.S.A.* 116 E3
Manning, *S.C., U.S.A.* 109 J5
Manning Prov. Park, *Canada* 104 D4
Mannington, *U.S.A.* 108 F5
Mannu →, *Italy* 30 C2
Mannu, C., *Italy* 30 B1
Mannum, *Australia* 95 E2
Mano, *S. Leone* 82 D2
Manokwari, *Indonesia* 63 E8
Manolás, *Greece* 38 C3
Manombo, *Madag.* 89 C7
Manono, *Dem. Rep. of the Congo* 86 D2
Manoppello, *Italy* 29 F11
Manosque, *France* 21 E9
Manouane, L., *Canada* 103 B5
Manpojin, *N. Korea* 57 D14
Manresa, *Spain* 32 D6
Mansa, *Gujarat, India* 68 H5
Mansa, *Punjab, India* 68 E6
Mansa, *Zambia* 87 E2
Månsåsen, *Sweden* 10 A8
Mansehra, *Pakistan* 68 B5
Mansel I., *Canada* 101 B12
Mansfield, *Australia* 95 F4
Mansfield, *U.K.* 12 D6
Mansfield, *La., U.S.A.* 113 J8
Mansfield, *Mass., U.S.A.* 111 D13
Mansfield, *Ohio, U.S.A.* 110 F2
Mansfield, *Pa., U.S.A.* 110 E7
Mansfield, *Wash., U.S.A.* 114 C4
Mansilla de las Mulas, *Spain* 34 C5
Mansle, *France* 20 C4
Mansoa, *Guinea-Biss.* 82 C1
Manson Creek, *Canada* 104 B4
Manta, *Ecuador* 124 D2
Mantalingajan, Mt., *Phil.* 61 G2
Mantare, *Tanzania* 86 C3
Manteca, *U.S.A.* 116 H5
Manteo, *U.S.A.* 109 H8
Mantes-la-Jolie, *France* 19 D8
Manthani, *India* 66 K11
Manti, *U.S.A.* 114 G8
Mantiqueira, Serra da, *Brazil* 127 A7
Manton, *U.S.A.* 108 C3
Mantorp, *Sweden* 11 F9
Mántova, *Italy* 28 C7
Mänttä, *Finland* 9 E21
Mantua = Mántova, *Italy* 28 C7
Manturovo, *Russia* 48 A7
Manu, *Peru* 124 F4
Manu →, *Peru* 124 F4
Manua Is., *Amer. Samoa* 91 B14
Manuae, *Cook Is.* 97 J12
Manuel Alves →, *Brazil* 125 F9
Manui, *Indonesia* 63 E6
Manuripi →, *Bolivia* 124 F5
Manville, *U.S.A.* 112 D2
Many, *U.S.A.* 113 K8
Manyara, L., *Tanzania* 86 C4
Manyas, *Turkey* 41 F11

Manych →, *Russia* 49 G5
Manych-Gudilo, Ozero, *Russia* 49 G6
Manyonga →, *Tanzania* 86 C3
Manyoni, *Tanzania* 86 D3
Manyoni □, *Tanzania* 86 D3
Manzai, *Pakistan* 68 C4
Manzala, Bahra el, *Egypt* 80 H7
Manzanares, *Spain* 35 F7
Manzaneda, *Spain* 34 C3
Manzanillo, *Cuba* 120 B4
Manzanillo, *Mexico* 118 D4
Manzanillo, Pta., *Panama* 120 E4
Manzano Mts., *U.S.A.* 115 J10
Manzarīyeh, *Iran* 71 C6
Manzhouli, *China* 60 B6
Manzini, *Swaziland* 89 D5
Mao, *Chad* 79 F9
Maó, *Spain* 37 B11
Maoke, Pegunungan, *Indonesia* 63 E9
Maolin, *China* 57 C12
Maoming, *China* 59 G8
Maowen, *China* 58 B4
Maoxing, *China* 57 B13
Mapam Yumco, *China* 60 C3
Mapastepec, *Mexico* 119 D6
Mapia, Kepulauan, *Indonesia* 63 D8
Mapimí, *Mexico* 118 B4
Mapimí, Bolsón de, *Mexico* 118 B4
Maping, *China* 59 B9
Mapinga, *Tanzania* 86 D4
Mapinhane, *Mozam.* 89 C6
Maple Creek, *Canada* 105 D7
Maple Valley, *U.S.A.* 116 C4
Mapleton, *U.S.A.* 114 D2
Mapuera →, *Brazil* 124 D7
Maputo, *Mozam.* 89 D5
Maputo, B. de, *Mozam.* 89 D5
Maqiaohe, *China* 57 B16
Maqnā, *Si. Arabia* 70 D2
Maqueda, *Spain* 34 E6
Maquela do Zombo, *Angola* 84 F3
Maquinchao, *Argentina* 128 E3
Maquoketa, *U.S.A.* 112 D9
Mar, Serra do, *Brazil* 127 B6
Mar Chiquita, L., *Argentina* 126 C3
Mar del Plata, *Argentina* 126 D4
Mar Menor, *Spain* 33 H4
Mara, *Tanzania* 86 C3
Mara □, *Tanzania* 86 C3
Maraã, *Brazil* 124 D5
Marabá, *Brazil* 125 E9
Maracá, I. de, *Brazil* 125 C8
Maracaibo, *Venezuela* 124 A4
Maracaibo, L. de, *Venezuela* 122 C3
Maracaju, *Brazil* 127 A4
Maracay, *Venezuela* 124 A5
Maracena, *Spain* 35 H7
Maradi, *Niger* 83 C6
Maradun, *Nigeria* 83 C6
Marāgheh, *Iran* 70 B5
Marāh, *Si. Arabia* 70 E5
Marajó, I. de, *Brazil* 122 D6
Marākand, *Iran* 70 B5
Maralal, *Kenya* 86 B4
Maralinga, *Australia* 93 F5
Marama, *Australia* 95 F3
Maramaraereğlisi, *Turkey* 41 F11
Marampa, *S. Leone* 82 D2
Maramureş □, *Romania* 43 C9
Maran, *Malaysia* 65 L4
Marana, *U.S.A.* 115 K8
Maranboy, *Australia* 92 B5
Maranchón, *Spain* 32 D2
Marand, *Iran* 70 B5
Marang, *Malaysia* 65 K4
Maranguape, *Brazil* 125 D11
Maranhão = São Luís, *Brazil* 125 D10
Maranhão □, *Brazil* 125 E9
Marano, L. di, *Italy* 29 C10
Maranoa →, *Australia* 95 D4
Marañón →, *Peru* 122 D3
Marão, *Mozam.* 89 C5
Maraş = Kahramanmaraş, *Turkey* 72 D7
Mărăşeşti, *Romania* 43 E12
Maratea, *Italy* 31 C8
Marateca, *Portugal* 35 G2
Marathasa □, *Cyprus* 36 E11
Marathókambos, *Greece* 39 D8
Marathon, *Australia* 94 C3
Marathon, *Canada* 102 C2
Marathón, *Greece* 38 C5
Marathon, *N.Y., U.S.A.* 111 D8
Marathon, *Tex., U.S.A.* 113 K3
Marathóvouno, *Cyprus* 36 D12
Maratua, *Indonesia* 63 D5
Maravatío, *Mexico* 118 D4
Marawi City, *Phil.* 61 H6
Marāwih, *U.A.E.* 71 E7
Marbella, *Spain* 35 J6
Marble Bar, *Australia* 92 D2
Marble Falls, *U.S.A.* 113 K5
Marblehead, *U.S.A.* 111 D14
Marburg, *Germany* 24 E4
Marcal →, *Hungary* 42 C2
Marcali, *Hungary* 42 D2
Marcaria, *Italy* 28 C7
Mărcăuţi, *Moldova* 43 B12
March, *U.K.* 13 E8
Marche, *France* 20 B5
Marche □, *Italy* 29 E10
Marche-en-Famenne, *Belgium* 17 D5
Marchena, *Spain* 35 H5
Marches = Marche □, *Italy* 29 E10
Marciana Marina, *Italy* 28 F7
Marcianise, *Italy* 31 A7
Marcigny, *France* 19 F11
Marcillat-en-Combraille, *France* 19 F9
Marck, *France* 19 B8
Marckolsheim, *France* 19 D14
Marcos Juárez, *Argentina* 126 C3
Mărculeşti, *Moldova* 43 C13
Marcus I. = Minami-Tori-Shima, *Pac. Oc.* 96 E7
Marcus Necker Ridge, *Pac. Oc.* 96 F9
Marcy, Mt., *U.S.A.* 111 B11
Mardan, *Pakistan* 68 B5
Mardie, *Australia* 92 D2
Mardin, *Turkey* 73 D9
Mårdsjön, *Sweden* 10 A9
Marécchia →, *Italy* 29 D9
Maree, L., *U.K.* 14 D3
Mareeba, *Australia* 94 B4
Maremma, *Italy* 29 F8
Maréna, *Mali* 82 C3
Marengo, *U.S.A.* 112 E8
Marennes, *France* 20 C2
Marenyi, *Kenya* 86 C4
Marerano, *Madag.* 89 C7
Maréttimo, *Italy* 30 E5
Mareuil, *France* 20 C4
Marfa, *U.S.A.* 113 K2
Marfa Pt., *Malta* 36 D1
Marganets = Marhanets, *Ukraine* 47 J8
Margaret →, *Australia* 92 C4
Margaret Bay, *Canada* 104 C3
Margaret L., *Canada* 104 B5
Margaret River, *Australia* 92 C4
Margarita, I. de, *Venezuela* 122 B4
Margarítion, *Greece* 38 B2
Margaritovo, *Russia* 54 C7
Margate, *S. Africa* 89 E5
Margate, *U.K.* 13 F9
Margeride, Mts. de la, *France* 20 D7
Margherita di Savóia, *Italy* 31 A9
Marghita, *Romania* 42 C7
Margonin, *Poland* 45 F4
Margosatubig, *Phil.* 61 H5
Marguerite, *Canada* 104 C4
Marhanets, *Ukraine* 47 J8
Mari El □, *Russia* 48 B8
Mari Republic □ = Mari El □, *Russia* 48 B8
María, Sa. de, *Spain* 33 H2
María Elena, *Chile* 126 A2
María Grande, *Argentina* 126 C4
Maria I., *N. Terr., Australia* 94 A2
Maria I., *Tas., Australia* 94 G4
Maria van Diemen, C., *N.Z.* 91 F4
Mariager, *Denmark* 11 H3
Mariager Fjord, *Denmark* 11 H4
Mariakani, *Kenya* 86 C4
Marian L., *Canada* 104 A5
Mariana Trench, *Pac. Oc.* 96 F6
Marianao, *Cuba* 120 B3
Marianna, *Ark., U.S.A.* 113 H9
Marianna, *Fla., U.S.A.* 109 K3
Mariannelund, *Sweden* 11 G9
Mariánské Lázně, *Czech Rep.* 26 B5
Marias →, *U.S.A.* 114 C8
Mariato, Punta, *Panama* 120 E3
Mariazell, *Austria* 26 D8
Maribo, *Denmark* 11 K5
Maribor, *Slovenia* 29 B12
Marico →, *Africa* 88 C4
Maricopa, *Ariz., U.S.A.* 115 K7
Maricopa, *Calif., U.S.A.* 117 K7
Marîdî, *Sudan* 81 G2
Maridi, Wadi →, *Sudan* 81 F2
Marié →, *Brazil* 124 D5
Marie Byrd Land, *Antarctica* 5 D14
Marie-Galante, *Guadeloupe* 121 C7
Mariecourt = Kangiqsujuaq, *Canada* 101 B12
Mariefred, *Sweden* 10 E11
Marieholm, *Sweden* 11 J7
Mariembourg, *Belgium* 17 D4
Marienbad = Mariánské Lázně, *Czech Rep.* 26 B5
Marienberg, *Germany* 24 E9
Mariental, *Namibia* 88 C2
Marienville, *U.S.A.* 110 E5
Mariestad, *Sweden* 11 F7
Marietta, *Ga., U.S.A.* 109 J3
Marietta, *Ohio, U.S.A.* 108 F5
Marieville, *Canada* 111 A11
Marignane, *France* 21 E9
Marihatag, *Phil.* 61 G7
Mariinsk, *Russia* 50 D9
Mariinskiy Posad, *Russia* 48 B8
Marijampolė, *Lithuania* 9 J20
Marijampolės □, *Lithuania* 44 D10
Marília, *Brazil* 127 A6
Marillana, *Australia* 92 D2
Marín, *Spain* 34 C2
Marina, *U.S.A.* 116 J5
Marina Plains, *Australia* 94 A3
Marinduque, *Phil.* 61 E5
Marine City, *U.S.A.* 108 D4
Marineo, *Italy* 30 E6
Marinette, *U.S.A.* 108 C2
Maringá, *Brazil* 127 A5
Marinha Grande, *Portugal* 34 F2
Marino, *Italy* 29 G9
Marion, *Ala., U.S.A.* 109 J2
Marion, *Ill., U.S.A.* 113 G10
Marion, *Ind., U.S.A.* 108 E3
Marion, *Iowa, U.S.A.* 112 D9
Marion, *Kans., U.S.A.* 112 F6
Marion, *Mich., U.S.A.* 108 C3
Marion, *N.C., U.S.A.* 109 H5
Marion, *Ohio, U.S.A.* 108 E4
Marion, *S.C., U.S.A.* 109 H6
Marion, *Va., U.S.A.* 109 G5
Marion, L., *U.S.A.* 109 J5
Mariposa, *U.S.A.* 116 H7
Mariscal Estigarribia, *Paraguay* 126 A3
Maritime Alps = Maritimes, Alpes, *Europe* 21 D11
Maritimes, Alpes, *Europe* 21 D11
Maritsa = Évros →, *Bulgaria* 72 B2
Maritsá, *Greece* 36 C10
Mariupol, *Ukraine* 47 J9
Marīvān, *Iran* 70 C5
Markam, *China* 58 C2
Markaryd, *Sweden* 11 H7
Markazī □, *Iran* 71 C6
Markdale, *Canada* 110 B4
Marked Tree, *U.S.A.* 113 H9
Markelsdorfer Huk, *Germany* 24 A7
Market Drayton, *U.K.* 12 E5
Market Harborough, *U.K.* 13 E7
Market Rasen, *U.K.* 12 D7
Markham, *Canada* 110 C5
Markham, Mt., *Antarctica* 5 E11
Markham L., *Canada* 105 A8
Marki, *Poland* 45 F8
Markkleeberg, *Germany* 24 D8
Markleeville, *U.S.A.* 116 G7
Markoupoulon, *Greece* 38 D5
Markovac, *Serbia, Yug.* 40 B5
Markovo, *Russia* 51 C17
Markoye, *Burkina Faso* 83 C5
Marks, *Russia* 48 E8
Marksville, *U.S.A.* 113 K8
Markt Schwaben, *Germany* 25 G7
Marktoberdorf, *Germany* 25 H6
Marktredwitz, *Germany* 25 E8
Marl, *Germany* 24 D3
Marla, *Australia* 95 D1
Marlboro, *U.S.A.* 111 D13
Marlborough, *Australia* 94 C4
Marlborough, *U.K.* 13 F6
Marlborough Downs, *U.K.* 13 F6
Marle, *France* 19 C10
Marlin, *U.S.A.* 113 K6
Marlow, *Germany* 24 A8
Marlow, *U.S.A.* 113 H6
Marmagao, *India* 66 M8
Marmande, *France* 20 D4
Marmara, *Turkey* 41 F11
Marmara, Sea of = Marmara Denizi, *Turkey* 41 F12
Marmara Denizi, *Turkey* 41 F12
Marmara Gölü, *Turkey* 39 C10
Marmaris, *Turkey* 39 E10
Marmaris Limanı, *Turkey* 39 E10
Marmarth, *U.S.A.* 112 B3
Marmion, Mt., *Australia* 93 E2
Marmion L., *Canada* 102 C1
Marmolada, Mte., *Italy* 29 B8
Marmolejo, *Spain* 35 G6
Marmora, *Canada* 102 D4
Mármora, La, *Italy* 30 C2
Marnay, *France* 19 E12
Marne, *Germany* 24 B5
Marne □, *France* 19 D11
Marne →, *France* 19 D9
Marneuli, *Georgia* 49 K7
Maroala, *Madag.* 89 B8
Maroantsetra, *Madag.* 89 B8
Maromandia, *Madag.* 89 A8
Marondera, *Zimbabwe* 87 F3
Maroni →, *Fr. Guiana* 125 B8
Marónia, *Greece* 41 F9
Maronne →, *France* 20 C5
Maroochydore, *Australia* 95 D5
Maroona, *Australia* 95 F3
Maros →, *Hungary* 42 D5
Marosakoa, *Madag.* 89 B8
Maróstica, *Italy* 29 C8
Maroua, *Cameroon* 83 C7
Marovoay, *Madag.* 89 B8
Marquard, *S. Africa* 88 D4
Marquesas Is. = Marquises, Is., *Pac. Oc.* 97 H14
Marquette, *U.S.A.* 108 B2
Marquise, *France* 19 B8
Marquises, Is., *Pac. Oc.* 97 H14
Marra, Gebel, *Sudan* 81 F2
Marracuene, *Mozam.* 89 D5
Marradi, *Italy* 29 D8
Marrakech, *Morocco* 78 B4
Marratxi, *Spain* 32 F7
Marrawah, *Australia* 94 G3
Marree, *Australia* 95 D2
Marrilla, *Australia* 92 D1
Marrimane, *Mozam.* 89 C5
Marromeu, *Mozam.* 89 B6
Marroquí, Punta, *Spain* 35 K5
Marrowie Cr. →, *Australia* 95 E4
Marrubane, *Mozam.* 87 F4
Marrúbiu, *Italy* 30 C1
Marrupa, *Mozam.* 87 E4
Marsá Matrûh, *Egypt* 80 A2
Marsabit, *Kenya* 86 B4
Marsabit □, *Kenya* 86 B4
Marsala, *Italy* 30 E5
Marsalforn, *Malta* 36 C1
Mârşani, *Romania* 43 F9
Marsberg, *Germany* 24 D4
Marsciano, *Italy* 29 F9
Marsden, *Australia* 95 E4
Marseillan, *France* 20 E7
Marseille, *France* 21 E9
Marseilles = Marseille, *France* 21 E9
Marsh I., *U.S.A.* 113 L9
Marsh L., *U.S.A.* 112 C7
Marshall, *Liberia* 82 D2
Marshall, *Ark., U.S.A.* 113 H8
Marshall, *Mich., U.S.A.* 108 D3
Marshall, *Minn., U.S.A.* 112 C7
Marshall, *Mo., U.S.A.* 112 F8
Marshall, *Tex., U.S.A.* 113 J7
Marshall →, *Australia* 94 C2
Marshall Is. ■, *Pac. Oc.* 96 G9
Marshalltown, *U.S.A.* 112 D8
Marshfield, *Mo., U.S.A.* 113 G8
Marshfield, *Wis., U.S.A.* 112 C9
Marshūn, *Iran* 71 B6
Màrsico Nuovo, *Italy* 31 B8
Märsta, *Sweden* 10 E11
Marstal, *Denmark* 11 K4
Marstrand, *Sweden* 11 G5
Mart, *U.S.A.* 113 K6
Marta →, *Italy* 29 F8
Martaban, *Burma* 67 L20
Martaban, G. of, *Burma* 67 L20
Martano, *Italy* 31 B11
Martapura, *Kalimantan, Indonesia* 62 E4
Martapura, *Sumatera, Indonesia* 62 E2
Marte, *Nigeria* 83 C7
Martel, *France* 20 D5
Martelange, *Belgium* 17 E5
Martellago, *Italy* 29 C9
Martés, Sierra, *Spain* 33 F4
Martfű, *Hungary* 42 C5
Martha's Vineyard, *U.S.A.* 111 E14
Martigné-Ferchaud, *France* 18 E5
Martigny, *Switz.* 25 J3
Martigues, *France* 21 E9
Martin, *Slovak Rep.* 27 B11
Martin, *S. Dak., U.S.A.* 112 D4
Martin, *Tenn., U.S.A.* 113 G10
Martín →, *Spain* 32 D4
Martin L., *U.S.A.* 109 J3
Martina Franca, *Italy* 31 B10
Martinborough, *N.Z.* 91 J5
Martinez, *U.S.A.* 116 G4
Martinique ■, *W. Indies* 121 D7
Martinique Passage, *W. Indies* 121 C7
Martínon, *Greece* 38 C5
Martinópolis, *Brazil* 127 A5
Martins Ferry, *U.S.A.* 110 F4
Martinsberg, *Austria* 26 C8
Martinsburg, *Pa., U.S.A.* 110 F6
Martinsburg, *W. Va., U.S.A.* 108 F7
Martinsicuro, *Italy* 29 F10
Martinsville, *Ind., U.S.A.* 108 F2
Martinsville, *Va., U.S.A.* 109 G6
Marton, *N.Z.* 91 J5
Martorell, *Spain* 32 D6
Martos, *Spain* 35 H7
Martuni, *Armenia* 49 K7
Maru, *Nigeria* 83 C6
Marudi, *Malaysia* 62 D4
Ma'ruf, *Afghan.* 66 D5
Marugame, *Japan* 55 G6
Marulan, *Australia* 95 E5
Marunga, *Angola* 88 B3
Marungu, Mts., *Dem. Rep. of the Congo* 86 D3
Marvast, *Iran* 71 D7
Marvejols, *France* 20 D7
Marwar, *India* 68 G5
Mary, *Turkmenistan* 50 F7
Mary Frances L., *Canada* 105 A7
Mary Kathleen, *Australia* 94 C2
Maryborough = Port Laoise, *Ireland* 15 C4
Maryborough, *Queens., Australia* 95 D5
Maryborough, *Vic., Australia* 95 F3
Maryfield, *Canada* 105 D8
Maryland □, *U.S.A.* 108 F7
Maryland Junction, *Zimbabwe* 87 F3
Maryport, *U.K.* 12 C4
Mary's Harbour, *Canada* 103 B8
Marystown, *Canada* 103 C8
Marysvale, *U.S.A.* 115 G7
Marysville, *Canada* 104 D5
Marysville, *Calif., U.S.A.* 116 F5
Marysville, *Kans., U.S.A.* 112 F6
Marysville, *Mich., U.S.A.* 110 D2
Marysville, *Ohio, U.S.A.* 108 E4
Marysville, *Wash., U.S.A.* 116 B4
Maryvale, *Australia* 95 D5
Maryville, *U.S.A.* 109 H4
Marzūq, *Libya* 79 C8
Masahunga, *Tanzania* 86 C3
Masai Steppe, *Tanzania* 86 C4
Masaka, *Uganda* 86 C3
Masalembo, Kepulauan, *Indonesia* 62 F4
Masalima, Kepulauan, *Indonesia* 62 F5
Masallı, *Azerbaijan* 73 C13
Masamba, *Indonesia* 63 E6
Masan, *S. Korea* 57 G15
Masasi, *Tanzania* 87 E4
Masasi □, *Tanzania* 87 E4
Masaya, *Nic.* 120 D2
Masba, *Nigeria* 83 C7
Masbate, *Phil.* 61 E5
Máscali, *Italy* 31 E8
Mascara, *Algeria* 78 A6
Mascota, *Mexico* 118 C4
Masela, *Indonesia* 63 F7
Maseru, *Lesotho* 88 D4
Mashaba, *Zimbabwe* 87 G3
Mashābih, *Si. Arabia* 70 E3
Mashan, *China* 58 F7
Masherbrum, *Pakistan* 69 B7
Mashhad, *Iran* 71 B8
Mashi, *Nigeria* 83 C6
Mashīz, *Iran* 71 D8
Mashkel, Hamun-i-, *Pakistan* 66 E3
Mashki Chāh, *Pakistan* 66 E3
Mashonaland Central □, *Zimbabwe* 89 B5
Mashonaland East □, *Zimbabwe* 89 B5
Mashonaland West □, *Zimbabwe* 89 B4
Mashtaga = Maştağa, *Azerbaijan* 49 K10
Masindi, *Uganda* 86 B3
Masindi Port, *Uganda* 86 B3
Masisi, *Dem. Rep. of the Congo* 86 C2
Masjed Soleyman, *Iran* 71 D6
Mask, L., *Ireland* 15 C2
Maslen Nos, *Bulgaria* 41 D11
Maslinica, *Croatia* 29 E13
Masnou = El Masnou, *Spain* 32 D7
Masoala, Tanjon' i, *Madag.* 89 B9
Masoarivo, *Madag.* 89 B7
Masomeloka, *Madag.* 89 C8
Mason, *Nev., U.S.A.* 116 G7
Mason, *Tex., U.S.A.* 113 K5
Mason City, *U.S.A.* 112 D8
Maspalomas, *Canary Is.* 37 G4
Maspalomas, Pta., *Canary Is.* 37 G4
Masqat, *Oman* 74 C6
Massa, *Italy* 28 D7
Massa Maríttima, *Italy* 28 E7
Massachusetts □, *U.S.A.* 111 D13
Massachusetts B., *U.S.A.* 111 D14
Massafra, *Italy* 31 B10
Massakory, *Chad* 79 F9
Massanella, *Spain* 37 B9
Massangena, *Mozam.* 89 C5
Massat, *France* 20 F5
Massawa = Mitsiwa, *Eritrea* 81 D4
Massena, *U.S.A.* 111 B10
Massénya, *Chad* 79 F9
Masset, *Canada* 104 C2
Masseube, *France* 20 E4
Massiac, *France* 20 C7
Massif Central, *France* 20 D7
Massillon, *U.S.A.* 110 F3
Massinga, *Mozam.* 89 C6
Mässlingen, *Sweden* 10 B6
Masson, *Canada* 111 A9
Masson I., *Antarctica* 5 C7
Maştağa, *Azerbaijan* 49 K10
Mastanli = Momchilgrad, *Bulgaria* 41 E9
Masterton, *N.Z.* 91 J5
Mástikho, Ákra, *Greece* 39 C8
Mastuj, *Pakistan* 69 A5
Mastung, *Pakistan* 66 E5
Mastūrah, *Si. Arabia* 80 C4
Masty, *Belarus* 46 F3
Masuda, *Japan* 55 G5
Masvingo, *Zimbabwe* 87 G3
Masvingo □, *Zimbabwe* 87 G3
Maswa □, *Tanzania* 86 C3
Maşyāf, *Syria* 70 C3
Maszewo, *Poland* 44 E2
Matabeleland North □, *Zimbabwe* 87 F2
Matabeleland South □, *Zimbabwe* 87 G2
Matachel →, *Spain* 35 G4
Matachewan, *Canada* 102 C3
Matad, *Mongolia* 60 B6
Matadi, *Dem. Rep. of the Congo* 84 F2
Matagalpa, *Nic.* 120 D2
Matagami, *Canada* 102 C4
Matagami, L., *Canada* 102 C4
Matagorda, *U.S.A.* 113 L7
Matagorda B., *U.S.A.* 113 L6
Matagorda I., *U.S.A.* 113 L6
Matak, *Indonesia* 65 L6
Matakana, *Australia* 95 E4
Mátala, *Greece* 36 E6
Matam, *Senegal* 82 B2
Matameye, *Niger* 83 C6
Matamoros, *Campeche, Mexico* 119 D6
Matamoros, *Coahuila, Mexico* 118 B4

Matamoros, *Puebla, Mexico* 119 D5
Matamoros, *Tamaulipas, Mexico* 119 B5
Ma'ṭan as Sarra, *Libya* 79 D10
Matandu →, *Tanzania* 87 D3
Matane, *Canada* 103 C6
Matang, *China* 58 F5
Matankari, *Niger* 83 C5
Matanzas, *Cuba* 120 B3
Matapan, C. = Taínaron, Ákra, *Greece* 38 E4
Matapédia, *Canada* 103 C6
Matara, *Sri Lanka* 66 S12
Mataram, *Indonesia* 62 F5
Matarani, *Peru* 124 G4
Mataranka, *Australia* 92 B5
Matarma, Râs, *Egypt* 75 E1
Mataró, *Spain* 32 D7
Matarraña →, *Spain* 32 D5
Mataruška Banja, *Serbia, Yug.* 40 C4
Matatiele, *S. Africa* 89 E4
Mataura, *N.Z.* 91 M2
Matehuala, *Mexico* 118 C4
Mateke Hills, *Zimbabwe* 87 G3
Matera, *Italy* 31 B9
Matese, Monti del, *Italy* 31 A7
Mátészalka, *Hungary* 42 C7
Matetsi, *Zimbabwe* 87 F2
Matfors, *Sweden* 10 B11
Matha, *France* 20 C3
Matheson Island, *Canada* 105 C9
Mathis, *U.S.A.* 113 L6
Mathráki, *Greece* 36 A3
Mathura, *India* 68 F7
Mati, *Phil.* 61 H7
Mati →, *Albania* 40 E3
Matías Romero, *Mexico* 119 D5
Matibane, *Mozam.* 87 E5
Matima, *Botswana* 88 C3
Matiri Ra., *N.Z.* 91 J4
Matlock, *U.K.* 12 D6
Matna, *Sudan* 81 E4
Mato Grosso □, *Brazil* 125 F8
Mato Grosso, Planalto do, *Brazil* 122 E5
Mato Grosso do Sul □, *Brazil* 125 G8
Matochkin Shar, *Russia* 50 B6
Matopo Hills, *Zimbabwe* 87 G2
Matopos, *Zimbabwe* 87 G2
Matosinhos, *Portugal* 34 D2
Matour, *France* 19 F11
Matsena, *Nigeria* 83 C7
Matsesta, *Russia* 49 J4
Matsu Tao, *Taiwan* 59 E13
Matsue, *Japan* 55 G6
Matsumae, *Japan* 54 D10
Matsumoto, *Japan* 55 F9
Matsusaka, *Japan* 55 G8
Matsuura, *Japan* 55 H4
Matsuyama, *Japan* 55 H6
Mattagami →, *Canada* 102 B3
Mattancheri, *India* 66 Q10
Mattawa, *Canada* 102 C4
Mattawamkeag, *U.S.A.* 103 C6
Matterhorn, *Switz.* 25 K3
Mattersburg, *Austria* 27 D9
Matthew Town, *Bahamas* 121 B5
Matthew's Ridge, *Guyana* 124 B6
Mattice, *Canada* 102 C3
Mattituck, *U.S.A.* 111 F12
Matuba, *Mozam.* 89 C5
Matucana, *Peru* 124 F3
Matun, *Afghan.* 68 C3
Maturín, *Venezuela* 124 B6
Matveyev Kurgan, *Russia* 47 J10
Matxitxako, C., *Spain* 32 B2
Mau, *India* 69 G10
Mau Escarpment, *Kenya* 86 C4
Mau Ranipur, *India* 69 G8
Maubeuge, *France* 19 B10
Maubourguet, *France* 20 E4
Maud, Pt., *Australia* 92 D1
Maude, *Australia* 95 E3
Maudin Sun, *Burma* 67 M19
Maués, *Brazil* 124 D7
Mauganj, *India* 67 G12
Maughold Hd., *U.K.* 12 C3
Mauguio, *France* 20 E7
Maui, *U.S.A.* 106 H16
Maulamyaing = Moulmein, *Burma* 67 L20
Maule □, *Chile* 126 D1
Mauléon-Licharre, *France* 20 E3
Maumee, *U.S.A.* 108 E4
Maumee →, *U.S.A.* 108 E4
Maumere, *Indonesia* 63 F6
Maumusson, Pertuis de, *France* 20 C2
Maun, *Botswana* 88 C3
Mauna Kea, *U.S.A.* 106 J17
Mauna Loa, *U.S.A.* 106 J17
Maungmagan Is., *Burma* 67 N20
Maungmagan Kyunzu, *Burma* 67 N20
Maupin, *U.S.A.* 114 D3
Maure-de-Bretagne, *France* 18 E5
Maurepas, L., *U.S.A.* 113 K9
Maures, *France* 21 E10
Mauriac, *France* 20 C6
Maurice, L., *Australia* 93 E5
Maurienne, *France* 21 C10
Mauritania ■, *Africa* 78 E3
Mauritius ■, *Ind. Oc.* 77 J9
Mauron, *France* 18 D4
Maurs, *France* 20 D6
Mauston, *U.S.A.* 112 D9
Mauterndorf, *Austria* 26 D6
Mauthen, *Austria* 26 E6
Mauvezin, *France* 20 E4
Mauzé-sur-le-Mignon, *France* 20 B3
Mavli, *India* 68 G5
Mavrova, *Albania* 40 F3
Mavuradonha Mts., *Zimbabwe* 87 F3
Mawa, *Dem. Rep. of the Congo* 86 B2
Mawana, *India* 68 E7
Mawand, *Pakistan* 68 E3
Mawk Mai, *Burma* 67 J20
Mawlaik, *Burma* 67 H19
Mawquq, *Si. Arabia* 70 E4
Mawson Coast, *Antarctica* 5 C6
Max, *U.S.A.* 112 B4
Maxcanú, *Mexico* 119 C6
Maxesibeni, *S. Africa* 89 E4
Maxhamish L., *Canada* 104 B4
Maxixe, *Mozam.* 89 C6
Maxville, *Canada* 111 A10
Maxwell, *U.S.A.* 116 F4
Maxwelton, *Australia* 94 C3
May Downs, *Australia* 94 C4
May Pen, *Jamaica* 120 C4
Maya →, *Russia* 51 D14
Maya Mts., *Belize* 119 D7
Mayaguana, *Bahamas* 121 B5
Mayagüez, *Puerto Rico* 121 C6
Mayahi, *Niger* 83 C6
Mayals = Maials, *Spain* 32 D5
Mayāmey, *Iran* 71 B7
Mayang, *China* 58 D7
Mayarí, *Cuba* 121 B4
Maybell, *U.S.A.* 114 F9
Maybole, *U.K.* 14 F4
Maychew, *Ethiopia* 81 E4
Maydān, *Iraq* 70 C5
Maydena, *Australia* 94 G4
Mayen, *Germany* 25 E3
Mayenne, *France* 18 D6
Mayenne □, *France* 18 D6
Mayenne →, *France* 18 E6
Mayer, *U.S.A.* 115 J7
Mayerthorpe, *Canada* 104 C5
Mayfield, *U.S.A.* 109 G1
Mayhill, *U.S.A.* 115 K11
Maykop, *Russia* 49 H5
Maymyo, *Burma* 64 A1
Maynard, *U.S.A.* 116 C4
Maynard Hills, *Australia* 93 E2
Mayne →, *Australia* 94 C3
Maynooth, *Ireland* 15 C5
Mayo, *Canada* 100 B6
Mayo □, *Ireland* 15 C2
Mayon Volcano, *Phil.* 61 E5
Mayor I., *N.Z.* 91 G6
Mayorga, *Spain* 34 C5
Mayotte, I., *Mayotte* 77 H8
Mayraira Pt., *Phil.* 61 B4
Mayskiy, *Russia* 49 J7
Mayson L., *Canada* 105 B7
Maysville, *U.S.A.* 108 F4
Mayu, *Indonesia* 63 D7
Mayville, *N. Dak., U.S.A.* 112 B6
Mayville, *N.Y., U.S.A.* 110 D5
Mayya, *Russia* 51 C14
Mazabuka, *Zambia* 87 F2
Mazagán = El Jadida, *Morocco* 78 B4
Mazagão, *Brazil* 125 D8
Mazamet, *France* 20 E6
Mazán, *Peru* 124 D4
Māzandarān □, *Iran* 71 B7
Mazapil, *Mexico* 118 C4
Mazara del Vallo, *Italy* 30 E5
Mazarrón, *Spain* 33 H3
Mazarrón, G. de, *Spain* 33 H3
Mazaruni →, *Guyana* 124 B7
Mazatán, *Mexico* 118 B2
Mazatenango, *Guatemala* 120 D1
Mazatlán, *Mexico* 118 C3
Mažeikiai, *Lithuania* 9 H20
Māzhān, *Iran* 71 C8
Mazīnān, *Iran* 71 B8
Mazoe, *Mozam.* 87 F3
Mazoe →, *Mozam.* 87 F3
Mazowe, *Zimbabwe* 87 F3
Mazrûb, *Sudan* 81 E2
Mazu Dao, *China* 59 D12
Mazurian Lakes = Mazurski, Pojezierze, *Poland* 44 E7
Mazurski, Pojezierze, *Poland* 44 E7
Mazyr, *Belarus* 47 F5
Mbaba, *Senegal* 82 C1
Mbabane, *Swaziland* 89 D5
Mbagne, *Mauritania* 82 B2
M'bahiakro, *Ivory C.* 82 D4
Mbaïki, *C.A.R.* 84 D3
Mbala, *Zambia* 87 D3
Mbale, *Uganda* 86 B3
Mbalmayo, *Cameroon* 83 E7
Mbamba Bay, *Tanzania* 87 E3
Mbandaka, *Dem. Rep. of the Congo* 84 D3
Mbanga, *Cameroon* 83 E6
Mbanza Congo, *Angola* 84 F2
Mbanza Ngungu, *Dem. Rep. of the Congo* 84 F2
Mbarara, *Uganda* 86 C3
Mbashe →, *S. Africa* 89 E4
Mbatto, *Ivory C.* 82 D4
Mbenkuru →, *Tanzania* 87 D4
Mberengwa, *Zimbabwe* 87 G2
Mberengwa, Mt., *Zimbabwe* 87 G2
Mberubu, *Nigeria* 83 D6
Mbesuma, *Zambia* 87 E3
Mbeya, *Tanzania* 87 D3
Mbeya □, *Tanzania* 86 D3
Mbinga, *Tanzania* 87 E4
Mbinga □, *Tanzania* 87 E4
Mbini □, *Eq. Guin.* 84 D2
Mboki, *C.A.R.* 81 F2
Mboro, *Senegal* 82 B1
Mboune, *Senegal* 82 C2
Mbour, *Senegal* 82 C1
Mbout, *Mauritania* 82 B2
Mbozi □, *Tanzania* 87 D3
Mbuji-Mayi, *Dem. Rep. of the Congo* 86 D1
Mbulu, *Tanzania* 86 C4
Mbulu □, *Tanzania* 86 C4
Mburucuyá, *Argentina* 126 B4
Mchinja, *Tanzania* 87 D4
Mchinji, *Malawi* 87 E3
Mead, L., *U.S.A.* 117 J12
Meade, *U.S.A.* 113 G4
Meadow, *Australia* 93 E1
Meadow Lake, *Canada* 105 C7
Meadow Lake Prov. Park, *Canada* 105 C7
Meadow Valley Wash →, *U.S.A.* 117 J12
Meadville, *U.S.A.* 110 E4
Meaford, *Canada* 102 D3
Mealhada, *Portugal* 34 E2
Mealy Mts., *Canada* 103 B8
Meander River, *Canada* 104 B5
Meares, C., *U.S.A.* 114 D2
Mearim →, *Brazil* 125 D10
Meath □, *Ireland* 15 C5
Meath Park, *Canada* 105 C7
Meaulne, *France* 19 F9
Meaux, *France* 19 D9
Mebechi-Gawa →, *Japan* 54 D10
Mecanhelas, *Mozam.* 87 F4
Mecca = Makkah, *Si. Arabia* 80 C4
Mecca, *U.S.A.* 117 M10
Mechanicsburg, *U.S.A.* 110 F8
Mechanicville, *U.S.A.* 111 D11
Mechara, *Ethiopia* 81 F5
Mechelen, *Belgium* 17 C4
Mecheria, *Algeria* 78 B5
Mechernich, *Germany* 24 E2
Mechetinskaya, *Russia* 49 G5
Mecidiye, *Turkey* 41 F10
Mecitözü, *Turkey* 72 B6
Mecklenburg-Vorpommern □, *Germany* 24 B8
Mecklenburger Bucht, *Germany* 24 A7
Meconta, *Mozam.* 87 E4
Mecsek, *Hungary* 42 D3
Meda, *Australia* 92 C3
Meda, *Portugal* 34 E3
Medan, *Indonesia* 62 D1
Medanosa, Pta., *Argentina* 128 F3
Mede, *Italy* 28 C5
Médéa, *Algeria* 78 A6
Mededa, *Bos.-H.* 42 G4
Medellín, *Colombia* 124 B3
Medelpad, *Sweden* 10 B10
Medemblik, *Neths.* 17 B5
Mederdra, *Mauritania* 82 B1
Medford, *Mass., U.S.A.* 111 D13
Medford, *Oreg., U.S.A.* 114 E2
Medford, *Wis., U.S.A.* 112 C9
Medgidia, *Romania* 43 F13
Medi, *Sudan* 81 F3
Media Agua, *Argentina* 126 C2
Media Luna, *Argentina* 126 C2
Mediaş, *Romania* 43 D9
Medical Lake, *U.S.A.* 114 C5
Medicina, *Italy* 29 D8
Medicine Bow, *U.S.A.* 114 F10
Medicine Bow Pk., *U.S.A.* 114 F10
Medicine Bow Ra., *U.S.A.* 114 F10
Medicine Hat, *Canada* 105 D6
Medicine Lake, *U.S.A.* 112 A2
Medicine Lodge, *U.S.A.* 113 G5
Medina = Al Madīnah, *Si. Arabia* 70 E3
Medina, *N. Dak., U.S.A.* 112 B5
Medina, *N.Y., U.S.A.* 110 C6
Medina, *Ohio, U.S.A.* 110 E3
Medina →, *U.S.A.* 113 L5
Medina de Pomar, *Spain* 34 C7
Medina de Ríoseco, *Spain* 34 D5
Medina del Campo, *Spain* 34 D6
Medina L., *U.S.A.* 113 L5
Medina Sidonia, *Spain* 35 J5
Medinaceli, *Spain* 32 D2
Medinipur, *India* 69 H12
Mediterranean Sea, *Europe* 6 H7
Medley, *Canada* 105 C6
Médoc, *France* 20 C3
Medstead, *Canada* 105 C7
Medulin, *Croatia* 29 D10
Medveđa, *Serbia, Yug.* 40 D5
Medvedevo, *Russia* 48 B8
Medveditsa →, *Tver, Russia* 46 D9
Medveditsa →, *Volgograd, Russia* 48 F6
Medvedok, *Russia* 48 B10
Medvezhi, Ostrava, *Russia* 51 B17
Medvezhyegorsk, *Russia* 50 C4
Medway →, *U.K.* 13 F8
Medway Towns □, *U.K.* 13 F8
Medzev, *Slovak Rep.* 27 C13
Medzilaborce, *Slovak Rep.* 27 B14
Medžitlija, *Macedonia* 40 F5
Meeberrie, *Australia* 93 E2
Meekatharra, *Australia* 93 E2
Meeker, *U.S.A.* 114 F10
Meersburg, *Germany* 25 H5
Meerut, *India* 68 E7
Meeteetse, *U.S.A.* 114 D9
Mega, *Ethiopia* 81 G4
Megálo Khorío, *Greece* 39 E9
Megálo Petalí, *Greece* 38 D6
Megalópolis, *Greece* 38 D4
Meganísi, *Greece* 38 C2
Mégara, *Greece* 38 D5
Megdhova →, *Greece* 38 B3
Megève, *France* 21 C10
Meghalaya □, *India* 67 G17
Meghezez, *Ethiopia* 81 F4
Mégiscane, L., *Canada* 102 C4
Megiste, *Greece* 39 E11
Megra, *Russia* 46 B9
Mehadia, *Romania* 42 F7
Mehedeby, *Sweden* 10 D11
Mehedinţi □, *Romania* 42 F7
Meheisa, *Sudan* 80 D3
Mehndawal, *India* 69 F10
Mehr Jān, *Iran* 71 C7
Mehrābād, *Iran* 70 B5
Mehrān, *Iran* 70 C5
Mehrīz, *Iran* 71 D7
Mehun-sur-Yèvre, *France* 19 E9
Mei Jiang →, *China* 59 E11
Mei Xian, *Guangdong, China* 59 E11
Mei Xian, *Shaanxi, China* 56 G4
Meicheng, *China* 59 C12
Meichengzhen, *China* 59 C8
Meichuan, *China* 59 B10
Meiktila, *Burma* 67 J19
Meinerzhagen, *Germany* 24 D3
Meiningen, *Germany* 24 E6
Meira, Serra de, *Spain* 34 B3
Meiringen, *Switz.* 25 J4
Meishan, *China* 58 B4
Meissen, *Germany* 24 D9
Meissner, *Germany* 24 D5
Meitan, *China* 58 D6
Mejillones, *Chile* 126 A1
Meka, *Australia* 93 E2
Mekdela, *Ethiopia* 81 E4
Mekele, *Ethiopia* 81 E4
Mekhtar, *Pakistan* 66 D6
Meknès, *Morocco* 78 B4
Meko, *Nigeria* 83 D5
Mekong →, *Asia* 65 H6
Mekongga, *Indonesia* 63 E6
Mekvari = Kür →, *Azerbaijan* 73 C13
Mel, *Italy* 29 B9
Melagiri Hills, *India* 66 N10
Melaka, *Malaysia* 65 L4
Melalap, *Malaysia* 62 C5
Mélambes, *Greece* 36 D6
Melanesia, *Pac. Oc.* 96 H7
Melbourne, *Australia* 95 F4
Melbourne, *U.S.A.* 109 L5
Melchor Múzquiz, *Mexico* 118 B4
Melchor Ocampo, *Mexico* 118 C4
Méldola, *Italy* 29 D9
Meldorf, *Germany* 24 A5
Melegnano, *Italy* 28 C6
Melenci, *Serbia, Yug.* 42 E5
Melenki, *Russia* 48 C5
Mélèzes →, *Canada* 101 C12
Melfi, *Italy* 31 B8
Melfort, *Canada* 105 C8
Melfort, *Zimbabwe* 87 F3
Melgaço, *Portugal* 34 C2
Melgar de Fernamental, *Spain* 34 C6
Melhus, *Norway* 8 E14
Melide, *Spain* 34 C2
Meligalá, *Greece* 38 D3
Melilla, *N. Afr.* 78 A5
Melilli, *Italy* 31 E8
Melipilla, *Chile* 126 C1
Mélissa, Ákra, *Greece* 36 D6
Mélissa Óros, *Greece* 39 D8
Melita, *Canada* 105 D8
Mélito di Porto Salvo, *Italy* 31 E8
Melitopol, *Ukraine* 47 J8
Melk, *Austria* 26 C8
Mellan Fryken, *Sweden* 10 E7
Mellansel, *Sweden* 8 E18
Mellbystrand, *Sweden* 11 H6
Melle, *France* 20 B3
Melle, *Germany* 24 C4
Mellen, *U.S.A.* 112 B9
Mellerud, *Sweden* 11 F6
Mellette, *U.S.A.* 112 C5
Mellid = Melide, *Spain* 34 C2
Mellieha, *Malta* 36 D1
Mellit, *Sudan* 81 E2
Mellrichstadt, *Germany* 24 E6
Mělník, *Czech Rep.* 26 A7
Melo, *Uruguay* 127 C5
Melolo, *Indonesia* 63 F6
Melouprey, *Cambodia* 64 F5
Melrose, *N.S.W., Australia* 95 E4
Melrose, *W. Austral., Australia* 93 E3
Melrose, *U.K.* 14 F6
Melrose, *U.S.A.* 113 H3
Melstone, *U.S.A.* 114 C10
Melsungen, *Germany* 24 D5
Melton Mowbray, *U.K.* 12 E7
Melun, *France* 19 D9
Melut, *Sudan* 81 E3
Melville, *Canada* 105 C8
Melville, C., *Australia* 94 A3
Melville, L., *Canada* 103 B8
Melville B., *Australia* 94 A2
Melville I., *Australia* 92 B5
Melville I., *Canada* 4 B2
Melville Pen., *Canada* 101 B11
Melvin →, *Canada* 104 B5
Mélykút, *Hungary* 42 D4
Memaliaj, *Albania* 40 F3
Memba, *Mozam.* 87 E5
Memboro, *Indonesia* 63 F5
Membrilla, *Spain* 35 G7
Memel = Klaipėda, *Lithuania* 9 J19
Memel, *S. Africa* 89 D4
Memmingen, *Germany* 25 H6
Mempawah, *Indonesia* 62 D3
Memphis, *Tenn., U.S.A.* 113 H10
Memphis, *Tex., U.S.A.* 113 H4
Mena, *Ukraine* 47 G7
Mena, *U.S.A.* 113 H7
Mena →, *Ethiopia* 81 F5
Menai Strait, *U.K.* 12 D3
Ménaka, *Mali* 83 B5
Menan = Chao Phraya →, *Thailand* 64 F3
Menarandra →, *Madag.* 89 D7
Menard, *U.S.A.* 113 K5
Menasha, *U.S.A.* 108 C1
Mendawai →, *Indonesia* 62 E4
Mende, *France* 20 D7
Mendebo, *Ethiopia* 81 F4
Menden, *Germany* 24 D3
Menderes, *Turkey* 39 C9
Mendez, *Mexico* 119 B5
Mendhar, *India* 69 C6
Mendi, *Ethiopia* 81 F4
Mendip Hills, *U.K.* 13 F5
Mendocino, *U.S.A.* 114 G2
Mendocino, C., *U.S.A.* 114 F1
Mendota, *Calif., U.S.A.* 116 J6
Mendota, *Ill., U.S.A.* 112 E10
Mendoza, *Argentina* 126 C2
Mendoza □, *Argentina* 126 C2
Mene Grande, *Venezuela* 124 B4
Menemen, *Turkey* 39 C9
Menen, *Belgium* 17 D3
Menfi, *Italy* 30 E5
Mengcheng, *China* 59 A11
Mengdingjie, *China* 58 F2
Mengeš, *Slovenia* 29 B11
Menggala, *Indonesia* 62 E3
Menghai, *China* 58 G3
Mengíbar, *Spain* 35 H7
Mengjin, *China* 56 G7
Mengla, *China* 58 G3
Menglian, *China* 58 F2
Mengshan, *China* 59 E8
Mengyin, *China* 57 G9
Mengzhe, *China* 58 F3
Mengzi, *China* 58 F4
Menihek L., *Canada* 103 B6
Menin = Menen, *Belgium* 17 D3
Menindee, *Australia* 95 E3
Menindee L., *Australia* 95 E3
Meningie, *Australia* 95 F2
Menlo Park, *U.S.A.* 116 H4
Menominee, *U.S.A.* 108 C2
Menominee →, *U.S.A.* 108 C2
Menomonie, *U.S.A.* 112 C9
Menongue, *Angola* 85 G3
Menorca, *Spain* 37 B11
Mentakab, *Malaysia* 65 L4
Mentawai, Kepulauan, *Indonesia* 62 E1
Menton, *France* 21 E11
Mentor, *U.S.A.* 110 E3
Menzies, *Australia* 93 E3
Me'ona, *Israel* 75 B4
Meoqui, *Mexico* 118 B3
Mepaco, *Mozam.* 87 F3
Meppel, *Neths.* 17 B6
Meppen, *Germany* 24 C3
Mequinenza, *Spain* 32 D5
Mequinenza, Embalse de, *Spain* 32 D5
Mer, *France* 18 E8
Mer Rouge, *U.S.A.* 113 J9
Merabéllou, Kólpos, *Greece* 36 D7
Meramangye, L., *Australia* 93 E5
Meran = Merano, *Italy* 29 B8
Merano, *Italy* 29 B8
Merate, *Italy* 28 C6
Merauke, *Indonesia* 63 F10
Merbein, *Australia* 95 E3
Merca, *Somali Rep.* 74 G3
Mercato Saraceno, *Italy* 29 E9
Merced, *U.S.A.* 116 H6
Merced Pk., *U.S.A.* 116 H7
Mercedes, *Buenos Aires, Argentina* 126 C4
Mercedes, *Corrientes, Argentina* 126 B4
Mercedes, *San Luis, Argentina* 126 C2
Mercedes, *Uruguay* 126 C4
Merceditas, *Chile* 126 B1
Mercer, *N.Z.* 91 G5
Mercer, *U.S.A.* 110 E4
Mercury, *U.S.A.* 117 J11

Mercy C., *Canada* 101 B13
Merdrignac, *France* 18 D4
Mere, *U.K.* 13 F5
Meredith, C., *Falk. Is.* 128 G4
Meredith, L., *U.S.A.* 113 H4
Merefa, *Ukraine* 47 H9
Merei, *Romania* 43 E11
Merga = Nukheila, *Sudan* 80 D2
Mergui, *Burma* 64 F2
Mergui Arch. = Myeik Kyunzu, *Burma* 65 G1
Meriç, *Turkey* 41 E10
Meriç →, *Turkey* 41 F10
Mérida, *Mexico* 119 C7
Mérida, *Spain* 35 G4
Mérida, *Venezuela* 124 B4
Mérida, Cord. de, *Venezuela* 122 C3
Meriden, *U.K.* 13 E6
Meriden, *U.S.A.* 111 E12
Meridian, *Calif., U.S.A.* 116 F5
Meridian, *Idaho, U.S.A.* 114 E5
Meridian, *Miss., U.S.A.* 109 J1
Meridian, *Tex., U.S.A.* 113 K6
Mérignac, *France* 20 D3
Mering, *Germany* 25 G6
Meriruma, *Brazil* 125 C8
Merkel, *U.S.A.* 113 J5
Mermaid Reef, *Australia* 92 C2
Merowe, *Sudan* 80 D3
Merredin, *Australia* 93 F2
Merrick, *U.K.* 14 F4
Merrickville, *Canada* 111 B9
Merrill, *Oreg., U.S.A.* 114 E3
Merrill, *Wis., U.S.A.* 112 C10
Merriman, *U.S.A.* 112 D4
Merritt, *Canada* 104 C4
Merriwa, *Australia* 95 E5
Merriwagga, *Australia* 95 E4
Merry I., *Canada* 102 A4
Merrygoen, *Australia* 95 E4
Merryville, *U.S.A.* 113 K8
Mersa Fatma, *Eritrea* 81 E5
Mersch, *Lux.* 17 E6
Merse →, *Italy* 29 E8
Mersea I., *U.K.* 13 F8
Merseburg, *Germany* 24 D7
Mersey →, *U.K.* 12 D4
Merseyside □, *U.K.* 12 D4
Mersin, *Turkey* 72 D6
Mersing, *Malaysia* 65 L4
Merta, *India* 68 F6
Merthyr Tydfil, *U.K.* 13 F4
Merthyr Tydfil □, *U.K.* 13 F4
Mértola, *Portugal* 35 H3
Mertzon, *U.S.A.* 113 K4
Méru, *France* 19 C9
Meru, *Kenya* 86 B4
Meru, *Tanzania* 86 C4
Meru □, *Kenya* 86 B4
Merville, *France* 19 B9
Méry-sur-Seine, *France* 19 D10
Merzifon, *Turkey* 72 B6
Merzig, *Germany* 25 F2
Mesa, *U.S.A.* 115 K8
Mesagne, *Italy* 31 B10
Mesanagrós, *Greece* 36 C9
Mesaoría □, *Cyprus* 36 D12
Mesarás, Kólpos, *Greece* 36 D6
Meschede, *Germany* 24 D4
Mescit, *Turkey* 73 B9
Mesfinto, *Ethiopia* 81 E4
Mesgouez, L., *Canada* 102 B5
Meshchovsk, *Russia* 46 E8
Meshed = Mashhad, *Iran* 71 B8
Meshoppen, *U.S.A.* 111 E8
Meshra er Req, *Sudan* 81 F2
Mesick, *U.S.A.* 108 C3
Mesilinka →, *Canada* 104 B4
Mesilla, *U.S.A.* 115 K10
Meslay-du-Maine, *France* 18 E6
Mesocco, *Switz.* 25 J5
Mesolóngion, *Greece* 38 C3
Mesopotamia = Al Jazirah, *Iraq* 70 C5
Mesopótamon, *Greece* 38 B2
Mesoraca, *Italy* 31 C9
Mésou Volímais = Volímai, *Greece* 38 D2
Mesquite, *U.S.A.* 115 H6
Mess Cr. →, *Canada* 104 B2
Messac, *France* 18 E5
Messalo →, *Mozam.* 87 E4
Méssaména, *Cameroon* 83 E7
Messeue, *Greece* 38 D3
Messina, *Italy* 31 D8
Messina, *S. Africa* 89 C5
Messina, Str. di, *Italy* 31 D8
Messíni, *Greece* 38 D4
Messínia □, *Greece* 38 D3
Messiniakós Kólpos, *Greece* 38 E4
Messkirch, *Germany* 25 H5
Messonghi, *Greece* 36 B3
Mesta →, *Bulgaria* 40 E7
Mestá, Ákra, *Greece* 39 C7
Mestanza, *Spain* 35 G6
Mestre, *Italy* 29 C9
Mesudiye, *Turkey* 72 B7
Meta →, *S. Amer.* 122 C4
Metairie, *U.S.A.* 113 L9
Metalici, Munţii, *Romania* 42 D7
Metaline Falls, *U.S.A.* 114 B5
Metallifere, Colline, *Italy* 28 E8
Metán, *Argentina* 126 B3
Metangula, *Mozam.* 87 E3
Metauro →, *Italy* 29 E10
Metema, *Ethiopia* 81 E4
Metengobalame, *Mozam.* 87 E3
Méthana, *Greece* 38 D5
Methóni, *Greece* 38 E3
Methven, *N.Z.* 91 K3
Methy L., *Canada* 105 B7
Metil, *Mozam.* 87 F4
Metkovets, *Bulgaria* 40 C7
Metković, *Croatia* 29 E14
Metlakatla, *U.S.A.* 104 B2
Metlika, *Slovenia* 29 C12
Metropolis, *U.S.A.* 113 G10
Métsovon, *Greece* 38 B3
Mettur Dam, *India* 66 P10
Metz, *France* 19 C13
Metzingen, *Germany* 25 G5
Meulaboh, *Indonesia* 62 D1
Meung-sur-Loire, *France* 19 E8
Meureudu, *Indonesia* 62 C1
Meurthe →, *France* 19 D13
Meurthe-et-Moselle □, *France* 19 D13
Meuse □, *France* 19 C12
Meuse →, *Europe* 17 D5
Meuselwitz, *Germany* 24 D8
Mexia, *U.S.A.* 113 K6
Mexiana, I., *Brazil* 125 D9
Mexicali, *Mexico* 118 A1
Mexican Plateau, *Mexico* 98 G9
México, *Mexico* 119 D5
Mexico, *Maine, U.S.A.* 111 B14
Mexico, *Mo., U.S.A.* 112 F9
México □, *Mexico* 118 D5
Mexico ■, *Cent. Amer.* 118 C4
Mexico, G. of, *Cent. Amer.* 119 C7
Meyenburg, *Germany* 24 B8
Meymac, *France* 20 C6
Meymaneh, *Afghan.* 66 B4
Meyrueis, *France* 20 D7
Meyssac, *France* 20 C5
Meyzieu, *France* 21 C8
Mezdra, *Bulgaria* 40 C7
Mèze, *France* 20 E7
Mezen, *Russia* 50 C5
Mezen →, *Russia* 50 C5
Mézenc, Mt., *France* 21 D8
Mezeş, Munţii, *Romania* 42 C8
Mezha →, *Russia* 46 E6
Mézidon-Canon, *France* 18 C6
Mézières-en-Brenne, *France* 20 B5
Mézilhac, *France* 21 D8
Mézin, *France* 20 D4
Mezőberény, *Hungary* 42 D6
Mezőfalva, *Hungary* 42 D3
Mezőhegyes, *Hungary* 42 D5
Mezőkövácsháza, *Hungary* 42 D5
Mezőkövesd, *Hungary* 42 C5
Mézos, *France* 20 D2
Mezőtúr, *Hungary* 42 C5
Mezquital, *Mexico* 118 C4
Mezzolombardo, *Italy* 28 B8
Mgeta, *Tanzania* 87 D4
Mglin, *Russia* 47 F7
Mhlaba Hills, *Zimbabwe* 87 F3
Mhow, *India* 68 H6
Miahuatlán, *Mexico* 119 D5
Miajadas, *Spain* 35 F5
Miallo, *Australia* 94 B4
Miami, *Ariz., U.S.A.* 115 K8
Miami, *Fla., U.S.A.* 109 N5
Miami, *Tex., U.S.A.* 113 H4
Miami →, *U.S.A.* 108 F3
Miami Beach, *U.S.A.* 109 N5
Mian Xian, *China* 56 H4
Mianchi, *China* 56 G6
Mīāndowāb, *Iran* 70 B5
Miandrivazo, *Madag.* 89 B8
Mīāneh, *Iran* 70 B5
Mianning, *China* 58 C4
Mianwali, *Pakistan* 68 C4
Mianyang, *Hubei, China* 59 B9
Mianyang, *Sichuan, China* 58 B5
Mianzhu, *China* 58 B5
Miaoli, *Taiwan* 59 E13
Miarinarivo, *Madag.* 89 B8
Miass, *Russia* 50 D7
Miasteczko Krajeńskie, *Poland* 45 E4
Miastko, *Poland* 44 E3
Micăsasa, *Romania* 43 D9
Michalovce, *Slovak Rep.* 27 C14
Michigan □, *U.S.A.* 108 C3
Michigan, L., *U.S.A.* 108 D2
Michigan City, *U.S.A.* 108 E2
Michikamau L., *Canada* 103 B7
Michipicoten, *Canada* 102 C3
Michipicoten I., *Canada* 102 C2
Michoacan □, *Mexico* 118 D4
Michurin, *Bulgaria* 41 D11
Michurinsk, *Russia* 48 D5
Miclere, *Australia* 94 C4
Mico, Pta., *Nic.* 120 D3
Micronesia, Federated States of ■, *Pac. Oc.* 96 G7
Midai, *Indonesia* 65 L6
Midale, *Canada* 105 D8
Middelburg, *Neths.* 17 C3
Middelburg, *Eastern Cape, S. Africa* 88 E4
Middelburg, *Mpumalanga, S. Africa* 89 D4
Middelfart, *Denmark* 11 J3
Middelwit, *S. Africa* 88 C4
Middle Alkali L., *U.S.A.* 114 F3
Middle Fork Feather →, *U.S.A.* 116 F5
Middle I., *Australia* 93 F3
Middle Loup →, *U.S.A.* 112 E5
Middleboro, *U.S.A.* 111 E14
Middleburg, *N.Y., U.S.A.* 111 D10
Middleburg, *Pa., U.S.A.* 110 F7
Middlebury, *U.S.A.* 111 B11
Middleport, *U.S.A.* 108 F4
Middlesboro, *U.S.A.* 109 G4
Middlesbrough, *U.K.* 12 C6
Middlesbrough □, *U.K.* 12 C6
Middlesex, *Belize* 120 C2
Middlesex, *U.S.A.* 111 F10
Middleton, *Australia* 94 C3
Middleton, *Canada* 103 D6
Middletown, *U.K.* 15 B5
Middletown, *Calif., U.S.A.* 116 G4
Middletown, *Conn., U.S.A.* 111 E12
Middletown, *N.Y., U.S.A.* 111 E10
Middletown, *Ohio, U.S.A.* 108 F3
Middletown, *Pa., U.S.A.* 111 F8
Midhurst, *U.K.* 13 G7
Midi, Canal du →, *France* 20 E5
Midi d'Ossau, Pic du, *France* 20 F3
Midi-Pyrénées □, *France* 20 E5
Midland, *Canada* 102 D4
Midland, *Calif., U.S.A.* 117 M12
Midland, *Mich., U.S.A.* 108 D3
Midland, *Pa., U.S.A.* 110 F4
Midland, *Tex., U.S.A.* 113 K3
Midlands □, *Zimbabwe* 87 F2
Midleton, *Ireland* 15 E3
Midlothian, *U.S.A.* 113 J6
Midlothian □, *U.K.* 14 F5
Midongy, Tangorombohitr' i, *Madag.* 89 C8
Midongy Atsimo, *Madag.* 89 C8
Midou →, *France* 20 E3
Midouze →, *France* 20 E3
Midsayap, *Phil.* 61 H6
Midu, *China* 58 E3
Midway Is., *Pac. Oc.* 96 E10
Midway Wells, *U.S.A.* 117 N11
Midwest, *U.S.A.* 107 B9
Midwest, *Wyo., U.S.A.* 114 E10
Midwest City, *U.S.A.* 113 H6
Midyat, *Turkey* 73 D9
Midzŏr, *Bulgaria* 40 C6
Mie □, *Japan* 55 G8
Miechów, *Poland* 45 H7
Miedwie, Jezioro, *Poland* 45 E1
Międzybórz, *Poland* 45 G4
Międzychód, *Poland* 45 F2
Międzylesie, *Poland* 45 H3
Międzyrzec Podlaski, *Poland* 45 G9
Międzyrzecz, *Poland* 45 F2
Międzyzdroje, *Poland* 44 E1
Miejska Górka, *Poland* 45 G3
Miélan, *France* 20 E4
Mielec, *Poland* 45 H8
Mienga, *Angola* 88 B2
Miercurea-Ciuc, *Romania* 43 D10
Miercurea Sibiului, *Romania* 43 E8
Mieres, *Spain* 34 B5
Mieroszów, *Poland* 45 H3
Mieso, *Ethiopia* 81 F5
Mieszkowice, *Poland* 45 F1
Mifflintown, *U.S.A.* 110 F7
Mifraz Hefa, *Israel* 75 C4
Migennes, *France* 19 E10
Migliarino, *Italy* 29 D8
Miguel Alemán, Presa, *Mexico* 119 D5
Miguelturra, *Spain* 35 G7
Mihăileni, *Romania* 43 C11
Mihăileşti, *Romania* 43 F10
Mihailovca, *Moldova* 43 D13
Mihalgazi, *Turkey* 39 A12
Mihaliççık, *Turkey* 72 C4
Mihara, *Japan* 55 G6
Miheşu de Cîmpie, *Romania* 43 D9
Mijas, *Spain* 35 J6
Mikese, *Tanzania* 86 D4
Mikha-Tskhakaya = Senaki, *Georgia* 49 J6
Mikhailovka = Mykhaylivka, *Ukraine* 47 J8
Mikhaylov, *Russia* 46 E10
Mikhaylovgrad = Montana, *Bulgaria* 40 C7
Mikhaylovka, *Russia* 48 E6
Mikhnevo, *Russia* 46 E9
Mikínai, *Greece* 38 D4
Mikkeli, *Finland* 9 F22
Mikkwa →, *Canada* 104 B6
Mikniya, *Sudan* 81 D3
Mikołajki, *Poland* 44 E8
Míkonos, *Greece* 39 D7
Mikrí Préspa, Límni, *Greece* 40 F5
Mikrón Dhérion, *Greece* 41 E10
Mikstat, *Poland* 45 G4
Mikulov, *Czech Rep.* 27 C9
Mikumi, *Tanzania* 86 D4
Mila, *Algeria* 78 A7
Milaca, *U.S.A.* 112 C8
Milagro, *Ecuador* 124 D3
Milagros, *Phil.* 61 E5
Milan = Milano, *Italy* 28 C6
Milan, *Mo., U.S.A.* 112 E8
Milan, *Tenn., U.S.A.* 109 H1
Milang, *Australia* 95 E2
Milange, *Mozam.* 87 F4
Milano, *Italy* 28 C6
Milâs, *Turkey* 39 D9
Milatos, *Greece* 36 D7
Milazzo, *Italy* 31 D8
Milbank, *U.S.A.* 112 C6
Milden, *Canada* 105 C7
Mildenhall, *U.K.* 13 E8
Mildmay, *Canada* 110 B3
Mildura, *Australia* 95 E3
Mile, *China* 58 E4
Miléai, *Greece* 38 B5
Miles, *Australia* 95 D5
Miles, *U.S.A.* 113 K4
Miles City, *U.S.A.* 112 B2
Mileşti, *Moldova* 43 C13
Milestone, *Canada* 105 D8
Mileto, *Italy* 31 D9
Miletto, Mte., *Italy* 31 A7
Miletus, *Turkey* 39 D9
Mileura, *Australia* 93 E2
Milevsko, *Czech Rep.* 26 B7
Milford, *Calif., U.S.A.* 116 E6
Milford, *Conn., U.S.A.* 111 E11
Milford, *Del., U.S.A.* 108 F8
Milford, *Mass., U.S.A.* 111 D13
Milford, *Pa., U.S.A.* 111 E10
Milford, *Utah, U.S.A.* 115 G7
Milford Haven, *U.K.* 13 F2
Milford Sd., *N.Z.* 91 L1
Milgun, *Australia* 93 D2
Milh, Bahr al, *Iraq* 70 C4
Milicz, *Poland* 45 G4
Miling, *Australia* 93 F2
Militello in Val di Catánia, *Italy* 31 E7
Milk →, *U.S.A.* 114 B10
Milk, Wadi el →, *Sudan* 80 D3
Milk River, *Canada* 104 D6
Mill City, *U.S.A.* 114 D2
Mill I., *Antarctica* 5 C8
Mill Valley, *U.S.A.* 116 H4
Millárs →, *Spain* 32 F4
Millau, *France* 20 D7
Millbridge, *Canada* 110 B7
Millbrook, *Canada* 110 B6
Mille Lacs, L. des, *Canada* 102 C1
Mille Lacs L., *U.S.A.* 112 B8
Milledgeville, *U.S.A.* 109 J4
Millen, *U.S.A.* 109 J5
Miller, *U.S.A.* 112 C5
Millerovo, *Russia* 49 F5
Millersburg, *Ohio, U.S.A.* 110 F3
Millersburg, *Pa., U.S.A.* 110 F8
Millerton, *U.S.A.* 111 E11
Millerton L., *U.S.A.* 116 J7
Millevaches, Plateau de, *France* 20 C6
Millicent, *Australia* 95 F3
Millinocket, *U.S.A.* 103 C6
Millmerran, *Australia* 95 D5
Millom, *U.K.* 12 C4
Mills L., *Canada* 104 A5
Millsboro, *U.S.A.* 110 G5
Milltown Malbay, *Ireland* 15 D2
Millville, *U.S.A.* 108 F8
Millwood L., *U.S.A.* 113 J8
Milna, *Croatia* 29 E13
Milne →, *Australia* 94 C2
Milnor, *U.S.A.* 112 B6
Milo, *Canada* 104 C6
Mílos, *Greece* 38 E6
Miłosław, *Poland* 45 F4
Milot, *Albania* 40 E3
Milparinka P.O., *Australia* 95 D3
Miltenberg, *Germany* 25 F5
Milton, *Canada* 110 C5
Milton, *N.Z.* 91 M2
Milton, *Calif., U.S.A.* 116 G6
Milton, *Fla., U.S.A.* 109 K2
Milton, *Pa., U.S.A.* 110 F8
Milton-Freewater, *U.S.A.* 114 D4
Milton Keynes, *U.K.* 13 E7
Milton Keynes □, *U.K.* 13 E7
Milverton, *Canada* 110 C4
Milwaukee, *U.S.A.* 108 D2
Milwaukee Deep, *Atl. Oc.* 121 C6
Milwaukie, *U.S.A.* 116 E4
Mim, *Ghana* 82 D4
Mimizan, *France* 20 D2
Mimoň, *Czech Rep.* 26 A7
Min Jiang →, *Fujian, China* 59 E12
Min Jiang →, *Sichuan, China* 58 C5
Min Xian, *China* 56 G3
Mina, *U.S.A.* 115 G4
Mina Pirquitas, *Argentina* 126 A2
Mīnā Su'ud, *Si. Arabia* 71 D6
Mīnā'al Ahmadī, *Kuwait* 71 D6
Mīnāb, *Iran* 71 E8
Minago →, *Canada* 105 C9
Minaki, *Canada* 105 D10
Minamata, *Japan* 55 H5
Minami-Tori-Shima, *Pac. Oc.* 96 E7
Minas, *Uruguay* 127 C4
Minas, Sierra de las, *Guatemala* 120 C2
Minas Basin, *Canada* 103 C7
Minas de Rio Tinto = Minas de Riotinto, *Spain* 35 H4
Minas de Riotinto, *Spain* 35 H4
Minas Gerais □, *Brazil* 125 G9
Minatitlán, *Mexico* 119 D6
Minbu, *Burma* 67 J19
Mincio →, *Italy* 28 C7
Minčol, *Slovak Rep.* 27 B13
Mindanao, *Phil.* 61 H6
Mindanao Sea = Bohol Sea, *Phil.* 63 C6
Mindanao Trench, *Pac. Oc.* 61 F7
Mindel →, *Germany* 25 G6
Mindelheim, *Germany* 25 G6
Minden, *Canada* 110 B6
Minden, *Germany* 24 C4
Minden, *La., U.S.A.* 113 J8
Minden, *Nev., U.S.A.* 116 G7
Mindiptana, *Indonesia* 63 F10
Mindoro, *Phil.* 61 E4
Mindoro Str., *Phil.* 61 E4
Mine, *Japan* 55 G5
Minehead, *U.K.* 13 F4
Mineola, *U.S.A.* 113 J7
Mineral King, *U.S.A.* 116 J8
Mineral Wells, *U.S.A.* 113 J5
Mineralnyye Vody, *Russia* 49 H6
Minersville, *Pa., U.S.A.* 111 F8
Minersville, *Utah, U.S.A.* 115 G7
Minerva, *U.S.A.* 110 F3
Minervino Murge, *Italy* 31 A9
Minetto, *U.S.A.* 111 C8
Mingäçevir, *Azerbaijan* 49 K8
Mingäçevir Su Anbarı, *Azerbaijan* 49 K8
Mingan, *Canada* 103 B7
Mingechaur = Mingäçevir, *Azerbaijan* 49 K8
Mingechaurskoye Vdkhr. = Mingäçevir Su Anbarı, *Azerbaijan* 49 K8
Mingela, *Australia* 94 B4
Mingenew, *Australia* 93 E2
Mingera Cr. →, *Australia* 94 C2
Minggang, *China* 59 A10
Mingin, *Burma* 67 H19
Mingir, *Moldova* 43 D13
Minglanilla, *Spain* 33 F3
Minglun, *China* 58 E7
Mingorria, *Spain* 34 E6
Mingt'iehkaitafan = Mintaka Pass, *Pakistan* 69 A6
Mingxi, *China* 59 D11
Mingyuegue, *China* 57 C15
Minho = Miño →, *Spain* 34 D2
Minhou, *China* 59 E12
Minićevo, *Serbia, Yug.* 42 G7
Minidoka, *U.S.A.* 114 E7
Minigwal, L., *Australia* 93 E3
Minilya, *Australia* 93 D1
Minilya →, *Australia* 93 D1
Minipi, L., *Canada* 103 B7
Mink L., *Canada* 104 A5
Minna, *Nigeria* 83 D6
Minneapolis, *Kans., U.S.A.* 112 F6
Minneapolis, *Minn., U.S.A.* 112 C8
Minnedosa, *Canada* 105 C9
Minnesota □, *U.S.A.* 112 B8
Minnie Creek, *Australia* 93 D2
Minnipa, *Australia* 95 E2
Minnitaki L., *Canada* 102 C1
Mino, *Japan* 55 G8
Miño, *Spain* 34 B2
Miño →, *Spain* 34 D2
Minoa, *Greece* 39 F7
Minorca = Menorca, *Spain* 37 B11
Minore, *Australia* 95 E4
Minot, *U.S.A.* 112 A4
Minqin, *China* 56 E2
Minqing, *China* 59 D12
Minsen, *Germany* 24 B3
Minsk, *Belarus* 46 F4
Mińsk Mazowiecki, *Poland* 45 F8
Mintaka Pass, *Pakistan* 69 A6
Minto, *Canada* 105 D8
Minturn, *U.S.A.* 114 G10
Minturno, *Italy* 30 A6
Minûf, *Egypt* 80 H7
Minusinsk, *Russia* 51 D10
Minutang, *India* 67 E20
Minya el Qamh, *Egypt* 80 H7
Mionica, *Bos.-H.* 42 F3
Mionica, *Serbia, Yug.* 40 B4
Mir, *Niger* 83 C7
Mīr Kūh, *Iran* 71 E8
Mīr Shahdād, *Iran* 71 E8
Mira, *Italy* 29 C9
Mira, *Portugal* 34 E2
Mira →, *Portugal* 35 H2
Mira por vos Cay, *Bahamas* 121 B5
Mirabella Eclano, *Italy* 31 A7
Miraj, *India* 66 L9
Miram Shah, *Pakistan* 68 C4
Miramar, *Argentina* 126 D4
Miramar, *Mozam.* 89 C6
Miramas, *France* 21 E8
Mirambeau, *France* 20 C3
Miramichi B., *Canada* 103 C7
Miramont-de-Guyenne, *France* 20 D4
Miranda, *Brazil* 125 H7
Miranda →, *Brazil* 124 G7
Miranda de Ebro, *Spain* 32 C2
Miranda do Corvo, *Spain* 34 E2
Miranda do Douro, *Portugal* 34 D4
Mirande, *France* 20 E4
Mirandela, *Portugal* 34 D3
Mirando City, *U.S.A.* 113 M5
Mirándola, *Italy* 28 D8
Mirandópolis, *Brazil* 127 A5
Mirango, *Malawi* 87 E3
Mirani, *Australia* 94 C4
Mirano, *Italy* 29 C9
Miras, *Albania* 40 F4
Mirassol, *Brazil* 127 A6
Mirbāţ, *Oman* 74 D5
Mirear, *Egypt* 80 C4

Mirebeau, *Côte-d'Or, France* 19 E12
Mirebeau, *Vienne, France* 18 F7
Mirecourt, *France* 19 D13
Mirgorod = Myrhorod, *Ukraine* 47 H7
Miri, *Malaysia* 62 D4
Miriam Vale, *Australia* 94 C5
Miribel, *France* 19 G11
Mirim, L., *S. Amer.* 127 C5
Mirnyy, *Russia* 51 C12
Miroč, *Serbia, Yug.* 40 B6
Mirond L., *Canada* 105 B8
Mirosławiec, *Poland* 44 E3
Mirpur, *Pakistan* 69 C5
Mirpur Bibiwari, *Pakistan* 68 E2
Mirpur Khas, *Pakistan* 68 G3
Mirpur Sakro, *Pakistan* 68 G2
Mirria, *Niger* 83 C6
Mirror, *Canada* 104 C6
Mirsk, *Poland* 45 H2
Miryang, *S. Korea* 57 G15
Mirzaani, *Georgia* 49 K8
Mirzapur, *India* 69 G10
Mirzapur-cum-Vindhyachal = Mirzapur, *India* 69 G10
Misantla, *Mexico* 119 D5
Misawa, *Japan* 54 D10
Miscou I., *Canada* 103 C7
Mish'āb, Ra's al, *Si. Arabia* 71 D6
Mishan, *China* 60 B8
Mishawaka, *U.S.A.* 108 E2
Mishbih, Gebel, *Egypt* 80 C3
Mishima, *Japan* 55 G9
Misión, *Mexico* 117 N10
Misiones □, *Argentina* 127 B5
Misiones □, *Paraguay* 126 B4
Miskah, *Si. Arabia* 70 E4
Miskitos, Cayos, *Nic.* 120 D3
Miskolc, *Hungary* 42 B5
Misoke, *Dem. Rep. of the Congo* 86 C2
Misool, *Indonesia* 63 E8
Misrātah, *Libya* 79 B9
Missanabie, *Canada* 102 C3
Missinaibi →, *Canada* 102 B3
Missinaibi L., *Canada* 102 C3
Mission, *S. Dak., U.S.A.* 112 D4
Mission, *Tex., U.S.A.* 113 M5
Mission City, *Canada* 104 D4
Mission Viejo, *U.S.A.* 117 M9
Missisa L., *Canada* 102 B2
Mississagi →, *Canada* 102 C3
Mississippi □, *U.S.A.* 113 J10
Mississippi →, *U.S.A.* 113 L10
Mississippi L., *Canada* 111 A8
Mississippi River Delta, *U.S.A.* 113 L9
Mississippi Sd., *U.S.A.* 113 K10
Missoula, *U.S.A.* 114 C7
Missouri □, *U.S.A.* 112 F8
Missouri →, *U.S.A.* 112 F9
Missouri Valley, *U.S.A.* 112 E7
Mist, *U.S.A.* 116 E3
Mistake B., *Canada* 105 A10
Mistassini →, *Canada* 103 C5
Mistassini L., *Canada* 102 B5
Mistastin L., *Canada* 103 A7
Mistatim, *Canada* 105 C8
Mistelbach, *Austria* 27 C9
Misterbianco, *Italy* 31 E8
Mistretta, *Italy* 31 E7
Misty L., *Canada* 105 B8
Misurata = Misrātah, *Libya* 79 B9
Mît Ghamr, *Egypt* 80 H7
Mitatib, *Sudan* 81 D4
Mitchell, *Australia* 95 D4
Mitchell, *Canada* 110 C3
Mitchell, *Ind., U.S.A.* 108 F2
Mitchell, *Nebr., U.S.A.* 112 E3
Mitchell, *Oreg., U.S.A.* 114 D3
Mitchell, *S. Dak., U.S.A.* 112 D6
Mitchell →, *Australia* 94 B3
Mitchell, Mt., *U.S.A.* 109 H4
Mitchell Ranges, *Australia* 94 A2
Mitchelstown, *Ireland* 15 D3
Mitha Tiwana, *Pakistan* 68 C5
Míthimna, *Greece* 39 B8
Mitilíni, *Greece* 39 B8
Mitilinoí, *Greece* 39 D8
Mito, *Japan* 55 F10
Mitrofanovka, *Russia* 47 H10
Mitrovica = Kosovska Mitrovica, *Serbia, Yug.* 40 D4
Mitsinjo, *Madag.* 89 B8
Mitsiwa, *Eritrea* 81 D4
Mitsiwa Channel, *Eritrea* 81 D5
Mitsukaidō, *Japan* 55 F9
Mittagong, *Australia* 95 E5
Mittelberg, *Austria* 26 D3
Mittelfranken □, *Germany* 25 F6
Mittellandkanal →, *Germany* 24 C4
Mittenwalde, *Germany* 24 C9
Mittersill, *Austria* 26 D5
Mitterteich, *Germany* 25 F8
Mittweida, *Germany* 24 E8
Mitú, *Colombia* 124 C4
Mitumba, *Tanzania* 86 D3
Mitumba, Mts., *Dem. Rep. of the Congo* 86 D2
Mitwaba, *Dem. Rep. of the Congo* 87 D2
Mityana, *Uganda* 86 B3
Mixteco →, *Mexico* 119 D5
Miyagi □, *Japan* 54 E10
Miyâh, W. el →, *Egypt* 80 C3
Miyah, W. el →, *Syria* 70 C3
Miyake-Jima, *Japan* 55 G9
Miyako, *Japan* 54 E10
Miyako-Jima, *Japan* 55 M2
Miyako-Rettō, *Japan* 55 M2
Miyakonojō, *Japan* 55 J5
Miyanoura-Dake, *Japan* 55 J5
Miyazaki, *Japan* 55 J5
Miyazaki □, *Japan* 55 H5
Miyazu, *Japan* 55 G7
Miyet, Bahr el = Dead Sea, *Asia* 75 D4
Miyi, *China* 58 D4
Miyoshi, *Japan* 55 G6
Miyun, *China* 56 D9
Miyun Shuiku, *China* 57 D9
Mizdah, *Libya* 79 B8
Mizen Hd., *Cork, Ireland* 15 E2
Mizen Hd., *Wick., Ireland* 15 D5
Mizhi, *China* 56 F6
Mizil, *Romania* 43 F11
Mizoram □, *India* 67 H18
Mizpe Ramon, *Israel* 75 E3
Mizusawa, *Japan* 54 E10
Mjällby, *Sweden* 11 H8
Mjöbäck, *Sweden* 11 G6
Mjölby, *Sweden* 11 F9
Mjörn, *Sweden* 11 G6
Mjøsa, *Norway* 9 F14
Mkata, *Tanzania* 86 D4
Mkokotoni, *Tanzania* 86 D4
Mkomazi, *Tanzania* 86 C4
Mkomazi →, *S. Africa* 89 E5
Mkulwe, *Tanzania* 87 D3
Mkumbi, Ras, *Tanzania* 86 D4
Mkushi, *Zambia* 87 E2
Mkushi River, *Zambia* 87 E2
Mkuze, *S. Africa* 89 D5
Mladá Boleslav, *Czech Rep.* 26 A7
Mladenovac, *Serbia, Yug.* 40 B4
Mlala Hills, *Tanzania* 86 D3
Mlange = Mulanje, *Malawi* 87 F4
Mlava →, *Serbia, Yug.* 40 B5
Mława, *Poland* 45 E7
Mlinište, *Bos.-H.* 29 D13
Mljet, *Croatia* 29 F14
Mljetski Kanal, *Croatia* 29 F14
Młynary, *Poland* 44 D6
Mmabatho, *S. Africa* 88 D4
Mme, *Cameroon* 83 D7
Mnichovo Hradiště, *Czech Rep.* 26 A7
Mo i Rana, *Norway* 8 C16
Moa, *Indonesia* 63 F7
Moa →, *S. Leone* 82 D2
Moab, *U.S.A.* 115 G9
Moala, *Fiji* 91 D8
Moalie Park, *Australia* 95 D3
Moate, *Ireland* 15 C4
Moba, *Dem. Rep. of the Congo* 86 D2
Mobārakābād, *Iran* 71 D7
Mobārakīyeh, *Iran* 71 C6
Mobaye, *C.A.R.* 84 D4
Mobayi, *Dem. Rep. of the Congo* 84 D4
Moberly, *U.S.A.* 112 F8
Moberly →, *Canada* 104 B4
Mobile, *U.S.A.* 109 K1
Mobile B., *U.S.A.* 109 K2
Mobridge, *U.S.A.* 112 C4
Mobutu Sese Seko, L. = Albert L., *Africa* 86 B3
Moc Chau, *Vietnam* 64 B5
Moc Hoa, *Vietnam* 65 G5
Mocabe Kasari, *Dem. Rep. of the Congo* 87 D2
Moçambique, *Mozam.* 87 F5
Moçâmedes = Namibe, *Angola* 85 H2
Mochudi, *Botswana* 88 C4
Mocimboa da Praia, *Mozam.* 87 E5
Mociu, *Romania* 43 D9
Möckeln, *Sweden* 11 H8
Mockfjärd, *Sweden* 10 D8
Moclips, *U.S.A.* 116 C2
Mocoa, *Colombia* 124 C3
Mococa, *Brazil* 127 A6
Mocorito, *Mexico* 118 B3
Moctezuma, *Mexico* 118 B3
Moctezuma →, *Mexico* 119 C5
Mocuba, *Mozam.* 87 F4
Mocúzari, Presa, *Mexico* 118 B3
Modane, *France* 21 C10
Modasa, *India* 68 H5
Modder →, *S. Africa* 88 D3
Modderrivier, *S. Africa* 88 D3
Módena, *Italy* 28 D7
Modena, *U.S.A.* 115 H7
Modesto, *U.S.A.* 116 H6
Módica, *Italy* 31 F7
Mödling, *Austria* 27 C9
Modo, *Sudan* 81 F3
Modra, *Slovak Rep.* 27 C10
Modriča, *Bos.-H.* 42 F3
Moe, *Australia* 95 F4
Moebase, *Mozam.* 87 F4
Moëlan-sur-Mer, *France* 18 E3
Moengo, *Surinam* 125 B8
Moffat, *U.K.* 14 F5
Moga, *India* 68 D6
Mogadishu = Muqdisho, *Somali Rep.* 74 G4
Mogador = Essaouira, *Morocco* 78 B4
Mogadouro, *Portugal* 34 D4
Mogalakwena →, *S. Africa* 89 C4
Mogami →, *Japan* 54 E10
Mogán, *Canary Is.* 37 G4
Mogaung, *Burma* 67 G20
Mogente = Moixent, *Spain* 33 G4
Mogho, *Ethiopia* 81 G5
Mogi das Cruzes, *Brazil* 127 A6
Mogi-Guaçu →, *Brazil* 127 A6
Mogi-Mirim, *Brazil* 127 A6
Mogielnica, *Poland* 45 G7
Mogilev = Mahilyow, *Belarus* 46 F6
Mogilev-Podolskiy = Mohyliv-Podilskyy, *Ukraine* 47 H4
Mogilno, *Poland* 45 F4
Mogincual, *Mozam.* 87 F5
Mogliano Véneto, *Italy* 29 C9
Mogocha, *Russia* 51 D12
Mogok, *Burma* 67 H20
Mógoro, *Italy* 30 C1
Moguer, *Spain* 35 H4
Mogumber, *Australia* 93 F2
Mohács, *Hungary* 42 E3
Mohales Hoek, *Lesotho* 88 E4
Mohall, *U.S.A.* 112 A4
Moḩammadābād, *Iran* 71 B8
Mohave, L., *U.S.A.* 117 K12
Mohawk →, *U.S.A.* 111 D11
Moheda, *Sweden* 11 G8
Möhne →, *Germany* 24 D3
Mohoro, *Tanzania* 86 D4
Mohyliv-Podilskyy, *Ukraine* 47 H4
Moia, *Sudan* 81 F2
Moidart, L., *U.K.* 14 E3
Moinești, *Romania* 43 D11
Moirans, *France* 21 C9
Moirans-en-Montagne, *France* 19 F12
Moíres, *Greece* 36 D6
Moisaküla, *Estonia* 9 G21
Moisie, *Canada* 103 B6
Moisie →, *Canada* 103 B6
Moissac, *France* 20 D5
Moita, *Portugal* 35 G2
Moixent, *Spain* 33 G4
Möja, *Sweden* 10 E12
Mojácar, *Spain* 33 H3
Mojados, *Spain* 34 D6
Mojave, *U.S.A.* 117 K8
Mojave Desert, *U.S.A.* 117 L10
Mojiang, *China* 58 F3
Mojkovac, *Montenegro, Yug.* 40 D3
Mojo, *Bolivia* 126 A2
Mojo, *Ethiopia* 81 F4
Mojokerto, *Indonesia* 63 G15
Mokai, *N.Z.* 91 H5
Mokambo, *Dem. Rep. of the Congo* 87 E2
Mokameh, *India* 69 G11
Mokelumne →, *U.S.A.* 116 G5
Mokelumne Hill, *U.S.A.* 116 G6
Mokhós, *Greece* 36 D7
Mokhotlong, *Lesotho* 89 D4
Möklinta, *Sweden* 10 D10
Mokokchung, *India* 67 F19
Mokolo →, *S. Africa* 89 C4
Mokpo, *S. Korea* 57 G14
Mokra Gora, *Serbia, Yug.* 40 D4
Mokronog, *Slovenia* 29 C12
Moksha →, *Russia* 48 C6
Mokshan, *Russia* 48 D7
Mol, *Belgium* 17 C5
Mola di Bari, *Italy* 31 A10
Moláoi, *Greece* 38 E4
Molara, *Italy* 30 B2
Molat, *Croatia* 29 D11
Molchanovo, *Russia* 50 D9
Mold, *U.K.* 12 D4
Moldava nad Bodvou, *Slovak Rep.* 27 C14
Moldavia = Moldova ■, *Europe* 43 C13
Moldavia, *Romania* 43 D12
Molde, *Norway* 8 E12
Moldova ■, *Europe* 43 C13
Moldova Nouă, *Romania* 42 F6
Moldoveana, Vf., *Romania* 43 E9
Moldovița, *Romania* 43 C10
Mole →, *U.K.* 13 F7
Molepolole, *Botswana* 88 C4
Molfetta, *Italy* 31 A9
Molina de Aragón, *Spain* 32 E3
Molina de Segura, *Spain* 33 G3
Moline, *U.S.A.* 112 E9
Molinella, *Italy* 29 D8
Molinos, *Argentina* 126 B2
Moliro, *Dem. Rep. of the Congo* 86 D3
Moliterno, *Italy* 31 B8
Molkom, *Sweden* 10 E7
Mollahat, *Bangla.* 69 H13
Mölle, *Sweden* 11 H6
Molledo, *Spain* 34 B6
Mollendo, *Peru* 124 G4
Mollerin, L., *Australia* 93 F2
Mollerussa, *Spain* 32 D5
Mollina, *Spain* 35 H6
Mölln, *Germany* 24 B6
Mölltorp, *Sweden* 11 F8
Mölnlycke, *Sweden* 11 G6
Molochansk, *Ukraine* 47 J8
Molochnoye, Ozero, *Ukraine* 47 J8
Molodechno = Maladzyechna, *Belarus* 46 E4
Molokai, *U.S.A.* 106 H16
Molong, *Australia* 95 E4
Molopo →, *Africa* 88 D3
Mólos, *Greece* 38 C4
Molotov = Perm, *Russia* 50 D6
Molsheim, *France* 19 D14
Molson L., *Canada* 105 C9
Molteno, *S. Africa* 88 E4
Molu, *Indonesia* 63 F8
Molucca Sea, *Indonesia* 63 E6
Moluccas = Maluku, *Indonesia* 63 E7
Moma, *Dem. Rep. of the Congo* 86 C1
Moma, *Mozam.* 87 F4
Mombasa, *Kenya* 86 C4
Mombetsu, *Japan* 54 B11
Mombuey, *Spain* 34 C4
Momchilgrad, *Bulgaria* 41 E9
Momi, *Dem. Rep. of the Congo* 86 C2
Mompós, *Colombia* 124 B4
Møn, *Denmark* 11 K6
Mon →, *Burma* 67 J19
Mona, Canal de la, *W. Indies* 121 C6
Mona, Isla, *Puerto Rico* 121 C6
Mona, Pta., *Costa Rica* 120 E3
Monaco ■, *Europe* 21 E11
Monadhliath Mts., *U.K.* 14 D4
Monaghan, *Ireland* 15 B5
Monaghan □, *Ireland* 15 B5
Monahans, *U.S.A.* 113 K3
Monapo, *Mozam.* 87 E5
Monar, L., *U.K.* 14 D3
Monarch Mt., *Canada* 104 C3
Monasterevin, *Ireland* 15 C4
Monastir = Bitola, *Macedonia* 40 E5
Moncada, *Phil.* 61 D4
Moncalieri, *Italy* 28 D4
Moncalvo, *Italy* 28 C5
Moncão, *Portugal* 34 C2
Moncarapacho, *Portugal* 35 H3
Moncayo, Sierra del, *Spain* 32 D3
Mönchengladbach, *Germany* 24 D2
Monchique, *Portugal* 35 H2
Monclova, *Mexico* 118 B4
Moncontour, *France* 18 D4
Moncton, *Canada* 103 C7
Mondariz, *Spain* 34 C2
Mondego →, *Portugal* 34 E2
Mondego, C., *Portugal* 34 E2
Mondeodo, *Indonesia* 63 E6
Mondeville, *France* 18 C6
Mondolfo, *Italy* 29 E10
Mondoñedo, *Spain* 34 B3
Mondovì, *Italy* 28 D4
Mondovi, *U.S.A.* 112 C9
Mondragon, *Phil.* 61 E6
Mondragone, *Italy* 30 A6
Mondrain I., *Australia* 93 F3
Monduli □, *Tanzania* 86 C4
Monemvasía, *Greece* 38 E5
Monessen, *U.S.A.* 110 F5
Monesterio, *Spain* 35 G4
Monestier-de-Clermont, *France* 21 D9
Monett, *U.S.A.* 113 G8
Moneymore, *U.K.* 15 B5
Monfalcone, *Italy* 29 C10
Monflanquin, *France* 20 D4
Monforte, *Portugal* 35 F3
Monforte de Lemos, *Spain* 34 C3
Mong Hsu, *Burma* 67 J21
Mong Kung, *Burma* 67 J20
Mong Nai, *Burma* 67 J20
Mong Pawk, *Burma* 67 H21
Mong Ton, *Burma* 67 J21
Mong Wa, *Burma* 67 J22
Mong Yai, *Burma* 67 H21
Mongalla, *Sudan* 81 F3
Mongers, L., *Australia* 93 E2
Monghyr = Munger, *India* 69 G12
Mongibello = Etna, *Italy* 31 E7
Mongo, *Chad* 79 F9
Mongolia ■, *Asia* 60 B5
Mongonu, *Nigeria* 83 C7
Mongu, *Zambia* 85 H4
Mônguа, *Angola* 88 B2
Monifieth, *U.K.* 14 E6
Monistrol-sur-Loire, *France* 21 C8
Monkey Bay, *Malawi* 87 E4
Monkey River, *Belize* 119 D7
Mońki, *Poland* 44 E9
Monkira, *Australia* 94 C3
Monkoto, *Dem. Rep. of the Congo* 84 E4
Monmouth, *U.K.* 13 F5
Monmouth, *U.S.A.* 112 E9
Monmouthshire □, *U.K.* 13 F5
Mono L., *U.S.A.* 116 H7
Monolith, *U.S.A.* 117 K8
Monólithos, *Greece* 36 C9
Monongahela, *U.S.A.* 110 F5
Monópoli, *Italy* 31 B10
Monor, *Hungary* 42 C4
Monóvar, *Spain* 33 G4
Monreal del Campo, *Spain* 32 E3
Monreale, *Italy* 30 D6
Monroe, *Ga., U.S.A.* 109 J4
Monroe, *La., U.S.A.* 113 J8
Monroe, *Mich., U.S.A.* 108 E4
Monroe, *N.C., U.S.A.* 109 H5
Monroe, *N.Y., U.S.A.* 111 E10
Monroe, *Utah, U.S.A.* 115 G7
Monroe, *Wash., U.S.A.* 116 C5
Monroe, *Wis., U.S.A.* 112 D10
Monroe City, *U.S.A.* 112 F9
Monroeville, *Ala., U.S.A.* 109 K2
Monroeville, *Pa., U.S.A.* 110 F5
Monrovia, *Liberia* 82 D2
Mons, *Belgium* 17 D3
Møns Klint, *Denmark* 11 K6
Monsaraz, *Portugal* 35 G3
Monse, *Indonesia* 63 E6
Monségur, *France* 20 D4
Monsélice, *Italy* 29 C8
Mönsterås, *Sweden* 11 G10
Mont Cenis, Col du, *France* 21 C10
Mont-de-Marsan, *France* 20 E3
Mont-Joli, *Canada* 103 C6
Mont-Laurier, *Canada* 102 C4
Mont-roig del Camp, *Spain* 32 D5
Mont-St-Michel, Le = Le Mont-St-Michel, *France* 18 D5
Mont Tremblant Prov. Park, *Canada* 102 C5
Montabaur, *Germany* 24 E3
Montagnac, *France* 20 E7
Montagnana, *Italy* 29 C8
Montagu, *S. Africa* 88 E3
Montagu I., *Antarctica* 5 B1
Montague, *Canada* 103 C7
Montague, *U.S.A.* 114 F2
Montague, I., *Mexico* 118 A2
Montague Ra., *Australia* 93 E2
Montague Sd., *Australia* 92 B4
Montaigu, *France* 18 F5
Montalbán, *Spain* 32 E4
Montalbano Iónico, *Italy* 31 B9
Montalbo, *Spain* 32 F2
Montalcino, *Italy* 29 E8
Montalegre, *Portugal* 34 D3
Montalto, *Italy* 31 D8
Montalto di Castro, *Italy* 29 F8
Montalto Uffugo, *Italy* 31 C9
Montalvo, *U.S.A.* 117 L7
Montamarta, *Spain* 34 D5
Montana, *Bulgaria* 40 C7
Montaña, *Peru* 124 E4
Montana □, *Bulgaria* 40 C7
Montana □, *U.S.A.* 114 C9
Montaña Clara, I., *Canary Is.* 37 E6
Montánchez, *Spain* 35 F4
Montargil, *Portugal* 35 F2
Montargis, *France* 19 E9
Montauban, *France* 20 D5
Montauk, *U.S.A.* 111 E13
Montauk Pt., *U.S.A.* 111 E13
Montbard, *France* 19 E11
Montbarrey, *France* 19 E12
Montbéliard, *France* 19 E13
Montblanc, *Spain* 32 D6
Montbrison, *France* 21 C8
Montcalm, Pic de, *France* 20 F5
Montceau-les-Mines, *France* 19 F11
Montcenis, *France* 21 B8
Montclair, *U.S.A.* 111 F10
Montcornet, *France* 19 C11
Montcuq, *France* 20 D5
Montdidier, *France* 19 C9
Monte Albán, *Mexico* 119 D5
Monte Alegre, *Brazil* 125 D8
Monte Azul, *Brazil* 125 G10
Monte Bello Is., *Australia* 92 D2
Monte-Carlo, *Monaco* 21 E11
Monte Caseros, *Argentina* 126 C4
Monte Comán, *Argentina* 126 C2
Monte Cristi, *Dom. Rep.* 121 C5
Monte Lindo →, *Paraguay* 126 A4
Monte Quemado, *Argentina* 126 B3
Monte Redondo, *Portugal* 34 F2
Monte Rio, *U.S.A.* 116 G4
Monte San Giovanni Campano, *Italy* 30 A6
Monte San Savino, *Italy* 29 E8
Monte Sant' Ángelo, *Italy* 29 G12
Monte Santu, C. di, *Italy* 30 B2
Monte Vista, *U.S.A.* 115 H10
Monteagudo, *Argentina* 127 B5
Montealegre del Castillo, *Spain* 33 G3
Montebello, *Canada* 102 C5
Montebello Iónico, *Italy* 31 E8
Montebelluna, *Italy* 29 C9
Montebourg, *France* 18 C5
Montecastrilli, *Italy* 29 F9
Montecatini Terme, *Italy* 28 E7
Montecito, *U.S.A.* 117 L7
Montecristo, *Italy* 28 F7
Montefalco, *Italy* 29 F9
Montefiascone, *Italy* 29 F9
Montefrío, *Spain* 35 H7
Montegiórgio, *Italy* 29 E10
Montego Bay, *Jamaica* 120 C4
Montehermoso, *Spain* 34 E4
Montejicar, *Spain* 35 H7
Montejinnie, *Australia* 92 C5
Montélimar, *France* 21 D8
Montella, *Italy* 31 B8
Montellano, *Spain* 35 J5
Montello, *U.S.A.* 112 D10
Montemor-o-Novo, *Portugal* 35 G2
Montemor-o-Velho, *Portugal* 34 E2
Montemorelos, *Mexico* 119 B5
Montendre, *France* 20 C3
Montenegro, *Brazil* 127 B5

Montenegro □, *Yugoslavia* 40 D3
Montenero di Bisáccia, *Italy* 29 G11
Montepuez, *Mozam.* 87 E4
Montepuez →, *Mozam.* 87 E5
Montepulciano, *Italy* 29 E8
Montereale, *Italy* 29 F10
Montereau-Faut-Yonne, *France* 19 D9
Monterey, *U.S.A.* 116 J5
Monterey B., *U.S.A.* 116 J5
Montería, *Colombia* 124 B3
Monteros, *Argentina* 126 B2
Monterotondo, *Italy* 29 F9
Monterrey, *Mexico* 118 B4
Montes Claros, *Brazil* 125 G10
Montesano, *U.S.A.* 116 D3
Montesano sulla Marcellana, *Italy* 31 B8
Montesárchio, *Italy* 31 A7
Montescaglioso, *Italy* 31 B9
Montesilvano, *Italy* 29 F11
Montevarchi, *Italy* 29 E8
Montevideo, *Uruguay* 127 C4
Montevideo, *U.S.A.* 112 C7
Montezuma, *U.S.A.* 112 E8
Montfaucon, *France* 18 E5
Montfaucon-d'Argonne, *France* 19 C12
Montfaucon-en-Velay, *France* 21 C8
Montfort, *France* 18 D5
Montfort-le-Gesnois, *France* 18 D7
Montgenèvre, *France* 21 D10
Montgomery = Sahiwal, *Pakistan* 68 D5
Montgomery, *U.K.* 13 E4
Montgomery, *Ala., U.S.A.* 109 J2
Montgomery, *W. Va., U.S.A.* 108 F5
Montguyon, *France* 20 C3
Monthermé, *France* 19 C11
Monthey, *Switz.* 25 J2
Monthois, *France* 19 C11
Monti, *Italy* 30 B2
Monticelli d'Ongina, *Italy* 28 C6
Monticello, *Ark., U.S.A.* 113 J9
Monticello, *Fla., U.S.A.* 109 K4
Monticello, *Ind., U.S.A.* 108 E2
Monticello, *Iowa, U.S.A.* 112 D9
Monticello, *Ky., U.S.A.* 109 G3
Monticello, *Minn., U.S.A.* 112 C8
Monticello, *Miss., U.S.A.* 113 K9
Monticello, *N.Y., U.S.A.* 111 E10
Monticello, *Utah, U.S.A.* 115 H9
Montichiari, *Italy* 28 C7
Montier-en-Der, *France* 19 D11
Montignac, *France* 20 C5
Montigny-les-Metz, *France* 19 C13
Montigny-sur-Aube, *France* 19 E11
Montijo, *Portugal* 35 G2
Montijo, *Spain* 35 G4
Montilla, *Spain* 35 H6
Montivilliers, *France* 18 C7
Montluçon, *France* 19 F9
Montmagny, *Canada* 103 C5
Montmarault, *France* 19 F9
Montmartre, *Canada* 105 C8
Montmédy, *France* 19 C12
Montmélian, *France* 21 C10
Montmirail, *France* 19 D10
Montmoreau-St-Cybard, *France* 20 C4
Montmorency, *Canada* 103 C5
Montmorillon, *France* 20 B4
Montmort-Lucy, *France* 19 D10
Monto, *Australia* 94 C5
Montoire-sur-le-Loir, *France* 18 E7
Montório al Vomano, *Italy* 29 F10
Montoro, *Spain* 35 G6
Montour Falls, *U.S.A.* 110 D8
Montpelier, *Idaho, U.S.A.* 114 E8
Montpelier, *Ohio, U.S.A.* 108 E3
Montpelier, *Vt., U.S.A.* 111 B12
Montpellier, *France* 20 E7
Montpezat-de-Quercy, *France* 20 D5
Montpon-Ménestérol, *France* 20 D4
Montréal, *Canada* 102 C5
Montréal, *Aude, France* 20 E6
Montréal, *Gers, France* 20 E4
Montreal L., *Canada* 105 C7
Montreal Lake, *Canada* 105 C7
Montredon-Labessonnié, *France* 20 E6
Montrésor, *France* 18 E8
Montret, *France* 19 F12
Montreuil, *Pas-de-Calais, France* 19 B8
Montreuil, *Seine-St-Denis, France* 19 D9
Montreuil-Bellay, *France* 18 E6
Montreux, *Switz.* 25 J2
Montrevel-en-Bresse, *France* 19 F12
Montrichard, *France* 18 E8
Montrose, *U.K.* 14 E6
Montrose, *Colo., U.S.A.* 115 G10
Montrose, *Pa., U.S.A.* 111 E9
Monts, Pte. des, *Canada* 103 C6
Montsalvy, *France* 20 D6
Montsant, Serra de, *Spain* 32 D6
Montsauche-les-Settons, *France* 19 E11
Montsech, Serra del, *Spain* 32 C5
Montserrat, *Spain* 32 D6
Montserrat ■, *W. Indies* 121 C7
Montuenga, *Spain* 34 D6
Montuiri, *Spain* 37 B9
Monywa, *Burma* 67 H19
Monza, *Italy* 28 C6
Monze, *Zambia* 87 F2
Monze, C., *Pakistan* 68 G2
Monzón, *Spain* 32 D5
Mooi River, *S. Africa* 89 D4
Moolawatana, *Australia* 95 D2
Mooliabeenee, *Australia* 93 F2
Mooloogool, *Australia* 93 E2
Moomin Cr. →, *Australia* 95 D4
Moonah →, *Australia* 94 C2
Moonbeam, *Canada* 102 C3
Moonda, L., *Australia* 94 D3
Moonie, *Australia* 95 D5
Moonie →, *Australia* 95 D4
Moonta, *Australia* 95 E2
Moora, *Australia* 93 F2
Mooraberree, *Australia* 94 D3
Moorarie, *Australia* 93 E2
Moorcroft, *U.S.A.* 112 C2
Moore →, *Australia* 93 F2
Moore, L., *Australia* 93 E2
Moore Reefs, *Australia* 94 B4
Moorefield, *U.S.A.* 108 F6
Moores Res., *U.S.A.* 111 B13
Mooresville, *U.S.A.* 109 H5
Moorfoot Hills, *U.K.* 14 F5
Moorhead, *U.S.A.* 112 B6
Moormerland, *Germany* 24 B3
Mooroopna, *Australia* 95 F4
Moorpark, *U.S.A.* 117 L8
Moorreesburg, *S. Africa* 88 E2
Moosburg, *Germany* 25 G7
Moose →, *Canada* 102 B3
Moose Factory, *Canada* 102 B3
Moose I., *Canada* 105 C9
Moose Jaw, *Canada* 105 C7
Moose Jaw →, *Canada* 105 C7
Moose Lake, *Canada* 105 C8
Moose Lake, *U.S.A.* 112 B8
Moose Mountain Cr. →, *Canada* 105 D8
Moose Mountain Prov. Park, *Canada* 105 D8
Moose River, *Canada* 102 B3
Moosehead L., *U.S.A.* 103 C6
Moosomin, *Canada* 105 C8
Moosonee, *Canada* 102 B3
Moosup, *U.S.A.* 111 E13
Mopeia Velha, *Mozam.* 87 F4
Mopipi, *Botswana* 88 C3
Mopoi, *C.A.R.* 86 A2
Mopti, *Mali* 82 C4
Moqatta, *Sudan* 81 E4
Moquegua, *Peru* 124 G4
Mór, *Hungary* 42 C3
Móra, *Portugal* 35 G2
Mora, *Spain* 35 F7
Mora, *Sweden* 10 C8
Mora, *Minn., U.S.A.* 112 C8
Mora, *N. Mex., U.S.A.* 115 J11
Mora de Ebro = Mòra d'Ebre, *Spain* 32 D5
Mora de Rubielos, *Spain* 32 E4
Mòra d'Ebre, *Spain* 32 D5
Mòra la Nova, *Spain* 32 D5
Morača →, *Montenegro, Yug.* 40 D3
Moradabad, *India* 69 E8
Morafenobe, *Madag.* 89 B7
Morąg, *Poland* 44 E6
Moral de Calatrava, *Spain* 35 G7
Moraleja, *Spain* 34 E4
Moramanga, *Madag.* 89 B8
Moran, *Kans., U.S.A.* 113 G7
Moran, *Wyo., U.S.A.* 114 E8
Moranbah, *Australia* 94 C4
Morano Cálabro, *Italy* 31 C9
Morant Cays, *Jamaica* 120 C4
Morant Pt., *Jamaica* 120 C4
Morar, L., *U.K.* 14 E3
Moratalla, *Spain* 33 G3
Moratuwa, *Sri Lanka* 66 R11
Morava →, *Slovak Rep.* 27 C9
Moravia, *U.S.A.* 112 E8
Moravian Hts. = Českomoravská Vrchovina, *Czech Rep.* 26 B8
Moravica →, *Serbia, Yug.* 40 C4
Moraviţa, *Romania* 42 E6
Moravská Třebová, *Czech Rep.* 27 B9
Moravské Budějovice, *Czech Rep.* 26 B8
Morawa, *Australia* 93 E2
Morawhanna, *Guyana* 124 B7
Moray □, *U.K.* 14 D5
Moray Firth, *U.K.* 14 D5
Morbach, *Germany* 25 F3
Morbegno, *Italy* 28 B6
Morbi, *India* 68 H4
Morbihan □, *France* 18 E4
Mörbylånga, *Sweden* 11 H10
Morcenx, *France* 20 D3
Morcone, *Italy* 31 A7
Mordelles, *France* 18 D5
Morden, *Canada* 105 D9
Mordoğan, *Turkey* 39 C8
Mordovian Republic □ = Mordvinia □, *Russia* 48 C7
Mordovo, *Russia* 48 D5
Mordvinia □, *Russia* 48 C7
Mordy, *Poland* 45 F9
Morea, *Australia* 95 F3
Morea, *Greece* 6 H10
Moreau →, *U.S.A.* 112 C4
Morecambe, *U.K.* 12 C5
Morecambe B., *U.K.* 12 C5
Moree, *Australia* 95 D4
Morehead, *U.S.A.* 108 F4
Morehead City, *U.S.A.* 109 H7
Morelia, *Mexico* 118 D4
Morella, *Australia* 94 C3
Morella, *Spain* 32 E4
Morelos, *Mexico* 118 B3
Morelos □, *Mexico* 119 D5
Morena, Sierra, *Spain* 35 G7
Morenci, *U.S.A.* 115 K9
Moreni, *Romania* 43 F10
Moreno Valley, *U.S.A.* 117 M10
Moresby I., *Canada* 104 C2
Morestel, *France* 21 C9
Moreton, *Australia* 94 A3
Moreton I., *Australia* 95 D5
Moreuil, *France* 19 C9
Morey, *Spain* 37 B10
Morez, *France* 19 F13
Morgan, *Australia* 95 E2
Morgan, *U.S.A.* 114 F8
Morgan City, *U.S.A.* 113 L9
Morgan Hill, *U.S.A.* 116 H5
Morganfield, *U.S.A.* 108 G2
Morganton, *U.S.A.* 109 H5
Morgantown, *U.S.A.* 108 F6
Morgenzon, *S. Africa* 89 D4
Morges, *Switz.* 25 J2
Morghak, *Iran* 71 D8
Morgongåva, *Sweden* 10 E10
Morhange, *France* 19 D13
Mori, *Italy* 28 C7
Morice L., *Canada* 104 C3
Moriki, *Nigeria* 83 C6
Morinville, *Canada* 104 C6
Morioka, *Japan* 54 E10
Moris, *Mexico* 118 B3
Morlaàs, *France* 20 E3
Morlaix, *France* 18 D3
Mörlunda, *Sweden* 11 G9
Mormanno, *Italy* 31 C8
Mormant, *France* 19 D9
Mornington, *Vic., Australia* 95 F4
Mornington, *W. Austral., Australia* 92 C4
Mornington, I., *Chile* 128 F1
Mornington I., *Australia* 94 B2
Mórnos →, *Greece* 38 C3
Moro, *Sudan* 81 E3
Moro G., *Phil.* 61 H5
Morocco ■, *N. Afr.* 78 B4
Morogoro, *Tanzania* 86 D4
Morogoro □, *Tanzania* 86 D4
Moroleón, *Mexico* 118 C4
Morombe, *Madag.* 89 C7
Moron, *Argentina* 126 C4
Morón, *Cuba* 120 B4
Mörön →, *Mongolia* 60 B6
Morón de Almazán, *Spain* 32 D2
Morón de la Frontera, *Spain* 35 H5
Morona →, *Peru* 124 D3
Morondava, *Madag.* 89 C7
Morondo, *Ivory C.* 82 D3
Morongo Valley, *U.S.A.* 117 L10
Moronou, *Ivory C.* 82 D4
Morotai, *Indonesia* 63 D7
Moroto, *Uganda* 86 B3
Moroto Summit, *Kenya* 86 B3
Morozov, *Bulgaria* 41 D9
Morozovsk, *Russia* 49 F5
Morpeth, *U.K.* 12 B6
Morphou, *Cyprus* 36 D11
Morphou Bay, *Cyprus* 36 D11
Morrilton, *U.S.A.* 113 H8
Morrinhos, *Brazil* 125 G9
Morrinsville, *N.Z.* 91 G5
Morris, *Canada* 105 D9
Morris, *Ill., U.S.A.* 108 E1
Morris, *Minn., U.S.A.* 112 C7
Morris, Mt., *Australia* 93 E5
Morrisburg, *Canada* 102 D4
Morrison, *U.S.A.* 112 E10
Morristown, *Ariz., U.S.A.* 115 K7
Morristown, *N.J., U.S.A.* 111 F10
Morristown, *S. Dak., U.S.A.* 112 C4
Morristown, *Tenn., U.S.A.* 109 G4
Morro, Pta., *Chile* 126 B1
Morro Bay, *U.S.A.* 116 K6
Morro del Jable, *Canary Is.* 37 F5
Morro Jable, Pta. de, *Canary Is.* 37 F5
Morrosquillo, G. de, *Colombia* 120 E4
Mörrum, *Sweden* 11 H8
Morrumbene, *Mozam.* 89 C6
Mörrumsån →, *Sweden* 11 H8
Mors, *Denmark* 11 H2
Morshansk, *Russia* 48 D5
Mörsil, *Sweden* 10 A7
Mortagne →, *France* 19 D13
Mortagne-au-Perche, *France* 18 D7
Mortagne-sur-Gironde, *France* 20 C3
Mortagne-sur-Sèvre, *France* 18 F6
Mortain, *France* 18 D6
Mortara, *Italy* 28 C5
Morteau, *France* 19 E13
Morteros, *Argentina* 126 C3
Mortlake, *Australia* 95 F3
Morton, *Tex., U.S.A.* 113 J3
Morton, *Wash., U.S.A.* 116 D4
Morundah, *Australia* 95 E4
Moruya, *Australia* 95 F5
Morvan, *France* 19 E11
Morven, *Australia* 95 D4
Morvern, *U.K.* 14 E3
Morwell, *Australia* 95 F4
Moryń, *Poland* 45 F1
Morzine, *France* 19 F13
Mosalsk, *Russia* 46 E8
Mosbach, *Germany* 25 F5
Mošćenice, *Croatia* 29 C11
Mosciano Sant' Ángelo, *Italy* 29 F10
Moscos Is. = Maungmagan Is., *Burma* 67 N20
Moscow = Moskva, *Russia* 46 E9
Moscow, *U.S.A.* 114 C5
Mosel →, *Europe* 19 B14
Moselle = Mosel →, *Europe* 19 B14
Moselle □, *France* 19 D13
Moses Lake, *U.S.A.* 114 C4
Mosgiel, *N.Z.* 91 L3
Moshi, *Tanzania* 86 C4
Moshi □, *Tanzania* 86 C4
Moshupa, *Botswana* 88 C4
Mosina, *Poland* 45 F3
Mosjøen, *Norway* 8 D15
Moskenesøya, *Norway* 8 C15
Moskenstraumen, *Norway* 8 C15
Moskva, *Russia* 46 E9
Moskva →, *Russia* 46 E10
Moslavačka Gora, *Croatia* 29 C13
Mosomane, *Botswana* 88 C4
Moson-magyaróvár, *Hungary* 42 C2
Mošorin, *Serbia, Yug.* 42 E5
Mospino, *Ukraine* 47 J9
Mosquera, *Colombia* 124 C3
Mosquero, *U.S.A.* 113 H3
Mosqueruela, *Spain* 32 E4
Mosquitia, *Honduras* 120 C3
Mosquitos, G. de los, *Panama* 120 E3
Moss, *Norway* 9 G14
Moss Vale, *Australia* 95 E5
Mossbank, *Canada* 105 D7
Mossburn, *N.Z.* 91 L2
Mosselbaai, *S. Africa* 88 E3
Mossendjo, *Congo* 84 E2
Mossgiel, *Australia* 95 E3
Mössingen, *Germany* 25 G5
Mossman, *Australia* 94 B4
Mossoró, *Brazil* 125 E11
Mossuril, *Mozam.* 87 E5
Mossy →, *Canada* 105 C8
Most, *Czech Rep.* 26 A6
Mosta, *Malta* 36 D1
Moşţafāābād, *Iran* 71 C7
Mostaganem, *Algeria* 78 A6
Mostar, *Bos.-H.* 42 G2
Mostardas, *Brazil* 127 C5
Mostiska = Mostyska, *Ukraine* 47 H2
Móstoles, *Spain* 34 E7
Mosty = Masty, *Belarus* 46 F3
Mostyska, *Ukraine* 47 H2
Mosul = Al Mawşil, *Iraq* 70 B4
Mosulpo, *S. Korea* 57 H14
Mota del Cuervo, *Spain* 33 F2
Mota del Marqués, *Spain* 34 D5
Motagua →, *Guatemala* 120 C2
Motala, *Sweden* 11 F9
Moţca, *Romania* 43 C11
Motherwell, *U.K.* 14 F5
Motihari, *India* 69 F11
Motilla del Palancar, *Spain* 33 F3
Motnik, *Slovenia* 29 B11
Motovun, *Croatia* 29 C10
Motozintla de Mendoza, *Mexico* 119 D6
Motril, *Spain* 35 J7
Motru, *Romania* 42 F7
Motru →, *Romania* 43 F8
Mott, *U.S.A.* 112 B3
Móttola, *Italy* 31 B10
Motueka, *N.Z.* 91 J4
Motueka →, *N.Z.* 91 J4
Motul, *Mexico* 119 C7
Mouchalagane →, *Canada* 103 B6
Moúdhros, *Greece* 39 B7
Mouding, *China* 58 E3
Moudjeria, *Mauritania* 82 B2
Moudon, *Switz.* 25 J2
Mouila, *Gabon* 84 E2
Moulamein, *Australia* 95 F3
Moulianá, *Greece* 36 D7
Moulins, *France* 19 F10
Moulmein, *Burma* 67 L20
Moulton, *U.S.A.* 113 L6
Moultrie, *U.S.A.* 109 K4
Moultrie, L., *U.S.A.* 109 J5
Mound City, *Mo., U.S.A.* 112 E7
Mound City, *S. Dak., U.S.A.* 112 C4
Moúnda, Ákra, *Greece* 38 C2
Moundou, *Chad* 79 G9
Moundsville, *U.S.A.* 110 G4
Moung, *Cambodia* 64 F4
Mount Airy, *U.S.A.* 109 G5
Mount Albert, *Canada* 110 B5
Mount Amherst, *Australia* 92 C4
Mount Angel, *U.S.A.* 114 D2
Mount Augustus, *Australia* 92 D2
Mount Barker, *S. Austral., Australia* 95 F2
Mount Barker, *W. Austral., Australia* 93 F2
Mount Carmel, *U.S.A.* 108 F2
Mount Clemens, *U.S.A.* 102 D3
Mount Coolon, *Australia* 94 C4
Mount Darwin, *Zimbabwe* 87 F3
Mount Desert I., *U.S.A.* 103 D6
Mount Dora, *U.S.A.* 109 L5
Mount Douglas, *Australia* 94 C4
Mount Eba, *Australia* 95 E2
Mount Edgecumbe, *U.S.A.* 104 B1
Mount Elizabeth, *Australia* 92 C4
Mount Fletcher, *S. Africa* 89 E4
Mount Forest, *Canada* 102 D3
Mount Gambier, *Australia* 95 F3
Mount Garnet, *Australia* 94 B4
Mount Hope, *N.S.W., Australia* 95 E4
Mount Hope, *S. Austral., Australia* 95 E2
Mount Hope, *U.S.A.* 108 G5
Mount Horeb, *U.S.A.* 112 D10
Mount Howitt, *Australia* 95 D3
Mount Isa, *Australia* 94 C2
Mount Keith, *Australia* 93 E3
Mount Laguna, *U.S.A.* 117 N10
Mount Larcom, *Australia* 94 C5
Mount Lofty Ra., *Australia* 95 E2
Mount Magnet, *Australia* 93 E2
Mount Margaret, *Australia* 95 D3
Mount Maunganui, *N.Z.* 91 G6
Mount Molloy, *Australia* 94 B4
Mount Monger, *Australia* 93 F3
Mount Morgan, *Australia* 94 C5
Mount Morris, *U.S.A.* 110 D7
Mount Mulligan, *Australia* 94 B3
Mount Narryer, *Australia* 93 E2
Mount Oxide Mine, *Australia* 94 B2
Mount Pearl, *Canada* 103 C9
Mount Perry, *Australia* 95 D5
Mount Phillips, *Australia* 92 D2
Mount Pleasant, *Iowa, U.S.A.* 112 E9
Mount Pleasant, *Mich., U.S.A.* 108 D3
Mount Pleasant, *Pa., U.S.A.* 110 F5
Mount Pleasant, *S.C., U.S.A.* 109 J6
Mount Pleasant, *Tenn., U.S.A.* 109 H2
Mount Pleasant, *Tex., U.S.A.* 113 J7
Mount Pleasant, *Utah, U.S.A.* 114 G8
Mount Pocono, *U.S.A.* 111 E9
Mount Rainier National Park, *U.S.A.* 116 D5
Mount Revelstoke Nat. Park, *Canada* 104 C5
Mount Robson Prov. Park, *Canada* 104 C5
Mount Sandiman, *Australia* 93 D2
Mount Shasta, *U.S.A.* 114 F2
Mount Signal, *U.S.A.* 117 N11
Mount Sterling, *Ill., U.S.A.* 112 F9
Mount Sterling, *Ky., U.S.A.* 108 F4
Mount Surprise, *Australia* 94 B3
Mount Union, *U.S.A.* 110 F7
Mount Vernon, *Australia* 92 D2
Mount Vernon, *Ind., U.S.A.* 112 F10
Mount Vernon, *N.Y., U.S.A.* 111 F11
Mount Vernon, *Ohio, U.S.A.* 110 F2
Mount Vernon, *Wash., U.S.A.* 116 B4
Mountain Ash, *U.K.* 13 F4
Mountain Center, *U.S.A.* 117 M10
Mountain City, *Nev., U.S.A.* 114 F6
Mountain City, *Tenn., U.S.A.* 109 G5
Mountain Grove, *U.S.A.* 113 G8
Mountain Home, *Ark., U.S.A.* 113 G8
Mountain Home, *Idaho, U.S.A.* 114 E6
Mountain Iron, *U.S.A.* 112 B8
Mountain Park, *Canada* 104 C5
Mountain Pass, *U.S.A.* 117 K11
Mountain View, *Ark., U.S.A.* 113 H8
Mountain View, *Calif., U.S.A.* 116 H4
Mountainair, *U.S.A.* 115 J10
Mountmellick, *Ireland* 15 C4
Mountrath, *Ireland* 15 D4
Moura, *Australia* 94 C4
Moura, *Brazil* 124 D6
Moura, *Portugal* 35 G3
Mourão, *Portugal* 35 G3
Mourdi, Dépression du, *Chad* 79 E10
Mourdiah, *Mali* 82 C3
Mourenx-Ville-Nouvelle, *France* 20 E3
Mouri, *Ghana* 83 D4
Mourilyan, *Australia* 94 B4
Mourmelon-le-Grand, *France* 19 C11
Mourne →, *U.K.* 15 B4

Mourne Mts., *U.K.* 15 B5
Mourniaí, *Greece* 36 D6
Mournies = Mourniaí, *Greece* 36 D6
Mouscron, *Belgium* 17 D3
Moussoro, *Chad* 79 F9
Mouthe, *France* 19 F13
Moutier, *Switz.* 25 H3
Moûtiers, *France* 21 C10
Moutohara, *N.Z.* 91 H6
Moutong, *Indonesia* 63 D6
Mouy, *France* 19 C9
Mouzáki, *Greece* 38 B3
Mouzon, *France* 19 C12
Movas, *Mexico* 118 B3
Moville, *Ireland* 15 A4
Moy →, *Ireland* 15 B2
Moyale, *Kenya* 81 G4
Moyamba, *S. Leone* 82 D2
Moyen Atlas, *Morocco* 78 B4
Moyo, *Indonesia* 62 F5
Moyobamba, *Peru* 124 E3
Moyyero →, *Russia* 51 C11
Moyynty, *Kazakstan* 50 E8
Mozambique = Moçambique, *Mozam.* 87 F5
Mozambique ■, *Africa* 87 F4
Mozambique Chan., *Africa* 89 B7
Mozdok, *Russia* 49 J7
Mozdūrān, *Iran* 71 B9
Mozhaysk, *Russia* 46 E9
Mozhga, *Russia* 48 B11
Mozhnābād, *Iran* 71 C9
Mozirje, *Slovenia* 29 B11
Mozyr = Mazyr, *Belarus* 47 F5
Mpanda, *Tanzania* 86 D3
Mpanda □, *Tanzania* 86 D3
Mpésoba, *Mali* 82 C3
Mpika, *Zambia* 87 E3
Mpulungu, *Zambia* 87 D3
Mpumalanga, *S. Africa* 89 D5
Mpumalanga □, *S. Africa* 89 B5
Mpwapwa, *Tanzania* 86 D4
Mpwapwa □, *Tanzania* 86 D4
Mqinvartsveri = Kazbek, *Russia* 49 J7
Mrągowo, *Poland* 44 E8
Mramor, *Serbia, Yug.* 40 C5
Mrkonjić Grad, *Bos.-H.* 42 F2
Mrkopalj, *Croatia* 29 C11
Mrocza, *Poland* 45 E4
Msambansovu, *Zimbabwe* 87 F3
Msoro, *Zambia* 87 E3
Msta →, *Russia* 46 C6
Mstislavl = Mstsislaw, *Belarus* 46 E6
Mstsislaw, *Belarus* 46 E6
Mszana Dolna, *Poland* 45 J7
Mszczonów, *Poland* 45 G7
Mtama, *Tanzania* 87 E4
Mtilikwe →, *Zimbabwe* 87 G3
Mtsensk, *Russia* 46 F9
Mtskheta, *Georgia* 49 K7
Mtubatuba, *S. Africa* 89 D5
Mtwara-Mikindani, *Tanzania* 87 E5
Mu Gia, Deo, *Vietnam* 64 D5
Mu Us Shamo, *China* 56 E5
Muang Chiang Rai, *Thailand* 64 C2
Muang Khong, *Laos* 64 E5
Muang Lamphun, *Thailand* 64 C2
Muang Pak Beng, *Laos* 64 C3
Muar, *Malaysia* 65 L4
Muarabungo, *Indonesia* 62 E2
Muaraenim, *Indonesia* 62 E2
Muarajuloi, *Indonesia* 62 E4
Muarakaman, *Indonesia* 62 E5
Muaratebo, *Indonesia* 62 E2
Muaratembesi, *Indonesia* 62 E2
Muaratewe, *Indonesia* 62 E4
Mubarakpur, *India* 69 F10
Mubarraz = Al Mubarraz, *Si. Arabia* 71 E6
Mubende, *Uganda* 86 B3
Mubi, *Nigeria* 83 C7
Mubur, Pulau, *Indonesia* 65 L6
Mucajaí →, *Brazil* 124 C6
Muchachos, Roque de los, *Canary Is.* 37 F2
Mücheln, *Germany* 24 D7
Muchinga Mts., *Zambia* 87 E3
Muchkapskiy, *Russia* 48 E6
Muck, *U.K.* 14 E2
Muckadilla, *Australia* 95 D4
Mucur, *Turkey* 72 C6
Mucuri, *Brazil* 125 G11
Mucusso, *Angola* 88 B3
Muda, *Canary Is.* 37 F6
Mudan Jiang →, *China* 57 A15
Mudanjiang, *China* 57 B15
Mudanya, *Turkey* 41 F12
Muddy Cr. →, *U.S.A.* 115 H8
Mudgee, *Australia* 95 E4
Mudjatik →, *Canada* 105 B7
Mudurnu, *Turkey* 72 B4
Muecate, *Mozam.* 87 E4
Mueda, *Mozam.* 87 E4
Mueller Ra., *Australia* 92 C4
Muende, *Mozam.* 87 E3
Muerto, Mar, *Mexico* 119 D6
Mufindi □, *Tanzania* 87 D4
Mufu Shan, *China* 59 C10
Mufulira, *Zambia* 87 E2
Mufumbiro Range, *Africa* 86 C2
Mugardos, *Spain* 34 B2
Muge →, *Portugal* 35 F2
Múggia, *Italy* 29 C10
Mughayrā', *Si. Arabia* 70 D3
Mugi, *Japan* 55 H7
Mugia = Muxía, *Spain* 34 B1
Mugila, Mts., *Dem. Rep. of the Congo* 86 D2
Muğla, *Turkey* 39 D10
Muğla □, *Turkey* 39 D10
Müglizh, *Bulgaria* 41 D9
Mugu, *Nepal* 69 E10
Muhammad, Râs, *Egypt* 80 B3
Muhammad Qol, *Sudan* 80 C4
Muhammadabad, *India* 69 F10
Muhesi →, *Tanzania* 86 D4
Muheza □, *Tanzania* 86 D4
Mühlacker, *Germany* 25 G4
Mühldorf, *Germany* 25 G8
Mühlhausen, *Germany* 24 D6
Mühlig Hofmann fjell, *Antarctica* 5 D3
Mühlviertel, *Austria* 26 C7
Muhos, *Finland* 8 D22
Muhu, *Estonia* 9 G20
Muhutwe, *Tanzania* 86 C3
Muikamachi, *Japan* 55 F9
Muine Bheag, *Ireland* 15 D5
Muir, L., *Australia* 93 F2
Mukacheve, *Ukraine* 47 H2
Mukachevo = Mukacheve, *Ukraine* 47 H2
Mukah, *Malaysia* 62 D4
Mukawwa, Geziret, *Egypt* 80 C4
Mukdahan, *Thailand* 64 D5
Mukden = Shenyang, *China* 57 D12
Mukhtolovo, *Russia* 48 C6
Mukhtuya = Lensk, *Russia* 51 C12
Mukinbudin, *Australia* 93 F2
Mukishi, *Dem. Rep. of the Congo* 87 D1
Mukomuko, *Indonesia* 62 E2
Mukomwenze, *Dem. Rep. of the Congo* 86 D2
Muktsar, *India* 68 D6
Mukur, *Afghan.* 68 C2
Mukutawa →, *Canada* 105 C9
Mukwela, *Zambia* 87 F2
Mula, *Spain* 33 G3
Mulange, *Dem. Rep. of the Congo* 86 C2
Mulanje, *Malawi* 87 F4
Mulchén, *Chile* 126 D1
Mulde →, *Germany* 24 D8
Mule Creek, *U.S.A.* 112 D2
Muleba, *Tanzania* 86 C3
Muleba □, *Tanzania* 86 C3
Muleshoe, *U.S.A.* 113 H3
Mulgathing, *Australia* 95 E1
Mulgrave, *Canada* 103 C7
Mulhacén, *Spain* 35 H7
Mülheim, *Germany* 24 D2
Mulhouse, *France* 19 E14
Muli, *China* 58 D3
Muling, *China* 57 B16
Mull, *U.K.* 14 E3
Mull, Sound of, *U.K.* 14 E3
Mullaittivu, *Sri Lanka* 66 Q12
Mullen, *U.S.A.* 112 D4
Mullengudgery, *Australia* 95 E4
Mullens, *U.S.A.* 108 G5
Muller, Pegunungan, *Indonesia* 62 D4
Mullet Pen., *Ireland* 15 B1
Mullewa, *Australia* 93 E2
Müllheim, *Germany* 25 H3
Mulligan →, *Australia* 94 D2
Mullin, *U.S.A.* 113 K5
Mullingar, *Ireland* 15 C4
Mullins, *U.S.A.* 109 H6
Mullsjö, *Sweden* 11 G7
Mullumbimby, *Australia* 95 D5
Mulobezi, *Zambia* 87 F2
Mulroy B., *Ireland* 15 A4
Multan, *Pakistan* 68 D4
Mulumbe, Mts., *Dem. Rep. of the Congo* 87 D2
Mulungushi Dam, *Zambia* 87 E2
Mulvane, *U.S.A.* 113 G6
Mulwad, *Sudan* 80 D3
Mulwala, *Australia* 95 F4
Mumbai, *India* 66 K8
Mumbwa, *Zambia* 87 F2
Mumra, *Russia* 49 H8
Mun →, *Thailand* 64 E5
Muna, *Indonesia* 63 F6
Munamagi, *Estonia* 9 H22
Münchberg, *Germany* 25 E7
Müncheberg, *Germany* 24 C10
München, *Germany* 25 G7
Munchen-Gladbach = Mönchengladbach, *Germany* 24 D2
Muncho Lake, *Canada* 104 B3
Munchŏn, *N. Korea* 57 E14
Muncie, *U.S.A.* 108 E3
Muncoonie, L., *Australia* 94 D2
Mundare, *Canada* 104 C6
Munday, *U.S.A.* 113 J5
Münden, *Germany* 24 D5
Mundiwindi, *Australia* 92 D3
Mundo →, *Spain* 33 G2
Mundo Novo, *Brazil* 125 F10
Mundra, *India* 68 H3
Mundrabilla, *Australia* 93 F4
Munera, *Spain* 33 F2
Mungallala, *Australia* 95 D4
Mungallala Cr. →, *Australia* 95 D4
Mungana, *Australia* 94 B3
Mungaoli, *India* 68 G8
Mungari, *Mozam.* 87 F3
Mungbere, *Dem. Rep. of the Congo* 86 B2
Munger, *India* 69 G12
Mungindi, *Australia* 95 D4
Munich = München, *Germany* 25 G7
Munising, *U.S.A.* 108 B2
Munka-Ljungby, *Sweden* 11 H6
Munkebo, *Denmark* 11 J4
Munkedal, *Sweden* 11 F5
Munkfors, *Sweden* 10 E7
Munku-Sardyk, *Russia* 51 D11
Münnerstadt, *Germany* 25 E6
Muñoz Gamero, Pen., *Chile* 128 G2
Munroe L., *Canada* 105 B9
Munsan, *S. Korea* 57 F14
Munster, *France* 19 D14
Munster, *Niedersachsen, Germany* 24 C6
Münster, *Nordrhein-Westfalen, Germany* 24 D3
Munster □, *Ireland* 15 D3
Muntadgin, *Australia* 93 F2
Muntele Mare, Vf., *Romania* 43 D8
Muntok, *Indonesia* 62 E3
Munyama, *Zambia* 87 F2
Munzur Dağları, *Turkey* 73 C8
Muong Beng, *Laos* 64 B3
Muong Boum, *Vietnam* 64 A4
Muong Et, *Laos* 64 B5
Muong Hai, *Laos* 64 B3
Muong Hiem, *Laos* 64 B4
Muong Houn, *Laos* 64 B3
Muong Hung, *Vietnam* 64 B4
Muong Kau, *Laos* 64 E5
Muong Khao, *Laos* 64 C4
Muong Khoua, *Laos* 64 B4
Muong Liep, *Laos* 64 C3
Muong May, *Laos* 64 E6
Muong Ngeun, *Laos* 64 B3
Muong Ngoi, *Laos* 64 B4
Muong Nhie, *Vietnam* 64 A4
Muong Nong, *Laos* 64 D6
Muong Ou Tay, *Laos* 64 A3
Muong Oua, *Laos* 64 C3
Muong Peun, *Laos* 64 B4
Muong Phalane, *Laos* 64 D5
Muong Phieng, *Laos* 64 C3
Muong Phine, *Laos* 64 D6
Muong Sai, *Laos* 64 B3
Muong Saiapoun, *Laos* 64 C3
Muong Sen, *Vietnam* 64 C5
Muong Sing, *Laos* 64 B3
Muong Son, *Laos* 64 B4
Muong Soui, *Laos* 64 C4
Muong Va, *Laos* 64 B4
Muong Xia, *Vietnam* 64 B5
Muonio, *Finland* 8 C20
Muonionjoki →, *Finland* 8 C20
Muping, *China* 57 F11
Muqaddam, Wadi →, *Sudan* 80 D3
Muqdisho, *Somali Rep.* 74 G4
Mur →, *Austria* 27 E9
Mur-de-Bretagne, *France* 18 D4
Muradiye, *Manisa, Turkey* 39 C9
Muradiye, *Van, Turkey* 73 C10
Murakami, *Japan* 54 E9
Murallón, Cerro, *Chile* 128 F2
Muranda, *Rwanda* 86 C2
Murang'a, *Kenya* 86 C4
Murashi, *Russia* 50 D5
Murat, *France* 20 C6
Murat →, *Turkey* 73 C9
Murat Dağı, *Turkey* 39 C11
Muratlı, *Turkey* 41 E11
Murato, *France* 21 F13
Murau, *Austria* 26 D7
Muravera, *Italy* 30 C2
Murayama, *Japan* 54 E10
Murban, *U.A.E.* 71 F7
Murça, *Portugal* 34 D3
Murchison →, *Australia* 93 E1
Murchison, Mt., *Antarctica* 5 D11
Murchison Falls, *Uganda* 86 B3
Murchison House, *Australia* 93 E1
Murchison Ra., *Australia* 94 C1
Murchison Rapids, *Malawi* 87 F3
Murcia, *Spain* 33 G3
Murcia □, *Spain* 33 H3
Murdo, *U.S.A.* 112 D4
Murdoch Pt., *Australia* 94 A3
Mürefte, *Turkey* 41 F11
Mureş □, *Romania* 43 D9
Mureş →, *Romania* 42 D5
Mureşul = Mureş →, *Romania* 42 D5
Muret, *France* 20 E5
Murfreesboro, *U.S.A.* 109 H2
Murgab = Murghob, *Tajikistan* 50 F8
Murgeni, *Romania* 43 D13
Murghob, *Tajikistan* 50 F8
Murgon, *Australia* 95 D5
Murgoo, *Australia* 93 E2
Muria, *Indonesia* 63 G14
Muriaé, *Brazil* 127 A7
Murias de Paredes, *Spain* 34 C4
Muriel Mine, *Zimbabwe* 87 F3
Müritz, *Germany* 24 B8
Murka, *Kenya* 86 C4
Murmansk, *Russia* 50 C4
Murnau, *Germany* 25 H7
Muro, *France* 21 F12
Muro, *Spain* 37 B10
Muro, C. de, *France* 21 G12
Muro de Alcoy, *Spain* 33 G4
Muro Lucano, *Italy* 31 B8
Murom, *Russia* 48 C6
Muroran, *Japan* 54 C10
Muros, *Spain* 34 C1
Muros y de Noya, Ría de, *Spain* 34 C1
Muroto, *Japan* 55 H7
Muroto-Misaki, *Japan* 55 H7
Murowana Goślina, *Poland* 45 F3
Murphy, *U.S.A.* 114 E5
Murphys, *U.S.A.* 116 G6
Murphysboro, *U.S.A.* 113 G10
Murrat, *Sudan* 80 D2
Murray, *Ky., U.S.A.* 109 G1
Murray, *Utah, U.S.A.* 114 F8
Murray →, *Australia* 95 F2
Murray →, *Canada* 104 B4
Murray, L., *U.S.A.* 109 H5
Murray Bridge, *Australia* 95 F2
Murray Downs, *Australia* 94 C1
Murray Harbour, *Canada* 103 C7
Murraysburg, *S. Africa* 88 E3
Murree, *Pakistan* 68 C5
Murrieta, *U.S.A.* 117 M9
Murrin Murrin, *Australia* 93 E3
Murro di Porco, Capo, *Italy* 31 F8
Murrumbidgee →, *Australia* 95 E3
Murrumburrah, *Australia* 95 E4
Murrurundi, *Australia* 95 E5
Murshid, *Sudan* 80 C3
Murshidabad, *India* 69 G13
Murska Sobota, *Slovenia* 29 B13
Murtle L., *Canada* 104 C5
Murtoa, *Australia* 95 F3
Murtosa, *Portugal* 34 E2
Murungu, *Tanzania* 86 C3
Murwara, *India* 69 H9
Murwillumbah, *Australia* 95 D5
Mürz →, *Austria* 26 D8
Mürzzuschlag, *Austria* 26 D8
Muş, *Turkey* 73 C9
Mûsa, Gebel, *Egypt* 80 J8
Musa Khel, *Pakistan* 68 D3
Mūsá Qal'eh, *Afghan.* 66 C4
Musaffargarh, *Pakistan* 66 D7
Musala, *Bulgaria* 40 D7
Musala, *Indonesia* 62 D1
Musan, *N. Korea* 57 C15
Musangu, *Dem. Rep. of the Congo* 87 E1
Musasa, *Tanzania* 86 C3
Musay'īd, *Qatar* 71 E6
Muscat = Masqat, *Oman* 74 C6
Muscat & Oman = Oman ■, *Asia* 74 C6
Muscatine, *U.S.A.* 112 E9
Musgrave, *Australia* 94 A3
Musgrave Ranges, *Australia* 93 E5
Mushie, *Dem. Rep. of the Congo* 84 E3
Mushin, *Nigeria* 83 D5
Musi →, *Indonesia* 62 E2
Muskeg →, *Canada* 104 A4
Muskegon, *U.S.A.* 108 D2
Muskegon →, *U.S.A.* 108 D2
Muskegon Heights, *U.S.A.* 108 D2
Muskogee, *U.S.A.* 113 H7
Muskwa →, *Canada* 104 B4
Muslīmiyah, *Syria* 70 B3
Musmar, *Sudan* 80 D4
Musofu, *Zambia* 87 E2
Musoma, *Tanzania* 86 C3
Musoma □, *Tanzania* 86 C3
Musquaro, L., *Canada* 103 B7
Musquodoboit Harbour, *Canada* 103 D7
Musselburgh, *U.K.* 14 F5
Musselshell →, *U.S.A.* 114 C10
Mussidan, *France* 20 C4
Mussomeli, *Italy* 30 E6
Mussoorie, *India* 68 D8
Mussuco, *Angola* 88 B2
Mustafakemalpaşa, *Turkey* 41 F12
Mustang, *Nepal* 69 E10
Musters, L., *Argentina* 128 F3
Musudan, *N. Korea* 57 D15
Muswellbrook, *Australia* 95 E5
Muszyna, *Poland* 45 J7
Mût, *Egypt* 80 B2
Mut, *Turkey* 72 D5
Mutanda, *Mozam.* 89 C5
Mutanda, *Zambia* 87 E2
Mutare, *Zimbabwe* 87 F3
Muting, *Indonesia* 63 F10
Mutoray, *Russia* 51 C11
Mutshatsha, *Dem. Rep. of the Congo* 87 E1
Mutsu, *Japan* 54 D10
Mutsu-Wan, *Japan* 54 D10
Muttaburra, *Australia* 94 C3
Muttalip, *Turkey* 39 B12
Mutton I., *Ireland* 15 D2
Mutuáli, *Mozam.* 87 E4
Muweilih, *Egypt* 75 E3
Muxía, *Spain* 34 B1
Muy Muy, *Nic.* 120 D2
Muyinga, *Burundi* 86 C3
Muynak, *Uzbekistan* 50 E6
Muzaffarabad, *Pakistan* 69 B5
Muzaffargarh, *Pakistan* 68 D4
Muzaffarnagar, *India* 68 E7
Muzaffarpur, *India* 69 F11
Muzhi, *Russia* 50 C7
Muzillac, *France* 18 E4
Muzon, C., *U.S.A.* 104 C2
Muztag, *China* 60 C3
Mvôlô, *Sudan* 81 F2
Mvuma, *Zimbabwe* 87 F3
Mvurwi, *Zimbabwe* 87 F3
Mwadui, *Tanzania* 86 C3
Mwambo, *Tanzania* 87 E5
Mwandi, *Zambia* 87 F1
Mwanza, *Dem. Rep. of the Congo* 86 D2
Mwanza, *Tanzania* 86 C3
Mwanza, *Zambia* 87 F1
Mwanza □, *Tanzania* 86 C3
Mwaya, *Tanzania* 87 D3
Mweelrea, *Ireland* 15 C2
Mweka, *Dem. Rep. of the Congo* 84 E4
Mwenezi, *Zimbabwe* 87 G3
Mwenezi →, *Mozam.* 87 G3
Mwenga, *Dem. Rep. of the Congo* 86 C2
Mweru, L., *Zambia* 87 D2
Mweza Range, *Zimbabwe* 87 G3
Mwilambwe, *Dem. Rep. of the Congo* 86 D2
Mwimbi, *Tanzania* 87 D3
Mwinilunga, *Zambia* 87 E1
My Tho, *Vietnam* 65 G6
Myajlar, *India* 68 F4
Myanaung, *Burma* 67 K19
Myanmar = Burma ■, *Asia* 67 J20
Myaungmya, *Burma* 67 L19
Myeik Kyunzu, *Burma* 65 G1
Myerstown, *U.S.A.* 111 F8
Myingyan, *Burma* 67 J19
Myitkyina, *Burma* 67 G20
Myjava, *Slovak Rep.* 27 C10
Mykhaylivka, *Ukraine* 47 J8
Mykines, *Færoe Is.* 8 E9
Mykolayiv, *Ukraine* 47 J7
Mymensingh, *Bangla.* 67 G17
Mynydd Du, *U.K.* 13 F4
Mýrdalsjökull, *Iceland* 8 E4
Myrhorod, *Ukraine* 47 H7
Myroodah, *Australia* 92 C3
Myrtle Beach, *U.S.A.* 109 J6
Myrtle Creek, *U.S.A.* 114 E2
Myrtle Point, *U.S.A.* 114 E1
Myrtou, *Cyprus* 36 D12
Mysia, *Turkey* 41 G11
Myślenice, *Poland* 45 J6
Myślibórz, *Poland* 45 F1
Mysłowice, *Poland* 45 H6
Mysore = Karnataka □, *India* 66 N10
Mysore, *India* 66 N10
Mystic, *U.S.A.* 111 E13
Myszków, *Poland* 45 H6
Myszyniec, *Poland* 44 E8
Mytishchi, *Russia* 46 E9
Myton, *U.S.A.* 114 F8
Mývatn, *Iceland* 8 D5
Mže →, *Czech Rep.* 26 B6
Mzimba, *Malawi* 87 E3
Mzimkulu →, *S. Africa* 89 E5
Mzimvubu →, *S. Africa* 89 E4
Mzuzu, *Malawi* 87 E3

N

N' Dioum, *Senegal* 82 B2
Na Hearadh = Harris, *U.K.* 14 D2
Na Noi, *Thailand* 64 C3
Na Phao, *Laos* 64 D5
Na Sam, *Vietnam* 64 A6
Na San, *Vietnam* 64 B5
Naab →, *Germany* 25 F8
Na'am, *Sudan* 81 F2
Naantali, *Finland* 9 F19
Naas, *Ireland* 15 C5
Nababiep, *S. Africa* 88 D2
Nabadwip = Navadwip, *India* 69 H13
Nabari, *Japan* 55 G8
Nabawa, *Australia* 93 E1
Nabberu, L., *Australia* 93 E3
Nabburg, *Germany* 25 F8
Naberezhnyye Chelny, *Russia* 48 C11
Nabeul, *Tunisia* 79 A8
Nabha, *India* 68 D7
Nabīd, *Iran* 71 D8
Nabire, *Indonesia* 63 E9
Nabisar, *Pakistan* 68 G3
Nabisipi →, *Canada* 103 B7
Nabiswera, *Uganda* 86 B3
Nablus = Nābulus, *West Bank* 75 C4
Naboomspruit, *S. Africa* 89 C4
Nabua, *Phil.* 61 E5
Nābulus, *West Bank* 75 C4
Nacala, *Mozam.* 87 E5
Nacala-Velha, *Mozam.* 87 E5
Nacaome, *Honduras* 120 D2
Nacaroa, *Mozam.* 87 E4
Naches, *U.S.A.* 114 C3
Naches →, *U.S.A.* 116 D6

Nachingwea, *Tanzania* 87 E4
Nachingwea □, *Tanzania* 87 E4
Nachna, *India* 68 F4
Náchod, *Czech Rep.* 26 A9
Nacimiento Reservoir, *U.S.A.* 116 K6
Nackara, *Australia* 95 E2
Naco, *Mexico* 118 A3
Naco, *U.S.A.* 115 L9
Nacogdoches, *U.S.A.* 113 K7
Nácori Chico, *Mexico* 118 B3
Nacozari, *Mexico* 118 A3
Nadi, *Sudan* 80 D3
Nadiad, *India* 68 H5
Nădlac, *Romania* 42 D5
Nadur, *Malta* 36 C1
Nadūshan, *Iran* 71 C7
Nadvirna, *Ukraine* 47 H3
Nadvornaya = Nadvirna, *Ukraine* 47 H3
Nadym, *Russia* 50 C8
Nadym →, *Russia* 50 C8
Nærbø, *Norway* 9 G11
Næstved, *Denmark* 11 J5
Nafada, *Nigeria* 83 C7
Naftshahr, *Iran* 70 C5
Nafud Desert = An Nafūd, *Si. Arabia* 70 D4
Nag Hammâdi, *Egypt* 80 B3
Naga, *Phil.* 61 E5
Nagagami →, *Canada* 102 C3
Nagahama, *Japan* 55 G8
Nagai, *Japan* 54 E10
Nagaland □, *India* 67 G19
Nagano, *Japan* 55 F9
Nagano □, *Japan* 55 F9
Nagaoka, *Japan* 55 F9
Nagappattinam, *India* 66 P11
Nagar Parkar, *Pakistan* 68 G4
Nagasaki, *Japan* 55 H4
Nagasaki □, *Japan* 55 H4
Nagato, *Japan* 55 G5
Nagaur, *India* 68 F5
Nagercoil, *India* 66 Q10
Nagina, *India* 69 E8
Nagīneh, *Iran* 71 C8
Nagir, *Pakistan* 69 A6
Naglarby, *Sweden* 10 D9
Nagold, *Germany* 25 G4
Nagold →, *Germany* 25 G4
Nagoorin, *Australia* 94 C5
Nagorno-Karabakh, *Azerbaijan* 73 C12
Nagornyy, *Russia* 51 D13
Nagoya, *Japan* 55 G8
Nagpur, *India* 66 J11
Nagua, *Dom. Rep.* 121 C6
Nagyatád, *Hungary* 42 D2
Nagyecsed, *Hungary* 42 C7
Nagykálló, *Hungary* 42 C6
Nagykanizsa, *Hungary* 42 D2
Nagykáta, *Hungary* 42 C4
Nagykőrös, *Hungary* 42 C4
Naha, *Japan* 55 L3
Nahanni Butte, *Canada* 104 A4
Nahanni Nat. Park, *Canada* 104 A4
Nahariyya, *Israel* 70 C2
Nahāvand, *Iran* 71 C6
Nahe →, *Germany* 25 F3
Nahîya, W. →, *Egypt* 80 J7
Nahlin, *Canada* 104 B2
Naicá, *Mexico* 118 B3
Naicam, *Canada* 105 C8
Naila, *Germany* 25 E7
Nain, *Canada* 103 A7
Nā'īn, *Iran* 71 C7
Naini Tal, *India* 69 E8
Nainpur, *India* 66 H12
Naintré, *France* 18 F7
Naipu, *Romania* 43 F10
Nairn, *U.K.* 14 D5
Nairobi, *Kenya* 86 C4
Naissaar, *Estonia* 9 G21
Naivasha, *Kenya* 86 C4
Naivasha, L., *Kenya* 86 C4
Najac, *France* 20 D5
Najafābād, *Iran* 71 C6
Nájera, *Spain* 32 C2
Najerilla →, *Spain* 32 C2
Najibabad, *India* 68 E8
Najin, *N. Korea* 57 C16
Najmah, *Si. Arabia* 71 E6
Naju, *S. Korea* 57 G14
Nakadōri-Shima, *Japan* 55 H4
Nakalagba, *Dem. Rep. of the Congo* 86 B2
Nakaminato, *Japan* 55 F10
Nakamura, *Japan* 55 H6
Nakano, *Japan* 55 F9
Nakano-Shima, *Japan* 55 K4
Nakashibetsu, *Japan* 54 C12
Nakfa, *Eritrea* 81 D4
Nakhichevan = Naxçıvan, *Azerbaijan* 73 C11
Nakhichevan Republic □ = Naxçıvan □, *Azerbaijan* 50 F5
Nakhl, *Egypt* 75 F2
Nakhl-e Taqī, *Iran* 71 E7
Nakhodka, *Russia* 54 C6
Nakhon Nayok, *Thailand* 64 E3
Nakhon Pathom, *Thailand* 64 F3
Nakhon Phanom, *Thailand* 64 D5
Nakhon Ratchasima, *Thailand* 64 E4
Nakhon Sawan, *Thailand* 64 E3
Nakhon Si Thammarat, *Thailand* 65 H3
Nakhon Thai, *Thailand* 64 D3
Nakina, *B.C., Canada* 104 B2
Nakina, *Ont., Canada* 102 B2
Nakło nad Noteią, *Poland* 45 E4
Nakodar, *India* 68 D6
Nakskov, *Denmark* 11 K5
Naktong →, *S. Korea* 57 G15
Nakuru, *Kenya* 86 C4
Nakuru □, *Kenya* 86 C4
Nakuru, L., *Kenya* 86 C4
Nakusp, *Canada* 104 C5
Nal →, *Pakistan* 68 G1
Nalchik, *Russia* 49 J6
Nałęczów, *Poland* 45 G9
Nalerigu, *Ghana* 83 C4
Nalgonda, *India* 66 L11
Nalhati, *India* 69 G12
Nallamalai Hills, *India* 66 M11
Nallıhan, *Turkey* 72 B4
Nalón →, *Spain* 34 B4
Nam Can, *Vietnam* 65 H5
Nam Co, *China* 60 C4
Nam Dinh, *Vietnam* 64 B6
Nam Du, Hon, *Vietnam* 65 H5
Nam Ngum Dam, *Laos* 64 C4
Nam-Phan = Cochin China, *Vietnam* 65 G6
Nam Phong, *Thailand* 64 D4
Nam Tha, *Laos* 64 B3
Nam Tok, *Thailand* 64 E2
Namacunde, *Angola* 88 B2
Namacurra, *Mozam.* 89 B6
Namak, Daryācheh-ye, *Iran* 71 C7
Namak, Kavir-e, *Iran* 71 C8
Namaland, *Namibia* 88 C2
Namangan, *Uzbekistan* 50 E8
Namapa, *Mozam.* 87 E4
Namaqualand, *S. Africa* 88 E2
Namasagali, *Uganda* 86 B3
Namber, *Indonesia* 63 E8
Nambour, *Australia* 95 D5
Nambucca Heads, *Australia* 95 E5
Namche Bazar, *Nepal* 69 F12
Namchonjŏm, *N. Korea* 57 E14
Namecunda, *Mozam.* 87 E4
Nameponda, *Mozam.* 87 F4
Náměšť nad Oslavou, *Czech Rep.* 27 B9
Námestovo, *Slovak Rep.* 27 B12
Nametil, *Mozam.* 87 F4
Namew L., *Canada* 105 C8
Namib Desert = Namibwoestyn, *Namibia* 88 C2
Namibe, *Angola* 85 H2
Namibe □, *Angola* 88 B1
Namibia ■, *Africa* 88 C2
Namibwoestyn, *Namibia* 88 C2
Namīn, *Iran* 73 C13
Namlea, *Indonesia* 63 E7
Namoi →, *Australia* 95 E4
Nampa, *U.S.A.* 114 E5
Nampo, *N. Korea* 57 E13
Nampō-Shotō, *Japan* 55 J10
Nampula, *Mozam.* 87 F4
Namrole, *Indonesia* 63 E7
Namse Shankou, *China* 67 E13
Namsen →, *Norway* 8 D14
Namsos, *Norway* 8 D14
Namtsy, *Russia* 51 C13
Namtu, *Burma* 67 H20
Namtumbo, *Tanzania* 87 E4
Namu, *Canada* 104 C3
Namur, *Belgium* 17 D4
Namur □, *Belgium* 17 D4
Namutoni, *Namibia* 88 B2
Namwala, *Zambia* 87 F2
Namwŏn, *S. Korea* 57 G14
Namysłów, *Poland* 45 G4
Nan, *Thailand* 64 C3
Nan →, *Thailand* 64 E3
Nan Xian, *China* 59 C9
Nana, *Romania* 43 F11
Nanaimo, *Canada* 104 D4
Nanam, *N. Korea* 57 D15
Nanan, *China* 59 E12
Nanango, *Australia* 95 D5
Nan'ao, *China* 59 F11
Nanao, *Japan* 55 F8
Nanbu, *China* 58 B6
Nanchang, *China* 59 C10
Nancheng, *China* 59 D11
Nanching = Nanjing, *China* 59 A12
Nanchong, *China* 58 B6
Nanchuan, *China* 58 C6
Nancy, *France* 19 D13
Nanda Devi, *India* 69 D8
Nandan, *China* 58 E6
Nandan, *Japan* 55 G7
Nanded, *India* 66 K10
Nandewar Ra., *Australia* 95 E5
Nandi, *Fiji* 91 C7
Nandi □, *Kenya* 86 B4
Nandurbar, *India* 66 J9
Nandyal, *India* 66 M11
Nanfeng, *Guangdong, China* 59 F8
Nanfeng, *Jiangxi, China* 59 D11
Nanga, *Australia* 93 E1
Nanga-Eboko, *Cameroon* 83 E7
Nanga Parbat, *Pakistan* 69 B6
Nangade, *Mozam.* 87 E4
Nangapinoh, *Indonesia* 62 E4
Nangarhár □, *Afghan.* 66 B7
Nangatayap, *Indonesia* 62 E4
Nangeya Mts., *Uganda* 86 B3
Nangis, *France* 19 D10
Nangong, *China* 56 F8
Nanhua, *China* 58 E3
Nanhuang, *China* 57 F11
Nanhui, *China* 59 B13
Nanjeko, *Zambia* 85 H4
Nanji Shan, *China* 59 D13
Nanjian, *China* 58 E3
Nanjiang, *China* 58 A6
Nanjing, *Fujian, China* 59 E11
Nanjing, *Jiangsu, China* 59 A12
Nanjirinji, *Tanzania* 87 D4
Nankana Sahib, *Pakistan* 68 D5
Nankang, *China* 59 E10
Nanking = Nanjing, *China* 59 A12
Nankoku, *Japan* 55 H6
Nanling, *China* 59 B12
Nanning, *China* 58 F7
Nannup, *Australia* 93 F2
Nanpan Jiang →, *China* 58 E6
Nanpara, *India* 69 F9
Nanpi, *China* 56 E9
Nanping, *Fujian, China* 59 D12
Nanping, *Henan, China* 59 C9
Nanri Dao, *China* 59 E12
Nanripe, *Mozam.* 87 E4
Nansei-Shotō = Ryūkyū-rettō, *Japan* 55 M3
Nansen Sd., *Canada* 4 A3
Nansio, *Tanzania* 86 C3
Nant, *France* 20 D7
Nanterre, *France* 19 D9
Nantes, *France* 18 E5
Nantiat, *France* 20 B5
Nanticoke, *U.S.A.* 111 E8
Nanton, *Canada* 104 C6
Nantong, *China* 59 A13
Nantua, *France* 19 F12
Nantucket I., *U.S.A.* 98 E12
Nantwich, *U.K.* 12 D5
Nanuque, *Brazil* 125 G10
Nanusa, Kepulauan, *Indonesia* 63 D7
Nanutarra, *Australia* 92 D2
Nanxiong, *China* 59 E10
Nanyang, *China* 56 H7
Nanyi Hu, *China* 59 B12
Nanyuan, *China* 56 E9
Nanyuki, *Kenya* 86 B4
Nanzhang, *China* 59 B8
Nao, C. de la, *Spain* 33 G5
Naococane L., *Canada* 103 B5
Naoetsu, *Japan* 55 F9
Náousa, *Imathía, Greece* 40 F6
Náousa, *Kikládhes, Greece* 39 D7
Naozhou Dao, *China* 59 G8
Napa, *U.S.A.* 116 G4
Napa →, *U.S.A.* 116 G4
Napanee, *Canada* 102 D4
Napanoch, *U.S.A.* 111 E10
Nape, *Laos* 64 C5
Nape Pass = Keo Neua, Deo, *Vietnam* 64 C5
Napier, *N.Z.* 91 H6
Napier Broome B., *Australia* 92 B4
Napier Downs, *Australia* 92 C3
Napier Pen., *Australia* 94 A2
Naples = Nápoli, *Italy* 31 B7
Naples, *U.S.A.* 109 M5
Napo, *China* 58 F5
Napo →, *Peru* 122 D3
Napoleon, *N. Dak., U.S.A.* 112 B5
Napoleon, *Ohio, U.S.A.* 108 E3
Nápoli, *Italy* 31 B7
Nápoli, G. di, *Italy* 31 B7
Napopo, *Dem. Rep. of the Congo* 86 B2
Nappa Merrie, *Australia* 95 D3
Naqâda, *Egypt* 80 B3
Naqadeh, *Iran* 73 D11
Naqqāsh, *Iran* 71 C6
Nara, *Japan* 55 G7
Nara, *Mali* 82 B3
Nara □, *Japan* 55 G8
Nara Canal, *Pakistan* 68 G3
Nara Visa, *U.S.A.* 113 H3
Naracoorte, *Australia* 95 F3
Naradhan, *Australia* 95 E4
Narasapur, *India* 67 L12
Narathiwat, *Thailand* 65 J3
Narayanganj, *Bangla.* 67 H17
Narayanpet, *India* 66 L10
Narbonne, *France* 20 E7
Narcea →, *Spain* 34 B4
Nardīn, *Iran* 71 B7
Nardò, *Italy* 31 B11
Narembeen, *Australia* 93 F2
Nares Str., *Arctic* 98 A13
Naretha, *Australia* 93 F3
Narew →, *Poland* 45 F7
Nari →, *Pakistan* 68 F2
Narin, *Afghan.* 66 A6
Narindra, Helodranon' i, *Madag.* 89 A8
Narita, *Japan* 55 G10
Närke, *Sweden* 10 E8
Narmada →, *India* 68 J5
Narman, *Turkey* 73 B9
Narmland, *Sweden* 9 F15
Narnaul, *India* 68 E7
Narni, *Italy* 29 F9
Naro, *Ghana* 82 C4
Naro Fominsk, *Russia* 46 E9
Narodnaya, *Russia* 6 B17
Narok, *Kenya* 86 C4
Narok □, *Kenya* 86 C4
Narón, *Spain* 34 B2
Narooma, *Australia* 95 F5
Narowal, *Pakistan* 68 C6
Narrabri, *Australia* 95 E4
Narran →, *Australia* 95 D4
Narrandera, *Australia* 95 E4
Narraway →, *Canada* 104 B5
Narrogin, *Australia* 93 F2
Narromine, *Australia* 95 E4
Narsimhapur, *India* 69 H8
Nartes, L. e, *Albania* 40 F3
Nartkala, *Russia* 49 J6
Naruto, *Japan* 55 G7
Narva, *Estonia* 46 C5
Narva →, *Russia* 9 G22
Narvik, *Norway* 8 B17
Narvskoye Vdkhr., *Russia* 46 C5
Narwana, *India* 68 E7
Naryan-Mar, *Russia* 50 C6
Naryilco, *Australia* 95 D3
Narym, *Russia* 50 D9
Naryn, *Kyrgyzstan* 50 E8
Nasa, *Norway* 8 C16
Nasarawa, *Nigeria* 83 D6
Năsăud, *Romania* 43 C9
Naseby, *N.Z.* 91 L3
Naselle, *U.S.A.* 116 D3
Naser, Buheirat en, *Egypt* 80 C3
Nashua, *Iowa, U.S.A.* 112 D8
Nashua, *Mont., U.S.A.* 114 B10
Nashua, *N.H., U.S.A.* 111 D13
Nashville, *Ark., U.S.A.* 113 J8
Nashville, *Ga., U.S.A.* 109 K4
Nashville, *Tenn., U.S.A.* 109 G2
Našice, *Croatia* 42 E3
Nasielsk, *Poland* 45 F7
Nasik, *India* 66 K8
Nasipit, *Phil.* 61 G6
Nasirabad, *India* 68 F6
Naskaupi →, *Canada* 103 B7
Naso, *Italy* 31 D7
Naşriān-e Pā'īn, *Iran* 70 C5
Nass →, *Canada* 104 C3
Nassau, *Bahamas* 120 A4
Nassau, *U.S.A.* 111 D11
Nassau, B., *Chile* 128 H3
Nasser, L. = Naser, Buheirat en, *Egypt* 80 C3
Nasser City = Kôm Ombo, *Egypt* 80 C3
Nassian, *Ivory C.* 82 D4
Nässjö, *Sweden* 11 G8
Nasugbu, *Phil.* 61 D4
Näsum, *Sweden* 11 H8
Näsviken, *Sweden* 10 C10
Nat Kyizin, *Burma* 67 M20
Nata, *Botswana* 88 C4
Natal, *Brazil* 125 E11
Natal, *Canada* 104 D6
Natal, *Indonesia* 62 D1
Natalinci, *Serbia, Yug.* 42 F5
Naţanz, *Iran* 71 C6
Natashquan, *Canada* 103 B7
Natashquan →, *Canada* 103 B7
Natchez, *U.S.A.* 113 K9
Natchitoches, *U.S.A.* 113 K8
Nathalia, *Australia* 95 F4
Nathdwara, *India* 68 G5
Nati, Pta., *Spain* 37 A10
Natimuk, *Australia* 95 F3
Nation →, *Canada* 104 B4
National City, *U.S.A.* 117 N9
Natitingou, *Benin* 83 C5
Natividad, I., *Mexico* 118 B1
Natoma, *U.S.A.* 112 F5
Natron, L., *Tanzania* 86 C4
Natrona Heights, *U.S.A.* 110 F5
Natrûn, W. el →, *Egypt* 80 H7
Nättraby, *Sweden* 11 H9
Natuna Besar, Kepulauan, *Indonesia* 65 L7
Natuna Is. = Natuna Besar, Kepulauan, *Indonesia* 65 L7
Natuna Selatan, Kepulauan, *Indonesia* 65 L7
Natural Bridge, *U.S.A.* 111 B9
Naturaliste, C., *Australia* 94 G4
Nau Qala, *Afghan.* 68 B3
Naubinway, *U.S.A.* 102 C2
Naucelle, *France* 20 D6
Nauders, *Austria* 26 E3
Nauen, *Germany* 24 C8
Naugatuck, *U.S.A.* 111 E11
Naujoji Akmenė, *Lithuania* 44 B9
Naumburg, *Germany* 24 D7
Nā'ūr at Tunayb, *Jordan* 75 D4
Nauru ■, *Pac. Oc.* 96 H8
Naushahra = Nowshera, *Pakistan* 66 C8
Nauta, *Peru* 124 D4
Nautanwa, *India* 67 F13
Nautla, *Mexico* 119 C5
Nava, *Mexico* 118 B4
Nava, *Spain* 34 B5
Nava del Rey, *Spain* 34 D5
Navadwip, *India* 69 H13
Navahermosa, *Spain* 35 F6
Navahrudak, *Belarus* 46 F3
Navajo Reservoir, *U.S.A.* 115 H10
Navalcarnero, *Spain* 34 E6
Navalmoral de la Mata, *Spain* 34 F5
Navalvillar de Pela, *Spain* 35 F5
Navan = An Uaimh, *Ireland* 15 C5
Navapolatsk, *Belarus* 46 E5
Navarino, I., *Chile* 128 H3
Navarra □, *Spain* 32 C3
Navarre, *U.S.A.* 110 F3
Navarro →, *U.S.A.* 116 F3
Navas de San Juan, *Spain* 35 G7
Navasota, *U.S.A.* 113 K6
Navassa, *W. Indies* 121 C5
Nävekvarn, *Sweden* 11 F10
Naver →, *U.K.* 14 C4
Navia, *Spain* 34 B4
Navia →, *Spain* 34 B4
Navia de Suarna, *Spain* 34 C3
Navidad, *Chile* 126 C1
Navlya, *Russia* 47 F8
Năvodari, *Romania* 43 F13
Navoi = Nawoiy, *Uzbekistan* 50 E7
Navojoa, *Mexico* 118 B3
Navolato, *Mexico* 118 C3
Návpaktos, *Greece* 38 C3
Návplion, *Greece* 38 D4
Navrongo, *Ghana* 83 C4
Navsari, *India* 66 J8
Nawa Kot, *Pakistan* 68 E4
Nawabganj, *Ut. P., India* 69 F9
Nawabganj, *Ut. P., India* 69 E8
Nawabshah, *Pakistan* 68 F3
Nawada, *India* 69 G11
Nawakot, *Nepal* 69 F11
Nawalgarh, *India* 68 F6
Nawanshahr, *India* 69 C6
Nawi, *Sudan* 80 D3
Nawoiy, *Uzbekistan* 50 E7
Naxçıvan, *Azerbaijan* 73 C11
Naxçıvan □, *Azerbaijan* 50 F5
Náxos, *Greece* 39 D7
Nay, *France* 20 E3
Nāy Band, *Iran* 71 E7
Nayakhan, *Russia* 51 C16
Nayarit □, *Mexico* 118 C4
Nayé, *Senegal* 82 C2
Nayong, *China* 58 D5
Nayoro, *Japan* 54 B11
Nayyāl, W. →, *Si. Arabia* 70 D3
Nazaré, *Brazil* 125 F11
Nazaré, *Portugal* 35 F1
Nazareth = Nazerat, *Israel* 75 C4
Nazas, *Mexico* 118 B4
Nazas →, *Mexico* 118 B4
Nazca, *Peru* 124 F4
Naze, The, *U.K.* 13 F9
Nazerat, *Israel* 75 C4
Nāzīk, *Iran* 70 B5
Nazilli, *Turkey* 39 D10
Nazir Hat, *Bangla.* 67 H17
Nazko, *Canada* 104 C4
Nazko →, *Canada* 104 C4
Nazret, *Ethiopia* 81 F4
Nchanga, *Zambia* 87 E2
Ncheu, *Malawi* 87 E3
Ndala, *Tanzania* 86 C3
Ndalatando, *Angola* 84 F2
Ndali, *Benin* 83 D5
Ndareda, *Tanzania* 86 C4
Ndélé, *C.A.R.* 84 C4
Ndjamena, *Chad* 79 F8
Ndola, *Zambia* 87 E2
Ndoto Mts., *Kenya* 86 B4
Nduguti, *Tanzania* 86 C3
Néa Alikarnassós, *Greece* 39 F7
Néa Ankhíalos, *Greece* 38 B4
Néa Epídhavros, *Greece* 38 D5
Néa Flippiás, *Greece* 38 B2
Néa Ionía, *Greece* 38 B4
Néa Kallikrátia, *Greece* 40 F7
Néa Mákri, *Greece* 38 C5
Néa Moudhaniá, *Greece* 40 F7
Néa Péramos, *Attikí, Greece* 38 C5
Néa Péramos, *Kavála, Greece* 41 F8
Néa Víssi, *Greece* 41 E10
Néa Zíkhna, *Greece* 40 E7
Neagh, Lough, *U.K.* 15 B5
Neah Bay, *U.S.A.* 116 B2
Neale, L., *Australia* 92 D5
Neamţ □, *Romania* 43 C11
Neápolis, *Kozáni, Greece* 40 F5
Neápolis, *Kríti, Greece* 36 D7
Neápolis, *Lakonía, Greece* 38 E5
Near Is., *U.S.A.* 100 C1
Neath, *U.K.* 13 F4
Neath Port Talbot □, *U.K.* 13 F4
Nebbou, *Burkina Faso* 83 C4
Nebine Cr. →, *Australia* 95 D4
Nebitdag, *Turkmenistan* 50 F6
Nebolchy, *Russia* 46 C7
Nebraska □, *U.S.A.* 112 E5
Nebraska City, *U.S.A.* 112 E7
Nébrodi, Monti, *Italy* 31 E7
Necedah, *U.S.A.* 112 C9
Nechako →, *Canada* 104 C4
Neches →, *U.S.A.* 113 L8
Neckar →, *Germany* 25 F4
Necochea, *Argentina* 126 D4
Neda, *Spain* 34 B2
Nedelino, *Bulgaria* 41 E9
Nedelišće, *Croatia* 29 B13
Nédha →, *Greece* 38 D3
Needles, *U.S.A.* 117 L12
Needles, The, *U.K.* 13 G6
Ñeembucú □, *Paraguay* 126 B4
Neemuch = Nimach, *India* 68 G6
Neenah, *U.S.A.* 108 C1
Neepawa, *Canada* 105 C9
Neftçala, *Azerbaijan* 73 C13
Neftegorsk, *Russia* 49 H4
Neftekumsk, *Russia* 49 H7
Nefyn, *U.K.* 12 E3

Negapatam = Nagappattinam, India 66 P11
Negaunee, U.S.A. 108 B2
Negele, Ethiopia 81 F4
Negev Desert = Hanegev, Israel 75 E4
Negoiul, Vf., Romania 43 E9
Negombo, Sri Lanka 66 R11
Negotin, Serbia, Yug. 40 B6
Negotino, Macedonia 40 E6
Negra, Peña, Spain 34 C4
Negra, Pta., Peru 122 D2
Negrais, C. = Maudin Sun, Burma 67 M19
Negreşti, Romania 43 D12
Negreşti-Oaş, Romania 43 C8
Negro →, Argentina 122 H4
Negro →, Brazil 122 D4
Negro →, Uruguay 127 C4
Negros, Phil. 61 G5
Negru Vodă, Romania 43 G13
Nehalem →, U.S.A. 116 E3
Nehāvand, Iran 71 C6
Nehbandān, Iran 71 D9
Nehoiu, Romania 43 E11
Nei Monggol Zizhiqu □, China 56 D7
Neidpath, Canada 105 C7
Neihart, U.S.A. 114 C8
Neijiang, China 58 C5
Neilton, U.S.A. 114 C2
Neiqiu, China 56 F8
Neiva, Colombia 124 C3
Neixiang, China 56 H6
Nejanilini L., Canada 105 B9
Nejo, Ethiopia 81 F4
Nekā, Iran 71 B7
Nekemte, Ethiopia 81 F4
Nêkheb, Egypt 80 B3
Neksø, Denmark 11 J9
Nelas, Portugal 34 E3
Nelia, Australia 94 C3
Nelidovo, Russia 46 D7
Neligh, U.S.A. 112 D5
Nelkan, Russia 51 D14
Nellore, India 66 M11
Nelson, Canada 104 D5
Nelson, N.Z. 91 J4
Nelson, U.K. 12 D5
Nelson, U.S.A. 115 J7
Nelson →, Canada 105 C9
Nelson, C., Australia 95 F3
Nelson, Estrecho, Chile 128 G2
Nelson Forks, Canada 104 B4
Nelson House, Canada 105 B9
Nelson L., Canada 105 B8
Nelspoort, S. Africa 88 E3
Nelspruit, S. Africa 89 D5
Néma, Mauritania 82 B3
Neman, Russia 9 J20
Neman →, Lithuania 9 J20
Neméa, Greece 38 D4
Nemeiben L., Canada 105 B7
Nemërçkës, Mal, Albania 40 F4
Nemira, Vf., Romania 43 D11
Nemours, France 19 D9
Nemšová, Slovak Rep. 27 C11
Nemunas = Neman →, Lithuania 9 J20
Nemuro, Japan 54 C12
Nemuro-Kaikyō, Japan 54 C12
Nen Jiang →, China 57 B13
Nenagh, Ireland 15 D3
Nenasi, Malaysia 65 L4
Nene →, U.K. 13 E8
Nénita, Greece 39 C8
Nenjiang, China 60 B7
Neno, Malawi 87 F3
Neodesha, U.S.A. 113 G7
Neokhórion, Aitolía kai Akarnanía, Greece 38 C3
Neokhórion, Árta, Greece 38 B2
Néon Karlovásion, Greece 39 D8
Néon Petrítsi, Greece 40 E7
Neosho, U.S.A. 113 G7
Neosho →, U.S.A. 113 H7
Nepal ■, Asia 69 F11
Nepalganj, Nepal 69 E9
Nephi, U.S.A. 114 G8
Nephin, Ireland 15 B2
Nepi, Italy 29 F9
Nepomuk, Czech Rep. 26 B6
Neptune, U.S.A. 111 F10
Nera →, Italy 29 F9
Nera →, Romania 42 F6
Nérac, France 20 D4
Neratovice, Czech Rep. 26 A7
Nerchinsk, Russia 51 D12
Nereju, Romania 43 E11
Nerekhta, Russia 46 D11
Néret L., Canada 103 B5
Neretvanski Kanal, Croatia 29 E14
Neringa, Lithuania 9 J19
Nerja, Spain 35 J7
Nerl →, Russia 46 D11
Nerpio, Spain 33 G2
Nerva, Spain 35 H4
Nervi, Italy 28 D6
Nesebŭr, Bulgaria 41 D11
Ness, L., U.K. 14 D4
Nesterov, Poland 47 G2
Nestórion, Greece 40 F5
Néstos →, Greece 41 E8
Nesvady, Slovak Rep. 27 D11
Nesvizh = Nyasvizh, Belarus 47 F4
Netanya, Israel 75 C3
Nete →, Belgium 17 C4
Netherdale, Australia 94 C4
Netherlands ■, Europe 17 C5
Netherlands Antilles ■, W. Indies 124 A5
Neto →, Italy 31 C10
Nettancourt, France 19 D11
Nettetal, Germany 24 D2
Nettilling L., Canada 101 B12
Nettuno, Italy 30 A5
Netzahualcoyotl, Presa, Mexico 119 D6
Neu-Isenburg, Germany 25 E4
Neu-Ulm, Germany 25 G6
Neubrandenburg, Germany 24 B9
Neubukow, Germany 24 A7
Neuburg, Germany 25 G7
Neuchâtel, Switz. 25 J2
Neuchâtel □, Switz. 25 J2
Neuchâtel, Lac de, Switz. 25 J2
Neudau, Austria 26 D9
Neuenhagen, Germany 24 C9
Neuenhaus, Germany 24 C2
Neuf-Brisach, France 19 D14
Neufahrn, Bayern, Germany 25 G8
Neufahrn, Bayern, Germany 25 G7
Neufchâteau, Belgium 17 E5
Neufchâteau, France 19 D12
Neufchâtel-en-Bray, France 18 C8
Neufchâtel-sur-Aisne, France 19 C11
Neuhaus, Germany 24 B6
Neuillé-Pont-Pierre, France 18 E7
Neuilly-St-Front, France 19 C10
Neukalen, Germany 24 B8
Neumarkt, Germany 25 F7
Neumünster, Germany 24 A5
Neung-sur-Beuvron, France 19 E8
Neunkirchen, Austria 26 D9
Neunkirchen, Germany 25 F3
Neuquén, Argentina 128 D3
Neuquén □, Argentina 126 D2
Neuruppin, Germany 24 C8
Neusäss, Germany 25 G6
Neuse →, U.S.A. 109 H7
Neusiedl, Austria 27 D9
Neusiedler See, Austria 27 D9
Neuss, Germany 24 D2
Neussargues-Moissac, France 20 C7
Neustadt, Bayern, Germany 25 F8
Neustadt, Bayern, Germany 25 G7
Neustadt, Bayern, Germany 25 F6
Neustadt, Bayern, Germany 25 E7
Neustadt, Brandenburg, Germany 24 C8
Neustadt, Hessen, Germany 24 E5
Neustadt, Niedersachsen, Germany 24 C5
Neustadt, Rhld-Pfz., Germany 25 F4
Neustadt, Sachsen, Germany 24 D10
Neustadt, Schleswig-Holstein, Germany 24 A6
Neustadt, Thüringen, Germany 24 E7
Neustrelitz, Germany 24 B9
Neuvic, France 20 C6
Neuville-sur-Saône, France 21 C8
Neuvy-le-Roi, France 18 E7
Neuvy-St-Sépulchre, France 19 F8
Neuvy-sur-Barangeon, France 19 E9
Neuwerk, Germany 24 B4
Neuwied, Germany 24 E3
Neva →, Russia 46 C6
Nevada, U.S.A. 113 G7
Nevada □, U.S.A. 114 G5
Nevada, Sierra, Spain 35 H7
Nevada, Sierra, U.S.A. 114 G3
Nevada City, U.S.A. 116 F6
Nevado, Cerro, Argentina 126 D2
Nevel, Russia 46 D5
Nevers, France 19 F10
Nevertire, Australia 95 E4
Nevesinje, Bos.-H. 40 C2
Neville, Canada 105 D7
Nevinnomyssk, Russia 49 H6
Nevis, W. Indies 121 C7
Nevrokop = Gotse Delchev, Bulgaria 40 E7
Nevşehir, Turkey 72 C6
New Albany, Ind., U.S.A. 108 F3
New Albany, Miss., U.S.A. 113 H10
New Albany, Pa., U.S.A. 111 E8
New Amsterdam, Guyana 124 B7
New Angledool, Australia 95 D4
New Bedford, U.S.A. 111 E14
New Bern, U.S.A. 109 H7
New Bethlehem, U.S.A. 110 F5
New Bloomfield, U.S.A. 110 F7
New Boston, U.S.A. 113 J7
New Braunfels, U.S.A. 113 L5
New Brighton, N.Z. 91 K4
New Brighton, U.S.A. 110 F4
New Britain, Papua N. G. 96 H7
New Britain, U.S.A. 111 E12
New Brunswick, U.S.A. 111 F10
New Brunswick □, Canada 103 C6
New Bussa, Nigeria 83 D5
New Caledonia ■, Pac. Oc. 96 K8
New Castle, Ind., U.S.A. 108 F3
New Castle, Pa., U.S.A. 110 F4
New City, U.S.A. 111 E11
New Cumberland, U.S.A. 110 F4
New Cuyama, U.S.A. 117 L7
New Delhi, India 68 E7
New Denver, Canada 104 D5
New Don Pedro Reservoir, U.S.A. 116 H6
New England, U.S.A. 112 B3
New England Ra., Australia 95 E5
New Forest, U.K. 13 G6
New Galloway, U.K. 14 F4
New Glasgow, Canada 103 C7
New Guinea, Oceania 96 H5
New Hamburg, Canada 110 C4
New Hampshire □, U.S.A. 111 C13
New Hampton, U.S.A. 112 D8
New Hanover, S. Africa 89 D5
New Haven, Conn., U.S.A. 111 E12
New Haven, Mich., U.S.A. 110 D2
New Hazelton, Canada 104 B3
New Hebrides = Vanuatu ■, Pac. Oc. 96 J8
New Iberia, U.S.A. 113 K9
New Ireland, Papua N. G. 96 H7
New Jersey □, U.S.A. 111 F10
New Kensington, U.S.A. 110 F5
New Lexington, U.S.A. 108 F4
New Liskeard, Canada 102 C4
New London, Conn., U.S.A. 111 E12
New London, Minn., U.S.A. 112 C7
New London, Ohio, U.S.A. 110 E2
New London, Wis., U.S.A. 112 C10
New Madrid, U.S.A. 113 G10
New Meadows, U.S.A. 114 D5
New Melones L., U.S.A. 116 H6
New Mexico □, U.S.A. 115 J10
New Milford, Conn., U.S.A. 111 E11
New Milford, Pa., U.S.A. 111 E9
New Norcia, Australia 93 F2
New Norfolk, Australia 94 G4
New Orleans, U.S.A. 113 L9
New Philadelphia, U.S.A. 110 F3
New Plymouth, N.Z. 91 H5
New Plymouth, U.S.A. 114 E5
New Providence, Bahamas 120 A4
New Quay, U.K. 13 E3
New Radnor, U.K. 13 E4
New Richmond, U.S.A. 112 C8
New Roads, U.S.A. 113 K9
New Rochelle, U.S.A. 111 F11
New Rockford, U.S.A. 112 B5
New Romney, U.K. 13 G8
New Ross, Ireland 15 D5
New Salem, U.S.A. 112 B4
New Scone, U.K. 14 E5
New Siberian I. = Novaya Sibir, Ostrov, Russia 51 B16
New Siberian Is. = Novosibirskiye Ostrova, Russia 51 B15
New Smyrna Beach, U.S.A. 109 L5
New South Wales □, Australia 95 E4
New Springs, Australia 93 E3
New Town, U.S.A. 112 B3
New Tredegar, U.K. 13 F4
New Ulm, U.S.A. 112 C7
New Waterford, Canada 103 C7
New Westminster, Canada 104 D4
New York □, U.S.A. 111 D9
New York City, U.S.A. 111 F11
New Zealand ■, Oceania 91 J6
Newala, Tanzania 87 E4
Newala □, Tanzania 87 E4
Newark, Del., U.S.A. 108 F8
Newark, N.J., U.S.A. 111 F10
Newark, N.Y., U.S.A. 110 C7
Newark, Ohio, U.S.A. 110 F2
Newark-on-Trent, U.K. 12 D7
Newaygo, U.S.A. 108 D3
Newberg, U.S.A. 114 D2
Newberry, Mich., U.S.A. 108 B3
Newberry, S.C., U.S.A. 109 H5
Newberry Springs, U.S.A. 117 L10
Newbridge = Droichead Nua, Ireland 15 C5
Newbrook, Canada 104 C6
Newburgh, U.S.A. 111 E10
Newbury, U.K. 13 F6
Newbury, U.S.A. 111 B12
Newburyport, U.S.A. 111 D14
Newcastle, Australia 95 E5
Newcastle, Canada 103 C6
Newcastle, S. Africa 89 D4
Newcastle, U.K. 15 B6
Newcastle, Calif., U.S.A. 116 G5
Newcastle, Wyo., U.S.A. 112 D2
Newcastle Emlyn, U.K. 13 E3
Newcastle Ra., Australia 92 C5
Newcastle-under-Lyme, U.K. 12 D5
Newcastle-upon-Tyne, U.K. 12 C6
Newcastle Waters, Australia 94 B1
Newcastle West, Ireland 15 D2
Newdegate, Australia 93 F2
Newell, U.S.A. 112 C3
Newfoundland □, Canada 103 B8
Newfoundland I., N. Amer. 98 E14
Newhalem, U.S.A. 104 D4
Newhall, U.S.A. 117 L8
Newhaven, U.K. 13 G8
Newkirk, U.S.A. 113 G6
Newlyn, U.K. 13 G2
Newman, Australia 92 D2
Newman, U.S.A. 116 H5
Newmarket, Canada 110 B5
Newmarket, Ireland 15 D2
Newmarket, U.K. 13 E8
Newmarket, U.S.A. 111 C14
Newnan, U.S.A. 109 J3
Newport, Ireland 15 C2
Newport, I. of W., U.K. 13 G6
Newport, Newp., U.K. 13 F5
Newport, Ark., U.S.A. 113 H9
Newport, Ky., U.S.A. 108 F3
Newport, N.H., U.S.A. 111 C12
Newport, Oreg., U.S.A. 114 D1
Newport, Pa., U.S.A. 110 F7
Newport, R.I., U.S.A. 111 E13
Newport, Tenn., U.S.A. 109 H4
Newport, Vt., U.S.A. 111 B12
Newport, Wash., U.S.A. 114 B5
Newport □, U.K. 13 F4
Newport Beach, U.S.A. 117 M9
Newport News, U.S.A. 108 G7
Newport Pagnell, U.K. 13 E7
Newquay, U.K. 13 G2
Newry, U.K. 15 B5
Newton, Iowa, U.S.A. 112 E8
Newton, Mass., U.S.A. 111 D13
Newton, Miss., U.S.A. 113 J10
Newton, N.C., U.S.A. 109 H5
Newton, N.J., U.S.A. 111 E10
Newton, Tex., U.S.A. 113 K8
Newton Abbot, U.K. 13 G4
Newton Aycliffe, U.K. 12 C6
Newton Boyd, Australia 95 D5
Newton Stewart, U.K. 14 G4
Newtonmore, U.K. 14 D4
Newtown, U.K. 13 E4
Newtownabbey, U.K. 15 B6
Newtownards, U.K. 15 B6
Newtownbarry = Bunclody, Ireland 15 D5
Newtownstewart, U.K. 15 B4
Newville, U.S.A. 110 F7
Nexon, France 20 C5
Neya, Russia 48 A6
Neyrīz, Iran 71 D7
Neyshābūr, Iran 71 B8
Nezhin = Nizhyn, Ukraine 47 G6
Nezperce, U.S.A. 114 C5
Ngabang, Indonesia 62 D3
Ngabordamlu, Tanjung, Indonesia 63 F8
Ngambé, Cameroon 83 D7
Ngami Depression, Botswana 88 C3
Ngamo, Zimbabwe 87 F2
Nganglong Kangri, China 67 C12
Ngao, Thailand 64 C2
Ngaoundéré, Cameroon 84 C2
Ngapara, N.Z. 91 L3
Ngara, Tanzania 86 C3
Ngara □, Tanzania 86 C3
Ngawi, Indonesia 63 G14
Nghia Lo, Vietnam 64 B5
Ngoma, Malawi 87 E3
Ngomahura, Zimbabwe 87 G3
Ngomba, Tanzania 87 D3
Ngop, Sudan 81 F3
Ngoring Hu, China 60 C4
Ngorkou, Mali 82 B4
Ngorongoro, Tanzania 86 C4
Ngozi, Burundi 86 C2
Ngudu, Tanzania 86 C3
Nguigmi, Niger 79 F8
Ngukurr, Australia 94 A1
Ngunga, Tanzania 86 C3
Nguru, Nigeria 83 C7
Nguru Mts., Tanzania 86 D4
Nguyen Binh, Vietnam 64 A5
Nha Trang, Vietnam 65 F7
Nhacoongo, Mozam. 89 C6
Nhamaabué, Mozam. 87 F4
Nhamundá →, Brazil 125 D7
Nhangutazi, L., Mozam. 89 C5
Nhill, Australia 95 F3
Nho Quan, Vietnam 64 B5
Nhulunbuy, Australia 94 A2
Nia-nia, Dem. Rep. of the Congo 86 B2
Niafounké, Mali 82 B4
Niagara, U.S.A. 108 C2
Niagara Falls, Canada 102 D4
Niagara Falls, U.S.A. 110 C6
Niagara-on-the-Lake, Canada 110 C5
Niah, Malaysia 62 D4
Niamey, Niger 83 C5
Nianforando, Guinea 82 D2
Niangara, Dem. Rep. of the Congo 86 B2
Nias, Indonesia 62 D1
Niassa □, Mozam. 87 E4
Nibe, Denmark 11 H3
Nicaragua ■, Cent. Amer. 120 D2
Nicaragua, L. de, Nic. 120 D2
Nicastro, Italy 31 D9
Nice, France 21 E11
Niceville, U.S.A. 109 K2
Nichinan, Japan 55 J5
Nicholás, Canal, W. Indies 120 B3
Nicholasville, U.S.A. 108 G3
Nichols, U.S.A. 111 D8
Nicholson, Australia 92 C4
Nicholson, U.S.A. 111 E9
Nicholson →, Australia 94 B2
Nicholson Ra., Australia 93 E2
Nicobar Is., Ind. Oc. 52 J13
Nicola, Canada 104 C4
Nicolet, Canada 102 C5
Nicolls Town, Bahamas 120 A4
Nicopolis, Greece 38 B2
Nicosia, Cyprus 36 D12
Nicosia, Italy 31 E7
Nicótera, Italy 31 D8
Nicoya, Costa Rica 120 D2
Nicoya, G. de, Costa Rica 120 E3
Nicoya, Pen. de, Costa Rica 120 E2
Nidd →, U.K. 12 D6
Nidda, Germany 25 E5
Nidda →, Germany 25 E4
Nidwalden □, Switz. 25 J4
Nidzica, Poland 45 E7
Niebüll, Germany 24 A4
Nied →, Germany 19 C13
Niederaula, Germany 24 E5
Niederbayern □, Germany 25 G8
Niederbronn-les-Bains, France 19 D14
Niedere Tauern, Austria 26 D7
Niederlausitz, Germany 24 D9
Niederösterreich □, Austria 26 C8
Niedersachsen □, Germany 24 C4
Niekerkshoop, S. Africa 88 D3
Niellé, Ivory C. 82 C3
Niemba, Dem. Rep. of the Congo 86 D2
Niemen = Neman →, Lithuania 9 J20
Niemodlin, Poland 45 H4
Nienburg, Germany 24 C5
Niepołomice, Poland 45 H7
Niers →, Germany 24 D1
Niesky, Germany 24 D10
Nieszawa, Poland 45 F5
Nieu Bethesda, S. Africa 88 E3
Nieuw Amsterdam, Surinam 125 B7
Nieuw Nickerie, Surinam 125 B7
Nieuwoudtville, S. Africa 88 E2
Nieuwpoort, Belgium 17 C2
Nieves, Pico de las, Canary Is. 37 G4
Nièvre □, France 19 E10
Niğde, Turkey 72 D6
Nigel, S. Africa 89 D4
Niger □, Nigeria 83 D6
Niger ■, W. Afr. 83 B7
Niger →, W. Afr. 83 D6
Nigeria ■, W. Afr. 83 D6
Nightcaps, N.Z. 91 L2
Nigríta, Greece 40 F7
Nihtaur, India 69 E8
Nii-Jima, Japan 55 G9
Niigata, Japan 54 F9
Niigata □, Japan 55 F9
Niihama, Japan 55 H6
Niihau, U.S.A. 106 H14
Niimi, Japan 55 G6
Niitsu, Japan 54 F9
Nîjar, Spain 33 J2
Nijil, Jordan 75 E4
Nijkerk, Neths. 17 B5
Nijmegen, Neths. 17 C5
Nijverdal, Neths. 17 B6
Nīk Pey, Iran 71 B6
Nike, Nigeria 83 D6
Nikiniki, Indonesia 63 F6
Nikísiani, Greece 41 F8
Nikítas, Greece 40 F7
Nikki, Benin 83 D5
Nikkō, Japan 55 F9
Nikolayev = Mykolayiv, Ukraine 47 J7
Nikolayevsk, Russia 48 E7
Nikolayevsk-na-Amur, Russia 51 D15
Nikolsk, Russia 48 D8
Nikolskoye, Russia 51 D17
Nikopol, Bulgaria 41 C8
Nikopol, Ukraine 47 J8
Niksar, Turkey 72 B7
Nīkshahr, Iran 71 E9
Nikšić, Montenegro, Yug. 40 D2
Nîl, Nahr en →, Africa 80 H7
Nîl el Abyad →, Sudan 81 D3
Nîl el Azraq →, Sudan 81 D3
Niland, U.S.A. 117 M11
Nile = Nîl, Nahr en →, Africa 80 H7
Nile Delta, Egypt 80 H7
Niles, U.S.A. 110 E4
Nilüfer →, Turkey 41 F12
Nimach, India 68 G6
Nimbahera, India 68 G6
Nîmes, France 21 E8
Nimfaíon, Ákra = Pínnes, Ákra, Greece 41 F8
Nimmitabel, Australia 95 F4
Nimule, Sudan 81 G3
Nin, Croatia 29 D12
Nīnawá, Iraq 70 B4
Nindigully, Australia 95 D4
Ninemile, U.S.A. 104 B2
Nineveh = Nīnawá, Iraq 70 B4
Ning Xian, China 56 G4
Ningaloo, Australia 92 D1
Ning'an, China 57 B15
Ningbo, China 59 C13
Ningcheng, China 57 D10
Ningde, China 59 D12
Ningdu, China 59 D10
Ninggang, China 59 D9
Ningguo, China 59 B12

Ninghai, *China* 59 C13
Ninghua, *China* 59 D11
Ningjin, *China* 56 F8
Ningjing Shan, *China* 58 C2
Ninglang, *China* 58 D3
Ningling, *China* 56 G8
Ningming, *China* 58 F6
Ningnan, *China* 58 D4
Ningpo = Ningbo, *China* 59 C13
Ningqiang, *China* 56 H4
Ningshan, *China* 56 H5
Ningsia Hui A.R. = Ningxia Huizu Zizhiqu □, *China* 56 F4
Ningwu, *China* 56 E7
Ningxia Huizu Zizhiqu □, *China* 56 F4
Ningxiang, *China* 59 C9
Ningyang, *China* 56 G9
Ningyuan, *China* 59 E8
Ninh Binh, *Vietnam* 64 B5
Ninh Giang, *Vietnam* 64 B6
Ninh Hoa, *Vietnam* 64 F7
Ninh Ma, *Vietnam* 64 F7
Ninove, *Belgium* 17 D4
Nioaque, *Brazil* 127 A4
Niobrara, *U.S.A.* 112 D6
Niobrara →, *U.S.A.* 112 D6
Niono, *Mali* 82 C3
Nioro du Rip, *Senegal* 82 C1
Nioro du Sahel, *Mali* 82 B3
Niort, *France* 20 B3
Nipawin, *Canada* 105 C8
Nipawin Prov. Park, *Canada* 105 C8
Nipfjället, *Sweden* 10 C6
Nipigon, *Canada* 102 C2
Nipigon, L., *Canada* 102 C2
Nipin →, *Canada* 105 B7
Nipishish L., *Canada* 103 B7
Nipissing L., *Canada* 102 C4
Nipomo, *U.S.A.* 117 K6
Nipton, *U.S.A.* 117 K11
Niquelândia, *Brazil* 125 F9
Nīr, *Iran* 70 B5
Nirasaki, *Japan* 55 G9
Nirmal, *India* 66 K11
Nirmali, *India* 69 F12
Niš, *Serbia, Yug.* 40 C5
Nisa, *Portugal* 35 F3
Nişāb, *Si. Arabia* 70 D5
Nişāb, *Yemen* 74 E4
Nišava →, *Serbia, Yug.* 40 C5
Niscemi, *Italy* 31 E7
Nishinomiya, *Japan* 55 G7
Nishino'omote, *Japan* 55 J5
Nishiwaki, *Japan* 55 G7
Nísíros, *Greece* 39 E9
Niška Banja, *Serbia, Yug.* 40 C6
Niskibi →, *Canada* 102 A2
Nisko, *Poland* 45 H9
Nisporeni, *Moldova* 43 C13
Nisqually →, *U.S.A.* 116 C4
Nissáki, *Greece* 36 A3
Nissan →, *Sweden* 11 H6
Nissum Bredning, *Denmark* 11 H2
Nissum Fjord, *Denmark* 11 H2
Nistru = Dnister →, *Europe* 47 J6
Nisutlin →, *Canada* 104 A2
Nitchequon, *Canada* 103 B5
Niterói, *Brazil* 127 A7
Nith →, *U.K.* 14 F5
Nitra, *Slovak Rep.* 27 C11
Nitra →, *Slovak Rep.* 27 D11
Nitriansky □, *Slovak Rep.* 27 C11
Nittenau, *Germany* 25 F8
Niuafo'ou, *Tonga* 91 B11
Niue, *Cook Is.* 97 J11
Niulan Jiang →, *China* 58 D4
Niut, *Indonesia* 62 D4
Niutou Shan, *China* 59 C13
Niuzhuang, *China* 57 D12
Nivala, *Finland* 8 E21
Nivelles, *Belgium* 17 D4
Nivernais, *France* 19 E10
Nixon, *U.S.A.* 113 L6
Nizamabad, *India* 66 K11
Nizamghat, *India* 67 E19
Nizhne Kolymsk, *Russia* 51 C17
Nizhnegorskiy = Nyzhnohirskyy, *Ukraine* 47 K8
Nizhnekamsk, *Russia* 48 C10
Nizhneudinsk, *Russia* 51 D10
Nizhnevartovsk, *Russia* 50 C8
Nizhniy Chir, *Russia* 49 F6
Nizhniy Lomov, *Russia* 48 D6
Nizhniy Novgorod, *Russia* 48 B7
Nizhniy Tagil, *Russia* 50 D6
Nizhyn, *Ukraine* 47 G6
Nizina Mazowiecka, *Poland* 45 F8
Nizip, *Turkey* 72 D7
Nízké Tatry, *Slovak Rep.* 27 C12
Nízký Jeseník, *Czech Rep.* 27 B10
Nizza Monferrato, *Italy* 28 D5
Njakwa, *Malawi* 87 E3
Njanji, *Zambia* 87 E3
Njegoš, *Montenegro, Yug.* 40 D2
Njinjo, *Tanzania* 87 D4
Njombe, *Tanzania* 87 D3
Njombe □, *Tanzania* 87 D3
Njombe →, *Tanzania* 86 D4
Njurundabommen, *Sweden* 10 B11
Nkambe, *Cameroon* 83 D7
Nkana, *Zambia* 87 E2
Nkawkaw, *Ghana* 83 D4
Nkayi, *Zimbabwe* 87 F2
Nkhotakota, *Malawi* 87 E3
Nkongsamba, *Cameroon* 83 E6
Nkurenkuru, *Namibia* 88 B2
Nkwanta, *Ghana* 82 D4
Nmai →, *Burma* 67 G20
Noakhali = Maijdi, *Bangla.* 67 H17
Nobel, *Canada* 110 A4
Nobeoka, *Japan* 55 H5
Noblejas, *Spain* 34 F7
Noblesville, *U.S.A.* 108 E3
Noce →, *Italy* 28 B8
Nocera Inferiore, *Italy* 31 B7
Nocera Umbra, *Italy* 29 E9
Noci, *Italy* 31 B10
Nockatunga, *Australia* 95 D3
Nocona, *U.S.A.* 113 J6
Nocrich, *Romania* 43 E9
Noda, *Japan* 55 G9
Noel, *U.S.A.* 113 G7
Nogales, *Mexico* 118 A2
Nogales, *U.S.A.* 115 L8
Nōgata, *Japan* 55 H5
Nogaro, *France* 20 E3
Nogat →, *Poland* 44 D6
Nōgata, *Japan* 55 H5
Nogent, *France* 19 D12
Nogent-le-Rotrou, *France* 18 D7
Nogent-sur-Seine, *France* 19 D10
Noggerup, *Australia* 93 F2
Noginsk, *Moskva, Russia* 46 E10
Noginsk, *Tunguska, Russia* 51 C10
Nogoa →, *Australia* 94 C4
Nogoyá, *Argentina* 126 C4
Nógrád □, *Hungary* 42 C4
Noguera Pallaresa →, *Spain* 32 D5
Noguera Ribagorzana →, *Spain* 32 D5
Nohar, *India* 68 E6
Nohfelden, *Germany* 25 F3
Noia, *Spain* 34 C2
Noire, Montagne, *France* 20 E6
Noire, Mt., *France* 18 D3
Noirétable, *France* 20 C7
Noirmoutier, Î. de, *France* 18 F4
Noirmoutier-en-l'Île, *France* 18 F4
Nojane, *Botswana* 88 C3
Nojima-Zaki, *Japan* 55 G9
Nok Kundi, *Pakistan* 66 E3
Nokaneng, *Botswana* 88 B3
Nokia, *Finland* 9 F20
Nokomis, *Canada* 105 C8
Nokomis L., *Canada* 105 B8
Nol, *Sweden* 11 G6
Nola, *C.A.R.* 84 D3
Nola, *Italy* 31 B7
Nolay, *France* 19 F11
Noli, C. di, *Italy* 28 D5
Nolinsk, *Russia* 48 B9
Noma Omuramba →, *Namibia* 88 B3
Noman L., *Canada* 105 A7
Nombre de Dios, *Panama* 120 E4
Nome, *U.S.A.* 100 B3
Nomo-Zaki, *Japan* 55 H4
Nonacho L., *Canada* 105 A7
Nonancourt, *France* 18 D8
Nonda, *Australia* 94 C3
None, *Italy* 28 D4
Nong Chang, *Thailand* 64 E2
Nong Het, *Laos* 64 C4
Nong Khai, *Thailand* 64 D4
Nong'an, *China* 57 B13
Nongoma, *S. Africa* 89 D5
Nonoava, *Mexico* 118 B3
Nonthaburi, *Thailand* 64 F3
Nontron, *France* 20 C4
Nonza, *France* 21 F13
Noonamah, *Australia* 92 B5
Noonan, *U.S.A.* 112 A3
Noondoo, *Australia* 95 D4
Noonkanbah, *Australia* 92 C3
Noord Brabant □, *Neths.* 17 C5
Noord Holland □, *Neths.* 17 B4
Noordbeveland, *Neths.* 17 C3
Noordoostpolder, *Neths.* 17 B5
Noordwijk, *Neths.* 17 B4
Nootka, *Canada* 104 D3
Nootka I., *Canada* 104 D3
Nora, *Eritrea* 81 D5
Nora, *Sweden* 10 E9
Noranda = Rouyn-Noranda, *Canada* 102 C4
Norberg, *Sweden* 10 D9
Nórcia, *Italy* 29 F10
Norco, *U.S.A.* 117 M9
Nord □, *France* 19 B10
Nord-Ostsee-Kanal, *Germany* 24 A5
Nord-Pas-de-Calais □, *France* 19 B9
Nordaustlandet, *Svalbard* 4 B9
Nordborg, *Denmark* 11 J3
Nordby, *Denmark* 11 J2
Norddeich, *Germany* 24 B3
Nordegg, *Canada* 104 C5
Norden, *Germany* 24 B3
Nordenham, *Germany* 24 B4
Norderney, *Germany* 24 B3
Norderstedt, *Germany* 24 B6
Nordfjord, *Norway* 9 F11
Nordfriesische Inseln, *Germany* 24 A4
Nordhausen, *Germany* 24 D6
Nordhorn, *Germany* 24 C3
Norðoyar, *Færoe Is.* 8 E9
Nordingrå, *Sweden* 10 B12
Nordjyllands Amtskommune □, *Denmark* 11 G4
Nordkapp, *Norway* 8 A21
Nordkapp, *Svalbard* 4 A9
Nordkinn = Kinnarodden, *Norway* 6 A11
Nordkinn-halvøya, *Norway* 8 A22
Nördlingen, *Germany* 25 G6
Nordrhein-Westfalen □, *Germany* 24 D3
Nordstrand, *Germany* 24 A4
Nordvik, *Russia* 51 B12
Nore →, *Ireland* 15 D4
Norembega, *Canada* 102 C3
Norfolk, *Nebr., U.S.A.* 112 D6
Norfolk, *Va., U.S.A.* 108 G7
Norfolk □, *U.K.* 13 E8
Norfolk I., *Pac. Oc.* 96 K8
Norfork Res., *U.S.A.* 113 G8
Norilsk, *Russia* 51 C9
Norley, *Australia* 95 D3
Norma, Mt., *Australia* 94 C3
Normal, *U.S.A.* 112 E10
Norman, *U.S.A.* 113 H6
Norman →, *Australia* 94 B3
Norman Wells, *Canada* 100 B7
Normanby →, *Australia* 94 A3
Normandin, *Canada* 102 C5
Normanhurst, Mt., *Australia* 93 E3
Normanton, *Australia* 94 B3
Norquay, *Canada* 105 C8
Norquinco, *Argentina* 128 E2
Norra Dellen, *Sweden* 10 C10
Norra Ulvön, *Sweden* 10 A12
Norrahammar, *Sweden* 11 G8
Norrbotten □, *Sweden* 8 C19
Nørre Åby, *Denmark* 11 J3
Nørre Alslev, *Denmark* 11 K5
Nørresundby, *Denmark* 11 G3
Norrhult, *Sweden* 11 G9
Norris, *U.S.A.* 114 D8
Norristown, *U.S.A.* 111 F9
Norrköping, *Sweden* 11 F10
Norrland, *Sweden* 9 E16
Norrsundet, *Sweden* 10 D11
Norrtälje, *Sweden* 10 E12
Norseman, *Australia* 93 F3
Norsk, *Russia* 51 D14
Norte, Pta. del, *Canary Is.* 37 G2
Norte, Serra do, *Brazil* 124
North Adams, *U.S.A.* 111 D11
North Ayrshire □, *U.K.* 14 F4
North Battleford, *Canada* 105 C7
North Bay, *Canada* 102 C4
North Belcher Is., *Canada* 102 A4
North Bend, *Canada* 104 D4
North Bend, *Oreg., U.S.A.* 114 E1
North Bend, *Pa., U.S.A.* 110 E7
North Bend, *Wash., U.S.A.* 116 C5
North Berwick, *U.K.* 14 E6
North Berwick, *U.S.A.* 111 C14
North C., *Canada* 103 C7
North C., *N.Z.* 91 F4
North Canadian →, *U.S.A.* 113 H7
North Cape = Nordkapp, *Norway* 8 A21
North Cape = Nordkapp, *Svalbard* 4 A9
North Caribou L., *Canada* 102 B1
North Carolina □, *U.S.A.* 109 H6
North Channel, *Canada* 102 C3
North Channel, *U.K.* 14 F3
North Charleston, *U.S.A.* 109 J6
North Chicago, *U.S.A.* 108 D2
North Dakota □, *U.S.A.* 112 B5
North Dandalup, *Australia* 93 F2
North Downs, *U.K.* 13 F8
North East, *U.S.A.* 110 D5
North East Frontier Agency = Arunachal Pradesh □, *India* 67 F19
North East Lincolnshire □, *U.K.* 12 D7
North East Providence Chan., *W. Indies* 120 A4
North Eastern □, *Kenya* 86 B5
North Esk →, *U.K.* 14 E6
North European Plain, *Europe* 6 E10
North Foreland, *U.K.* 13 F9
North Fork, *U.S.A.* 116 H7
North Fork American →, *U.S.A.* 116 G5
North Fork Feather →, *U.S.A.* 116 F5
North Frisian Is. = Nordfriesische Inseln, *Germany* 24 A4
North Henik L., *Canada* 105 A9
North Highlands, *U.S.A.* 116 G5
North Horr, *Kenya* 86 B4
North I., *Kenya* 86 B4
North I., *N.Z.* 91 H5
North Kingsville, *U.S.A.* 110 E4
North Knife →, *Canada* 105 B10
North Koel →, *India* 69 G10
North Korea ■, *Asia* 57 E14
North Lakhimpur, *India* 67 F19
North Lanarkshire □, *U.K.* 14 F5
North Las Vegas, *U.S.A.* 117 J11
North Lincolnshire □, *U.K.* 12 D7
North Little Rock, *U.S.A.* 113 H8
North Loup →, *U.S.A.* 112 E5
North Magnetic Pole, *Canada* 4 B2
North Minch, *U.K.* 14 C3
North Nahanni →, *Canada* 104 A4
North Olmsted, *U.S.A.* 110 E3
North Ossetia □, *Russia* 49 J7
North Pagai, I. = Pagai Utara, Pulau, *Indonesia* 62 E2
North Palisade, *U.S.A.* 116 H8
North Platte, *U.S.A.* 112 E4
North Platte →, *U.S.A.* 112 E4
North Pole, *Arctic* 4 A
North Portal, *Canada* 105 D8
North Powder, *U.S.A.* 114 D5
North Pt., *Canada* 103 C7
North Rhine Westphalia □ = Nordrhein-Westfalen □, *Germany* 24 D3
North Ronaldsay, *U.K.* 14 B6
North Saskatchewan →, *Canada* 105 C7
North Sea, *Europe* 6 D6
North Somerset □, *U.K.* 13 F5
North Sporades = Vóriai Sporádhes, *Greece* 38 B5
North Sydney, *Canada* 103 C7
North Taranaki Bight, *N.Z.* 91 H5
North Thompson →, *Canada* 104 C4
North Tonawanda, *U.S.A.* 110 C6
North Troy, *U.S.A.* 111 B12
North Truchas Pk., *U.S.A.* 115 J11
North Twin I., *Canada* 102 B4
North Tyne →, *U.K.* 12 B5
North Uist, *U.K.* 14 D1
North Vancouver, *Canada* 104 D4
North Vernon, *U.S.A.* 108 F3
North Wabasca L., *Canada* 104 B6
North Walsham, *U.K.* 12 E9
North-West □, *S. Africa* 88 D4
North West C., *Australia* 92 D1
North West Christmas I. Ridge, *Pac. Oc.* 97 G11
North West Frontier □, *Pakistan* 68 C4
North West Highlands, *U.K.* 14 D4
North West Providence Channel, *W. Indies* 120 A4
North West River, *Canada* 103 B7
North Western □, *Zambia* 87 E2
North York Moors, *U.K.* 12 C7
North Yorkshire □, *U.K.* 12 C6
Northallerton, *U.K.* 12 C6
Northam, *S. Africa* 88 C4
Northampton, *Australia* 93 E1
Northampton, *U.K.* 13 E7
Northampton, *Mass., U.S.A.* 111 D12
Northampton, *Pa., U.S.A.* 111 F9
Northampton Downs, *Australia* 94 C4
Northamptonshire □, *U.K.* 13 E7
Northbridge, *U.S.A.* 111 D13
Northcliffe, *Australia* 93 F2
Northeim, *Germany* 24 D6
Northern □, *Malawi* 87 E3
Northern □, *Uganda* 86 B3
Northern □, *Zambia* 87 E3
Northern Cape □, *S. Africa* 88 D3
Northern Circars, *India* 67 L13
Northern Indian L., *Canada* 105 B9
Northern Ireland □, *U.K.* 15 B5
Northern Light, L., *Canada* 102 C1
Northern Marianas ■, *Pac. Oc.* 96 F6
Northern Province □, *S. Leone* 82 D2
Northern Territory □, *Australia* 92 D5
Northern Transvaal □, *S. Africa* 89 C4
Northfield, *U.S.A.* 112 C8
Northland □, *N.Z.* 91 F4
Northome, *U.S.A.* 112 B7
Northport, *Ala., U.S.A.* 109 J2
Northport, *Mich., U.S.A.* 108 C3
Northport, *Wash., U.S.A.* 114 B5
Northumberland □, *U.K.* 12 B6
Northumberland, C., *Australia* 95 F3
Northumberland Is., *Australia* 94 C4
Northumberland Str., *Canada* 103 C7
Northwest Territories □, *Canada* 100 B9
Northwood, *Iowa, U.S.A.* 112 D8
Northwood, *N. Dak., U.S.A.* 112 B6
Norton, *U.S.A.* 112 F5
Norton, *Zimbabwe* 87 F3
Norton Sd., *U.S.A.* 100 B3
Nortorf, *Germany* 24 A5
Norwalk, *Calif., U.S.A.* 117 M8
Norwalk, *Conn., U.S.A.* 111 E11
Norwalk, *Ohio, U.S.A.* 110 E2
Norway, *U.S.A.* 108 C2
Norway ■, *Europe* 8 E14
Norway House, *Canada* 105 C9
Norwegian Sea, *Atl. Oc.* 4 C8
Norwich, *Canada* 110 D4
Norwich, *U.K.* 13 E9
Norwich, *Conn., U.S.A.* 111 E12
Norwich, *N.Y., U.S.A.* 111 D9
Norwood, *Canada* 110 B7
Noshiro, *Japan* 54 D10
Nosivka, *Ukraine* 47 G6
Nosovka = Nosivka, *Ukraine* 47 G6
Noss Hd., *U.K.* 14 C5
Nossebro, *Sweden* 11 F6
Nossob →, *S. Africa* 88 D3
Nosy Be, *Madag.* 85 G9
Nosy Boraha, *Madag.* 89 B8
Nosy Varika, *Madag.* 89 C8
Noteć →, *Poland* 45 F2
Notigi Dam, *Canada* 105 B9
Notikewin →, *Canada* 104 B5
Notios Evvoïkos Kólpos, *Greece* 38 C5
Noto, *Italy* 31 F8
Noto, G. di, *Italy* 31 F8
Notodden, *Norway* 9 G13
Notre-Dame, *Canada* 103 C7
Notre Dame B., *Canada* 103 C8
Notre Dame de Koartac = Quaqtaq, *Canada* 101 B13
Notre Dame d'Ivugivic = Ivujivik, *Canada* 101 B12
Notsé, *Togo* 83 D5
Nottaway →, *Canada* 102 B4
Nottingham, *U.K.* 12 E6
Nottingham, City of □, *U.K.* 12 E6
Nottinghamshire □, *U.K.* 12 D6
Nottoway →, *U.S.A.* 108 G7
Notwane →, *Botswana* 88 C4
Nouâdhibou, *Mauritania* 78 D2
Nouâdhibou, Ras, *Mauritania* 78 D2
Nouakchott, *Mauritania* 82 B1
Nouméa, *N. Cal.* 96 K8
Noupoort, *S. Africa* 88 E3
Nouveau Comptoir = Wemindji, *Canada* 102 B4
Nouvelle-Calédonie = New Caledonia ■, *Pac. Oc.* 96 K8
Nouzonville, *France* 19 C11
Nová Baňa, *Slovak Rep.* 27 C11
Nová Bystřice, *Czech Rep.* 26 B8
Nova Casa Nova, *Brazil* 125 E10
Nova Esperança, *Brazil* 127 A5
Nova Friburgo, *Brazil* 127 A7
Nova Gaia = Cambundi-Catembo, *Angola* 84 G3
Nova Gorica, *Slovenia* 29 C10
Nova Gradiška, *Croatia* 42 E2
Nova Iguaçu, *Brazil* 127 A7
Nova Iorque, *Brazil* 125 E10
Nova Kakhovka, *Ukraine* 47 J7
Nova Lamego, *Guinea-Biss.* 82 C2
Nova Lima, *Brazil* 127 A7
Nova Lisboa = Huambo, *Angola* 85 G3
Nova Lusitânia, *Mozam.* 87 F3
Nova Mambone, *Mozam.* 89 C6
Nova Odesa, *Ukraine* 47 J6
Nová Paka, *Czech Rep.* 26 A8
Nova Pavova, *Serbia, Yug.* 42 F5
Nova Scotia □, *Canada* 103 C7
Nova Siri, *Italy* 31 B9
Nova Sofala, *Mozam.* 89 C5
Nova Varoš, *Serbia, Yug.* 40 C3
Nova Venécia, *Brazil* 125 G10
Nova Zagora, *Bulgaria* 41 D10
Novaci, *Macedonia* 40 E5
Novaci, *Romania* 43 E8
Novafeltria, *Italy* 29 E9
Novaleksandrovskaya = Novoaleksandrovsk, *Russia* 49 H5
Novannenskiy = Novoannenskiy, *Russia* 48 E6
Novara, *Italy* 28 C5
Novato, *U.S.A.* 116 G4
Novaya Kakhovka = Nova Kakhovka, *Ukraine* 47 J7
Novaya Kazanka, *Kazakstan* 49 F9
Novaya Ladoga, *Russia* 46 B7
Novaya Lyalya, *Russia* 50 D7
Novaya Sibir, Ostrov, *Russia* 51 B16
Novaya Zemlya, *Russia* 50 B6
Nové Město, *Slovak Rep.* 27 C10
Nové Město na Moravě, *Czech Rep.* 26 B9
Nové Město nad Metují, *Czech Rep.* 27 A9
Nové Zámky, *Slovak Rep.* 27 C11
Novelda, *Spain* 33 G4
Novellara, *Italy* 28 D7
Noventa Vicentina, *Italy* 29 C8
Novgorod, *Russia* 46 C6
Novgorod-Severskiy = Novhorod-Siverskyy, *Ukraine* 47 G7
Novhorod-Siverskyy, *Ukraine* 47 G7
Novi Bečej, *Serbia, Yug.* 42 E5
Novi Iskar, *Bulgaria* 40 D7
Novi Kneževac, *Serbia, Yug.* 42 D5
Novi Lígure, *Italy* 28 D5
Novi Pazar, *Bulgaria* 41 C11
Novi Pazar, *Serbia, Yug.* 40 C4
Novi Sad, *Serbia, Yug.* 42 E4
Novi Slankamen, *Serbia, Yug.* 42 E5
Novi Travnik, *Bos.-H.* 42 F2
Novi Vinodolski, *Croatia* 29 C11

Novigrad, *Istra, Croatia* .. 29 C10
Novigrad, *Zadar, Croatia* . 29 D12
Novigradsko More, *Croatia* 29 D12
Nôvo Hamburgo, *Brazil* .. 127 B5
Novo Mesto, *Slovenia* 29 C12
Novo Miloševo, *Serbia, Yug.* 42 E5
Novo Remanso, *Brazil* ... 125 E10
Novoaleksandrovsk, *Russia* 49 H5
Novoannenskiy, *Russia* ... 48 E6
Novoataysk, *Russia* 50 D9
Novoazovsk, *Ukraine* 47 J10
Novocheboksarsk, *Russia* . 48 B8
Novocherkassk, *Russia* ... 49 G5
Novodevichye, *Russia* 48 D9
Novogrudok = Navahrudak, *Belarus* ... 46 F3
Novohrad-Volynskyy, *Ukraine* 47 G4
Novokachalinsk, *Russia* ... 54 B6
Novokazalinsk = Zhangaqazaly, *Kazakstan* 50 E7
Novokhopersk, *Russia* 48 E5
Novokuybyshevsk, *Russia* . 48 D9
Novokuznetsk, *Russia* 50 D9
Novomirgorod, *Ukraine* .. 47 H6
Novomoskovsk, *Russia* .. 46 E10
Novomoskovsk, *Ukraine* .. 47 H8
Novopolotsk = Navapolatsk, *Belarus* ... 46 E5
Novorossiysk, *Russia* 47 K9
Novorybnoye, *Russia* 51 B11
Novorzhev, *Russia* 46 D5
Novosej, *Albania* 40 E4
Novoselytsya, *Ukraine* 47 H4
Novoshakhtinsk, *Russia* .. 47 J10
Novosibirsk, *Russia* 50 D9
Novosibirskiye Ostrova, *Russia* 51 B15
Novosil, *Russia* 47 F9
Novosokolniki, *Russia* 46 D6
Novotitarovskaya, *Russia* . 49 H4
Novotroitsk, *Russia* 50 D6
Novoukrayinka, *Ukraine* .. 47 H6
Novouljanovsk, *Russia* ... 48 C9
Novouzensk, *Russia* 48 E9
Novovolynsk, *Ukraine* 47 G3
Novovoronezhskiy, *Russia* 47 G10
Novozybkov, *Russia* 47 F6
Novska, *Croatia* 29 C14
Nový Bor, *Czech Rep.* ... 26 A7
Novy Bug = Novyy Buh, *Ukraine* 47 J7
Nový Bydžov, *Czech Rep.* 26 A8
Novy Dwór Mazowiecki, *Poland* 45 F7
Nový Jičín, *Czech Rep.* ... 27 B11
Novyy Afon, *Georgia* 49 J5
Novyy Buh, *Ukraine* 47 J7
Novyy Oskol, *Russia* 47 G9
Novyy Port, *Russia* 50 C8
Now Shahr, *Iran* 71 B6
Nowa Deba, *Poland* 45 H8
Nowa Ruda, *Poland* 45 H3
Nowa Sarzyna, *Poland* ... 45 H9
Nowa Sól, *Poland* 45 G2
Nowbarān, *Iran* 71 C6
Nowe, *Poland* 44 E5
Nowe Miasteczko, *Poland* 45 G2
Nowe Miasto, *Poland* 45 G7
Nowe Miasto Lubawskie, *Poland* 44 E6
Nowe Skalmierzyce, *Poland* 45 G4
Nowe Warpno, *Poland* ... 44 E1
Nowghāb, *Iran* 71 C8
Nowgong, *India* 67 F18
Nowogard, *Poland* 44 E2
Nowogród, *Poland* 45 E8
Nowogród Bobrzanski, *Poland* 45 G2
Nowogrodziec, *Poland* ... 45 G2
Nowra, *Australia* 95 E5
Nowshera, *Pakistan* 66 C8
Nowy Dwór Gdański, *Poland* 44 D6
Nowy Sącz, *Poland* 45 J7
Nowy Sącz □, *Poland* 45 J7
Nowy Staw, *Poland* 44 D6
Nowy Targ, *Poland* 45 J7
Nowy Tomyśl, *Poland* ... 45 F3
Nowy Wiśnicz, *Poland* ... 45 J7
Noxen, *U.S.A.* 111 E8
Noxon, *U.S.A.* 114 C6
Noyant, *France* 18 E7
Noyers, *France* 19 E10
Noyes I., *U.S.A.* 104 B2
Noyon, *France* 19 C9
Noyon, *Mongolia* 56 C2
Nozay, *France* 18 E5
Nsanje, *Malawi* 87 F4
Nsawam, *Ghana* 83 D4
Nsomba, *Zambia* 87 E2
Nsukka, *Nigeria* 83 D6
Nu Jiang →, *China* 58 C1
Nu Shan, *China* 58 E2
Nuba Mts. = Nubah, Jibalan, *Sudan* 81 E3
Nubah, Jibalan, *Sudan* ... 81 E3
Nubia, *Africa* 76 D7
Nubian Desert = Nûbîya, Es Sahrâ en, *Sudan* 80 C3
Nûbîya, Es Sahrâ en, *Sudan* 80 C3
Ñuble □, *Chile* 126 D1
Nubledo, *Spain* 34 B5
Nuboai, *Indonesia* 63 E9
Nubra →, *India* 69 B7
Nucet, *Romania* 42 D7
Nueces →, *U.S.A.* 113 M6
Nueltin L., *Canada* 105 A9
Nueva Asunción □, *Paraguay* 126 A3
Nueva Carteya, *Spain* 35 H6
Nueva Gerona, *Cuba* 120 B3
Nueva Palmira, *Uruguay* .. 126 C4
Nueva Rosita, *Mexico* 118 B4
Nueva San Salvador, *El Salv.* 120 D2
Nueva Tabarca, *Spain* 33 G4
Nuéve de Julio, *Argentina* 126 D3
Nuevitas, *Cuba* 120 B4
Nuevo, G., *Argentina* 128 E4
Nuevo Guerrero, *Mexico* . 119 B5
Nuevo Laredo, *Mexico* ... 119 B5
Nuevo León □, *Mexico* ... 118 C5
Nuevo Rocafuerte, *Ecuador* 124 D3
Nugget Pt., *N.Z.* 91 M2
Nugrus, Gebel, *Egypt* 80 C3
Nuhaka, *N.Z.* 91 H6
Nuits-St-Georges, *France* . 19 E11
Nukey Bluff, *Australia* ... 95 E2
Nukheila, *Sudan* 80 D2
Nukhuyb, *Iraq* 73 F10
Nuku'alofa, *Tonga* 91 E12
Nukus, *Uzbekistan* 50 E6
Nules, *Spain* 32 F4
Nullagine →, *Australia* ... 92 D3
Nullarbor, *Australia* 93 F5
Nullarbor Plain, *Australia* . 93 F4
Numalla, L., *Australia* 95 D3
Numan, *Nigeria* 83 D7
Numata, *Japan* 55 F9
Numatinna →, *Sudan* 81 F2
Numazu, *Japan* 55 G9
Numbulwar, *Australia* 94 A2
Numfoor, *Indonesia* 63 E8
Numurkah, *Australia* 95 F4
Nunaksaluk I., *Canada* ... 103 A7
Nunavut □, *Canada* 101 B11
Nungo, *Mozam.* 87 E4
Nungwe, *Tanzania* 86 C3
Nunivak I., *U.S.A.* 100 C3
Nunkun, *India* 69 C7
Núoro, *Italy* 30 B2
Nūrābād, *Iran* 71 E8
Nure →, *Italy* 28 C6
Nuremberg = Nürnberg, *Germany* 25 F7
Nuri, *Mexico* 118 B3
Nurina, *Australia* 93 F4
Nuriootpa, *Australia* 95 E2
Nurlat, *Russia* 48 C10
Nurmes, *Finland* 8 E23
Nürnberg, *Germany* 25 F7
Nurra, La, *Italy* 30 B1
Nurran, L. = Terewah, L., *Australia* 95 D4
Nurrari Lakes, *Australia* .. 93 E5
Nurri, *Italy* 30 C2
Nürtingen, *Germany* 25 G5
Nurzec →, *Poland* 45 F9
Nus, *Italy* 28 C4
Nusa Barung, *Indonesia* .. 63 H15
Nusa Kambangan, *Indonesia* 63 G13
Nusa Tenggara Barat □, *Indonesia* 62 F5
Nusa Tenggara Timur □, *Indonesia* 63 F6
Nusaybin, *Turkey* 73 D9
Nushki, *Pakistan* 68 E2
Nutwood Downs, *Australia* 94 B1
Nuuk, *Greenland* 4 C5
Nuwakot, *Nepal* 69 E10
Nuweiba', *Egypt* 80 B3
Nuweveldberge, *S. Africa* . 88 E3
Nuyts, C., *Australia* 93 F5
Nuyts Arch., *Australia* 95 E1
Nxau-Nxau, *Botswana* 88 B3
Nyaake, *Liberia* 82 E3
Nyack, *U.S.A.* 111 E11
Nyah West, *Australia* 95 F3
Nyahanga, *Tanzania* 86 C3
Nyahua, *Tanzania* 86 D3
Nyahururu, *Kenya* 86 B4
Nyainqentanglha Shan, *China* 60 C4
Nyakanazi, *Tanzania* 86 C3
Nyakrom, *Ghana* 83 D4
Nyâlâ, *Sudan* 81 E1
Nyamandhlovu, *Zimbabwe* 87 F2
Nyambiti, *Tanzania* 86 C3
Nyamwaga, *Tanzania* 86 C3
Nyandekwa, *Tanzania* 86 C3
Nyanding →, *Sudan* 81 F3
Nyandoma, *Russia* 46 B11
Nyangana, *Namibia* 88 B3
Nyanguge, *Tanzania* 86 C3
Nyankpala, *Ghana* 83 D4
Nyanza, *Rwanda* 86 C2
Nyanza □, *Kenya* 86 C3
Nyanza-Lac, *Burundi* 86 C2
Nyarling →, *Canada* 104 A6
Nyasa, L., *Africa* 87 E3
Nyasvizh, *Belarus* 47 F4
Nyazura, *Zimbabwe* 87 F3
Nyazwidzi →, *Zimbabwe* . 87 G3
Nyborg, *Denmark* 11 J4
Nybro, *Sweden* 11 H9
Nyda, *Russia* 50 C8
Nyeri, *Kenya* 86 C4
Nyerol, *Sudan* 81 F3
Nyhammar, *Sweden* 10 D8
Nyiel, *Sudan* 81 F3
Nyinahin, *Ghana* 82 D4
Nyíradony, *Hungary* 42 C6
Nyirbátor, *Hungary* 42 C7
Nyíregyháza, *Hungary* 42 C6
Nykøbing, *Storstrøm, Denmark* 11 K5
Nykøbing, *Vestsjælland, Denmark* 11 J5
Nykøbing, *Viborg, Denmark* 11 H2
Nyköping, *Sweden* 11 F11
Nykroppa, *Sweden* 10 E8
Nykvarn, *Sweden* 10 E11
Nyland, *Sweden* 10 A11
Nylstroom, *S. Africa* 89 C4
Nymagee, *Australia* 95 E4
Nymburk, *Czech Rep.* 26 A8
Nynäshamn, *Sweden* 11 F11
Nyngan, *Australia* 95 E4
Nyoman = Neman →, *Lithuania* 9 J20
Nyon, *Switz.* 25 J2
Nyong →, *Cameroon* 83 E6
Nyons, *France* 21 D9
Nyou, *Burkina Faso* 83 C4
Nýrsko, *Czech Rep.* 26 B6
Nysa, *Poland* 45 H4
Nysa →, *Europe* 24 C10
Nysa Kłodzka →, *Poland* 45 H4
Nysäter, *Sweden* 10 E6
Nyssa, *U.S.A.* 114 E5
Nysted, *Denmark* 11 K5
Nyunzu, *Dem. Rep. of the Congo* 86 D2
Nyurba, *Russia* 51 C12
Nyzhnohirskyy, *Ukraine* .. 47 K8
Nzega, *Tanzania* 86 C3
Nzega □, *Tanzania* 86 C3
N'zérékoré, *Guinea* 82 D3
Nzeto, *Angola* 84 F2
Nzilo, Chutes de, *Dem. Rep. of the Congo* 87 E2
Nzubuka, *Tanzania* 86 C3

O

O Barco, *Spain* 34 C4
O Carballiño, *Spain* 34 C2
O Corgo, *Spain* 34 C3
O Pino, *Spain* 34 C2
O Porriño, *Spain* 34 C2
Ō-Shima, *Nagasaki, Japan* 55 G4
Ō-Shima, *Shizuoka, Japan* 55 G9
Oa, Mull of, *U.K.* 14 F2
Oacoma, *U.S.A.* 112 D5
Oahe, L., *U.S.A.* 112 C4
Oahe Dam, *U.S.A.* 112 C4
Oahu, *U.S.A.* 106 H16
Oak Creek, *U.S.A.* 114 F10
Oak Harbor, *U.S.A.* 116 B4
Oak Hill, *U.S.A.* 108 G5
Oak Park, *U.S.A.* 108 E2
Oak Ridge, *U.S.A.* 109 G3
Oak View, *U.S.A.* 117 L7
Oakan-Dake, *Japan* 54 C12
Oakbank, *Australia* 95 E3
Oakdale, *Calif., U.S.A.* .. 116 H6
Oakdale, *La., U.S.A.* 113 K8
Oakes, *U.S.A.* 112 B5
Oakesdale, *U.S.A.* 114 C5
Oakey, *Australia* 95 D5
Oakham, *U.K.* 13 E7
Oakhurst, *U.S.A.* 116 H7
Oakland, *Calif., U.S.A.* .. 116 H4
Oakland, *Oreg., U.S.A.* .. 114 E2
Oakland City, *U.S.A.* 108 F2
Oakley, *Idaho, U.S.A.* 114 E7
Oakley, *Kans., U.S.A.* 112 F4
Oakover →, *Australia* 92 D3
Oakridge, *U.S.A.* 114 E2
Oakville, *U.S.A.* 116 D3
Oamaru, *N.Z.* 91 L3
Oancea, *Romania* 43 E12
Oasis, *Calif., U.S.A.* 117 M10
Oasis, *Nev., U.S.A.* 116 H9
Oates Land, *Antarctica* .. 5 C11
Oatman, *U.S.A.* 117 K12
Oaxaca, *Mexico* 119 D5
Oaxaca □, *Mexico* 119 D5
Ob →, *Russia* 50 C7
Oba, *Canada* 102 C3
Obala, *Cameroon* 83 E7
Obama, *Japan* 55 G7
Oban, *U.K.* 14 E3
Obbia, *Somali Rep.* 74 F4
Obed, *Canada* 104 C5
Obera, *Argentina* 127 B4
Oberammergau, *Germany* . 25 H7
Oberasbach, *Germany* 25 F6
Oberbayern □, *Germany* . 25 G7
Oberdrauburg, *Austria* ... 26 E5
Oberfranken □, *Germany* 25 E7
Oberhausen, *Germany* 24 D2
Oberkirch, *Germany* 25 G4
Oberlausitz, *Germany* 24 D10
Oberlin, *Kans., U.S.A.* ... 112 F4
Oberlin, *La., U.S.A.* 113 K8
Oberlin, *Ohio, U.S.A.* ... 110 E2
Obernai, *France* 19 D14
Oberndorf, *Germany* 25 G4
Oberon, *Australia* 95 E4
Oberösterreich □, *Austria* 26 C7
Oberpfalz □, *Germany* ... 25 F8
Oberpfälzer Wald, *Germany* 25 F8
Oberstdorf, *Germany* 25 H6
Oberursel, *Germany* 25 E4
Oberwart, *Austria* 27 D9
Obi, Kepulauan, *Indonesia* 63 E7
Obi Is. = Obi, Kepulauan, *Indonesia* 63 E7
Obiaruku, *Nigeria* 83 D6
Óbidos, *Brazil* 125 D7
Óbidos, *Portugal* 35 F1
Obihiro, *Japan* 54 C11
Obilatu, *Indonesia* 63 E7
Obilnoye, *Russia* 49 G7
Obing, *Germany* 25 G8
Objat, *France* 20 C5
Obluchye, *Russia* 51 E14
Obninsk, *Russia* 46 E9
Obo, *C.A.R.* 86 A2
Obo, *Ethiopia* 81 G4
Oboa, Mt., *Uganda* 86 B3
Obock, *Djibouti* 81 E5
Oborniki, *Poland* 45 F3
Oborniki Śląskie, *Poland* . 45 G3
Oboyan, *Russia* 47 G9
Obozerskaya = Obozerskiy, *Russia* 50 C5
Obozerskiy, *Russia* 50 C5
Obrenovac, *Serbia, Yug.* .. 40 B4
Obrovac, *Croatia* 29 D12
Obruk, *Turkey* 72 C5
Obrzycko, *Poland* 45 F3
Observatory Inlet, *Canada* 104 B3
Obshchi Syrt, *Russia* 6 E16
Obskaya Guba, *Russia* ... 50 C8
Obuasi, *Ghana* 83 D4
Obubra, *Nigeria* 83 D6
Obwalden □, *Switz.* 25 J4
Obzor, *Bulgaria* 41 D11
Ocala, *U.S.A.* 109 L4
Ocampo, *Mexico* 118 B3
Ocaña, *Spain* 34 F7
Ocanomowoc, *U.S.A.* 112 D10
Ocate, *U.S.A.* 113 G2
Occidental, Cordillera, *Colombia* 122 C3
Ocean City, *N.J., U.S.A.* . 108 F8
Ocean City, *Wash., U.S.A.* 116 C2
Ocean I. = Banaba, *Kiribati* 96 H8
Ocean Park, *U.S.A.* 116 D2
Oceano, *U.S.A.* 117 K6
Oceanport, *U.S.A.* 111 F10
Oceanside, *U.S.A.* 117 M9
Ochagavía, *Spain* 32 C3
Ochakiv, *Ukraine* 47 J6
Ochamchira, *Georgia* 49 J5
Ochil Hills, *U.K.* 14 E5
Ochre River, *Canada* 105 C9
Ochsenfurt, *Germany* 25 F6
Ochsenhausen, *Germany* . 25 G5
Ocilla, *U.S.A.* 109 K4
Ockelbo, *Sweden* 10 D10
Ocmulgee →, *U.S.A.* 109 K4
Ocna Mureş, *Romania* ... 43 D8
Ocna Sibiului, *Romania* .. 43 E9
Ocnele Mari, *Romania* ... 43 E9
Ocniţa, *Moldova* 43 B12
Oconee →, *U.S.A.* 109 K4
Oconto, *U.S.A.* 108 C2
Oconto Falls, *U.S.A.* 108 C1
Ocosingo, *Mexico* 119 D6
Ocotal, *Nic.* 120 D2
Ocotlán, *Mexico* 118 C4
Ocreza →, *Portugal* 35 F3
Ócsa, *Hungary* 42 C4
Octave, *U.S.A.* 115 J7
Octeville, *France* 18 C5
Oda, *Ghana* 83 D4
Ōda, *Japan* 55 G6
Oda, J., *Sudan* 80 C4
Ódáðahraun, *Iceland* 8 D5
Ödåkra, *Sweden* 11 H6
Odate, *Japan* 54 D10
Odawara, *Japan* 55 G9
Odda, *Norway* 9 F12
Odder, *Denmark* 11 J4
Odei →, *Canada* 105 B9
Odemira, *Portugal* 35 H2
Ödemiş, *Turkey* 39 C9
Odendaalsrus, *S. Africa* .. 88 D4
Odensbacken, *Sweden* 10 E9
Odense, *Denmark* 11 J4
Odenwald, *Germany* 25 F5
Oder →, *Europe* 24 B10
Oder-Havel Kanal, *Germany* 24 C10
Oderzo, *Italy* 29 C9
Odesa, *Ukraine* 47 J6
Ödeshög, *Sweden* 11 F8
Odessa = Odesa, *Ukraine* 47 J6
Odessa, *Canada* 111 B8
Odessa, *Tex., U.S.A.* 113 K3
Odessa, *Wash., U.S.A.* ... 114 C4
Odiakwe, *Botswana* 88 C4
Odiel →, *Spain* 35 H4
Odienné, *Ivory C.* 82 D3
Odintsovo, *Russia* 46 E9
Odiongan, *Phil.* 61 E4
Odobeşti, *Romania* 43 E12
Odolanów, *Poland* 45 G4
O'Donnell, *U.S.A.* 113 J4
Odorheiu Secuiesc, *Romania* 43 D10
Odoyevo, *Russia* 46 F9
Odra = Oder →, *Europe* 24 B10
Odra →, *Spain* 34 C6
Odžaci, *Serbia, Yug.* 42 E4
Odžak, *Bos.-H.* 42 E3
Odzi, *Zimbabwe* 89 B5
Oebisfelde, *Germany* 24 C6
Oeiras, *Brazil* 125 E10
Oeiras, *Portugal* 35 G1
Oelrichs, *U.S.A.* 112 D3
Oelsnitz, *Germany* 25 E8
Oelwein, *U.S.A.* 112 D9
Oenpelli, *Australia* 92 B5
Oetz, *Austria* 26 D3
Of, *Turkey* 73 B9
Ofanto →, *Italy* 31 A9
Offa, *Nigeria* 83 D5
Offaly □, *Ireland* 15 C4
Offenbach, *Germany* 25 E4
Offenburg, *Germany* 25 G3
Offida, *Italy* 29 F10
Ofidhousa, *Greece* 39 E8
Ofotfjorden, *Norway* 8 B17
Ōfunato, *Japan* 54 E10
Oga, *Japan* 54 E9
Oga-Hantō, *Japan* 54 E9
Ogahalla, *Canada* 102 B2
Ōgaki, *Japan* 55 G8
Ogallala, *U.S.A.* 112 E4
Ogasawara Gunto, *Pac. Oc.* 96 E6
Ogbomosho, *Nigeria* 83 D5
Ogden, *Iowa, U.S.A.* 112 D8
Ogden, *Utah, U.S.A.* 114 F7
Ogdensburg, *U.S.A.* 111 B9
Ogeechee →, *U.S.A.* 109 K5
Ogilby, *U.S.A.* 117 N12
Oglio →, *Italy* 28 C7
Ogmore, *Australia* 94 C4
Ognon →, *France* 19 E12
Ogoja, *Nigeria* 83 D6
Ogoki →, *Canada* 102 B2
Ogoki L., *Canada* 102 B2
Ogoki Res., *Canada* 102 B2
Ogooué →, *Gabon* 84 E1
Ogosta →, *Bulgaria* 40 C7
Ogowe = Ogooué →, *Gabon* 84 E1
Ogr = Sharafa, *Sudan* 81 E2
Ograźden, *Macedonia* 40 E6
Ogre, *Latvia* 9 H21
Ogrein, *Sudan* 80 D3
Ogulin, *Croatia* 29 C12
Ogun □, *Nigeria* 83 D5
Oguta, *Nigeria* 83 D6
Ogwashi-Uku, *Nigeria* ... 83 D6
Ogwe, *Nigeria* 83 E6
Ohai, *N.Z.* 91 L2
Ohakune, *N.Z.* 91 H5
Ohata, *Japan* 54 D10
Ohau, L., *N.Z.* 91 L2
Ohio □, *U.S.A.* 108 E3
Ohio →, *U.S.A.* 108 G1
Ohře →, *Czech Rep.* 26 A7
Ohre →, *Germany* 24 C7
Ohrid, *Macedonia* 40 E4
Ohridsko Jezero, *Macedonia* 40 E4
Ohrigstad, *S. Africa* 89 C5
Öhringen, *Germany* 25 F5
Oiapoque, *Brazil* 125
Oikou, *China* 57 E9
Oil City, *U.S.A.* 110 E5
Oildale, *U.S.A.* 117 K7
Oinousa, *Greece* 39 C8
Oise □, *France* 19 C9
Oise →, *France* 19 C9
Ōita, *Japan* 55 H5
Ōita □, *Japan* 55 H5
Oiticica, *Brazil* 125 E10
Ojai, *U.S.A.* 117 L7
Ojinaga, *Mexico* 118 B4
Ojiya, *Japan* 55 F9
Ojos del Salado, Cerro, *Argentina* 126 B2
Oka →, *Russia* 48 B7
Okaba, *Indonesia* 63 F9
Okahandja, *Namibia* 88 C2
Okahukura, *N.Z.* 91 H5
Okanagan L., *Canada* 104 D5
Okanogan, *U.S.A.* 114 B4
Okanogan →, *U.S.A.* 114 B4
Okány, *Hungary* 42 D6
Okaputa, *Namibia* 88 C2
Okara, *Pakistan* 68 D5
Okarito, *N.Z.* 91 K3
Okaukuejo, *Namibia* 88 B2
Okavango Swamps, *Botswana* 88 B3
Okaya, *Japan* 55 F9
Okayama, *Japan* 55 G6
Okayama □, *Japan* 55 G6
Okazaki, *Japan* 55 G8
Oke-Iho, *Nigeria* 83 D5
Okeechobee, *U.S.A.* 109 M5
Okeechobee, L., *U.S.A.* .. 109 M5
Okefenokee Swamp, *U.S.A.* 109 K4
Okehampton, *U.K.* 13 G4
Okene, *Nigeria* 83 D6
Oker →, *Germany* 24 C6
Okha, *Russia* 51 D15
Ókhi Óros, *Greece* 38 C6
Okhotsk, *Russia* 51 D15
Okhotsk, Sea of, *Asia* 51 D15
Okhotskiy Perevoz, *Russia* 51 C14
Okhtyrka, *Ukraine* 47 G8
Oki-Shotō, *Japan* 55 F6
Okiep, *S. Africa* 88 D2
Okigwi, *Nigeria* 83 D6

Okija, *Nigeria* 83 D6
Okinawa □, *Japan* 55 L4
Okinawa-Guntō, *Japan* 55 L4
Okinawa-Jima, *Japan* 55 L4
Okino-erabu-Shima, *Japan* 55 L4
Okitipupa, *Nigeria* 83 D5
Oklahoma □, *U.S.A.* 113 H6
Oklahoma City, *U.S.A.* 113 H6
Okmulgee, *U.S.A.* 113 H7
Oknitsa = Ocniţa, *Moldova* 43 B12
Okolo, *Uganda* 86 B3
Okolona, *U.S.A.* 113 J10
Okonek, *Poland* 44 E3
Okrika, *Nigeria* 83 E6
Oksibil, *Indonesia* 63 E10
Oktabrsk = Oktyabrsk, *Kazakstan* 50 E6
Oktyabrsk, *Kazakstan* 50 E6
Oktyabrsk, *Russia* 48 D9
Oktyabrskiy = Aktsyabrski, *Belarus* 47 F5
Oktyabrskiy, *Russia* 49 G5
Oktyabrskoy Revolyutsii, Ostrov, *Russia* 51 B10
Oktyabrskoye = Zhovtneve, *Ukraine* 47 J7
Okulovka, *Russia* 46 C7
Okuru, *N.Z.* 91 K2
Okushiri-Tō, *Japan* 54 C9
Okuta, *Nigeria* 83 D5
Okwa →, *Botswana* 88 C3
Ola, *U.S.A.* 113 H8
Ólafsfjörður, *Iceland* 8 C4
Ólafsvík, *Iceland* 8 D2
Olaine, *Latvia* 44 B10
Olancha, *U.S.A.* 117 J8
Olancha Pk., *U.S.A.* 117 J8
Olanchito, *Honduras* 120 C2
Öland, *Sweden* 11 H10
Ölands norra udde, *Sweden* 11 G11
Ölands södra udde, *Sweden* 11 H10
Olargues, *France* 20 E6
Olary, *Australia* 95 E3
Olascoaga, *Argentina* 126 D3
Olathe, *U.S.A.* 112 F7
Olavarría, *Argentina* 126 D3
Oława, *Poland* 45 H4
Olbernhau, *Germany* 24 E9
Ólbia, *Italy* 30 B2
Ólbia, G. di, *Italy* 30 B2
Olching, *Germany* 25 G7
Old Bahama Chan. = Bahama, Canal Viejo de, *W. Indies* 120 B4
Old Baldy Pk. = San Antonio, Mt., *U.S.A.* 117 L9
Old Cork, *Australia* 94 C3
Old Crow, *Canada* 100 B6
Old Dale, *U.S.A.* 117 L11
Old Dongola, *Sudan* 80 D3
Old Forge, *N.Y., U.S.A.* 111 C10
Old Forge, *Pa., U.S.A.* 111 E9
Old Fort →, *Canada* 105 B6
Old Shinyanga, *Tanzania* 86 C3
Old Speck Mt., *U.S.A.* 111 B14
Old Town, *U.S.A.* 103 D6
Old Wives L., *Canada* 105 C7
Oldbury, *U.K.* 13 F5
Oldcastle, *Ireland* 15 C4
Oldeani, *Tanzania* 86 C4
Oldenburg, *Niedersachsen, Germany* 24 B4
Oldenburg, *Schleswig-Holstein, Germany* 24 A6
Oldenzaal, *Neths.* 17 B6
Oldham, *U.K.* 12 D5
Oldman →, *Canada* 104 D6
Oldmeldrum, *U.K.* 14 D6
Olds, *Canada* 104 C6
Olean, *U.S.A.* 110 D6
Olecko, *Poland* 44 D9
Oléggio, *Italy* 28 C5
Oleiros, *Portugal* 34 F3
Oleiros, *Spain* 34 B2
Olekma →, *Russia* 51 C13
Olekminsk, *Russia* 51 C13
Oleksandriya, *Kirovohrad, Ukraine* 47 H7
Oleksandriya, *Rivne, Ukraine* 47 G4
Oleksandrovka, *Ukraine* 47 H7
Olema, *U.S.A.* 116 G4
Olenek, *Russia* 51 C12
Olenek →, *Russia* 51 B13
Olenino, *Russia* 46 D7
Oléron, Î. d', *France* 20 C2
Oleśnica, *Poland* 45 G4
Olesno, *Poland* 45 H5
Olevsk, *Ukraine* 47 G4
Olga, *Russia* 51 E14
Olga, L., *Canada* 102 C4
Olga, Mt., *Australia* 93 E5
Ølgod, *Denmark* 11 J2
Olhão, *Portugal* 35 H3
Olib, *Croatia* 29 D11
Oliena, *Italy* 30 B2
Oliete, *Spain* 32 D4
Olifants →, *Africa* 89 C5
Olifantshoek, *S. Africa* 88 D3
Ólimbos, *Greece* 39 F9
Ólimbos, Óros, *Greece* 40 F6
Olímpia, *Brazil* 127 A6
Olinda, *Brazil* 125 E12
Olite, *Spain* 32 C3
Oliva, *Argentina* 126 C3
Oliva, *Spain* 33 G4
Oliva, Punta del, *Spain* 34 B5
Oliva de la Frontera, *Spain* 35 G4
Olivares, *Spain* 32 F2
Olivehurst, *U.S.A.* 116 F5
Oliveira de Azeméis, *Portugal* 34 E2
Oliveira do Douro, *Portugal* 34 D2
Olivenza, *Spain* 35 G3
Oliver, *Canada* 104 D5
Oliver L., *Canada* 105 B8
Olivet, *France* 19 E8
Olkhovka, *Russia* 48 F7
Olkusz, *Poland* 45 H6
Ollagüe, *Chile* 126 A2
Olmedo, *Spain* 34 D6
Olmeto, *France* 21 G12
Olney, *Ill., U.S.A.* 108 F1
Olney, *Tex., U.S.A.* 113 J5
Olofström, *Sweden* 11 H8
Oloma, *Cameroon* 83 E7
Olomane →, *Canada* 103 B7
Olomouc, *Czech Rep.* 27 B10
Olonets, *Russia* 46 B7
Olongapo, *Phil.* 61 D4
Olonne-sur-Mer, *France* 20 B2
Oloron, Gave d' →, *France* 20 E2
Oloron-Ste-Marie, *France* 20 E3
Olot, *Spain* 32 C7
Olovo, *Bos.-H.* 42 F3
Olovyannaya, *Russia* 51 D12
Oloy →, *Russia* 51 C16
Olsberg, *Germany* 24 D4
Olshammar, *Sweden* 11 F8
Olshanka, *Ukraine* 47 H6
Olshany, *Ukraine* 47 G8
Olsztyn, *Poland* 44 E7
Olsztyn □, *Poland* 44 E7
Olsztynek, *Poland* 44 E7
Olt □, *Romania* 43 F9
Olt →, *Romania* 43 G9
Olten, *Switz.* 25 H3
Olteniţa, *Romania* 43 F11
Olton, *U.S.A.* 113 H3
Oltu, *Turkey* 73 B9
Olula del Rio, *Spain* 33 H2
Olur, *Turkey* 73 B10
Olutanga, *Phil.* 61 H5
Olvega, *Spain* 32 D2
Olvera, *Spain* 35 J5
Olymbos, *Cyprus* 36 D12
Olympia, *Greece* 38 D3
Olympia, *U.S.A.* 116 D4
Olympic Mts., *U.S.A.* 116 C3
Olympic Nat. Park, *U.S.A.* 116 C3
Olympus, *Cyprus* 36 E11
Olympus, Mt. = Ólimbos, Óros, *Greece* 40 F6
Olympus, Mt. = Uludağ, *Turkey* 41 F13
Olympus, Mt., *U.S.A.* 116 C3
Olyphant, *U.S.A.* 111 E9
Om →, *Russia* 50 D8
Om Hajer, *Eritrea* 81 E4
Om Koi, *Thailand* 64 D2
Ōma, *Japan* 54 D10
Ōmachi, *Japan* 55 F8
Omae-Zaki, *Japan* 55 G9
Ōmagari, *Japan* 54 E10
Omagh, *U.K.* 15 B4
Omagh □, *U.K.* 15 B4
Omaha, *U.S.A.* 112 E7
Omak, *U.S.A.* 114 B4
Omalos, *Greece* 36 D5
Oman ■, *Asia* 74 C6
Oman, G. of, *Asia* 71 E8
Omaruru, *Namibia* 88 C2
Omaruru →, *Namibia* 88 C1
Omate, *Peru* 124 G4
Ombai, Selat, *Indonesia* 63 F6
Omboué, *Gabon* 84 E1
Ombrone →, *Italy* 28 F8
Omdurmân, *Sudan* 81 D3
Omegna, *Italy* 28 C5
Omeonga, *Dem. Rep. of the Congo* 86 C1
Ometepe, I. de, *Nic.* 120 D2
Ometepec, *Mexico* 119 D5
Ominato, *Japan* 54 D10
Omineca →, *Canada* 104 B4
Omiš, *Croatia* 29 E13
Omišalj, *Croatia* 29 C11
Omitara, *Namibia* 88 C2
Ōmiya, *Japan* 55 G9
Omme Å →, *Denmark* 11 J2
Ommen, *Neths.* 17 B6
Ömnögovĭ □, *Mongolia* 56 C3
Omo →, *Ethiopia* 81 F4
Omodeo, L., *Italy* 30 B1
Omodhos, *Cyprus* 36 E11
Omolon →, *Russia* 51 C16
Omono-Gawa →, *Japan* 54 E10
Omsk, *Russia* 50 D8
Omsukchan, *Russia* 51 C16
Ōmu, *Japan* 54 B11
Omul, Vf., *Romania* 43 E10
Omulew →, *Poland* 45 E8
Ōmura, *Japan* 55 H4
Omuramba Omatako →, *Namibia* 85 H4
Omurtag, *Bulgaria* 41 C10
Ōmuta, *Japan* 55 H5
Oña, *Spain* 34 C7
Onaga, *U.S.A.* 112 F6
Onalaska, *U.S.A.* 112 D9
Onamia, *U.S.A.* 112 B8
Onancock, *U.S.A.* 108 G8
Onang, *Indonesia* 63 E5
Onaping L., *Canada* 102 C3
Oñati, *Spain* 32 B2
Onavas, *Mexico* 118 B3
Onawa, *U.S.A.* 112 D6
Onaway, *U.S.A.* 108 C3
Oncócua, *Angola* 88 B1
Onda, *Spain* 32 F4
Ondaejin, *N. Korea* 57 D15
Ondangua, *Namibia* 88 B2
Ondarroa, *Spain* 32 B2
Ondava →, *Slovak Rep.* 27 C14
Ondjiva, *Angola* 88 B2
Ondo, *Nigeria* 83 D5
Ondo □, *Nigeria* 83 D6
Öndörhaan, *Mongolia* 60 B6
Öndörshil, *Mongolia* 56 B5
Öndverðarnes, *Iceland* 8 D1
Onega, *Russia* 50 C4
Onega →, *Russia* 6 C13
Onega, L. = Onezhskoye Ozero, *Russia* 46 B8
Onehunga, *N.Z.* 91 G5
Oneida, *U.S.A.* 111 C9
Oneida L., *U.S.A.* 111 C9
O'Neill, *U.S.A.* 112 D5
Onekotan, Ostrov, *Russia* 51 E16
Onema, *Dem. Rep. of the Congo* 86 C1
Oneonta, *Ala., U.S.A.* 109 J2
Oneonta, *N.Y., U.S.A.* 111 D9
Oneşti, *Romania* 43 D11
Onezhskoye Ozero, *Russia* 46 B8
Ongarue, *N.Z.* 91 H5
Ongerup, *Australia* 93 F2
Ongjin, *N. Korea* 57 F13
Ongkharak, *Thailand* 64 E3
Ongniud Qi, *China* 57 C10
Ongoka, *Dem. Rep. of the Congo* 86 C2
Ongole, *India* 66 M12
Ongon, *Mongolia* 56 B7
Oni, *Georgia* 49 J6
Onida, *U.S.A.* 112 C4
Onilahy →, *Madag.* 89 C7
Onitsha, *Nigeria* 83 D6
Onoda, *Japan* 55 G5
Onpyŏng-ni, *S. Korea* 57 H14
Ons, I. de, *Spain* 34 C2
Onslow, *Australia* 92 D2
Onslow B., *U.S.A.* 109 H7
Ontake-San, *Japan* 55 G8
Ontario, *Calif., U.S.A.* 117 L9
Ontario, *Oreg., U.S.A.* 114 D5
Ontario □, *Canada* 102 B2
Ontario, L., *U.S.A.* 102 D4
Ontinyent, *Spain* 33 G4
Ontonagon, *U.S.A.* 112 B10
Ontur, *Spain* 33 G3
Onyx, *U.S.A.* 117 K8
Oodnadatta, *Australia* 95 D2
Ooldea, *Australia* 93 F5
Oombulgurri, *Australia* 92 C4
Oona River, *Canada* 104 C2
Oorindi, *Australia* 94 C3
Oost-Vlaanderen □, *Belgium* 17 C3
Oostende, *Belgium* 17 C2
Oosterhout, *Neths.* 17 C4
Oosterschelde, *Neths.* 17 C4
Oosterwolde, *Neths.* 17 B6
Ootacamund = Udagamandalam, *India* 66 P10
Ootsa L., *Canada* 104 C3
Opaka, *Bulgaria* 41 C10
Opala, *Dem. Rep. of the Congo* 86 C1
Opalenica, *Poland* 45 F3
Opan, *Bulgaria* 41 D9
Opanake, *Sri Lanka* 66 R12
Opasatika, *Canada* 102 C3
Opasquia, *Canada* 105 C10
Opatija, *Croatia* 29 C11
Opatów, *Poland* 45 H8
Opava, *Czech Rep.* 27 B10
Opelousas, *U.S.A.* 113 K8
Opémisca, L., *Canada* 102 C5
Opheim, *U.S.A.* 114 B10
Ophthalmia Ra., *Australia* 92 D2
Opi, *Nigeria* 83 D6
Opinaca →, *Canada* 102 B4
Opinaca L., *Canada* 102 B4
Opiskotish, L., *Canada* 103 B6
Opobo, *Nigeria* 83 E6
Opochka, *Russia* 46 D5
Opoczno, *Poland* 45 G7
Opol, *Phil.* 61 G6
Opole, *Poland* 45 H4
Opole □, *Poland* 45 H4
Opole Lubelskie, *Poland* 45 G8
Oporto = Porto, *Portugal* 34 D2
Opotiki, *N.Z.* 91 H6
Opp, *U.S.A.* 109 K2
Oppdal, *Norway* 9 E13
Óppido Mamertina, *Italy* 31 D8
Oprişor, *Romania* 42 F8
Oprtalj, *Croatia* 29 C10
Opua, *N.Z.* 91 F5
Opunake, *N.Z.* 91 H4
Opuzen, *Croatia* 29 E14
Ora, *Cyprus* 36 E12
Ora Banda, *Australia* 93 F3
Oracle, *U.S.A.* 115 K8
Oradea, *Romania* 42 C6
Öræfajökull, *Iceland* 8 D5
Orahovac, *Serbia, Yug.* 40 D4
Orahovica, *Croatia* 42 E2
Orai, *India* 69 G8
Oraison, *France* 21 E9
Oral = Zhayyq →, *Kazakstan* 50 E6
Oral, *Kazakstan* 48 E10
Oran, *Algeria* 78 A5
Oran, *Argentina* 126 A3
Orange, *Australia* 95 E4
Orange, *France* 21 D8
Orange, *Calif., U.S.A.* 117 M9
Orange, *Mass., U.S.A.* 111 D12
Orange, *Tex., U.S.A.* 113 K8
Orange, *Va., U.S.A.* 108 F6
Orange →, *S. Africa* 88 D2
Orange, C., *Brazil* 122 C5
Orange Cove, *U.S.A.* 116 J7
Orange Free State □ = Free State □, *S. Africa* 88 D4
Orange Grove, *U.S.A.* 113 M6
Orange Walk, *Belize* 119 D7
Orangeburg, *U.S.A.* 109 J5
Orangeville, *Canada* 102 D3
Orani, *Phil.* 61 D4
Oranienburg, *Germany* 24 C9
Oranje = Orange →, *S. Africa* 88 D2
Oranje Vrystaat □ = Free State □, *S. Africa* 88 D4
Oranjemund, *Namibia* 88 D2
Oranjerivier, *S. Africa* 88 D3
Oras, *Phil.* 61 E6
Orašje, *Bos.-H.* 42 E3
Orăştie, *Romania* 43 E8
Oraşul Stalin = Braşov, *Romania* 43 E10
Orava →, *Slovak Rep.* 27 B12
Orava, Vodna nádrž, *Slovak Rep.* 27 B12
Oraviţa, *Romania* 42 E6
Orb →, *France* 20 E7
Orba →, *Italy* 28 D5
Ørbæk, *Denmark* 11 J4
Orbe, *Switz.* 25 J2
Orbec, *France* 18 C7
Orbetello, *Italy* 29 F8
Órbigo →, *Spain* 34 C5
Orbost, *Australia* 95 F4
Örbyhus, *Sweden* 10 D11
Orce, *Spain* 33 H2
Orce →, *Spain* 33 H2
Orchies, *France* 19 B10
Orchila, I., *Venezuela* 124 A5
Órcia →, *Italy* 29 F8
Orco →, *Italy* 28 C4
Orcutt, *U.S.A.* 117 L6
Ord →, *Australia* 92 C4
Ord, Mt., *Australia* 92 C4
Ordenes = Ordes, *Spain* 34 B2
Orderville, *U.S.A.* 115 H7
Ordes, *Spain* 34 B2
Ording = St-Peter-Ording, *Germany* 24 A4
Ordos = Mu Us Shamo, *China* 56 E5
Ordu, *Turkey* 72 B7
Ordubad, *Azerbaijan* 73 C12
Orduña, *Álava, Spain* 32 C2
Orduña, *Granada, Spain* 35 H7
Ordway, *U.S.A.* 112 F3
Ordzhonikidze = Vladikavkaz, *Russia* 49 J7
Ordzhonikidze, *Ukraine* 47 J8
Ore, *Dem. Rep. of the Congo* 86 B2
Ore Mts. = Erzgebirge, *Germany* 24 E8
Orebić, *Croatia* 29 F14
Örebro, *Sweden* 10 E9
Örebro län □, *Sweden* 10 E8
Oregon, *U.S.A.* 112 D10
Oregon □, *U.S.A.* 114 E3
Oregon City, *U.S.A.* 116 E4
Öregrund, *Sweden* 10 D12
Öregrundsgrepen, *Sweden* 10 D12
Orekhov = Orikhiv, *Ukraine* 47 J8
Orekhovo-Zuyevo, *Russia* 46 E10
Orel, *Russia* 47 F9
Orel →, *Ukraine* 47 H8
Orellana, *Spain* 35 F5
Orellana, Canal de, *Spain* 35 F5
Orellana, Embalse de, *Spain* 35 F5
Orem, *U.S.A.* 114 F8
Ören, *Turkey* 39 D9
Orenburg, *Russia* 50 D6
Örencik, *Turkey* 39 B11
Orense = Ourense, *Spain* 34 C3
Orense □, *Spain* 34 C3
Orepuki, *N.Z.* 91 M1
Orestiás, *Greece* 41 E10
Øresund, *Europe* 11 J6
Orford Ness, *U.K.* 13 E9
Organà = Organyà, *Spain* 32 C6
Organos, Pta. de los, *Canary Is.* 37 F2
Organyà, *Spain* 32 C6
Orgaz, *Spain* 35 F7
Orgeyev = Orhei, *Moldova* 43 C13
Orhaneli, *Turkey* 41 G12
Orhaneli →, *Turkey* 41 G12
Orhangazi, *Turkey* 41 F13
Orhei, *Moldova* 43 C13
Orhon Gol →, *Mongolia* 60 A5
Ória, *Italy* 31 B10
Orient, *Australia* 95 D3
Oriental, Cordillera, *Colombia* 122 C3
Oriente, *Argentina* 126 D3
Orihuela, *Spain* 33 G4
Orihuela del Tremedal, *Spain* 32 E3
Orikhiv, *Ukraine* 47 J8
Oriku, *Albania* 40 F3
Orinoco →, *Venezuela* 122 C4
Orissa □, *India* 67 K14
Orissaare, *Estonia* 9 G20
Oristano, *Italy* 30 C1
Oristano, G. di, *Italy* 30 C1
Orizaba, *Mexico* 119 D5
Orizare, *Bulgaria* 41 D11
Orjen, *Bos.-H.* 40 D2
Orjiva, *Spain* 35 J7
Orkanger, *Norway* 8 E13
Örkelljunga, *Sweden* 11 H7
Örken, *Sweden* 11 G9
Örkény, *Hungary* 42 C4
Orkla →, *Norway* 8 E13
Orkney, *S. Africa* 88 D4
Orkney □, *U.K.* 14 B5
Orkney Is., *U.K.* 14 B6
Orland, *U.S.A.* 116 F4
Orlando, *U.S.A.* 109 L5
Orlando, C. d', *Italy* 31 D7
Orléanais, *France* 19 E9
Orléans, *France* 19 E8
Orleans, *U.S.A.* 111 B12
Orléans, I. d', *Canada* 103 C5
Orlice →, *Czech Rep.* 27 A8
Orlov, *Slovak Rep.* 27 B13
Orlov Gay, *Russia* 48 E9
Orlová, *Czech Rep.* 27 B11
Orlovat, *Serbia, Yug.* 42 E5
Ormara, *Pakistan* 66 G4
Ormea, *Italy* 28 D4
Ormília, *Greece* 40 F7
Ormoc, *Phil.* 61 F6
Ormond, *N.Z.* 91 H6
Ormond Beach, *U.S.A.* 109 L5
Ormož, *Slovenia* 29 B13
Ormskirk, *U.K.* 12 D5
Ormstown, *Canada* 111 A11
Ornans, *France* 19 E13
Orne □, *France* 18 D7
Orne →, *France* 18 C6
Orneta, *Poland* 44 D7
Ornö, *Sweden* 10 E12
Örnsköldsvik, *Sweden* 10 A12
Oro, *N. Korea* 57 D14
Oro →, *Mexico* 118 B3
Oro Grande, *U.S.A.* 117 L9
Orobie, Alpi, *Italy* 28 B6
Orocué, *Colombia* 124 C4
Orodo, *Nigeria* 83 D6
Orogrande, *U.S.A.* 115 K10
Orol Dengizi = Aral Sea, *Asia* 50 E7
Oromocto, *Canada* 103 C6
Oron, *Nigeria* 83 E6
Orono, *Canada* 110 C6
Oronsay, *U.K.* 14 E2
Oropesa, *Spain* 34 F5
Oroquieta, *Phil.* 61 G5
Orosei, *Italy* 30 B2
Orosei, G. di, *Italy* 30 B2
Orosháza, *Hungary* 42 D5
Oroszlány, *Hungary* 42 C3
Orotukan, *Russia* 51 C16
Oroville, *Calif., U.S.A.* 116 F5
Oroville, *Wash., U.S.A.* 114 B4
Oroville, L., *U.S.A.* 116 F5
Orrefors, *Sweden* 11 H9
Orroroo, *Australia* 95 E2
Orrviken, *Sweden* 10 A8
Orrville, *U.S.A.* 110 F3
Orsa, *Sweden* 10 C8
Orsara di Púglia, *Italy* 31 A8
Orsasjön, *Sweden* 10 C8
Orsha, *Belarus* 46 E6
Örsjö, *Sweden* 11 H9
Orsk, *Russia* 50 D6
Orşova, *Romania* 42 F7
Ørsted, *Denmark* 11 H4
Örsundsbro, *Sweden* 10 E11
Orta, L. d', *Italy* 28 C5
Orta Nova, *Italy* 31 A8
Ortaca, *Turkey* 39 E10
Ortakent, *Turkey* 39 D9
Ortaklar, *Turkey* 39 D9
Ortaköy, *Çorum, Turkey* 72 B6
Ortaköy, *Niğde, Turkey* 72 C6
Orte, *Italy* 29 F9
Ortegal, C., *Spain* 34 B3
Orthez, *France* 20 E3
Ortigueira, *Spain* 34 B3
Orting, *U.S.A.* 116 C4
Ortisei, *Italy* 29 B8
Ortles, *Italy* 28 B7
Ortón →, *Bolivia* 124 F5
Ortona, *Italy* 29 F11
Orūmīyeh, *Iran* 70 B5
Orūmīyeh, Daryācheh-ye, *Iran* 70 B5
Orune, *Italy* 30 B2
Oruro, *Bolivia* 124 G5
Orust, *Sweden* 11 F5
Oruzgān □, *Afghan.* 66 C5
Orvault, *France* 18 E5
Orvieto, *Italy* 29 F9
Orwell, *U.S.A.* 110 E4
Orwell →, *U.K.* 13 F9
Oryakhovo, *Bulgaria* 40 C7
Orzinuovi, *Italy* 28 C6

Orzyc →, *Poland* 45 F8
Orzysz, *Poland* 44 E8
Osa →, *Poland* 44 E5
Osa, Pen. de, *Costa Rica* 120 E3
Osage, *Iowa, U.S.A.* 112 D8
Osage, *Wyo., U.S.A.* 112 D2
Osage →, *U.S.A.* 112 F9
Osage City, *U.S.A.* 112 F7
Ōsaka, *Japan* 55 G7
Osan, *S. Korea* 57 F14
Osawatomie, *U.S.A.* 112 F7
Osborne, *U.S.A.* 112 F5
Osby, *Sweden* 11 H7
Osceola, *Ark., U.S.A.* 113 H10
Osceola, *Iowa, U.S.A.* 112 E8
Oschatz, *Germany* 24 D9
Oschersleben, *Germany* 24 C7
Óschiri, *Italy* 30 B2
Oscoda, *U.S.A.* 110 B1
Osečina, *Serbia, Yug.* 40 B3
Ösel = Saaremaa, *Estonia* 9 G20
Osery, *Russia* 46 E10
Osh, *Kyrgyzstan* 50 E8
Oshawa, *Canada* 102 D4
Oshkosh, *Nebr., U.S.A.* 112 E3
Oshkosh, *Wis., U.S.A.* 112 C10
Oshmyany = Ashmyany, *Belarus* 9 J21
Oshnovīyeh, *Iran* 70 B5
Oshogbo, *Nigeria* 83 D5
Oshtorīnān, *Iran* 71 C6
Oshwe, *Dem. Rep. of the Congo* 84 E3
Osieczna, *Poland* 45 G3
Osijek, *Croatia* 42 E3
Ósilo, *Italy* 30 B1
Ósimo, *Italy* 29 E10
Osintorf, *Belarus* 46 E6
Osipenko = Berdyansk, *Ukraine* 47 J9
Osipovichi = Asipovichy, *Belarus* 46 F5
Osizweni, *S. Africa* 89 D5
Oskaloosa, *U.S.A.* 112 E8
Oskarshamn, *Sweden* 11 G10
Oskarström, *Sweden* 11 H6
Oskélanéo, *Canada* 102 C4
Öskemen, *Kazakstan* 50 E9
Oskol →, *Ukraine* 47 H9
Oslo, *Norway* 9 G14
Oslob, *Phil.* 61 G5
Oslofjorden, *Norway* 9 G14
Osmanabad, *India* 66 K10
Osmancık, *Turkey* 72 B6
Osmaniye, *Turkey* 72 D7
Osmanlı, *Turkey* 41 E10
Ösmo, *Sweden* 10 F11
Osnabrück, *Germany* 24 C4
Ośno Lubuskie, *Poland* 45 F1
Osoblaha, *Czech Rep.* 27 A10
Osogovska Planina, *Macedonia* 40 D6
Osor, *Italy* 29 D11
Osorio, *Brazil* 127 B5
Osorno, *Chile* 128 E2
Osorno, *Spain* 34 C6
Osoyoos, *Canada* 104 D5
Osøyro, *Norway* 9 F11
Ospika →, *Canada* 104 B4
Osprey Reef, *Australia* 94 A4
Oss, *Neths.* 17 C5
Ossa, Mt., *Australia* 94 G4
Óssa, Óros, *Greece* 38 B4
Ossa de Montiel, *Spain* 33 G2
Ossabaw I., *U.S.A.* 109 K5
Osse →, *France* 20 D4
Ossi, *Italy* 30 B1
Ossining, *U.S.A.* 111 E11
Ossipee, *U.S.A.* 111 C13
Ossokmanuan L., *Canada* 103 B7
Ossora, *Russia* 51 D17
Ostashkov, *Russia* 46 D7
Östavall, *Sweden* 10 B9
Oste →, *Germany* 24 B5
Ostend = Oostende, *Belgium* 17 C2
Oster, *Ukraine* 47 G6
Osterburg, *Germany* 24 C7
Osterburken, *Germany* 25 F5
Österbybruk, *Sweden* 10 D11
Österbymo, *Sweden* 11 G9
Österdalälven, *Sweden* 10 C7
Østerdalen, *Norway* 9 F14
Österfärnebo, *Sweden* 10 D10
Österforse, *Sweden* 10 A11
Östergötlands län □, *Sweden* 11 F9
Osterholz-Scharmbeck, *Germany* 24 B4
Østerild, *Denmark* 11 G2
Osterode, *Germany* 24 D6
Östersund, *Sweden* 10 A8
Östervåla, *Sweden* 10 D11
Ostfriesische Inseln, *Germany* 24 B3
Ostfriesland, *Germany* 24 B3
Östhammar, *Sweden* 10 D12
Óstia, Lido di, *Italy* 29 G9
Ostíglia, *Italy* 29 C8
Östmark, *Sweden* 10 D6
Östra Husby, *Sweden* 11 F10
Ostrava, *Czech Rep.* 27 B11
Ostróda, *Poland* 44 E6
Ostrogozhsk, *Russia* 47 G10
Ostroh, *Ukraine* 47 G4
Ostrołęka, *Poland* 45 E8
Ostrołęka □, *Poland* 45 F8
Ostrov, *Bulgaria* 41 C8
Ostrov, *Czech Rep.* 26 A5
Ostrov, *Romania* 43 F12
Ostrov, *Russia* 46 D5
Ostrów Lubelski, *Poland* 45 G9
Ostrów Mazowiecka, *Poland* 45 F8
Ostrów Wielkopolski, *Poland* 45 G4
Ostrowiec-Świętokrzyski, *Poland* 45 H8
Ostrožac, *Bos.-H.* 42 G2
Ostrzeszów, *Poland* 45 G4
Ostseebad Kühlungsborn, *Germany* 24 A7
Osttirol □, *Austria* 26 E5
Ostuni, *Italy* 31 B10
Osŭm →, *Bulgaria* 41 C8
Osumi →, *Albania* 40 F4
Ōsumi-Kaikyō, *Japan* 55 J5
Ōsumi-Shotō, *Japan* 55 J5
Osun □, *Nigeria* 83 D5
Osuna, *Spain* 35 H5
Oswego, *U.S.A.* 111 C8
Oswestry, *U.K.* 12 E4
Oświęcim, *Poland* 45 H6
Otaci, *Moldova* 43 B12
Otago □, *N.Z.* 91 L2
Otago Harbour, *N.Z.* 91 L3
Ōtake, *Japan* 55 G6
Otaki, *N.Z.* 91 J5
Otaru, *Japan* 54 C10
Otaru-Wan = Ishikari-Wan, *Japan* 54 C10
Otava →, *Czech Rep.* 26 B7
Otavalo, *Ecuador* 124 C3
Otavi, *Namibia* 88 B2
Otchinjau, *Angola* 88 B1
Otelec, *Romania* 42 E5
Oţelu Roşu, *Romania* 42 E7
Otero de Rey = Outeiro de Rei, *Spain* 34 B3
Othello, *U.S.A.* 114 C4
Othonoí, *Greece* 38 B1
Óthris, Óros, *Greece* 38 B4
Otira Gorge, *N.Z.* 91 K3
Otis, *U.S.A.* 112 E3
Otjiwarongo, *Namibia* 88 C2
Otmuchów, *Poland* 45 H4
Otočac, *Croatia* 29 D12
Otoineppu, *Japan* 54 B11
Otok, *Croatia* 29 E13
Otorohanga, *N.Z.* 91 H5
Otoskwin →, *Canada* 102 B2
Otosquen, *Canada* 105 C8
Otra →, *Norway* 9 G13
Otradnyy, *Russia* 48 D10
Otranto, *Italy* 31 B11
Otranto, C. d', *Italy* 31 B11
Otranto, Str. of, *Italy* 31 B11
Otrokovice, *Czech Rep.* 27 B10
Otse, *S. Africa* 88 D4
Ōtsu, *Japan* 55 G7
Ōtsuki, *Japan* 55 G9
Ottawa = Outaouais →, *Canada* 102 C5
Ottawa, *Canada* 102 C4
Ottawa, *Ill., U.S.A.* 112 E10
Ottawa, *Kans., U.S.A.* 112 F7
Ottawa Is., *Canada* 101 C11
Ottélé, *Cameroon* 83 E7
Ottensheim, *Austria* 26 C7
Otter L., *Canada* 105 B8
Otter Rapids, *Ont., Canada* 102 B3
Otter Rapids, *Sask., Canada* 105 B8
Otterndorf, *Germany* 24 B4
Otterup, *Denmark* 11 J4
Otterville, *Canada* 110 D4
Ottery St. Mary, *U.K.* 13 G4
Otto Beit Bridge, *Zimbabwe* 87 F2
Ottosdal, *S. Africa* 88 D4
Ottumwa, *U.S.A.* 112 E8
Otu, *Nigeria* 83 D5
Otukpa, *Nigeria* 83 D6
Oturkpo, *Nigeria* 83 D6
Otway, B., *Chile* 128 G2
Otway, C., *Australia* 95 F3
Otwock, *Poland* 45 F8
Ötztaler Ache →, *Austria* 26 D3
Ötztaler Alpen, *Austria* 26 E3
Ou →, *Laos* 64 B4
Ou Neua, *Laos* 64 A3
Ou-Sammyaku, *Japan* 54 E10
Ouachita →, *U.S.A.* 113 K9
Ouachita, L., *U.S.A.* 113 H8
Ouachita Mts., *U.S.A.* 113 H7
Ouagadougou, *Burkina Faso* 83 C4
Ouahigouya, *Burkina Faso* 82 C4
Ouahran = Oran, *Algeria* 78 A5
Oualâta, *Mauritania* 82 B3
Ouallene, *Algeria* 78 D6
Ouargla, *Algeria* 78 B7
Ouarzazate, *Morocco* 78 B4
Ouatagouna, *Mali* 83 B5
Oubangi →, *Dem. Rep. of the Congo* 84 E3
Ouche →, *France* 19 E12
Ouddorp, *Neths.* 17 C3
Oude Rijn →, *Neths.* 17 B4
Oudenaarde, *Belgium* 17 D3
Oudon →, *France* 18 E6
Oudtshoorn, *S. Africa* 88 E3
Ouellé, *Ivory C.* 82 D4
Ouessa, *Burkina Faso* 82 C4
Ouessant, Î. d', *France* 18 D1
Ouesso, *Congo* 84 D3
Ouest, Pte., *Canada* 103 C7
Ouezzane, *Morocco* 78 B4
Oughterard, *Ireland* 15 C2
Ouidah, *Benin* 83 D5
Ouistreham, *France* 18 C6
Oujda, *Morocco* 78 B5
Oulainen, *Finland* 8 D21
Ould Yenjé, *Mauritania* 82 B2
Oullins, *France* 21 C8
Oulu, *Finland* 8 D21
Oulujärvi, *Finland* 8 D22
Oulujoki →, *Finland* 8 D21
Oulx, *Italy* 28 C3
Oum Chalouba, *Chad* 79 E10
Oum Hadjer, *Chad* 79 F9
Oumé, *Ivory C.* 82 D3
Ounasjoki →, *Finland* 8 C21
Ounguati, *Namibia* 88 C2
Ounianga Sérir, *Chad* 79 E10
Our →, *Lux.* 17 E6
Ouranópolis, *Greece* 40 F7
Ouray, *U.S.A.* 115 G10
Ourcq →, *France* 19 C10
Ourense, *Spain* 34 C3
Ouricuri, *Brazil* 125 E10
Ourinhos, *Brazil* 127 A6
Ourique, *Portugal* 35 H2
Ouro Fino, *Brazil* 127 A6
Ouro Prêto, *Brazil* 127 A7
Ouro Sogui, *Senegal* 82 B2
Oursi, *Burkina Faso* 83 C4
Ourthe →, *Belgium* 17 D5
Ouse, *Australia* 94 G4
Ouse →, *E. Susx., U.K.* 13 G8
Ouse →, *N. Yorks., U.K.* 12 D7
Oust, *France* 20 F5
Oust →, *France* 18 E4
Outaouais →, *Canada* 102 C5
Outardes →, *Canada* 103 C6
Outeiro de Rei, *Spain* 34 B3
Outer Hebrides, *U.K.* 14 D1
Outer I., *Canada* 103 B8
Outes = Serra de Outes, *Spain* 34 C2
Outjo, *Namibia* 88 C2
Outlook, *Canada* 105 C7
Outlook, *U.S.A.* 112 A2
Outokumpu, *Finland* 8 E23
Outreau, *France* 19 B8
Ouvèze →, *France* 21 E8
Ouyen, *Australia* 95 F3
Ouzouer-le-Marché, *France* 19 E8
Ovada, *Italy* 28 D5
Ovalau, *Fiji* 91 C8
Ovalle, *Chile* 126 C1
Ovamboland, *Namibia* 88 B2
Ovar, *Portugal* 34 E2
Overath, *Germany* 24 E3
Overflakkee, *Neths.* 17 C4
Overijssel □, *Neths.* 17 B6
Overland Park, *U.S.A.* 112 F7
Overton, *U.S.A.* 117 J12
Övertorneå, *Sweden* 8 C20
Överum, *Sweden* 11 F10
Ovid, *U.S.A.* 112 E3
Ovidiopol, *Ukraine* 47 J6
Ovidiu, *Romania* 43 F13
Oviedo, *Spain* 34 B5
Oviksfjällen, *Sweden* 10 A7
Oviši, *Latvia* 9 H19
Övör Hangay □, *Mongolia* 56 B2
Ovoro, *Nigeria* 83 D6
Øvre Årdal, *Norway* 9 F12
Övre Fryken, *Sweden* 10 E7
Ovruch, *Ukraine* 47 G5
Owaka, *N.Z.* 91 M2
Owambo = Ovamboland, *Namibia* 88 B2
Owase, *Japan* 55 G8
Owatonna, *U.S.A.* 112 C8
Owbeh, *Afghan.* 66 B3
Owego, *U.S.A.* 111 D8
Owen Falls Dam, *Uganda* 86 B3
Owen Sound, *Canada* 102 D3
Owens →, *U.S.A.* 116 J9
Owens L., *U.S.A.* 117 J9
Owensboro, *U.S.A.* 108 G2
Owensville, *U.S.A.* 112 F9
Owerri, *Nigeria* 83 D6
Owl →, *Canada* 105 B10
Owo, *Nigeria* 83 D6
Owosso, *U.S.A.* 108 D3
Owyhee, *U.S.A.* 114 F5
Owyhee →, *U.S.A.* 114 E5
Owyhee, L., *U.S.A.* 114 E5
Ox Mts. = Slieve Gamph, *Ireland* 15 B3
Öxarfjörður, *Iceland* 8 C5
Oxelösund, *Sweden* 11 F11
Oxford, *N.Z.* 91 K4
Oxford, *U.K.* 13 F6
Oxford, *Miss., U.S.A.* 113 H10
Oxford, *N.C., U.S.A.* 109 G6
Oxford, *Ohio, U.S.A.* 108 F3
Oxford L., *Canada* 105 C9
Oxfordshire □, *U.K.* 13 F6
Oxía, *Greece* 38 C3
Oxie, *Sweden* 11 J7
Oxílithos, *Greece* 38 C6
Oxley, *Australia* 95 E3
Oxnard, *U.S.A.* 117 L7
Oxsjövålen, *Sweden* 10 B7
Oxus = Amudarya →, *Uzbekistan* 50 E6
Oya, *Malaysia* 62 D4
Oyama, *Japan* 55 F9
Oyem, *Gabon* 84 D2
Oyen, *Canada* 105 C6
Oykel →, *U.K.* 14 D4
Oymyakon, *Russia* 51 C15
Oyo, *Nigeria* 83 D5
Oyo □, *Nigeria* 83 D5
Oyonnax, *France* 19 F12
Oyster Bay, *U.S.A.* 111 F11
Ōyūbari, *Japan* 54 C11
Özalp, *Turkey* 73 C10
Ozamiz, *Phil.* 61 G5
Ozark, *Ala., U.S.A.* 109 K3
Ozark, *Ark., U.S.A.* 113 H8
Ozark, *Mo., U.S.A.* 113 G8
Ozark Plateau, *U.S.A.* 113 G9
Ozarks, L. of the, *U.S.A.* 112 F8
Ożarów, *Poland* 45 H8
Ózd, *Hungary* 42 B5
Ozernoye, *Russia* 48 E10
Ozette L., *U.S.A.* 116 B2
Ozieri, *Italy* 30 B2
Ozimek, *Poland* 45 H5
Ozinki, *Russia* 48 E9
Ozona, *U.S.A.* 113 K4
Ozorków, *Poland* 45 G6
Ozren, *Bos.-H.* 42 G3
Ozuluama, *Mexico* 119 C5
Ozun, *Romania* 43 E10
Ozurgeti, *Georgia* 49 K5

P

Pa, *Burkina Faso* 82 C4
Pa-an, *Burma* 67 L20
Pa Mong Dam, *Thailand* 64 D4
Paamiut = Frederikshåb, *Greenland* 4 C5
Paar →, *Germany* 25 G7
Paarl, *S. Africa* 88 E2
Paauilo, *U.S.A.* 106 H17
Pab Hills, *Pakistan* 68 F2
Pabbay, *U.K.* 14 D1
Pabianice, *Poland* 45 G6
Pabna, *Bangla.* 67 G16
Pabo, *Uganda* 86 B3
Pacaja →, *Brazil* 125 D8
Pacaraima, Sierra, *Venezuela* 122 C4
Pacasmayo, *Peru* 124 E3
Paceco, *Italy* 30 E5
Pachhar, *India* 68 G7
Pachino, *Italy* 31 F8
Pachitea →, *Peru* 124 E4
Pachpadra, *India* 66 G8
Pachuca, *Mexico* 119 C5
Pacific, *Canada* 104 C3
Pacific-Antarctic Ridge, *Pac. Oc.* 97 M16
Pacific Grove, *U.S.A.* 116 J5
Pacific Ocean, *Pac. Oc.* 97 G14
Pacifica, *U.S.A.* 116 H4
Pacitan, *Indonesia* 63 H14
Packwood, *U.S.A.* 116 D5
Pacov, *Czech Rep.* 26 B8
Pacy-sur-Eure, *France* 18 C8
Padaido, Kepulauan, *Indonesia* 63 E9
Padang, *Indonesia* 62 E2
Padang Endau, *Malaysia* 65 L4
Padangpanjang, *Indonesia* 62 E2
Padangsidempuan, *Indonesia* 62 D1
Padborg, *Denmark* 11 K3
Paddockwood, *Canada* 105 C7
Paderborn, *Germany* 24 D4
Padeş, Vf., *Romania* 42 E7
Padina, *Romania* 43 F12
Pádova, *Italy* 29 C8
Padra, *India* 68 H5
Padrauna, *India* 69 F10
Padre I., *U.S.A.* 113 M6
Padrón, *Spain* 34 C2
Padstow, *U.K.* 13 G3
Padua = Pádova, *Italy* 29 C8
Paducah, *Ky., U.S.A.* 108 G1
Paducah, *Tex., U.S.A.* 113 H4
Padul, *Spain* 35 H7
Paengnyong-do, *S. Korea* 57 F13
Paeroa, *N.Z.* 91 G5
Paesana, *Italy* 28 D4
Pafúri, *Mozam.* 89 C5
Pag, *Croatia* 29 D12
Paga, *Ghana* 83 C4
Pagadian, *Phil.* 61 H5
Pagai Selatan, Pulau, *Indonesia* 62 E2
Pagai Utara, Pulau, *Indonesia* 62 E2
Pagalu = Annobón, *Atl. Oc.* 77 G4
Pagastikós Kólpos, *Greece* 38 B5
Pagatan, *Indonesia* 62 E5
Page, *Ariz., U.S.A.* 115 H8
Page, *N. Dak., U.S.A.* 112 B6
Pagėgiai, *Lithuania* 44 C8
Pago Pago, *Amer. Samoa* 91 B13
Pagosa Springs, *U.S.A.* 115 H10
Pagwa River, *Canada* 102 B2
Pahala, *U.S.A.* 106 J17
Pahang →, *Malaysia* 65 L4
Pahiatua, *N.Z.* 91 J5
Pahokee, *U.S.A.* 109 M5
Pahrump, *U.S.A.* 117 J11
Pahute Mesa, *U.S.A.* 116 H10
Pai, *Thailand* 64 C2
Paia, *U.S.A.* 106 H16
Paicines, *U.S.A.* 116 J5
Paide, *Estonia* 9 G21
Paignton, *U.K.* 13 G4
Paiho, *Taiwan* 59 F13
Päijänne, *Finland* 9 F21
Pailin, *Cambodia* 64 F4
Paimpol, *France* 18 D3
Painan, *Indonesia* 62 E2
Painesville, *U.S.A.* 110 E3
Paint Hills = Wemindji, *Canada* 102 B4
Paint L., *Canada* 105 B9
Paint Rock, *U.S.A.* 113 K5
Painted Desert, *U.S.A.* 115 J8
Paintsville, *U.S.A.* 108 G4
País Vasco □, *Spain* 32 C2
Paisley, *Canada* 110 B3
Paisley, *U.K.* 14 F4
Paisley, *U.S.A.* 114 E3
Paita, *Peru* 124 E2
Paiva →, *Portugal* 34 D2
Paizhou, *China* 59 B9
Pajares, *Spain* 34 B5
Pajares, Puerto de, *Spain* 34 C5
Pajęczno, *Poland* 45 G5
Pak Lay, *Laos* 64 C3
Pak Phanang, *Thailand* 65 H3
Pak Sane, *Laos* 64 C4
Pak Song, *Laos* 64 E6
Pak Suong, *Laos* 64 C4
Pákhnes, *Greece* 36 D6
Pakistan ■, *Asia* 68 E4
Pakkading, *Laos* 64 C4
Pakokku, *Burma* 67 J19
Pakość, *Poland* 45 F5
Pakpattan, *Pakistan* 68 D5
Pakrac, *Croatia* 42 E2
Pakruojis, *Lithuania* 44 C10
Paks, *Hungary* 42 D3
Paktīā □, *Afghan.* 66 C6
Pakwach, *Uganda* 86 B3
Pakxe, *Laos* 64 E5
Pala, *Chad* 79 G9
Pala, *Dem. Rep. of the Congo* 86 D2
Pala, *U.S.A.* 117 M9
Palabek, *Uganda* 86 B3
Palacios, *U.S.A.* 113 L6
Palafrugell, *Spain* 32 D8
Palagiano, *Italy* 31 B10
Palagonía, *Italy* 31 E7
Palagruža, *Croatia* 29 F13
Palaiókastron, *Greece* 36 D8
Palaiokhóra, *Greece* 36 D5
Pálairos, *Greece* 38 C2
Palaiseau, *France* 19 D9
Palam, *India* 66 K10
Palamás, *Greece* 38 B4
Palamòs, *Spain* 32 D8
Palampur, *India* 68 C7
Palamut, *Turkey* 39 C9
Palana, *Australia* 94 F4
Palana, *Russia* 51 D16
Palanan, *Phil.* 61 C5
Palanan Pt., *Phil.* 61 C5
Palandri, *Pakistan* 69 C5
Palanga, *Lithuania* 9 J19
Palangkaraya, *Indonesia* 62 E4
Palani Hills, *India* 66 P10
Palanpur, *India* 68 G5
Palapye, *Botswana* 88 C4
Palas, *Pakistan* 69 B5
Palas de Rei, *Spain* 34 C3
Palatka, *Russia* 51 C16
Palatka, *U.S.A.* 109 L5
Palau, *Italy* 30 A2
Palau ■, *Pac. Oc.* 96 G5
Palauk, *Burma* 64 F2
Palawan, *Phil.* 61 G3
Palayankottai, *India* 66 Q10
Palazzo, Pte., *France* 21 F12
Palazzo San Gervásio, *Italy* 31 B8
Palazzolo Acréide, *Italy* 31 E7
Paldiski, *Estonia* 9 G21
Pale, *Bos.-H.* 42 G3
Paleleh, *Indonesia* 63 D6
Palembang, *Indonesia* 62 E2
Palencia, *Spain* 34 C6
Palencia □, *Spain* 34 C6
Paleokastrítsa, *Greece* 36 A3
Paleometokho, *Cyprus* 36 D12
Palermo, *Italy* 30 D6
Palermo, *U.S.A.* 114 G3
Palestina, *Chile* 128 A3
Palestine, *Asia* 75 D4
Palestine, *U.S.A.* 113 K7
Palestrina, *Italy* 29 G9
Paletwa, *Burma* 67 J18
Palghat, *India* 66 P10
Palgrave, Mt., *Australia* 92 D2
Pali, *India* 68 G5
Palinuro, *Italy* 31 B8
Palinuro, C., *Italy* 31 B8
Palioúrion, Ákra, *Greece* 40 G7
Palisade, *U.S.A.* 112 E4
Paliseul, *Belgium* 17 E5
Palitana, *India* 68 J4
Palizada, *Mexico* 119 D6
Palk Bay, *Asia* 66 Q11
Palk Strait, *Asia* 66 Q11
Palkānah, *Iraq* 70 C5
Palla Road = Dinokwe, *Botswana* 88 C4
Pallanza = Verbánia, *Italy* 28 C5

Pallasovka, *Russia* 48 E8
Pallës, Bishti i, *Albania* 40 E3
Pallisa, *Uganda* 86 B3
Pallu, *India* 68 E6
Palm Bay, *U.S.A.* 109 L5
Palm Beach, *U.S.A.* 109 M6
Palm Desert, *U.S.A.* 117 M10
Palm Is., *Australia* 94 B4
Palm Springs, *U.S.A.* 117 M10
Palma, *Mozam.* 87 E5
Palma, B. de, *Spain* 37 B9
Palma de Mallorca, *Spain* 37 B9
Palma del Río, *Spain* 35 H5
Palma di Montechiaro, *Italy* 30 E6
Palma Soriano, *Cuba* 120 B4
Palmares, *Brazil* 125 E11
Palmarola, *Italy* 30 B5
Palmas, *Brazil* 127 B5
Palmas, C., *Liberia* 82 E3
Pálmas, G. di, *Italy* 30 D1
Palmdale, *U.S.A.* 117 L8
Palmeira dos Índios, *Brazil* 125 E11
Palmela, *Portugal* 35 G2
Palmer, *U.S.A.* 100 B5
Palmer →, *Australia* 94 B3
Palmer Arch., *Antarctica* 5 C17
Palmer Lake, *U.S.A.* 112 F2
Palmer Land, *Antarctica* 5 D18
Palmerston, *Canada* 110 C4
Palmerston, *N.Z.* 91 L3
Palmerston North, *N.Z.* 91 J5
Palmerton, *U.S.A.* 111 F9
Palmetto, *U.S.A.* 109 M4
Palmi, *Italy* 31 D8
Palmira, *Argentina* 126 C2
Palmira, *Colombia* 124 C3
Palmyra = Tudmur, *Syria* 70 C3
Palmyra, *Mo., U.S.A.* 112 F9
Palmyra, *N.Y., U.S.A.* 110 C7
Palmyra Is., *Pac. Oc.* 97 G11
Palo Alto, *U.S.A.* 116 H4
Palo Verde, *U.S.A.* 117 M12
Palompon, *Phil.* 61 F6
Palopo, *Indonesia* 63 E6
Palos, C. de, *Spain* 33 H4
Palos de la Frontera, *Spain* 35 H4
Palos Verdes, *U.S.A.* 117 M8
Palos Verdes, Pt., *U.S.A.* 117 M8
Palouse, *U.S.A.* 114 C5
Palparara, *Australia* 94 C3
Pålsboda, *Sweden* 10 E9
Palu, *Indonesia* 63 E5
Palu, *Turkey* 73 C9
Paluzza, *Italy* 29 B10
Palwal, *India* 68 E7
Pama, *Burkina Faso* 83 C5
Pamanukan, *Indonesia* 63 G12
Pamiers, *France* 20 E5
Pamir, *Tajikistan* 50 F8
Pamlico →, *U.S.A.* 109 H7
Pamlico Sd., *U.S.A.* 109 H8
Pampa, *U.S.A.* 113 H4
Pampa de las Salinas, *Argentina* 126 C2
Pampanua, *Indonesia* 63 E6
Pampas, *Argentina* 126 D3
Pampas, *Peru* 124 F4
Pamphylia, *Turkey* 72 D4
Pamplona, *Colombia* 124 B4
Pamplona, *Spain* 32 C3
Pampoenpoort, *S. Africa* 88 E3
Pamukçu, *Turkey* 39 B9
Pamukkale, *Turkey* 39 D11
Pan Xian, *China* 58 E5
Pana, *U.S.A.* 112 F10
Panabo, *Phil.* 61 H6
Panaca, *U.S.A.* 115 H6
Panagyurishte, *Bulgaria* 41 D8
Panaitan, *Indonesia* 63 G11
Panaji, *India* 66 M8
Panamá, *Panama* 120 E4
Panama ■, *Cent. Amer.* 120 E4
Panamá, G. de, *Panama* 120 E4
Panama Canal, *Panama* 120 E4
Panama City, *U.S.A.* 109 K3
Panamint Range, *U.S.A.* 117 J9
Panamint Springs, *U.S.A.* 117 J9
Panão, *Peru* 124 E3
Panaon I., *Phil.* 61 F6
Panare, *Thailand* 65 J3
Panarea, *Italy* 31 D8
Panaro →, *Italy* 29 D8
Panay, *Phil.* 61 F5
Panay, G., *Phil.* 63 B6
Pancake Range, *U.S.A.* 115 G6
Pančevo, *Serbia, Yug.* 42 F5
Panciu, *Romania* 43 E12
Pancorbo, Desfiladero, *Spain* 34 C7
Pâncota, *Romania* 42 D6
Pandan, *Antique, Phil.* 61 F5
Pandan, *Catanduanes, Phil.* 61 D6
Pandegelang, *Indonesia* 63 G12
Pandharpur, *India* 66 L9
Pando, *Uruguay* 127 C4
Pando, L. = Hope, L., *Australia* 95 D2
Pandokrátor, *Greece* 36 A3
Pandora, *Costa Rica* 120 E3
Pandrup, *Denmark* 11 G3
Panevėžys, *Lithuania* 9 J21
Panfilov, *Kazakstan* 50 E9
Panfilovo, *Russia* 48 E6
Pang-Long, *Burma* 67 H21
Pang-Yang, *Burma* 67 H21
Panga, *Dem. Rep. of the Congo* 86 B2
Pangaíon Óros, *Greece* 41 F8
Pangalanes, Canal des, *Madag.* 89 C8
Pangani, *Tanzania* 86 D4
Pangani □, *Tanzania* 86 D4
Pangani →, *Tanzania* 86 D4
Pangfou = Bengbu, *China* 57 H9
Pangil, *Dem. Rep. of the Congo* 86 C2
Pangkah, Tanjung, *Indonesia* 63 G15
Pangkajene, *Indonesia* 63 E5
Pangkalanbrandan, *Indonesia* 62 D1
Pangkalanbuun, *Indonesia* 62 E4
Pangkalpinang, *Indonesia* 62 E3
Pangnirtung, *Canada* 101 B13
Panguitch, *U.S.A.* 115 H7
Pangutaran Group, *Phil.* 61 H4
Panhandle, *U.S.A.* 113 H4
Pani Mines, *India* 68 H5
Pania-Mutombo, *Dem. Rep. of the Congo* 86 D1
Panipat, *India* 68 E7
Panjal Range, *India* 68 C7
Panjgur, *Pakistan* 66 F4
Panjim = Panaji, *India* 66 M8
Panjinad Barrage, *Pakistan* 66 E7
Panjwai, *Afghan.* 68 D1
Pankshin, *Nigeria* 83 D6
Panmunjŏm, *N. Korea* 57 F14
Panna, *India* 69 G9
Panna Hills, *India* 69 G9
Pano Lefkara, *Cyprus* 36 E12
Pano Panayia, *Cyprus* 36 E11
Panorama, *Brazil* 127 A5
Pánormon, *Greece* 36 D6
Panshan, *China* 57 D12
Panshi, *China* 57 C14
Pantanal, *Brazil* 124 H7
Pantar, *Indonesia* 63 F6
Pante Macassar, *Indonesia* 63 F6
Pantelleria, *Italy* 30 F4
Pantón, *Spain* 34 C3
Pánuco, *Mexico* 119 C5
Panyam, *Nigeria* 83 D6
Panyu, *China* 59 F9
Páola, *Italy* 31 C9
Paola, *Malta* 36 D2
Paola, *U.S.A.* 112 F7
Paonia, *U.S.A.* 115 G10
Paoting = Baoding, *China* 56 E8
Paot'ou = Baotou, *China* 56 D6
Paoua, *C.A.R.* 84 C3
Pápa, *Hungary* 42 C2
Papa Stour, *U.K.* 14 A7
Papa Westray, *U.K.* 14 B6
Papagayo →, *Mexico* 119 D5
Papagayo, G. de, *Costa Rica* 120 D2
Papakura, *N.Z.* 91 G5
Papantla, *Mexico* 119 C5
Papar, *Malaysia* 62 C5
Pápas, Ákra, *Greece* 38 C3
Papenburg, *Germany* 24 B3
Paphlagonia, *Turkey* 72 B5
Paphos, *Cyprus* 36 E11
Papien Chiang = Da →, *Vietnam* 64 B5
Papigochic →, *Mexico* 118 B3
Paposo, *Chile* 126 B1
Papoutsa, *Cyprus* 36 E12
Papua New Guinea ■, *Oceania* 96 H6
Papudo, *Chile* 126 C1
Papuk, *Croatia* 42 E2
Papun, *Burma* 67 K20
Papunya, *Australia* 92 D5
Pará = Belém, *Brazil* 125 D9
Pará □, *Brazil* 125 D8
Paraburdoo, *Australia* 92 D2
Paracale, *Phil.* 61 D5
Paracatu, *Brazil* 125 G9
Paracel Is., *S. China Sea* 62 A4
Parachilna, *Australia* 95 E2
Parachinar, *Pakistan* 68 C4
Paraćin, *Serbia, Yug.* 40 C5
Paradas, *Spain* 35 H5
Paradela, *Spain* 34 C3
Paradhísi, *Greece* 36 C10
Paradip, *India* 67 J15
Paradise, *Calif., U.S.A.* 116 F5
Paradise, *Mont., U.S.A.* 114 C6
Paradise, *Nev., U.S.A.* 117 J11
Paradise →, *Canada* 103 B8
Paradise Valley, *U.S.A.* 114 F5
Parado, *Indonesia* 63 F5
Paragould, *U.S.A.* 113 G9
Paragua →, *Venezuela* 124 B6
Paraguaçu →, *Brazil* 125 F11
Paraguaçu Paulista, *Brazil* 127 A5
Paraguaná, Pen. de, *Venezuela* 124 A5
Paraguarí, *Paraguay* 126 B4
Paraguarí □, *Paraguay* 126 B4
Paraguay ■, *S. Amer.* 126 A4
Paraguay →, *Paraguay* 126 B4
Paraíba = João Pessoa, *Brazil* 125 E12
Paraíba □, *Brazil* 125 E11
Paraíba do Sul →, *Brazil* 127 A7
Parainen, *Finland* 9 F20
Paraiso, *Mexico* 119 D6
Parak, *Iran* 71 E7
Parakhino Paddubye, *Russia* 46 C7
Parakou, *Benin* 83 D5
Paralimni, *Cyprus* 36 D12
Parálion-Astrous, *Greece* 38 D4
Paramaribo, *Surinam* 125 B7
Paramithiá, *Greece* 38 B2
Paramushir, Ostrov, *Russia* 51 D16
Paran →, *Israel* 75 E4
Paraná, *Argentina* 126 C3
Paranã, *Brazil* 125 F9
Paraná □, *Brazil* 127 A5
Paraná →, *Argentina* 126 C4
Paranaguá, *Brazil* 127 B6
Paranaíba, *Brazil* 125 G8
Paranaíba →, *Brazil* 125 H8
Paranapanema →, *Brazil* 127 A5
Paranapiacaba, Serra do, *Brazil* 127 A6
Paranavaí, *Brazil* 127 A5
Parang, *Jolo, Phil.* 61 J4
Parang, *Mindanao, Phil.* 63 C6
Parângul Mare, Vf., *Romania* 43 E8
Parapóla, *Greece* 38 E5
Paraspóri, Ákra, *Greece* 39 F9
Paratoo, *Australia* 95 E2
Parattah, *Australia* 94 G4
Paray-le-Monial, *France* 19 F11
Parbati →, *India* 68 G7
Parbhani, *India* 66 K10
Parchim, *Germany* 24 B7
Parczew, *Poland* 45 G9
Pardes Hanna-Karkur, *Israel* 75 C3
Pardilla, *Spain* 34 D7
Pardo →, *Bahia, Brazil* 125 G11
Pardo →, *Mato Grosso, Brazil* 127 A5
Pardubice, *Czech Rep.* 26 A8
Pare, *Indonesia* 63 G15
Pare □, *Tanzania* 86 C4
Pare Mts., *Tanzania* 86 C4
Parecis, Serra dos, *Brazil* 124 F7
Paredes de Nava, *Spain* 34 C6
Pareh, *Iran* 70 B5
Paren, *Russia* 51 C17
Parent, *Canada* 102 C5
Parent, L., *Canada* 102 C4
Parentis-en-Born, *France* 20 D2
Parepare, *Indonesia* 63 E5
Parfino, *Russia* 46 D6
Párga, *Greece* 38 B2
Pargo, Pta. do, *Madeira* 37 D2
Pariaguán, *Venezuela* 124 B6
Paricutín, Cerro, *Mexico* 118 D4
Parigi, *Indonesia* 63 E6
Parika, *Guyana* 124 B7
Parikkala, *Finland* 46 B5
Parima, Serra, *Brazil* 124 C6
Parinari, *Peru* 124 D4
Pariñas, Pta., *S. Amer.* 122 D2
Parincea, *Romania* 43 D12
Parintins, *Brazil* 125 D7
Pariparit Kyun, *Burma* 67 M18
Paris, *Canada* 102 D3
Paris, *France* 19 D9
Paris, *Idaho, U.S.A.* 114 E8
Paris, *Ky., U.S.A.* 108 F3
Paris, *Tenn., U.S.A.* 109 G1
Paris, *Tex., U.S.A.* 113 J7
Paris, Ville de □, *France* 19 D9
Parish, *U.S.A.* 111 C8
Park, *U.S.A.* 116 B4
Park City, *U.S.A.* 114 F8
Park Falls, *U.S.A.* 112 C9
Park Range, *U.S.A.* 114 G10
Park Rapids, *U.S.A.* 112 B7
Park River, *U.S.A.* 112 A6
Park Rynie, *S. Africa* 89 E5
Parkā Bandar, *Iran* 71 E8
Parkano, *Finland* 9 E20
Parker, *Ariz., U.S.A.* 117 L12
Parker, *S. Dak., U.S.A.* 112 D6
Parker Dam, *U.S.A.* 117 L12
Parkersburg, *U.S.A.* 108 F5
Parkerview, *Canada* 105 C8
Parkes, *Australia* 95 E4
Parkfield, *U.S.A.* 116 K6
Parkland, *U.S.A.* 116 C4
Parkside, *Canada* 105 C7
Parkston, *U.S.A.* 112 D6
Parksville, *Canada* 104 D4
Parla, *Spain* 34 E7
Pârliţa, *Moldova* 43 C12
Parma, *Italy* 28 D7
Parma, *Idaho, U.S.A.* 114 E5
Parma, *Ohio, U.S.A.* 110 E3
Parma →, *Italy* 28 D7
Parnaguá, *Brazil* 125 F10
Parnaíba, *Brazil* 125 D10
Parnaíba →, *Brazil* 122 D6
Parnassós, *Greece* 38 C4
Párnis, *Greece* 38 C5
Párnon Óros, *Greece* 38 D4
Pärnu, *Estonia* 9 G21
Paroo →, *Australia* 95 E3
Páros, *Greece* 39 D7
Parowan, *U.S.A.* 115 H7
Parpaillon, *France* 21 D10
Parral, *Chile* 126 D1
Parramatta, *Australia* 95 E5
Parras, *Mexico* 118 B4
Parrett →, *U.K.* 13 F4
Parris I., *U.S.A.* 109 J5
Parrsboro, *Canada* 103 C7
Parry Is., *Canada* 4 B2
Parry Sound, *Canada* 102 C4
Parsberg, *Germany* 25 F7
Parsęta →, *Poland* 44 D2
Parshall, *U.S.A.* 112 B3
Parsnip →, *Canada* 104 B4
Parsons, *U.S.A.* 113 G7
Parsons Ra., *Australia* 94 A2
Partanna, *Italy* 30 E5
Parthenay, *France* 18 F6
Partinico, *Italy* 30 D6
Partizánske, *Slovak Rep.* 27 C11
Paru →, *Brazil* 125 D8
Parvān □, *Afghan.* 66 B6
Parvatipuram, *India* 67 K13
Påryd, *Sweden* 11 H9
Parys, *S. Africa* 88 D4
Pas, Pta. des, *Spain* 37 C7
Pas-de-Calais □, *France* 19 B9
Pasada, *Spain* 34 B5
Pasadena, *Calif., U.S.A.* 117 L8
Pasadena, *Tex., U.S.A.* 113 L7
Pasaje →, *Argentina* 126 B3
Paşalimanı, *Turkey* 41 F11
Pasay, *Phil.* 61 D4
Pascagoula, *U.S.A.* 113 K10
Pascagoula →, *U.S.A.* 113 K10
Paşcani, *Romania* 43 C11
Pasco, *U.S.A.* 114 C4
Pasco, Cerro de, *Peru* 124 F3
Pascua, I. de, *Pac. Oc.* 97 K17
Pasewalk, *Germany* 24 B9
Pasfield L., *Canada* 105 B7
Pasha →, *Russia* 46 B7
Pashiwari, *Pakistan* 69 B6
Pashmakli = Smolyan, *Bulgaria* 41 E8
Pasinler, *Turkey* 73 C9
Pasir Mas, *Malaysia* 65 J4
Pasirian, *Indonesia* 63 H15
Pasirkuning, *Indonesia* 62 E2
Påskallavik, *Sweden* 11 G10
Paskūh, *Iran* 71 E9
Pasłęk, *Poland* 44 D6
Pasłęka →, *Poland* 44 D6
Pasley, C., *Australia* 93 F3
Pašman, *Croatia* 29 E12
Pasni, *Pakistan* 66 G3
Paso Cantinela, *Mexico* 117 N11
Paso de Indios, *Argentina* 128 E3
Paso de los Libres, *Argentina* 126 B4
Paso de los Toros, *Uruguay* 126 C4
Paso Robles, *U.S.A.* 115 J3
Paspébiac, *Canada* 103 C6
Pasrur, *Pakistan* 68 C6
Passage West, *Ireland* 15 E3
Passaic, *U.S.A.* 111 F10
Passau, *Germany* 25 G9
Passero, C., *Italy* 31 F8
Passo Fundo, *Brazil* 127 B5
Passos, *Brazil* 125 H9
Passow, *Germany* 24 B10
Passy, *France* 21 C10
Pastavy, *Belarus* 9 J22
Pastaza →, *Peru* 124 D3
Pasto, *Colombia* 124 C3
Pastrana, *Spain* 32 E2
Pasuruan, *Indonesia* 63 G15
Pasym, *Poland* 44 E7
Pásztó, *Hungary* 42 C4
Patagonia, *Argentina* 122 H4
Patagonia, *U.S.A.* 115 L8
Patambar, *Iran* 71 D9
Patan, *India* 66 H8
Patan, *Maharashtra, India* 68 H5
Patan, *Nepal* 67 F14
Patani, *Indonesia* 63 D7
Pătârlagele, *Romania* 43 E11
Pataudi, *India* 68 E7
Patchewollock, *Australia* 95 F3
Patchogue, *U.S.A.* 111 F11
Patea, *N.Z.* 91 H5
Pategi, *Nigeria* 83 D6
Patensie, *S. Africa* 88 E3
Paterna, *Spain* 33 F4
Paternion, *Austria* 26 E6
Paternò, *Italy* 31 E7
Pateros, *U.S.A.* 114 B4
Paterson, *U.S.A.* 111 F10
Paterson Ra., *Australia* 92 D3
Pathankot, *India* 68 C6
Pathfinder Reservoir, *U.S.A.* 114 E10
Pathiu, *Thailand* 65 G2
Pathum Thani, *Thailand* 64 E3
Pati, *Indonesia* 63 G14
Patía →, *Colombia* 124 C3
Patiala, *India* 68 D7
Patine Kouka, *Senegal* 82 C2
Patitírion, *Greece* 38 B5
Patkai Bum, *India* 67 F19
Pátmos, *Greece* 39 D8
Patna, *India* 69 G11
Patnos, *Turkey* 73 C10
Pato Branco, *Brazil* 128 B6
Patonga, *Uganda* 86 B3
Patos, *Brazil* 125 E11
Patos, L. dos, *Brazil* 127 C5
Patos de Minas, *Brazil* 125 G9
Patosi, *Albania* 40 F3
Patquía, *Argentina* 126 C2
Pátrai, *Greece* 38 C3
Pátraikós Kólpos, *Greece* 38 C3
Patras = Pátrai, *Greece* 38 C3
Patrocínio, *Brazil* 125 G9
Patta, *Kenya* 86 C5
Pattada, *Italy* 30 B2
Pattani, *Thailand* 65 J3
Patten, *U.S.A.* 103 C6
Patterson, *Calif., U.S.A.* 116 H5
Patterson, *La., U.S.A.* 113 L9
Patterson, Mt., *U.S.A.* 116 G7
Patti, *India* 68 D6
Patti, *Italy* 31 D7
Pattoki, *Pakistan* 68 D5
Patton, *U.S.A.* 110 F6
Patuakhali, *Bangla.* 67 H17
Patuca →, *Honduras* 120 C3
Patuca, Punta, *Honduras* 120 C3
Pătulele, *Romania* 42 F7
Pátzcuaro, *Mexico* 118 D4
Pau, *France* 20 E3
Pau, Gave de →, *France* 20 E2
Pauillac, *France* 20 C3
Pauk, *Burma* 67 J19
Paul I., *Canada* 103 A7
Paulhan, *France* 20 E7
Paulis = Isiro, *Dem. Rep. of the Congo* 86 B2
Paulistana, *Brazil* 125 E10
Paullina, *U.S.A.* 112 D7
Paulo Afonso, *Brazil* 125 E11
Paulpietersburg, *S. Africa* 89 D5
Pauls Valley, *U.S.A.* 113 H6
Pauma Valley, *U.S.A.* 117 M10
Pāveh, *Iran* 70 C5
Pavelets, *Russia* 46 F10
Pavia, *Italy* 28 C6
Pavilly, *France* 18 C7
Pāvilosta, *Latvia* 9 H19
Pavlikeni, *Bulgaria* 41 C9
Pavlodar, *Kazakstan* 50 D8
Pavlograd = Pavlohrad, *Ukraine* 47 H8
Pavlohrad, *Ukraine* 47 H8
Pavlovo, *Russia* 48 C6
Pavlovsk, *Russia* 48 E5
Pavlovskaya, *Russia* 49 G4
Pavlovskiy-Posad, *Russia* 46 E10
Pavullo nel Frignano, *Italy* 28 D7
Pawhuska, *U.S.A.* 113 G6
Pawling, *U.S.A.* 111 E11
Pawnee, *U.S.A.* 113 G6
Pawnee City, *U.S.A.* 112 E6
Pawtucket, *U.S.A.* 111 E13
Paximádhia, *Greece* 36 E6
Paxoí, *Greece* 38 B2
Paxton, *Ill., U.S.A.* 108 E1
Paxton, *Nebr., U.S.A.* 112 E4
Payakumbuh, *Indonesia* 62 E2
Payerne, *Switz.* 25 J2
Payette, *U.S.A.* 114 D5
Paymogo, *Spain* 35 H3
Payne Bay = Kangirsuk, *Canada* 101 C13
Paynes Find, *Australia* 93 E2
Paynesville, *Liberia* 82 D2
Paynesville, *U.S.A.* 112 C7
Pays de la Loire □, *France* 18 E6
Paysandú, *Uruguay* 126 C4
Payson, *Ariz., U.S.A.* 115 J8
Payson, *Utah, U.S.A.* 114 F8
Paz →, *Guatemala* 120 D1
Paz, B. la, *Mexico* 118 C2
Pāzanān, *Iran* 71 D6
Pazar, *Turkey* 73 B9
Pazarcık, *Turkey* 72 D7
Pazardzhik, *Bulgaria* 41 D8
Pazarköy, *Turkey* 39 B9
Pazarlar, *Turkey* 39 C11
Pazaryeri, *Turkey* 39 B11
Pazaryolu, *Turkey* 73 B9
Pazin, *Croatia* 29 C10
Pčinja →, *Macedonia* 40 E5
Pe Ell, *U.S.A.* 116 D3
Peabody, *U.S.A.* 111 D14
Peace →, *Canada* 104 B6
Peace Point, *Canada* 104 B6
Peace River, *Canada* 104 B5
Peach Springs, *U.S.A.* 115 J7
Peak, The = Kinder Scout, *U.K.* 12 D6
Peak Downs, *Australia* 94 C4
Peak Downs Mine, *Australia* 94 C4
Peak Hill, *N.S.W., Australia* 95 E4
Peak Hill, *W. Austral., Australia* 93 E2
Peak Ra., *Australia* 94 C4
Peake, *Australia* 95 F2
Peake Cr. →, *Australia* 95 D2
Peal de Becerro, *Spain* 35 H7
Peale, Mt., *U.S.A.* 115 G9
Pearblossom, *U.S.A.* 117 L9
Pearl →, *U.S.A.* 113 K10
Pearl City, *U.S.A.* 106 H16
Pearsall, *U.S.A.* 113 L5
Pearse I., *Canada* 104 C2
Peary Land, *Greenland* 4 A6
Pease →, *U.S.A.* 113 H5
Pebane, *Mozam.* 87 F4
Pebas, *Peru* 124 D4
Pebble Beach, *U.S.A.* 116 J5
Peć, *Serbia, Yug.* 40 D4
Péccioli, *Italy* 28 E7
Pechea, *Romania* 43 E12
Pechenga, *Russia* 50 C4
Pechenizhyn, *Ukraine* 47 H3
Pechiguera, Pta., *Canary Is.* 37 F6
Pechnezhskoye Vdkhr., *Ukraine* 47 G9
Pechora →, *Russia* 50 C6
Pechorskaya Guba, *Russia* 50 C6
Pecica, *Romania* 42 D6
Pecka, *Serbia, Yug.* 40 B3

Pécora, C., *Italy* 30 C1
Pečory, *Russia* 9 H22
Pecos, *U.S.A.* 113 K3
Pecos →, *U.S.A.* 113 L3
Pécs, *Hungary* 42 D3
Pedder, L., *Australia* 94 G4
Peddie, *S. Africa* 89 E4
Pédernales, *Dom. Rep.* 121 C5
Pedieos →, *Cyprus* 36 D12
Pedirka, *Australia* 95 D2
Pedra Azul, *Brazil* 125 G10
Pedreguer, *Spain* 33 G5
Pedreiras, *Brazil* 125 D10
Pedro Afonso, *Brazil* 125 E9
Pedro Cays, *Jamaica* 120 C4
Pedro de Valdivia, *Chile* 126 A2
Pedro Juan Caballero, *Paraguay* 127 A4
Pedro Muñoz, *Spain* 35 F8
Pedrógão Grande, *Portugal* 34 F2
Peebinga, *Australia* 95 E3
Peebles, *U.K.* 14 F5
Peekskill, *U.S.A.* 111 E11
Peel, *U.K.* 12 C3
Peel →, *Australia* 95 E5
Peel →, *Canada* 100 B6
Peene →, *Germany* 24 A9
Peera Peera Poolanna L., *Australia* 95 D2
Peers, *Canada* 104 C5
Pegasus Bay, *N.Z.* 91 K4
Peggau, *Austria* 26 D8
Pegnitz, *Germany* 25 F7
Pegnitz →, *Germany* 25 F6
Pego, *Spain* 33 G4
Pegu, *Burma* 67 L20
Pegu Yoma, *Burma* 67 K20
Pehčevo, *Macedonia* 40 E6
Pehlıvanköy, *Turkey* 41 E10
Pehuajó, *Argentina* 126 D3
Pei Xian, *China* 56 G9
Peichiang, *Taiwan* 59 F13
Peine, *Chile* 126 A2
Peine, *Germany* 24 C6
Peip'ing = Beijing, *China* 56 E9
Peipus, L. = Chudskoye, Oz., *Russia* 9 G22
Peissenberg, *Germany* 25 H7
Peitz, *Germany* 24 D10
Peixe, *Brazil* 125 F9
Peixe →, *Brazil* 125 H8
Pek →, *Serbia, Yug.* 40 B5
Pekalongan, *Indonesia* 63 G13
Pekan, *Malaysia* 65 L4
Pekanbaru, *Indonesia* 62 D2
Pekin, *U.S.A.* 112 E10
Peking = Beijing, *China* 56 E9
Pelabuhan Kelang, *Malaysia* 65 L3
Pelabuhan Ratu, Teluk, *Indonesia* 63 G12
Pelabuhanratu, *Indonesia* 63 G12
Pélagos, *Greece* 38 B6
Pelaihari, *Indonesia* 62 E4
Pelat, Mt., *France* 21 D10
Pełczyce, *Poland* 45 E2
Peleaga, Vf., *Romania* 42 E7
Pelée, Mt., *Martinique* 121 D7
Pelee, Pt., *Canada* 102 D3
Pelee I., *Canada* 102 D3
Pelekech, *Kenya* 86 B4
Peleng, *Indonesia* 63 E6
Pelham, *U.S.A.* 109 K3
Pelhřimov, *Czech Rep.* 26 B8
Pelican L., *Canada* 105 C8
Pelican Narrows, *Canada* 105 B8
Pelican Rapids, *Canada* 105 C8
Pelješac, *Croatia* 29 F14
Pelkosenniemi, *Finland* 8 C22
Pella, *Greece* 40 F6
Pella, *S. Africa* 88 D2
Pella, *U.S.A.* 112 E8
Pélla □, *Greece* 40 F6
Pello, *Finland* 8 C21
Pellworm, *Germany* 24 A4
Pelly →, *Canada* 100 B6
Pelly Bay, *Canada* 101 B11
Peloponnese = Pelopónnisos □, *Greece* 38 D4
Pelopónnisos □, *Greece* 38 D4
Peloritani, Monti, *Italy* 31 D8
Pelorus Sd., *N.Z.* 91 J4
Pelotas, *Brazil* 127 C5
Pelovo, *Bulgaria* 41 C8
Pelplin, *Poland* 44 E5
Pelvoux, Massif du, *France* 21 D10
Pemalang, *Indonesia* 63 G13
Pematangsiantar, *Indonesia* 62 D1
Pemba, *Mozam.* 87 E5
Pemba, *Zambia* 87 F2
Pemba Channel, *Tanzania* 86 D4
Pemba I., *Tanzania* 86 D4
Pemberton, *Australia* 93 F2
Pemberton, *Canada* 104 C4
Pembina, *U.S.A.* 112 A6
Pembina →, *U.S.A.* 105 D9
Pembine, *U.S.A.* 108 C2
Pembroke, *Canada* 102 C4
Pembroke, *U.K.* 13 F3
Pembroke, *U.S.A.* 109 J5
Pembrokeshire □, *U.K.* 13 F3
Pen-y-Ghent, *U.K.* 12 C5
Peña, Sierra de la, *Spain* 32 C4
Peña de Francia, Sierra de la, *Spain* 34 E4
Penafiel, *Portugal* 34 D2
Peñafiel, *Spain* 34 D6
Peñaflor, *Spain* 35 H5
Peñalara, *Spain* 34 E7
Penamacôr, *Portugal* 34 E3
Penang = Pinang, *Malaysia* 65 K3
Penápolis, *Brazil* 127 A6
Peñaranda de Bracamonte, *Spain* 34 E5
Peñarroya, *Spain* 32 E4
Peñarroya-Pueblonuevo, *Spain* 35 G5
Penarth, *U.K.* 13 F4
Peñas, C. de, *Spain* 34 B5
Penas, G. de, *Chile* 122 H3
Peñas de San Pedro, *Spain* 33 G3
Peñas del Chache, *Canary Is.* 37 E6
Peñausende, *Spain* 34 D5
Pench'i = Benxi, *China* 57 D12
Pend Oreille →, *U.S.A.* 114 B5
Pend Oreille L., *U.S.A.* 114 C5
Pendálofon, *Greece* 40 F5
Pendembu, *S. Leone* 82 D2
Pender B., *Australia* 92 C3
Pendik, *Turkey* 41 F13
Pendleton, *Calif., U.S.A.* 117 M9
Pendleton, *Oreg., U.S.A.* 114 D4
Penedo, *Brazil* 125 F11
Penetanguishene, *Canada* 102 D4
Peng Xian, *China* 58 B4
Pengalengan, *Indonesia* 63 G12
Penge, *Kasai Or., Dem. Rep. of the Congo* 86 D1
Penge, *Kivu, Dem. Rep. of the Congo* 86 C2
Penglai, *China* 57 F11
Pengshui, *China* 58 C7
Penguin, *Australia* 94 G4
Pengxi, *China* 58 B5
Pengze, *China* 59 C11
Penhalonga, *Zimbabwe* 87 F3
Peniche, *Portugal* 35 F1
Penicuik, *U.K.* 14 F5
Penida, *Indonesia* 62 F5
Peninnes, Alpes = Pennine, Alpi, *Alps* 25 J3
Peninsular Malaysia □, *Malaysia* 65 L4
Peñíscola, *Spain* 32 E5
Penitente, Serra dos, *Brazil* 125 E9
Penkridge, *U.K.* 12 E5
Penmarch, *France* 18 E2
Penmarch, Pte. de, *France* 18 E2
Penn Hills, *U.S.A.* 110 F5
Penn Yan, *U.S.A.* 110 D7
Penna, Punta della, *Italy* 29 F11
Pennant, *Canada* 105 C7
Penne, *Italy* 29 F10
Penner →, *India* 66 M12
Pennine, Alpi, *Alps* 25 J3
Pennines, *U.K.* 12 C5
Pennington, *U.S.A.* 116 F5
Pennino, Mte., *Italy* 29 E9
Pennsylvania □, *U.S.A.* 108 E7
Penny, *Canada* 104 C4
Peno, *Russia* 46 D7
Penola, *Australia* 95 F3
Penong, *Australia* 93 F5
Penonomé, *Panama* 120 E3
Penrith, *Australia* 95 E5
Penrith, *U.K.* 12 C5
Penryn, *U.K.* 13 G2
Pensacola, *U.S.A.* 109 K2
Pensacola Mts., *Antarctica* 5 E1
Pense, *Canada* 105 C8
Penshurst, *Australia* 95 F3
Penticton, *Canada* 104 D5
Pentland, *Australia* 94 C4
Pentland Firth, *U.K.* 14 C5
Pentland Hills, *U.K.* 14 F5
Penylan L., *Canada* 105 A7
Penza, *Russia* 48 D7
Penzance, *U.K.* 13 G2
Penzberg, *Germany* 25 H7
Penzhino, *Russia* 51 C17
Penzhinskaya Guba, *Russia* 51 C17
Penzlin, *Germany* 24 B9
Peoria, *Ariz., U.S.A.* 115 K7
Peoria, *Ill., U.S.A.* 112 E10
Peqini, *Albania* 40 E3
Pera Hd., *Australia* 94 A3
Perabumulih, *Indonesia* 62 E2
Perak →, *Malaysia* 65 K3
Perakhóra, *Greece* 38 C4
Perales de Alfambra, *Spain* 32 E4
Perales del Puerto, *Spain* 34 E4
Pérama, *Kérkira, Greece* 36 A3
Pérama, *Kríti, Greece* 36 D6
Peräpohjola, *Finland* 8 C22
Perast, *Montenegro, Yug.* 40 D2
Percé, *Canada* 103 C7
Perche, *France* 18 D8
Perchtoldsdorf, *Austria* 27 C9
Percival Lakes, *Australia* 92 D4
Percy, *France* 18 D5
Percy Is., *Australia* 94 C5
Perdido, Mte., *Spain* 32 C5
Perdu, Mt. = Perdido, Mte., *Spain* 32 C5
Pereira, *Colombia* 124 C3
Perekerten, *Australia* 95 E3
Perelazovskiy, *Russia* 49 F6
Perenjori, *Australia* 93 E2
Peresecina, *Moldova* 43 C13
Pereslavl-Zalesskiy, *Russia* 46 D10
Peretu, *Romania* 43 F10
Pereyaslav-Khmelnytskyy, *Ukraine* 47 G6
Pérez, I., *Mexico* 119 C7
Perg, *Austria* 26 C7
Pergamino, *Argentina* 126 C3
Pergau →, *Malaysia* 65 K3
Pérgine Valsugana, *Italy* 29 B8
Pérgola, *Italy* 29 E9
Perham, *U.S.A.* 112 B7
Periam, *Romania* 42 D5
Péribonca →, *Canada* 103 C5
Péribonca, L., *Canada* 103 B5
Perico, *Argentina* 126 A2
Pericos, *Mexico* 118 B3
Périers, *France* 18 C5
Périgord, *France* 20 D4
Périgueux, *France* 20 C4
Perijá, Sierra de, *Colombia* 124 B4
Peristéra, *Greece* 38 B5
Peristerona →, *Cyprus* 36 D12
Perito Moreno, *Argentina* 128 F2
Perivol = Dragovishtitsa, *Bulgaria* 40 D6
Perković, *Croatia* 29 E13
Perlas, Arch. de las, *Panama* 120 E4
Perlas, Punta de, *Nic.* 120 D3
Perleberg, *Germany* 24 B7
Perlez, *Serbia, Yug.* 42 E5
Perm, *Russia* 50 D6
Përmeti, *Albania* 40 F4
Pernambuco = Recife, *Brazil* 125 E12
Pernambuco □, *Brazil* 125 E11
Pernatty Lagoon, *Australia* 95 E2
Pernik, *Bulgaria* 40 D7
Peron, C., *Australia* 93 E1
Peron Is., *Australia* 92 B5
Peron Pen., *Australia* 93 E1
Péronne, *France* 19 C9
Perosa Argentina, *Italy* 28 D4
Perow, *Canada* 104 C3
Perpendicular Pt., *Australia* 95 E5
Perpignan, *France* 20 F6
Perris, *U.S.A.* 117 M9
Perros-Guirec, *France* 18 D3
Perry, *Fla., U.S.A.* 109 K4
Perry, *Ga., U.S.A.* 109 J4
Perry, *Iowa, U.S.A.* 112 E7
Perry, *Maine, U.S.A.* 109 C12
Perry, *Okla., U.S.A.* 113 G6
Perryton, *U.S.A.* 113 G4
Perryville, *U.S.A.* 113 G10
Persan, *France* 19 C9
Persberg, *Sweden* 10 E8
Perşembe, *Turkey* 72 B7
Pershotravensk, *Ukraine* 47 G4
Persia = Iran ■, *Asia* 71 C7
Persian Gulf = Gulf, The, *Asia* 71 E6
Perstorp, *Sweden* 11 H7
Pertek, *Turkey* 73 C8
Perth, *Australia* 93 F2
Perth, *Canada* 102 D4
Perth, *U.K.* 14 E5
Perth & Kinross □, *U.K.* 14 E5
Perth Amboy, *U.S.A.* 111 F10
Pertuis, *France* 21 E9
Pertusato, C., *France* 21 G13
Peru, *Ill., U.S.A.* 112 E10
Peru, *Ind., U.S.A.* 108 E2
Peru ■, *S. Amer.* 124 D4
Peru-Chile Trench, *Pac. Oc.* 124 G3
Perúgia, *Italy* 29 E9
Perušić, *Croatia* 29 D12
Pervomaysk, *Russia* 48 C6
Pervomaysk, *Ukraine* 47 H6
Pervouralsk, *Russia* 50 D6
Pésaro, *Italy* 29 E9
Pescara, *Italy* 29 F11
Pescara →, *Italy* 29 F11
Peschanokopskoye, *Russia* 49 G5
Péscia, *Italy* 28 E7
Pescina, *Italy* 29 F10
Peshawar, *Pakistan* 68 B4
Peshkopi, *Albania* 40 E4
Peshtera, *Bulgaria* 41 D8
Peshtigo, *U.S.A.* 108 C2
Peski, *Russia* 48 E6
Pêso da Régua, *Portugal* 34 D3
Pesqueira, *Brazil* 125 E11
Pessac, *France* 20 D3
Pest □, *Hungary* 42 C4
Pestovo, *Russia* 46 C8
Pestravka, *Russia* 48 D9
Péta, *Greece* 38 B3
Petah Tiqwa, *Israel* 75 C3
Petalídhion, *Greece* 38 E3
Petaling Jaya, *Malaysia* 65 L3
Petaloudhes, *Greece* 36 C10
Petaluma, *U.S.A.* 116 G4
Pétange, *Lux.* 17 E5
Petatlán, *Mexico* 118 D4
Petauke, *Zambia* 87 E3
Petawawa, *Canada* 102 C4
Petén Itzá, L., *Guatemala* 120 C2
Peter I.s Øy, *Antarctica* 5 C16
Peter Pond L., *Canada* 105 B7
Peterbell, *Canada* 102 C3
Peterborough, *Australia* 95 E2
Peterborough, *Canada* 110 B6
Peterborough, *U.K.* 13 E7
Peterborough, *U.S.A.* 111 D13
Peterborough □, *U.K.* 13 E7
Peterculter, *U.K.* 14 D6
Peterhead, *U.K.* 14 D7
Peterlee, *U.K.* 12 C6
Petermann Bjerg, *Greenland* 98 B17
Petersburg, *Alaska, U.S.A.* 104 B2
Petersburg, *Ind., U.S.A.* 108 F2
Petersburg, *Va., U.S.A.* 108 G7
Petersburg, *W. Va., U.S.A.* 108 F6
Petersfield, *U.K.* 13 F7
Petershagen, *Germany* 24 C4
Petford, *Australia* 94 B3
Petília Policastro, *Italy* 31 C9
Petit Bois I., *U.S.A.* 109 K1
Petit-Cap, *Canada* 103 C7
Petit Goâve, *Haiti* 121 C5
Petit Lac Manicouagan, *Canada* 103 B6
Petit Saint Bernard, Col du, *Italy* 21 C10
Petitcodiac, *Canada* 103 C6
Petite Baleine →, *Canada* 102 A4
Petite Saguenay, *Canada* 103 C5
Petitsikapau, L., *Canada* 103 B6
Petlad, *India* 68 H5
Peto, *Mexico* 119 C7
Petone, *N.Z.* 91 J5
Petoskey, *U.S.A.* 108 C3
Petra, *Jordan* 75 E4
Petra, *Spain* 37 B10
Petra, Ostrova, *Russia* 4 B13
Petra Velikogo, Zaliv, *Russia* 54 C6
Petrel = Petrer, *Spain* 33 G4
Petrella, Monte, *Italy* 30 A6
Petrer, *Spain* 33 G4
Petreto-Bicchisano, *France* 21 G12
Petrich, *Bulgaria* 40 E7
Petrijanec, *Croatia* 29 B13
Petrikov = Pyetrikaw, *Belarus* 47 F5
Petrila, *Romania* 43 E8
Petrinja, *Croatia* 29 C13
Petrodvorets, *Russia* 46 C5
Petrograd = Sankt-Peterburg, *Russia* 46 C6
Petrolândia, *Brazil* 125 E11
Petrolia, *Canada* 102 D3
Petrolina, *Brazil* 125 E10
Petropavl, *Kazakstan* 50 D7
Petropavlovsk = Petropavl, *Kazakstan* 50 D7
Petropavlovsk-Kamchatskiy, *Russia* 51 D16
Petropavlovskiy = Akhtubinsk, *Russia* 49 F8
Petrópolis, *Brazil* 127 A7
Petroşani, *Romania* 43 E8
Petrova Gora, *Croatia* 29 C12
Petrovac, *Montenegro, Yug.* 40 D2
Petrovac, *Serbia, Yug.* 40 B5
Petrovaradin, *Serbia, Yug.* 42 E4
Petrovsk, *Russia* 48 D7
Petrovsk-Zabaykalskiy, *Russia* 51 D11
Petrovskaya, *Russia* 47 K9
Petrovskoye = Svetlograd, *Russia* 49 H6
Petrozavodsk, *Russia* 46 B8
Petrus Steyn, *S. Africa* 89 D4
Petrusburg, *S. Africa* 88 D4
Petzeck, *Austria* 26 E5
Peumo, *Chile* 126 C1
Peureulak, *Indonesia* 62 D1
Pevek, *Russia* 51 C18
Peveragno, *Italy* 28 D4
Peyrehorade, *France* 20 E2
Peyruis, *France* 21 D9
Pézenas, *France* 20 E7
Pezinok, *Slovak Rep.* 27 C10
Pfaffenhofen, *Germany* 25 G7
Pfarrkirchen, *Germany* 25 G8
Pfeffenhausen, *Germany* 25 G7
Pforzheim, *Germany* 25 G4
Pfullendorf, *Germany* 25 H5
Pfungstadt, *Germany* 25 F4
Phagwara, *India* 66 D9
Phaistós, *Greece* 36 D6
Phala, *Botswana* 88 C4
Phalera = Phulera, *India* 68 F6
Phalodi, *India* 68 F5
Phalsbourg, *France* 19 D14
Phan, *Thailand* 64 C2
Phan Rang, *Vietnam* 65 G7
Phan Ri = Hoa Da, *Vietnam* 65 G7
Phan Thiêt, *Vietnam* 65 G7
Phanae, *Greece* 39 C7
Phanat Nikhom, *Thailand* 64 F3
Phangan, Ko, *Thailand* 65 H3
Phangnga, *Thailand* 65 H2
Phanh Bho Ho Chi Minh, *Vietnam* 65 G6
Phanom Sarakham, *Thailand* 64 F3
Pharenda, *India* 69 F10
Phatthalung, *Thailand* 65 J3
Phayao, *Thailand* 64 C2
Phelps, *N.Y., U.S.A.* 110 D7
Phelps, *Wis., U.S.A.* 112 B10
Phelps L., *Canada* 105 B8
Phenix City, *U.S.A.* 109 J3
Phet Buri, *Thailand* 64 F2
Phetchabun, *Thailand* 64 D3
Phetchabun, Thiu Khao, *Thailand* 64 E3
Phetchaburi = Phet Buri, *Thailand* 64 F2
Phi Phi, Ko, *Thailand* 65 J2
Phiafay, *Laos* 64 E6
Phibun Mangsahan, *Thailand* 64 E5
Phichai, *Thailand* 64 D3
Phichit, *Thailand* 64 D3
Philadelphia, *Miss., U.S.A.* 113 J10
Philadelphia, *N.Y., U.S.A.* 111 B9
Philadelphia, *Pa., U.S.A.* 111 G9
Philip, *U.S.A.* 112 C4
Philippeville, *Belgium* 17 D4
Philippi, *Greece* 41 E8
Philippi L., *Australia* 94 C2
Philippines ■, *Asia* 61 F5
Philippolis, *S. Africa* 88 E4
Philippopolis = Plovdiv, *Bulgaria* 41 D8
Philipsburg, *Mont., U.S.A.* 114 C7
Philipsburg, *Pa., U.S.A.* 110 F6
Philipstown = Daingean, *Ireland* 15 C4
Philipstown, *S. Africa* 88 E3
Phillip I., *Australia* 95 F4
Phillips, *Tex., U.S.A.* 113 H4
Phillips, *Wis., U.S.A.* 112 C9
Phillipsburg, *Kans., U.S.A.* 112 F5
Phillipsburg, *N.J., U.S.A.* 111 F9
Phillott, *Australia* 95 D4
Philmont, *U.S.A.* 111 D11
Philomath, *U.S.A.* 114 D2
Phimai, *Thailand* 64 E4
Phitsanulok, *Thailand* 64 D3
Phnom Dangrek, *Thailand* 62 B2
Phnom Penh, *Cambodia* 65 G5
Phnum Penh = Phnom Penh, *Cambodia* 65 G5
Phoenix, *Ariz., U.S.A.* 115 K7
Phoenix, *N.Y., U.S.A.* 111 C8
Phoenix Is., *Kiribati* 96 H10
Phoenixville, *U.S.A.* 111 F9
Phon, *Thailand* 64 E4
Phon Tiou, *Laos* 64 D5
Phong →, *Thailand* 64 D4
Phong Saly, *Laos* 64 B4
Phong Tho, *Vietnam* 64 A4
Phonhong, *Laos* 64 C4
Phonum, *Thailand* 65 H2
Phosphate Hill, *Australia* 94 C2
Photharam, *Thailand* 64 F2
Phra Nakhon Si Ayutthaya, *Thailand* 64 E3
Phra Thong, Ko, *Thailand* 65 H2
Phrae, *Thailand* 64 C3
Phrom Phiram, *Thailand* 64 D3
Phrygia, *Turkey* 72 C4
Phu Dien, *Vietnam* 64 C5
Phu Loi, *Laos* 64 B4
Phu Ly, *Vietnam* 64 B5
Phu Quoc, Dao, *Vietnam* 65 G4
Phu Tho, *Vietnam* 64 B5
Phuc Yen, *Vietnam* 64 B5
Phuket, *Thailand* 65 J2
Phuket, Ko, *Thailand* 65 J2
Phulera, *India* 68 F6
Phun Phin, *Thailand* 65 H2
Piacenza, *Italy* 28 C6
Pialba, *Australia* 95 D5
Pian Cr. →, *Australia* 95 E4
Piana, *France* 21 F12
Pianella, *Italy* 29 F11
Pianosa, *Puglia, Italy* 29 F12
Pianosa, *Toscana, Italy* 28 F7
Piapot, *Canada* 105 D7
Pias, *Portugal* 35 G3
Piaseczno, *Poland* 45 F8
Piaski, *Poland* 45 G9
Piastów, *Poland* 45 F7
Piatra, *Romania* 43 G10
Piatra Neamţ, *Romania* 43 D11
Piatra Olt, *Romania* 43 F9
Piauí □, *Brazil* 125 E10
Piaui →, *Brazil* 125 E10
Piave →, *Italy* 29 C9
Piazza Ármerina, *Italy* 31 E7
Pibor →, *Sudan* 81 F3
Pibor Post, *Sudan* 81 F3
Picardie, *France* 19 C10
Picardie, Plaine de, *France* 19 C9
Picardy = Picardie, *France* 19 C10
Picayune, *U.S.A.* 113 K10
Picerno, *Italy* 31 B8
Pichilemu, *Chile* 126 C1
Pickerel L., *Canada* 102 C1
Pickering, *U.K.* 12 C7
Pickering, Vale of, *U.K.* 12 C7
Pickle Lake, *Canada* 102 B1
Pico Truncado, *Argentina* 128 F3
Picos, *Brazil* 125 E10
Picton, *Australia* 95 E5
Picton, *Canada* 102 D4
Picton, *N.Z.* 91 J5
Pictou, *Canada* 103 C7
Picture Butte, *Canada* 104 D6
Picún Leufú, *Argentina* 128 D3
Pidurutalagala, *Sri Lanka* 66 R12
Piechowice, *Poland* 45 H2
Piedmont = Piemonte □, *Italy* 28 D5
Piedmont, *U.S.A.* 109 J3
Piedmont Plateau, *U.S.A.* 109 J5
Piedmonte Matese, *Italy* 31 A7
Piedra →, *Spain* 32 D3
Piedrabuena, *Spain* 35 G6
Piedrahita, *Spain* 34 E5
Piedralaves, *Spain* 34 E6
Piedras Blancas, *Spain* 34 B5
Piedras Negras, *Mexico* 118 B4
Piekary Śląskie, *Poland* 45 H5
Pieksämäki, *Finland* 9 E22
Piemonte □, *Italy* 28 D5

Pieniężno, *Poland* 44 D7
Pieńsk, *Poland* 45 G2
Pierce, *U.S.A.* 114 C6
Piercefield, *U.S.A.* 111 B10
Piería □, *Greece* 40 F6
Pierre, *U.S.A.* 112 C4
Pierre-Buffière, *France* 20 C5
Pierre-de-Bresse, *France* 19 F12
Pierrefontaine-les-Varans, *France* 19 E13
Pierrefort, *France* 20 D6
Pierrelatte, *France* 21 D8
Pieštany, *Slovak Rep.* 27 C10
Piesting →, *Austria* 27 C9
Pieszyce, *Poland* 45 H3
Piet Retief, *S. Africa* 89 D5
Pietarsaari, *Finland* 8 E20
Pietermaritzburg, *S. Africa* 89 D5
Pietersburg, *S. Africa* 89 C4
Pietragalla, *Italy* 31 B8
Pietrasanta, *Italy* 28 E7
Pietroşiţa, *Romania* 43 E10
Pietrosul, Vf., *Maramureş, Romania* 43 C9
Pietrosul, Vf., *Suceava, Romania* 43 C10
Pieve di Cadore, *Italy* 29 B9
Pieve di Teco, *Italy* 28 D4
Pievepélago, *Italy* 28 D7
Pigadhítsa, *Greece* 40 G5
Pigeon, *U.S.A.* 108 D4
Piggott, *U.S.A.* 113 G9
Pigna, *Italy* 28 E4
Pigüe, *Argentina* 126 D3
Pihani, *India* 69 F9
Pihlajavesi, *Finland* 9 F23
Pikalevo, *Russia* 46 C8
Pikes Peak, *U.S.A.* 112 F2
Piketberg, *S. Africa* 88 E2
Pikeville, *U.S.A.* 108 G4
Pikou, *China* 57 E12
Pikwitonei, *Canada* 105 B9
Piła, *Poland* 45 E3
Pila, *Spain* 33 G3
Piła □, *Poland* 45 E3
Pilaía, *Greece* 40 F6
Pilani, *India* 68 E6
Pilar, *Paraguay* 126 B4
Pilar de la Horadada, *Spain* 33 H4
Pilawa, *Poland* 45 G8
Pilaya →, *Bolivia* 124 H6
Pilcomayo →, *Paraguay* 126 B4
Pilcomayo →, *Paraguay* 126 B4
Pilgrimstad, *Sweden* 10 B9
Píli, *Greece* 39 E9
Pilibhit, *India* 69 E8
Pilica →, *Poland* 45 G8
Pilion, *Greece* 38 B5
Pilis, *Hungary* 42 C4
Pilisvörösvár, *Hungary* 42 C3
Pilkhawa, *India* 68 E7
Pílos, *Greece* 38 E3
Pilot Mound, *Canada* 105 D9
Pilot Point, *U.S.A.* 113 J6
Pilot Rock, *U.S.A.* 114 D4
Pilsen = Plzeň, *Czech Rep.* 26 B6
Pilštanj, *Slovenia* 29 B12
Piltene, *Latvia* 44 A8
Pilzno, *Poland* 45 J8
Pima, *U.S.A.* 115 K9
Pimba, *Australia* 95 E2
Pimenta Bueno, *Brazil* 124 F6
Pimentel, *Peru* 124 E3
Pina de Ebro, *Spain* 32 D4
Pinamalayan, *Phil.* 61 E4
Pinang, *Malaysia* 65 K3
Pinar, C. des, *Spain* 37 B10
Pinar del Río, *Cuba* 120 B3
Pınarbaşı, *Çanakkale, Turkey* 39 B8
Pinarbaşi, *Kayseri, Turkey* 72 C7
Pınarhisar, *Turkey* 41 E11
Pincehely, *Hungary* 42 D3
Pinchang, *China* 58 B6
Pincher Creek, *Canada* 104 D6
Pinchi L., *Canada* 104 C4
Pinckneyville, *U.S.A.* 112 F10
Pińczów, *Poland* 45 H7
Pind Dadan Khan, *Pakistan* 68 C5
Pindar, *Australia* 93 E2
Pindi Gheb, *Pakistan* 68 C5
Pindiga, *Nigeria* 83 D7
Pindos Óros, *Greece* 38 B3
Pindus Mts. = Pindos Óros, *Greece* 38 B3
Pine, *U.S.A.* 115 J8
Pine →, *Canada* 105 B7
Pine, C., *Canada* 103 C9
Pine Bluff, *U.S.A.* 113 H9
Pine City, *U.S.A.* 112 C8
Pine Falls, *Canada* 105 C9
Pine Flat L., *U.S.A.* 116 J7
Pine Pass, *Canada* 104 B4
Pine Point, *Canada* 104 A6
Pine Ridge, *U.S.A.* 112 D3
Pine River, *Canada* 105 C8
Pine River, *U.S.A.* 112 B7
Pine Valley, *U.S.A.* 117 N10
Pinecrest, *U.S.A.* 116 G6
Pineda de Mar, *Spain* 32 D7
Pinedale, *U.S.A.* 116 J7
Pinega →, *Russia* 50 C5
Pinehill, *Australia* 94 C4
Pinerolo, *Italy* 28 D4
Pineto, *Italy* 29 F11
Pinetop, *U.S.A.* 115 J9
Pinetown, *S. Africa* 89 D5
Pinetree, *U.S.A.* 114 E11
Pineville, *Ky., U.S.A.* 109 G4
Pineville, *La., U.S.A.* 113 K8
Piney, *France* 19 D11
Ping →, *Thailand* 64 E3
Pingaring, *Australia* 93 F2
Pingba, *China* 58 D6
Pingchuan, *China* 58 D3
Pingding, *China* 56 F7
Pingdingshan, *China* 56 H7
Pingdong, *Taiwan* 59 F13
Pingdu, *China* 57 F10
Pingelly, *Australia* 93 F2
Pingguo, *China* 58 F6
Pinghe, *China* 59 E11
Pinghu, *China* 59 B13
Pingjiang, *China* 59 C9
Pingle, *China* 59 E8
Pingli, *China* 58 A7
Pingliang, *China* 56 G4
Pinglu, *China* 56 E7
Pingluo, *China* 56 E4
Pingnan, *Fujian, China* 59 D12
Pingnan, *Guangxi Zhuangzu, China* 59 F8
Pingquan, *China* 57 D10
Pingrup, *Australia* 93 F2
Pingtan, *China* 59 E12
Pingtang, *China* 58 E6
P'ingtung, *Taiwan* 59 F13
Pingwu, *China* 56 H3
Pingxiang, *Guangxi Zhuangzu, China* 58 F6
Pingxiang, *Jiangxi, China* 59 D9
Pingyao, *China* 56 F7
Pingyi, *China* 57 G9
Pingyin, *China* 56 F9
Pingyuan, *Guangdong, China* 59 E10
Pingyuan, *Shandong, China* 56 F9
Pingyuanjie, *China* 58 F4
Pinhal, *Brazil* 127 A6
Pinhal Novo, *Portugal* 35 G2
Pinheiro, *Brazil* 125 D9
Pinhel, *Portugal* 34 E3
Pini, *Indonesia* 62 D1
Piniós →, *Ilía, Greece* 38 D3
Piniós →, *Tríkkala, Greece* 38 B4
Pinjarra, *Australia* 93 F2
Pink →, *Canada* 105 B8
Pinkafeld, *Austria* 27 D9
Pinnacles, *Australia* 93 E3
Pinnacles, *U.S.A.* 116 J5
Pinnaroo, *Australia* 95 F3
Pinneberg, *Germany* 24 B5
Pínnes, Ákra, *Greece* 41 F8
Pinon Hills, *U.S.A.* 117 L9
Pinos, *Mexico* 118 C4
Pinos, Mt., *U.S.A.* 117 L7
Pinos Pt., *U.S.A.* 115 H3
Pinos Puente, *Spain* 35 H7
Pinotepa Nacional, *Mexico* 119 D5
Pinrang, *Indonesia* 63 E5
Pinsk, *Belarus* 47 F4
Pintados, *Chile* 124 H5
Pintumba, *Australia* 93 F5
Pinyang, *China* 59 D13
Pinyug, *Russia* 50 C5
Pioche, *U.S.A.* 115 H6
Piombino, *Italy* 28 F7
Piombino, Canale di, *Italy* 28 F7
Pioner, Ostrov, *Russia* 51 B10
Pionki, *Poland* 45 G8
Piorini, L., *Brazil* 124 D6
Piotrków Trybunalski, *Poland* 45 G6
Piotrków Trybunalski □, *Poland* 45 G6
Piove di Sacco, *Italy* 29 C9
Pīp, *Iran* 71 E9
Pipar, *India* 68 F5
Piparia, *India* 68 H8
Pipéri, *Greece* 38 B6
Pipestone, *U.S.A.* 112 D6
Pipestone →, *Canada* 102 B2
Pipestone Cr. →, *Canada* 105 D8
Pipmuacan, Rés., *Canada* 103 C5
Pippingarra, *Australia* 92 D2
Pipriac, *France* 18 E5
Piqua, *U.S.A.* 108 E3
Piquiri →, *Brazil* 127 A5
Pīr Sohrāb, *Iran* 71 E9
Piracicaba, *Brazil* 127 A6
Piracuruca, *Brazil* 125 D10
Piræus = Piraiévs, *Greece* 38 D5
Piraiévs, *Greece* 38 D5
Pirajuí, *Brazil* 127 A6
Piran, *Slovenia* 29 C10
Pirané, *Argentina* 126 B4
Pirano = Piran, *Slovenia* 29 C10
Pirapora, *Brazil* 125 G10
Pirdop, *Bulgaria* 41 D8
Pírgos, *Ilía, Greece* 38 D3
Pírgos, *Kríti, Greece* 39 F7
Pirgovo, *Bulgaria* 41 C9
Piribebuy, *Paraguay* 126 B4
Pirin Planina, *Bulgaria* 40 E7
Píríneos = Pyrénées, *Europe* 20 F4
Piripiri, *Brazil* 125 D10
Pirmasens, *Germany* 25 F3
Pirna, *Germany* 24 E9
Pirot, *Serbia, Yug.* 40 C6
Piru, *Indonesia* 63 E7
Piru, *U.S.A.* 117 L8
Piryatin = Pyryatyn, *Ukraine* 47 G7
Piryí, *Greece* 39 C7
Pisa, *Italy* 28 E7
Pisa →, *Poland* 45 E8
Pisagne, *Italy* 28 C7
Pisagua, *Chile* 124 G4
Pisarovina, *Croatia* 29 C12
Pisco, *Peru* 124 F3
Piscu, *Romania* 43 E12
Písek, *Czech Rep.* 26 B7
Pishan, *China* 60 C2
Pishin Lora →, *Pakistan* 68 E1
Pisidia, *Turkey* 72 D4
Pising, *Indonesia* 63 F6
Pismo Beach, *U.S.A.* 117 K6
Pissis, Cerro, *Argentina* 126 B2
Pissos, *France* 20 D3
Pissouri, *Cyprus* 36 E11
Pisticci, *Italy* 31 B9
Pistóia, *Italy* 28 E7
Pistol B., *Canada* 105 A10
Pisuerga →, *Spain* 34 D6
Pisz, *Poland* 44 E8
Pitarpunga, L., *Australia* 95 E3
Pitcairn I., *Pac. Oc.* 97 K14
Pite älv →, *Sweden* 8 D19
Piteå, *Sweden* 8 D19
Piterka, *Russia* 48 E8
Piteşti, *Romania* 43 F9
Pithapuram, *India* 67 L13
Pithara, *Australia* 93 F2
Píthion, *Greece* 41 E10
Pithiviers, *France* 19 D9
Pitigliano, *Italy* 29 F8
Pitkyaranta, *Russia* 46 B6
Pitlochry, *U.K.* 14 E5
Pitsilia □, *Cyprus* 36 E12
Pitt I., *Canada* 104 C3
Pittsburg, *Kans., U.S.A.* 113 G7
Pittsburg, *Tex., U.S.A.* 113 J7
Pittsburgh, *U.S.A.* 110 F5
Pittsfield, *Ill., U.S.A.* 112 F9
Pittsfield, *Maine, U.S.A.* 111 D11
Pittsfield, *N.H., U.S.A.* 111 C13
Pittston, *U.S.A.* 111 E9
Pittsworth, *Australia* 95 D5
Pituri →, *Australia* 94 C2
Piura, *Peru* 124 E2
Piva →, *Montenegro, Yug.* 40 C2
Piwniczna, *Poland* 45 J7
Pixley, *U.S.A.* 116 K7
Piyai, *Greece* 38 B3
Pizarra, *Spain* 35 J6
Pizzo, *Italy* 31 D9
Placentia, *Canada* 103 C9
Placentia B., *Canada* 103 C9
Placer, *Phil.* 61 F5
Placerville, *U.S.A.* 116 G6
Placetas, *Cuba* 120 B4
Plačkovica, *Macedonia* 40 E6
Plain Dealing, *U.S.A.* 113 J8
Plainfield, *U.S.A.* 111 F10
Plains, *Kans., U.S.A.* 113 G4
Plains, *Mont., U.S.A.* 114 C6
Plains, *Tex., U.S.A.* 113 J3
Plainview, *Nebr., U.S.A.* 112 D6
Plainview, *Tex., U.S.A.* 113 H4
Plainville, *U.S.A.* 112 F5
Plainwell, *U.S.A.* 108 D3
Plaisance, *France* 20 E4
Pláka, *Greece* 39 B7
Pláka, Ákra, *Greece* 36 D8
Plakenska Planina, *Macedonia* 40 E5
Planá, *Czech Rep.* 26 B5
Plana Cays, *Bahamas* 121 B5
Planada, *U.S.A.* 116 H6
Plancoët, *France* 18 D4
Plandište, *Serbia, Yug.* 42 E6
Plankinton, *U.S.A.* 112 D5
Plano, *U.S.A.* 113 J6
Plant City, *U.S.A.* 109 M4
Plaquemine, *U.S.A.* 113 K9
Plasencia, *Spain* 34 E4
Plaški, *Croatia* 29 C12
Plaster City, *U.S.A.* 117 N11
Plaster Rock, *Canada* 103 C6
Plastun, *Russia* 54 B8
Plasy, *Czech Rep.* 26 B6
Plata, Río de la, *S. Amer.* 126 C4
Plátani →, *Italy* 30 E6
Plátanos, *Greece* 36 D5
Plateau □, *Nigeria* 83 D6
Plateau du Coteau du Missouri, *U.S.A.* 112 B4
Platí, Ákra, *Greece* 41 F8
Platte, *U.S.A.* 112 D5
Platte →, *Mo., U.S.A.* 112 F7
Platte →, *Nebr., U.S.A.* 98 E10
Platteville, *U.S.A.* 112 E2
Plattling, *Germany* 25 G8
Plattsburgh, *U.S.A.* 111 B11
Plattsmouth, *U.S.A.* 112 E7
Plau, *Germany* 24 B8
Plauen, *Germany* 24 E8
Plauer See, *Germany* 24 B8
Plav, *Montenegro, Yug.* 40 D3
Plavinas, *Latvia* 9 H21
Plavnica, *Montenegro, Yug.* 40 D3
Plavno, *Croatia* 29 D13
Plavsk, *Russia* 46 F9
Playa Blanca, *Canary Is.* 37 F6
Playa Blanca Sur, *Canary Is.* 37 F6
Playa de las Americas, *Canary Is.* 37 F3
Playa de Mogán, *Canary Is.* 37 G4
Playa del Inglés, *Canary Is.* 37 G4
Playa Esmerelda, *Canary Is.* 37 F5
Playgreen L., *Canada* 105 C9
Pleasant Bay, *Canada* 103 C7
Pleasant Hill, *Calif., U.S.A.* 116 H4
Pleasant Hill, *Mo., U.S.A.* 112 F7
Pleasanton, *U.S.A.* 113 L5
Pleasantville, *U.S.A.* 108 F8
Pléaux, *France* 20 C6
Plei Ku, *Vietnam* 64 F7
Plélan-le-Grand, *France* 18 D4
Pléneuf-Val-André, *France* 18 D4
Pleniţa, *Romania* 43 F8
Plenty →, *Australia* 94 C2
Plenty, B. of, *N.Z.* 91 G6
Plentywood, *U.S.A.* 112 A2
Plérin, *France* 18 D4
Plessisville, *Canada* 103 C5
Plestin-les-Grèves, *France* 18 D3
Pleszew, *Poland* 45 G4
Pleternica, *Croatia* 42 E2
Pletipi L., *Canada* 103 B5
Pleven, *Bulgaria* 41 C8
Plevlja, *Montenegro, Yug.* 40 C3
Pljesevica, *Croatia* 29 D12
Ploaghe, *Italy* 30 B1
Plo'ana, *Slovak Rep.* 27 C12
Ploče, *Croatia* 29 E14
Płock, *Poland* 45 F6
Płock □, *Poland* 45 F6
Plöckenpass, *Italy* 29 B9
Plöckenstein, *Germany* 25 G9
Ploemeur, *France* 18 E3
Ploërmel, *France* 18 E4
Ploieşti, *Romania* 43 F11
Plomárion, *Greece* 39 C8
Plombières-les-Bains, *France* 19 E13
Plomin, *Croatia* 29 C11
Plön, *Germany* 24 A6
Plonge, Lac la, *Canada* 105 B7
Płońsk, *Poland* 45 F7
Plopeni, *Romania* 43 E10
Plopişului, Munţii, *Romania* 42 C7
Płoty, *Poland* 44 E2
Plouaret, *France* 18 D3
Plouay, *France* 18 E3
Ploučnice →, *Czech Rep.* 26 A7
Ploudalmézeau, *France* 18 D2
Plouescat, *France* 18 D2
Plougasnou, *France* 18 D3
Plougastel-Daoulas, *France* 18 D2
Plouguerneau, *France* 18 D2
Plouha, *France* 18 D4
Plouhinec, *France* 18 E2
Plovdiv, *Bulgaria* 41 D8
Plovdiv □, *Bulgaria* 41 D8
Plum, *U.S.A.* 110 F5
Plum I., *U.S.A.* 111 E12
Plumas, *U.S.A.* 116 F7
Plummer, *U.S.A.* 114 C5
Plumtree, *Zimbabwe* 87 G2
Plungė, *Lithuania* 9 J19
Pluvigner, *France* 18 E3
Plymouth, *U.K.* 13 G3
Plymouth, *Calif., U.S.A.* 116 G6
Plymouth, *Ind., U.S.A.* 108 E2
Plymouth, *Mass., U.S.A.* 111 E14
Plymouth, *N.C., U.S.A.* 109 H7
Plymouth, *N.H., U.S.A.* 111 C13
Plymouth, *Pa., U.S.A.* 111 E9
Plymouth, *Wis., U.S.A.* 108 D2
Plynlimon = Pumlumon Fawr, *U.K.* 13 E4
Plyusa, *Russia* 46 C5
Plyusa →, *Russia* 46 C5
Plyussa = Plyusa, *Russia* 46 C5
Plyussa → = Plyusa →, *Russia* 46 C5
Plzeň, *Czech Rep.* 26 B6
Pniewy, *Poland* 45 F3
Pô, *Burkina Faso* 83 C4
Po →, *Italy* 29 D9
Po, Foci del, *Italy* 29 D9
Po Hai = Bo Hai, *China* 57 E10
Pobé, *Benin* 83 D5
Pobeda, *Russia* 51 C15
Pobedy, Pik, *Kyrgyzstan* 50 E8
Pobiedziska, *Poland* 45 F4
Pobla de Segur, *Spain* 32 C5
Pobladura del Valle, *Spain* 34 C5
Pobra de Trives, *Spain* 34 C3
Pocahontas, *Ark., U.S.A.* 113 G9
Pocahontas, *Iowa, U.S.A.* 112 D7
Pocatello, *U.S.A.* 114 E7
Počátky, *Czech Rep.* 26 B8
Pochep, *Russia* 47 F7
Pochinki, *Russia* 48 C7
Pochinok, *Russia* 46 E7
Pöchlarn, *Austria* 26 C8
Pochutla, *Mexico* 119 D5
Pocito Casas, *Mexico* 118 B2
Pocking, *Germany* 25 G9
Pocomoke City, *U.S.A.* 108 F8
Poços de Caldas, *Brazil* 127 A6
Podbořany, *Czech Rep.* 26 A6
Poddębice, *Poland* 45 G5
Poděbrady, *Czech Rep.* 26 A8
Podensac, *France* 20 D3
Podenzano, *Italy* 28 D6
Podgorač, *Croatia* 42 E3
Podgorica, *Montenegro, Yug.* 40 D3
Podgorie, *Albania* 40 F4
Podilska Vysochyna, *Ukraine* 47 H4
Podkova, *Bulgaria* 41 E9
Podlapača, *Croatia* 29 D12
Podoleni, *Romania* 43 D11
Podolínec, *Slovak Rep.* 27 B13
Podolsk, *Russia* 46 E9
Podor, *Senegal* 82 B1
Podporozhy, *Russia* 46 B8
Podu Iloaiei, *Romania* 43 C12
Podu Turcului, *Romania* 43 D12
Podujevo, *Serbia, Yug.* 40 D5
Poel, *Germany* 24 B6
Pofadder, *S. Africa* 88 D2
Pogamasing, *Canada* 102 C3
Poggiardo, *Italy* 31 B11
Poggibonsi, *Italy* 28 E8
Póggio Mirteto, *Italy* 29 F9
Pogoanele, *Romania* 43 F12
Pogorzela, *Poland* 45 G4
Pogradeci, *Albania* 40 F4
Pogranitšnyi, *Russia* 54 B5
Poh, *Indonesia* 63 E6
Pohang, *S. Korea* 57 F15
Pohjanmaa, *Finland* 8 E20
Pohnpei, *Pac. Oc.* 96 G7
Pohorelá, *Slovak Rep.* 27 C13
Pohořelice, *Czech Rep.* 27 C9
Pohorje, *Slovenia* 29 B12
Poiana Mare, *Romania* 42 G8
Poiana Ruscăi, Munţii, *Romania* 42 E7
Poiana Stampei, *Romania* 43 C10
Poinsett, C., *Antarctica* 5 C8
Point Edward, *Canada* 102 D3
Point Pedro, *Sri Lanka* 66 Q12
Point Pleasant, *N.J., U.S.A.* 111 F10
Point Pleasant, *W. Va., U.S.A.* 108 F4
Pointe-à-la Hache, *U.S.A.* 113 L10
Pointe-à-Pitre, *Guadeloupe* 121 C7
Pointe-Noire, *Congo* 84 E2
Poio, *Spain* 34 C2
Poirino, *Italy* 28 D4
Poisonbush Ra., *Australia* 92 D3
Poitiers, *France* 18 F7
Poitou, *France* 20 B3
Poitou-Charentes □, *France* 20 B4
Poix-de-Picardie, *France* 19 C8
Poix-Terron, *France* 19 C11
Pojoaque Valley, *U.S.A.* 115 J11
Pokaran, *India* 66 F7
Pokataroo, *Australia* 95 D4
Pokhara, *Nepal* 69 E10
Pokhvistnevo, *Russia* 48 D11
Poko, *Dem. Rep. of the Congo* 86 B2
Poko, *Sudan* 81 F3
Pokrov, *Russia* 46 E10
Pokrovsk = Engels, *Russia* 48 E8
Pokrovsk, *Russia* 51 C13
Pokrovskoye, *Russia* 47 J10
Pola = Pula, *Croatia* 29 D10
Pola, *Russia* 46 D7
Pola de Allande, *Spain* 34 B4
Pola de Lena, *Spain* 34 B5
Pola de Siero, *Spain* 34 B5
Pola de Somiedo, *Spain* 34 B4
Polacca, *U.S.A.* 115 J8
Polan, *Iran* 71 E9
Poland ■, *Europe* 45 G3
Polanica-Zdrój, *Poland* 45 H3
Połaniec, *Poland* 45 H8
Polanów, *Poland* 44 D3
Polatlı, *Turkey* 72 C5
Polatsk, *Belarus* 46 E5
Polcura, *Chile* 126 D1
Połczyn-Zdrój, *Poland* 44 E3
Polessk, *Russia* 9 J19
Polesye = Pripet Marshes, *Europe* 47 F5
Polgar, *Hungary* 42 C6
Pŏlgyo-ri, *S. Korea* 57 G14
Políaigos, *Greece* 38 E6
Policastro, G. di, *Italy* 31 C8
Police, *Poland* 44 E1
Polička, *Czech Rep.* 27 B9
Policoro, *Italy* 31 B9
Polignano a Mare, *Italy* 31 A9
Poligny, *France* 19 F12
Políkhnitas, *Greece* 39 B8
Polillo Is., *Phil.* 61 D5
Polillo Strait, *Phil.* 61 D4
Polis, *Cyprus* 36 D11
Polístena, *Italy* 31 D9
Políyiros, *Greece* 40 F7
Polk, *U.S.A.* 110 E5
Polkowice, *Poland* 45 G3
Polla, *Italy* 31 B8
Pollachi, *India* 66 P10
Pollença, *Spain* 37 B10
Pollença, B. de, *Spain* 37 B10
Póllica, *Italy* 31 B8
Pollino, Mte., *Italy* 31 C9
Pollock, *U.S.A.* 112 C4
Polna, *Russia* 46 C5
Polnovat, *Russia* 50 C7
Polo, *U.S.A.* 112 E10
Pology, *Ukraine* 47 J9
Polonne, *Ukraine* 47 G4
Polonnoye = Polonne, *Ukraine* 47 G4
Polski Trŭmbesh, *Bulgaria* 41 C9
Polsko Kosovo, *Bulgaria* 41 C9
Polson, *U.S.A.* 114 C6

Poltár, *Slovak Rep.* 27 C12
Poltava, *Ukraine* 47 H8
Põltsamaa, *Estonia* 9 G21
Polunochnoye, *Russia* 50 C7
Põlva, *Estonia* 9 G22
Polynesia, *Pac. Oc.* 97 J11
Polynésie française = French Polynesia ■, *Pac. Oc.* 97 K13
Pomarance, *Italy* 28 E7
Pomaro, *Mexico* 118 D4
Pombal, *Portugal* 34 F2
Pómbia, *Greece* 36 E6
Pomeroy, *Ohio, U.S.A.* 108 F4
Pomeroy, *Wash., U.S.A.* 114 C5
Pomézia, *Italy* 30 A5
Pomichna, *Ukraine* 47 H6
Pomona, *U.S.A.* 117 L9
Pomorie, *Bulgaria* 41 D11
Pomorskie, Pojezierze, *Poland* 44 E3
Pomos, *Cyprus* 36 D11
Pomos, C., *Cyprus* 36 D11
Pompano Beach, *U.S.A.* 109 M5
Pompei, *Italy* 31 B7
Pompey, *France* 19 D13
Pompeys Pillar, *U.S.A.* 114 D10
Ponape = Pohnpei, *Pac. Oc.* 96 G7
Ponask, L., *Canada* 102 B1
Ponass L., *Canada* 105 C8
Ponca, *U.S.A.* 112 D6
Ponca City, *U.S.A.* 113 G6
Ponce, *Puerto Rico* 121 C6
Ponchatoula, *U.S.A.* 113 K9
Poncheville, L., *Canada* 102 B4
Pond, *U.S.A.* 117 K7
Pond Inlet, *Canada* 101 A12
Pondicherry, *India* 66 P11
Ponds, I. of, *Canada* 103 B8
Ponferrada, *Spain* 34 C4
Pongo, Wadi →, *Sudan* 81 F2
Poniatowa, *Poland* 45 G9
Poniec, *Poland* 45 G3
Ponikva, *Slovenia* 29 B12
Ponnani, *India* 66 P9
Ponnyadaung, *Burma* 67 J19
Ponoka, *Canada* 104 C6
Ponorogo, *Indonesia* 63 G14
Pons = Ponts, *Spain* 32 D6
Pons, *France* 20 C3
Ponsul →, *Portugal* 34 F3
Pont-à-Mousson, *France* 19 D13
Pont-Audemer, *France* 18 C7
Pont-Aven, *France* 18 E3
Pont Canavese, *Italy* 28 C4
Pont-d'Ain, *France* 19 F12
Pont-de-Roide, *France* 19 E13
Pont-de-Salars, *France* 20 D6
Pont-de-Vaux, *France* 19 F11
Pont-de-Veyle, *France* 19 F11
Pont-du-Château, *France* 19 G10
Pont-l'Abbé, *France* 18 E2
Pont-l'Évêque, *France* 18 C7
Pont-St-Esprit, *France* 21 D8
Pont-St-Martin, *Italy* 28 C4
Pont-Ste-Maxence, *France* 19 C9
Pont-sur-Yonne, *France* 19 D10
Ponta do Sol, *Madeira* 37 D2
Ponta Grossa, *Brazil* 127 B5
Ponta Pora, *Brazil* 127 A4
Pontacq, *France* 20 E3
Pontailler-sur-Saône, *France* 19 E12
Pontarlier, *France* 19 F13
Pontassieve, *Italy* 29 E8
Pontaumur, *France* 20 C6
Pontcharra, *France* 21 C10
Pontchartrain L., *U.S.A.* 113 K10
Pontchâteau, *France* 18 E4
Ponte da Barca, *Portugal* 34 D2
Ponte de Sor, *Portugal* 35 F2
Ponte dell'Ólio, *Italy* 28 D6
Ponte di Legno, *Italy* 28 B7
Ponte do Lima, *Portugal* 34 D2
Ponte do Pungué, *Mozam.* 87 F3
Ponte-Leccia, *France* 21 F13
Ponte nelle Alpi, *Italy* 29 B9
Ponte Nova, *Brazil* 127 A7
Ponteareas, *Spain* 34 C2
Pontebba, *Italy* 29 B10
Ponteceso, *Spain* 34 B2
Pontecorvo, *Italy* 30 A6
Pontedeume, *Spain* 34 B2
Ponteix, *Canada* 105 D7
Pontevedra, *Spain* 34 C2
Pontevedra □, *Spain* 34 C2
Pontevedra, R. de →, *Spain* 34 C2
Pontevico, *Italy* 28 C7
Pontiac, *Ill., U.S.A.* 112 E10
Pontiac, *Mich., U.S.A.* 108 D4
Pontian Kecil, *Malaysia* 65 M4
Pontianak, *Indonesia* 62 E3
Pontine Is. = Ponziane, Ísole, *Italy* 30 B5
Pontine Mts. = Kuzey Anadolu Dağları, *Turkey* 72 B7
Pontínia, *Italy* 30 A6
Pontivy, *France* 18 D4
Pontoise, *France* 19 C9
Ponton →, *Canada* 104 B5
Pontorson, *France* 18 D5
Pontrémoli, *Italy* 28 D6
Pontrieux, *France* 18 D3
Ponts, *Spain* 32 D6
Pontypool, *Canada* 110 B6
Pontypool, *U.K.* 13 F4
Ponza, *Italy* 30 B5
Ponziane, Ísole, *Italy* 30 B5
Poochera, *Australia* 95 E1
Poole, *U.K.* 13 G6
Poole □, *U.K.* 13 G6
Pooley I., *Canada* 104 C3
Poona = Pune, *India* 66 K8
Pooncarie, *Australia* 95 E3
Poopelloe L., *Australia* 95 E3
Poopó, L. de, *Bolivia* 122 E4
Popanyinning, *Australia* 93 F2
Popayán, *Colombia* 124 C3
Poperinge, *Belgium* 17 D2
Popilta, L., *Australia* 95 E3
Popina, *Bulgaria* 41 B10
Popio L., *Australia* 95 E3
Poplar, *U.S.A.* 112 A2
Poplar →, *Man., Canada* 105 C9
Poplar →, *N.W.T., Canada* 104 A4
Poplar Bluff, *U.S.A.* 113 G9
Poplarville, *U.S.A.* 113 K10
Popocatépetl, Volcán, *Mexico* 119 D5
Popokabaka, *Dem. Rep. of the Congo* 84 F3
Pópoli, *Italy* 29 F10
Popovača, *Croatia* 29 C13
Popovo, *Bulgaria* 41 C10
Poppberg, *Germany* 25 F7
Poppi, *Italy* 29 E8
Poprad, *Slovak Rep.* 27 B13
Poprad →, *Slovak Rep.* 27 B13
Porali →, *Pakistan* 68 G2
Porbandar, *India* 68 J3
Porcher I., *Canada* 104 C2
Porcuna, *Spain* 35 H6
Porcupine →, *Canada* 105 B8
Porcupine →, *U.S.A.* 100 B5
Pordenone, *Italy* 29 C9
Pordim, *Bulgaria* 41 C8
Poreč, *Croatia* 29 C10
Poretskoye, *Russia* 48 C8
Pori, *Finland* 9 F19
Porí, *Greece* 38 F5
Porkhov, *Russia* 46 D5
Porlamar, *Venezuela* 124 A6
Porlezza, *Italy* 28 B6
Porma →, *Spain* 34 C5
Pornic, *France* 18 E4
Poronaysk, *Russia* 51 E15
Póros, *Greece* 38 D5
Poroshiri-Dake, *Japan* 54 C11
Poroszló, *Hungary* 42 C5
Poroto Mts., *Tanzania* 87 D3
Porpoise B., *Antarctica* 5 C9
Porquerolles, Î. de, *France* 21 F10
Porrentruy, *Switz.* 25 H3
Porreres, *Spain* 37 B10
Porsangen, *Norway* 8 A21
Porsgrunn, *Norway* 9 G13
Port Adelaide, *Australia* 95 E2
Port Alberni, *Canada* 104 D4
Port Alfred, *Canada* 103 C5
Port Alfred, *S. Africa* 88 E4
Port Alice, *Canada* 104 C3
Port Allegany, *U.S.A.* 110 E6
Port Allen, *U.S.A.* 113 K9
Port Alma, *Australia* 94 C5
Port Angeles, *U.S.A.* 116 B3
Port Antonio, *Jamaica* 120 C4
Port Aransas, *U.S.A.* 113 M6
Port Arthur = Lüshun, *China* 57 E11
Port Arthur, *Australia* 94 G4
Port Arthur, *U.S.A.* 113 L8
Port au Port B., *Canada* 103 C8
Port-au-Prince, *Haiti* 121 C5
Port Augusta, *Australia* 95 E2
Port Augusta West, *Australia* 95 E2
Port Austin, *U.S.A.* 102 D3
Port Bell, *Uganda* 86 B3
Port Bergé Vaovao, *Madag.* 89 B8
Port Blandford, *Canada* 103 C9
Port Bouët, *Ivory C.* 82 D4
Port Bradshaw, *Australia* 94 A2
Port Broughton, *Australia* 95 E2
Port Burwell, *Canada* 102 D3
Port Canning, *India* 69 H13
Port-Cartier, *Canada* 103 B6
Port Chalmers, *N.Z.* 91 L3
Port Chester, *U.S.A.* 111 F11
Port Clements, *Canada* 104 C2
Port Clinton, *U.S.A.* 108 E4
Port Colborne, *Canada* 102 D4
Port Coquitlam, *Canada* 104 D4
Port Credit, *Canada* 110 C5
Port Curtis, *Australia* 94 C5
Port d'Alcúdia, *Spain* 37 B10
Port Dalhousie, *Canada* 110 C5
Port Darwin, *Australia* 92 B5
Port Darwin, *Falk. Is.* 128 G5
Port Davey, *Australia* 94 G4
Port-de-Bouc, *France* 21 E8
Port-de-Paix, *Haiti* 121 C5
Port de Pollença, *Spain* 37 B10
Port de Sóller, *Spain* 37 B9
Port Dickson, *Malaysia* 65 L3
Port Douglas, *Australia* 94 B4
Port Dover, *Canada* 110 D4
Port Edward, *Canada* 104 C2
Port Elgin, *Canada* 102 D3
Port Elizabeth, *S. Africa* 88 E4
Port Ellen, *U.K.* 14 F2
Port-en-Bessin, *France* 18 C6
Port Erin, *U.K.* 12 C3
Port Essington, *Australia* 92 B5
Port Etienne = Nouâdhibou, *Mauritania* 78 D2
Port Fairy, *Australia* 95 F3
Port Fouâd = Bûr Fuad, *Egypt* 80 H8
Port Gamble, *U.S.A.* 116 C4
Port-Gentil, *Gabon* 84 E1
Port Gibson, *U.S.A.* 113 K9
Port Glasgow, *U.K.* 14 F4
Port Harcourt, *Nigeria* 83 E6
Port Hardy, *Canada* 104 C3
Port Harrison = Inukjuak, *Canada* 101 C12
Port Hawkesbury, *Canada* 103 C7
Port Hedland, *Australia* 92 D2
Port Henry, *U.S.A.* 111 B11
Port Hood, *Canada* 103 C7
Port Hope, *Canada* 102 D4
Port Hueneme, *U.S.A.* 117 L7
Port Huron, *U.S.A.* 108 D4
Port Iliç, *Azerbaijan* 73 C13
Port Isabel, *U.S.A.* 113 M6
Port Jefferson, *U.S.A.* 111 F11
Port Jervis, *U.S.A.* 111 E10
Port-Joinville, *France* 18 F4
Port Katon, *Russia* 47 J10
Port Kelang = Pelabuhan Kelang, *Malaysia* 65 L3
Port Kembla, *Australia* 95 E5
Port Kenny, *Australia* 95 E1
Port-la-Nouvelle, *France* 20 E7
Port Lairge = Waterford, *Ireland* 15 D4
Port Laoise, *Ireland* 15 C4
Port Lavaca, *U.S.A.* 113 L6
Port Lincoln, *Australia* 95 E2
Port Loko, *S. Leone* 82 D2
Port Louis, *France* 18 E3
Port Lyautey = Kenitra, *Morocco* 78 B4
Port MacDonnell, *Australia* 95 F3
Port Macquarie, *Australia* 95 E5
Port Maria, *Jamaica* 120 C4
Port Mellon, *Canada* 104 D4
Port-Menier, *Canada* 103 C7
Port Morant, *Jamaica* 120 C4
Port Moresby, *Papua N. G.* 96 H6
Port Mouton, *Canada* 103 D7
Port Musgrave, *Australia* 94 A3
Port-Navalo, *France* 18 E4
Port Nelson, *Canada* 105 B10
Port Nolloth, *S. Africa* 88 D2
Port Nouveau-Québec = Kangiqsualujjuaq, *Canada* 101 C13
Port O'Connor, *U.S.A.* 113 L6
Port of Spain, *Trin. & Tob.* 121 D7
Port Orchard, *U.S.A.* 116 C4
Port Orford, *U.S.A.* 114 E1
Port Pegasus, *N.Z.* 91 M1
Port Perry, *Canada* 102 D4
Port Phillip B., *Australia* 95 F3
Port Pirie, *Australia* 95 E2
Port Radium = Echo Bay, *Canada* 100 B8
Port Renfrew, *Canada* 104 D4
Port Roper, *Australia* 94 A2
Port Rowan, *Canada* 102 D3
Port Safaga = Bûr Safâga, *Egypt* 80 B3
Port Said = Bûr Sa'îd, *Egypt* 80 H8
Port St. Joe, *U.S.A.* 109 L3
Port St. Johns, *S. Africa* 89 E4
Port-St-Louis-du-Rhône, *France* 21 E8
Port-Ste-Marie, *France* 20 D4
Port Sanilac, *U.S.A.* 102 D3
Port Saunders, *Canada* 103 B8
Port Severn, *Canada* 110 B5
Port Shepstone, *S. Africa* 89 E5
Port Simpson, *Canada* 104 C2
Port Stanley = Stanley, *Falk. Is.* 128 G5
Port Stanley, *Canada* 102 D3
Port Sudan = Bûr Sûdân, *Sudan* 80 D4
Port-sur-Saône, *France* 19 E13
Port Talbot, *U.K.* 13 F4
Port Taufiq = Bûr Taufiq, *Egypt* 80 J8
Port Townsend, *U.S.A.* 116 B4
Port-Vendres, *France* 20 F7
Port Wakefield, *Australia* 95 E2
Port Washington, *U.S.A.* 108 D2
Port Weld = Kuala Sepetang, *Malaysia* 65 K3
Portadown, *U.K.* 15 B5
Portaferry, *U.K.* 15 B6
Portage, *U.S.A.* 112 D10
Portage La Prairie, *Canada* 105 D9
Portageville, *U.S.A.* 113 G10
Portalegre, *Portugal* 35 F3
Portalegre □, *Portugal* 35 F3
Portales, *U.S.A.* 113 H3
Portarlington, *Ireland* 15 C4
Portbou, *Spain* 32 C8
Portel, *Portugal* 35 G3
Porter L., *N.W.T., Canada* 105 A7
Porter L., *Sask., Canada* 105 B7
Porterville, *S. Africa* 88 E2
Porterville, *U.S.A.* 116 J8
Portes-lès-Valence, *France* 21 D8
Porthcawl, *U.K.* 13 F4
Porthill, *U.S.A.* 114 B5
Porthmadog, *U.K.* 12 E3
Portile de Fier, *Europe* 42 F7
Portimão, *Portugal* 35 H2
Portishead, *U.K.* 13 F5
Portiţei, Gura, *Romania* 43 F14
Portknockie, *U.K.* 14 D6
Portland, *N.S.W., Australia* 95 E5
Portland, *Vic., Australia* 95 F3
Portland, *Canada* 111 B8
Portland, *Conn., U.S.A.* 111 E12
Portland, *Maine, U.S.A.* 103 D5
Portland, *Mich., U.S.A.* 108 D3
Portland, *Oreg., U.S.A.* 116 E4
Portland, I. of, *U.K.* 13 G5
Portland B., *Australia* 95 F3
Portland Bill, *U.K.* 13 G5
Portlands Roads, *Australia* 94 A3
Portmadoc = Porthmadog, *U.K.* 12 E3
Portneuf, *Canada* 103 C5
Porto, *France* 21 F12
Porto, *Portugal* 34 D2
Porto □, *Portugal* 34 D2
Porto, G. de, *France* 21 F12
Pôrto Alegre, *Brazil* 127 C5
Porto Amboim = Gunza, *Angola* 84 G2
Porto Azzurro, *Italy* 28 F7
Porto Cristo, *Spain* 37 B10
Pôrto de Móz, *Brazil* 125 D8
Porto Empédocle, *Italy* 30 E6
Pôrto Esperança, *Brazil* 124 G7
Pôrto Franco, *Brazil* 125 E9
Pórto Lágos, *Greece* 41 E9
Porto Mendes, *Brazil* 127 A5
Porto Moniz, *Madeira* 37 D2
Pôrto Murtinho, *Brazil* 124 H7
Pôrto Nacional, *Brazil* 125 F9
Porto-Novo, *Benin* 83 D5
Porto Petro, *Spain* 37 B10
Porto San Giórgio, *Italy* 29 E10
Porto Sant' Elpídio, *Italy* 29 E10
Porto Santo, *Madeira* 78 B2
Porto Santo Stéfano, *Italy* 28 F8
Pôrto São José, *Brazil* 127 A5
Pôrto Seguro, *Brazil* 125 G11
Porto Tolle, *Italy* 29 D9
Porto Tórres, *Italy* 30 B1
Pôrto União, *Brazil* 127 B5
Pôrto Válter, *Brazil* 124 E4
Porto-Vecchio, *France* 21 G13
Pôrto Velho, *Brazil* 124 E6
Portobelo, *Panama* 120 E4
Portoferráio, *Italy* 28 F7
Portogruaro, *Italy* 29 C9
Portola, *U.S.A.* 116 F6
Portomaggiore, *Italy* 29 D8
Portoscuso, *Italy* 30 C1
Portovénere, *Italy* 28 D6
Portoviejo, *Ecuador* 124 D2
Portpatrick, *U.K.* 14 G3
Portree, *U.K.* 14 D2
Portrush, *U.K.* 15 A5
Portsmouth, *Domin.* 121 C7
Portsmouth, *U.K.* 13 G6
Portsmouth, *N.H., U.S.A.* 111 C14
Portsmouth, *Ohio, U.S.A.* 108 F4
Portsmouth, *R.I., U.S.A.* 111 E13
Portsmouth, *Va., U.S.A.* 108 G7
Portsmouth □, *U.K.* 13 G6
Portsoy, *U.K.* 14 D6
Portstewart, *U.K.* 15 A5
Porttipahtan tekojärvi, *Finland* 8 B22
Portugal ■, *Europe* 34 F3
Portugalete, *Spain* 32 B1
Portumna, *Ireland* 15 C3
Portville, *U.S.A.* 110 D6
Porvenir, *Chile* 128 G2
Porvoo, *Finland* 9 F21
Porzuna, *Spain* 35 F6
Posada, *Italy* 30 B2
Posada →, *Italy* 30 B2
Posadas, *Argentina* 127 B4
Posadas, *Spain* 35 H5
Poschiavo, *Switz.* 25 J6
Posets, *Spain* 32 C5
Poshan = Boshan, *China* 57 F9
Posht-e-Badam, *Iran* 71 C7
Posídhion, Ákra, *Greece* 40 G7
Posidium, *Greece* 39 F9
Poso, *Indonesia* 63 E6
Posong, *S. Korea* 57 G14
Posse, *Brazil* 125 F9
Possession I., *Antarctica* 5 D11
Pössneck, *Germany* 24 E7
Post, *U.S.A.* 113 J4
Post Falls, *U.S.A.* 114 C5
Postavy = Pastavy, *Belarus* 9 J22
Postmasburg, *S. Africa* 88 D3
Postojna, *Slovenia* 29 C11
Poston, *U.S.A.* 117 M12
Potamós, *Andikíthira, Greece* 38 F5
Potamós, *Kíthira, Greece* 38 E4
Potchefstroom, *S. Africa* 88 D4
Potcoava, *Romania* 43 F9
Poteau, *U.S.A.* 113 H7
Poteet, *U.S.A.* 113 L5
Potenza, *Italy* 31 B8
Potenza →, *Italy* 29 E10
Potenza Picena, *Italy* 29 E10
Poteriteri, L., *N.Z.* 91 M1
Potgietersrus, *S. Africa* 89 C4
Poti, *Georgia* 49 J5
Potiskum, *Nigeria* 83 C7
Potlogi, *Romania* 43 F10
Potomac →, *U.S.A.* 108 G7
Potosí, *Bolivia* 124 G5
Potosi Mt., *U.S.A.* 117 K11
Pototan, *Phil.* 61 F5
Potrerillos, *Chile* 126 B2
Potsdam, *Germany* 24 C9
Potsdam, *U.S.A.* 111 B10
Pottenstein, *Germany* 25 F7
Potter, *U.S.A.* 112 E3
Pottery Hill = Abû Ballas, *Egypt* 80 C2
Pottstown, *U.S.A.* 111 F9
Pottsville, *U.S.A.* 111 F8
Pottuvil, *Sri Lanka* 66 R12
P'otzu, *Taiwan* 59 F13
Pouancé, *France* 18 E5
Pouce Coupé, *Canada* 104 B4
Poughkeepsie, *U.S.A.* 111 E11
Pouilly-sur-Loire, *France* 19 E9
Poulaphouca Res., *Ireland* 15 C5
Poulsbo, *U.S.A.* 116 C4
Poulton-le-Fylde, *U.K.* 12 D5
Pouso Alegre, *Brazil* 127 A6
Pouthisat, *Cambodia* 64 F4
Pouzauges, *France* 18 F6
Pova de Sta. Iria, *Portugal* 35 G1
Považská Bystrica, *Slovak Rep.* 27 B11
Poverty B., *N.Z.* 91 H7
Povlen, *Serbia, Yug.* 40 B3
Póvoa de Lanhosa, *Portugal* 34 D2
Póvoa de Varzim, *Portugal* 34 D2
Povorino, *Russia* 48 E6
Powassan, *Canada* 102 C4
Poway, *U.S.A.* 117 N9
Powder →, *U.S.A.* 112 B2
Powder River, *U.S.A.* 114 E10
Powell, *U.S.A.* 114 D9
Powell, L., *U.S.A.* 115 H8
Powell River, *Canada* 104 D4
Powers, *Mich., U.S.A.* 108 C2
Powers, *Oreg., U.S.A.* 114 E1
Powers Lake, *U.S.A.* 112 A3
Powys □, *U.K.* 13 E4
Poyang Hu, *China* 59 C11
Poyarkovo, *Russia* 51 E13
Poysdorf, *Austria* 27 C9
Poza de la Sal, *Spain* 34 C7
Poza Rica, *Mexico* 119 C5
Pozanti, *Turkey* 72 D6
Požarevac, *Serbia, Yug.* 40 B5
Pozazal, Puerto, *Spain* 34 C6
Požega, *Croatia* 42 E2
Požega, *Serbia, Yug.* 40 C4
Poznań, *Poland* 45 F3
Poznań □, *Poland* 45 F3
Pozo, *U.S.A.* 117 K6
Pozo Alcón, *Spain* 35 H8
Pozo Almonte, *Chile* 124 H5
Pozo Colorado, *Paraguay* 126 A4
Pozo del Dátil, *Mexico* 118 B2
Pozoblanco, *Spain* 35 G6
Pozzallo, *Italy* 31 F7
Pozzomaggiore, *Italy* 30 B1
Pozzuoli, *Italy* 31 B7
Pra →, *Ghana* 83 D4
Prabuty, *Poland* 44 E6
Prača, *Bos.-H.* 42 G3
Prachatice, *Czech Rep.* 26 B6
Prachin Buri, *Thailand* 64 F3
Prachuap Khiri Khan, *Thailand* 65 G2
Pradelles, *France* 20 D7
Prades, *France* 20 F6
Prado, *Brazil* 125 G11
Prado del Rey, *Spain* 35 J5
Præstø, *Denmark* 11 J6
Pragersko, *Slovenia* 29 B12
Prague = Praha, *Czech Rep.* 26 A7
Praha, *Czech Rep.* 26 A7
Prahecq, *France* 20 B3
Prahova □, *Romania* 43 E10
Prahova →, *Romania* 43 F10
Prahovo, *Serbia, Yug.* 40 B6
Praia, *C. Verde Is.* 77 E1
Práia a Mare, *Italy* 31 C8
Praid, *Romania* 43 D10
Prainha, *Amazonas, Brazil* 124 E6
Prainha, *Pará, Brazil* 125 D8
Prairie, *Australia* 94 C3
Prairie →, *U.S.A.* 113 H5
Prairie City, *U.S.A.* 114 D4
Prairie du Chien, *U.S.A.* 112 D9
Pramánda, *Greece* 38 B3
Pran Buri, *Thailand* 64 F2
Prang, *Ghana* 83 D4
Prapat, *Indonesia* 62 D1
Prasonísi, Ákra, *Greece* 36 D9
Prästmon, *Sweden* 10 A11
Praszka, *Poland* 45 G5
Prata, *Brazil* 125 G9
Pratapgarh, *India* 68 G6
Prato, *Italy* 28 E8
Prátola Peligna, *Italy* 29 F10
Prats-de-Mollo-la-Preste, *France* 20 F6
Pratt, *U.S.A.* 113 G5
Prattville, *U.S.A.* 109 J2
Pravdinsk, *Russia* 48 B6
Pravets, *Bulgaria* 40 D7
Pravia, *Spain* 34 B4
Praya, *Indonesia* 62 F5
Pré-en-Pail, *France* 18 D6
Precordillera, *Argentina* 126 C2

Predáppio, Italy 29 D8
Predazzo, Italy 29 B8
Predeal, Romania 43 E10
Predejane, Serbia, Yug. 40 D6
Preeceville, Canada 105 C8
Preetz, Germany 24 A6
Pregrada, Croatia 29 B12
Preiļi, Latvia 9 H22
Preko, Croatia 29 D12
Prelate, Canada 105 C7
Prelog, Croatia 29 B13
Prémery, France 19 E10
Premià de Mar, Spain 32 D7
Premier, Canada 104 B3
Premont, U.S.A. 113 M5
Premuda, Croatia 29 D11
Prenjasi, Albania 40 E4
Prentice, U.S.A. 112 C9
Prenzlau, Germany 24 B9
Preobrazheniye, Russia 54 C6
Preparis North Channel, Ind. Oc. 67 M18
Preparis South Channel, Ind. Oc. 67 M18
Přerov, Czech Rep. 27 B10
Prescott, Canada 102 D4
Prescott, Ariz., U.S.A. 115 J7
Prescott, Ark., U.S.A. 113 J8
Preservation Inlet, N.Z. 91 M1
Preševo, Serbia, Yug. 40 D5
Presho, U.S.A. 112 D4
Presicce, Italy 31 C11
Presidencia de la Plaza, Argentina 126 B4
Presidencia Roque Saenz Peña, Argentina 126 B3
Presidente Epitácio, Brazil 125 H8
Presidente Hayes □, Paraguay 126 A4
Presidente Prudente, Brazil 127 A5
Presidio, Mexico 118 B4
Presidio, U.S.A. 113 L2
Preslav, Bulgaria 41 C10
Preslavska Planina, Bulgaria 41 C10
Prešov, Slovak Rep. 27 B14
Prešovský □, Slovak Rep. 27 B13
Prespa, Bulgaria 41 E8
Prespa, L. = Prespansko Jezero, Macedonia 40 F5
Prespansko Jezero, Macedonia 40 F5
Presque Isle, U.S.A. 103 C6
Prestatyn, U.K. 12 D4
Prestea, Ghana 82 D4
Presteigne, U.K. 13 E5
Přeštice, Czech Rep. 26 B6
Preston, Canada 110 C4
Preston, U.K. 12 D5
Preston, Idaho, U.S.A. 114 E8
Preston, Minn., U.S.A. 112 D8
Preston, Nev., U.S.A. 114 G6
Preston, C., Australia 92 D2
Prestwick, U.K. 14 F4
Pretoria, S. Africa 89 D4
Preuilly-sur-Claise, France 18 F7
Préveza, Greece 38 C2
Préveza □, Greece 38 B2
Prey Veng, Cambodia 65 G5
Priazovskoye, Ukraine 47 J8
Pribilof Is., U.S.A. 4 D17
Priboj, Serbia, Yug. 40 C3
Příbram, Czech Rep. 26 B7
Price, U.S.A. 114 G8
Price I., Canada 104 C3
Prichard, U.S.A. 109 K1
Priego, Spain 32 E2
Priego de Córdoba, Spain 35 H6
Priekule, Latvia 9 H19
Prien, Germany 25 H8
Prienai, Lithuania 44 D10
Prieska, S. Africa 88 D3
Priest →, U.S.A. 114 B5
Priest L., U.S.A. 114 B5
Priest Valley, U.S.A. 116 J6
Priestly, Canada 104 C3
Prievidza, Slovak Rep. 27 C11
Prignitz, Germany 24 B7
Prijedor, Bos.-H. 29 D13
Prijepolje, Serbia, Yug. 40 C3
Prikaspiyskaya Nizmennost = Caspian Depression, Eurasia 49 G9
Prikubanskaya Nizmennost, Russia 47 K10
Prilep, Macedonia 40 E5
Priluki = Pryluky, Ukraine 47 G7
Prime Seal I., Australia 94 G4
Primorsk, Russia 46 B5
Primorsko, Bulgaria 41 D11
Primorsko-Akhtarsk, Russia 47 J10
Primorskoye, Ukraine 47 J9
Primrose L., Canada 105 C7
Prince Albert, Canada 105 C7
Prince Albert, S. Africa 88 E3
Prince Albert Mts., Antarctica 5 D11
Prince Albert Nat. Park, Canada 105 C7
Prince Albert Pen., Canada 100 A8
Prince Albert Sd., Canada 100 A8
Prince Alfred, C., Canada 4 B1
Prince Charles I., Canada 101 B12
Prince Charles Mts., Antarctica 5 D6
Prince Edward I. □, Canada 103 C7
Prince Edward Is., Ind. Oc. 3 G11
Prince George, Canada 104 C4
Prince of Wales, C., U.S.A. 98 C3
Prince of Wales I., Australia 94 A3
Prince of Wales I., Canada 4 B3
Prince of Wales I., U.S.A. 104 B2
Prince Patrick I., Canada 4 B2
Prince Regent Inlet, Canada 4 B3
Prince Rupert, Canada 104 C2
Princess Charlotte B., Australia 94 A3
Princess May Ranges, Australia 92 C4
Princess Royal I., Canada 104 C3
Princeton, Canada 104 D4
Princeton, Calif., U.S.A. 116 F4
Princeton, Ill., U.S.A. 112 E10
Princeton, Ind., U.S.A. 108 F2
Princeton, Ky., U.S.A. 108 G2
Princeton, Mo., U.S.A. 112 E8
Princeton, N.J., U.S.A. 111 F10
Princeton, W. Va., U.S.A. 108 G5
Principe, I. de, Atl. Oc. 76 F4
Principe Chan., Canada 104 C3
Principe da Beira, Brazil 124 F6
Prineville, U.S.A. 114 D3
Prins Harald Kyst, Antarctica 5 D4
Prinsesse Astrid Kyst, Antarctica 5 D3
Prinsesse Ragnhild Kyst, Antarctica 5 D4
Prinzapolca, Nic. 120 D3
Prior, C., Spain 34 B2
Priozersk, Russia 46 B6
Pripet → = Prypyat →, Europe 47 G6
Pripet Marshes, Europe 47 F5
Pripyat Marshes = Pripet Marshes, Europe 47 F5
Pripyats = Prypyat →, Europe 47 G6
Prislop, Pasul, Romania 43 C9
Pristen, Russia 47 G9
Priština, Serbia, Yug. 40 D5
Pritzwalk, Germany 24 B8
Privas, France 21 D8
Priverno, Italy 30 A6
Privolzhsk, Russia 48 B5
Privolzhskaya Vozvyshennost, Russia 48 E7
Privolzhskiy, Russia 48 E8
Privolzhye, Russia 48 D9
Priyutnoye, Russia 49 G6
Prizren, Serbia, Yug. 40 D4
Prizzi, Italy 30 E6
Prnjavor, Bos.-H. 42 F2
Probolinggo, Indonesia 63 G15
Prochowice, Poland 45 G3
Proddatur, India 66 M11
Prodhromos, Cyprus 36 E11
Proença-a-Nova, Portugal 34 F3
Profítis Ilías, Greece 36 C9
Profondeville, Belgium 17 D4
Progreso, Mexico 119 C7
Prokhladnyy, Russia 49 J7
Prokletije, Albania 40 D3
Prokopyevsk, Russia 50 D9
Prokuplje, Serbia, Yug. 40 C5
Proletarsk, Russia 49 G5
Prome = Pyè, Burma 67 K19
Prophet →, Canada 104 B4
Propriá, Brazil 125 F11
Propriano, France 21 G12
Proserpine, Australia 94 C4
Prosna →, Poland 45 F4
Prosser, U.S.A. 114 C4
Prostějov, Czech Rep. 27 B10
Prostki, Poland 44 E9
Proston, Australia 95 D5
Proszowice, Poland 45 H7
Protection, U.S.A. 113 G5
Próti, Greece 38 D3
Provadiya, Bulgaria 41 C11
Provence, France 21 E9
Provence-Alpes-Côte d'Azur □, France 21 D10
Providence, Ky., U.S.A. 108 G2
Providence, R.I., U.S.A. 111 E13
Providence Bay, Canada 102 C3
Providence Mts., U.S.A. 115 J6
Providencia, I. de, Colombia 120 D3
Provideniya, Russia 51 C19
Provins, France 19 D10
Provo, U.S.A. 114 F8
Provost, Canada 105 C6
Prozor, Bos.-H. 42 G2
Prud'homme, Canada 105 C7
Prudnik, Poland 45 H4
Prüm, Germany 25 E2
Prundu, Romania 43 F11
Pruszcz Gdański, Poland 44 D5
Pruszków, Poland 45 F7
Prut →, Romania 43 E13
Pruzhany, Belarus 47 F3
Prvič, Croatia 29 D11
Prydz B., Antarctica 5 C6
Pryluky, Ukraine 47 G7
Pryor, U.S.A. 113 G7
Prypyat →, Europe 47 G6
Przasnysz, Poland 45 E7
Przedbórz, Poland 45 G6
Przedecz, Poland 45 F5
Przemków, Poland 45 G2
Przemyśl, Poland 45 J9
Przemyśl □, Poland 45 J9
Przeworsk, Poland 45 H9
Przewóz, Poland 45 G1
Przhevalsk, Kyrgyzstan 50 E8
Przysucha, Poland 45 G7
Psakhná, Greece 38 C5
Psará, Greece 39 C7
Psathoúra, Greece 38 B6
Psel →, Ukraine 47 H7
Pserimos, Greece 39 E9
Psíra, Greece 36 D7
Pskov, Russia 46 D5
Pskovskoye, Ozero, Russia 9 H22
Psunj, Croatia 42 E2
Pteleón, Greece 38 B4
Ptich = Ptsich →, Belarus 47 F5
Ptolemaís, Greece 40 F5
Ptsich →, Belarus 47 F5
Ptuj, Slovenia 29 B12
Ptujska Gora, Slovenia 29 B12
Pu Xian, China 56 F6
Pua, Thailand 64 C3
Puán, Argentina 126 D3
Pu'an, China 58 E5
Puan, S. Korea 57 G14
Pubei, China 58 F7
Pucallpa, Peru 124 E4
Pucheng, China 59 D12
Pucheni, Romania 43 E10
Puchheim, Germany 25 G7
Púchov, Slovak Rep. 27 B11
Pucioasa, Romania 43 E10
Pučišća, Croatia 29 E13
Puck, Poland 44 D5
Pucka, Zatoka, Poland 44 D5
Puçol, Spain 33 F4
Pudasjärvi, Finland 8 D22
Puding, China 58 D5
Pudozh, Russia 46 B9
Pudukkottai, India 66 P11
Puebla, Mexico 119 D5
Puebla □, Mexico 119 D5
Puebla de Alcocer, Spain 35 G5
Puebla de Don Fadrique, Spain 33 H2
Puebla de Don Rodrigo, Spain 35 F6
Puebla de Guzmán, Spain 35 H3
Puebla de la Calzada, Spain 35 G4
Puebla de Sanabria, Spain 34 C4
Puebla de Trives = Pobra de Trives, Spain 34 C3
Pueblo, U.S.A. 112 F2
Pueblo Hundido, Chile 126 B1
Puelches, Argentina 126 D2
Puelén, Argentina 126 D2
Puente Alto, Chile 126 C1
Puente-Genil, Spain 35 H6
Puente la Reina, Spain 32 C3
Puenteareas = Ponteareas, Spain 34 C2
Puentedeume = Pontedeume, Spain 34 B2
Puentes de Garcia Rodriguez = As Pontes de García Rodríquez, Spain 34 B3
Pu'er, China 58 F3
Puerco →, U.S.A. 115 J10
Puerto, Canary Is. 37 F2
Puerto Aisén, Chile 128 F2
Puerto Ángel, Mexico 119 D5
Puerto Arista, Mexico 119 D6
Puerto Armuelles, Panama 120 E3
Puerto Ayacucho, Venezuela 124 B5
Puerto Barrios, Guatemala 120 C2
Puerto Bermejo, Argentina 126 B4
Puerto Bermúdez, Peru 124 F4
Puerto Bolívar, Ecuador 124 D3
Puerto Cabello, Venezuela 124 A5
Puerto Cabezas, Nic. 120 D3
Puerto Cabo Gracias á Dios, Nic. 120 D3
Puerto Carreño, Colombia 124 B5
Puerto Castilla, Honduras 120 C2
Puerto Chicama, Peru 124 E3
Puerto Coig, Argentina 128 G3
Puerto Cortés, Costa Rica 120 E3
Puerto Cortés, Honduras 120 C2
Puerto Cumarebo, Venezuela 124 A5
Puerto de Alcudia = Port d'Alcúdia, Spain 37 B10
Puerto de Andraitx, Spain 37 B9
Puerto de Cabrera, Spain 37 B9
Puerto de Gran Tarajal, Canary Is. 37 F5
Puerto de la Cruz, Canary Is. 37 F3
Puerto de Mazarrón, Spain 33 H3
Puerto de Pozo Negro, Canary Is. 37 F6
Puerto de Sóller = Port de Sóller, Spain 37 B9
Puerto de Somosierra, Spain 34 D7
Puerto del Carmen, Canary Is. 37 F6
Puerto del Rosario, Canary Is. 37 F6
Puerto Deseado, Argentina 128 F3
Puerto Heath, Bolivia 124 F5
Puerto Inírida, Colombia 124 C5
Puerto Juárez, Mexico 119 C7
Puerto La Cruz, Venezuela 124 A6
Puerto Leguízamo, Colombia 124 D4
Puerto Limón, Colombia 124 C4
Puerto Lobos, Argentina 128 E3
Puerto Lumbreras, Spain 33 H3
Puerto Madryn, Argentina 128 E3
Puerto Maldonado, Peru 124 F5
Puerto Manotí, Cuba 120 B4
Puerto Mazarrón = Puerto de Mazarrón, Spain 33 H3
Puerto Montt, Chile 128 E2
Puerto Morelos, Mexico 119 C7
Puerto Natales, Chile 128 G2
Puerto Padre, Cuba 120 B4
Puerto Páez, Venezuela 124 B5
Puerto Peñasco, Mexico 118 A2
Puerto Pinasco, Paraguay 126 A4
Puerto Plata, Dom. Rep. 121 C5
Puerto Pollensa = Port de Pollença, Spain 37 B10
Puerto Princesa, Phil. 61 G3
Puerto Quepos, Costa Rica 120 E3
Puerto Real, Spain 35 J4
Puerto Rico, Canary Is. 37 G4
Puerto Rico ■, W. Indies 121 C6
Puerto Rico Trench, Atl. Oc. 121 C6
Puerto San Julián, Argentina 128 F3
Puerto Sastre, Paraguay 126 A4
Puerto Serrano, Spain 35 J5
Puerto Suárez, Bolivia 124 G7
Puerto Vallarta, Mexico 118 C3
Puerto Wilches, Colombia 124 B4
Puertollano, Spain 35 G6
Pueyrredón, L., Argentina 128 F2
Puffin I., Ireland 15 E1
Pugachev, Russia 48 D9
Puge, China 58 D4
Puge, Tanzania 86 C3
Puget Sound, U.S.A. 114 C2
Puget-Théniers, France 21 E10
Púglia □, Italy 31 A9
Pugŏdong, N. Korea 57 C16
Pugu, Tanzania 86 D4
Pūgūnzī, Iran 71 E8
Pui, Romania 42 E8
Puieşti, Romania 43 D12
Puig Major, Spain 37 B9
Puigcerdà, Spain 32 C6
Puigmal, Spain 32 C7
Puigpunyent, Spain 37 B9
Puisaye, Collines de la, France 19 E10
Puiseaux, France 19 D9
Pujols, France 20 D3
Pujon-chosuji, N. Korea 57 D14
Puka, Albania 40 D3
Pukaki L., N.Z. 91 L3
Pukapuka, Cook Is. 97 J11
Pukatawagan, Canada 105 B8
Pukchin, N. Korea 57 D13
Pukchŏng, N. Korea 57 D15
Pukekohe, N.Z. 91 G5
Pukou, China 59 A12
Pula, Croatia 29 D10
Pula, Italy 30 C1
Pulacayo, Bolivia 124 H5
Pulaski, N.Y., U.S.A. 111 C8
Pulaski, Tenn., U.S.A. 109 H2
Pulaski, Va., U.S.A. 108 G5
Puławy, Poland 45 G8
Pulga, U.S.A. 116 F5
Pulicat, L., India 66 N12
Pullman, U.S.A. 114 C5
Pulog, Phil. 61 C4
Pułtusk, Poland 45 F8
Pülümür, Turkey 73 C8
Pumlumon Fawr, U.K. 13 E4
Puná, I., Ecuador 124 D2
Punakha, Bhutan 67 F16
Punasar, India 68 F5
Punata, Bolivia 124 G5
Punch, India 69 C6
Pune, India 66 K8
Pungsan, N. Korea 57 D15
Pungue, Ponte de, Mozam. 87 F3
Puning, China 59 F11
Punjab □, India 68 D7
Punjab □, Pakistan 68 E6
Puno, Peru 124 G4
Punta Alta, Argentina 128 D4
Punta Arenas, Chile 128 G2
Punta de Díaz, Chile 126 B1
Punta Gorda, Belize 119 D7
Punta Gorda, U.S.A. 109 M5
Punta Prieta, Mexico 118 B2
Punta Prima, Spain 37 B11
Punta Umbría, Spain 35 H4
Puntabie, Australia 95 E1
Puntarenas, Costa Rica 120 E3
Punto Fijo, Venezuela 124 A4
Punxsatawney, U.S.A. 110 F6
Puqi, China 59 C9
Puquio, Peru 124 F4
Pur →, Russia 50 C8
Purace, Vol., Colombia 124 C3
Puračić, Bos.-H. 42 F3
Puralia = Puruliya, India 69 H12
Purbeck, Isle of, U.K. 13 G6
Purcell, U.S.A. 113 H6
Puri, India 67 K14
Purmerend, Neths. 17 B4
Purnia, India 69 G12
Pursat = Pouthisat, Cambodia 64 F4
Purukcahu, Indonesia 62 E4
Puruliya, India 69 H12
Purus →, Brazil 122 D4
Puruvesi, Finland 46 B5
Pŭrvomay, Bulgaria 41 D9
Purwakarta, Indonesia 63 G12
Purwodadi, Indonesia 63 G14
Purwokerto, Indonesia 63 G13
Puryŏng, N. Korea 57 C15
Pusan, S. Korea 57 G15
Pushkin, Russia 46 C6
Pushkino, Moskva, Russia 46 D9
Pushkino, Saratov, Russia 48 E8
Püspökladány, Hungary 42 C6
Pustoshka, Russia 46 D5
Puszczykowo, Poland 45 F3
Putahow L., Canada 105 B8
Putao, Burma 67 F20
Putaruru, N.Z. 91 H5
Putbus, Germany 24 A9
Puthein Myit →, Burma 67 M19
Putian, China 59 E12
Putignano, Italy 31 B10
Puting, Tanjung, Indonesia 62 E4
Putlitz, Germany 24 B8
Putna, Romania 43 C10
Putna →, Romania 43 E12
Putnam, U.S.A. 111 E13
Putnok, Hungary 42 B5
Putorana, Gory, Russia 51 C10
Puttalam, Sri Lanka 66 Q11
Puttgarden, Germany 24 A7
Püttlingen, Germany 25 F2
Putumayo →, S. Amer. 122 D4
Putuo, China 59 C14
Putussibau, Indonesia 62 D4
Puy-de-Dôme, France 20 C6
Puy-de-Dôme □, France 20 C7
Puy-l'Évêque, France 20 D5
Puyallup, U.S.A. 116 C4
Puyang, China 56 G8
Puylaurens, France 20 E6
Pūzeh Rīg, Iran 71 E8
Pwani □, Tanzania 86 D4
Pweto, Dem. Rep. of the Congo 87 D2
Pwllheli, U.K. 12 E3
Pyana →, Russia 48 C8
Pyapon, Burma 67 L19
Pyasina →, Russia 51 B9
Pyatigorsk, Russia 49 H6
Pyatykhatky, Ukraine 47 H7
Pydna, Greece 40 F6
Pyè, Burma 67 K19
Pyetrikaw, Belarus 47 F5
Pyhäjoki, Finland 8 D21
Pyinmana, Burma 67 K20
Pyla, C., Cyprus 36 E12
Pyŏktong, N. Korea 57 D13
Pyŏnggang, N. Korea 57 E14
P'yŏngtaek, S. Korea 57 F14
P'yŏngyang, N. Korea 57 E13
Pyote, U.S.A. 113 K3
Pyramid L., U.S.A. 114 G4
Pyramid Pk., U.S.A. 117 J10
Pyramids, Egypt 80 J7
Pyrénées, Europe 20 F4
Pyrénées-Atlantiques □, France 20 E3
Pyrénées-Orientales □, France 20 F6
Pyryatyn, Ukraine 47 G7
Pyrzyce, Poland 45 E1
Pyskowice, Poland 45 H5
Pytalovo, Russia 46 D4
Pyu, Burma 67 K20
Pyzdry, Poland 45 F4

Q

Qaanaaq = Thule, Greenland 4 B4
Qabirri →, Azerbaijan 49 K8
Qachasnek, S. Africa 89 E4
Qa'el Jafr, Jordan 75 E5
Qa'emābād, Iran 71 D9
Qā'emshahr, Iran 71 B7
Qagan Nur, China 56 C8
Qahar Youyi Zhongqi, China 56 D7
Qahremānshahr = Bākhtarān, Iran 70 C5
Qaidam Pendi, China 60 C4
Qajarīyeh, Iran 71 D6
Qala, Ras il, Malta 36 C1
Qala-i-Jadid, Afghan. 68 D2
Qala Yangi, Afghan. 68 B2
Qal'at al Akhḑar, Si. Arabia 70 E3
Qal'at Dīzah, Iraq 73 D11
Qal'at Sukkar, Iraq 70 D5
Qal'eh Darreh, Iran 70 B5
Qal'eh Shaharak, Afghan. 66 B4
Qalyûb, Egypt 80 H7
Qamdo, China 58 B1
Qamruddin Karez, Pakistan 68 D3
Qandahār, Afghan. 66 D4
Qandahār □, Afghan. 66 D4
Qapān, Iran 71 B7
Qapshaghay, Kazakstan 50 E8
Qaqortoq = Julianehåb, Greenland 4 C5
Qâra, Egypt 80 B2
Qara Qash →, India 69 B8
Qarabutaq, Kazakstan 50 E7

Qaraçala, *Azerbaijan* 49 L9
Qaraghandy, *Kazakstan* 50 E8
Qārah, *Si. Arabia* 70 D4
Qarataū, *Kazakstan* 50 E8
Qardud, *Sudan* 81 E2
Qareh →, *Iran* 70 B5
Qareh Tekān, *Iran* 71 B6
Qarqan, *China* 60 C3
Qarqan He →, *China* 60 C3
Qarqaraly, *Kazakstan* 50 E8
Qarrasa, *Sudan* 81 E3
Qarshi, *Uzbekistan* 50 F7
Qartabā, *Lebanon* 75 A4
Qaryat al Gharab, *Iraq* 70 D5
Qaryat al 'Ulyā, *Si. Arabia* 70 E5
Qasr 'Amra, *Jordan* 70 D3
Qaşr-e Qand, *Iran* 71 E9
Qasr Farâfra, *Egypt* 80 B2
Qatanā, *Syria* 75 B5
Qatar ■, *Asia* 71 E6
Qatlīsh, *Iran* 71 B8
Qattâra, *Egypt* 80 A2
Qattâra, Munkhafed el, *Egypt* 80 B2
Qattâra Depression = Qattâra, Munkhafed el, *Egypt* 80 B2
Qawām al Ḥamzah, *Iraq* 70 D5
Qāyen, *Iran* 71 C8
Qazaqstan = Kazakstan ■, *Asia* 50 E8
Qazimämmäd, *Azerbaijan* 49 K9
Qazvin, *Iran* 71 B6
Qena, *Egypt* 80 B3
Qena, W. →, *Egypt* 80 B3
Qeqertarsuaq = Disko, *Greenland* 4 C5
Qeqertarsuaq = Godhavn, *Greenland* 4 C5
Qeshlāq, *Iran* 70 C5
Qeshm, *Iran* 71 E8
Qezi'ot, *Israel* 75 E3
Qi Xian, *China* 56 G8
Qian Gorlos, *China* 57 B13
Qian Xian, *China* 56 G5
Qiancheng, *China* 58 D7
Qianjiang, *Guangxi Zhuangzu, China* 58 F7
Qianjiang, *Hubei, China* 59 B9
Qianjiang, *Sichuan, China* 58 C7
Qianshan, *China* 59 B11
Qianwei, *China* 58 C4
Qianxi, *China* 58 D6
Qianyang, *Hunan, China* 59 D8
Qianyang, *Shaanxi, China* 56 G4
Qianyang, *Zhejiang, China* 59 B12
Qiaojia, *China* 58 D4
Qibā', *Si. Arabia* 70 E5
Qichun, *China* 59 B10
Qidong, *Hunan, China* 59 D9
Qidong, *Jiangsu, China* 59 B13
Qijiang, *China* 58 C6
Qila Safed, *Pakistan* 66 E2
Qila Saifullāh, *Pakistan* 68 D3
Qilian Shan, *China* 60 C4
Qimen, *China* 59 C11
Qin He →, *China* 56 G7
Qin Jiang →, *China* 59 D10
Qin Ling = Qinling Shandi, *China* 56 H5
Qin'an, *China* 56 G3
Qing Xian, *China* 56 E9
Qingcheng, *China* 57 F9
Qingdao, *China* 57 F11
Qingfeng, *China* 56 G8
Qinghai □, *China* 60 C4
Qinghai Hu, *China* 60 C5
Qinghecheng, *China* 57 D13
Qinghemen, *China* 57 D11
Qingjian, *China* 56 F6
Qingjiang, *Jiangsu, China* 57 H10
Qingjiang, *Jiangxi, China* 59 C10
Qingliu, *China* 59 D11
Qinglong, *China* 58 E5
Qingping, *China* 58 D6
Qingpu, *China* 59 B13
Qingshui, *China* 56 G4
Qingshuihe, *China* 56 E6
Qingtian, *China* 59 C13
Qingtongxia Shuiku, *China* 56 F3
Qingxi, *China* 58 D7
Qingxu, *China* 56 F7
Qingyang, *Anhui, China* 59 B11
Qingyang, *Gansu, China* 56 F4
Qingyi Jiang →, *China* 58 C4
Qingyuan, *Guangdong, China* 59 F9
Qingyuan, *Liaoning, China* 57 C13
Qingyuan, *Zhejiang, China* 59 D12
Qingyun, *China* 57 F9
Qingzhen, *China* 58 D6
Qinhuangdao, *China* 57 E10
Qinling Shandi, *China* 56 H5
Qinshui, *China* 56 G7
Qinyang, *China* 56 G7
Qinyuan, *China* 56 F7
Qinzhou, *China* 58 G7
Qionghai, *China* 64 C8
Qionglai, *China* 58 B4
Qionglai Shan, *China* 58 B4
Qiongzhou Haixia, *China* 64 B8
Qiqihar, *China* 60 B7
Qirâiya, W. →, *Egypt* 75 E3
Qiryat Ata, *Israel* 75 C4
Qiryat Gat, *Israel* 75 D3
Qiryat Mal'akhi, *Israel* 75 D3
Qiryat Shemona, *Israel* 75 B4
Qiryat Yam, *Israel* 75 C4
Qishan, *China* 56 G4
Qitai, *China* 60 B3
Qiubei, *China* 58 E5
Qixia, *China* 57 F11
Qiyang, *China* 59 D8
Qızılağac Körfäzi, *Azerbaijan* 73 C13
Qojūr, *Iran* 70 B5
Qom, *Iran* 71 C6
Qomsheh, *Iran* 71 D6
Qorveh, *Iran* 73 E12
Qostanay, *Kazakstan* 50 D7
Qoṭūr, *Iran* 73 C11
Qu Jiang →, *China* 58 B6
Qu Xian, *Sichuan, China* 58 B6
Qu Xian, *Zhejiang, China* 59 C12
Quairading, *Australia* 93 F2
Quakenbrück, *Germany* 24 C3
Quakertown, *U.S.A.* 111 F9
Qualeup, *Australia* 93 F2
Quambatook, *Australia* 95 F3
Quambone, *Australia* 95 E4
Quamby, *Australia* 94 C3
Quan Long = Ca Mau, *Vietnam* 65 H5
Quanah, *U.S.A.* 113 H5
Quandialla, *Australia* 95 E4
Quang Ngai, *Vietnam* 64 E7
Quang Tri, *Vietnam* 64 D6
Quang Yen, *Vietnam* 64 B6
Quannan, *China* 59 E10
Quantock Hills, *U.K.* 13 F4
Quanzhou, *Fujian, China* 59 E12
Quanzhou, *Guangxi Zhuangzu, China* 59 E8
Quaqtaq, *Canada* 101 B13
Quaraí, *Brazil* 126 C4
Quarré-les-Tombes, *France* 19 E11
Quarteira, *Portugal* 35 H2
Quartu Sant'Élena, *Italy* 30 C2
Quartzsite, *U.S.A.* 117 M12
Quatsino, *Canada* 104 C3
Quatsino Sd., *Canada* 104 C3
Quba, *Azerbaijan* 49 K9
Qūchān, *Iran* 71 B8
Queanbeyan, *Australia* 95 F4
Québec, *Canada* 103 C5
Québec □, *Canada* 103 C6
Quedlinburg, *Germany* 24 D7
Queen Alexandra Ra., *Antarctica* 5 E11
Queen Charlotte, *Canada* 104 C2
Queen Charlotte Is., *Canada* 104 C2
Queen Charlotte Sd., *Canada* 104 C3
Queen Elizabeth Is., *Canada* 98 B10
Queen Elizabeth Nat. Park, *Uganda* 86 C3
Queen Mary Land, *Antarctica* 5 D7
Queen Maud G., *Canada* 100 B9
Queen Maud Land, *Antarctica* 5 D3
Queen Maud Mts., *Antarctica* 5 E13
Queens Chan., *Australia* 92 C4
Queenscliff, *Australia* 95 F3
Queensland □, *Australia* 94 C3
Queenstown, *Australia* 94 G4
Queenstown, *N.Z.* 91 L2
Queenstown, *S. Africa* 88 E4
Queets, *U.S.A.* 116 C2
Queguay Grande →, *Uruguay* 126 C4
Queimadas, *Brazil* 125 F11
Quelimane, *Mozam.* 87 F4
Quellón, *Chile* 128 E2
Quelpart = Cheju Do, *S. Korea* 57 H14
Queluz, *Portugal* 35 G1
Quemado, *N. Mex., U.S.A.* 115 J9
Quemado, *Tex., U.S.A.* 113 L4
Quemoy = Chinmen, *Taiwan* 59 E13
Quemú-Quemú, *Argentina* 126 D3
Quequén, *Argentina* 126 D4
Querétaro, *Mexico* 118 C4
Querétaro □, *Mexico* 118 C5
Querfurt, *Germany* 24 D7
Quérigut, *France* 20 F6
Querqueville, *France* 18 C5
Quesada, *Spain* 35 H7
Queshan, *China* 56 H8
Quesnel, *Canada* 104 C4
Quesnel →, *Canada* 104 C4
Quesnel L., *Canada* 104 C4
Questa, *U.S.A.* 115 H11
Questembert, *France* 18 E4
Quetico Prov. Park, *Canada* 102 C1
Quetta, *Pakistan* 68 D2
Quezaltenango, *Guatemala* 120 D1
Quezon City, *Phil.* 61 D4
Qufār, *Si. Arabia* 70 E4
Qui Nhon, *Vietnam* 64 F7
Quibaxe, *Angola* 84 F2
Quibdo, *Colombia* 124 B3
Quiberon, *France* 18 E3
Quiberon, Presqu'île de, *France* 18 E3
Quick, *Canada* 104 C3
Quickborn, *Germany* 24 B5
Quiet L., *Canada* 104 A2
Quiindy, *Paraguay* 126 B4
Quila, *Mexico* 118 C3
Quilán, C., *Chile* 128 E2
Quilcene, *U.S.A.* 116 C4
Quilimarí, *Chile* 126 C1
Quilino, *Argentina* 126 C3
Quillabamba, *Peru* 124 F4
Quillagua, *Chile* 126 A2
Quillaicillo, *Chile* 126 C1
Quillan, *France* 20 F6
Quillota, *Chile* 126 C1
Quilmes, *Argentina* 126 C4
Quilon, *India* 66 Q10
Quilpie, *Australia* 95 D3
Quilpué, *Chile* 126 C1
Quilua, *Mozam.* 87 F4
Quimilí, *Argentina* 126 B3
Quimper, *France* 18 E2
Quimperlé, *France* 18 E3
Quinault →, *U.S.A.* 116 C2
Quincy, *Calif., U.S.A.* 116 F6
Quincy, *Fla., U.S.A.* 109 K3
Quincy, *Ill., U.S.A.* 112 F9
Quincy, *Mass., U.S.A.* 111 D14
Quincy, *Wash., U.S.A.* 114 C4
Quines, *Argentina* 126 C2
Quinga, *Mozam.* 87 F5
Quingey, *France* 19 E12
Quintana de la Serena, *Spain* 35 G5
Quintana Roo □, *Mexico* 119 D7
Quintanar de la Orden, *Spain* 35 F7
Quintanar de la Sierra, *Spain* 32 D2
Quintanar del Rey, *Spain* 33 F3
Quintero, *Chile* 126 C1
Quintin, *France* 18 D4
Quinto, *Spain* 32 D4
Quinyambie, *Australia* 95 E3
Quípar →, *Spain* 33 G3
Quirihue, *Chile* 126 D1
Quirindi, *Australia* 95 E5
Quirinópolis, *Brazil* 125 G8
Quiroga, *Spain* 34 C3
Quissac, *France* 21 E8
Quissanga, *Mozam.* 87 E5
Quitilipi, *Argentina* 126 B3
Quitman, *Ga., U.S.A.* 109 K4
Quitman, *Miss., U.S.A.* 109 J1
Quitman, *Tex., U.S.A.* 113 J7
Quito, *Ecuador* 124 D3
Quixadá, *Brazil* 125 D11
Quixaxe, *Mozam.* 87 F5
Qujing, *China* 58 E4
Qul'ân, Jazâ'ir, *Egypt* 80 C4
Qumbu, *S. Africa* 89 E4
Quneitra, *Syria* 75 B4
Qŭnghirot, *Uzbekistan* 50 E6
Quoin I., *Australia* 92 B4
Quoin Pt., *S. Africa* 88 E2
Quondong, *Australia* 95 E3
Quorn, *Australia* 95 E2
Qŭqon, *Uzbekistan* 50 E8
Qurein, *Sudan* 81 E3
Qurnat as Sawdā', *Lebanon* 75 A5
Qûs, *Egypt* 80 B3
Qusar, *Azerbaijan* 49 K9
Qusaybah, *Iraq* 70 C4
Quseir, *Egypt* 80 B3
Qūshchī, *Iran* 70 B5
Quthing, *Lesotho* 89 E4
Qūṭīābād, *Iran* 71 C6
Quwo, *China* 56 G6
Quyang, *China* 56 E8
Quynh Nhai, *Vietnam* 64 B4
Quzi, *China* 56 F4
Qvareli, *Georgia* 49 K7
Qytet Stalin = Kuçovë, *Albania* 40 F3
Qyzylorda, *Kazakstan* 50 E7

R

Ra, Ko, *Thailand* 65 H2
Raab, *Austria* 26 C6
Raahe, *Finland* 8 D21
Raalte, *Neths.* 17 B6
Raasay, *U.K.* 14 D2
Raasay, Sd. of, *U.K.* 14 D2
Rab, *Croatia* 29 D11
Raba, *Indonesia* 63 F5
Rába →, *Hungary* 42 C2
Raba →, *Poland* 45 H7
Rabaçal →, *Portugal* 34 D3
Rabah, *Nigeria* 83 C6
Rabai, *Kenya* 86 C4
Rabastens, *France* 20 E5
Rabastens-de-Bigorre, *France* 20 E4
Rabat, *Malta* 36 D1
Rabat, *Morocco* 78 B4
Rabaul, *Papua N. G.* 96 H7
Rabbit →, *Canada* 104 B3
Rabbit Lake, *Canada* 105 C7
Rabbitskin →, *Canada* 104 A4
Rabka, *Poland* 45 J6
Râbniţa, *Moldova* 43 C14
Rābor, *Iran* 71 D8
Rača, *Serbia, Yug.* 40 B4
Răcăciuni, *Romania* 43 D11
Răcăşdia, *Romania* 42 F6
Racconigi, *Italy* 28 D4
Race, C., *Canada* 103 C9
Rach Gia, *Vietnam* 65 G5
Raciąż, *Poland* 45 F7
Racibórz, *Poland* 45 H5
Racine, *U.S.A.* 108 D2
Rackerby, *U.S.A.* 116 F5
Radama, Nosy, *Madag.* 89 A8
Radama, Saikanosy, *Madag.* 89 A8
Radan, *Serbia, Yug.* 40 D5
Rădăuţi, *Romania* 43 C10
Rădăuţi-Prut, *Romania* 43 B11
Radbuza →, *Czech Rep.* 26 B6
Radebeul, *Germany* 24 D9
Radeburg, *Germany* 24 D9
Radeče, *Slovenia* 29 B12
Radekhiv, *Ukraine* 47 G3
Radekhov = Radekhiv, *Ukraine* 47 G3
Radenthein, *Austria* 26 E6
Radew →, *Poland* 44 D2
Radford, *U.S.A.* 108 G5
Radhanpur, *India* 68 H4
Radika →, *Macedonia* 40 E4
Radisson, *Canada* 105 C7
Radium Hot Springs, *Canada* 104 C5
Radlje ob Dravi, *Slovenia* 29 B12
Radnevo, *Bulgaria* 41 D9
Radnice, *Czech Rep.* 26 B6
Radnor Forest, *U.K.* 13 E4
Radolfzell, *Germany* 25 H4
Radom, *Poland* 45 G8
Radom □, *Poland* 45 G8
Radomir, *Bulgaria* 40 D6
Radomka →, *Poland* 45 G8
Radomsko, *Poland* 45 G6
Radomyshl, *Ukraine* 47 G5
Radomyśl Wielki, *Poland* 45 H8
Radoszyce, *Poland* 45 G7
Radoviš, *Macedonia* 40 E6
Radovljica, *Slovenia* 29 B11
Radstadt, *Austria* 26 D6
Radstock, C., *Australia* 95 E1
Răducăneni, *Romania* 43 D12
Raduša, *Serbia, Yug.* 40 D5
Radviliškis, *Lithuania* 9 J20
Radville, *Canada* 105 D8
Radymno, *Poland* 45 J9
Radzanów, *Poland* 45 F7
Radziejów, *Poland* 45 F5
Radzyń Chełmiński, *Poland* 44 E5
Radzyń Podlaski, *Poland* 45 G9
Rae, *Canada* 104 A5
Rae Bareli, *India* 69 F9
Rae Isthmus, *Canada* 101 B11
Raeren, *Belgium* 17 D6
Raeside, L., *Australia* 93 E3
Raetihi, *N.Z.* 91 H5
Rafaela, *Argentina* 126 C3
Rafah, *Gaza Strip* 75 D3
Rafai, *C.A.R.* 86 B1
Raffadali, *Italy* 30 E6
Rafḩā, *Si. Arabia* 70 D4
Rafsanjān, *Iran* 71 D8
Raft Pt., *Australia* 92 C3
Ragachow, *Belarus* 47 F6
Ragag, *Sudan* 81 E1
Ragama, *Sri Lanka* 66 R11
Ragged, Mt., *Australia* 93 F3
Raglan, *Australia* 94 C5
Raglan, *N.Z.* 91 G5
Ragusa, *Italy* 31 F7
Raha, *Indonesia* 63 E6
Rahad, Nahr ed →, *Sudan* 81 E3
Rahaeng = Tak, *Thailand* 64 D2
Rahden, *Germany* 24 C4
Raheita, *Eritrea* 81 E5
Raḩīmah, *Si. Arabia* 71 E6
Rahimyar Khan, *Pakistan* 68 E4
Rāhjerd, *Iran* 71 C6
Raichur, *India* 66 L10
Raiganj, *India* 69 G13
Raigarh, *India* 67 J13
Raijua, *Indonesia* 63 F6
Railton, *Australia* 94 G4
Rainbow Lake, *Canada* 104 B5
Rainier, *U.S.A.* 116 D4
Rainier, Mt., *U.S.A.* 116 D5
Rainy L., *Canada* 105 D10
Rainy River, *Canada* 105 D10
Raippaluoto, *Finland* 8 E19
Raipur, *India* 67 J12
Raisio, *Finland* 9 F20
Raj Nandgaon, *India* 67 J12
Raja, Ujung, *Indonesia* 62 D1
Raja Ampat, Kepulauan, *Indonesia* 63 E8
Rajahmundry, *India* 67 L12
Rajang →, *Malaysia* 62 D4
Rajapalaiyam, *India* 66 Q10
Rajasthan □, *India* 68 F5
Rajasthan Canal, *India* 68 F5
Rajauri, *India* 69 C6
Rajgarh, *Mad. P., India* 68 G7
Rajgarh, *Raj., India* 68 E6
Rajgród, *Poland* 44 E9
Rajkot, *India* 68 H4
Rajmahal Hills, *India* 69 G12
Rajpipla, *India* 66 J8
Rajpura, *India* 68 D7
Rajshahi, *Bangla.* 67 G16
Rajshahi □, *Bangla.* 69 G13
Rakaia, *N.Z.* 91 K4
Rakaia →, *N.Z.* 91 K4
Rakan, Ra's, *Qatar* 71 E6
Rakaposhi, *Pakistan* 69 A6
Rakata, Pulau, *Indonesia* 62 F3
Rakhiv, *Ukraine* 47 H3
Rakhni, *Pakistan* 68 D3
Rakitnoye, *Russia* 54 B7
Rakitovo, *Bulgaria* 41 E8
Rakoniewice, *Poland* 45 F3
Rakops, *Botswana* 88 C3
Rakovica, *Croatia* 29 D12
Rakovník, *Czech Rep.* 26 A6
Rakovski, *Bulgaria* 41 D8
Rakvere, *Estonia* 9 G22
Raleigh, *U.S.A.* 109 H6
Raleigh B., *U.S.A.* 109 H7
Ralja, *Serbia, Yug.* 40 B4
Ralls, *U.S.A.* 113 J4
Ram →, *Canada* 104 A4
Rām Allāh, *West Bank* 75 D4
Ram Hd., *Australia* 95 F4
Rama, *Nic.* 120 D3
Ramacca, *Italy* 31 E7
Ramales de la Victoria, *Spain* 34 B7
Raman, *Thailand* 65 J3
Ramanathapuram, *India* 66 Q11
Ramanetaka, B. de, *Madag.* 89 A8
Ramat Gan, *Israel* 75 C3
Ramatlhabama, *S. Africa* 88 D4
Ramban, *India* 69 C6
Rambervillers, *France* 19 D13
Rambipuji, *Indonesia* 63 H15
Rambouillet, *France* 19 D8
Ramea, *Canada* 103 C8
Ramechhap, *Nepal* 69 F12
Ramenskoye, *Russia* 46 E10
Ramgarh, *Bihar, India* 69 H11
Ramgarh, *Raj., India* 68 F6
Ramgarh, *Raj., India* 68 F4
Rāmhormoz, *Iran* 71 D6
Ramīān, *Iran* 71 B7
Ramingining, *Australia* 94 A2
Ramla, *Israel* 75 D3
Ramlu, *Eritrea* 81 E5
Râmna →, *Romania* 43 E12
Ramnad = Ramanathapuram, *India* 66 Q11
Ramnagar, *India* 69 C6
Ramnäs, *Sweden* 10 E10
Râmnicu Sărat, *Romania* 43 E12
Râmnicu Vâlcea, *Romania* 43 E9
Ramon, *Russia* 47 G10
Ramona, *U.S.A.* 117 M10
Ramonville-St-Agne, *France* 20 E5
Ramore, *Canada* 102 C3
Ramotswa, *Botswana* 88 C4
Rampur, *H.P., India* 68 D7
Rampur, *Mad. P., India* 68 H5
Rampur, *Ut. P., India* 69 E8
Rampur Hat, *India* 69 G12
Rampura, *India* 68 G6
Ramree I. = Ramree Kyun, *Burma* 67 K19
Ramree Kyun, *Burma* 67 K19
Rāmsar, *Iran* 71 B6
Ramsey, *Canada* 102 C3
Ramsey, *U.K.* 12 C3
Ramsgate, *U.K.* 13 F9
Ramsjö, *Sweden* 10 B9
Ramstein, *Germany* 25 F3
Ramtek, *India* 66 J11
Ramvik, *Sweden* 10 B11
Ranaghat, *India* 69 H13
Ranahu, *Pakistan* 68 G3
Ranau, *Malaysia* 62 C5
Rancagua, *Chile* 126 C1
Rance →, *France* 18 D5
Rancheria →, *Canada* 104 A3
Ranchester, *U.S.A.* 114 D10
Ranchi, *India* 69 H11
Rancho Cucamonga, *U.S.A.* 117 L9
Randalstown, *U.K.* 15 B5
Randan, *France* 19 F10
Randazzo, *Italy* 31 E7
Randers, *Denmark* 11 H4
Randers Fjord, *Denmark* 11 H4
Randfontein, *S. Africa* 89 D4
Randle, *U.S.A.* 116 D5
Randolph, *Mass., U.S.A.* 111 D13
Randolph, *N.Y., U.S.A.* 110 D6
Randolph, *Utah, U.S.A.* 114 F8
Randolph, *Vt., U.S.A.* 111 C12
Råne älv →, *Sweden* 8 D20
Rangae, *Thailand* 65 J3
Rangaunu B., *N.Z.* 91 F4
Rangeley, *U.S.A.* 111 B14
Rangely, *U.S.A.* 114 F9
Ranger, *U.S.A.* 113 J5
Rangia, *India* 67 F17
Rangiora, *N.Z.* 91 K4
Rangitaiki →, *N.Z.* 91 G6
Rangitata →, *N.Z.* 91 K3
Rangkasbitung, *Indonesia* 63 G12
Rangon →, *Burma* 67 L20
Rangoon, *Burma* 67 L20
Rangpur, *Bangla.* 67 G16
Rangsit, *Thailand* 64 F3
Ranibennur, *India* 66 M9
Raniganj, *India* 69 H12
Raniwara, *India* 66 G8
Rāniyah, *Iraq* 70 B5
Ranken →, *Australia* 94 C2
Rankin, *U.S.A.* 113 K4
Rankin Inlet, *Canada* 100 B10
Rankins Springs, *Australia* 95 E4
Rankweil, *Austria* 26 D2

Rannoch, L., *U.K.* 14 E4
Rannoch Moor, *U.K.* 14 E4
Ranobe, Helodranon' i, *Madag.* 89 C7
Ranohira, *Madag.* 89 C8
Ranomafana, *Toamasina, Madag.* 89 B8
Ranomafana, *Toliara, Madag.* 89 C8
Ranong, *Thailand* 65 H2
Rānsa, *Iran* 71 C6
Ransiki, *Indonesia* 63 E8
Rantauprapat, *Indonesia* 62 D1
Rantemario, *Indonesia* 63 E5
Rantoul, *U.S.A.* 108 E1
Ranum, *Denmark* 11 H3
Raon l'Étape, *France* 19 D13
Raoyang, *China* 56 E8
Rapa, *Pac. Oc.* 97 K13
Rapallo, *Italy* 28 D6
Rāpch, *Iran* 71 E8
Rapid →, *Canada* 104 B3
Rapid City, *U.S.A.* 112 D3
Rapid River, *U.S.A.* 108 C2
Rapides des Joachims, *Canada* 102 C4
Rapla, *Estonia* 9 G21
Rapu Rapu I., *Phil.* 61 E6
Rarotonga, *Cook Is.* 97 K12
Ra's al 'Ayn, *Syria* 70 B4
Ra's al Khaymah, *U.A.E.* 71 E8
Ra's an Naqb, *Jordan* 75 F4
Ras Dashen, *Ethiopia* 81 E4
Râs Ghârib, *Egypt* 80 J8
Ras Mallap, *Egypt* 80 J8
Râs Timirist, *Mauritania* 82 B1
Rasca, Pta. de la, *Canary Is.* 37 G3
Rășcani, *Moldova* 43 C12
Raseiniai, *Lithuania* 9 J20
Rashad, *Sudan* 81 E3
Rashîd, *Egypt* 80 H7
Rashîd, Masabb, *Egypt* 80 H7
Rasht, *Iran* 71 B6
Rasi Salai, *Thailand* 64 E5
Raška, *Serbia, Yug.* 40 C4
Râsnov, *Romania* 43 E10
Rason L., *Australia* 93 E3
Rașova, *Romania* 43 F12
Rasovo, *Bulgaria* 40 C7
Rasra, *India* 69 G10
Rasskazovo, *Russia* 48 D5
Rast, *Romania* 43 G8
Rastatt, *Germany* 25 G4
Rastede, *Germany* 24 B4
Răstolița, *Romania* 43 D9
Raszków, *Poland* 45 G4
Rat Buri, *Thailand* 64 F2
Rat Islands, *U.S.A.* 100 C1
Rat River, *Canada* 104 A6
Ratangarh, *India* 68 E6
Rätansbyn, *Sweden* 10 B8
Raṭāwī, *Iraq* 70 D5
Rath, *India* 69 G8
Rath Luirc, *Ireland* 15 D3
Rathdrum, *Ireland* 15 D5
Rathenow, *Germany* 24 C8
Rathkeale, *Ireland* 15 D3
Rathlin I., *U.K.* 15 A5
Rathmelton, *Ireland* 15 A4
Ratibor = Racibórz, *Poland* 45 H5
Rätikon, *Austria* 26 D2
Ratingen, *Germany* 24 D2
Ratlam, *India* 68 H6
Ratnagiri, *India* 66 L8
Raton, *U.S.A.* 113 G2
Rattaphum, *Thailand* 65 J3
Ratten, *Austria* 26 D8
Rattray Hd., *U.K.* 14 D7
Rättvik, *Sweden* 10 D9
Ratz, Mt., *Canada* 104 B2
Ratzeburg, *Germany* 24 B6
Raub, *Malaysia* 65 L3
Rauch, *Argentina* 126 D4
Raufarhöfn, *Iceland* 8 C6
Raufoss, *Norway* 9 F14
Raukumara Ra., *N.Z.* 91 H6
Rauma, *Finland* 9 F19
Raurkela, *India* 69 H11
Rausu-Dake, *Japan* 54 B12
Răut →, *Moldova* 43 C14
Rava-Ruska, *Poland* 47 G2
Rava Russkaya = Rava-Ruska, *Poland* 47 G2
Ravānsar, *Iran* 70 C5
Ravanusa, *Italy* 30 E6
Rāvar, *Iran* 71 D8
Ravena, *U.S.A.* 111 D11
Ravenna, *Italy* 29 D9
Ravenna, *Nebr., U.S.A.* 112 E5
Ravenna, *Ohio, U.S.A.* 110 E3
Ravensburg, *Germany* 25 H5
Ravenshoe, *Australia* 94 B4
Ravensthorpe, *Australia* 93 F3
Ravenswood, *Australia* 94 C4
Ravenswood, *U.S.A.* 108 F5
Ravi →, *Pakistan* 68 D4
Ravna Gora, *Croatia* 29 C11
Ravna Reka, *Serbia, Yug.* 40 B5
Ravne na Koroškem, *Slovenia* 29 B11
Rawa Mazowiecka, *Poland* 45 G7
Rawalpindi, *Pakistan* 68 C5
Rawāndūz, *Iraq* 70 B5
Rawang, *Malaysia* 65 L3
Rawdon, *Canada* 102 C5
Rawene, *N.Z.* 91 F4
Rawicz, *Poland* 45 G3
Rawka →, *Poland* 45 F7
Rawlinna, *Australia* 93 F4
Rawlins, *U.S.A.* 114 F10
Rawlinson Ra., *Australia* 93 D4
Rawson, *Argentina* 128 E3
Ray, *U.S.A.* 112 A3
Ray, C., *Canada* 103 C8
Rayadurg, *India* 66 M10
Rayagada, *India* 67 K13
Raychikhinsk, *Russia* 51 E13
Rāyen, *Iran* 71 D8
Rayleigh, *U.K.* 13 F8
Raymond, *Canada* 104 D6
Raymond, *Calif., U.S.A.* 116 H7
Raymond, *Wash., U.S.A.* 116 D3
Raymondville, *U.S.A.* 113 M6
Raymore, *Canada* 105 C8
Rayne, *U.S.A.* 113 K8
Rayón, *Mexico* 118 B2
Rayong, *Thailand* 64 F3
Rayville, *U.S.A.* 113 J9
Raz, Pte. du, *France* 18 D2
Razan, *Iran* 71 C6
Ražana, *Serbia, Yug.* 40 B3
Ražanj, *Serbia, Yug.* 40 C5
Razdelna, *Bulgaria* 41 C11
Razdel'naya = Rozdilna, *Ukraine* 47 J6
Razdolnoye, *Russia* 54 C5
Razdolnoye, *Ukraine* 47 K7
Razeh, *Iran* 71 C6
Razgrad, *Bulgaria* 41 C10
Razim, Lacul, *Romania* 43 F14
Razlog, *Bulgaria* 40 E7
Razmak, *Pakistan* 68 C3
Ré, Î. de, *France* 20 B2
Reading, *U.K.* 13 F7
Reading, *U.S.A.* 111 F9
Reading □, *U.K.* 13 F7
Realicó, *Argentina* 126 D3
Réalmont, *France* 20 E6
Ream, *Cambodia* 65 G4
Reata, *Mexico* 118 B4
Reay Forest, *U.K.* 14 C4
Rebais, *France* 19 D10
Rebecca, L., *Australia* 93 F3
Rebi, *Indonesia* 63 F8
Rebiana, *Libya* 79 D10
Rebun-Tō, *Japan* 54 B10
Recanati, *Italy* 29 E10
Recaș, *Romania* 42 E6
Recco, *Italy* 28 D6
Recherche, Arch. of the, *Australia* 93 F3
Rechytsa, *Belarus* 47 F6
Recife, *Brazil* 125 E12
Recklinghausen, *Germany* 24 D3
Reconquista, *Argentina* 126 B4
Recreo, *Argentina* 126 B2
Recz, *Poland* 45 E2
Red →, *La., U.S.A.* 113 K9
Red →, *N. Dak., U.S.A.* 112 A6
Red Bank, *U.S.A.* 111 F10
Red Bay, *Canada* 103 B8
Red Bluff, *U.S.A.* 114 F2
Red Bluff L., *U.S.A.* 113 K3
Red Cliffs, *Australia* 95 E3
Red Cloud, *U.S.A.* 112 E5
Red Deer, *Canada* 104 C6
Red Deer →, *Alta., Canada* 105 C7
Red Deer →, *Man., Canada* 105 C8
Red Deer L., *Canada* 105 C8
Red Indian L., *Canada* 103 C8
Red Lake, *Canada* 105 C10
Red Lake Falls, *U.S.A.* 112 B6
Red Lodge, *U.S.A.* 114 D9
Red Mountain, *U.S.A.* 117 K9
Red Oak, *U.S.A.* 112 E7
Red Rock, *Canada* 102 C2
Red Rock, L., *U.S.A.* 112 E8
Red Rocks Pt., *Australia* 93 F4
Red Sea, *Asia* 74 C2
Red Slate Mt., *U.S.A.* 116 H8
Red Sucker L., *Canada* 105 C10
Red Tower Pass = Turnu Roșu, P., *Romania* 43 E9
Red Wing, *U.S.A.* 112 C8
Reda, *Poland* 44 D5
Redange, *Lux.* 17 E5
Redcar, *U.K.* 12 C6
Redcar & Cleveland □, *U.K.* 12 C7
Redcliff, *Canada* 105 C6
Redcliffe, *Australia* 95 D5
Redcliffe, Mt., *Australia* 93 E3
Reddersburg, *S. Africa* 88 D4
Redding, *U.S.A.* 114 F2
Redditch, *U.K.* 13 E6
Redfield, *U.S.A.* 112 C5
Redkino, *Russia* 46 D9
Redknife →, *Canada* 104 A5
Redlands, *U.S.A.* 117 M9
Redmond, *Australia* 93 F2
Redmond, *Oreg., U.S.A.* 114 D3
Redmond, *Wash., U.S.A.* 116 C4
Redon, *France* 18 E4
Redonda, *Antigua* 121 C7
Redondela, *Spain* 34 C2
Redondo, *Portugal* 35 G3
Redondo Beach, *U.S.A.* 117 M8
Redrock Pt., *Canada* 104 A5
Redruth, *U.K.* 13 G2
Redvers, *Canada* 105 D8
Redwater, *Canada* 104 C6
Redwood, *U.S.A.* 111 B9
Redwood City, *U.S.A.* 116 H4
Redwood Falls, *U.S.A.* 112 C7
Ree, L., *Ireland* 15 C3
Reed, L., *Canada* 105 C8
Reed City, *U.S.A.* 108 D3
Reeder, *U.S.A.* 112 B3
Reedley, *U.S.A.* 116 J7
Reedsburg, *U.S.A.* 112 D9
Reedsport, *U.S.A.* 114 E1
Reefton, *N.Z.* 91 K3
Rees, *Germany* 24 D2
Refahiye, *Turkey* 73 C8
Reftele, *Sweden* 11 G7
Refugio, *U.S.A.* 113 L6
Rega →, *Poland* 44 D2
Regalbuto, *Italy* 31 E7
Regen, *Germany* 25 G9
Regen →, *Germany* 25 F8
Regensburg, *Germany* 25 F8
Regenstauf, *Germany* 25 F8
Reggello, *Italy* 29 E8
Réggio di Calábria, *Italy* 31 D8
Réggio nell'Emília, *Italy* 28 D7
Reghin, *Romania* 43 D9
Regina, *Canada* 105 C8
Registro, *Brazil* 127 A6
Reguengos de Monsaraz, *Portugal* 35 G3
Rehar →, *India* 69 H10
Rehoboth, *Namibia* 88 C2
Rehovot, *Israel* 75 D3
Reichenbach, *Germany* 24 E8
Reid, *Australia* 93 F4
Reid River, *Australia* 94 B4
Reidsville, *U.S.A.* 109 G6
Reigate, *U.K.* 13 F7
Reillo, *Spain* 32 F3
Reims, *France* 19 C11
Reina Adelaida, Arch., *Chile* 128 G2
Reinbeck, *U.S.A.* 112 D8
Reinbek, *Germany* 24 B6
Reindeer →, *Canada* 105 B8
Reindeer I., *Canada* 105 C9
Reindeer L., *Canada* 105 B8
Reinga, C., *N.Z.* 91 F4
Reinosa, *Spain* 34 B6
Reitz, *S. Africa* 89 D4
Reivilo, *S. Africa* 88 D3
Rejmyre, *Sweden* 11 F9
Rejowiec Fabryczny, *Poland* 45 G10
Reka →, *Slovenia* 29 C11
Rekovac, *Serbia, Yug.* 40 C5
Reliance, *Canada* 105 A7
Rémalard, *France* 18 D7
Remarkable, Mt., *Australia* 95 E2
Rembang, *Indonesia* 63 G14
Remedios, *Panama* 120 E3
Remeshk, *Iran* 71 E8
Remetea, *Romania* 43 D10
Remich, *Lux.* 17 E6
Remiremont, *France* 19 D13
Remo, *Ethiopia* 81 F5
Remontnoye, *Russia* 49 G6
Remoulins, *France* 21 E8
Remscheid, *Germany* 24 D3
Ren Xian, *China* 56 F8
Rende, *Italy* 31 C9
Rendína, *Greece* 38 B3
Rendsburg, *Germany* 24 A5
Renfrew, *Canada* 102 C4
Renfrewshire □, *U.K.* 14 F4
Rengat, *Indonesia* 62 E2
Rengo, *Chile* 126 C1
Renhua, *China* 59 E9
Renhuai, *China* 58 D6
Reni, *Ukraine* 47 K5
Renk, *Sudan* 81 E3
Renmark, *Australia* 95 E3
Rennell Sd., *Canada* 104 C2
Renner Springs T.O., *Australia* 94 B1
Rennes, *France* 18 D5
Reno, *U.S.A.* 116 F7
Reno →, *Italy* 29 D9
Renovo, *U.S.A.* 110 E7
Renqiu, *China* 56 E9
Rens, *Denmark* 11 K3
Rensselaer, *Ind., U.S.A.* 108 E2
Rensselaer, *N.Y., U.S.A.* 111 D11
Rentería, *Spain* 32 B3
Renton, *U.S.A.* 116 C4
Réo, *Burkina Faso* 82 C4
Reocín, *Spain* 34 B6
Reotipur, *India* 69 G10
Répcelak, *Hungary* 42 C2
Republic, *Mich., U.S.A.* 108 B2
Republic, *Wash., U.S.A.* 114 B4
Republican →, *U.S.A.* 112 F6
Republican City, *U.S.A.* 112 E5
Repulse Bay, *Canada* 101 B11
Requena, *Peru* 124 E4
Requena, *Spain* 33 F3
Réquista, *France* 20 D6
Reșadiye = Datça, *Turkey* 39 E9
Reșadiye, *Turkey* 72 B7
Reșadiye Yarımadası, *Turkey* 39 E9
Resavica, *Serbia, Yug.* 40 B5
Resen, *Macedonia* 40 E5
Reserve, *Canada* 105 C8
Reserve, *U.S.A.* 115 K9
Resht = Rasht, *Iran* 71 B6
Resistencia, *Argentina* 126 B4
Reșița, *Romania* 42 E6
Resko, *Poland* 44 E2
Resolution I., *Canada* 101 B13
Resolution I., *N.Z.* 91 L1
Ressano Garcia, *Mozam.* 89 D5
Reston, *Canada* 105 D8
Reszel, *Poland* 44 D8
Retalhuleu, *Guatemala* 120 D1
Retenue, L. de, *Dem. Rep. of the Congo* 87 E2
Retezat, Munții, *Romania* 42 E8
Retford, *U.K.* 12 D7
Rethel, *France* 19 C11
Rethem, *Germany* 24 C5
Réthímnon, *Greece* 36 D6
Réthímnon □, *Greece* 36 D6
Retiche, Alpi, *Switz.* 25 J6
Retiers, *France* 18 E5
Retortillo, *Spain* 34 E4
Retournac, *France* 21 C8
Rétság, *Hungary* 42 C4
Réunion ■, *Ind. Oc.* 77 J9
Reus, *Spain* 32 D6
Reuterstadt Stavenhagen, *Germany* 24 B8
Reutlingen, *Germany* 25 G5
Reutte, *Austria* 26 D3
Reval = Tallinn, *Estonia* 9 G21
Revel, *France* 20 E6
Revelganj, *India* 69 G11
Revelstoke, *Canada* 104 C5
Reventazón, *Peru* 124 E2
Revigny-sur-Ornain, *France* 19 D11
Revilla Gigedo, Is., *Pac. Oc.* 97 F16
Revillagigedo I., *U.S.A.* 104 B2
Revin, *France* 19 C11
Revúca, *Slovak Rep.* 27 C13
Revuè →, *Mozam.* 87 F3
Rewa, *India* 69 G9
Rewari, *India* 68 E7
Rexburg, *U.S.A.* 114 E8
Rey, *Iran* 71 C6
Rey, I. del, *Panama* 120 E4
Rey, Rio del →, *Nigeria* 83 E6
Rey Malabo, *Eq. Guin.* 83 E6
Reyðarfjörður, *Iceland* 8 D6
Reyes, Pt., *U.S.A.* 116 H3
Reyhanlı, *Turkey* 72 D7
Reykjahlið, *Iceland* 8 D5
Reykjanes, *Iceland* 8 E2
Reykjavík, *Iceland* 8 D3
Reynolds, *Canada* 105 D9
Reynolds Ra., *Australia* 92 D5
Reynoldsville, *U.S.A.* 110 E6
Reynosa, *Mexico* 119 B5
Rēzekne, *Latvia* 9 H22
Rezina, *Moldova* 43 C13
Rezovo, *Bulgaria* 41 D12
Rezvān, *Iran* 71 E8
Rgotina, *Serbia, Yug.* 40 B6
Rhamnus, *Greece* 38 C6
Rhayader, *U.K.* 13 E4
Rheda-Wiedenbrück, *Germany* 24 D4
Rhede, *Germany* 24 D2
Rhein, *Canada* 105 C8
Rhein →, *Europe* 17 C6
Rhein-Main-Donau-Kanal, *Germany* 25 F7
Rheinbach, *Germany* 24 E2
Rheine, *Germany* 24 C3
Rheinfelden, *Germany* 25 H3
Rheinhessen-Pfalz □, *Germany* 25 F3
Rheinland-Pfalz □, *Germany* 25 E2
Rheinsberg, *Germany* 24 B8
Rhin = Rhein →, *Europe* 17 C6
Rhine = Rhein →, *Europe* 17 C6
Rhineland-Palatinate □ = Rheinland-Pfalz □, *Germany* 25 E2
Rhinelander, *U.S.A.* 112 C10
Rhinns Pt., *U.K.* 14 F2
Rhino Camp, *Uganda* 86 B3
Rho, *Italy* 28 C6
Rhode Island □, *U.S.A.* 111 E13
Rhodes = Ródhos, *Greece* 36 C10
Rhodesia = Zimbabwe ■, *Africa* 87 F3
Rhodope Mts. = Rhodopi Planina, *Bulgaria* 41 E8
Rhodopi Planina, *Bulgaria* 41 E8
Rhön = Rhön, *Germany* 24 E5
Rhön, *Germany* 24 E5
Rhondda, *U.K.* 13 F4
Rhondda Cynon Taff □, *U.K.* 13 F4
Rhône □, *France* 21 C8
Rhône →, *France* 21 E8
Rhône-Alpes □, *France* 21 C9
Rhum, *U.K.* 14 E2
Rhyl, *U.K.* 12 D4
Ri-Aba, *Eq. Guin.* 83 E6
Riachão, *Brazil* 125 E9
Riaño, *Spain* 34 C6
Rians, *France* 21 E9
Riansáres →, *Spain* 35 F7
Riasi, *India* 69 C6
Riau □, *Indonesia* 62 E2
Riau, Kepulauan, *Indonesia* 62 D2
Riau Arch. = Riau, Kepulauan, *Indonesia* 62 D2
Riaza, *Spain* 34 D7
Riaza →, *Spain* 34 D7
Riba de Saelices, *Spain* 32 E2
Riba-Roja de Turia, *Spain* 33 F4
Ribadavia, *Spain* 34 C2
Ribadeo, *Spain* 34 B3
Ribadesella, *Spain* 34 B5
Ribas = Ribes de Freser, *Spain* 32 C7
Ribas do Rio Pardo, *Brazil* 125 H8
Ribble →, *U.K.* 12 D5
Ribe, *Denmark* 11 J2
Ribe Amtskommune □, *Denmark* 11 J2
Ribeauvillé, *France* 19 D14
Ribécourt-Dreslincourt, *France* 19 C9
Ribeira = Santa Uxía, *Spain* 34 C2
Ribeira Brava, *Madeira* 37 D2
Ribeirão Prêto, *Brazil* 127 A6
Ribemont, *France* 19 C10
Ribera, *Italy* 30 E6
Ribérac, *France* 20 C4
Riberalta, *Bolivia* 124 F5
Ribes de Freser, *Spain* 32 C7
Ribnica, *Slovenia* 29 C11
Ribnitz-Damgarten, *Germany* 24 A8
Říčany, *Czech Rep.* 26 B7
Riccarton, *N.Z.* 91 K4
Ríccia, *Italy* 31 A7
Riccione, *Italy* 29 E9
Rice, *U.S.A.* 117 L12
Rice L., *Canada* 110 B6
Rice Lake, *U.S.A.* 112 C9
Rich Hill, *U.S.A.* 113 F7
Richards Bay, *S. Africa* 89 D5
Richards L., *Canada* 105 B7
Richardson →, *Canada* 105 B6
Richardson Springs, *U.S.A.* 116 F5
Richardton, *U.S.A.* 112 B3
Riche, C., *Australia* 93 F2
Richelieu, *France* 18 E7
Richey, *U.S.A.* 112 B2
Richfield, *Idaho, U.S.A.* 114 E6
Richfield, *Utah, U.S.A.* 115 G8
Richford, *U.S.A.* 111 B12
Richibucto, *Canada* 103 C7
Richland, *Ga., U.S.A.* 109 J3
Richland, *Oreg., U.S.A.* 114 D5
Richland, *Wash., U.S.A.* 114 C4
Richland Center, *U.S.A.* 112 D9
Richlands, *U.S.A.* 108 G5
Richmond, *N.S.W., Australia* 95 E5
Richmond, *Queens., Australia* 94 C3
Richmond, *N.Z.* 91 J4
Richmond, *U.K.* 12 C6
Richmond, *Calif., U.S.A.* 116 H4
Richmond, *Ind., U.S.A.* 108 F3
Richmond, *Ky., U.S.A.* 108 G3
Richmond, *Mich., U.S.A.* 110 D2
Richmond, *Mo., U.S.A.* 112 F8
Richmond, *Tex., U.S.A.* 113 L7
Richmond, *Utah, U.S.A.* 114 F8
Richmond, *Va., U.S.A.* 108 G7
Richmond Ra., *Australia* 95 D5
Richton, *U.S.A.* 109 K1
Richwood, *U.S.A.* 108 F5
Ricla, *Spain* 32 D3
Ridder = Leninogorsk, *Kazakstan* 50 D9
Ridgecrest, *U.S.A.* 117 K9
Ridgedale, *Canada* 105 C8
Ridgefield, *U.S.A.* 116 E4
Ridgeland, *U.S.A.* 109 J5
Ridgelands, *Australia* 94 C5
Ridgetown, *Canada* 102 D3
Ridgewood, *U.S.A.* 111 F10
Ridgway, *U.S.A.* 110 E6
Riding Mountain Nat. Park, *Canada* 105 C9
Ridley, Mt., *Australia* 93 F3
Ried, *Austria* 26 C6
Riedlingen, *Germany* 25 G5
Riedstadt, *Germany* 25 F4
Rienza →, *Italy* 29 B8
Riesa, *Germany* 24 D9
Riesi, *Italy* 31 E7
Riet →, *S. Africa* 88 D3
Rietavas, *Lithuania* 44 C8
Rieti, *Italy* 29 F9
Rieupeyroux, *France* 20 D6
Riez, *France* 21 E10
Riffe L., *U.S.A.* 116 D4
Rifle, *U.S.A.* 114 G10
Rift Valley □, *Kenya* 86 B4
Rīga, *Latvia* 9 H21
Riga, G. of, *Latvia* 9 H20
Rīgān, *Iran* 71 D8
Rīgas Jūras Līcis = Riga, G. of, *Latvia* 9 H20
Rigaud, *Canada* 111 A10
Rigby, *U.S.A.* 114 E8
Rīgestān □, *Afghan.* 66 D4
Riggins, *U.S.A.* 114 D5
Rignac, *France* 20 D6
Rigolet, *Canada* 103 B8
Riihimäki, *Finland* 9 F21
Riiser-Larsen-halvøya, *Antarctica* 5 C4
Rijau, *Nigeria* 83 C6
Rijeka, *Croatia* 29 C11
Rijeka Crnojevića, *Montenegro, Yug.* 40 D3
Rijssen, *Neths.* 17 B6
Rike, *Ethiopia* 81 E4
Rikuzentakada, *Japan* 54 E10

Rila, *Bulgaria* 40 D7
Rila Planina, *Bulgaria* 40 D7
Riley, *U.S.A.* 114 E4
Rima →, *Nigeria* 83 C6
Rimah, Wadi ar →, *Si. Arabia* 70 E4
Rimavská Sobota, *Slovak Rep.* 27 C13
Rimbey, *Canada* 104 C6
Rimbo, *Sweden* 10 E12
Rimforsa, *Sweden* 11 F9
Rimi, *Nigeria* 83 C6
Rímini, *Italy* 29 D9
Rimouski, *Canada* 103 C6
Rimrock, *U.S.A.* 116 D5
Rinca, *Indonesia* 63 F5
Rincón de la Victoria, *Spain* 35 J6
Rincón de Romos, *Mexico* 118 C4
Rinconada, *Argentina* 126 A2
Ringarum, *Sweden* 11 F10
Ringe, *Denmark* 11 J4
Ringim, *Nigeria* 83 C6
Ringkøbing, *Denmark* 11 H2
Ringkøbing Amtskommune □, *Denmark* 11 H2
Ringkøbing Fjord, *Denmark* 11 H2
Ringling, *U.S.A.* 114 C8
Ringsjön, *Sweden* 11 J7
Ringsted, *Denmark* 11 J5
Ringvassøy, *Norway* 8 B18
Rinía, *Greece* 39 D7
Rinjani, *Indonesia* 62 F5
Rinteln, *Germany* 24 C5
Río, Punta del, *Spain* 33 J2
Rio Branco, *Brazil* 124 E5
Río Branco, *Uruguay* 127 C5
Rio Brilhante, *Brazil* 127 A5
Rio Claro, *Brazil* 127 A6
Rio Claro, *Trin. & Tob.* 121 D7
Río Colorado, *Argentina* 128 D4
Río Cuarto, *Argentina* 126 C3
Rio das Pedras, *Mozam.* 89 C6
Rio de Janeiro, *Brazil* 127 A7
Rio de Janeiro □, *Brazil* 127 A7
Rio do Sul, *Brazil* 127 B6
Río Gallegos, *Argentina* 128 G3
Río Grande, *Argentina* 128 G3
Rio Grande, *Brazil* 127 C5
Río Grande, *Mexico* 118 C4
Río Grande, *Nic.* 120 D3
Rio Grande →, *U.S.A.* 113 N6
Rio Grande City, *U.S.A.* 113 M5
Río Grande del Norte →, *N. Amer.* 107 E7
Rio Grande do Norte □, *Brazil* 125 E11
Rio Grande do Sul □, *Brazil* 127 C5
Río Hato, *Panama* 120 E3
Río Lagartos, *Mexico* 119 C7
Rio Largo, *Brazil* 125 E11
Rio Maior, *Portugal* 35 F2
Rio Marina, *Italy* 28 F7
Río Mulatos, *Bolivia* 124 G5
Río Muni = Mbini □, *Eq. Guin.* 84 D2
Rio Negro, *Brazil* 127 B6
Rio Pardo, *Brazil* 127 C5
Río Segundo, *Argentina* 126 C3
Río Tercero, *Argentina* 126 C3
Rio Tinto, *Portugal* 34 D2
Rio Verde, *Brazil* 125 G8
Río Verde, *Mexico* 119 C5
Rio Vista, *U.S.A.* 116 G5
Ríobamba, *Ecuador* 124 D3
Ríohacha, *Colombia* 124 A4
Riom, *France* 20 C7
Riom-ès-Montagnes, *France* 20 C6
Rion-des-Landes, *France* 20 E3
Rionero in Vúlture, *Italy* 31 B8
Rioni →, *Georgia* 49 J5
Riós, *Spain* 34 D3
Ríosucio, *Colombia* 124 B3
Riou L., *Canada* 105 B7
Rioz, *France* 19 E13
Ripatransone, *Italy* 29 F10
Ripley, *Canada* 110 B3
Ripley, *Calif., U.S.A.* 117 M12
Ripley, *N.Y., U.S.A.* 110 D5
Ripley, *Tenn., U.S.A.* 113 H10
Ripoll, *Spain* 32 C7
Ripon, *U.K.* 12 C6
Ripon, *Calif., U.S.A.* 116 H5
Ripon, *Wis., U.S.A.* 108 D1
Riposto, *Italy* 31 E8
Risalpur, *Pakistan* 68 B4
Risan, *Montenegro, Yug.* 40 D2
Riscle, *France* 20 E3
Rishā', W. ar →, *Si. Arabia* 70 E5
Rishiri-Tō, *Japan* 54 B10
Rishon le Ẕiyyon, *Israel* 75 D3
Risle →, *France* 18 C7
Rison, *U.S.A.* 113 J8
Risør, *Norway* 9 G13
Riti, *Nigeria* 83 D6
Rittman, *U.S.A.* 110 F3
Ritzville, *U.S.A.* 114 C4
Riva del Garda, *Italy* 28 C7
Riva Lígure, *Italy* 28 E4
Rivadavia, *Buenos Aires, Argentina* 126 D3
Rivadavia, *Mendoza, Argentina* 126 C2
Rivadavia, *Salta, Argentina* 126 A3
Rivadavia, *Chile* 126 B1
Rivarolo Canavese, *Italy* 28 C4
Rivas, *Nic.* 120 D2
Rive-de-Gier, *France* 21 C8
River Cess, *Liberia* 82 D3
Rivera, *Argentina* 128 D4
Rivera, *Uruguay* 127 C4
Riverdale, *U.S.A.* 116 J7
Riverhead, *U.S.A.* 111 F12
Riverhurst, *Canada* 105 C7
Riverina, *Australia* 93 E3
Rivers, *Canada* 105 C8
Rivers □, *Nigeria* 83 E6
Rivers, L. of the, *Canada* 105 D7
Rivers Inlet, *Canada* 104 C3
Riversdale, *S. Africa* 88 E3
Riverside, *Calif., U.S.A.* 117 M9
Riverside, *Wyo., U.S.A.* 114 F10
Riversleigh, *Australia* 94 B2
Riverton, *Australia* 95 E2
Riverton, *Canada* 105 C9
Riverton, *N.Z.* 91 M2
Riverton, *U.S.A.* 114 E9
Riverton Heights, *U.S.A.* 116 C4
Rives, *France* 21 C9
Rivesaltes, *France* 20 F6
Riviera di Levante, *Italy* 28 D6
Riviera di Ponente, *Italy* 28 D5
Rivière-à-Pierre, *Canada* 103 C5
Rivière-au-Renard, *Canada* 103 C7
Rivière-du-Loup, *Canada* 103 C6
Rivière-Pentecôte, *Canada* 103 C6
Rivière-Pilote, *Martinique* 121 D7
Rivne, *Ukraine* 47 G4
Rívoli, *Italy* 28 C4
Rivoli B., *Australia* 95 F3
Rixheim, *France* 19 E14
Riyadh = Ar Riyāḍ, *Si. Arabia* 70 E5
Rize, *Turkey* 73 B9
Rizhao, *China* 57 G10
Rizokarpaso, *Cyprus* 36 D13
Rizzuto, C., *Italy* 31 D10
Rjukan, *Norway* 9 G13
Ro, *Greece* 39 E11
Roa, *Spain* 34 D7
Road Town, *Virgin Is.* 121 C7
Roanne, *France* 19 F11
Roanoke, *Ala., U.S.A.* 109 J3
Roanoke, *Va., U.S.A.* 108 G6
Roanoke →, *U.S.A.* 109 H7
Roanoke I., *U.S.A.* 109 H8
Roanoke Rapids, *U.S.A.* 109 G7
Roatán, *Honduras* 120 C2
Robbins I., *Australia* 94 G4
Róbbio, *Italy* 28 C5
Robe →, *Australia* 92 D2
Röbel, *Germany* 24 B8
Robert Lee, *U.S.A.* 113 K4
Roberts, *U.S.A.* 114 E7
Robertsganj, *India* 69 G10
Robertson, *S. Africa* 88 E2
Robertson I., *Antarctica* 5 C18
Robertson Ra., *Australia* 92 D3
Robertsport, *Liberia* 82 D2
Robertstown, *Australia* 95 E2
Roberval, *Canada* 103 C5
Robeson Chan., *Greenland* 4 A4
Robinson →, *Australia* 94 B2
Robinson Ra., *Australia* 93 E2
Robinson River, *Australia* 94 B2
Robinvale, *Australia* 95 E3
Robledo, *Spain* 33 G2
Roblin, *Canada* 105 C8
Roboré, *Bolivia* 124 G7
Robson, Mt., *Canada* 104 C5
Robstown, *U.S.A.* 113 M6
Roca, C. da, *Portugal* 35 G1
Roca Partida, I., *Mexico* 118 D2
Rocamadour, *France* 20 D5
Rocas, I., *Brazil* 125 D12
Rocca San Casciano, *Italy* 29 D8
Roccadáspide, *Italy* 31 B8
Roccastrada, *Italy* 29 F8
Roccella Iónica, *Italy* 31 D9
Rocha, *Uruguay* 127 C5
Rochdale, *U.K.* 12 D5
Rochechouart, *France* 20 C4
Rochefort, *Belgium* 17 D5
Rochefort, *France* 20 C3
Rochefort-en-Terre, *France* 18 E4
Rochelle, *U.S.A.* 112 E10
Rocher River, *Canada* 104 A6
Rocheservière, *France* 18 F5
Rochester, *Canada* 104 C6
Rochester, *U.K.* 13 F8
Rochester, *Ind., U.S.A.* 108 E2
Rochester, *Minn., U.S.A.* 112 C8
Rochester, *N.H., U.S.A.* 111 C14
Rochester, *N.Y., U.S.A.* 110 C7
Rociu, *Romania* 43 F10
Rock →, *Canada* 104 A3
Rock Hill, *U.S.A.* 109 H5
Rock Island, *U.S.A.* 112 E9
Rock Rapids, *U.S.A.* 112 D6
Rock River, *U.S.A.* 114 F11
Rock Sound, *Bahamas* 120 B4
Rock Springs, *Mont., U.S.A.* 114 C10
Rock Springs, *Wyo., U.S.A.* 114 F9
Rock Valley, *U.S.A.* 112 D6
Rockall, *Atl. Oc.* 6 D3
Rockdale, *Tex., U.S.A.* 113 K6
Rockdale, *Wash., U.S.A.* 116 C5
Rockefeller Plateau, *Antarctica* 5 E14
Rockford, *U.S.A.* 112 D10
Rockglen, *Canada* 105 D7
Rockhampton, *Australia* 94 C5
Rockhampton Downs, *Australia* 94 B2
Rockingham, *Australia* 93 F2
Rockingham B., *Australia* 94 B4
Rocklake, *U.S.A.* 112 A5
Rockland, *Canada* 111 A9
Rockland, *Idaho, U.S.A.* 114 E7
Rockland, *Maine, U.S.A.* 103 D6
Rockland, *Mich., U.S.A.* 112 B10
Rocklin, *U.S.A.* 116 G5
Rockmart, *U.S.A.* 109 H3
Rockport, *Mo., U.S.A.* 112 E7
Rockport, *Tex., U.S.A.* 113 L6
Rocksprings, *U.S.A.* 113 K4
Rockville, *Conn., U.S.A.* 111 E12
Rockville, *Md., U.S.A.* 108 F7
Rockwall, *U.S.A.* 113 J6
Rockwell City, *U.S.A.* 112 D7
Rockwood, *U.S.A.* 109 H3
Rocky Ford, *U.S.A.* 112 F3
Rocky Gully, *Australia* 93 F2
Rocky Lane, *Canada* 104 B5
Rocky Mount, *U.S.A.* 109 H7
Rocky Mountain House, *Canada* 104 C6
Rocky Mts., *N. Amer.* 104 C4
Rockyford, *Canada* 104 C6
Rocroi, *France* 19 C11
Rod, *Pakistan* 66 E3
Rødby, *Denmark* 11 K5
Rødbyhavn, *Denmark* 11 K5
Roddickton, *Canada* 103 B8
Rødding, *Denmark* 11 J3
Rödeby, *Sweden* 11 H9
Rødekro, *Denmark* 11 J3
Rodenkirchen, *Germany* 24 B4
Roderick I., *Canada* 104 C3
Rodez, *France* 20 D6
Rodholívas, *Greece* 40 F7
Rodhópi □, *Greece* 41 E9
Rodhopoú, *Greece* 36 D5
Ródhos, *Greece* 36 C10
Rodi Gargánico, *Italy* 29 G12
Rodna, *Romania* 43 C9
Rodnei, Munţii, *Romania* 43 C9
Rodney, *Canada* 110 D3
Rodney, C., *N.Z.* 91 G5
Rodniki, *Russia* 48 B5
Rodonit, Kepi i, *Albania* 40 E3
Rodriguez, *Ind. Oc.* 3 E13
Roe →, *U.K.* 15 A5
Roebling, *U.S.A.* 111 F10
Roebourne, *Australia* 92 D2
Roebuck B., *Australia* 92 C3
Roebuck Plains, *Australia* 92 C3
Roermond, *Neths.* 17 C6
Roes Welcome Sd., *Canada* 101 B11
Roeselare, *Belgium* 17 D3
Rogachev = Ragachow, *Belarus* 47 F6
Rogačica, *Serbia, Yug.* 40 B3
Rogagua, L., *Bolivia* 124 F5
Rogaška Slatina, *Slovenia* 29 B12
Rogatec, *Slovenia* 29 B12
Rogatica, *Bos.-H.* 42 G4
Rogatyn, *Ukraine* 47 H3
Rogdhia, *Greece* 36 D7
Rogers, *U.S.A.* 113 G7
Rogers City, *U.S.A.* 108 C4
Rogerson, *U.S.A.* 114 E6
Rogersville, *U.S.A.* 109 G4
Roggan River, *Canada* 102 B4
Roggeveldberge, *S. Africa* 88 E3
Roggiano Gravina, *Italy* 31 C9
Rogliano, *France* 21 F13
Rogliano, *Italy* 31 C9
Rogoaguado, L., *Bolivia* 124 F5
Rogoźno, *Poland* 45 F3
Rogue →, *U.S.A.* 114 E1
Rohan, *France* 18 D4
Róhda, *Greece* 36 A3
Rohnert Park, *U.S.A.* 116 G4
Rohri, *Pakistan* 68 F3
Rohri Canal, *Pakistan* 68 F3
Rohtak, *India* 68 E7
Roi Et, *Thailand* 64 D4
Roja, *Latvia* 9 H20
Rojas, *Argentina* 126 C3
Rojişte, *Romania* 43 F8
Rojo, C., *Mexico* 119 C5
Rokan →, *Indonesia* 62 D2
Rokeby, *Australia* 94 A3
Rokiškis, *Lithuania* 9 J21
Rokitno, *Russia* 47 G8
Rokycany, *Czech Rep.* 26 B6
Rolândia, *Brazil* 127 A5
Rolette, *U.S.A.* 112 A5
Rolla, *Kans., U.S.A.* 113 G4
Rolla, *Mo., U.S.A.* 113 G9
Rolla, *N. Dak., U.S.A.* 112 A5
Rolleston, *Australia* 94 C4
Rollingstone, *Australia* 94 B4
Rom, *Sudan* 81 F3
Roma, *Australia* 95 D4
Roma, *Italy* 29 G9
Roma, *Sweden* 11 G12
Roman, *Bulgaria* 40 C7
Roman, *Romania* 43 D11
Roman-Kosh, Gora, *Ukraine* 47 K8
Romanche →, *France* 21 C9
Romang, *Indonesia* 63 F7
Românî, *Egypt* 75 E1
Romania ■, *Europe* 43 D10
Romanija, *Bos.-H.* 42 G3
Romano, Cayo, *Cuba* 120 B4
Romanovka = Basarabeasca, *Moldova* 43 D13
Romans-sur-Isère, *France* 21 C9
Romanshorn, *Switz.* 25 H5
Romblon, *Phil.* 61 E5
Rombo □, *Tanzania* 86 C4
Rome = Roma, *Italy* 29 G9
Rome, *Ga., U.S.A.* 109 H3
Rome, *N.Y., U.S.A.* 111 C9
Rometta, *Italy* 31 D8
Romilly-sur-Seine, *France* 19 D10
Romney, *U.S.A.* 108 F6
Romney Marsh, *U.K.* 13 F8
Romny, *Ukraine* 47 G7
Rømø, *Denmark* 11 J2
Romodan, *Ukraine* 47 G7
Romodanovo, *Russia* 48 C7
Romont, *Switz.* 25 J2
Romorantin-Lanthenay, *France* 19 E8
Romsdalen, *Norway* 9 E12
Romsey, *U.K.* 13 G6
Ron, *Vietnam* 64 D6
Rona, *U.K.* 14 D3
Ronan, *U.S.A.* 114 C6
Roncador, Cayos, *Caribbean* 120 D3
Roncador, Serra do, *Brazil* 125 F8
Ronceverte, *U.S.A.* 108 G5
Ronciglione, *Italy* 29 F9
Ronco →, *Italy* 29 D9
Ronda, *Spain* 35 J5
Ronda, Serranía de, *Spain* 35 J5
Rondane, *Norway* 9 F13
Rondônia □, *Brazil* 124 F6
Rondonópolis, *Brazil* 125 G8
Rong Jiang →, *China* 58 E7
Rong Xian, *Guangxi Zhuangzu, China* 59 F8
Rong Xian, *Sichuan, China* 58 C5
Rong'an, *China* 58 E7
Rongchang, *China* 58 C5
Ronge, L. la, *Canada* 105 B7
Rongjiang, *China* 58 E7
Rongshui, *China* 58 E7
Rønne, *Denmark* 11 J8
Ronne Ice Shelf, *Antarctica* 5 D18
Ronneby, *Sweden* 11 H9
Ronnebyån →, *Sweden* 11 H9
Rönneshytta, *Sweden* 11 F9
Ronsard, C., *Australia* 93 D1
Ronse, *Belgium* 17 D3
Roodepoort, *S. Africa* 89 D4
Roof Butte, *U.S.A.* 115 H9
Roorkee, *India* 68 E7
Roosendaal, *Neths.* 17 C4
Roosevelt, *Minn., U.S.A.* 112 A7
Roosevelt, *Utah, U.S.A.* 114 F8
Roosevelt →, *Brazil* 122 D4
Roosevelt, Mt., *Canada* 104 B3
Roosevelt I., *Antarctica* 5 D12
Roosevelt Res., *U.S.A.* 115 K8
Ropczyce, *Poland* 45 H8
Roper →, *Australia* 94 A2
Ropesville, *U.S.A.* 113 J3
Roque Pérez, *Argentina* 126 D4
Roquefort, *France* 20 D3
Roquemaure, *France* 21 D8
Roquetas de Mar, *Spain* 33 J2
Roquetes, *Spain* 32 E5
Roquevaire, *France* 21 E9
Roraima □, *Brazil* 124 C6
Roraima, Mt., *Venezuela* 122 C4
Rorketon, *Canada* 105 C9
Røros, *Norway* 9 E14
Rorschach, *Switz.* 25 H5
Rosa, *Zambia* 87 D3
Rosa, Monte, *Italy* 28 C4
Rosal de la Frontera, *Spain* 35 H3
Rosalia, *U.S.A.* 114 C5
Rosamond, *U.S.A.* 117 L8
Rosans, *France* 21 D9
Rosario, *Argentina* 126 C3
Rosário, *Brazil* 125 D10
Rosario, *Baja Calif., Mexico* 118 B1
Rosario, *Sinaloa, Mexico* 118 C3
Rosario, *Paraguay* 126 A4
Rosario de la Frontera, *Argentina* 126 B3
Rosario de Lerma, *Argentina* 126 A2
Rosario del Tala, *Argentina* 126 C4
Rosário do Sul, *Brazil* 127 C5
Rosarito, *Mexico* 117 N9
Rosarno, *Italy* 31 D8
Rosas = Roses, *Spain* 32 C8
Roscoe, *U.S.A.* 112 C5
Roscoff, *France* 18 D3
Roscommon, *Ireland* 15 C3
Roscommon, *U.S.A.* 108 C3
Roscommon □, *Ireland* 15 C3
Roscrea, *Ireland* 15 D4
Rose →, *Australia* 94 A2
Rose Blanche, *Canada* 103 C8
Rose Harbour, *Canada* 104 C2
Rose Pt., *Canada* 104 C2
Rose Valley, *Canada* 105 C8
Roseau, *Domin.* 121 C7
Roseau, *U.S.A.* 112 A7
Rosebery, *Australia* 94 G4
Rosebud, *U.S.A.* 113 K6
Roseburg, *U.S.A.* 114 E2
Rosedale, *Australia* 94 C5
Rosedale, *U.S.A.* 113 J9
Roseland, *U.S.A.* 116 G4
Rosemary, *Canada* 104 C6
Rosenberg, *U.S.A.* 113 L7
Rosendaël, *France* 19 A9
Rosenheim, *Germany* 25 H8
Roses, *Spain* 32 C8
Roses, G. de, *Spain* 32 C8
Roseto degli Abruzzi, *Italy* 29 F11
Rosetown, *Canada* 105 C7
Rosetta = Rashîd, *Egypt* 80 H7
Roseville, *U.S.A.* 116 G5
Rosewood, *N. Terr., Australia* 92 C4
Rosewood, *Queens., Australia* 95 D5
Roshkhvār, *Iran* 71 C8
Rosières-en-Santerre, *France* 19 C9
Rosignano Maríttimo, *Italy* 28 E7
Rosignol, *Guyana* 124 B7
Roşiori de Vede, *Romania* 43 F10
Rositsa, *Bulgaria* 41 C11
Rositsa →, *Bulgaria* 41 C9
Roskilde, *Denmark* 11 J6
Roskilde Amtskommune □, *Denmark* 11 J6
Roskovec, *Albania* 40 F3
Roslavl, *Russia* 46 F7
Roslyn, *Australia* 95 E4
Rosmaninhal, *Portugal* 34 F3
Rosmead, *S. Africa* 88 E4
Røsnæs, *Denmark* 11 J4
Rosolini, *Italy* 31 F7
Rosporden, *France* 18 E3
Ross, *Australia* 94 G4
Ross, *N.Z.* 91 K3
Ross I., *Antarctica* 5 D11
Ross Ice Shelf, *Antarctica* 5 E12
Ross L., *U.S.A.* 114 B3
Ross-on-Wye, *U.K.* 13 F5
Ross Sea, *Antarctica* 5 D11
Rossall Pt., *U.K.* 12 D4
Rossan Pt., *Ireland* 15 B3
Rossano, *Italy* 31 C9
Rossburn, *Canada* 105 C8
Rosseau, *Canada* 110 A5
Rosses, The, *Ireland* 15 A3
Rossignol, L., *Canada* 102 B5
Rossignol Res., *Canada* 103 D6
Rossland, *Canada* 104 D5
Rosslare, *Ireland* 15 D5
Rosslau, *Germany* 24 D8
Rosso, *Mauritania* 82 B1
Rosso, C., *France* 21 F12
Rossosh, *Russia* 47 G10
Rossport, *Canada* 102 C2
Røssvatnet, *Norway* 8 D16
Rossville, *Australia* 94 B4
Røst, *Norway* 8 C15
Rosthern, *Canada* 105 C7
Rostock, *Germany* 24 A8
Rostov, *Don, Russia* 47 J10
Rostov, *Yaroslavl, Russia* 46 D10
Rostrenen, *France* 18 D3
Roswell, *Ga., U.S.A.* 109 H3
Roswell, *N. Mex., U.S.A.* 113 J2
Rota, *Spain* 35 J4
Rotan, *U.S.A.* 113 J4
Rotenburg, *Hessen, Germany* 24 E5
Rotenburg, *Niedersachsen, Germany* 24 B5
Roth, *Germany* 25 F7
Rothaargebirge, *Germany* 24 D4
Rothenburg ob der Tauber, *Germany* 25 F6
Rother →, *U.K.* 13 G8
Rotherham, *U.K.* 12 D6
Rothes, *U.K.* 14 D5
Rothesay, *Canada* 103 C6
Rothesay, *U.K.* 14 F3
Roti, *Indonesia* 63 F6
Rotja, Pta., *Spain* 33 G6
Roto, *Australia* 95 E4
Rotoroa, L., *N.Z.* 91 J4
Rotorua, *N.Z.* 91 H6
Rotorua, L., *N.Z.* 91 H6
Rott →, *Germany* 25 G9
Rottenburg, *Germany* 25 G4
Rottenmann, *Austria* 26 D7
Rotterdam, *Neths.* 17 C4
Rottne, *Sweden* 11 G8
Rottnest I., *Australia* 93 F2
Rottumeroog, *Neths.* 17 A6
Rottweil, *Germany* 25 G4
Rotuma, *Fiji* 96 J9
Roubaix, *France* 19 B10
Roudnice nad Labem, *Czech Rep.* 26 A7
Rouen, *France* 18 C8
Rouergue, *France* 20 D5
Rouillac, *France* 20 C3
Rouleau, *Canada* 105 C8
Round Mountain, *U.S.A.* 114 G5
Round Mt., *Australia* 95 E5
Roundup, *U.S.A.* 114 C9
Rousay, *U.K.* 14 B5
Rouses Point, *U.S.A.* 111 B11
Roussillon, *Isère, France* 21 C8
Roussillon, *Pyrénées-Or., France* 20 F6
Rouxville, *S. Africa* 88 E4
Rouyn-Noranda, *Canada* 102 C4
Rovaniemi, *Finland* 8 C21

Rovato, *Italy* 28 C7
Rovenki, *Ukraine* 47 H10
Rovereto, *Italy* 28 C8
Rovigo, *Italy* 29 C8
Rovinj, *Croatia* 29 C10
Rovno = Rivne, *Ukraine* 47 G4
Rovnoye, *Russia* 48 E8
Rovuma = Ruvuma →, *Tanzania* 87 E5
Row'ān, *Iran* 71 C6
Rowena, *Australia* 95 D4
Rowley Shoals, *Australia* 92 C2
Roxa, *Guinea-Biss.* 82 C1
Roxas, *Capiz, Phil.* 61 F5
Roxas, *Isabela, Phil.* 61 C4
Roxas, *Mindoro, Phil.* 61 E4
Roxboro, *U.S.A.* 109 G6
Roxborough Downs, *Australia* 94 C2
Roxburgh, *N.Z.* 91 L2
Roxen, *Sweden* 11 F9
Roy, *Mont., U.S.A.* 114 C9
Roy, *N. Mex., U.S.A.* 113 H2
Roy Hill, *Australia* 92 D2
Royal Canal, *Ireland* 15 C4
Royal Leamington Spa, *U.K.* 13 E6
Royal Tunbridge Wells, *U.K.* 13 F8
Royan, *France* 20 C2
Roye, *France* 19 C9
Royston, *U.K.* 13 E7
Rožaj, *Montenegro, Yug.* 40 D4
Różan, *Poland* 45 F8
Rozay-en-Brie, *France* 19 D9
Rozdilna, *Ukraine* 47 J6
Rozhyshche, *Ukraine* 47 G3
Rožmitál pod Třemšínem, *Czech Rep.* 26 B6
Rožňava, *Slovak Rep.* 27 C13
Rozogi, *Poland* 44 E8
Rozoy-sur-Serre, *France* 19 C11
Rozzano, *Italy* 28 C6
Rrësheni, *Albania* 40 E3
Rrogozhino, *Albania* 40 E3
Rtanj, *Serbia, Yug.* 40 C5
Rtishchevo, *Russia* 48 D6
Rúa = A Rúa, *Spain* 34 C3
Ruacaná, *Angola* 88 B1
Ruahine Ra., *N.Z.* 91 H6
Ruapehu, *N.Z.* 91 H5
Ruapuke I., *N.Z.* 91 M2
Ruâq, W. →, *Egypt* 75 F2
Rub' al Khālī, *Si. Arabia* 74 D4
Rubeho Mts., *Tanzania* 86 D4
Rubezhnoye = Rubizhne, *Ukraine* 47 H10
Rubh a' Mhail, *U.K.* 14 F2
Rubha Hunish, *U.K.* 14 D2
Rubha Robhanais = Lewis, Butt of, *U.K.* 14 C2
Rubi, *Spain* 32 D7
Rubicon →, *U.S.A.* 116 G5
Rubicone →, *Italy* 29 D9
Rubik, *Albania* 40 E3
Rubino, *Ivory C.* 82 D4
Rubio, *Venezuela* 124 B4
Rubizhne, *Ukraine* 47 H10
Rubtsovsk, *Russia* 50 D9
Ruby L., *U.S.A.* 114 F6
Ruby Mts., *U.S.A.* 114 F6
Rucheng, *China* 59 E9
Ruciane-Nida, *Poland* 44 E8
Rūd Sar, *Iran* 71 B6
Ruda, *Sweden* 11 G10
Ruda Śląska, *Poland* 45 H5
Rudall, *Australia* 95 E2
Rudall →, *Australia* 92 D3
Rüdersdorf, *Germany* 24 C9
Rudewa, *Tanzania* 87 E3
Rudkøbing, *Denmark* 11 K4
Rudna, *Poland* 45 G3
Rudnik, *Bulgaria* 41 D11
Rudnik, *Poland* 45 H9
Rudnik, *Serbia, Yug.* 40 B4
Rudnya, *Russia* 46 E6
Rudnyy, *Kazakstan* 50 D7
Rudo, *Bos.-H.* 42 G4
Rudolfa, Ostrov, *Russia* 50 A6
Rudolstadt, *Germany* 24 E7
Rudong, *China* 59 A13
Rudozem, *Bulgaria* 41 E8
Rudyard, *U.S.A.* 108 B3
Rue, *France* 19 B8
Rufa'a, *Sudan* 81 E3
Rufiji □, *Tanzania* 86 D4
Rufiji →, *Tanzania* 86 D4
Rufino, *Argentina* 126 C3
Rufisque, *Senegal* 82 C1
Rufunsa, *Zambia* 87 F2
Rugao, *China* 59 A13
Rugby, *U.K.* 13 E6
Rugby, *U.S.A.* 112 A5
Rügen, *Germany* 24 A9
Rugles, *France* 18 D7
Ruhengeri, *Rwanda* 86 C2
Ruhla, *Germany* 24 E6
Ruhland, *Germany* 24 D9
Ruhnu, *Estonia* 9 H20
Ruhr →, *Germany* 24 D2
Ruhuhu →, *Tanzania* 87 E3
Rui'an, *China* 59 D13
Ruichang, *China* 59 C10
Ruidosa, *U.S.A.* 113 L2
Ruidoso, *U.S.A.* 115 K11
Ruili, *China* 58 E1
Ruivo, Pico, *Madeira* 37 D3
Ruj, *Bulgaria* 40 D6
Rujen, *Macedonia* 40 D6
Rujm Tal'at al Jamā'ah, *Jordan* 75 E4
Ruk, *Pakistan* 68 F3
Rukwa □, *Tanzania* 86 D3
Rukwa, L., *Tanzania* 86 D3
Rulhieres, C., *Australia* 92 B4
Rum = Rhum, *U.K.* 14 E2
Rum Cay, *Bahamas* 121 B5
Rum Jungle, *Australia* 92 B5
Ruma, *Serbia, Yug.* 42 E4
Rumāḥ, *Si. Arabia* 70 E5
Rumania = Romania ■, *Europe* 43 D10
Rumaylah, *Iraq* 70 D5
Rumbalara, *Australia* 94 D1
Rumbêk, *Sudan* 81 F2
Rumburk, *Czech Rep.* 26 A7
Rumford, *U.S.A.* 111 B14
Rumia, *Poland* 44 D5
Rumilly, *France* 21 C9
Rumoi, *Japan* 54 C10
Rumonge, *Burundi* 86 C2
Rumsey, *Canada* 104 C6
Rumula, *Australia* 94 B4
Rumuruti, *Kenya* 86 B4
Runan, *China* 56 H8
Runanga, *N.Z.* 91 K3
Runaway, C., *N.Z.* 91 G6
Runcorn, *U.K.* 12 D5
Rungwa, *Tanzania* 86 D3
Rungwa →, *Tanzania* 86 D3
Rungwe, *Tanzania* 87 D3
Rungwe □, *Tanzania* 87 D3
Runka, *Nigeria* 83 C6
Runn, *Sweden* 10 D9
Runton Ra., *Australia* 92 D3
Ruokolahti, *Finland* 46 B5
Ruoqiang, *China* 60 C3
Rupa, *India* 67 F18
Rupar, *India* 68 D7
Rupat, *Indonesia* 62 D2
Rupea, *Romania* 43 D10
Rupert →, *Canada* 102 B4
Rupert House = Waskaganish, *Canada* 102 B4
Rur →, *Germany* 24 D1
Rurrenabaque, *Bolivia* 124 F5
Rus →, *Spain* 33 F2
Rusambo, *Zimbabwe* 87 F3
Rusape, *Zimbabwe* 87 F3
Ruschuk = Ruse, *Bulgaria* 41 C9
Ruse, *Bulgaria* 41 C9
Ruse □, *Bulgaria* 41 C10
Ruşeţu, *Romania* 43 F12
Rush, *Ireland* 15 C5
Rushan, *China* 57 F11
Rushden, *U.K.* 13 E7
Rushford, *U.S.A.* 112 D9
Rushville, *Ill., U.S.A.* 112 E9
Rushville, *Ind., U.S.A.* 108 F3
Rushville, *Nebr., U.S.A.* 112 D3
Rushworth, *Australia* 95 F4
Russas, *Brazil* 125 D11
Russell, *Canada* 105 C8
Russell, *U.S.A.* 112 F5
Russell L., *Man., Canada* 105 B8
Russell L., *N.W.T., Canada* 104 A5
Russellkonda, *India* 67 K14
Russellville, *Ala., U.S.A.* 109 H2
Russellville, *Ark., U.S.A.* 113 H8
Russellville, *Ky., U.S.A.* 109 G2
Rüsselsheim, *Germany* 25 F4
Russi, *Italy* 29 D9
Russia ■, *Eurasia* 51 C11
Russian →, *U.S.A.* 116 G3
Russkoye Ustie, *Russia* 4 B15
Rust, *Austria* 27 D9
Rustam, *Pakistan* 68 B5
Rustam Shahr, *Pakistan* 68 F2
Rustavi, *Georgia* 49 K7
Rustenburg, *S. Africa* 88 D4
Ruston, *U.S.A.* 113 J8
Rutana, *Burundi* 86 C3
Rute, *Spain* 35 H6
Ruteng, *Indonesia* 63 F6
Ruth, *Mich., U.S.A.* 110 C2
Ruth, *Nev., U.S.A.* 114 G6
Rutherford, *U.S.A.* 116 G4
Rutland □, *U.K.* 13 E7
Rutland Plains, *Australia* 94 B3
Rutland Water, *U.K.* 13 E7
Rutledge →, *Canada* 105 A6
Rutledge L., *Canada* 105 A6
Rutqa, W. →, *Syria* 73 E9
Rutshuru, *Dem. Rep. of the Congo* 86 C2
Ruvo di Púglia, *Italy* 31 A9
Ruvu, *Tanzania* 86 D4
Ruvu →, *Tanzania* 86 D4
Ruvuma □, *Tanzania* 87 E4
Ruvuma →, *Tanzania* 87 E5
Ruwais, *U.A.E.* 71 E7
Ruwenzori, *Africa* 86 B2
Ruyigi, *Burundi* 86 C3
Ruyuan, *China* 59 E9
Ruzayevka, *Russia* 48 C7
Rūzhevo Konare, *Bulgaria* 41 D8
Ružomberok, *Slovak Rep.* 27 B12
Rwanda ■, *Africa* 86 C3
Ryakhovo, *Bulgaria* 41 C10
Ryan, L., *U.K.* 14 G3
Ryazan, *Russia* 46 E10
Ryazhsk, *Russia* 46 F11
Rybache = Rybachye, *Kazakstan* 50 E9
Rybachye = Ysyk-Köl, *Kyrgyzstan* 52 E11
Rybachye, *Kazakstan* 50 E9
Rybinsk, *Russia* 46 C10
Rybinskoye Vdkhr., *Russia* 46 C10
Rybnik, *Poland* 45 H5
Rybnitsa = Râbniţa, *Moldova* 43 C14
Rybnoye, *Russia* 46 E10
Rychnov nad Kněžnou, *Czech Rep.* 27 A9
Rychwał, *Poland* 45 F5
Ryd, *Sweden* 11 H8
Rydaholm, *Sweden* 11 H8
Ryde, *U.K.* 13 G6
Ryderwood, *U.S.A.* 116 D3
Rydzyna, *Poland* 45 G3
Rye, *U.K.* 13 G8
Rye →, *U.K.* 12 C7
Rye Bay, *U.K.* 13 G8
Rye Patch Reservoir, *U.S.A.* 114 F4
Ryegate, *U.S.A.* 114 C9
Ryki, *Poland* 45 G8
Rylsk, *Russia* 47 G8
Rylstone, *Australia* 95 E4
Rymanów, *Poland* 45 J8
Ryn, *Poland* 44 E8
Ryn Peski, *Kazakstan* 49 G9
Ryōthu, *Japan* 54 E9
Rypin, *Poland* 45 E6
Ryssby, *Sweden* 11 H8
Ryūgasaki, *Japan* 55 G10
Ryūkyū Is. = Ryūkyū-rettō, *Japan* 55 M3
Ryūkyū-rettō, *Japan* 55 M3
Rzepin, *Poland* 45 F1
Rzeszów, *Poland* 45 H8
Rzeszów □, *Poland* 45 J8
Rzhev, *Russia* 46 D8

S

Sa, *Thailand* 64 C3
Sa Canal, *Spain* 37 C7
Sa Conillera, *Spain* 37 C7
Sa Dec, *Vietnam* 65 G5
Sa Dragonera, , *Spain* 37 B9
Sa Mesquida, *Spain* 37 B11
Sa Pobla, *Spain* 32 F8
Sa Savina, *Spain* 37 C7
Sa'ādatābād, *Fārs, Iran* 71 D7
Sa'ādatābād, *Kermān, Iran* 71 D7
Saale →, *Germany* 24 D7
Saaler Bodden, *Germany* 24 A8
Saalfeld, *Germany* 24 E7
Saalfelden, *Austria* 26 D5
Saane →, *Switz.* 25 H3
Saar →, *Europe* 17 E6
Saarbrücken, *Germany* 25 F2
Saarburg, *Germany* 25 F2
Saaremaa, *Estonia* 9 G20
Saarijärvi, *Finland* 9 E21
Saariselkä, *Finland* 8 B23
Saarland □, *Germany* 25 F2
Saarlouis, *Germany* 25 F2
Sab 'Ābar, *Syria* 70 C3
Saba, *W. Indies* 121 C7
Šabac, *Serbia, Yug.* 40 B3
Sabadell, *Spain* 32 D7
Sabah □, *Malaysia* 62 C5
Sabak Bernam, *Malaysia* 65 L3
Sabalān, Kūhhā-ye, *Iran* 73 C12
Sabalana, Kepulauan, *Indonesia* 63 F5
Sábana de la Mar, *Dom. Rep.* 121 C6
Sábanalarga, *Colombia* 124 A4
Sabang, *Indonesia* 62 C1
Săbăoani, *Romania* 43 C11
Sabará, *Brazil* 125 G10
Sabattis, *U.S.A.* 111 B10
Sabáudia, *Italy* 30 A6
Saberania, *Indonesia* 63 E9
Sabhah, *Libya* 79 C8
Sabie, *S. Africa* 89 D5
Sabinal, *Mexico* 118 A3
Sabinal, *U.S.A.* 113 L5
Sabiñánigo, *Spain* 32 C4
Sabinar, Punta del, *Spain* 33 J2
Sabinas, *Mexico* 118 B4
Sabinas →, *Mexico* 118 B4
Sabinas Hidalgo, *Mexico* 118 B4
Sabine →, *U.S.A.* 113 L8
Sabine L., *U.S.A.* 113 L8
Sabine Pass, *U.S.A.* 113 L8
Sabinov, *Slovak Rep.* 27 B14
Sabirabad, *Azerbaijan* 49 K9
Sabkhet el Bardawîl, *Egypt* 75 D2
Sablayan, *Phil.* 61 E4
Sable, C., *Canada* 103 D6
Sable, C., *U.S.A.* 107 E10
Sable I., *Canada* 103 D8
Sablé-sur-Sarthe, *France* 18 E6
Sabor →, *Portugal* 34 D3
Sabou, *Burkina Faso* 82 C4
Sabres, *France* 20 D3
Sabrina Coast, *Antarctica* 5 C9
Sabugal, *Portugal* 34 E3
Sabulubbek, *Indonesia* 62 E1
Sabuncu, *Turkey* 39 B12
Sabzevār, *Iran* 71 B8
Sabzvārān, *Iran* 71 D8
Sac City, *U.S.A.* 112 D7
Sacedón, *Spain* 32 E2
Săcele, *Romania* 43 E10
Sachigo →, *Canada* 102 A2
Sachigo, L., *Canada* 102 B1
Sachkhere, *Georgia* 49 J6
Sachsen □, *Germany* 24 E9
Sachsen-Anhalt □, *Germany* 24 D7
Sacile, *Italy* 29 C9
Sackets Harbor, *U.S.A.* 111 C8
Saco, *Maine, U.S.A.* 109 D10
Saco, *Mont., U.S.A.* 114 B10
Sacramento, *U.S.A.* 116 G5
Sacramento →, *U.S.A.* 116 G5
Sacramento Mts., *U.S.A.* 115 K11
Sacramento Valley, *U.S.A.* 116 G5
Sacratif, C., *Spain* 35 J7
Săcueni, *Romania* 42 C7
Sada, *Spain* 34 B2
Sádaba, *Spain* 32 C3
Sadani, *Tanzania* 86 D4
Sadao, *Thailand* 65 J3
Sadd el Aali, *Egypt* 80 C3
Saddle Mt., *U.S.A.* 116 E3
Sade, *Nigeria* 83 C7
Sadimi, *Dem. Rep. of the Congo* 87 D1
Sa'dīyah, Hawr as, *Iraq* 73 F12
Sado, *Japan* 54 F9
Sado →, *Portugal* 35 G2
Sadon, *Burma* 67 G20
Sadon, *Russia* 49 J6
Sæby, *Denmark* 11 G4
Saegerstown, *U.S.A.* 110 E4
Saelices, *Spain* 32 F2
Safaalan, *Turkey* 41 E12
Safaga, *Egypt* 80 B3
Şafājah, *Si. Arabia* 70 E3
Šafárikovo = Tornal'a, *Slovak Rep.* 27 C13
Säffle, *Sweden* 10 E6
Safford, *U.S.A.* 115 K9
Saffron Walden, *U.K.* 13 E8
Safi, *Morocco* 78 B4
Şafīābād, *Iran* 71 B8
Safīd Dasht, *Iran* 71 C6
Safīd Kūh, *Afghan.* 66 B3
Safonovo, *Russia* 46 E7
Safranbolu, *Turkey* 72 B5
Safwān, *Iraq* 70 D5
Sag Harbor, *U.S.A.* 111 F12
Saga, *Japan* 55 H5
Saga □, *Japan* 55 H5
Sagae, *Japan* 54 E10
Sagala, *Mali* 82 C3
Sagar, *India* 66 M9
Sagara, L., *Tanzania* 86 D3
Sagay, *Phil.* 61 F5
Sagil, *Mongolia* 60 A4
Saginaw, *U.S.A.* 108 D4
Saginaw B., *U.S.A.* 108 D4
Sagleipie, *Liberia* 82 D3
Saglouc = Salluit, *Canada* 101 B12
Sagŏ-ri, *S. Korea* 57 G14
Sagone, *France* 21 F12
Sagone, G. de, *France* 21 F12
Sagres, *Portugal* 35 J2
Sagua la Grande, *Cuba* 120 B3
Saguache, *U.S.A.* 115 G10
Saguenay →, *Canada* 103 C5
Sagunt, *Spain* 32 F4
Sagunto = Sagunt, *Spain* 32 F4
Sahaba, *Sudan* 80 D3
Sahagún, *Spain* 34 C5
Saḥam al Jawlān, *Syria* 75 C4
Sahand, Kūh-e, *Iran* 70 B5
Sahara, *Africa* 78 D6
Saharan Atlas = Saharien, Atlas, *Algeria* 78 B6
Saharanpur, *India* 68 E7
Saharien, Atlas, *Algeria* 78 B6
Sahasinaka, *Madag.* 89 C8
Sahaswan, *India* 69 E8
Sahel, Canal du, *Mali* 82 C3
Sahibganj, *India* 69 G12
Sāḥilīyah, *Iraq* 70 C4
Sahiwal, *Pakistan* 68 D5
Şaḥneh, *Iran* 70 C5
Sahtaneh →, *Canada* 104 B4
Sahuaripa, *Mexico* 118 B3
Sahuarita, *U.S.A.* 115 L8
Sahuayo, *Mexico* 118 C4
Šahy, *Slovak Rep.* 27 C11
Sai Buri, *Thailand* 65 J3
Sa'id Bundas, *Sudan* 79 G10
Sa'īdābād, *Kermān, Iran* 71 D7
Sa'īdābād, *Semnān, Iran* 71 B7
Sa'īdīyeh, *Iran* 71 B6
Saidpur, *Bangla.* 67 G16
Saidu, *Pakistan* 69 B5
Saignes, *France* 20 C6
Saigon = Phanh Bho Ho Chi Minh, *Vietnam* 65 G6
Saijō, *Japan* 55 H6
Saikhoa Ghat, *India* 67 F19
Saiki, *Japan* 55 H5
Saillans, *France* 21 D9
Sailolof, *Indonesia* 63 E8
Saimaa, *Finland* 9 F23
Saimbeyli, *Turkey* 72 D7
Şa'in Dezh, *Iran* 70 B5
St. Abb's Head, *U.K.* 14 F6
St-Affrique, *France* 20 E6
St-Agrève, *France* 21 C8
St-Aignan, *France* 18 E8
St. Alban's, *Canada* 103 C8
St. Albans, *U.K.* 13 F7
St. Albans, *Vt., U.S.A.* 111 B11
St. Albans, *W. Va., U.S.A.* 108 F5
St. Alban's Head, *U.K.* 13 G5
St. Albert, *Canada* 104 C6
St-Amand-en-Puisaye, *France* 19 E10
St-Amand-les-Eaux, *France* 19 B10
St-Amand-Montrond, *France* 19 F9
St-Amarin, *France* 19 E14
St-Amour, *France* 19 F12
St-André-de-Cubzac, *France* 20 D3
St-André-les-Alpes, *France* 21 E10
St. Andrew's, *Canada* 103 C8
St. Andrews, *U.K.* 14 E6
St-Anicet, *Canada* 111 A10
St. Ann B., *Canada* 103 C7
St. Ann's Bay, *Jamaica* 120 C4
St. Anthony, *Canada* 103 B8
St. Anthony, *U.S.A.* 114 E8
St-Antonin-Noble-Val, *France* 20 D5
St. Arnaud, *Australia* 95 F3
St. Arthur, *Canada* 103 C6
St-Astier, *France* 20 C4
St-Aubin-du-Cormier, *France* 18 D5
St-Augustin-Saguenay, *Canada* 103 B8
St. Augustine, *U.S.A.* 109 L5
St-Aulaye, *France* 20 C4
St. Austell, *U.K.* 13 G3
St-Avold, *France* 19 C13
St-Barthélemy, *W. Indies* 121 C7
St-Béat, *France* 20 F4
St. Bees Hd., *U.K.* 12 C4
St-Benoît-du-Sault, *France* 20 B5
St. Boniface, *Canada* 105 D9
St-Bonnet, *France* 21 D10
St-Brévin-les-Pins, *France* 18 E4
St-Brice-en-Coglès, *France* 18 D5
St. Bride's, *Canada* 103 C9
St. Brides B., *U.K.* 13 F2
St-Brieuc, *France* 18 D4
St-Calais, *France* 18 E7
St-Cast-le-Guildo, *France* 18 D4
St. Catharines, *Canada* 102 D4
St. Catherines I., *U.S.A.* 109 K5
St. Catherine's Pt., *U.K.* 13 G6
St-Céré, *France* 20 D5
St-Cergue, *Switz.* 25 J2
St-Cernin, *France* 20 C6
St-Chamond, *France* 21 C8
St. Charles, *Ill., U.S.A.* 108 E1
St. Charles, *Mo., U.S.A.* 112 F9
St-Chély-d'Apcher, *France* 20 D7
St-Chinian, *France* 20 E6
St. Christopher = St. Kitts, *W. Indies* 121 C7
St. Christopher-Nevis ■ = St. Kitts & Nevis ■, *W. Indies* 121 C7
St-Ciers-sur-Gironde, *France* 20 C3
St. Clair, *Mich., U.S.A.* 110 D2
St. Clair, *Pa., U.S.A.* 111 F8
St. Clair, L., *Canada* 102 D3
St. Clairsville, *U.S.A.* 110 F4
St-Claud, *France* 20 C4
St. Claude, *Canada* 105 D9
St-Claude, *France* 19 F12
St. Cloud, *Fla., U.S.A.* 109 L5
St. Cloud, *Minn., U.S.A.* 112 C7
St-Coeur de Marie, *Canada* 103 C5
St. Cricq, C., *Australia* 93 E1
St. Croix, *Virgin Is.* 121 C7
St. Croix →, *U.S.A.* 112 C8
St. Croix Falls, *U.S.A.* 112 C8
St-Cyprien, *France* 20 F7
St-Cyr-sur-Mer, *France* 21 E9
St. David's, *Canada* 103 C8
St. David's, *U.K.* 13 F2
St. David's Head, *U.K.* 13 F2
St-Denis, *France* 19 D9
St-Dié, *France* 19 D13
St-Dizier, *France* 19 D11
St-Égrève, *France* 21 C9
St. Elias, Mt., *U.S.A.* 100 B5
St. Elias Mts., *Canada* 104 A1
St-Eloy-les-Mines, *France* 19 F9
St-Émilion, *France* 20 D3
St-Étienne, *France* 21 C8
St-Étienne-de-Tinée, *France* 21 D10
St-Étienne-du-Rouvray, *France* 18 C8
St. Eugène, *Canada* 111 A10
St. Eustatius, *W. Indies* 121 C7
St-Fargeau, *France* 19 E10
St-Félicien, *Canada* 102 C5
St-Florent, *France* 21 F13
St-Florent, G. de, *France* 21 F13
St-Florent-sur-Cher, *France* 19 F9
St-Florentin, *France* 19 E10
St-Flour, *France* 20 C7
St. Francis, *U.S.A.* 112 F4
St. Francis →, *U.S.A.* 113 H9
St. Francis, C., *S. Africa* 88 E3
St. Francisville, *U.S.A.* 113 K9
St-François, L., *Canada* 111 A10
St-Fulgent, *France* 18 F5
St-Gabriel-de-Brandon, *Canada* 102 C5
St. Gallen = Sankt Gallen, *Switz.* 25 H5

St-Galmier, *France* 19 G11
St-Gaudens, *France* 20 E4
St-Gaultier, *France* 18 F8
St-Gengoux-le-National, *France* 19 F11
St-Geniez-d'Olt, *France* 20 D6
St. George, *Australia* 95 D4
St. George, *Canada* 103 C6
St. George, *S.C., U.S.A.* 109 J5
St. George, *Utah, U.S.A.* 115 H7
St. George, C., *Canada* 103 C8
St. George, C., *U.S.A.* 109 L3
St. George Ra., *Australia* 92 C4
St. George's, *Canada* 103 C8
St-Georges, *Canada* 103 C5
St. George's, *Grenada* 121 D7
St. George's B., *Canada* 103 C8
St. Georges Basin, *Australia* 92 C4
St. George's Channel, *Europe* 15 E6
St. Georges Hd., *Australia* 95 F5
St-Georges-lès-Baillargeaux, *France* 20 B4
St-Germain-de-Calberte, *France* 20 D7
St-Germain-en-Laye, *France* 19 D9
St-Germain-Lembron, *France* 20 C7
St-Gervais-d'Auvergne, *France* 19 F9
St-Gervais-les-Bains, *France* 21 C10
St-Gildas, Pte. de, *France* 18 E4
St-Gilles, *France* 21 E8
St-Girons, *Ariège, France* 20 F5
St-Girons, *Landes, France* 20 E2
St. Gotthard P. = San Gottardo, P. del, *Switz.* 25 J4
St. Helena, *U.S.A.* 114 G2
St. Helena ■, *Atl. Oc.* 77 H3
St. Helena, Mt., *U.S.A.* 116 G4
St. Helena B., *S. Africa* 88 E2
St. Helens, *Australia* 94 G4
St. Helens, *U.K.* 12 D5
St. Helens, *U.S.A.* 116 E4
St. Helens, Mt., *U.S.A.* 116 D4
St. Helier, *U.K.* 13 H5
St-Herblain, *France* 18 E5
St-Hilaire-du-Harcouët, *France* 18 D5
St-Hippolyte, *France* 19 E13
St-Hippolyte-du-Fort, *France* 20 E7
St-Honoré-les-Bains, *France* 19 F10
St-Hubert, *Belgium* 17 D5
St-Hyacinthe, *Canada* 102 C5
St. Ignace, *U.S.A.* 108 C3
St. Ignace I., *Canada* 102 C2
St. Ignatius, *U.S.A.* 114 C6
St-Imier, *Switz.* 25 H2
St. Ives, *U.K.* 13 G2
St-James, *France* 18 D5
St. James, *U.S.A.* 112 D7
St-Jean, *Canada* 102 C5
St-Jean →, *Canada* 103 B7
St-Jean, L., *Canada* 103 C5
St. Jean Baptiste, *Canada* 105 D9
St-Jean-d'Angély, *France* 20 C3
St-Jean-de-Braye, *France* 19 E8
St-Jean-de-Luz, *France* 20 E2
St-Jean-de-Maurienne, *France* 21 C10
St-Jean-de-Monts, *France* 18 F4
St-Jean-du-Gard, *France* 20 D7
St-Jean-en-Royans, *France* 21 C9
St-Jean-Pied-de-Port, *France* 20 E2
St-Jean-Port-Joli, *Canada* 103 C5
St-Jérôme, *Qué., Canada* 102 C5
St-Jérôme, *Qué., Canada* 103 C5
St. John, *Canada* 103 C6
St. John, *Kans., U.S.A.* 113 G5
St. John, *N. Dak., U.S.A.* 112 A5
St. John →, *U.S.A.* 103 C6
St. John, C., *Canada* 103 C8
St. John's, *Antigua* 121 C7
St. John's, *Canada* 103 C9
St. Johns, *Ariz., U.S.A.* 115 J9
St. Johns, *Mich., U.S.A.* 108 D3
St. Johns →, *U.S.A.* 109 K5
St. John's Pt., *Ireland* 15 B3
St. Johnsbury, *U.S.A.* 111 B12
St. Johnsville, *U.S.A.* 111 D10
St. Joseph, *La., U.S.A.* 113 K9
St. Joseph, *Mich., U.S.A.* 108 D2
St. Joseph, *Mo., U.S.A.* 112 F7
St. Joseph →, *U.S.A.* 108 D2
St. Joseph, I., *Canada* 102 C3
St. Joseph, L., *Canada* 102 B1
St-Jovite, *Canada* 102 C5
St-Juéry, *France* 20 E6
St-Julien-Chapteuil, *France* 21 C8
St-Julien-de-Vouvantes, *France* 18 E5
St-Julien-en-Genevois, *France* 19 F13
St-Junien, *France* 20 C4
St-Just-en-Chaussée, *France* 19 C9
St-Just-en-Chevalet, *France* 20 C7
St. Kilda, *N.Z.* 91 L3
St. Kitts, *W. Indies* 121 C7
St. Kitts & Nevis ■, *W. Indies* 121 C7
St. Laurent, *Canada* 105 C9
St-Laurent-de-la-Salanque, *France* 20 F6
St-Laurent-du-Pont, *France* 21 C9
St-Laurent-en-Grandvaux, *France* 19 F12
St-Laurent-et-Benon, *France* 20 C3
St. Lawrence, *Australia* 94 C4
St. Lawrence, *Canada* 103 C8
St. Lawrence →, *Canada* 103 C6
St. Lawrence, Gulf of, *Canada* 103 C7
St. Lawrence I., *U.S.A.* 100 B3
St. Leonard, *Canada* 103 C6
St-Léonard-de-Noblat, *France* 20 C5
St. Lewis →, *Canada* 103 B8
St-Lô, *France* 18 C5
St-Louis, *France* 19 E14
St. Louis, *Senegal* 82 B1
St. Louis, *Mich., U.S.A.* 108 D3
St. Louis, *Mo., U.S.A.* 112 F9
St. Louis →, *U.S.A.* 112 B8
St-Loup-sur-Semouse, *France* 19 E13
St. Lucia ■, *W. Indies* 121 D7
St. Lucia, L., *S. Africa* 89 D5
St. Lucia Channel, *W. Indies* 121 D7
St. Lunaire-Griquet, *Canada* 103 B8
St. Maarten, *W. Indies* 121 C7
St. Magnus B., *U.K.* 14 A7
St-Maixent-l'École, *France* 20 B3
St-Malo, *France* 18 D4
St-Malo, G. de, *France* 18 D4
St-Mandrier-sur-Mer, *France* 21 E9
St-Marc, *Haiti* 121 C5
St-Marcellin, *France* 21 C9
St-Marcouf, Îs., *France* 18 C5
St. Maries, *U.S.A.* 114 C5
St-Martin, *W. Indies* 121 C7
St. Martin, L., *Canada* 105 C9
St-Martin-de-Crau, *France* 21 E8
St-Martin-de-Ré, *France* 20 B2
St-Martin-d'Hères, *France* 21 C9
St-Martin-Vésubie, *France* 21 D11
St. Martins, *Canada* 103 C6
St. Martinville, *U.S.A.* 113 K9
St-Martory, *France* 20 E4
St. Mary Pk., *Australia* 95 E2
St. Marys, *Australia* 94 G4
St. Marys, *Canada* 110 C3
St. Mary's, *Corn., U.K.* 13 H1
St. Mary's, *Orkney, U.K.* 14 C6
St. Marys, *U.S.A.* 110 E6
St. Mary's, C., *Canada* 103 C9
St. Mary's B., *Canada* 103 C9
St. Marys Bay, *Canada* 103 D6
St-Mathieu, Pte., *France* 18 D2
St. Matthews, I. = Zadetkyi Kyun, *Burma* 65 H2
St-Maurice →, *Canada* 102 C5
St-Maximin-la-Ste-Baume, *France* 21 E9
St-Médard-en-Jalles, *France* 20 D3
St-Méen-le-Grand, *France* 18 D4
St-Mihiel, *France* 19 D12
St. Moritz, *Switz.* 25 J5
St-Nazaire, *France* 18 E4
St. Neots, *U.K.* 13 E7
St-Nicolas-de-Port, *France* 19 D13
St-Niklaas, *Belgium* 17 C4
St-Omer, *France* 19 B9
St-Pacome, *Canada* 103 C6
St-Palais-sur-Mer, *France* 20 C2
St-Pamphile, *Canada* 103 C6
St-Pardoux-la-Rivière, *France* 20 C4
St. Pascal, *Canada* 103 C6
St. Paul, *Canada* 104 C6
St-Paul, *France* 21 D10
St. Paul, *Minn., U.S.A.* 112 C8
St. Paul, *Nebr., U.S.A.* 112 E5
St. Paul, I., *Ind. Oc.* 3 F13
St-Paul-de-Fenouillet, *France* 20 F6
St. Paul I., *Canada* 103 C7
St-Paul-lès-Dax, *France* 20 E2
St-Péray, *France* 21 D8
St. Peter, *U.S.A.* 112 C8
St-Peter-Ording, *Germany* 24 A4
St. Peter Port, *U.K.* 13 H5
St. Peters, *N.S., Canada* 103 C7
St. Peters, *P.E.I., Canada* 103 C7
St. Petersburg = Sankt-Peterburg, *Russia* 46 C6
St. Petersburg, *U.S.A.* 109 M4
St-Philbert-de-Grand-Lieu, *France* 18 E5
St-Pierre, *St- P. & M.* 103 C8
St-Pierre, L., *Canada* 102 C5
St-Pierre-d'Oléron, *France* 20 C2
St-Pierre-en-Port, *France* 18 C7
St-Pierre et Miquelon □, *St- P. & M.* 103 C8
St-Pierre-le-Moûtier, *France* 19 F10
St-Pierre-sur-Dives, *France* 18 C6
St-Pol-de-Léon, *France* 18 D3
St-Pol-sur-Mer, *France* 19 A9
St-Pol-sur-Ternoise, *France* 19 B9
St-Pons, *France* 20 E6
St-Pourçain-sur-Sioule, *France* 19 F10
St-Priest, *France* 21 C8
St-Quay-Portrieux, *France* 18 D4
St-Quentin, *France* 19 C10
St-Rambert-d'Albon, *France* 21 C8
St-Raphaël, *France* 21 E10
St. Regis, *U.S.A.* 114 C6
St-Renan, *France* 18 D2
St-Saëns, *France* 18 C8
St-Savin, *France* 20 B4
St-Savinien, *France* 20 C3
St. Sebastien, Tanjon' i, *Madag.* 89 A8
St-Seine-l'Abbaye, *France* 19 E11
St-Sernin-sur-Rance, *France* 20 E6
St-Sever, *France* 20 E3
St-Siméon, *Canada* 103 C6
St. Stephen, *Canada* 103 C6
St-Sulpice, *France* 20 E5
St-Sulpice-Laurière, *France* 20 B5
St-Sulpice-les-Feuilles, *France* 20 B5
St-Syprien = St-Cyprien, *France* 20 F7
St-Thégonnec, *France* 18 D3
St. Thomas, *Canada* 102 D3
St. Thomas I., *Virgin Is.* 121 C7
St-Tite, *Canada* 102 C5
St-Tropez, *France* 21 E10
St. Troud = St. Truiden, *Belgium* 17 D5
St. Truiden, *Belgium* 17 D5
St-Vaast-la-Hougue, *France* 18 C5
St-Valery-en-Caux, *France* 18 C7
St-Valéry-sur-Somme, *France* 19 B8
St-Vallier, *France* 19 F11
St-Vallier-de-Thiey, *France* 21 E10
St-Varent, *France* 18 F6
St-Vaury, *France* 20 B5
St. Vincent, *Italy* 28 C4
St. Vincent, *W. Indies* 121 D7
St. Vincent, G., *Australia* 95 F2
St. Vincent & the Grenadines ■, *W. Indies* 121 D7
St-Vincent-de-Tyrosse, *France* 20 E2
St. Vincent Passage, *W. Indies* 121 D7
St-Vith, *Belgium* 17 D6
St-Vivien-de-Médoc, *France* 20 C2
St-Yrieix-la-Perche, *France* 20 C5
Ste-Adresse, *France* 18 C7
Ste-Agathe-des-Monts, *Canada* 102 C5
Ste-Anne de Beaupré, *Canada* 103 C5
Ste-Anne-des-Monts, *Canada* 103 C6
Ste-Croix, *Switz.* 25 J2
Ste-Enimie, *France* 20 D7
Ste-Foy-la-Grande, *France* 20 D4
Ste. Genevieve, *U.S.A.* 112 G9
Ste-Hermine, *France* 20 B2
Ste-Livrade-sur-Lot, *France* 20 D4
Ste-Marguerite →, *Canada* 103 B6
Ste-Marie, *Martinique* 121 D7
Ste-Marie-aux-Mines, *France* 19 D14
Ste-Marie de la Madeleine, *Canada* 103 C5
Ste-Maure-de-Touraine, *France* 18 E7
Ste-Maxime, *France* 21 E10
Ste-Menehould, *France* 19 C11
Ste-Mère-Église, *France* 18 C5
Ste-Rose, *Guadeloupe* 121 C7
Ste. Rose du Lac, *Canada* 105 C9
Ste-Savine, *France* 19 D11
Ste-Sigolène, *France* 21 C8
Saintes, *France* 20 C3
Saintes, I. des, *Guadeloupe* 121 C7
Stes-Maries-de-la-Mer, *France* 21 E8
Saintfield, *U.K.* 15 B6
Saintonge, *France* 20 C3
Saipan, *Pac. Oc.* 96 F6
Sairang, *India* 67 H18
Sairecábur, Cerro, *Bolivia* 126 A2
Saitama □, *Japan* 55 F9
Saiţi, *Moldova* 43 D14
Sajama, *Bolivia* 124 G5
Sajan, *Serbia, Yug.* 42 E5
Sajó →, *Hungary* 42 C6
Sajószentpéter, *Hungary* 42 B5
Sajum, *India* 69 C8
Sak →, *S. Africa* 88 E3
Sakai, *Japan* 55 G7
Sakaide, *Japan* 55 G6
Sakaiminato, *Japan* 55 G6
Sakākah, *Si. Arabia* 70 D4
Sakakawea, L., *U.S.A.* 112 B4
Sakami, L., *Canada* 102 B4
Sakania, *Dem. Rep. of the Congo* 87 E2
Sakarya = Adapazarı, *Turkey* 72 B4
Sakarya →, *Turkey* 72 B4
Sakashima-Guntō, *Japan* 55 M2
Sakata, *Japan* 54 E9
Sakchu, *N. Korea* 57 D13
Sakeny →, *Madag.* 89 C8
Sakété, *Benin* 83 D5
Sakha □, *Russia* 51 C14
Sakhalin, *Russia* 51 D15
Sakhalinskiy Zaliv, *Russia* 51 D15
Şaki, *Azerbaijan* 49 K8
Šakiai, *Lithuania* 9 J20
Sakon Nakhon, *Thailand* 64 D5
Sakrand, *Pakistan* 68 F3
Sakrivier, *S. Africa* 88 E3
Sakskøbing, *Denmark* 11 K5
Sakuma, *Japan* 55 G8
Sakurai, *Japan* 55 G7
Saky, *Ukraine* 47 K7
Sal →, *Russia* 49 G5
Šal'a, *Slovak Rep.* 27 C10
Sala, *Sweden* 10 E10
Sala Consilina, *Italy* 31 B8
Sala-y-Gómez, *Pac. Oc.* 97 K17
Salaberry-de-Valleyfield, *Canada* 102 C5
Saladas, *Argentina* 126 B4
Saladillo, *Argentina* 126 D4
Salado →, *Buenos Aires, Argentina* 126 D4
Salado →, *La Pampa, Argentina* 128 D3
Salado →, *Santa Fe, Argentina* 126 C3
Salado →, *Mexico* 118 B5
Salaga, *Ghana* 83 D4
Şalāh, *Syria* 75 C5
Sălaj □, *Romania* 42 C8
Sálakhos, *Greece* 36 C9
Salala, *Liberia* 82 D2
Salala, *Sudan* 80 C4
Salālah, *Oman* 74 D5
Salamanca, *Chile* 126 C1
Salamanca, *Spain* 34 E5
Salamanca, *U.S.A.* 110 D6
Salamanca □, *Spain* 34 E5
Salāmatābād, *Iran* 70 C5
Salamis, *Cyprus* 36 D12
Salamís, *Greece* 38 D5
Salar de Atacama, *Chile* 126 A2
Salar de Uyuni, *Bolivia* 124 H5
Sălard, *Romania* 42 C7
Salas, *Spain* 34 B4
Salas de los Infantes, *Spain* 34 C7
Salatiga, *Indonesia* 63 G14
Salaverry, *Peru* 124 E3
Salawati, *Indonesia* 63 E8
Salayar, *Indonesia* 63 F6
Salazar →, *Spain* 32 C3
Salbris, *France* 19 E9
Salcia, *Romania* 43 G9
Sălciua, *Romania* 43 D8
Salcombe, *U.K.* 13 G4
Saldaña, *Spain* 34 C6
Saldanha, *S. Africa* 88 E2
Saldanha B., *S. Africa* 88 E2
Saldus, *Latvia* 9 H20
Saldus □, *Latvia* 44 B9
Sale, *Australia* 95 F4
Sale, *Italy* 28 D5
Salé, *Morocco* 78 B4
Sale, *U.K.* 12 D5
Salekhard, *Russia* 50 C7
Salem, *India* 66 P11
Salem, *Ind., U.S.A.* 108 F2
Salem, *Mass., U.S.A.* 111 D14
Salem, *Mo., U.S.A.* 113 G9
Salem, *N.J., U.S.A.* 108 F8
Salem, *Ohio, U.S.A.* 110 F4
Salem, *Oreg., U.S.A.* 114 D2
Salem, *S. Dak., U.S.A.* 112 D6
Salem, *Va., U.S.A.* 108 G5
Salemi, *Italy* 30 E5
Sälen, *Sweden* 10 C7
Salernes, *France* 21 E10
Salerno, *Italy* 31 B7
Salerno, G. di, *Italy* 31 B7
Salford, *U.K.* 12 D5
Salgir →, *Ukraine* 47 K8
Salgótarján, *Hungary* 42 B4
Salgueiro, *Brazil* 125 E11
Salida, *U.S.A.* 106 C5
Salies-de-Béarn, *France* 20 E3
Salihli, *Turkey* 72 C3
Salihorsk, *Belarus* 47 F4
Salima, *Malawi* 85 G6
Salina, *Italy* 31 D7
Salina, *U.S.A.* 112 F6
Salina Cruz, *Mexico* 119 D5
Salinas, *Brazil* 125 G10
Salinas, *Chile* 126 A2
Salinas, *Ecuador* 124 D2
Salinas, *U.S.A.* 116 J5
Salinas →, *Guatemala* 119 D6
Salinas →, *U.S.A.* 116 J5
Salinas, B. de, *Nic.* 120 D2
Salinas, Pampa de las, *Argentina* 126 C2
Salinas Ambargasta, *Argentina* 126 B3
Salinas de Hidalgo, *Mexico* 118 C4
Salinas Grandes, *Argentina* 126 C3
Saline →, *Ark., U.S.A.* 113 J8
Saline →, *Kans., U.S.A.* 112 F6
Salines, *Spain* 37 B10
Salines, C. de ses, *Spain* 37 B10
Salinópolis, *Brazil* 125 D9
Salins-les-Bains, *France* 19 F12
Salir, *Portugal* 35 H2
Salisbury = Harare, *Zimbabwe* 87 F3
Salisbury, *Australia* 95 E2
Salisbury, *U.K.* 13 F6
Salisbury, *Md., U.S.A.* 108 F8
Salisbury, *N.C., U.S.A.* 109 H5
Salisbury Plain, *U.K.* 13 F6
Săliște, *Romania* 43 E8
Salka, *Nigeria* 83 C5
Şalkhad, *Syria* 75 C5
Salla, *Finland* 8 C23
Sallanches, *France* 21 C10
Sallent, *Spain* 32 D6
Salles, *France* 20 D3
Salles-Curan, *France* 20 D6
Salling, *Denmark* 11 H2
Sallisaw, *U.S.A.* 113 H7
Sallom Junction, *Sudan* 80 D4
Salluit, *Canada* 101 B12
Salmās, *Iran* 70 B5
Salmerón, *Spain* 32 E2
Salmo, *Canada* 104 D5
Salmon, *U.S.A.* 114 D7
Salmon →, *Canada* 104 C4
Salmon →, *U.S.A.* 114 D5
Salmon Arm, *Canada* 104 C5
Salmon Falls, *U.S.A.* 114 E6
Salmon Gums, *Australia* 93 F3
Salmon Res., *Canada* 103 C8
Salmon River Mts., *U.S.A.* 114 D6
Salo, *Finland* 9 F20
Salò, *Italy* 28 C7
Salobreña, *Spain* 35 J7
Salome, *U.S.A.* 117 M13
Salon-de-Provence, *France* 21 E9
Salonica = Thessaloníki, *Greece* 40 F6
Salonta, *Romania* 42 D6
Salor →, *Spain* 35 F3
Salou, *Spain* 32 D6
Salou, C. de, *Spain* 32 D6
Salpausselkä, *Finland* 9 F22
Salsacate, *Argentina* 126 C2
Salses, *France* 20 F6
Salsk, *Russia* 49 G5
Salso →, *Italy* 30 E6
Salsomaggiore Terme, *Italy* 28 D6
Salt, *Spain* 32 D7
Salt →, *Canada* 104 B6
Salt →, *U.S.A.* 115 K7
Salt Creek, *Australia* 95 F2
Salt Fork Arkansas →, *U.S.A.* 113 G6
Salt Lake City, *U.S.A.* 114 F8
Salt Range, *Pakistan* 68 C5
Salta, *Argentina* 126 A2
Salta □, *Argentina* 126 A2
Saltara, *Italy* 29 E9
Saltash, *U.K.* 13 G3
Saltburn by the Sea, *U.K.* 12 C7
Saltcoats, *U.K.* 14 F4
Saltee Is., *Ireland* 15 D5
Saltfjellet, *Norway* 8 C16
Saltfjorden, *Norway* 8 C16
Saltholm, *Denmark* 11 J6
Saltillo, *Mexico* 118 B4
Salto, *Argentina* 126 C3
Salto, *Uruguay* 126 C4
Salto del Guaíra, *Paraguay* 128 A6
Salton City, *U.S.A.* 117 M11
Salton Sea, *U.S.A.* 117 M11
Saltpond, *Ghana* 83 D4
Saltsjöbaden, *Sweden* 10 E12
Saltville, *U.S.A.* 108 G5
Saluda →, *U.S.A.* 109 J5
Salûm, *Egypt* 80 A2
Salûm, Khâlig el, *Egypt* 80 A2
Salur, *India* 67 K13
Saluzzo, *Italy* 28 D4
Salvador, *Brazil* 125 F11
Salvador, *Canada* 105 C7
Salvador, L., *U.S.A.* 113 L9
Salvaterra de Magos, *Portugal* 35 F2
Sálvora, I. de, *Spain* 34 C2
Salween →, *Burma* 67 L20
Salyan, *Azerbaijan* 73 C13
Salyersville, *U.S.A.* 108 G4
Salza →, *Austria* 26 D7
Salzach →, *Austria* 26 C5
Salzburg, *Austria* 26 D6
Salzburg □, *Austria* 26 D6
Salzgitter, *Germany* 24 C6
Salzkotten, *Germany* 24 D4
Salzwedel, *Germany* 24 C7
Sam Neua, *Laos* 64 B5
Sam Ngao, *Thailand* 64 D2
Sam Rayburn Reservoir, *U.S.A.* 113 K7
Sam Son, *Vietnam* 64 C5
Sam Teu, *Laos* 64 C5
Sama de Langreo = Langreo, *Spain* 34 B5
Samagaltay, *Russia* 51 D10
Samales Group, *Phil.* 61 J5
Samalût, *Egypt* 80 J7
Samana, *India* 68 D7
Samana Cay, *Bahamas* 121 B5
Samandağı, *Turkey* 72 D6
Samandıra, *Turkey* 41 F13
Samanga, *Tanzania* 87 D4
Samangwa, *Dem. Rep. of the Congo* 86 C1
Samani, *Japan* 54 C11
Samanli Dağları, *Turkey* 41 F13
Samar, *Phil.* 61 F6
Samara, *Russia* 48 D10
Samara →, *Russia* 48 D10
Samara →, *Ukraine* 47 H8
Samaria = Shōmrōn, *West Bank* 75 C4
Samariá, *Greece* 36 D5
Samarinda, *Indonesia* 62 E5
Samarkand = Samarqand, *Uzbekistan* 50 F7
Samarqand, *Uzbekistan* 50 F7
Sāmarrā, *Iraq* 70 C4
Samastipur, *India* 69 G11
Şamaxi, *Azerbaijan* 49 K9

Samba, Dem. Rep. of the Congo 86 C2
Samba, India 69 C6
Sambalpur, India 67 J14
Sambar, Tanjung, Indonesia 62 E4
Sambas, Indonesia 62 D3
Sambava, Madag. 89 A9
Sambawizi, Zimbabwe 87 F2
Sambhal, India 69 E8
Sambhar, India 68 F6
Sambiase, Italy 31 D9
Sambir, Ukraine 47 H2
Sambor, Cambodia 64 F6
Sambuca di Sicília, Italy 30 E6
Samburu □, Kenya 86 B4
Samchŏk, S. Korea 57 F15
Samchonpo, S. Korea 57 G15
Same, Tanzania 86 C4
Samer, France 19 B8
Samfya, Zambia 87 E2
Sámi, Greece 38 C2
Şämkir, Azerbaijan 49 K8
Şamlı, Turkey 39 B9
Samnah, Si. Arabia 70 E3
Samo Alto, Chile 126 C1
Samobor, Croatia 29 C12
Samoëns, France 19 F13
Samokov, Bulgaria 40 D7
Samoorombón, B., Argentina 126 D4
Šamorín, Slovak Rep. 27 C10
Samorogouan, Burkina Faso 82 C4
Sámos, Greece 39 D8
Samoš, Serbia, Yug. 42 E5
Samos, Spain 34 C3
Sámos □, Greece 39 D8
Samothráki = Mathráki, Greece 36 A3
Samothráki, Greece 41 F9
Samoylovka, Russia 48 E6
Sampa, Ghana 82 D4
Sampacho, Argentina 126 C3
Sampang, Indonesia 63 G15
Samper de Calanda, Spain 32 D4
Sampéyre, Italy 28 D4
Sampit, Indonesia 62 E4
Sampit, Teluk, Indonesia 62 E4
Samrong, Cambodia 64 E4
Samrong, Thailand 64 E3
Samsø, Denmark 11 J4
Samsø Bælt, Denmark 11 J4
Samsun, Turkey 72 B7
Samtredia, Georgia 49 J6
Samui, Ko, Thailand 65 H3
Samur →, Russia 49 K9
Samurskiy Khrebet, Russia 49 K8
Samusole, Dem. Rep. of the Congo 87 E1
Samut Prakan, Thailand 64 F3
Samwari, Pakistan 68 E2
San, Mali 82 C4
San →, Cambodia 64 F5
San →, Poland 45 H8
San Adrián, Spain 32 C3
San Adrián, C. de, Spain 34 B2
San Agustin, C., Phil. 61 H7
San Agustín de Valle Fértil, Argentina 126 C2
San Ambrosio, Pac. Oc. 122 F3
San Andreas, U.S.A. 116 G6
San Andrés, I. de, Caribbean 120 D3
San Andrês del Rabanedo, Spain 34 C5
San Andres Mts., U.S.A. 115 K10
San Andrés Tuxtla, Mexico 119 D5
San Angelo, U.S.A. 113 K4
San Anselmo, U.S.A. 116 H4
San Antonio, Belize 119 D7
San Antonio, Chile 126 C1
San Antonio, Phil. 61 D4
San Antonio, N. Mex., U.S.A. 115 K10
San Antonio, Tex., U.S.A. 113 L5
San Antonio →, U.S.A. 113 L6
San Antonio, C., Argentina 126 D4
San Antonio, C., Cuba 120 B3
San Antonio, C. de, Spain 33 G5
San Antonio, Mt., U.S.A. 117 L9
San Antonio de los Baños, Cuba 120 B3
San Antonio de los Cobres, Argentina 126 A2
San Antonio Oeste, Argentina 128 E4
San Arcángelo, Italy 31 B9
San Ardo, U.S.A. 116 J6
San Augustín, Canary Is. 37 G4
San Augustine, U.S.A. 113 K7
San Bartolomé, Canary Is. 37 F6
San Bartolomé de Tirajana, Canary Is. 37 G4
San Bartolomeo in Galdo, Italy 31 A8
San Benedetto del Tronto, Italy 29 F10
San Benedetto Po, Italy 28 C7
San Benedicto, I., Mexico 118 D2
San Benito, U.S.A. 113 M6
San Benito →, U.S.A. 116 J5
San Benito Mt., U.S.A. 116 J6
San Bernardino, U.S.A. 117 L9
San Bernardino Mts., U.S.A. 117 L10
San Bernardino Str., Phil. 61 E6
San Bernardo, Chile 126 C1
San Bernardo, I. de, Colombia 124 B3
San Blas, Mexico 118 B3
San Blas, Arch. de, Panama 120 E4
San Blas, C., U.S.A. 109 L3
San Bonifacio, Italy 29 C8
San Borja, Bolivia 124 F5
San Buenaventura, Mexico 118 B4
San Carlos = Butuku-Luba, Eq. Guin. 83 E6
San Carlos = Sant Carles, Spain 37 B8
San Carlos, Argentina 126 C2
San Carlos, Chile 126 D1
San Carlos, Mexico 118 B4
San Carlos, Nic. 120 D3
San Carlos, Negros, Phil. 61 F5
San Carlos, Pangasinan, Phil. 61 D4
San Carlos, Uruguay 127 C5
San Carlos, U.S.A. 115 K8
San Carlos, Cojedes, Venezuela 124 B5
San Carlos, Cojedes, Venezuela 124 B5
San Carlos de Bariloche, Argentina 128 E2
San Carlos de Bolívar, Argentina 128 D4
San Carlos de la Rápita = Sant Carles de la Ràpita, Spain 32 E5
San Carlos del Zulia, Venezuela 124 B4
San Carlos L., U.S.A. 115 K8
San Cataldo, Italy 30 E6
San Celoni = Sant Celoni, Spain 32 D7
San Clemente, Chile 126 D1
San Clemente, Spain 33 F2
San Clemente, U.S.A. 117 M9
San Clemente I., U.S.A. 117 N8
San Cristóbal = Es Migjorn Gran, Spain 37 B11
San Cristóbal, Argentina 126 C3
San Cristóbal, Dom. Rep. 121 C5
San Cristóbal, Mexico 119 D6
San Cristóbal, Venezuela 124 B4
San Damiano d'Asti, Italy 28 D5
San Daniele del Friuli, Italy 29 B10
San Diego, Calif., U.S.A. 117 N9
San Diego, Tex., U.S.A. 113 M5
San Diego, C., Argentina 128 G3
San Diego de la Unión, Mexico 118 C4
San Dimitri, Ras, Malta 36 C1
San Donà di Piave, Italy 29 C9
San Estanislao, Paraguay 126 A4
San Esteban de Gormaz, Spain 32 D1
San Felice Circeo, Italy 30 A6
San Felice sul Panaro, Italy 29 D8
San Felipe, Chile 126 C1
San Felipe, Mexico 118 A2
San Felipe, Venezuela 124 A5
San Felipe →, U.S.A. 117 M11
San Félix, Pac. Oc. 122 F2
San Fernando = Sant Ferran, Spain 37 C7
San Fernando, Chile 126 C1
San Fernando, Mexico 118 B1
San Fernando, La Union, Phil. 61 C4
San Fernando, Pampanga, Phil. 61 D4
San Fernando, Spain 35 J4
San Fernando, Trin. & Tob. 121 D7
San Fernando, U.S.A. 117 L8
San Fernando →, Mexico 118 C5
San Fernando de Apure, Venezuela 124 B5
San Fernando de Atabapo, Venezuela 124 C5
San Fernando di Púglia, Italy 31 A9
San Francisco, Argentina 126 C3
San Francisco, U.S.A. 116 H4
San Francisco →, U.S.A. 115 K9
San Francisco, Paso de, S. Amer. 126 B2
San Francisco de Macorîs, Dom. Rep. 121 C5
San Francisco del Monte de Oro, Argentina 126 C2
San Francisco del Oro, Mexico 118 B3
San Francisco Javier = Sant Francesc de Formentera, Spain 37 C7
San Francisco Solano, Pta., Colombia 122 C3
San Fratello, Italy 31 D7
San Gavino Monreale, Italy 30 C1
San Gimignano, Italy 28 E8
San Giórgio di Nogaro, Italy 29 C10
San Giórgio Iónico, Italy 31 B10
San Giovanni Bianco, Italy 28 C6
San Giovanni in Fiore, Italy 31 C9
San Giovanni in Persiceto, Italy 29 D8
San Giovanni Rotondo, Italy 29 G12
San Giovanni Valdarno, Italy 29 E8
San Giuliano Terme, Italy 28 E7
San Gorgonio Mt., U.S.A. 117 L10
San Gottardo, P. del, Switz. 25 J4
San Gregorio, Uruguay 127 C4
San Gregorio, U.S.A. 116 H4
San Guiseppe Jato, Italy 30 E6
San Ignacio, Belize 119 D7
San Ignacio, Bolivia 124 G6
San Ignacio, Mexico 118 B2
San Ignacio, Paraguay 126 B4
San Ignacio, L., Mexico 118 B2
San Ildefonso, C., Phil. 61 D5
San Isidro, Argentina 126 C4
San Jacinto, U.S.A. 117 M10
San Jaime = Sant Jaume, Spain 37 B11
San Javier, Misiones, Argentina 127 B4
San Javier, Santa Fe, Argentina 126 C4
San Javier, Bolivia 124 G6
San Javier, Chile 126 D1
San Javier, Spain 33 H4
San Jeronimo Taviche, Mexico 119 D5
San Joaquin, U.S.A. 116 J6
San Joaquin →, U.S.A. 116 G5
San Joaquin Valley, U.S.A. 116 J6
San Jordi = Sant Jordi, Spain 37 B9
San Jorge, Argentina 126 C3
San Jorge, Spain 37 C7
San Jorge, B. de, Mexico 118 A2
San Jorge, G., Argentina 128 F3
San Jorge, G. of, Argentina 122 H4
San José = San Josep, Spain 37 C7
San José, Costa Rica 120 E3
San José, Guatemala 120 D1
San José, Mexico 118 C2
San Jose, Luzon, Phil. 61 D4
San Jose, Mindoro, Phil. 61 E4
San Jose, U.S.A. 116 H5
San Jose →, U.S.A. 115 J10
San José de Chiquitos, Bolivia 124 G6
San José de Feliciano, Argentina 126 C4
San José de Jáchal, Argentina 126 C2
San José de Mayo, Uruguay 126 C4
San José del Cabo, Mexico 118 C3
San José del Guaviare, Colombia 124 C4
San Josep, Spain 37 C7
San Juan, Argentina 126 C2
San Juan, Mexico 118 C4
San Juan, Phil. 61 G7
San Juan, Puerto Rico 121 C6
San Juan □, Argentina 126 C2
San Juan →, Argentina 126 C2
San Juan →, Nic. 120 D3
San Juan →, U.S.A. 115 H8
San Juan Bautista = Sant Joan Baptista, Spain 37 B8
San Juan Bautista, Paraguay 126 B4
San Juan Bautista, U.S.A. 116 J5
San Juan Bautista Valle Nacional, Mexico 119 D5
San Juan Capistrano, U.S.A. 117 M9
San Juan Cr. →, U.S.A. 116 J5
San Juan de Alicante, Spain 33 G4
San Juan de Guadalupe, Mexico 118 C4
San Juan de los Morros, Venezuela 124 B5
San Juan del Norte, Nic. 120 D3
San Juan del Norte, B. de, Nic. 120 D3
San Juan del Río, Mexico 119 C5
San Juan del Sur, Nic. 120 D2
San Juan I., U.S.A. 116 B3
San Juan Mts., U.S.A. 115 H10
San Just, Sierra de, Spain 32 E4
San Justo, Argentina 126 C3
San Kamphaeng, Thailand 64 C2
San Lázaro, C., Mexico 118 C2
San Lázaro, Sa., Mexico 118 C3
San Leandro, U.S.A. 116 H4
San Leonardo de Yagüe, Spain 32 D1
San Lorenzo = Sant Llorenç des Cardassar, Spain 37 B10
San Lorenzo, Argentina 126 C3
San Lorenzo, Ecuador 124 C3
San Lorenzo, Paraguay 126 B4
San Lorenzo →, Mexico 118 C3
San Lorenzo, I., Mexico 118 B2
San Lorenzo, Mt., Argentina 128 F2
San Lorenzo de la Parrilla, Spain 32 F2
San Lorenzo de Morunys = Sant Llorenç de Morunys, Spain 32 C6
San Lucas, Bolivia 124 H5
San Lucas, Baja Calif. S., Mexico 118 C3
San Lucas, Baja Calif. S., Mexico 118 B2
San Lucas, U.S.A. 116 J5
San Lucas, C., Mexico 118 C3
San Lúcido, Italy 31 C9
San Luis, Argentina 126 C2
San Luis, Cuba 120 B3
San Luis, Guatemala 120 C2
San Luis, U.S.A. 115 H11
San Luis □, Argentina 126 C2
San Luis, I., Mexico 118 B2
San Luis, Sierra de, Argentina 126 C2
San Luis de la Paz, Mexico 118 C4
San Luis Obispo, U.S.A. 117 K6
San Luis Potosí, Mexico 118 C4
San Luis Potosí □, Mexico 118 C4
San Luis Reservoir, U.S.A. 116 H5
San Luis Río Colorado, Mexico 118 A2
San Marco, C., Italy 30 C1
San Marco Argentano, Italy 31 C9
San Marco in Lámis, Italy 29 G12
San Marcos, Guatemala 120 D1
San Marcos, Mexico 118 B2
San Marcos, U.S.A. 113 L6
San Marino, San Marino 29 E9
San Marino ■, Europe 29 E9
San Martín, Argentina 126 C2
San Martín →, Bolivia 124 F6
San Martín, L., Argentina 128 F2
San Martín de la Vega, Spain 34 E7
San Martin de los Andes, Argentina 128 E2
San Martín de Valdeiglesias, Spain 34 E6
San Mateo = Sant Mateu, Baleares, Spain 37 B7
San Mateo = Sant Mateu, Valencia, Spain 32 E5
San Mateo, Phil. 61 C4
San Mateo, U.S.A. 116 H4
San Matías, Bolivia 124 G7
San Matías, G., Argentina 122 H4
San Miguel = Sant Miquel, Spain 37 B7
San Miguel, El Salv. 120 D2
San Miguel, Panama 120 E4
San Miguel, U.S.A. 116 K6
San Miguel →, Bolivia 124 F6
San Miguel de Tucumán, Argentina 126 B2
San Miguel del Monte, Argentina 126 D4
San Miguel I., U.S.A. 117 L6
San Miniato, Italy 28 E7
San Narciso, Phil. 61 D4
San Nicolás, Canary Is. 37 G4
San Nicolas, Phil. 61 B4
San Nicolás de los Arroyas, Argentina 126 C3
San Nicolas I., U.S.A. 117 M7
San Onofre, U.S.A. 117 M9
San Pablo, Bolivia 126 A2
San Pablo, Phil. 61 D4
San Páolo di Civitate, Italy 29 G12
San Pedro, Buenos Aires, Argentina 127 B5
San Pedro, Jujuy, Argentina 126 A3
San Pedro, Ivory C. 82 E3
San Pedro, Mexico 118 C2
San Pedro □, Paraguay 126 A4
San Pedro →, Chihuahua, Mexico 118 B3
San Pedro →, Michoacan, Mexico 118 D4
San Pedro →, Nayarit, Mexico 118 C3
San Pedro →, U.S.A. 115 K8
San Pedro, Pta., Chile 126 B1
San Pedro, Sierra de, Spain 35 F4
San Pedro Channel, U.S.A. 117 M8
San Pedro de Atacama, Chile 126 A2
San Pedro de Jujuy, Argentina 126 A3
San Pedro de las Colonias, Mexico 118 B4
San Pedro de Macorís, Dom. Rep. 121 C6
San Pedro del Norte, Nic. 120 D3
San Pedro del Paraná, Paraguay 126 B4
San Pedro del Pinatar, Spain 33 H4
San Pedro Mártir, Sierra, Mexico 118 A1
San Pedro Mixtepec, Mexico 119 D5
San Pedro Ocampo = Melchor Ocampo, Mexico 118 C4
San Pedro Sula, Honduras 120 C2
San Pietro, Italy 30 C1
San Pietro Vernótico, Italy 31 B11
San Quintín, Mexico 118 A1
San Rafael, Argentina 126 C2
San Rafael, Calif., U.S.A. 116 H4
San Rafael, N. Mex., U.S.A. 115 J10
San Rafael Mt., U.S.A. 117 L7
San Rafael Mts., U.S.A. 117 L7
San Ramón de la Nueva Orán, Argentina 126 A3
San Remo, Italy 28 E4
San Roque, Argentina 126 B4
San Roque, Spain 35 J5
San Rosendo, Chile 126 D1
San Saba, U.S.A. 113 K5
San Salvador, Bahamas 121 B5
San Salvador, El Salv. 120 D2
San Salvador, Spain 37 B10
San Salvador de Jujuy, Argentina 126 A3
San Salvador I., Bahamas 121 B5
San Salvo, Italy 29 F11
San Sebastián = Donostia-San Sebastián, Spain 32 B3
San Sebastián, Argentina 128 G3
San Sebastian de la Gomera, Canary Is. 37 F2
San Serra = Son Serra, Spain 37 B10
San Serverino Marche, Italy 29 E10
San Severo, Italy 29 G12
San Simeon, U.S.A. 116 K5
San Simon, U.S.A. 115 K9
San Stéfano di Cadore, Italy 29 B9
San Stino di Livenza, Italy 29 C9
San Telmo = Sant Telm, Spain 37 B9
San Telmo, Mexico 118 A1
San Tiburcio, Mexico 118 C4
San Valentin, Mte., Chile 122 H3
San Vicente, Phil. 61 B5
San Vicente de Alcántara, Spain 35 F3
San Vicente de la Barquera, Spain 34 B6
San Vincente del Raspeig, Spain 33 G4
San Vincenzo, Italy 28 E7
San Vito, Italy 30 C2
San Vito, C., Italy 30 D5
San Vito al Tagliamento, Italy 29 C9
San Vito Chietino, Italy 29 F11
San Vito dei Normanni, Italy 31 B10
San Ygnacio, U.S.A. 113 M5
Sana', Yemen 74 D3
Sana →, Bos.-H. 29 C13
Sanaba, Burkina Faso 82 C4
Şanāfīr, Si. Arabia 80 B3
Sanaga →, Cameroon 83 E6
Sanaloa, Presa, Mexico 118 C3
Sanana, Indonesia 63 E7
Sanand, India 68 H5
Sanandaj, Iran 70 C5
Sanandita, Bolivia 126 A3
Sanary-sur-Mer, France 21 E9
Sanawad, India 68 H7
Sancellas = Sencelles, Spain 37 B9
Sancergues, France 19 E9
Sancerre, France 19 E9
Sancerrois, Collines du, France 19 E9
Sancha He →, China 58 D6
Sanchahe, China 57 B14
Sánchez, Dom. Rep. 121 C6
Sanchor, India 68 G4
Sancoins, France 19 F9
Sancti Spíritus, Cuba 120 B4
Sancy, Puy de, France 20 C6
Sand →, S. Africa 89 C5
Sand Springs, U.S.A. 113 G6
Sanda, Japan 55 G7
Sandakan, Malaysia 62 C5
Sandan = Sambor, Cambodia 64 F6
Sandanski, Bulgaria 40 E7
Sandaré, Mali 82 C2
Sandared, Sweden 11 G6
Sandarne, Sweden 10 C11
Sanday, U.K. 14 B6
Sandefjord, Norway 9 G14
Sanders, U.S.A. 115 J9
Sanderson, U.S.A. 113 K3
Sandfly L., Canada 105 B7
Sandgate, Australia 95 D5
Sandhammaren, C., Sweden 11 J8
Sandía, Peru 124 F5
Sandıklı, Turkey 39 C12
Sandnes, Norway 9 G11
Sandnessjøen, Norway 8 C15
Sandoa, Dem. Rep. of the Congo 84 F4
Sandomierz, Poland 45 H8
Sândominic, Romania 43 D10
Sandover →, Australia 94 C2
Sandoway, Burma 67 K19
Sandoy, Færoe Is. 8 F9
Sandpoint, U.S.A. 114 B5
Sandray, U.K. 14 E1
Sandringham, U.K. 12 E8
Sandspit, Canada 104 C2
Sandstone, Australia 93 E2
Sandu, China 58 E6
Sandusky, Mich., U.S.A. 102 D3
Sandusky, Ohio, U.S.A. 110 E2
Sandvig, Sweden 11 J8
Sandviken, Sweden 10 D10
Sandwich, C., Australia 94 B4
Sandwich B., Canada 103 B8
Sandwich B., Namibia 88 C1
Sandwip Chan., Bangla. 67 H17
Sandy, Nev., U.S.A. 117 K11
Sandy, Oreg., U.S.A. 116 E4
Sandy, Utah, U.S.A. 114 F8
Sandy Bight, Australia 93 F3
Sandy C., Queens., Australia 94 C5
Sandy C., Tas., Australia 94 G3
Sandy Cay, Bahamas 121 B4
Sandy Cr. →, U.S.A. 114 F9

Sandy L., *Canada* 102 B1
Sandy Lake, *Canada* 102 B1
Sandy Narrows, *Canada* 105 B8
Sanford, *Fla., U.S.A.* 109 L5
Sanford, *Maine, U.S.A.* 111 C14
Sanford, *N.C., U.S.A.* 109 H6
Sanford →, *Australia* 93 E2
Sanford, Mt., *U.S.A.* 100 B5
Sang-i-Masha, *Afghan.* 68 C2
Sanga, *Mozam.* 87 E4
Sanga →, *Congo* 84 E3
Sangamner, *India* 66 K9
Sangar, *Afghan.* 68 C1
Sangar, *Russia* 51 C13
Sangar Sarai, *Afghan.* 68 B4
Sangatte, *France* 19 B8
Sangay, *Ecuador* 124 D3
Sange, *Dem. Rep. of the Congo* 86 D2
Sangeang, *Indonesia* 63 F5
Sângeorz-Băi, *Romania* 43 C9
Sanger, *U.S.A.* 116 J7
Sângera, *Moldova* 43 D13
Sangerhausen, *Germany* 24 D7
Sanggan He →, *China* 56 E9
Sanggau, *Indonesia* 62 D4
Sangihe, Kepulauan, *Indonesia* 63 D7
Sangihe, Pulau, *Indonesia* 63 D7
Sangju, *S. Korea* 57 F15
Sangkapura, *Indonesia* 62 F4
Sangkhla, *Thailand* 64 E2
Sangli, *India* 66 L9
Sangmélima, *Cameroon* 83 E7
Sangre de Cristo Mts., *U.S.A.* 113 G2
Sangro →, *Italy* 29 F11
Sangudo, *Canada* 104 C6
Sangue →, *Brazil* 124 F7
Sangüesa, *Spain* 32 C3
Sanguinaires, Îs., *France* 21 G12
Sangzhi, *China* 59 C8
Sanhala, *Ivory C.* 82 C3
Sanje, *Uganda* 86 C3
Sanjiang, *China* 58 E7
Sanjo, *Japan* 54 F9
Sankt Andrä, *Austria* 26 E7
Sankt Augustin, *Germany* 24 E3
Sankt Blasien, *Germany* 25 H4
Sankt Gallen, *Switz.* 25 H5
Sankt Gallen □, *Switz.* 25 H5
Sankt Goar, *Germany* 25 E3
Sankt Ingbert, *Germany* 25 F3
Sankt Johann im Pongau, *Austria* 26 D6
Sankt Johann in Tirol, *Austria* 26 D5
Sankt-Peterburg, *Russia* 46 C6
Sankt Pölten, *Austria* 26 C8
Sankt Ulrich = Ortisei, *Italy* 29 B8
Sankt Valentin, *Austria* 26 C7
Sankt Veit an der Glan, *Austria* 26 E7
Sankt Wendel, *Germany* 25 F3
Sankt Wolfgang, *Austria* 26 D6
Sankuru →, *Dem. Rep. of the Congo* 84 E4
Sanliurfa, *Turkey* 73 D8
Sanlúcar de Barrameda, *Spain* 35 J4
Sanluri, *Italy* 30 C1
Sânmartin, *Romania* 43 D10
Sanmenxia, *China* 56 G6
Sanming, *China* 59 D11
Sannaspos, *S. Africa* 88 D4
Sannicandro Gargánico, *Italy* 29 G12
Sânnicolau Mare, *Romania* 42 D5
Sannieshof, *S. Africa* 88 D4
Sannīn, J., *Lebanon* 75 B4
Sanok, *Poland* 45 J9
Sanquhar, *U.K.* 14 F5
Sansanding Dam, *Mali* 82 C3
Sansepolcro, *Italy* 29 E9
Sansha, *China* 59 D13
Sanshui, *China* 59 F9
Sanski Most, *Bos.-H.* 29 D13
Sansui, *China* 58 D7
Sant Antoni Abat, *Spain* 37 C7
Sant Boi de Llobregat, *Spain* 32 D7
Sant Carles, *Spain* 37 B8
Sant Carles de la Ràpita, *Spain* 32 E5
Sant Celoni, *Spain* 32 D7
Sant Feliu de Guíxols, *Spain* 32 D8
Sant Feliu de Llobregat, *Spain* 32 D7
Sant Ferran, *Spain* 37 C7
Sant Francesc de Formentera, *Spain* 37 C7
Sant Jaume, *Spain* 37 B11
Sant Joan Baptista, *Spain* 37 B8
Sant Jordi, *Spain* 37 B9
Sant Jordi, G. de, *Spain* 32 E6
Sant Llorenç de Morunys, *Spain* 32 C6
Sant Llorenç des Cardassar, *Spain* 37 B10
Sant Mateu, *Baleares, Spain* 37 B7
Sant Mateu, *Valencia, Spain* 32 E5
Sant Miquel, *Spain* 37 B7
Sant Telm, *Spain* 37 B9
Sant' Ágata Militello, *Italy* 31 D7
Santa Agnés, *Spain* 37 B7
Santa Ana, *Bolivia* 124 F5
Santa Ana, *El Salv.* 120 D2
Santa Ana, *Mexico* 118 A2
Santa Ana, *U.S.A.* 117 M9
Sant' Ángelo Lodigiano, *Italy* 28 C6
Sant' Antíoco, *Italy* 30 C1
Santa Barbara, *Honduras* 120 D2
Santa Bárbara, *Mexico* 118 B3
Santa Bárbara, *Spain* 32 E5
Santa Barbara, *U.S.A.* 117 L7
Santa Bárbara, Mt., *Spain* 33 H2
Santa Barbara Channel, *U.S.A.* 117 L7
Santa Barbara I., *U.S.A.* 117 M7
Santa Catalina, *Mexico* 118 B2
Santa Catalina, Gulf of, *U.S.A.* 117 N9
Santa Catalina I., *U.S.A.* 117 M8
Santa Catarina □, *Brazil* 127 B6
Santa Catarina, I. de, *Brazil* 127 B6
Santa Caterina di Pittinuri, *Italy* 30 B1
Santa Caterina Villarmosa, *Italy* 31 E7
Santa Cecília, *Brazil* 127 B5
Santa Clara, *Cuba* 120 B4
Santa Clara, *Calif., U.S.A.* 116 H5
Santa Clara, *Utah, U.S.A.* 115 H7
Santa Clara de Olimar, *Uruguay* 127 C5
Santa Clotilde, *Peru* 124 D4
Santa Coloma de Farners, *Spain* 32 D7
Santa Coloma de Gramenet, *Spain* 32 D7
Santa Comba, *Spain* 34 B2
Santa Croce Camerina, *Italy* 31 F7
Santa Croce di Magliano, *Italy* 29 G11
Santa Cruz, *Argentina* 128 G3
Santa Cruz, *Bolivia* 124 G6
Santa Cruz, *Chile* 126 C1
Santa Cruz, *Costa Rica* 120 D2
Santa Cruz, *Madeira* 37 D3
Santa Cruz, *Phil.* 61 D4
Santa Cruz, *U.S.A.* 116 J4
Santa Cruz →, *Argentina* 128 G3
Santa Cruz de la Palma, *Canary Is.* 37 F2
Santa Cruz de Mudela, *Spain* 35 G7
Santa Cruz de Tenerife, *Canary Is.* 37 F3
Santa Cruz del Norte, *Cuba* 120 B3
Santa Cruz del Retamar, *Spain* 34 E6
Santa Cruz del Sur, *Cuba* 120 B4
Santa Cruz do Rio Pardo, *Brazil* 127 A6
Santa Cruz do Sul, *Brazil* 127 B5
Santa Cruz I., *U.S.A.* 117 M7
Santa Cruz Is., *Solomon Is.* 96 J8
Santa Domingo, Cay, *Bahamas* 120 B4
Sant' Egídio alla Vibrata, *Italy* 29 F10
Santa Elena, *Argentina* 126 C4
Santa Elena, C., *Costa Rica* 120 D2
Sant' Eufémia, G. di, *Italy* 31 D9
Santa Eugenia, Pta., *Mexico* 118 B1
Santa Eulàlia des Riu, *Spain* 37 C8
Santa Fe, *Argentina* 126 C3
Santa Fe, *Spain* 35 H7
Santa Fe, *U.S.A.* 115 J11
Santa Fé □, *Argentina* 126 C3
Santa Fé do Sul, *Brazil* 125 H8
Santa Filomena, *Brazil* 125 E9
Santa Fiora, *Italy* 29 F8
Santa Gertrudis, *Spain* 37 C7
Santa Giustina, *Italy* 29 B9
Santa Inês, *Brazil* 125 F11
Santa Inés, *Spain* 35 G5
Santa Inés, I., *Chile* 122 J3
Santa Isabel = Rey Malabo, *Eq. Guin.* 83 E6
Santa Isabel, *Argentina* 126 D2
Santa Isabel, Pico, *Eq. Guin.* 83 E6
Santa Isabel do Morro, *Brazil* 125 F8
Santa Lucía, *Corrientes, Argentina* 126 B4
Santa Lucía, *San Juan, Argentina* 126 C2
Santa Lucía, *Spain* 33 H4
Santa Lucía, *Uruguay* 126 C4
Santa Lucia Range, *U.S.A.* 116 K5
Santa Magdalena, I., *Mexico* 118 C2
Santa Margarita, *Argentina* 126 D3
Santa Margarita, *Mexico* 118 C2
Santa Margarita, *Spain* 37 B10
Santa Margarita, *U.S.A.* 116 K6
Santa Margarita →, *U.S.A.* 117 M9
Santa Margherita, *Italy* 30 D1
Santa Margherita Ligure, *Italy* 28 D6
Santa María, *Argentina* 126 B2
Santa Maria, *Brazil* 127 B5
Santa Maria, *Phil.* 61 C4
Santa Maria, *U.S.A.* 117 L6
Santa María →, *Mexico* 118 A3
Santa María, B. de, *Mexico* 118 B3
Santa Maria, C. de, *Portugal* 35 J3
Santa Maria Cápua Vétere, *Italy* 31 A7
Santa Maria da Feira, *Portugal* 34 E2
Santa Maria da Vitória, *Brazil* 125 F10
Santa Maria del Camí, *Spain* 37 B9
Santa Maria di Léuca, C., *Italy* 31 C11
Santa María la Real de Nieva, *Spain* 34 D6
Santa Marinella, *Italy* 29 F8
Santa Marta, *Colombia* 124 A4
Santa Marta, Sierra Nevada de, *Colombia* 122 B3
Santa Marta de Tormes, *Spain* 34 E5
Santa Marta Grande, C., *Brazil* 127 B6
Santa Marta Ortigueira, Ría de, *Spain* 34 B3
Santa Monica, *U.S.A.* 117 M8
Santa Olalla, *Huelva, Spain* 35 H4
Santa Olalla, *Toledo, Spain* 34 E6
Santa Pola, *Spain* 33 G4
Santa Ponsa, *Spain* 37 B9
Santa Rita, *U.S.A.* 115 K10
Santa Rosa, *La Pampa, Argentina* 126 D3
Santa Rosa, *San Luis, Argentina* 126 C2
Santa Rosa, *Brazil* 127 B5
Santa Rosa, *Calif., U.S.A.* 116 G4
Santa Rosa, *N. Mex., U.S.A.* 113 H2
Santa Rosa de Copán, *Honduras* 120 D2
Santa Rosa de Río Primero, *Argentina* 126 C3
Santa Rosa del Sara, *Bolivia* 124 G6
Santa Rosa I., *Calif., U.S.A.* 117 M6
Santa Rosa I., *Fla., U.S.A.* 109 K2
Santa Rosa Range, *U.S.A.* 114 F5
Santa Rosalía, *Mexico* 118 B2
Santa Sylvina, *Argentina* 126 B3
Santa Tecla = Nueva San Salvador, *El Salv.* 120 D2
Santa Teresa, *Argentina* 126 C3
Santa Teresa, *Mexico* 119 B5
Santa Teresa di Riva, *Italy* 31 E8
Santa Teresa Gallura, *Italy* 30 A2
Santa Uxía, *Spain* 34 C2
Santa Vitória do Palmar, *Brazil* 127 C5
Santa Ynez →, *U.S.A.* 117 L6
Santa Ynez Mts., *U.S.A.* 117 L6
Santa Ysabel, *U.S.A.* 117 M10
Santadi, *Italy* 30 C1
Santaella, *Spain* 35 H6
Santai, *China* 58 B5
Santana, *Madeira* 37 D3
Sântana, *Romania* 42 D6
Santana, Coxilha de, *Brazil* 127 C4
Santana do Livramento, *Brazil* 127 C4
Santander, *Spain* 34 B7
Santander Jiménez, *Mexico* 119 C5
Santanyí, *Spain* 37 B10
Santaquin, *U.S.A.* 114 G8
Santarcángelo di Romagna, *Italy* 29 D9
Santarém, *Brazil* 125 D8
Santarém, *Portugal* 35 F2
Santarém □, *Portugal* 35 F2
Santaren Channel, *W. Indies* 120 B4
Santee, *U.S.A.* 117 N10
Santéramo in Colle, *Italy* 31 B9
Santerno →, *Italy* 29 D8
Santhià, *Italy* 28 C5
Santiago, *Brazil* 127 B5
Santiago, *Chile* 126 C1
Santiago, *Panama* 120 E3
Santiago, *Phil.* 61 C4
Santiago □, *Chile* 126 C1
Santiago →, *Mexico* 98 G9
Santiago →, *Peru* 124 D3
Santiago, Punta de, *Eq. Guin.* 83 E6
Santiago de Compostela, *Spain* 34 C2
Santiago de Cuba, *Cuba* 120 C4
Santiago de los Cabelleros, *Dom. Rep.* 121 C5
Santiago del Estero, *Argentina* 126 B3
Santiago del Estero □, *Argentina* 126 B3
Santiago del Teide, *Canary Is.* 37 F3
Santiago do Cacém, *Portugal* 35 G2
Santiago Ixcuintla, *Mexico* 118 C3
Santiago Papasquiaro, *Mexico* 118 C3
Santiaguillo, L. de, *Mexico* 118 C4
Santillana, *Spain* 34 B6
Santisteban del Puerto, *Spain* 35 G7
Santo Amaro, *Brazil* 125 F11
Santo Anastácio, *Brazil* 127 A5
Santo André, *Brazil* 127 A6
Santo Ângelo, *Brazil* 127 B5
Santo Antonio, *Brazil* 125 G7
Santo Antônio do Içá, *Brazil* 124 D5
Santo Domingo, *Dom. Rep.* 121 C6
Santo Domingo, *Baja Calif., Mexico* 118 A1
Santo Domingo, *Baja Calif. S., Mexico* 118 B2
Santo Domingo, *Nic.* 120 D3
Santo Domingo de la Calzada, *Spain* 32 C2
Santo Domingo de los Colorados, *Ecuador* 124 D3
Santo Stéfano di Camastro, *Italy* 31 D7
Santo Tirso, *Portugal* 34 D2
Santo Tomás, *Mexico* 118 A1
Santo Tomás, *Peru* 124 F4
Santo Tomé, *Argentina* 127 B4
Santo Tomé de Guayana = Ciudad Guayana, *Venezuela* 124 B6
Santomera, *Spain* 33 G3
Santoña, *Spain* 34 B7
Santoríni = Thíra, *Greece* 39 E7
Santos, *Brazil* 127 A6
Santos, Sierra de los, *Spain* 35 G5
Santos Dumont, *Brazil* 127 A7
Sanxenxo, *Spain* 34 C2
Sanyuan, *China* 56 G5
São Anastácio, *Brazil* 127 A5
São Bartolomeu de Messines, *Portugal* 35 H2
São Bernardo do Campo, *Brazil* 127 A6
São Borja, *Brazil* 127 B4
São Brás de Alportel, *Portugal* 35 H3
São Carlos, *Brazil* 127 A6
São Cristóvão, *Brazil* 125 F11
São Domingos, *Brazil* 125 F9
São Francisco, *Brazil* 125 G10
São Francisco →, *Brazil* 122 E7
São Francisco do Sul, *Brazil* 127 B6
São Gabriel, *Brazil* 127 C5
São Gonçalo, *Brazil* 127 A7
Sao Hill, *Tanzania* 87 D4
São João da Boa Vista, *Brazil* 127 A6
São João da Madeira, *Portugal* 34 E2
São João da Pesqueira, *Portugal* 34 D3
São João del Rei, *Brazil* 127 A7
São João do Araguaia, *Brazil* 125 E9
São João do Piauí, *Brazil* 125 E10
São Jorge, Pta. de, *Madeira* 37 D3
São José do Rio Prêto, *Brazil* 127 A6
São José dos Campos, *Brazil* 127 A6
São Leopoldo, *Brazil* 127 B5
São Lourenço, *Brazil* 127 A6
São Lourenço →, *Brazil* 125 G7
São Lourenço, Pta. de, *Madeira* 37 D3
São Luís, *Brazil* 125 D10
São Luís Gonzaga, *Brazil* 127 B5
São Marcos →, *Brazil* 125 G9
São Marcos, B. de, *Brazil* 125 D10
São Martinho da Cortiça, *Portugal* 34 E2
São Mateus, *Brazil* 125 G11
São Paulo, *Brazil* 127 A6
São Paulo □, *Brazil* 127 A6
São Paulo, I., *Atl. Oc.* 2 D8
São Paulo de Olivença, *Brazil* 124 D5
São Pedro do Sul, *Portugal* 34 E2
São Roque, *Madeira* 37 D3
São Roque, C. de, *Brazil* 122 D7
São Sebastião, I. de, *Brazil* 127 A6
São Sebastião do Paraíso, *Brazil* 127 A6
São Teotónio, *Portugal* 35 H2
São Tomé, *Atl. Oc.* 76 F4
São Tomé, C. de, *Brazil* 127 A7
São Tomé & Principe ■, *Africa* 77 F4
São Vicente, *Brazil* 127 A6
São Vicente, *Madeira* 37 D2
São Vicente, C. de, *Portugal* 35 H1
Saona, I., *Dom. Rep.* 121 C6
Saône →, *France* 19 G11
Saône-et-Loire □, *France* 19 F11
Saonek, *Indonesia* 63 E8
Sápai, *Greece* 41 E9
Sapanca, *Turkey* 72 B4
Saparua, *Indonesia* 63 E7
Sapele, *Nigeria* 83 D6
Sapelo I., *U.S.A.* 109 K5
Şaphane, *Turkey* 39 B11
Sapiéntza, *Greece* 38 E3
Sapone, *Burkina Faso* 83 C4
Saposoa, *Peru* 124 E3
Sapozhok, *Russia* 48 D5
Sappho, *U.S.A.* 116 B2
Sapporo, *Japan* 54 C10
Sapri, *Italy* 31 B8
Sapulpa, *U.S.A.* 113 H7
Saqqez, *Iran* 70 B5
Sar Dasht, *Iran* 71 C6
Sar Gachīneh, *Iran* 71 D6
Sar Planina, *Macedonia* 40 E4
Sara, *Burkina Faso* 82 C4
Sara, *Phil.* 61 F5
Sara Buri = Saraburi, *Thailand* 64 E3
Sarāb, *Iran* 70 B5
Sarabadi, *Iraq* 70 C5
Saraburi, *Thailand* 64 E3
Sarada →, *India* 67 F12
Saragossa = Zaragoza, *Spain* 32 D4
Saraguro, *Ecuador* 124 D3
Saraiu, *Romania* 43 F13
Sarajevo, *Bos.-H.* 42 G3
Saran, Gunung, *Indonesia* 62 E4
Saranac Lake, *U.S.A.* 111 B10
Saranda, *Tanzania* 86 D3
Sarandë, *Albania* 40 G3
Sarandí del Yi, *Uruguay* 127 C4
Sarandí Grande, *Uruguay* 126 C4
Sarangani B., *Phil.* 61 J6
Sarangani Is., *Phil.* 61 J6
Sarangarh, *India* 67 J13
Saransk, *Russia* 48 C7
Sarapul, *Russia* 50 D6
Sarasota, *U.S.A.* 109 M4
Saratoga, *Calif., U.S.A.* 116 H4
Saratoga, *Wyo., U.S.A.* 114 F10
Saratoga Springs, *U.S.A.* 111 C11
Saratov, *Russia* 48 E7
Saravane, *Laos* 64 E6
Sarawak □, *Malaysia* 62 D4
Saray, *Tekirdağ, Turkey* 41 E11
Saray, *Van, Turkey* 73 C11
Saraya, *Senegal* 82 C2
Saraycık, *Turkey* 39 B11
Sarayköy, *Turkey* 39 D10
Saraylar, *Turkey* 41 F11
Sarayönü, *Turkey* 72 C5
Sarbāz, *Iran* 71 E9
Sarbīsheh, *Iran* 71 C8
Sárbogárd, *Hungary* 42 D3
Sarca →, *Italy* 28 C7
Sarcelles, *France* 19 D9
Sarda → = Sarada →, *India* 67 F12
Sardarshahr, *India* 68 E6
Sardegna □, *Italy* 30 B1
Sardhana, *India* 68 E7
Sardina, Pta., *Canary Is.* 37 F4
Sardinia = Sardegna □, *Italy* 30 B1
Sardis, *Turkey* 39 C10
Sārdūīyeh = Dar Mazār, *Iran* 71 D8
S'Arenal, *Spain* 37 B9
Sarentino, *Italy* 29 B8
Saréyamou, *Mali* 82 B4
Sargent, *U.S.A.* 112 E5
Sargodha, *Pakistan* 68 C5
Sarh, *Chad* 79 G9
Sārī, *Iran* 71 B7
Sari d'Orcino, *France* 21 F12
Sária, *Greece* 39 F9
Sarıbeyler, *Turkey* 39 B9
Sarıgöl, *Turkey* 72 C3
Sarikamiş, *Turkey* 73 B10
Sarıkaya, *Turkey* 72 C6
Sarikei, *Malaysia* 62 D4
Sarıköy, *Turkey* 41 F11
Sarina, *Australia* 94 C4
Sariñena, *Spain* 32 D4
Sarita, *U.S.A.* 113 M6
Sariwŏn, *N. Korea* 57 E13
Sariyar Baraji, *Turkey* 72 B4
Sariyer, *Turkey* 41 E13
Sark, *U.K.* 13 H5
Sarkad, *Hungary* 42 D6
Şarkışla, *Turkey* 72 C7
Şarköy, *Turkey* 41 F11
Sarlat-la-Canéda, *France* 20 D5
Sarles, *U.S.A.* 112 A5
Sărmăşag, *Romania* 42 C7
Sărmaşu, *Romania* 43 D9
Sarmi, *Indonesia* 63 E9
Sarmiento, *Argentina* 128 F3
Sarmizegetusa, *Romania* 42 E7
Särna, *Sweden* 10 C7
Sarnano, *Italy* 29 E10
Sarnen, *Switz.* 25 J4
Sarnia, *Canada* 102 D3
Sarno, *Italy* 31 B7
Sarnthein = Sarentino, *Italy* 29 B8
Särö, *Sweden* 11 G5
Sarolangun, *Indonesia* 62 E2
Saronikós Kólpos, *Greece* 38 D5
Saronno, *Italy* 28 C6
Saros Körfezi, *Turkey* 41 F10
Sárospatak, *Hungary* 42 B6
Sarpsborg, *Norway* 9 G14
Sarracín, *Spain* 34 C7
Sarralbe, *France* 19 D14
Sarre = Saar →, *Europe* 17 E6
Sarre, *Italy* 28 C4
Sarre-Union, *France* 19 D14
Sarrebourg, *France* 19 D14
Sarreguemines, *France* 19 C14

Sarria, *Spain* 34 C3
Sarrión, *Spain* 32 E4
Sarro, *Mali* 82 C3
Sarstedt, *Germany* 24 C5
Sartène, *France* 21 G12
Sarthe □, *France* 18 D7
Sarthe →, *France* 18 E6
Sartilly, *France* 18 D5
Saruhanlı, *Turkey* 39 C9
Sărulești, *Romania* 43 F11
Sárvár, *Hungary* 42 C1
Sarvestān, *Iran* 71 D7
Särvfjället, *Sweden* 10 B7
Sárviz →, *Hungary* 42 D3
Sary-Tash, *Kyrgyzstan* 50 F8
Sarych, Mys, *Ukraine* 47 K7
Saryshagan, *Kazakstan* 50 E8
Sarzana, *Italy* 28 D6
Sarzeau, *France* 18 E4
Sasaram, *India* 69 G11
Sasebo, *Japan* 55 H4
Saser, *India* 69 B7
Saskatchewan □, *Canada* 105 C7
Saskatchewan →, *Canada* 105 C8
Saskatoon, *Canada* 105 C7
Saskylakh, *Russia* 51 B12
Sasolburg, *S. Africa* 89 D4
Sasovo, *Russia* 48 C5
Sassandra, *Ivory C.* 82 E3
Sassandra →, *Ivory C.* 82 E3
Sássari, *Italy* 30 B1
Sassnitz, *Germany* 24 A9
Sasso Marconi, *Italy* 29 D8
Sassocorvaro, *Italy* 29 E9
Sassoferrato, *Italy* 29 E9
Sasstown, *Liberia* 82 E3
Sassuolo, *Italy* 28 D7
Sástago, *Spain* 32 D4
Sasumua Dam, *Kenya* 86 C4
Sasyk, Ozero, *Ukraine* 47 K5
Sata-Misaki, *Japan* 55 J5
Satadougou, *Mali* 82 C2
Satakunta, *Finland* 9 F20
Satanta, *U.S.A.* 113 G4
Satara, *India* 66 L8
Såtenäs, *Sweden* 11 F6
Säter, *Sweden* 10 D9
Satilla →, *U.S.A.* 109 K5
Satmala Hills, *India* 66 J9
Satna, *India* 69 G9
Šator, *Bos.-H.* 29 D13
Sátoraljaújhely, *Hungary* 42 B6
Satpura Ra., *India* 68 J7
Satrup, *Germany* 24 A5
Satsuna-Shotō, *Japan* 55 K5
Sattahip, *Thailand* 64 F3
Satu Mare, *Romania* 42 C7
Satu Mare □, *Romania* 42 C8
Satui, *Indonesia* 62 E5
Satun, *Thailand* 65 J3
Saturnina →, *Brazil* 124 F7
Sauce, *Argentina* 126 C4
Sauceda, *Mexico* 118 B4
Saucillo, *Mexico* 118 B3
Sauda, *Norway* 9 G12
Sauðarkrókur, *Iceland* 8 D4
Saudi Arabia ■, *Asia* 74 B3
Saugeen →, *Canada* 110 B3
Saugerties, *U.S.A.* 111 D11
Saugues, *France* 20 D7
Saujon, *France* 20 C3
Sauk Centre, *U.S.A.* 112 C7
Sauk Rapids, *U.S.A.* 112 C7
Saulgau, *Germany* 25 G5
Saulieu, *France* 19 E11
Sault, *France* 21 D9
Sault Ste. Marie, *Canada* 102 C3
Sault Ste. Marie, *U.S.A.* 108 B3
Saumlaki, *Indonesia* 63 F8
Saumur, *France* 18 E6
Saunders C., *N.Z.* 91 L3
Saunders I., *Antarctica* 5 B1
Saunders Point, *Australia* 93 E4
Sauri, *Nigeria* 83 C6
Saurimo, *Angola* 84 F4
Sausalito, *U.S.A.* 116 H4
Sauveterre-de-Béarn, *France* 20 E3
Sauzé-Vaussais, *France* 20 B4
Savá, *Honduras* 120 C2
Sava, *Italy* 31 B10
Sava →, *Serbia, Yug.* 42 F5
Savage, *U.S.A.* 112 B2
Savage I. = Niue, *Cook Is.* 97 J11
Savai'i, *W. Samoa* 91 A12
Savalou, *Benin* 83 D5
Savane, *Mozam.* 87 F4
Savanna, *U.S.A.* 112 D9
Savanna-la-Mar, *Jamaica* 120 C4
Savannah, *Ga., U.S.A.* 109 J5
Savannah, *Mo., U.S.A.* 112 F7
Savannah, *Tenn., U.S.A.* 109 H1
Savannah →, *U.S.A.* 109 J5
Savannakhet, *Laos* 64 D5
Savant L., *Canada* 102 B1
Savant Lake, *Canada* 102 B1
Savanur, *India* 66 M9
Săvârșin, *Romania* 42 D7
Savaştepe, *Turkey* 39 B9
Savé, *Benin* 83 D5
Save →, *France* 20 E5
Save →, *Mozam.* 89 C5
Sāveh, *Iran* 71 C6
Savelugu, *Ghana* 83 D4
Savenay, *France* 18 E5
Săveni, *Romania* 43 C11
Saverdun, *France* 20 E5
Saverne, *France* 19 D14
Savigliano, *Italy* 28 D4
Savigny-sur-Braye, *France* 18 E7
Sávio →, *Italy* 29 D9
Šavnik, *Montenegro, Yug.* 40 D3
Savo, *Finland* 8 E22
Savoie □, *France* 21 C10
Savona, *Italy* 28 D5
Savonlinna, *Finland* 46 B5
Şavşat, *Turkey* 73 B10
Sävsjö, *Sweden* 11 G8
Sawahlunto, *Indonesia* 62 E2
Sawai, *Indonesia* 63 E7
Sawai Madhopur, *India* 68 G7
Sawang Daen Din, *Thailand* 64 D4
Sawankhalok, *Thailand* 64 D2
Sawara, *Japan* 55 G10
Sawatch Mts., *U.S.A.* 115 G10
Sawel Mt., *U.K.* 15 B4
Sawi, *Thailand* 65 G2
Sawmills, *Zimbabwe* 87 F2
Sawu, *Indonesia* 63 F6
Sawu Sea, *Indonesia* 63 F6
Saxby →, *Australia* 94 B3
Saxmundham, *U.K.* 13 E9
Saxony, Lower = Niedersachsen □, *Germany* 24 C4
Saxton, *U.S.A.* 110 F6
Say, *Niger* 83 C5
Saya, *Nigeria* 83 D5
Sayabec, *Canada* 103 C6
Sayaboury, *Laos* 64 C3
Sayán, *Peru* 124 F3
Sayan, Vostochnyy, *Russia* 51 D10
Sayan, Zapadnyy, *Russia* 51 D10
Saydā, *Lebanon* 75 B4
Sayhan-Ovoo, *Mongolia* 56 B2
Sayhandulaan, *Mongolia* 56 B5
Sayḩūt, *Yemen* 74 D5
Saykhin, *Kazakstan* 49 F8
Saynshand, *Mongolia* 56 B6
Sayre, *Okla., U.S.A.* 113 H5
Sayre, *Pa., U.S.A.* 111 E8
Sayula, *Mexico* 118 D4
Sazanit, *Albania* 40 F3
Sázava →, *Czech Rep.* 26 B7
Sazin, *Pakistan* 69 B5
Sazlika →, *Bulgaria* 41 E9
Scaër, *France* 18 D3
Scafell Pike, *U.K.* 12 C4
Scalea, *Italy* 31 C8
Scalloway, *U.K.* 14 A7
Scalpay, *U.K.* 14 D3
Scandia, *Canada* 104 C6
Scandiano, *Italy* 28 D7
Scandicci, *Italy* 29 E8
Scandinavia, *Europe* 6 C8
Scansano, *Italy* 29 F8
Scapa Flow, *U.K.* 14 C5
Scappoose, *U.S.A.* 116 E4
Scarámia, Capo, *Italy* 31 F7
Scarba, *U.K.* 14 E3
Scarborough, *Trin. & Tob.* 121 D7
Scarborough, *U.K.* 12 C7
Scariff I., *Ireland* 15 E1
Scarp, *U.K.* 14 C1
Scebeli, Wabi →, *Somali Rep.* 81 G5
Šćedro, *Croatia* 29 E13
Scenic, *U.S.A.* 112 D3
Schaal See, *Germany* 24 B6
Schaffhausen, *Switz.* 25 H4
Schagen, *Neths.* 17 B4
Schärding, *Austria* 26 C6
Scharhörn, *Germany* 24 B4
Scheessel, *Germany* 24 B5
Schefferville, *Canada* 103 B6
Scheibbs, *Austria* 26 C8
Schelde →, *Belgium* 17 C4
Schell Creek Ra., *U.S.A.* 114 G6
Schenectady, *U.S.A.* 111 D11
Scherfede, *Germany* 24 D5
Schesslitz, *Germany* 25 F7
Schiedam, *Neths.* 17 C4
Schiermonnikoog, *Neths.* 17 A6
Schiltigheim, *France* 19 D14
Schio, *Italy* 29 C8
Schladming, *Austria* 26 D6
Schlanders = Silandro, *Italy* 28 B7
Schlei →, *Germany* 24 A5
Schleiden, *Germany* 24 E2
Schleiz, *Germany* 24 E7
Schleswig, *Germany* 24 A5
Schleswig-Holstein □, *Germany* 24 A5
Schlüchtern, *Germany* 25 E5
Schmalkalden, *Germany* 24 E6
Schmölln, *Germany* 24 E8
Schneeberg, *Austria* 26 D8
Schneeberg, *Germany* 24 E8
Schneverdingen, *Germany* 24 B5
Schofield, *U.S.A.* 112 C10
Scholls, *U.S.A.* 116 E4
Schönberg, *Mecklenburg-Vorpommern, Germany* 24 B6
Schönberg, *Schleswig-Holstein, Germany* 24 A6
Schönebeck, *Germany* 24 C7
Schongau, *Germany* 25 H6
Schöningen, *Germany* 24 C6
Schopfheim, *Germany* 25 H3
Schorndorf, *Germany* 25 G5
Schortens, *Germany* 24 B3
Schouten I., *Australia* 94 G4
Schouten Is. = Supiori, *Indonesia* 63 E9
Schouwen, *Neths.* 17 C3
Schramberg, *Germany* 25 G4
Schrankogel, *Austria* 26 D4
Schreiber, *Canada* 102 C2
Schrems, *Austria* 26 C8
Schrobenhausen, *Germany* 25 G7
Schruns, *Austria* 26 D2
Schuler, *Canada* 105 C6
Schumacher, *Canada* 102 C3
Schurz, *U.S.A.* 114 G4
Schuyler, *U.S.A.* 112 E6
Schuylkill Haven, *U.S.A.* 111 F8
Schwabach, *Germany* 25 F7
Schwaben □, *Germany* 25 G6
Schwäbisch Gmünd, *Germany* 25 G5
Schwäbisch Hall, *Germany* 25 F5
Schwäbische Alb, *Germany* 25 G5
Schwabmünchen, *Germany* 25 G6
Schwalmstadt, *Germany* 24 E5
Schwandorf, *Germany* 25 F8
Schwaner, Pegunungan, *Indonesia* 62 E4
Schwanewede, *Germany* 24 B4
Schwarmstedt, *Germany* 24 C5
Schwarze Elster →, *Germany* 24 D8
Schwarzenberg, *Germany* 24 E8
Schwarzwald, *Germany* 25 G4
Schwaz, *Austria* 26 D4
Schwechat, *Austria* 27 C9
Schwedt, *Germany* 24 B10
Schweinfurt, *Germany* 25 E6
Schweizer-Reneke, *S. Africa* 88 D4
Schwenningen = Villingen-Schwenningen, *Germany* 25 G4
Schwerin, *Germany* 24 B7
Schweriner See, *Germany* 24 B7
Schwetzingen, *Germany* 25 F4
Schwyz, *Switz.* 25 H4
Schwyz □, *Switz.* 25 H4
Sciacca, *Italy* 30 E6
Scicli, *Italy* 31 F7
Scilla, *Italy* 31 D8
Scilly, Isles of, *U.K.* 13 H1
Ścinawa, *Poland* 45 G3
Scione, *Greece* 40 G7
Scioto →, *U.S.A.* 108 F4
Scobey, *U.S.A.* 112 A2
Scone, *Australia* 95 E5
Scordia, *Italy* 31 E7
Scoresbysund, *Greenland* 4 B6
Scornicești, *Romania* 43 F9
Scotia, *Calif., U.S.A.* 114 F1
Scotia, *N.Y., U.S.A.* 111 D11
Scotia Sea, *Antarctica* 5 B18
Scotland, *U.S.A.* 112 D6
Scotland □, *U.K.* 14 E5
Scotland Neck, *U.S.A.* 109 G7
Scott, C., *Australia* 92 B4
Scott City, *U.S.A.* 112 F4
Scott Glacier, *Antarctica* 5 C8
Scott I., *Antarctica* 5 C11
Scott Is., *Canada* 104 C3
Scott L., *Canada* 105 B7
Scott Reef, *Australia* 92 B3
Scottburgh, *S. Africa* 89 E5
Scottdale, *U.S.A.* 110 F5
Scottish Borders □, *U.K.* 14 F6
Scottsbluff, *U.S.A.* 112 E3
Scottsboro, *U.S.A.* 109 H3
Scottsburg, *U.S.A.* 108 F3
Scottsdale, *Australia* 94 G4
Scottsdale, *U.S.A.* 115 K7
Scottsville, *Ky., U.S.A.* 109 G2
Scottsville, *N.Y., U.S.A.* 110 C7
Scottville, *U.S.A.* 108 D2
Scranton, *U.S.A.* 111 E9
Scugog, L., *Canada* 110 B6
Sculeni, *Moldova* 43 C12
Scunthorpe, *U.K.* 12 D7
Scuol, *Switz.* 25 J6
Scutari = Üsküdar, *Turkey* 41 F13
Seabrook, L., *Australia* 93 F2
Seaford, *U.K.* 13 G8
Seaford, *U.S.A.* 108 F8
Seaforth, *Canada* 102 D3
Seaforth, L., *U.K.* 14 D2
Seagraves, *U.S.A.* 113 J3
Seaham, *U.K.* 12 C6
Seal →, *Canada* 105 B10
Seal Cove, *Canada* 103 C8
Seal L., *Canada* 103 B7
Sealy, *U.S.A.* 113 L6
Searchlight, *U.S.A.* 117 K12
Searcy, *U.S.A.* 113 H9
Searles L., *U.S.A.* 117 K9
Seascale, *U.K.* 12 C4
Seaside, *Calif., U.S.A.* 116 J5
Seaside, *Oreg., U.S.A.* 116 E3
Seaspray, *Australia* 95 F4
Seattle, *U.S.A.* 116 C4
Seaview Ra., *Australia* 94 B4
Sebastián Vizcaíno, B., *Mexico* 118 B2
Sebastopol = Sevastopol, *Ukraine* 47 K7
Sebastopol, *U.S.A.* 116 G4
Sebderat, *Eritrea* 81 D4
Seben, *Turkey* 72 B4
Sebeş, *Romania* 43 E8
Sebeşului, Munţii, *Romania* 43 E8
Sebewaing, *U.S.A.* 108 D4
Sebezh, *Russia* 46 D5
Sebha = Sabhah, *Libya* 79 C8
Sébi, *Mali* 82 B4
Şebinkarahisar, *Turkey* 73 B8
Sebiş, *Romania* 42 D7
Sebkhet Te-n-Dghâmcha, *Mauritania* 82 B1
Sebnitz, *Germany* 24 E10
Sebring, *Fla., U.S.A.* 109 M5
Sebring, *Ohio, U.S.A.* 110 F3
Sebringville, *Canada* 110 C3
Sebta = Ceuta, *N. Afr.* 78 A4
Sebuku, *Indonesia* 62 E5
Sebuku, Teluk, *Malaysia* 62 D5
Sečanj, *Serbia, Yug.* 42 E5
Secchia →, *Italy* 28 C8
Sechelt, *Canada* 104 D4
Sechura, Desierto de, *Peru* 124 E2
Seclin, *France* 19 B10
Secondigny, *France* 18 F6
Sečovce, *Slovak Rep.* 27 C14
Secretary I., *N.Z.* 91 L1
Secunderabad, *India* 66 L11
Sedalia, *U.S.A.* 112 F8
Sedan, *Australia* 95 E2
Sedan, *France* 19 C11
Sedan, *U.S.A.* 113 G6
Sedano, *Spain* 34 C7
Seddon, *N.Z.* 91 J5
Seddonville, *N.Z.* 91 J4
Sedeh, *Fārs, Iran* 71 D7
Sedeh, *Khorāsān, Iran* 71 C8
Séderon, *France* 21 D9
Sederot, *Israel* 75 D3
Sedgewick, *Canada* 104 C6
Sédhiou, *Senegal* 82 C1
Sedico, *Italy* 29 B9
Sedlčany, *Czech Rep.* 26 B7
Sedley, *Canada* 105 C8
Sedova, Pik, *Russia* 50 B6
Sedro Woolley, *U.S.A.* 116 B4
Šeduva, *Lithuania* 44 C10
Sędziszów, *Poland* 45 H7
Sędziszów Małapolski, *Poland* 45 H8
Seebad Ahlbeck, *Germany* 24 B10
Seefeld in Tirol, *Austria* 26 D4
Seehausen, *Germany* 24 C7
Seeheim, *Namibia* 88 D2
Seeheim-Jugenheim, *Germany* 25 F4
Seekoei →, *S. Africa* 88 E4
Seelow, *Germany* 24 C10
Sées, *France* 18 D7
Seesen, *Germany* 24 D6
Seevetal, *Germany* 24 B6
Sefadu, *S. Leone* 82 D2
Seferihisar, *Turkey* 39 C8
Séfeto, *Mali* 82 C3
Sefwi Bekwai, *Ghana* 82 D4
Segamat, *Malaysia* 65 L4
Şegarcea, *Romania* 43 F8
Segbwema, *S. Leone* 82 D2
Seget, *Indonesia* 63 E8
Segonzac, *France* 20 C3
Segorbe, *Spain* 32 F4
Ségou, *Mali* 82 C3
Segovia = Coco →, *Cent. Amer.* 120 D3
Segovia, *Spain* 34 E6
Segovia □, *Spain* 34 E6
Segré, *France* 18 E6
Segre →, *Spain* 32 D5
Séguéla, *Ivory C.* 82 D3
Seguin, *U.S.A.* 113 L6
Segundo →, *Argentina* 126 C3
Segura →, *Spain* 33 G4
Segura, Sierra de, *Spain* 33 G2
Seh Qal'eh, *Iran* 71 C8
Sehitwa, *Botswana* 88 C3
Sehore, *India* 68 H7
Sehwan, *Pakistan* 68 F2
Şeica Mare, *Romania* 43 D9
Seil, *U.K.* 14 E3
Seiland, *Norway* 8 A20
Seilhac, *France* 20 C5
Seiling, *U.S.A.* 113 G5
Seille →, *Moselle, France* 19 C13
Seille →, *Saône-et-Loire, France* 19 F11
Sein, Î. de, *France* 18 D2
Seinäjoki, *Finland* 9 E20
Seine →, *France* 18 C7
Seine, B. de la, *France* 18 C6
Seine-et-Marne □, *France* 19 D10
Seine-Maritime □, *France* 18 C7
Seine-St-Denis □, *France* 19 D9
Seini, *Romania* 43 C8
Seirijai, *Lithuania* 44 D10
Seistan, *Iran* 71 D9
Seistan, Daryācheh-ye, *Iran* 66 D2
Sejerø, *Denmark* 11 J5
Sejerø Bugt, *Denmark* 11 J5
Sejny, *Poland* 44 D10
Seka, *Ethiopia* 81 F4
Sekayu, *Indonesia* 62 E2
Seke, *Tanzania* 86 C3
Sekenke, *Tanzania* 86 C3
Seki, *Turkey* 39 E11
Sekondi-Takoradi, *Ghana* 82 E4
Seksna, *Russia* 46 C10
Sekuma, *Botswana* 88 C3
Selah, *U.S.A.* 114 C3
Selama, *Malaysia* 65 K3
Selárgius, *Italy* 30 C2
Selaru, *Indonesia* 63 F8
Selb, *Germany* 25 E8
Selby, *U.K.* 12 D6
Selby, *U.S.A.* 112 C4
Selca, *Croatia* 29 E13
Selçuk, *Turkey* 39 D9
Selden, *U.S.A.* 112 F4
Sele →, *Italy* 31 B7
Selebi-Pikwe, *Botswana* 89 C4
Selemdzha →, *Russia* 51 D13
Selendi, *Manisa, Turkey* 39 C10
Selendi, *Manisa, Turkey* 39 C9
Selenga = Selenge Mörön →, *Asia* 60 A5
Selenge Mörön →, *Asia* 60 A5
Selenica, *Albania* 40 F3
Selenter See, *Germany* 24 A6
Sélestat, *France* 19 D14
Seletan, Tanjung, *Indonesia* 62 E4
Selevac, *Serbia, Yug.* 40 B4
Selfridge, *U.S.A.* 112 B4
Sélibabi, *Mauritania* 82 B2
Seliger, Ozero, *Russia* 46 D7
Seligman, *U.S.A.* 115 J7
Şelim, *Turkey* 73 B10
Selîma, El Wâhât el, *Sudan* 80 C2
Selimiye, *Turkey* 39 D9
Selinda Spillway, *Botswana* 88 B3
Selinoús, *Greece* 38 D3
Selizharovo, *Russia* 46 D7
Selkirk, *Canada* 105 C9
Selkirk, *U.K.* 14 F6
Selkirk I., *Canada* 105 C9
Selkirk Mts., *Canada* 104 C5
Selliá, *Greece* 36 D6
Sellières, *France* 19 F12
Sells, *U.S.A.* 115 L8
Sellye, *Hungary* 42 E2
Selma, *Ala., U.S.A.* 109 J2
Selma, *Calif., U.S.A.* 116 J7
Selma, *N.C., U.S.A.* 109 H6
Selmer, *U.S.A.* 109 H1
Selongey, *France* 19 E12
Selowandoma Falls, *Zimbabwe* 87 G3
Selpele, *Indonesia* 63 E8
Selsey Bill, *U.K.* 13 G7
Seltso, *Russia* 46 F8
Seltz, *France* 19 D15
Selu, *Indonesia* 63 F8
Sélune →, *France* 18 D5
Selva = La Selva del Camp, *Spain* 32 D6
Selva, *Argentina* 126 B3
Selvas, *Brazil* 122 D4
Selwyn, *Australia* 94 C3
Selwyn L., *Canada* 105 B8
Selwyn Ra., *Australia* 94 C3
Semani →, *Albania* 40 F3
Semarang, *Indonesia* 63 G14
Sembabule, *Uganda* 86 C3
Şemdinli, *Turkey* 73 D11
Sémé, *Senegal* 82 B2
Semeih, *Sudan* 81 E3
Semenov, *Russia* 48 B7
Semenovka, *Chernihiv, Ukraine* 47 F7
Semenovka, *Kremenchuk, Ukraine* 47 H7
Semeru, *Indonesia* 63 H15
Semey, *Kazakstan* 50 D9
Semikarakorskiy, *Russia* 49 G5
Semiluki, *Russia* 47 G10
Seminoe Reservoir, *U.S.A.* 114 F10
Seminole, *Okla., U.S.A.* 113 H6
Seminole, *Tex., U.S.A.* 113 J3
Semipalatinsk = Semey, *Kazakstan* 50 D9
Semirara Is., *Phil.* 61 F4
Semitau, *Indonesia* 62 D4
Semiyarka, *Kazakstan* 50 D8
Semiyarskoye = Semiyarka, *Kazakstan* 50 D8
Semmering P., *Austria* 26 D8
Semnān, *Iran* 71 C7
Semnān □, *Iran* 71 C7
Semporna, *Malaysia* 63 D5
Semuda, *Indonesia* 62 E4
Semur-en-Auxois, *France* 19 E11
Senā, *Iran* 71 D6
Sena, *Mozam.* 87 F4
Sena Madureira, *Brazil* 124 E5
Senador Pompeu, *Brazil* 125 E11
Senaki, *Georgia* 49 J6
Senanga, *Zambia* 88 B3
Senatobia, *U.S.A.* 113 H10
Sencelles, *Spain* 37 B9
Sendafa, *Ethiopia* 81 F4
Sendai, *Kagoshima, Japan* 55 J5
Sendai, *Miyagi, Japan* 54 E10
Sendai-Wan, *Japan* 54 E10
Senden, *Bayern, Germany* 25 G6
Senden, *Nordrhein-Westfalen, Germany* 24 D3
Senec, *Slovak Rep.* 27 C10
Seneca, *Oreg., U.S.A.* 114 D4
Seneca, *S.C., U.S.A.* 109 H4
Seneca Falls, *U.S.A.* 111 D8
Seneca L., *U.S.A.* 110 D8
Senegal ■, *W. Afr.* 82 C2
Senegal →, *W. Afr.* 82 B1
Senegambia, *Africa* 76 E2
Senekal, *S. Africa* 89 D4

Senftenberg, *Germany* 24 D10
Senga Hill, *Zambia* 87 D3
Senge Khambab = Indus →, *Pakistan* 68 G2
Sengerema □, *Tanzania* 86 C3
Sengiley, *Russia* 48 D9
Sengua →, *Zimbabwe* 87 F2
Senhor-do-Bonfim, *Brazil* 125 F10
Senica, *Slovak Rep.* 27 C10
Senigállia, *Italy* 29 E10
Senio →, *Italy* 29 D9
Senirkent, *Turkey* 39 C12
Senise, *Italy* 31 B9
Senj, *Croatia* 29 D11
Senja, *Norway* 8 B17
Senlis, *France* 19 C9
Senmonorom, *Cambodia* 64 F6
Sennâr, *Sudan* 81 E3
Senneterre, *Canada* 102 C4
Senniquelle, *Liberia* 82 D3
Senno, *Belarus* 46 E5
Sénnori, *Italy* 30 B1
Seno, *Laos* 64 D5
Senonches, *France* 18 D8
Senorbì, *Italy* 30 C2
Senožeče, *Slovenia* 29 C11
Sens, *France* 19 D10
Senta, *Serbia, Yug.* 42 E5
Sentani, *Indonesia* 63 E10
Sentery, *Dem. Rep. of the Congo* 86 D2
Sentinel, *U.S.A.* 115 K7
Šentjur, *Slovenia* 29 B12
Senya Beraku, *Ghana* 83 D4
Seo de Urgel = La Seu d'Urgell, *Spain* 32 C6
Seohara, *India* 69 E8
Seoni, *India* 69 H8
Seoul = Sŏul, *S. Korea* 57 F14
Separation Point, *Canada* 103 B8
Sepīdān, *Iran* 71 D7
Sepo-ri, *N. Korea* 57 E14
Sępólno Krajeńskie, *Poland* 44 E4
Sepone, *Laos* 64 D6
Sępopol, *Poland* 44 D8
Sept-Îles, *Canada* 103 B6
Septemvri, *Bulgaria* 41 D8
Sepúlveda, *Spain* 34 D7
Sequeros, *Spain* 34 E4
Sequim, *U.S.A.* 116 B3
Sequoia National Park, *U.S.A.* 116 J8
Serafimovich, *Russia* 48 F6
Seraing, *Belgium* 17 D5
Seraja, *Indonesia* 65 L7
Serakhis →, *Cyprus* 36 D11
Seram, *Indonesia* 63 E7
Seram Sea, *Indonesia* 63 E7
Serang, *Indonesia* 63 G12
Serasan, *Indonesia* 65 L7
Seravezza, *Italy* 28 E7
Şerbettar, *Turkey* 41 E10
Serbia □, *Yugoslavia* 40 C5
Şercaia, *Romania* 43 E10
Serdo, *Ethiopia* 81 E5
Serdobsk, *Russia* 48 D7
Sered', *Slovak Rep.* 27 C10
Seredka, *Russia* 46 C5
Şereflikoçhisar, *Turkey* 72 C5
Seregno, *Italy* 28 C6
Seremban, *Malaysia* 65 L3
Serengeti □, *Tanzania* 86 C3
Serengeti Plain, *Tanzania* 86 C4
Serenje, *Zambia* 87 E3
Sereth = Siret →, *Romania* 43 E12
Sergach, *Russia* 48 C7
Sergen, *Turkey* 41 E11
Sergipe □, *Brazil* 125 F11
Sergiyev Posad, *Russia* 46 D10
Seria, *Brunei* 62 D4
Serian, *Malaysia* 62 D4
Seriate, *Italy* 28 C6
Seribu, Kepulauan, *Indonesia* 62 F3
Sérifontaine, *France* 19 C8
Sérifos, *Greece* 38 D6
Sérignan, *France* 20 E7
Serik, *Turkey* 72 D4
Seringapatam Reef, *Australia* 92 B3
Serinhisar, *Turkey* 39 D11
Sermaize-les-Bains, *France* 19 D11
Sermata, *Indonesia* 63 F7
Sérmide, *Italy* 29 D8
Sernovodsk, *Russia* 48 D10
Sernur, *Russia* 48 B9
Serock, *Poland* 45 F8
Serón, *Spain* 33 H2
Seròs, *Spain* 32 D5
Serov, *Russia* 50 D7
Serowe, *Botswana* 88 C4
Serpa, *Portugal* 35 H3
Serpeddí, Punta, *Italy* 30 C2
Serpentara, *Italy* 30 C2
Serpentine, *Australia* 93 F2
Serpentine Lakes, *Australia* 93 E4
Serpis →, *Spain* 33 G4
Serpukhov, *Russia* 46 E9
Serra de Outes, *Spain* 34 C2
Serra do Navio, *Brazil* 125 C8
Serra San Bruno, *Italy* 31 D9
Serradilla, *Spain* 34 F4
Sérrai, *Greece* 40 E7
Sérrai □, *Greece* 40 E7
Serramanna, *Italy* 30 C1
Serravalle Scrívia, *Italy* 28 D5
Serre-Ponçon, L. de, *France* 21 D10
Serres, *France* 21 D9
Serrezuela, *Argentina* 126 C2
Serrinha, *Brazil* 125 F11
Sersale, *Italy* 31 C9
Sertã, *Portugal* 34 F2
Sertanópolis, *Brazil* 127 A5
Sêrtar, *China* 58 A3
Serua, *Indonesia* 63 F8
Serui, *Indonesia* 63 E9
Serule, *Botswana* 88 C4
Sérvia, *Greece* 40 F6
Serzedelo, *Portugal* 34 D2
Sese Is., *Uganda* 86 C3
Sesepe, *Indonesia* 63 E7
Sesfontein, *Namibia* 88 B1
Sesheke, *Zambia* 88 B3
Sésia →, *Italy* 28 C5
Sesimbra, *Portugal* 35 G1
S'Espalmador, *Spain* 37 C7
S'Espardell, *Spain* 37 C7
Sessa Aurunca, *Italy* 30 A6
S'Estanyol, *Spain* 37 B9
Sestao, *Spain* 32 B2
Sesto Calende, *Italy* 28 C5
Sesto San Giovanni, *Italy* 28 C6
Sestri Levante, *Italy* 28 D6
Sestriere, *Italy* 28 D3
Sestroretsk, *Russia* 46 B6
Sestrunj, *Croatia* 29 D11
Sestu, *Italy* 30 C2
Setana, *Japan* 54 C9
Sète, *France* 20 E7
Sete Lagôas, *Brazil* 125 G10
Sétif, *Algeria* 78 A7
Seto, *Japan* 55 G8
Setonaikai, *Japan* 55 G6
Settat, *Morocco* 78 B4
Séttimo Torinese, *Italy* 28 C4
Setting L., *Canada* 105 C9
Settle, *U.K.* 12 C5
Settlement Pt., *Bahamas* 109 M6
Setúbal, *Portugal* 35 G2
Setúbal □, *Portugal* 35 G2
Setúbal, B. de, *Portugal* 35 G2
Seugne →, *France* 20 C3
Seurre, *France* 19 F12
Sevan, *Armenia* 49 K7
Sevan, Ozero = Sevana Lich, *Armenia* 49 K7
Sevana Lich, *Armenia* 49 K7
Sevastopol, *Ukraine* 47 K7
Seven Emu, *Australia* 94 B2
Seven Sisters, *Canada* 104 C3
Sever →, *Spain* 35 F3
Sévérac-le-Château, *France* 20 D7
Severn →, *Canada* 102 A2
Severn →, *U.K.* 13 F5
Severn L., *Canada* 102 B1
Severnaya Zemlya, *Russia* 51 B11
Severo-Kurilsk, *Russia* 51 D16
Severo-Yeniseyskiy, *Russia* 51 C10
Severočeský □, *Czech Rep.* 26 A7
Severodonetsk = Syeverodonetsk, *Ukraine* 47 H10
Severodvinsk, *Russia* 50 C4
Severomoravský □, *Czech Rep.* 27 B10
Sevier, *U.S.A.* 115 G7
Sevier →, *U.S.A.* 115 G7
Sevier L., *U.S.A.* 114 G7
Sevilla, *Spain* 35 H5
Sevilla □, *Spain* 35 H5
Seville = Sevilla, *Spain* 35 H5
Sevlievo, *Bulgaria* 41 C9
Sevnica, *Slovenia* 29 B12
Sèvre-Nantaise →, *France* 18 E5
Sèvre-Niortaise →, *France* 20 B3
Sevsk, *Russia* 47 F8
Seward, *Alaska, U.S.A.* 100 B5
Seward, *Nebr., U.S.A.* 112 E6
Seward Peninsula, *U.S.A.* 100 B3
Sewell, *Chile* 126 C1
Sewer, *Indonesia* 63 F8
Sewickley, *U.S.A.* 110 F4
Sexsmith, *Canada* 104 B5
Seychelles ■, *Ind. Oc.* 52 K9
Seyðisfjörður, *Iceland* 8 D6
Seydişehir, *Turkey* 72 D4
Seydvān, *Iran* 70 B5
Seyhan →, *Turkey* 72 D6
Seyhan Barajı, *Turkey* 72 D6
Seyitgazi, *Turkey* 39 B12
Seyitömer, *Turkey* 39 B11
Seym →, *Ukraine* 47 G7
Seymen, *Turkey* 41 E11
Seymour, *Australia* 95 F4
Seymour, *S. Africa* 89 E4
Seymour, *Conn., U.S.A.* 111 E11
Seymour, *Ind., U.S.A.* 108 F3
Seymour, *Tex., U.S.A.* 113 J5
Seymour, *Wis., U.S.A.* 108 C1
Seyne, *France* 21 D10
Seyssel, *France* 21 C9
Sežana, *Slovenia* 29 C10
Sézanne, *France* 19 D10
Sezze, *Italy* 30 A6
Sfântu Gheorghe, *Covasna, Romania* 43 E10
Sfântu Gheorghe, *Tulcea, Romania* 43 F14
Sfântu Gheorghe, Braţul →, *Romania* 43 F14
Sfax, *Tunisia* 79 B8
Sha Xi →, *China* 59 D12
Sha Xian, *China* 59 D11
Shaanxi □, *China* 56 G5
Shaba □, *Dem. Rep. of the Congo* 86 D2
Shabla, *Bulgaria* 41 C12
Shabunda, *Dem. Rep. of the Congo* 86 C2
Shache, *China* 60 C2
Shackleton Ice Shelf, *Antarctica* 5 C8
Shackleton Inlet, *Antarctica* 5 E11
Shādegān, *Iran* 71 D6
Shadi, *China* 59 D10
Shadi, *India* 69 C7
Shadrinsk, *Russia* 50 D7
Shaffa, *Nigeria* 83 C7
Shafter, *Calif., U.S.A.* 117 K7
Shafter, *Tex., U.S.A.* 113 L2
Shaftesbury, *U.K.* 13 F5
Shagamu, *Nigeria* 83 D5
Shagram, *Pakistan* 69 A5
Shah Bunder, *Pakistan* 68 G2
Shahabad, *Punjab, India* 68 D7
Shahabad, *Raj., India* 68 G7
Shahabad, *Ut. P., India* 69 F8
Shahadpur, *Pakistan* 68 G3
Shahba, *Syria* 75 C5
Shahdād, *Iran* 71 D8
Shahdadkot, *Pakistan* 68 F2
Shahe, *China* 56 F8
Shahganj, *India* 69 F10
Shahgarh, *India* 66 F6
Shahjahanpur, *India* 69 F8
Shahpur, *India* 68 H7
Shahpur, *Pakistan* 68 E3
Shahpura, *India* 69 H9
Shahr-e Kord, *Iran* 71 C6
Shāhrakht, *Iran* 71 C9
Shahrig, *Pakistan* 68 D2
Shahukou, *China* 56 D7
Shaikhabad, *Afghan.* 68 B3
Shajapur, *India* 68 H7
Shakargarh, *Pakistan* 68 C6
Shakawe, *Botswana* 88 B3
Shaker Heights, *U.S.A.* 110 E3
Shakhty, *Russia* 49 G5
Shakhunya, *Russia* 48 B8
Shaki, *Nigeria* 83 D5
Shala, L., *Ethiopia* 81 F4
Shali, *Russia* 49 J7
Shallow Lake, *Canada* 110 B3
Shalqar, *Kazakstan* 50 E6
Shalskiy, *Russia* 46 B8
Shaluli Shan, *China* 58 B2
Shām, *Iran* 71 E8
Shamâl Dârfûr □, *Sudan* 81 E2
Shamâl Kordofân □, *Sudan* 81 E3
Shamattawa, *Canada* 105 B10
Shamattawa →, *Canada* 102 A2
Shambe, *Sudan* 81 F3
Shambu, *Ethiopia* 81 F4
Shamīl, *Iran* 71 E8
Shamkhor = Şämkir, *Azerbaijan* 49 K8
Shāmkūh, *Iran* 71 C8
Shamli, *India* 68 E7
Shamo = Gobi, *Asia* 56 C6
Shamo, L., *Ethiopia* 81 F4
Shamokin, *U.S.A.* 111 F8
Shamrock, *U.S.A.* 113 H4
Shamva, *Zimbabwe* 87 F3
Shan □, *Burma* 67 J21
Shan Xian, *China* 56 G9
Shanan →, *Ethiopia* 81 F5
Shanchengzhen, *China* 57 C13
Shāndak, *Iran* 71 D9
Shandon, *U.S.A.* 116 K6
Shandong □, *China* 57 G10
Shandong Bandao, *China* 57 F11
Shang Xian, *China* 56 H5
Shangalowe, *Dem. Rep. of the Congo* 87 E2
Shangani →, *Zimbabwe* 87 F2
Shangbancheng, *China* 57 D10
Shangcai, *China* 59 A10
Shangcheng, *China* 59 B10
Shangchuan Dao, *China* 59 G9
Shangdu, *China* 56 D7
Shanggao, *China* 59 C10
Shanghai, *China* 59 B13
Shanghang, *China* 59 E11
Shanghe, *China* 57 F9
Shangjin, *China* 59 A8
Shanglin, *China* 58 F7
Shangnan, *China* 56 H6
Shangqiu, *China* 56 G8
Shangrao, *China* 59 C11
Shangshui, *China* 56 H8
Shangsi, *China* 58 F6
Shangyou, *China* 59 E10
Shangzhi, *China* 57 B14
Shanhetun, *China* 57 B14
Shani, *Nigeria* 83 C7
Shaniko, *U.S.A.* 114 D3
Shannon, *N.Z.* 91 J5
Shannon →, *Ireland* 15 D2
Shannon, Mouth of the, *Ireland* 15 D2
Shannon Airport, *Ireland* 15 D3
Shansi = Shanxi □, *China* 56 F7
Shantar, Ostrov Bolshoy, *Russia* 51 D14
Shantipur, *India* 69 H13
Shantou, *China* 59 F11
Shantung = Shandong □, *China* 57 G10
Shanxi □, *China* 56 F7
Shanyang, *China* 56 H5
Shanyin, *China* 56 E7
Shaoguan, *China* 59 E9
Shaowu, *China* 59 D11
Shaoxing, *China* 59 C13
Shaoyang, *Hunan, China* 59 D8
Shaoyang, *Hunan, China* 59 D8
Shap, *U.K.* 12 C5
Shapinsay, *U.K.* 14 B6
Shaqra', *Si. Arabia* 70 E5
Shaqrā', *Yemen* 74 E4
Sharafa, *Sudan* 81 E2
Sharafkhāneh, *Iran* 73 C11
Sharbot Lake, *Canada* 111 B8
Shari, *Japan* 54 C12
Sharjah = Ash Shāriqah, *U.A.E.* 71 E7
Shark B., *Australia* 93 E1
Sharm el Sheikh, *Egypt* 80 B3
Sharon, *Mass., U.S.A.* 111 D13
Sharon, *Pa., U.S.A.* 110 E4
Sharon Springs, *U.S.A.* 112 F4
Sharp Pt., *Australia* 94 A3
Sharpe L., *Canada* 105 C10
Sharpsville, *U.S.A.* 110 E4
Sharq el Istiwa'iya □, *Sudan* 81 G3
Sharya, *Russia* 48 A7
Shasha, *Ethiopia* 81 F4
Shashemene, *Ethiopia* 81 F4
Shashi, *Botswana* 89 C4
Shashi, *China* 59 B9
Shashi →, *Africa* 87 G2
Shasta, Mt., *U.S.A.* 114 F2
Shasta L., *U.S.A.* 114 F2
Shatsk, *Russia* 48 C5
Shatt al'Arab →, *Iraq* 71 D6
Shattuck, *U.S.A.* 113 G5
Shatura, *Russia* 46 E10
Shaumyani = Shulaveri, *Georgia* 49 K7
Shaunavon, *Canada* 105 D7
Shaver L., *U.S.A.* 116 H7
Shaw →, *Australia* 92 D2
Shaw I., *Australia* 94 C4
Shawan, *China* 60 B3
Shawanaga, *Canada* 110 A4
Shawano, *U.S.A.* 108 C1
Shawinigan, *Canada* 102 C5
Shawnee, *U.S.A.* 113 H6
Shaybārā, *Si. Arabia* 70 E3
Shayib el Banat, Gebel, *Egypt* 80 B3
Shaykh Sa'īd, *Iraq* 70 C5
Shchekino, *Russia* 46 E9
Shcherbakov = Rybinsk, *Russia* 46 C10
Shchigry, *Russia* 47 G9
Shchors, *Ukraine* 47 G6
Shchuchinsk, *Kazakstan* 50 D8
She Xian, *Anhui, China* 59 C12
She Xian, *Hebei, China* 56 F7
Shebekino, *Russia* 47 G9
Shebele = Scebeli, Wabi →, *Somali Rep.* 81 G5
Sheboygan, *U.S.A.* 108 D2
Shediac, *Canada* 103 C7
Sheelin, L., *Ireland* 15 C4
Sheep Haven, *Ireland* 15 A4
Sheerness, *U.K.* 13 F8
Sheet Harbour, *Canada* 103 D7
Sheffield, *U.K.* 12 D6
Sheffield, *Ala., U.S.A.* 109 H2
Sheffield, *Mass., U.S.A.* 111 D11
Sheffield, *Pa., U.S.A.* 110 E5
Sheffield, *Tex., U.S.A.* 113 K4
Sheho, *Canada* 105 C8
Shehojele, *Ethiopia* 81 E4
Shehong, *China* 58 B5
Sheikhpura, *India* 69 G11
Shek Hasan, *Ethiopia* 81 E4
Shekhupura, *Pakistan* 68 D5
Sheki = Şaki, *Azerbaijan* 49 K8
Shelburne, *N.S., Canada* 103 D6
Shelburne, *Ont., Canada* 102 D3
Shelburne, *U.S.A.* 111 B11
Shelburne B., *Australia* 94 A3
Shelburne Falls, *U.S.A.* 111 D12
Shelby, *Mich., U.S.A.* 108 D2
Shelby, *Mont., U.S.A.* 114 B8
Shelby, *N.C., U.S.A.* 109 H5
Shelby, *Ohio, U.S.A.* 110 F2
Shelbyville, *Ill., U.S.A.* 112 F10
Shelbyville, *Ind., U.S.A.* 108 F3
Shelbyville, *Tenn., U.S.A.* 109 H2
Sheldon, *U.S.A.* 112 D7
Sheldrake, *Canada* 103 B7
Shelikhova, Zaliv, *Russia* 51 D16
Shell Lake, *Canada* 105 C7
Shell Lakes, *Australia* 93 E4
Shellbrook, *Canada* 105 C7
Shellharbour, *Australia* 95 E5
Shelon →, *Russia* 46 C6
Shelton, *Conn., U.S.A.* 111 E11
Shelton, *Wash., U.S.A.* 116 C3
Shemakha = Şamaxi, *Azerbaijan* 49 K9
Shen Xian, *China* 56 F8
Shenandoah, *Iowa, U.S.A.* 112 E7
Shenandoah, *Pa., U.S.A.* 111 F8
Shenandoah, *Va., U.S.A.* 108 F6
Shenandoah →, *U.S.A.* 108 F7
Shenchi, *China* 56 E7
Shendam, *Nigeria* 83 D6
Shendî, *Sudan* 81 D3
Sheng Xian, *China* 59 C13
Shengfang, *China* 56 E9
Shëngjergji, *Albania* 40 E4
Shëngjin, *Albania* 40 E3
Shenjingzi, *China* 57 B13
Shenmëria, *Albania* 40 D4
Shenmu, *China* 56 E6
Shennongjia, *China* 59 B8
Shenqiu, *China* 56 H8
Shenqiucheng, *China* 56 H8
Shensi = Shaanxi □, *China* 56 G5
Shenyang, *China* 57 D12
Shenzhen, *China* 59 F10
Sheopur Kalan, *India* 66 G10
Shepetivka, *Ukraine* 47 G4
Shepparton, *Australia* 95 F4
Sheppey, I. of, *U.K.* 13 F8
Shepton Mallet, *U.K.* 13 F5
Sheqi, *China* 56 H7
Sher Qila, *Pakistan* 69 A6
Sherborne, *U.K.* 13 G5
Sherbro I., *S. Leone* 82 D2
Sherbrooke, *Canada* 103 C5
Shereik, *Sudan* 80 D3
Sheridan, *Ark., U.S.A.* 113 H8
Sheridan, *Wyo., U.S.A.* 114 D10
Sheringham, *U.K.* 12 E9
Sherkin I., *Ireland* 15 E2
Sherkot, *India* 69 E8
Sherman, *U.S.A.* 113 J6
Sherridon, *Canada* 105 B8
Sherwood, *N. Dak., U.S.A.* 112 A4
Sherwood, *Tex., U.S.A.* 113 K4
Sherwood Forest, *U.K.* 12 D6
Sheslay, *Canada* 104 B2
Sheslay →, *Canada* 104 B2
Shethanei L., *Canada* 105 B9
Shetland □, *U.K.* 14 A7
Shetland Is., *U.K.* 14 A7
Shewa □, *Ethiopia* 81 F4
Shewa Gimira, *Ethiopia* 81 F4
Sheyenne, *U.S.A.* 112 B5
Sheyenne →, *U.S.A.* 112 B6
Shibām, *Yemen* 74 D4
Shibata, *Japan* 54 F9
Shibecha, *Japan* 54 C12
Shibetsu, *Japan* 54 B11
Shibîn el Kôm, *Egypt* 80 H7
Shibîn el Qanâtir, *Egypt* 80 H7
Shibing, *China* 58 D7
Shibogama L., *Canada* 102 B2
Shibushi, *Japan* 55 J5
Shicheng, *China* 59 D11
Shickshock Mts. = Chic-Chocs, Mts., *Canada* 103 C6
Shidao, *China* 57 F12
Shidian, *China* 58 E2
Shido, *Japan* 55 G7
Shiel, L., *U.K.* 14 E3
Shield, C., *Australia* 94 A2
Shiga □, *Japan* 55 G8
Shigu, *China* 58 D2
Shiguaigou, *China* 56 D6
Shihchiachuangi = Shijiazhuang, *China* 56 E8
Shijaku, *Albania* 40 E3
Shijiazhuang, *China* 56 E8
Shijiu Hu, *China* 59 B12
Shikarpur, *India* 68 E8
Shikarpur, *Pakistan* 68 F3
Shikoku □, *Japan* 55 H6
Shikoku-Sanchi, *Japan* 55 H6
Shiliguri, *India* 67 F16
Shilka, *Russia* 51 D12
Shilka →, *Russia* 51 D13
Shillelagh, *Ireland* 15 D5
Shillong, *India* 67 G17
Shilo, *West Bank* 75 C4
Shilong, *China* 59 F9
Shilou, *China* 56 F6
Shilovo, *Russia* 48 C5
Shimabara, *Japan* 55 H5
Shimada, *Japan* 55 G9
Shimane □, *Japan* 55 G6
Shimanovsk, *Russia* 51 D13
Shimen, *China* 59 C8
Shimenjie, *China* 59 C11
Shimian, *China* 58 C4
Shimizu, *Japan* 55 G9
Shimodate, *Japan* 55 F9
Shimoga, *India* 66 N9
Shimoni, *Kenya* 86 C4
Shimonoseki, *Japan* 55 H5
Shimpuru Rapids, *Angola* 88 B2
Shimsk, *Russia* 46 C6
Shin, L., *U.K.* 14 C4
Shin-Tone →, *Japan* 55 G10
Shinan, *China* 58 F7
Shinano →, *Japan* 55 F9
Shīndand, *Afghan.* 66 C3
Shingleton, *U.S.A.* 102 C2
Shingū, *Japan* 55 H7
Shinjō, *Japan* 54 E10
Shinkafe, *Nigeria* 83 C6
Shinshār, *Syria* 75 A5
Shinyanga, *Tanzania* 86 C3
Shinyanga □, *Tanzania* 86 C3
Shiogama, *Japan* 54 E10
Shiojiri, *Japan* 55 F8
Ship I., *U.S.A.* 113 K10
Shipchenski Prokhod, *Bulgaria* 41 D9
Shiping, *China* 58 F4
Shipki La, *India* 66 D11
Shippegan, *Canada* 103 C7
Shippensburg, *U.S.A.* 110 F7

Shiprock, *U.S.A.* 115 H9
Shiqian, *China* 58 D7
Shiqma, N. →, *Israel* 75 D3
Shiquan, *China* 56 H5
Shīr Kūh, *Iran* 71 D7
Shiragami-Misaki, *Japan* 54 D10
Shirakawa, *Fukushima, Japan* 55 F10
Shirakawa, *Gifu, Japan* 55 F8
Shirane-San, *Gumma, Japan* 55 F9
Shirane-San, *Yamanashi, Japan* 55 G9
Shiraoi, *Japan* 54 C10
Shīrāz, *Iran* 71 D7
Shirbin, *Egypt* 80 H7
Shire →, *Africa* 87 F4
Shiretoko-Misaki, *Japan* 54 B12
Shirinab →, *Pakistan* 68 D2
Shiriya-Zaki, *Japan* 54 D10
Shiroishi, *Japan* 54 F10
Shīrvān, *Iran* 71 B8
Shirwa, L. = Chilwa, L., *Malawi* 87 F4
Shishou, *China* 59 C9
Shitai, *China* 59 B11
Shivpuri, *India* 68 G7
Shixian, *China* 57 C15
Shixing, *China* 59 E10
Shiyan, *China* 59 A8
Shiyata, *Egypt* 80 B2
Shizhu, *China* 58 C7
Shizong, *China* 58 E5
Shizuishan, *China* 56 E4
Shizuoka, *Japan* 55 G9
Shizuoka □, *Japan* 55 G9
Shklov = Shklow, *Belarus* 46 E6
Shklow, *Belarus* 46 E6
Shkoder = Shkodra, *Albania* 40 D3
Shkodra, *Albania* 40 D3
Shkumbini →, *Albania* 40 E3
Shmidta, Ostrov, *Russia* 51 A10
Shō-Gawa →, *Japan* 55 F8
Shoal Lake, *Canada* 105 C8
Shōdo-Shima, *Japan* 55 G7
Sholapur = Solapur, *India* 66 L9
Shologontsy, *Russia* 51 C12
Shōmrōn, *West Bank* 75 C4
Shoreham by Sea, *U.K.* 13 G7
Shoshone, *Calif., U.S.A.* 117 K10
Shoshone, *Idaho, U.S.A.* 114 E6
Shoshone L., *U.S.A.* 114 D8
Shoshone Mts., *U.S.A.* 114 G5
Shoshong, *Botswana* 88 C4
Shoshoni, *U.S.A.* 114 E9
Shostka, *Ukraine* 47 G7
Shou Xian, *China* 59 A11
Shouchang, *China* 59 C12
Shouguang, *China* 57 F10
Shouning, *China* 59 D12
Shouyang, *China* 56 F7
Show Low, *U.S.A.* 115 J9
Shpola, *Ukraine* 47 H6
Shreveport, *U.S.A.* 113 J8
Shrewsbury, *U.K.* 13 E5
Shrirampur, *India* 69 H13
Shropshire □, *U.K.* 13 E5
Shu, *Kazakstan* 50 E8
Shu →, *Kazakstan* 52 E10
Shuangbai, *China* 58 E3
Shuangcheng, *China* 57 B14
Shuangfeng, *China* 59 D9
Shuanggou, *China* 57 G9
Shuangjiang, *China* 58 F2
Shuangliao, *China* 57 C12
Shuangshanzi, *China* 57 D10
Shuangyang, *China* 57 C13
Shuangyashan, *China* 60 B8
Shucheng, *China* 59 B11
Shugozero, *Russia* 46 C8
Shuguri Falls, *Tanzania* 87 D4
Shuiji, *China* 59 D12
Shuiye, *China* 56 F8
Shujalpur, *India* 68 H7
Shukpa Kunzang, *India* 69 B8
Shulan, *China* 57 B14
Shulaveri, *Georgia* 49 K7
Shule, *China* 60 C2
Shumagin Is., *U.S.A.* 100 C4
Shumen, *Bulgaria* 41 C10
Shumerlya, *Russia* 48 C8
Shumikha, *Russia* 50 D7
Shunchang, *China* 59 D11
Shunde, *China* 59 F9
Shungay, *Kazakstan* 49 F8
Shuo Xian, *China* 56 E7
Shūr →, *Iran* 71 D7
Shūr Āb, *Iran* 71 C6
Shūr Gaz, *Iran* 71 D8
Shūrāb, *Iran* 71 C8
Shūrjestān, *Iran* 71 D7
Shurugwi, *Zimbabwe* 87 F3
Shūsf, *Iran* 71 D9
Shūsh, *Iran* 73 F13
Shūshtar, *Iran* 71 D6
Shuswap L., *Canada* 104 C5
Shuya, *Russia* 48 B5
Shuyang, *China* 57 G10
Shūzū, *Iran* 71 D7
Shwebo, *Burma* 67 H19
Shwegu, *Burma* 67 G20
Shweli →, *Burma* 67 H20
Shymkent, *Kazakstan* 50 E7
Shyok, *India* 69 B8
Shyok →, *Pakistan* 69 B6
Si Chon, *Thailand* 65 H2
Si Kiang = Xi Jiang →, *China* 59 F9
Si-ngan = Xi'an, *China* 56 G5
Si Prachan, *Thailand* 64 E3
Si Racha, *Thailand* 64 F3
Si Xian, *China* 57 H9
Siahan Range, *Pakistan* 66 F4
Siaksriindrapura, *Indonesia* 62 D2
Sialkot, *Pakistan* 68 C6
Siam = Thailand ■, *Asia* 64 E4
Sianów, *Poland* 44 D3
Siantan, *Indonesia* 62 D3
Sīāreh, *Iran* 71 D9
Siargao, *Phil.* 61 G7
Siari, *Pakistan* 69 B7
Siasi, *Phil.* 63 C6
Siasi I., *Phil.* 61 J4
Siátista, *Greece* 40 F5
Siau, *Indonesia* 63 D7
Šiauliai, *Lithuania* 9 J20
Šiauliai □, *Lithuania* 44 C10
Siaya □, *Kenya* 86 C3
Siazan = Siyäzän, *Azerbaijan* 49 K9
Sibâi, Gebel el, *Egypt* 80 B3
Sibayi, L., *S. Africa* 89 D5
Šibenik, *Croatia* 29 E12
Siberia, *Russia* 4 D13
Siberut, *Indonesia* 62 E1
Sibi, *Pakistan* 68 E2
Sibil = Oksibil, *Indonesia* 63 E10
Sibiti, *Congo* 84 E2
Sibiu, *Romania* 43 E9
Sibiu □, *Romania* 43 E9
Sibley, *Iowa, U.S.A.* 112 D7
Sibley, *La., U.S.A.* 113 J8
Sibolga, *Indonesia* 62 D1
Sibsagar, *India* 67 F19
Sibu, *Malaysia* 62 D4
Sibuco, *Phil.* 61 H5
Sibuguey B., *Phil.* 61 H5
Sibut, *C.A.R.* 84 C3
Sibutu, *Phil.* 63 D5
Sibutu Group, *Phil.* 61 J3
Sibutu Passage, *E. Indies* 63 D6
Sibuyan, *Phil.* 61 E5
Sibuyan Sea, *Phil.* 61 E5
Sic, *Romania* 43 D8
Sicamous, *Canada* 104 C5
Sichuan □, *China* 58 B5
Sicilia, *Italy* 31 E7
Sicily = Sicilia, *Italy* 31 E7
Sicuani, *Peru* 124 F4
Šid, *Serbia, Yug.* 42 E4
Sidamo □, *Ethiopia* 81 G4
Sidaouet, *Niger* 83 B6
Sidári, *Greece* 36 A3
Siddhapur, *India* 68 H5
Siddipet, *India* 66 K11
Sidensjö, *Sweden* 10 A12
Sidéradougou, *Burkina Faso* 82 C4
Siderno, *Italy* 31 D9
Sídheros, Ákra, *Greece* 36 D8
Sidhirókastron, *Greece* 40 E7
Sîdi Abd el Rahmân, *Egypt* 80 H6
Sîdi Barrâni, *Egypt* 80 A2
Sidi-bel-Abbès, *Algeria* 78 A5
Sidi Haneish, *Egypt* 80 A2
Sidi Omar, *Egypt* 80 A1
Sidlaw Hills, *U.K.* 14 E5
Sidley, Mt., *Antarctica* 5 D14
Sidmouth, *U.K.* 13 G4
Sidmouth, C., *Australia* 94 A3
Sidney, *Canada* 104 D4
Sidney, *Mont., U.S.A.* 112 B2
Sidney, *N.Y., U.S.A.* 111 D9
Sidney, *Nebr., U.S.A.* 112 E3
Sidney, *Ohio, U.S.A.* 108 E3
Sidoarjo, *Indonesia* 63 G15
Sidon = Saydā, *Lebanon* 75 B4
Sidra, G. of = Surt, Khalīj, *Libya* 79 B9
Siedlce, *Poland* 45 F9
Siedlce □, *Poland* 45 F9
Sieg →, *Germany* 24 E3
Siegburg, *Germany* 24 E3
Siegen, *Germany* 24 E4
Siem Pang, *Cambodia* 64 E6
Siem Reap = Siemreab, *Cambodia* 64 F4
Siemiatycze, *Poland* 45 F9
Siemreab, *Cambodia* 64 F4
Siena, *Italy* 29 E8
Sieniawa, *Poland* 45 H9
Sieradz, *Poland* 45 G5
Sieradz □, *Poland* 45 G5
Sieraków, *Poland* 45 F3
Sierck-les-Bains, *France* 19 C13
Sierning, *Austria* 26 C7
Sierpc, *Poland* 45 F6
Sierra Blanca, *U.S.A.* 115 L11
Sierra Blanca Peak, *U.S.A.* 115 K11
Sierra City, *U.S.A.* 116 F6
Sierra Colorada, *Argentina* 128 E3
Sierra de Yeguas, *Spain* 35 H6
Sierra Gorda, *Chile* 126 A2
Sierra Leone ■, *W. Afr.* 82 D2
Sierra Madre, *Mexico* 119 D6
Sierra Mojada, *Mexico* 118 B4
Sierraville, *U.S.A.* 116 F6
Sierre, *Switz.* 25 J3
Sífnos, *Greece* 38 E6
Sifton, *Canada* 105 C8
Sifton Pass, *Canada* 104 B3
Sigean, *France* 20 E6
Sighetu-Marmației, *Romania* 43 C8
Sighișoara, *Romania* 43 D9
Sigli, *Indonesia* 62 C1
Siglufjörður, *Iceland* 8 C4
Sigmaringen, *Germany* 25 G5
Signa, *Italy* 28 E8
Signakhi = Tsnori, *Georgia* 49 K7
Signal, *U.S.A.* 117 L13
Signal Pk., *U.S.A.* 117 M12
Signy-l'Abbaye, *France* 19 C11
Sigsig, *Ecuador* 124 D3
Sigüenza, *Spain* 32 D2
Siguiri, *Guinea* 82 C3
Sigulda, *Latvia* 9 H21
Sigurd, *U.S.A.* 115 G8
Sihanoukville = Kampong Saom, *Cambodia* 65 G4
Sihui, *China* 59 F9
Siikajoki →, *Finland* 8 D21
Siilinjärvi, *Finland* 8 E22
Siirt, *Turkey* 73 D9
Sijarira Ra., *Zimbabwe* 87 F2
Sikao, *Thailand* 65 J2
Sikar, *India* 68 F6
Sikasso, *Mali* 82 C3
Sikeston, *U.S.A.* 113 G10
Sikhote Alin, Khrebet, *Russia* 54 B8
Sikhote Alin Ra. = Sikhote Alin, Khrebet, *Russia* 54 B8
Sikiá., *Greece* 40 F7
Síkinos, *Greece* 39 E7
Sikkani Chief →, *Canada* 104 B4
Sikkim □, *India* 67 F16
Siklós, *Hungary* 42 E3
Sikotu-Ko, *Japan* 54 C10
Sil →, *Spain* 34 C3
Silacayoapan, *Mexico* 119 D5
Šilalė, *Lithuania* 44 C9
Silandro, *Italy* 28 B7
Silay, *Phil.* 61 F5
Silba, *Croatia* 29 D11
Silchar, *India* 67 G18
Silcox, *Canada* 105 B10
Şile, *Turkey* 41 E13
Siler City, *U.S.A.* 109 H6
Silgarhi Doti, *Nepal* 69 E9
Silghat, *India* 67 F18
Silifke, *Turkey* 72 D5
Siliguri = Shiliguri, *India* 67 F16
Siling Co, *China* 60 C3
Silistea Nouă, *Romania* 43 F10
Silistra, *Bulgaria* 41 B11
Silivri, *Turkey* 41 E12
Siljan, *Sweden* 10 D8
Siljansnäs, *Sweden* 10 D8
Silkeborg, *Denmark* 11 H3
Silla, *Spain* 33 F4
Sillajhuay, Cordillera, *Chile* 124 G5
Sillamäe, *Estonia* 9 G22
Sillé-le-Guillaume, *France* 18 D6
Silleda, *Spain* 34 C2
Silloth, *U.K.* 12 C4
Sílo, *Greece* 41 E9
Siloam Springs, *U.S.A.* 113 G7
Silopi, *Turkey* 73 D10
Silsbee, *U.S.A.* 113 K7
Šilutė, *Lithuania* 9 J19
Silva Porto = Kuito, *Angola* 85 G3
Silvan, *Turkey* 73 C9
Silver City, *N. Mex., U.S.A.* 115 K9
Silver City, *Nev., U.S.A.* 114 G4
Silver Cr. →, *U.S.A.* 114 E4
Silver Creek, *U.S.A.* 110 D5
Silver L., *Calif., U.S.A.* 116 G6
Silver L., *Calif., U.S.A.* 117 K10
Silver Lake, *U.S.A.* 114 E3
Silver Streams, *S. Africa* 88 D3
Silverdalen, *Sweden* 11 G9
Silverton, *Colo., U.S.A.* 115 H10
Silverton, *Tex., U.S.A.* 113 H4
Silves, *Portugal* 35 H2
Silvi Marina, *Italy* 29 F11
Silvies →, *U.S.A.* 114 E4
Silvrettahorn, *Switz.* 28 B7
Silwa Bahari, *Egypt* 80 C3
Silz, *Austria* 26 D3
Simanggang = Bandar Sri Aman, *Malaysia* 62 D4
Simao, *China* 58 F3
Simard, L., *Canada* 102 C4
Şimareh →, *Iran* 73 F12
Simav, *Turkey* 39 B10
Simav →, *Turkey* 41 F12
Simav Dağları, *Turkey* 39 B10
Simba, *Tanzania* 86 C4
Simbach, *Germany* 25 G9
Simbirsk, *Russia* 48 C9
Simbo, *Tanzania* 86 C2
Simcoe, *Canada* 102 D3
Simcoe, L., *Canada* 102 D4
Simeonovgrad, *Bulgaria* 41 D9
Simeria, *Romania* 42 E8
Simeto →, *Italy* 31 E8
Simeulue, *Indonesia* 62 D1
Simferopol, *Ukraine* 47 K8
Sími, *Greece* 39 E9
Simi Valley, *U.S.A.* 117 L8
Simikot, *Nepal* 69 E9
Simitli, *Bulgaria* 40 E7
Simla, *India* 68 D7
Simlångsdalen, *Sweden* 11 H7
Şimleu-Silvaniei, *Romania* 42 C7
Simmern, *Germany* 25 F3
Simmie, *Canada* 105 D7
Simmler, *U.S.A.* 117 K7
Simnas, *Lithuania* 44 D10
Simojoki →, *Finland* 8 D21
Simojovel, *Mexico* 119 D6
Simonette →, *Canada* 104 B5
Simonstown, *S. Africa* 88 E2
Simontornya, *Hungary* 42 D3
Simplon P., *Switz.* 25 J4
Simplontunnel, *Switz.* 25 J4
Simpson Desert, *Australia* 94 D2
Simpungdong, *N. Korea* 57 D15
Simrishamn, *Sweden* 11 J8
Simushir, Ostrov, *Russia* 51 E16
Sinabang, *Indonesia* 62 D1
Sinadogo, *Somali Rep.* 74 F4
Sinai = Es Sînâ', *Egypt* 80 J8
Sinai, Mt. = Mûsa, Gebel, *Egypt* 80 J8
Sinai Peninsula, *Egypt* 75 F3
Sinaia, *Romania* 43 E10
Sinaloa □, *Mexico* 118 C3
Sinaloa de Leyva, *Mexico* 118 B3
Sinalunga, *Italy* 29 E8
Sinan, *China* 58 D7
Sînandrei, *Romania* 42 E6
Sinarádhes, *Greece* 36 A3
Sincan, *Turkey* 72 B5
Sincanlı, *Turkey* 39 C12
Sincelejo, *Colombia* 124 B3
Sinchang, *N. Korea* 57 D15
Sinchang-ni, *N. Korea* 57 E14
Sinclair, *U.S.A.* 114 F10
Sinclair Mills, *Canada* 104 C4
Sinclair's B., *U.K.* 14 C5
Sincorá, Serra do, *Brazil* 125 F10
Sind, *Pakistan* 68 G3
Sind □, *Pakistan* 68 G3
Sind →, *India* 69 B6
Sind Sagar Doab, *Pakistan* 68 D4
Sindal, *Denmark* 11 G4
Sindangan, *Phil.* 61 G5
Sindangbarang, *Indonesia* 63 G12
Sinde, *Zambia* 87 F2
Sindelfingen, *Germany* 25 G4
Sındırgı, *Turkey* 39 B10
Sinegorskiy, *Russia* 49 G5
Sinekli, *Turkey* 41 E12
Sinelnikovo = Synelnykove, *Ukraine* 47 H8
Sines, *Portugal* 35 H2
Sines, C. de, *Portugal* 35 H2
Sineu, *Spain* 37 B10
Sinfra, *Ivory C.* 82 D3
Sing Buri, *Thailand* 64 E3
Singa, *Sudan* 81 E3
Singapore ■, *Asia* 65 M4
Singapore, Straits of, *Asia* 65 M5
Singaraja, *Indonesia* 62 F5
Singen, *Germany* 25 H4
Singida, *Tanzania* 86 C3
Singida □, *Tanzania* 86 D3
Singitikós Kólpos, *Greece* 40 F7
Singkaling Hkamti, *Burma* 67 G19
Singkang, *Indonesia* 63 E6
Singkawang, *Indonesia* 62 D3
Singleton, *Australia* 95 E5
Singleton, Mt., *N. Terr., Australia* 92 D5
Singleton, Mt., *W. Austral., Australia* 93 E2
Singö, *Sweden* 10 D12
Singoli, *India* 68 G6
Singora = Songkhla, *Thailand* 65 J3
Singosan, *N. Korea* 57 E14
Sinhung, *N. Korea* 57 D14
Sînî □, *Egypt* 75 F3
Siniátsikon, Óros, *Greece* 40 F5
Siniscóla, *Italy* 30 B2
Sinj, *Croatia* 29 E13
Sinjai, *Indonesia* 63 F6
Sinjajevina, *Montenegro, Yug.* 40 D3
Sinjār, *Iraq* 70 B4
Sinkat, *Sudan* 80 D4
Sinkiang Uighur = Xinjiang Uygur Zizhiqu □, *China* 60 B3
Sinmak, *N. Korea* 57 E14
Sínnai, *Italy* 30 C2
Sinnamary, *Fr. Guiana* 125 B8
Sinni →, *Italy* 31 B9
Sinnuris, *Egypt* 80 J7
Sinoie, Lacul, *Romania* 43 F13
Sinop, *Turkey* 72 A6
Sinpo, *N. Korea* 57 E15
Sinsheim, *Germany* 25 F4
Sinsk, *Russia* 51 C13
Sint Eustatius, I., *Neth. Ant.* 121 C7
Sint Maarten, I., *W. Indies* 121 C7
Sintang, *Indonesia* 62 D4
Sinton, *U.S.A.* 113 L6
Sintra, *Portugal* 35 G1
Sinŭiju, *N. Korea* 57 D13
Sinyukha →, *Ukraine* 47 H6
Sinzig, *Germany* 24 E3
Sio →, *Hungary* 42 D3
Siocon, *Phil.* 61 H5
Siófok, *Hungary* 42 D3
Sioma, *Zambia* 88 B3
Sion, *Switz.* 25 J3
Sion Mills, *U.K.* 15 B4
Sioux City, *U.S.A.* 112 D6
Sioux Falls, *U.S.A.* 112 D6
Sioux Lookout, *Canada* 102 B1
Sipalay, *Phil.* 61 G5
Šipan, *Croatia* 40 D1
Siping, *China* 57 C13
Sipiwesk L., *Canada* 105 B9
Šipovo, *Bos.-H.* 42 F2
Sipura, *Indonesia* 62 E1
Siquia →, *Nic.* 120 D3
Siquijor, *Phil.* 61 G5
Siquirres, *Costa Rica* 120 D3
Sir Edward Pellew Group, *Australia* 94 B2
Sir Graham Moore Is., *Australia* 92 B4
Sira →, *Norway* 9 G12
Siracusa, *Italy* 31 E8
Sirajganj, *Bangla.* 69 G13
Sirakoro, *Mali* 82 C3
Şiran, *Turkey* 73 B8
Sirasso, *Ivory C.* 82 D3
Sīrdān, *Iran* 71 B6
Sirdaryo = Syrdarya →, *Kazakstan* 50 E7
Sirer, *Spain* 37 C7
Siret, *Romania* 43 C11
Siret →, *Romania* 43 E12
Şiria, *Romania* 42 D6
Sirino, Mte., *Italy* 31 B8
Sírna, *Greece* 39 E8
Şirnak, *Turkey* 73 D10
Sirohi, *India* 68 G5
Sironj, *India* 68 G7
Síros, *Greece* 38 D6
Sirretta Pk., *U.S.A.* 117 K8
Sirsa, *India* 68 E6
Siruela, *Spain* 35 G5
Sisak, *Croatia* 29 C13
Sisaket, *Thailand* 64 E5
Sisante, *Spain* 33 F2
Sisargas, Is., *Spain* 34 B2
Sishen, *S. Africa* 88 D3
Sishui, *Henan, China* 56 G7
Sishui, *Shandong, China* 57 G9
Sisipuk L., *Canada* 105 B8
Sisophon, *Cambodia* 64 F4
Sisseton, *U.S.A.* 112 C6
Sissonne, *France* 19 C10
Sīstān va Balūchestān □, *Iran* 71 E9
Sisteron, *France* 21 D9
Sisters, *U.S.A.* 114 D3
Sitamarhi, *India* 69 F11
Sitapur, *India* 69 F9
Siteki, *Swaziland* 89 D5
Sitges, *Spain* 32 D6
Sithoniá, *Greece* 40 F7
Sitía, *Greece* 36 D8
Sitka, *U.S.A.* 100 C6
Sitoti, *Botswana* 88 C3
Sitra, *Egypt* 80 B2
Sittang Myit →, *Burma* 67 L20
Sittard, *Neths.* 17 C5
Sittensen, *Germany* 24 B5
Sittingbourne, *U.K.* 13 F8
Sittona, *Eritrea* 81 E4
Sittwe, *Burma* 67 J18
Siuna, *Nic.* 120 D3
Siuri, *India* 69 H12
Siutghiol, Lacul, *Romania* 43 F13
Sivana, *India* 68 E8
Sīvand, *Iran* 71 D7
Sivas, *Turkey* 72 C7
Sivaslı, *Turkey* 39 C11
Siverek, *Turkey* 73 D8
Sivrihisar, *Turkey* 72 C4
Siwa, *Egypt* 80 B2
Sîwa, El Wâhât es, *Egypt* 80 B2
Siwa Oasis, *Egypt* 76 D6
Siwalik Range, *Nepal* 69 F10
Siwan, *India* 69 F11
Sixmilebridge, *Ireland* 15 D3
Siyâl, Jazâ'ir, *Egypt* 80 C4
Siyäzän, *Azerbaijan* 49 K9
Siziwang Qi, *China* 56 D6
Sjælland, *Denmark* 11 J5
Sjællands Odde, *Denmark* 11 J5
Sjenica, *Serbia, Yug.* 40 C3
Sjöbo, *Sweden* 11 J7
Sjötofta, *Sweden* 11 G7
Sjötorp, *Sweden* 11 F8
Sjumen = Shumen, *Bulgaria* 41 C10
Sjuntorp, *Sweden* 11 F6
Skadarsko Jezero, *Montenegro, Yug.* 40 D3
Skadovsk, *Ukraine* 47 J7
Skælskør, *Denmark* 11 J5
Skærbæk, *Denmark* 11 J2
Skaftafell, *Iceland* 8 D5
Skagafjörður, *Iceland* 8 D4
Skagastølstindane, *Norway* 9 F12
Skagaströnd, *Iceland* 8 D3
Skagen, *Denmark* 11 G4
Skagern, *Sweden* 11 F8
Skagerrak, *Denmark* 11 G2
Skagit →, *U.S.A.* 116 B4
Skagway, *U.S.A.* 104 B1
Skala-Podilska, *Ukraine* 47 H4
Skala Podolskaya = Skala-Podilska, *Ukraine* 47 H4
Skalat, *Ukraine* 47 H3
Skalbmierz, *Poland* 45 H7
Skälderviken, *Sweden* 11 H6
Skalica, *Slovak Rep.* 27 C10
Skallingen, *Denmark* 11 J2

Skalni Dol = Kamenyak, *Bulgaria* 41 C10
Skanderborg, *Denmark* 11 H3
Skåne, *Sweden* 11 J7
Skänninge, *Sweden* 11 F9
Skanör med Falsterbo, *Sweden* 11 J6
Skantzoúra, *Greece* 38 B6
Skara, *Sweden* 11 F7
Skaraborgs län □, *Sweden* 11 F7
Skärblacka, *Sweden* 11 F9
Skardu, *Pakistan* 69 B6
Skåre, *Sweden* 10 E7
Skärhamn, *Sweden* 11 G5
Skarszewy, *Poland* 44 D5
Skaryszew, *Poland* 45 G8
Skarżysko-Kamienna, *Poland* 45 G7
Skattkärr, *Sweden* 10 E7
Skattungbyn, *Sweden* 10 C8
Skawina, *Poland* 45 J6
Skebobruk, *Sweden* 10 E12
Skeena →, *Canada* 104 C2
Skeena Mts., *Canada* 104 B3
Skegness, *U.K.* 12 D8
Skeldon, *Guyana* 124 B7
Skellefte älv →, *Sweden* 8 D19
Skellefteå, *Sweden* 8 D19
Skelleftehamn, *Sweden* 8 D19
Skender Vakuf, *Bos.-H.* 42 F2
Skerries, The, *U.K.* 12 D3
Skhíza, *Greece* 38 E3
Skhoinoúsa, *Greece* 39 E7
Ski, *Norway* 9 G14
Skíathos, *Greece* 38 B5
Skibbereen, *Ireland* 15 E2
Skiddaw, *U.K.* 12 C4
Skídhra, *Greece* 40 F6
Skien, *Norway* 9 G13
Skierniewice, *Poland* 45 G7
Skierniewice □, *Poland* 45 G7
Skikda, *Algeria* 78 A7
Skillingaryd, *Sweden* 11 G8
Skillinge, *Sweden* 11 J8
Skilloura, *Cyprus* 36 D12
Skinári, Ákra, *Greece* 38 D2
Skinnskatteberg, *Sweden* 10 E9
Skipton, *Australia* 95 F3
Skipton, *U.K.* 12 D5
Skirmish Pt., *Australia* 94 A1
Skiropoúla, *Greece* 38 C6
Skíros, *Greece* 38 C6
Skivarp, *Sweden* 11 J7
Skive, *Denmark* 11 H3
Skjálfandafljót →, *Iceland* 8 D5
Skjálfandi, *Iceland* 8 C5
Skjern, *Denmark* 11 J2
Skoczów, *Poland* 45 J5
Škofja Loka, *Slovenia* 29 B11
Skoghall, *Sweden* 10 E7
Skogstorp, *Sweden* 10 E10
Skoki, *Poland* 45 F4
Skole, *Ukraine* 47 H2
Skópelos, *Greece* 38 B5
Skopí, *Greece* 36 D8
Skopin, *Russia* 46 F10
Skopje, *Macedonia* 40 D5
Skórcz, *Poland* 44 E5
Skørping, *Denmark* 11 H3
Skövde, *Sweden* 11 F7
Skovorodino, *Russia* 51 D13
Skowhegan, *U.S.A.* 103 D6
Skownan, *Canada* 105 C9
Skradin, *Croatia* 29 E12
Skrea, *Sweden* 11 H6
Skrunda, *Latvia* 44 B9
Skrwa →, *Poland* 45 F6
Skull, *Ireland* 15 E2
Skultorp, *Sweden* 11 F7
Skultuna, *Sweden* 10 E10
Skunk →, *U.S.A.* 112 E9
Skuodas, *Lithuania* 9 H19
Skurup, *Sweden* 11 J7
Skutskär, *Sweden* 10 D11
Skvyra, *Ukraine* 47 H5
Skwierzyna, *Poland* 45 F2
Skye, *U.K.* 14 D2
Skykomish, *U.S.A.* 114 C3
Skyttorp, *Sweden* 10 D11
Slættaratindur, *Færoe Is.* 8 E9
Slagelse, *Denmark* 11 J5
Slamet, *Indonesia* 63 G13
Slaney →, *Ireland* 15 D5
Slănic, *Romania* 43 E10
Slano, *Croatia* 40 D1
Slantsy, *Russia* 46 C5
Slaný, *Czech Rep.* 26 A7
Slätbaken, *Sweden* 11 F10
Slate Is., *Canada* 102 C2
Slatina, *Croatia* 42 E2
Slatina, *Romania* 43 F9
Slatina Timiş, *Romania* 42 E7
Slaton, *U.S.A.* 113 J4
Slave →, *Canada* 104 A6
Slave Coast, *W. Afr.* 83 D5
Slave Lake, *Canada* 104 B6
Slave Pt., *Canada* 104 A5
Slavgorod, *Russia* 50 D8
Slavinja, *Serbia, Yug.* 40 C6
Slavkov u Brna, *Czech Rep.* 27 B9
Slavonija, *Europe* 42 E2
Slavonski Brod, *Croatia* 42 E3
Slavuta, *Ukraine* 47 G4
Slavyanka, *Russia* 54 C5
Slavyanovo, *Bulgaria* 41 C8
Slavyansk = Slovyansk, *Ukraine* 47 H9
Slavyansk-na-Kubani, *Russia* 47 K10
Sława, *Poland* 45 G3
Slawharad, *Belarus* 46 F6
Sławno, *Poland* 44 D3
Sławoborze, *Poland* 44 E2
Sleaford, *U.K.* 12 D7
Sleaford B., *Australia* 95 E2
Sleat, Sd. of, *U.K.* 14 D3
Sleeper Is., *Canada* 101 C11
Sleepy Eye, *U.S.A.* 112 C7
Slemon L., *Canada* 104 A5
Ślesin, *Poland* 45 F5
Slidell, *U.S.A.* 113 K10
Sliema, *Malta* 36 D2
Slieve Aughty, *Ireland* 15 C3
Slieve Bloom, *Ireland* 15 C4
Slieve Donard, *U.K.* 15 B6
Slieve Gamph, *Ireland* 15 B3
Slieve Gullion, *U.K.* 15 B5
Slieve Mish, *Ireland* 15 D2
Slievenamon, *Ireland* 15 D4
Sligeach = Sligo, *Ireland* 15 B3
Sligo, *Ireland* 15 B3
Sligo □, *Ireland* 15 B3
Sligo B., *Ireland* 15 B3
Slite, *Sweden* 11 G12
Sliven, *Bulgaria* 41 D10
Slivnitsa, *Bulgaria* 40 D7
Sljeme, *Croatia* 29 C12
Sloan, *U.S.A.* 117 K11
Sloansville, *U.S.A.* 111 D10
Slobozia, *Moldova* 43 D14
Slobozia, *Argeş, Romania* 43 F10
Slobozia, *Ialomiţa, Romania* 43 F12
Slocan, *Canada* 104 D5
Słomniki, *Poland* 45 H7
Slonim, *Belarus* 47 F3
Slough, *U.K.* 13 F7
Slough □, *U.K.* 13 F7
Sloughhouse, *U.S.A.* 116 G5
Slovak Rep. ■, *Europe* 27 C13
Slovakia = Slovak Rep. ■, *Europe* 27 C13
Slovakian Ore Mts. = Slovenské Rudohorie, *Slovak Rep.* 27 C12
Slovenia ■, *Europe* 29 C11
Slovenija = Slovenia ■, *Europe* 29 C11
Slovenj Gradec, *Slovenia* 29 B12
Slovenska Bistrica, *Slovenia* 29 B12
Slovenske Konjice, *Slovenia* 29 B12
Slovenské Rudohorie, *Slovak Rep.* 27 C12
Slovyansk, *Ukraine* 47 H9
Słubice, *Poland* 45 F1
Sluch →, *Ukraine* 47 G4
Sluis, *Neths.* 17 C3
Slŭnchev Bryag, *Bulgaria* 41 D11
Slunj, *Croatia* 29 C12
Słupca, *Poland* 45 F4
Słupia →, *Poland* 44 D3
Słupsk, *Poland* 44 D4
Słupsk □, *Poland* 44 D4
Slurry, *S. Africa* 88 D4
Slutsk, *Belarus* 47 F4
Slyne Hd., *Ireland* 15 C1
Slyudyanka, *Russia* 51 D11
Småland, *Sweden* 11 G9
Smålandsfarvandet, *Denmark* 11 J5
Smålandsstenar, *Sweden* 11 G7
Smalltree L., *Canada* 105 A8
Smallwood Res., *Canada* 103 B7
Smara, *Morocco* 78 B4
Smarhon, *Belarus* 46 E4
Smarje, *Slovenia* 29 B12
Smartt Syndicate Dam, *S. Africa* 88 E3
Smartville, *U.S.A.* 116 F5
Smeaton, *Canada* 105 C8
Smedby, *Sweden* 11 H10
Smederevo, *Serbia, Yug.* 40 B4
Smederevska Palanka, *Serbia, Yug.* 40 B4
Smedjebacken, *Sweden* 10 D9
Smela = Smila, *Ukraine* 47 H6
Smerwick Harbour, *Ireland* 15 D1
Smethport, *U.S.A.* 110 E6
Smidovich, *Russia* 51 E14
Śmigiel, *Poland* 45 F3
Smila, *Ukraine* 47 H6
Smiley, *Canada* 105 C7
Smilyan, *Bulgaria* 41 E8
Smith, *Canada* 104 B6
Smith →, *Canada* 104 B3
Smith Center, *U.S.A.* 112 F5
Smith Sund, *Greenland* 4 B4
Smithburne →, *Australia* 94 B3
Smithers, *Canada* 104 C3
Smithfield, *S. Africa* 89 E4
Smithfield, *N.C., U.S.A.* 109 H6
Smithfield, *Utah, U.S.A.* 114 F8
Smiths Falls, *Canada* 102 D4
Smithton, *Australia* 94 G4
Smithtown, *Australia* 95 E5
Smithville, *Canada* 110 C5
Smithville, *U.S.A.* 113 K6
Smoky →, *Canada* 104 B5
Smoky Bay, *Australia* 95 E1
Smoky Falls, *Canada* 102 B3
Smoky Hill →, *U.S.A.* 112 F6
Smoky Lake, *Canada* 104 C6
Smøla, *Norway* 8 E13
Smolensk, *Russia* 46 E7
Smolikas, Óros, *Greece* 40 F4
Smolník, *Slovak Rep.* 27 C13
Smolyan, *Bulgaria* 41 E8
Smooth Rock Falls, *Canada* 102 C3
Smoothstone L., *Canada* 105 C7
Smorgon = Smarhon, *Belarus* 46 E4
Smulţi, *Romania* 43 E12
Smyadovo, *Bulgaria* 41 C11
Smygehamn, *Sweden* 11 J7
Smyrna = İzmir, *Turkey* 39 C9
Snæfell, *Iceland* 8 D6
Snaefell, *U.K.* 12 C3
Snæfellsjökull, *Iceland* 8 D2
Snake →, *U.S.A.* 114 C4
Snake I., *Australia* 95 F4
Snake L., *Canada* 105 B7
Snake Range, *U.S.A.* 114 G6
Snake River Plain, *U.S.A.* 114 E7
Snasahögarna, *Sweden* 10 A6
Snåsavatnet, *Norway* 8 D14
Snedsted, *Denmark* 11 H2
Sneek, *Neths.* 17 A5
Sneeuberge, *S. Africa* 88 E3
Snejbjerg, *Denmark* 11 H2
Snelling, *U.S.A.* 116 H6
Snezhnoye, *Ukraine* 47 J10
Snežnik, *Slovenia* 29 C11
Śniadowo, *Poland* 45 E8
Śniardwy, Jezioro, *Poland* 44 E8
Śnieżka, *Europe* 26 A8
Snigirevka = Snihurivka, *Ukraine* 47 J7
Snihurivka, *Ukraine* 47 J7
Snina, *Slovak Rep.* 27 C15
Snizort, L., *U.K.* 14 D2
Snøhetta, *Norway* 9 E13
Snohomish, *U.S.A.* 116 C4
Snoul, *Cambodia* 65 F6
Snow Hill, *U.S.A.* 108 F8
Snow Lake, *Canada* 105 C8
Snow Mt., *U.S.A.* 116 F4
Snowbird L., *Canada* 105 A8
Snowdon, *U.K.* 12 D3
Snowdrift →, *Canada* 105 A6
Snowflake, *U.S.A.* 115 J8
Snowshoe Pk., *U.S.A.* 114 B6
Snowtown, *Australia* 95 E2
Snowville, *U.S.A.* 114 F7
Snowy →, *Australia* 95 F4
Snowy Mts., *Australia* 95 F4
Snug Corner, *Bahamas* 121 B5
Snyatyn, *Ukraine* 47 H3
Snyder, *Okla., U.S.A.* 113 H5
Snyder, *Tex., U.S.A.* 113 J4
Soahanina, *Madag.* 89 B7
Soalala, *Madag.* 89 B8
Soan →, *Pakistan* 68 C4
Soanierana-Ivongo, *Madag.* 89 B8
Soap Lake, *U.S.A.* 114 C4
Şoarş, *Romania* 43 E9
Sobat, Nahr →, *Sudan* 81 F3
Soběslav, *Czech Rep.* 26 B7
Sobhapur, *India* 68 H8
Sobinka, *Russia* 46 E11
Sobótka, *Poland* 45 H3
Sobra, *Croatia* 29 F14
Sobradinho, Reprêsa de, *Brazil* 125 E10
Sobral, *Brazil* 125 D10
Sobrance, *Slovak Rep.* 27 C15
Sobreira Formosa, *Portugal* 34 F3
Soc Giang, *Vietnam* 64 A6
Soc Trang, *Vietnam* 65 H5
Soča →, *Europe* 26 E6
Sochaczew, *Poland* 45 F7
Soch'e = Shache, *China* 60 C2
Sochi, *Russia* 49 J4
Société, Is. de la, *Pac. Oc.* 97 J12
Society Is. = Société, Is. de la, *Pac. Oc.* 97 J12
Socompa, Portezuelo de, *Chile* 126 A2
Socorro, *U.S.A.* 115 J10
Socorro, I., *Mexico* 118 D2
Socotra, *Ind. Oc.* 74 E5
Socovos, *Spain* 33 G3
Socuéllamos, *Spain* 33 F2
Soda L., *U.S.A.* 115 J5
Soda Plains, *India* 69 B8
Soda Springs, *U.S.A.* 114 E8
Sodankylä, *Finland* 8 C22
Söderala, *Sweden* 10 C10
Söderbärke, *Sweden* 10 D9
Söderfors, *Sweden* 10 D11
Söderhamn, *Sweden* 10 C11
Söderköping, *Sweden* 11 F10
Södermanland, *Sweden* 9 G17
Södermanlands län □, *Sweden* 10 E10
Södertälje, *Sweden* 10 E11
Sodiri, *Sudan* 81 E2
Sodo, *Ethiopia* 81 F4
Södra Dellen, *Sweden* 10 C10
Södra Finnskoga, *Sweden* 10 D6
Södra Sandby, *Sweden* 11 J7
Södra Ulvön, *Sweden* 10 B12
Södra Vi, *Sweden* 11 G9
Sodražica, *Slovenia* 29 C11
Sodus, *U.S.A.* 110 C7
Soekmekaar, *S. Africa* 89 C4
Soest, *Germany* 24 D4
Soest, *Neths.* 17 B5
Sofádhes, *Greece* 38 B4
Sofara, *Mali* 82 C4
Sofia = Sofiya, *Bulgaria* 40 D7
Sofia →, *Madag.* 89 B8
Sofievka, *Ukraine* 47 H7
Sofikón, *Greece* 38 D5
Sofiya, *Bulgaria* 40 D7
Sofiya □, *Bulgaria* 40 D7
Sōfu-Gan, *Japan* 55 K10
Sogakofe, *Ghana* 83 D5
Sogamoso, *Colombia* 124 B4
Sogār, *Iran* 71 E8
Sögel, *Germany* 24 C3
Sogndalsfjøra, *Norway* 9 F12
Søgne, *Norway* 9 G12
Sognefjorden, *Norway* 9 F11
Söğüt, *Bilecik, Turkey* 39 A12
Söğüt, *Burdur, Turkey* 39 D11
Söğüt Dağı, *Turkey* 39 D11
Söğütköy, *Turkey* 39 E10
Sŏgwi-po, *S. Korea* 57 H14
Soh, *Iran* 71 C6
Sohâg, *Egypt* 80 B3
Sŏhori, *N. Korea* 57 D15
Soignies, *Belgium* 17 D4
Soira, *Eritrea* 81 E4
Soissons, *France* 19 C10
Sōja, *Japan* 55 G6
Sojat, *India* 68 G5
Sok →, *Russia* 48 D10
Sokal, *Ukraine* 47 G3
Söke, *Turkey* 39 D9
Sokelo, *Dem. Rep. of the Congo* 87 D1
Sokhós, *Greece* 40 F7
Sokhumi, *Georgia* 49 J5
Soko Banja, *Serbia, Yug.* 40 C5
Sokodé, *Togo* 83 D5
Sokol, *Russia* 46 C11
Sokolac, *Bos.-H.* 42 G3
Sokółka, *Poland* 44 E10
Sokolo, *Mali* 82 C3
Sokolov, *Czech Rep.* 26 A5
Sokołów Małpolski, *Poland* 45 H9
Sokołów Podlaski, *Poland* 45 F9
Sokoły, *Poland* 45 F9
Sokoto, *Nigeria* 83 C6
Sokoto □, *Nigeria* 83 C6
Sokoto →, *Nigeria* 83 C5
Sol Iletsk, *Russia* 50 D6
Sola →, *Poland* 45 H6
Solai, *Kenya* 86 B4
Solano, *Phil.* 61 C4
Solapur, *India* 66 L9
Solca, *Romania* 43 C10
Solda Gölü, *Turkey* 39 D11
Soldăneşti, *Moldova* 43 C13
Soléa □, *Cyprus* 36 D12
Solec Kujawski, *Poland* 45 E5
Soledad, *Colombia* 124 A4
Soledad, *U.S.A.* 116 J5
Soledad, *Venezuela* 124 B6
Solent, The, *U.K.* 13 G6
Solenzara, *France* 21 G13
Solesmes, *France* 19 B10
Solfonn, *Norway* 9 F12
Solhan, *Turkey* 73 C9
Soligorsk = Salihorsk, *Belarus* 47 F4
Solihull, *U.K.* 13 E6
Solikamsk, *Russia* 50 D6
Solila, *Madag.* 89 C8
Solimões = Amazonas →, *S. Amer.* 122 D5
Solin, *Croatia* 29 E13
Solingen, *Germany* 24 D3
Sollebrunn, *Sweden* 11 F6
Sollefteå, *Sweden* 10 A11
Sollentuna, *Sweden* 10 E11
Sóller, *Spain* 37 B9
Sollerön, *Sweden* 10 D8
Solling, *Germany* 24 D5
Solnechnogorsk, *Russia* 46 D9
Solofra, *Italy* 31 B7
Sologne, *France* 19 E8
Solok, *Indonesia* 62 E2
Sololá, *Guatemala* 120 D1
Solomon, N. Fork →, *U.S.A.* 112 F5
Solomon, S. Fork →, *U.S.A.* 112 F5
Solomon Is. ■, *Pac. Oc.* 96 H7
Solon, *China* 60 B7
Solon Springs, *U.S.A.* 112 B9
Solor, *Indonesia* 63 F6
Solotcha, *Russia* 46 E10
Solothurn, *Switz.* 25 H3
Solothurn □, *Switz.* 25 H3
Solsona, *Spain* 32 C6
Solt, *Hungary* 42 D4
Šolta, *Croatia* 29 E13
Solṭānābād, *Khorāsān, Iran* 71 C8
Solṭānābād, *Khorāsān, Iran* 71 B8
Solṭānābād, *Markazī, Iran* 71 C6
Soltau, *Germany* 24 C5
Soltsy, *Russia* 46 C6
Solunska Glava, *Macedonia* 40 E5
Solvang, *U.S.A.* 117 L6
Solvay, *U.S.A.* 111 C8
Sölvesborg, *Sweden* 11 H8
Solway Firth, *U.K.* 12 C4
Solwezi, *Zambia* 87 E2
Sōma, *Japan* 54 F10
Soma, *Turkey* 39 B9
Somali Pen., *Africa* 76 F8
Somali Rep. ■, *Africa* 74 F4
Somalia = Somali Rep. ■, *Africa* 74 F4
Sombernon, *France* 19 E11
Sombor, *Serbia, Yug.* 42 E4
Sombra, *Canada* 110 D2
Sombrerete, *Mexico* 118 C4
Sombrero, *Anguilla* 121 C7
Şomcuta Mare, *Romania* 43 C8
Somers, *U.S.A.* 114 B6
Somerset, *Canada* 105 D9
Somerset, *Colo., U.S.A.* 115 G10
Somerset, *Ky., U.S.A.* 108 G3
Somerset, *Mass., U.S.A.* 111 E13
Somerset, *Pa., U.S.A.* 110 F5
Somerset □, *U.K.* 13 F5
Somerset East, *S. Africa* 88 E4
Somerset I., *Canada* 4 B3
Somerset West, *S. Africa* 88 E2
Somerton, *U.S.A.* 115 K6
Somerville, *U.S.A.* 111 F10
Someş →, *Romania* 42 C7
Someşul Mare →, *Romania* 43 C8
Sommariva, *Australia* 95 D4
Somme □, *France* 19 C9
Somme →, *France* 19 B8
Somme, B. de la, *France* 18 B8
Sommen, *Jönköping, Sweden* 11 F8
Sommen, *Östergötland, Sweden* 11 F9
Sommepy-Tahure, *France* 19 C11
Sömmerda, *Germany* 24 D7
Sommesous, *France* 19 D11
Sommières, *France* 21 E8
Somogy □, *Hungary* 42 D2
Somogyszob, *Hungary* 42 D2
Somoto, *Nic.* 120 D2
Sompolno, *Poland* 45 F5
Somport, Puerto de, *Spain* 32 C4
Son Ha, *Vietnam* 64 E7
Son Hoa, *Vietnam* 64 F7
Son La, *Vietnam* 64 B4
Son Serra, *Spain* 37 B10
Son Servera, *Spain* 32 F8
Son Tay, *Vietnam* 64 B5
Soná, *Panama* 120 E3
Sonamarg, *India* 69 B6
Sonamukhi, *India* 69 H12
Sŏnchŏn, *N. Korea* 57 E13
Sondags →, *S. Africa* 88 E4
Sóndalo, *Italy* 28 B7
Sondar, *India* 69 C6
Sønder Felding, *Denmark* 11 J2
Sønder Omme, *Denmark* 11 J2
Sønderborg, *Denmark* 11 K3
Sønderjyllands Amtskommune □, *Denmark* 11 J3
Sondershausen, *Germany* 24 D6
Sóndrio, *Italy* 28 B6
Sone, *Mozam.* 87 F3
Sonepur, *India* 67 J13
Song, *Thailand* 64 C3
Song Cau, *Vietnam* 64 F7
Song Xian, *China* 56 G7
Songchŏn, *N. Korea* 57 E14
Songea, *Tanzania* 87 E4
Songea □, *Tanzania* 87 E4
Songeons, *France* 19 C8
Songhua Hu, *China* 57 C14
Songhua Jiang →, *China* 60 B8
Songjiang, *China* 59 B13
Songjin, *N. Korea* 57 D15
Songjŏng-ni, *S. Korea* 57 G14
Songkan, *China* 58 C6
Songkhla, *Thailand* 65 J3
Songming, *China* 58 E4
Songnim, *N. Korea* 57 E13
Songpan, *China* 58 A4
Songtao, *China* 58 C7
Songwe, *Dem. Rep. of the Congo* 86 C2
Songwe →, *Africa* 87 D3
Songxi, *China* 59 D12
Songzi, *China* 59 B8
Sonid Youqi, *China* 56 C7
Sonipat, *India* 68 E7
Sonkovo, *Russia* 46 D9
Sonmiani, *Pakistan* 68 G2
Sonnino, *Italy* 30 A6
Sono →, *Brazil* 125 E9
Sonora, *Calif., U.S.A.* 116 H6
Sonora, *Tex., U.S.A.* 113 K4
Sonora □, *Mexico* 118 B2
Sonora →, *Mexico* 118 B2
Sonora Desert, *U.S.A.* 117 L12
Sonoyta, *Mexico* 118 A2
Sonqor, *Iran* 73 E12
Sŏnsan, *S. Korea* 57 F15
Sonseca, *Spain* 35 F7
Sonsonate, *El Salv.* 120 D2
Sonstorp, *Sweden* 11 F9
Sonthofen, *Germany* 25 H6
Soochow = Suzhou, *China* 59 B13
Sop Hao, *Laos* 64 B5
Sop Prap, *Thailand* 64 D2
Sopelana, *Spain* 32 B2
Sopi, *Indonesia* 63 D7
Sopo, Nahr →, *Sudan* 81 F2
Sopot, *Bulgaria* 41 D8
Sopot, *Poland* 44 D4
Sopot, *Serbia, Yug.* 40 B4
Sopotnica, *Macedonia* 40 E5
Sopron, *Hungary* 42 C1
Sop's Arm, *Canada* 103 C8

Sopur, *India* 69 B6
Sør-Rondane, *Antarctica* 5 D4
Sora, *Italy* 29 G10
Sorah, *Pakistan* 68 F3
Söråker, *Sweden* 10 B11
Sorano, *Italy* 29 F8
Sorbas, *Spain* 33 H2
Sörbygden, *Sweden* 10 B10
Sore, *France* 20 D3
Sorel, *Canada* 102 C5
Soresina, *Italy* 28 C6
Sörforsa, *Sweden* 10 C10
Sórgono, *Italy* 30 B2
Sorgues, *France* 21 D8
Sorgun, *Turkey* 72 C6
Soria, *Spain* 32 D2
Soria □, *Spain* 32 D2
Soriano, *Uruguay* 126 C4
Soriano nel Cimino, *Italy* 29 F9
Sorkh, Kuh-e, *Iran* 71 C8
Sorø, *Denmark* 11 J5
Soro, *Guinea* 82 C3
Soroca, *Moldova* 43 B13
Sorocaba, *Brazil* 127 A6
Soroki = Soroca, *Moldova* 43 B13
Soron, *India* 69 F8
Sorong, *Indonesia* 63 E8
Soroní, *Greece* 36 C10
Soroti, *Uganda* 86 B3
Sørøya, *Norway* 8 A20
Sørøysundet, *Norway* 8 A20
Sorraia →, *Portugal* 35 G2
Sorrento, *Australia* 95 F3
Sorrento, *Italy* 31 B7
Sorsele, *Sweden* 8 D17
Sörsjön, *Sweden* 10 C7
Sorso, *Italy* 30 B1
Sorsogon, *Phil.* 61 E6
Sortavala, *Russia* 46 B6
Sortino, *Italy* 31 E8
Sortland, *Norway* 8 B16
Sorvizhi, *Russia* 48 B9
Sos = Sos del Rey Católico, *Spain* 32 C3
Sos del Rey Católico, *Spain* 32 C3
Sŏsan, *S. Korea* 57 F14
Soscumica, L., *Canada* 102 B4
Sösdala, *Sweden* 11 H7
Sosna →, *Russia* 47 F10
Sosnovka, *Kirov, Russia* 48 B10
Sosnovka, *Tambov, Russia* 48 D5
Sosnovyy Bor, *Russia* 46 C5
Sosnowiec, *Poland* 45 H6
Sospel, *France* 21 E11
Šoštanj, *Slovenia* 29 B12
Sŏsura, *N. Korea* 57 C16
Sotkamo, *Finland* 8 D23
Soto del Barco, *Spain* 34 B4
Soto la Marina →, *Mexico* 119 C5
Soto y Amío, *Spain* 34 C5
Sotrondio, *Spain* 34 B5
Sotuta, *Mexico* 119 C7
Souanké, *Congo* 84 D2
Soúdha, *Greece* 36 D6
Soúdhas, Kólpos, *Greece* 36 D6
Souflíon, *Greece* 41 E10
Souillac, *France* 20 D5
Souilly, *France* 19 C12
Soukhouma, *Laos* 64 E5
Sŏul, *S. Korea* 57 F14
Soulac-sur-Mer, *France* 20 C2
Soultz-sous-Forêts, *France* 19 D14
Sound, The = Øresund, *Europe* 11 J6
Sound, The, *U.K.* 13 G3
Soúnion, Ákra, *Greece* 38 D6
Sources, Mt. aux, *Lesotho* 89 D4
Soure, *Brazil* 125 D9
Soure, *Portugal* 34 E2
Souris, *Man., Canada* 105 D8
Souris, *P.E.I., Canada* 103 C7
Souris →, *Canada* 112 A5
Soúrpi, *Greece* 38 B4
Sousa, *Brazil* 125 E11
Sousel, *Portugal* 35 G3
Sousse, *Tunisia* 79 A8
Soustons, *France* 20 E2
South Africa ■, *Africa* 88 E3
South Atlantic Ocean 122 H7
South Aulatsivik I., *Canada* 103 A7
South Australia □, *Australia* 95 E2
South Ayrshire □, *U.K.* 14 F4
South Baldy, *U.S.A.* 115 J10
South Bend, *Ind., U.S.A.* 108 E2
South Bend, *Wash., U.S.A.* 116 D3
South Boston, *U.S.A.* 109 G6
South Branch, *Canada* 103 C8
South Brook, *Canada* 103 C8
South Carolina □, *U.S.A.* 109 J5
South Charleston, *U.S.A.* 108 F5
South China Sea, *Asia* 62 C4
South Dakota □, *U.S.A.* 112 C5
South Downs, *U.K.* 13 G7
South East C., *Australia* 94 G4
South East Is., *Australia* 93 F3
South Esk →, *U.K.* 14 E6
South Foreland, *U.K.* 13 F9
South Fork →, *U.S.A.* 114 C7
South Fork, American →, *U.S.A.* 116 G5
South Fork, Feather →, *U.S.A.* 116 F5
South Georgia, *Antarctica* 5 B1
South Gloucestershire □, *U.K.* 13 F5
South Haven, *U.S.A.* 108 D2
South Henik, L., *Canada* 105 A9
South Honshu Ridge, *Pac. Oc.* 96 E6
South Horr, *Kenya* 86 B4
South I., *Kenya* 86 B4
South I., *N.Z.* 91 L3
South Invercargill, *N.Z.* 91 M2
South Knife →, *Canada* 105 B10
South Korea ■, *Asia* 57 G15
South Lake Tahoe, *U.S.A.* 116 G6
South Lanarkshire □, *U.K.* 14 F5
South Loup →, *U.S.A.* 112 E5
South Magnetic Pole, *Antarctica* 5 C9
South Milwaukee, *U.S.A.* 108 D2
South Molton, *U.K.* 13 F4
South Nahanni →, *Canada* 104 A4
South Natuna Is. = Natuna Selatan, Kepulauan, *Indonesia* 65 L7
South Negril Pt., *Jamaica* 120 C4
South Orkney Is., *Antarctica* 5 C18
South Ossetia □, *Georgia* 49 J7
South Pagai, I. = Pagai Selatan, Pulau, *Indonesia* 62 E2
South Pass, *U.S.A.* 114 E9
South Pittsburg, *U.S.A.* 109 H3
South Platte →, *U.S.A.* 112 E4
South Pole, *Antarctica* 5 E
South Porcupine, *Canada* 102 C3
South River, *Canada* 102 C4
South River, *U.S.A.* 111 F10
South Ronaldsay, *U.K.* 14 C6
South Sandwich Is., *Antarctica* 5 B1
South Saskatchewan →, *Canada* 105 C7
South Seal →, *Canada* 105 B9
South Shetland Is., *Antarctica* 5 C18
South Shields, *U.K.* 12 C6
South Sioux City, *U.S.A.* 112 D6
South Taranaki Bight, *N.Z.* 91 H5
South Thompson →, *Canada* 104 C4
South Twin I., *Canada* 102 B4
South Tyne →, *U.K.* 12 C5
South Uist, *U.K.* 14 D1
South West Africa = Namibia ■, *Africa* 88 C2
South West C., *Australia* 94 G4
South Yorkshire □, *U.K.* 12 D6
Southampton, *Canada* 102 D3
Southampton, *U.K.* 13 G6
Southampton, *U.S.A.* 111 F12
Southampton □, *U.K.* 13 G6
Southampton I., *Canada* 4 C3
Southbridge, *N.Z.* 91 K4
Southbridge, *U.S.A.* 111 D12
Southend, *Canada* 105 B8
Southend-on-Sea, *U.K.* 13 F8
Southend-on-Sea □, *U.K.* 13 F8
Southern □, *Malawi* 87 F4
Southern □, *S. Leone* 82 D2
Southern □, *Uganda* 86 C3
Southern □, *Zambia* 87 F2
Southern Alps, *N.Z.* 91 K3
Southern Cross, *Australia* 93 F2
Southern Hills, *Australia* 93 F3
Southern Indian L., *Canada* 105 B9
Southern Ocean, *Antarctica* 5 C6
Southern Pines, *U.S.A.* 109 H6
Southern Uplands, *U.K.* 14 F5
Southington, *U.S.A.* 111 E12
Southold, *U.S.A.* 111 E12
Southport, *Australia* 95 D5
Southport, *U.K.* 12 D4
Southport, *U.S.A.* 109 J6
Southwest C., *N.Z.* 91 M1
Southwold, *U.K.* 13 E9
Soutpansberg, *S. Africa* 89 C4
Souvigny, *France* 19 F10
Sovata, *Romania* 43 D10
Soverato, *Italy* 31 D9
Sovetsk, *Kaliningd., Russia* 9 J19
Sovetsk, *Kirov, Russia* 48 B9
Sovetskaya Gavan = Vanino, *Russia* 51 E15
Sovicille, *Italy* 29 E8
Soweto, *S. Africa* 89 D4
Sōya-Kaikyō = La Perouse Str., *Asia* 54 B11
Sōya-Misaki, *Japan* 54 B10
Soyaux, *France* 20 C4
Sozh →, *Belarus* 47 F6
Sozopol, *Bulgaria* 41 D11
Spa, *Belgium* 17 D5
Spain ■, *Europe* 7 H5
Spalding, *Australia* 95 E2
Spalding, *U.K.* 12 E7
Spalding, *U.S.A.* 112 E5
Spangler, *U.S.A.* 110 F6
Spaniard's Bay, *Canada* 103 C9
Spanish, *Canada* 102 C3
Spanish Fork, *U.S.A.* 114 F8
Spanish Town, *Jamaica* 120 C4
Sparks, *U.S.A.* 116 F7
Sparreholm, *Sweden* 10 E10
Sparta = Spárti, *Greece* 38 D4
Sparta, *Ga., U.S.A.* 109 J4
Sparta, *Wis., U.S.A.* 112 D9
Spartanburg, *U.S.A.* 109 H5
Spartansburg, *U.S.A.* 110 E5
Spárti, *Greece* 38 D4
Spartivento, C., *Calabria, Italy* 31 E9
Spartivento, C., *Sard., Italy* 30 D1
Spas-Demensk, *Russia* 46 E7
Spas-Klepiki, *Russia* 46 E11
Spassk Dalniy, *Russia* 54 B6
Spassk-Ryazanskiy, *Russia* 46 E11
Spátha, Ákra, *Greece* 36 D5
Spatsizi →, *Canada* 104 B3
Spean →, *U.K.* 14 E4
Spearfish, *U.S.A.* 112 C3
Spearman, *U.S.A.* 113 G4
Speers, *Canada* 105 C7
Speia, *Moldova* 43 D14
Speightstown, *Barbados* 121 D8
Speke Gulf, *Tanzania* 86 C3
Spello, *Italy* 29 F9
Spencer, *Idaho, U.S.A.* 114 D7
Spencer, *Iowa, U.S.A.* 112 D7
Spencer, *N.Y., U.S.A.* 111 D8
Spencer, *Nebr., U.S.A.* 112 D5
Spencer, *W. Va., U.S.A.* 108 F5
Spencer, C., *Australia* 95 F2
Spencer B., *Namibia* 88 D1
Spencer G., *Australia* 95 E2
Spencerville, *Canada* 111 B9
Spences Bridge, *Canada* 104 C4
Spennymoor, *U.K.* 12 C6
Spenser Mts., *N.Z.* 91 K4
Spentrup, *Denmark* 11 H4
Sperkhiós →, *Greece* 38 C4
Sperrin Mts., *U.K.* 15 B5
Spessart, *Germany* 25 F5
Spétsai, *Greece* 38 D5
Spey →, *U.K.* 14 D5
Speyer, *Germany* 25 F4
Spezzano Albanese, *Italy* 31 C9
Spiekeroog, *Germany* 24 B3
Spiez, *Switz.* 25 J3
Spíli, *Greece* 36 D6
Spilimbergo, *Italy* 29 B9
Spin Baldak = Qala-i-Jadid, *Afghan.* 68 D2
Spinalónga, *Greece* 36 D7
Spinazzola, *Italy* 31 B9
Spineni, *Romania* 43 F9
Spirit Lake, *Idaho, U.S.A.* 114 C5
Spirit Lake, *Wash., U.S.A.* 116 D4
Spirit River, *Canada* 104 B5
Spiritwood, *Canada* 105 C7
Spišská Nová Ves, *Slovak Rep.* 27 C13
Spišské Podhradie, *Slovak Rep.* 27 B13
Spital, *Austria* 26 D7
Spithead, *U.K.* 13 G6
Spittal an der Drau, *Austria* 26 E6
Spitzbergen = Svalbard, *Arctic* 4 B8
Spjelkavik, *Norway* 9 E12
Split, *Croatia* 29 E13
Split L., *Canada* 105 B9
Splitski Kanal, *Croatia* 29 E13
Splügenpass, *Switz.* 25 J5
Spofford, *U.S.A.* 113 L4
Spokane, *U.S.A.* 114 C5
Spoleto, *Italy* 29 F9
Spooner, *U.S.A.* 112 C9
Sporyy Navolok, Mys, *Russia* 50 B7
Spragge, *Canada* 102 C3
Sprague, *U.S.A.* 114 C5
Sprague River, *U.S.A.* 114 E3
Spratly Is., *S. China Sea* 62 C4
Spray, *U.S.A.* 114 D4
Spreča →, *Bos.-H.* 42 F3
Spree →, *Germany* 24 C9
Spreewald, *Germany* 24 D9
Spremberg, *Germany* 24 D10
Sprengisandur, *Iceland* 8 D5
Spring City, *U.S.A.* 114 G8
Spring Garden, *U.S.A.* 116 F6
Spring Mts., *U.S.A.* 115 H6
Spring Valley, *Calif., U.S.A.* 117 N10
Spring Valley, *Minn., U.S.A.* 112 D8
Springbok, *S. Africa* 88 D2
Springdale, *Canada* 103 C8
Springdale, *Ark., U.S.A.* 113 G7
Springdale, *Wash., U.S.A.* 114 B5
Springe, *Germany* 24 C5
Springer, *U.S.A.* 113 G2
Springerville, *U.S.A.* 115 J9
Springfield, *Canada* 110 D4
Springfield, *N.Z.* 91 K3
Springfield, *Colo., U.S.A.* 113 G3
Springfield, *Ill., U.S.A.* 112 F10
Springfield, *Mass., U.S.A.* 111 D12
Springfield, *Mo., U.S.A.* 113 G8
Springfield, *Ohio, U.S.A.* 108 F4
Springfield, *Oreg., U.S.A.* 114 D2
Springfield, *Tenn., U.S.A.* 109 G2
Springfield, *Vt., U.S.A.* 111 C12
Springfontein, *S. Africa* 88 E4
Springhill, *Canada* 103 C7
Springhouse, *Canada* 104 C4
Springhurst, *Australia* 95 F4
Springs, *S. Africa* 89 D4
Springsure, *Australia* 94 C4
Springvale, *Queens., Australia* 94 C3
Springvale, *W. Austral., Australia* 92 C4
Springvale, *U.S.A.* 111 C14
Springville, *Calif., U.S.A.* 116 J8
Springville, *N.Y., U.S.A.* 110 D6
Springville, *Utah, U.S.A.* 114 F8
Springwater, *Canada* 105 C7
Spruce-Creek, *U.S.A.* 110 F6
Spur, *U.S.A.* 113 J4
Spurn Hd., *U.K.* 12 D8
Spuž, *Montenegro, Yug.* 40 D3
Spuzzum, *Canada* 104 D4
Squam L., *U.S.A.* 111 C13
Squamish, *Canada* 104 D4
Square Islands, *Canada* 103 B8
Squillace, G. di, *Italy* 31 D9
Squinzano, *Italy* 31 B11
Squires, Mt., *Australia* 93 E4
Srbac, *Bos.-H.* 42 E2
Srbija = Serbia □, *Yugoslavia* 40 C5
Srbobran, *Serbia, Yug.* 42 E4
Sre Ambel, *Cambodia* 65 G4
Sre Khtum, *Cambodia* 65 F6
Sre Umbell = Sre Ambel, *Cambodia* 65 G4
Srebrenica, *Bos.-H.* 42 F4
Sredinny Ra. = Sredinnyy Khrebet, *Russia* 51 D17
Sredinnyy Khrebet, *Russia* 51 D17
Središče, *Slovenia* 29 B13
Sredna Gora, *Bulgaria* 41 D8
Srednekolymsk, *Russia* 51 C16
Sredni Rodopi, *Bulgaria* 41 E8
Srednogorie, *Bulgaria* 41 D8
Śrem, *Poland* 45 F4
Sremska Mitrovica, *Serbia, Yug.* 42 F4
Sremski Karlovci, *Serbia, Yug.* 42 E4
Srepok →, *Cambodia* 64 F6
Sretensk, *Russia* 51 D12
Sri Lanka ■, *Asia* 66 R12
Srikakulam, *India* 67 K13
Srinagar, *India* 69 B6
Środa Śląska, *Poland* 45 G3
Środa Wielkopolski, *Poland* 45 F4
Srpska Crnja, *Serbia, Yug.* 42 E5
Srpski Itebej, *Serbia, Yug.* 42 E5
Staaten →, *Australia* 94 B3
Staberhuk, *Germany* 24 A7
Stade, *Germany* 24 B5
Stadskanaal, *Neths.* 17 A6
Stadtallendorf, *Germany* 24 E5
Stadthagen, *Germany* 24 C5
Stadtlohn, *Germany* 24 D2
Stadtroda, *Germany* 24 E7
Staffa, *U.K.* 14 E2
Staffanstorp, *Sweden* 11 J7
Stafford, *U.K.* 12 E5
Stafford, *U.S.A.* 113 G5
Stafford Springs, *U.S.A.* 111 E12
Staffordshire □, *U.K.* 12 E5
Stagnone, *Italy* 30 E5
Staines, *U.K.* 13 F7
Stainz, *Austria* 26 E8
Stakhanov, *Ukraine* 47 H10
Stalać, *Serbia, Yug.* 40 C5
Stalingrad = Volgograd, *Russia* 49 F7
Staliniri = Tskhinvali, *Georgia* 49 J7
Stalino = Donetsk, *Ukraine* 47 J9
Stalinogorsk = Novomoskovsk, *Russia* 46 E10
Stalis, *Greece* 36 D7
Stallarholmen, *Sweden* 10 E11
Ställdalen, *Sweden* 10 E8
Stalowa Wola, *Poland* 45 H9
Stalybridge, *U.K.* 12 D5
Stamford, *Australia* 94 C3
Stamford, *U.K.* 13 E7
Stamford, *Conn., U.S.A.* 111 E11
Stamford, *Tex., U.S.A.* 113 J5
Stamps, *U.S.A.* 113 J8
Stanberry, *U.S.A.* 112 E7
Stančevo = Kalipetrovo, *Bulgaria* 41 B11
Standerton, *S. Africa* 89 D4
Standish, *U.S.A.* 108 D4
Stanford, *U.S.A.* 114 C8
Stånga, *Sweden* 11 G12
Stanger, *S. Africa* 89 D5
Stanišić, *Serbia, Yug.* 42 E4
Stanislaus →, *U.S.A.* 116 H5
Stanislav = Ivano-Frankivsk, *Ukraine* 47 H3
Stanisławów, *Poland* 45 F8
Stanley, *Australia* 94 G4
Stanley, *N.B., Canada* 103 C6
Stanley, *Sask., Canada* 105 B8
Stanley, *Falk. Is.* 128 G5
Stanley, *U.K.* 12 C6
Stanley, *Idaho, U.S.A.* 114 D6
Stanley, *N. Dak., U.S.A.* 112 A3
Stanley, *N.Y., U.S.A.* 110 D7
Stanley, *Wis., U.S.A.* 112 C9
Stanovoy Khrebet, *Russia* 51 D14
Stanovoy Ra. = Stanovoy Khrebet, *Russia* 51 D14
Stansmore Ra., *Australia* 92 D4
Stanthorpe, *Australia* 95 D5
Stanton, *U.S.A.* 113 J4
Stanwood, *U.S.A.* 116 B4
Staples, *U.S.A.* 112 B7
Stapleton, *U.S.A.* 112 E4
Stąporków, *Poland* 45 G7
Star City, *Canada* 105 C8
Stará L'ubovňa, *Slovak Rep.* 27 B13
Stara Moravica, *Serbia, Yug.* 42 E4
Stara Pazova, *Serbia, Yug.* 42 F5
Stara Planina, *Bulgaria* 40 C7
Stará Turá, *Slovak Rep.* 27 C10
Stara Zagora, *Bulgaria* 41 D9
Starachowice, *Poland* 45 G8
Staraya Russa, *Russia* 46 D6
Starbuck I., *Kiribati* 97 H12
Starchiojd, *Romania* 43 E11
Stargard Szczeciński, *Poland* 44 E2
Stari Bar, *Montenegro, Yug.* 40 D3
Stari Trg, *Slovenia* 29 C12
Staritsa, *Russia* 46 D8
Starke, *U.S.A.* 109 L4
Starkville, *Colo., U.S.A.* 113 G2
Starkville, *Miss., U.S.A.* 109 J1
Starnberg, *Germany* 25 H7
Starnberger See, *Germany* 25 H7
Starobilsk, *Ukraine* 47 H10
Starodub, *Russia* 47 F7
Starogard Gdański, *Poland* 44 E5
Starokonstantinov = Starokonstyantyniv, *Ukraine* 47 H4
Starokonstyantyniv, *Ukraine* 47 H4
Starominskaya, *Russia* 47 J10
Staroshcherbinovskaya, *Russia* 47 J10
Start Pt., *U.K.* 13 G4
Stary Sącz, *Poland* 45 J7
Staryy Biryuzyak, *Russia* 49 H8
Staryy Chartoriysk, *Ukraine* 47 G3
Staryy Krym, *Ukraine* 47 K8
Staryy Oskol, *Russia* 47 G9
Stassfurt, *Germany* 24 D7
Staszów, *Poland* 45 H8
State College, *U.S.A.* 110 F7
Stateline, *U.S.A.* 116 G7
Staten, I. = Estados, I. de Los, *Argentina* 122 J4
Staten I., *U.S.A.* 111 F10
Statesboro, *U.S.A.* 109 J5
Statesville, *U.S.A.* 109 H5
Stauffer, *U.S.A.* 117 L7
Staunton, *Ill., U.S.A.* 112 F10
Staunton, *Va., U.S.A.* 108 F6
Stavanger, *Norway* 9 G11
Staveley, *N.Z.* 91 K3
Stavelot, *Belgium* 17 D5
Stavern, *Norway* 9 G14
Stavoren, *Neths.* 17 B5
Stavropol, *Russia* 49 H6
Stavros, *Cyprus* 36 D11
Stavrós, *Greece* 36 D6
Stavros, Ákra, *Greece* 36 D6
Stavroúpolis, *Greece* 41 E8
Stawell, *Australia* 95 F3
Stawell →, *Australia* 94 C3
Stawiski, *Poland* 44 E9
Stawiszyn, *Poland* 45 G5
Stayner, *Canada* 110 B4
Steamboat Springs, *U.S.A.* 114 F10
Stebleva, *Albania* 40 E4
Steele, *U.S.A.* 112 B5
Steelton, *U.S.A.* 110 F8
Steelville, *U.S.A.* 113 G9
Steen River, *Canada* 104 B5
Steenkool = Bintuni, *Indonesia* 63 E8
Steenwijk, *Neths.* 17 B6
Steep Pt., *Australia* 93 E1
Steep Rock, *Canada* 105 C9
Ştefan Vodă, *Moldova* 43 D14
Ştefăneşti, *Romania* 43 C12
Stefanie L. = Chew Bahir, *Ethiopia* 81 G4
Stefansson Bay, *Antarctica* 5 C5
Stege, *Denmark* 11 K6
Ştei, *Romania* 42 D7
Steiermark □, *Austria* 26 D8
Steigerwald, *Germany* 25 F6
Steilacoom, *U.S.A.* 116 C4
Steinbach, *Canada* 105 D9
Steinfurt, *Germany* 24 C3
Steinheim, *Germany* 24 D5
Steinhuder Meer, *Germany* 24 C5
Steinkjer, *Norway* 8 D14
Steinkopf, *S. Africa* 88 D2
Stellarton, *Canada* 103 C7
Stellenbosch, *S. Africa* 88 E2
Stelvio, Paso dello, *Italy* 28 B7
Stenay, *France* 19 C12
Stendal, *Germany* 24 C7
Stende, *Latvia* 44 A9
Stenhamra, *Sweden* 10 E11
Stenstorp, *Sweden* 11 F7
Stenungsund, *Sweden* 11 F5
Steornabhaigh = Stornoway, *U.K.* 14 C2
Stepanakert = Xankändi, *Azerbaijan* 73 C12
Stepanavan, *Armenia* 49 K7
Stephen, *U.S.A.* 112 A6
Stephens Creek, *Australia* 95 E3
Stephens I., *Canada* 104 C2
Stephenville, *Canada* 103 C8
Stephenville, *U.S.A.* 113 J5
Stepnica, *Poland* 44 E1
Stepnoi = Elista, *Russia* 49 G7
Steppe, *Asia* 52 D9
Stereá Ellas □, *Greece* 38 C4
Sterkstroom, *S. Africa* 88 E4

Sterling, *Colo., U.S.A.* . . . 112 E3
Sterling, *Ill., U.S.A.* 112 E10
Sterling, *Kans., U.S.A.* . . . 112 F5
Sterling City, *U.S.A.* 113 K4
Sterling Run, *U.S.A.* 110 E6
Sterlitamak, *Russia* 50 D6
Sternberg, *Germany* 24 B7
Šternberk, *Czech Rep.* . . . 27 B10
Stérnes, *Greece* 36 D6
Sterzing = Vipiteno, *Italy* . 29 B8
Stettin = Szczecin, *Poland* 44 E1
Stettiner Haff, *Germany* . . 24 B10
Stettler, *Canada* 104 C6
Steubenville, *U.S.A.* 110 F4
Stevenage, *U.K.* 13 F7
Stevens Point, *U.S.A.* 112 C10
Stevenson, *U.S.A.* 116 E5
Stevenson L., *Canada* 105 C9
Stevns Klint, *Denmark* . . . 11 J6
Stewart, *Canada* 104 B3
Stewart, *U.S.A.* 116 F7
Stewart, C., *Australia* 94 A1
Stewart, I., *Chile* 128 G2
Stewart I., *N.Z.* 91 M1
Stewarts Point, *U.S.A.* . . . 116 G3
Stewiacke, *Canada* 103 C7
Steynsburg, *S. Africa* 88 E4
Steyr, *Austria* 26 C7
Steyr →, *Austria* 26 C7
Steytlerville, *S. Africa* 88 E3
Stia, *Italy* 29 E8
Stigler, *U.S.A.* 113 H7
Stigliano, *Italy* 31 B9
Stigtomta, *Sweden* 11 F10
Stikine →, *Canada* 104 B2
Stilfontein, *S. Africa* 88 D4
Stilís, *Greece* 38 C4
Stillwater, *N.Z.* 91 K3
Stillwater, *Minn., U.S.A.* . 112 C8
Stillwater, *N.Y., U.S.A.* . . 111 D11
Stillwater, *Okla., U.S.A.* . . 113 G6
Stillwater Range, *U.S.A.* . . 114 G4
Stilo, Pta., *Italy* 31 D9
Stilwell, *U.S.A.* 113 H7
Štip, *Macedonia* 40 E6
Stíra, *Greece* 38 C6
Stirling, *Australia* 94 B3
Stirling, *Canada* 104 D6
Stirling, *U.K.* 14 E5
Stirling □, *U.K.* 14 E4
Stirling Ra., *Australia* 93 F2
Stittsville, *Canada* 111 A9
Stjernøya, *Norway* 8 A20
Stjørdalshalsen, *Norway* . . 8 E14
Stockach, *Germany* 25 H5
Stockaryd, *Sweden* 11 G8
Stockerau, *Austria* 27 C9
Stockett, *U.S.A.* 114 C8
Stockholm, *Sweden* 10 E12
Stockholms län □, *Sweden* 10 E12
Stockport, *U.K.* 12 D5
Stocksbridge, *U.K.* 12 D6
Stockton, *Calif., U.S.A.* . . 116 H5
Stockton, *Kans., U.S.A.* . . 112 F5
Stockton, *Mo., U.S.A.* . . . 113 G8
Stockton-on-Tees, *U.K.* . . 12 C6
Stockton-on-Tees □, *U.K.* 12 C6
Stoczek Łukowski, *Poland* 45 G8
Stöde, *Sweden* 10 B10
Stoeng Treng, *Cambodia* . 64 F5
Stoer, Pt. of, *U.K.* 14 C3
Stogovo, *Macedonia* 40 E4
Stoholm, *Denmark* 11 H3
Stoke-on-Trent, *U.K.* 12 D5
Stoke-on-Trent □, *U.K.* . . 12 D5
Stokes Bay, *Canada* 102 D3
Stokes Pt., *Australia* 94 G3
Stokes Ra., *Australia* 92 C5
Stokksnes, *Iceland* 8 D6
Stokmarknes, *Norway* 8 B16
Stolac, *Bos.-H.* 40 C1
Stolberg, *Germany* 24 E2
Stolbovoy, Ostrov, *Russia* 51 D17
Stolbtsy = Stowbtsy, *Belarus* 46 F4
Stolin, *Belarus* 47 G4
Stöllet, *Sweden* 10 D7
Stolnici, *Romania* 43 F9
Stomíon, *Greece* 36 D5
Ston, *Croatia* 29 F14
Stone, *U.K.* 12 E5
Stonehaven, *U.K.* 14 E6
Stonehenge, *Australia* 94 C3
Stonehenge, *U.K.* 13 F6
Stonewall, *Canada* 105 C9
Stony L., *Man., Canada* . . 105 B9
Stony L., *Ont., Canada* . . . 110 B6
Stony Rapids, *Canada* 105 B7
Stony Tunguska = Tunguska, Podkamennaya →, *Russia* 51 C10
Stonyford, *U.S.A.* 116 F4
Stopnica, *Poland* 45 H7
Storå, *Sweden* 10 E9
Storå →, *Denmark* 11 H2
Stora Gla, *Sweden* 10 E6
Stora Le, *Sweden* 10 E5
Stora Lulevatten, *Sweden* . 8 C18
Storavan, *Sweden* 8 D18
Stord, *Norway* 9 G11
Store Bælt, *Denmark* 11 J4
Store Creek, *Australia* 95 E4
Store Heddinge, *Denmark* 11 J6
Storebro, *Sweden* 11 G9
Storfors, *Sweden* 10 E8
Storlien, *Sweden* 10 A6
Storm B., *Australia* 94 G4
Storm Lake, *U.S.A.* 112 D7
Stormberge, *S. Africa* 88 E4
Stormsrivier, *S. Africa* 88 E3
Stornoway, *U.K.* 14 C2
Storo, *Italy* 28 C7
Storozhinets = Storozhynets, *Ukraine* . . 47 H3
Storozhynets, *Ukraine* 47 H3
Storsjön, *Gävleborg, Sweden* 10 D10
Storsjön, *Jämtland, Sweden* 10 B7
Storsjön, *Jämtland, Sweden* 10 A8
Storstrøms Amtskommune □, *Denmark* 11 J5
Storuman, *Sweden* 8 D17
Storuman, sjö, *Sweden* . . . 8 D17
Storvätteshågna, *Sweden* . . 10 B6
Storvik, *Sweden* 10 D10
Storvreta, *Sweden* 10 E11
Stoughton, *Canada* 105 D8
Stour →, *Dorset, U.K.* 13 G6
Stour →, *Kent, U.K.* 13 F9
Stour →, *Suffolk, U.K.* . . . 13 F9
Stourbridge, *U.K.* 13 E5
Stout, L., *Canada* 105 C10
Stove Pipe Wells Village, *U.S.A.* 117 J9
Støvring, *Denmark* 11 H3
Stowbtsy, *Belarus* 46 F4
Stowmarket, *U.K.* 13 E9
Strabane, *U.K.* 15 B4
Stracin, *Macedonia* 40 D6
Stradella, *Italy* 28 C6
Strahan, *Australia* 94 G4
Strajitsa, *Bulgaria* 41 C9
Strakonice, *Czech Rep.* . . . 26 B6
Straldzha, *Bulgaria* 41 D10
Stralsund, *Germany* 24 A9
Strand, *S. Africa* 88 E2
Stranda, *Møre og Romsdal, Norway* 9 E12
Stranda, *Nord-Trøndelag, Norway* 8 E14
Strandby, *Denmark* 11 G4
Strangford L., *U.K.* 15 B6
Strängnäs, *Sweden* 10 E11
Strangsville, *U.S.A.* 110 E3
Stranraer, *U.K.* 14 G3
Strasbourg, *Canada* 105 C8
Strasbourg, *France* 19 D14
Strasburg, *Germany* 24 B9
Strasburg, *U.S.A.* 112 B4
Străşeni, *Moldova* 43 C13
Stråssa, *Sweden* 10 E9
Stratford, *Canada* 102 D3
Stratford, *N.Z.* 91 H5
Stratford, *Calif., U.S.A.* . . 116 J7
Stratford, *Conn., U.S.A.* . . 111 E11
Stratford, *Tex., U.S.A.* . . . 113 G3
Stratford-upon-Avon, *U.K.* 13 E6
Strath Spey, *U.K.* 14 D5
Strathalbyn, *Australia* 95 F2
Strathaven, *U.K.* 14 F4
Strathcona Prov. Park, *Canada* 104 D3
Strathmore, *Australia* 94 B3
Strathmore, *Canada* 104 C6
Strathmore, *U.K.* 14 E5
Strathmore, *U.S.A.* 116 J7
Strathnaver, *Canada* 104 C4
Strathpeffer, *U.K.* 14 D4
Strathroy, *Canada* 102 D3
Strathy Pt., *U.K.* 14 C4
Stratton, *U.S.A.* 112 F3
Straubing, *Germany* 25 G8
Straumnes, *Iceland* 8 C2
Strausberg, *Germany* 24 C9
Strawberry Reservoir, *U.S.A.* 114 F8
Strawn, *U.S.A.* 113 J5
Strážnice, *Czech Rep.* 27 C10
Streaky B., *Australia* 95 E1
Streaky Bay, *Australia* 95 E1
Streator, *U.S.A.* 112 E10
Středočeský □, *Czech Rep.* 26 B7
Streeter, *U.S.A.* 112 B5
Streetsville, *Canada* 110 C5
Strehaia, *Romania* 43 F8
Strelcha, *Bulgaria* 41 D8
Strelka, *Russia* 51 D10
Streng →, *Cambodia* 64 F4
Stresa, *Italy* 28 C5
Streymoy, *Færoe Is.* 8 E9
Strezhevoy, *Russia* 50 C8
Stříbro, *Czech Rep.* 26 A6
Strimón →, *Greece* 40 F7
Strimonikós Kólpos, *Greece* 40 F7
Strofádhes, *Greece* 38 D3
Stroma, *U.K.* 14 C5
Strómboli, *Italy* 31 D8
Stromeferry, *U.K.* 14 D3
Stromness, *U.K.* 14 C5
Strömsbruk, *Sweden* 10 C11
Stromsburg, *U.S.A.* 112 E6
Strömsnäsbruk, *Sweden* . . . 11 H7
Strömstad, *Sweden* 11 F5
Strömsund, *Sweden* 8 E16
Strongilí, *Greece* 39 E11
Strongoli, *Italy* 31 C10
Stronie Śląskie, *Poland* 45 H3
Stronsay, *U.K.* 14 B6
Stropkov, *Slovak Rep.* 27 B14
Stroud, *U.K.* 13 F5
Stroud Road, *Australia* . . . 95 E5
Stroudsburg, *U.S.A.* 111 F9
Stroumbi, *Cyprus* 36 E11
Struer, *Denmark* 11 H2
Struga, *Macedonia* 40 E4
Strugi Krasnyye, *Russia* . . 46 C5
Strumica, *Macedonia* 40 E6
Strumica →, *Europe* 40 E7
Struthers, *Canada* 102 C2
Struthers, *U.S.A.* 110 E4
Stryama, *Bulgaria* 41 D8
Stryker, *U.S.A.* 114 B6
Stryków, *Poland* 45 G6
Stryy, *Ukraine* 47 H2
Strzegom, *Poland* 45 H3
Strzelce Krajeńskie, *Poland* 45 F2
Strzelce Opolskie, *Poland* . 45 H5
Strzelecki Cr. →, *Australia* 95 D2
Strzelin, *Poland* 45 H4
Strzelno, *Poland* 45 F5
Strzybnica, *Poland* 45 H5
Strzyżów, *Poland* 45 J8
Stuart, *Fla., U.S.A.* 109 M5
Stuart, *Nebr., U.S.A.* 112 D5
Stuart →, *Canada* 104 C4
Stuart Bluff Ra., *Australia* . 92 D5
Stuart L., *Canada* 104 C4
Stuart Ra., *Australia* 95 D1
Stubbekøbing, *Denmark* . . . 11 K6
Stuben, *Austria* 26 D3
Studen Kladenets, Yazovir, *Bulgaria* 41 E9
Studenka, *Czech Rep.* 27 B11
Stugun, *Sweden* 10 A9
Stuhr, *Germany* 24 B4
Stull, L., *Canada* 102 B1
Stung Treng = Stoeng Treng, *Cambodia* 64 F5
Stupart →, *Canada* 105 B10
Stupava, *Slovak Rep.* 27 C10
Stupino, *Russia* 46 E10
Sturgeon B., *Canada* 105 C9
Sturgeon Bay, *U.S.A.* 108 C2
Sturgeon Falls, *Canada* . . . 102 C4
Sturgeon L., *Alta., Canada* 104 B5
Sturgeon L., *Ont., Canada* 102 C1
Sturgeon L., *Ont., Canada* 110 B6
Sturgis, *Mich., U.S.A.* 108 E3
Sturgis, *S. Dak., U.S.A.* . . . 112 C3
Sturkö, *Sweden* 11 H9
Štúrovo, *Slovak Rep.* 27 D11
Sturt Cr. →, *Australia* 92 C4
Sturt Creek, *Australia* 92 C4
Stutterheim, *S. Africa* 88 E4
Stuttgart, *Germany* 25 G5
Stuttgart, *U.S.A.* 113 H9
Stuyvesant, *U.S.A.* 111 D11
Stykkishólmur, *Iceland* . . . 8 D2
Styria = Steiermark □, *Austria* 26 D8
Styrsö, *Sweden* 11 G5
Su Xian, *China* 56 H9
Suakin, *Sudan* 80 D4
Suan, *N. Korea* 57 E14
Suaqui, *Mexico* 118 B3
Subang, *Indonesia* 63 G12
Subansiri →, *India* 67 F18
Subayhah, *Si. Arabia* 70 D3
Subcetate, *Romania* 42 E8
Subi, *Indonesia* 65 L7
Subiaco, *Italy* 29 G10
Subotica, *Serbia, Yug.* 42 D4
Success, *Canada* 105 C7
Suceava, *Romania* 43 C11
Suceava □, *Romania* 43 C10
Suceava →, *Romania* 43 C11
Sucha-Beskidzka, *Poland* . . 45 J6
Suchań, *Poland* 45 E2
Suchan, *Russia* 54 C6
Suchedniów, *Poland* 45 G7
Suchitoto, *El Salv.* 120 D2
Suchou = Suzhou, *China* . . 59 B13
Süchow = Xuzhou, *China* . 57 G9
Suchowola, *Poland* 44 E10
Suck →, *Ireland* 15 C3
Sucre, *Bolivia* 124 G5
Sućuraj, *Croatia* 29 E14
Sucuriú →, *Brazil* 125 H8
Sud, Pte., *Canada* 103 C7
Sud-Ouest, Pte. du, *Canada* 103 C7
Suda →, *Russia* 46 C9
Sudak, *Ukraine* 47 K8
Sudan, *U.S.A.* 113 H3
Sudan ■, *Africa* 81 E3
Sudbury, *Canada* 102 C3
Sudbury, *U.K.* 13 E8
Sûdd, *Sudan* 81 F3
Süderbrarup, *Germany* 24 A5
Süderlügum, *Germany* 24 A4
Süderoogsand, *Germany* . . . 24 A4
Sudeten Mts. = Sudety, *Europe* 27 A9
Sudety, *Europe* 27 A9
Suðuroy, *Færoe Is.* 8 F9
Sudi, *Tanzania* 87 E4
Sudirman, Pegunungan, *Indonesia* 63 E9
Sudiţi, *Romania* 43 F12
Sudogda, *Russia* 48 C5
Sudr, *Egypt* 80 J8
Sudzha, *Russia* 47 G8
Sueca, *Spain* 33 F4
Suedinenie, *Bulgaria* 41 D8
Suez = El Suweis, *Egypt* . 80 J8
Suez, G. of = Suweis, Khalîg el, *Egypt* 80 J8
Suez Canal = Suweis, Qanâ es, *Egypt* 80 H8
Suffield, *Canada* 105 C6
Suffolk, *U.S.A.* 108 G7
Suffolk □, *U.K.* 13 E9
Şugag, *Romania* 43 E8
Sugar City, *U.S.A.* 112 F3
Suğla Gölü, *Turkey* 72 D5
Sugluk = Salluit, *Canada* . 101 B12
Suhaia, Lacul, *Romania* . . 43 G10
Şuḩār, *Oman* 71 E8
Sühbaatar, *Mongolia* 60 A5
Sühbaatar □, *Mongolia* . . . 56 B8
Suhl, *Germany* 24 E6
Şuhut, *Turkey* 39 C12
Sui Xian, *Henan, China* . . . 56 G8
Sui Xian, *Henan, China* . . . 59 B9
Šuica, *Bos.-H.* 42 G2
Suichang, *China* 59 C12
Suichuan, *China* 59 D10
Suide, *China* 56 F6
Suifenhe, *China* 57 B16
Suihua, *China* 60 B7
Suijiang, *China* 58 C4
Suining, *Hunan, China* 59 D8
Suining, *Jiangsu, China* . . . 57 H9
Suining, *Sichuan, China* . . . 58 B5
Suiping, *China* 56 H7
Suippes, *France* 19 C11
Suir →, *Ireland* 15 D4
Suixi, *China* 59 G8
Suiyang, *Guizhou, China* . . 58 D6
Suiyang, *Heilongjiang, China* 57 B16
Suizhong, *China* 57 D11
Sujangarh, *India* 68 F6
Sukabumi, *Indonesia* 63 G12
Sukadana, *Indonesia* 62 E4
Sukagawa, *Japan* 55 F10
Sukaraja, *Indonesia* 62 E4
Sukarnapura = Jayapura, *Indonesia* 63 E10
Sukchŏn, *N. Korea* 57 E13
Sukhindol, *Bulgaria* 41 C9
Sukhinichi, *Russia* 46 E8
Sukhona →, *Russia* 50 D4
Sukhothai, *Thailand* 64 D2
Sukhumi = Sokhumi, *Georgia* 49 J5
Sukkur, *Pakistan* 68 F3
Sukkur Barrage, *Pakistan* . 68 F3
Sukovo, *Serbia, Yug.* 40 C6
Sukumo, *Japan* 55 H6
Sukunka →, *Canada* 104 B4
Sula →, *Ukraine* 47 H7
Sula, Kepulauan, *Indonesia* 63 E7
Sulaco →, *Honduras* 120 C2
Sulaiman Range, *Pakistan* 68 D3
Sulak →, *Russia* 49 J8
Sūlār, *Iran* 71 D6
Sulawesi □, *Indonesia* 63 E6
Sulawesi Sea = Celebes Sea, *Indonesia* 63 D6
Sulechów, *Poland* 45 F2
Sulęcin, *Poland* 45 F2
Sulejów, *Poland* 45 G6
Sulejówek, *Poland* 45 F8
Süleymanlı, *Turkey* 39 C9
Sulima, *S. Leone* 82 D2
Sulina, *Romania* 43 E14
Sulina, Braţul →, *Romania* 43 E14
Sulingen, *Germany* 24 C4
Suliţa, *Romania* 43 C11
Sulitjelma, *Norway* 8 C17
Sułkowice, *Poland* 45 J6
Sullana, *Peru* 124 D2
Süller, *Turkey* 39 C11
Sullivan, *Ill., U.S.A.* 112 F10
Sullivan, *Ind., U.S.A.* 108 F2
Sullivan, *Mo., U.S.A.* 112 F9
Sullivan Bay, *Canada* 104 C3
Sullivan I. = Lambi Kyun, *Burma* 65 G2
Sully-sur-Loire, *France* . . . 19 E9
Sulmierzyce, *Poland* 45 G4
Sulmona, *Italy* 29 F10
Süloğlu, *Turkey* 41 E10
Sulphur, *La., U.S.A.* 113 K8
Sulphur, *Okla., U.S.A.* . . . 113 H6
Sulphur Pt., *Canada* 104 A6
Sulphur Springs, *U.S.A.* . . 113 J7
Sulphur Springs Draw →, *U.S.A.* 113 J4
Sultan, *Canada* 102 C3
Sultan, *U.S.A.* 116 C5
Sultan Dağları, *Turkey* . . . 72 C4
Sultanhisar, *Turkey* 39 D10
Sultaniça, *Turkey* 41 F10
Sultaniye, *Turkey* 41 F12
Sultanpur, *India* 69 F10
Sulu Arch., *Phil.* 61 J4
Sulu Sea, *E. Indies* 61 H4
Sülüklü, *Turkey* 72 C5
Sululta, *Ethiopia* 81 F4
Suluova, *Turkey* 72 B6
Suluq, *Libya* 79 B10
Sulzbach, *Germany* 25 F3
Sulzbach-Rosenberg, *Germany* 25 F7
Sulzberger Ice Shelf, *Antarctica* 5 D10
Sumalata, *Indonesia* 63 D6
Sumampa, *Argentina* 126 B3
Sumatera □, *Indonesia* . . . 62 D2
Sumatra = Sumatera □, *Indonesia* 62 D2
Sumatra, *U.S.A.* 114 C10
Sumba, *Indonesia* 63 F5
Sumba, Selat, *Indonesia* . . 63 F5
Sumbawa, *Indonesia* 62 F5
Sumbawa Besar, *Indonesia* 62 F5
Sumbawanga □, *Tanzania* 86 D3
Sumbe, *Angola* 84 G2
Sumburgh Hd., *U.K.* 14 B7
Sumdo, *India* 69 B8
Sumedang, *Indonesia* 63 G12
Sümeg, *Hungary* 42 D2
Šumen = Shumen, *Bulgaria* 41 C10
Sumenep, *Indonesia* 63 G15
Sumgait = Sumqayıt, *Azerbaijan* 49 K9
Summer L., *U.S.A.* 114 E3
Summerland, *Canada* 104 D5
Summerside, *Canada* 103 C7
Summerville, *Ga., U.S.A.* . 109 H3
Summerville, *S.C., U.S.A.* 109 J5
Summit Lake, *Canada* 104 C4
Summit Peak, *U.S.A.* 115 H10
Sumner, *Iowa, U.S.A.* 112 D8
Sumner, *Wash., U.S.A.* . . . 116 C4
Sumoto, *Japan* 55 G7
Šumperk, *Czech Rep.* 27 B9
Sumqayıt, *Azerbaijan* 49 K9
Sumter, *U.S.A.* 109 J5
Sumy, *Ukraine* 47 G8
Sun City, *Ariz., U.S.A.* . . . 115 K7
Sun City, *Calif., U.S.A.* . . 117 M9
Sunagawa, *Japan* 54 C10
Sunan, *N. Korea* 57 E13
Sunart, L., *U.K.* 14 E3
Sunburst, *U.S.A.* 114 B8
Sunbury, *Australia* 95 F3
Sunbury, *U.S.A.* 111 F8
Sunchales, *Argentina* 126 C3
Suncho Corral, *Argentina* . 126 B3
Sunchon, *S. Korea* 57 G14
Suncook, *U.S.A.* 111 C13
Sunda, Selat, *Indonesia* . . . 62 F3
Sunda Is., *Indonesia* 96 H2
Sunda Str. = Sunda, Selat, *Indonesia* 62 F3
Sundance, *U.S.A.* 112 C2
Sundarbans, The, *Asia* . . . 67 J16
Sundargarh, *India* 67 H14
Sundays = Sondags →, *S. Africa* 88 E4
Sunderland, *Canada* 110 B5
Sunderland, *U.K.* 12 C6
Sundre, *Canada* 104 C6
Sundridge, *Canada* 102 C4
Sunds, *Denmark* 11 H3
Sundsvall, *Sweden* 10 B11
Sundsvallsbukten, *Sweden* 10 B11
Sung Hei, *Vietnam* 65 G6
Sungai Kolok, *Thailand* . . 65 J3
Sungai Lembing, *Malaysia* 65 L4
Sungai Petani, *Malaysia* . . 65 K3
Sungaigerong, *Indonesia* . . 62 E2
Sungailiat, *Indonesia* 62 E3
Sungaipenuh, *Indonesia* . . 62 E2
Sungari = Songhua Jiang →, *China* 60 B8
Sunghua Chiang = Songhua Jiang →, *China* 60 B8
Sungikai, *Sudan* 81 E2
Sungurlu, *Turkey* 72 B6
Sunja, *Croatia* 29 C13
Sunnansjö, *Sweden* 10 D8
Sunndalsøra, *Norway* 9 E13
Sunne, *Sweden* 10 E7
Sunnemo, *Sweden* 10 E7
Sunnyside, *Utah, U.S.A.* . . 114 G8
Sunnyside, *Wash., U.S.A.* . 114 C3
Sunnyvale, *U.S.A.* 116 H4
Sunray, *U.S.A.* 113 G4
Suntar, *Russia* 51 C12
Sunyani, *Ghana* 82 D4
Suomenselkä, *Finland* 8 E21
Suomussalmi, *Finland* 8 D23
Suoyarvi, *Russia* 46 A7
Supai, *U.S.A.* 115 H7
Supaul, *India* 69 F12
Superior, *Ariz., U.S.A.* . . . 115 K8
Superior, *Mont., U.S.A.* . . 114 C6
Superior, *Nebr., U.S.A.* . . 112 E5
Superior, *Wis., U.S.A.* . . . 112 B8
Superior, L., *U.S.A.* 102 C2
Supetar, *Croatia* 29 E13
Suphan Buri, *Thailand* . . . 64 E3
Suphan Dağı, *Turkey* 73 C10
Supiori, *Indonesia* 63 E9
Supraśl, *Poland* 45 E10
Supraśl →, *Poland* 45 E9
Supung Shuiku, *China* 57 D13
Sūq Suwayq, *Si. Arabia* . . 70 E3
Suqian, *China* 57 H10
Sūr, *Lebanon* 75 B4
Sur, Pt., *U.S.A.* 116 J5
Sura →, *Russia* 48 C8
Surab, *Pakistan* 68 E2
Surabaja = Surabaya, *Indonesia* 63 G15
Surabaya, *Indonesia* 63 G15
Surahammar, *Sweden* 10 E10
Suraia, *Romania* 43 E12
Surakarta, *Indonesia* 63 G14
Surakhany, *Azerbaijan* . . . 49 K10
Šurany, *Slovak Rep.* 27 C11
Surat, *Australia* 95 D4
Surat, *India* 66 J8
Surat Thani, *Thailand* 65 H2
Suratgarh, *India* 68 E5

Suraż, *Poland* 45 F9
Surazh, *Belarus* 46 E6
Surazh, *Russia* 47 F7
Surduc, *Romania* 43 C8
Surduc Pasul, *Romania* 43 E8
Surdulica, *Serbia, Yug.* 40 D6
Surendranagar, *India* 68 H4
Surf, *U.S.A.* 117 L6
Surgères, *France* 20 B3
Surgut, *Russia* 50 C8
Sùria, *Spain* 32 D6
Suriapet, *India* 66 L11
Surigao, *Phil.* 61 G6
Surigao Strait, *Phil.* 61 F6
Surin, *Thailand* 64 E4
Surin Nua, Ko, *Thailand* 65 H1
Surinam ■, *S. Amer.* 125 C7
Suriname = Surinam ■, *S. Amer.* 125 C7
Suriname →, *Surinam* 125 B7
Sūrmaq, *Iran* 71 D7
Sürmene, *Turkey* 73 B9
Surovikino, *Russia* 49 F6
Surprise L., *Canada* 104 B2
Surrey □, *U.K.* 13 F7
Sursee, *Switz.* 25 H4
Sursk, *Russia* 48 D7
Surskoye, *Russia* 48 C8
Surt, *Libya* 79 B9
Surt, Khalīj, *Libya* 79 B9
Surte, *Sweden* 11 G6
Surtsey, *Iceland* 8 E3
Sürüç, *Turkey* 73 D8
Suruga-Wan, *Japan* 55 G9
Susa, *Italy* 28 C4
Suså →, *Denmark* 11 J5
Sušac, *Croatia* 29 F13
Susak, *Croatia* 29 D11
Susaki, *Japan* 55 H6
Sūsangerd, *Iran* 71 D6
Susanville, *U.S.A.* 114 F3
Susch, *Switz.* 25 J6
Suşehri, *Turkey* 73 B8
Sušice, *Czech Rep.* 26 B6
Susleni, *Moldova* 43 C13
Susong, *China* 59 B11
Susquehanna →, *U.S.A.* 111 G8
Susquehanna Depot, *U.S.A.* 111 E9
Susques, *Argentina* 126 A2
Sussex, *Canada* 103 C6
Sussex, *U.S.A.* 111 E10
Sussex, E. □, *U.K.* 13 G8
Sussex, W. □, *U.K.* 13 G7
Sustut →, *Canada* 104 B3
Susuman, *Russia* 51 C15
Susunu, *Indonesia* 63 E8
Susurluk, *Turkey* 39 B10
Susuz, *Turkey* 73 B10
Susz, *Poland* 44 E6
Sütçüler, *Turkey* 72 D4
Şuţeşti, *Romania* 43 E12
Sutherland, *S. Africa* 88 E3
Sutherland, *U.S.A.* 112 E4
Sutherland Falls, *N.Z.* 91 L1
Sutherlin, *U.S.A.* 114 E2
Sutlej →, *Pakistan* 68 E4
Sutter, *U.S.A.* 116 F5
Sutter Creek, *U.S.A.* 116 G6
Sutton, *Canada* 111 A12
Sutton, *U.S.A.* 112 E6
Sutton →, *Canada* 102 A3
Sutton Coldfield, *U.K.* 13 E6
Sutton in Ashfield, *U.K.* 12 D6
Suttor →, *Australia* 94 C4
Suttsu, *Japan* 54 C10
Suva, *Fiji* 91 D8
Suva Gora, *Macedonia* 40 E5
Suva Planina, *Serbia, Yug.* 40 C6
Suva Reka, *Serbia, Yug.* 40 D4
Suvorov, *Russia* 46 E9
Suvorov Is. = Suwarrow Is., *Cook Is.* 97 J11
Suvorovo, *Bulgaria* 41 C11
Suwałki, *Poland* 44 D9
Suwałki □, *Poland* 44 E9
Suwannaphum, *Thailand* 64 E4
Suwannee →, *U.S.A.* 109 L4
Suwanose-Jima, *Japan* 55 K4
Suwarrow Is., *Cook Is.* 97 J11
Suwayq aş Şuqban, *Iraq* 70 D5
Suweis, Khalîg el, *Egypt* 80 J8
Suweis, Qanâ es, *Egypt* 80 H8
Suwŏn, *S. Korea* 57 F14
Suzdal, *Russia* 46 D11
Suzhou, *China* 59 B13
Suzu, *Japan* 55 F8
Suzu-Misaki, *Japan* 55 F8
Suzuka, *Japan* 55 G8
Suzzara, *Italy* 28 D7
Svalbard, *Arctic* 4 B8
Svalöv, *Sweden* 11 J7
Svaneke, *Denmark* 11 J9
Svängsta, *Sweden* 11 H8
Svanskog, *Sweden* 10 E6
Svappavaara, *Sweden* 8 C19
Svärdsjö, *Sweden* 10 D9
Svartå, *Sweden* 10 E8
Svartisen, *Norway* 8 C15
Svartvik, *Sweden* 10 B11
Svatove, *Ukraine* 47 H10
Svatovo = Svatove, *Ukraine* 47 H10
Svay Chek, *Cambodia* 64 F4
Svay Rieng, *Cambodia* 65 G5
Svealand □, *Sweden* 10 D9
Svedala, *Sweden* 11 J7
Sveg, *Sweden* 10 B8
Svendborg, *Denmark* 11 J4
Svenljunga, *Sweden* 11 G7
Svenstavik, *Sweden* 10 B8
Svenstrup, *Denmark* 11 H3
Sverdlovsk = Yekaterinburg, *Russia* 50 D7
Sverdlovsk, *Ukraine* 47 H10
Sverdrup Is., *Canada* 4 B3
Svetac, *Croatia* 29 E12
Sveti Nikola, Prokhad, *Europe* 40 C6
Sveti Nikole, *Macedonia* 40 E5
Sveti Rok, *Croatia* 29 D12
Svetlaya, *Russia* 54 A9
Svetlogorsk = Svyetlahorsk, *Belarus* 47 F5
Svetlograd, *Russia* 49 H6
Svetlovodsk = Svitlovodsk, *Ukraine* 47 H7
Svidník, *Slovak Rep.* 27 B14
Svilaja Planina, *Croatia* 29 E13
Svilajnac, *Serbia, Yug.* 40 B5
Svilengrad, *Bulgaria* 41 E10
Svir →, *Russia* 46 B7
Sviritsa, *Russia* 46 B7
Svishtov, *Bulgaria* 41 C9
Svislach, *Belarus* 47 F3
Svitava →, *Czech Rep.* 27 B9
Svitavy, *Czech Rep.* 27 B9
Svitlovodsk, *Ukraine* 47 H7
Svobodnyy, *Russia* 51 D13
Svoge, *Bulgaria* 40 D7
Svolvær, *Norway* 8 B16
Svratka →, *Czech Rep.* 27 B9
Svrljig, *Serbia, Yug.* 40 C6
Svyetlahorsk, *Belarus* 47 F5
Swabian Alps = Schwäbische Alb, *Germany* 25 G5
Swainsboro, *U.S.A.* 109 J4
Swakopmund, *Namibia* 88 C1
Swale →, *U.K.* 12 C6
Swan Hill, *Australia* 95 F3
Swan Hills, *Canada* 104 C5
Swan Is., *W. Indies* 120 C3
Swan L., *Canada* 105 C8
Swan River, *Canada* 105 C8
Swanage, *U.K.* 13 G6
Swansea, *Australia* 95 E5
Swansea, *U.K.* 13 F4
Swansea □, *U.K.* 13 F3
Swar →, *Pakistan* 69 B5
Swartberge, *S. Africa* 88 E3
Swartmodder, *S. Africa* 88 D3
Swartruggens, *S. Africa* 88 D4
Swarzędz, *Poland* 45 F4
Swastika, *Canada* 102 C3
Swatow = Shantou, *China* 59 F11
Swaziland ■, *Africa* 89 D5
Sweden ■, *Europe* 9 G16
Swedru, *Ghana* 83 D4
Sweet Home, *U.S.A.* 114 D2
Sweetwater, *Nev., U.S.A.* 116 G7
Sweetwater, *Tex., U.S.A.* 113 J4
Sweetwater →, *U.S.A.* 114 E10
Swellendam, *S. Africa* 88 E3
Swider →, *Poland* 45 F8
Świdnica, *Poland* 45 H3
Świdnik, *Poland* 45 G9
Świdwin, *Poland* 44 E2
Świebodzice, *Poland* 45 H3
Świebodzin, *Poland* 45 F2
Świecie, *Poland* 44 E5
Świerzawa, *Poland* 45 G2
Świętokrzyskie, Góry, *Poland* 45 H7
Swift Current, *Canada* 105 C7
Swiftcurrent →, *Canada* 105 C7
Swilly, L., *Ireland* 15 A4
Swindle, I., *Canada* 104 C3
Swindon, *U.K.* 13 F6
Swindon □, *U.K.* 13 F6
Swinemünde = Świnoujście, *Poland* 44 E1
Swinford, *Ireland* 15 C3
Świnoujście, *Poland* 44 E1
Switzerland ■, *Europe* 25 J4
Swords, *Ireland* 15 C5
Syasstroy, *Russia* 46 B7
Sychevka, *Russia* 46 E8
Syców, *Poland* 45 G4
Sydney, *Australia* 95 E5
Sydney, *Canada* 103 C7
Sydney Mines, *Canada* 103 C7
Sydprøven, *Greenland* 4 C5
Sydra, G. of = Surt, Khalīj, *Libya* 79 B9
Syeverodonetsk, *Ukraine* 47 H10
Syke, *Germany* 24 C4
Syktyvkar, *Russia* 50 C6
Sylacauga, *U.S.A.* 109 J2
Sylarna, *Sweden* 8 E15
Sylhet, *Bangla.* 67 G17
Sylt, *Germany* 24 A4
Sylvan Lake, *Canada* 104 C6
Sylvania, *U.S.A.* 109 J5
Sylvester, *U.S.A.* 109 K4
Sym, *Russia* 50 C9
Symón, *Mexico* 118 C4
Synelnykove, *Ukraine* 47 H8
Synnott Ra., *Australia* 92 C4
Syracuse, *Kans., U.S.A.* 113 G4
Syracuse, *N.Y., U.S.A.* 111 C8
Syrdarya →, *Kazakstan* 50 E7
Syria ■, *Asia* 70 C3
Syrian Desert = Ash Shām, Bādiyat, *Asia* 52 F7
Sysslebäck, *Sweden* 10 D6
Syzran, *Russia* 48 D9
Szabolcs-Szatmár-Bereg □, *Hungary* 42 B6
Szadek, *Poland* 45 G5
Szamocin, *Poland* 45 E4
Szamos →, *Hungary* 42 B7
Szamotuły, *Poland* 45 F3
Száraz →, *Hungary* 42 D6
Szarvas, *Hungary* 42 D5
Százhalombatta, *Hungary* 42 C3
Szczawnica, *Poland* 45 J7
Szczebrzeszyn, *Poland* 45 H9
Szczecin, *Poland* 44 E1
Szczecin □, *Poland* 44 E1
Szczecinek, *Poland* 44 E3
Szczeciński, Zalew = Stettiner Haff, *Germany* 24 B10
Szczekociny, *Poland* 45 H6
Szczucin, *Poland* 45 H8
Szczuczyn, *Poland* 44 E9
Szczyrk, *Poland* 45 J6
Szczytna, *Poland* 45 H3
Szczytno, *Poland* 44 E7
Szechwan = Sichuan □, *China* 58 B5
Szécsény, *Hungary* 42 B4
Szeged, *Hungary* 42 D5
Szeghalom, *Hungary* 42 C6
Székesfehérvár, *Hungary* 42 C3
Szekszárd, *Hungary* 42 D3
Szendrő, *Hungary* 42 B5
Szentendre, *Hungary* 42 C4
Szentes, *Hungary* 42 D5
Szentgotthárd, *Hungary* 42 D1
Szentlőrinc, *Hungary* 42 D3
Szerencs, *Hungary* 42 B6
Szigetszentmiklós, *Hungary* 42 C4
Szigetvár, *Hungary* 42 D2
Szikszó, *Hungary* 42 B5
Szklarska Poreba, *Poland* 45 H2
Szkwa →, *Poland* 45 E8
Szlichtyngowa, *Poland* 45 G3
Szob, *Hungary* 42 C3
Szolnok, *Hungary* 42 C5
Szombathely, *Hungary* 42 C1
Szprotawa, *Poland* 45 G2
Sztum, *Poland* 44 E6
Sztutowo, *Poland* 44 D6
Szubin, *Poland* 45 E4
Szydłowiec, *Poland* 45 G7
Szypliszki, *Poland* 44 D10

T

Ta Khli Khok, *Thailand* 64 E3
Ta Lai, *Vietnam* 65 G6
Tab, *Hungary* 42 D3
Tabacal, *Argentina* 126 A3
Tabaco, *Phil.* 61 E5
Tabagné, *Ivory C.* 82 D4
Ţābah, *Si. Arabia* 70 E4
Ţabas, *Khorāsān, Iran* 71 C9
Ţabas, *Khorāsān, Iran* 71 C8
Tabasará, Serranía de, *Panama* 120 E3
Tabasco □, *Mexico* 119 D6
Tabatinga, Serra da, *Brazil* 125 F10
Tabāzīn, *Iran* 71 D8
Taber, *Canada* 104 D6
Taberg, *Sweden* 11 G8
Tablas, *Phil.* 61 E5
Tablas Strait, *Phil.* 61 E4
Table B. = Tafelbaai, *S. Africa* 88 E2
Table B., *Canada* 103 B8
Table Mt., *S. Africa* 88 E2
Tableland, *Australia* 92 C4
Tabletop, Mt., *Australia* 94 C4
Tábor, *Czech Rep.* 26 B7
Tabora, *Tanzania* 86 D3
Tabora □, *Tanzania* 86 D3
Tabou, *Ivory C.* 82 E3
Tabrīz, *Iran* 70 B5
Tabuaeran, *Pac. Oc.* 97 G12
Tabuelan, *Phil.* 61 F5
Tabuenca, *Spain* 32 D3
Tabūk, *Si. Arabia* 70 D3
Täby, *Sweden* 10 E12
Tacámbaro de Codallos, *Mexico* 118 D4
Tacheng, *China* 60 B3
Tachia, *Taiwan* 59 E13
Tach'ing Shan = Daqing Shan, *China* 56 D6
Tachov, *Czech Rep.* 26 B5
Tácina →, *Italy* 31 D9
Tacloban, *Phil.* 61 F6
Tacna, *Peru* 124 G4
Tacoma, *U.S.A.* 116 C4
Tacuarembó, *Uruguay* 127 C4
Tademaït, Plateau du, *Algeria* 78 C6
Tadjoura, *Djibouti* 81 E5
Tadjoura, Golfe de, *Djibouti* 81 E5
Tadmor, *N.Z.* 91 J4
Tadoule, L., *Canada* 105 B9
Tadoussac, *Canada* 103 C6
Tadzhikistan = Tajikistan ■, *Asia* 50 F8
Taechŏn-ni, *S. Korea* 57 F14
Taegu, *S. Korea* 57 G15
Taegwan, *N. Korea* 57 D13
Taejŏn, *S. Korea* 57 F14
Tafalla, *Spain* 32 C3
Tafar, *Sudan* 81 F2
Tafelbaai, *S. Africa* 88 E2
Tafermaar, *Indonesia* 63 F8
Tafí Viejo, *Argentina* 126 B2
Tafīhān, *Iran* 71 D7
Tafiré, *Ivory C.* 82 D3
Taft, *Iran* 71 D7
Taft, *Phil.* 61 F6
Taft, *Calif., U.S.A.* 117 K7
Taft, *Tex., U.S.A.* 113 M6
Taga Dzong, *Bhutan* 67 F16
Taganrog, *Russia* 47 J10
Taganrogskiy Zaliv, *Russia* 47 J10
Tagânt, *Mauritania* 82 B2
Tagatay, *Phil.* 61 D4
Tagbilaran, *Phil.* 61 G5
Tággia, *Italy* 28 E4
Tagish, *Canada* 104 A2
Tagish L., *Canada* 104 A2
Tagliacozzo, *Italy* 29 F10
Tagliamento →, *Italy* 29 C10
Táglio di Po, *Italy* 29 D9
Tago, *Phil.* 61 G7
Tagomago, *Spain* 37 B8
Taguatinga, *Brazil* 125 F10
Tagudin, *Phil.* 61 C4
Tagum, *Phil.* 61 H6
Tagus = Tejo →, *Europe* 35 F2
Tahakopa, *N.Z.* 91 M2
Tahan, Gunong, *Malaysia* 65 K4
Tahat, *Algeria* 78 D7
Tāherī, *Iran* 71 E7
Tahiti, *Pac. Oc.* 97 J13
Tahoe, L., *U.S.A.* 116 G6
Tahoe City, *U.S.A.* 116 F6
Taholah, *U.S.A.* 116 C2
Tahoua, *Niger* 83 C6
Tahta, *Egypt* 80 B3
Tahtaköprü, *Turkey* 41 G13
Tahtalı Dağları, *Turkey* 72 C7
Tahulandang, *Indonesia* 63 D7
Tahuna, *Indonesia* 63 D7
Taï, *Ivory C.* 82 D3
Tai Hu, *China* 60 C7
Tai Shan, *China* 57 F9
Tai Xian, *China* 59 A13
Tai'an, *China* 57 F9
Taibei = T'aipei, *Taiwan* 59 E13
Taibique, *Canary Is.* 37 G2
Taibus Qi, *China* 56 D8
T'aichung, *Taiwan* 59 E13
Taieri →, *N.Z.* 91 M3
Taigu, *China* 56 F7
Taihang Shan, *China* 56 G7
Taihape, *N.Z.* 91 H5
Taihe, *Anhui, China* 56 H8
Taihe, *Jiangxi, China* 59 D10
Taihu, *China* 59 B11
Taijiang, *China* 58 D7
Taikang, *China* 56 G8
Tailem Bend, *Australia* 95 F2
Tailfingen, *Germany* 25 G5
Taimyr Peninsula = Taymyr, Poluostrov, *Russia* 51 B11
Tain, *U.K.* 14 D4
T'ainan, *Taiwan* 59 F13
Taínaron, Ákra, *Greece* 38 E4
Taining, *China* 59 D11
T'aipei, *Taiwan* 59 E13
Taiping, *China* 59 B12
Taiping, *Malaysia* 65 K3
Taipingzhen, *China* 56 H6
Tairbeart = Tarbert, *U.K.* 14 D2
Taishan, *China* 59 F9
Taishun, *China* 59 D12
Taita □, *Kenya* 86 C4
Taita Hills, *Kenya* 86 C4
Taitao, Pen. de, *Chile* 122 H3
T'aitung, *Taiwan* 59 F13
Taivalkoski, *Finland* 8 D23
Taiwan ■, *Asia* 59 F13
Taixing, *China* 59 A13
Taïyetos Óros, *Greece* 38 D4
Taiyiba, *Israel* 75 C4
Taiyuan, *China* 56 F7
Taizhong = T'aichung, *Taiwan* 59 E13
Taizhou, *China* 59 A12
Taizhou Liedao, *China* 59 C13
Ta'izz, *Yemen* 74 E3
Tājābād, *Iran* 71 D7
Tajikistan ■, *Asia* 50 F8
Tajima, *Japan* 55 F9
Tajo = Tejo →, *Europe* 35 F2
Tajrīsh, *Iran* 71 C6
Tak, *Thailand* 64 D2
Takāb, *Iran* 70 B5
Takachiho, *Japan* 55 H5
Takada, *Japan* 55 F9
Takahagi, *Japan* 55 F10
Takaka, *N.Z.* 91 J4
Takamatsu, *Japan* 55 G7
Takaoka, *Japan* 55 F8
Takapuna, *N.Z.* 91 G5
Takasaki, *Japan* 55 F9
Takatsuki, *Japan* 55 G7
Takaungu, *Kenya* 86 C4
Takayama, *Japan* 55 F8
Take-Shima, *Japan* 55 J5
Takefu, *Japan* 55 G8
Takengon, *Indonesia* 62 D1
Takeo, *Japan* 55 H5
Tåkern, *Sweden* 11 F8
Tākestān, *Iran* 71 C6
Taketa, *Japan* 55 H5
Takev, *Cambodia* 65 G5
Takh, *India* 69 C7
Takikawa, *Japan* 54 C10
Takla L., *Canada* 104 B3
Takla Landing, *Canada* 104 B3
Takla Makan = Taklamakan Shamo, *China* 52 F12
Taklamakan Shamo, *China* 52 F12
Taku →, *Canada* 104 B2
Takum, *Nigeria* 83 D6
Tal Halāl, *Iran* 71 D7
Tala, *Uruguay* 127 C4
Talachyn, *Belarus* 46 E5
Talacogan, *Phil.* 61 G6
Talagante, *Chile* 126 C1
Talak, *Niger* 83 B6
Talamanca, Cordillera de, *Cent. Amer.* 120 E3
Talant, *France* 19 E11
Talara, *Peru* 124 D2
Talas, *Kyrgyzstan* 50 E8
Talas, *Turkey* 72 C6
Talâta, *Egypt* 75 E1
Talata Mafara, *Nigeria* 83 C6
Talaud, Kepulauan, *Indonesia* 63 D7
Talaud Is. = Talaud, Kepulauan, *Indonesia* 63 D7
Talavera de la Reina, *Spain* 34 F6
Talavera la Real, *Spain* 35 G4
Talawana, *Australia* 92 D3
Talayan, *Phil.* 61 H6
Talayuela, *Spain* 34 F5
Talbert, Sillon de, *France* 18 D3
Talbot, C., *Australia* 92 B4
Talbragar →, *Australia* 95 E4
Talca, *Chile* 126 D1
Talca □, *Chile* 126 D1
Talcahuano, *Chile* 126 D1
Talcher, *India* 67 J14
Talcho, *Niger* 83 C5
Taldy Kurgan = Taldyqorghan, *Kazakstan* 50 E8
Taldyqorghan, *Kazakstan* 50 E8
Tālesh, *Iran* 71 B6
Ţalesh, Kūhhā-ye, *Iran* 71 B6
Talguharai, *Sudan* 80 D4
Tali Post, *Sudan* 81 F3
Talibon, *Phil.* 63 B6
Talibong, Ko, *Thailand* 65 J2
Talihina, *U.S.A.* 113 H7
Talisayan, *Phil.* 61 G6
Taliwang, *Indonesia* 62 F5
Tall 'Afar, *Iraq* 73 D10
Tall Kalakh, *Syria* 75 A5
Talla, *Egypt* 80 J7
Talladega, *U.S.A.* 109 J2
Tallahassee, *U.S.A.* 109 K3
Tallangatta, *Australia* 95 F4
Tallard, *France* 21 D10
Tallarook, *Australia* 95 F4
Tällberg, *Sweden* 10 D9
Tallering Pk., *Australia* 93 E2
Tallinn, *Estonia* 9 G21
Tallulah, *U.S.A.* 113 J9
Tălmaciu, *Romania* 43 E9
Talmont-St-Hilaire, *France* 20 B2
Talne, *Ukraine* 47 H6
Talnoye = Talne, *Ukraine* 47 H6
Talodi, *Sudan* 81 E3
Talovaya, *Russia* 48 E5
Taloyoak, *Canada* 100 B10
Talpa de Allende, *Mexico* 118 C4
Talsi, *Latvia* 9 H20
Talsi □, *Latvia* 44 A9
Taltal, *Chile* 126 B1
Taltson →, *Canada* 104 A6
Talwood, *Australia* 95 D4
Talyawalka Cr. →, *Australia* 95 E3
Tam Chau, *Vietnam* 65 G5
Tam Ky, *Vietnam* 64 E7
Tam Quan, *Vietnam* 64 E7
Tama, *U.S.A.* 112 E8
Tamala, *Australia* 93 E1
Tamale, *Ghana* 83 D4
Taman, *Russia* 47 K9
Tamano, *Japan* 55 G6
Tamanrasset, *Algeria* 78 D7
Tamaqua, *U.S.A.* 111 F9
Tamar →, *U.K.* 13 G3
Tamarang, *Australia* 95 E5
Tamarinda, *Spain* 37 B10
Tamarite de Litera, *Spain* 32 D5
Tamashima, *Japan* 55 G6
Tamási, *Hungary* 42 D3
Tamaské, *Niger* 83 C6
Tamaulipas □, *Mexico* 119 C5
Tamaulipas, Sierra de, *Mexico* 119 C5
Tamazula, *Mexico* 118 C3
Tamazunchale, *Mexico* 119 C5
Tamba-Dabatou, *Guinea* 82 C2
Tambacounda, *Senegal* 82 C2
Tambelan, Kepulauan, *Indonesia* 62 D3
Tambellup, *Australia* 93 F2
Tambo, *Australia* 94 C4
Tambo de Mora, *Peru* 124 F3
Tambohorano, *Madag.* 89 B7

Tambora, *Indonesia* 62 F5
Tambov, *Russia* 48 D5
Tambre →, *Spain* 34 C2
Tambuku, *Indonesia* 63 G15
Tamburâ, *Sudan* 81 F2
Tâmchekket, *Mauritania* 82 B2
Tâmega →, *Portugal* 34 D2
Tamenglong, *India* 67 G18
Tamiahua, L. de, *Mexico* 119 C5
Tamil Nadu □, *India* 66 P10
Tamis →, *Serbia, Yug.* 42 F5
Tamluk, *India* 69 H12
Tammerfors = Tampere, *Finland* 9 F20
Tammisaari, *Finland* 9 F20
Tämnaren, *Sweden* 10 D11
Tamo Abu, Pegunungan, *Malaysia* 62 D5
Tampa, *U.S.A.* 109 M4
Tampa B., *U.S.A.* 109 M4
Tampere, *Finland* 9 F20
Tampico, *Mexico* 119 C5
Tampin, *Malaysia* 65 L4
Tamsagbulag, *Mongolia* 60 B6
Tamsweg, *Austria* 26 D6
Tamu, *Burma* 67 G19
Tamuja →, *Spain* 35 F4
Tamworth, *Australia* 95 E5
Tamworth, *U.K.* 13 E6
Tamyang, *S. Korea* 57 G14
Tan An, *Vietnam* 65 G6
Tana →, *Kenya* 86 C5
Tana →, *Norway* 8 A23
Tana, L., *Ethiopia* 81 E4
Tana River, *Kenya* 86 C4
Tanabe, *Japan* 55 H7
Tanafjorden, *Norway* 8 A23
Tanaga, Pta., *Canary Is.* 37 G1
Tanahbala, *Indonesia* 62 E1
Tanahgrogot, *Indonesia* 62 E5
Tanahjampea, *Indonesia* 63 F6
Tanahmasa, *Indonesia* 62 E1
Tanahmerah, *Indonesia* 63 F10
Tanakura, *Japan* 55 F10
Tanami, *Australia* 92 C4
Tanami Desert, *Australia* 92 C5
Tanana →, *U.S.A.* 100 B4
Tananarive = Antananarivo, *Madag.* 89 B8
Tánaro →, *Italy* 28 D5
Tanbar, *Australia* 94 D3
Tancheng, *China* 57 G10
Tanchŏn, *N. Korea* 57 D15
Tanda, *Ut. P., India* 69 F10
Tanda, *Ut. P., India* 69 E8
Tanda, *Ivory C.* 82 D4
Tandag, *Phil.* 61 G7
Tandaia, *Tanzania* 87 D3
Tăndărei, *Romania* 43 F12
Tandaué, *Angola* 88 B2
Tandil, *Argentina* 126 D4
Tandil, Sa. del, *Argentina* 126 D4
Tandlianwala, *Pakistan* 68 D5
Tando Adam, *Pakistan* 68 G3
Tandou L., *Australia* 95 E3
Tandragee, *U.K.* 15 B5
Tandsjöborg, *Sweden* 10 C8
Tane-ga-Shima, *Japan* 55 J5
Taneatua, *N.Z.* 91 H6
Tanen Tong Dan, *Burma* 67 L21
Tanew →, *Poland* 45 H9
Tanezrouft, *Algeria* 78 D6
Tang, Koh, *Cambodia* 65 G4
Tang Krasang, *Cambodia* 64 F5
Tanga, *Tanzania* 86 D4
Tanga □, *Tanzania* 86 D4
Tanganyika, L., *Africa* 86 D3
Tanger = Tangier, *Morocco* 78 A4
Tangerang, *Indonesia* 63 G12
Tangerhütte, *Germany* 24 C7
Tangermünde, *Germany* 24 C7
Tanggu, *China* 57 E9
Tanggula Shan, *China* 60 C4
Tanghe, *China* 56 H7
Tangier, *Morocco* 78 A4
Tangorin P.O., *Australia* 94 C3
Tangshan, *China* 57 E10
Tangtou, *China* 57 G10
Tanguiéta, *Benin* 83 C5
Tangxi, *China* 59 C12
Tangyan He →, *China* 58 C7
Tanimbar, Kepulauan, *Indonesia* 63 F8
Tanimbar Is. = Tanimbar, Kepulauan, *Indonesia* 63 F8
Taninthari, *Burma* 65 F2
Tanjay, *Phil.* 61 G5
Tanjong Malim, *Malaysia* 65 L3
Tanjore = Thanjavur, *India* 66 P11
Tanjung, *Indonesia* 62 E5
Tanjungbalai, *Indonesia* 62 D1
Tanjungbatu, *Indonesia* 62 D5
Tanjungkarang Telukbetung, *Indonesia* 62 F3
Tanjungpandan, *Indonesia* 62 E3
Tanjungpinang, *Indonesia* 62 D2
Tanjungredeb, *Indonesia* 62 D5
Tanjungselor, *Indonesia* 62 D5
Tank, *Pakistan* 68 C4
Tännäs, *Sweden* 10 B6
Tannis Bugt, *Denmark* 11 G4
Tannu-Ola, *Russia* 51 D10
Tano →, *Ghana* 82 D4
Tanon Str., *Phil.* 61 F5
Tanout, *Niger* 83 C6
Tanshui, *Taiwan* 59 E13
Tanta, *Egypt* 80 H7
Tantoyuca, *Mexico* 119 C5
Tantung = Dandong, *China* 57 D13
Tanumshede, *Sweden* 11 F5
Tanunda, *Australia* 95 E2
Tanus, *France* 20 D6
Tanzania ■, *Africa* 86 D3
Tanzilla →, *Canada* 104 B2
Tao, Ko, *Thailand* 65 G2
Tao'an, *China* 57 B12
Tao'er He →, *China* 57 B13
Taohua Dao, *China* 59 C14
Taolanaro, *Madag.* 89 D8
Taole, *China* 56 E4
Taormina, *Italy* 31 E8
Taos, *U.S.A.* 115 H11
Taoudenni, *Mali* 78 D5
Taoyuan, *China* 59 C8
T'aoyüan, *Taiwan* 59 E13
Tapa, *Estonia* 9 G21
Tapa Shan = Daba Shan, *China* 58 B7
Tapachula, *Mexico* 119 E6
Tapah, *Malaysia* 65 K3
Tapajós →, *Brazil* 122 D5
Tapaktuan, *Indonesia* 62 D1
Tapanahoni →, *Surinam* 125 C8
Tapanui, *N.Z.* 91 L2
Tapauá →, *Brazil* 124 E6
Tapeta, *Liberia* 82 D3
Taphan Hin, *Thailand* 64 D3
Tapi →, *India* 66 J8
Tapia de Casariego, *Spain* 34 B4
Tapirapecó, Serra, *Venezuela* 124 C6
Tapolca, *Hungary* 42 D2
Tappahannock, *U.S.A.* 108 G7
Tapuaenuku, Mt., *N.Z.* 91 K4
Tapul Group, *Phil.* 61 J4
Tapurucuará, *Brazil* 124 D5
Taqīābād, *Iran* 71 C8
Țaqṭaq, *Iraq* 70 C5
Taquara, *Brazil* 127 B5
Taquari →, *Brazil* 124 G7
Tara, *Australia* 95 D5
Tara, *Canada* 110 B3
Tara, *Russia* 50 D8
Tara, *Zambia* 87 F2
Tara →, *Montenegro, Yug.* 40 C2
Taraba □, *Nigeria* 83 D7
Tarabagatay, Khrebet, *Kazakstan* 50 E9
Tarābulus, *Lebanon* 75 A4
Tarābulus, *Libya* 79 B8
Taraclia, *Moldova* 43 D14
Taraclia, *Moldova* 43 E13
Tarajalejo, *Canary Is.* 37 F5
Tarakan, *Indonesia* 62 D5
Tarakit, Mt., *Kenya* 86 B4
Taralga, *Australia* 95 E4
Tarama-Jima, *Japan* 55 M2
Taran, Mys, *Russia* 9 J18
Taranagar, *India* 68 E6
Taranaki □, *N.Z.* 91 H5
Tarancón, *Spain* 32 E1
Taranga, *India* 68 H5
Taranga Hill, *India* 68 H5
Taransay, *U.K.* 14 D1
Táranto, *Italy* 31 B10
Táranto, G. di, *Italy* 31 B10
Tarapacá, *Colombia* 124 D5
Tarapacá □, *Chile* 126 A2
Tarapoto, *Peru* 124 E3
Tarare, *France* 21 C8
Tararua Ra., *N.Z.* 91 J5
Tarascon, *France* 21 E8
Tarascon-sur-Ariège, *France* 20 F5
Tarashcha, *Ukraine* 47 H6
Tarauacá, *Brazil* 124 E4
Tarauacá →, *Brazil* 124 E5
Taravo →, *France* 21 G12
Tarawera, *N.Z.* 91 H6
Tarawera L., *N.Z.* 91 H6
Tarazona, *Spain* 32 D3
Tarazona de la Mancha, *Spain* 33 F3
Tarbat Ness, *U.K.* 14 D5
Tarbela Dam, *Pakistan* 68 B5
Tarbert, *Arg. & Bute, U.K.* 14 F3
Tarbert, *W. Isles, U.K.* 14 D2
Tarbes, *France* 20 E4
Tarboro, *U.S.A.* 109 H7
Tarbrax, *Australia* 94 C3
Tărcău, Munții, *Romania* 43 D11
Tarcento, *Italy* 29 B10
Tarcoola, *Australia* 95 E1
Tarcoon, *Australia* 95 E4
Tardets-Sorholus, *France* 20 E3
Tardoire →, *France* 20 C4
Taree, *Australia* 95 E5
Tarfa, W. el →, *Egypt* 80 J7
Tarfaya, *Morocco* 78 C3
Târgoviște, *Romania* 43 F10
Târgu Bujor, *Romania* 43 E12
Târgu Cărbunești, *Romania* 43 F8
Târgu Frumos, *Romania* 43 C12
Târgu-Jiu, *Romania* 43 E8
Târgu Lăpuș, *Romania* 43 C8
Târgu Mureș, *Romania* 43 D9
Târgu Neamț, *Romania* 43 C11
Târgu Ocna, *Romania* 43 D11
Târgu Secuiesc, *Romania* 43 E11
Târgușor, *Romania* 43 F13
Tărhăus, Vf., *Romania* 43 D11
Tarifa, *Spain* 35 J5
Tarija, *Bolivia* 126 A3
Tarija □, *Bolivia* 126 A3
Tariku →, *Indonesia* 63 E9
Tarim Basin = Tarim Pendi, *China* 60 C3
Tarim He →, *China* 60 C3
Tarim Pendi, *China* 60 C3
Tarime □, *Tanzania* 86 C3
Taritatu →, *Indonesia* 63 E9
Tarka →, *S. Africa* 88 E4
Tarkastad, *S. Africa* 88 E4
Tarkhankut, Mys, *Ukraine* 47 K7
Tarko Sale, *Russia* 50 C8
Tarkwa, *Ghana* 82 D4
Tarlac, *Phil.* 61 D4
Tarlton Downs, *Australia* 94 C2
Tarm, *Denmark* 11 J2
Tarma, *Peru* 124 F3
Tarn □, *France* 20 E6
Tarn →, *France* 20 D5
Tarn-et-Garonne □, *France* 20 D5
Tarna →, *Hungary* 42 C4
Târnava Mare →, *Romania* 43 D8
Târnava Mică →, *Romania* 43 D8
Târnăveni, *Romania* 43 D9
Tarnica, *Poland* 45 J9
Tarnobrzeg, *Poland* 45 H8
Tarnobrzeg □, *Poland* 45 H8
Tarnogród, *Poland* 45 H9
Tarnos, *France* 20 E2
Târnova, *Moldova* 43 B12
Târnova, *Romania* 42 E6
Tarnów, *Poland* 45 H8
Tarnów □, *Poland* 45 J7
Tarnowskie Góry, *Poland* 45 H5
Tärnsjö, *Sweden* 10 D10
Táro →, *Italy* 28 C7
Taroom, *Australia* 95 D4
Taroudannt, *Morocco* 78 B4
Tarp, *Germany* 24 A5
Tarpon Springs, *U.S.A.* 109 L4
Tarquínia, *Italy* 29 F8
Tarragona, *Spain* 32 D6
Tarragona □, *Spain* 32 D6
Tarrasa = Terrassa, *Spain* 32 D7
Tàrrega, *Spain* 32 D6
Tarrytown, *U.S.A.* 111 E11
Târs, *Denmark* 11 G4
Tarshiha = Me'ona, *Israel* 75 B4
Tarso Emissi, *Chad* 79 D9
Tarsus, *Turkey* 72 D6
Tartagal, *Argentina* 126 A3
Tärtär, *Azerbaijan* 49 K8
Tärtär →, *Azerbaijan* 49 K8
Tartas, *France* 20 E3
Tartu, *Estonia* 9 G22
Ṭarṭūs, *Syria* 70 C2
Tarumizu, *Japan* 55 J5
Tarussa, *Russia* 46 E9
Tarutao, Ko, *Thailand* 65 J2
Tarutung, *Indonesia* 62 D1
Tarvísio, *Italy* 29 B10
Taschereau, *Canada* 102 C4
Taseko →, *Canada* 104 C4
Tash-Kömür, *Kyrgyzstan* 50 E8
Tash-Kumyr = Tash-Kömür, *Kyrgyzstan* 50 E8
Tashauz = Dashhowuz, *Turkmenistan* 50 E6
Tashi Chho Dzong = Thimphu, *Bhutan* 67 F16
Tashkent = Toshkent, *Uzbekistan* 50 E7
Tashtagol, *Russia* 50 D9
Tasikmalaya, *Indonesia* 63 G13
Tåsinge, *Denmark* 11 J4
Tåsjön, *Sweden* 8 D16
Taskan, *Russia* 51 C16
Taşköprü, *Turkey* 72 B6
Taşlâc, *Moldova* 43 C14
Tasman B., *N.Z.* 91 J4
Tasman Mts., *N.Z.* 91 J4
Tasman Pen., *Australia* 94 G4
Tasman Sea, *Pac. Oc.* 96 L8
Tasmania □, *Australia* 94 G4
Tășnad, *Romania* 42 C7
Tassili n'Ajjer, *Algeria* 76 D4
Tasu Sd., *Canada* 104 C2
Tata, *Hungary* 42 C3
Tatabánya, *Hungary* 42 C3
Tatar Republic □ = Tatarstan □, *Russia* 48 C10
Tatarbunary, *Ukraine* 47 K5
Tatarsk, *Russia* 50 D8
Tatarstan □, *Russia* 48 C10
Tateyama, *Japan* 55 G9
Tathlina L., *Canada* 104 A5
Tathra, *Australia* 95 F4
Tatinnai L., *Canada* 105 A9
Tatlısu, *Turkey* 41 F11
Tatnam, C., *Canada* 105 B10
Tatra = Tatry, *Slovak Rep.* 27 B13
Tatry, *Slovak Rep.* 27 B13
Tatsuno, *Japan* 55 G7
Tatta, *Pakistan* 68 G2
Tatuí, *Brazil* 127 A6
Tatum, *U.S.A.* 113 J3
Tat'ung = Datong, *China* 56 D7
Tatvan, *Turkey* 73 C10
Taubaté, *Brazil* 127 A6
Tauberbischofsheim, *Germany* 25 F5
Taucha, *Germany* 24 D8
Tauern-tunnel, *Austria* 26 D6
Taufikia, *Sudan* 81 F3
Taulé, *France* 18 D3
Taumarunui, *N.Z.* 91 H5
Taumaturgo, *Brazil* 124 E4
Taung, *S. Africa* 88 D3
Taungdwingyi, *Burma* 67 J19
Taunggyi, *Burma* 67 J20
Taungup, *Burma* 67 K19
Taungup Pass, *Burma* 67 K19
Taungup Taunggya, *Burma* 67 K18
Taunsa Barrage, *Pakistan* 68 D4
Taunton, *U.K.* 13 F4
Taunton, *U.S.A.* 111 E13
Taunus, *Germany* 25 E4
Taupo, *N.Z.* 91 H6
Taupo, L., *N.Z.* 91 H5
Tauragė, *Lithuania* 9 J20
Tauragė □, *Lithuania* 44 C9
Tauranga, *N.Z.* 91 G6
Tauranga Harb., *N.Z.* 91 G6
Taurianova, *Italy* 31 D9
Taurus Mts. = Toros Dağları, *Turkey* 72 D5
Tauste, *Spain* 32 D3
Tauz = Tovuz, *Azerbaijan* 49 K7
Tavas, *Turkey* 39 D11
Tavda, *Russia* 50 D7
Tavda →, *Russia* 50 D7
Tavernes de la Valldigna, *Spain* 33 F4
Taveta, *Tanzania* 86 C4
Taveuni, *Fiji* 91 C9
Taviano, *Italy* 31 C11
Tavignano →, *France* 21 F13
Tavira, *Portugal* 35 H3
Tavistock, *Canada* 110 C4
Tavistock, *U.K.* 13 G3
Tavolara, *Italy* 30 B2
Távora →, *Portugal* 34 D3
Tavoy = Dawei, *Burma* 64 E2
Tavşanlı, *Turkey* 39 B11
Taw →, *U.K.* 13 F3
Tawas City, *U.S.A.* 108 C4
Tawau, *Malaysia* 62 D5
Tawitawi, *Phil.* 61 J4
Taxila, *Pakistan* 68 C5
Tay →, *U.K.* 14 E5
Tay, Firth of, *U.K.* 14 E5
Tay, L., *Australia* 93 F3
Tay, L., *U.K.* 14 E4
Tay Ninh, *Vietnam* 65 G6
Tayabamba, *Peru* 124 E3
Tayabas Bay, *Phil.* 61 E4
Taylakova, *Russia* 50 D8
Taylakovy = Taylakova, *Russia* 50 D8
Taylor, *Canada* 104 B4
Taylor, *Nebr., U.S.A.* 112 E5
Taylor, *Pa., U.S.A.* 111 E9
Taylor, *Tex., U.S.A.* 113 K6
Taylor, Mt., *U.S.A.* 115 J10
Taylorville, *U.S.A.* 112 F10
Taymā, *Si. Arabia* 70 E3
Taymyr, Oz., *Russia* 51 B11
Taymyr, Poluostrov, *Russia* 51 B11
Tayport, *U.K.* 14 E6
Tayshet, *Russia* 51 D10
Taytay, *Phil.* 61 F3
Taz →, *Russia* 50 C8
Taza, *Morocco* 78 B5
Tāzah Khurmātū, *Iraq* 70 C5
Tazawa-Ko, *Japan* 54 E10
Tazin L., *Canada* 105 B7
Tazovskiy, *Russia* 50 C8
Tbilisi, *Georgia* 49 K7
Tchad = Chad ■, *Africa* 79 F8
Tchad, L., *Chad* 79 F8
Tchaourou, *Benin* 83 D5
Tch'eng-tou = Chengdu, *China* 58 B5
Tchentlo L., *Canada* 104 B4
Tchibanga, *Gabon* 84 E2
Tchien, *Liberia* 82 D3
Tchin Tabaraden, *Niger* 83 B6
Tch'ong-k'ing = Chongqing, *China* 58 C6
Tczew, *Poland* 44 D5
Te Anau, L., *N.Z.* 91 L1
Te Aroha, *N.Z.* 91 G5
Te Awamutu, *N.Z.* 91 H5
Te Kuiti, *N.Z.* 91 H5
Te Puke, *N.Z.* 91 G6
Te Waewae B., *N.Z.* 91 M1
Tea Tree, *Australia* 94 C1
Teaca, *Romania* 43 D9
Teague, *U.S.A.* 113 K6
Teano, *Italy* 31 A7
Teapa, *Mexico* 119 D6
Teba, *Spain* 35 J6
Tebakang, *Malaysia* 62 D4
Teberda, *Russia* 49 J5
Tébessa, *Algeria* 78 A7
Tebicuary →, *Paraguay* 126 B4
Tebingtinggi, *Indonesia* 62 D1
Tebulos, *Georgia* 49 J7
Tecate, *Mexico* 117 N10
Tecer Dağları, *Turkey* 72 C7
Tech →, *France* 20 F7
Techiman, *Ghana* 82 D4
Techirghiol, *Romania* 43 F13
Tecka, *Argentina* 128 E2
Tecomán, *Mexico* 118 D4
Tecopa, *U.S.A.* 117 K10
Tecoripa, *Mexico* 118 B3
Tecuala, *Mexico* 118 C3
Tecuci, *Romania* 43 E12
Tecumseh, *U.S.A.* 108 D4
Tedzhen = Tejen, *Turkmenistan* 50 F7
Tees →, *U.K.* 12 C6
Tees B., *U.K.* 12 C6
Teeswater, *Canada* 110 C3
Tefé, *Brazil* 124 D6
Tefenni, *Turkey* 39 D11
Tegal, *Indonesia* 63 G13
Tegernsee, *Germany* 25 H7
Teggiano, *Italy* 31 B8
Teghra, *India* 69 G11
Tegid, L. = Bala, L., *U.K.* 12 E4
Tegina, *Nigeria* 83 C6
Tegucigalpa, *Honduras* 120 D2
Tehachapi, *U.S.A.* 117 K8
Tehachapi Mts., *U.S.A.* 117 L8
Tehamiyam, *Sudan* 80 D4
Tehilla, *Sudan* 80 D4
Téhini, *Ivory C.* 82 D4
Tehoru, *Indonesia* 63 E7
Tehrān, *Iran* 71 C6
Tehuacán, *Mexico* 119 D5
Tehuantepec, *Mexico* 119 D5
Tehuantepec, G. de, *Mexico* 119 D5
Tehuantepec, Istmo de, *Mexico* 119 D6
Teide, *Canary Is.* 37 F3
Teifi →, *U.K.* 13 E3
Teign →, *U.K.* 13 G4
Teignmouth, *U.K.* 13 G4
Teiuș, *Romania* 43 D8
Teixeira Pinto, *Guinea-Biss.* 82 C1
Tejen, *Turkmenistan* 50 F7
Tejo →, *Europe* 35 F2
Tejon Pass, *U.S.A.* 117 L8
Tekamah, *U.S.A.* 112 E6
Tekapo, L., *N.Z.* 91 K3
Tekax, *Mexico* 119 C7
Teke, *Turkey* 41 E13
Tekeli, *Kazakstan* 50 E8
Tekeze →, *Ethiopia* 81 E4
Tekija, *Serbia, Yug.* 40 B6
Tekirdağ, *Turkey* 41 F11
Tekirdağ □, *Turkey* 41 E11
Tekirova, *Turkey* 39 E12
Tekkali, *India* 67 K14
Tekke, *Turkey* 72 B7
Tekman, *Turkey* 73 C9
Tekoa, *U.S.A.* 114 C5
Tel Aviv-Yafo, *Israel* 75 C3
Tel Lakhish, *Israel* 75 D3
Tel Megiddo, *Israel* 75 C4
Tela, *Honduras* 120 C2
Telanaipura = Jambi, *Indonesia* 62 E2
Telavi, *Georgia* 49 J7
Telč, *Czech Rep.* 26 B8
Telciu, *Romania* 43 C9
Telde, *Canary Is.* 37 G4
Telegraph Creek, *Canada* 104 B2
Telekhany = Tsyelyakhany, *Belarus* 47 F3
Telemark, *Norway* 9 G12
Telén, *Argentina* 126 D2
Teleneşti, *Moldova* 43 C13
Teleng, *Iran* 71 E9
Teleño, *Spain* 34 C4
Teleorman □, *Romania* 43 G10
Teleorman →, *Romania* 43 G10
Teles Pires →, *Brazil* 122 D5
Telescope Pk., *U.S.A.* 117 J9
Teletaye, *Mali* 83 B5
Telford, *U.K.* 13 E5
Telford and Wrekin □, *U.K.* 12 E5
Telfs, *Austria* 26 D4
Télimélé, *Guinea* 82 C2
Telkwa, *Canada* 104 C3
Tell City, *U.S.A.* 108 G2
Tellicherry, *India* 66 P9
Telluride, *U.S.A.* 115 H10
Teloloapán, *Mexico* 119 D5
Telpos Iz, *Russia* 6 C17
Telsen, *Argentina* 128 E3
Telšiai, *Lithuania* 9 H20
Telšiai □, *Lithuania* 44 C9
Teltow, *Germany* 24 C9
Teluk Anson = Teluk Intan, *Malaysia* 65 K3
Teluk Betung = Tanjungkarang Telukbetung, *Indonesia* 62 F3
Teluk Intan, *Malaysia* 65 K3
Telukbutun, *Indonesia* 65 K7
Telukdalem, *Indonesia* 62 D1
Tema, *Ghana* 83 D5
Temapache, *Mexico* 119 C5
Temax, *Mexico* 119 C7
Temba, *S. Africa* 89 D4
Tembe, *Dem. Rep. of the Congo* 86 C2
Tembleque, *Spain* 34 F7
Temblor Range, *U.S.A.* 117 K7
Teme →, *U.K.* 13 E5
Temecula, *U.S.A.* 117 M9
Temerloh, *Malaysia* 62 D2
Temir, *Kazakstan* 50 E6
Temirtau, *Kazakstan* 50 D8
Temirtau, *Russia* 50 D9
Témiscaming, *Canada* 102 C4
Temma, *Australia* 94 G3
Temnikov, *Russia* 48 C6
Temo →, *Italy* 30 B1

Temora, *Australia* 95 E4
Temosachic, *Mexico* 118 B3
Tempe, *U.S.A.* 115 K8
Tempe Downs, *Australia* 92 D5
Témpio Pausánia, *Italy* 30 B2
Tempiute, *U.S.A.* 116 H11
Temple, *U.S.A.* 113 K6
Temple B., *Australia* 94 A3
Templemore, *Ireland* 15 D4
Templeton, *U.S.A.* 116 K6
Templeton →, *Australia* 94 C2
Templin, *Germany* 24 B9
Tempoal, *Mexico* 119 C5
Temryuk, *Russia* 47 K9
Temska →, *Serbia, Yug.* 40 C6
Temuco, *Chile* 128 D2
Temuka, *N.Z.* 91 L3
Tenabo, *Mexico* 119 C6
Tenaha, *U.S.A.* 113 K7
Tenali, *India* 66 L12
Tenancingo, *Mexico* 119 D5
Tenango, *Mexico* 119 D5
Tenasserim = Taninthari, *Burma* 65 F2
Tenasserim □, *Burma* 64 F2
Tenby, *U.K.* 13 F3
Tenda, Colle di, *France* 21 D11
Tendaho, *Ethiopia* 81 E5
Tende, *France* 21 D11
Tendelti, *Sudan* 81 E3
Tendrovskaya Kosa, *Ukraine* 47 J6
Teneida, *Egypt* 80 B2
Ténéré, *Niger* 83 B7
Tenerife, *Canary Is.* 37 F3
Tenerife, Pico, *Canary Is.* 37 G1
Teng Xian, *Guangxi Zhuangzu, China* 59 F8
Teng Xian, *Shandong, China* 57 G9
Tengah □, *Indonesia* 63 E6
Tengah, Kepulauan, *Indonesia* 62 F5
Tengchong, *China* 58 E2
Tengchowfu = Penglai, *China* 57 F11
Tenggara □, *Indonesia* 63 E6
Tenggarong, *Indonesia* 62 E5
Tenggol, Pulau, *Malaysia* 65 K4
Tengiz, Ozero, *Kazakstan* 50 D7
Tenhult, *Sweden* 11 G8
Tenino, *U.S.A.* 116 D4
Tenkasi, *India* 66 Q10
Tenke, *Shaba, Dem. Rep. of the Congo* 87 E2
Tenke, *Shaba, Dem. Rep. of the Congo* 87 E2
Tenkodogo, *Burkina Faso* 83 C4
Tenna →, *Italy* 29 E10
Tennant Creek, *Australia* 94 B1
Tennessee □, *U.S.A.* 109 H2
Tennessee →, *U.S.A.* 108 G1
Tennille, *U.S.A.* 109 J4
Teno, Pta. de, *Canary Is.* 37 F3
Tenom, *Malaysia* 62 C5
Tenosique, *Mexico* 119 D6
Tenryū-Gawa →, *Japan* 55 G8
Tent L., *Canada* 105 A7
Tenterden, *U.K.* 13 F8
Tenterfield, *Australia* 95 D5
Teo, *Spain* 34 C2
Teófilo Otoni, *Brazil* 125 G10
Teotihuacán, *Mexico* 119 D5
Tepa, *Indonesia* 63 F7
Tepalcatepec →, *Mexico* 118 D4
Tepecik, *Bursa, Turkey* 41 F12
Tepecik, *Kütahya, Turkey* 39 B11
Tepehuanes, *Mexico* 118 B3
Tepelena, *Albania* 40 F4
Tepetongo, *Mexico* 118 C4
Tepic, *Mexico* 118 C4
Teplá, *Czech Rep.* 26 B5
Teplice, *Czech Rep.* 26 A6
Tepoca, C., *Mexico* 118 A2
Tequila, *Mexico* 118 C4
Ter →, *Spain* 32 C8
Ter Apel, *Neths.* 17 B7
Téra, *Niger* 83 C5
Tera →, *Spain* 34 D5
Teraina, *Kiribati* 97 G11
Téramo, *Italy* 29 F10
Terang, *Australia* 95 F3
Tercan, *Turkey* 73 C9
Tercero →, *Argentina* 126 C3
Terebovlya, *Ukraine* 47 H3
Teregova, *Romania* 42 E7
Terek →, *Russia* 49 J8
Tereshka →, *Russia* 48 E8
Teresina, *Brazil* 125 E10
Terespol, *Poland* 45 F10
Terewah, L., *Australia* 95 D4
Terges →, *Portugal* 35 H3
Tergnier, *France* 19 C10
Teridgerie Cr. →, *Australia* 95 E4
Terlizzi, *Italy* 31 A9
Terme, *Turkey* 72 B7
Termez = Termiz, *Uzbekistan* 50 F7
Términi Imerese, *Italy* 30 E6
Términos, L. de, *Mexico* 119 D6
Termiz, *Uzbekistan* 50 F7
Térmoli, *Italy* 29 F12
Ternate, *Indonesia* 63 D7
Terneuzen, *Neths.* 17 C3
Terney, *Russia* 54 B8
Terni, *Italy* 29 F9
Ternitz, *Austria* 26 D9
Ternopil, *Ukraine* 47 H3
Ternopol = Ternopil, *Ukraine* 47 H3
Terowie, *N.S.W., Australia* 95 E4
Terowie, *S. Austral., Australia* 95 E2
Terpní, *Greece* 40 F7
Terra Bella, *U.S.A.* 117 K7
Terrace, *Canada* 104 C3
Terrace Bay, *Canada* 102 C2
Terracina, *Italy* 30 A6
Terralba, *Italy* 30 C1
Terranova = Ólbia, *Italy* 30 B2
Terrasini, *Italy* 30 D6
Terrassa, *Spain* 32 D7
Terrasson-la-Villedieu, *France* 20 C5
Terre Haute, *U.S.A.* 108 F2
Terrebonne B., *U.S.A.* 113 L9
Terrell, *U.S.A.* 113 J6
Terrenceville, *Canada* 103 C9
Terrick Terrick, *Australia* 94 C4
Terry, *U.S.A.* 112 B2
Terschelling, *Neths.* 17 A5
Tersko-Kumskiy Kanal →, *Russia* 49 H7
Tertenía, *Italy* 30 C2
Terter → = Tärtär →, *Azerbaijan* 49 K8
Teruel, *Spain* 32 E3
Teruel □, *Spain* 32 E4
Tervel, *Bulgaria* 41 C11
Tervola, *Finland* 8 C21
Teryaweyna L., *Australia* 95 E3
Tešanj, *Bos.-H.* 42 F3
Teseney, *Eritrea* 81 D4
Tesha →, *Russia* 48 C6
Teshio, *Japan* 54 B10
Teshio-Gawa →, *Japan* 54 B10
Tešica, *Serbia, Yug.* 40 C5
Tesiyn Gol →, *Mongolia* 60 A4
Teslić, *Bos.-H.* 42 F2
Teslin, *Canada* 104 A2
Teslin →, *Canada* 104 A2
Teslin L., *Canada* 104 A2
Tessalit, *Mali* 83 A5
Tessaoua, *Niger* 83 C6
Tessin, *Germany* 24 A8
Tessit, *Mali* 83 B5
Test →, *U.K.* 13 G6
Testa del Gargano, *Italy* 29 G13
Tét, *Hungary* 42 C2
Têt →, *France* 20 F7
Tetachuck L., *Canada* 104 C3
Tetas, Pta., *Chile* 126 A1
Tete, *Mozam.* 87 F3
Tete □, *Mozam.* 87 F3
Teterev →, *Ukraine* 47 G6
Teterow, *Germany* 24 B8
Teteven, *Bulgaria* 41 D8
Tethul →, *Canada* 104 A6
Tetiyev, *Ukraine* 47 H5
Teton →, *U.S.A.* 114 C8
Tétouan, *Morocco* 78 A4
Tetovo, *Macedonia* 40 D4
Tetyukhe Pristan, *Russia* 54 B7
Tetyushi, *Russia* 48 C9
Teuco →, *Argentina* 126 B3
Teulada, *Italy* 30 D1
Teulon, *Canada* 105 C9
Teun, *Indonesia* 63 F7
Teutoburger Wald, *Germany* 24 C4
Tevere →, *Italy* 29 G9
Teverya, *Israel* 75 C4
Teviot →, *U.K.* 14 F6
Tewantin, *Australia* 95 D5
Tewkesbury, *U.K.* 13 F5
Texada I., *Canada* 104 D4
Texarkana, *Ark., U.S.A.* 113 J8
Texarkana, *Tex., U.S.A.* 113 J7
Texas, *Australia* 95 D5
Texas □, *U.S.A.* 113 K5
Texas City, *U.S.A.* 113 L7
Texel, *Neths.* 17 A4
Texhoma, *U.S.A.* 113 G4
Texline, *U.S.A.* 113 G3
Texoma, L., *U.S.A.* 113 J6
Teykovo, *Russia* 46 D11
Teza →, *Russia* 48 B5
Tezin, *Afghan.* 68 B3
Teziutlán, *Mexico* 119 D5
Tezpur, *India* 67 F18
Tezzeron L., *Canada* 104 C4
Tha-anne →, *Canada* 105 A10
Tha Deua, *Laos* 64 D4
Tha Deua, *Laos* 64 C3
Tha Pla, *Thailand* 64 D3
Tha Rua, *Thailand* 64 E3
Tha Sala, *Thailand* 65 H2
Tha Song Yang, *Thailand* 64 D1
Thaba Putsoa, *Lesotho* 89 D4
Thabana Ntlenyana, *Lesotho* 89 D4
Thabazimbi, *S. Africa* 89 C4
Thai Binh, *Vietnam* 64 B6
Thai Muang, *Thailand* 65 H2
Thai Nguyen, *Vietnam* 64 B5
Thailand ■, *Asia* 64 E4
Thailand, G. of, *Asia* 65 G3
Thakhek, *Laos* 64 D5
Thal, *Pakistan* 68 C4
Thal Desert, *Pakistan* 68 D4
Thala La, *Burma* 67 E20
Thalabarivat, *Cambodia* 64 F5
Thallon, *Australia* 95 D4
Thalwil, *Switz.* 25 H4
Thames, *N.Z.* 91 G5
Thames →, *Canada* 102 D3
Thames →, *U.K.* 13 F8
Thames →, *U.S.A.* 111 E12
Thames Estuary, *U.K.* 13 F8
Thamesford, *Canada* 110 C4
Thamesville, *Canada* 110 D3
Than Uyen, *Vietnam* 64 B4
Thane, *India* 66 K8
Thanesar, *India* 68 D7
Thanet, I. of, *U.K.* 13 F9
Thangoo, *Australia* 92 C3
Thangool, *Australia* 94 C5
Thanh Hoa, *Vietnam* 64 C5
Thanh Hung, *Vietnam* 65 H5
Thanh Pho Ho Chi Minh = Phanh Bho Ho Chi Minh, *Vietnam* 65 G6
Thanh Thuy, *Vietnam* 64 A5
Thanjavur, *India* 66 P11
Thann, *France* 19 E14
Thaon-les-Vosges, *France* 19 D13
Thap Sakae, *Thailand* 65 G2
Thap Than, *Thailand* 64 E2
Thar Desert, *India* 68 F5
Tharad, *India* 68 G4
Thargomindah, *Australia* 95 D3
Tharrawaddy, *Burma* 67 L19
Tharthār, Mileh, *Iraq* 70 C4
Tharthār, W. ath →, *Iraq* 70 C4
Thasopoúla, *Greece* 41 F8
Thásos, *Greece* 41 F8
That Khe, *Vietnam* 64 A6
Thatcher, *Ariz., U.S.A.* 115 K9
Thatcher, *Colo., U.S.A.* 113 G2
Thaton, *Burma* 67 L20
Thau, Bassin de, *France* 20 E7
Thaungdut, *Burma* 67 G19
Thayer, *U.S.A.* 113 G9
Thayetmyo, *Burma* 67 K19
Thazi, *Burma* 67 J20
The Alberga →, *Australia* 95 D2
The Bight, *Bahamas* 121 B4
The Coorong, *Australia* 95 F2
The Dalles, *U.S.A.* 114 D3
The English Company's Is., *Australia* 94 A2
The Frome →, *Australia* 95 D2
The Grampians, *Australia* 95 F3
The Great Divide = Great Dividing Ra., *Australia* 94 C4
The Hague = 's-Gravenhage, *Neths.* 17 B4
The Hamilton →, *Australia* 95 D2
The Macumba →, *Australia* 95 D2
The Neales →, *Australia* 95 D2
The Officer →, *Australia* 93 E5
The Pas, *Canada* 105 C8
The Range, *Zimbabwe* 87 F3
The Rock, *Australia* 95 F4
The Salt L., *Australia* 95 E3
The Stevenson →, *Australia* 95 D2
The Warburton →, *Australia* 95 D2
Thebes = Thívai, *Greece* 38 C5
Thebes, *Egypt* 80 B3
Thedford, *Canada* 110 C3
Thedford, *U.S.A.* 112 E4
Theebine, *Australia* 95 D5
Thekulthili L., *Canada* 105 A7
Thelon →, *Canada* 105 A8
Thénezay, *France* 18 F6
Thenon, *France* 20 C5
Theodore, *Australia* 94 C5
Thepha, *Thailand* 65 J3
Thérain →, *France* 19 C9
Theresa, *U.S.A.* 111 B9
Thermaïkós Kólpos, *Greece* 40 F6
Thermí, *Greece* 39 B8
Thermopolis, *U.S.A.* 114 E9
Thermopylae P., *Greece* 38 C4
Thesprotía □, *Greece* 38 B2
Thessalía □, *Greece* 38 B4
Thessalon, *Canada* 102 C3
Thessaloníki, *Greece* 40 F6
Thessaloníki □, *Greece* 40 F7
Thessaloniki, Gulf of = Thermaïkós Kólpos, *Greece* 40 F6
Thessaly = Thessalía □, *Greece* 38 B4
Thetford, *U.K.* 13 E8
Thetford Mines, *Canada* 103 C5
Theun →, *Laos* 64 C5
Theunissen, *S. Africa* 88 D4
Thevenard, *Australia* 95 E1
Thiámis →, *Greece* 38 B2
Thiberville, *France* 18 C7
Thibodaux, *U.S.A.* 113 L9
Thicket Portage, *Canada* 105 B9
Thief River Falls, *U.S.A.* 112 A6
Thiel Mts., *Antarctica* 5 E16
Thiene, *Italy* 29 C8
Thiérache, *France* 19 C10
Thiers, *France* 20 C7
Thiès, *Senegal* 82 C1
Thiesi, *Italy* 30 B1
Thiet, *Sudan* 81 F2
Thika, *Kenya* 86 C4
Thikombia, *Fiji* 91 B9
Thille-Boubacar, *Senegal* 82 B1
Thimphu, *Bhutan* 67 F16
þingvallavatn, *Iceland* 8 D3
Thionville, *France* 19 C13
Thíra, *Greece* 39 E7
Thirasía, *Greece* 39 E7
Thirsk, *U.K.* 12 C6
Thisted, *Denmark* 11 H2
Thistle I., *Australia* 95 F2
Thívai, *Greece* 38 C5
Thiviers, *France* 20 C4
Thizy, *France* 19 F11
þjórsá →, *Iceland* 8 E3
Thlewiaza →, *Man., Canada* 105 B8
Thlewiaza →, *N.W.T., Canada* 105 A10
Thmar Puok, *Cambodia* 64 F4
Tho Vinh, *Vietnam* 64 C5
Thoa →, *Canada* 105 A7
Thoen, *Thailand* 64 D2
Thoeng, *Thailand* 64 C3
Tholdi, *Pakistan* 69 B7
Thomas, *Okla., U.S.A.* 113 H5
Thomas, *W. Va., U.S.A.* 108 F6
Thomas, L., *Australia* 95 D2
Thomaston, *U.S.A.* 109 J3
Thomasville, *Ala., U.S.A.* 109 K2
Thomasville, *Ga., U.S.A.* 109 K4
Thomasville, *N.C., U.S.A.* 109 H5
Thompson, *Canada* 105 B9
Thompson, *U.S.A.* 115 G9
Thompson →, *Canada* 104 C4
Thompson →, *U.S.A.* 112 F8
Thompson Falls, *U.S.A.* 114 C6
Thompson Landing, *Canada* 105 A6
Thompson Pk., *U.S.A.* 114 F2
Thomson's Falls = Nyahururu, *Kenya* 86 B4
Thônes, *France* 21 C10
Thonon-les-Bains, *France* 19 F13
Thorez, *Ukraine* 47 H10
þórisvatn, *Iceland* 8 D4
Thornaby on Tees, *U.K.* 12 C6
Thornbury, *Canada* 110 B4
Thorne, *U.K.* 12 D7
Thorold, *Canada* 110 C5
þórshöfn, *Iceland* 8 C6
Thouarcé, *France* 18 E6
Thouars, *France* 18 F6
Thouet →, *France* 18 E6
Thouin, C., *Australia* 92 D2
Thousand Oaks, *U.S.A.* 117 L8
Thrace, *Turkey* 41 F10
Thrakikón Pélagos, *Greece* 41 F8
Three Forks, *U.S.A.* 114 D8
Three Hills, *Canada* 104 C6
Three Hummock I., *Australia* 94 G3
Three Lakes, *U.S.A.* 112 C10
Three Points, C., *Ghana* 82 E4
Three Rivers, *Australia* 93 E2
Three Rivers, *Calif., U.S.A.* 116 J8
Three Rivers, *Tex., U.S.A.* 113 L5
Three Sisters, *U.S.A.* 114 D3
Throssell, L., *Australia* 93 E3
Throssell Ra., *Australia* 92 D3
Thuan Hoa, *Vietnam* 65 H5
Thubun Lakes, *Canada* 105 A6
Thueyts, *France* 21 D8
Thuin, *Belgium* 17 D4
Thuir, *France* 20 F6
Thule, *Greenland* 4 B4
Thun, *Switz.* 25 J3
Thundelarra, *Australia* 93 E2
Thunder B., *U.S.A.* 110 B1
Thunder Bay, *Canada* 102 C2
Thunersee, *Switz.* 25 J3
Thung Song, *Thailand* 65 H2
Thunkar, *Bhutan* 67 F17
Thuong Tra, *Vietnam* 64 D6
Thur →, *Switz.* 25 H5
Thurgau □, *Switz.* 25 H5
Thüringen □, *Germany* 24 D6
Thüringer Wald, *Germany* 24 E6
Thurles, *Ireland* 15 D4
Thurloo Downs, *Australia* 95 D3
Thurn P., *Austria* 26 D5
Thurrock □, *U.K.* 13 F8
Thursday I., *Australia* 94 A3
Thurso, *Canada* 102 C4
Thurso, *U.K.* 14 C5
Thurso →, *U.K.* 14 C5
Thurston I., *Antarctica* 5 D16
Thury-Harcourt, *France* 18 D6
Thutade L., *Canada* 104 B3
Thy, *Denmark* 11 H2
Thyborøn, *Denmark* 11 H2
Thylungra, *Australia* 95 D3
Thyolo, *Malawi* 87 F4
Thysville = Mbanza Ngungu, *Dem. Rep. of the Congo* 84 F2
Ti-n-Barraouene, O. →, *Africa* 83 B5
Tia, *Australia* 95 E5
Tian Shan, *Asia* 60 B3
Tianchang, *China* 59 A12
Tiandong, *China* 58 F6
Tian'e, *China* 58 E6
Tianhe, *China* 58 E7
Tianjin, *China* 57 E9
Tiankoura, *Burkina Faso* 82 C4
Tianlin, *China* 58 E6
Tianmen, *China* 59 B9
Tianquan, *China* 58 B4
Tianshui, *China* 56 G3
Tiantai, *China* 59 C13
Tianyang, *China* 58 F6
Tianzhen, *China* 56 D8
Tianzhu, *China* 58 D7
Tianzhuangtai, *China* 57 D12
Tiaret, *Algeria* 78 A6
Tiassalé, *Ivory C.* 82 D4
Tibagi, *Brazil* 127 A5
Tibagi →, *Brazil* 127 A5
Tibati, *Cameroon* 83 D7
Tiber = Tevere →, *Italy* 29 G9
Tiber Reservoir, *U.S.A.* 114 B8
Tiberias = Teverya, *Israel* 75 C4
Tiberias, L. = Yam Kinneret, *Israel* 75 C4
Tibesti, *Chad* 79 D9
Tibet = Xizang Zizhiqu □, *China* 60 C3
Tibet, Plateau of, *Asia* 52 F12
Tibiao, *Phil.* 61 F5
Tibiri, *Niger* 83 C6
Ţibleş, Vf., *Romania* 43 C9
Ţibleşului, Munţii, *Romania* 43 C9
Tibnī, *Syria* 70 C3
Tibooburra, *Australia* 95 D3
Tibro, *Sweden* 11 F8
Tiburón, *Mexico* 118 B2
Ticao I., *Phil.* 61 E5
Tîchît, *Mauritania* 82 B3
Ticho, *Ethiopia* 81 F4
Ticino □, *Switz.* 25 J4
Ticino →, *Italy* 25 K5
Ticleni, *Romania* 43 F8
Ticonderoga, *U.S.A.* 111 C11
Ticul, *Mexico* 119 C7
Tidaholm, *Sweden* 11 F7
Tidan, *Sweden* 11 F8
Tiddim, *Burma* 67 H18
Tidjikja, *Mauritania* 82 B2
Tidore, *Indonesia* 63 D7
Tiébissou, *Ivory C.* 82 D3
Tiel, *Neths.* 17 C5
Tiel, *Senegal* 82 C1
Tieling, *China* 57 C12
Tielt, *Belgium* 17 C3
Tien Shan = Tian Shan, *Asia* 60 B3
Tien-tsin = Tianjin, *China* 57 E9
Tien Yen, *Vietnam* 64 B6
T'ienching = Tianjin, *China* 57 E9
Tienen, *Belgium* 17 D4
Tiénigbé, *Ivory C.* 82 D3
Tientsin = Tianjin, *China* 57 E9
Tierp, *Sweden* 10 D11
Tierra Amarilla, *Chile* 126 B1
Tierra Amarilla, *U.S.A.* 115 H10
Tierra Colorada, *Mexico* 119 D5
Tierra de Barros, *Spain* 35 G4
Tierra de Campos, *Spain* 34 C6
Tierra del Fuego, I. Gr. de, *Argentina* 122 J4
Tiétar →, *Spain* 34 F4
Tieté →, *Brazil* 127 A5
Tieyon, *Australia* 95 D1
Tiffin, *U.S.A.* 108 E4
Tiflis = Tbilisi, *Georgia* 49 K7
Tifton, *U.S.A.* 109 K4
Tifu, *Indonesia* 63 E7
Tighina, *Moldova* 43 D14
Tigil, *Russia* 51 D16
Tignish, *Canada* 103 C7
Tigray □, *Ethiopia* 81 E4
Tigre →, *Peru* 124 D4
Tigre →, *Venezuela* 124 B6
Tigris = Dijlah, Nahr →, *Asia* 70 D5
Tigveni, *Romania* 43 E9
Tigyaing, *Burma* 67 H20
Tîh, Gebel el, *Egypt* 80 J8
Tijuana, *Mexico* 117 N9
Tikal, *Guatemala* 120 C2
Tikamgarh, *India* 69 G8
Tikhoretsk, *Russia* 49 H5
Tikhvin, *Russia* 46 C7
Tiko, *Cameroon* 83 E6
Tikrīt, *Iraq* 70 C4
Tiksi, *Russia* 51 B13
Tilamuta, *Indonesia* 63 D6
Tilburg, *Neths.* 17 C5
Tilbury, *Canada* 102 D3
Tilbury, *U.K.* 13 F8
Tilcara, *Argentina* 126 A2
Tilden, *Nebr., U.S.A.* 112 D6
Tilden, *Tex., U.S.A.* 113 L5
Tilemses, *Niger* 83 B5
Tilemsi, Vallée du, *Mali* 83 B5
Tilhar, *India* 69 F8
Tilichiki, *Russia* 51 C17
Tílissos, *Greece* 36 D7
Till →, *U.K.* 12 B5
Tillabéri, *Niger* 83 C5
Tillamook, *U.S.A.* 114 D2
Tillberga, *Sweden* 10 E10
Tillia, *Niger* 83 B5
Tillsonburg, *Canada* 102 D3
Tillyeria □, *Cyprus* 36 D11
Tílos, *Greece* 39 E9
Tilpa, *Australia* 95 E3
Tilsit = Sovetsk, *Russia* 9 J19
Tilt →, *U.K.* 14 E5
Tilton, *U.S.A.* 111 C13
Tim, *Denmark* 11 H2

Timagami L., *Canada* 102 C3
Timaru, *N.Z.* 91 L3
Timashevo, *Russia* 48 D10
Timashevsk, *Russia* 49 H4
Timau, *Kenya* 86 B4
Timbákion, *Greece* 36 D6
Timbedgha, *Mauritania* 82 B3
Timber Lake, *U.S.A.* 112 C4
Timber Mt., *U.S.A.* 116 H10
Timboon, *Australia* 95 F3
Timbuktu = Tombouctou, *Mali* 82 B4
Timétrine Montagnes, *Mali* 83 B4
Timfi Óros, *Greece* 38 B2
Timfristós, Óros, *Greece* 38 C3
Timi, *Cyprus* 36 E11
Tîmia, *Niger* 83 B6
Timimoun, *Algeria* 78 C6
Timiş = Tamis →, *Serbia, Yug.* 42 F5
Timiş □, *Romania* 42 E6
Timişoara, *Romania* 42 E6
Timmersdala, *Sweden* 11 F7
Timmins, *Canada* 102 C3
Timok →, *Serbia, Yug.* 40 B6
Timor, *Indonesia* 63 F7
Timor Sea, *Ind. Oc.* 92 B4
Timor Timur □, *Indonesia* 63 F7
Timrå, *Sweden* 10 B11
Tin Gornai, *Mali* 83 B4
Tin Mt., *U.S.A.* 116 J9
Tîna, Khalîg el, *Egypt* 80 H8
Tinaca Pt., *Phil.* 61 J6
Tinajo, *Canary Is.* 37 E6
Tinca, *Romania* 42 D6
Tindouf, *Algeria* 78 C4
Tinée →, *France* 21 E11
Tineo, *Spain* 34 B4
Ting Jiang →, *China* 59 E11
Tinggi, Pulau, *Malaysia* 65 L5
Tinglev, *Denmark* 11 K3
Tingo Maria, *Peru* 124 E3
Tingsryd, *Sweden* 11 H9
Tingstäde, *Sweden* 11 G12
Tinh Bien, *Vietnam* 65 G5
Tinkurrin, *Australia* 93 F2
Tinnevelly = Tirunelveli, *India* 66 Q10
Tinogasta, *Argentina* 126 B2
Tínos, *Greece* 39 D7
Tiñoso, C., *Spain* 33 H3
Tintina, *Argentina* 126 B3
Tintinara, *Australia* 95 F3
Tinto →, *Spain* 35 H4
Tioga, *U.S.A.* 110 E7
Tioman, Pulau, *Malaysia* 65 L5
Tione di Trento, *Italy* 28 B7
Tionesta, *U.S.A.* 110 E5
Tior, *Sudan* 81 F3
Tipongpani, *India* 67 F19
Tipperary, *Ireland* 15 D3
Tipperary □, *Ireland* 15 D4
Tipton, *Calif., U.S.A.* 116 J7
Tipton, *Ind., U.S.A.* 108 E2
Tipton, *Iowa, U.S.A.* 112 E9
Tipton Mt., *U.S.A.* 117 K12
Tiptonville, *U.S.A.* 113 G10
Tīrān, *Iran* 71 C6
Tīrān, *Si. Arabia* 80 B3
Tirana, *Albania* 40 E3
Tiranë = Tirana, *Albania* 40 E3
Tirano, *Italy* 28 B7
Tiraspol, *Moldova* 43 D14
Tirdout, *Mali* 83 B4
Tire, *Turkey* 39 C9
Tirebolu, *Turkey* 73 B8
Tiree, *U.K.* 14 E2
Tiree, Passage of, *U.K.* 14 E2
Tîrgovişte = Târgovişte, *Romania* 43 F10
Tîrgu-Jiu = Târgu-Jiu, *Romania* 43 E8
Tîrgu Mureş = Târgu Mureş, *Romania* 43 D9
Tirich Mir, *Pakistan* 66 A7
Tiriolo, *Italy* 31 D9
Tírnavos, *Greece* 38 B4
Tirodi, *India* 66 J11
Tirol □, *Austria* 26 D3
Tirschenreuth, *Germany* 25 F8
Tirso →, *Italy* 30 C1
Tirstrup, *Denmark* 11 H4
Tiruchchirappalli, *India* 66 P11
Tirunelveli, *India* 66 Q10
Tirupati, *India* 66 N11
Tiruppur, *India* 66 P10
Tiruvannamalai, *India* 66 N11
Tisa →, *Serbia, Yug.* 42 E5
Tisdale, *Canada* 105 C8
Tishomingo, *U.S.A.* 113 H6
Tisjön, *Sweden* 10 D7
Tisnaren, *Sweden* 11 F9
Tišnov, *Czech Rep.* 27 B9
Tisovec, *Slovak Rep.* 27 C12
Tisza = Tisa →, *Serbia, Yug.* 42 E5
Tiszaföldvár, *Hungary* 42 D5
Tiszafüred, *Hungary* 42 C5
Tiszalök, *Hungary* 42 B6
Tiszavasvári, *Hungary* 42 C6
Tit-Ary, *Russia* 51 B13
Titaguas, *Spain* 32 F3
Titel, *Serbia, Yug.* 42 E5
Tithwal, *Pakistan* 69 B5
Titicaca, L., *S. Amer.* 122 E4
Titisee, *Germany* 25 H4
Titiwa, *Nigeria* 83 C7
Tito, *Italy* 31 B8
Titograd = Podgorica, *Montenegro, Yug.* 40 D3
Titova Korenica, *Croatia* 29 D12
Titu, *Romania* 43 F10
Titule, *Dem. Rep. of the Congo* 86 B2
Titusville, *Fla., U.S.A.* 109 L5
Titusville, *Pa., U.S.A.* 110 E5
Tivaouane, *Senegal* 82 C1
Tivat, *Montenegro, Yug.* 40 D2
Tiverton, *U.K.* 13 G4
Tívoli, *Italy* 29 G9
Tiyo, *Eritrea* 81 E5
Tizi-Ouzou, *Algeria* 78 A6
Tizimín, *Mexico* 119 C7
Tjæreborg, *Denmark* 11 J2
Tjällmo, *Sweden* 11 F9
Tjeggelvas, *Sweden* 8 C17
Tjirebon = Cirebon, *Indonesia* 63 G13
Tjörn, *Sweden* 11 F5
Tkibuli = Tqibuli, *Georgia* 49 J6
Tkvarcheli = Tqvarcheli, *Georgia* 49 J5
Tlacotalpan, *Mexico* 119 D5
Tlahualilo, *Mexico* 118 B4
Tlaquepaque, *Mexico* 118 C4
Tlaxcala, *Mexico* 119 D5
Tlaxcala □, *Mexico* 119 D5
Tlaxiaco, *Mexico* 119 D5
Tlell, *Canada* 104 C2
Tlemcen, *Algeria* 78 B5
Tłuszcz, *Poland* 45 F8
Tlyarata, *Russia* 49 J8
To Bong, *Vietnam* 64 F7
Toad →, *Canada* 104 B4
Toamasina, *Madag.* 89 B8
Toamasina □, *Madag.* 89 B8
Toay, *Argentina* 126 D3
Toba, *Japan* 55 G8
Toba, Danau, *Indonesia* 62 D1
Toba Kakar, *Pakistan* 68 D3
Toba Tek Singh, *Pakistan* 68 D5
Tobago, *W. Indies* 121 D7
Tobarra, *Spain* 33 G3
Tobelo, *Indonesia* 63 D7
Tobermorey, *Australia* 94 C2
Tobermory, *Canada* 102 C3
Tobermory, *U.K.* 14 E2
Tobin, *U.S.A.* 116 F5
Tobin, L., *Australia* 92 D4
Tobin L., *Canada* 105 C8
Toblach = Dobbiaco, *Italy* 29 B9
Toboali, *Indonesia* 62 E3
Tobol →, *Russia* 50 D7
Toboli, *Indonesia* 63 E6
Tobolsk, *Russia* 50 D7
Tobruk = Tubruq, *Libya* 79 B10
Tobyhanna, *U.S.A.* 111 E9
Tobyl = Tobol →, *Russia* 50 D7
Tocantinópolis, *Brazil* 125 E9
Tocantins □, *Brazil* 125 F9
Tocantins →, *Brazil* 122 D6
Toccoa, *U.S.A.* 109 H4
Toce →, *Italy* 28 C5
Tochigi, *Japan* 55 F9
Tochigi □, *Japan* 55 F9
Tocina, *Spain* 35 H5
Töcksfors, *Sweden* 10 E5
Tocopilla, *Chile* 126 A1
Tocumwal, *Australia* 95 F4
Tocuyo →, *Venezuela* 124 A5
Todd →, *Australia* 94 C2
Todeli, *Indonesia* 63 E6
Todenyang, *Kenya* 86 B4
Todi, *Italy* 29 F9
Todos os Santos, B. de, *Brazil* 125 F11
Todos Santos, *Mexico* 118 C2
Todtnau, *Germany* 25 H3
Toe Hd., *U.K.* 14 D1
Toecé, *Burkina Faso* 83 C4
Tofield, *Canada* 104 C6
Tofino, *Canada* 104 D3
Tofua, *Tonga* 91 D11
Tōgane, *Japan* 55 G10
Togba, *Mauritania* 82 B2
Togian, Kepulauan, *Indonesia* 63 E6
Togliatti, *Russia* 48 D9
Togo ■, *W. Afr.* 83 D5
Togtoh, *China* 56 D6
Tohma →, *Turkey* 72 C7
Tōhoku □, *Japan* 54 E10
Toinya, *Sudan* 81 F2
Tojikiston = Tajikistan ■, *Asia* 50 F8
Tojo, *Indonesia* 63 E6
Tōjō, *Japan* 55 G6
Tokachi-Dake, *Japan* 54 C11
Tokachi-Gawa →, *Japan* 54 C11
Tokaj, *Hungary* 42 B6
Tokala, *Indonesia* 63 E6
Tōkamachi, *Japan* 55 F9
Tokanui, *N.Z.* 91 M2
Tokar, *Sudan* 80 D4
Tokara-Rettō, *Japan* 55 K4
Tokarahi, *N.Z.* 91 L3
Tokashiki-Shima, *Japan* 55 L3
Tokat, *Turkey* 72 B7
Tŏkchŏn, *N. Korea* 57 E14
Tokeland, *U.S.A.* 116 D3
Tokelau Is., *Pac. Oc.* 96 H10
Tokmak, *Kyrgyzstan* 50 E8
Tokmak, *Ukraine* 47 J8
Toko Ra., *Australia* 94 C2
Tokoro-Gawa →, *Japan* 54 B12
Toku, *Japan* 55 L4
Tokushima, *Japan* 55 G7
Tokushima □, *Japan* 55 H7
Tokuyama, *Japan* 55 G5
Tōkyō, *Japan* 55 G9
Tolaga Bay, *N.Z.* 91 H7
Tolbukhin = Dobrich, *Bulgaria* 41 C11
Toledo, *Spain* 34 F6
Toledo, *Ohio, U.S.A.* 108 E4
Toledo, *Oreg., U.S.A.* 114 D2
Toledo, *Wash., U.S.A.* 114 C2
Toledo, Montes de, *Spain* 35 F6
Tolentino, *Italy* 29 E10
Tolfa, *Italy* 29 F8
Toliara, *Madag.* 89 C7
Toliara □, *Madag.* 89 C8
Tolima, *Colombia* 124 C3
Tolitoli, *Indonesia* 63 D6
Tolkmicko, *Poland* 44 D6
Tollarp, *Sweden* 11 J7
Tollensesee, *Germany* 24 B9
Tollhouse, *U.S.A.* 116 H7
Tolmachevo, *Russia* 46 C5
Tolmezzo, *Italy* 29 B10
Tolmin, *Slovenia* 29 B10
Tolna, *Hungary* 42 D3
Tolna □, *Hungary* 42 D3
Tolo, Teluk, *Indonesia* 63 E6
Tolochin = Talachyn, *Belarus* 46 E5
Tolosa, *Spain* 32 B2
Tolox, *Spain* 35 J6
Toluca, *Mexico* 119 D5
Tom Burke, *S. Africa* 89 C4
Tom Price, *Australia* 92 D2
Tomah, *U.S.A.* 112 D9
Tomahawk, *U.S.A.* 112 C10
Tomai, *Moldova* 43 D13
Tomakomai, *Japan* 54 C10
Tomales, *U.S.A.* 116 G4
Tomales B., *U.S.A.* 116 G3
Tomar, *Portugal* 35 F2
Tómaros, Óros, *Greece* 38 B2
Tomarza, *Turkey* 72 C6
Tomaszów Lubelski, *Poland* 45 H10
Tomaszów Mazowiecki, *Poland* 45 G7
Tomatlán, *Mexico* 118 D3
Tombador, Serra do, *Brazil* 124 F7
Tombé, *Sudan* 81 F3
Tombigbee →, *U.S.A.* 109 K2
Tombouctou, *Mali* 82 B4
Tombstone, *U.S.A.* 115 L8
Tombua, *Angola* 88 B1
Tomé, *Chile* 126 D1
Tomelilla, *Sweden* 11 J7
Tomelloso, *Spain* 35 F7
Tomingley, *Australia* 95 E4
Tomini, *Indonesia* 63 D6
Tomini, Teluk, *Indonesia* 63 E6
Tominian, *Mali* 82 C4
Tomiño, *Spain* 34 D2
Tomintoul, *U.K.* 14 D5
Tomislavgrad, *Bos.-H.* 42 G2
Tomkinson Ranges, *Australia* 93 E4
Tommot, *Russia* 51 D13
Tomnop Ta Suos, *Cambodia* 65 G5
Tomo →, *Colombia* 124 B5
Toms Place, *U.S.A.* 116 H8
Toms River, *U.S.A.* 111 G10
Tomsk, *Russia* 50 D9
Tomtabacken, *Sweden* 11 G8
Tona, *Spain* 32 D7
Tonalá, *Mexico* 119 D6
Tonale, Passo del, *Italy* 28 B7
Tonalea, *U.S.A.* 115 H8
Tonantins, *Brazil* 124 D5
Tonasket, *U.S.A.* 114 B4
Tonawanda, *U.S.A.* 110 D6
Tonbridge, *U.K.* 13 F8
Tondano, *Indonesia* 63 D6
Tondela, *Portugal* 34 E2
Tønder, *Denmark* 11 K2
Tondi Kiwindi, *Niger* 83 C5
Tondibi, *Mali* 83 B4
Tonekābon, *Iran* 71 B6
Tong Xian, *China* 56 E9
Tonga ■, *Pac. Oc.* 91 D11
Tonga Trench, *Pac. Oc.* 96 J10
Tongaat, *S. Africa* 89 D5
Tong'an, *China* 59 E12
Tongareva, *Cook Is.* 97 H12
Tongatapu, *Tonga* 91 E12
Tongbai, *China* 59 A9
Tongcheng, *Anhui, China* 59 B11
Tongcheng, *Hubei, China* 59 C9
Tongchŏn-ni, *N. Korea* 57 E14
Tongchuan, *China* 56 G5
Tongdao, *China* 58 D7
Tongeren, *Belgium* 17 D5
Tonggu, *China* 59 C10
Tongguan, *China* 56 G6
Tonghai, *China* 58 E4
Tonghua, *China* 57 D13
Tongjiang, *Heilongjiang, China* 60 B8
Tongjiang, *Sichuan, China* 58 B6
Tongjosŏn Man, *N. Korea* 57 E15
Tongking, G. of = Tonkin, G. of, *Asia* 64 C7
Tongliang, *China* 58 C6
Tongliao, *China* 57 C12
Tongling, *China* 59 B11
Tonglu, *China* 59 C12
Tongnae, *S. Korea* 57 G15
Tongnan, *China* 58 B5
Tongobory, *Madag.* 89 C7
Tongoy, *Chile* 126 C1
Tongren, *China* 58 D7
Tongres = Tongeren, *Belgium* 17 D5
Tongsa Dzong, *Bhutan* 67 F17
Tongue, *U.K.* 14 C4
Tongue →, *U.S.A.* 112 B2
Tongwei, *China* 56 G3
Tongxin, *China* 56 F3
Tongyang, *N. Korea* 57 E14
Tongyu, *China* 57 B12
Tongzi, *China* 58 C6
Tonj, *Sudan* 81 F2
Tonk, *India* 68 F6
Tonkawa, *U.S.A.* 113 G6
Tonkin = Bac Phan, *Vietnam* 64 B5
Tonkin, G. of, *Asia* 64 C7
Tonle Sap, *Cambodia* 64 F5
Tonnay-Charente, *France* 20 C3
Tonneins, *France* 20 D4
Tonnerre, *France* 19 E10
Tönning, *Germany* 24 A4
Tono, *Japan* 54 E10
Tonopah, *U.S.A.* 115 G5
Tonosí, *Panama* 120 E3
Tønsberg, *Norway* 9 G14
Tonya, *Turkey* 73 B8
Tooele, *U.S.A.* 114 F7
Toompine, *Australia* 95 D3
Toonpan, *Australia* 94 B4
Toora, *Australia* 95 F4
Toora-Khem, *Russia* 51 D10
Toowoomba, *Australia* 95 D5
Topalu, *Romania* 43 F13
Topaz, *U.S.A.* 116 G7
Topeka, *U.S.A.* 112 F7
Topl'a →, *Slovak Rep.* 27 C14
Topley, *Canada* 104 C3
Toplica →, *Serbia, Yug.* 40 C5
Topliţa, *Romania* 43 D10
Topocalma, Pta., *Chile* 126 C1
Topock, *U.S.A.* 117 L12
Topola, *Serbia, Yug.* 40 B4
Topolčani, *Macedonia* 40 E5
Topol'čany, *Slovak Rep.* 27 C11
Topolnitsa →, *Bulgaria* 41 D8
Topolobampo, *Mexico* 118 B3
Topoloveni, *Romania* 43 F10
Topolovgrad, *Bulgaria* 41 D10
Topolvăţu Mare, *Romania* 42 E6
Toppenish, *U.S.A.* 114 C3
Topraisar, *Romania* 43 F13
Topusko, *Croatia* 29 C12
Torà, *Spain* 32 D6
Tora Kit, *Sudan* 81 E3
Toraka Vestale, *Madag.* 89 B7
Torata, *Peru* 124 G4
Torbalı, *Turkey* 39 C9
Torbay, *Canada* 103 C9
Torbay □, *U.K.* 13 G4
Torbjörntorp, *Sweden* 11 F7
Tordesillas, *Spain* 34 D6
Töreboda, *Sweden* 11 F8
Torekov, *Sweden* 11 H6
Torellò, *Spain* 32 C7
Toreno, *Spain* 34 C4
Torfaen □, *U.K.* 13 F4
Torgau, *Germany* 24 D8
Torgelow, *Germany* 24 B10
Torhamn, *Sweden* 11 H9
Torhout, *Belgium* 17 C3
Tori, *Ethiopia* 81 F3
Tori-Shima, *Japan* 55 J10
Torigni-sur-Vire, *France* 18 C6
Torija, *Spain* 32 E1
Torin, *Mexico* 118 B2
Torino, *Italy* 28 C4
Torit, *Sudan* 81 G3
Torkamān, *Iran* 73 D12
Torkovichi, *Russia* 46 C6
Tormac, *Romania* 42 E6
Tormes →, *Spain* 34 D4
Tornado Mt., *Canada* 104 D6
Tornal'a, *Slovak Rep.* 27 C13
Torne älv →, *Sweden* 8 D21
Torneå = Tornio, *Finland* 8 D21
Torneträsk, *Sweden* 8 B18
Tornio, *Finland* 8 D21
Tornionjoki →, *Finland* 8 D21
Tornquist, *Argentina* 126 D3
Toro, *Baleares, Spain* 37 B11
Toro, *Zamora, Spain* 34 D5
Torö, *Sweden* 11 F11
Toro, Cerro del, *Chile* 126 B2
Toro Pk., *U.S.A.* 117 M10
Törökszentmiklós, *Hungary* 42 C5
Toronîos Kólpos, *Greece* 40 F7
Toronto, *Australia* 95 E5
Toronto, *Canada* 102 D4
Toronto, *U.S.A.* 110 F4
Toropets, *Russia* 46 D6
Tororo, *Uganda* 86 B3
Toros Dağları, *Turkey* 72 D5
Torquay, *Canada* 105 D8
Torquay, *U.K.* 13 G4
Torquemada, *Spain* 34 C6
Torrance, *U.S.A.* 117 M8
Torrão, *Portugal* 35 G2
Torre Annunziata, *Italy* 31 B7
Torre de Moncorvo, *Portugal* 34 D3
Torre del Campo, *Spain* 35 H7
Torre del Greco, *Italy* 31 B7
Torre del Mar, *Spain* 35 J6
Torre-Pacheco, *Spain* 33 H4
Torre Péllice, *Italy* 28 D4
Torreblanca, *Spain* 32 E5
Torrecampo, *Spain* 35 G6
Torrecilla en Cameros, *Spain* 32 C2
Torredembarra, *Spain* 32 D6
Torredonjimeno, *Spain* 35 H7
Torrejón de Ardoz, *Spain* 34 E7
Torrejoncillo, *Spain* 34 F4
Torrelaguna, *Spain* 34 E7
Torrelavega, *Spain* 34 B6
Torremaggiore, *Italy* 29 G12
Torremolinos, *Spain* 35 J6
Torrens, L., *Australia* 95 E2
Torrens Cr. →, *Australia* 94 C4
Torrens Creek, *Australia* 94 C4
Torrent, *Spain* 33 F4
Torrenueva, *Spain* 35 G7
Torreón, *Mexico* 118 B4
Torreperogil, *Spain* 35 G7
Torres, *Mexico* 118 B2
Torres Novas, *Portugal* 35 F2
Torres Strait, *Australia* 96 H6
Torres Vedras, *Portugal* 35 F1
Torrevieja, *Spain* 33 H4
Torrey, *U.S.A.* 115 G8
Torridge →, *U.K.* 13 G3
Torridon, L., *U.K.* 14 D3
Torrijos, *Spain* 34 F6
Tørring, *Denmark* 11 J3
Torrington, *Conn., U.S.A.* 111 E11
Torrington, *Wyo., U.S.A.* 112 D2
Torroella de Montgrì, *Spain* 32 C8
Torrox, *Spain* 35 J7
Torsås, *Sweden* 11 H9
Torsby, *Sweden* 10 D6
Torshälla, *Sweden* 10 E10
Tórshavn, *Færoe Is.* 8 E9
Torslanda, *Sweden* 11 G5
Torsö, *Sweden* 11 F7
Tortola, *Virgin Is.* 121 C7
Tórtoles de Esgueva, *Spain* 34 D6
Tortolì, *Italy* 30 C2
Tortona, *Italy* 28 D5
Tortorici, *Italy* 31 D7
Tortosa, *Spain* 32 E5
Tortosa, C., *Spain* 32 E5
Tortosendo, *Portugal* 34 E3
Tortue, I. de la, *Haiti* 121 B5
Tortum, *Turkey* 73 B9
Ţorūd, *Iran* 71 C7
Torul, *Turkey* 73 B8
Toruń, *Poland* 45 E5
Toruń □, *Poland* 45 E5
Tory I., *Ireland* 15 A3
Torysa →, *Slovak Rep.* 27 C14
Torzhok, *Russia* 46 D8
Torzym, *Poland* 45 F2
Tosa, *Japan* 55 H6
Tosa-Shimizu, *Japan* 55 H6
Tosa-Wan, *Japan* 55 H6
Toscana □, *Italy* 28 E8
Toscano, Arcipelago, *Italy* 28 F7
Toshkent, *Uzbekistan* 50 E7
Tosno, *Russia* 46 C6
Tossa de Mar, *Spain* 32 D7
Tösse, *Sweden* 11 F6
Tostado, *Argentina* 126 B3
Tostedt, *Germany* 24 B5
Tostón, Pta. de, *Canary Is.* 37 F5
Tosu, *Japan* 55 H5
Tosya, *Turkey* 72 B6
Toszek, *Poland* 45 H5
Totana, *Spain* 33 H3
Totebo, *Sweden* 11 G10
Toteng, *Botswana* 88 C3
Tôtes, *France* 18 C8
Tótkomlós, *Hungary* 42 D5
Totma, *Russia* 50 D5
Totnes, *U.K.* 13 G4
Totness, *Surinam* 125 B7
Totonicapán, *Guatemala* 120 D1
Totten Glacier, *Antarctica* 5 C8
Tottenham, *Australia* 95 E4
Tottenham, *Canada* 110 B5
Tottori, *Japan* 55 G7
Tottori □, *Japan* 55 G7
Touba, *Ivory C.* 82 D3
Toubkal, Djebel, *Morocco* 78 B4
Toucy, *France* 19 E10
Tougan, *Burkina Faso* 82 C4
Touggourt, *Algeria* 78 B7
Tougué, *Guinea* 82 C2
Toul, *France* 19 D12
Toulepleu, *Ivory C.* 82 D3
Toulon, *France* 21 E9
Toulouse, *France* 20 E5
Toummo, *Niger* 79 D8
Toumodi, *Ivory C.* 82 D3
Tounan, *Taiwan* 59 F13
Toungoo, *Burma* 67 K20
Touques →, *France* 18 C7
Touraine, *France* 18 E7
Tourane = Da Nang, *Vietnam* 64 D7
Tourcoing, *France* 19 B10
Touriñán, C., *Spain* 34 B1
Tournai, *Belgium* 17 D3
Tournan-en-Brie, *France* 19 D9

Tournay, *France* 20 E4
Tournon-St-Martin, *France* 18 F7
Tournon-sur-Rhône, *France* 21 C8
Tournus, *France* 19 F11
Tours, *France* 18 E7
Touwsrivier, *S. Africa* 88 E3
Tovarkovskiy, *Russia* 46 F10
Tovuz, *Azerbaijan* 49 K7
Towada, *Japan* 54 D10
Towada-Ko, *Japan* 54 D10
Towamba, *Australia* 95 F4
Towanda, *U.S.A.* 111 E8
Towang, *India* 67 F17
Tower, *U.S.A.* 112 B8
Towerhill Cr. →, *Australia* 94 C3
Towner, *U.S.A.* 112 A4
Townsend, *U.S.A.* 114 C8
Townshend I., *Australia* 94 C5
Townsville, *Australia* 94 B4
Towson, *U.S.A.* 108 F7
Toya-Ko, *Japan* 54 C10
Toyah, *U.S.A.* 113 K3
Toyahvale, *U.S.A.* 113 K3
Toyama, *Japan* 55 F8
Toyama □, *Japan* 55 F8
Toyama-Wan, *Japan* 55 F8
Toyohashi, *Japan* 55 G8
Toyokawa, *Japan* 55 G8
Toyonaka, *Japan* 55 G7
Toyooka, *Japan* 55 G7
Toyota, *Japan* 55 G8
Tozeur, *Tunisia* 78 B7
Tqibuli, *Georgia* 49 J6
Tqvarcheli, *Georgia* 49 J5
Trá Li = Tralee, *Ireland* 15 D2
Tra On, *Vietnam* 65 H5
Trabancos →, *Spain* 34 D5
Traben-Trarbach, *Germany* 25 F3
Trabzon, *Turkey* 73 B8
Tracadie, *Canada* 103 C7
Tracy, *Calif., U.S.A.* 116 H5
Tracy, *Minn., U.S.A.* 112 C7
Tradate, *Italy* 28 C5
Trafalgar, C., *Spain* 35 J4
Traian, *Brăila, Romania* 43 E12
Traian, *Tulcea, Romania* 43 E13
Trail, *Canada* 104 D5
Trainor L., *Canada* 104 A4
Trákhonas, *Cyprus* 36 D12
Tralee, *Ireland* 15 D2
Tralee B., *Ireland* 15 D2
Tramore, *Ireland* 15 D4
Tramore B., *Ireland* 15 D4
Tran Ninh, Cao Nguyen, *Laos* 64 C4
Tranås, *Sweden* 11 F8
Tranbjerg, *Denmark* 11 H4
Trancas, *Argentina* 126 B2
Trancoso, *Portugal* 34 E3
Tranebjerg, *Denmark* 11 J4
Tranemo, *Sweden* 11 G7
Trang, *Thailand* 65 J2
Trangahy, *Madag.* 89 B7
Trangan, *Indonesia* 63 F8
Trangie, *Australia* 95 E4
Trångsviken, *Sweden* 10 A7
Trani, *Italy* 31 A9
Tranoroa, *Madag.* 89 C8
Tranqueras, *Uruguay* 127 C4
Trans Nzoia □, *Kenya* 86 B4
Transantarctic Mts., *Antarctica* 5 E12
Transcona, *Canada* 105 D9
Transilvania, *Romania* 43 D9
Transilvanian Alps = Carpații Meridionali, *Romania* 43 E9
Transtrand, *Sweden* 10 C7
Transtrandsfjällen, *Sweden* 10 C6
Transylvania = Transilvania, *Romania* 43 D9
Trápani, *Italy* 30 D5
Trapper Pk., *U.S.A.* 114 D6
Traralgon, *Australia* 95 F4
Trarza, *Mauritania* 82 B2
Trasacco, *Italy* 29 G10
Trăscău, Munții, *Romania* 43 D8
Trasimeno, L., *Italy* 29 E9
Träslövsläge, *Sweden* 11 G6
Trasvase Tajo-Segura, Canal de, *Spain* 32 E2
Trat, *Thailand* 65 F4
Traun, *Austria* 26 C7
Traunreut, *Germany* 25 H8
Traunsee, *Austria* 26 D6
Traunstein, *Germany* 25 H8
Traveller's L., *Australia* 95 E3
Travemünde, *Germany* 24 B6
Travers, Mt., *N.Z.* 91 K4
Traverse City, *U.S.A.* 108 C3
Travnik, *Bos.-H.* 42 F2
Trayning, *Australia* 93 F2
Trbovlje, *Slovenia* 29 B12
Trébbia →, *Italy* 28 C6
Trebel →, *Germany* 24 B9
Trébeurden, *France* 18 D3
Třebíč, *Czech Rep.* 26 B8
Trebinje, *Bos.-H.* 40 D2
Trebisacce, *Italy* 31 C9
Trebišnjica →, *Bos.-H.* 40 D2
Trebišov, *Slovak Rep.* 27 C14
Trebižat →, *Bos.-H.* 29 E14
Trebnje, *Slovenia* 29 C12
Třeboň, *Czech Rep.* 26 B7
Trebujena, *Spain* 35 J4
Trecate, *Italy* 28 C5
Trece Martires, *Phil.* 61 D4
Tregaron, *U.K.* 13 E4
Tregnago, *Italy* 29 C8
Tregrosse Is., *Australia* 94 B5
Tréguier, *France* 18 D3
Trégunc, *France* 18 E3
Treherne, *Canada* 105 D9
Tréia, *Italy* 29 E10
Treignac, *France* 20 C5
Treinta y Tres, *Uruguay* 127 C5
Treis-karden, *Germany* 25 E3
Treklyano, *Bulgaria* 40 D6
Trélazé, *France* 18 E6
Trelew, *Argentina* 128 E3
Trélissac, *France* 20 C4
Trelleborg, *Sweden* 11 J7
Tremadog Bay, *U.K.* 12 E3
Trémiti, *Italy* 29 F12
Tremonton, *U.S.A.* 114 F7
Tremp, *Spain* 32 C5
Trenche →, *Canada* 102 C5
Trenčiansky □, *Slovak Rep.* 27 C11
Trenčín, *Slovak Rep.* 27 C11
Trenggalek, *Indonesia* 63 H14
Trenque Lauquen, *Argentina* 126 D3
Trent →, *U.K.* 12 D7
Trentino-Alto Adige □, *Italy* 29 B8
Trento, *Italy* 28 B8
Trenton, *Canada* 102 D4
Trenton, *Mo., U.S.A.* 112 E8
Trenton, *N.J., U.S.A.* 111 F10
Trenton, *Nebr., U.S.A.* 112 E4
Trenton, *Tenn., U.S.A.* 113 H10
Trepassey, *Canada* 103 C9
Trepuzzi, *Italy* 31 B11
Tres Arroyos, *Argentina* 126 D3
Três Corações, *Brazil* 127 A6
Três Lagoas, *Brazil* 125 H8
Tres Marías, *Mexico* 118 C3
Tres Montes, C., *Chile* 128 F1
Tres Pinos, *U.S.A.* 116 J5
Três Pontas, *Brazil* 127 A6
Tres Puentes, *Chile* 126 B1
Tres Puntas, C., *Argentina* 128 F3
Três Rios, *Brazil* 127 A7
Tres Valles, *Mexico* 119 D5
Tresco, *U.K.* 13 H1
Treska →, *Macedonia* 40 E5
Treskavica, *Bos.-H.* 42 G3
Trespaderne, *Spain* 34 C7
Trets, *France* 21 E9
Treuchtlingen, *Germany* 25 G6
Treuenbrietzen, *Germany* 24 C8
Trevi, *Italy* 29 F9
Trevíglio, *Italy* 28 C6
Trevínca, Peña, *Spain* 34 C4
Treviso, *Italy* 29 C9
Trévoux, *France* 21 C8
Trgovište, *Serbia, Yug.* 40 D6
Triabunna, *Australia* 94 G4
Triánda, *Greece* 36 C10
Triaucourt-en-Argonne, *France* 19 D12
Tribsees, *Germany* 24 A8
Tribulation, C., *Australia* 94 B4
Tribune, *U.S.A.* 112 F4
Tricárico, *Italy* 31 B9
Tricase, *Italy* 31 C11
Trichinopoly = Tiruchchirappalli, *India* 66 P11
Trichur, *India* 66 P10
Trida, *Australia* 95 E4
Trier, *Germany* 25 F2
Trieste, *Italy* 29 C10
Trieste, G. di, *Italy* 29 C10
Trieux →, *France* 18 D3
Triggiano, *Italy* 31 A9
Triglav, *Slovenia* 29 B10
Trigno →, *Italy* 29 F11
Trigueros, *Spain* 35 H4
Tríkeri, *Greece* 38 B5
Trikhonis, Límni, *Greece* 38 C3
Tríkkala, *Greece* 38 B3
Tríkkala □, *Greece* 38 B3
Trikomo, *Cyprus* 36 D12
Trikora, Puncak, *Indonesia* 63 E9
Trilj, *Croatia* 29 E13
Trillo, *Spain* 32 E2
Trim, *Ireland* 15 C5
Trincomalee, *Sri Lanka* 66 Q12
Trindade, *Brazil* 125 G9
Trindade, I., *Atl. Oc.* 2 F8
Třinec, *Czech Rep.* 27 B11
Trinidad, *Bolivia* 124 F6
Trinidad, *Bolivia* 124 F6
Trinidad, *Cuba* 120 B4
Trinidad, *Uruguay* 126 C4
Trinidad, *U.S.A.* 113 G2
Trinidad, *W. Indies* 121 D7
Trinidad →, *Mexico* 119 D5
Trinidad & Tobago ■, *W. Indies* 121 D7
Trinitápoli, *Italy* 31 A9
Trinity, *Canada* 103 C9
Trinity, *U.S.A.* 113 K7
Trinity →, *Calif., U.S.A.* 114 F2
Trinity →, *Tex., U.S.A.* 113 L7
Trinity B., *Canada* 103 C9
Trinity Range, *U.S.A.* 114 F4
Trinkitat, *Sudan* 80 D4
Trino, *Italy* 28 C5
Trion, *U.S.A.* 109 H3
Trionto, C., *Italy* 31 C9
Triora, *Italy* 28 D4
Tripoli = Tarābulus, *Lebanon* 75 A4
Tripoli = Tarābulus, *Libya* 79 B8
Trípolis, *Greece* 38 D4
Tripolitania, *Libya* 76 C5
Tripp, *U.S.A.* 112 D6
Tripura □, *India* 67 H18
Tripylos, *Cyprus* 36 E11
Trischen, *Germany* 24 A4
Tristan da Cunha, *Atl. Oc.* 77 K2
Trivandrum, *India* 66 Q10
Trivento, *Italy* 29 G11
Trnava, *Slovak Rep.* 27 C10
Trnavský □, *Slovak Rep.* 27 C10
Troarn, *France* 18 C6
Trochu, *Canada* 104 C6
Trodely I., *Canada* 102 B4
Troezen, *Greece* 38 D5
Trogir, *Croatia* 29 E13
Troglav, *Croatia* 29 E13
Tróia, *Italy* 31 A8
Troilus, L., *Canada* 102 B5
Troina, *Italy* 31 E7
Trois-Pistoles, *Canada* 103 C6
Trois-Rivières, *Canada* 102 C5
Troisdorf, *Germany* 24 E3
Troitsk, *Russia* 50 D7
Troitsko Pechorsk, *Russia* 50 C6
Trölladyngja, *Iceland* 8 D5
Trollhättan, *Sweden* 11 F6
Trollheimen, *Norway* 8 E13
Trombetas →, *Brazil* 125 D7
Tromsø, *Norway* 8 B18
Trona, *U.S.A.* 117 K9
Tronador, *Argentina* 128 E2
Trøndelag, *Norway* 8 D14
Trondheim, *Norway* 8 E14
Trondheimsfjorden, *Norway* 8 E14
Trönninge, *Sweden* 11 H6
Tronto →, *Italy* 29 F10
Troodos, *Cyprus* 36 E11
Troon, *U.K.* 14 F4
Tropea, *Italy* 31 D8
Tropic, *U.S.A.* 115 H7
Tropoja, *Albania* 40 D4
Trosa, *Sweden* 11 F11
Trostan, *U.K.* 15 A5
Trostberg, *Germany* 25 G8
Trostyanets, *Ukraine* 47 G8
Troup, *U.S.A.* 113 J7
Trout →, *Canada* 104 A5
Trout L., *N.W.T., Canada* 104 A4
Trout L., *Ont., Canada* 105 C10
Trout Lake, *Mich., U.S.A.* 102 C2
Trout Lake, *Wash., U.S.A.* 116 E5
Trout River, *Canada* 103 C8
Trouville-sur-Mer, *France* 18 C7
Trowbridge, *U.K.* 13 F5
Troy, *Turkey* 39 B8
Troy, *Ala., U.S.A.* 109 K3
Troy, *Idaho, U.S.A.* 114 C5
Troy, *Kans., U.S.A.* 112 F7
Troy, *Mo., U.S.A.* 112 F9
Troy, *Mont., U.S.A.* 114 B6
Troy, *N.Y., U.S.A.* 111 D11
Troy, *Ohio, U.S.A.* 108 E3
Troyan, *Bulgaria* 41 D8
Troyes, *France* 19 D11
Trpanj, *Croatia* 29 E14
Trstenik, *Serbia, Yug.* 40 C5
Trubchevsk, *Russia* 47 F7
Trucial States = United Arab Emirates ■, *Asia* 71 F7
Truckee, *U.S.A.* 116 F6
Trudfront, *Russia* 49 H8
Trudovoye, *Russia* 54 C6
Trujillo, *Honduras* 120 C2
Trujillo, *Peru* 124 E3
Trujillo, *Spain* 35 F5
Trujillo, *U.S.A.* 113 H2
Trujillo, *Venezuela* 124 B4
Truk, *Pac. Oc.* 96 G7
Trumann, *U.S.A.* 113 H9
Trumbull, Mt., *U.S.A.* 115 H7
Trŭn, *Bulgaria* 40 D6
Trun, *France* 18 D7
Trundle, *Australia* 95 E4
Trung-Phan = Annam, *Vietnam* 64 E7
Truro, *Canada* 103 C7
Truro, *U.K.* 13 G2
Truskavets, *Ukraine* 47 H2
Truslove, *Australia* 93 F3
Trŭstenik, *Bulgaria* 41 C8
Trustrup, *Denmark* 11 H4
Truth or Consequences, *U.S.A.* 115 K10
Trutnov, *Czech Rep.* 26 A8
Truyère →, *France* 20 D6
Tryavna, *Bulgaria* 41 D9
Tryon, *U.S.A.* 109 H4
Tryonville, *U.S.A.* 110 E5
Trzcianka, *Poland* 45 E3
Trzciel, *Poland* 45 F2
Trzcińsko Zdrój, *Poland* 45 F1
Trzebiatów, *Poland* 44 D2
Trzebiez, *Poland* 44 E1
Trzebnica, *Poland* 45 G4
Trzemeszno, *Poland* 45 F4
Tržič, *Slovenia* 29 B11
Tsagan Aman, *Russia* 49 G8
Tsamandás, *Greece* 38 B2
Tsaratanana, *Madag.* 89 B8
Tsaratanana, Mt. de, *Madag.* 89 A8
Tsarevo = Michurin, *Bulgaria* 41 D11
Tsarevo, *Bulgaria* 41 D9
Tsaritsáni, *Greece* 38 B4
Tsau, *Botswana* 88 C3
Tsebrykove, *Ukraine* 47 J6
Tselinograd = Aqmola, *Kazakstan* 50 D8
Tsetserleg, *Mongolia* 60 B5
Tshabong, *Botswana* 88 D3
Tshane, *Botswana* 88 C3
Tshela, *Dem. Rep. of the Congo* 84 E2
Tshesebe, *Botswana* 89 C4
Tshibeke, *Dem. Rep. of the Congo* 86 C2
Tshibinda, *Dem. Rep. of the Congo* 86 C2
Tshikapa, *Dem. Rep. of the Congo* 84 F4
Tshilenge, *Dem. Rep. of the Congo* 86 D1
Tshinsenda, *Dem. Rep. of the Congo* 87 E2
Tshofa, *Dem. Rep. of the Congo* 86 D2
Tshwane, *Botswana* 88 C3
Tsigara, *Botswana* 88 C4
Tsihombe, *Madag.* 89 D8
Tsimlyansk, *Russia* 49 G6
Tsimlyansk Res. = Tsimlyanskoye Vdkhr., *Russia* 49 F6
Tsimlyanskoye Vdkhr., *Russia* 49 F6
Tsinan = Jinan, *China* 56 F9
Tsineng, *S. Africa* 88 D3
Tsínga, *Greece* 41 E8
Tsinghai = Qinghai □, *China* 60 C4
Tsingtao = Qingdao, *China* 57 F11
Tsinjomitondraka, *Madag.* 89 B8
Tsiroanomandidy, *Madag.* 89 B8
Tsiteli-Tsqaro, *Georgia* 49 K8
Tsivilsk, *Russia* 48 C8
Tsivory, *Madag.* 89 C8
Tskhinvali, *Georgia* 49 J7
Tsna →, *Russia* 48 C6
Tsnori, *Georgia* 49 K7
Tso Moriri, L., *India* 69 C8
Tsodilo Hill, *Botswana* 88 B3
Tsogttsetsiy, *Mongolia* 56 C3
Tsolo, *S. Africa* 89 E4
Tsomo, *S. Africa* 89 E4
Tsu, *Japan* 55 G8
Tsu L., *Canada* 104 A6
Tsuchiura, *Japan* 55 F10
Tsugaru-Kaikyō, *Japan* 54 D10
Tsumeb, *Namibia* 88 B2
Tsumis, *Namibia* 88 C2
Tsuruga, *Japan* 55 G8
Tsurugi-San, *Japan* 55 H7
Tsuruoka, *Japan* 54 E9
Tsushima, *Gifu, Japan* 55 G8
Tsushima, *Nagasaki, Japan* 55 G4
Tsvetkovo, *Ukraine* 47 H6
Tsyelyakhany, *Belarus* 47 F3
Tua →, *Portugal* 34 D3
Tual, *Indonesia* 63 F8
Tuam, *Ireland* 15 C3
Tuamotu Arch. = Tuamotu Is., *Pac. Oc.* 97 J13
Tuamotu Is., *Pac. Oc.* 97 J13
Tuamotu Ridge, *Pac. Oc.* 97 K14
Tuanfeng, *China* 59 B10
Tuanxi, *China* 58 D6
Tuao, *Phil.* 61 C4
Tuapse, *Russia* 49 H4
Tuatapere, *N.Z.* 91 M1
Tuba City, *U.S.A.* 115 H8
Tuban, *Indonesia* 63 G15
Tubarão, *Brazil* 127 B6
Tūbās, *West Bank* 75 C4
Tübingen, *Germany* 25 G5
Tubruq, *Libya* 79 B10
Tubuai Is., *Pac. Oc.* 97 K13
Tuc Trung, *Vietnam* 65 G6
Tucacas, *Venezuela* 124 A5
T'uch'ang, *Taiwan* 59 E13
Tuchodi →, *Canada* 104 B4
Tuchola, *Poland* 44 E4
Tuchów, *Poland* 45 J8
Tucson, *U.S.A.* 115 K8
Tucumán □, *Argentina* 126 B2
Tucumcari, *U.S.A.* 113 H3
Tucupita, *Venezuela* 124 B6
Tucuruí, *Brazil* 125 D9
Tucuruí, Reprêsa de, *Brazil* 125 D9
Tuczno, *Poland* 45 E3
Tudela, *Spain* 32 C3
Tudmur, *Syria* 70 C3
Tudor, L., *Canada* 103 A6
Tudora, *Romania* 43 C11
Tuella →, *Portugal* 34 D3
Tuen, *Australia* 95 D4
Tugela →, *S. Africa* 89 D5
Tuguegarao, *Phil.* 61 C4
Tugur, *Russia* 51 D14
Tui, *Spain* 34 C2
Tuineje, *Canary Is.* 37 F5
Tukangbesi, Kepulauan, *Indonesia* 63 F6
Tukarak I., *Canada* 102 A4
Tukayyid, *Iraq* 70 D5
Tûkh, *Egypt* 80 H7
Tukobo, *Ghana* 82 D4
Tuktoyaktuk, *Canada* 100 B6
Tukums, *Latvia* 9 H20
Tukums □, *Latvia* 44 B10
Tukuyu, *Tanzania* 87 D3
Tula, *Hidalgo, Mexico* 119 C5
Tula, *Tamaulipas, Mexico* 119 C5
Tula, *Nigeria* 83 D7
Tula, *Russia* 46 E9
Tulancingo, *Mexico* 119 C5
Tulare, *Serbia, Yug.* 40 D5
Tulare, *U.S.A.* 116 J7
Tulare Lake Bed, *U.S.A.* 116 K7
Tularosa, *U.S.A.* 115 K10
Tulbagh, *S. Africa* 88 E2
Tulcán, *Ecuador* 124 C3
Tulcea, *Romania* 43 E13
Tulcea □, *Romania* 43 E13
Tulchyn, *Ukraine* 47 H5
Tüleh, *Iran* 71 C7
Tulemalu L., *Canada* 105 A9
Tulgheș, *Romania* 43 D10
Tuli, *Zimbabwe* 87 G2
Tulia, *U.S.A.* 113 H4
Tuliszków, *Poland* 45 F5
Tulita, *Canada* 100 B7
Ţūlkarm, *West Bank* 75 C4
Tulla, *Ireland* 15 D3
Tullahoma, *U.S.A.* 109 H2
Tullamore, *Australia* 95 E4
Tullamore, *Ireland* 15 C4
Tulle, *France* 20 C5
Tullibigeal, *Australia* 95 E4
Tulln, *Austria* 26 C9
Tullow, *Ireland* 15 D5
Tullus, *Sudan* 81 E1
Tully, *Australia* 94 B4
Tulmur, *Australia* 94 C3
Tulnici, *Romania* 43 E11
Tulovo, *Bulgaria* 41 D9
Tulsa, *U.S.A.* 113 G7
Tulsequah, *Canada* 104 B2
Tulu Milki, *Ethiopia* 81 F4
Tulu Welel, *Ethiopia* 81 F3
Tulua, *Colombia* 124 C3
Tulucești, *Romania* 43 E13
Tulun, *Russia* 51 D11
Tulungagung, *Indonesia* 63 H14
Tuma, *Russia* 46 E11
Tuma →, *Nic.* 120 D3
Tumaco, *Colombia* 124 C3
Tumatumari, *Guyana* 124 B7
Tumba, *Sweden* 10 E11
Tumba, L., *Dem. Rep. of the Congo* 84 E3
Tumbarumba, *Australia* 95 F4
Tumbaya, *Argentina* 126 A2
Tumbes, *Peru* 124 D2
Tumbwe, *Dem. Rep. of the Congo* 87 E2
Tumby Bay, *Australia* 95 E2
Tumd Youqi, *China* 56 D6
Tumen, *China* 57 C15
Tumen Jiang →, *China* 57 C16
Tumeremo, *Venezuela* 124 B6
Tumkur, *India* 66 N10
Tump, *Pakistan* 66 F3
Tumpat, *Malaysia* 65 J4
Tumu, *Ghana* 82 C4
Tumucumaque, Serra, *Brazil* 122 C5
Tumut, *Australia* 95 F4
Tumwater, *U.S.A.* 114 C2
Tunadal, *Sweden* 10 B11
Tunas de Zaza, *Cuba* 120 B4
Tunbridge Wells = Royal Tunbridge Wells, *U.K.* 13 F8
Tunçbilek, *Turkey* 39 B11
Tunceli, *Turkey* 73 C8
Tuncurry, *Australia* 95 E5
Tunduru, *Tanzania* 87 E4
Tunduru □, *Tanzania* 87 E4
Tundzha →, *Bulgaria* 41 E10
Tunga Pass, *India* 67 E19
Tungabhadra →, *India* 66 M11
Tungaru, *Sudan* 81 E3
Tungla, *Nic.* 120 D3
Tungshih, *Taiwan* 59 E13
Tungsten, *Canada* 104 A3
Tunguska, Nizhnyaya →, *Russia* 51 C9
Tunguska, Podkamennaya →, *Russia* 51 C10
Tunica, *U.S.A.* 113 H9
Tunis, *Tunisia* 79 A8
Tunisia ■, *Africa* 79 A7
Tunja, *Colombia* 124 B4
Tunkhannock, *U.S.A.* 111 E9
Tunliu, *China* 56 F7
Tunnsjøen, *Norway* 8 D15
Tunø, *Denmark* 11 J4
Tunungayualok I., *Canada* 103 A7
Tunuyán, *Argentina* 126 C2
Tunuyán →, *Argentina* 126 C2
Tunxi, *China* 59 C12
Tuo Jiang →, *China* 58 C5
Tuolumne, *U.S.A.* 116 H6
Tuolumne →, *U.S.A.* 116 H5
Tūp Āghāj, *Iran* 70 B5
Tupã, *Brazil* 127 A5
Tupelo, *U.S.A.* 109 H1
Tupik, *Russia* 46 E7
Tupinambaranas, *Brazil* 124 D7
Tupiza, *Bolivia* 126 A2
Tupižnica, *Serbia, Yug.* 40 C6
Tupman, *U.S.A.* 117 K7

Tupper, *Canada* 104 B4
Tupper Lake, *U.S.A.* 111 B10
Tupungato, Cerro, *S. Amer.* 126 C2
Tuquan, *China* 57 B11
Túquerres, *Colombia* 124 C3
Tura, *Russia* 51 C11
Turabah, *Si. Arabia* 70 D4
Tūrān, *Iran* 71 C8
Turan, *Russia* 51 D10
Turayf, *Si. Arabia* 70 D3
Turbacz, *Poland* 45 J7
Turbe, *Bos.-H.* 42 F2
Turčianske Teplice, *Slovak Rep.* 27 C11
Turcoaia, *Romania* 43 E13
Turda, *Romania* 43 D8
Turek, *Poland* 45 F5
Turen, *Venezuela* 124 B5
Turfan = Turpan, *China* 60 B3
Turfan Depression = Turpan Hami, *China* 60 B3
Tŭrgovishte, *Bulgaria* 41 C10
Turgut, *Turkey* 39 D10
Turgutlu, *Turkey* 39 C9
Turhal, *Turkey* 72 B7
Turia →, *Spain* 33 F4
Turiaçu, *Brazil* 125 D9
Turiaçu →, *Brazil* 125 D9
Turiec →, *Slovak Rep.* 27 B11
Turin = Torino, *Italy* 28 C4
Turin, *Canada* 104 D6
Turkana □, *Kenya* 86 B4
Turkana, L., *Africa* 86 B4
Türkeli, *Turkey* 41 F11
Turkestan = Türkistan, *Kazakstan* 50 E7
Túrkeve, *Hungary* 42 C5
Turkey ■, *Eurasia* 72 C7
Turkey Creek, *Australia* 92 C4
Turki, *Russia* 48 D6
Türkistan, *Kazakstan* 50 E7
Türkmenbashi, *Turkmenistan* 50 F6
Turkmenistan ■, *Asia* 50 F6
Türkmenli, *Turkey* 39 B8
Türkoğlu, *Turkey* 72 D7
Turks & Caicos Is. ■, *W. Indies* 121 B5
Turks Island Passage, *W. Indies* 121 B5
Turku, *Finland* 9 F20
Turkwel →, *Kenya* 86 B4
Turlock, *U.S.A.* 116 H6
Turnagain →, *Canada* 104 B3
Turnagain, C., *N.Z.* 91 J6
Turneffe Is., *Belize* 119 D7
Turner, *Australia* 92 C4
Turner, *U.S.A.* 114 B9
Turner Pt., *Australia* 94 A1
Turner Valley, *Canada* 104 C6
Turners Falls, *U.S.A.* 111 D12
Turnhout, *Belgium* 17 C4
Türnitz, *Austria* 26 D8
Turnor L., *Canada* 105 B7
Turnov, *Czech Rep.* 26 A8
Tŭrnovo = Veliko Tŭrnovo, *Bulgaria* 41 C9
Turnu Măgurele, *Romania* 43 G9
Turnu Roşu, P., *Romania* 43 E9
Turobin, *Poland* 45 H9
Turon, *U.S.A.* 113 G5
Turpan, *China* 60 B3
Turpan Hami, *China* 60 B3
Turrës, Kalaja e, *Albania* 40 E3
Turriff, *U.K.* 14 D6
Tursāq, *Iraq* 70 C5
Tursi, *Italy* 31 B9
Turtle Head I., *Australia* 94 A3
Turtle L., *Canada* 105 C7
Turtle Lake, *N. Dak., U.S.A.* 112 B4
Turtle Lake, *Wis., U.S.A.* 112 C8
Turtleford, *Canada* 105 C7
Turukhansk, *Russia* 51 C9
Turzovka, *Slovak Rep.* 27 B11
Tuscaloosa, *U.S.A.* 109 J2
Tuscánia, *Italy* 29 F8
Tuscany = Toscana □, *Italy* 28 E8
Tuscola, *Ill., U.S.A.* 108 F1
Tuscola, *Tex., U.S.A.* 113 J5
Tuscumbia, *U.S.A.* 109 H2
Tuskegee, *U.S.A.* 109 J3
Tustin, *U.S.A.* 117 M9
Tuszyn, *Poland* 45 G6
Tutak, *Turkey* 73 C10
Tutayev, *Russia* 46 D10
Tuticorin, *India* 66 Q11
Tutin, *Serbia, Yug.* 40 D4
Tutóia, *Brazil* 125 D10
Tutong, *Brunei* 62 D4
Tutova →, *Romania* 43 D12
Tutrakan, *Bulgaria* 41 B10
Tutshi L., *Canada* 104 B2
Tuttle, *U.S.A.* 112 B5
Tuttlingen, *Germany* 25 H4
Tutuala, *Indonesia* 63 F7
Tutuila, *Amer. Samoa* 91 B13
Tututepec, *Mexico* 119 D5
Tuva □, *Russia* 51 D10
Tuvalu ■, *Pac. Oc.* 96 H9
Tuxer Alpen, *Austria* 26 D4
Tuxpan, *Mexico* 119 C5
Tuxtla Gutiérrez, *Mexico* 119 D6
Tuy = Tui, *Spain* 34 C2
Tuy An, *Vietnam* 64 F7
Tuy Duc, *Vietnam* 65 F6
Tuy Hoa, *Vietnam* 64 F7
Tuy Phong, *Vietnam* 65 G7
Tuya L., *Canada* 104 B2
Tuyen Hoa, *Vietnam* 64 D6
Tuyen Quang, *Vietnam* 64 B5
Tūysarkān, *Iran* 71 C6
Tuz Gölü, *Turkey* 72 C5
Ţūz Khurmātū, *Iraq* 70 C5
Tuzi, *Montenegro, Yug.* 40 D3
Tuzla, *Bos.-H.* 42 F3
Tuzlov →, *Russia* 47 J10
Tuzluca, *Turkey* 73 B10
Tvååker, *Sweden* 11 G6
Tvardiţa, *Moldova* 43 D13
Tver, *Russia* 46 D8
Tvrdošin, *Slovak Rep.* 27 B12
Tvrdošovce, *Slovak Rep.* 27 C11
Tvŭrditsa, *Bulgaria* 41 D9
Twain, *U.S.A.* 116 E5
Twain Harte, *U.S.A.* 116 G6
Twardogóra, *Poland* 45 G4
Tweed, *Canada* 110 B7
Tweed →, *U.K.* 14 F6
Tweed Heads, *Australia* 95 D5
Tweedsmuir Prov. Park, *Canada* 104 C3
Twentynine Palms, *U.S.A.* 117 L10
Twillingate, *Canada* 103 C9
Twin Bridges, *U.S.A.* 114 D7
Twin Falls, *U.S.A.* 114 E6
Twin Valley, *U.S.A.* 112 B6
Twisp, *U.S.A.* 114 B3
Twistringen, *Germany* 24 C4
Two Harbors, *U.S.A.* 112 B9
Two Hills, *Canada* 104 C6
Two Rivers, *U.S.A.* 108 C2
Twofold B., *Australia* 95 F4
Tyachiv, *Ukraine* 47 H2
Tychy, *Poland* 45 H5
Tyczyn, *Poland* 45 J9
Tykocin, *Poland* 45 E9
Tyler, *U.S.A.* 107 D7
Tyler, *Minn., U.S.A.* 112 C6
Tyler, *Tex., U.S.A.* 113 J7
Tyligul →, *Ukraine* 47 J6
Týn nad Vltavou, *Czech Rep.* 26 B7
Tynda, *Russia* 51 D13
Tyne →, *U.K.* 12 C6
Tyne & Wear □, *U.K.* 12 B6
Týnec nad Sázavou, *Czech Rep.* 26 B7
Tynemouth, *U.K.* 12 B6
Tyre = Sūr, *Lebanon* 75 B4
Tyrifjorden, *Norway* 9 F14
Tyringe, *Sweden* 11 H7
Tyrnyauz, *Russia* 49 J6
Tyrol = Tirol □, *Austria* 26 D3
Tyrone, *U.S.A.* 110 F6
Tyrone □, *U.K.* 15 B4
Tyrrell →, *Australia* 95 F3
Tyrrell, L., *Australia* 95 F3
Tyrrell Arm, *Canada* 105 A9
Tyrrell L., *Canada* 105 A7
Tyrrhenian Sea, *Medit. S.* 6 G8
Tysfjorden, *Norway* 8 B17
Tystberga, *Sweden* 11 F11
Tytuvėnai, *Lithuania* 44 C10
Tyub Karagan, Mys, *Kazakstan* 49 H10
Tyuleni, Ostrova, *Kazakstan* 49 H10
Tyuleniy, *Russia* 49 H8
Tyuleniy, Mys, *Azerbaijan* 49 K10
Tyumen, *Russia* 50 D7
Tywi →, *U.K.* 13 F3
Tywyn, *U.K.* 13 E3
Tzaneen, *S. Africa* 89 C5
Tzermiádhes, *Greece* 36 D7
Tzoumérka, Óros, *Greece* 38 B3
Tzukong = Zigong, *China* 58 C5

U

U Taphao, *Thailand* 64 F3
U.S.A. = United States of America ■, *N. Amer.* 106 C7
Uanda, *Australia* 94 C3
Uasin □, *Kenya* 86 B4
Uatumã →, *Brazil* 124 D7
Uaupés, *Brazil* 124 D5
Uaupés →, *Brazil* 124 C5
Uaxactún, *Guatemala* 120 C2
Ub, *Serbia, Yug.* 40 B4
Ubá, *Brazil* 127 A7
Ubaitaba, *Brazil* 125 F11
Ubangi = Oubangi →, *Dem. Rep. of the Congo* 84 E3
Ubauro, *Pakistan* 68 E3
Ubaye →, *France* 21 D10
Ubayyiḍ, W. al →, *Iraq* 73 F10
Ube, *Japan* 55 H5
Úbeda, *Spain* 35 G7
Uberaba, *Brazil* 125 G9
Uberlândia, *Brazil* 125 G9
Überlingen, *Germany* 25 H5
Ubiaja, *Nigeria* 83 D6
Ubolratna Res., *Thailand* 64 D4
Ubombo, *S. Africa* 89 D5
Ubon Ratchathani, *Thailand* 64 E5
Ubondo, *Dem. Rep. of the Congo* 86 C2
Ubort →, *Belarus* 47 F5
Ubrique, *Spain* 35 J5
Ubundu, *Dem. Rep. of the Congo* 86 C2
Ucayali →, *Peru* 122 D3
Uchi Lake, *Canada* 105 C10
Uchiura-Wan, *Japan* 54 C10
Uchte, *Germany* 24 C4
Uchur →, *Russia* 51 D14
Uckermark, *Germany* 24 B9
Ucluelet, *Canada* 104 D3
Uda →, *Russia* 51 D14
Udagamandalam, *India* 66 P10
Udaipur, *India* 68 G5
Udaipur Garhi, *Nepal* 69 F12
Udbina, *Croatia* 29 D12
Uddeholm, *Sweden* 10 D7
Uddevalla, *Sweden* 11 F5
Uddjaur, *Sweden* 8 D17
Uden, *Neths.* 17 C5
Udgir, *India* 66 K10
Udhampur, *India* 69 C6
Udi, *Nigeria* 83 D6
Údine, *Italy* 29 B10
Udmurtia □, *Russia* 50 D6
Udon Thani, *Thailand* 64 D4
Udupi, *India* 66 N9
Udvoy Balkan, *Bulgaria* 41 D10
Udzungwa Range, *Tanzania* 87 D4
Ueckermünde, *Germany* 24 B10
Ueda, *Japan* 55 F9
Uedineniya, Os., *Russia* 4 B12
Uele →, *Dem. Rep. of the Congo* 84 D4
Uelen, *Russia* 51 C19
Uelzen, *Germany* 24 C6
Uetersen, *Germany* 24 B5
Uetze, *Germany* 24 C6
Ufa, *Russia* 50 D6
Uffenheim, *Germany* 25 F6
Ugab →, *Namibia* 88 C1
Ugalla →, *Tanzania* 86 D3
Uganda ■, *Africa* 86 B3
Ugento, *Italy* 31 C11
Ugep, *Nigeria* 83 D6
Ugie, *S. Africa* 89 E4
Ugíjar, *Spain* 35 J7
Ugine, *France* 21 C10
Uglegorsk, *Russia* 51 E15
Uglich, *Russia* 46 D10
Ugljan, *Croatia* 29 D12
Ugljane, *Croatia* 29 E13
Ugra →, *Russia* 46 E9
Uğurchin, *Bulgaria* 41 C8
Uh →, *Slovak Rep.* 27 C15
Uherské Hradiště, *Czech Rep.* 27 B10
Uherský Brod, *Czech Rep.* 27 B10
Úhlava →, *Czech Rep.* 26 B6
Uhrichsville, *U.S.A.* 110 F3
Uibhist a Deas = South Uist, *U.K.* 14 D1
Uibhist a Tuath = North Uist, *U.K.* 14 D1
Uig, *U.K.* 14 D2
Uíge, *Angola* 84 F2
Uijŏngbu, *S. Korea* 57 F14
Ŭiju, *N. Korea* 57 D13
Uinta Mts., *U.S.A.* 114 F8
Uitenhage, *S. Africa* 88 E4
Uithuizen, *Neths.* 17 A6
Ujazd, *Poland* 45 H5
Újfehértó, *Hungary* 42 C6
Ujhani, *India* 69 F8
Uji-guntō, *Japan* 55 J4
Ujjain, *India* 68 H6
Ujście, *Poland* 45 E3
Újszász, *Hungary* 42 C5
Ujung Pandang, *Indonesia* 63 F5
Uka, *Russia* 51 D17
Ukara I., *Tanzania* 86 C3
Uke-Shima, *Japan* 55 K4
Ukerewe □, *Tanzania* 86 C3
Ukerewe I., *Tanzania* 86 C3
Ukholovo, *Russia* 48 D5
Ukhrul, *India* 67 G19
Ukhta, *Russia* 50 C6
Ukiah, *U.S.A.* 116 F3
Ukki Fort, *India* 69 C7
Ukmergė, *Lithuania* 9 J21
Ukraine ■, *Europe* 47 H7
Ukwi, *Botswana* 88 C3
Ulaanbaatar, *Mongolia* 60 B5
Ulaangom, *Mongolia* 60 A4
Ulamba, *Dem. Rep. of the Congo* 87 D1
Ulan Bator = Ulaanbaatar, *Mongolia* 60 B5
Ulan Erge, *Russia* 49 G7
Ulan Khol, *Russia* 49 H8
Ulan Ude, *Russia* 51 D11
Ulanga □, *Tanzania* 87 D4
Ulanów, *Poland* 45 H9
Ulaş, *Sivas, Turkey* 72 C7
Ulaş, *Tekirdağ, Turkey* 41 E11
Ulaya, *Morogoro, Tanzania* 86 D4
Ulaya, *Tabora, Tanzania* 86 C3
Ulcinj, *Montenegro, Yug.* 40 E3
Ulco, *S. Africa* 88 D3
Ulefoss, *Norway* 9 G13
Ulëza, *Albania* 40 E3
Ulfborg, *Denmark* 11 H2
Ulhasnagar, *India* 66 K8
Uljma, *Serbia, Yug.* 42 E6
Ulla →, *Spain* 34 C2
Ulladulla, *Australia* 95 F5
Ullapool, *U.K.* 14 D3
Ullared, *Sweden* 11 G6
Ulldecona, *Spain* 32 E5
Ullswater, *U.K.* 12 C5
Ullung-do, *S. Korea* 57 F16
Ulm, *Germany* 25 G5
Ulmarra, *Australia* 95 D5
Ulmeni, *Buzău, Romania* 43 E11
Ulmeni, *Maramureş, Romania* 43 C8
Ulonguè, *Mozam.* 87 E3
Ulricehamn, *Sweden* 11 G7
Ulrika, *Sweden* 11 F9
Ulsan, *S. Korea* 57 G15
Ulsta, *U.K.* 14 A7
Ulster □, *U.K.* 15 B5
Ulstrem, *Bulgaria* 41 D10
Ulubaria, *India* 69 H13
Ulubat Gölü, *Turkey* 41 F12
Ulubey, *Turkey* 39 C11
Uluborlu, *Turkey* 39 C12
Uluçinar, *Turkey* 72 D6
Uludağ, *Turkey* 41 F13
Uludere, *Turkey* 73 D10
Uluguru Mts., *Tanzania* 86 D4
Ulukışla, *Turkey* 72 D6
Ulungur He →, *China* 60 B3
Uluru = Ayers Rock, *Australia* 93 E5
Ulutau, *Kazakstan* 50 E7
Ulva, *U.K.* 14 E2
Ulverston, *U.K.* 12 C4
Ulverstone, *Australia* 94 G4
Ulya, *Russia* 51 D15
Ulyanovsk = Simbirsk, *Russia* 48 C9
Ulyasutay, *Mongolia* 60 B4
Ulysses, *U.S.A.* 113 G4
Umag, *Croatia* 29 C10
Umala, *Bolivia* 124 G5
Uman, *Ukraine* 47 H6
Umaria, *India* 67 H12
Umarkot, *Pakistan* 66 G6
Umatilla, *U.S.A.* 114 D4
Umbértide, *Italy* 29 E9
Umbrella Mts., *N.Z.* 91 L2
Umbria □, *Italy* 29 F9
Ume älv →, *Sweden* 8 E19
Umeå, *Sweden* 8 E19
Umera, *Indonesia* 63 E7
Umfuli →, *Zimbabwe* 87 F2
Umgusa, *Zimbabwe* 87 F2
Umka, *Serbia, Yug.* 40 B4
Umkomaas, *S. Africa* 89 E5
Umm ad Daraj, J., *Jordan* 75 C4
Umm al Qaywayn, *U.A.E.* 71 E7
Umm al Qittayn, *Jordan* 75 C5
Umm Arda, *Sudan* 81 D3
Umm Bāb, *Qatar* 71 E6
Umm Bel, *Sudan* 81 E2
Umm Dubban, *Sudan* 81 D3
Umm el Fahm, *Israel* 75 C4
Umm Koweika, *Sudan* 81 E3
Umm Lajj, *Si. Arabia* 70 E3
Umm Merwa, *Sudan* 80 D3
Umm Ruwaba, *Sudan* 81 E3
Umm Sidr, *Sudan* 81 E2
Umnak I., *U.S.A.* 100 C3
Umniati →, *Zimbabwe* 87 F2
Umpqua →, *U.S.A.* 114 E1
Umreth, *India* 68 H5
Umtata, *S. Africa* 89 E4
Umuahia, *Nigeria* 83 D6
Umuarama, *Brazil* 127 A5
Umurbey, *Turkey* 41 F10
Umvukwe Ra., *Zimbabwe* 87 F3
Umzimvubu = Port St. Johns, *S. Africa* 89 E4
Umzingwane →, *Zimbabwe* 87 G2
Umzinto, *S. Africa* 89 E5
Una, *India* 68 J4
Una →, *Bos.-H.* 29 D13
Unac →, *Bos.-H.* 29 D13
Unadilla, *U.S.A.* 111 D9
Unalaska, *U.S.A.* 100 C3
'Unayzah, *Si. Arabia* 70 E4
'Unāzah, J., *Asia* 73 F8
Uncastillo, *Spain* 32 C3
Uncía, *Bolivia* 124 G5
Uncompahgre Peak, *U.S.A.* 115 G10
Unden, *Sweden* 11 F8
Underbool, *Australia* 95 F3
Undersaker, *Sweden* 10 A7
Unecha, *Russia* 47 F7
Ungarie, *Australia* 95 E4
Ungarra, *Australia* 95 E2
Ungava, Pén. d', *Canada* 101 C12
Ungava B., *Canada* 101 C13
Ungeny = Ungheni, *Moldova* 43 C12
Unggi, *N. Korea* 57 C16
Ungheni, *Moldova* 43 C12
Ungwatiri, *Sudan* 81 D4
Uni, *Russia* 48 B10
União da Vitória, *Brazil* 127 B5
Uničov, *Czech Rep.* 27 B10
Uniejów, *Poland* 45 G5
Unije, *Croatia* 29 D11
Unimak I., *U.S.A.* 100 C3
Union, *Miss., U.S.A.* 113 J10
Union, *Mo., U.S.A.* 112 F9
Union, *S.C., U.S.A.* 109 H5
Union, Mt., *U.S.A.* 115 J7
Union City, *Calif., U.S.A.* 116 H4
Union City, *N.J., U.S.A.* 111 F10
Union City, *Pa., U.S.A.* 110 E5
Union City, *Tenn., U.S.A.* 113 G10
Union Gap, *U.S.A.* 114 C3
Union Springs, *U.S.A.* 109 J3
Uniondale, *S. Africa* 88 E3
Uniontown, *U.S.A.* 108 F6
Unionville, *U.S.A.* 112 E8
Unirea, *Romania* 43 F12
United Arab Emirates ■, *Asia* 71 F7
United Kingdom ■, *Europe* 7 E5
United States of America ■, *N. Amer.* 106 C7
Unity, *Canada* 105 C7
Universales, Mtes., *Spain* 32 E3
Unjha, *India* 68 H5
Unna, *Germany* 24 D3
Unnao, *India* 69 F9
Uno, Ilha, *Guinea-Biss.* 82 C1
Unst, *U.K.* 14 A8
Unstrut →, *Germany* 24 D7
Unterfranken □, *Germany* 25 F5
Unterschleissheim, *Germany* 25 G7
Unuk →, *Canada* 104 B2
Ünye, *Turkey* 72 B7
Unzha, *Russia* 48 A7
Unzha →, *Russia* 48 B6
Uozu, *Japan* 55 F8
Upata, *Venezuela* 124 B6
Upemba, L., *Dem. Rep. of the Congo* 87 D2
Upernavik, *Greenland* 4 B5
Upington, *S. Africa* 88 D3
Upleta, *India* 68 J4
Upolu, *W. Samoa* 91 A13
Upper Alkali Lake, *U.S.A.* 114 F3
Upper Arrow L., *Canada* 104 C5
Upper Austria = Oberösterreich □, *Austria* 26 C7
Upper Foster L., *Canada* 105 B7
Upper Hutt, *N.Z.* 91 J5
Upper Klamath L., *U.S.A.* 114 E3
Upper Lake, *U.S.A.* 116 F4
Upper Musquodoboit, *Canada* 103 C7
Upper Red L., *U.S.A.* 112 A7
Upper Sandusky, *U.S.A.* 108 E4
Upper Volta = Burkina Faso ■, *Africa* 82 C4
Upphärad, *Sweden* 11 F6
Uppland, *Sweden* 10 E11
Upplands-Väsby, *Sweden* 10 E11
Uppsala, *Sweden* 10 E11
Uppsala län □, *Sweden* 10 D11
Upshi, *India* 69 C7
Upstart, C., *Australia* 94 B4
Upton, *U.S.A.* 112 C2
Ur, *Iraq* 70 D5
Uracara, *Brazil* 124 D7
Urad Qianqi, *China* 56 D5
Urakawa, *Japan* 54 C11
Ural = Zhayyq →, *Kazakstan* 50 E6
Ural, *Australia* 95 E4
Ural Mts. = Uralskie Gory, *Eurasia* 50 D6
Uralla, *Australia* 95 E5
Uralsk = Oral, *Kazakstan* 48 E10
Uralskie Gory, *Eurasia* 50 D6
Urambo, *Tanzania* 86 D3
Urambo □, *Tanzania* 86 D3
Urandangi, *Australia* 94 C2
Uranium City, *Canada* 105 B7
Uranquinty, *Australia* 95 F4
Uraricoera →, *Brazil* 124 C6
Urawa, *Japan* 55 G9
Uray, *Russia* 50 C7
'Uray'irah, *Si. Arabia* 71 E6
Urbana, *Ill., U.S.A.* 108 E1
Urbana, *Ohio, U.S.A.* 108 E4
Urbánia, *Italy* 29 E9
Urbel →, *Spain* 34 C7
Urbino, *Italy* 29 E9
Urbión, Picos de, *Spain* 32 C2
Urcos, *Peru* 124 F4
Urdinarrain, *Argentina* 126 C4
Urdos, *France* 20 F3
Urdzhar, *Kazakstan* 50 E9
Ure →, *U.K.* 12 C6
Uren, *Russia* 48 B7
Ures, *Mexico* 118 B2
Urfa = Sanliurfa, *Turkey* 73 D8
Urganch, *Uzbekistan* 50 E7
Urgench = Urganch, *Uzbekistan* 50 E7
Uri, *India* 69 B6
Uri □, *Switz.* 25 J4
Uribia, *Colombia* 124 A4
Uricani, *Romania* 42 E8
Uriondo, *Bolivia* 126 A3
Urique, *Mexico* 118 B3
Urique →, *Mexico* 118 B3
Urk, *Neths.* 17 B5
Urla, *Turkey* 39 C8
Urlaţi, *Romania* 43 F11
Urmia = Orūmīyeh, *Iran* 70 B5
Urmia, L. = Orūmīyeh, Daryācheh-ye, *Iran* 70 B5
Uroševac, *Serbia, Yug.* 40 D5
Urshult, *Sweden* 11 H8
Uruaçu, *Brazil* 125 F9
Uruapan, *Mexico* 118 D4

Urubamba →, *Peru* 124 F4
Uruçuí, *Brazil* 125 E10
Uruguai →, *Brazil* 127 B5
Uruguaiana, *Brazil* 126 B4
Uruguay ■, *S. Amer.* 126 C4
Uruguay →, *S. Amer.* 126 C4
Urumchi = Ürümqi, *China* 60 B3
Ürümqi, *China* 60 B3
Urup →, *Russia* 49 H5
Urup, Ostrov, *Russia* 51 E16
Uryupinsk, *Russia* 48 E5
Urzhum, *Russia* 48 B9
Urziceni, *Romania* 43 F11
Uşak, *Turkey* 39 C11
Uşak □, *Turkey* 39 C11
Usakos, *Namibia* 88 C2
Ušće, *Serbia, Yug.* 40 C4
Usedom, *Germany* 24 B10
'Usfān, *Si. Arabia* 80 C4
Ush-Tobe, *Kazakstan* 50 E8
Ushakova, Ostrov, *Russia* 4 A12
Ushant = Ouessant, Î. d', *France* 18 D1
Ushashi, *Tanzania* 86 C3
Ushat, *Sudan* 81 F2
Ushibuka, *Japan* 55 H5
Ushuaia, *Argentina* 128 G3
Ushumun, *Russia* 51 D13
Usk →, *U.K.* 13 F5
Üsküdar, *Turkey* 41 F13
Uslar, *Germany* 24 D5
Usman, *Russia* 47 F10
Usoke, *Tanzania* 86 D3
Usolye Sibirskoye, *Russia* 51 D11
Usoro, *Nigeria* 83 D6
Uspallata, P. de, *Argentina* 126 C2
Uspenskiy, *Kazakstan* 50 E8
Ussel, *France* 20 C6
Usson-du-Poitou, *France* 20 B4
Ussuri →, *Asia* 54 A7
Ussuriysk, *Russia* 54 C5
Ussurka, *Russia* 54 B6
Ust-Aldan = Batamay, *Russia* 51 C13
Ust Amginskoye = Khandyga, *Russia* 51 C14
Ust-Bolsheretsk, *Russia* 51 D16
Ust Buzulukskaya, *Russia* 48 E6
Ust Chaun, *Russia* 51 C18
Ust-Donetskiy, *Russia* 49 G5
Ust Ilimpeya = Yukta, *Russia* 51 C11
Ust-Ilimsk, *Russia* 51 D11
Ust Ishim, *Russia* 50 D8
Ust-Kamchatsk, *Russia* 51 D17
Ust-Kamenogorsk = Öskemen, *Kazakstan* 50 E9
Ust Khayryuzovo, *Russia* 51 D16
Ust-Kut, *Russia* 51 D11
Ust Kuyga, *Russia* 51 B14
Ust-Labinsk, *Russia* 49 H4
Ust Luga, *Russia* 46 C5
Ust Maya, *Russia* 51 C14
Ust-Mil, *Russia* 51 D14
Ust-Nera, *Russia* 51 C15
Ust-Nyukzha, *Russia* 51 D13
Ust Olenek, *Russia* 51 B12
Ust-Omchug, *Russia* 51 C15
Ust Port, *Russia* 50 C9
Ust Tsilma, *Russia* 50 C6
Ust Urt = Ustyurt Plateau, *Asia* 50 E6
Ustaritz, *France* 20 E2
Uster, *Switz.* 25 H4
Ústí nad Labem, *Czech Rep.* 26 A7
Ústí nad Orlicí, *Czech Rep.* 27 B9
Ústica, *Italy* 30 D6
Ustinov = Izhevsk, *Russia* 50 D6
Ustka, *Poland* 44 D3
Ustroń, *Poland* 45 J5
Ustrzyki Dolne, *Poland* 45 J9
Ustyurt Plateau, *Asia* 50 E6
Ustyuzhna, *Russia* 46 C9
Usu, *China* 60 B3
Usuki, *Japan* 55 H5
Usulután, *El Salv.* 120 D2
Usumacinta →, *Mexico* 119 D6
Usumbura = Bujumbura, *Burundi* 86 C2
Usure, *Tanzania* 86 C3
Uta, *Indonesia* 63 E9
Utah □, *U.S.A.* 114 G8
Utah L., *U.S.A.* 114 F8
Utansjö, *Sweden* 10 B11
Ute Creek →, *U.S.A.* 113 H3
Utebo, *Spain* 32 D3
Utena, *Lithuania* 9 J21
Utete, *Tanzania* 86 D4
Uthai Thani, *Thailand* 64 E3
Uthal, *Pakistan* 68 G2
Utiariti, *Brazil* 124 F7
Utica, *N.Y., U.S.A.* 111 C9
Utica, *Ohio, U.S.A.* 110 F2
Utiel, *Spain* 33 F3
Utik L., *Canada* 105 B9
Utikuma L., *Canada* 104 B5
Utö, *Sweden* 10 F12
Utrecht, *Neths.* 17 B5
Utrecht, *S. Africa* 89 D5
Utrecht □, *Neths.* 17 B5
Utrera, *Spain* 35 H5
Utsjoki, *Finland* 8 B22
Utsunomiya, *Japan* 55 F9
Uttar Pradesh □, *India* 69 F9
Uttaradit, *Thailand* 64 D3
Uttoxeter, *U.K.* 12 E6
Uummannarsuaq = Farvel, Kap, *Greenland* 4 D5
Uusikaarlepyy, *Finland* 8 E20
Uusikaupunki, *Finland* 9 F19
Uva, *Russia* 48 B11
Uvac →, *Serbia, Yug.* 40 C3
Uvalde, *U.S.A.* 113 L5
Uvarovo, *Russia* 48 E6
Uvat, *Russia* 50 D7
Uvinza, *Tanzania* 86 D3
Uvira, *Dem. Rep. of the Congo* 86 C2
Uvs Nuur, *Mongolia* 60 A4
Uwajima, *Japan* 55 H6
Uweinat, Jebel, *Sudan* 80 C1
Uxbridge, *Canada* 110 B5
Uxin Qi, *China* 56 E5
Uxmal, *Mexico* 119 C7
Uyo, *Nigeria* 83 D6
Üyüklü Tepe, *Turkey* 39 D9
Uyûn Mûsa, *Egypt* 75 F1
Uyuni, *Bolivia* 124 H5
Uzbekistan ■, *Asia* 50 E7
Uzen, Bolshoi →, *Kazakstan* 49 F9
Uzen, Mal →, *Kazakstan* 49 F9
Uzerche, *France* 20 C5
Uzès, *France* 21 D8
Uzh →, *Ukraine* 47 G6
Uzhgorod = Uzhhorod, *Ukraine* 47 H2
Uzhhorod, *Ukraine* 47 H2
Užice, *Serbia, Yug.* 40 C3
Uzlovaya, *Russia* 46 F10
Üzümlü, *Turkey* 39 E11
Uzunköprü, *Turkey* 41 E10
Uzunkuyu, *Turkey* 39 C8

V

Vaal →, *S. Africa* 88 D3
Vaal Dam, *S. Africa* 89 D4
Vaalwater, *S. Africa* 89 C4
Vaasa, *Finland* 8 E19
Vabre, *France* 20 E6
Vác, *Hungary* 42 C4
Vacaria, *Brazil* 127 B5
Vacaville, *U.S.A.* 116 G5
Vaccarès, Étang de, *France* 21 E8
Vach → = Vakh →, *Russia* 50 C8
Vache, Î. à, *Haiti* 121 C5
Väckelsång, *Sweden* 11 H8
Väddö, *Sweden* 10 D12
Väderstad, *Sweden* 11 F8
Vadnagar, *India* 68 H5
Vado Lígure, *Italy* 28 D5
Vadodara, *India* 68 H5
Vadsø, *Norway* 8 A23
Vadstena, *Sweden* 11 F8
Vaduz, *Liech.* 25 H5
Værøy, *Norway* 8 C15
Vágar, *Færoe Is.* 8 E9
Vaggeryd, *Sweden* 11 G8
Vagney, *France* 19 D13
Vagnhärad, *Sweden* 11 F11
Vagos, *Portugal* 34 E2
Vågsfjorden, *Norway* 8 B17
Váh →, *Slovak Rep.* 27 D11
Vahsel B., *Antarctica* 5 D1
Váï, *Greece* 36 D8
Vaigach, *Russia* 50 B6
Vaiges, *France* 18 D6
Vaihingen, *Germany* 25 G4
Vailly-sur-Aisne, *France* 19 C10
Vaison-la-Romaine, *France* 21 D9
Vakarel, *Bulgaria* 40 D7
Vakfikebir, *Turkey* 73 B8
Vakh →, *Russia* 50 C8
Vakhtan, *Russia* 48 B8
Vál, *Hungary* 42 C3
Val-de-Marne □, *France* 19 D9
Val-d'Isère, *France* 21 C10
Val-d'Oise □, *France* 19 C9
Val-d'Or, *Canada* 102 C4
Val Marie, *Canada* 105 D7
Valaam, *Russia* 46 B6
Valadares, *Portugal* 34 D2
Valahia, *Romania* 43 F9
Valais □, *Switz.* 25 J3
Valais, Alpes du, *Switz.* 25 J3
Valandovo, *Macedonia* 40 E6
Valašské Meziříčí, *Czech Rep.* 27 B10
Valáxa, *Greece* 38 C6
Vålberg, *Sweden* 10 E7
Valbo, *Sweden* 10 D10
Valbondione, *Italy* 28 B7
Vălcani, *Romania* 42 D5
Vâlcea □, *Romania* 43 F9
Valcheta, *Argentina* 128 E3
Valdagno, *Italy* 29 C8
Valdahon, *France* 19 E13
Valday, *Russia* 46 D7
Valdayskaya Vozvyshennost, *Russia* 46 D7
Valdeazogues →, *Spain* 35 G6
Valdecañas, Embalse de, *Spain* 34 F5
Valdemarsvik, *Sweden* 11 F10
Valdemoro, *Spain* 34 E7
Valdepeñas, *Spain* 35 G7
Valderaduey →, *Spain* 34 D5
Valdérice, *Italy* 30 D5
Valderrobres, *Spain* 32 E5
Valdés, Pen., *Argentina* 122 H4
Valdez, *U.S.A.* 100 B5
Valdivia, *Chile* 128 D2
Valdobbiádene, *Italy* 29 C8
Valdosta, *U.S.A.* 109 K4
Valdoviño, *Spain* 34 B2
Valdres, *Norway* 9 F13
Vale, *Georgia* 49 K6
Vale, *U.S.A.* 114 E5
Vale of Glamorgan □, *U.K.* 13 F4
Valea lui Mihai, *Romania* 42 C7
Valea Mărului, *Romania* 43 E12
Valença, *Brazil* 125 F11
Valença, *Portugal* 34 C2
Valença do Piauí, *Brazil* 125 E10
Valençay, *France* 19 E8
Valence = Valence d'Agen, *France* 20 D4
Valence, *France* 21 D8
Valence d'Agen, *France* 20 D4
Valencia, *Spain* 33 F4
Valencia, *Venezuela* 124 A5
Valencia □, *Spain* 33 F4
Valencia, G. de, *Spain* 33 F5
Valencia de Alcántara, *Spain* 35 F3
Valencia de Don Juan, *Spain* 34 C5
Valencia I., *Ireland* 15 E1
Valenciennes, *France* 19 B10
Văleni, *Romania* 43 F9
Vălenii de Munte, *Romania* 43 E11
Valensole, *France* 21 E9
Valentigney, *France* 19 E13
Valentim, Sa. do, *Brazil* 125 E10
Valentin, *Russia* 54 C7
Valentine, *Nebr., U.S.A.* 112 D4
Valentine, *Tex., U.S.A.* 113 K2
Valenza, *Italy* 28 C5
Valera, *Venezuela* 124 B4
Valga, *Estonia* 9 H22
Valguarnera Caropepe, *Italy* 31 E7
Valier, *U.S.A.* 114 B7
Valinco, G. de, *France* 21 G12
Valjevo, *Serbia, Yug.* 40 B3
Valka, *Latvia* 9 H21
Valkeakoski, *Finland* 9 F20
Valkenswaard, *Neths.* 17 C5
Vall de Uxó = La Vall d'Uixó, *Spain* 32 F4
Valla, *Sweden* 10 E10
Valladolid, *Mexico* 119 C7
Valladolid, *Spain* 34 D6
Valladolid □, *Spain* 34 D6
Vallata, *Italy* 31 A8
Valldemossa, *Spain* 37 B9
Valle d'Aosta □, *Italy* 28 C4
Valle de Arán, *Spain* 32 C5
Valle de la Pascua, *Venezuela* 124 B5
Valle de las Palmas, *Mexico* 117 N10
Valle de Santiago, *Mexico* 118 C4
Valle de Suchil, *Mexico* 118 C4
Valle de Zaragoza, *Mexico* 118 B3
Valle Fértil, Sierra del, *Argentina* 126 C2
Valle Hermoso, *Mexico* 119 B5
Valledupar, *Colombia* 124 A4
Vallehermoso, *Canary Is.* 37 F2
Vallejo, *U.S.A.* 116 G4
Vallenar, *Chile* 126 B1
Vallentuna, *Sweden* 10 E12
Valleraugue, *France* 20 D7
Vallet, *France* 18 E5
Valletta, *Malta* 36 D2
Valley Center, *U.S.A.* 117 M9
Valley City, *U.S.A.* 112 B6
Valley Falls, *U.S.A.* 114 E3
Valley Springs, *U.S.A.* 116 G6
Valley Wells, *U.S.A.* 117 K11
Valleyview, *Canada* 104 B5
Valli di Comácchio, *Italy* 29 D9
Vallimanca, Arroyo, *Argentina* 126 D4
Vallo della Lucánia, *Italy* 31 B8
Vallon-Pont-d'Arc, *France* 21 D8
Vallorbe, *Switz.* 25 J2
Valls, *Spain* 32 D6
Valmaseda = Balmaseda, *Spain* 32 B1
Valmiera, *Latvia* 9 H21
Valnera, *Spain* 34 B7
Valognes, *France* 18 C5
Valona = Vlóra, *Albania* 40 F3
Valongo, *Portugal* 34 D2
Valozhyn, *Belarus* 46 E4
Valpaços, *Portugal* 34 D3
Valparaíso, *Chile* 126 C1
Valparaíso, *Mexico* 118 C4
Valparaiso, *U.S.A.* 108 E2
Valparaíso □, *Chile* 126 C1
Valpovo, *Croatia* 42 E3
Valréas, *France* 21 D9
Vals, *Switz.* 25 J5
Vals →, *S. Africa* 88 D4
Vals, Tanjung, *Indonesia* 63 F9
Vals-les-Bains, *France* 21 D8
Valsad, *India* 66 J8
Valtellina, *Italy* 28 B6
Valuyki, *Russia* 47 G10
Valverde, *Canary Is.* 37 G2
Valverde del Camino, *Spain* 35 H4
Valverde del Fresno, *Spain* 34 E4
Vama, *Romania* 43 C10
Vamdrup, *Denmark* 11 J3
Våmhus, *Sweden* 10 C8
Vammala, *Finland* 9 F20
Vámos, *Greece* 36 D6
Van, *Turkey* 73 C10
Van, L. = Van Gölü, *Turkey* 73 C10
Van Alstyne, *U.S.A.* 113 J6
Van Blommestein Meer, *Surinam* 125 C7
Van Bruyssel, *Canada* 103 C5
Van Buren, *Canada* 103 C6
Van Buren, *Ark., U.S.A.* 113 H7
Van Buren, *Maine, U.S.A.* 109 B11
Van Buren, *Mo., U.S.A.* 113 G9
Van Canh, *Vietnam* 64 F7
Van Diemen, C., *N. Terr., Australia* 92 B5
Van Diemen, C., *Queens., Australia* 94 B2
Van Diemen G., *Australia* 92 B5
Van Gölü, *Turkey* 73 C10
Van Horn, *U.S.A.* 113 K2
Van Ninh, *Vietnam* 64 F7
Van Rees, Pegunungan, *Indonesia* 63 E9
Van Tassell, *U.S.A.* 112 D2
Van Wert, *U.S.A.* 108 E3
Van Yen, *Vietnam* 64 B5
Vanadzor, *Armenia* 49 K7
Vanavara, *Russia* 51 C11
Vancouver, *Canada* 104 D4
Vancouver, *U.S.A.* 116 E4
Vancouver, C., *Australia* 93 G2
Vancouver I., *Canada* 104 D3
Vandalia, *Ill., U.S.A.* 112 F10
Vandalia, *Mo., U.S.A.* 112 F9
Vandenburg, *U.S.A.* 117 L6
Vanderbijlpark, *S. Africa* 89 D4
Vandergrift, *U.S.A.* 110 F5
Vanderhoof, *Canada* 104 C4
Vanderkloof Dam, *S. Africa* 88 E3
Vanderlin I., *Australia* 94 B2
Vandyke, *Australia* 94 C4
Vänern, *Sweden* 11 F7
Vänersborg, *Sweden* 11 F6
Vang Vieng, *Laos* 64 C4
Vanga, *Kenya* 86 C4
Vangaindrano, *Madag.* 89 C8
Vanguard, *Canada* 105 D7
Vanier, *Canada* 102 C4
Vanino, *Russia* 51 E15
Vânju Mare, *Romania* 42 F7
Vankleek Hill, *Canada* 102 C5
Vanna, *Norway* 8 A18
Vännäs, *Sweden* 8 E18
Vannes, *France* 18 E4
Vanoise, *France* 21 C10
Vanrhynsdorp, *S. Africa* 88 E2
Vanrook, *Australia* 94 B3
Vansbro, *Sweden* 10 D8
Vansittart B., *Australia* 92 B4
Vantaa, *Finland* 9 F21
Vanthli, *India* 68 J4
Vanua Levu, *Fiji* 91 C8
Vanua Mbalavu, *Fiji* 91 C9
Vanuatu ■, *Pac. Oc.* 96 J8
Vanwyksvlei, *S. Africa* 88 E3
Vanzylsrus, *S. Africa* 88 D3
Vapnyarka, *Ukraine* 47 H5
Var □, *France* 21 E10
Var →, *France* 21 E11
Vara, *Sweden* 11 F6
Varades, *France* 18 E5
Varáita →, *Italy* 28 D4
Varallo, *Italy* 28 C5
Varanasi, *India* 69 G10
Varanger-halvøya, *Norway* 8 A23
Varangerfjorden, *Norway* 8 A23
Varano, Lago di, *Italy* 29 G12
Varaždin, *Croatia* 29 B13
Varazze, *Italy* 28 D5
Varberg, *Sweden* 11 G6
Vardar = Axiós →, *Greece* 40 F6
Varde, *Denmark* 11 J2
Varde Å →, *Denmark* 11 J2
Vardø, *Norway* 8 A24
Varel, *Germany* 24 B4
Varella, Mui, *Vietnam* 64 F7
Varèna, *Lithuania* 9 J21
Varennes-sur-Allier, *France* 19 F10
Varennes-Vauzelles, *France* 19 E10
Vareš, *Bos.-H.* 42 F3
Varese, *Italy* 28 C5
Vârfurile, *Romania* 42 D7
Vårgårda, *Sweden* 11 F6
Varginha, *Brazil* 127 A6
Vargön, *Sweden* 11 F6
Variadero, *U.S.A.* 113 H2
Varillas, *Chile* 126 A1
Varkaus, *Finland* 9 E22
Värmdölandet, *Sweden* 10 E12
Värmeln, *Sweden* 10 E6
Värmlands Bro, *Sweden* 10 E7
Värmlands län □, *Sweden* 10 E6
Varna, *Bulgaria* 41 C11
Varna □, *Bulgaria* 41 C11
Värnamo, *Sweden* 11 G8
Varnsdorf, *Czech Rep.* 26 A7
Várpalota, *Hungary* 42 C3
Vars, *Canada* 111 A9
Vars, *France* 21 D10
Varto, *Turkey* 73 C9
Varvarin, *Serbia, Yug.* 40 C5
Varzaneh, *Iran* 71 C7
Varzi, *Italy* 28 D6
Varzo, *Italy* 28 B5
Varzy, *France* 19 E10
Vas □, *Hungary* 42 C1
Vasa Barris →, *Brazil* 125 F11
Vásárosnamény, *Hungary* 42 B7
Vascão →, *Portugal* 35 H3
Vaşcău, *Romania* 42 D7
Vascongadas = País Vasco □, *Spain* 32 C2
Vasht = Khāsh, *Iran* 66 E2
Vasilevichi, *Belarus* 47 F5
Vasilikón, *Greece* 38 C5
Vasilkov = Vasylkiv, *Ukraine* 47 G6
Vaslui, *Romania* 43 D12
Vaslui □, *Romania* 43 D12
Väsman, *Sweden* 10 D9
Vassar, *Canada* 105 D9
Vassar, *U.S.A.* 108 D4
Västerås, *Sweden* 10 E10
Västerbotten, *Sweden* 8 D18
Västerdalälven →, *Sweden* 10 D8
Västergötland, *Sweden* 11 F7
Västerhaninge, *Sweden* 10 E12
Västervik, *Sweden* 11 G10
Västmanland, *Sweden* 9 G16
Västmanlands län □, *Sweden* 10 E10
Vasto, *Italy* 29 F11
Vasvár, *Hungary* 42 C1
Vasylkiv, *Ukraine* 47 G6
Vatan, *France* 19 E8
Vatersay, *U.K.* 14 E1
Váthia, *Greece* 38 E4
Vatican City ■, *Europe* 29 G9
Vaticano, C., *Italy* 31 D8
Vatili, *Cyprus* 36 D12
Vatin, *Serbia, Yug.* 42 E6
Vatnajökull, *Iceland* 8 D5
Vatoa, *Fiji* 91 D9
Vatólakkos, *Greece* 36 D5
Vatoloha, *Madag.* 89 B8
Vatomandry, *Madag.* 89 B8
Vatra-Dornei, *Romania* 43 C10
Vättern, *Sweden* 11 F8
Vaucluse □, *France* 21 E9
Vaucouleurs, *France* 19 D12
Vaud □, *Switz.* 25 J2
Vaughn, *Mont., U.S.A.* 114 C8
Vaughn, *N. Mex., U.S.A.* 115 J11
Vaupés = Uaupés →, *Brazil* 124 C5
Vaupes □, *Colombia* 124 C4
Vauvert, *France* 21 E8
Vauxhall, *Canada* 104 C6
Vava'u, *Tonga* 91 D12
Vavoua, *Ivory C.* 82 D3
Vawkavysk, *Belarus* 47 F3
Vaxholm, *Sweden* 10 E12
Växjö, *Sweden* 11 H8
Våxtorp, *Sweden* 11 H7
Vaygach, Ostrov, *Russia* 50 C7
Váyia, *Greece* 38 C5
Váyia, Ákra, *Greece* 36 C10
Vechelde, *Germany* 24 C6
Vechta, *Germany* 24 C4
Vechte →, *Neths.* 17 B6
Vecsés, *Hungary* 42 C4
Veddige, *Sweden* 11 G6
Vedea →, *Romania* 43 G10
Vedia, *Argentina* 126 C3
Vedum, *Sweden* 11 F7
Veendam, *Neths.* 17 A6
Veenendaal, *Neths.* 17 B5
Vefsna →, *Norway* 8 D15
Vega, *Norway* 8 D14
Vega, *U.S.A.* 113 H3
Vegadeo, *Spain* 34 B3
Vegorrítis, Límni, *Greece* 40 F5
Vegreville, *Canada* 104 C6
Veinge, *Sweden* 11 H7
Veisiejai, *Lithuania* 44 D10
Vejbystrand, *Sweden* 11 H6
Vejen, *Denmark* 11 J3
Vejer de la Frontera, *Spain* 35 J5
Vejle, *Denmark* 11 J3
Vejle Amtskommune □, *Denmark* 11 J3
Vejle Fjord, *Denmark* 11 J3
Vela Luka, *Croatia* 29 F13
Velas, C., *Costa Rica* 120 D2
Velasco, Sierra de, *Argentina* 126 B2
Velay, Mts. du, *France* 20 D7
Velbert, *Germany* 24 D3
Velddrif, *S. Africa* 88 E2
Velebit Planina, *Croatia* 29 D12
Velebitski Kanal, *Croatia* 29 D11
Veleka →, *Bulgaria* 41 D11
Velencei-tó, *Hungary* 42 C3
Velenje, *Slovenia* 29 B12
Veles, *Macedonia* 40 E5
Velestínon, *Greece* 38 B4
Vélez-Málaga, *Spain* 35 J6
Vélez Rubio, *Spain* 33 H2
Velhas →, *Brazil* 125 G10

Velika, *Croatia* 42 E2
Velika Gorica, *Croatia* 29 C13
Velika Kapela, *Croatia* 29 C12
Velika Kladuša, *Bos.-H.* 29 C12
Velika Morava →, *Serbia, Yug.* 40 B5
Velika Plana, *Serbia, Yug.* 40 B5
Velikaya →, *Russia* 46 D5
Velikaya Kema, *Russia* 54 B8
Velikaya Lepetikha, *Ukraine* 47 J7
Veliké Kapušany, *Slovak Rep.* 27 C15
Velike Lašče, *Slovenia* 29 C11
Veliki Jastrebac, *Serbia, Yug.* 40 C5
Veliki Kanal, *Serbia, Yug.* 42 E4
Veliki Popović, *Serbia, Yug.* 40 B5
Velikiye Luki, *Russia* 46 D6
Veliko Gradište, *Serbia, Yug.* 40 B5
Veliko Tŭrnovo, *Bulgaria* 41 C9
Velikonda Range, *India* 66 M11
Velingrad, *Bulgaria* 40 D7
Velino, Mte., *Italy* 29 F10
Velizh, *Russia* 46 E6
Velké Karlovice, *Czech Rep.* 27 B11
Velké Meziříčí, *Czech Rep.* 26 B9
Vel'ký Javorník, *Slovak Rep.* 27 B11
Vel'ký Krtíš, *Slovak Rep.* 27 C12
Vel'ký Meder, *Slovak Rep.* 27 D10
Vel'ký Tribeč, *Slovak Rep.* 27 C11
Velletri, *Italy* 30 A5
Vellinge, *Sweden* 11 J6
Vellmar, *Germany* 24 D5
Vellore, *India* 66 N11
Velsk, *Russia* 46 B11
Velten, *Germany* 24 C9
Velva, *U.S.A.* 112 A4
Velvendós, *Greece* 40 F6
Vemb, *Denmark* 11 H2
Vemdalen, *Sweden* 10 B7
Ven, *Sweden* 11 J6
Venaco, *France* 21 F13
Venado Tuerto, *Argentina* 126 C3
Venafro, *Italy* 31 A7
Venarey-les-Laumes, *France* 19 E11
Venaría, *Italy* 28 C4
Venčane, *Serbia, Yug.* 40 B4
Vence, *France* 21 E11
Vendas Novas, *Portugal* 35 G2
Vendée □, *France* 18 F5
Vendée →, *France* 18 F5
Vendéen, Bocage, *France* 20 B2
Vendeuvre-sur-Barse, *France* 19 D11
Vendôme, *France* 18 E8
Vendrell = El Vendrell, *Spain* 32 D6
Vendsyssel, *Denmark* 11 G4
Venelles, *France* 21 E9
Véneta, L., *Italy* 29 C9
Véneto □, *Italy* 29 C9
Venev, *Russia* 46 E10
Venézia, *Italy* 29 C9
Venézia, G. di, *Italy* 29 C10
Venezuela ■, *S. Amer.* 124 B5
Venezuela, G. de, *Venezuela* 122 B3
Vengurla, *India* 66 M8
Venice = Venézia, *Italy* 29 C9
Vénissieux, *France* 21 C8
Venjansjön, *Sweden* 10 D8
Venkatapuram, *India* 67 K12
Venlo, *Neths.* 17 C6
Vennesla, *Norway* 9 G12
Venosa, *Italy* 31 B8
Venray, *Neths.* 17 C6
Venta, *Lithuania* 44 B9
Venta →, *Latvia* 44 A8
Venta de Baños, *Spain* 34 D6
Venta de Cardeña = Cardeña, *Spain* 35 G6
Ventana, Punta de la, *Mexico* 118 C3
Ventana, Sa. de la, *Argentina* 126 D3
Ventersburg, *S. Africa* 88 D4
Venterstad, *S. Africa* 88 E4
Ventimíglia, *Italy* 28 E4
Ventnor, *U.K.* 13 G6
Ventoténe, *Italy* 30 B6
Ventoux, Mt., *France* 21 D9
Ventspils, *Latvia* 9 H19
Ventspils □, *Latvia* 44 A8
Ventuarí →, *Venezuela* 124 C5
Ventucopa, *U.S.A.* 117 L7
Ventura, *U.S.A.* 117 L7
Venus B., *Australia* 95 F4
Vera, *Argentina* 126 B3
Vera, *Spain* 33 H3
Veracruz, *Mexico* 119 D5
Veracruz □, *Mexico* 119 D5
Veraval, *India* 68 J4
Verbánia, *Italy* 28 C5
Verbicaro, *Italy* 31 C8
Verbier, *Switz.* 25 J3
Vercelli, *Italy* 28 C5
Verchovchevo, *Ukraine* 47 H8
Verdalsøra, *Norway* 8 E14
Verde →, *Argentina* 128 E3
Verde →, *Goiás, Brazil* 125 G8
Verde →, *Mato Grosso do Sul, Brazil* 125 H8
Verde →, *Chihuahua, Mexico* 118 B3
Verde →, *Oaxaca, Mexico* 119 D5
Verde →, *Veracruz, Mexico* 118 C4
Verde →, *Paraguay* 126 A4
Verde, Cay, *Bahamas* 120 B4
Verde Island Pass, *Phil.* 61 E4
Verden, *Germany* 24 C5
Verdhikoúsa, *Greece* 38 B3
Verdi, *U.S.A.* 116 F7
Verdigre, *U.S.A.* 112 D6
Verdon →, *France* 21 E9
Verdun, *France* 19 C12
Verdun-sur-le-Doubs, *France* 19 F12
Vereeniging, *S. Africa* 89 D4
Vérendrye, Parc Prov. de la, *Canada* 102 C4
Verga, C., *Guinea* 82 C2
Vergato, *Italy* 28 D8
Vergemont, *Australia* 94 C3
Vergemont Cr. →, *Australia* 94 C3
Vergennes, *U.S.A.* 111 B11
Vergt, *France* 20 C4
Verín, *Spain* 34 D3
Verkhnedvinsk = Vyerkhnyadzvinsk, *Belarus* 46 E4
Verkhnevilyuysk, *Russia* 51 C13
Verkhniy Baskunchak, *Russia* 49 F8
Verkhovye, *Russia* 47 F9
Verkhoyansk, *Russia* 51 C14
Verkhoyansk Ra. = Verkhoyanskiy Khrebet, *Russia* 51 C13
Verkhoyanskiy Khrebet, *Russia* 51 C13
Verlo, *Canada* 105 C7
Vermenton, *France* 19 E10
Vermilion, *Canada* 105 C6
Vermilion →, *Alta., Canada* 105 C6
Vermilion →, *Qué., Canada* 102 C5
Vermilion, B., *U.S.A.* 113 L9
Vermilion Bay, *Canada* 105 D10
Vermilion Chutes, *Canada* 104 B6
Vermilion L., *U.S.A.* 112 B8
Vermillion, *U.S.A.* 112 D6
Vermont □, *U.S.A.* 111 C12
Vermosh, *Albania* 40 D3
Vernal, *U.S.A.* 114 F9
Vernalis, *U.S.A.* 116 H5
Vernazza, *Italy* 28 D6
Verner, *Canada* 102 C3
Verneuil-sur-Avre, *France* 18 D7
Verneukpan, *S. Africa* 88 E3
Vernier, *Switz.* 25 J2
Vérnio, *Italy* 28 D8
Vernon, *Canada* 104 C5
Vernon, *France* 18 C8
Vernon, *U.S.A.* 113 H5
Vernonia, *U.S.A.* 116 E3
Vernouillet, *France* 18 D8
Vero Beach, *U.S.A.* 109 M5
Véroia, *Greece* 40 F6
Véroli, *Italy* 29 G10
Verona, *Italy* 28 C7
Verrès, *Italy* 28 C4
Versailles, *France* 19 D9
Versmold, *Germany* 24 C4
Vert, C., *Senegal* 82 C1
Vertou, *France* 18 E5
Vertus, *France* 19 D11
Verulam, *S. Africa* 89 D5
Verviers, *Belgium* 17 D5
Vervins, *France* 19 C10
Veržej, *Slovenia* 29 B13
Verzy, *France* 19 C11
Vescovato, *France* 21 F13
Veselí nad Lužnicí, *Czech Rep.* 26 B7
Veselie, *Bulgaria* 41 D11
Veselovskoye Vdkhr., *Russia* 49 G5
Veshenskaya, *Russia* 48 F5
Vesle →, *France* 19 C10
Vesoul, *France* 19 E13
Vessigebro, *Sweden* 11 H6
Vesterålen, *Norway* 8 B16
Vestfjorden, *Norway* 8 C15
Vestmannaeyjar, *Iceland* 8 E3
Vestsjællands Amtskommune □, *Denmark* 11 J5
Vestspitsbergen, *Svalbard* 4 B8
Vestvågøy, *Norway* 8 B15
Vesuvio, *Italy* 31 B7
Vesuvius, Mt. = Vesuvio, *Italy* 31 B7
Vesyegonsk, *Russia* 46 C9
Veszprém, *Hungary* 42 C2
Veszprém □, *Hungary* 42 C2
Vésztő, *Hungary* 42 D6
Vetlanda, *Sweden* 11 G9
Vetluga, *Russia* 48 B7
Vetlugu →, *Russia* 48 B8
Vetluzhskiy, *Kostroma, Russia* 48 A7
Vetluzhskiy, *Nizhniy Novgorod, Russia* 48 B7
Vetovo, *Bulgaria* 41 C10
Vetralla, *Italy* 29 F9
Vetren, *Bulgaria* 41 D8
Vettore, Mte., *Italy* 29 F10
Veurne, *Belgium* 17 C2
Vevey, *Switz.* 25 J2
Vévi, *Greece* 40 F5
Veynes, *France* 21 D9
Veys, *Iran* 71 D6
Vézelay, *France* 19 E10
Vézelise, *France* 19 D13
Vézère →, *France* 20 D4
Vezhen, *Bulgaria* 41 D8
Vezirköprü, *Turkey* 72 B6
Vezzani, *France* 21 F13
Vi Thanh, *Vietnam* 65 H5
Viacha, *Bolivia* 124 G5
Viadana, *Italy* 28 D7
Viamão, *Brazil* 127 C5
Viana, *Brazil* 125 D10
Viana, *Spain* 32 C2
Viana do Alentejo, *Portugal* 35 G3
Viana do Bolo, *Spain* 34 C3
Viana do Castelo, *Portugal* 34 D2
Viana do Castelo □, *Portugal* 34 D2
Vianden, *Lux.* 17 E6
Vianópolis, *Brazil* 125 G9
Viar →, *Spain* 35 H5
Viaréggio, *Italy* 28 E7
Viaur →, *France* 20 D5
Vibank, *Canada* 105 C8
Vibble, *Sweden* 11 G12
Vibo Valéntia, *Italy* 31 D9
Viborg, *Denmark* 11 H3
Viborg Amtskommune □, *Denmark* 11 H3
Vibraye, *France* 18 D7
Vic, *Spain* 32 D7
Vic, Étang de, *France* 20 E7
Vic-en-Bigorre, *France* 20 E4
Vic-Fézensac, *France* 20 E4
Vic-le-Comte, *France* 19 G10
Vic-sur-Cère, *France* 20 D6
Vícar, *Spain* 33 J2
Vicenza, *Italy* 29 C8
Vich = Vic, *Spain* 32 D7
Vichada →, *Colombia* 124 C5
Vichuga, *Russia* 48 B5
Vichy, *France* 19 F10
Vicksburg, *Ariz., U.S.A.* 117 M13
Vicksburg, *Mich., U.S.A.* 108 D3
Vicksburg, *Miss., U.S.A.* 113 J9
Vico, *France* 21 F12
Vico, L. di, *Italy* 29 F9
Vico del Gargano, *Italy* 29 G12
Vicovu de Sus, *Romania* 43 C10
Victor, *India* 68 J4
Victor, *Colo., U.S.A.* 112 F2
Victor, *N.Y., U.S.A.* 110 D7
Victor Harbor, *Australia* 95 F2
Victoria = Labuan, *Malaysia* 62 C5
Victoria, *Argentina* 126 C3
Victoria, *Canada* 104 D4
Victoria, *Chile* 128 D2
Victoria, *Guinea* 82 C2
Victoria, *Malta* 36 C1
Victoria, *Phil.* 61 D4
Victoria, *Romania* 43 E9
Victoria, *Kans., U.S.A.* 112 F5
Victoria, *Tex., U.S.A.* 113 L6
Victoria □, *Australia* 95 F3
Victoria →, *Australia* 92 C4
Victoria, Grand L., *Canada* 102 C4
Victoria, L., *Africa* 86 C3
Victoria, L., *Australia* 95 E3
Victoria Beach, *Canada* 105 C9
Victoria de Durango = Durango, *Mexico* 118 C4
Victoria de las Tunas, *Cuba* 120 B4
Victoria Falls, *Zimbabwe* 87 F2
Victoria Harbour, *Canada* 102 D4
Victoria I., *Canada* 100 A8
Victoria Ld., *Antarctica* 5 D11
Victoria Nile →, *Uganda* 86 B3
Victoria Res., *Canada* 103 C8
Victoria River Downs, *Australia* 92 C5
Victoria Taungdeik, *Burma* 67 J18
Victoria West, *S. Africa* 88 E3
Victorias, *Phil.* 61 F5
Victoriaville, *Canada* 103 C5
Victorica, *Argentina* 126 D2
Victorville, *U.S.A.* 117 L9
Vicuña, *Chile* 126 C1
Vicuña Mackenna, *Argentina* 126 C3
Vidal, *U.S.A.* 117 L12
Vidal Junction, *U.S.A.* 117 L12
Vidalia, *U.S.A.* 109 J4
Vidauban, *France* 21 E10
Videbæk, *Denmark* 11 H2
Videle, *Romania* 43 F10
Vídho, *Greece* 36 A3
Vidigueira, *Portugal* 35 G3
Vidin, *Bulgaria* 40 C6
Vidio, C., *Spain* 34 B4
Vidisha, *India* 68 H7
Vidra, *Romania* 43 E11
Viduša, *Bos.-H.* 40 D2
Vidzy, *Belarus* 9 J22
Viechtach, *Germany* 25 F8
Viedma, *Argentina* 128 E4
Viedma, L., *Argentina* 128 F2
Vieira do Minho, *Portugal* 34 D2
Vielha, *Spain* 32 C5
Viella = Vielha, *Spain* 32 C5
Vielsalm, *Belgium* 17 D5
Vienenburg, *Germany* 24 D6
Vieng Pou Kha, *Laos* 64 B3
Vienna = Wien, *Austria* 27 C9
Vienna, *U.S.A.* 113 G10
Vienne, *France* 21 C8
Vienne □, *France* 20 B4
Vienne →, *France* 18 E7
Vientiane, *Laos* 64 D4
Vientos, Paso de los, *Caribbean* 121 C5
Viernheim, *Germany* 25 F4
Viersen, *Germany* 24 D2
Vierwaldstättersee, *Switz.* 25 J4
Vierzon, *France* 19 E9
Vieste, *Italy* 29 G13
Vietnam ■, *Asia* 64 C6
Vieux-Boucau-les-Bains, *France* 20 E2
Vif, *France* 21 C9
Vigan, *Phil.* 61 C4
Vigévano, *Italy* 28 C5
Vigia, *Brazil* 125 D9
Vigía Chico, *Mexico* 119 D7
Víglas, Ákra, *Greece* 36 D9
Vignemalle, *France* 20 F3
Vigneulles-lès-Hattonchâtel, *France* 19 D12
Vignola, *Italy* 28 D8
Vigo, *Spain* 34 C2
Vigo, Ría de, *Spain* 34 C2
Vigsø Bugt, *Denmark* 11 G2
Vihiers, *France* 18 E6
Vijayawada, *India* 67 L12
Vík, *Iceland* 8 E4
Vika, *Sweden* 10 D8
Vikarbyn, *Sweden* 10 D9
Vikeke, *Indonesia* 63 F7
Viken, *Malmöhus, Sweden* 11 H6
Viken, *Skaraborg, Sweden* 11 F8
Viking, *Canada* 104 C6
Vikmanshyttan, *Sweden* 10 D9
Vikna, *Norway* 8 D14
Vila da Maganja, *Mozam.* 87 F4
Vila de João Belo = Xai-Xai, *Mozam.* 89 D5
Vila de Rei, *Portugal* 34 F2
Vila do Bispo, *Portugal* 35 H2
Vila do Chibuto, *Mozam.* 89 C5
Vila do Conde, *Portugal* 34 D2
Vila Franca de Xira, *Portugal* 35 G2
Vila Gamito, *Mozam.* 87 E3
Vila Gomes da Costa, *Mozam.* 89 C5
Vila Machado, *Mozam.* 87 F3
Vila Mouzinho, *Mozam.* 87 E3
Vila Nova de Famalicão, *Portugal* 34 D2
Vila Nova de Fos Côa, *Portugal* 34 D3
Vila Nova de Foscôa = Vila Nova de Fos Côa, *Portugal* 34 D3
Vila Nova de Gaia, *Portugal* 34 D2
Vila Nova de Ourém, *Portugal* 34 F2
Vila Pouca de Aguiar, *Portugal* 34 D3
Vila Real, *Portugal* 34 D3
Vila Real □, *Portugal* 34 D3
Vila-real de los Infantes, *Spain* 32 F4
Vila Real de Santo António, *Portugal* 35 H3
Vila Vasco da Gama, *Mozam.* 87 E3
Vila Velha, *Brazil* 127 A7
Vila Viçosa, *Portugal* 35 G3
Vilafranca del Maestrat, *Spain* 32 E4
Vilafranca del Penedès, *Spain* 32 D6
Vilagarcía de Arousa, *Spain* 34 C2
Vilaine →, *France* 18 E4
Vilanandro, Tanjona, *Madag.* 89 B7
Vilanculos, *Mozam.* 89 C6
Vilanova de Castelló, *Spain* 33 F4
Vilanova i la Geltrú, *Spain* 32 D6
Vilar Formosa, *Portugal* 34 E4
Vilaseca, *Spain* 32 D6
Vilaseca-Salou = Vilaseca, *Spain* 32 D6
Vilbjerg, *Denmark* 11 H2
Vilches, *Spain* 35 G7
Vileyka, *Belarus* 46 E4
Vilhelmina, *Sweden* 8 D17
Vilhena, *Brazil* 124 F6
Viliga, *Russia* 51 C16
Viliya →, *Lithuania* 9 J21
Viljandi, *Estonia* 9 G21
Vilkaviškis, *Lithuania* 44 D10
Vilkija, *Lithuania* 44 C10
Vilkitskogo, Proliv, *Russia* 51 B11
Vilkovo = Vylkove, *Ukraine* 47 K5
Villa Abecia, *Bolivia* 126 A2
Villa Ahumada, *Mexico* 118 A3
Villa Ana, *Argentina* 126 B4
Villa Ángela, *Argentina* 126 B3
Villa Bella, *Bolivia* 124 F5
Villa Bens = Tarfaya, *Morocco* 78 C3
Villa Cañás, *Argentina* 126 C3
Villa Cisneros = Dakhla, *W. Sahara* 78 D2
Villa Colón, *Argentina* 126 C2
Villa Constitución, *Argentina* 126 C3
Villa de María, *Argentina* 126 B3
Villa del Rio, *Spain* 35 H6
Villa Dolores, *Argentina* 126 C2
Villa Frontera, *Mexico* 118 B4
Villa Guillermina, *Argentina* 126 B4
Villa Hayes, *Paraguay* 126 B4
Villa Iris, *Argentina* 126 D3
Villa Juárez, *Mexico* 118 B4
Villa María, *Argentina* 126 C3
Villa Mazán, *Argentina* 126 B2
Villa Minozzo, *Italy* 28 D7
Villa Montes, *Bolivia* 126 A3
Villa Ocampo, *Argentina* 126 B4
Villa Ocampo, *Mexico* 118 B3
Villa Ojo de Agua, *Argentina* 126 B3
Villa San Giovanni, *Italy* 31 D8
Villa San José, *Argentina* 126 C4
Villa San Martín, *Argentina* 126 B3
Villa Santina, *Italy* 29 B9
Villa Unión, *Mexico* 118 C3
Villablino, *Spain* 34 C4
Villacarlos, *Spain* 37 B11
Villacarriedo, *Spain* 34 B7
Villacarrillo, *Spain* 35 G7
Villacastín, *Spain* 34 E6
Villach, *Austria* 26 E6
Villacidro, *Italy* 30 C1
Villada, *Spain* 34 C6
Villadiego, *Spain* 34 C6
Villadóssola, *Italy* 28 B5
Villafeliche, *Spain* 32 D3
Villafranca, *Spain* 32 C3
Villafranca de los Barros, *Spain* 35 G4
Villafranca de los Caballeros, *Baleares, Spain* 37 B10
Villafranca de los Caballeros, *Toledo, Spain* 35 F7
Villafranca del Cid = Vilafranca del Maestrat, *Spain* 32 E4
Villafranca del Panadés = Vilafranca del Penedès, *Spain* 32 D6
Villafranca di Verona, *Italy* 28 C7
Villafranca Tirrena, *Italy* 31 D8
Villagrán, *Mexico* 119 C5
Villaguay, *Argentina* 126 C4
Villaharta, *Spain* 35 G6
Villahermosa, *Mexico* 119 D6
Villahermosa, *Spain* 33 G2
Villaines-la-Juhel, *France* 18 D6
Villajoyosa, *Spain* 33 G4
Villalba, *Spain* 34 B3
Villalba de Guardo, *Spain* 34 C6
Villalón de Campos, *Spain* 34 C5
Villalpando, *Spain* 34 D5
Villaluenga, *Spain* 34 E7
Villamanán, *Spain* 34 C5
Villamartín, *Spain* 35 J5
Villamayor de Santiago, *Spain* 32 F2
Villamblard, *France* 20 C4
Villanova Monteleone, *Italy* 30 B1
Villanueva, *U.S.A.* 115 J11
Villanueva de Castellón = Vilanova de Castelló, *Spain* 33 F4
Villanueva de Córdoba, *Spain* 35 G6
Villanueva de la Fuente, *Spain* 33 G2
Villanueva de la Serena, *Spain* 35 G5
Villanueva de la Sierra, *Spain* 34 E4
Villanueva de los Castillejos, *Spain* 35 H3
Villanueva de los Infantes, *Spain* 35 G7
Villanueva del Arzobispo, *Spain* 33 G2
Villanueva del Fresno, *Spain* 35 G3
Villanueva y Geltrú = Vilanova i la Geltrú, *Spain* 32 D6
Villaputzu, *Italy* 30 C2
Villaquilambre, *Spain* 34 C5
Villar del Arzobispo, *Spain* 32 F4
Villar del Rey, *Spain* 35 F4
Villard-de-Lans, *France* 21 C9
Villarramiel, *Spain* 34 C6
Villarreal = Vila-real de los Infantes, *Spain* 32 F4
Villarrica, *Chile* 128 D2
Villarrica, *Paraguay* 126 B4
Villarrobledo, *Spain* 33 F2
Villarroya de la Sierra, *Spain* 32 D3

Villarrubia de los Ojos, Spain 35 F7
Villars-les-Dombes, France 19 F12
Villasayas, Spain 32 D2
Villaseca de los Gamitos = Villaseco de los Gamitos, Spain 34 D4
Villaseco de los Gamitos, Spain 34 D4
Villasimíus, Italy 30 C2
Villastar, Spain 32 E3
Villatobas, Spain 34 F7
Villavicencio, Argentina 126 C2
Villavicencio, Colombia 124 C4
Villaviciosa, Spain 34 B5
Villazón, Bolivia 126 A2
Ville-Marie, Canada 102 C4
Ville Platte, U.S.A. 113 K8
Villedieu-les-Poêles, France 18 D5
Villefort, France 20 D7
Villefranche-de-Lauragais, France 20 E5
Villefranche-de-Rouergue, France 20 D6
Villefranche-du-Périgord, France 20 D5
Villefranche-sur-Saône, France 21 C8
Villel, Spain 32 E3
Villemur-sur-Tarn, France 20 E5
Villena, Spain 33 G4
Villenauxe-la-Grande, France 19 D10
Villenave-d'Ornon, France 20 D3
Villeneuve-d'Ascq, France 19 B10
Villeneuve-l'Archevêque, France 19 D10
Villeneuve-lès-Avignon, France 21 E8
Villeneuve-sur-Allier, France 19 F10
Villeneuve-sur-Lot, France 20 D4
Villeneuve-sur-Yonne, France 19 D10
Villeréal, France 20 D4
Villers-Bocage, France 18 C6
Villers-Cotterêts, France 19 C10
Villers-sur-Mer, France 18 C6
Villersexel, France 19 E13
Villerupt, France 19 C12
Villeurbanne, France 21 C8
Villiers, S. Africa 89 D4
Villingen-Schwenningen, Germany 25 G4
Villisca, U.S.A. 112 E7
Vilna, Canada 104 C6
Vilnius, Lithuania 9 J21
Vils, Austria 26 D3
Vils →, Bayern, Germany 25 G9
Vils →, Bayern, Germany 25 F7
Vilsbiburg, Germany 25 G8
Vilshofen, Germany 25 G9
Vilusi, Montenegro, Yug. 40 D2
Vilvoorde, Belgium 17 D4
Vilyuy →, Russia 51 C13
Vilyuysk, Russia 51 C13
Vimianzo, Spain 34 B1
Vimioso, Portugal 34 D4
Vimmerby, Sweden 11 G9
Vimoutiers, France 18 D7
Vimperk, Czech Rep. 26 B6
Viña del Mar, Chile 126 C1
Vinarós, Spain 32 E5
Vincennes, U.S.A. 108 F2
Vincent, U.S.A. 117 L8
Vinchina, Argentina 126 B2
Vindelälven →, Sweden 8 E18
Vindeln, Sweden 8 D18
Vinderup, Denmark 11 H2
Vindhya Ra., India 68 H7
Vineland, U.S.A. 108 F8
Vineuil, France 18
Vinga, Romania 42 D6
Vingåker, Sweden 10 E9
Vinh, Vietnam 64 C5
Vinh Linh, Vietnam 64 D6
Vinh Long, Vietnam 65 G5
Vinh Yen, Vietnam 64 B5
Vinhais, Portugal 34 D3
Vinica, Croatia 29 B13
Vinica, Macedonia 40 E6
Vinica, Slovenia 29 C12
Vinita, U.S.A. 113 G7
Vinkovci, Croatia 42 E3
Vinnitsa = Vinnytsya, Ukraine 47 H5
Vinnytsya, Ukraine 47 H5
Vinslöv, Sweden 11 H7
Vintjärn, Sweden 10 D10
Vinton, Calif., U.S.A. 116 F6
Vinton, Iowa, U.S.A. 112 D8
Vinton, La., U.S.A. 113 K8
Vințu de Jos, Romania 43 D8
Viöl, Germany 24 A5
Vipava, Slovenia 29 C10
Vipiteno, Italy 29 B8
Vir, Croatia 29 D12
Virac, Phil. 61 E6
Virachei, Cambodia 64 F6
Virago Sd., Canada 104 C2
Viramgam, India 68 H5
Viranşehir, Turkey 73 D8
Virbalis, Lithuania 44 D9
Virden, Canada 105 D8
Vire, France 18 D6
Vire →, France 18 C5
Vírgenes, C., Argentina 128 G3
Virgin →, Canada 105 B7
Virgin →, U.S.A. 115 H6
Virgin Gorda, Virgin Is. 121 C7
Virgin Is. (British) ■, W. Indies 121 C7
Virgin Is. (U.S.) ■, W. Indies 121 C7
Virginia, S. Africa 88 D4
Virginia, U.S.A. 112 B8
Virginia □, U.S.A. 108 G7
Virginia Beach, U.S.A. 108 G8
Virginia City, Mont., U.S.A. 114 D8
Virginia City, Nev., U.S.A. 116 F7
Virginia Falls, Canada 104 A3
Virginiatown, Canada 102 C4
Virje, Croatia 29 B13
Viroqua, U.S.A. 112 D9
Virovitica, Croatia 42 E2
Virpazar, Montenegro, Yug. 40 D3
Virserum, Sweden 11 G9
Virton, Belgium 17 E5
Virudunagar, India 66 Q10
Vis, Croatia 29 E13
Visalia, U.S.A. 116 J7
Visayan Sea, Phil. 61 F5
Visby, Sweden 11 G12
Viscount Melville Sd., Canada 4 B2
Visé, Belgium 17 D5
Višegrad, Bos.-H. 42 G4
Viseu, Brazil 125 D9
Viseu, Portugal 34 E3
Viseu □, Portugal 34 E3
Vișeu de Sus, Romania 43 C9
Vishakhapatnam, India 67 L13
Vișina, Romania 43 G9
Vișinești, Moldova 43 D13
Visingsö, Sweden 11 F8
Viskafors, Sweden 11 G6
Viskan →, Sweden 11 G6
Viški Kanal, Croatia 29 E13
Vislanda, Sweden 11 H8
Visnagar, India 68 H5
Višnja Gora, Slovenia 29 C11
Viso, Mte., Italy 28 D4
Viso del Marqués, Spain 35 G7
Visoko, Bos.-H. 42 G3
Visokoi I., Antarctica 5 B1
Visp, Switz. 25 J3
Vissefjärda, Sweden 11 H9
Visselhövede, Germany 24 C5
Vissenbjerg, Denmark 11 J4
Vista, U.S.A. 117 M9
Vistonikos, Ormos = Vistonís, Límni, Greece 41 E9
Vistonís, Límni, Greece 41 E9
Vistula = Wisła →, Poland 44 D5
Vit →, Bulgaria 41 C8
Vitanje, Slovenia 29 B12
Vitebsk = Vitsyebsk, Belarus 46 E6
Viterbo, Italy 29 F9
Vitez, Bos.-H. 42 F2
Viti Levu, Fiji 91 C7
Vitigudino, Spain 34 D4
Vitim, Russia 51 D12
Vitim →, Russia 51 D12
Vitina, Bos.-H. 29 E14
Vitína, Greece 38 D4
Vítkov, Czech Rep. 27 B10
Vitória, Brazil 125 H10
Vitória da Conquista, Brazil 125 F10
Vitória de São Antão, Brazil 125 E11
Vitoria-Gasteiz, Spain 32 C2
Vitré, France 18 D5
Vitry-le-François, France 19 D11
Vitry-sur-Seine, France 19 D9
Vitsand, Sweden 10 D7
Vitsi, Óros, Greece 40 F5
Vitsyebsk, Belarus 46 E6
Vittaryd, Sweden 11 H7
Vitteaux, France 19 E11
Vittel, France 19 D12
Vittória, Italy 31 F7
Vittório Véneto, Italy 29 C9
Vittsjö, Sweden 11 H7
Viveiro, Spain 34 B3
Viviers, France 21 D8
Vivonne, France 20 B4
Vizcaíno, Desierto de, Mexico 118 B2
Vizcaíno, Sierra, Mexico 118 B2
Vizcaya □, Spain 32 B2
Vize, Turkey 41 E11
Vizianagaram, India 67 K13
Vizille, France 21 C9
Viziñada, Croatia 29 C10
Viziru, Romania 43 E12
Vizzini, Italy 31 E7
Vjosa →, Albania 40 F3
Vlaardingen, Neths. 17 C4
Vlădeasa, Vf., Romania 42 D7
Vladičin Han, Serbia, Yug. 40 D6
Vladikavkaz, Russia 49 J7
Vladimir, Russia 46 D11
Vladimir Volynskiy = Volodymyr-Volynskyy, Ukraine 47 G3
Vladimirci, Serbia, Yug. 40 B3
Vladimirovac, Serbia, Yug. 42 E5
Vladimirovka, Russia 49 F8
Vladimirovo, Bulgaria 40 C7
Vladimorvka, Kazakstan 48 E10
Vladislavovka, Ukraine 47 K8
Vladivostok, Russia 54 C5
Vlăhița, Romania 43 D10
Vlakhiótis, Greece 38 E4
Vlasenica, Bos.-H. 42 F3
Vlašić, Bos.-H. 42 F2
Vlašim, Czech Rep. 26 B7
Vlasinsko Jezero, Serbia, Yug. 40 D6
Vlasotince, Serbia, Yug. 40 D6
Vlieland, Neths. 17 A4
Vlissingen, Neths. 17 C3
Vlóra, Albania 40 F3
Vlorës, Gjiri i, Albania 40 F3
Vltava →, Czech Rep. 26 A7
Vo Dat, Vietnam 65 G6
Vobarno, Italy 28 C7
Voćin, Croatia 42 E2
Vöcklabruck, Austria 26 C6
Vodice, Croatia 29 E12
Vodňany, Czech Rep. 26 B7
Vodnjan, Croatia 29 D10
Voe, U.K. 14 A7
Vogelkop = Doberai, Jazirah, Indonesia 63 E8
Vogelsberg, Germany 24 E5
Voghera, Italy 28 D6
Vohibinany, Madag. 89 B8
Vohimarina = Iharana, Madag. 89 A9
Vohimena, Tanjon' i, Madag. 89 D8
Vohipeno, Madag. 89 C8
Voi, Kenya 86 C4
Void-Vacon, France 19 D12
Voinești, Iași, Romania 43 C12
Voinești, Prahova, Romania 43 E10
Voiotía □, Greece 38 C5
Voiron, France 21 C9
Voisey B., Canada 103 A7
Voitsberg, Austria 26 D8
Vojens, Denmark 11 J3
Vojmsjön, Sweden 8 D17
Vojnić, Croatia 29 C12
Vojnik, Italy 29 B12
Vojvodina □, Serbia, Yug. 42 E5
Vokhtoga, Russia 46 C11
Volary, Czech Rep. 26 C6
Volborg, U.S.A. 112 C2
Volcano Is. = Kazan-Rettō, Pac. Oc. 96 E6
Volchansk = Vovchansk, Ukraine 47 G9
Volchya →, Ukraine 47 H8
Volda, Norway 9 E12
Volga, Russia 46 C10
Volga →, Russia 49 G9
Volga Hts. = Privolzhskaya Vozvyshennost, Russia 48 E7
Volgo-Baltiyskiy Kanal, Russia 46 B9
Volgo-Donskoy Kanal, Russia 49 F7
Volgodonsk, Russia 49 G6
Volgograd, Russia 49 F7
Volgogradskoye Vdkhr., Russia 48 E8
Volgorechensk, Russia 48 B5
Volímai, Greece 38 D2
Volintiri, Moldova 43 D14
Volissós, Greece 39 C7
Volkach, Germany 25 F6
Völkermarkt, Austria 26 E7
Volkhov, Russia 46 C7
Volkhov →, Russia 46 B7
Völklingen, Germany 25 F2
Volkovysk = Vawkavysk, Belarus 47 F3
Volksrust, S. Africa 89 D4
Volnansk, Ukraine 47 H8
Volnovakha, Ukraine 47 J9
Volochanka, Russia 51 B10
Volodarsk, Russia 48 B6
Volodymyr-Volynskyy, Ukraine 47 G3
Vologda, Russia 46 C10
Volokolamsk, Russia 46 D8
Volokonovka, Russia 47 G9
Vólos, Greece 38 B4
Volosovo, Russia 46 C5
Volovets, Ukraine 47 H2
Volovo, Russia 46 F10
Volozhin = Valozhyn, Belarus 46 E4
Volsk, Russia 48 D8
Volta →, Ghana 83 D5
Volta, L., Ghana 83 D5
Volta Blanche = White Volta →, Ghana 83 D4
Volta Redonda, Brazil 127 A7
Voltaire, C., Australia 92 B4
Volterra, Italy 28 E7
Voltri, Italy 28 D5
Volturno →, Italy 30 A6
Vólvi, L., Greece 40 F7
Volvo, Australia 95 E3
Volyně, Czech Rep. 26 B6
Volzhsk, Russia 48 C9
Volzhskiy, Russia 49 F7
Vondrozo, Madag. 89 C8
Vónitsa, Greece 38 C2
Vopnafjörður, Iceland 8 D6
Vorarlberg □, Austria 26 D2
Vóras Óros, Greece 40 F5
Vorbasse, Denmark 11 J3
Vorchdorf, Austria 26 C6
Vorderrhein →, Switz. 25 J5
Vordingborg, Denmark 11 J5
Vorë, Albania 40 E3
Voreppe, France 21 C9
Vóriai Sporádhes, Greece 38 B5
Vórios Aiyaíon □, Greece 39 C7
Vórios Evvoïkos Kólpos, Greece 38 C5
Vorkuta, Russia 50 C7
Vormsi, Estonia 9 G20
Vorona →, Russia 48 E6
Voronezh, Russia 47 G10
Voronezh, Ukraine 47 G7
Voronezh →, Russia 47 G10
Vorontsovo-Aleksandrovskoye = Zelenokumsk, Russia 49 H6
Voroshilovgrad = Luhansk, Ukraine 47 H10
Voroshilovsk = Alchevsk, Ukraine 47 H10
Vórroi, Greece 38 F6
Vorskla →, Ukraine 47 H8
Võrts Järv, Estonia 9 G22
Võru, Estonia 9 H22
Vosges, France 19 D14
Vosges □, France 19 D13
Voskopoja, Albania 40 F4
Voskresensk, Russia 46 E10
Voskresenskoye, Russia 48 B7
Voss, Norway 9 F12
Vostok I., Kiribati 97 J12
Votice, Czech Rep. 26 B7
Vouga →, Portugal 34 E2
Vouillé, France 18 F7
Voúxa, Ákra, Greece 36 D5
Vouzela, Portugal 34 E2
Vouziers, France 19 C11
Vovchansk, Ukraine 47 G9
Vozhe Ozero, Russia 46 B10
Vozhega, Russia 46 B11
Voznesensk, Ukraine 47 J6
Voznesenye, Russia 46 B8
Vrå, Denmark 11 G3
Vráble, Slovak Rep. 27 C11
Vraćevšnica, Serbia, Yug. 40 B4
Vrakhnéïka, Greece 38 C3
Vrancea □, Romania 43 E11
Vrancei, Munții, Romania 43 E11
Vrangelya, Ostrov, Russia 51 B19
Vranica, Bos.-H. 42 G2
Vranje, Serbia, Yug. 40 D5
Vranjska Banja, Serbia, Yug. 40 D6
Vranov nad Topľou, Slovak Rep. 27 C14
Vransko, Slovenia 29 B11
Vransko Jezero, Croatia 29 E12
Vrapčište, Macedonia 40 E4
Vratsa, Bulgaria 40 C7
Vrbas, Serbia, Yug. 42 E4
Vrbas →, Bos.-H. 42 E2
Vrbnik, Croatia 29 C11
Vrbovec, Croatia 29 C13
Vrbovsko, Croatia 29 C12
Vrchlabí, Czech Rep. 26 A8
Vrede, S. Africa 89 D4
Vredefort, S. Africa 88 D4
Vreden, Germany 24 C2
Vredenburg, S. Africa 88 E2
Vredendal, S. Africa 88 E2
Vretstorp, Sweden 10 E8
Vrgorac, Croatia 29 E14
Vrhnika, Slovenia 29 C11
Vridi, Ivory C. 82 D4
Vrigstad, Sweden 11 G8
Vrindavan, India 68 F7
Vríses, Greece 36 D6
Vrnograč, Bos.-H. 29 C12
Vrondádhes, Greece 39 C8
Vrpolje, Croatia 42 E3
Vršac, Serbia, Yug. 42 E6
Vrsacki Kanal, Serbia, Yug. 42 E5
Vrútky, Slovak Rep. 27 B11
Vryburg, S. Africa 88 D3
Vryheid, S. Africa 89 D5
Vsetín, Czech Rep. 27 B11
Vu Liet, Vietnam 64 C5
Vŭcha →, Bulgaria 41 D8
Vučitrn, Serbia, Yug. 40 D4
Vukovar, Croatia 42 E3
Vulcan, Canada 104 C6
Vulcan, Romania 43 E8
Vulcan, U.S.A. 108 C2
Vulcanești, Moldova 43 E13
Vulcano, Italy 31 D7
Vŭlchedruma, Bulgaria 40 C7
Vulkaneshty = Vulcanești, Moldova 43 E13
Vunduzi →, Mozam. 87 F3
Vung Tau, Vietnam 65 G6
Vŭrbitsa, Bulgaria 41 D10
Vurshets, Bulgaria 40 C7
Vutcani, Romania 43 D12
Vyartsilya, Russia 46 A6
Vyatka = Kirov, Russia 50 D5
Vyatka →, Russia 48 C10
Vyatskiye Polyany, Russia 48 B10
Vyazemskiy, Russia 51 E14
Vyazma, Russia 46 E8
Vyazniki, Russia 48 B6
Vyborg, Russia 46 B5
Vychegda →, Russia 50 C5
Vychodné Beskydy, Europe 27 B15
Východočeský □, Czech Rep. 26 E8
Vyerkhnyadzvinsk, Belarus 46 E4
Vyksa, Russia 48 C6
Vylkove, Ukraine 47 K5
Vynohradiv, Ukraine 47 H2
Vyrnwy, L., U.K. 12 E4
Vyshniy Volochek, Russia 46 D8
Vyškov, Czech Rep. 27 B9
Vysoké Mýto, Czech Rep. 27 B9
Vysokovsk, Russia 46 D9
Vyšší Brod, Czech Rep. 26 C7
Vytegra, Russia 46 B9

W

W.A.C. Bennett Dam, Canada 104 B4
Wa, Ghana 82 C4
Waal →, Neths. 17 C5
Waalwijk, Neths. 17 C5
Wabakimi L., Canada 102 B2
Wabana, Canada 103 C9
Wabasca, Canada 104 B6
Wabash, U.S.A. 108 E3
Wabash →, U.S.A. 108 G1
Wabeno, U.S.A. 108 C1
Wabi →, Ethiopia 81 F5
Wabigoon L., Canada 105 D10
Wabowden, Canada 105 C9
Wąbrzeźno, Poland 45 E5
Wabu Hu, China 59 A11
Wabuk Pt., Canada 102 A2
Wabush, Canada 103 B6
Wabuska, U.S.A. 114 G4
Wąchock, Poland 45 G8
Wächtersbach, Germany 25 E5
Waco, U.S.A. 113 K6
Waconichi, L., Canada 102 B5
Wad, Pakistan 68 F2
Wad Ban Naqa, Sudan 81 D3
Wad Banda, Sudan 81 E2
Wad el Haddad, Sudan 81 E3
Wad en Nau, Sudan 81 E3
Wad Hamid, Sudan 81 D3
Wâd Medanî, Sudan 81 E3
Wadai, Africa 76 E5
Wadayama, Japan 55 G7
Waddeneilanden, Neths. 17 A5
Waddenzee, Neths. 17 A5
Wadderin Hill, Australia 93 F2
Waddington, U.S.A. 111 B9
Waddington, Mt., Canada 104 C3
Waddy Pt., Australia 95 C5
Wadebridge, U.K. 13 G3
Wadena, Canada 105 C8
Wadena, U.S.A. 112 B7
Wädenswil, Switz. 25 H4
Wadern, Germany 25 F2
Wadesboro, U.S.A. 109 H5
Wadhams, Canada 104 C3
Wādī as Sīr, Jordan 75 D4
Wadi Gemâl, Egypt 80 C4
Wadi Halfa, Sudan 80 C3
Wadian, China 59 A9
Wadlew, Poland 45 G6
Wadowice, Poland 45 J6
Wadsworth, U.S.A. 114 G4
Waegwan, S. Korea 57 G15
Wafrah, Si. Arabia 70 D5
Wageningen, Neths. 17 C5
Wager B., Canada 101 B11
Wagga Wagga, Australia 95 F4
Waghete, Indonesia 63 E9
Wagin, Australia 93 F2
Wagon Mound, U.S.A. 113 G2
Wagoner, U.S.A. 113 H7
Wągrowiec, Poland 45 F4
Wah, Pakistan 68 C5
Wahai, Indonesia 63 E7
Wahiawa, U.S.A. 106 H15
Wâḩid, Egypt 75 E1
Wahnai, Afghan. 68 C1
Wahoo, U.S.A. 112 E6
Wahpeton, U.S.A. 112 B6
Wai, Koh, Cambodia 65 H4
Waiau →, N.Z. 91 K4
Waibeem, Indonesia 63 E8
Waiblingen, Germany 25 G5
Waidhofen an der Thaya, Austria 26 C8
Waidhofen an der Ybbs, Austria 26 D7
Waigeo, Indonesia 63 E8
Waihi, N.Z. 91 G5
Waihou →, N.Z. 91 G5
Waika, Dem. Rep. of the Congo 86 C2
Waikabubak, Indonesia 63 F5
Waikari, N.Z. 91 K4
Waikato →, N.Z. 91 G5
Waikerie, Australia 95 E3
Waikokopu, N.Z. 91 H6
Waikouaiti, N.Z. 91 L3
Waimakariri →, N.Z. 91 K4
Waimate, N.Z. 91 L3
Wainganga →, India 66 K11
Waingapu, Indonesia 63 F6

Waini →, *Guyana* 124 **B7**
Wainwright, *Canada* 105 **C6**
Waiouru, *N.Z.* 91 **H5**
Waipara, *N.Z.* 91 **K4**
Waipawa, *N.Z.* 91 **H6**
Waipiro, *N.Z.* 91 **H7**
Waipu, *N.Z.* 91 **F5**
Waipukurau, *N.Z.* 91 **J6**
Wairakei, *N.Z.* 91 **H6**
Wairarapa, L., *N.Z.* 91 **J5**
Wairoa, *N.Z.* 91 **H6**
Waitaki →, *N.Z.* 91 **L3**
Waitara, *N.Z.* 91 **H5**
Waitsburg, *U.S.A.* 114 **C5**
Waiuku, *N.Z.* 91 **G5**
Wajima, *Japan* 55 **F8**
Wajir, *Kenya* 86 **B5**
Wajir □, *Kenya* 86 **B5**
Wakasa, *Japan* 55 **G7**
Wakasa-Wan, *Japan* 55 **G7**
Wakatipu, L., *N.Z.* 91 **L2**
Wakaw, *Canada* 105 **C7**
Wakayama, *Japan* 55 **G7**
Wakayama-ken □, *Japan* 55 **H7**
Wake Forest, *U.S.A.* 109 **H6**
Wake I., *Pac. Oc.* 96 **F8**
Wakefield, *N.Z.* 91 **J4**
Wakefield, *U.K.* 12 **D6**
Wakefield, *Mass., U.S.A.* 111 **D13**
Wakefield, *Mich., U.S.A.* 112 **B10**
Wakema, *Burma* 67 **L19**
Wakkanai, *Japan* 54 **B10**
Wakkerstroom, *S. Africa* 89 **D5**
Wakool, *Australia* 95 **F3**
Wakool →, *Australia* 95 **F3**
Wakre, *Indonesia* 63 **E8**
Wakuach L., *Canada* 103 **A6**
Walamba, *Zambia* 87 **E2**
Wałbrzych, *Poland* 45 **H3**
Walbury Hill, *U.K.* 13 **F6**
Walcha, *Australia* 95 **E5**
Walcheren, *Neths.* 17 **C3**
Walcott, *U.S.A.* 114 **F10**
Wałcz, *Poland* 45 **E3**
Waldbröl, *Germany* 24 **E3**
Waldburg Ra., *Australia* 92 **D2**
Waldeck, *Germany* 24 **D5**
Walden, *Colo., U.S.A.* 114 **F10**
Walden, *N.Y., U.S.A.* 111 **E10**
Waldkirch, *Germany* 25 **G3**
Waldkirchen, *Germany* 25 **G9**
Waldkraiburg, *Germany* 25 **G8**
Waldport, *U.S.A.* 114 **D1**
Waldron, *U.S.A.* 113 **H7**
Waldviertel, *Austria* 26 **C8**
Walembele, *Ghana* 82 **C4**
Walensee, *Switz.* 25 **H5**
Wales □, *U.K.* 13 **E3**
Walewale, *Ghana* 83 **C4**
Walgett, *Australia* 95 **E4**
Walgreen Coast, *Antarctica* 5 **D15**
Walhalla, *Australia* 95 **F4**
Walhalla, *U.S.A.* 105 **D9**
Walker, *U.S.A.* 112 **B7**
Walker L., *Man., Canada* 105 **C9**
Walker L., *Qué., Canada* 103 **B6**
Walker L., *U.S.A.* 114 **G4**
Walkerston, *Australia* 94 **C4**
Walkerton, *Canada* 110 **B3**
Wall, *U.S.A.* 112 **D3**
Walla Walla, *U.S.A.* 114 **C4**
Wallabadah, *Australia* 94 **B3**
Wallace, *Idaho, U.S.A.* 114 **C6**
Wallace, *N.C., U.S.A.* 109 **H7**
Wallace, *Nebr., U.S.A.* 112 **E4**
Wallaceburg, *Canada* 102 **D3**
Wallachia = Valahia, *Romania* 43 **F9**
Wallal, *Australia* 95 **D4**
Wallal Downs, *Australia* 92 **C3**
Wallambin, L., *Australia* 93 **F2**
Wallaroo, *Australia* 95 **E2**
Walldürn, *Germany* 25 **F5**
Wallenhorst, *Germany* 24 **C4**
Wallerawang, *Australia* 95 **E5**
Wallhallow, *Australia* 94 **B2**
Wallingford, *U.S.A.* 111 **E12**
Wallis & Futuna, Is., *Pac. Oc.* 96 **J10**
Wallowa, *U.S.A.* 114 **D5**
Wallowa Mts., *U.S.A.* 114 **D5**
Walls, *U.K.* 14 **A7**
Wallsend, *Australia* 95 **E5**
Wallula, *U.S.A.* 114 **C4**
Wallumbilla, *Australia* 95 **D4**
Walmsley, L., *Canada* 105 **A7**
Walney, I. of, *U.K.* 12 **C4**
Walnut Creek, *U.S.A.* 116 **H4**
Walnut Ridge, *U.S.A.* 113 **G9**
Wals, *Austria* 26 **D5**
Walsall, *U.K.* 13 **E6**
Walsenburg, *U.S.A.* 113 **G2**
Walsh, *U.S.A.* 113 **G3**
Walsh →, *Australia* 94 **B3**
Walsh P.O., *Australia* 94 **B3**
Walsrode, *Germany* 24 **C5**
Walterboro, *U.S.A.* 109 **J5**
Walters, *U.S.A.* 113 **H5**
Waltershausen, *Germany* 24 **E6**
Waltham, *U.S.A.* 111 **D13**
Waltham Station, *Canada* 102 **C4**
Waltman, *U.S.A.* 114 **E10**
Walton, *U.S.A.* 111 **D9**
Walton-on-the-Naze, *U.K.* 13 **F9**
Walvis Bay, *Namibia* 88 **C1**
Walvisbaai = Walvis Bay, *Namibia* 88 **C1**
Wamba, *Dem. Rep. of the Congo* 86 **B2**
Wamba, *Kenya* 86 **B4**
Wamego, *U.S.A.* 112 **F6**
Wamena, *Indonesia* 63 **E9**
Wamulan, *Indonesia* 63 **E7**
Wan Xian, *China* 56 **E8**
Wana, *Pakistan* 68 **C3**
Wanaaring, *Australia* 95 **D3**
Wanaka, *N.Z.* 91 **L2**
Wanaka L., *N.Z.* 91 **L2**
Wan'an, *China* 59 **D10**
Wanapitei L., *Canada* 102 **C3**
Wanbi, *Australia* 95 **E3**
Wandarrie, *Australia* 93 **E2**
Wandel Sea = McKinley Sea, *Arctic* 4 **A7**
Wanderer, *Zimbabwe* 87 **F3**
Wandoan, *Australia* 95 **D4**
Wanfu, *China* 57 **D12**
Wang →, *Thailand* 64 **D2**
Wang Kai, *Sudan* 81 **F2**
Wang Noi, *Thailand* 64 **E3**
Wang Saphung, *Thailand* 64 **D3**
Wang Thong, *Thailand* 64 **D3**
Wanga, *Dem. Rep. of the Congo* 86 **B2**
Wangal, *Indonesia* 63 **F8**
Wanganella, *Australia* 95 **F3**
Wanganui, *N.Z.* 91 **H5**
Wangaratta, *Australia* 95 **F4**
Wangary, *Australia* 95 **E2**
Wangcang, *China* 58 **A6**
Wangdu, *China* 56 **E8**
Wangen, *Germany* 25 **H5**
Wangerooge, *Germany* 24 **B3**
Wangi, *Kenya* 86 **C5**
Wangiwangi, *Indonesia* 63 **F6**
Wangjiang, *China* 59 **B11**
Wangmo, *China* 58 **E6**
Wangqing, *China* 57 **C15**
Wankaner, *India* 68 **H4**
Wanless, *Canada* 105 **C8**
Wannian, *China* 59 **C11**
Wanning, *Taiwan* 64 **C8**
Wanon Niwat, *Thailand* 64 **D4**
Wanquan, *China* 56 **D8**
Wanrong, *China* 56 **G6**
Wanshan, *China* 58 **D7**
Wanshengchang, *China* 58 **C6**
Wantage, *U.K.* 13 **F6**
Wanxian, *China* 58 **B7**
Wanyuan, *China* 58 **A7**
Wanzai, *China* 59 **C10**
Wapakoneta, *U.S.A.* 108 **E3**
Wapato, *U.S.A.* 114 **C3**
Wapawekka L., *Canada* 105 **C8**
Wapikopa L., *Canada* 102 **B2**
Wappingers Falls, *U.S.A.* 111 **E11**
Wapsipinicon →, *U.S.A.* 112 **E9**
Warangal, *India* 66 **L11**
Waratah, *Australia* 94 **G4**
Waratah B., *Australia* 95 **F4**
Warburg, *Germany* 24 **D5**
Warburton, *Vic., Australia* 95 **F4**
Warburton, *W. Austral., Australia* 93 **E4**
Warburton Ra., *Australia* 93 **E4**
Ward, *N.Z.* 91 **J5**
Ward →, *Australia* 95 **D4**
Ward Cove, *U.S.A.* 104 **B2**
Ward Mt., *U.S.A.* 116 **H8**
Warden, *S. Africa* 89 **D4**
Wardha, *India* 66 **J11**
Wardha →, *India* 66 **K11**
Wardlow, *Canada* 104 **C6**
Ware, *Canada* 104 **B3**
Ware, *U.S.A.* 111 **D12**
Waregem, *Belgium* 17 **D3**
Wareham, *U.S.A.* 111 **E14**
Waremme, *Belgium* 17 **D5**
Waren, *Germany* 24 **B8**
Warendorf, *Germany* 24 **D4**
Warialda, *Australia* 95 **D5**
Wariap, *Indonesia* 63 **E8**
Warin Chamrap, *Thailand* 64 **E5**
Warka, *Poland* 45 **G8**
Warkopi, *Indonesia* 63 **E8**
Warm Springs, *U.S.A.* 115 **G5**
Warman, *Canada* 105 **C7**
Warmbad, *Namibia* 88 **D2**
Warmbad, *S. Africa* 89 **C4**
Warminster, *U.K.* 13 **F5**
Warnambool Downs, *Australia* 94 **C3**
Warnemünde, *Germany* 24 **A8**
Warner, *Canada* 104 **D6**
Warner Mts., *U.S.A.* 114 **F3**
Warner Robins, *U.S.A.* 109 **J4**
Warnow →, *Germany* 24 **A8**
Waroona, *Australia* 93 **F2**
Warracknabeal, *Australia* 95 **F3**
Warragul, *Australia* 95 **F4**
Warrawagine, *Australia* 92 **D3**
Warrego →, *Australia* 95 **E4**
Warrego Ra., *Australia* 94 **C4**
Warren, *Australia* 95 **E4**
Warren, *Ark., U.S.A.* 113 **J8**
Warren, *Mich., U.S.A.* 108 **D4**
Warren, *Minn., U.S.A.* 112 **A6**
Warren, *Ohio, U.S.A.* 110 **E4**
Warren, *Pa., U.S.A.* 110 **E5**
Warrenpoint, *U.K.* 15 **B5**
Warrensburg, *U.S.A.* 112 **F8**
Warrenton, *S. Africa* 88 **D3**
Warrenton, *U.S.A.* 116 **D3**
Warrenville, *Australia* 95 **D4**
Warri, *Nigeria* 83 **D6**
Warrina, *Australia* 95 **D2**
Warrington, *U.K.* 12 **D5**
Warrington, *U.S.A.* 109 **K2**
Warrington □, *U.K.* 12 **D5**
Warrnambool, *Australia* 95 **F3**
Warroad, *U.S.A.* 112 **A7**
Warsa, *Indonesia* 63 **E9**
Warsaw = Warszawa, *Poland* 45 **F8**
Warsaw, *Ind., U.S.A.* 108 **E3**
Warsaw, *N.Y., U.S.A.* 110 **D6**
Warsaw, *Ohio, U.S.A.* 110 **F3**
Warstein, *Germany* 24 **D4**
Warszawa, *Poland* 45 **F8**
Warszawa □, *Poland* 45 **F7**
Warta, *Poland* 45 **G5**
Warta →, *Poland* 45 **F1**
Warthe = Warta →, *Poland* 45 **F1**
Waru, *Indonesia* 63 **E8**
Warwick, *Australia* 95 **D5**
Warwick, *U.K.* 13 **E6**
Warwick, *U.S.A.* 111 **E13**
Warwickshire □, *U.K.* 13 **E6**
Wasaga Beach, *Canada* 110 **B4**
Wasatch Ra., *U.S.A.* 114 **F8**
Wasbank, *S. Africa* 89 **D5**
Wasco, *Calif., U.S.A.* 117 **K7**
Wasco, *Oreg., U.S.A.* 114 **D3**
Waseca, *U.S.A.* 112 **C8**
Wasekamio L., *Canada* 105 **B7**
Wash, The, *U.K.* 12 **E8**
Washago, *Canada* 110 **B5**
Washburn, *N. Dak., U.S.A.* 112 **B4**
Washburn, *Wis., U.S.A.* 112 **B9**
Washim, *India* 66 **J10**
Washington, *U.K.* 12 **C6**
Washington, *D.C., U.S.A.* 108 **F7**
Washington, *Ga., U.S.A.* 109 **J4**
Washington, *Ind., U.S.A.* 108 **F2**
Washington, *Iowa, U.S.A.* 112 **E9**
Washington, *Mo., U.S.A.* 112 **F9**
Washington, *N.C., U.S.A.* 109 **H7**
Washington, *N.J., U.S.A.* 111 **F10**
Washington, *Pa., U.S.A.* 110 **F4**
Washington, *Utah, U.S.A.* 115 **H7**
Washington □, *U.S.A.* 114 **C3**
Washington, Mt., *U.S.A.* 111 **B13**
Washington I., *U.S.A.* 108 **C2**
Washougal, *U.S.A.* 116 **E4**
Wasian, *Indonesia* 63 **E8**
Wasilków, *Poland* 45 **E10**
Wasior, *Indonesia* 63 **E8**
Waskaganish, *Canada* 102 **B4**
Waskaiowaka, L., *Canada* 105 **B9**
Waskesiu Lake, *Canada* 105 **C7**
Wasserburg, *Germany* 25 **G8**
Wasserkuppe, *Germany* 24 **E5**
Wassy, *France* 19 **D11**
Waswanipi, *Canada* 102 **C4**
Waswanipi, L., *Canada* 102 **C4**
Watampone, *Indonesia* 63 **E6**
Water Park Pt., *Australia* 94 **C5**
Water Valley, *U.S.A.* 113 **H10**
Waterberge, *S. Africa* 89 **C4**
Waterbury, *Conn., U.S.A.* 111 **E11**
Waterbury, *Vt., U.S.A.* 111 **B12**
Waterbury L., *Canada* 105 **B8**
Waterdown, *Canada* 110 **C5**
Waterford, *Canada* 110 **D4**
Waterford, *Ireland* 15 **D4**
Waterford, *U.S.A.* 116 **H6**
Waterford □, *Ireland* 15 **D4**
Waterford Harbour, *Ireland* 15 **D5**
Waterhen L., *Man., Canada* 105 **C9**
Waterhen L., *Sask., Canada* 105 **C7**
Waterloo, *Belgium* 17 **D4**
Waterloo, *Ont., Canada* 102 **D3**
Waterloo, *Qué., Canada* 111 **A12**
Waterloo, *S. Leone* 82 **D2**
Waterloo, *Ill., U.S.A.* 112 **F9**
Waterloo, *Iowa, U.S.A.* 112 **D8**
Waterloo, *N.Y., U.S.A.* 110 **D8**
Watersmeet, *U.S.A.* 112 **B10**
Waterton-Glacier International Peace Park, *U.S.A.* 114 **B7**
Watertown, *Conn., U.S.A.* 111 **E11**
Watertown, *N.Y., U.S.A.* 111 **C9**
Watertown, *S. Dak., U.S.A.* 112 **C6**
Watertown, *Wis., U.S.A.* 112 **D10**
Waterval-Boven, *S. Africa* 89 **D5**
Waterville, *Canada* 111 **A13**
Waterville, *Maine, U.S.A.* 103 **D6**
Waterville, *N.Y., U.S.A.* 111 **D9**
Waterville, *Pa., U.S.A.* 110 **E7**
Waterville, *Wash., U.S.A.* 114 **C3**
Watervliet, *U.S.A.* 111 **D11**
Wates, *Indonesia* 63 **G14**
Watford, *Canada* 110 **D3**
Watford, *U.K.* 13 **F7**
Watford City, *U.S.A.* 112 **B3**
Wathaman →, *Canada* 105 **B8**
Watheroo, *Australia* 93 **F2**
Wating, *China* 56 **G4**
Watkins Glen, *U.S.A.* 110 **D8**
Watling I. = San Salvador, *Bahamas* 121 **B5**
Watonga, *U.S.A.* 113 **H5**
Watrous, *Canada* 105 **C7**
Watrous, *U.S.A.* 113 **H2**
Watsa, *Dem. Rep. of the Congo* 86 **B2**
Watseka, *U.S.A.* 108 **E2**
Watson, *Australia* 93 **F5**
Watson, *Canada* 105 **C8**
Watson Lake, *Canada* 104 **A3**
Watsonville, *U.S.A.* 116 **J5**
Wattiwarriganna Cr. →, *Australia* 95 **D2**
Wattwil, *Switz.* 25 **H5**
Watuata = Batuata, *Indonesia* 63 **F6**
Watubela, Kepulauan, *Indonesia* 63 **E8**
Watubela Is. = Watubela, Kepulauan, *Indonesia* 63 **E8**
Wau, *Sudan* 77 **F6**
Waubamik, *Canada* 110 **A4**
Waubay, *U.S.A.* 112 **C6**
Waubra, *Australia* 95 **F3**
Wauchope, *Australia* 95 **E5**
Wauchula, *U.S.A.* 109 **M5**
Waugh, *Canada* 105 **D9**
Waukarlycarly, L., *Australia* 92 **D3**
Waukegan, *U.S.A.* 108 **D2**
Waukesha, *U.S.A.* 108 **D1**
Waukon, *U.S.A.* 112 **D9**
Wauneta, *U.S.A.* 112 **E4**
Waupaca, *U.S.A.* 112 **C10**
Waupun, *U.S.A.* 112 **D10**
Waurika, *U.S.A.* 113 **H6**
Wausau, *U.S.A.* 112 **C10**
Wautoma, *U.S.A.* 112 **C10**
Wauwatosa, *U.S.A.* 108 **D2**
Wave Hill, *Australia* 92 **C5**
Waveney →, *U.K.* 13 **E9**
Waverley, *N.Z.* 91 **H5**
Waverly, *Iowa, U.S.A.* 112 **D8**
Waverly, *N.Y., U.S.A.* 111 **E8**
Wavre, *Belgium* 17 **D4**
Wâw, *Sudan* 81 **F2**
Wāw al Kabīr, *Libya* 79 **C9**
Wawa, *Canada* 102 **C3**
Wawa, *Nigeria* 83 **D5**
Wawa, *Sudan* 80 **C3**
Wawanesa, *Canada* 105 **D9**
Wawona, *U.S.A.* 116 **H7**
Waxahachie, *U.S.A.* 113 **J6**
Way, L., *Australia* 93 **E3**
Wayatinah, *Australia* 94 **G4**
Waycross, *U.S.A.* 109 **K4**
Wayi, *Sudan* 81 **F3**
Wayne, *Nebr., U.S.A.* 112 **D6**
Wayne, *W. Va., U.S.A.* 108 **F4**
Waynesboro, *Ga., U.S.A.* 109 **J4**
Waynesboro, *Miss., U.S.A.* 109 **K1**
Waynesboro, *Pa., U.S.A.* 108 **F7**
Waynesboro, *Va., U.S.A.* 108 **F6**
Waynesburg, *U.S.A.* 108 **F5**
Waynesville, *U.S.A.* 109 **H4**
Waynoka, *U.S.A.* 113 **G5**
Wazirabad, *Pakistan* 68 **C6**
Wda →, *Poland* 44 **E5**
We, *Indonesia* 62 **C1**
Weald, The, *U.K.* 13 **F8**
Wear →, *U.K.* 12 **C6**
Weatherford, *Okla., U.S.A.* 113 **H5**
Weatherford, *Tex., U.S.A.* 113 **J6**
Weaverville, *U.S.A.* 114 **F2**
Webb City, *U.S.A.* 113 **G7**
Webo = Nyaake, *Liberia* 82 **E3**
Webster, *Mass., U.S.A.* 111 **D13**
Webster, *N.Y., U.S.A.* 110 **C7**
Webster, *S. Dak., U.S.A.* 112 **C6**
Webster, *Wis., U.S.A.* 112 **C8**
Webster City, *U.S.A.* 112 **D8**
Webster Green, *U.S.A.* 112 **F9**
Webster Springs, *U.S.A.* 108 **F5**
Weda, *Indonesia* 63 **D7**
Weda, Teluk, *Indonesia* 63 **D7**
Weddell I., *Falk. Is.* 128 **G4**
Weddell Sea, *Antarctica* 5 **D1**
Wedderburn, *Australia* 95 **F3**
Wedel, *Germany* 24 **B5**
Wedemark, *Germany* 24 **C5**
Wedgeport, *Canada* 103 **D6**
Wedza, *Zimbabwe* 87 **F3**
Wee Waa, *Australia* 95 **E4**
Weed, *U.S.A.* 114 **F2**
Weed Heights, *U.S.A.* 116 **G7**
Weedsport, *U.S.A.* 111 **C8**
Weedville, *U.S.A.* 110 **E6**
Weemelah, *Australia* 95 **D4**
Weenen, *S. Africa* 89 **D5**
Weener, *Germany* 24 **B3**
Weert, *Neths.* 17 **C5**
Węgierska-Górka, *Poland* 45 **J6**
Wegliniec, *Poland* 45 **G2**
Węgorzewo, *Poland* 44 **D8**
Węgorzyno, *Poland* 44 **E2**
Węgrów, *Poland* 45 **F9**
Wei He →, *Hebei, China* 56 **F8**
Wei He →, *Shaanxi, China* 56 **G6**
Weichang, *China* 57 **D9**
Weichuan, *China* 56 **G7**
Weida, *Germany* 24 **E8**
Weiden, *Germany* 25 **F8**
Weifang, *China* 57 **F10**
Weihai, *China* 57 **F12**
Weil, *Germany* 25 **H3**
Weilburg, *Germany* 24 **E4**
Weilheim, *Germany* 25 **H7**
Weimar, *Germany* 24 **E7**
Weinan, *China* 56 **G5**
Weingarten, *Germany* 25 **F4**
Weinheim, *Germany* 25 **F4**
Weining, *China* 58 **D5**
Weipa, *Australia* 94 **A3**
Weir →, *Australia* 95 **D4**
Weir →, *Canada* 105 **B10**
Weir River, *Canada* 105 **B10**
Weirton, *U.S.A.* 110 **F4**
Weiser, *U.S.A.* 114 **D5**
Weishan, *Shandong, China* 57 **G9**
Weishan, *Yunnan, China* 58 **E3**
Weissenburg, *Germany* 25 **F6**
Weissenfels, *Germany* 24 **D7**
Weisswasser, *Germany* 24 **D10**
Wéitra, *Austria* 26 **C7**
Weixi, *China* 58 **D2**
Weixin, *China* 58 **D5**
Weiyuan, *China* 56 **G3**
Weiz, *Austria* 26 **D8**
Weizhou Dao, *China* 58 **G7**
Wejherowo, *Poland* 44 **D5**
Wekusko L., *Canada* 105 **C9**
Welbourn Hill, *Australia* 95 **D1**
Welch, *U.S.A.* 108 **G5**
Weldya, *Ethiopia* 81 **E4**
Welega □, *Ethiopia* 81 **F3**
Welkite, *Ethiopia* 81 **F4**
Welkom, *S. Africa* 88 **D4**
Welland, *Canada* 102 **D4**
Welland →, *U.K.* 13 **E7**
Wellesley Is., *Australia* 94 **B2**
Wellingborough, *U.K.* 13 **E7**
Wellington, *Australia* 95 **E4**
Wellington, *Canada* 102 **D4**
Wellington, *N.Z.* 91 **J5**
Wellington, *S. Africa* 88 **E2**
Wellington, *Somst., U.K.* 13 **G4**
Wellington, *Telford & Wrekin, U.K.* 13 **E5**
Wellington, *Colo., U.S.A.* 112 **E2**
Wellington, *Kans., U.S.A.* 113 **G6**
Wellington, *Nev., U.S.A.* 116 **G7**
Wellington, *Ohio, U.S.A.* 110 **E2**
Wellington, *Tex., U.S.A.* 113 **H4**
Wellington, I., *Chile* 122 **H3**
Wellington, L., *Australia* 95 **F4**
Wells, *U.K.* 13 **F5**
Wells, *Maine, U.S.A.* 111 **C14**
Wells, *Minn., U.S.A.* 112 **D8**
Wells, *Nev., U.S.A.* 114 **F6**
Wells, L., *Australia* 93 **E3**
Wells Gray Prov. Park, *Canada* 104 **C4**
Wells-next-the-Sea, *U.K.* 12 **E8**
Wells River, *U.S.A.* 111 **B12**
Wellsboro, *U.S.A.* 110 **E7**
Wellsburg, *U.S.A.* 110 **F4**
Wellsville, *Mo., U.S.A.* 112 **F9**
Wellsville, *N.Y., U.S.A.* 110 **D7**
Wellsville, *Ohio, U.S.A.* 110 **F4**
Wellsville, *Utah, U.S.A.* 114 **F8**
Wellton, *U.S.A.* 115 **K6**
Welmel, Wabi →, *Ethiopia* 81 **F5**
Welo □, *Ethiopia* 81 **E4**
Wels, *Austria* 26 **C7**
Welshpool, *U.K.* 13 **E4**
Welwyn Garden City, *U.K.* 13 **F7**
Wem, *U.K.* 12 **E5**
Wembere →, *Tanzania* 86 **C3**
Wemindji, *Canada* 102 **B4**
Wen Xian, *Gansu, China* 56 **H3**
Wen Xian, *Henan, China* 56 **G7**
Wenatchee, *U.S.A.* 114 **C3**
Wenchang, *China* 64 **C8**
Wencheng, *China* 59 **D13**
Wenchi, *Ghana* 82 **D4**
Wenchow = Wenzhou, *China* 59 **D13**
Wenchuan, *China* 58 **B4**
Wendell, *U.S.A.* 114 **E6**
Wenden, *U.S.A.* 117 **M13**
Wendeng, *China* 57 **F12**
Wendesi, *Indonesia* 63 **E8**
Wendo, *Ethiopia* 81 **F4**
Wendover, *U.S.A.* 114 **F6**
Weng'an, *China* 58 **D6**
Wengcheng, *China* 59 **E9**
Wengyuan, *China* 59 **E10**
Wenjiang, *China* 58 **B4**
Wenling, *China* 59 **C13**
Wenlock →, *Australia* 94 **A3**
Wenshan, *China* 58 **F5**
Wenshang, *China* 56 **G9**
Wenshui, *Guizhou, China* 58 **C6**
Wenshui, *Shanxi, China* 56 **F7**
Wensleydale, *U.K.* 12 **C6**
Wensu, *China* 60 **B3**
Wensum →, *U.K.* 12 **E8**
Wentworth, *Australia* 95 **E3**
Wenut, *Indonesia* 63 **E8**
Wenxi, *China* 56 **G6**
Wenzhou, *China* 59 **D13**
Weott, *U.S.A.* 114 **F2**
Wepener, *S. Africa* 88 **D4**
Werda, *Botswana* 88 **D3**
Werdau, *Germany* 24 **E8**
Werder, *Germany* 24 **C8**
Werdohl, *Germany* 24 **D3**
Wereilu, *Ethiopia* 81 **E4**
Weri, *Indonesia* 63 **E8**
Werneck, *Germany* 25 **F6**
Wernigerode, *Germany* 24 **D6**
Werra →, *Germany* 24 **D5**

Werribee, *Australia* 95 F3
Werrimull, *Australia* 95 E3
Werris Creek, *Australia* 95 E5
Wertach →, *Germany* 25 G6
Wertheim, *Germany* 25 F5
Wertingen, *Germany* 25 G6
Wesel, *Germany* 24 D2
Weser →, *Germany* 24 B4
Weser-Ems □, *Germany* 24 C3
Weserbergland, *Germany* 24 C5
Wesiri, *Indonesia* 63 F7
Wesley Vale, *U.S.A.* 115 J10
Wesleyville, *Canada* 103 C9
Wesleyville, *U.S.A.* 110 D4
Wessel, C., *Australia* 94 A2
Wessel Is., *Australia* 94 A2
Wesselburen, *Germany* 24 A4
Wessington, *U.S.A.* 112 C5
Wessington Springs, *U.S.A.* 112 C5
West, *U.S.A.* 113 K6
West Allis, *U.S.A.* 108 D1
West B., *U.S.A.* 113 L10
West Baines →, *Australia* 92 C4
West Bank □, *Asia* 75 C4
West Bend, *U.S.A.* 108 D1
West Bengal □, *India* 69 H13
West Berkshire □, *U.K.* 13 F6
West Beskids = Západné Beskydy, *Europe* 27 B12
West Branch, *U.S.A.* 108 C3
West Bromwich, *U.K.* 13 E6
West Burra, *U.K.* 14 A7
West Cape Howe, *Australia* 93 G2
West Chazy, *U.S.A.* 111 B11
West Chester, *U.S.A.* 108 F8
West Columbia, *U.S.A.* 113 L7
West Covina, *U.S.A.* 117 L9
West Des Moines, *U.S.A.* 112 E8
West Dunbartonshire □, *U.K.* 14 F4
West End, *Bahamas* 120 A4
West Falkland, *Falk. Is.* 122 J4
West Fjord = Vestfjorden, *Norway* 8 C15
West Frankfort, *U.S.A.* 112 G10
West Hartford, *U.S.A.* 111 E12
West Haven, *U.S.A.* 111 E12
West Helena, *U.S.A.* 113 H9
West Ice Shelf, *Antarctica* 5 C7
West Indies, *Cent. Amer.* 121 D7
West Lorne, *Canada* 110 D3
West Lothian □, *U.K.* 14 F5
West Lunga →, *Zambia* 87 E1
West Memphis, *U.S.A.* 113 H9
West Midlands □, *U.K.* 13 E6
West Mifflin, *U.S.A.* 110 F5
West Monroe, *U.S.A.* 113 J8
West Newton, *U.S.A.* 110 F5
West Nicholson, *Zimbabwe* 87 G2
West Palm Beach, *U.S.A.* 109 M5
West Plains, *U.S.A.* 113 G9
West Point, *Ga., U.S.A.* 109 J3
West Point, *Miss., U.S.A.* 109 J1
West Point, *Nebr., U.S.A.* 112 E6
West Point, *Va., U.S.A.* 108 G7
West Pokot □, *Kenya* 86 B4
West Pt. = Ouest, Pte., *Canada* 103 C7
West Pt., *Australia* 95 F2
West Road →, *Canada* 104 C4
West Rutland, *U.S.A.* 111 C11
West Schelde = Westerschelde →, *Neths.* 17 C3
West Seneca, *U.S.A.* 110 D6
West Siberian Plain, *Russia* 52 C11
West Sussex □, *U.K.* 13 G7
West-Terschelling, *Neths.* 17 A5
West Valley City, *U.S.A.* 114 F8
West Virginia □, *U.S.A.* 108 F5
West-Vlaanderen □, *Belgium* 17 D2
West Walker →, *U.S.A.* 116 G7
West Wyalong, *Australia* 95 E4
West Yellowstone, *U.S.A.* 114 D8
West Yorkshire □, *U.K.* 12 D6
Westall Pt., *Australia* 95 E1
Westbrook, *Maine, U.S.A.* 109 D10
Westbrook, *Tex., U.S.A.* 113 J4
Westbury, *Australia* 94 G4
Westby, *U.S.A.* 112 A2
Westend, *U.S.A.* 117 K9
Westerland, *Germany* 9 J13
Western □, *Kenya* 86 B3
Western □, *Uganda* 86 B3
Western □, *Zambia* 87 F1
Western Australia □, *Australia* 93 E2
Western Cape □, *S. Africa* 88 E3
Western Dvina = Daugava →, *Latvia* 9 H21
Western Ghats, *India* 66 N9
Western Isles □, *U.K.* 14 D1
Western Sahara ■, *Africa* 78 D3
Western Samoa ■, *Pac. Oc.* 91 B13
Westernport, *U.S.A.* 108 F6
Westerschelde →, *Neths.* 17 C3
Westerstede, *Germany* 24 B3
Westerwald, *Germany* 24 E3
Westfield, *Mass., U.S.A.* 111 D12
Westfield, *N.Y., U.S.A.* 110 D5
Westfield, *Pa., U.S.A.* 110 E7
Westhill, *U.K.* 14 D6
Westhope, *U.S.A.* 112 A4
Westland Bight, *N.Z.* 91 K3
Westlock, *Canada* 104 C6
Westmeath □, *Ireland* 15 C4
Westminster, *U.S.A.* 108 F7
Westmorland, *U.S.A.* 115 K6
Weston, *Oreg., U.S.A.* 114 D4
Weston, *W. Va., U.S.A.* 108 F5
Weston I., *Canada* 102 B4
Weston-super-Mare, *U.K.* 13 F5
Westport, *Canada* 111 B8
Westport, *Ireland* 15 C2
Westport, *N.Z.* 91 J3
Westport, *Oreg., U.S.A.* 116 D3
Westport, *Wash., U.S.A.* 114 C1
Westray, *Canada* 105 C8
Westray, *U.K.* 14 B5
Westree, *Canada* 102 C3
Westville, *Calif., U.S.A.* 116 F6
Westville, *Ill., U.S.A.* 108 E2
Westville, *Okla., U.S.A.* 113 H7
Westwood, *U.S.A.* 114 F3
Wetar, *Indonesia* 63 F7
Wetaskiwin, *Canada* 104 C6
Wetherby, *U.K.* 12 D6
Wethersfield, *U.S.A.* 111 E12
Wetteren, *Belgium* 17 D3
Wetzlar, *Germany* 24 E4
Wewoka, *U.S.A.* 113 H6
Wexford, *Ireland* 15 D5
Wexford □, *Ireland* 15 D5
Wexford Harbour, *Ireland* 15 D5
Weyburn, *Canada* 105 D8
Weyburn L., *Canada* 104 A5
Weyer Markt, *Austria* 26 D7
Weyhe, *Germany* 24 C4
Weyib →, *Ethiopia* 81 F5
Weymouth, *Canada* 103 D6
Weymouth, *U.K.* 13 G5
Weymouth, *U.S.A.* 111 D14
Weymouth, C., *Australia* 94 A3
Wha Ti, *Canada* 100 B8
Whakatane, *N.Z.* 91 G6
Whale →, *Canada* 103 A6
Whale Cove, *Canada* 105 A10
Whales, B. of, *Antarctica* 5 D12
Whalsay, *U.K.* 14 A8
Whangamomona, *N.Z.* 91 H5
Whangarei, *N.Z.* 91 F5
Whangarei Harb., *N.Z.* 91 F5
Wharfe →, *U.K.* 12 D6
Wharfedale, *U.K.* 12 C5
Wharton, *N.J., U.S.A.* 111 F10
Wharton, *Pa., U.S.A.* 110 E6
Wharton, *Tex., U.S.A.* 113 L6
Wheatland, *Calif., U.S.A.* 116 F5
Wheatland, *Wyo., U.S.A.* 112 D2
Wheatley, *Canada* 110 D2
Wheaton, *U.S.A.* 112 C6
Wheelbarrow Pk., *U.S.A.* 116 H10
Wheeler, *Oreg., U.S.A.* 114 D2
Wheeler, *Tex., U.S.A.* 113 H4
Wheeler →, *Canada* 105 B7
Wheeler Pk., *N. Mex., U.S.A.* 115 H11
Wheeler Pk., *Nev., U.S.A.* 115 G6
Wheeler Ridge, *U.S.A.* 117 L8
Wheeling, *U.S.A.* 110 F4
Whernside, *U.K.* 12 C5
Whidbey I., *U.S.A.* 104 D4
Whiskey Gap, *Canada* 104 D6
Whiskey Jack L., *Canada* 105 B8
Whistleduck Cr. →, *Australia* 94 C2
Whitby, *Canada* 110 C6
Whitby, *U.K.* 12 C7
White →, *Ark., U.S.A.* 113 J9
White →, *Ind., U.S.A.* 108 F2
White →, *S. Dak., U.S.A.* 112 D5
White →, *Utah, U.S.A.* 114 F9
White →, *Wash., U.S.A.* 116 C4
White, L., *Australia* 92 D4
White B., *Canada* 103 C8
White Bear Res., *Canada* 103 C8
White Bird, *U.S.A.* 114 D5
White Butte, *U.S.A.* 112 B3
White City, *U.S.A.* 112 F6
White Cliffs, *Australia* 95 E3
White Deer, *U.S.A.* 113 H4
White Hall, *U.S.A.* 112 F9
White Haven, *U.S.A.* 111 E9
White Horse, Vale of, *U.K.* 13 F6
White I., *N.Z.* 91 G6
White L., *Canada* 111 A8
White L., *U.S.A.* 113 L8
White Mts., *Calif., U.S.A.* 116 H8
White Mts., *N.H., U.S.A.* 111 B13
White Nile = Nîl el Abyad →, *Sudan* 81 D3
White Nile Dam = Khazzân Jabal el Awliyâ, *Sudan* 81 D3
White Otter L., *Canada* 102 C1
White Pass, *Canada* 104 B1
White Pass, *U.S.A.* 116 D5
White Plains, *U.S.A.* 111 E11
White River, *Canada* 102 C2
White River, *S. Africa* 89 D5
White River, *U.S.A.* 112 D4
White Russia = Belarus ■, *Europe* 46 F4
White Sea = Beloye More, *Russia* 50 C4
White Sulphur Springs, *Mont., U.S.A.* 114 C8
White Sulphur Springs, *W. Va., U.S.A.* 108 G5
White Swan, *U.S.A.* 116 D6
White Volta →, *Ghana* 83 D4
Whitecliffs, *N.Z.* 91 K3
Whitecourt, *Canada* 104 C5
Whiteface, *U.S.A.* 113 J3
Whitefield, *U.S.A.* 111 B13
Whitefish, *U.S.A.* 114 B6
Whitefish L., *Canada* 105 A7
Whitefish Point, *U.S.A.* 108 B3
Whitegull, L., *Canada* 103 A7
Whitehall, *Mich., U.S.A.* 108 D2
Whitehall, *Mont., U.S.A.* 114 D7
Whitehall, *N.Y., U.S.A.* 111 C11
Whitehall, *Wis., U.S.A.* 112 C9
Whitehaven, *U.K.* 12 C4
Whitehorse, *Canada* 104 A1
Whitemark, *Australia* 94 G4
Whitemouth, *Canada* 105 D9
Whiteplains, *Liberia* 82 D2
Whitesboro, *N.Y., U.S.A.* 111 C9
Whitesboro, *Tex., U.S.A.* 113 J6
Whiteshell Prov. Park, *Canada* 105 D9
Whitetail, *U.S.A.* 112 A2
Whiteville, *U.S.A.* 109 H6
Whitewater, *U.S.A.* 108 D1
Whitewater Baldy, *U.S.A.* 115 K9
Whitewater L., *Canada* 102 B2
Whitewood, *Australia* 94 C3
Whitewood, *Canada* 105 C8
Whitfield, *Australia* 95 F4
Whithorn, *U.K.* 14 G4
Whitianga, *N.Z.* 91 G5
Whitman, *U.S.A.* 111 D14
Whitmire, *U.S.A.* 109 H5
Whitney, *Canada* 102 C4
Whitney, Mt., *U.S.A.* 116 J8
Whitney Point, *U.S.A.* 111 D9
Whitstable, *U.K.* 13 F9
Whitsunday I., *Australia* 94 C4
Whittier, *U.S.A.* 117 M8
Whittlesea, *Australia* 95 F4
Whitwell, *U.S.A.* 109 H3
Wholdaia L., *Canada* 105 A8
Whyalla, *Australia* 95 E2
Whyjonta, *Australia* 95 D3
Wiarton, *Canada* 102 D3
Wiawso, *Ghana* 82 D4
Wiay, *U.K.* 14 D1
Wiązów, *Poland* 45 H4
Wibaux, *U.S.A.* 112 B2
Wichian Buri, *Thailand* 64 E3
Wichita, *U.S.A.* 113 G6
Wichita Falls, *U.S.A.* 113 J5
Wick, *U.K.* 14 C5
Wickenburg, *U.S.A.* 115 K7
Wickepin, *Australia* 93 F2
Wickham, C., *Australia* 94 F3
Wickliffe, *U.S.A.* 110 E3
Wicklow, *Ireland* 15 D5
Wicklow □, *Ireland* 15 D5
Wicklow Hd., *Ireland* 15 D6
Wicklow Mts., *Ireland* 15 C5
Widawa, *Poland* 45 G5
Widawka →, *Poland* 45 G5
Widgiemooltha, *Australia* 93 F3
Widnes, *U.K.* 12 D5
Więcbork, *Poland* 45 E4
Wiehl, *Germany* 24 E3
Wiek, *Germany* 24 A9
Wielbark, *Poland* 44 E7
Wieleń, *Poland* 45 F3
Wielichowo, *Poland* 45 F3
Wieliczka, *Poland* 45 J7
Wieluń, *Poland* 45 G5
Wien, *Austria* 27 C9
Wiener Neustadt, *Austria* 27 D9
Wieprz →, *Poland* 45 G8
Wieprza →, *Poland* 44 D3
Wieruszów, *Poland* 45 G5
Wiesbaden, *Germany* 25 E4
Wiesental, *Germany* 25 F4
Wiesloch, *Germany* 25 F4
Wiesmoor, *Germany* 24 B3
Wieżyca, *Poland* 44 D5
Wigan, *U.K.* 12 D5
Wiggins, *Colo., U.S.A.* 112 E2
Wiggins, *Miss., U.S.A.* 113 K10
Wight, I. of □, *U.K.* 13 G6
Wigry, Jezioro, *Poland* 44 D10
Wigston, *U.K.* 13 E6
Wigton, *U.K.* 12 C4
Wigtown, *U.K.* 14 G4
Wigtown B., *U.K.* 14 G4
Wil, *Switz.* 25 H5
Wilamowice, *Poland* 45 J6
Wilber, *U.S.A.* 112 E6
Wilberforce, *Canada* 110 A6
Wilberforce, C., *Australia* 94 A2
Wilburton, *U.S.A.* 113 H7
Wilcannia, *Australia* 95 E3
Wilcox, *U.S.A.* 110 E6
Wildbad, *Germany* 25 G4
Wildeshausen, *Germany* 24 C4
Wildon, *Austria* 26 E8
Wildrose, *Calif., U.S.A.* 117 J9
Wildrose, *N. Dak., U.S.A.* 112 A3
Wildspitze, *Austria* 26 E3
Wildwood, *U.S.A.* 108 F8
Wilga →, *Poland* 45 G8
Wilge →, *S. Africa* 89 D4
Wilhelm II Coast, *Antarctica* 5 C7
Wilhelmsburg, *Austria* 26 C8
Wilhelmshaven, *Germany* 24 B4
Wilhelmstal, *Namibia* 88 C2
Wilkes-Barre, *U.S.A.* 111 E9
Wilkesboro, *U.S.A.* 109 G5
Wilkie, *Canada* 105 C7
Wilkinsburg, *U.S.A.* 110 F5
Wilkinson Lakes, *Australia* 93 E5
Willamina, *U.S.A.* 114 D2
Willandra Billabong Creek →, *Australia* 95 E4
Willapa B., *U.S.A.* 114 C2
Willapa Hills, *U.S.A.* 116 D3
Willard, *N. Mex., U.S.A.* 115 J10
Willard, *Utah, U.S.A.* 114 F7
Willcox, *U.S.A.* 115 K9
Willemstad, *Neth. Ant.* 121 D6
Willeroo, *Australia* 92 C5
William →, *Canada* 105 B7
William Creek, *Australia* 95 D2
Williambury, *Australia* 93 D2
Williams, *Australia* 93 F2
Williams, *Ariz., U.S.A.* 115 J7
Williams, *Calif., U.S.A.* 116 F4
Williams Lake, *Canada* 104 C4
Williamsburg, *Ky., U.S.A.* 109 G3
Williamsburg, *Pa., U.S.A.* 110 F6
Williamsburg, *Va., U.S.A.* 108 G7
Williamson, *N.Y., U.S.A.* 110 C7
Williamson, *W. Va., U.S.A.* 108 G4
Williamsport, *U.S.A.* 110 E7
Williamston, *U.S.A.* 109 H7
Williamstown, *Australia* 95 F3
Williamstown, *Mass., U.S.A.* 111 D11
Williamstown, *N.Y., U.S.A.* 111 C9
Williamsville, *U.S.A.* 113 G9
Willimantic, *U.S.A.* 111 E12
Willis Group, *Australia* 94 B5
Williston, *S. Africa* 88 E3
Williston, *Fla., U.S.A.* 109 L4
Williston, *N. Dak., U.S.A.* 112 A3
Williston L., *Canada* 104 B4
Willits, *U.S.A.* 114 G2
Willmar, *U.S.A.* 112 C7
Willoughby, *U.S.A.* 110 E3
Willow Bunch, *Canada* 105 D7
Willow L., *Canada* 104 A5
Willow Lake, *U.S.A.* 112 C6
Willow Springs, *U.S.A.* 113 G9
Willow Wall, The, *China* 57 C12
Willowlake →, *Canada* 104 A4
Willowmore, *S. Africa* 88 E3
Willows, *Australia* 94 C4
Willows, *U.S.A.* 116 F4
Willowvale = Gatyana, *S. Africa* 89 E4
Wills, L., *Australia* 92 D4
Wills Cr. →, *Australia* 94 C3
Wills Point, *U.S.A.* 113 J7
Willunga, *Australia* 95 F2
Wilmette, *U.S.A.* 108 D2
Wilmington, *Australia* 95 E2
Wilmington, *Del., U.S.A.* 108 F8
Wilmington, *Ill., U.S.A.* 108 E1
Wilmington, *N.C., U.S.A.* 109 H7
Wilmington, *Ohio, U.S.A.* 108 F4
Wilmslow, *U.K.* 12 D5
Wilpena Cr. →, *Australia* 95 E2
Wilsall, *U.S.A.* 114 D8
Wilson, *U.S.A.* 109 H7
Wilson →, *Queens., Australia* 95 D3
Wilson →, *W. Austral., Australia* 92 C4
Wilson Bluff, *Australia* 93 F4
Wilsons Promontory, *Australia* 95 F4
Wilster, *Germany* 24 B5
Wilton, *U.S.A.* 112 B4
Wilton →, *Australia* 94 A1
Wiltshire □, *U.K.* 13 F6
Wiltz, *Lux.* 17 E5
Wiluna, *Australia* 93 E3
Wimborne Minster, *U.K.* 13 G6
Wimereux, *France* 19 B8
Wimmera →, *Australia* 95 F3
Winam G., *Kenya* 86 C3
Winburg, *S. Africa* 88 D4
Winchendon, *U.S.A.* 111 D12
Winchester, *U.K.* 13 F6
Winchester, *Conn., U.S.A.* 111 E11
Winchester, *Idaho, U.S.A.* 114 C5
Winchester, *Ind., U.S.A.* 108 E3
Winchester, *Ky., U.S.A.* 108 G3
Winchester, *N.H., U.S.A.* 111 D12
Winchester, *Nev., U.S.A.* 117 J11
Winchester, *Tenn., U.S.A.* 109 H2
Winchester, *Va., U.S.A.* 108 F6
Wind →, *U.S.A.* 114 E9
Wind River Range, *U.S.A.* 114 E9
Windau = Ventspils, *Latvia* 9 H19
Windber, *U.S.A.* 110 F6
Windermere, *U.K.* 12 C5
Windfall, *Canada* 104 C5
Windflower L., *Canada* 104 A5
Windhoek, *Namibia* 88 C2
Windischgarsten, *Austria* 26 D7
Windom, *U.S.A.* 112 D7
Windorah, *Australia* 94 D3
Window Rock, *U.S.A.* 115 J9
Windrush →, *U.K.* 13 F6
Windsor, *Australia* 95 E5
Windsor, *N.S., Canada* 103 D7
Windsor, *Nfld., Canada* 103 C8
Windsor, *Ont., Canada* 102 D3
Windsor, *U.K.* 13 F7
Windsor, *Colo., U.S.A.* 112 E2
Windsor, *Conn., U.S.A.* 111 E12
Windsor, *Mo., U.S.A.* 112 F8
Windsor, *N.Y., U.S.A.* 111 D9
Windsor, *Vt., U.S.A.* 111 C12
Windsor & Maidenhead □, *U.K.* 13 F7
Windsorton, *S. Africa* 88 D3
Windward Is., *W. Indies* 121 D7
Windward Passage = Vientos, Paso de los, *Caribbean* 121 C5
Windy L., *Canada* 105 A8
Winefred L., *Canada* 105 B6
Winejok, *Sudan* 81 F2
Winfield, *U.S.A.* 113 G6
Wingate Mts., *Australia* 92 B5
Wingen, *Australia* 95 E5
Wingham, *Australia* 95 E5
Wingham, *Canada* 102 D3
Winifred, *U.S.A.* 114 C9
Winisk, *Canada* 102 A2
Winisk →, *Canada* 102 A2
Winisk L., *Canada* 102 B2
Wink, *U.S.A.* 113 K3
Winkler, *Canada* 105 D9
Winklern, *Austria* 26 E5
Winlock, *U.S.A.* 116 D4
Winneba, *Ghana* 83 D4
Winnebago, *U.S.A.* 112 D7
Winnebago, L., *U.S.A.* 108 D1
Winnecke Cr. →, *Australia* 92 C5
Winnemucca, *U.S.A.* 114 F5
Winnemucca L., *U.S.A.* 114 F4
Winner, *U.S.A.* 112 D5
Winnett, *U.S.A.* 114 C9
Winnfield, *U.S.A.* 113 K8
Winnibigoshish, L., *U.S.A.* 112 B7
Winning, *Australia* 92 D1
Winnipeg, *Canada* 105 D9
Winnipeg →, *Canada* 105 C9
Winnipeg, L., *Canada* 105 C9
Winnipeg Beach, *Canada* 105 C9
Winnipegosis, *Canada* 105 C9
Winnipegosis L., *Canada* 105 C9
Winnipesaukee, L., *U.S.A.* 111 C13
Winnsboro, *La., U.S.A.* 113 J9
Winnsboro, *S.C., U.S.A.* 109 H5
Winnsboro, *Tex., U.S.A.* 113 J7
Winokapau, L., *Canada* 103 B7
Winona, *Minn., U.S.A.* 112 C9
Winona, *Miss., U.S.A.* 113 J10
Winooski, *U.S.A.* 111 B11
Winschoten, *Neths.* 17 A7
Winsen, *Germany* 24 B6
Winsford, *U.K.* 12 D5
Winslow, *Ariz., U.S.A.* 115 J8
Winslow, *Wash., U.S.A.* 116 C4
Winsted, *U.S.A.* 111 E11
Winston-Salem, *U.S.A.* 109 G5
Winter Garden, *U.S.A.* 109 L5
Winter Haven, *U.S.A.* 109 M5
Winter Park, *U.S.A.* 109 L5
Winterberg, *Germany* 24 D4
Winterhaven, *U.S.A.* 117 N12
Winters, *Calif., U.S.A.* 116 G5
Winters, *Tex., U.S.A.* 113 K5
Winterset, *U.S.A.* 112 E8
Wintersville, *U.S.A.* 110 F4
Winterswijk, *Neths.* 17 C6
Winterthur, *Switz.* 25 H4
Winthrop, *Minn., U.S.A.* 112 C7
Winthrop, *Wash., U.S.A.* 114 B3
Winton, *Australia* 94 C3
Winton, *N.Z.* 91 M2
Winton, *U.S.A.* 109 G7
Wipper →, *Germany* 24 D7
Wirrulla, *Australia* 95 E1
Wisbech, *U.K.* 13 E8
Wisconsin □, *U.S.A.* 112 C10
Wisconsin →, *U.S.A.* 112 D9
Wisconsin Dells, *U.S.A.* 112 D10
Wisconsin Rapids, *U.S.A.* 112 C10
Wisdom, *U.S.A.* 114 D7
Wishaw, *U.K.* 14 F5
Wishek, *U.S.A.* 112 B5
Wisła, *Poland* 45 J5
Wisła →, *Poland* 44 D5
Wisłok →, *Poland* 45 H9
Wisłoka →, *Poland* 45 H8
Wismar, *Germany* 24 B7
Wisner, *U.S.A.* 112 E6
Wissant, *France* 19 B8
Wissembourg, *France* 19 C14
Wisznice, *Poland* 45 G10
Witbank, *S. Africa* 89 D4
Witdraai, *S. Africa* 88 D3
Witham, *U.K.* 13 F8
Witham →, *U.K.* 12 E7
Withernsea, *U.K.* 12 D8
Witkowo, *Poland* 45 F4
Witney, *U.K.* 13 F6
Witnica, *Poland* 45 F1
Witnossob →, *Namibia* 88 D3
Wittdün, *Germany* 24 A4
Witten, *Germany* 24 D3
Wittenberge, *Germany* 24 B7
Wittenburg, *Germany* 24 B7
Wittenheim, *France* 19 E14
Wittenoom, *Australia* 92 D2
Wittingen, *Germany* 24 C6
Wittlich, *Germany* 25 F2
Wittmund, *Germany* 24 B3
Wittow, *Germany* 24 A9
Wittstock, *Germany* 24 B8
Witzenhausen, *Germany* 24 D5
Wkra →, *Poland* 45 F7
Władysławowo, *Poland* 44 D5

Wleń, *Poland* 45 G2
Wlingi, *Indonesia* 63 H15
Włocławek, *Poland* 45 F6
Włocławek □, *Poland* 45 F6
Włodawa, *Poland* 45 G10
Włoszczowa, *Poland* 45 H6
Woburn, *U.S.A.* 111 D13
Wodian, *China* 56 H7
Wodonga, *Australia* 95 F4
Wodzisław Śląski, *Poland* 45 H5
Wœrth, *France* 19 D14
Woinbogoin, *China* 58 A2
Woippy, *France* 19 C13
Wojcieszow, *Poland* 45 H2
Wokam, *Indonesia* 63 F8
Woking, *U.K.* 13 F7
Wokingham □, *U.K.* 13 F7
Wolbrom, *Poland* 45 H6
Wołczyn, *Poland* 45 G5
Woldegk, *Germany* 24 B9
Wolf →, *Canada* 104 A2
Wolf Creek, *U.S.A.* 114 C7
Wolf L., *Canada* 104 A2
Wolf Point, *U.S.A.* 112 A2
Wolfe I., *Canada* 102 D4
Wolfen, *Germany* 24 D8
Wolfenbüttel, *Germany* 24 C6
Wolfratshausen, *Germany* 25 H7
Wolfsberg, *Austria* 26 E7
Wolfsburg, *Germany* 24 C6
Wolgast, *Germany* 24 A9
Wolhusen, *Switz.* 25 H4
Wolin, *Poland* 44 E1
Wollaston, Is., *Chile* 128 H3
Wollaston L., *Canada* 105 B8
Wollaston Pen., *Canada* 100 B8
Wollogorang, *Australia* 94 B2
Wollongong, *Australia* 95 E5
Wolmaransstad, *S. Africa* 88 D4
Wolmirstedt, *Germany* 24 C7
Wołomin, *Poland* 45 F8
Wołów, *Poland* 45 G3
Wolseley, *Australia* 95 F3
Wolseley, *Canada* 105 C8
Wolseley, *S. Africa* 88 E2
Wolstenholme, C., *Canada* 98 C12
Wolsztyn, *Poland* 45 F3
Wolvega, *Neths.* 17 B6
Wolverhampton, *U.K.* 13 E5
Wonarah, *Australia* 94 B2
Wondai, *Australia* 95 D5
Wongalarroo L., *Australia* 95 E3
Wongan Hills, *Australia* 93 F2
Wongawol, *Australia* 93 E3
Wŏnju, *S. Korea* 57 F14
Wonosari, *Indonesia* 63 G14
Wŏnsan, *N. Korea* 57 E14
Wonthaggi, *Australia* 95 F4
Woocalla, *Australia* 95 E2
Wood Buffalo Nat. Park, *Canada* 104 B6
Wood Is., *Australia* 92 C3
Wood L., *Canada* 105 B8
Wood Lake, *U.S.A.* 112 D4
Woodah I., *Australia* 94 A2
Woodanilling, *Australia* 93 F2
Woodbridge, *Canada* 110 C5
Woodbridge, *U.K.* 13 E9
Woodburn, *Australia* 95 D5
Woodenbong, *Australia* 95 D5
Woodend, *Australia* 95 F3
Woodfords, *U.S.A.* 116 G7
Woodgreen, *Australia* 94 C1
Woodlake, *U.S.A.* 116 J7
Woodland, *U.S.A.* 116 G5
Woodlands, *Australia* 92 D2
Woodpecker, *Canada* 104 C4
Woodridge, *Canada* 105 D9
Woodroffe, Mt., *Australia* 93 E5
Woodruff, *Ariz., U.S.A.* 115 J8
Woodruff, *Utah, U.S.A.* 114 F8
Woods, L., *Australia* 94 B1
Woods, L., *Canada* 103 B6
Woods, L. of the, *Canada* 105 D10
Woodstock, *Queens., Australia* 94 B4
Woodstock, *W. Austral., Australia* 92 D2
Woodstock, *N.B., Canada* 103 C6
Woodstock, *Ont., Canada* 102 D3
Woodstock, *U.K.* 13 F6
Woodstock, *Ill., U.S.A.* 112 D10
Woodstock, *Vt., U.S.A.* 111 C12
Woodsville, *U.S.A.* 111 B13
Woodville, *N.Z.* 91 J5
Woodville, *U.S.A.* 113 K7
Woodward, *U.S.A.* 113 G5
Woody, *U.S.A.* 117 K8
Woolamai, C., *Australia* 95 F4
Wooler, *U.K.* 12 B5
Woolgoolga, *Australia* 95 E5
Woombye, *Australia* 95 D5
Woomera, *Australia* 95 E2
Woonsocket, *R.I., U.S.A.* 111 E13
Woonsocket, *S. Dak., U.S.A.* 112 C5
Wooramel, *Australia* 93 E1
Wooramel →, *Australia* 93 E1
Wooroloo, *Australia* 93 F2
Wooster, *U.S.A.* 110 F3
Worcester, *S. Africa* 88 E2
Worcester, *U.K.* 13 E5
Worcester, *Mass., U.S.A.* 111 D13
Worcester, *N.Y., U.S.A.* 111 D10
Worcestershire □, *U.K.* 13 E5
Wörgl, *Austria* 26 D5
Workington, *U.K.* 12 C4
Worksop, *U.K.* 12 D6
Workum, *Neths.* 17 B5
Worland, *U.S.A.* 114 D10
Wormhout, *France* 19 B9
Worms, *Germany* 25 F4
Wörth, *Germany* 25 F8
Wortham, *U.S.A.* 113 K6
Wörther See, *Austria* 26 E7
Worthing, *U.K.* 13 G7
Worthington, *U.S.A.* 112 D7
Wosi, *Indonesia* 63 E7
Wou-han = Wuhan, *China* 59 B10
Wousi = Wuxi, *China* 59 B13
Wowoni, *Indonesia* 63 E6
Woy Woy, *Australia* 95 E5
Wrangel I. = Vrangelya, Ostrov, *Russia* 51 B19
Wrangell, *U.S.A.* 100 C6
Wrangell I., *U.S.A.* 104 B2
Wrangell Mts., *U.S.A.* 100 B5
Wrath, C., *U.K.* 14 C3
Wray, *U.S.A.* 112 E3
Wrekin, The, *U.K.* 13 E5
Wrens, *U.S.A.* 109 J4
Wrexham, *U.K.* 12 D4
Wrexham □, *U.K.* 12 D5
Wriezen, *Germany* 24 C10
Wright, *Canada* 104 C4
Wright, *Phil.* 61 F6
Wrightson Mt., *U.S.A.* 115 L8
Wrightwood, *U.S.A.* 117 L9
Wrigley, *Canada* 100 B7
Wrocław, *Poland* 45 G4
Wrocław □, *Poland* 45 G4
Wronki, *Poland* 45 F3
Września, *Poland* 45 F4
Wschowa, *Poland* 45 G3
Wu Jiang →, *China* 58 C6
Wu'an, *China* 56 F8
Wubin, *Australia* 93 F2
Wubu, *China* 56 F6
Wuchang, *China* 57 B14
Wucheng, *China* 56 F9
Wuchuan, *Guangdong, China* 59 G8
Wuchuan, *Guizhou, China* 58 C7
Wuchuan, *Nei Mongol Zizhiqu, China* 56 D6
Wudi, *China* 57 F9
Wuding, *China* 58 E4
Wuding He →, *China* 56 F6
Wudu, *China* 56 H3
Wufeng, *China* 59 B8
Wugang, *China* 59 D8
Wugong Shan, *China* 59 D10
Wuhan, *China* 59 B10
Wuhe, *China* 57 H9
Wuhsi = Wuxi, *China* 59 B13
Wuhu, *China* 59 B12
Wujiang, *China* 59 B13
Wukari, *Nigeria* 83 D6
Wulajie, *China* 57 B14
Wulanbulang, *China* 56 D6
Wulehe, *Ghana* 83 D5
Wulian, *China* 57 G10
Wuliang Shan, *China* 58 E3
Wuliaru, *Indonesia* 63 F8
Wulumuchi = Ürümqi, *China* 60 B3
Wum, *Cameroon* 83 D7
Wuming, *China* 58 F7
Wuning, *China* 59 C10
Wunnummin L., *Canada* 102 B2
Wunsiedel, *Germany* 25 E8
Wunstorf, *Germany* 24 C5
Wuntho, *Burma* 67 H19
Wuping, *China* 59 E11
Wuppertal, *Germany* 24 D3
Wuppertal, *S. Africa* 88 E2
Wuqing, *China* 57 E9
Wurung, *Australia* 94 B3
Würzburg, *Germany* 25 F5
Wurzen, *Germany* 24 D8
Wushan, *Gansu, China* 56 G3
Wushan, *Sichuan, China* 58 B7
Wusuli Jiang = Ussuri →, *Asia* 54 A7
Wutach →, *Germany* 25 H4
Wutai, *China* 56 E7
Wuting = Huimin, *China* 57 F9
Wutong, *China* 59 E8
Wutonghaolai, *China* 57 C11
Wutongqiao, *China* 58 C4
Wuwei, *Anhui, China* 59 B11
Wuwei, *Gansu, China* 60 C5
Wuxi, *Jiangsu, China* 59 B13
Wuxi, *Sichuan, China* 58 B7
Wuxiang, *China* 56 F7
Wuxing, *China* 59 B13
Wuxuan, *China* 58 F7
Wuyang, *China* 56 H7
Wuyi, *Hebei, China* 56 F8
Wuyi, *Zhejiang, China* 59 C12
Wuyi Shan, *China* 59 D11
Wuyo, *Nigeria* 83 C7
Wuyuan, *Jiangxi, China* 59 C11
Wuyuan, *Nei Mongol Zizhiqu, China* 56 D5
Wuzhai, *China* 56 E6
Wuzhi Shan, *China* 60 E5
Wuzhong, *China* 56 E4
Wuzhou, *China* 59 F8
Wyaaba Cr. →, *Australia* 94 B3
Wyalkatchem, *Australia* 93 F2
Wyalusing, *U.S.A.* 111 E8
Wyandotte, *U.S.A.* 108 D4
Wyandra, *Australia* 95 D4
Wyangala Res., *Australia* 95 E4
Wyara, L., *Australia* 95 D3
Wycheproof, *Australia* 95 F3
Wye →, *U.K.* 13 F5
Wyemandoo, *Australia* 93 E2
Wyk, *Germany* 24 A4
Wymondham, *U.K.* 13 E9
Wymore, *U.S.A.* 112 E6
Wynbring, *Australia* 95 E1
Wyndham, *Australia* 92 C4
Wyndham, *N.Z.* 91 M2
Wyndmere, *U.S.A.* 112 B6
Wynne, *U.S.A.* 113 H9
Wynnum, *Australia* 95 D5
Wynyard, *Australia* 94 G4
Wynyard, *Canada* 105 C8
Wyola, L., *Australia* 93 E5
Wyoming □, *U.S.A.* 114 E10
Wyong, *Australia* 95 E5
Wyrzysk, *Poland* 45 E4
Wyśmierzyce, *Poland* 45 G7
Wysoka, *Poland* 45 E4
Wysokie, *Poland* 45 H9
Wysokie Mazowieckie, *Poland* 45 F9
Wyszków, *Poland* 45 F8
Wyszogród, *Poland* 45 F7
Wytheville, *U.S.A.* 108 G5
Wyżyna Małopolska, *Poland* 45 H7

X

Xaçmaz, *Azerbaijan* 49 K9
Xai-Xai, *Mozam.* 89 D5
Xainza, *China* 60 C3
Xangongo, *Angola* 88 B2
Xankändi, *Azerbaijan* 73 C12
Xanlar, *Azerbaijan* 49 K8
Xanten, *Germany* 24 D2
Xánthi, *Greece* 41 E8
Xánthi □, *Greece* 41 E8
Xanthos, *Turkey* 39 E11
Xapuri, *Brazil* 124 F5
Xar Moron He →, *China* 57 C11
Xarrë, *Albania* 40 G4
Xátiva, *Spain* 33 G4
Xau, L., *Botswana* 88 C3
Xavantina, *Brazil* 127 A5
Xenia, *U.S.A.* 108 F4
Xeropotamos →, *Cyprus* 36 E11
Xertigny, *France* 19 D13
Xhora, *S. Africa* 89 E4
Xhumo, *Botswana* 88 C3
Xi Jiang →, *China* 59 F9
Xi Xian, *Henan, China* 59 A10
Xi Xian, *Shanxi, China* 56 F6
Xia Xian, *China* 56 G6
Xiachengzi, *China* 57 B16
Xiachuan Dao, *China* 59 G9
Xiaguan, *China* 58 E3
Xiajiang, *China* 59 D10
Xiajin, *China* 56 F9
Xiamen, *China* 59 E12
Xi'an, *China* 56 G5
Xian Xian, *China* 56 E9
Xianfeng, *China* 58 C7
Xiang Jiang →, *China* 59 C9
Xiangcheng, *Henan, China* 56 H8
Xiangcheng, *Henan, China* 56 H7
Xiangcheng, *Sichuan, China* 58 C2
Xiangdu, *China* 58 F6
Xiangfan, *China* 59 A9
Xianghuang Qi, *China* 56 C7
Xiangning, *China* 56 G6
Xiangquan, *China* 56 F7
Xiangshan, *China* 59 C13
Xiangshui, *China* 57 G10
Xiangtan, *China* 59 D9
Xiangxiang, *China* 59 D9
Xiangyin, *China* 59 C9
Xiangyun, *China* 58 E3
Xiangzhou, *China* 58 F7
Xianju, *China* 59 C13
Xianning, *China* 59 C10
Xianshui He →, *China* 58 B3
Xianyang, *China* 56 G5
Xianyou, *China* 59 E12
Xiao Hinggan Ling, *China* 60 B7
Xiao Xian, *China* 56 G9
Xiaofeng, *China* 59 B12
Xiaogan, *China* 59 B9
Xiaojin, *China* 58 B4
Xiaolan, *China* 59 F9
Xiaoshan, *China* 59 B13
Xiaoyi, *China* 56 F6
Xiapu, *China* 59 D12
Xiawa, *China* 57 C11
Xiayi, *China* 56 G9
Xichang, *China* 58 D4
Xichong, *China* 58 B5
Xichuan, *China* 56 H6
Xiemahe, *China* 59 B8
Xieng Khouang, *Laos* 64 C4
Xifei He →, *China* 56 H9
Xifeng, *Guizhou, China* 58 D6
Xifeng, *Liaoning, China* 57 C13
Xifengzhen, *China* 56 G4
Xigazê, *China* 60 D3
Xihe, *China* 56 G3
Xihua, *China* 56 H8
Xilaganí, *Greece* 41 F9
Xiliao He →, *China* 57 C12
Xilin, *China* 58 E5
Xilókastron, *Greece* 38 C4
Xin Jiang →, *China* 59 C11
Xin Xian, *China* 56 E7
Xinavane, *Mozam.* 89 D5
Xinbin, *China* 57 D13
Xincai, *China* 59 A10
Xinchang, *China* 59 C13
Xincheng, *Guangxi Zhuangzu, China* 58 E7
Xincheng, *Jiangxi, China* 59 D10
Xinfeng, *Guangdong, China* 59 E10
Xinfeng, *Jiangxi, China* 59 D11
Xinfeng, *Jiangxi, China* 59 E10
Xing Xian, *China* 56 E6
Xing'an, *Guangxi Zhuangzu, China* 59 E8
Xingan, *Jiangxi, China* 59 D10
Xingcheng, *China* 57 D11
Xingguo, *China* 59 D10
Xinghe, *China* 56 D7
Xinghua, *China* 57 H10
Xinghua Wan, *China* 59 E12
Xinglong, *China* 57 D9
Xingning, *China* 59 E10
Xingping, *China* 56 G5
Xingren, *China* 58 E5
Xingshan, *China* 59 B8
Xingtai, *China* 56 F8
Xingu →, *Brazil* 122 D5
Xingyang, *China* 56 G7
Xinhe, *China* 56 F8
Xinhua, *China* 59 D8
Xinhuang, *China* 58 D7
Xinhui, *China* 59 F9
Xining, *China* 60 C5
Xinjiang, *China* 56 G6
Xinjiang Uygur Zizhiqu □, *China* 60 B3
Xinjie, *China* 58 D3
Xinjin, *Liaoning, China* 57 E11
Xinjin, *Sichuan, China* 58 B4
Xinkai He →, *China* 57 C12
Xinle, *China* 56 E8
Xinlitun, *China* 57 D12
Xinlong, *China* 58 B3
Xinmin, *China* 57 D12
Xinning, *China* 59 D8
Xinping, *China* 58 E3
Xinshao, *China* 59 D8
Xintai, *China* 57 G9
Xintian, *China* 59 E9
Xinxiang, *China* 56 G7
Xinxing, *China* 59 F9
Xinyang, *China* 59 A10
Xinye, *China* 59 A9
Xinyi, *China* 59 F8
Xinyu, *China* 59 D10
Xinzhan, *China* 57 C14
Xinzheng, *China* 56 G7
Xinzhou, *China* 59 B10
Xinzo de Limia, *Spain* 34 C3
Xiong Xian, *China* 56 E9
Xiongyuecheng, *China* 57 D12
Xiping, *Henan, China* 56 H8
Xiping, *Henan, China* 56 H6
Xiping, *Zhejiang, China* 59 C12
Xique-Xique, *Brazil* 125 F10
Xisha Qundao = Paracel Is., *S. China Sea* 62 A4
Xishui, *China* 59 B10
Xituozhen, *China* 58 B7
Xiuning, *China* 59 C12
Xiuren, *China* 59 E8
Xiushan, *China* 58 C7
Xiushui, *China* 59 C10
Xiuwen, *China* 58 D6
Xiuyan, *China* 57 D12
Xixabangma Feng, *China* 67 E14
Xixia, *China* 56 H6
Xixiang, *China* 56 H4
Xiyang, *China* 56 F7
Xizang Zizhiqu □, *China* 60 C3
Xlendi, *Malta* 36 C1
Xu Jiang →, *China* 59 D11
Xuan Loc, *Vietnam* 65 G6
Xuancheng, *China* 59 B12
Xuan'en, *China* 58 C7
Xuanhan, *China* 58 B6
Xuanhua, *China* 56 D8
Xuchang, *China* 56 G7
Xudat, *Azerbaijan* 49 K9
Xuefeng Shan, *China* 59 D8
Xuejiaping, *China* 59 B8
Xun Jiang →, *China* 59 F8
Xun Xian, *China* 56 G8
Xundian, *China* 58 E4
Xunwu, *China* 59 E10
Xunyang, *China* 56 H5
Xunyi, *China* 56 G5
Xupu, *China* 59 D8
Xúquer →, *Spain* 33 F4
Xushui, *China* 56 E8
Xuwen, *China* 59 G8
Xuyen Moc, *Vietnam* 65 G6
Xuyong, *China* 58 C5
Xuzhou, *China* 57 G9
Xylophagou, *Cyprus* 36 E12

Y

Ya Xian, *China* 64 C7
Yaamba, *Australia* 94 C5
Ya'an, *China* 58 C4
Yaapeet, *Australia* 95 F3
Yabassi, *Cameroon* 83 E6
Yabelo, *Ethiopia* 81 G4
Yablanitsa, *Bulgaria* 41 C8
Yablonovy Ra. = Yablonovyy Khrebet, *Russia* 51 D12
Yablonovyy Khrebet, *Russia* 51 D12
Yabrai Shan, *China* 56 E2
Yabrūd, *Syria* 75 B5
Yacheng, *China* 64 C7
Yacuiba, *Bolivia* 126 A3
Yacuma →, *Bolivia* 124 F5
Yadgir, *India* 66 L10
Yadkin →, *U.S.A.* 109 H5
Yadrin, *Russia* 48 C8
Yagaba, *Ghana* 83 C4
Yağcılar, *Turkey* 39 B10
Yagodnoye, *Russia* 51 C15
Yahila, *Dem. Rep. of the Congo* 86 B1
Yahk, *Canada* 104 D5
Yahotyn, *Ukraine* 47 G6
Yahuma, *Dem. Rep. of the Congo* 84 D4
Yahyalı, *Turkey* 72 C6
Yaita, *Japan* 55 F9
Yaiza, *Canary Is.* 37 F6
Yajiang, *China* 58 B3
Yajua, *Nigeria* 83 C7
Yakima, *U.S.A.* 114 C3
Yakima →, *U.S.A.* 114 C3
Yako, *Burkina Faso* 82 C4
Yakoruda, *Bulgaria* 40 D7
Yakovlevka, *Russia* 54 B6
Yaku-Shima, *Japan* 55 J5
Yakutat, *U.S.A.* 100 C6
Yakutia = Sakha □, *Russia* 51 C14
Yakutsk, *Russia* 51 C13
Yala, *Thailand* 65 J3
Yalbalgo, *Australia* 93 E1
Yalboroo, *Australia* 94 C4
Yale, *U.S.A.* 110 C2
Yalgoo, *Australia* 93 E2
Yalinga, *C.A.R.* 84 C4
Yalkubul, Punta, *Mexico* 119 C7
Yalleroi, *Australia* 94 C4
Yalobusha →, *U.S.A.* 113 J9
Yalong Jiang →, *China* 58 D3
Yalova, *Turkey* 41 F13
Yalta, *Ukraine* 47 K8
Yalu Jiang →, *China* 57 E13
Yalvaç, *Turkey* 72 C4
Yam Ha Melaḥ = Dead Sea, *Asia* 75 D4
Yam Kinneret, *Israel* 75 C4
Yamada, *Japan* 55 H5
Yamagata, *Japan* 54 E10
Yamagata □, *Japan* 54 E10
Yamaguchi, *Japan* 55 G5
Yamaguchi □, *Japan* 55 G5
Yamal, Poluostrov, *Russia* 50 B8
Yamal Pen. = Yamal, Poluostrov, *Russia* 50 B8
Yamanashi □, *Japan* 55 G9
Yamba, *N.S.W., Australia* 95 D5
Yamba, *S. Austral., Australia* 95 E3
Yambah, *Australia* 94 C1
Yambarran Ra., *Australia* 92 C5
Yâmbiô, *Sudan* 81 G2
Yambol, *Bulgaria* 41 D10
Yamdena, *Indonesia* 63 F8
Yame, *Japan* 55 H5
Yamethin, *Burma* 67 J20
Yamil, *Nigeria* 83 C6
Yamma-Yamma, L., *Australia* 95 D3
Yamoussoukro, *Ivory C.* 82 D3
Yampa →, *U.S.A.* 114 F9
Yampi Sd., *Australia* 92 C3
Yampil, *Moldova* 47 H5
Yampol = Yampil, *Moldova* 47 H5
Yamrat, *Nigeria* 83 C6
Yamrukchal = Botev, *Bulgaria* 41 D8
Yamuna →, *India* 69 G9
Yamzho Yumco, *China* 60 D4
Yan, *Nigeria* 83 C7
Yana →, *Russia* 51 B14
Yanac, *Australia* 95 F3
Yanagawa, *Japan* 55 H5
Yanai, *Japan* 55 H6
Yan'an, *China* 56 F5
Yanbian, *China* 58 D3
Yanbu 'al Baḥr, *Si. Arabia* 70 F3
Yancannia, *Australia* 95 E3
Yanchang, *China* 56 F6
Yancheng, *Henan, China* 56 H8
Yancheng, *Jiangsu, China* 57 H11
Yanchi, *China* 56 F4
Yanchuan, *China* 56 F6
Yanco Cr. →, *Australia* 95 F4
Yandal, *Australia* 93 E3
Yandanooka, *Australia* 93 E2
Yandaran, *Australia* 94 C5
Yandoon, *Burma* 67 L19
Yanfeng, *China* 58 E3

Yanfolila, *Mali* 82 C3
Yang Xian, *China* 56 H4
Yangambi, *Dem. Rep. of the Congo* 86 B1
Yangbi, *China* 58 E2
Yangcheng, *China* 56 G7
Yangch'ü = Taiyuan, *China* 56 F7
Yangchun, *China* 59 F8
Yanggao, *China* 56 D7
Yanggu, *China* 56 F8
Yangjiang, *China* 59 G8
Yangliuqing, *China* 57 E9
Yangon = Rangoon, *Burma* 67 L20
Yangping, *China* 59 B8
Yangpingguan, *China* 56 H4
Yangquan, *China* 56 F7
Yangshan, *China* 59 E9
Yangshuo, *China* 59 E8
Yangtse = Chang Jiang →, *China* 59 B13
Yangtze Kiang = Chang Jiang →, *China* 59 B13
Yangxin, *China* 59 C10
Yangyang, *S. Korea* 57 E15
Yangyuan, *China* 56 D8
Yangzhou, *China* 59 A12
Yanhe, *China* 58 C7
Yanji, *China* 57 C15
Yanjin, *China* 58 C5
Yanjing, *China* 58 C2
Yankton, *U.S.A.* 112 D6
Yanna, *Australia* 95 D4
Yanonge, *Dem. Rep. of the Congo* 86 B1
Yanqi, *China* 60 B3
Yanqing, *China* 56 D8
Yanshan, *Hebei, China* 57 E9
Yanshan, *Jiangxi, China* 59 C11
Yanshan, *Yunnan, China* 58 F5
Yanshou, *China* 57 B15
Yantabulla, *Australia* 95 D4
Yantai, *China* 57 F11
Yanting, *China* 58 B5
Yantra →, *Bulgaria* 41 C9
Yanwa, *China* 58 D2
Yanyuan, *China* 58 D3
Yanzhou, *China* 56 G9
Yao Xian, *China* 56 G5
Yao Yai, Ko, *Thailand* 65 J2
Yao'an, *China* 58 E3
Yaodu, *China* 58 A5
Yaoundé, *Cameroon* 83 E7
Yaowan, *China* 57 G10
Yap I., *Pac. Oc.* 96 G5
Yapen, *Indonesia* 63 E9
Yapen, Selat, *Indonesia* 63 E9
Yappar →, *Australia* 94 B3
Yaqui →, *Mexico* 118 B2
Yar-Sale, *Russia* 50 C8
Yaraka, *Australia* 94 C3
Yaransk, *Russia* 48 B8
Yarbasan, *Turkey* 39 C10
Yardea P.O., *Australia* 95 E2
Yardımcı Burnu, *Turkey* 39 E12
Yare →, *U.K.* 13 E9
Yaremcha, *Ukraine* 47 H3
Yarensk, *Russia* 50 C5
Yarí →, *Colombia* 124 D4
Yarkand = Shache, *China* 60 C2
Yarker, *Canada* 111 B8
Yarkhun →, *Pakistan* 69 A5
Yarmouth, *Canada* 103 D6
Yarmūk →, *Syria* 75 C4
Yaroslavl, *Russia* 46 D10
Yarqa, W. →, *Egypt* 75 F2
Yarra Yarra Lakes, *Australia* 93 E2
Yarraden, *Australia* 94 A3
Yarraloola, *Australia* 92 D2
Yarram, *Australia* 95 F4
Yarraman, *Australia* 95 D5
Yarranvale, *Australia* 95 D4
Yarras, *Australia* 95 E5
Yarrowmere, *Australia* 94 C4
Yartsevo, *Sib., Russia* 51 C10
Yartsevo, *Smolensk, Russia* 46 E7
Yarumal, *Colombia* 124 B3
Yasawa Group, *Fiji* 91 C7
Yaselda, *Belarus* 47 F4
Yashi, *Nigeria* 83 C6
Yashkul, *Russia* 49 G7
Yasin, *Pakistan* 69 A5
Yasinovataya, *Ukraine* 47 H9
Yasinski, L., *Canada* 102 B4
Yasinya, *Ukraine* 47 H3
Yasothon, *Thailand* 64 E5
Yass, *Australia* 95 E4
Yatağan, *Turkey* 39 D10
Yates Center, *U.S.A.* 113 G7
Yathkyed L., *Canada* 105 A9
Yatsushiro, *Japan* 55 H5
Yatta Plateau, *Kenya* 86 C4
Yavari →, *Peru* 124 D4
Yavatmal, *India* 66 J11
Yavne, *Israel* 75 D3
Yavoriv, *Ukraine* 47 H2
Yavorov = Yavoriv, *Ukraine* 47 H2
Yavuzeli, *Turkey* 72 D7
Yawatahama, *Japan* 55 H6
Yawri B., *S. Leone* 82 D2
Yaxi, *China* 58 D6
Yayama-Rettō, *Japan* 55 M1
Yazd, *Iran* 71 D7
Yazd □, *Iran* 71 D7
Yazıköy, *Turkey* 39 E9
Yazoo →, *U.S.A.* 113 J9
Yazoo City, *U.S.A.* 113 J9
Ybbs, *Austria* 26 C8
Yding Skovhøj, *Denmark* 11 J3
Ye Xian, *Henan, China* 56 H7
Ye Xian, *Shandong, China* 57 F10
Yealering, *Australia* 93 F2
Yebyu, *Burma* 67 M21
Yechŏn, *S. Korea* 57 F15
Yecla, *Spain* 33 G3
Yécora, *Mexico* 118 B3
Yedintsy = Edineţ, *Moldova* 43 B12
Yeeda, *Australia* 92 C3
Yeelanna, *Australia* 95 E2
Yefremov, *Russia* 46 F10
Yeghegnadzor, *Armenia* 73 C11
Yegorlyk →, *Russia* 49 G5
Yegorlykskaya, *Russia* 49 G5
Yegoryevsk, *Russia* 46 E10
Yegros, *Paraguay* 126 B4
Yehuda, Midbar, *Israel* 75 D4
Yei, *Sudan* 81 G3
Yei, Nahr →, *Sudan* 81 F3
Yejmiadzin, *Armenia* 49 K7
Yekaterinburg, *Russia* 50 D7
Yekaterinodar = Krasnodar, *Russia* 49 H4
Yelabuga, *Russia* 48 C11
Yelan, *Russia* 48 E6
Yelarbon, *Australia* 95 D5
Yelatma, *Russia* 48 C5
Yelets, *Russia* 47 F10
Yélimané, *Mali* 82 B2
Yelizavetgrad = Kirovohrad, *Ukraine* 47 H7
Yell, *U.K.* 14 A7
Yell Sd., *U.K.* 14 A7
Yellow Sea, *China* 57 G12
Yellowhead Pass, *Canada* 104 C5
Yellowknife, *Canada* 104 A6
Yellowknife →, *Canada* 104 A6
Yellowstone →, *U.S.A.* 112 B3
Yellowstone L., *U.S.A.* 114 D8
Yellowstone National Park, *U.S.A.* 114 D9
Yellowtail Res., *U.S.A.* 114 D9
Yelnya, *Russia* 46 E7
Yelsk, *Belarus* 47 G5
Yelvertoft, *Australia* 94 C2
Yelwa, *Nigeria* 83 C5
Yemen ■, *Asia* 74 E3
Yen Bai, *Vietnam* 64 B5
Yenakiyeve, *Ukraine* 47 H10
Yenakiyevo = Yenakiyeve, *Ukraine* 47 H10
Yenangyaung, *Burma* 67 J19
Yenbo = Yanbu 'al Baḥr, *Si. Arabia* 70 F3
Yenda, *Australia* 95 E4
Yendéré, *Ivory C.* 82 C4
Yendi, *Ghana* 83 D4
Yenice, *Ankara, Turkey* 72 C5
Yenice, *Aydın, Turkey* 39 D10
Yenice, *Çanakkale, Turkey* 39 B9
Yenice, *Edirne, Turkey* 41 F10
Yenice →, *Turkey* 72 D6
Yenifoça, *Turkey* 39 C8
Yenihisar, *Turkey* 39 D9
Yeniköy, *Bursa, Turkey* 41 F13
Yeniköy, *Çanakkale, Turkey* 39 B8
Yeniköy, *Kütahya, Turkey* 39 C11
Yenipazar, *Turkey* 39 D10
Yenisaía, *Greece* 41 E8
Yenişehir, *Turkey* 41 F13
Yenisey →, *Russia* 50 B9
Yeniseysk, *Russia* 51 D10
Yeniseyskiy Zaliv, *Russia* 50 B9
Yennádhi, *Greece* 36 C9
Yenne, *France* 21 C9
Yenotayevka, *Russia* 49 G8
Yenyuka, *Russia* 51 D13
Yeo →, *U.K.* 13 G5
Yeo, L., *Australia* 93 E3
Yeola, *India* 66 J9
Yeoryioúpolis, *Greece* 36 D6
Yeovil, *U.K.* 13 G5
Yepes, *Spain* 34 F7
Yeppoon, *Australia* 94 C5
Yeráki, *Greece* 38 D4
Yerbent, *Turkmenistan* 50 F6
Yerbogachen, *Russia* 51 C11
Yerevan, *Armenia* 49 K7
Yerilla, *Australia* 93 E3
Yerkesik, *Turkey* 39 D10
Yerköy, *Turkey* 72 C6
Yermak, *Kazakstan* 50 D8
Yermo, *U.S.A.* 117 L10
Yerólakkos, *Cyprus* 36 D12
Yeropol, *Russia* 51 C17
Yeropótamos →, *Greece* 36 D6
Yeroskipos, *Cyprus* 36 E11
Yershov, *Russia* 48 E9
Yerushalayim = Jerusalem, *Israel* 75 D4
Yerville, *France* 18 C7
Yes Tor, *U.K.* 13 G4
Yesan, *S. Korea* 57 F14
Yeşilhisar, *Turkey* 72 C6
Yeşilırmak →, *Turkey* 72 B7
Yeşilkent, *Turkey* 72 D7
Yeşilköy, *Turkey* 41 F12
Yeşilova, *Turkey* 39 D11
Yeşilyurt, *Manisa, Turkey* 39 C10
Yeşilyurt, *Muğla, Turkey* 39 D10
Yesnogorsk, *Russia* 46 E9
Yeso, *U.S.A.* 113 H2
Yessentuki, *Russia* 49 H6
Yessey, *Russia* 51 C11
Yeste, *Spain* 33 G2
Yeu, Î. d', *France* 18 F4
Yevlakh = Yevlax, *Azerbaijan* 49 K8
Yevlax, *Azerbaijan* 49 K8
Yevpatoriya, *Ukraine* 47 K7
Yeya →, *Russia* 47 J10
Yeysk, *Russia* 47 J10
Yezd = Yazd, *Iran* 71 D7
Yezerishche, *Belarus* 46 E5
Yhati, *Paraguay* 126 B4
Yhú, *Paraguay* 127 B4
Yi →, *Uruguay* 126 C4
Yi 'Allaq, G., *Egypt* 75 E2
Yi He →, *China* 57 G10
Yi Xian, *Anhui, China* 59 C11
Yi Xian, *Hebei, China* 56 E8
Yi Xian, *Liaoning, China* 57 D11
Yialí, *Greece* 39 E9
Yialiás →, *Cyprus* 36 D12
Yi'allaq, G., *Egypt* 80 H8
Yialousa, *Cyprus* 36 D13
Yiáltra, *Greece* 38 C4
Yianisádhes, *Greece* 36 D8
Yiannitsa, *Greece* 40 F6
Yibin, *China* 58 C5
Yichang, *China* 59 B8
Yicheng, *Henan, China* 59 B9
Yicheng, *Shanxi, China* 56 G6
Yichuan, *China* 56 F6
Yichun, *Heilongjiang, China* 60 B7
Yichun, *Jiangxi, China* 59 D10
Yidu, *Hubei, China* 59 B8
Yidu, *Shandong, China* 57 F10
Yidun, *China* 58 B2
Yihuang, *China* 59 D11
Yijun, *China* 56 G5
Yıldız Dağları, *Turkey* 41 E11
Yıldızeli, *Turkey* 72 C7
Yiliang, *Yunnan, China* 58 D5
Yiliang, *Yunnan, China* 58 E4
Yilong, *China* 58 B6
Yimen, *China* 58 E4
Yimianpo, *China* 57 B15
Yinchuan, *China* 56 E4
Yindarlgooda, L., *Australia* 93 F3
Ying He →, *China* 56 H9
Ying Xian, *China* 56 E7
Yingcheng, *China* 59 B9
Yingde, *China* 59 E9
Yingjiang, *China* 58 E1
Yingjing, *China* 58 C4
Yingkou, *China* 57 D12
Yingshan, *Henan, China* 59 B9
Yingshan, *Hubei, China* 59 B10
Yingshan, *Sichuan, China* 58 B6
Yingshang, *China* 59 A11
Yingtan, *China* 60 D6
Yining, *China* 60 B3
Yinjiang, *China* 58 C7
Yinmabin, *Burma* 67 H19
Yinnietharra, *Australia* 92 D2
Yiofiros →, *Greece* 36 D7
Yioúra, *Nótios Aiyaíon, Greece* 38 D6
Yioúra, *Thessalía, Greece* 38 B6
Yipinglang, *China* 58 E3
Yirga Alem, *Ethiopia* 81 F4
Yishan, *China* 58 E7
Yishui, *China* 57 G10
Yíthion, *Greece* 38 E4
Yitiaoshan, *China* 56 F3
Yitong, *China* 57 C13
Yiwu, *China* 59 C13
Yixing, *China* 59 B12
Yiyang, *Henan, China* 56 G7
Yiyang, *Hunan, China* 59 C9
Yiyang, *Jiangxi, China* 59 C11
Yizhang, *China* 59 E9
Yizheng, *China* 59 A12
Yli-Kitka, *Finland* 8 C23
Ylitornio, *Finland* 8 C20
Ylivieska, *Finland* 8 D21
Yngaren, *Sweden* 11 F10
Yoakum, *U.S.A.* 113 L6
Yobe □, *Nigeria* 83 C7
Yog Pt., *Phil.* 63 B6
Yogan, *Togo* 83 D5
Yoğuntaş, *Turkey* 41 E11
Yogyakarta, *Indonesia* 63 G14
Yoho Nat. Park, *Canada* 104 C5
Yojoa, L. de, *Honduras* 120 D2
Yŏju, *S. Korea* 57 F14
Yokadouma, *Cameroon* 84 D2
Yokkaichi, *Japan* 55 G8
Yoko, *Cameroon* 83 D7
Yokohama, *Japan* 55 G9
Yokosuka, *Japan* 55 G9
Yokote, *Japan* 54 E10
Yola, *Nigeria* 83 D7
Yolaina, Cordillera de, *Nic.* 120 D3
Yonago, *Japan* 55 G6
Yonaguni-Jima, *Japan* 55 M1
Yŏnan, *N. Korea* 57 F14
Yonezawa, *Japan* 54 F10
Yong Peng, *Malaysia* 65 M4
Yong Sata, *Thailand* 65 J2
Yongampo, *N. Korea* 57 E13
Yong'an, *China* 59 E11
Yongcheng, *China* 56 H9
Yŏngchŏn, *S. Korea* 57 G15
Yongchuan, *China* 58 C5
Yongchun, *China* 59 E12
Yongdeng, *China* 56 F2
Yongding, *China* 59 E11
Yŏngdŏk, *S. Korea* 57 F15
Yŏngdŭngpo, *S. Korea* 57 F14
Yongfeng, *China* 59 D10
Yongfu, *China* 58 E7
Yonghe, *China* 56 F6
Yŏnghŭng, *N. Korea* 57 E14
Yongji, *China* 56 G6
Yŏngju, *S. Korea* 57 F15
Yongkang, *Yunnan, China* 58 E2
Yongkang, *Zhejiang, China* 59 C13
Yongnian, *China* 56 F8
Yongning, *Guangxi Zhuangzu, China* 58 F7
Yongning, *Ningxia Huizu, China* 56 E4
Yongping, *China* 58 E2
Yongqing, *China* 56 E9
Yongren, *China* 58 D3
Yongshan, *China* 58 C4
Yongsheng, *China* 58 D3
Yongshun, *China* 58 C7
Yongtai, *China* 59 E12
Yŏngwŏl, *S. Korea* 57 F15
Yongxin, *China* 59 D10
Yongxing, *China* 59 D9
Yongxiu, *China* 59 C10
Yonibana, *S. Leone* 82 D2
Yonkers, *U.S.A.* 111 F11
Yonne □, *France* 19 E10
Yonne →, *France* 19 D9
York, *Australia* 93 F2
York, *U.K.* 12 D6
York, *Ala., U.S.A.* 109 J1
York, *Nebr., U.S.A.* 112 E6
York, *Pa., U.S.A.* 108 F7
York, C., *Australia* 94 A3
York, City of □, *U.K.* 12 D6
York, Kap, *Greenland* 4 B4
York, Vale of, *U.K.* 12 C6
York Sd., *Australia* 92 C4
Yorke Pen., *Australia* 95 E2
Yorkshire Wolds, *U.K.* 12 C7
Yorkton, *Canada* 105 C8
Yorktown, *U.S.A.* 113 L6
Yorkville, *U.S.A.* 116 G3
Yornup, *Australia* 93 F2
Yoro, *Honduras* 120 C2
Yoron-Jima, *Japan* 55 L4
Yos Sudarso, Pulau = Dolak, Pulau, *Indonesia* 63 F9
Yosemite National Park, *U.S.A.* 116 H7
Yosemite Village, *U.S.A.* 116 H7
Yoshkar Ola, *Russia* 48 B8
Yŏsu, *S. Korea* 57 G14
Yotvata, *Israel* 75 F4
You Xian, *China* 59 D9
Youbou, *Canada* 104 D4
Youghal, *Ireland* 15 E4
Youghal B., *Ireland* 15 E4
Youkounkoun, *Guinea* 82 C2
Young, *Australia* 95 E4
Young, *Canada* 105 C7
Young, *Uruguay* 126 C4
Younghusband, L., *Australia* 95 E2
Younghusband Pen., *Australia* 95 F2
Youngstown, *Canada* 105 C6
Youngstown, *N.Y., U.S.A.* 110 C5
Youngstown, *Ohio, U.S.A.* 110 E4
Youngsville, *U.S.A.* 110 E5
Youxi, *China* 59 D12
Youyang, *China* 58 C7
Youyu, *China* 56 D7
Yoweragabbie, *Australia* 93 E2
Yozgat, *Turkey* 72 C6
Ypané →, *Paraguay* 126 A4
Yport, *France* 18 C7
Ypres = Ieper, *Belgium* 17 D2
Ypsilanti, *U.S.A.* 108 D4
Yreka, *U.S.A.* 114 F2
Ysleta, *U.S.A.* 115 L10
Yssingeaux, *France* 21 C8
Ystad, *Sweden* 11 J7
Ysyk-Köl, *Kyrgyzstan* 52 E11
Ysyk-Köl, Ozero, *Kyrgyzstan* 50 E8
Ythan →, *U.K.* 14 D7
Ytterhogdal, *Sweden* 10 B8
Ytyk Kyuyel, *Russia* 51 C14
Yu Jiang →, *China* 60 D6
Yu Xian, *Hebei, China* 56 E8
Yu Xian, *Henan, China* 56 G7
Yu Xian, *Shanxi, China* 56 E7
Yuan Jiang →, *Hunan, China* 59 C8
Yuan Jiang →, *Yunnan, China* 58 F4
Yuan'an, *China* 59 B8
Yuanjiang, *Hunan, China* 59 C9
Yuanjiang, *Yunnan, China* 58 F4
Yüanli, *Taiwan* 59 E13
Yüanlin, *Taiwan* 59 F13
Yuanlin, *Taiwan* 59 F13
Yuanling, *China* 59 C8
Yuanmou, *China* 58 E3
Yuanqu, *China* 56 G6
Yuanyang, *Henan, China* 56 G7
Yuanyang, *Yunnan, China* 58 F4
Yuba →, *U.S.A.* 116 F5
Yuba City, *U.S.A.* 116 F5
Yūbari, *Japan* 54 C10
Yūbetsu, *Japan* 54 B11
Yucatán □, *Mexico* 119 C7
Yucatán, Canal de, *Caribbean* 120 B2
Yucatán, Península de, *Mexico* 98 H11
Yucatán Basin, *Cent. Amer.* 98 H11
Yucatan Str. = Yucatán, Canal de, *Caribbean* 120 B2
Yucca, *U.S.A.* 117 L12
Yucca Valley, *U.S.A.* 117 L10
Yucheng, *China* 56 F9
Yuci, *China* 56 F7
Yudu, *China* 59 E10
Yuendumu, *Australia* 92 D5
Yueqing, *China* 59 C13
Yueqing Wan, *China* 59 C13
Yuexi, *Anhui, China* 59 B11
Yuexi, *Sichuan, China* 58 C4
Yueyang, *China* 59 C9
Yugan, *China* 59 C11
Yugoslavia ■, *Europe* 40 C4
Yuhuan, *China* 59 C13
Yujiang, *China* 59 C11
Yukhnov, *Russia* 46 E8
Yukon →, *U.S.A.* 100 B3
Yukon Territory □, *Canada* 100 B6
Yüksekova, *Turkey* 73 D11
Yukta, *Russia* 51 C11
Yukuhashi, *Japan* 55 H5
Yule →, *Australia* 92 D2
Yuli, *Nigeria* 83 D7
Yulin, *Guangxi Zhuangzu, China* 59 F8
Yulin, *Shaanxi, China* 56 E5
Yulin, *Shensi, China* 64 C7
Yuma, *Ariz., U.S.A.* 117 N12
Yuma, *Colo., U.S.A.* 112 E3
Yuma, B. de, *Dom. Rep.* 121 C6
Yumbe, *Uganda* 86 B3
Yumbi, *Dem. Rep. of the Congo* 86 C2
Yumen, *China* 60 C4
Yumurtalık, *Turkey* 72 D6
Yun Ho →, *China* 57 E9
Yun Xian, *Hubei, China* 59 A8
Yun Xian, *Yunnan, China* 58 E3
Yunak, *Turkey* 72 C4
Yunan, *China* 59 F8
Yuncheng, *Henan, China* 56 G8
Yuncheng, *Shanxi, China* 56 G6
Yundamindra, *Australia* 93 E3
Yunfu, *China* 59 F9
Yungas, *Bolivia* 124 G5
Yungay, *Chile* 126 D1
Yunhe, *China* 59 C12
Yunlin, *Taiwan* 59 F13
Yunling, *China* 58 D2
Yunlong, *China* 58 E2
Yunmeng, *China* 59 B9
Yunnan □, *China* 58 E4
Yunquera de Henares, *Spain* 32 E1
Yunt Dağı, *Turkey* 39 C9
Yunta, *Australia* 95 E2
Yunxi, *China* 56 H6
Yunxiao, *China* 59 F11
Yunyang, *China* 58 B7
Yuping, *China* 58 D7
Yupyongdong, *N. Korea* 57 D15
Yuqing, *China* 58 D6
Yurga, *Russia* 50 D9
Yurimaguas, *Peru* 124 E3
Yuryev-Polskiy, *Russia* 46 D10
Yuryevets, *Russia* 48 B6
Yuryung Kaya, *Russia* 51 B12
Yuscarán, *Honduras* 120 D2
Yushanzhen, *China* 58 C7
Yushe, *China* 56 F7
Yushu, *Jilin, China* 57 B14
Yushu, *Qinghai, China* 60 C4
Yusufeli, *Turkey* 73 B9
Yutai, *China* 56 G9
Yutian, *China* 57 E9
Yuxarı Qarabağ = Nagorno-Karabakh, *Azerbaijan* 73 C12
Yuxi, *China* 58 E4
Yuyao, *China* 59 B13
Yuzawa, *Japan* 54 E10
Yuzha, *Russia* 48 B6
Yuzhno-Sakhalinsk, *Russia* 51 E15
Yvelines □, *France* 19 D8
Yverdon, *Switz.* 25 J2
Yvetot, *France* 18 C7
Yzeure, *France* 19 F10

Z

Zaanstad, *Neths.* 17 B4
Zāb al Kabīr →, *Iraq* 70 C4
Zāb aş Şagīr →, *Iraq* 70 C4
Žabalj, *Serbia, Yug.* 42 E5
Žabari, *Serbia, Yug.* 40 B5
Zabarjad, *Egypt* 80 C4
Zabaykalsk, *Russia* 51 E12
Zabki, *Poland* 45 F8
Ząbkowice Śląskie, *Poland* 45 H3
Žabljak, *Montenegro, Yug.* 40 C3

Zabłudów, *Poland* 45 F9
Zabno, *Poland* 45 H7
Zābol, *Iran* 71 D9
Zābolī, *Iran* 71 E9
Zabré, *Burkina Faso* 83 C4
Zábřeh, *Czech Rep.* 27 B9
Zabrze, *Poland* 45 H5
Zacapa, *Guatemala* 120 D2
Zacapu, *Mexico* 118 D4
Zacatecas, *Mexico* 118 C4
Zacatecas □, *Mexico* 118 C4
Zacatecoluca, *El Salv.* 120 D2
Zacoalco, *Mexico* 118 C4
Zacualtipán, *Mexico* 119 C5
Zadar, *Croatia* 29 D12
Zadawa, *Nigeria* 83 C7
Zadetkyi Kyun, *Burma* 65 H2
Zadonsk, *Russia* 47 F10
Zafarqand, *Iran* 71 C7
Zafora, *Greece* 39 E8
Zafra, *Spain* 35 G4
Żagań, *Poland* 45 G2
Žagarė, *Lithuania* 44 B10
Zagazig, *Egypt* 80 H7
Zāgheh, *Iran* 71 C6
Zaglivérion, *Greece* 40 F7
Zagnanado, *Benin* 83 D5
Zagorá, *Greece* 38 B5
Zagorje, *Slovenia* 29 B11
Zagórów, *Poland* 45 F4
Zagorsk = Sergiyev Posad, *Russia* 46 D10
Zagórz, *Poland* 45 J9
Zagreb, *Croatia* 29 C12
Zāgros, Kūhhā-ye, *Iran* 71 C6
Zagros Mts. = Zāgros, Kūhhā-ye, *Iran* 71 C6
Žagubica, *Serbia, Yug.* 40 B5
Zaguinaso, *Ivory C.* 82 C3
Zagyva →, *Hungary* 42 C5
Zāhedān, *Fārs, Iran* 71 D7
Zāhedān, *Sīstān va Balūchestān, Iran* 71 D9
Zahlah, *Lebanon* 75 B4
Zahna, *Germany* 24 D8
Záhony, *Hungary* 42 B7
Zainsk, *Russia* 48 C11
Zaïre = Congo, Dem. Rep. of the ■, *Africa* 84 E4
Zaïre → = Congo →, *Africa* 84 F2
Zaječar, *Serbia, Yug.* 40 C6
Zakamensk, *Russia* 51 D11
Zakataly = Zaqatala, *Azerbaijan* 49 K8
Zakháro, *Greece* 38 D3
Zakhodnaya Dzvina = Daugava →, *Latvia* 9 H21
Zākhū, *Iraq* 70 B4
Zákinthos, *Greece* 38 D2
Zákinthos □, *Greece* 38 D2
Zakopane, *Poland* 45 J6
Zakroczym, *Poland* 45 F7
Zákros, *Greece* 36 D8
Zala □, *Hungary* 42 D1
Zala →, *Hungary* 42 D2
Zalaegerszeg, *Hungary* 42 D1
Zalakomár, *Hungary* 42 D2
Zalalövő, *Hungary* 42 D1
Zalamea de la Serena, *Spain* 35 G5
Zalamea la Real, *Spain* 35 H4
Zalău, *Romania* 42 C8
Žalec, *Slovenia* 29 B12
Zaleshchiki = Zalishchyky, *Ukraine* 47 H3
Zalew Wiślany, *Poland* 44 D6
Zalewo, *Poland* 44 E6
Zalingei, *Sudan* 79 F10
Zalishchyky, *Ukraine* 47 H3
Zambeke, *Dem. Rep. of the Congo* 86 B2
Zambeze →, *Africa* 87 F4
Zambezi = Zambeze →, *Africa* 87 F4
Zambezi, *Zambia* 85 G4
Zambezia □, *Mozam.* 87 F4
Zambia ■, *Africa* 87 F2
Zamboanga, *Phil.* 61 H5
Zamboanguita, *Phil.* 61 G5
Zambrów, *Poland* 45 F9
Zametchino, *Russia* 48 D6
Zamora, *Mexico* 118 D4
Zamora, *Spain* 34 D5
Zamora □, *Spain* 34 D5
Zamość, *Poland* 45 H10
Zamość □, *Poland* 45 H10
Zan, *Ghana* 83 D4
Záncara →, *Spain* 33 F1
Zandvoort, *Neths.* 17 B4
Zanesville, *U.S.A.* 110 G2
Zangābād, *Iran* 70 B5
Zangue →, *Mozam.* 87 F4
Zanjān, *Iran* 71 B6
Zanjān □, *Iran* 71 B6
Zannone, *Italy* 30 B6
Zante = Zákinthos, *Greece* 38 D2
Zanthus, *Australia* 93 F3
Zanzibar, *Tanzania* 86 D4
Zaouiet El-Kala = Bordj Omar Driss, *Algeria* 78 C7
Zaouiet Reggane, *Algeria* 78 C6
Zaoyang, *China* 59 A9
Zaozhuang, *China* 57 G9
Zap Suyu = Zāb al Kabīr →, *Iraq* 70 C4
Zapadna Morava →, *Serbia, Yug.* 40 C5
Zapadnaya Dvina, *Russia* 46 D7
Zapadnaya Dvina → = Daugava →, *Latvia* 9 H21
Západné Beskydy, *Europe* 27 B12
Zapadni Rodopi, *Bulgaria* 40 E7
Západočeský □, *Czech Rep.* 26 B6
Zapala, *Argentina* 128 D2
Zapaleri, Cerro, *Bolivia* 126 A2
Zapata, *U.S.A.* 113 M5
Zapatón →, *Spain* 35 F4
Zaporizhzhya, *Ukraine* 47 J8
Zaporozhye = Zaporizhzhya, *Ukraine* 47 J8
Zaqatala, *Azerbaijan* 49 K8
Zara, *Turkey* 72 C7
Zaragoza, *Coahuila, Mexico* 118 B4
Zaragoza, *Nuevo León, Mexico* 119 C5
Zaragoza, *Spain* 32 D4
Zaragoza □, *Spain* 32 D4
Zarand, *Kermān, Iran* 71 D8
Zarand, *Markazī, Iran* 71 C6
Zărandului, Munţii, *Romania* 42 D7
Zaranj, *Afghan.* 66 D2
Zarasai, *Lithuania* 9 J22
Zarate, *Argentina* 126 C4
Zarautz, *Spain* 32 B2
Zaraysk, *Russia* 46 E10
Zāreh, *Iran* 71 C6
Zarembo I., *U.S.A.* 104 B2
Zaria, *Nigeria* 83 C6
Żarki, *Poland* 45 H6
Zárkon, *Greece* 38 B4
Zarneh, *Iran* 70 C5
Zărneşti, *Romania* 43 E10
Zarós, *Greece* 36 D6
Żarów, *Poland* 45 H3
Zarqā', Nahr az →, *Jordan* 75 C4
Zarrīn, *Iran* 71 C7
Zaruma, *Ecuador* 124 D3
Żary, *Poland* 45 G2
Zarza de Granadilla, *Spain* 34 E4
Zarzis, *Tunisia* 79 B8
Zas, *Spain* 34 B2
Zaskar →, *India* 69 B7
Zaskar Mts., *India* 69 C7
Zastron, *S. Africa* 88 E4
Žatec, *Czech Rep.* 26 A6
Zaterechnyy, *Russia* 49 H7
Zator, *Poland* 45 J6
Zavala, *Bos.-H.* 40 D1
Zavāreh, *Iran* 71 C7
Zavetnoye, *Russia* 49 G6
Zavidovići, *Bos.-H.* 42 F3
Zavitinsk, *Russia* 51 D13
Zavodovski, I., *Antarctica* 5 B1
Zavolzhsk, *Russia* 48 B6
Zavolzhye, *Russia* 48 B6
Zawadzkie, *Poland* 45 H5
Zawichost, *Poland* 45 H8
Zawidów, *Poland* 45 G2
Zawiercie, *Poland* 45 H6
Zāwiyat al Bayḍā = Al Bayḍā, *Libya* 79 B10
Zâwyet Shammas, *Egypt* 80 A2
Zâwyet Um el Rakham, *Egypt* 80 A2
Zâwyet Ungeîla, *Egypt* 80 A2
Zāyā, *Iraq* 70 C5
Zaysan, *Kazakstan* 50 E9
Zaysan, Oz., *Kazakstan* 50 E9
Zayü, *China* 58 C1
Zázrivá, *Slovak Rep.* 27 B12
Zbarazh, *Ukraine* 47 H3
Zbąszyń, *Poland* 45 F2
Zbąszynek, *Poland* 45 F2
Zblewo, *Poland* 44 E5
Žďár nad Sázavov, *Czech Rep.* 26 B8
Zdolbuniv, *Ukraine* 47 G4
Ždrelo, *Serbia, Yug.* 40 B5
Zduńska Wola, *Poland* 45 G5
Zduny, *Poland* 45 G4
Zeballos, *Canada* 104 D3
Zebediela, *S. Africa* 89 C4
Zeebrugge, *Belgium* 17 C3
Zeehan, *Australia* 94 G4
Zeeland □, *Neths.* 17 C3
Zeerust, *S. Africa* 88 D4
Zefat, *Israel* 75 C4
Zege, *Ethiopia* 81 E4
Zégoua, *Mali* 82 C3
Zehdenick, *Germany* 24 C9
Zeil, Mt., *Australia* 92 D5
Zeila, *Somali Rep.* 74 E3
Zeist, *Neths.* 17 B5
Zeitz, *Germany* 24 D8
Żelechów, *Poland* 45 G8
Zelengora, *Bos.-H.* 40 C2
Zelenodolsk, *Russia* 48 C9
Zelenogorsk, *Russia* 46 B5
Zelenograd, *Russia* 46 D9
Zelenogradsk, *Russia* 9 J19
Zelenokumsk, *Russia* 49 H6
Železná Ruda, *Czech Rep.* 26 B6
Železnik, *Serbia, Yug.* 40 B4
Želiezovce, *Slovak Rep.* 27 C11
Zelina, *Croatia* 29 C13
Zell, *Baden-W., Germany* 25 H3
Zell, *Rhld-Pfz., Germany* 25 E3
Zell am See, *Austria* 26 D5
Zella-Mehlis, *Germany* 24 E6
Zelów, *Poland* 45 G6
Zeltweg, *Austria* 26 D7
Zémio, *C.A.R.* 86 A2
Zempléni-hegység, *Hungary* 42 B6
Zemplínska šírava, *Slovak Rep.* 27 C15
Zemun, *Serbia, Yug.* 40 B4
Zengbe, *Cameroon* 83 D7
Zengcheng, *China* 59 F9
Zenica, *Bos.-H.* 42 F2
Žepče, *Bos.-H.* 42 F3
Zeraf, Bahr ez →, *Sudan* 81 F3
Zerbst, *Germany* 24 D8
Żerków, *Poland* 45 F4
Zermatt, *Switz.* 25 J3
Zernez, *Switz.* 25 J6
Zernograd, *Russia* 49 G5
Zerqani, *Albania* 40 E4
Zestaponi, *Georgia* 49 J6
Zetel, *Germany* 24 B3
Zeulenroda, *Germany* 24 E7
Zeven, *Germany* 24 B5
Zevenaar, *Neths.* 17 C6
Zévio, *Italy* 28 C8
Zeya, *Russia* 51 D13
Zeya →, *Russia* 51 D13
Zeytinbaği, *Turkey* 41 F12
Zeytindağ, *Turkey* 39 C9
Zghartā, *Lebanon* 75 A4
Zgierz, *Poland* 45 G6
Zgorzelec, *Poland* 45 G2
Zguriţa, *Moldova* 43 B13
Zhabinka, *Belarus* 47 F3
Zhailma, *Kazakstan* 50 D7
Zhambyl, *Kazakstan* 50 E8
Zhangaly, *Kazakstan* 49 G10
Zhangaqazaly, *Kazakstan* 50 E7
Zhangbei, *China* 56 D8
Zhangguangcai Ling, *China* 57 B15
Zhangjiakou, *China* 56 D8
Zhangping, *China* 59 E11
Zhangpu, *China* 59 E11
Zhangwu, *China* 57 C12
Zhangye, *China* 60 C5
Zhangzhou, *China* 59 E11
Zhanhua, *China* 57 F10
Zhanjiang, *China* 59 G8
Zhannetty, Ostrov, *Russia* 51 B16
Zhanyi, *China* 58 E4
Zhanyu, *China* 57 B12
Zhao Xian, *China* 56 F8
Zhao'an, *China* 59 F11
Zhaocheng, *China* 56 F6
Zhaojue, *China* 58 C4
Zhaoping, *China* 59 E8
Zhaoqing, *China* 59 F9
Zhaotong, *China* 58 D4
Zhaoyuan, *Heilongjiang, China* 57 B13
Zhaoyuan, *Shandong, China* 57 F11
Zharkovskiy, *Russia* 46 E7
Zhashkiv, *Ukraine* 47 H6
Zhashui, *China* 56 H5
Zhayyq →, *Kazakstan* 50 E6
Zhdanov = Mariupol, *Ukraine* 47 J9
Zhecheng, *China* 56 G8
Zhegao, *China* 59 B11
Zhejiang □, *China* 59 C13
Zheleznogorsk, *Russia* 47 F8
Zheleznogorsk-Ilimskiy, *Russia* 51 D11
Zheltyye Vody = Zhovti Vody, *Ukraine* 47 H7
Zhen'an, *China* 56 H5
Zhenfeng, *China* 58 E5
Zheng'an, *China* 58 C6
Zhengding, *China* 56 E8
Zhenghe, *China* 59 D12
Zhengyang, *China* 59 A10
Zhengyangguan, *China* 59 A11
Zhengzhou, *China* 56 G7
Zhenhai, *China* 59 C13
Zhenjiang, *China* 59 A12
Zhenlai, *China* 57 B12
Zhenning, *China* 58 D5
Zhenping, *Henan, China* 56 H7
Zhenping, *Shaanxi, China* 58 B7
Zhenxiong, *China* 58 D5
Zhenyuan, *Gansu, China* 56 G4
Zhenyuan, *Guizhou, China* 58 D7
Zherdevka, *Russia* 48 E5
Zherong, *China* 59 D12
Zhetiqara, *Kazakstan* 50 D7
Zhezqazghan, *Kazakstan* 50 E7
Zhidan, *China* 56 F5
Zhigansk, *Russia* 51 C13
Zhigulevsk, *Russia* 48 D9
Zhijiang, *Hubei, China* 59 B8
Zhijiang, *Hunan, China* 58 D7
Zhijin, *China* 58 D5
Zhilinda, *Russia* 51 C12
Zhirnovsk, *Russia* 48 E7
Zhitomir = Zhytomyr, *Ukraine* 47 G5
Zhizdra, *Russia* 46 F8
Zhlobin, *Belarus* 47 F6
Zhmerinka = Zhmerynka, *Ukraine* 47 H5
Zhmerynka, *Ukraine* 47 H5
Zhob, *Pakistan* 68 D3
Zhodino = Zhodzina, *Belarus* 46 E5
Zhodzina, *Belarus* 46 E5
Zhokhova, Ostrov, *Russia* 51 B16
Zhong Xian, *China* 58 B7
Zhongdian, *China* 58 D2
Zhongdong, *China* 58 F6
Zhongdu, *China* 58 E7
Zhongning, *China* 56 F3
Zhongshan, *Guangdong, China* 59 F9
Zhongshan, *Guangxi Zhuangzu, China* 59 E8
Zhongtiao Shan, *China* 56 G6
Zhongwei, *China* 56 F3
Zhongxiang, *China* 59 B9
Zhongyang, *China* 56 F6
Zhoucun, *China* 57 F9
Zhouning, *China* 59 D12
Zhoushan Dao, *China* 59 C14
Zhouzhi, *China* 56 G5
Zhovti Vody, *Ukraine* 47 H7
Zhovtneve, *Ukraine* 47 J7
Zhovtnevoye = Zhovtneve, *Ukraine* 47 J7
Zhuanghe, *China* 57 E12
Zhucheng, *China* 57 G10
Zhugqu, *China* 56 H3
Zhuhai, *China* 59 F9
Zhuji, *China* 59 C13
Zhukovka, *Russia* 46 F7
Zhumadian, *China* 56 H8
Zhuo Xian, *China* 56 E8
Zhuolu, *China* 56 D8
Zhuozi, *China* 56 D7
Zhushan, *China* 59 A8
Zhuxi, *China* 58 A7
Zhuzhou, *China* 59 D9
Zhytomyr, *Ukraine* 47 G5
Zi Shui →, *China* 59 C9
Žiar nad Hronom, *Slovak Rep.* 27 C11
Zīārān, *Iran* 71 B6
Ziarat, *Pakistan* 68 D2
Zibo, *China* 57 F10
Zichang, *China* 56 F5
Zidarovo, *Bulgaria* 41 D11
Ziębice, *Poland* 45 H4
Zielona Góra, *Poland* 45 G2
Zielona Góra □, *Poland* 45 G2
Zierikzee, *Neths.* 17 C3
Ziesar, *Germany* 24 C8
Zifta, *Egypt* 80 H7
Zigey, *Chad* 79 F9
Zigong, *China* 58 C5
Zigui, *China* 58 B8
Ziguinchor, *Senegal* 82 C1
Zihuatanejo, *Mexico* 118 D4
Zijin, *China* 59 F10
Zile, *Turkey* 72 B6
Žilina, *Slovak Rep.* 27 B11
Žilinský □, *Slovak Rep.* 27 B12
Zillah, *Libya* 79 C9
Zillertaler Alpen, *Austria* 26 D4
Zima, *Russia* 51 D11
Zimapán, *Mexico* 119 C5
Zimba, *Zambia* 87 F2
Zimbabwe, *Zimbabwe* 87 G3
Zimbabwe ■, *Africa* 87 F3
Zimnicea, *Romania* 43 G10
Zimovniki, *Russia* 49 G6
Zinder, *Niger* 83 C6
Zinga, *Tanzania* 87 D4
Zingst, *Germany* 24 A8
Ziniaré, *Burkina Faso* 83 C4
Zinnowitz, *Germany* 24 A9
Zion National Park, *U.S.A.* 115 H7
Zirbitzkogel, *Austria* 26 D7
Zirc, *Hungary* 42 C2
Žiri, *Slovenia* 29 B11
Žirje, *Croatia* 29 E12
Zirl, *Austria* 26 D4
Zirndorf, *Germany* 25 F6
Ziros, *Greece* 36 D8
Zisterdorf, *Austria* 27 C9
Zitácuaro, *Mexico* 118 D4
Žitava →, *Slovak Rep.* 27 C11
Žitište, *Serbia, Yug.* 42 E5
Zítsa, *Greece* 38 B2
Zittau, *Germany* 24 E10
Zitundo, *Mozam.* 89 D5
Živinice, *Bos.-H.* 42 F3
Ziway, L., *Ethiopia* 81 F4
Zixi, *China* 59 D11
Zixing, *China* 59 E9
Ziyang, *Shaanxi, China* 56 H5
Ziyang, *Sichuan, China* 58 B5
Ziyun, *China* 58 E6
Zizhixian, *China* 59 E8
Zizhong, *China* 58 C5
Zlarin, *Croatia* 29 E12
Zlatar, *Croatia* 29 B13
Zlatar, *Serbia, Yug.* 40 C3
Zlataritsa, *Bulgaria* 41 C9
Zlaté Moravce, *Slovak Rep.* 27 C11
Zlatibor, *Serbia, Yug.* 40 C3
Zlatitsa, *Bulgaria* 41 D8
Zlatna, *Romania* 43 D8
Zlatna Panega, *Bulgaria* 41 C8
Zlatni Pyasŭtsi, *Bulgaria* 41 C12
Zlatograd, *Bulgaria* 41 E9
Zlatoust, *Russia* 50 D6
Zletovo, *Macedonia* 40 E6
Zlín, *Czech Rep.* 27 B10
Złocieniec, *Poland* 44 E3
Złoczew, *Poland* 45 G5
Zlot, *Serbia, Yug.* 40 B5
Złotoryja, *Poland* 45 G2
Złotów, *Poland* 44 E4
Zmeinogorsk, *Kazakstan* 50 D9
Żmigród, *Poland* 45 G3
Zmiyev, *Ukraine* 47 H9
Znamenka = Znamyanka, *Ukraine* 47 H7
Znamyanka, *Ukraine* 47 H7
Żnin, *Poland* 45 F4
Znojmo, *Czech Rep.* 26 C9
Zobeyrī, *Iran* 70 C5
Zobia, *Dem. Rep. of the Congo* 86 B2
Zoetermeer, *Neths.* 17 B4
Zogang, *China* 58 C1
Zogno, *Italy* 28 C6
Zogqên, *China* 58 A2
Zolochiv, *Ukraine* 47 H3
Zolotonosha, *Ukraine* 47 H7
Zomba, *Malawi* 87 F4
Zongo, *Dem. Rep. of the Congo* 84 D3
Zonguldak, *Turkey* 72 B4
Zonqor Pt., *Malta* 36 D2
Zonza, *France* 21 G13
Zorgo, *Burkina Faso* 83 C4
Zorita, *Spain* 35 F5
Zorleni, *Romania* 43 D12
Zornitsa, *Bulgaria* 41 D10
Zorritos, *Peru* 124 D2
Żory, *Poland* 45 H5
Zorzor, *Liberia* 82 D3
Zossen, *Germany* 24 C9
Zou Xiang, *China* 56 G9
Zouar, *Chad* 79 D9
Zouérate = Zouîrât, *Mauritania* 78 D3
Zouîrât, *Mauritania* 78 D3
Zoushan Dao, *China* 59 B14
Zoutkamp, *Neths.* 17 A6
Zrenjanin, *Serbia, Yug.* 42 E5
Zuarungu, *Ghana* 83 C4
Zuba, *Nigeria* 83 D6
Zubayr, *Yemen* 81 D5
Zubtsov, *Russia* 46 D8
Zuénoula, *Ivory C.* 82 D3
Zuera, *Spain* 32 D4
Zufār, *Oman* 74 D5
Zug □, *Switz.* 25 H4
Zugdidi, *Georgia* 49 J5
Zugersee, *Switz.* 25 H4
Zugspitze, *Germany* 25 H6
Zuid-Holland □, *Neths.* 17 C4
Zuidbeveland, *Neths.* 17 C3
Zuidhorn, *Neths.* 17 A6
Zújar, *Spain* 35 H8
Zújar →, *Spain* 35 F5
Żukowo, *Poland* 44 D5
Zula, *Eritrea* 81 D4
Zülpich, *Germany* 24 E2
Zumaia, *Spain* 32 B2
Zumárraga, *Spain* 32 B2
Zumbo, *Mozam.* 87 F3
Zummo, *Nigeria* 83 D7
Zumpango, *Mexico* 119 D5
Zungeru, *Nigeria* 83 D6
Zunhua, *China* 57 D9
Zuni, *U.S.A.* 115 J9
Zunyi, *China* 58 D6
Zuoquan, *China* 56 F7
Zuozhou, *China* 58 F6
Županja, *Croatia* 42 E3
Žur, *Serbia, Yug.* 40 D4
Zurbātīyah, *Iraq* 70 C5
Zürich, *Switz.* 25 H4
Zürich □, *Switz.* 25 H4
Zürichsee, *Switz.* 25 H4
Żuromin, *Poland* 45 E6
Zuru, *Nigeria* 83 C6
Žut, *Croatia* 29 E12
Zutphen, *Neths.* 17 B6
Zuwārah, *Libya* 79 B8
Zūzan, *Iran* 71 C8
Žužemberk, *Slovenia* 29 C11
Zvenigorodka = Zvenyhorodka, *Ukraine* 47 H6
Zvenyhorodka, *Ukraine* 47 H6
Zverinogolovskoye, *Russia* 50 D7
Zvezdets, *Bulgaria* 41 D11
Zvishavane, *Zimbabwe* 87 G3
Zvolen, *Slovak Rep.* 27 C12
Zvonce, *Serbia, Yug.* 40 D6
Zvornik, *Bos.-H.* 42 F4
Zwedru = Tchien, *Liberia* 82 D3
Zweibrücken, *Germany* 25 F3
Zwenkau, *Germany* 24 D8
Zwettl, *Austria* 26 C8
Zwickau, *Germany* 24 E8
Zwierzyniec, *Poland* 45 H9
Zwiesel, *Germany* 25 F9
Zwoleń, *Poland* 45 G8
Zwolle, *Neths.* 17 B6
Zwolle, *U.S.A.* 113 K8
Żychlin, *Poland* 45 F6
Zymoetz →, *Canada* 104 C3
Żyrardów, *Poland* 45 F7
Zyryan, *Kazakstan* 50 E9
Zyryanka, *Russia* 51 C16
Zyryanovsk = Zyryan, *Kazakstan* 50 E9
Żywiec, *Poland* 45 J6
Zyyi, *Cyprus* 36 E12

KEY TO WORLD MAP PAGES

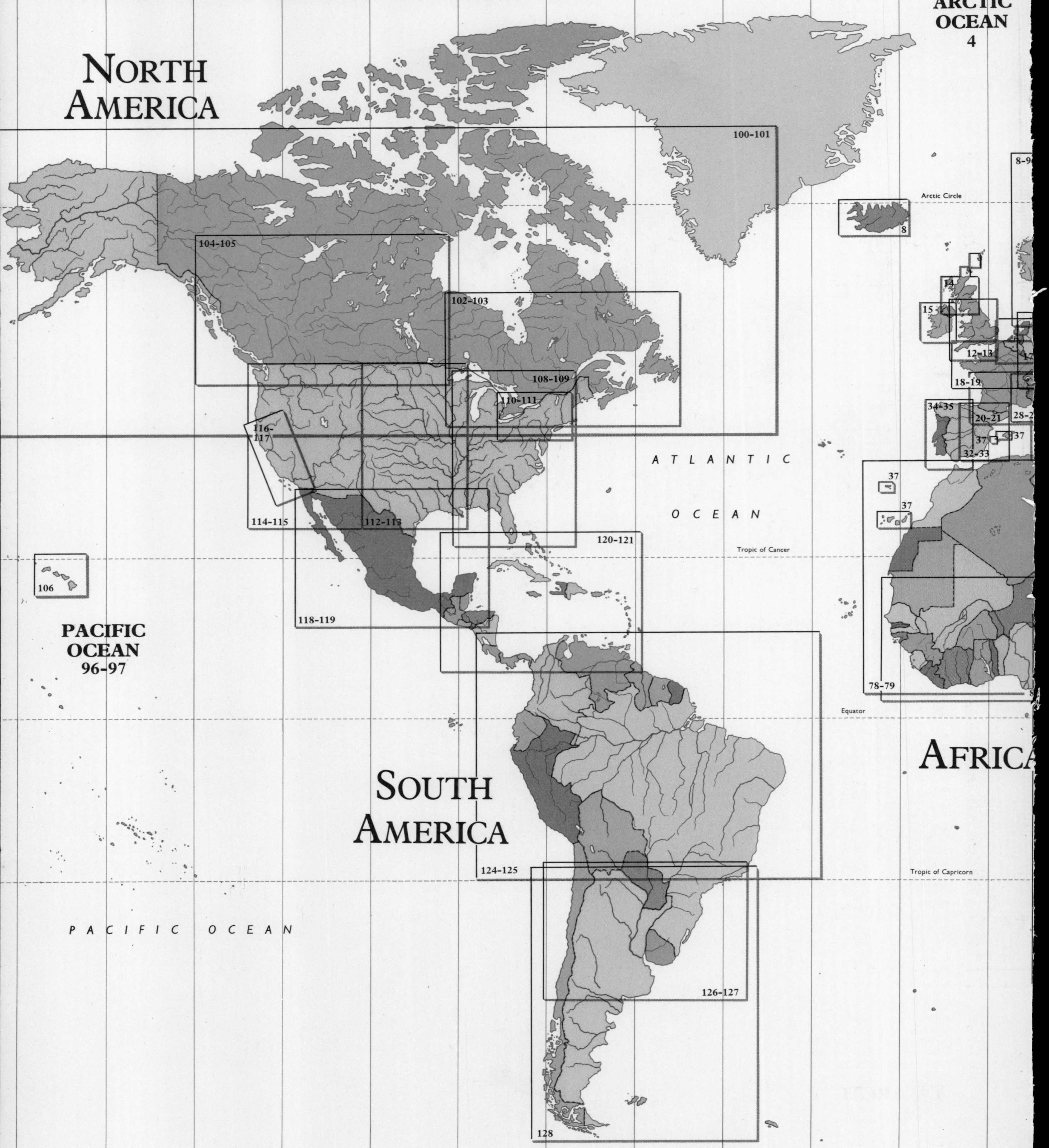